LIFE-SPAN DEVELOPMENT

SIXTH CANADIAN EDITION

John W. Santrock
University of Texas at Dallas

Anne MacKenzie-Rivers
George Brown College (retired)

Verna Pangman
University of Manitoba

LIFE-SPAN DEVELOPMENT
Sixth Canadian Edition

ISBN-13: 978-1-25-936943-8
ISBN-10: 1-25-936943-9

4 5 6 7 8 9 10 11 12 13 WEB 22 21 20 19

Printed and bound in Canada.

Portfolio and Program Manager: Karen Fozard
Product Manager: Scott Hardie
Associate Marketing Manager: Kelli Legros
Product Developer: Sarah Fulton
Photo/Permissions Research: Mary Rose MacLachlan
Senior Product Team Associate: Marina Seguin
Supervising Editor: Joanne Limebeer
Copy Editor: Janice Dyer
Plant Production Coordinator: Michelle Saddler
Manufacturing Production Coordinator: Sheryl MacAdam
Cover Design: Michelle Losier
Cover Image: David Malan/Getty Images
Interior Design: Jennifer Stimson
Composition and Page Layout: SPi Global
Printer: Webcom Inc.

With special appreciation to my mother, Ruth Santrock, and my father, John Santrock.
—John W. Santrock

With appreciation to my husband, Ray, for his love and support; to the many students, friends, and family from whom I learn; and to the editorial staff at McGraw-Hill Education for their collegiality and diligence.
—Anne MacKenzie-Thompson

To students, who have inspired me; to my husband, Clare, who has lovingly supported me; and to my colleagues and friends for their assistance and patience.
—Verna Pangman

About the Authors

John W. Santrock received his Ph.D. from the University of Minnesota. He taught at the University of Charleston and the University of Georgia before joining the Program in Psychology and Human Development at the University of Texas at Dallas, where he currently teaches a number of undergraduate courses and was recently given the University's Effective Teaching Award. In 2010, he created the UT-Dallas Santrock undergraduate scholarship, an annual award that is given to outstanding undergraduate students majoring in developmental psychology to enable them to attend research conventions.

John has been a member of the editorial boards of *Child Development* and *Developmental Psychology*. His research on father custody is widely cited and used in expert witness testimony to promote flexibility and alternative considerations in custody disputes. John also has authored these exceptional McGraw-Hill texts: *Children* (13th edition), *Adolescence* (15th edition), *A Topical Approach to Life-Span Development* (7th edition), and *Educational Psychology* (5th edition).

For many years, John was involved in tennis as a player, teaching professional, and coach of professional tennis players. At the University of Miami (FL), the tennis team on which he played still holds the NCAA Division I record for most consecutive wins (137) in any sport. His wife, Mary Jo, has a Master's degree in special education and has worked as a teacher and a realtor. He has two daughters—Tracy, who also is a realtor, and Jennifer, who is a medical sales specialist. He has one granddaughter, Jordan, age 21, currently a graduate in Cox School of Business at Southern Methodist University, and two grandsons, Alex, age 9, and Luke, age 7. In the last two decades, John has also spent time painting expressionist art.

Anne MacKenzie-Rivers retired from a rewarding career as teacher and administrator at George Brown College. Her interest in psychology focuses on social psychology, positive psychology, and contemporary research on the brain. Throughout her career, both as faculty and an administrator, she has participated in the design and delivery of a diverse number of courses and programs, ranging from Interdisciplinary Studies, the School of Labour, the Aboriginal Centre, and Community Services, to Nursing. Her degrees are in English and educational psychology. As well as spending time with her children and grandchildren, Anne and her husband enjoy volunteering, theatre, art, music, writing, and gardening.

Verna Pangman is a Senior Scholar in the College of Nursing, University of Manitoba. She has taught Human Growth and Development for a number of years at the undergraduate level. Verna is the primary author of the leadership textbook *Nursing Leadership from a Canadian Perspective*. In addition, she has been invited to insert Canadian data in several textbooks and chapters. She is the recipient of the Excellence in Professional Nursing Award from the College of Registered Nurses of Manitoba. She serves as a Research Affiliate at the Centre on Aging, University of Manitoba. Verna and her husband reside in a city on the prairies, but during the summer they have a mobile home in a small harbour town on the shores of Lake Winnipeg. They both enjoy outdoor activities and community life.

Brief Contents

Preface xxiii

SECTION 1 The Life-Span Developmental Perspective 1

1 The Life-Span Perspective **1**

2 Prominent Approaches in Life-Span Development **46**

SECTION 2 Beginnings 80

3 Biological Beginnings **80**

4 Prenatal Development and Birth **111**

SECTION 3 Infancy 148

5 Physical and Cognitive Development in Infancy **148**

6 Socio-Emotional Development in Infancy **191**

SECTION 4 Early Childhood 223

7 Physical and Cognitive Development in Early Childhood **223**

8 Socio-Emotional Development in Early Childhood **259**

SECTION 5 Middle and Late Childhood 288

9 Physical and Cognitive Development in Middle and Late Childhood **288**

10 Socio-Emotional Development in Middle and Late Childhood **335**

SECTION 6 Adolescence 369

11 Physical and Cognitive Development in Adolescence **369**

12 Socio-Emotional Development in Adolescence **409**

SECTION 7 Early Adulthood 442

13 Physical and Cognitive Development in Early Adulthood **442**

14 Socio-Emotional Development in Early Adulthood **477**

SECTION 8 Middle Adulthood 512

15 Physical and Cognitive Development in Middle Adulthood **512**

16 Socio-Emotional Development in Middle Adulthood **545**

SECTION 9 Late Adulthood 576

17 Physical and Cognitive Development in Late Adulthood **576**

18 Socio-Emotional Development in Late Adulthood **625**

SECTION 10 Endings 658

19 Death and Grieving **658**

Glossary GL-1
References RE-1
Name Index NI-1
Subject Index SI-1

Contents

Preface xxiii

SECTION 1 THE LIFE-SPAN DEVELOPMENTAL PERSPECTIVE

CHAPTER 1

THE LIFE-SPAN PERSPECTIVE 1

Our Amazing Brain Over the Life Span 3

The Life-Span Perspective 7

Life-Span Development 7

The Importance of Studying Life-Span Development 7

The Role of Context 10

CRITICAL THINKING 13

Developmental Processes 14

Biological, Cognitive, and Socio-Emotional Processes 15

Periods of Development 16

The Periods of Development 16

The Concept of Age 17

CRITICAL THINKING 17

Issues in Life-Span Development 19

CRITICAL THINKING 20

Interactional Model 21

Continuity and Discontinuity 21

Stability and Change 22

Evaluating Developmental Issues 23

CONNECTING THROUGH SOCIAL POLICY *Dr. J. Douglas Willms and Dr. Lucia Tramonte* 23

Some Contemporary Concerns 25

Health and Well-Being 25

Education 25

Socio-Cultural Contexts 26

Social Policy 28

CRITICAL THINKING 29

Research Methods and Challenges 30

Methods of Collecting Data 31

Research Designs 33

CRITICAL THINKING 36

CONNECTING THROUGH RESEARCH *Longitudinal Studies* 37

Research Challenges 38

CONNECTING DEVELOPMENT TO LIFE *Gender Makes a Difference* 40

Reach Your Learning Outcomes 42
review connect reflect 45

CHAPTER 2

PROMINENT APPROACHES IN LIFE-SPAN DEVELOPMENT 46

Brief Historical Overview of Psychology 48
The Psychoanalytic Approach 49
Characteristics of the Psychoanalytic Approach 49
Sigmund Freud 50
Erik Erikson 52

CRITICAL THINKING 53

Other Psychoanalytic Theories 53
Evaluating the Psychoanalytic Approach 55
The Cognitive Approach 55
Piaget's Cognitive Developmental Theory 55

CONNECTING THROUGH RESEARCH *The Magic Brain—Neuroplasticity* 57

Vygotsky's Socio-Cultural Cognitive Theory 58
The Information-Processing Approach 59
Evaluating the Cognitive Approach 59
The Behavioural and Social Cognitive Approach 60

CRITICAL THINKING 60

Pavlov's Classical Conditioning 60
Skinner's Operant Conditioning 60
Bandura's Social Cognitive Theory 61

CRITICAL THINKING 62

Evaluating the Behavioural and Social Cognitive Approach 63
The Ethological Approach 63
Charles Darwin 63
Konrad Lorenz 63
John Bowlby 64
Jane Goodall 65
Evaluating the Ethological Approach 65
The Humanist Approach 66
Carl Rogers 66
Abraham Maslow 66

CRITICAL THINKING 67

Evaluating the Humanist Approach 67
The Bio-Ecological Approach 68
Urie Bronfenbrenner 68
Evaluating the Bio-Ecological Approach 70

CRITICAL THINKING 70

Contemporary Approaches to Psychology 70
Positive Psychology 70
Neuroscience and Neuroplasticity 72
Dynamic Systems 72
Evolutionary Psychology 72

CONNECTING DEVELOPMENT TO LIFE *Applying the Approaches 73*

An Eclectic Theoretical Orientation 74
The Eclectic Approach 74
Reach Your Learning Outcomes 75
review connect reflect 79

SECTION 2 BEGINNINGS

CHAPTER 3

BIOLOGICAL BEGINNINGS 80

Three Dilemmas 81
The Evolutionary Perspective 82
Natural Selection and Adaptive Behaviour 83
Evolutionary Psychology 84
Genetic Foundations 86
The Collaborative Gene 87
Genes and Chromosomes 89

CRITICAL THINKING 90

Genetic Principles 90
Chromosome and Gene-Linked Variations 92

CONNECTING THROUGH SOCIAL POLICY *Eugenics and Social Policy 95*

The Human Genome Project 96
Reproduction Challenges and Choices 97
Prenatal Diagnostic Tests 97
Infertility and Reproductive Technology 99

CRITICAL THINKING 100

Adoption 101
Heredity–Environment Interaction: The Nature–Nurture Debate 102
Behaviour Genetics 102

CONNECTING THROUGH RESEARCH *Ethical Considerations of Stem Cell Research and Genetic Screening: An Overview* 102

Heredity–Environment Correlations 104
Shared and Non-shared Environmental Experiences 105
The Epigenetic View 105

CONNECTING DEVELOPMENT TO LIFE *Segun's Life Journey 106*

Conclusions about Heredity–Environment Interaction 107
Reach Your Learning Outcomes 107
review connect reflect 110

CHAPTER 4

PRENATAL DEVELOPMENT AND BIRTH 111

Birth: Yesterday, Today, and Tomorrow 112
Prenatal Development 113
The Course of Prenatal Development 114
Teratology and Hazards to Prenatal Development 118

CRITICAL THINKING 120
CRITICAL THINKING 125

Prenatal Care 131
Positive Prenatal Development 131
Birth 131
The Birth Process 131

CONNECTING THROUGH SOCIAL POLICY *Home or Hospital: Where Would You Like to Give Birth?* 134
CRITICAL THINKING 136

Special Neonatal Considerations 136
Measures of Neonatal Health and Responsiveness 139
The Postpartum Period 140
What Is the Postpartum Period? 140
Physical Adjustments 141
Emotional and Psychological Adjustments 142

CRITICAL THINKING 143
CONNECTING DEVELOPMENT TO LIFE *Global Responses to Pregnancy and Attachment after Birth* 143

Reach Your Learning Outcomes 145
review connect reflect 147

SECTION 3 INFANCY

CHAPTER 5

PHYSICAL AND COGNITIVE DEVELOPMENT IN INFANCY 148

Bottle- and Breastfeeding in Africa and Canada 150
Physical Development and Health 151
Physical Growth 152
Brain 152
Sleep 157
Health 159

CRITICAL THINKING 159

Motor, Sensory, and Perceptual Development 161
Motor Development 161

CRITICAL THINKING 164

CONNECTING DEVELOPMENT TO LIFE *The Effect of Maternal Mental Health and Childbearing Context on the Development of Children* 167

Sensory and Perceptual Development 167

Cognitive Development 173

Piaget's Sensorimotor Stage 173

Information Processing 177

CRITICAL THINKING 181

Infant Intelligence 181

Language Development 181

Language Acquisition 182

Biological Foundations of Language 184

Behavioural and Environmental Influences 186

CRITICAL THINKING 187

Reach Your Learning Outcomes 188

review connect reflect 190

CHAPTER 6

SOCIO-EMOTIONAL DEVELOPMENT IN INFANCY 191

Tom and His Father 192

Emotional Development 193

Defining Emotion 194

Biological and Environmental Influences 194

Early Emotions 194

Emotion Expression and Social Relationships 196

Emotion Regulation and Coping 198

Temperament and Personality Development 199

Temperament 199

CRITICAL THINKING 200

Personality Development 203

Social Orientation/Understanding and Attachment 205

Social Orientation/Understanding 205

Attachment and Its Development 207

Individual Differences in Attachment 209

Caregiving Styles and Attachment Classifications 210

CRITICAL THINKING 211

Attachment, Temperament, and the Wider Social World 211

Social Contexts 213

The Family 213

CONNECTING THROUGH RESEARCH *Singing in the Crib: Sandra Trehub's Research on Maternal Singing* 214

CRITICAL THINKING 216

Child Care 216

CONNECTING DEVELOPMENT TO LIFE *Comparing Child Care Policies in the Canadian Provinces (Pasoli, 2015) 217*
CRITICAL THINKING 217

Infants with Special Needs 218
Reach Your Learning Outcomes 219
review connect reflect 222

SECTION 4 EARLY CHILDHOOD

CHAPTER 7

PHYSICAL AND COGNITIVE DEVELOPMENT IN EARLY CHILDHOOD 223

The Reggio Emilia Approach 225
Physical Development 226
Body Growth 226
The Brain 226
Motor and Perceptual Development 228
Health and Wellness 231
Sleep 231
Nutrition and Exercise 231
Wellness in Canada 232

CRITICAL THINKING 233

Wellness in Other Countries 234
Cognitive Development 234
Piaget's Preoperational Stage 234
Vygotsky's Theory 238
Information Processing 242

CRITICAL THINKING 245
CONNECTING THROUGH RESEARCH *Carole Peterson, Narrative Researcher* 248

Language Development 249
Early Childhood Education 252
Variations in Early Childhood Education 253

CRITICAL THINKING 253

Developmentally Appropriate Practices 254
Young Children's Literacy and Numeracy 254
Education for Children Who Are Disadvantaged 254
Reach Your Learning Outcomes 255
review connect reflect 258

CHAPTER 8

SOCIO-EMOTIONAL DEVELOPMENT IN EARLY CHILDHOOD 259

Is the Sky the Limit for a Parent's Love? 260
The Self and Emotional Development 261
The Self 261

Emotional Development 263
CRITICAL THINKING 264
Moral Development and Gender 265
Moral Development 266
Gender 267
CONNECTING THROUGH DEVELOPMENT *Gender Identity – Variations* 268
CRITICAL THINKING 269
The Changing Family in a Changing Society 272
Parenting 272
CRITICAL THINKING 275
CONNECTING DEVELOPMENT TO LIFE *Parental Attitudes of the Sami* 276
CRITICAL THINKING 276
Divorce 276
CRITICAL THINKING 280
Sibling Relationships and Birth Order 280
Peer Relations, Play, and Social Media 281
Peer Relations 281
Play 282
Media/Screen Time 283
Reach Your Learning Outcomes 284
review connect reflect 286

SECTION 5 MIDDLE AND LATE CHILDHOOD

CHAPTER 9

PHYSICAL AND COGNITIVE DEVELOPMENT IN MIDDLE AND LATE CHILDHOOD 288
Gandhi's Glasses 290
Physical Changes and Health 290
Body Growth and Change 290
The Brain 291
Motor Development 292
CRITICAL THINKING 292
Exercise 292
CRITICAL THINKING 293
Health, Illness, and Disease 293
CRITICAL THINKING 294
Cognitive Development 295
Piaget's Concrete Operational Stage 295
Information Processing 298
CONNECTING DEVELOPMENT TO LIFE *Strategies for Increasing Children's Creative Thinking* 303
Intelligence 306
CONNECTING DEVELOPMENT TO LIFE *The "Flynn Effect": Are We Smarter than Our Grandparents?* 311

CRITICAL THINKING 314

CRITICAL THINKING 315

Language Development 317

Vocabulary, Grammar, and Metalinguistic Awareness 317

Reading 317

Writing 318

Bilingualism 319

Educational Approaches and Issues 320

Approaches to Student Learning 320

CRITICAL THINKING 321

Educational Issues 321

CONNECTING THROUGH SOCIAL POLICY *How Inclusive is Canada's Education?* 321

CRITICAL THINKING 323

Private Schools and Home Education 324

CRITICAL THINKING 324

Children with Disabilities 324

Learning Disabilities 325

CRITICAL THINKING 326

Attention Deficit Hyperactivity Disorder (ADHD) 326

Autism Spectrum Disorders 328

Physical Disabilities 328

Children's Disabilities and the Family 329

Educational Issues 329

Reach Your Learning Outcomes 330

review connect reflect 333

CHAPTER 10

SOCIO-EMOTIONAL DEVELOPMENT IN MIDDLE AND LATE CHILDHOOD 335

Meeting my Dad 336

Emotional and Personality Development 338

The Self 338

CRITICAL THINKING 339

CRITICAL THINKING 340

CONNECTING DEVELOPMENT TO LIFE *Increasing Children's Self-Esteem* 341

CRITICAL THINKING 341

Emotional Development 343

CONNECTING THROUGH SOCIAL POLICY *Challenges Facing Immigrants and Refugees* 345

Moral Development and Gender 346

Moral Development 346

CRITICAL THINKING 349

CONNECTING THROUGH RESEARCH *Morality and Modesty* 350

Gender 352

CRITICAL THINKING 354

CRITICAL THINKING 355

Families 356

Developmental Changes in Parent–Child Relationships 357

Child Maltreatment: Prevalence and Consequences 358

Peers, Bullying, and Social Media 360

Friends 360

Peer Statuses 361

Social Cognition 362

Bullying 363

Social Media 364

CRITICAL THINKING 365

Reach Your Learning Outcomes 366

review connect reflect 368

SECTION 6 ADOLESCENCE

CHAPTER 11

PHYSICAL AND COGNITIVE DEVELOPMENT IN ADOLESCENCE 369

Adolescence: A Time of Firsts 371

The Nature of Adolescence 371

CRITICAL THINKING 372

Physical Changes during Puberty 372

Sexual Maturation, Height, and Weight 373

Hormonal Changes 375

Body Image 375

Teen Perspectives on Maturity 376

CRITICAL THINKING 376

The Brain 377

Adolescent Sexuality 379

Developing a Sexual Identity 380

The Timing of Adolescent Sexual Behaviours 381

Risk Factors and Sexual Problems 382

Adolescent Pregnancy and Health 383

CRITICAL THINKING 383

Adolescent Health Problems and Wellness 385

Nutrition, Exercise, and Sleep 385

CRITICAL THINKING 386

Eating Disorders 386

CONNECTING THROUGH SOCIAL POLICY *Dr. Roger Tonkin, Pioneer and Visionary in Adolescent Health Care* 387

Risk and Vulnerability 390

Substance Use and Addiction 391

CRITICAL THINKING 394

Teen Depression 394

CONNECTING DEVELOPMENT TO LIFE *Suicide* 395

Adolescent Cognition 397

Piaget's Theory 398

Adolescent Egocentrism 400

Information Processing 400

Education 401

CRITICAL THINKING 402

Reach Your Learning Outcomes 404

review connect reflect 408

CHAPTER 12

SOCIO-EMOTIONAL DEVELOPMENT IN ADOLESCENCE 409

The Challenges of Being an Adolescent 410

Self-Esteem and Identity Development 411

Self-Esteem 411

Identity 412

CRITICAL THINKING 414

CONNECTING DEVELOPMENT TO LIFE *Child or Adult? The Case of Omar Khadr* 415

Identity: Family, Religion, Race, Ethnicity, Culture, and Sexual Orientation 416

Families 417

CRITICAL THINKING 420

Religion 422

CRITICAL THINKING 422

Racial, Ethnic, and Cultural Identity 423

CRITICAL THINKING 425

Traditions and Changes in Adolescence around the World 426

Sexual Orientation and Identity 429

Friendship 429

Adolescent Groups versus Children's Groups 430

Peer Groups 430

Dating and Romantic Relationships 431

Adolescent Problems 433

Young Offenders 434

Causes of Delinquency 435

CRITICAL THINKING 435

Successful Prevention and Intervention Programs 437

CRITICAL THINKING 437

Reach Your Learning Outcomes 438

review connect reflect 441

SECTION 7 EARLY ADULTHOOD

CHAPTER 13

PHYSICAL AND COGNITIVE DEVELOPMENT IN EARLY ADULTHOOD 442
Winning Gold: Canada's Women's Hockey Team, Olympics 2010–2014 444
The Transition from Adolescence to Adulthood 445
CRITICAL THINKING 445
The Criteria for Becoming an Adult 446
CRITICAL THINKING 446
The Transition from High School to College, University, or Work 447
Physical Development, Health, and Wellness 448
Health 449
Eating and Weight 450
Regular Exercise 453
Substance Abuse 453
CRITICAL THINKING 457
Sexuality 457
Sexual Activity in Emerging Adulthood 458
Sexually Transmitted Infections 460
CRITICAL THINKING 462
Violence against Women 463
CRITICAL THINKING 463
CONNECTING DEVELOPMENT TO LIFE *Violence against Aboriginal Women—A Continuing Outrage* 464
Cognitive Development 465
Piaget's View 465
Creativity 466
Careers and Work 469
Developmental Changes 469
CRITICAL THINKING 469
Values and Careers 469
CONNECTING THROUGH SOCIAL POLICY *Dr. Samantha Nutt* 470
CRITICAL THINKING 471
The Occupational Outlook 471
The Impact of Work 471
Reach Your Learning Outcomes 473
review connect reflect 476

CHAPTER 14

SOCIO-EMOTIONAL DEVELOPMENT IN EARLY ADULTHOOD 477
Variations: Do Any of These Scenarios Resemble Someone You Know? 479
Stability and Change from Childhood to Adulthood 480
Temperament 480

Attachment 482

CONNECTING THROUGH RESEARCH *Dr. Susan Johnson, Psychologist, Counsellor, Researcher, and Co-Developer of Emotionally Focused Therapy* 482

Attraction, Love, and Close Relationships 485

Attraction 486

The Faces of Love 487

Falling Out of Love 489

CONNECTING THROUGH RESEARCH *Personal Growth Following a Romantic Relationship Breakup* 490

Friendship 491

CRITICAL THINKING 491

Loneliness 492

CRITICAL THINKING 492

Intimate Relationships: Marriage and the Family Life Cycle 493

Marital Trends in Canada 493

Social Contexts 493

Making Marriage Work 494

CRITICAL THINKING 495

Benefits of a Good Marriage 495

The Family Life Cycle 496

Parenting Myths and Realities 499

The Diversity of Adult Lifestyles 499

Single Adults 500

Cohabiting Adults 500

Divorced Adults 501

Remarried Adults 502

CRITICAL THINKING 503

Parenting Adults 503

CRITICAL THINKING 503

Lone-Parent Adults 503

Gay and Lesbian Adults 504

Gender, Relationships, and Moral Development 505

Moral Development 505

Women's Development 506

Men's Development 507

Reach Your Learning Outcomes 508

review connect reflect 511

SECTION 8 MIDDLE ADULTHOOD

CHAPTER 15

PHYSICAL AND COGNITIVE DEVELOPMENT IN MIDDLE ADULTHOOD 512

Middle Age 514

The Nature of Middle Adulthood 514

Changing Midlife 515
Physical Development 515
Physical Changes 516
Health Concerns and Wellness Strategies 520
CONNECTING DEVELOPMENT TO LIFE *The Thin Door* 522
CRITICAL THINKING 522
Culture, Relationships, and Health 523
CRITICAL THINKING 523
Mortality Rates 523
Sexuality 524
Cognitive Development 527
Intelligence 527
CONNECTING THROUGH RESEARCH *K. Warner Schaie, Professor of Human Development* 530
Information Processing 531
CRITICAL THINKING 532
CONNECTING THROUGH RESEARCH *Mihaly Csikszentmihalyi* 534
Careers, Work, and Leisure 535
Work in Midlife 535
Career Challenges and Changes 537
CRITICAL THINKING 538
Leisure 538
Meaning in Life 538
Meditation, Religion, and Spirituality 539
CRITICAL THINKING 540
Meaning in Life 540
Health and Well-Being 541
Reach Your Learning Outcomes 542
review connect reflect 544

CHAPTER 16

SOCIO-EMOTIONAL DEVELOPMENT IN MIDDLE ADULTHOOD 545
Chantal Petitclerc 546
Personality Theories and Development in Middle Adulthood 547
Stages of Adulthood 547
CRITICAL THINKING 549
CRITICAL THINKING 549
The Life-Events Approach 552
CRITICAL THINKING 554
Stress and Personal Control in Midlife 554
CRITICAL THINKING 555
Contexts of Midlife Development 555
CRITICAL THINKING 556

CONNECTING DEVELOPMENT TO LIFE *Immigrants Define Canada: "The Land of the Second Chance"—Nellie McClung (1873–1951)* 558

Stability and Change 559

Longitudinal Studies 559

CRITICAL THINKING 561

Conclusions 562

Close Relationships 563

Love and Marriage at Midlife 563

CRITICAL THINKING 566

The Empty Nest and Its Refilling 566

Sibling Relationships and Friendships 566

Grandparenting 567

CONNECTING DEVELOPMENT TO LIFE *Elders—The Glue That Binds* 568

Intergenerational Relationships 569

Reach Your Learning Outcomes 572

review connect reflect 574

SECTION 9 LATE ADULTHOOD

CHAPTER 17

PHYSICAL AND COGNITIVE DEVELOPMENT IN LATE ADULTHOOD 575

Seniors Making a Difference 577

Longevity and Biological Theories of Aging 578

Life Expectancy and Life Span 578

CRITICAL THINKING 581

The Young Old, the Old Old, and the Oldest Old 581

The Robust Oldest Old 581

Biological Theories of Aging 581

CRITICAL THINKING 584

The Course of Physical Development in Late Adulthood 584

The Aging Brain 585

CONNECTING THROUGH RESEARCH *Does Staying Intellectually Challenged Affect One's Quality of Life and Longevity?* 588

Sleep 589

The Immune System 589

Physical Appearance and Movement 589

CRITICAL THINKING 590

Sensory Development 590

CRITICAL THINKING 592

The Circulatory System and Lungs 593

Sexuality 593

Physical and Mental Health and Wellness 594

Health Problems 595

Exercise, Nutrition, and Weight 596
The Nature of Mental Health in Late Adulthood 600
CRITICAL THINKING 602
Dementia, Alzheimer's Disease, and Related Disorders 602
Health Promotion 605
CONNECTING THROUGH RESEARCH *Ursula Franklin (1921–2016)* 606
CRITICAL THINKING 607
CONNECTING DEVELOPMENT TO LIFE *Health Care Providers and Older Adults* 608
Cognitive Functioning in Older Adults 609
The Multi-Dimensional, Multi-Directional Nature of Cognition 609
Education, Work, and Health: Links to Cognitive Functioning 614
Promoting Cognitive Skills in Later Life: Use It or Lose It 615
Cognitive Neuroscience and Aging 616
Meditation, Religion, and Spirituality in Late Adulthood 618
Reach Your Learning Outcomes 619
review connect reflect 624

CHAPTER 18

SOCIO-EMOTIONAL DEVELOPMENT IN LATE ADULTHOOD 625
The Honourable Michaëlle Jean 627
Theories of Socio-Emotional Development 628
Erikson's Theory 628
Activity Theory 630
Socio-Emotional Selectivity Theory 630
CRITICAL THINKING 632
Selective Optimization with Compensation Theory 632
Social Determinants of Health 633
Personality, the Self, and Society 634
Personality 634
The Self 635
Older Adults in Society 636
CRITICAL THINKING 639
Families and Social Relationships 640
The Aging Couple 640
Older Adult Parents and Their Adult Children 642
Grandparenting and Great-Grandparenting 642
Friendship 643
Fear of Victimization, Crime, and Elder Maltreatment 644
CRITICAL THINKING 645
CONNECTING THROUGH RESEARCH *Elder Abuse* 647
Social Integration 648
Social Support and Social Integration 648

CONNECTING DEVELOPMENT TO LIFE *Intergenerational Programs* 649

Altruism and Volunteerism 650
Gender 651

CRITICAL THINKING 651

Ethnicity 651
Culture 652
Successful Aging 652

CRITICAL THINKING 653

Reach Your Learning Outcomes 654
review connect reflect 657

SECTION 10 ENDINGS

CHAPTER 19

DEATH AND GRIEVING 658

National Mourning 660
Defining Death and Life/Death Issues 661
Issues in Determining Death 661
Decisions Regarding Life, Death, and Health Care 661

CRITICAL THINKING 663

CRITICAL THINKING 665

Death and Socio-Historical, Cultural Contexts 667
Changing Historical Circumstances 667
Death in Different Cultures 668

CRITICAL THINKING 669

A Developmental Perspective on Death 669
Causes of Death and Expectations about Death 670
Understanding Death from a Life-Span Perspective 670

CRITICAL THINKING 672

Facing One's Own Death 673
Kübler-Ross's Stages of Dying 673
Perceived Control and Denial 675

CRITICAL THINKING 675

The Contexts in Which People Die 675
Coping with the Death of Someone Else 676
Communicating with a Dying Person 676
Grieving 677

CONNECTING THROUGH RESEARCH *Life after Death* 678

Making Sense of the World 680

CRITICAL THINKING 680

Losing a Life Partner 680

The Funeral 681

CONNECTING DEVELOPMENT TO LIFE *Personalizing Funerals* 682

CRITICAL THINKING 683

Reach Your Learning Outcomes 683

review connect reflect 686

Glossary GL-1

References RE-1

Name Index NI-1

Subject Index SI-1

Preface

The sixth Canadian edition builds on the traditions of the Santrock legacy through the integration of more current research, much of it Canadian, and the addition of intellectually engaging content, presented where relevant in a Canadian context. In this sixth edition, the authors thread throughout the chapters the challenges faced by immigrants and refugees who resettle in Canada, linking these life events to theories of development. Student-friendly writing style and pedagogy, enticing illustrations, and increased emphasis on discussions relevant to the Canadian student work to more fully integrate the Canadian experience.

Like the previous edition, this edition includes a Connections theme to provide a systematic, integrative approach to the course material. This theme was developed by John Santrock based on feedback from his students, who said that highlighting connections among the different aspects of life-span development would help them to better understand the concepts. This Connections theme is presented through the use of the following boxes:

- **Connecting through Research.** To provide students with the best and most recent theory and research in the world today about each of the periods of human life span.
- **Connecting through Social Policy.** To provide students with insights about how contemporary research shapes policy.
- **Connecting Development to Life.** To help students understand ways to apply content about the human life span to the real world and improve people's lives; and to motivate them to think deeply about their own personal journey through life and better understand who they were, are, and will be.

Connecting with Today's Students

In *Life-Span Development*, we recognize that today's students are as different in some ways from the learners of the last generation as today's discipline of the life-span development is different from the field 30 years ago. Students now learn in multiple modalities; rather than sitting down and reading traditional printed chapters in linear fashion from beginning to end, their work preferences tend to be more visual and more interactive, and their reading and study often occur in short bursts. For many students, a traditionally formatted, printed textbook is no longer enough when they have instant, 24/7 access to news and information from around the globe. Two features that specifically support today's students are the adaptive ebook, Smartbook (discussed in more detail under Supplements), and the learning outcomes system.

The Learning Outcomes System

CHAPTER OUTLINE

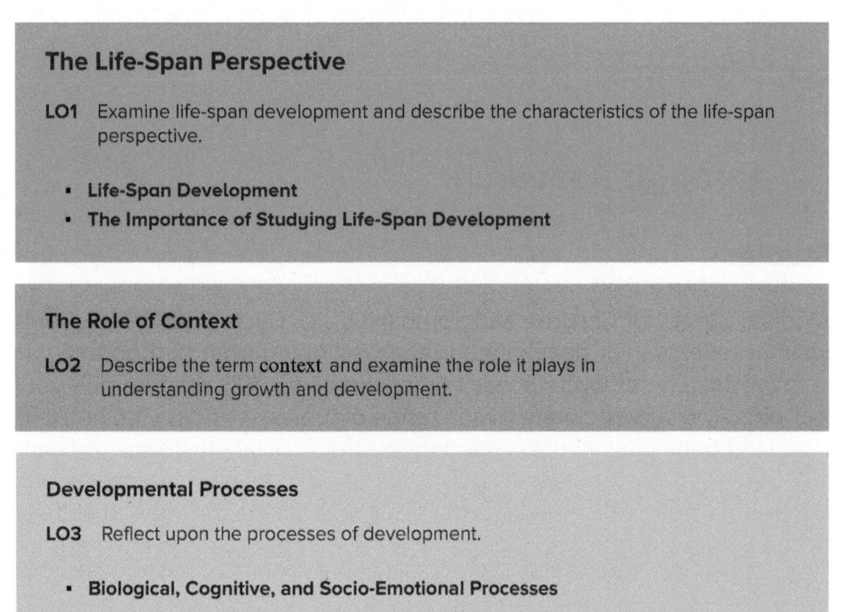

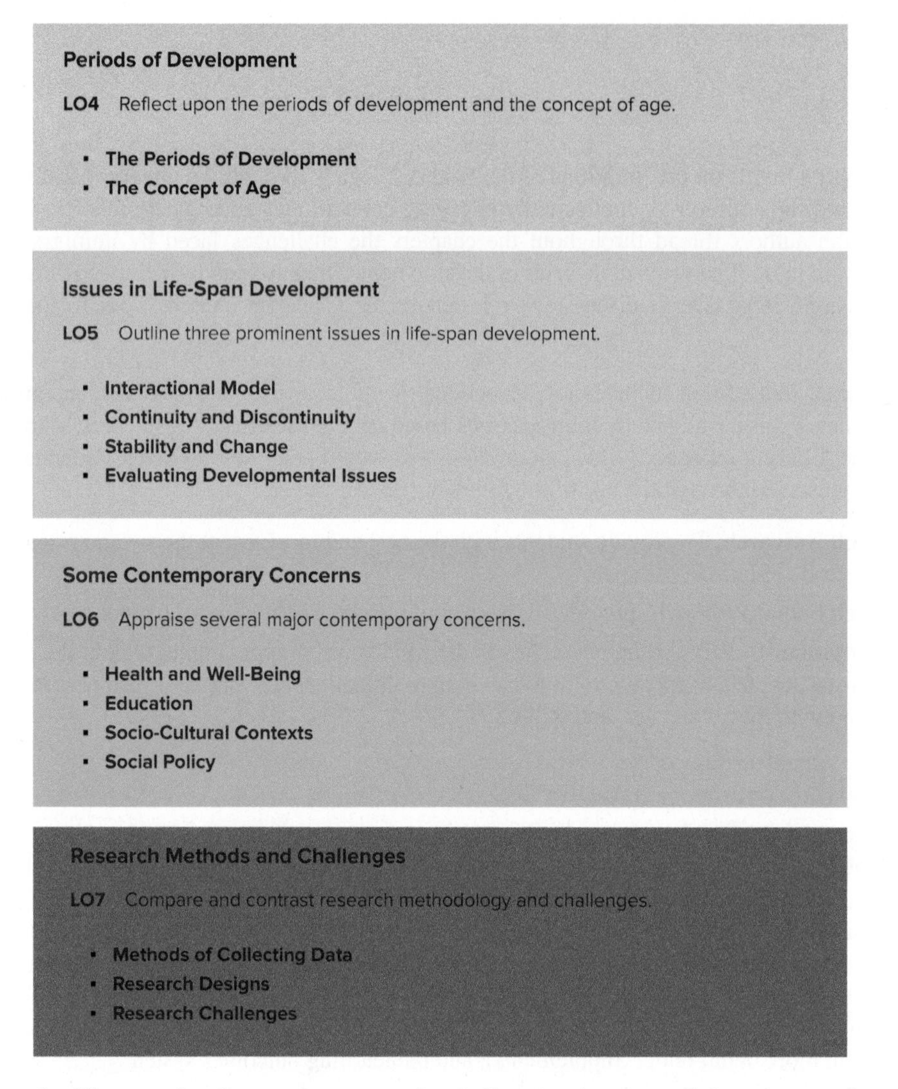

Periods of Development

LO4 Reflect upon the periods of development and the concept of age.

- **The Periods of Development**
- **The Concept of Age**

Issues in Life-Span Development

LO5 Outline three prominent issues in life-span development.

- **Interactional Model**
- **Continuity and Discontinuity**
- **Stability and Change**
- **Evaluating Developmental Issues**

Some Contemporary Concerns

LO6 Appraise several major contemporary concerns.

- **Health and Well-Being**
- **Education**
- **Socio-Cultural Contexts**
- **Social Policy**

Research Methods and Challenges

LO7 Compare and contrast research methodology and challenges.

- **Methods of Collecting Data**
- **Research Designs**
- **Research Challenges**

Students often report the life-span development course to be challenging because of the amount of material covered. To help today's students focus on the key ideas, the Learning Outcomes System developed for *Life-Span Development* provides extensive learning connections throughout the chapters. The learning system connects the chapter opening outline, learning outcomes for the chapter, mini-chapter maps that open each main section of the chapter, and Reach Your Learning Outcomes and Review, Connect, Reflect at the end of each chapter. Key terms are defined as they appear in the text and in a glossary.

Connecting through Research

CONNECTING through Research

Longitudinal Studies

The National Longitudinal Survey of Children and Youth (NLSCY), Cycle 8 (2008–2009) is a comprehensive survey of Canadians that reflects their development and well-being from birth to early adulthood (Statistics Canada, 2010). The initial sample for Cycle 8 was comprised of 35 795 children and youths aged from 0–7 years and 14–25-year-olds. The survey covers a wide range of topics, including the health of children, physical development, learning and behaviour, and as well data on their social environment (family, friends, schools, and communities). The study collects data concerning factors that influence a child's social, emotional, and behavioural development. The survey monitors the impact of these factors on the child's development over time. Information from the NLSCY will help shape social policy to help children and their families avoid, or rise out of, the conditions and choices that lead to vulnerability.

This boxed feature looks closely at specific areas of research involving experts in related fields and current research. Connecting through Research describes a study or program to illustrate how research in life-span development is conducted and how it influences our understanding of the discipline.

Connecting through Social Policy

CONNECTING through Social Policy

Eugenics and Social Policy

You will find *Connecting Through Social Policy* boxes throughout this text, and you might ask, "Just what is social policy and where does it come from?" There is no simple answer to this question, as the definition, the source, and the implementation of social policy are multifaceted and complex. Generally, Canadian social policy attempts to address factors that affect the daily lives of citizens, including health, education, poverty, employment, safety, and housing. The development of policy is a lengthy zig-zagging process that involves problem identification, research, legislation, adoption, implementation, evaluation, and adaptation. Often policy changes are prompted by legal challenges to present laws and rest on Supreme Court decisions. Two examples of major policy shifts in the past two decades include the decriminalization of abortion and the legalization of same-sex marriages. Another couple of highly-charged policy considerations under discussion today are the implementation of physician-assisted death, which you will read more about in Chapter 19, and current research in the field of eugenics, which is discussed in this chapter.

Connecting development to social policy helps students connect to the social policies that mould our development throughout life. These Connecting through Social Policy boxes highlight life-span development research activities and their influence on social policy and students lives.

Connecting Development to Life

CONNECTING development to life

Gender Makes a Difference

Four prominent clinical psychoanalysts have significantly influenced the field of psychology. Arguing that the primary framework in the field, put forward by Freud, Jung, Erikson, Kohlberg, and others, is a framework designed by and for men, Karen Horney, Jean Baker Miller, Carol Gilligan, and Harriet Lerner have made an enormous contribution.

Karen Horney (1885–1952) was the first woman to challenge prevalent thinking by proposing that cultural and experiential factors are primary determinants of personality for both men and women. While Horney agreed with much of Freud's work, she firmly disagreed with what she thought to be a preoccupation with male genitalia. Arguing "anatomy is not destiny," Horney proposed that men should experience womb-envy rather than women experiencing penis envy because women are the bearers of future generations—something men cannot do. Horney founded the American Institute for Psychoanalysis so that research and training would not be constrained by prevalent thought. Her major contribution to the field was her theory of neurosis, the struggle between our real self and our idealized self. She also argued that neglect, not abuse, is the single most damaging factor in a child's development, because the child has no way to rail against neglect.

In addition to helping students make research and developmental connections, *Life-Span Development* shows the important connections between the concepts discussed and the real world. Students in life-span development have increasingly said that they want more of this type of information. In this edition, real-life connections are explicitly made through the chapters' Opening Vignettes and the Connecting Development to Life boxes.

Each chapter begins with a **vignette** designed to increase students' interest and motivation to read the chapter. Each vignette establishes the Canadian or international context and uses personal stories to set the tone for the content that follows. The **Connecting Development to Life** feature can be found within the chapter and describes the influence of development in a real-world context with special attention to culture, ethnicity, and gender.

review → connect → reflect

review

1. What is meant by the concept of development? LO1
2. List several characteristics of development. LO1
3. Why is the study of life-span development important? LO1
4. How is context related to growth and development? Provide an example. LO2
5. What are the three key developmental processes of development? LO3
6. How is age related to development? LO4
7. What are three main developmental issues? LO5
8. What are some contemporary concerns in life-span development? LO6
9. What research designs are used to study development? LO7
10. What are the researchers' ethical responsibilities to the individuals they study? LO7

connect

Reflect upon your own experience. How do you think biology and culture interact to affect development?

reflect

Your Own Personal Journey of Life

You and your parents grew up at different points in time. Consider some of the ways you are different from your parents. What are several differences that may be caused by cohort effects?

Critical Thinking boxes occur throughout each chapter to encourage students to critically consider what they have just read and challenge students to discuss and debate contemporary issues of concern to Canadians. To further emphasize important concepts and encourage students to make personal connections to content in the text, **Review, Connect & Reflect: Your Own Personal Journey of Life** questions appear in the end-of-chapter review in each chapter.

What's New in the Sixth Canadian Edition?

The sixth Canadian edition has been thoroughly revised and updated throughout to continue meeting the needs of Canadian instructors and students.

Chapter 1

- New data and updates have been added throughout, including new information regarding cross-cultural study, immigration status, truth and reconciliation, health care in Canada, Generation X, and homelessness.
- A new *Connecting Through Social Policy* box on Dr. J. Douglas Willms and Dr. Lucia Tremonte is provided, and *Connecting Through Research* boxes have been updated to facilitate understanding of critical concepts.

Chapter 2

- A new chapter opening vignette provides an historical overview of the history of psychology leading up to contemporary approaches.
- A new *Connecting Development to Life* box (on challenges facing new immigrants) and a revised *Connecting through Research* box (on neuroplasticity) illustrate the concepts of the chapter.

Chapter 3

- To highlight the chapter's concepts, the opening vignette, Three Dilemmas, has been revised.
- Two new boxes have been added. A new *Connecting Through Social Policy* box clarifies how social policy comes about and the implications for eugenics. The new *Connecting Development to Life* box applies theory to context through a true account of one immigrant Canadian's difficult journey through adolescence to adulthood.
- New and updated information is provided throughout, including information on the Genome Project and on research related to identical twins.

Chapter 4

- New and updated material is provided throughout, including coverage of physical and emotional adjustment, anencephaly, Caesarean section, diabetes, marijuana use, positive prenatal development, preterm and low birth weight, radiation, syphilis, emotional states and stress, genetic susceptibility, and use of alcohol and cocaine.
- New material has been added covering the Ballard Scale.
- New material has been added covering opioid dependency in pregnancy.

Chapter 5

- An updated discussion of babbling and other vocalizations is provided, along with new information on conceptual categories, behaviour and environmental influences, SIDS, and vision.
- New and updated data have been added on visual expectations, hearing loss, intermodal perceptions, perceptual motor coupling, causality, violations in expectations, methods, habituation, memory, early deprivation and brain activity, sleep patterns, bed sharing, dynamic systems theory, breast feeding, and gross motor skills.

Chapter 6

- New and updated material has been provided on autism, child care, maternal and paternal caregiving, provincial policies, emotions, and stability and change.
- Updated research has been added to discussions about concepts such as brain development, social orientation, intention, and goal-directed behaviour.
- A new figure has been added showing types of child care arrangements for children aged 4 and under in Canada, by region.

Chapter 7

- A new opening vignette details a remarkable approach to the education of young children that was developed by Reggio Emilia in Italy.
- The discussion of Vygotsky and language development has been revised.

- Updated coverage of nutrition and exercise has been added, including information about obesity in Canadian children as well as the role of nutrition in brain development.

Chapter 8

- A new *Connecting Development to Life* box has been added about variations in gender identity.
- Expanded and updated Canadian content on shyness and gender identity has been included.
- Coverage of parenting styles has been expanded to include research findings on immigrant and refugee families, gay and lesbian parenting, and co-parenting.
- Updated information is provided on the changing nature of families, including challenges to stepfamilies and blended families.
- Updated information has been added on child maltreatment.
- New data have been included on adolescent use of media/screen time.

Chapter 9

- Revised and updated coverage has been provided for a number of topics, including memory, executive functioning, intelligence, intelligence testing, extremes in intelligence, language development, writing, and bilingualism.
- Updated information has been provided on education systems, including provincial variations in legislation regarding the provision of bilingualism and inclusivity.
- New and revised information exploring the challenges faced by immigrant families, families with children who have various disabilities, and Aboriginal children has been provided.
- A new *Connecting Through Social Policy* box highlights the challenges of inclusive education.

Chapter 10

- This chapter begins with a new opening vignette written by Eivan Berhane, the son of an Eritrean journalist who sought asylum in Canada.
- Information on families has been revised and updated to include data related to the role of parents in blended or stepfamilies.
- The child maltreatment section has been revised and updated to include the impact of alcohol, social media, and parental role modelling, and long-term consequences such as leaving home to live on the streets, difficulty in establishing and maintaining relationships, substance abuse, and anxiety and depression.
- The bullying section has been revised and updated to include the four roles of bullying—bully, bullied, bystander, and upstander—and updated coverage of cyberbullying and the impact of bullying on the victim, the bully, and others has been provided.
- The impact of poverty has been threaded throughout the chapter, including data on the use of food banks and the dropout rate among Aboriginal children.
- Coverage of the Syrian refugee crisis and Canada's response, and a new *Connecting Through Social Policy* box highlighting parenting challenges that immigrant families may encounter, have been provided.

Chapter 11

- Updated and new content covering body image, body art, sleep patterns, disordered eating conditions, and depression has been provided.
- New research and data on the brain, adolescent sexual behaviours, STIs, and adolescent pregnancy and its consequences have been included.
- The information about service learning, Katimavik, and trends in the dropout and employment rates of young people has been updated and revised.

Chapter 12

- New updated data has been added throughout, including in the coverage of self-esteem, identity formation, Elkind's Age Dynamism, autonomy and attachment, parent–adolescent conflict, peers, religious and spiritual development, rites of passage, health, education, and work.
- A new section has been added on adolescent time allocation to different activities.

- Updated coverage has been provided about sexual orientation and identity, peer groups, peer pressure, street youth, and causes of delinquency, and new information has been added about successful intervention programs.
- The *Connecting Development to Life* box, Child or Adult: The Case of Omar Khadr, has been updated with the latest developments in Mr. Khadr's case.

Chapter 13

- A revised and updated opening vignette on Canada's women's hockey team has been included.
- An updated *Connecting Development to Life* box spotlights violence against Aboriginal women.
- Revised data on post-secondary education, impact of work, occupational outlooks, violence against women, protection against STIs, the continuum of sexual orientation, addiction relapses, gambling, e-cigarettes, binge drinking, and eating disorders have been provided.

Chapter 14

- A seventh stage has been added to the Family Life Cycle (Figure 14.4): Families nearing the end of life.
- New, current research on marriage, fidelity, and attachment has been provided.
- Updated statistics and content in the Diversity of Adult Lifestyles section have been added.
- The section on men's development has been completely revised, incorporating the effects of fatherhood and violence against women.

Chapter 15

- A revised opening vignette contextualizing middle adulthood within the family life cycle has been provided.
- Expanded and updated information about stress related to poverty and immigration has been added.
- Expanded and new information on hormonal changes in middle-aged men has been included.

Chapter 16

- A new opening vignette spotlights Canadian Senator Chantal Petitclerc, linking the implications of a life-altering accident to Erikson's theory.
- Expanded, revised information about changes in Canadian families has been provided.

Chapter 17

- A new opening vignette discusses three notable Canadians, now in their seventies, who continue to make significant contributions to their fields.
- The chapter introduces the Healthy Adjusted Life Expectancy (HALE) measurement, which differentiates between quantity and quality of longevity.
- Expanded, new, and updated research related to key mental health issues, such as social isolation, depression, and substance abuse, as well as cognitive disorders such as dementia, Alzheimer's disease, and related disorders, has been provided.

Chapter 18

- A new opening vignette spotlights Canada's former Governor General, the Honourable Michaëlle Jean, who came to Canada as a refugee.
- A new *Connecting Development to Life* box highlights intergenerational programs in senior residences.
- Revised and updated content has been provided throughout, including expanded coverage of elder abuse.

Chapter 19

- Substantially revised and updated coverage of advance care planning and physician assisted dying has been provided, reflecting the current legislation in Canada.
- New coverage of the role of spirituality for those facing an incurable illness has been included.

Supplements

MARKET LEADING TECHNOLOGY

connect

Learn without LimitsfConnect Key Features:

McGraw-Hill Connect® is an award-winning digital teaching and learning platform that gives students the means to better connect with their coursework, with their instructors, and with the important concepts that they will need to know for success now and in the future. With Connect, instructors can take advantage of McGraw-Hill's trusted content to seamlessly deliver assignments, quizzes, and tests online. McGraw-Hill Connect is a learning platform that continually adapts to each student, delivering precisely what they need, when they need it, so class time is more engaging and effective. Connect makes teaching and learning personal, easy, and proven.

Connect Key Features:

SmartBook®

As the first and only adaptive reading experience, SmartBook is changing the way students read and learn. SmartBook creates a personalized reading experience by highlighting the most important concepts a student needs to learn at that moment in time. As a student engages with SmartBook, the reading experience continuously adapts by highlighting content based on what each student knows and doesn't know. This ensures that he or she is focused on the content needed to close specific knowledge gaps, while it simultaneously promotes long-term learning.

Connect Insight®

Connect Insight is Connect's new one-of-a-kind visual analytics dashboard—now available for instructors—that provides at-a-glance information regarding student performance, which is immediately actionable. By presenting assignment, assessment, and topical performance results together with a time metric that is easily visible for aggregate or individual results, Connect Insight gives instructors the ability to take a just-in-time approach to teaching and learning, which was never before available. Connect Insight presents data that helps instructors improve class performance in a way that is efficient and effective.

Simple Assignment Management

With Connect, creating assignments is easier than ever, so instructors can spend more time teaching and less time managing.

- Assign SmartBook learning modules.
- Edit existing questions and create their own questions.
- Draw from a variety of text specific questions, resources, and test bank material to assign online.
- Streamline lesson planning, student progress reporting, and assignment grading to make classroom management more efficient than ever.

Smart Grading

When it comes to studying, time is precious. Connect helps students learn more efficiently by providing feedback and practice material when they need it, where they need it.

- Automatically score assignments, giving students immediate feedback on their work and comparisons with correct answers.
- Access and review each response; manually change grades or leave comments for students to review.
- Track individual student performance—by question, assignment or in relation to the class overall—with detailed grade reports.
- Reinforce classroom concepts with practice tests and instant quizzes.
- Integrate grade reports easily with Learning Management Systems including Blackboard, D2L, and Moodle.

Instructor Library

The Connect Instructor Library is a repository for additional resources to improve student engagement in and out of the class. It provides all the critical resources instructors need to build their course.

- Access instructor resources.
- View assignments and resources created for past sections.
- Post your own resources for students to use.

Instructor Resources

Connect is a one-stop shop for instructor resources, including:

Instructor's Manual Revised by the text authors, Verna Pangman, University of Winnipeg, and Anne MacKenzie-Rivers, this comprehensive guide includes an overview of each chapter, learning outcomes, suggestions and resources for lecture topics, classroom activities, projects, and suggestions for video and multimedia lecture enhancements.

Test Bank The Test Bank provides a wide variety of book-specific test questions. Revised and updated by the text author, Verna Pangman, University of Winnipeg, accuracy-checked to ensure it meets our highest standards of excellence, and available as Word files, the questions in the Test Bank are also provided in an easy-to-use electronic testing program. It accommodates a wide range of question types and allows instructors to add their own questions. The program is available for Windows and Macintosh environments.

NEW Case Study Test Bank: Written by co-author Anne MacKenzie-Rivers, the new case study test bank features an original and fully developed scenario for each chapter accompanied by a series of auto-gradable questions designed to assess students' comprehension of key chapter concepts, important development theories, and ongoing themes throughout the text. Uniquely cumulative in nature, case study test bank touches upon not just the chapter's content in isolation, but contextualizes it within the larger framework of what has come before. As with the main test bank, the case study test bank is available in Connect as well as paper-based test bank files.

Microsoft® PowerPoint® Presentations These presentations cover the key points of the chapter and include graphics. Revised by Karen Catney, Clinical Director of Alliance Youth Service, Inc., the presentation slides can be used as-is or modified to meet the instructor's needs.

Superior Learning Solutions and Support

The McGraw-Hill Education team is ready to help instructors assess and integrate any of our products, technology, and services into your course for optimal teaching and learning performance. Whether it's helping your students improve their grades, or putting your entire course online, the McGraw-Hill Education team is here to help you do it. Contact your Learning Solutions Consultant today to learn how to maximize all of McGraw-Hill Education's resources.

For more information, please visit us online:http://www.mheducation.ca/he/solutions

Acknowledgements

The Canadian authors would like to thank Scott Hardie, Product Manager; Sarah Fulton May, Product Developer; Joanne Limebeer, Supervising Editor; Janice Dyer, Copy Editor and Proofreader; Mary Rose MacLachlan, Permissions Editor; and the helpful, thoughtful team of people at McGraw-Hill Education Canada whose professionalism, insights, suggestions, and cheerfulness made working on this text a pleasure.

Last, but not least, we extend our thanks to those instructors whose thoughtful reviews informed the text:

Delphine Collin-Vezina, McGill University
Lucia New, Saskatchewan Polytechnic
Fiona Gironella, Grant MacEwan University
Verna Raab, Mount Royal University

Anne MacKenzie-Rivers and Verna Pangman

SECTION 1

The Life-Span Developmental Perspective

CHAPTER 1

The Life-Span Perspective

CHAPTER OUTLINE

The Life-Span Perspective

LO1 Examine life-span development and describe the characteristics of the life-span perspective.

- **Life-Span Development**
- **The Importance of Studying Life-Span Development**

The Role of Context

LO2 Describe the term *context* and examine the role it plays in understanding growth and development.

Developmental Processes

LO3 Reflect upon the processes of development.

- **Biological, Cognitive, and Socio-Emotional Processes**

Periods of Development

LO4 Reflect upon the periods of development and the concept of age.

- **The Periods of Development**
- **The Concept of Age**

Issues in Life-Span Development

LO5 Outline three prominent issues in life-span development.

- **Interactional Model**
- **Continuity and Discontinuity**
- **Stability and Change**
- **Evaluating Developmental Issues**

Some Contemporary Concerns

LO6 Appraise several major contemporary concerns.

- **Health and Well-Being**
- **Education**
- **Socio-Cultural Contexts**
- **Social Policy**

Research Methods and Challenges

LO7 Compare and contrast research methodology and challenges.

- **Methods of Collecting Data**
- **Research Designs**
- **Research Challenges**

"We reach backward to our parents and forward to our children, and through our children to a future we will never see, but about which we need to care."

—CARL JUNG, TWENTIETH-CENTURY SWISS PSYCHIATRIST

© Geri Lavrov/Getty Images

Our Amazing Brain Over the Life Span

Undoubtedly you have observed changes in yourself over the years. How different are you now from your baby pictures? How does your behaviour today differ from when you were 10 years old? 15 years old? How do you account for these changes? Not as obvious as some of the physical and behavioural changes, but equally important, is the growth and development of our brain over the course of our lives. From the moment of conception and throughout our life span, changes in the brain enable us to understand and respond to the world around us. Neuroscientists are just beginning to understand the magnitude of these changes.

Fetus Development

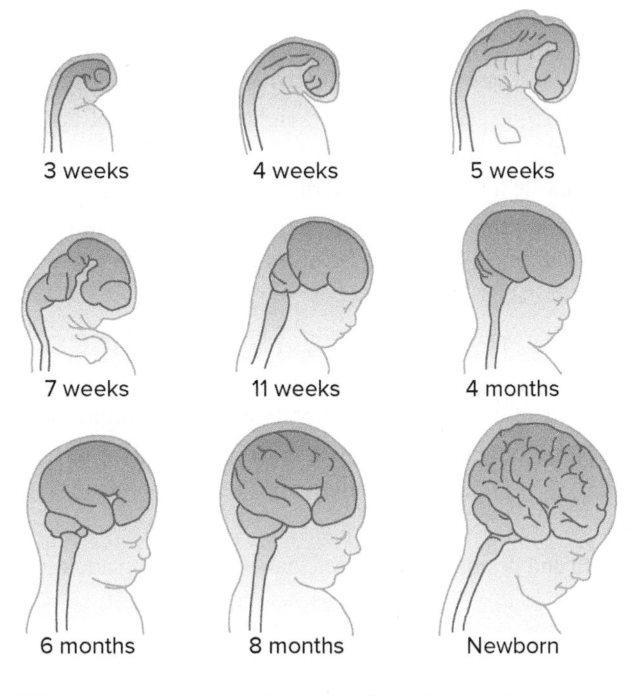

Warning! Take special care: cell explosions!

- Approximately 250 000 new nerve cells are created every minute. One billion are created by the time of birth.
- At the end of four weeks, the zygote's brain emerges.
- At the end of four weeks, the neurons begin to take on specialized tasks.
- Before birth, genes mainly direct the brain's development.

From Birth to Approximately 8–10 Years of Age:

Comstock/PictureQuest

Caution! Work in progress—will begin to interact with the world!

- After birth, environmental experiences associated with the five senses direct the brain's development.
- At birth, the infant's brain weighs 25 percent of its adult weight. By 2 years of age, the brain weighs 75 percent of its adult weight; by 6 years, 90 percent.
- The younger the brain, the more plastic it is; therefore, learning new things, such as language, is easier and more natural.
- The prefrontal cortex, which plays an important role in higher-order cognitive functioning such as decision making, attention, and memory, develops extensively between 3 and 6 years.

From Approximately 8–10 Years of Age Through Ages 20–25:

- As the brain adds the last 10 percent of its weight, its ability to regulate emotions increases.
- The amygdala, which processes emotion, matures earlier than the prefrontal cortex.
- Magnetic resonance imaging (MRI) shows that activity level in the amygdala of teens is considerably higher than in adults.
- Researchers call the rapid growth and pruning of synapses that occurs during adolescence *exuberance*.

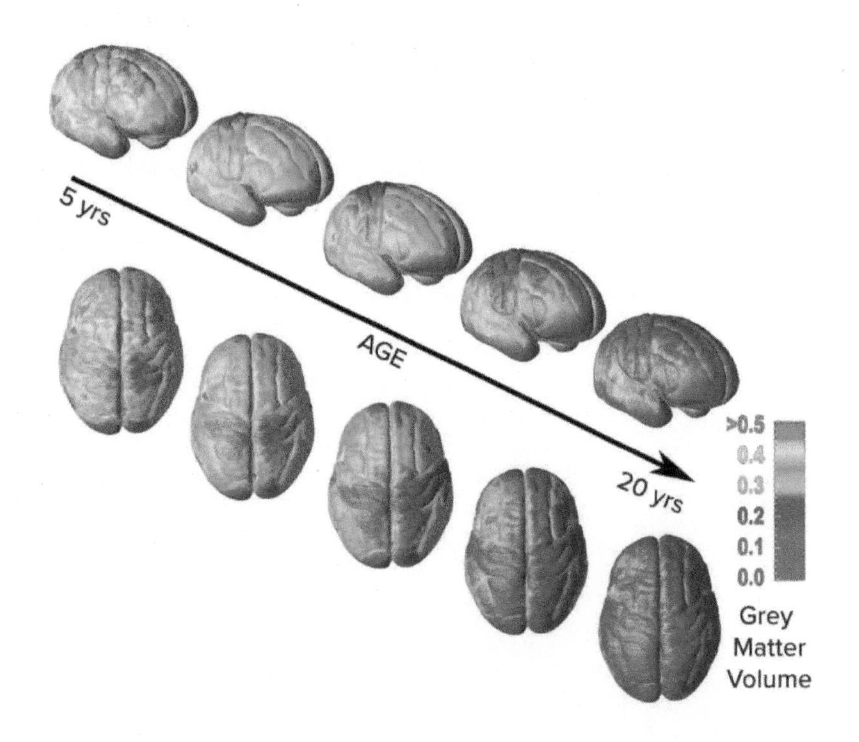

Image courtesy of Paul Thompson (USC) and Judith Rapoport (NIMH), and previously published in PNAS (2008)

Under Renovation: Much growth and exuberance! Please excuse our dust!

From Approximately 20–25 Years of Age Through Ages 60–65:

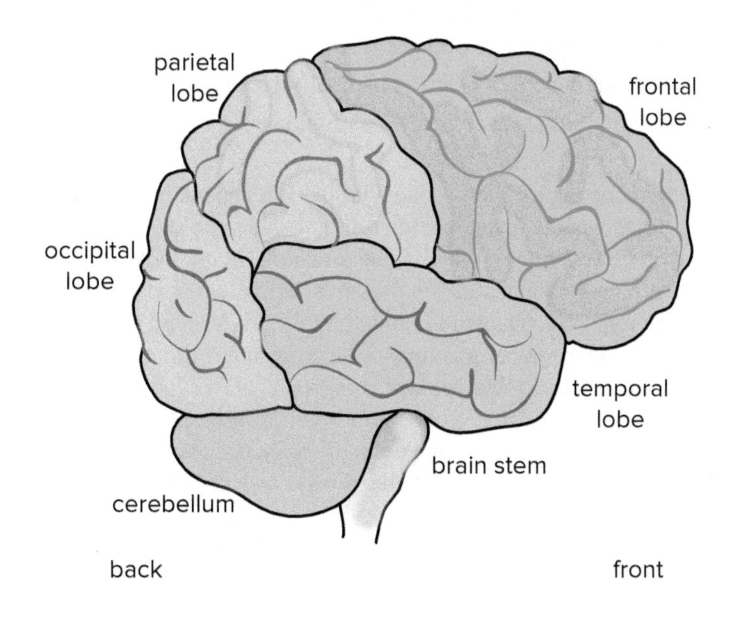

Primalchaos/Wikimedia Commons from National Institutes of Health

Welcome! Newly renovated and fully functioning!

- The exuberance of the adolescent brain is not completed until somewhere between the ages of 20 and 25.
- The myelin sheath, the layer of fat cells that insulates nerve cells and enables nerve impulses to travel rapidly, plays an important role in inhibiting behaviour. Myelination of the prefrontal cortex is not completed until our early twenties.
- Athleticism and physical strength peak in early adulthood.
- Creativity, which requires patience and practice and considerable self-regulation, peaks in middle adulthood.
- Unless compromised by disease, the adult brain remains plastic and grows more efficient.

From Approximately 60–65 Years of Age Through Age 120

monkeybusinessimages/Getty Images

Welcome! Please be mindful of possible loose connections!

- Physical, mental, and social activity, as well as a sense of purpose, are associated with healthy brain activity in late adulthood. A subject of contemporary research is to determine whether the brain remains healthy because of these activities or whether disengagement is an early sign of dementia.
- The first system of the brain to show age is memory. The prefrontal cortex loses its ability to hold information.
- Active brains maintain their capacity for abstract and analytical thinking.

With conception, when one heroic sperm among millions—one with its own genetic makeup and cultural legacy—manages to penetrate an ovum, with its own unique genetic makeup and cultural legacy, the story of prenatal development begins to unfold. The details of the story depend, however, on the individual situation. Many individuals who are unable to conceive through sexual intercourse turn to alternative methods of reproductive technologies to fulfill their parental desires. A few questions may arise, such as: Was the pregnancy planned? Is this the first pregnancy? Has the couple been taking fertility treatments? Is the mother a teenager? How is the father reacting to the pregnancy? Equally important are the responses from the prospective grandparents, brothers and sisters, relatives, and friends. Whatever the situation, everyone involved will be bubbling over with myriad thoughts and emotions. Everyone's brain will also be highly engaged, working night and day, celebrating, planning, worrying, and anticipating. At the same time, the brain of the unborn fetus continues to explode as the actual brain starts to become a fully fledged organ with specialized parts and hemispheres. Our brain continues to change throughout the life span.

The sketches and fast facts above highlight some of the significant changes in the brain at various points in the life span.

Throughout the text, you will learn about the growth and development of the brain. You will read more about the lightning-speed rate of growth during the prenatal and infancy stages, the consolidation in childhood, the restructuring in adolescence, the further consolidation in adulthood, and the changes in connectivity in late adulthood. You will also read about how the brain is affected by chemical substances, injury, and disease. Our brain's ability to respond consciously and unconsciously to myriad stimuli, to accommodate injury, heal, and much more, is truly inspiring.

But here's the most inspiring of insights about the brain: We can enhance our brain's performance by our own efforts. Thus, learning about the brain provides a wonderful mix of instruction, amazement, and self-improvement. As you gain knowledge, you're in a better position to improve its functioning and thereby increase the quality of your life.

—Dr. Richard Restak, neurologist, psychologist, and author of many books about the brain (Sweeney, 2009, p. 152).

Family photographs of your grandmother or grandfather's wedding, like those of yourself as a baby, illustrate some of the changes that take place over a lifetime. The changes we see in photographs show the more obvious physical or biological changes. We are also well aware of accompanying emotional changes; certainly, a baby does not have the same emotional response to a loved one as newlyweds have to each other, and we have more strategies to help us cope with disappointment than we did when we were four years old. As the opening vignette illustrates, the physiology of our brain, and thus our capacity for thinking, understanding, and creating meaning, changes throughout our lives. The neuroplasticity of the brain enables us to heal, accommodate injury, make decisions, and sustain ourselves.

The Life-Span Perspective

LO1 Examine life-span development and describe the characteristics of the life-span perspective.

- **Life-Span Development**
- **The Importance of Studying Life-Span Development**

Life-Span Development

Each life is a unique and fascinating biography. Understanding the rhythms and patterns of growth and development allows us to better understand and weave together the portrait of our present, our past, and, to some extent, our future.

How might we benefit from examining life-span development? Perhaps you are, or will be, a parent, social worker, law-enforcement officer, nurse, or teacher. If so, understanding others is, or will be, a part of your everyday life. The more you learn about them, the more rewarding your relationships will be. Most development involves growth, but it also includes decline (as in dying). In exploring development, we will examine the life span from the point of conception until the time when life (at least, life as we know it) ends. You will see yourself as an infant, as a child, and as an adolescent, and be stimulated to think about how those years influenced the kind of individual you are today. Not only will you gain greater insights about yourself and those with whom you interact professionally and socially, you may better understand the challenges facing the loved ones in your life as well.

Although growth and development are dramatic during the first two decades of life, they continue throughout the life span. The life-span approach emphasizes developmental change throughout adulthood as well as childhood (Baltes, 2009; Park & Schwarz, 2009; Schaie, 2007). **Life-span development** is the pattern of movement or change that begins at conception and continues through the human life span.

The Importance of Studying Life-Span Development

Characteristics of the Life-Span Perspective

The belief that development occurs throughout life is central to the life-span perspective on human development, but this perspective has other characteristics as well. According to life-span development expert Paul Baltes (1939–2006), the **life-span perspective** views development as lifelong, multidimensional, multidirectional, plastic, multidisciplinary, and contextual, and as a process that involves growth, maintenance, and regulation of loss (Baltes, 2003, 2009; Baltes,

Lindenberger, & Staudinger, 2006). In Baltes's view, it is important to understand that development is constructed through biological, socio-cultural, and individual factors working together (Baltes, Reuter-Lorenz, & Rösler, 2006). Let's look at each of these characteristics.

DEVELOPMENT IS LIFELONG

Is early adulthood the endpoint of development? According to the life-span perspective, it is not. In addition, no age period dominates development. Researchers are increasingly studying the experiences and psychological orientations of adults at different points in their development. Later in this chapter, we will describe the age periods of development and their characteristics.

DEVELOPMENT IS MULTIDIMENSIONAL

Development consists of biological, cognitive, and socio-emotional processes (later in the chapter, we will explore these key processes of life-span development). Even within a process such as cognition, various components such as opportunity, internalization, and support play a vital role.

DEVELOPMENT IS MULTIDIRECTIONAL

During early adulthood, as individuals establish romantic relationships, the time spent with their friends may decrease. During late adulthood, older adults might become wiser by being able to call on experience to guide their intellectual decision making, but they perform more poorly on tasks that require speed in processing information (Baltes, 2009; Baltes & Kunzmann, 2007; Salthouse, 2009b).

Courtesy of Paul Baltes, Margaret Baltes Foundation

Paul Baltes (1939–2006) was a leading architect of the life-span perspective of development. Here he is seen conversing with one of the long-time research participants in the Berlin Aging Study that he directed. She joined the study in the early 1990s and participated six times in extensive physical, medical, psychological, and social assessments. In her professional life, she was a medical doctor. At the time of this picture, she was 96 years of age.

DEVELOPMENT IS PLASTIC

A key developmental research agenda item is the search for plasticity and its constraints (Baltes, Lindenberger, & Staudinger, 2006). **Plasticity** means the capacity for change. For example, can intellectual skills still be improved through education for individuals in their seventies or eighties? Is there a possibility that these intellectual abilities are cast in stone by the time people are in their thirties so that further improvement is impossible? In one research study, the reasoning abilities of older adults were improved through retraining (Kramer & Morrow, 2009). However, it is possible that we possess less capacity for change when we become older (Baltes, Reuter-Lorenz, & Rösler, 2006). The search for plasticity and its constraints is a key element on the contemporary agenda for developmental research; in fact, the contemporary studies of neuroplasticity and neuropsychology have developed around this concept (Kramer & Morrow, 2009).

DEVELOPMENT IS MULTIDISCIPLINARY

Psychologists, sociologists, anthropologists, neuroscientists, and medical researchers all study human development and share an interest in unlocking the mysteries of development through the life span. What constraints on intelligence are set by the individual's heredity and health status? How universal are cognitive and socio-emotional changes? How do environmental contexts influence intellectual development?

DEVELOPMENT INVOLVES GROWTH, MAINTENANCE, AND REGULATION

Baltes and his colleagues (Baltes, Staudinger, & Lindenberger, 2006) believe that the mastery of life often involves conflict and competition among three goals of human development: growth, maintenance, and regulation. As individuals enter middle and late adulthood, the maintenance and regulation of their capacities take centre stage away from growth. Thus, a 70-year-old woman may aim not to improve her tennis shot, but to maintain her independence and continue to play. As we age, the goal to seek growth in intellectual capacities (such as memory) or physical capacities may yield to maintenance of skills or minimizing deterioration. In Section 9, "Late Adulthood," we will discuss these ideas in greater depth.

DEVELOPMENT IS A CO-CONSTRUCTION OF BIOLOGY, CULTURE, AND THE INDIVIDUAL

Development is a co-construction of biological, cultural, and individual factors working together (Baltes, 2009). For example, our brain shapes and interprets culture, but it is also shaped by culture and the experiences that we have or pursue. We can author a unique developmental path by actively choosing from the environment the things that optimize our lives (Rathunde & Csikszentmihalyi, 2006).

DEVELOPMENT IS CONTEXTUAL

All development occurs within a **context**, or a setting. Contexts include families, socio-economic status, schools, peer groups, churches, cities, neighbourhoods, university laboratories, countries, and so on. Each of these settings is influenced by historical, economic, geological, social, and cultural factors (Matsumoto & Juang, 2008; Mehrotra & Wagner, 2009).

Walter Hodges/Corbis/Getty Images

How might growth versus maintenance and regulation be reflected in the development of this grandmother and her granddaughter?

To this point, we have discussed the life-span perspective. For a review, see the Reach Your Learning Outcomes section at the end of this chapter.

The Role of Context

LO2 Describe the term *context* and examine the role it plays in understanding growth and development.

Context

As we just noted, all development occurs within a context; however, like individuals, contexts also can change. Thus, individuals are changing beings in a changing world. As a result of these changes, contexts exert three types of influences (Baltes, 2003): (1) normative age-graded influences, (2) normative history-graded influences, and (3) non-normative or highly individualized life events. Each of these types can have a biological or environmental impact on development.

NORMATIVE AGE-GRADED INFLUENCES

Normative age-graded influences are similar for individuals in a particular age group. These influences include biological processes such as puberty and menopause. They also include socio-cultural and environmental processes such as beginning formal education (usually at about age 5 in Canada), and retirement (which often occurs in the fifties or sixties). Forty or fifty years ago, Canadians married in their late teens or early twenties and rarely lived together prior to marriage. Now, couples typically cohabitate, postponing marriage until closer to age 30.

NORMATIVE HISTORY-GRADED INFLUENCES

Normative history-graded influences are common to people of a particular generation because of historical circumstances. For example, in their youth, North American baby boomers shared the experience of the Separatist Movement in Quebec, Trudeau-mania, and the British invasion. Other examples of normative history-graded influences include economic, political, and social upheavals such as the war in Afghanistan, the LGBTQ rights movements of the 1990s, the terrorist attacks of 9/11/2001, as well as the integration of computers and cell phones into everyday life (Schaie, 2007). In Canada in 2013, tropical storm Leslie could be considered a non-normative history-graded influence, as the storm affected thousands of lives on the eastern coastline. The Canadian Hurricane Centre warned the people of Newfoundland and Labrador to expect 12 hours of intense weather over the land; people had to cope with power outages and road hazards, which influenced their lives.

Mark Pearson/Alamy Stock Photo

What are some of the personal, historical, and cultural factors that are changed by a normative history-graded influence, such as the natural disaster in Haiti pictured here?

NON-NORMATIVE LIFE EVENTS

Non-normative life events are occurrences that are not anticipated but have a major impact on an individual's life. For example, most of us anticipate that we will outlive our parents; however, a parent who dies unexpectedly when a child is young illustrates a non-normative life event. Non-normative life events can also be positive events, such as winning the lottery or getting an unexpected career opportunity with special privileges. An important aspect of understanding the role of non-normative life events is to focus on how people adapt to them.

Life Expectancy

Life expectancy refers to the number of years an individual is expected to live starting from birth. Life expectancy is based on specific mortality statistics for a given observation period, typically three years. In 2009–2011, life expectancy for Canadians averaged 82 years. Males and females averaged 79.3 and 83.6 years, respectively. During that same period (2009–2011), males continued to have a lower life expectancy than females. The life expectancy difference in years between males and females has become smaller, from a difference of 4.5 years in 2007–2009 to 4.3 years in 2009–2011 (Statistics Canada, 2013).

For both men and women, life expectancy has been significantly higher in urban areas compared to rural areas (CIHR, 2006). Higher overall mortality rates seem to be driven by higher death rates from causes such as circulatory disease, injury, and suicide rates. On the other hand, more rural residents than urban residents report a strong sense of community belonging, a measure of social capital (DesMeules et al., 2012).

Perhaps more than any other single factor, context plays a vital role in life expectancy because context determines access to water, hygiene, health care, and social services. The country and community in which we live plays a determining factor in personal safety. Here again, context is critical, as life expectancy represents one of the planet's greatest disparities. In some parts of the world, many children do not live long enough to even go to school, and many young women die during childbirth.

The 2015 Human Development Report, published by the United Nations Development Programme (UNDP), indicates that substantial progress has been made in many aspects of human development. Today people are living longer, more children are going to school, and more people have access to clean water and basic sanitation. Work by artists, musicians, and writers is enriching human lives. The context of work is changing, with implications for human development. Driving the transformation of work are globalization and technological advancements, particularly the digital revolution. In the past 10 years, global trade in goods and services almost doubled—reaching nearly $23 trillion in 2014, up from $13 trillion in 2005. At the same time, knowledge has become central to production. Now is the time to be a worker with specific skills and the right education. Social entrepreneurs are also emerging as a new workforce committed to addressing social problems. One of the UN's sustainable goals is to end poverty in all its forms everywhere (United Nations, 2015).

The Human Development Index (HDI) combines data related to life expectancy, educational levels, and per capita income to measure the overall well-being of individuals. Additional related factors, such as the availability of fresh water, a healthy childhood, nutritious foods, hygiene, sanitation, and access to health care, further contribute to overall health (United Nations, 2015). In examining the HDI 2014 trend, Canada ranks 9th among 188 countries; Norway ranks first, and the lowest ranking country is Niger. However, there have been large improvements in life expectancy, school enrolment, literacy, and income in all countries (United Nations, 2015). See Figure 1.1 for an illustration of life expectancy in different parts of the world.

Figure 1.1

World Variations in Life Expectancy

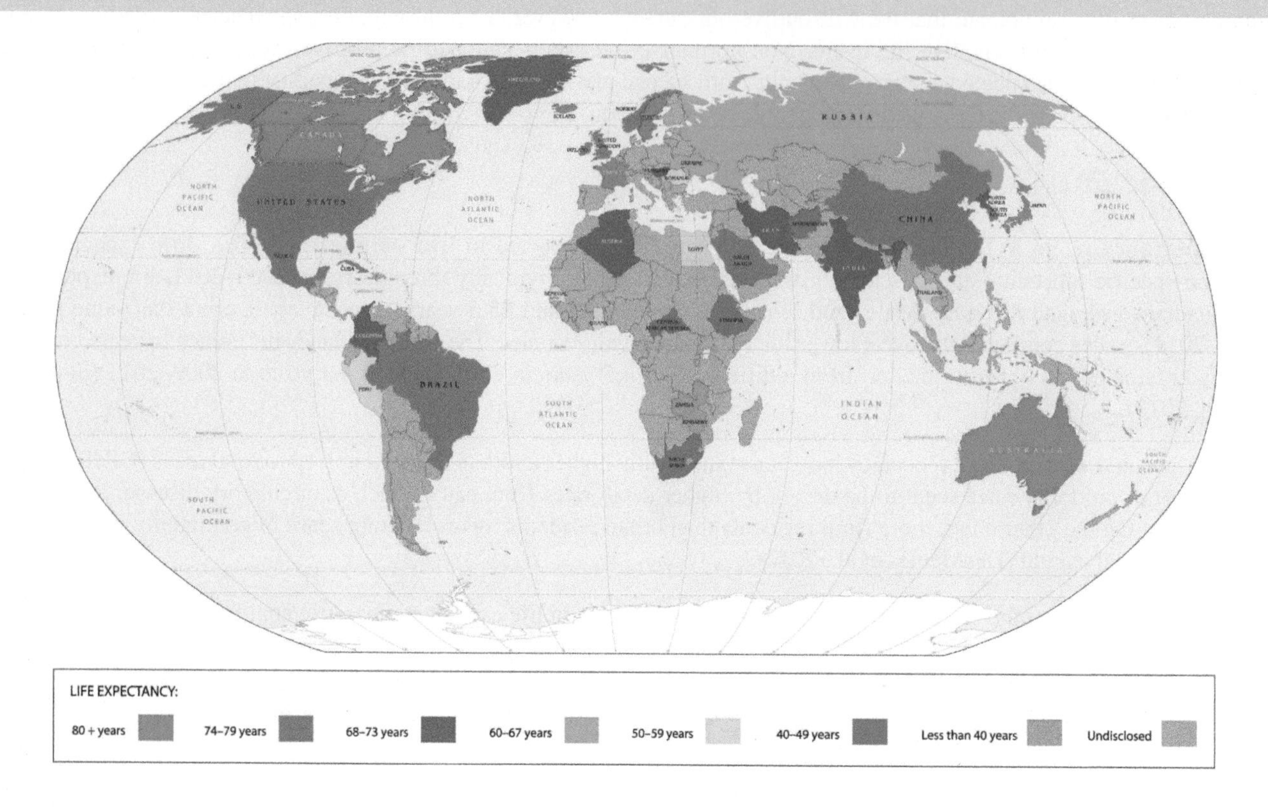

The World Factbook 2013-14. Washington, DC: Central Intelligence Agency, 2013.

This map illustrates the disparities in life expectancy around the world. Notice the many areas where the average of life expectancy is undisclosed. *What factors might contribute to this? What factors contribute to those areas of the world where life expectancy is less than 50 years?*

Today, most people live longer, are more educated, and have more access to goods and services than ever before. Even in economically impoverished countries, the health and education of their people have improved greatly. Progress has been credited, at least in part, to individuals who now exercise their voices to select leaders, influence public decisions, and share knowledge to improve their quality of life. However, not all countries have seen rapid progress, and the variations are striking. People in the former Soviet Union and in Southern Africa, for example, have endured times of regress, especially in health matters (United Nations, 2015).

Although consistently ranked among the healthiest countries of the world, disparities occur in our peaceful nation, particularly in the northern areas inhabited by Aboriginal Canadians. The life expectancy for Aboriginal Canadians, although improving, remains lower than that of the rest of the Canadian population. For example, the prevalence of obesity is significantly higher among Aboriginal compared to non-Aboriginal populations, particularly in Alberta, Manitoba, Ontario, and Quebec; however, this is not the case in Nunavut (CIHI, 2011).

Median Age and Centenarians

Between the 2006 and 2011 censuses, Canada's population increased 5.9 percent compared with the 5.4 percent increase during the previous five-year period (Statistics Canada, 2012h). In fact, between 2006 and 2011, Canada's population increased at a faster rate than the population of any other member of the G8 group of industrialized nations. During roughly the first decade of the 21st century, net international migration (the difference between the number of immigrants and emigrants) accounted for two-thirds of Canada's population growth. Meanwhile, natural increase (the difference between births and deaths) was accountable for only about one-third (Statistics Canada, 2012h).

In July 2011, the median age of Canada's population was estimated at 39.9 years, up 0.2 years from the same date a year earlier. Two major factors believed to have contributed to the increase in median age are decreased fertility rates and increased life expectancy (Statistics Canada, 2011a). Interestingly, as a result of gains in life expectancy, an increasing number of Canadians, called centenarians, are reaching the age of 100 (Statistics Canada, 2013b). The 2011 census counted 4 870 women and 955 men aged 100 and over. More women than men reach the age of 100 because, compared to men, women experience a lower probability of dying at all ages (Statistics Canada, 2013b). In the United States, the rate of centenarians was slightly lower than it was in Canada. Japan had the highest rate at nearly at 37 centenarians per 100 000 persons. Meanwhile, Russia had only 4 centenarians per 100 000 persons (Statistics in Canada, 2013b). These demographic estimates are interesting because they portray the life-span development of individuals from birth to death. See Figure 1.2 for an illustration of the aging population in Canada.

Figure 1.2

The Aging Senior Population in Canada

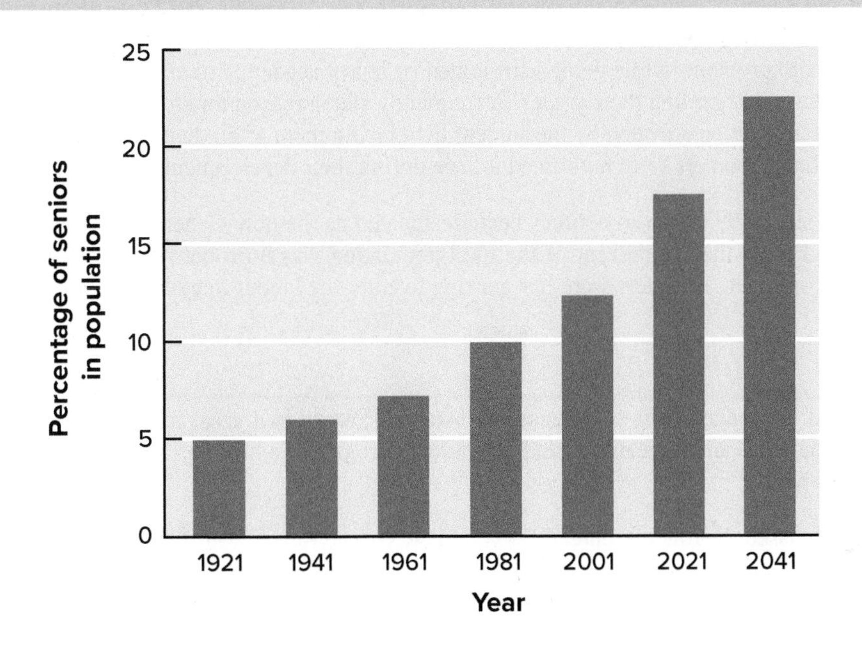

Source: Adapted from Statistics Canada, Age Groups (13) and Sex (3) for the Population of Canada, Provinces and Territories, 1921 to 2006 Censuses - 100% Data 97-551-XCB 2006005 Census Year 2006 Released July 17, 2007; Population Projections for Canada, Provinces and Territories 2009 to 2036 91-520-XWE 2010001 2009 to 2036, Released May 26, 2010

The percentage of seniors in the general population has been increasing.

Generations in Canada

In 2011, many generations comprised the Canadian population. The best-known generation is the baby boomers. The largest annual increase in the number of births since 1921 occurred between 1945 and 1946. This particular period of time showed an increase of about 15 percent in the population, and it marked the beginning of the baby boom period (Statistics Canada, 2011a). In the near future, many baby boomers will reach the age of 65; the result will be an acceleration of the aging population in Canada. By 2031, all baby boomers will have reached the age of 65, and the proportion of seniors is expected to reach 23 percent compared to 15 percent in 2011 (Statistics Canada, 2011c).

critical thinking

A natural implication of an increasing median age is that the population of those under 25 is decreasing. What do you think are the personal, social, economic, and political implications of our aging population? Compare and contrast relevant characteristics (housing, communication, and possible others) between the young population (under 25) and the aging population in Canada. Draw a representation of a centenarian's perception about his/her quality of life today. Specify the social environment of your centenarian.

The second significant generation is that of the parents of the baby boomers. This generation can be defined as all individuals born during the 22-year inter-war period (1919–1940). In 2016, these people were between 76 and 97 years of age.

According to Statistics Canada (2011a), 27 percent of the total population belongs to the children of the baby boomers, best known as Generation X. This generation may also be called Generation Y or "echo of the baby boom." Generation X is smaller than the baby boom generation because the baby boomers had fewer children than their parents did. Generation X individuals grew up in a world of mind-blowing technological invention. Not only did Generation X experience the impact of personal computers and other advanced technology throughout their developmental years, but in addition many experienced a tense environment of separation and divorce, two-parent working families, and institutional daycare, as well as more permissive parenting (Sudheimer, 2009).

It is interesting to consider whether the stresses experienced by current university students might be rooted in the events that have occurred in their lives. Results of a 2011 survey of 1600 students at the University of Alberta indicated that 51 percent of students reported that within the past 12 months they "felt things were hopeless." A shocking 7 percent admitted that they had "seriously considered suicide," and about 1 percent had attempted it (Lunau, 2012). A discussion paper delivered in June 2011 at Queen's University in Ontario offered a range of explanations. One such explanation claimed that students are grappling with mental health problems while being surrounded by heavy academic demands. Another explanation had to do with their parents' expectations regarding their grades. A frequently stated reason for student stress seems to be the looming recognition of a tough job market, aggravated by the student debt facing them at graduation (Lunau, 2012). It can be argued that these are factors the baby boomers were not forced to face during their developmental years.

Finally, individuals born since 1993 have sometimes been designated as the new Generation Z, or the Internet Generation. Canada's 2011 census indicated that 22 percent of the total population was born between 1993 and 2011. In 2011, these people were 18 years old or under, and a few were just starting to enter the labour market (Statistics Canada, 2011c).

Socio-Economic Status (SES)

Another major contextual influence is our socio-economic status. Poverty is a great inhibitor to growth and development because access to health services and recreational and educational programs is limited. You will read more about the impact of poverty throughout the text.

To this point, we have discussed the role of context. For a review, see the Reach Your Learning Outcomes section at the end of this chapter.

Developmental Processes

LO3 Reflect upon the processes of development.

Each of us develops partly like all other individuals, partly like some other individuals, and partly like no other individual. Most of the time, our attention is directed to an individual's uniqueness. But psychologists who study life-span development are drawn to our shared, as well as to our unique, characteristics. Most of us—Leonardo da Vinci, Sir John A. Macdonald, Justin Trudeau, Clara Hughes, Terry Fox, you—walked at about 1 year of age, engaged in fantasy play as a young child, and became more independent as a youth. Each of us, if we live long enough, will experience the aging process and the deaths of family members and friends.

At the beginning of this chapter, we defined life-span development as the pattern of change that begins at conception and continues through the life span. The opening vignette illustrates how the brain changes throughout the course of life; however, the patterns are incredibly complex because our growth and development reflect the integrative and fluid product of biological, cognitive, and socio-emotional processes (see Figure 1.3). The following discussion provides brief definitions of these processes around which this text is organized. As you read, you will learn how these processes develop at different stages of the life span.

Figure 1.3
Processes and Periods of Development

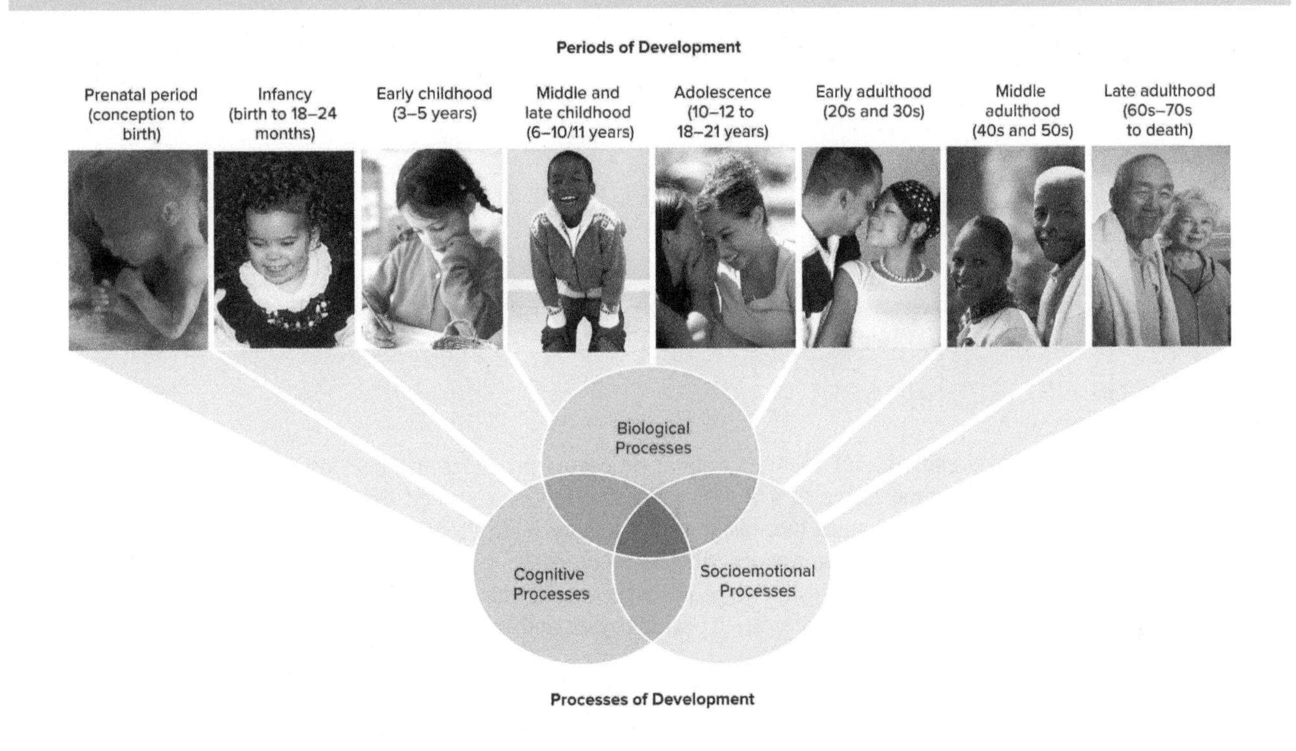

From L to R © Brand X Pictures/PunchStock; © Digital Vision; © PhotoAlto sas / Alamy Stock Photo; © George Doyle/Stockbyte/Getty Images; © SW Productions/Getty Images; © Blue Moon Stock/Alamy Stock Photo; © Doug Menuez/Getty Images; © Ryan McVay/Getty Images

The unfolding of life's periods of development is influenced by the interaction of biological, cognitive, and socio-emotional processes.

Biological, Cognitive, and Socio-Emotional Processes

Biological processes produce changes in an individual's physical nature. Genes inherited from parents, the development of the brain, height and weight gains, changes in motor skills, the hormonal changes of puberty, and cardiovascular decline all reflect the role of biological processes in development.

Cognitive processes refer to changes in the individual's thought, intelligence, and language. Watching a colourful mobile swinging above the crib, putting together a two-word sentence, memorizing a poem, imagining what it would be like to be a movie star, and solving a crossword puzzle all involve cognitive processes.

Socio-emotional processes involve changes in the individual's relationships with other people, changes in emotions, and changes in personality. An infant's smile in response to her mother's touch, a young boy's aggressive attack on a playmate, a girl's development of assertiveness, an older sibling's concern for a younger sibling, an adolescent's joy at the senior prom, and the affection of an elderly couple all reflect the role of the socio-emotional processes in development.

In many instances, biological, cognitive, and socio-emotional processes are bidirectional. For example, biological processes can influence cognitive processes and vice versa. Thus, although usually we will study the different processes of development (biological, cognitive, and socio-emotional) in separate locations, keep in mind that we are talking about the development of an integrated individual with a mind and body that are interdependent.

To this point, we have discussed developmental processes. For a review, see the Reach Your Learning Outcomes section at the end of this chapter.

Periods of Development

LO4 Reflect upon the periods of development and concept of age.

- **The Periods of Development**
- **The Concept of Age**

The Periods of Development

The interplay of biological, cognitive, and socio-emotional processes produces the periods of the human life span. A developmental period refers to a time frame in a person's life that is characterized by certain features. For example, in the opening vignette you read about changes that occur to our brains at different periods in our lives. For the purposes of organization and understanding, we commonly describe development in terms of these periods. The most widely used classification of developmental periods involves the eight-period sequence shown in Figure 1.3. Approximate age ranges are listed for the periods to provide a general idea of when a period begins and ends.

The *prenatal period* is the time from conception to birth. It involves tremendous growth—from a single cell to an organism complete with brain and behavioural capabilities, produced in approximately a nine-month period.

Infancy is the developmental period extending from birth to 18 or 24 months. Infancy is a time of extreme dependence upon adults. Many psychological activities are just beginning—language, symbolic thought, sensorimotor coordination, and social learning, for example.

Early childhood is the developmental period extending from the end of infancy to about 5 or 6 years of age. This period is sometimes called the "preschool years." During this time, young children learn to become more self-sufficient and to care for themselves, develop school readiness skills (following instructions, identifying letters), and spend many hours in play with peers. Grade 1 typically marks the end of early childhood.

Middle and late childhood is the developmental period extending from about 6 to 11 years of age. This period is sometimes called the "elementary school years." The fundamental skills of reading, writing, and arithmetic are mastered. The child is formally exposed to the larger world and its culture. Achievement becomes a more central theme of the child's world, and self-control increases.

Adolescence is the developmental period of transition from childhood to early adulthood, entered at approximately 10 to 12 years of age and ending at 18 to 21 years of age. Adolescence begins with rapid physical changes—dramatic gains in height and weight, changes in body contour, and the development of sexual characteristics, such as enlargement of the breasts, development of pubic and facial hair, and deepening of the voice. At this point in development, the pursuit of independence and an identity is prominent. Thought is more logical, abstract, and idealistic. More time is spent outside of the family with a peer group.

Early adulthood is the developmental period beginning in the late teens or early twenties and lasting through the thirties. It is a time of establishing personal and economic independence, career development, and, for many, selecting a mate, learning to live with someone in an intimate way, starting a family, and rearing children.

Middle adulthood is the developmental period beginning at approximately 40 years of age and extending to about age 60. It is a time of expanding personal and social involvement and responsibility; of assisting the next generation in becoming competent, mature individuals; and of reaching and maintaining satisfaction in a career.

Late adulthood has the longest span of any period of development, and as noted earlier, the number of people in this age group has been increasing dramatically. As a result, life-span developmentalists have been paying more attention to differences within late adulthood (Scheibe, Freund, & Baltes, 2007). Paul Baltes and Jacqui Smith (2003) argue that a major change takes place in older adults' lives as they become the "oldest-old," on average at about 85 years of age. For example, the "young-old" (classified as 65 through 84 in this analysis) have substantial potential for physical and cognitive fitness, retain much of their cognitive capacity, and can develop strategies to cope with the gains and losses of aging. In contrast, the oldest-old (85 and older) show considerable loss in cognitive skills, experience an increase in chronic stress, and are more frail (Baltes & Smith, 2003).

Thus, Baltes and Smith conclude that considerable plasticity and adaptability characterize adults from their sixties until their mid-eighties, but that the oldest-old have reached the limits of their functional capacity, which makes interventions to improve their lives difficult. Nonetheless, as will be described in later chapters, considerable variation exists in how much the oldest-old retain their capabilities (Barrett, 2012).

Life-span developmentalists who focus on adult development and aging increasingly describe life-span development in terms of four "ages" (Baltes, 2006; Willis & Schaie, 2006):

- *First age:* Childhood and adolescence
- *Second age:* Prime adulthood, twenties through fifties
- *Third age:* Approximately 60 to 79 years of age
- *Fourth age:* Approximately 80 years and older

The major emphasis in this conceptualization is on the third and fourth ages, especially the increasing evidence that individuals in the third age are healthier and can lead more active, productive lives than their predecessors in earlier generations. However, when older adults reach their eighties, especially 85 and over (fourth age), health and well-being decline.

The Concept of Age

In our description of the periods of the life span, we linked approximate age ranges with the periods. But we also have noted that there are variations in the capabilities of individuals of the same age, and we have seen how changes with age can be exaggerated. How important is age when we try to understand an individual? Are age and happiness related?

critical thinking

What different responses might a person have to a major disappointment if the person were 4 years old? 10 years? 16 years? 22 years? 35 years? 50 years? 70 years? Would the reactions differ if the individual were male or female? In what ways would you respond to a major celebration in your life today? Would the response be different in another 10 years?

Age and Happiness

Consider a 2008 large-scale, U.S. study of approximately 28 000 individuals from age 18 to 88 years that revealed happiness increases with age (Yang, 2008). For example, about 33 percent reported being very happy at 88 years of age, compared with only about 24 percent in their late teens and early twenties. Why might older people report as much or more happiness and life satisfaction as younger people? Despite the increase in physical problems and losses older adults experience, they are more content with what they have in their lives, have better relationships with the people who matter to them, are less pressured to achieve, have more time for leisurely pursuits, and have many years of experience that may help them better adapt to their circumstances with wisdom compared to younger adults (Cornwell, Laumann, & Schumm, 2008; Ram et al., 2008).

The study also stated that baby boomers (those born from 1944 to 1964) report being less happy than individuals born earlier, possibly because they are not lowering their aspirations and idealistic hopes as they age as earlier generations did. Because growing older is a certain outcome of living, it is good to know that we are likely to be just as happy or happier as older adults as when we were younger.

A prime example of an older Canadian adult who has been successful is Jean Chrétien. His public life spanned a course of 40 years. During that time, he served as prime minister of Canada for a decade and led his party to three successive majority governments. He was the fourth Canadian to be honoured with the Order of Merit, considered to be a personal gift from Queen Elizabeth. Jean Chrétien married Aline Chaîné on September 10, 1957.

Another example of a Canadian who is experiencing outstanding success is the current prime minister, Justin Trudeau. Mr. Trudeau is a representative of Generation X who is university educated, socially active, balanced, happy, and family oriented (Schroer, 2016). Prime Minister Trudeau won a Liberal government majority in the fall election of 2015. He is the 23rd Canadian prime minister, identifies himself as a feminist, and he defends women's rights. Furthermore, he met with hundreds of chiefs at the Assembly of First Nations and laid out his philosophy and commitments to Canada's indigenous people to assure them that he would make a significant investment in education programs, increase general funding, and launch an enquiry into missing and murdered indigenous women (Toronto Star, 2015). The Trudeau philosophy includes the promotion of freedom and diversity, as well as a highly democratic government that represents all of Canada. He has opened the doors of Canada to the acceptance of Syrian refugees. He is married to Sophie Grégoire, a Canadian television host and social justice advocate. Together, they have three children and reside (temporarily) at Rideau Cottage while 24 Sussex Drive, the official residence of the prime minister, is renovated (Annett, 2015).

THE CANADIAN PRESS/Adrian Wyld

Conceptions of Age

Like happiness, age can be defined in different ways. The clichés "You're only as old as you feel" or "She is wise beyond her years" illustrate, to some degree, the different connotations of age. The five ways psychologists define age are *chronological, biological, mental, psychological,* and *social.*

CHRONOLOGICAL AGE

Chronological age is the number of years that have elapsed since a person's birth. Many people consider chronological age synonymous with the concept of age. However, some developmentalists argue that chronological age is not relevant to understanding a person's psychological development. A person's age does not cause an individual's development. Rather, events and experiences that accumulate over the years contribute to shaping us. Time is a crude index of many events and experiences and is not in itself a causal factor.

BIOLOGICAL AGE

Biological age is a person's age in terms of biological health. Determining biological age involves knowing the functional capacities of a person's vital organ system. One person's vital capacities may be better or worse than those of others of comparable age. The younger the person's biological age, the longer the person is expected to live, regardless of chronological age.

MENTAL AGE

Mental age is an individual's ability to solve problems on a standardized instrument compared with others of the same chronological age. A child's mental age is used to understand the child's intelligence quotient (IQ). Binet first developed testing instruments in response to educators who wished to provide appropriate guidance to families about children's academic progress.

PSYCHOLOGICAL AGE

Psychological age is an individual's adaptive capacities relative to those of other individuals of the same chronological age. Thus, older adults who continue to learn may be more flexible and motivated. These and other attributes, such as emotional control and lucid thinking, mean that the individual has more strategies available with which to effectively adapt to change. The adaptability of these older adults contrasts sharply with that of chronological age mates who are not motivated, do not continue to learn, are rigid, and do not control their emotions or think clearly.

SOCIAL AGE

According to Marsh and colleagues (2009), **social age** refers to the social understandings and significance that are attached to a person's age. In fact, age-relevant behaviours are probably more influenced by social rules/norms than by biological ones. For example, in predicting the behaviour of an adult woman, it is probably more relevant to know that she is the mother of a 3-year-old child than to know whether she is 20 or 30 years of age.

To this point, we have discussed the periods of development. For a review, see the Reach Your Learning Outcomes section at the end of this chapter.

Issues in Life-Span Development

LO5 Outline three prominent issues in life-span development.

- **Interactional Model**
- **Continuity and Discontinuity**
- **Stability and Change**
- **Evaluating Developmental Issues**

Are we born with specific intellectual capacities, or do life experiences sculpt our talents? When you consider your family members, is one more mathematical than another? More musical? More athletic? Is one more extraverted? More conscientious? If so, why do you suppose that is? Do early experiences determine our later lives? Are our journeys through life marked out ahead of time, or can our experiences change our paths? Are the experiences we have early in our journeys more important than later ones? These questions point to three issues about the nature of development: the roles played by nature and nurture, stability and change, and continuity and discontinuity.

Dawn Russel, competing in the long jump in a Senior Olympics competition in Oregon.

A sedentary, overweight middle-aged man. *Even if Dawn Russel's chronological age is older, might her biological age be younger than the middle-aged man's?*

critical thinking

Siblings differ considerably; one may be extroverted, seeking the limelight, while another may be introverted, preferring books to people. The oldest may excel in math, a middle child in sports, and the youngest in art. One may be intellectually brilliant, another socially intuitive and skilled. Each family member is unique. In what ways does the dynamic interplay that results from the interaction of environment and biological processes shape human development over time? What makes the various aspects that you have identified in your development stand out for you?

Interactional Model

Developmentalists have, for some time now, debated the question of whether developmental change is due to **nature** (hereditary factors) or to **nurture** (environmental factors). This historical debate is called the **nature–nurture controversy** (Berger, 2011). In essence, nature always affects nurture and nurture affects nature. This tendency prompted developmentalists to shift toward an understanding that development could not be understood as a result of separate personal and situational factors. Rather, they claimed, development is a product of a reciprocal interaction between biological and situational factors (Mischel, Shoda, & Ayduk, 2008).

Many theorists have adopted the interactionist view that considers development to be the result of an ongoing dynamic interaction of individual differences and particular conditions and not caused entirely by the individual or the context (Berger, 2011). The proposed interactionists' models are a vast improvement over the either/or theories of depression, for example. Wade and colleagues (2007) argue that by understanding the causes of depression as an interaction among a person's biology, ways of thinking, and experiences, a person is then able to understand why the same precipitating event, such as a minor setback or even the loss of a loved one, might evoke feelings of sadness in one person and extreme depression in another.

Continuity and Discontinuity

Think about your development for a moment. Did you become the person you are gradually, like the slow, cumulative way a seedling grows into a giant oak? Or did you experience sudden, distinct changes in your growth, like the way a caterpillar changes into a butterfly? (See Figure 1.4.)

Figure 1.4
Continuity and Discontinuity in Development

Is our development like that of a seedling gradually growing into a giant oak? Or is it more like that of a caterpillar suddenly becoming a butterfly?

The **continuity–discontinuity issue** focuses on the extent to which development involves gradual, cumulative change (continuity) or distinct stages (discontinuity). In terms of continuity, a child's first word, though seemingly an abrupt, discontinuous event, is actually the result of weeks and months of growth and practice. Puberty, though also seemingly an abrupt, discontinuous occurrence, is actually a gradual process occurring over several years.

In terms of discontinuity, each person is described as passing through a sequence of stages in which change occurs qualitatively, rather than quantitatively. As the oak moves from seedling to giant oak, it becomes *more* oak—its development is continuous. As the caterpillar changes to a butterfly, it is not just more caterpillar; it is a *different kind of organism*—its development is discontinuous. For example, at some point a child moves from the limits of concrete thinking to being able to think abstractly about the world. This is a qualitative, discontinuous change in development, not a quantitative, continuous change.

Stability and Change

Another important developmental topic is the **stability–change issue**, which addresses whether development is best described by stability or by change. The stability–change issue involves the degree to which we become older renditions of our early experience or, instead, develop into someone different from who we were at an earlier point in development. Will the shy child who hides behind the sofa when visitors arrive be a wallflower at college or university parties, or will this child become a sociable, talkative individual?

Many developmentalists who emphasize stability in development argue that stability is the result of heredity and possibly early experiences in life. For example, many argue that if an individual is shy throughout life, this stability is due to heredity and possibly early experiences in which the infant or young child encountered considerable stress when interacting with people.

Developmentalists who emphasize change take the more optimistic view that later experiences can produce change. Recall that in the life-span perspective, plasticity—the potential for change—exists throughout the life span. Experts such as Paul Baltes (2003) argue that with increasing age, and on average, older adults often show less capacity for change in the sense of learning new things than younger adults. However, many older adults continue to be good at practising what they have learned in earlier times.

What is the nature of the early/later experience issue in development?

The roles of early and later experience are an aspect of the stability–change issue that has long been hotly debated. Some argue that unless infants experience a warm, nurturing caregiver in the first year or so of life, their development will never be optimal (George, Cummings, & Davies, 2010). The later-experience advocates see children as malleable throughout development, and believe that later sensitive caregiving is equally important to earlier sensitive caregiving.

Evaluating Developmental Issues

Most life-span developmentalists acknowledge that development is a reciprocal dynamic interaction among an individual's genetic heritage and social experiences and not caused entirely by nature or nurture separately (Berger, 2011; Mischel, Shoda, & Ayduk, 2008).

How can we answer questions about the roles of interactional model, stability and change, and continuity and discontinuity in development? How can we determine, for example, whether memory decline in older adults can be prevented, or whether special care can repair the harm inflicted by child neglect? Research using the scientific method is the best tool we have to answer such questions.

CONNECTING through Social Policy

Courtesy of Douglas Willms

J. DOUGLAS WILLMS, PH.D.

Dr. J. Douglas Willms is a professor and co-director (with Dr. Lucia Tramonte) of the Canadian Research Institute for Social Policy at the University of New Brunswick (UNB). He also holds the Canada Research Chair in Literacy and Human Development. He is a member of the U.S. National Academy of Education, a fellow of the Royal Society of Canada, and president-elect and fellow of the International Academy of Education.

Dr. Willms has published over 200 research articles and monographs pertaining to youth literacy, children's health, the accountability of schooling systems, and the assessment of national reforms. He is the editor of *Vulnerable Children: Findings from Canada's National Longitudinal Study of Children and Youth*, (University of Alberta Press, 2002), which received the Canadian Policy Research Award in 2002, and the author of *Student engagement at school: A sense of belonging and participation* (Paris: Organization for Economic Cooperation and Development), and *Monitoring School Performance: A Guide for Educators* (Falmer Press, 1992).

Dr. Willms played a lead role in developing the questionnaires for Canada's National Longitudinal Survey of Children and Youth (NLSCY) and the OECD's Programme for International Student Assessment (PISA). Willms and his colleagues also designed the Early Years Evaluation (EYE), an instrument for the direct assessment of children's developmental skills at ages 3 to 6 years, and *Tell Them from Me*, an evaluation system for the continuous monitoring of school climate and student engagement and wellness.

Dr. Willms is known for his training of new investigators in the analysis of complex multilevel data. He regularly conducts workshops on multilevel modelling across Canada and throughout Asia, Europe, and South America. He also established the New Investigators Network, an interdisciplinary, collaborative network of Canada's top social science researchers in the field of human development. Dr. Willms's current interests include the examination of family, school, and community factors that contribute to the health and well-being of children and adolescents, and the use of continuous monitoring for evaluating school reforms.

He lives in Fredericton, New Brunswick with his wife, Ann, and three children, Alison, Maya, and Andrew (Canadian Research Institute for Social Policy, 2016).

Courtesy of Lucia Tramonte

LUCIA TRAMONTE, PH.D.

Dr. Lucia Tramonte is an associate professor of sociology at the University of New Brunswick and the co-director of the Canadian Research Institute for Social Policy (CRISP). After completing a Ph.D. in Sociology at the Universita' degli Studi di Milan, Milan, Italy, she joined the University of New Brunswick in 2005 as a post-doctoral fellow at CRISP. From 2006 to 2009, she worked as a research associate at CRISP and led the Successful Transition Project. This project comprised a two-and-a-half year program of longitudinal research on the developmental outcomes of Canadian children and youth. The research team analyzed longitudinal data from the National Longitudinal Survey of Children and Youth (NLSCY). As the lead analyst, Dr. Tramonte developed the methodology, produced the analysis, and coauthored a series of 16 topic specific papers. In 2009, she joined the Department of Sociology at UNB, and since 2012 she has been a tenured associate professor in the department.

Dr. Tramonte conducts research in the areas of comparative sociology of education, social inequalities, and childhood development. Since 2004, she has consulted for large international organizations, in particular OECD and Unesco, international governments, and international universities on questionnaire construction, secondary data analysis, measurement, and multilevel modelling of cross-sectional and longitudinal data. She has been a member of the scientific board of the Interdisciplinary Ph.D. Program in Evaluation of Processes and Educational Systems at the Dipartimento di Scienze della Formazione (DISFOR) since 2007. She has collaborated with the Inter-American Development Bank (IADB) since 2011 on the Inequities and Inequalities in Education project, an initiative sponsored by the IADB to support efforts by Latin America and the Caribbean countries to reduce poverty and inequality. Dr. Tramonte has published a number of peer-reviewed articles, reports, and book chapters related to her work on the social determinants of school achievement, emotional development and school achievement, inequities and inequalities in education, and life trajectories. She is also a co-applicant on a number of grants sponsored by the Social Sciences and Humanities Research Council of Canada (SSHRC) and the Canadian Institutes of Health Research (CIHR) (Canadian Research for Social Policy, 2016).

To this point, we have discussed issues in life-span development. For a review, see the Reach Your Learning Outcomes section at the end of this chapter.

Some Contemporary Concerns

LO6 Appraise several major contemporary concerns.

- **Health and Well-Being**
- **Education**
- **Socio-Cultural Contexts**
- **Social Policy**

Using the Internet, you might read a blog about a political figure, Skype with a family member who is out of the country, play a game with someone from another part of the world, or text a friend. You can also read the news in your local or national newspaper, or online. You might read about how to improve your memory, about a test to predict Alzheimer's disease, or about Aboriginal land claims. These are some of the areas of contemporary concern. Further, research on these areas and others, including health and well-being, parenting, education, and socio-cultural contexts, influences social policy. One example of research influencing social policy is research on the adolescent brain that is being used to help determine whether or not a youth should be tried in an adult or juvenile court.

Health and Well-Being

Health and well-being have been important goals for just about everyone for most of human history. Just as Asian physicians in 2600 BCE and Greek physicians in 500 BCE recognized that good habits are essential for good health, professionals today recognize the power of lifestyles and psychological states in health and well-being (Fahey, Insel, & Roth, 2009; Hahn, Payne, & Lucas, 2009). In every chapter of this book, issues of health and well-being—such as genetic counselling, school health programs, breast- versus bottle-feeding, and geriatric concerns, including dementia and Alzheimer's disease—are integrated into our discussion.

Education

A sound education is an important ingredient of a democratic society. Research in education includes curriculum development to ensure currency and to provide an appropriate knowledge base for children who are gifted, as well as for those who are intellectually challenged. Research also supports programs aimed at addressing social needs such as dropout rates, the influence of computers on the brain, and bullying. Approaches to education such as school hours, the age to start kindergarten, the ethnic or racial composition of a school, or the constructivist approach to learning, which you will read about in later chapters, are some of the issues rooted in research.

The use of social media has revolutionized education and communication. The Internet and online communication tools including Facebook and instant messaging (IM) have become common ways for young people to communicate with peers, friends, and family. Social media has shifted the modes and speed of communication dramatically, allowing information "data" to be collected, analyzed, and used differently than was possible a decade ago. To meaningfully engage with the current generation of students in any faculty, teaching needs to be presented in a context that is relevant to the social media generation. The explosion of available information needs to be communicated in a way that will help students to learn and to think critically about issues (Ratzan, 2011).

For example, the results of a study conducted with Canadian and Israeli undergraduate participants concluded that IM was used primarily, but not exclusively, to maintain existing ties with close friends rather than to develop new ties (Mesch, Talmud, & Quan-Haase, 2012). These researchers argue that as this study is limited to university students, future studies need to examine the development of IM relational patterns over the life span.

Children learn to love when they are loved.

Socio-Cultural Contexts

The tapestry of Canadian culture has changed dramatically in recent years. Nowhere is the change more dramatic than in the increasing ethnic diversity of Canada's citizens. This changing demographic landscape promises not only the richness that diversity produces, but also difficult challenges in extending support and equal opportunity to all individuals.

Socio-cultural contexts include five important concepts: context, culture, ethnicity, gender, and race. Recall that a *context* is the setting in which development occurs. This setting is influenced by historical, political, economic, geographic, social, and cultural factors. Every person's development occurs against the backdrop of cultural contexts. These contexts or settings include homes, schools, peer groups, churches, workplaces, shelters, cities, neighbourhoods, university laboratories, as well as the larger society. Each of these settings has meaningful historical, economic, social, and cultural legacies (Reeskin & Wright, 2011).

Culture is the behaviour patterns, beliefs, and all other products of a particular group of people that are passed on from generation to generation. Culture results from the interaction of people over many years. A cultural group can be as large as a country, such as Canada, or as small as an isolated town, such as Rankin Inlet. Regardless of its size, a group's culture influences the behaviour of its members (Taylor & Whittaker, 2009). Since culture influences behaviour, it also impacts our understanding of human development.

Cross-cultural studies involve a comparison of a culture with one or more other cultures. The comparison provides information about the degree to which development is similar, or universal, across cultures or is instead culture-specific. For example, researchers from Canada and the United Kingdom drew samples of Canadian and English children and adolescents from three separate, regional studies that conducted comparable school based assessments (2006–2011). For each age-sex group, the researchers assessed between-country differences for body composition, cardiorespiratory fitness, strength (handgrip), and physical activity. The findings indicated that at all ages, Canadian boys and girls were taller, heavier, and showed greater Basal Metabolic Indices (BMI) and waist circumferences. English children had higher cardiorespiratory fitness than Canadians, which was explained by differences in body composition and physical activity. Canadian children were significantly stronger, partly due to greater body size. Interestingly, Canadian adolescent girls reported greater physical activity than did their English counterparts. However, neither physical activity nor body size could explain why Canadian adolescent girls had greater cardiorespiratory fitness and strength. The researchers concluded that future cross-cultural studies on physical activity should include indices of growth and fitness to better understand the relationships between physical activity and health outcomes (Voss et al., 2014).

Ethnicity is based on cultural heritage, nationality characteristics, race, religion, and language (the word "ethnic" comes from the Greek word for nation). Not only is there diversity within a country such as Canada, or a racial group such as Caucasian, there also is diversity within each ethnic group. For example, not all Aboriginal peoples live in low-income circumstances, and not all Italian-Canadians are Catholic. It is easy to fall into the trap of stereotyping an ethnic group by thinking that all its members are alike, whereas in reality each grouping represents a diverse group of people (Banks, 2008; Kim et al., 2009; Gollnick & Chinn, 2009).

Race is often used to refer to a group of people regarded as distinct from other groups on the basis of appearance, typically skin colour. Since race is a social construction that continues to lead to racism, some social scientists believe that the term race must be abandoned. For example, ethnic and cultural differences may be significant for development, but racial differences are not (Stassen Berger, & Chuang, 2014).

Gender is the socio-cultural dimension of being female or male. Sex refers to the biological dimension of being female or male. Few aspects of our development are more central to our identity and social relationships than gender (Blakemore, Berenbaum, & Liben, 2009; Matlin, 2008; Zosuls, Lurye, & Ruble, 2008). Society's gender attitudes are changing. But by how much?

The twentieth century has witnessed a growing equality between women and men in many countries, including Canada. One indicator of the worldwide progress of women is the annual computation of the Gender Inequality Index (GII) provided by the United Nations. This index is a composite measure reflecting inequality in achievements between men and women along three dimensions: reproductive health, empowerment, and the labour market (United Nations, 2015). According to the United Nations Human Development Report 2015, Canada ranked ninth among 188 nations included in the GII. Meanwhile, most of the highest-rated gender egalitarian countries, and those that ranked well above Canada, were situated in northern Europe (e.g., Norway ranked first and Switzerland ranked third).

Classrooms today have become more diverse, especially those in urban centres.

Canadian women, it seems, still have a considerable way to go before they achieve top-level equality with men. For example, although the gender gap in earnings is shrinking, the gap is expected to disappear only in 2085 in Canada, provided the difference continues to diminish at a consistent rate (Brym et al., 2013). Canadians can take some encouragement in two significant developments in recent decades: The number of Canadian women in politics has increased significantly, and birth control technology has enabled women to experience greater control over reproductive issues (Macionis, Jansson, & Benoit, 2013).

Social Policy

Social policy is a national government's course of action designed to influence the welfare of its citizens. A current trend is to conduct developmental research that will lead to effective social policy. Given that 1 child in 10 is living in poverty (Campaign 2000, 2009), low income is related to children's poor health and academic performance (Campaign 2000, 2012), children and young adolescents are giving birth, the use and abuse of drugs is widespread, the spectre of AIDS is present, and the provision of health care for the elderly is inadequate, our nation needs responsible and progressive social policies. Research conducted by the Canadian Research Institute for Social Policy is an example of how research shapes social policy in Canada. (See the Connecting through Research box "Longitudinal Studies" later in this chapter for more information.)

Social policy is responsive to demographics such as median age, life expectancy, immigration rates, fertility rates, gender, and sexual orientation. Many data are gathered from hospital admission charts or census forms. You may have noted that typically these forms ask participants to identify as either male or female. After the last census, an Internet campaign circulated requesting that the gender identifier be changed to include more inclusive identifiers, such as transsexual or intersexed. Without more inclusive identifiers, all findings can be classified only as belonging to either male or female groups, which is not helpful when tracking social trends and health conditions of the LBGQTI communities.

ABORIGINAL PEOPLES

An example of how social policy impacts individuals is evidenced in the Canadian government's relationship with the Aboriginal peoples of Canada. In an effort to address some of the concerns, the Royal Commission on Aboriginal Peoples was established in 1991. The Commission held 178 days of public hearings, visited 96 communities, consulted dozens of experts, commissioned scores of research studies, and reviewed numerous past inquiries and reports. The Commission's summary of its central conclusion was that "The main policy direction, pursued for more than 150 years, first by colonial then by Canadian governments, has been wrong" (Department of Indian and Northern Affairs Canada, 1996).

In 2006, the Government of Canada announced the approval of a final Indian Residential Schools Settlement Agreement. Involved in this agreement were the four churches responsible (United, Anglican, Presbyterian, and Catholic), the federal government, and residential school survivors (Czyzewski, 2011). The Settlement Agreement included the establishment of a Truth and Reconciliation Commission (TRC) to deal with the Indian Residential School (IRS) system (Stanton, 2011). In 2008, then Prime Minister Stephen Harper made a "Statement of Apology" to the Aboriginal people for Canada's role in the Residential School System debacle (Quinn, 2011). The TRC of Canada was finally appointed on June 1, 2008, with a five-year mandate ("Schedule N," 2011). The TRC Secretariat has been working hard to carry out the goals of the TRC through a series of national and community events, through the gathering of statements, as well as through a rigorous research and documentation effort (Quinn, 2011). Although the TRC's mandate ended in 2015, the work of truth and reconciliation will carry on (Nagy, 2014). It is important for people in all parts of the broader society to begin to support the work of the TRC by promoting a deeper understanding of what it can do and how it might begin to do that, and by engaging in its activities.

The shape and scope of social policy is strongly tied to our political system. Our country's policy agenda and the welfare of the nation's citizens are influenced by demographics, the values held by individual lawmakers, the nation's economic strengths and weaknesses, and partisan politics.

HEALTH CARE

Health care, more than any other major social institution, exemplifies the impact of politics, demographics, and competing values. Saskatchewan Premier Tommy Douglas (1904–1986) fought for universal health care, the forerunner of the healthcare system that Canadians enjoy today. The Romanow Commission, headed by Roy Romanow and established in 2001 to engage Canadians in a national dialogue about health care, released its findings in 2002 (Romanow, 2002). Recommendations for change were made that would ensure the sustainability of a publicly-funded universal healthcare system in spite of rising costs, an aging population, and privatization arguments modelled by the practices and policies of the United States. The Commission continues to fuel the debate about whether Canada should have a privatized and multi-tiered healthcare system.

Although the report is dated, the information contained there remains relevant. In 2004, the First Ministers' Meeting on the Future of Health Care announced a 10-year plan to strengthen health care. This plan expired in March 2014, with no comparable federal agreements to take its place. The Conservative federal government at the time did hand down a 10-year funding agreement; but other than setting finances aside, it did not take an active role in coordinating health care policy (Kelly & Quesnelle, 2016). At present, according to Prime Minister Justin Trudeau, the current Liberal government will modernize health care, negotiate a new Health Accord with the provinces and territories, and draft a new, long-term agreement on funding (CBC News, 2015).

According to the Conference Board of Canada (2016), Canada's health care system is a source of national pride and a hallmark of Canadian society. The future of health and health care in Canada will be dominated by technology, big data, new health care roles, outcome/value-based health care, participatory medicine, and scientific breakthroughs that will enable all Canadians to live longer, healthier lives (Canadian Conference Board, 2016). One of the new healthcare roles is the development of the role of the advanced practice nurse, the nurse practitioner (NP). NPs are in an excellent position to address current shortcomings in health care through increasing points of access to the healthcare system. They are able to provide an emphasis on education and disease prevention. In addition, NPs can deliver high-quality, cost-effective care in a multitude of practice settings (Archibald & Fraser, 2013).

critical thinking

Health care expenses continue to skyrocket at the same time that the population is aging and more are in need of care. How do you think taxpayers can meet the increasing demands of universal health care? Select one or two disparities and design a plan based on one or two relevant factors (location, cost, need, resources, etc.). Compare and contrast universal health care and privatization in Canada.

GENERATIONAL INEQUITY

Who should get the bulk of government dollars for improved well-being? Children? Their parents? Their grandparents or their great-grandparents? **Generational inequity**, a social policy concern, is the possible condition in which an aging society is being unfair to its younger members. This occurs because older adults pile up advantages by receiving inequitably large allocations of resources; for example, seniors are more likely to require assisted living facilities or medications. Generational inequity raises questions about whether the young should have to pay for the old and whether an "advantaged" older population is using up resources that should go to disadvantaged children.

If Canada were like many countries of the world where no social insurance systems exist, many adults would have to bear the financial burden of supporting their elderly parents, leaving fewer of their resources for educating their children. Our aging demographic spawns a host of social concerns ranging from health care, retirement age, and pension plans, to elder abuse. However, an interesting trend regarding aging is becoming prevalent in Canada. Aging baby boomers, with relatively high purchasing powers, will be able to pay more out-of-pocket for their health care either within Canada, or outside Canada as health care tourists. The lower income strata will then receive health care in what remains of the single-payer public system. The end result will increase economic and health care divides, resulting in social and political unrest in society (Wister & Speechley, 2015).

A somewhat uncomfortable ambiguity has persisted in Canadian society regarding home care for the elderly (Firbank, 2011). This prime contentious issue has been debated by governments for quite some time. The controversy in social policy formation has been evident in regard to informal caregivers and home support services. The possibility of designing a national "standard model" of home care is the logical first step for seeking federal/provincial consensus (Firbank, 2011). However, developing and applying such a model may prove to be considerably more difficult than is sometimes acknowledged.

IMMIGRATION

A shift in ethnicity, another demographic determinant, affects all levels of society, especially when it is fuelled by immigration. Canada has long been recognized as a world leader in international humanitarianism efforts due largely to its refugee sponsorship system, which empowers private groups to resettle refugees on their own. As of this text's writing, Prime Minister Justin Trudeau is determined to take in tens of thousands of refugees from Syria (Holtz, 2015). The Canadian Council for Refugees (CCR) appreciates the commitments made by the new government and is willing to assist by providing detailed information about the resulting changes due to immigration and their impacts. Intensive recommendations are being made on ways to meet the challenges. Some of the recommendations include: making status in Canada secure, providing access to protection, ensuring speedy family reunification, and promoting welcoming communities and rights and dignity for all (Canadian Council for Refugees, 2015).

HOMELESSNESS

Available estimates suggest that, in Canada, 150 000 to 300 000 people will experience homelessness during the course of a year (Aubry, Klodawsky, & Coulombe, 2012). Despite these high numbers, the population of homeless people indicates greater diversity. No longer is homelessness characterized simply as a problem among single men. In particular, the number of people experiencing homelessness includes a significant number of women, families, and youth (Klodawsky, 2006). Homelessness is a serious social problem in Canada (Figueiredo, Hwant & Quinonez, 2013). One of the fastest growing subpopulations is that of homeless youth (Hudson, et al., 2010). School drop-out, unemployment, drug abuse, pregnancy, mental illness, and arrests are higher among homeless youth aged 16–24 years, compared to youths who have a home (Smid, Bourgois, & Auerswald, 2010). The illegal activities engaged in by youth include panhandling, theft, sex trade work, various forms of vandalism, drug dealing, and mischief (Ferguson et al., 2011). According to Canadian researchers, adolescence is a critical time in terms of the effects of peer influence (Fielding & Forchuk, 2013). Many youths, homeless or not, become rebellious against adult supervision and follow the opinions and activities of their friends. Unfortunately, this period of development can have long-term consequences—especially for homeless youth who are already disengaged from conventional culture.

Given this growing diversity, developing effective social policies will facilitate meaningful advances in housing and shelter to help combat the different aspects of problems (Aubry, Klodawsky, & Coulombe, 2012). The promotion of health equity requires the promotion of social policy to strengthen the quality of social determinants of health (Raphael, 2010). Calling for housing security, as well as affordable child care, universal health care, living wages, and improved food and income are all essential means of promoting health equity. Canadian action on improving health equity by addressing the social determinants of health has been profoundly lacking. The housing crisis in Canada has seen explosive increases in homelessness. Researchers have noted that it is well within the reach of Canadian governments to end the homelessness crisis by increasing their allocation for housing by 1 percent. However, few Canadian governments seem willing to make such a commitment.

To this point, we have discussed some contemporary concerns. For a review, see the Reach Your Learning Outcomes section at the end of this chapter.

Research Methods and Challenges

LO7 Compare and contrast research methodology and challenges.

- **Methods of Collecting Data**
- **Research Designs**
- **Research Challenges**

As you can see from the prominent issues and contemporary concerns, as well as in this chapter's opening vignette, research is vital to the field of psychology. In fact, the study of life-span development is a science based on theories and systematic investigative strategies to explain human development and behaviour. Life-span development is a provocative, intriguing interdisciplinary field filled with information about who we are, how we have come to be this way, and where our futures may take us.

Generally, research in life-span development is designed to test **hypotheses** that, in some cases, are derived from the theories you will read about in Chapter 2. Through research, theories are modified to reflect new data, and occasionally new theories arise. What types of research are conducted in life-span development? If researchers want to study people of different ages, what research designs can they use? These are questions we will examine next.

Methods of Collecting Data

Whether we are interested in studying attachment in infants, the cognitive skills of children, or social relationships in older adults, we can choose from several ways of collecting data. Here we outline the measures most often used, beginning with observation.

Observation

Scientific **observation** requires an important set of skills (Rosnow & Rosenthal, 2008; Wiersma & Jurs, 2009). For observations to be effective, they have to be systematic. We have to have some idea of what we are looking for. We have to know whom we are observing, when and where we will observe, how the observations will be made, and how they will be recorded. Where should we make our observations? We have two choices: the laboratory and the everyday world.

When we observe scientifically, we often need to control certain factors that determine behaviour but are not the focus of our inquiry (McMillan, 2008). For this reason, some research in life-span development is conducted in a **laboratory**, a controlled setting where many of the complex factors of the "real world" are absent. For example, suppose you want to observe how children react when they see other people act aggressively. If you observe children in their homes or schools, you have no control over how much aggression the children observe, what kind of aggression they see, which people they see acting aggressively, or how other people treat the children. In contrast, if you observe the children in a laboratory, you can control these and other factors and therefore have more confidence about how to interpret your observations.

Laboratory research does have some drawbacks, however, including the following:

- It is almost impossible to conduct research without the participants knowing they are being studied.
- The laboratory setting is unnatural and therefore can cause the participants to behave unnaturally.
- People who are willing to come to a university laboratory may not fairly represent groups from diverse cultural backgrounds.
- People who are unfamiliar with university settings, and with the idea of "helping science," may be intimidated by the laboratory setting.

Naturalistic observation provides insights that we sometimes cannot achieve in the laboratory (Jackson, 2008). **Naturalistic observation** means observing behaviour in real-world settings, making no effort to manipulate or control the situation. Life-span researchers conduct naturalistic observations at sporting events, in child care centres, in work settings, in malls, and in other places where people live and frequent.

For example, naturalistic observation was used in one study that focused on conversations in a children's science museum (Crowley et al., 2001). When visiting exhibits at the science museum, parents were far more likely to engage boys than girls in explanatory talk. This finding suggests a gender bias that encourages boys more than girls to be interested in science (see Figure 1.5). Similarly, a team of researchers from Canadian universities in Ontario has been observing mother–infant interactions in the more convenient and natural home settings rather than in a laboratory (Bailey et al., 2007). In what ways would the home interaction be more realistic than a laboratory observation?

Figure 1.5

Parents' Explanations of Science to Sons and Daughters at a Science Museum

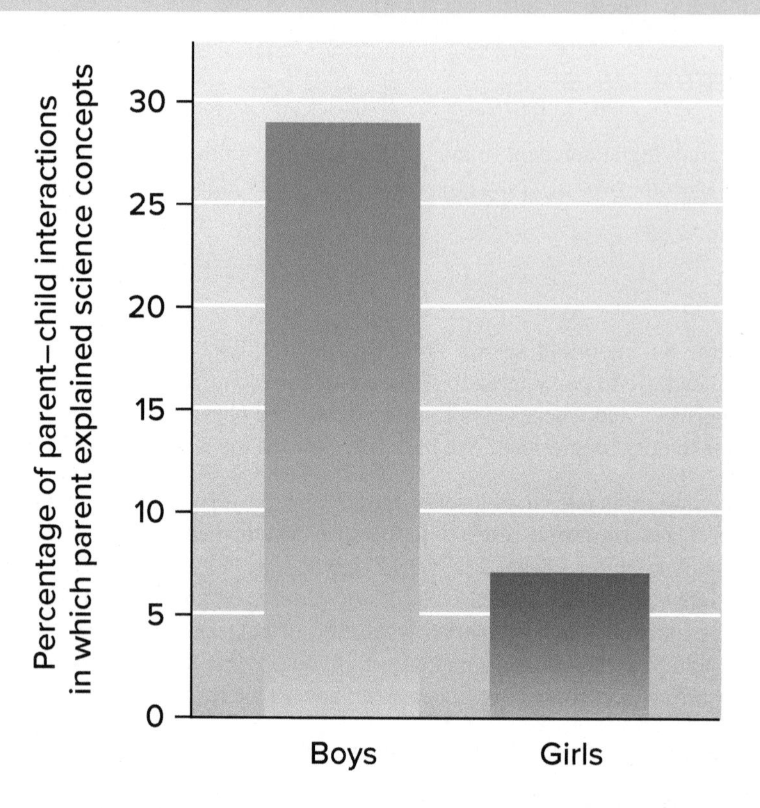

In a naturalistic observation study at a children's science museum, parents were three times more likely to explain science to boys than to girls (Crowley et al., 2001). The gender difference occurred regardless of whether the father, the mother, or both parents were with the child, although the gender difference was greatest for fathers' science explanations to sons and daughters.

Survey and Interview

Sometimes the best and quickest way to get information about people is to ask them for it. One technique is to interview them directly. A related method is the survey (sometimes referred to as a questionnaire), which is especially useful when information from many people is needed. A standard set of questions is used to obtain people's self-reported attitudes or beliefs about a particular topic. In a good survey the questions are clear and unbiased, allowing respondents to answer unambiguously.

Surveys and interviews can be used to study a wide range of topics, from religious beliefs to sexual habits to attitudes about gun control to beliefs about how to improve schools. Surveys and interviews may be conducted in person, over the telephone, and over the Internet.

One problem with surveys and interviews is the tendency of participants to answer questions in a way that they think is socially acceptable or desirable, rather than to say what they truly think or feel (Creswell, 2008). For example, on a survey or in an interview, some individuals might say that they do not take drugs even though they do.

Standardized Test

A **standardized test** has uniform procedures for administration and scoring. Many standardized tests compare a person's performance with that of other individuals; thus, they provide information about individual differences among people (Kingston, 2008). One example is the Stanford-Binet intelligence test, which is described in Chapter 9. Your score on the Stanford-Binet test tells you how your performance compares with that of thousands of other people who have taken the test (Bart & Peterson, 2008).

One criticism of standardized tests is that they assume a person's behaviour is consistent and stable, yet personality and intelligence—two primary targets of standardized testing—can vary with the situation. For example, a person may perform poorly on a standardized intelligence test in an office setting but score much higher at home, where the person is less anxious.

Case Study

A **case study** is an in-depth look at a single individual. Case studies are performed mainly by mental health professionals when, for either practical or ethical reasons, the unique aspects of an individual's life cannot be duplicated and tested in other individuals. A case study provides information about one person's experiences; it may focus on nearly any aspect of the subject's life that helps the researcher understand the person's mind, behaviour, or other attributes. A researcher may gather information for a case study from interviews and medical records.

A case study can provide a dramatic, in-depth portrayal of an individual's life, but we must be cautious when generalizing from this information. The subject of a case study is unique, with a genetic makeup and personal history that no one else shares. In addition, case studies involve judgments of unknown reliability. Researchers who conduct case studies rarely check to see if other professionals agree with their observations or findings.

Physiological Measures

Researchers increasingly are using physiological measures when they study development at different points in the life span. One physiological measure that is increasingly being used is neuroimaging, especially functional magnetic resonance imaging (fMRI), in which electromagnetic waves are used to construct images of a person's brain tissue and biochemical activity (Hofheimer & Lester, 2008; Moulson & Nelson, 2008). We will have much more to say about neuroimaging and other physiological measures in later chapters.

Research Designs

In addition to methods of collecting data, researchers also need a research design. The three basic types of research design are descriptive, correlational, and experimental. Each has strengths and weaknesses.

Descriptive Research

Some important theories have grown out of **descriptive research**, which is used to observe and record behaviour. For example, a psychologist might observe the extent to which people are altruistic or aggressive toward each other. By itself, descriptive research cannot prove what causes some phenomenon, but it can reveal important information about people's behaviour and attitudes. Descriptive research methods include observation, surveys and interviews, standardized tests, case studies, and life-history records (LoBiondo, Haber, & Singh, 2013).

Correlational Research

In contrast to descriptive research, correlational research goes beyond describing phenomena; it provides information that will help us to predict how people will behave. In **correlational research**, the goal is to describe the strength of the relationship between two or more events or characteristics. The more strongly the two events are correlated (or related or associated), the more effectively we can predict one event from the other (Jackson, 2008; Kraska, 2008; Howell, 2014).

For example, to study whether children of permissive parents have less self-control than other children, you would need to carefully record observations of parents' permissiveness and their children's self-control. You might observe that the higher a parent was in permissiveness, the lower the child was in self-control. You would then analyze these data statistically to yield a numerical measure, called a correlation coefficient, a number based on a statistical analysis that is used to describe the degree of association between two variables. The correlation coefficient ranges from +1.00 to –1.00. A negative number means an inverse relation. In this example, you might find an inverse correlation between permissive parenting and children's self-control with a coefficient of, say, –.30. By contrast, you might find a positive correlation of +.30 between parental monitoring of children and children's self-control.

The higher the correlation coefficient (whether positive or negative), the stronger the association between the two variables. A correlation of 0 means there is no association between the variables. A correlation of –.40 is stronger than a correlation of +.20 because we disregard whether the correlation is positive or negative in determining the strength of the correlation.

A note of caution is in order, however: Correlation does not equal causation (Aron, Aron, & Coupos, 2008). Figure 1.6 illustrates the possible interpretations of correlational data.

Figure 1.6

Possible Explanations for Correlational Data

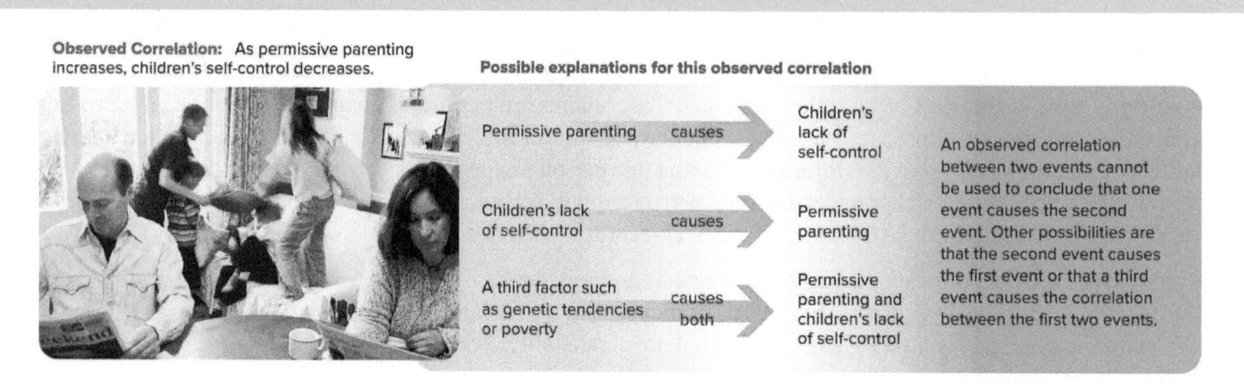

An observed correlation between two events cannot be used to conclude that one event caused the other. Some possibilities are that the second event caused the first event, or that a third, unknown event caused the correlation between the first two events.

Experimental Research

An **experiment** is a carefully regulated procedure in which one or more factors believed to influence the behaviour being studied are manipulated, while all other factors are held constant. If the behaviour under study changes when a factor is manipulated, we say that the manipulated factor has caused the behaviour to change (Kirk, 2003). In other words, the experiment has demonstrated cause and effect. The cause is the factor that was manipulated. The effect is the behaviour that changed because of the manipulation (see Figure 1.7). Non-experimental research methods (descriptive and correlational research) cannot establish cause and effect because they do not involve manipulating factors in a controlled way. Other chapters will cite studies that have been conducted using empirical methodology.

Figure 1.7

Principles of Experimental Research

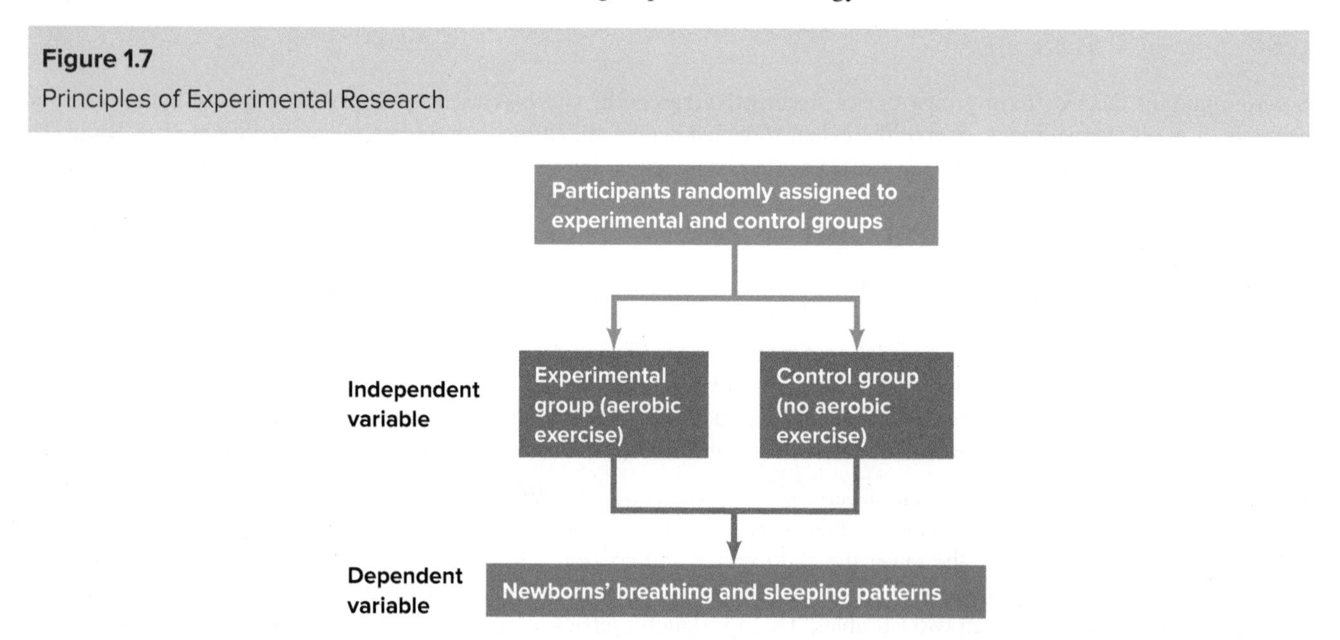

Imagine that you decide to conduct an experimental study of the effects of aerobic exercise by pregnant women on their newborns' breathing and sleeping patterns. You would randomly assign pregnant women to experimental and control groups. The experimental group women would engage in aerobic exercise over a specified number of sessions and weeks. The control group would not. Then, when the infants are born, you would assess their breathing and sleeping patterns. If the breathing and sleeping patterns of the newborns whose mothers were in the experimental group are more positive than those of the control group, you would conclude that aerobic exercise caused the positive effects.

INDEPENDENT AND DEPENDENT VARIABLES

Experiments include two types of changeable factors, or variables: independent and dependent. An *independent variable* is a manipulated, influential, experimental factor. It is a potential cause. The label "independent" is used because this variable can be manipulated independently of other factors to determine its effect. Researchers have a vast array of options open to them in selecting independent variables, and one experiment may include several independent variables.

A *dependent variable* is a factor that can change in an experiment, in response to changes in the independent variable. As researchers manipulate the independent variable, they measure the dependent variable for any resulting effect.

EXPERIMENTAL AND CONTROL GROUPS

Experiments can involve one or more experimental groups and one or more control groups. An *experimental group* is a group whose experience is manipulated. A *control group* is a comparison group that is as much like the experimental group as possible and is treated in every way like the experimental group except for the manipulated factor (independent variable). The control group serves as a baseline against which the effects of the manipulated condition can be compared.

Random assignment is an important principle for deciding whether each participant will be placed in the experimental group or in the control group. *Random assignment* means that researchers assign participants to experimental and control groups by chance. It reduces the likelihood that the experiment's results will be due to any pre-existing differences between groups (Polit & Beck, 2010). Figure 1.7 illustrates the nature of experimental research.

Time Span of Research

A special concern of developmentalists is the time span of a research investigation. Studies that focus on the relation of age to some other variable are common in life-span development. We have several options: researchers can study different individuals of different ages and compare them; they can study the same individuals as they age over time; or they can use some combination of these two approaches.

CROSS-SECTIONAL APPROACH

The **cross-sectional approach** is a research strategy in which individuals of different ages are compared at one time. A typical cross-sectional study might include a group of 5-year-olds, 8-year-olds, and 11-year-olds. Another might include a group of 15-year-olds, 25-year-olds, and 45-year-olds. The different groups can be compared with respect to a variety of dependent variables: IQ, memory, peer relations, attachment to parents, hormonal changes, and so on. All of this can be accomplished in a short time. In some studies, data are collected in a single day. Even in large-scale cross-sectional studies with hundreds of subjects, data collection does not usually take longer than several months to complete.

The main advantage of the cross-sectional study is that the researcher does not have to wait for the individuals to grow up or become older. Despite its time efficiency, the cross-sectional approach has its drawbacks. It gives no information about how individuals change or about the stability of their characteristics. The increases and decreases of development—the hills and valleys of growth and development—can become obscured in the cross-sectional approach. For example, in a cross-sectional approach to perceptions of life satisfaction, average increases and decreases might be revealed. But the study would not show how the life satisfaction of individual adults waxed and waned over the years. It also would not tell us whether adults who had positive or negative perceptions of life satisfaction as young adults maintained their relative degree of life satisfaction as middle-aged or older adults.

LONGITUDINAL APPROACH

The **longitudinal approach** is a research strategy in which the same individuals are studied over a period of time, usually several years or more. For example, if a study of life satisfaction were conducted longitudinally, the same adults might be assessed periodically over a 70-year time span—at the ages of 20, 35, 45, 65, and 90, for example. Figure 1.8 compares the cross-sectional and longitudinal approaches.

Figure 1.8
A Comparison of Cross-Sectional and Longitudinal Approaches

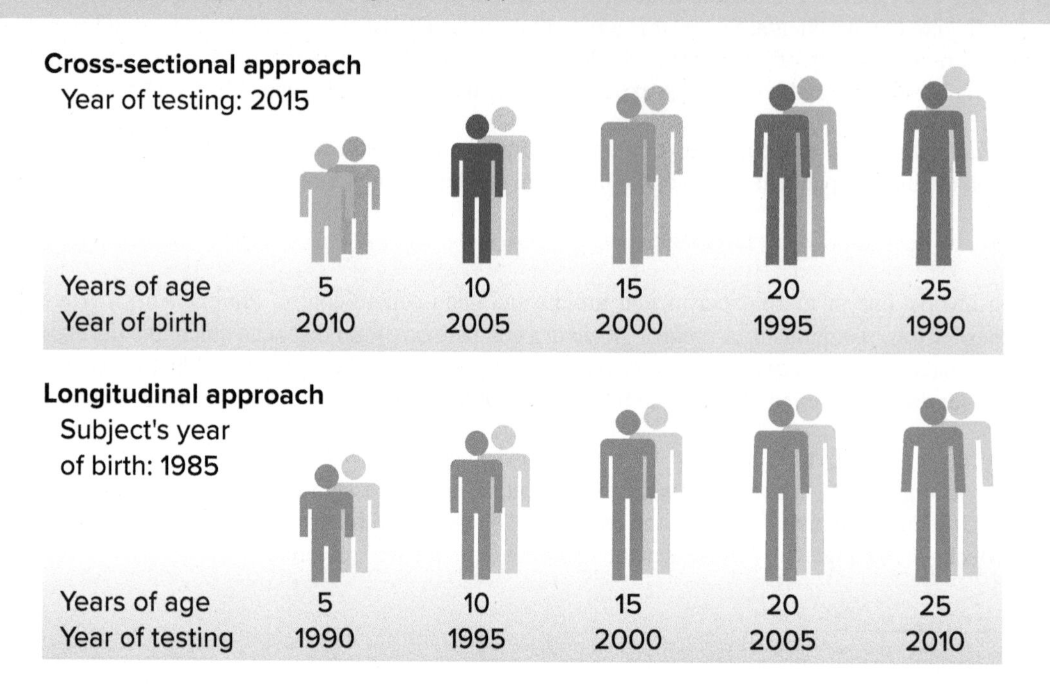

Although longitudinal studies provide a wealth of information about such important issues as stability and change in development and the importance of early experience for later development, they are not without their problems (Polit & Black, 2010). They are expensive and time consuming. The longer the study lasts, the more participants drop out—they move, get sick, lose interest, and so forth. Participants can bias the outcome of a study because those who remain may be dissimilar to those who drop out. Those individuals who remain in a longitudinal study over a number of years may be more compulsive and conformity-oriented, for example, or they might have more stable lives.

critical thinking

Life-span researchers are especially concerned about cohort effects because they shape an individual's understanding of the world, including what might be taken as common sense. For example, a woman born in Canada in 1998 might assume she would make an economic contribution to her family by having a career outside the home, whereas her grandmother may have shaped her identity around being a mother and homemaker. The individual born in the mid-70s may find some of the newer technologies more challenging than an individual born in 1990. The child born in Canada in 2015 will have a very different view of the world than a child born in Zimbabwe in 2015. What changes can you foresee that may shape the development of your children and grandchildren? In what ways do you believe that you can contribute to the development of your children and grandchildren? Write a detailed narrative, providing specifics, of your developmental plans and activities for when you are older as you might describe them to a friend.

COHORT EFFECTS

A *cohort* is a group of people who were born at a similar point in history and share similar experiences as a result, such as growing up in the same city around the same time. For example, cohorts can differ in years of education, child-rearing practices, health, attitudes toward sex, religious values, and economic status. In life-span development research, **cohort effects** are due to a person's time of birth or generation but not to actual age. Cohort effects are important because they can powerfully affect the dependent measures in a study ostensibly concerned with age. Researchers have shown it is especially important to be aware of cohort effects in the assessment of adult intelligence (Schaie, 2013). Individuals born in different decades, for example, may have had varying opportunities for education.

Cross-sectional studies can show how different cohorts respond, but they can confuse age changes and cohort effects. Longitudinal studies are effective in studying age changes, but only within one cohort. With sequential studies, age changes in one cohort can be examined and compared with age changes in another cohort.

An important point to make is that theories often are linked with a particular research method or methods. Thus, the methods researchers use are associated with their particular theoretical approach. Figure 1.9 illustrates the connections between research methods and theories.

Figure 1.9

Connections between Research Methods and Theories

Research Method	Theory
Observation	▪ All theories emphasize some form of observation. ▪ Behavioural and social cognitive theories place the strongest emphasis on laboratory observation. ▪ Ethological theory places the strongest emphasis on naturalistic observation.
Survey/interview	▪ Psychoanalytic and cognitive studies (Piaget, Vygotsky) often used interviews. ▪ Behavioural, social cognitive, and ethological theories are the least likely to use this method.
Case study	▪ Psychoanalytic theories (Freud, Erikson) were the most likely to use this method.
Correlational	▪ All of the theories use this research method, although psychoanalytic theories are the least likely to use it.
Experimental research	▪ The behavioural and social cognitive theories and the information-processing theories are the most likely to use this method. ▪ Psychoanalytic theories are the least likely to use it.
Cross-sectional/ longitudinal/sequential methods	▪ National Longitudinal Survey of Children and Youth (NLSCY) is an example of this method. ▪ The sequential method is the least likely to be used by any theory.

CONNECTING through Research

Longitudinal Studies

The National Longitudinal Survey of Children and Youth (NLSCY), Cycle 8 (2008–2009) is a comprehensive survey of Canadians that reflects their development and well-being from birth to early adulthood (Statistics Canada, 2010). The initial sample for Cycle 8 was comprised of 35 795 children and youths aged from 0–7 years and 14–25-year-olds. The survey covers a wide range of topics, including the health of children, physical development, learning and behaviour, and as well data on their social environment (family, friends, schools, and communities). The study collects data concerning factors that influence a child's social, emotional, and behavioural development. The survey monitors the impact of these factors on the child's development over time. Information from the NLSCY will help shape social policy to help children and their families avoid, or rise out of, the conditions and choices that lead to vulnerability.

Another longitudinal study, the Youth in Transition Survey (YITS), focuses on the transition from school to work by young adults in more than 50 countries. This study, a project of the Organisation for Economic Co-operation and Development (OECD), is designed to provide policy-oriented international indicators of the skills and knowledge base of 15-year-old students in the domains of reading, math, and science (OECD, 2010). This research not only is designed to discover and understand the challenges facing children growing up in various countries and the dynamics between social context and individual action in determining positive or negative outcomes, but also aims to shape social policy.

In Canada, social policy has attempted to create a nation in which people have equal opportunity to achieve positive life experiences. Where differences or difficulties exist, social policy sets up programs, agencies, and institutions to attempt to facilitate solutions to the problem or direct assistance to meet the basics for equal outcome.

Research Challenges

Conducting ethical research and minimizing bias are vital to protecting the rights of participants and representing information accurately.

Conducting Ethical Research

Ethics in research may affect you personally if you ever serve as a participant in a study. In that event, you need to know your rights as a participant and the responsibilities of researchers to ensure that these rights are safeguarded.

If you ever become a researcher in life-span development yourself, you will need an even deeper understanding of ethics. Even if you only carry out experimental projects in psychology courses, you must consider the rights of the participants in those projects. A student might think, "I volunteer in a home for people with intellectual disabilities several hours per week. I can use the residents of the home in my study to see if a particular treatment helps improve their memory for everyday tasks." But without proper permissions, the most well-meaning, kind, and considerate studies still violate the rights of the participants.

For the protection of human participants in research in Canada, the collaboration of the three major funding agencies—the Canadian Institutes of Health Research (CIHR), the Natural Sciences and Engineering Research Council of Canada (NSERC), and the Social Sciences and Humanities Research Council (SSHRC)—has led to a joint development of the document *Tri-Council Policy Statement: Ethical Conduct for Research Involving Humans* (Canadian Institutes of Health Research et al., 2010). The second edition of the *Tri-Council Policy Statement: Ethical Conduct for Research Involving Humans* (TCPS 2) was developed to keep pace with changes in research and society at large. The document continues to be based on respect for human dignity, and includes a consolidated set of three core principles identified as follows (Canadian Institutes of Health Research et al., 2010):

- *Respect for persons:* Both the intrinsic value of human beings and the respect and consideration to which they are entitled are recognized. Respect for persons is critical because it incorporates the dual moral obligations to respect autonomy and to protect those with developing, impaired, or diminished autonomy. One highly important research mechanism that strives to respect participants' autonomy is the requirement to obtain their free, informed, and ongoing consent.
- *Concern for welfare:* Welfare in research refers to the impact of factors such as a participant's physical, mental, and spiritual health or their well-being. Additional factors that must be considered are the participant's physical, economic, and social circumstances. For example, relevant determinants of welfare could be housing, community membership, and the extent of social participation in various aspects of life. Therefore, researchers must plan to protect the welfare of participants regarding any foreseeable risks associated with that research.
- *Justice:* Justice refers to the obligation of the researcher to treat participants fairly and equitably. Fairness entails treating all people with equal respect and concern. Equity requires distributing the burdens and benefits of research participation in such a way that no segment of the population is unduly burdened by any harm that might arise during the research project. In addition, participants must not be denied any benefits of knowledge generated from the investigation. Individuals or groups whose circumstances cause them to be vulnerable or marginalized must be afforded special attention in order that they are treated justly in research. Vulnerability is often created by one's limited capacity, or a limited access to social goods such as rights, opportunities, and power (Canadian Institutes of Health Research et al., 2010).

One of the most valuable assets realized for developing the second edition of TCPS is the feature included in Chapter 9 with Aboriginal partners. This feature discusses the latest thinking about ethical research involving Canada's Aboriginal peoples. The chapter emphasizes the need for equitable partnerships, and it explains safeguards specific to First Nations, Inuit, and Métis people (Macionis, Jansson, & Benoit, 2013).

© Anthony CassidyThe Image Bank/Getty Images

© Punchstock/Digital Vision

Look at these two photographs, one of all white males, the other of a diverse group of females and males from different ethnic groups, including some white individuals. Consider a topic in psychology, such as parenting, love, or cultural values. *If you were conducting research on this topic, might the results of the study be different depending on whether the participants in your study were the individuals in the top photograph or the bottom one?*

Minimizing Bias

Studies of life-span development are most useful when they are conducted without bias or prejudice toward any particular group of people. Of special concern are bias based on gender and bias based on culture or ethnicity.

GENDER BIAS

Sociological research frowns upon the process of using data from one gender to draw conclusions about populations. Consequently, approaching research problems from an exclusively male perspective is less common today (Brym et al., 2013). Pohlhaus and colleagues (2011) conducted an analysis of sex differences in National Institutes of Health (NIH) award programs. The findings of this cross-sectional analysis indicated that women and men are equally successful at all career stages. Meanwhile, the results of the longitudinal analysis revealed that men with previous experiences as NIH grantees have higher application and funding rates than women at similar career points. The researchers concluded that while greater participation of women in NIH programs is underway, further action will be required to eradicate remaining sex differences.

In the recent report, *Women in Canada: A Gender-Based Statistical Report* (2010–2011), a deeper understanding of the roles of women in Canadian society is presented with indications of ways in which these roles have changed over time. One example from the report focuses on women in the labour markets. The authors indicated that 77 percent of women under age 25 with a non-university, post-secondary certificate or diploma were employed in 2009, compared with 73 percent of men (Statistics Canada, 2010d). A significant question is generated by such a finding: What accounts for the differences in the age group under 25?

Fortunately, studies pioneered by Karen Horney, Erich Fromm, and, more recently, Carol Gilligan, Betty Jean Miller, and Harriet Lerner have opened the doors to wide examination of gender differences. See the Connecting Development to Life box "Gender Makes a Difference" for more information.

ETHNIC AND CULTURAL BIAS

The developmental and educational problems experienced by ethnic groups have been viewed as "confounds" or "noise" in the data. It now appears obvious that more individuals and groups from different ethnic backgrounds need to be included in cultural research (Mehrotra & Wagner, 2009). In 2008, the Multiculturalism and Human Rights Branch of the Department of Canadian Heritage commissioned six academic investigators to conduct a socio-economic scan of the regions of Canada and to identify and specify significant research themes related to Canadian multiculturalism. Consequently, two of the ten research themes for 2008–2010 were patterns of ethnic community formation, and racism and discrimination (Minister of Public Works and Government Services Canada, 2010).

CONNECTING development to life

Gender Makes a Difference

Four prominent clinical psychoanalysts have significantly influenced the field of psychology. Arguing that the primary framework in the field, put forward by Freud, Jung, Erikson, Kohlberg, and others, is a framework designed by and for men, Karen Horney, Jean Baker Miller, Carol Gilligan, and Harriet Lerner have made an enormous contribution.

Karen Horney (1885–1952) was the first woman to challenge prevalent thinking by proposing that cultural and experiential factors are primary determinants of personality for both men and women. While Horney agreed with much of Freud's work, she firmly disagreed with what she thought to be a preoccupation with male genitalia. Arguing "anatomy is not destiny," Horney proposed that men should experience womb-envy rather than women experiencing penis envy because women are the bearers of future generations—something men cannot do. Horney founded the American Institute for Psychoanalysis so that research and training would not be constrained by prevalent thought. Her major contribution to the field was her theory of neurosis, the struggle between our real self and our idealized self. She also argued that neglect, not abuse, is the single most damaging factor in a child's development, because the child has no way to rail against neglect.

Jean Baker Miller (1927–2006) was the founding director of the Jean Baker Miller Training Institute at Wellesley College. In her groundbreaking book *Toward a New Psychology of Women,* first published in 1970, she argues that "all life has been underdeveloped and distorted because our past explanations have been created by only one half of the human species." Miller believed that the dominant–subordinate grouping is inadequate because it defines and distorts members of both groups in different ways. Dominant groups define oppressed groups falsely, just as oppressed groups define dominant groups falsely. This distortion undermines the development of both groups and can be applied to all political contexts, including gender.

Carol Gilligan (1936–), psychoanalyst, ethicist, and feminist, was a colleague of Erikson and Kohlberg. She disagrees with Kohlberg, who believed that men have superior moral reasoning capacities. Gilligan asserts that men and women have different but equal moral and psychological tendencies. In her text *In a Different Voice: Psychological Theory and Women's Development* (1982), Gilligan observed that because of socialization, women not only define themselves in the context of relationships, but also judge themselves in terms of their ability to provide care and nurturance (p. 17). In addition, women alter their feelings and judgments in deference to others (pp. 95–101).

Harriet Lerner (1944–) is best known for her work on the psychology of women and the process of change in families. Lerner proposes that the rigidity of corporate culture disadvantages both male and female ability to manage and sustain relationships, thereby undermining the family unit. Lerner advocates that the corporate world demonstrate its valuing of family life by offering parental leaves, leaves to care for elderly parents or sick children, flexible hours, convenient daycare settings, and flexible work settings. These ideas are either very new to us or somewhere on the horizon (Lerner, 1998).

In different ways, Gilligan, Horney, Lerner, and Miller suggest that societal conventions and norms surrounding female identity, work, social, familial, and intimate relationships are strengthened when women and men both have healthy self-esteem and an equal voice.

Researchers also have tended to practise what is called "ethnic gloss" when they select and describe ethnic minority samples (Banks, 2008). Ethnic gloss involves using a superficial label that makes an ethnic group look more homogeneous than it really is. Ethnic gloss can cause researchers to obtain samples of ethnic groups that either are not representative or conceal the group's diversity, which can lead to overgeneralization and stereotyping.

The World Health Organization (WHO) notes the lack of research in underdeveloped nations, where people are suffering the traumas of war, famine, acquired immune deficiency syndrome (AIDS), and diseases related to the lack of fresh water and immunization. Today's concerns differ widely from the concerns of the researchers and analysts who lay the formative foundations of psychology. Current researchers, building on the theories of the past, are equally excited about new discoveries. Unlike their historical predecessors, however, they concern themselves with sensitive ethical dilemmas, rigorous scientific procedures, and critical issues that influence social policy.

THE CANADIAN PSYCHOLOGICAL ASSOCIATION (CPA)

The Canadian Psychological Association (CPA) publishes and periodically updates ethical guidelines for both clinical and research psychologists in this country. Now in its third edition, the *Canadian Code of Ethics for Psychologists* (CPA, 2000) states that the primary professional goal for psychologists is "to respect the dignity of all persons with whom they come in contact in their role as psychologists." A review of the 2000 Code was begun by the Canadian Psychological Association Committee on Ethics in 2010 (CPA, 2016).

To this point, we have discussed research methods and challenges. For a review, see the Reach Your Learning Outcomes section at the end of this chapter.

Reach Your **Learning Outcomes**

The Life-Span Perspective

LO1 Examine life-span development and describe the characteristics of the life-span perspective.

Life-Span Development	Life-span development is the pattern of movement or change that begins at conception and continues throughout the human life span.
The Importance of Studying Life-Span Development	Studying life-span development provides insights that will enrich both personal and professional understanding of self and others. According to Paul Baltes, life-span development is: ▪ multidimensional ▪ multidirectional ▪ multidisciplinary ▪ plastic ▪ contextual ▪ concerned with growth, maintenance, and regulation ▪ a co-construct of biology, culture, and the individual

The Role of Context

LO2 Describe the term *context* and examine the role it plays in understanding growth and development.

Context influences major aspects of growth and development including life expectancy, median age, and the demographics related to baby boomers. Major contextual influences include:

- normative age-graded influences
- normative history-graded influences
- non-normative life events

Socio-economic status (SES) is a major aspect of context.

Developmental Processes

LO3 Reflect upon processes of development.

Biological, Cognitive, and Socio-Emotional Processes	Three intricate and complex processes of development are: ▪ biological/physical ▪ cognitive ▪ socio-emotional These processes interact in a fluid manner, each shaping the growth and development of the other.

Periods of Development

LO4 **Describe the periods of development and the concept of age.**

The Periods of Development	Periods of development refer to the time frames in life that are characterized by certain features. The periods of development include: ▪ prenatal ▪ infancy ▪ early childhood ▪ middle and late childhood ▪ adolescence ▪ early adulthood ▪ middle adulthood ▪ late adulthood
The Concept of Age	There are five conceptions of age: ▪ chronological ▪ biological ▪ mental ▪ psychological ▪ social

Issues in Life-Span Development

LO5 **Outline three prominent issues in life-span development.**

Interactional Model	▪ Are we primarily influenced by the reciprocal interaction of both our biological inheritance or by our environment?
Continuity and Discontinuity	▪ Do we change gradually or in distinct stages?
Stability and Change	▪ Do we become older renditions of our childhood selves?
Evaluating Developmental Issues	▪ Life-span developmentalists do not take extreme positions on the three developmental issues.

Some Contemporary Concerns

LO6 **Appraise several major contemporary concerns.**

Health and Well-Being	▪ Research is a major focus of health and well-being, encompassing many areas of concern from genetics to geriatrics. ▪ Fitness, nutrition, mental health, stress, and dementia are some of the research areas.
Education	▪ Research in the area of education focuses on a wide range of topics from curriculum development, dropout rates, approaches to education, and neuroplasticity of the brain. ▪ Social media is drawing much attention to enhance critical thinking as well as enhancing relatedness.
Socio-Cultural Contexts	▪ Culture refers to patterns of behaviour and beliefs, as well as other products of a group that are passed on from generation to generation. ▪ Research in this area focuses primarily on cross-cultural studies, ethnicity, race, and gender.
Social Policy	▪ Social policy refers to a national government's course of action designed to influence the welfare of its citizens (e.g., Canada's approach to First Nations or Aboriginal peoples; generational inequity—the economic fairness to younger people who may shoulder the tax burden of facilities to care for older people, although aging baby boomers may have resource capital; homecare support for the elderly; the infrastructure needed to provide support to immigrants; housing security for the homeless).

Research Methods and Challenges

LO7 Compare and contrast research methodology and challenges.

Methods of Collecting Data	▪ Theory is an interrelated, coherent set of ideas that help explain and make predictions. ▪ Data are collected by observation, both naturalistic and observational, survey and interview, standardized tests, case studies, and physiological measures, including functional magnetic resonance imaging (fMRI).
Research Designs	▪ Descriptive research has the purpose of observing and recording data. ▪ Correlational research has as its goal the explanation or description of the strength of the relationship between two or more events or characteristics. ▪ Experimental research uses both independent and dependent variables to conduct an experiment to determine cause and effect. The independent variable is the manipulated, influential, experimental factor. The dependent variable responds to changes in the independent variable. ▪ Cross-sectional approach is a research strategy in which individuals of different ages are compared at one time. ▪ Longitudinal approach is a research strategy in which individuals are studied over a period of time, usually several years or more. ▪ Sequential approach combines the methods of both cross-sectional and longitudinal approaches. ▪ Cohort effects are the effects related to the historical time or generational time of an individual's birth, but not to actual age.

Research Challenges	- Conduct ethical research. According to the Canadian Psychological Association (CPA), the primary goal for psychologists is "to respect the dignity of all persons with whom they come in contact. . . ." Guidelines to ensure that research complies with this goal are established and reviewed periodically. - Minimize bias. Researchers make every effort to guard against gender, cultural, and ethnic biases in research. Individuals from varied ethnic background need to be included as participants in lifespan research. Overgeneralization about diverse and minority members within a group must be avoided.

review → connect → reflect

review

1. What is meant by the concept of development? LO1
2. List several characteristics of development. LO1
3. Why is the study of life-span development important? LO1
4. How is context related to growth and development? Provide an example. LO2
5. What are the three key developmental processes of development? LO3
6. How is age related to development? LO4
7. What are three main developmental issues? LO5
8. What are some contemporary concerns in life-span development? LO6
9. What research designs are used to study development? LO7
10. What are the researchers' ethical responsibilities to the individuals they study? LO7

connect

Reflect upon your own experience. How do you think biology and culture interact to affect development?

reflect

Your Own Personal Journey of Life

You and your parents grew up at different points in time. Consider some of the ways you are different from your parents. What are several differences that may be caused by cohort effects?

CHAPTER 2

Prominent Approaches in Life-Span Development

CHAPTER OUTLINE

The Psychoanalytic Approach

LO1 Describe the psychoanalytic approach and the contributions of major theorists.

- **Characteristics of the Psychoanalytic Approach**
- **Sigmund Freud**
- **Erik Erikson**
- **Other Psychoanalytic Theories**
- **Evaluating the Psychoanalytic Approach**

The Cognitive Approach

LO2 Compare and contrast the theories within the cognitive approach.

- **Piaget's Cognitive Developmental Theory**
- **Vygotsky's Socio-Cultural Cognitive Theory**
- **The Information-Processing Approach**
- **Evaluating the Cognitive Approach**

The Behavioural and Social Cognitive Approach

LO3 Discuss and examine the behavioural and social cognitive approach, including the contributions of Pavlov, Skinner, and Bandura.

- **Pavlov's Classical Conditioning**
- **Skinner's Operant Conditioning**
- **Bandura's Social Cognitive Theory**
- **Evaluating the Behavioural and Social Cognitive Approach**

The Ethological Approach

LO4 Describe the ethological approach and distinguish among the major contributions of Darwin, Lorenz, Bowlby, and Goodall.

- **Charles Darwin**
- **Konrad Lorenz**
- **John Bowlby**
- **Jane Goodall**
- **Evaluating the Ethological Approach**

The Humanist Approach

LO5 Describe and evaluate the humanist approach, including the contributions of Rogers and Maslow.

- **Carl Rogers**
- **Abraham Maslow**
- **Evaluating the Humanist Approach**

The Bio-Ecological Approach

LO6 Describe Bronfenbrenner's bio-ecological approach and illustrate how each system affects human growth and development.

- **Urie Bronfenbrenner**
- **Evaluating the Bio-Ecological Approach**

Contemporary Approaches to Psychology

LO7 Compare and contrast four contemporary approaches to human growth and development.

- **Positive Psychology**
- **Neuroscience and Neuroplasticity**
- **Dynamic Systems**
- **Evolutionary Psychology**

An Eclectic Theoretical Orientation

LO8 Discuss the eclectic approach.

- **The Eclectic Approach**

"A man is but the product of his thoughts—what he thinks, he becomes."

MAHATMA GANDHI, FATHER OF INDIAN INDEPENDENCE MOVEMENT

Bettmann/Getty Images

Brief Historical Overview of Psychology

Prior to World War I (1914–1918), psychology was concerned with curing mental illness, enabling people to be productive, as well as identifying and nurturing talent. Following World II, (1939–1945) the field shifted its primary focus to mental illness, depression, anger, and suicide (Cherry, 2015). By understanding these elements, psychologists hoped to understand personality growth and development, uncover the deep-rooted causes, and find cures, or at least help people cope.

A prominent figure leading the discussions at this time was Sigmund Freud, who founded the psychoanalytic approach to psychology, and who many believe to be the Father of Psychology. Freud believed we are motivated by both unconscious and conscious drives. We repress events too painful to remember or trauma that occurred in infancy; however, these events become indelibly woven in our brains. In their search for understanding, psychologists have focused on traumatic events, deeply buried memories, and causes for sadness, anger, and depression. In other words, traditional psychology has searched for ways to heal, rather than studying the factors that make life worth living.

As controversial as he is today, Freud's belief that the mind changes in relationship to conscious or repressed entities anticipated prevalent theories in neurology (Doidge, 2006). Eric Kandel, a contemporary proponent of Freud's theories, won the Nobel Prize in 2000 for proving that the process of thinking changes brain structure. Further validation of Freud's theories is illustrated by brain scans of infants who have endured trauma. These scans show structural changes that become encoded in an individual's implicit memory systems, even though the individual does not consciously recall the incident in later years (Doidge, 2006).

Psychoanalytic, humanist, and cognitive theorists broke with Freud in the early 1950s, citing more social and cultural approaches to development. Abraham Maslow and other humanists, such as Carl Rogers, focused their research on strengths and potential. They sought to understand the elements of motivation that created happiness and well-being, and that enabled the personality to flourish, thereby paving the way for today's approach of positive psychology.

Martin Seligman and Mihaly Csikszentmihalyi, two prominent psychologists, met by chance on a beach in Hawaii. Naturally, conversation turned to their lives' passion and work—the science of happiness and creativity. Although Seligman was noted for his research on depression, and Csikszentmihalyi for his research on creativity and flow, both wanted to shift the paradigm of current thinking. In 1996, a year after this fortuitous meeting, Seligman became president of the American Psychology Association and, like every APA president before him, he chose a theme; in this instance, he chose positive psychology (Cherry, 2015).

Theories of positive psychological perspectives are now being used to drive the plasticity of the brain in a positive direction. Improvements in brain chemistry, architecture, and performance associated with lifestyle choices are being studied and documented (Shaffer, 2012). By focusing on what makes us happy rather than what depresses us, we train our minds, and in doing so, we strengthen our resilience and sense of well-being. Such refocusing of our brains has applications in all sorts of activities ranging from health, sports, classrooms, and personal daily lives, to the workplace. For example, when a person decides to stop smoking, defining himself or herself as "a non-smoker" rather than "a smoker-trying-to-quit" may make quitting easier.

Dr. Jamie Gruman of the University of Guelph was instrumental in the founding of the Canadian Positive Psychology Association (CPPA) in 2012. He has conducted extensive research in positive organizational psychology, which explores factors of workplace well-being, employee engagement, and psychological capital: hope, optimism, confidence, and resilience (University of Guelph, 2012).

As you read this chapter, you will get an overview of these theories.

The Psychoanalytic Approach

LO1 Describe the psychoanalytic approach and the contributions of major theorists.

- **Characteristics of the Psychoanalytic Approach**
- **Sigmund Freud**
- **Erik Erikson**
- **Other Psychoanalytic Theories**
- **Evaluating the Psychoanalytic Approach**

Characteristics of the Psychoanalytic Approach

The **psychoanalytic approach** describes development as primarily unconscious—that is, beyond awareness—and as heavily coloured by emotion. Psychoanalytic theorists emphasize that behaviour is merely a surface characteristic and that to truly understand development requires analyzing the symbolic meanings of behaviour and the deep inner workings of the mind.

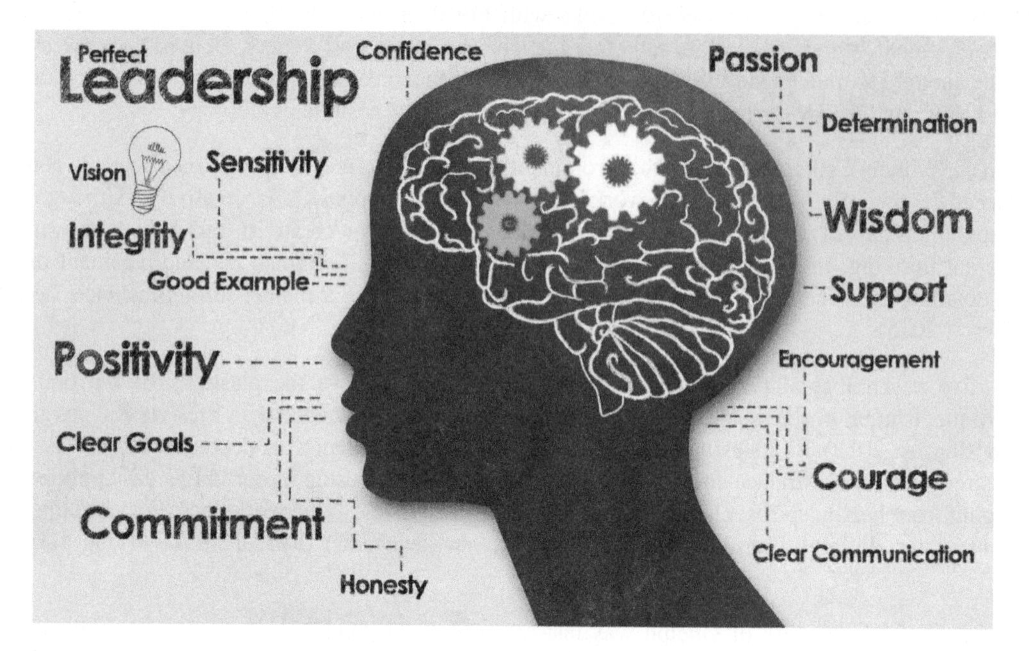

Characteristics of the psychoanalytic approach

Sigmund Freud

The revolutionary founder of psychoanalytic theory, Sigmund Freud's (1856–1939) major contributions include the exploration of the unconscious, from which his personality theory emerged; dream analysis; defence mechanisms; and the five psychosexual stages of development. Though famed for his work in psychoanalysis, few realize that Freud was a trained neurologist and spent as many hours in a laboratory studying neurons as he did in an office practising psychoanalysis (Doidge, 2006).

In 1917, Freud proposed that personality has three structures: the *id*, the *ego*, and the *superego*. The **id** consists of instincts, which are an individual's reservoir of psychic energy. In Freud's view, the id is totally unconscious and not concerned with reality. Early experiences with parents extensively shape development. As children experience the demands and constraints of their worlds, a new structure of personality emerges—the ego, which deals with the demands of reality. The **ego** is called the "executive branch" of the psyche because it uses reasoning to make decisions. The id and the ego are not moral entities. The moral branch of the personality is the **superego**, which takes into account whether something is right or wrong. The superego is what we often refer to as our "conscience."

In Freud's view, the rational ego must resolve conflicts between the demands of reality, the wishes and dreams of the id, and the constraints of the superego. Such conflicts cause anxiety that alerts the ego to use protective measures to resolve the conflict. These protective measures are called defence mechanisms, and they reduce anxiety and conflict by unconsciously distorting reality. As Freud listened to, probed, and analyzed his patients, he became convinced that their problems were the result of traumatic experiences early in life that they had repressed. Freud believed that *repression* is the most powerful and pervasive defence mechanism, because it pushes unacceptable id impulses (such as intense sexual and aggressive desires) into the unconscious mind. He further believed that dreams provide insights into repressed experiences.

Freud's five psychosexual stages illustrate discontinuity as development is accomplished in stages. The theory is that as children grow up, their focus of pleasure and sexual impulses shifts from the *oral stage* to the *anal stage*, followed by the *phallic stage*, the *latency period*, and finally the *genital stage* (see Figure 2.1). Each stage provides a **critical period** during which an individual resolves conflicts between sources of pleasure and the demands of reality. The adult personality is determined by how these conflicts are resolved. Freud believed that the individual is capable of developing a mature love relationship and functioning independently as an adult only when unresolved conflicts from childhood and adolescence are resolved.

Freud's theory has been significantly revised by a number of psychoanalytic theorists. Many of today's psychoanalytic theorists maintain that Freud overemphasized sexual instincts. Theorists such as Erikson, Adler, Horney, Maslow, Bronfenbrenner, Seligman, and Csikszentmihayi placed more emphasis on social and cultural experiences as determinants of an individual's development. Next, we will outline the ideas of one of the most influential revisionists of Freud's ideas—Erik Erikson.

Figure 2.1

Comparison of Freud's Five Psychosexual Stages and Erikson's Eight Psychosocial Stages

Age of Freud's Stages	Freud's Psychosexual Stages of Development	Age of Erikson's Stages	Erikson's Psychosocial Stages of Development
Birth–18 months	Oral stage: Pleasure centres around the mouth: chewing, sucking, and biting.	Birth–12 months	Trust vs. mistrust: Trust emerges when baby feels comfortable and safe. Needs are responded to lovingly. Resolution: Hope
15 months –3 years	Anal: Pleasure centres around the anus muscles and from elimination. Conflict occurs when child is punished too harshly or neglected.	1–3 years	Autonomy vs. shame and doubt: Toddler exercises will and independence. Shame and doubt result when toddler is restrained too much or punished too harshly. Resolution: Will
3–6 years	Phallic: Children discover that manipulation of their own genitals brings pleasure. During this stage, the Oedipus complex for boys and the Electra complex for girls occurs. This is when children first come face to face with the realities of their family life and a conscience emerges as they learn some things are taboo.	Preschool–4 or 5 years	Initiative vs. guilt: As children enter a wider social world, they learn to take responsibility for their toys, their behaviour, their bodies, etc. Their behaviour becomes more purposeful and a sense of accomplishment becomes more important. Guilt is quickly overcome when the child is able to accomplish something. Resolution: Purpose
6 years–puberty	Latency: The child represses interests in sexuality and develops social and intellectual skills.	Grades K–6	Industry vs. inferiority: Children enthusiastically pursue mastery of skills: spelling, multiplication tables, sports, etc. Children enjoy using their creativity and imagination. A sense of inferiority emerges when the child is unproductive or made to feel incompetent. Resolution: Competence
Puberty–late adulthood	Genital: Reawakening of sexual pleasure. The source of sexual pleasure becomes someone outside the family.	Adolescence	Identity vs. identity confusion: Self-discovery occurs at this stage. Resolution: Fidelity

Age of Freud's Stages	Freud's Psychosexual Stages of Development	Age of Erikson's Stages	Erikson's Psychosocial Stages of Development
		Early Adulthood	Intimacy vs. isolation: With a sense of self, the individual is able to commit to a relationship and to responsibilities such as managing one's own resources: health, time, money, relationships. Resolution: Love
		Middle Adulthood	Generativity vs. stagnation: Concern for the next generation. Stagnation occurs when the adult believes they can't contribute to the next generation. Resolution: Care
		Late Adulthood	Integrity vs. despair: In their senior years, individuals reflect on their lives and conclude that their life has or has not been well spent. Resolution: Wisdom

Erik Erikson

Unlike Freud, who believed that motivation is sexual in nature, Erik Erikson (1902–1994) believed that motivation is highly social by nature and reflects a desire to affiliate with others. Both theorists believed development occurs in stages (discontinuity); however, Erikson believed that development occurs over the life span, whereas Freud believed our basic personalities are formed by five years of age. Additionally, in contrast to Freud's five *psychosexual stages*, **Erikson's theory** identified eight stages and called them *psychosocial stages* (see Figure 2.1).

Each stage consists of a unique developmental task that confronts individuals with a crisis that must be faced. According to Erikson, the crisis is more of a turning point and is indicative of both increased vulnerability and enhanced potential. Like Freud, Erikson believed that the more successfully individuals resolve the crises or turning points, the healthier development will be (Hopkins, 2000).

Erikson believed that the resolution of a stage is not always completely positive. Some of the negative aspects to conflict are inevitable—you cannot trust all people under all circumstances and survive, for example. Nonetheless, balance is achieved in the healthy resolution to a stage crisis and virtues, or emotional strengths, emerge.

Historical time provides a context that influences thinking and behaviour. Attitudes and beliefs about a variety of concepts such as gender and human rights undergo major paradigm shifts and influence thought. For example, although Canadians hold dear their right to vote, it wasn't until 1960 that First Nations peoples were given that right. Same-sex marriage illustrates another major paradigm shift. Although some provinces had granted the right to marry earlier, 2005 marks the year that Canada as a nation extended the right for couples of the same sex to marry. Our thinking, laws, and norms change with time. Scholars such as Freud and Erikson developed their theories within a historical and social milieu as well. For example, Freud's argument that wars were the result of pent-up aggression may have been influenced by the historic World Wars I and II that took place in Europe and affected his life directly. Similarly, Erikson's belief that the key elements of women's identity were that of mother and wife were developed in the 1950s, a time when women did not enter the workforce as they do today and one income was sufficient to support a family.

Erik Erikson generated one of the most important developmental theories of the twentieth century. *Which stage of Erikson's theory are you in? Does Erikson's description of this stage characterize you?*

critical thinking

A number of psychoanalysts and psychologists have taken exception to the stages proposed by both Freud and Erikson, arguing that the progression from stage to stage differs for men and women or that development does not occur in stages. Do you believe your personal growth has progressed from one stage to the next, or have you developed more continuously? Do you think the cultural variables in your life, including your gender, have influenced your growth and development? If so, how?

Other Psychoanalytic Theories

The term *neo-Freudians* refers to psychologists who have contributed further to the psychoanalytic approach initiated by Freud. Some psychoanalysts thought that Freud's view of human nature was too negative and overly concerned with sex and aggression. Others believed that environmental, social, and biological factors, as well as both conscious and unconscious forces, influence personality development. A myriad of divergent ideas sprung forth from this group, including Alfred Adler, Carl Jung, Karen Horney, and Freud's own daughter, Anna Freud. None of these prominent theorists proposed a stage theory; instead, they looked at personality development more holistically. Figure 2.2 provides a synopsis of the contributions of the neo-Freudians.

Figure 2.2

Major Contributions of the Neo-Freudian Psychoanalytic Theorists

Neo-Freudian	**Theory**
Alfred Adler 1870–1937	Alfred Adler developed *individual psychology* because he believed each person is unique and is striving toward emotional health and well-being. He identified the inferiority complex to describe our feelings of lack of self-worth; we struggle to overcome our inferiority (Fisher, 2001).
Carl Jung 1875–1961	Carl Jung believed the psyche includes three parts: the *ego*, or the conscious mind; the *personal unconscious*, which includes everything not presently conscious, and the *collective unconscious*, or "psychic inheritance." *Déjà vu*, love at first sight, and immediate responses to various symbols are examples of the collective unconscious (Boeree, 2006). Jung developed a personality typology that distinguished between introversion and extraversion and identified preferred ways of dealing with the world. This typology is the groundwork for the Myers-Briggs Personality Inventory.
Karen Horney 1885–1952	Horney, a student of Freud's, criticized his work on the grounds of gender and cultural differences. Well-known for her work on neurosis, Horney identified ten neurotic trends that she believed result from parental indifference and that she called the "basic evil." The child's reaction to parental indifference, basic hostility, and basic anxiety leads the child to develop coping strategies; as the individual matures, neuroses may develop.
Anna Freud 1895–1982	Sigmund Freud's daughter, Anna Freud, made significant contributions to the fields of child psychoanalysis and child development psychology from her work in the analysis of children and adolescents. She was concerned with the ego, its conflicts with reality, and the defence mechanisms.
Eric Fromm 1900–1980	Fromm believed human nature is influenced by dysfunctional social patterns, such as poverty, war, power, and capitalistic greed, as well as biological factors. He endorsed the concepts of feminism and supported Horney's assertions of gender differences by arguing that men have to prove themselves in the world and thus are driven to acquire wealth and power at the expense of people and environment. Women, on the other hand, fear being abandoned and submit to male power. Fromm, who studied the theories of Karl Marx, believed that capitalistic societies alienate citizens, particularly those most marginalized or impoverished. Thus, he, along with Horney, was one of the first to consider the influence of racism, sexism, and economic inequities on personality growth.

Evaluating the Psychoanalytic Approach

Contributions of psychoanalytic theories include an emphasis on a developmental framework, family relationships, and the unconscious aspects of the mind. Criticisms include a lack of scientific rigour, too much emphasis on sexual underpinnings, and a relatively negative view of human nature.

To this point, we have discussed the various theories of the psychoanalytic approach. For a review, see the Reach Your Learning Outcomes section at the end of this chapter.

The Cognitive Approach

LO2 Compare and contrast the theories within the cognitive approach.

- **Piaget's Cognitive Developmental Theory**
- **Vygotsky's Socio-Cultural Cognitive Theory**
- **The Information-Processing Approach**
- **Evaluating the Cognitive Approach**

Whereas psychoanalytic theories stress the importance of unconscious thoughts, **cognitive theories** emphasize conscious thoughts. Three important cognitive theories are Piaget's cognitive development theory, Vygotsky's socio-cultural cognitive theory, and the information-processing approach.

Piaget's Cognitive Developmental Theory

Swiss psychologist Jean Piaget (1896–1980) proposed an important theory of cognitive development that illustrates discontinuity. **Piaget's theory** states that children actively construct their understanding of the world and go through four stages of cognitive development. Two processes underlie this cognitive construction of the world: organization and adaptation. To make sense of our world, we organize our experiences (Carpendale, Muller, & Bibok, 2008). For example, we separate important ideas from less important ideas and we connect one idea to another. But not only do we organize our observations and experiences, we also adapt our thinking to include new ideas because additional information furthers understanding (Byrnes, 2008). Piaget (1954) believed that we adapt in two ways: assimilation and accommodation.

Assimilation occurs when individuals incorporate new information into their existing knowledge. Accommodation occurs when individuals adjust to new information, for example when an infant drops a rattle over the side of the crib and learns gravity (Elkind, 1997–2012). Consider the circumstance in which a 9-year-old girl is given a hammer and nails to hang a picture on the wall. She has never used a hammer, but from observation she realizes that a hammer is an object to be held, that it is swung by the handle to hit the nail, and that it is usually swung a number of times. Recognizing each of these things, she fits her behaviour to the information she already has (assimilation). However, the hammer is heavy, and so she holds it near the top. She swings too hard and the nail bends, so she adjusts the pressure of her strikes. These adjustments reveal her ability to slightly alter her conception of the world, also known as **accommodation**. Learning progresses from one stage to the next, including from reflex to determined behaviour, as information is first assimilated and then accommodated.

Piaget thought that assimilation and accommodation operate in the very young infant's life. Newborns reflexively suck everything that touches their lips (assimilation), but after several months of experience they construct their understanding of the world differently. Some objects, such as fingers and the mother's breast, can be sucked, but others, such as fuzzy blankets, should not be sucked (accommodation).

Each of the four stages we go through as we seek an understanding of the world around us is age-related and consists of distinct ways of thinking (see Figure 2.3). According to Piaget, it is the different way of understanding the world that makes one stage more advanced than another; knowing more information does not make the child's thinking more advanced. This is what Piaget meant when he said the child's cognition is qualitatively different in one stage than in another (Vidal, 2000).

Figure 2.3

Piaget's Four Stages of Cognitive Development

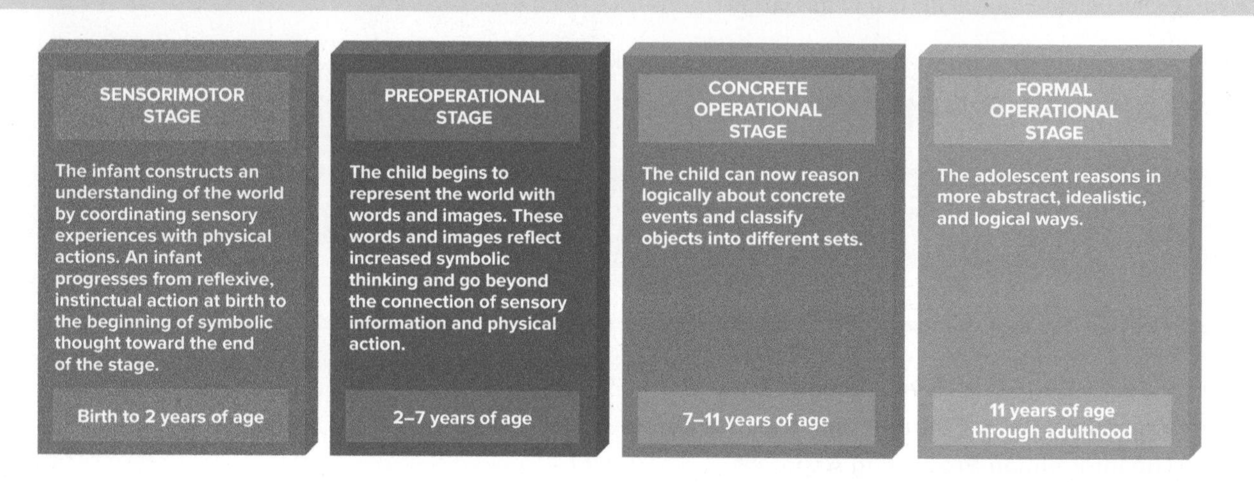

The *sensorimotor stage*, from birth to about 2 years of age, is the first Piagetian stage. In this stage, infants construct an understanding of the world by coordinating sensory experiences (such as seeing and hearing) with physical, motoric actions—hence the term sensorimotor. At the beginning of this stage, newborns have little more than reflexive patterns with which to work. At the end of the stage, 2-year-olds have complex sensorimotor patterns and are beginning to operate with primitive symbols.

The *preoperational stage*, from approximately 2 to 7 years of age, is the second Piagetian stage. In this stage, children begin to represent the world with words, images, and drawings. However, although preschool children can symbolically represent the world, according to Piaget they still lack the ability to perform operations, the Piagetian term for internalized mental actions that allow children to do mentally what they previously did physically.

The *concrete operational stage*, from approximately 7 to 11 years of age, is the third Piagetian stage. In this stage, children can perform operations and logical reasoning replaces intuitive thought, as long as reasoning can be applied to specific or concrete examples. For instance, concrete operational thinkers cannot imagine the steps necessary to complete an algebraic equation because manipulating unknowns is too abstract at this stage of development.

The *formal operational stage*, which appears between the ages of 11 and 15 years, is the fourth and final Piagetian stage. In this stage, individuals move beyond concrete experiences and think in abstract and more logical terms. As part of thinking more abstractly, adolescents develop images of ideal circumstances. They begin to entertain possibilities for the future and are fascinated with what they can be. In solving problems, they become more systematic, developing hypotheses about why something is happening the way it is and then testing these hypotheses.

Since Piaget's time, researchers have broadened Piaget's theories to include ideas from other traditions. Robbie Case (1994–2000), Director of the University of Toronto's Institute of Child Study prior to his death, is considered the quintessential neo-Piagetian. Case broadened Piaget's stages by incorporating Vygotsky's social-constructivist theory, information processing, linguistics, and current findings in neuroscience (Jackson, 2003).

Jean Piaget, the famous Swiss developmental psychologist, changed the way we think about the development of children's minds. *What are some key ideas in Piaget's theory?*

CONNECTING through research

The Magic Brain—Neuroplasticity

The brain is an incredible organ, with physiological properties that lend themselves to the development of complex, dynamic, and flexible human minds. It can produce new neurons or nerves ("neuro"), resulting in a brain that is malleable or adaptable ("plastic"), hence the word *neuroplasticity* (Doidge, 2007; Wexler, 2006). When one part of the brain is damaged—by stroke, accident, or trauma, for example—it is able to recruit capacity from another area of the brain to increase processing power (Doidge, 2007; Wexler, 2006). With intensive therapeutic treatment, patients have regained eyesight, recovered functioning after strokes, and ameliorated learning disorders (Doidge, 2007).

Rehabilitation training and aerobic exercise optimize learning and memory and promote neuroplasticity to facilitate the acquisition and retention of motor skills for post-stroke patients (Mang et al., 2013). Patients with brain injuries also receive rehabilitation intervention; however, the role of genetic expression influences the progress of such interventions. Motor recovery after brain damage requires that the individual participates in repetitive, intensive, and salient practice. Virtual reality systems using webcams and computer screens may assist in balance retraining, executive functioning, pain management, and upper-limb rehabilitation for both children and adults. The rapid changes in technology undermine available equipment and applications (Levin, 2011).

As neuroscience progresses, the potential for understanding and healing traumatic experiences (conscious or not) and degenerative diseases such as Alzheimer's disease becomes more plausible (Doidge, 2007). As brain imaging becomes more refined and sophisticated, therapists will be able to more effectively help individuals who have been diagnosed with mental illnesses or are facing difficult emotional circumstances (Pugh, 2004). In other words, as the body of knowledge grows, we will come to understand how the brain is changed by such things as emotional experiences, addictions, and learning experiences, as well as cultural factors such as technology (Doidge, 2007).

Vygotsky's Socio-Cultural Cognitive Theory

Like Piaget, the Russian psychologist Lev Vygotsky (1896–1934) also believed that children actively construct their knowledge. However, Vygotsky gave social interaction and culture far more important roles than did Piaget (Gauvain, 2013). **Vygotsky's theory** is a socio-cultural cognitive theory that emphasizes how culture and social interaction guide cognitive development. Vygotsky was born the same year as Piaget, but he died much earlier, from tuberculosis at the age of 37. Again, the social-political context emerged, this time in Russia, and the Russian government repudiated Vygotsky's theories. Fortunately, they were recovered in 1957 and are widely considered by psychologists, educators, and parents today.

A.R. Lauria/Dr. Michael Cole, Laboratory of Human Cognition, University of California, San Diego

There is considerable interest today in Lev Vygotsky's socio-cultural cognitive theory of child development. *What were Vygotsky's three basic claims about children's development?*

Vygotsky portrayed child development as inseparable from social and cultural activities (Gauvain, 2013). He believed that the development of *memory, attention, and reasoning* involves learning to use the inventions of society, such as language, mathematical systems, and memory strategies. In one culture, this might consist of learning to count with the help of a calculator. In another, it might consist of counting on one's fingers or using beads. Vygotsky's theory has stimulated considerable interest in the view that knowledge is *situated and collaborative* (Tudge, 2004). In this view, knowledge is not generated from within the individual, but instead is constructed through interaction with other people and objects in the culture, such as books and social media. This suggests that knowing can best be advanced through interaction with others in cooperative activities. According to Vygotsky, children's social interaction with more-skilled adults and peers is indispensable to their cognitive development (Mahn & John-Steiner, 2013). Through this interaction, they learn to use the tools that will help them adapt and be successful in their culture.

The Information-Processing Approach

The **information-processing approach** emphasizes that individuals manipulate information, monitor it, and strategize about it. The processes of memory and thinking are central to this approach. According to this approach, individuals develop a gradually increasing capacity for processing information, which allows them to acquire increasingly complex knowledge and skills (Halford, 2008; Vallotton & Fischer, 2008). Like Vygotsky's theory, the information-processing approach does not describe development as being stage-like.

Robert Siegler (2006, 2007), a leading expert on children's information processing, believes that thinking is information processing. He says that when individuals perceive, encode, represent, store, and retrieve information, they are thinking. Siegler believes that an important aspect of development is learning good strategies for processing information. For example, becoming a better reader might involve learning to monitor the key themes of the material being read. Robinson and Dube of the University of Regina study how students in grades 5 and 6 process multiplication and division. Their findings suggest that multiplication is committed to memory and more quickly retrieved on small problems than is division, which generally relies on skill for retrieval. Further, a "left to right" orientation, reinforced by reading, coupled with the focus on skills related to long division, may further contribute to the difficulty children have in acquiring concepts that are integral for understanding arithmetic in later years (Robinson, interview, 2016; Robinson & Dube, 2008, 2009).

Dr. Kang Lee (2010) notes that telling lies involves processing and manipulating information while at the same time keeping the truth in mind. Although most conscious lying starts at about 3 years of age, some very intelligent, perhaps gifted, children start telling lies at as young as 2 years old. As children mature they get better at lying, and their skills peak at age 12. About age 16, the tendency to tell lies falls off. Lee's studies have indicated that telling lies illustrates brain activity and does not mean the child is to become deceptive or will cheat; rather, because it is developmental and involves so much brain activity, lying serves as a predictor of future success (Alleyene, 2010).

Evaluating the Cognitive Approach

Contributions of the cognitive theories include a positive view of development and an emphasis on the active construction of understanding. Criticisms include skepticism about the pureness of Piaget's stages and insufficient attention to individual variations.

To this point, we have studied a number of ideas about the cognitive approach. For a review, see the Reach Your Learning Outcomes section at the end of this chapter.

The Behavioural and Social Cognitive Approach

LO3 Discuss and examine the behavioural and social cognitive approach, including the contributions of Pavlov, Skinner, and Bandura.

- **Pavlov's Classical Conditioning**
- **Skinner's Operant Conditioning**
- **Bandura's Social Cognitive Theory**
- **Evaluating the Behavioural and Social Cognitive Approach**

critical thinking

Imagine that you were to create a scrapbook of your life to date. Which of these theories do you think reflects your personal growth and development? What examples might you use to illustrate the theories you have chosen?

At about the same time that Freud was interpreting patients' unconscious minds through their early childhood experiences, Ivan Pavlov and John B. Watson were conducting detailed observations of behaviour in controlled laboratory settings. Their work provided the foundations of *behaviourism*, which essentially holds that only what can be directly observed and measured can be studied in a scientific way. Out of the behavioural tradition grew the belief that development is observable behaviour that can be learned through experience with the environment (Chance, 2014; Levy, 2013). In terms of the continuity–discontinuity issue discussed in Chapter 1, the behavioural and social cognitive theories emphasize continuity in development and argue that development does not occur in stage-like fashion. The three versions of the behavioural approach that we will explore are Pavlov's classical conditioning, Skinner's operant conditioning, and Bandura's social cognitive theory.

Pavlov's Classical Conditioning

In the early 1900s, Russian physiologist Ivan Pavlov (1927) knew that dogs innately salivate when they taste food. He became curious when he observed that dogs salivate in reaction to various sights and sounds even before eating their food. For example, when the ringing of a bell was paired with the food, the bell ringing alone subsequently elicited the dog's salivation. As a result, Pavlov discovered the principle of *classical conditioning*, in which a neutral stimulus (in this case, ringing a bell) acquires the ability to produce a response originally produced by another stimulus (in this example, food).

Many of our fears—fear of the dentist following a painful experience, fear of driving after being in an automobile accident, fear of heights—may have been learned through classical conditioning. As well, many of our stereotypical assumptions or fears may have been learned. For example, does the pairing of a word such as "terrorist" to a particular group stir up negative stereotypical images and create fear?

Skinner's Operant Conditioning

Classical conditioning may explain how we develop many involuntary responses such as fear, but B. F. Skinner (1904–1990) argued that a second type of conditioning accounts for the development of types of behaviour. According to Skinner's theory of *operant conditioning* (1938), the consequences of a behaviour produce changes in the probability of the behaviour's future occurrence. If a behaviour is followed by a rewarding stimulus, it is more likely to recur, but if a behaviour is followed by a punishing stimulus, it is less likely to recur. For example, when a person smiles at a child after the child has done something, the child is more likely to engage in the activity than if the person gives the child a disapproving look.

In Skinner's view (1938), such rewards and punishments shape individuals' development. For example, Skinner's approach argues that shy people learned to be shy because of the environmental experiences they had while growing up. It follows that modifications to an environment can help a shy person become more socially oriented. Skinner emphasized that behavioural changes are brought about by rewards and punishments, not by thoughts and feelings.

Bandura's Social Cognitive Theory

Some psychologists believe that the behaviourists are basically right when they say development is learned and is influenced strongly by environmental experiences. However, they also see cognition as important in understanding development (Mischel, 2004; Mischel et al., 2011). The **behavioural and social cognitive approach** is the view of psychologists who emphasize behaviour, environment, and cognition as the key factors in development.

Canadian-born psychologist Albert Bandura (1925–) was one of the leading architects of social cognitive theory. Bandura (1986, 2001, 2004, 2006, 2008, 2009a) emphasizes that cognitive processes have important links with environment and behaviour. Bandura's early research focused heavily on observational learning. Observational learning is also referred to as imitation or modelling. For example, a toddler may observe his older brother playing hockey and imitate his movements. Social cognitive theorists stress that people acquire a wide range of behaviours, thoughts, and feelings through observing the behaviour of others, and that these observations form an important part of life-span development.

Bandura believes that people cognitively represent the behaviour of others and then sometimes adopt this behaviour themselves. For example, a parent who often tells her child that he has three options, a, b, or c, may hear her child resolve a conflict with a friend by saying, "Tristan, we have three options. . . ." These observations form an important part of life-span development.

Bandura's (2001, 2004, 2006) most recent model of learning and development involves three elements: behaviour, the person, and the environment. An individual's confidence that he can control his success is an example of a person factor; strategies to do so are an example of a cognitive factor. As shown in Figure 2.4, behaviour, personal (and cognitive), and environmental factors operate interactively. Behaviour can influence personal factors and vice versa. The person's cognitive activities can influence the environment, the environment can change the person's cognition, and so on.

Figure 2.4
Bandura's Social Cognitive Model

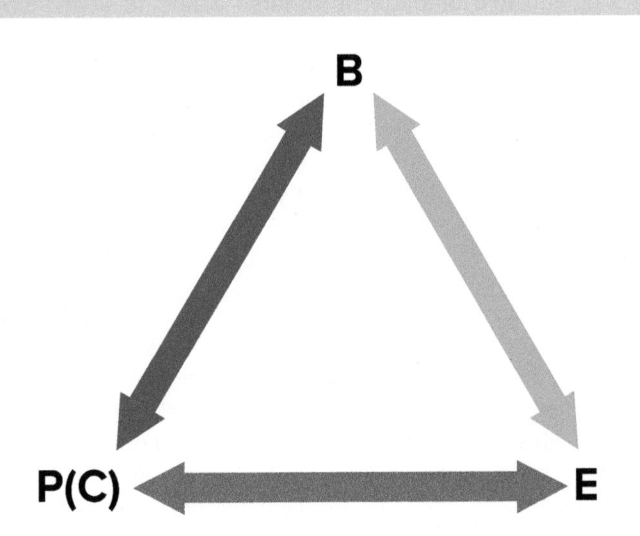

P(C) stands for personal and cognitive factors, *B* for behaviour, and *E* for environment. The arrows reflect how relations among these factors are reciprocal, rather than unidirectional.

Albert Bandura has been one of the leading architects of social cognitive theory. *How does Bandura's theory differ from Skinner's?*

critical thinking

The Children's Aid Society placed two teenaged brothers, 17 and 18 years old, in a group home. Their aunt and uncle had adopted them when they were 3 and 4 years of age because their mother, who has since died, was unable to care for them due to her drug and alcohol dependency. The boys were caged for 13 years and deprived of food, sanitation, and nurturing. In January 2004, their adoptive parents pleaded guilty to forcible confinement, assault with a weapon, and failure to provide the necessities of life. Based on your readings, observations, and experiences, how do you think the boys' physical, mental, and emotional growth would be affected? Imagine that you may interact with one or both of the brothers either professionally or as a neighbour. How might you understand them? Which of the theories discussed so far would be most useful to you? Which do you think would not be helpful?

Consider how Bandura's model might work in the case of a university student's achievement behaviour. As the student diligently studies and gets good grades, her behaviour produces positive thoughts about her abilities. As part of her effort to make good grades, she plans and develops a number of strategies to make her studying more efficient. In these ways, her behaviour has influenced her thoughts, and her thoughts have influenced her behaviour. At the beginning of the term, her school made a special effort to involve students in a study skills program, and she decided to join it. Her success, along with that of other students who attended the program, has led the university to expand the program next semester. In these ways, environment influenced behaviour, and behaviour changed the environment. The administrators' expectations that the study skills program would work made it possible in the first place. The program's success has spurred expectations that this type of program could work in other universities. In these ways, cognition changed the environment, and the environment changed cognition.

Evaluating the Behavioural and Social Cognitive Approach

Contributions of the behavioural and social cognitive theories include an emphasis on scientific research and environmental determinants of behaviour. Criticisms include too little emphasis on cognition and too much attention on environmental determinants.

To this point, we have discussed the behavioural and social cognitive approach. For a review, see the Reach Your Learning Outcomes section at the end of this chapter.

The Ethological Approach

LO4 Describe the ethological approach and distinguish among the major contributions of Darwin, Lorenz, Bowlby, and Goodall.

- **Charles Darwin**
- **Konrad Lorenz**
- **John Bowlby**
- **Jane Goodall**
- **Evaluating the Ethological Approach**

Ethology is the study of animals to discover their responses to the environment, their physiological makeup, their communication abilities, and their evolutionary aspects. For example, ethologists might study a trait such as dominance, mating, or aggression in many different types of animals to understand whether the behaviour is innate or learned. Ethologists believe behaviour is influenced by biology and that a critical or sensitive period is essential for healthy development. The presence or absence of certain experiences has a long-lasting influence on individuals.

Ethologists use three methods of study to understand the origins of non-verbal behaviours, social grooming, and other innate behaviours. They compare the behaviour of closely related species, for example humans and apes. They also study the responses of healthy children with those who have physical or intellectual challenges, such as deafness or blindness. Additionally, ethologists consider whether behaviours occur in more than one culture, as the more universally a behaviour is observed, the stronger the possibility that it is innate. Research shows that many non-verbal behaviours, such as smiles, raised eyebrows, and even flirting, are similar among cultures, and are therefore thought to be innate. Let's look at the contribution of four ethological theorists.

Charles Darwin

Charles Darwin (1809–1882), a British naturalist, was one of the first to theorize about the connection between humans and the rest of the animal kingdom. His theories of evolution, natural selection, and survival of the fittest were based on years of scientific study and observation. You will read more about the evolutionary approach in Chapter 3.

Konrad Lorenz

Zoologist Konrad Lorenz (1903–1989) is often called the "father of ethology" because of his studies of the innate behaviour of animals, especially imprinting in young birds. Through an elaborate set of experiments, mostly with greylag geese, Lorenz (1965) determined that newly hatched goslings attach themselves to the first "mother" figure they see. In fact, the goslings that were hatched in an incubator followed Lorenz everywhere because he was the first "mother" figure they saw, whereas those hatched in their natural habitat by their mother immediately bonded with her. He called this process *imprinting*, the rapid, innate learning within a limited critical period of time that involves attachment to the first moving object seen.

Operation Migration, founded in 1995 by William Lishman and John Duff, two Canadian artists turned naturalists, aims to save endangered species and uses the strategies introduced by Lorenz. A sculptor and environmentalist, Lishman dreamed of flying with the birds as a child, and in his teens, he pioneered ultralight aircrafts, planes described by some as chairs with wings and small engines. When a batch of goslings hatched near his Ontario home, the first moving object they saw was Lishman's ultralight aircraft, and naturally they attached themselves to it. Similar to the methods used by Lorenz more than two decades earlier, Lishman and his three children incubated eggs until they hatched, then trained the goslings who had attached themselves to Lishman and his children to follow them on foot, on motorcycles, and ultimately in an ultralight aircraft. Each time he led small groups of geese on local migratory flights, Lishman, or "Father Goose" as he is now widely known, felt the excitement and wonder of flying with the birds that he had imagined as a child. In 1993, he teamed up with photographer and ultralight pilot John Duff, and together they successfully led 18 geese on their migratory route from Ontario to Virginia. Duff's film, "Fly Away Home," documents this flight. Operation Migration uses imprinting principles to teach birds their natural migration routes so they may be reintroduced to their natural habitat (McKenzie, 2016; *McLean's,* 1996; Operation Migration, 2016).

Photo by Nina Leen/Life Magazine. © Time, Inc.

Konrad Lorenz, a pioneering student of animal behaviour, is followed through the water by three imprinted greylag geese. *Describe Lorenz's experiment with the geese. Do you think his experiment would have the same results with human babies? Explain.*

John Bowlby

John Bowlby (1907–1990), the "Father of Attachment Theory," contributed one of the most important applications of the ethological approach to human development. Bowlby stressed that all infants form enduring emotional bonds with their caregivers beyond the need for physical nourishment. The caregiver's role to protect the infant from harm ensures the survival of the species. Smiling, crying, and cooing are all part of the infant's innate repertoire of behaviours that elicit caregiver responses. The infant's senses—touch, smell, taste, sight, and hearing—all become intimately bound with the nurturer. In this manner, an infant elicits loving, protective responses from the caregiver, which in turn strengthen attachment. If the attachment is negative and insecure, life-span development will likely not be optimal.

As the infant grows and develops, he seeks the proximity of the caregiver, usually the mother. The child may wander off, but he frequently checks back with or returns to the mother or primary caregiver, thus ensuring availability and attentiveness. The young child does not seek out any caregiver, but only the one with whom a strong bond has been established. In a sense, this has been imprinted, thereby reducing the number of people the child will seek out.

A secure attachment during the critical period of the first two years of life contributes to the child's ability to develop a sense of self. According to Bowlby, there is no such thing as responding too much in the first 18 months. Responding reinforces attachment, and this strong bond enables the child to develop healthy relationships later in life. Secure attachments are associated with lower levels of depression, closer friendships, and more stable romantic relationships.

Jane Goodall

Jane Goodall (1934–), a well-known animal activist and scientist, has been dedicated to learning about animals since childhood. She studied chimpanzees in Tanzania and, gaining their trust, was able to document the complex social system of the chimps, including their ability to communicate, to make tools, and to comfort each other, along with their social status signs and gender roles. Through her programs and writings, she challenged scientists to redefine their long-held ideas on differences between humans and other primates. In recognition of her work she has received many awards, and was appointed a United Nations Messenger of Peace in 2002.

Jane Goodall is a well-known ethologist and animal activist whose studies of chimpanzees challenged previous ideas of how humans differed from other species.

Evaluating the Ethological Approach

Contributions of the ethological approach include a focus on biological and evolutionary bases of development, the role of sensitive or critical periods, and the use of careful observations in naturalistic settings. Criticisms include too much emphasis on biological foundations and the rigid time frame for the sensitive or critical periods.

To this point, we have discussed the ethological approach. For a review, see the Reach Your Learning Outcomes section at the end of this chapter.

The Humanist Approach

LO5 Describe and evaluate the humanist approach, including the contributions of Rogers and Maslow.

- **Carl Rogers**
- **Abraham Maslow**
- **Evaluating the Humanist Approach**

In the various schools of thought that you have read about so far, behaviour is rooted in either unconscious drives or biological processes. That there are other schools of thought should come as no surprise, because neither biology nor empirical behaviour could fully satisfy many prominent psychologists. As such, Abraham Maslow and Carl Rogers, believing they were onto a new frontier of understanding, founded the humanist school of thought.

The **humanists** believe that people work hard to become the best they can possibly become. Abraham Maslow called this striving self-actualization, whereas Rogers called it an actualizing tendency. These terms differ in that Maslow believed very few of us self-actualize, while Rogers believed all of us tend to self-actualize. Putting this difference aside, they agreed that all human behaviour is intrinsically motivated toward self-improvement and that values, intentions, and meaning play important roles in growth and development.

Carl Rogers

Carl Rogers (1902–1987) believed that in order for growth, individuals need an environment that provides openness, acceptance, and empathy. Given those three components, individuals can flourish and become fully functioning. He defined **congruence** as a state when our "ideal self" and our real self are consistent with each other. Another core concept is that our actualizing tendency refers to our efforts to reduce incongruity, the gap between the *real self* (the "I am") and the *ideal self* (the "I should be"). Rogers referred to this gap as **incongruity**.

Rogers believed that human nature strives to be healthy and that mental illness, criminality, and other human problems are distortions of the motivation toward health. According to Rogers (1961), a healthy, fully functioning person has the following characteristics: openness; existential living or engagement in the present; reliance on gut instincts when making decisions; freedom to experiment and assume responsibility; creativity; reliability and constructiveness for maintaining balance; and living a rich, full life (McLeod, 2012; Rogers, 1961).

Abraham Maslow

Abraham Maslow's (1908–1970) *hierarchy of needs* (1943) has been widely used to understand and explain human motivation. Maslow believed that human nature was either neutral or inherently good. His argument that some needs take precedence over others was based on observation and critical analysis. He noted things such as the fact that when we are critically ill, our need for sleep overtakes our need for self-esteem; once we are rested and healthy, we can resume fulfilling our esteem needs and return to work. In Canada, the hierarchy of needs is realized in accordance with Canadian norms and standards of living, which are quite different from those in many parts of the world. For example, people in many countries do not have universal health care, nor is water so readily available.

Maslow applied the principle of *homeostasis*—the body's desire to maintain balance—to explain his theory. Homeostasis functions as an internal monitor, alerting us when we need to put on a sweater or quench our thirst. Similarly, the first four needs in the hierarchy (physiological, safety and security, love and belonging, esteem needs) are primarily physical in nature and go relatively unnoticed in Canadian life unless they are not met.

According to Maslow, the esteem needs have a "lower" and "higher" order. The lower-order esteem needs are satisfied when we experience respect and recognition from others. Because recognition from others is often temporary and elusive, it can be lost just as easily as it was gained. The higher-order self-esteem needs, however, are not so easily lost as they are based on the respect we have for ourselves. Feelings of self-confidence, competence, autonomy, and freedom characterize this higher order. If our esteem needs are not met, we may suffer from inferiority complexes. Maslow called these needs *D-needs*, or *deficit needs*. When one is not met, an individual experiences anxiety and is motivated to find a way to fulfill this need.

Maslow believed that the primarily physical needs become dormant once they are met, leaving us free to pursue more psychological needs. Being intelligent and restless by nature, we strive to use our capacities and develop to our fullest potential. Thus, Maslow expanded his original hierarchy to include cognitive and aesthetic needs as well as self-actualizing needs. He called these growth needs *being needs*, or *B-needs*. He believed that failure to develop and use our capacities results in atrophy, anxiety, and neuroses.

Believing that we turn from ugliness and that we feel calmer and healthier in beautiful surroundings, Maslow further postulated that we strive for what he termed aesthetic needs. When the earlier needs are met, we wish to create and surround ourselves with beauty. The creation of music, art, architecture, and museums, as well as our appreciation of nature, illustrate this need (Maslow, 1970).

Self-actualization is the individualized expression of self in terms of reaching one's fullest potential without concern for praise or rewards. He regarded self-actualization as peak moments during which we are able to transcend physical and social conventions. The more completely the earlier needs are satisfied, the more peak moments we can experience. If forced to live without the freedom to be one's authentic self, the self-actualizer is vulnerable to depression, despair, disgust, alienation, and a degree of cynicism. Maslow believed that only 2 percent of the population and few, if any, young people could attain self-actualization because social and economic pressures keep our internal monitors directed at filling deficits (Maslow, 1954, 1968, 1970).

Maslow postulated that "a desire to understand, to systematize, to organize, to analyze, to look for relations and meanings" is an innate cognitive need (Maslow, 1970, p. 385). He attempted to distinguish between, yet also rank in order of importance, the desire for information and the desire for understanding, and wrote, "insight is usually a bright, happy, emotional spot in any person's life, perhaps even a high spot in the life span" (Maslow, 1970, p. 158).

critical thinking

To what degree do you act in accordance with Maslow's hierarchy of needs? Can you think of times when you acted in a way that was consistent with this theory, and others when you did not? Do you think the theory holds true for most people in most situations? If you were living in a war-torn country such as Syria, how might Maslow's hierarchy of needs apply?

Evaluating the Humanist Approach

The contributions of the humanist approach are the positive regard for human nature and the consideration of the environment on development. Criticisms include that the interpretation is too subjective and the approach lacks scientific rigour. Recent studies suggest that perception is integral to human motivation and that perception of time alters goals. When time is perceived as limited, for example when faced with mortality, both younger and older people change their goals (Gawande, 2014).

To this point, we have discussed the humanist approach. For a review, see the Reach Your Learning Outcomes section at the end of this chapter.

The Bio-Ecological Approach

LO6 Describe Bronfenbrenner's bio-ecological approach and illustrate how each system affects human growth and development.

- **Urie Bronfenbrenner**
- **Evaluating the Bio-Ecological Approach**

Urie Bronfenbrenner

Urie Bronfenbrenner(1917–2005), co-founder of the Head Start program, developed a **bio-ecological approach** (1986, 2000, 2004) that holds that development reflects the influence of five environmental systems (see Figure 2.5).

Figure 2.5

Bio-Ecological Theory of Development

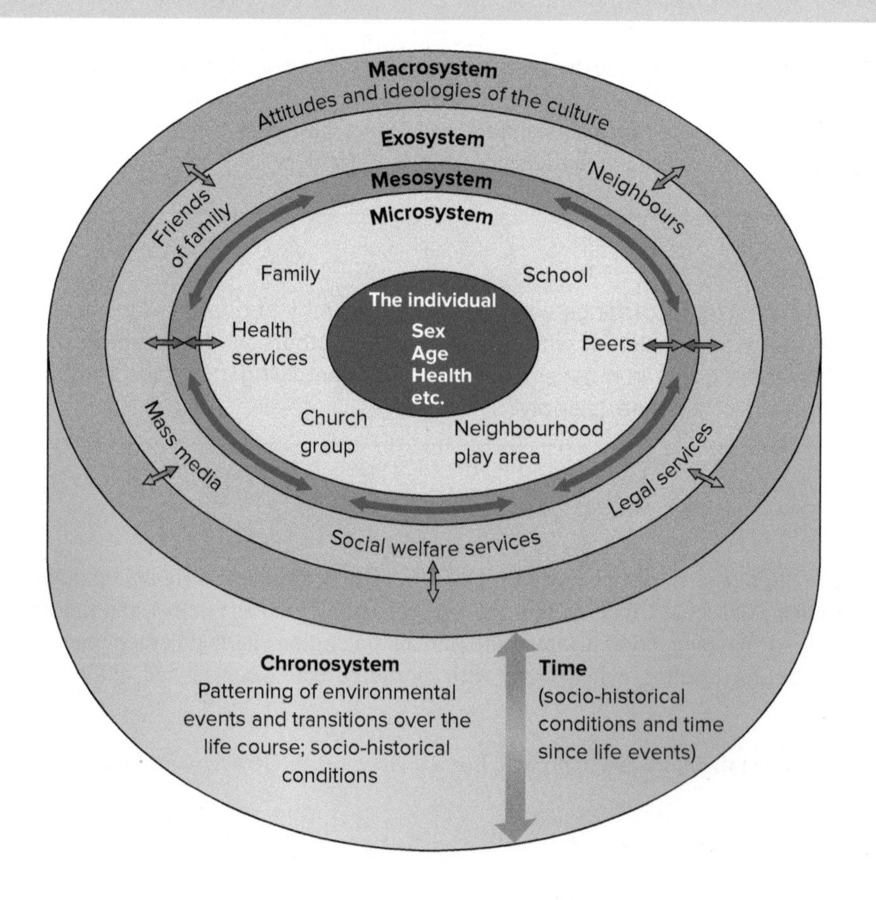

A.R. Lauria/Dr. Michael Cole, Laboratory of Human Cognition, University of California, San Diego

Bronfenbrenner's bio-ecological theory consists of five environmental systems: microsystem, mesosystem, exosystem, macrosystem, and chronosystem.

Courtesy of Urie Brofenbrenner

Urie Bronfenbrenner developed the bio-ecological approach, a perspective that is receiving increased attention. His theory emphasizes the importance of both the micro- and macro-dimensions of the environment in which an individual lives.

The five environmental systems are:

- *Microsystem:* This system represents the setting in which the individual lives. These contexts include the person's unique physical makeup, family, peers, school, and neighbourhood. It is in the microsystem that the most direct interactions with social agents take place—with parents, peers, and teachers, for example. The individual is viewed not as a passive recipient of experiences in these settings, but as someone who helps construct them.
- *Mesosystem:* This system involves relations between microsystems or connections between contexts. Examples are the relation of family experiences to school experiences, school experiences to church experiences, and family experiences to peer experiences. For example, children whose parents have rejected them may have difficulty developing positive relations with teachers.
- *Exosystem:* This system is involved when experiences in another social setting in which the individual does not have an active role influence what the individual experiences in an immediate context. For example, work experiences can affect a woman's relationship with her husband and their child. The mother might receive a promotion that requires more travel, which might increase marital conflict and change patterns of parent–child interaction.
- *Macrosystem:* This system represents the culture in which individuals live. Remember from Chapter 1 that culture refers to the behaviour patterns, beliefs, and all other products of a group of people that are passed on from generation to generation. Remember also that cross-cultural studies—the comparison of one culture with one or more other cultures—provide information about the generality of development. For example, most Canadians believe paying taxes is vital to support education and health care.
- *Chronosystem:* This system involves the patterning of environmental events and transitions over the life course, as well as socio-historical circumstances. For example, the socio-historical aspects of social media differ remarkably depending on determinants such as age, education, socio-economic status, and geography. Babies born today in societies where

Internet access is readily available will never experience the technological revolution in the same way as their parents or grandparents or those born in regions or countries without such access. Every year, technologies are redefining each of the systems, including personal space, individual behaviour, family life, education, health, community relationships, and work life, as well as legal boundaries and political systems.

These five systems integrate concepts of psychology, anthropology, economics, political structures, and sociology with human growth and development. Although Bronfenbrenner added biological influences to his theory, environmental contexts dominate (Bronfenbrenner & Morris, 1998, 2006; Ceci, 2000).

Evaluating the Bio-Ecological Approach

Contributions of the bio-ecological approach include a systematic examination of the macro- and micro-dimensions of environmental systems and attention to connections between environmental settings and historical influences. A further contribution of Bronfenbrenner's theory is an emphasis on a range of social contexts beyond the family, such as neighbourhood, religion, school, and workplace, as influential in children's development (Gauvain, 2013). Criticism includes giving inadequate attention to biological and cognitive factors.

critical thinking

Urie Bronfenbrenner argued that every child should have a champion, someone who would defend the child no matter what. How would having such a champion enable the individual to cope with the various systems as an adult?

To this point, we have discussed the bio-ecological approach. For a review, see the Reach Your Learning Outcomes section at the end of this chapter.

Contemporary Approaches to Psychology

LO7 Compare and contrast four contemporary approaches to human growth and development.

- **Positive Psychology**
- **Neuroscience and Neuroplasticity**
- **Dynamic Systems**
- **Evolutionary Psychology**

The historical approaches we have discussed thus far are quite divergent; nevertheless, they have provided an important springboard for contemporary research. Traditionally, the processes of our biological, cognitive, and socio-emotional development (see Chapter 1) have been considered separately; however, contemporary researchers are seeking frameworks that integrate these processes and explain our development in a more coherent way. Four relatively new approaches are positive psychology, neuroscience/neuroplasticity, evolutionary psychology, and dynamic systems.

Positive Psychology

As noted in the opening vignette, psychology has traditionally been concerned with illness—identifying, understanding, and treating conditions such as anxiety, stress, sadness, depression, delusions, neurosis, psychosis, and so forth. In doing so, the prominent approaches you just read about have contributed a wealth of information, enabling us to better understand our motivations and cope with a host of disorders. Contemporary psychologists agree that all of this is important and helpful; however, in the words of "father of positive psychology" Martin Seligman, as a science "psychology can do better" (Seligman, 2004). He and Hungarian-born Mihaly Csikszentmihalyi, highly regarded for his work on creativity and flow, championed research on positive psychology (APA, 2012). "Positive psychology is the scientific study of the strengths that enable individuals and communities to thrive" (Penn Arts & Sciences, 2016). It does not deny human flaws, but rather opens up an alternative manner of obtaining health. For example, rather than analyze the psychology underlying alcoholism, positive psychologists study the resilience of those who have recovered, such as through Alcoholics Anonymous. Lab experiments and research focuses on conditions that foster generosity, courage, creativity, and laughter (Lambert, 2007).

Javier Hernandez El Pais Photos/Newscom

Martin Seligman, called the father of positive psychology, said, "Life inflicts the same setbacks and tragedies on the optimist as on the pessimist, but the optimist weathers them better." *Do you agree with this view? If so, what can we learn from optimism? If not, why not?*

According to Seligman, we experience three kinds of happiness: (1) pleasure and gratification, (2) embodiment of strengths and virtues, and (3) meaning and purpose. The research of Seligman and Dr. Christopher Peterson, another expert in the field, identified six virtues that are universally valued: (1) wisdom & knowledge, (2) courage, (3) love and humanity, (4) justice, (5) temperance, and (6) spirituality and transcendence (Seligman, 2016). This shift toward positive psychology has led to an explosion of work on happiness, optimism, emotions, and healthy character traits.

So far, the findings indicate that we are most happy when what we are doing captivates our attention fully. Csikszentmihalyi defined this heightened state as "flow." Athletes, musicians, artists, and others sometimes refer to this state of total concentration as being "in the zone," or "in the moment." Time becomes inconsequential because purpose and the pleasure of the activity engage us completely. This heightened state usually, but not always, has three ingredients: pleasure, meaningfulness, and engagement. Frequently, pleasure comes last.

Neuroscience and Neuroplasticity

Fascinating discoveries about our brain, its development, and its ability to accommodate and heal have opened doorways to relatively new and interrelated areas of study: *neuroscience* (the study of the brain, the nervous system, and the spinal column) and *neuroplasticity* (the brain's ability to compensate for injury and disease). Thanks to modern imaging technology, contemporary neuroscientists can now observe how events trigger the formation of patterns in the brain in a self-organizing manner. Scientists are learning more and more about how the brain maps our personal narratives by connecting our experiences with neurotransmitters such as serotonin and dopamine (Lewis, 2000).

Research in the field is mushrooming, and for good reason. According to Brain Canada, "1 in 3 Canadians will be affected by a disease, disorder or injury of the brain, spinal cord or nervous system at some point in their lives" (Brain Canada, 2012, n.p.). Motivated by his own experience as a former addict, Dr. Marc Lewis, formerly of the University of Toronto and Radboud University in the Netherlands, uses neuroscience to understand the brain's link to addictions. He proposes that the brain is attentive to all experiences and our emotional responses to them (Lewis, 2012).

Other areas of investigation include the causes and treatments of Parkinson's disease, Alzheimer's disease, autism, multiple sclerosis, and eating and sleep disorders (Canadian Association for Neuroscience, 2012). See the box, Connecting Through Research, from earlier in the chapter for more information about neuroplasticity.

Dynamic Systems

The dynamic systems (DS) approach attempts to encompass all that explains human growth and development. Esther Thelen of the University of Indiana (1941–2004) brought an entirely new approach to Piaget's learning theory by conducting a number of experiments investigating how babies learn to manage movement. Her experiments showed that instead of isolated brain development, learning is connected firmly to physical experience.

Based on her experiments, Thelen concluded that skill development, such as walking and later abstract thinking and formal operations, results from "perceiving the world and activity in it throughout life." In her presidential address to the Society for Research in Child Development, Thelen described how we might acquire skills via an embedded system—the nervous system—interacting with the rest of the body, which interacts with the world outside the body (Fausto-Sterling, 2011). This interaction among the nervous system, the rest of the body, and the surrounding environment helps us to make sense of the world and is called self-organization (Lewis, 2000).

According to Dr. Marc Lewis, self-organization has four dominant characteristics (Lewis, 2000):

1. It allows developmental spontaneity and novelty.
2. It becomes more complex and sophisticated with experience.
3. Phase transition, or points of instability and turbulence, lead to new levels of complexity.
4. Self-organizing systems are both intrinsic and extrinsic due to the coupling of feedback with other systems, for example a toddler shifting from crawling to walking in response to the texture of the ground.

The dynamic systems approach is being applied to a diverse range of activities, from coaching athletes to parenting.

Evolutionary Psychology

Natural selection and survival of the fittest—Darwin's signature theories put forward in his 1869 book *On the Origin of Species*—remain vital to today's discourse, forming the basis of the *nature versus nurture* debate that you read about in Chapter 1. Have we evolved from earlier and more primitive species? If so, how? Are we the product of our genetic makeup, our environment, or both? If both, which influence dominates? What adaptations have we made? How closely linked are these adaptations to our mate selection? How closely is mate selection linked to our survival? Evolutionary psychology synthesizes modern evolutionary biology and psychology in the search for meaning to life's penetrating mysteries: Why is sex so important? Why is the world riddled with so much conflict? You will read more about genetic influence in Chapter 3.

CONNECTING development to life

Applying the Approaches

THE CANADIAN PRESS/Chris Young

Canada has a tradition of welcoming newcomers, be they immigrants or refugees. People who come to Canada bring their cultures, traditions, languages, cuisines, fashions, skills, values, assumptions of common sense, parenting approaches, and other assumptions, many of which may be quite different from those of Canadians. For example, in many cultures, a student would never look her teacher in the eye because it would be rude, whereas here, failure to look someone in the eyes when speaking indicates shame, shyness, or at worst, dishonesty.

Arriving in Canada, newcomers must adjust not only to the language and climate, but also to all kinds of subtleties that are very much a way of life here. Additionally, refugees have experienced unthinkable traumas and arrive here feeling alienated, with no family support. Family practices, approaches to medical treatment, gender roles, as well as parenting approaches that may be the norm elsewhere are not acceptable here; for example, spanking a child, beating a wife, practising polygamy, and female genital mutilation are not lawful in Canada and may result in completely unexpected legal complexities, including criminal charges, restraining orders, or deportation.

All of this makes adjustment quite challenging. Consider the theories presented in this chapter, including an eclectic approach. Imagine your role in the field you are studying to enter. Which theory or theories are most helpful to you in understanding and providing professional help to a newcomer? To a friend? What assumptions might you have that may be completely foreign to a client, patient, or friend? Why? Which theories do you find the least useful? And, again, why?

To this point, we have discussed contemporary approaches to psychology. For a review, see the Reach Your Learning Outcomes section at the end of this chapter.

An Eclectic Theoretical Orientation

LO8 Discuss the eclectic approach.

- **The Eclectic Approach**

The Eclectic Approach

No single theory described so far can entirely explain the rich complexity of life-span development, but each has contributed to our understanding. Psychoanalytic theory best explains the unconscious mind. Erikson's theory best describes the changes that occur in adult development. The views of Piaget, Vygotsky, and the information-processing approach provide the most complete description of cognitive development. The behavioural and social cognitive approaches of Pavlov, Skinner, and Bandura give an adept examination of the environmental determinants of development. On the other hand, the ethological approach of Darwin, Lorenz, and Bowlby has heightened our awareness of biology's role and the importance of sensitive periods in development. The humanist approach of Rogers and Maslow contributes a more optimistic framework by theorizing that individuals strive to be the best they can possibly be. Bronfenbrenner's bio-ecological approach examines the role society plays in our development. And the more contemporary approaches, such as positive psychology, neuroscience and neuroplasticity, dynamic systems, and evolutionary psychology further complement our understanding of learning, motivation, and development.

In short, although theories are helpful guides, relying on a single theory to explain development is probably a mistake. This book instead takes an **eclectic theoretical orientation**, which does not follow any one theoretical approach but rather selects the best features from each theory. In this way, you can view the study of development as it actually exists—with different theorists making different assumptions, stressing different empirical problems, and using different strategies to discover information.

The theories that we have discussed so far were developed at different points in history. Figure 2.6 shows when these theories were proposed.

These theoretical perspectives, along with the research methods and challenges discussed in Chapter 1, provide a sense of the scientific nature in the field of psychology. Context plays a major role in the formation of theories. For example, each generation is influenced by the building blocks provided by the generation before and contributes to the generations that follow. In 1935, Freud stated that he had reached the very climax of his psychoanalytic work in 1912, a year before Karen Horney received her medical degree (Horney, 1967). By the time Horney began publishing her findings, social and cultural paradigms, especially those related to women and culture, had shifted considerably.

Imagine the kind of debates Freud and Erikson may have had about whether personality is shaped more by psychosexual drives and repression or by social experiences. Perhaps Maslow and Rogers argued into the wee hours of the morning about whether all creatures strive for fulfillment, or whether only a few whose more basic needs have been met can realize their potential. Today, researchers such as Czikszentmihalyi, Elkind, Gilligan, Seligman, and many others continue the study of human growth and development, building on the insights of past generations and opening up new avenues of debate, inquiry, and thought for today and for generations to come.

To this point, we have discussed an eclectic theoretical orientation. For a review, see the Reach Your Learning Outcomes section at the end of this chapter.

Figure 2.6
Timeline for Major Developmental Theories

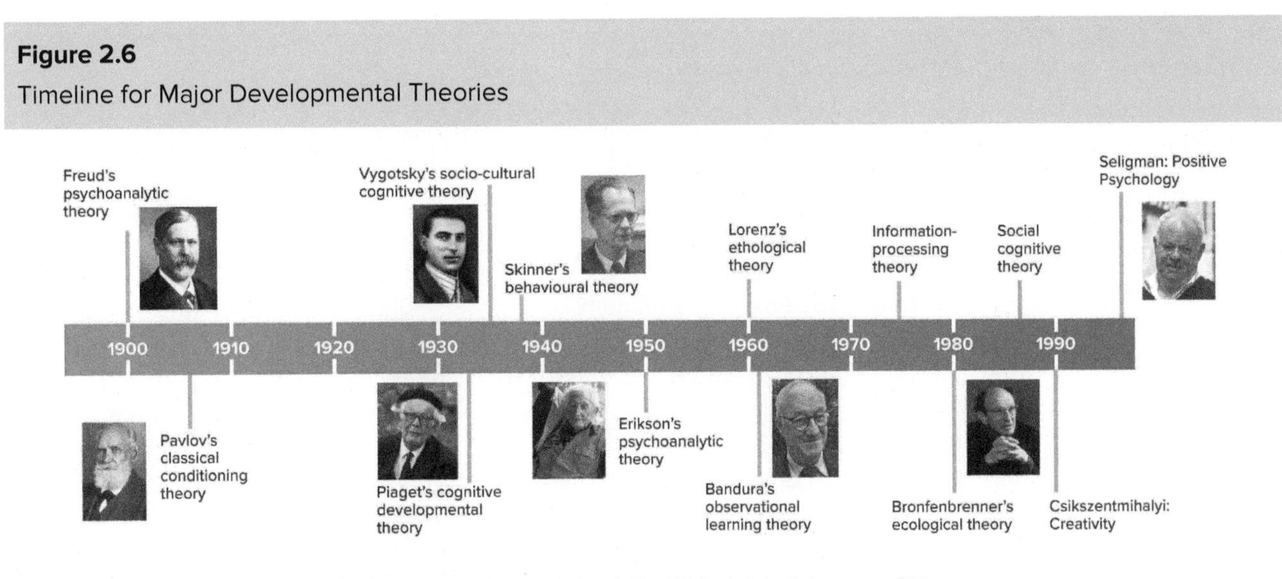

Top l to r © Bettmann Archives; A.R. Lauria/Dr. Michael Cole, Laboratory of Human Cognition; Copyright © 2016 The President and Fellows of Harvard College; Javier Hernandez El Pais Photos/NewsCom; Bottom l to r US National Library of Medicine; ©Yves de Braine/ Black Star/Stock Photo; ©Bettmann/Corbis; Courtesy Stanford University News Service; Courtesy of Urie Bronfenbrenner.

Reach Your **Learning Outcomes**

The Psychoanalytic Approach

LO1 Describe the psychoanalytic approach and the contributions of major theorists.

Characteristics of the Psychoanalytic Approach	• Development is primarily unconscious and influenced largely by emotion and biological factors. • Theorists attempt to analyze the symbolic meanings of behaviour to understand the inner workings of the mind.
Sigmund Freud (1856–1939)	Freud's theory included the following: • Personality is made up of the id, the ego, and the superego. • Conflicting demands of these structures produce anxiety and trigger defence mechanisms. • Individuals go through five psychosexual stages: oral, anal, phallic, latent, and genital.
Erik Erikson (1902–1994)	Erikson emphasized eight psychosocial stages of development: • trust versus mistrust • autonomy versus shame and doubt • initiative versus guilt • industry versus inferiority • identity versus identity confusion • intimacy versus isolation • generativity versus stagnation • integrity versus despair No stage is completely resolved; however, when balance is achieved virtues, or emotional strengths, emerge in the healthy personality.

Other Psychoanalytic Theories (the Neo-Freudians)	**Alfred Adler (1870–1937)** ▪ Developed individual psychology and believed that striving for perfection to fulfill one's potential is the single motivating drive behind all behaviour. **Carl Jung (1875–1961)** ▪ Believed the psyche had three parts: the ego or the conscious mind, the personal unconscious, and the collective unconscious. **Karen Horney (1885–1952)** ▪ Criticized Freud's argument on the grounds of gender and cultural differences. **Anna Freud (1895–1982)** ▪ Opened the field of psychoanalysis to include children and adolescents. **Eric Fromm (1900–1980)** ▪ Believed human nature to be influenced by dysfunctional social patterns.
Evaluating the Psychoanalytic Approach	▪ Contributions include an emphasis on a developmental framework, the role of parents or caregivers, and the role of the unconscious in personality growth and development. ▪ Criticisms are that the theories lack scientific rigour, portray human nature negatively, and place too much emphasis on sexual underpinnings.

The Cognitive Approach

LO2 **Compare and contrast the theories within the cognitive approach.**

Piaget's Cognitive Developmental Theory	▪ Children play an active role in their cognitive development. ▪ Children use the processes of assimilation and accommodation to understand their world. ▪ Children go through four cognitive stages: sensorimotor, preoperational, concrete operational, and formal operational. ▪ Neo-Piagetian Robbie Case extended Piaget's theory to include aspects of culture, information processing, linguistics, and neuroscience.
Vygotsky's Socio-Cultural Cognitive Theory	▪ Social and cultural contexts are primary factors in a child's development. ▪ Knowledge is situated and collaborative. ▪ Interaction with skillful adults or peers is essential for cognitive development.
The Information-Processing Approach	▪ Emphasizes that individuals manipulate information, monitor it, and strategize about it. ▪ Thinking is a form of information processing.
Evaluating the Cognitive Approach	▪ Contributions include an emphasis on the active construction of understanding. ▪ One criticism is that the approach gives too little attention to individual variation.

The Behavioural and Social Cognitive Approach

LO3 **Discuss and examine the behavioural and social cognitive approach, including the contributions of Pavlov, Skinner, and Bandura.**

Pavlov's Classical Conditioning (1849–1936)	▪ Demonstrated that a neutral stimulus acquires the ability to produce a response originally produced by another stimulus.
Skinner's Operant Conditioning (1904–1990)	▪ Demonstrated that the consequences of a behaviour produce changes in the probability of the behaviour's future occurrence.
Bandura's Social Cognitive Theory (1925–)	▪ Emphasized that cognitive processes are important mediators of environment–behaviour connections. ▪ Observational learning, or imitation and modelling, is cognitive in that individuals sometimes adopt the behaviours of others.
Evaluating the Behavioural and Social Cognitive Approach	▪ Contributions include an emphasis on scientific research and the role of environmental determinants of behaviour. ▪ Criticisms include too little emphasis on cognition and inadequate attention to developmental changes.

The Ethological Approach

LO4 **Describe the ethological approach and distinguish among the major contributions of Darwin, Lorenz, Bowlby, and Goodall.**

Charles Darwin (1809–1882)	▪ One of the first theorists to note the connection between animal behaviour and human behaviour. ▪ Developed the theory of evolution and natural selection.
Konrad Lorenz (1903–1989)	▪ Called "the father of ethology" for his study establishing the key concepts of imprinting and critical periods.
John Bowlby (1907–1990)	▪ Often called the "father of attachment theory" for his work on the innate bond between infant and caregiver.
Jane Goodall (1934–)	▪ Ethologist and animal activist who has documented behaviours in chimpanzees previously believed to be specific to humans.
Evaluating the Ethological Approach	▪ Contributions include a focus on the biological and evolutionary bases of development. ▪ Criticisms include a belief that the critical and sensitive period concepts are too rigid.

The Humanist Approach

LO5 **Describe and evaluate the humanist approach, including the contributions of Rogers and Maslow.**

Carl Rogers (1902–1987)	▪ Believed all living creatures worked hard to realize their fullest potential.
Abraham Maslow (1908–1970)	▪ Defined a hierarchy of needs: physiological, safety and security, love and belonging, esteem, and self-actualization.
Evaluating the Humanist Approach	▪ Contributed to establishing a positive regard for human nature. ▪ Criticisms include unscientific methods of study.

The Bio-Ecological Approach

LO6 **Describe Bronfenbrenner's bio-ecological approach and illustrate how each system affects human growth and development.**

Urie Bronfenbrenner (1917–2005)	▪ Identified five environmental systems that impact individual growth and development: microsystem, mesosystem, exosystem, macrosystem, and chronosystem.
Evaluating the Bio-Ecological Approach	▪ Contributions include a systematic explanation of environmental systems and the connections between these systems. ▪ One criticism is that inadequate attention is given to biological and cognitive factors.

Contemporary Approaches to Psychology

LO7 Compare and contrast four contemporary approaches to human growth and development.

Positive Psychology	▪ Emphasizes that understanding happiness can facilitate human growth and development.
Neuroscience and Neuroplasticity	▪ Focuses on the scientific study of the brain, the nervous system, and the spinal cord in an effort to understand how these organs and systems work, as well as how to respond when they malfunction.
Dynamic Systems	▪ This approach posits that human growth and development is linked to physical experience, which becomes embedded in the nervous system.
Evolutionary Psychology	▪ Scientific study in this approach synthesizes modern evolutionary biology and psychology in a search for meaning to life's penetrating mysteries, such as why sex is so important and why the world is riddled with so much conflict.

An Eclectic Theoretical Orientation

LO8 Discuss the eclectic approach.

The Eclectic Approach	▪ Because of the diversity of theories, many psychologists (and this text) select one or a combination of approaches depending what fits best in a particular context.

review → connect → reflect

review

1. What are the main psychoanalytic theories? LO1
2. What are some contributions and criticisms of psychoanalytic theories? LO1
3. What are three main cognitive theories? LO2
4. What are some contributions and criticisms of cognitive theories? LO2
5. What are two main bahavioural and social cognitive theories? LO3
6. What are some contributions and criticisms of behavioural and social cognitive theories? LO3
7. What is the nature of ethological theory? LO4
8. Which psychologists contributed to the humanistic theory? LO5
9. What are some contributions and criticisms of Bronfenbrenner's bio-ecological theory? LO6
10. What differentiates the approach of the neuroscience theory and the dynamic systems approach? LO7
11. What is an eclectic theoretical orientation? LO8

connect

Karen Horney considers child neglect the most damaging type of child maltreatment because the child cannot fight back. Imagine that you believe a child you know, perhaps one in your neighbourhood, is being neglected. On what evidence do you base your suspicion? What might be the long-term implications of this neglect? What theories outlined in this chapter might be useful in helping this child?

reflect

Your Own Personal Journey of Life

Imagine what your development would have been like in a culture that offers fewer or distinctly different choices. How might your development have been different if your family had been significantly richer or poorer?

available, including support groups for parents and families. However, much of it is not government subsidized. Both realize that their careers may be jeopardized in order to provide adequate home care and support for their child. They worry about their financial strength. The thought that "Every child brings his or her own special love" echoes in Stephanie's mind; Ray, on the other hand, is not so sure.

Moira and Joanne are considering in vitro fertilization. Moira's parents are thrilled at the prospect of becoming grandparents, but Joanne's parents are anxious because they will have to acknowledge their daughter's lesbian relationship; plus, they harbour concerns about a child raised by homosexual parents. Everyone involved worries about the safety and expenses of the procedure.

Environmental experiences and biological foundations work together to make us who we are. Our coverage of life's biological beginnings in this chapter focuses on theories and research about evolution, genetic foundations, reproduction challenges and choices, and the interaction of heredity and environment.

© Blend Images/Alamy Stock Photo

If parents could choose the genetic makeup of their child, would they choose the child's gender, physical attractiveness, intelligence, and strength? What are some traits that you might choose?

How much of a child's looks, personality, and aptitudes are a product of genetics and how much the result of environment? The evolutionary perspective may help us understand how our physical, cognitive, and socio-emotional elements are interconnected and function to influence growth and development.

The Evolutionary Perspective

LO1 Discuss the evolutionary perspective on life-span development.

- **Natural Selection and Adaptive Behaviour**
- **Evolutionary Psychology**

On the Origin of Species, written by Charles Darwin in 1856, introduced the theory of evolution by natural selection. This theory fell out of favour as a reaction to fascism following World War II, but has since resurfaced and become popular with social theorists. As noted in Chapter 2, **evolutionary psychology**, emphasizes the importance of adaptation, reproduction, and "survival of the fittest" in shaping behaviour. "Fit" in this sense refers to the ability to bear offspring that survive long enough to bear offspring of their own. In this view, natural selection favours behaviours that increase reproductive success—the ability to pass your genes to the next generation (Durrant & Ellis, 2013).

Natural Selection and Adaptive Behaviour

Natural selection is the evolutionary process that favours individuals of a species that are best adapted to survive and reproduce. Darwin noted that most organisms reproduce at rates that would cause enormous increases in populations, and yet species remain nearly constant. He reasoned that an intense, constant struggle for food, water, and resources must occur among the young because many do not survive. Those that do survive pass on their genes to the next generation (Hoefnagels, 2015). Over the course of many generations, this could produce a gradual modification of the whole population. When dramatic environmental changes and non-normative events, such as earthquakes, floods, and war, occur, other characteristics emerge or become favoured, and the process of natural selection can move the species in a different direction (Mader, 2014). Adaptive behaviour is behaviour that promotes an organism's survival in the natural habitat and is fundamental for survival of all organisms (Brooker et al., 2015; Johnson, 2015). For example, attachment between a caregiver and a baby ensures the infant's closeness to a caregiver for feeding and protection from danger, thus increasing the infant's chances of survival. For an illustration of the brain sizes of various primates and humans in relation to the length of the childhood period, see Figure 3.1.

Figure 3.1

The Brain Sizes of Various Primates and Humans in Relation to the Length of the Childhood Period

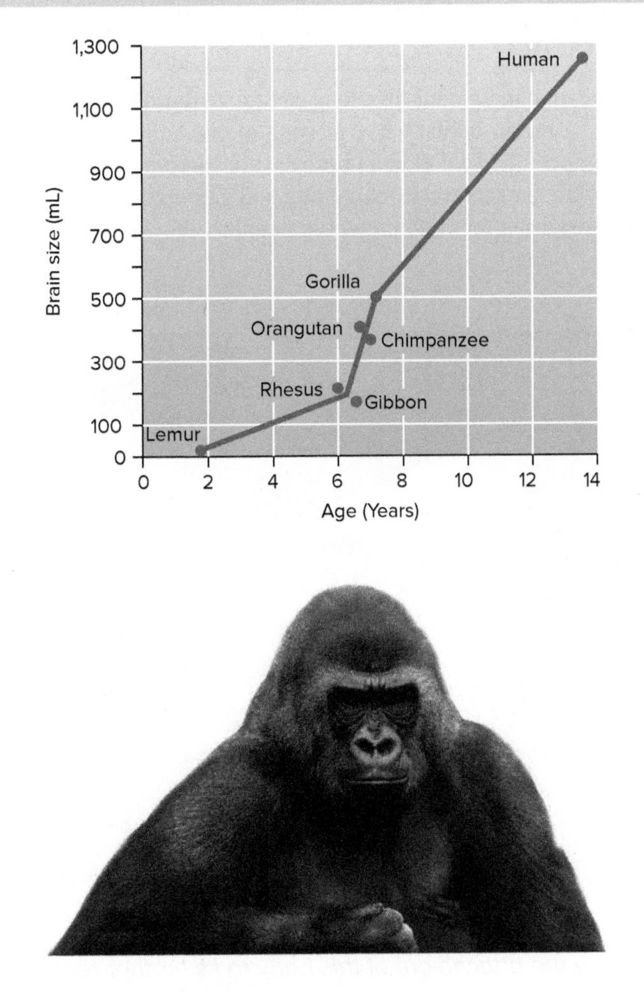

Compared with other primates, humans have both a larger brain and a longer childhood period. *What conclusions can you draw from the relationship indicated by this graph?*

Evolutionary Psychology

David Buss (1999, 2000, 2008, 2012) has been influential in stimulating new interest in the theory of evolution's explanation of human behaviour. He reasons that just as evolution shapes our physical features, it also influences how we make decisions, how aggressive we are, our fears, and our mating patterns. For example, assume that our ancestors were hunters and gatherers on the plains and that men did most of the hunting and women stayed close to home gathering seeds and plants for food. If you have to travel some distance from your home in an effort to find and slay a fleeing animal, you need certain physical traits as well as the ability for certain types of spatial thinking. Men born with these traits would be more likely to survive than men without them, and would also be considered attractive mates—and thus reproduce and pass on these characteristics to their children. Consequently, over many generations, men with good spatial thinking skills might become more numerous in the population. Critics point out that this scenario might or might not have actually happened.

Here's another example. An extended childhood period may have evolved in humans because we require time to develop large brains in order to learn the complexity of human societies. This is especially true as our economies have shifted from hunting and gathering, to agriculture, to manufacturing, and, most recently, to technology. Humans take longer to become reproductively mature than any other mammal (see Figure 3.1). During this extended childhood period, humans develop a large brain and gain experiences needed to become competent adults in a complex society.

Many of our evolved psychological mechanisms are domain-specific. That is, the mechanisms apply only to a specific aspect of a person's psychological makeup. According to evolutionary psychology, rather than a general-purpose device that can be applied equally to a vast array of problems, specialized modules in the mind have evolved to process information related to recurring activities and problems. For example, such specialized modules might include a module for physical knowledge for tracking animals, a module for mathematical knowledge for trading, and a module for language.

Connecting Evolution and Life-Span Development

In evolutionary theory, what matters is that individuals live long enough to reproduce and pass on their genetic characteristics (Starr, Evers, & Starr, 2015). Why, then, do humans live so long after viable reproduction? Perhaps evolution favoured longevity because the work and presence of social elders improves the survival rates of babies. For example, the ability of grandparents to care for the young while parents were out hunting and gathering food created an evolutionary advantage. In contemporary terms, grandparents are caring for children whose parents have died from the AIDS pandemic or whose lives are severely affected by poverty.

© Blend Images/Getty Images

How does the attachment of this baby to its mother reflect the evolutionary process of adaptive behaviour?

According to psychologist Paul Baltes (2003), the benefits of evolutionary selection decrease with age. Natural selection has not weeded out many conditions and non-adaptive characteristics that mostly affect older adults, such as dementia and arthritis. Why? Natural selection operates primarily on characteristics that are tied to reproductive fitness, which extends through the earlier part of adulthood. Thus, says Baltes, selection primarily operates during the first half of life.

Unaided by evolutionary pressures against non-adaptive conditions, we suffer the aches, pains, and infirmities of aging. And as the benefits of evolutionary selection decrease with age, argues Baltes, the need for culture-based resources (such as cognitive skills, literacy, and medical technology) and social support (such as help and training from other people to maintain their cognitive skills) increases (Knight & Sayegh, 2010). (See Figure 3.2.)

Figure 3.2
Baltes's View of Evolution and Culture across the Life Span

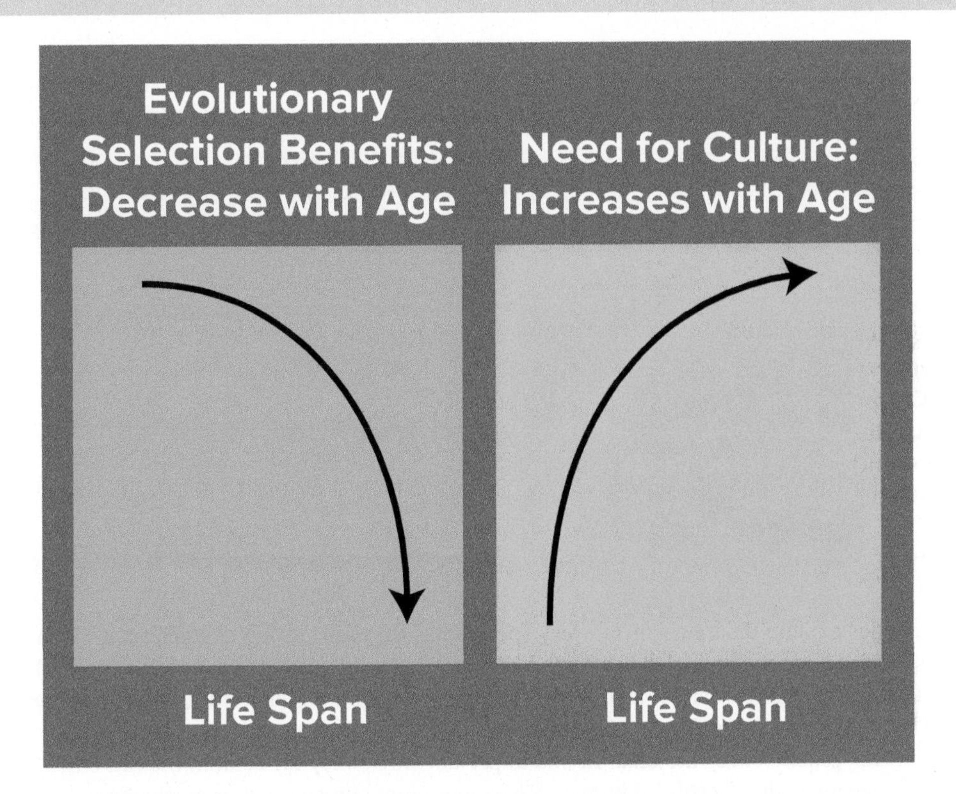

Baltes, P.B., Staudinger, U.M., & Lindenberger, U., 1999, "Lifespan Psychology," *Annual Review of Psychology*, 50, p. 474, Figure 1. Reprinted with permission, from the *Annual Review of Psychology*, Volume 50. Copyright © 1999 by Annual Reviews, www.annualreview.org.

Benefits derived from evolutionary selection decrease as we age, whereas the need for culture increases with age.

A concrete example of a decrease in evolutionary-selection benefits in older adults involves Alzheimer's disease, a progressive, irreversible brain disorder characterized by gradual deterioration. This disease does not typically appear before age 70. If the disease struck 20-year-olds, perhaps natural selection would have eliminated it eons before the birth of Dr. Alois Alzheimer, the German physician who first discovered the anatomical changes in the brain associated with it (Alzheimer Society, 2009a). Possibly, diseases such as Alzheimer's emerge in later life because evolutionary pressures based on reproductive fitness do not select against individuals prone to them.

Evaluating Evolutionary Psychology

Evolutionary psychology is one theoretical approach, and like other approaches, it has limitations, weaknesses, and critics (Hyde, 2014). Albert Bandura (1998), whose social cognitive theory was described in Chapter 2, acknowledges the important influence of evolution on human adaptation and change. However, he rejects what he calls "one-sided evolutionism," which sees social behaviour as the product of evolved biology. An alternative is the *bidirectional view*, in which environment and biological conditions influence each other. Evolutionary pressures created changes in biological structures for the use of tools, which enabled organisms to manipulate, alter, and construct new environmental conditions. Increasingly complex environmental innovations in turn produced new selection pressures for the evolution of specialized biological systems for consciousness, thought, and language.

Human evolution gave us bodily structures and biological potentialities, but it does not dictate behaviour. Having evolved, advanced biological capacities can be used to produce diverse cultures—aggressive, pacific, egalitarian, or autocratic. The "big picture" idea of natural selection leading to the development of human traits and behaviours is difficult to refute or test because it is on a time scale that does not lend itself to empirical study. Thus, studying specific genes in humans and other species—and their links to traits and behaviours—may be a more effective approach for testing ideas emanating from evolutionary psychology.

To this point, we have discussed the evolutionary perspective. For a review, see the Reach Your Learning Outcomes section at the end of this chapter.

Genetic Foundations

LO2 Describe what genes are and how they influence human development.

The Collaborative Gene
Genes and Chromosomes
Genetic Principles
Chromosome and Gene-Linked Variations
The Human Genome Project

The principles of genetics explain the mechanism every species has for transmitting characteristics from one generation to the next. Each of us carries a genetic code that is retained in our DNA, which is located within every cell in our bodies. Our DNA is not just inherited from our parents; it includes what we inherit from our ancestors. Genetic influences on behaviour evolve over time. The many traits and characteristics that are genetically influenced have a long evolutionary history that is retained in our DNA. Our genetic codes are alike in one important way—they all contain the ingredients for being human. Because of the human genetic code, a fertilized human egg cannot grow into an egret or an elephant.

Genetics is a fascinating, complex field and researchers are discovering new intricacies almost daily. Darwin's cousin, Francis Galton, engaged in twin studies and their relationship to heredity in 1876 (Minnesota Centre, 2012). About a century later, in 1979, the Minnesota Study of Twins Reared Apart, undertaken by Thomas Bouchard and his colleagues, brought identical twins (twins that resulted from the same fertilized egg) and fraternal twins (that come from different fertilized eggs) who had been separated at birth or shortly thereafter to Minneapolis from all over the world in order to investigate their lives (Bouchard et al., 1990). This ground-breaking study found genetically identical twins who had been separated as infants showed striking similarities in their tastes and habits and choices, including the names they chose for their children, the types of jobs they held, the names of their spouses, and unique behaviours they exhibited. Can we conclude that their genes caused the development of those similar tastes and habits and choices? Other possible causes need to be considered.

The twins shared not only the same genes, but also many common experiences. Some of the separated twins lived together for several months prior to their adoption; others had been reunited prior to testing (in some cases, many years earlier); adoption agencies often place twins in similar homes; and even strangers who spend several hours together and start comparing their lives are likely to come up with some coincidental similarities (Joseph, 2006).

The assumption at the time was that identical twins inherited identical genetic codes, and that fraternal twins were genetically no more similar than other siblings. But if identical twins are totally identical, then if one twin had schizophrenia, wouldn't the other suffer from the same disease? Studies of twins where one had been diagnosed with schizophrenia—conducted by Dr. Shiva Singh and Dr. Richard O'Reilly of Western University—revealed that "identical" twins, in fact, are not genetically identical. According to Dr. Singh, "Cells are dividing as we develop and differentiate [mitosis and meiosis, discussed later in this chapter]. More importantly, these cells may lose or acquire additional DNA. The genome is not static. The implication of their study is that each of us, including identical twins, have a unique human genome sequence; hence, everybody is different" (Shanks, 2011; Stone, 2011).

Several issues complicate the interpretation of twin studies. For example, adults might stress the similarities of identical twins more than those of fraternal twins, and identical twins might perceive themselves as a "set" and play together more than fraternal twins do. If so, the influence of the environment on the observed similarities between identical and fraternal twins might be very significant. In any case, these studies continue to further our understanding of evolution and genetic individuality, showing that each of us is unique (Maiti et al., 2011).

The Collaborative Gene

Each of us began life as a single cell weighing about one-fifty-millionth of a gram. Imagine! This tiny piece of matter housed our genetic code—instructions that orchestrate growth from that single cell to a person made of trillions of cells, each containing information that replicates the original genetic code. That code is carried by DNA, which includes all of our 20 000 genes. To understand genes and what do they do, we need to look into our cells. Describing the complexities of genes, Michael Kobo, from the Department of Medical Genetics at the University of British Columbia and the Centre for Molecular Medicine and Therapeutics (CMMT), says, "Each gene has its own dimmer switch, like a light bulb dimmer, to regulate the amount of protein produced from it. Genes can be turned all the way on or all the way off, or can be set anywhere in between" (Amos, 2011).

The nucleus of each human cell contains **chromosomes**, which are threadlike structures made up of deoxyribonucleic acid, or DNA. **DNA** is a complex molecule that has a double helix shape (like a spiral staircase), and contains genetic information. **Genes**, the units of hereditary information, are short segments composed of DNA. Genes act as a blueprint for cells to reproduce themselves and manufacture the proteins that maintain life. Proteins are the building blocks of cells as well as the regulators that direct the body's processes (Cowan, 2015; Willey, Sherwood, & Woolverton, 2014). As noted earlier, chromosomes, DNA, and genes change during meiosis and mitosis. Figure 3.3 will help you turn mystery to understanding.

Figure 3.3

Cells, Chromosomes, Genes, and DNA

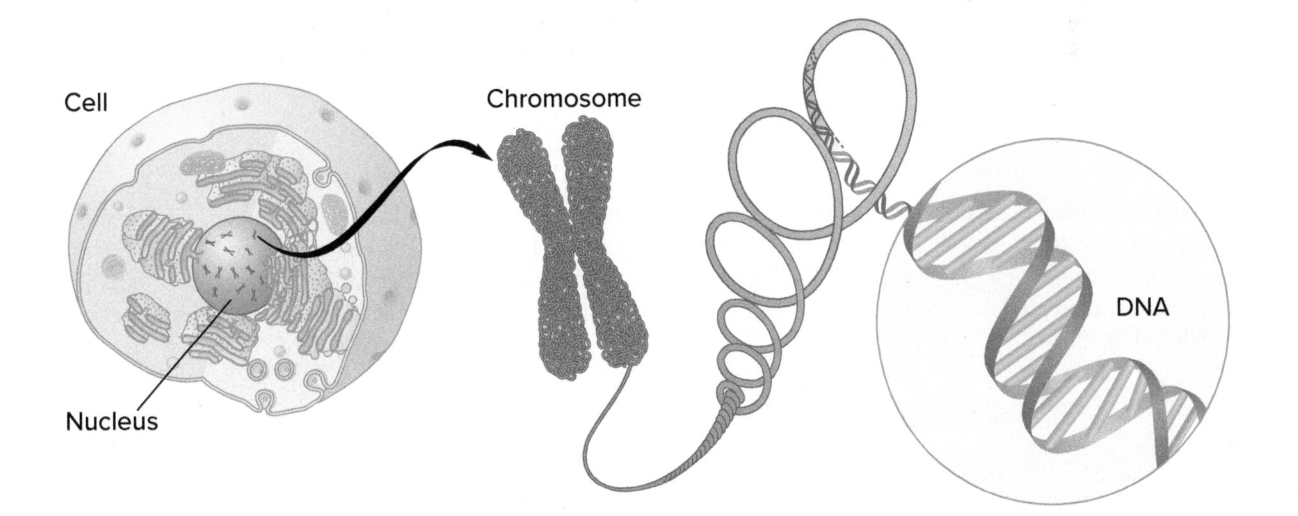

The body contains trillions of cells, which are the basic structural units of life. Each cell contains a central structure, the nucleus. Chromosomes and genes are located in the nucleus of the cell. Chromosomes are made up of threadlike structures composed of DNA molecules. A gene is a segment of DNA that contains the hereditary code. The structure of DNA is a spiralled double chain.

Each gene has its own location—its own designated place on a particular chromosome. Today, there is a great deal of enthusiasm about efforts to discover the specific locations of genes that are linked to certain functions and developmental outcomes (Mason et al., 2015; Raven et al., 2014). An important step in this direction is the Human Genome Project's efforts to map the human genome—the complete genetic content of our cells, which includes developmental information used for creating proteins that contribute to the making of a human organism (Brooker, 2015; Cummings, 2014).

Among the major approaches to gene identification and discovery that are being used are the genome-wide association method, linkage analysis, next-generation sequencing, and the Thousand Genomes Project. Let's have a brief look at each approach.

Genome-Wide Association Method

The Human Genome Project has led to use of the genome-wide association method to identify genetic variations and specific DNA variations. These variations are linked to an increased risk of particular diseases, such as Huntington disease (in which the central nervous system deteriorates), obesity, cancer, asthma, diabetes, hypertension, cardiovascular disease, and Alzheimer's disease (Brown et al., 2014; Guo et al., 2014; Cruchaga et al., 2014; Huang et al., 2014; Su et al., 2013). To conduct a genome-wide association study, researchers obtain DNA from individuals who have the disease and from others who don't have it. Then, each participant's complete set of DNA, or genome, is purified from the blood or other cells and scanned on machines to determine markers of genetic variation. If the genetic variations occur more frequently in people who have the disease, the variations point to the region in the human genome with the disease.

Genome-wide association studies have recently been conducted for childhood obesity (Zhao et al., 2014), cardiovascular disease (Malik et al., 2014), Alzheimer's disease (Liu et al., 2014; Raj et al., 2014; Cohen-Woods, Craig, & McGuffin, 2012), and depression (He et al., 2014; Major Depressive Disorder Working Group of the Psychiatric GWAS Consortium, 2013). Other gene-linkage studies include attention deficit hyperactivity disorder (Caylak, 2012) and autism (Warrier, Baron-Cohen, & Chakrabarti, 2014). Dr. Yingfu Li, Canada Research Chair, specializes in the study of DNA enzymes. Along with his team of researchers, he has developed a litmus test that would facilitate early detection of a wide range of diseases, including the genetic sequences for cancer cells. Dr. Li's research goals are to determine ways to destroy or repair cancer cells (Li, 2016).

Linkage Analysis

Linkage analysis, in which the goal is to discover the location of a gene (or genes) in relation to a marker gene (whose position is already known), is often used in the search for disease-related genes (Lyon & Wang, 2012). Genes transmitted to offspring tend to be in close proximity to each other so that the genes involved in the disease are usually located near the marker gene.

Next-Generation Sequencing

Next-generation sequencing (NGS), or high-throughput sequencing, is a term used to describe a number of different modern technologies used to study biological systems. NGS enables researchers to gain more complex genetic data in greater scope and depth. These technologies have not only generated information more quickly and at a much reduced cost, but they have also considerably increased our understanding about genetic influences on development (Kassahn, Scott, & Fletcher, 2014; Lango Allen et al., 2014).

Thousand Genomes Project

The human genome varies between individuals in small but very important ways. Understanding these variations requires examining the whole genomes of many individuals. Beginning in 2008, the Thousand Genomes Project is the most detailed study of human genetic variation to date. This project has the goal of determining the genomic sequences of at least 1000 individuals from different ethnic groups around the world (Abyzov et al., 2013; Shibata et al., 2012). By compiling complete descriptions of the genetic variations of many people, studies of genetic variations in disease can be conducted in a more detailed manner. For example, researchers of the University of British Columbia found that 15–20 percent of children in any population account for more than half of childhood illnesses and paediatric health care use. This group of children is not only more susceptible to injuries and common illness, but is also more susceptible to major behavioural problems and mental health issues in later life.

The Gene Expression Collaborative for Kids Only Project (GECKO) is a research initiative aimed at understanding these phenomena. Researchers collect DNA samples and conduct a series of tests to measure how 400 children between the ages of 7 and 11 respond to stress in terms of their brain activity and development (Amos, 2011). Other research is examining the role of environment and genetics on such conditions as mood disorders, Alzheimer's disease, Parkinson's disease, and stroke (Mowafaghian, 2014).

Genes and Chromosomes

Genes are not only collaborative; they are enduring. How do the genes manage to get passed from generation to generation and end up in all of the trillion cells in the body? Three processes explain the heart of the story: mitosis, meiosis, and fertilization.

Mitosis, Meiosis, and Fertilization

All cells in your body, except the sperm and egg, have 46 chromosomes arranged in 23 pairs. These cells reproduce by a process called mitosis. During **mitosis**, the cell's nucleus—including the chromosomes—duplicates itself and the cell divides. Two new cells are formed, each containing the same DNA as the original cell, arranged in the same 23 pairs of chromosomes.

However, a different type of cell division—meiosis—forms eggs and sperm (or gametes). During **meiosis**, a cell of the testes (in men) or ovaries (in women) duplicates its chromosomes but then divides twice, thus forming four cells, each of which has only half of the genetic material of the parent cell. By the end of meiosis, each egg or sperm has 23 unpaired chromosomes.

During **fertilization**, an egg and a sperm fuse to create a single cell, called a **zygote** (see Figure 3.4). In the zygote, the 23 unpaired chromosomes from the egg and the 23 unpaired chromosomes from the sperm combine to form one set of 23 paired chromosomes—one chromosome of each pair from the mother's egg and the other from the father's sperm. In this manner, each parent contributes half of the offspring's genetic material.

Figure 3.4
Union of Sperm and Egg

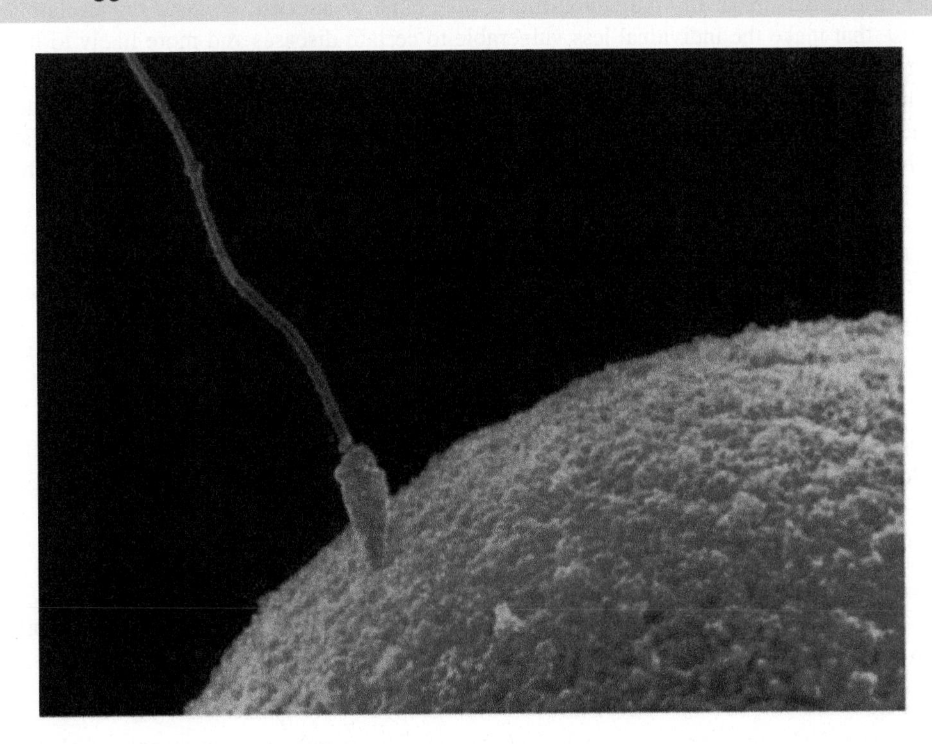

Sources of Variability

Combining the genes of two parents in offspring increases genetic variability in the population, which is valuable for a species because it provides more characteristics for natural selection. In fact, the human genetic process creates several important sources of variability.

First, the chromosomes in the zygote are not exact copies of those in the mother's ovaries and the father's testes. During the formation of the sperm and egg in meiosis, the members of each pair of chromosomes are separated, but which chromosome in the pair goes to the gamete is a matter of chance. In addition, before the pairs separate, pieces of the two chromosomes in each pair are exchanged, creating a new combination of genes on each chromosome (Mader, 2011). Thus, when chromosomes from the mother's egg and the father's sperm are brought together in the zygote, the result is a truly unique combination of genes (Starr, Evers, & Starr, 2010).

If each zygote is unique, how do identical twins exist? *Identical twins* (also called monozygotic twins) develop from a single zygote that splits into two identical replicas, each of which becomes a person. *Fraternal twins* (called dizygotic twins) develop from separate eggs and separate sperm, making them genetically no more similar than ordinary siblings. Identical or fraternal, the developmental changes that occur through mitosis and meiosis make each individual unique.

critical thinking

Although Genome Canada (2012) is funding a host of exciting research initiatives, some have warned that many of these initiatives raise complex ethical issues, including questions around the nature of life. What might be the advantages and disadvantages of using genetic modification to prevent genetic diseases? What are the arguments for and against developments such as cloning, genetic screening, genetically modified foods, and genetically modified people? Should we weed out undesirable genetic traits? If so, who decides which traits are desirable and which are not?

A second source of variability comes from DNA. Chance, a mistake by cellular machinery or damage from an environmental agent such as radiation, may produce a *mutated gene*, which is a permanently altered segment of DNA (Bauman, 2015).

Susceptibility genes, those that make the individual more vulnerable to specific diseases or acceleration of aging, and longevity genes, those that make the individual less vulnerable to certain diseases and more likely to live to an older age, are of increasing interest (Howard & Rogers, 2014; Stadler et al., 2014; Wei et al., 2014). The difference between genotypes and phenotypes helps us to understand this source of variability. All of a person's genetic material makes up his or her **genotype**. However, not all of the genetic material is apparent in our observed and measurable characteristics. A **phenotype** consists of observable characteristics. Phenotypes include physical characteristics (such as height, weight, and hair colour) and psychological characteristics (such as personality and intelligence).

For each genotype, a range of phenotypes can be expressed, providing another source of variability (Solomon et al., 2015). An individual can inherit the genetic potential to grow very large, for example, but good nutrition, among other things, will be essential to achieving that potential.

Genetic Principles

Genetic determination is a complex affair, and much is unknown about the way genes work (Moore, 2013). Three genetic principles such as dominant–recessive genes, sex-linked genes, and polygenically-inherited characteristics are outlined here.

Dominant–Recessive Genes Principle

A recessive gene exerts its influence only if both genes of a pair are recessive. If you inherit a recessive gene for a trait from both your parents, you will show the trait. In this way, two brown-eyed parents may have a blue-eyed child. If you inherit a recessive gene from only one parent, you may never know you carry the gene. Brown eyes, farsightedness, and dimples rule over blue eyes, nearsightedness, and freckles in the world of dominant–recessive genes.

Figure 3.5 shows 23 paired chromosomes of a male and female. The members of each pair of chromosomes are both similar and different: each chromosome in the pair contains varying forms of the same genes, at the same location on the chromosome. A gene for hair colour, for example, is located in the same place on both members of the same pairing. However, one of those chromosomes might carry the gene for blond hair and the other for brown hair.

Figure 3.5

The Genetic Difference between Males and Females

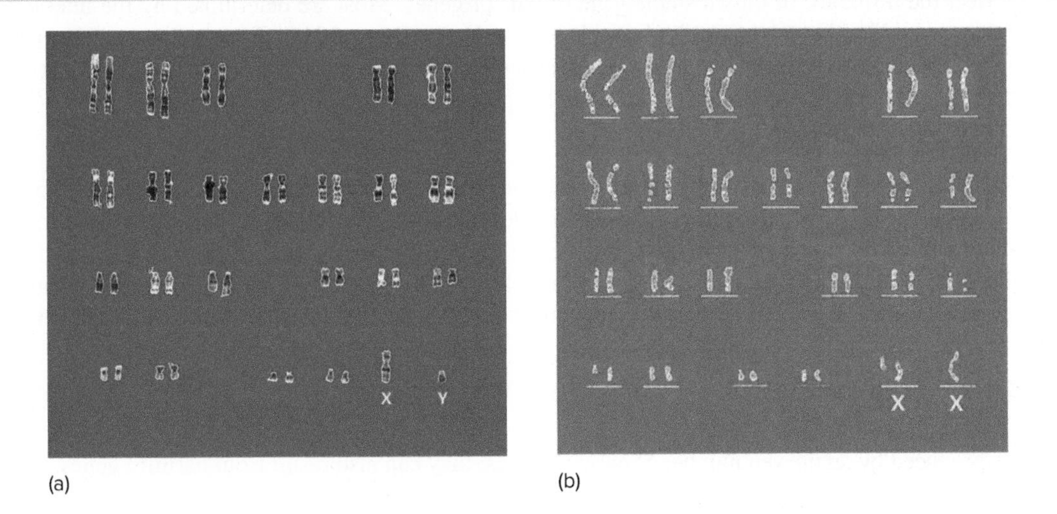

Set (a) shows the chromosome structure of a male, and set (b) shows the chromosome structure of a female. The last pair of 23 pairs of chromosomes is in the bottom right box of each set. Note that the Y chromosome of the male is smaller than the X chromosome of the female. To obtain this kind of chromosomal picture, a cell is removed from a person's body, usually from the inside of the mouth. The chromosomes are stained by chemical treatment, magnified, and then photographed.

Do you notice any differences between the male and female chromosomes in Figure 3.5? The difference lies in the 23rd pair. Ordinarily, in females this pair consists of two chromosomes called X chromosomes; in males, the 23rd pair consists of an X and a Y chromosome. The presence of a Y chromosome is what makes an individual male. Every two days, or in approximately one of every 1500 births, a child is born with a range of variations in their chromosome, hormone, and reproductive systems (Rainbow Health Ontario, 2011).

Sex-Linked Genes

Most mutated genes are recessive. When a mutated gene is carried on the X chromosome, the result is called *X-linked inheritance.* The implications for males may be very different than for females (Guffanti et al., 2013; McClelland, Bowles, & Koopman, 2012). Remember that males have only one X chromosome. Thus, if there is an altered, disease-creating gene on the X chromosome, males have no "backup" copy to counter the harmful gene and therefore may carry an X-linked disease. However, females have a second X chromosome, which is likely to be unchanged. As a result, they are not likely to have the X-linked disease. Thus, most individuals who have X-linked diseases are males. Females who have one changed copy of the X gene are known as "carriers," and they usually do not show any signs of the X-linked disease. Thus, they may not realize they are carriers until they have male children. Hemophilia and fragile X syndrome are examples of X-linked inheritance (Bartel, Weinstein, & Schaffer, 2012).

Genetic Imprinting

Genetic imprinting occurs when genes have differing effects depending on whether they are inherited from the mother or the father (Schneider et al., 2014). A chemical process "silences" one member of the gene pair. For example, as a result of imprinting, only the maternally derived copy of a gene might be active, while the paternally derived copy of the same gene is silenced—or vice versa (Court et al., 2014). Only a small percentage of human genes appear to undergo imprinting, but it is a normal and important aspect of development. When imprinting goes awry, development is disturbed, as in the case of Beckwith-Wiedemann syndrome, a growth variation, and Wilms' tumour, a type of cancer (Okun et al., 2014).

POLYGENIC INHERITANCE

Genetic transmission is usually more complex than the simple examples we have examined (Moore, 2013). Few characteristics reflect the influence of only a single gene or pair of genes. Most are determined by the interaction of many different genes; they are said to be polygenically determined (Lu, Yu, & Deng, 2012). Even a simple characteristic such as height, for example, reflects the interaction of many genes, as well as the influence of the environment. Most diseases, such as cancer and diabetes, develop as a consequence of complex gene interactions and environmental factors (Dastani et al., 2012; Ekeblad, 2010; Vimaleswaran & Loos, 2010).

The term gene–gene interaction is increasingly used to describe studies that focus on the interdependence of two or more genes in influencing characteristics, behaviours, diseases, and development (Hu, Wang, & Wang, 2014; Sarlos et al., 2014). For example, studies have documented gene–gene interaction in children's immune system functioning (Reijmerink et al., 2011), asthma (Lee et al., 2014), alcoholism (Yokoyama et al., 2013), cancer (Mandal, Abebe, & Chaudhary, 2014), cardiovascular disease (Kumar et al., 2014), arthritis (Freytag et al., 2014), and Alzheimer's disease (Koran et al., 2014).

Chromosome and Gene-Linked Variations

Variations can be produced by an uneven number of chromosomes; they can also result from harmful genes.

Chromosome Variations

When gametes are formed, the 46 chromosomes do not always divide evenly. In this case, the resulting sperm and ovum do not have their normal 23 chromosomes. The most notable instances when this occurs involve Down syndrome and gene-linked variations (see Figure 3.6).

Figure 3.6
Some Chromosome Variations

Name	Description	Treatment	Incidence
Down syndrome	Extra or altered 21st chromosome causes mild to severe retardation and physical variations	Surgery, early intervention, infant stimulation, and special learning programs	1 in 1900 births at maternal age 20; 1 in 300 births at maternal age 35; 1 in 30 births at maternal age 45
Klinefelter syndrome	An extra X chromosome causes physical variations	Hormone therapy can be effective	1 in 800 males
Fragile X syndrome	A variation in the X chromosome can cause intellectual disabilities or short attention span	Special education, speech and language therapy	1 in 1500 males; 1 in 2500 females
Turner syndrome	A missing X chromosome in females can cause intellectual disabilities and sexual underdevelopment	Hormone therapy in childhood and puberty	1 in 3000 female births
XYY syndrome	An extra Y chromosome can cause above-average height	No special treatment required	1 in 1000 male births

Other diseases that result from genetic variations include cystic fibrosis, diabetes, hemophilia, Huntington disease, spina bifida, and Tay-Sachs disease. Some day, scientists may identify why these and other genetic variations occur and discover cures. The Human Genome Project has already linked specific DNA variations with increased risk of a number of diseases and conditions, including Huntington disease (in which the central nervous system deteriorates), some forms of cancer, asthma, diabetes, hypertension, and Alzheimer's disease.

These athletes, some of whom have Down syndrome, are participating in a Special Olympics competition.

Approximately 1 in 800 Canadian children are born with Down syndrome. The prevalence increases for mothers over 35 years of age. Down syndrome is associated with the presence of extra chromosome 21 material and is characterized by well-defined phenotype, intellectual delay, as well as other major and minor anomalies such as congenital heart and gastrointestinal conditions (Kohut & Rouleau, 2013).

Gene-Linked Variations

Variations can not only be produced by an uneven number of chromosomes, but can also result from harmful genes (Croyle, 2000). Apart from the single pair of sex chromosomes, the 22 other pairs of chromosomes are referred to as autosomes and account for most of the genetic disorders. The inheritance of the disorders follows one of two paths, either *autosomal-dominant* or *autosomal-recessive*. In the autosomal-dominant pattern, one parent will usually be affected with the disorder. If only one parent has the dominant gene, then half the children will exhibit the disorder. If both parents have the gene, then all the children will have the disorder. Examples of disorders generated by the autosomal-dominant gene include achondroplasia, a bone growth disorder; hereditary colon cancer; and neurofibromatosis I, which causes light brown birthmarks and soft skin lumps over peripheral nerves.

In the autosomal-recessive pattern, if both parents are carriers but not affected by the disorder, each offspring will have a one-in-four chance of being affected. If both parents are affected, then all their children will be as well. If one is affected and the other not at all (and is not a carrier), then their children will be unaffected but will be carriers. If one parent is affected and the other is a carrier, then half their offspring will be affected. Phenylketonuria, sickle-cell anemia, Tay-Sachs disease, and cystic fibrosis are autosomal-recessive disorders. In both patterns, male and female babies are equally affected. More than 7000 such genetic variations have been identified, although most of them are rare. Other genetic anomalies include diabetes, hemophilia, Huntington disease, and spina bifida. Figure 3.7 provides further information about the genetic variations we have discussed.

Figure 3.7
Some Gene-Linked Variations

Name	Description	Treatment	Incidence
Cystic fibrosis	Glandular dysfunction that interferes with mucus production; breathing and digestion are hampered, resulting in a shortened life span	Physical and oxygen therapy, synthetic enzymes, and antibiotics; most individuals live to middle age	1 in 2000 births
Diabetes	Body does not produce enough insulin, which causes abnormal metabolism of sugar	Early onset can be fatal unless treated with insulin	1 in 2500 births
Hemophilia	Delayed blood clotting causes internal and external bleeding	Blood transfusions/ injections can reduce or prevent damage due to internal bleeding	1 in 10 000 males
Huntington disease	Central nervous system deteriorates, producing problems in muscle coordination and mental deterioration	Does not usually appear until age 35 or older; death likely 10 to 20 years after symptoms appear	1 in 20 000 births
Phenylketonuria (PKU)	Metabolic disorder that, left untreated, causes intellectual disabilities	Special diet can result in average intelligence and normal life span	1 in 14 000 births
Sickle-cell anemia	Blood disorder that limits the body's oxygen supply; can cause joint swelling, sickle-cell crises, heart and kidney failure	Penicillin, medication for pain, antibiotics, and blood transfusions	1 in 400 North American children of African descent (lower among other groups)
Spina bifida	Neural tube disorder that causes brain and spine variations	Corrective surgery at birth, orthopedic devices, and physical/medical therapy	2 in 1000 births
Tay-Sachs disease	Deceleration of mental and physical development caused by an accumulation of lipids in the nervous system	Medication and special diet are used, but death is likely by five years of age	1 in 30 North American Jews is a carrier

Every individual carries DNA variations that might predispose the person to serious physical disease or mental disorder. But not all individuals who carry a genetic disorder display the disorder. Other genes or developmental events sometimes compensate for genetic variations (Gottlieb, 2004; Gottlieb, Wahlsten, & Lickliter, 2006). Thus, genes are not destiny, but genes that are missing, non-functional, or mutated can be associated with disorders (Fujita et al., 2014; Moore, 2013). Identifying such genetic variations could enable doctors to predict an individual's risks, recommend healthy practices, and prescribe the safest and most effective drugs (Bennetts, 2014; Kassahn, Scott, & Fletcher, 2014).

A decade or two from now, parents of a newborn baby may be able to leave the hospital with a full genome analysis of their offspring that reveals disease risks. However, this knowledge might bring important costs as well as benefits. Who would have access to a person's genetic profile? Would an individual's ability to land and hold jobs or obtain insurance be threatened if it is known that a person is considered at risk for some disease? For example, should an individual who wishes to become an airline pilot or a neurosurgeon, but whose genetic makeup is predisposed to developing a disorder that makes the person's hands shake, be refused entry to the field? Genetic counsellors, usually physicians or biologists who are well versed in the field of medical genetics, understand the kinds of situations just described, the odds of encountering them, and helpful strategies for offsetting some of their effects (Mollee, 2014; Swanson, Ramos, & Snyder, 2014).

CONNECTING through Social Policy

Eugenics and Social Policy

You will find *Connecting Through Social Policy* boxes throughout this text, and you might ask, "Just what is social policy and where does it come from?" There is no simple answer to this question, as the definition, the source, and the implementation of social policy are multifaceted and complex. Generally, Canadian social policy attempts to address factors that affect the daily lives of citizens, including health, education, poverty, employment, safety, and housing. The development of policy is a lengthy zig-zagging process that involves problem identification, research, legislation, adoption, implementation, evaluation, and adaptation. Often policy changes are prompted by legal challenges to present laws and rest on Supreme Court decisions. Two examples of major policy shifts in the past two decades include the decriminalization of abortion and the legalization of same-sex marriages. Another couple of highly-charged policy considerations under discussion today are the implementation of physician-assisted death, which you will read more about in Chapter 19, and current research in the field of eugenics, which is discussed in this chapter.

What we learn and believe about ourselves, and the world around us, is informed by our families, communities, religious and political beliefs, and assumptions. Advances in scientific knowledge often challenge these understandings and the ensuing debates influence social policy, for better and for worse. For example, when Darwin's cousin, Francis Galton, proposed the idea of eugenics in the late 1880s, he perceived it as a science that would promote improvement of the human race. His ideas quickly caught on, resulting in many countries promoting laws to either sterilize, incarcerate, or otherwise prevent those deemed defective from reproducing (Lombardo, 2008). Who were those deemed defective? They were the poor, the criminal, those viewed as immoral (the alcoholic, the prostitute), the mentally ill, the disabled, the chronically ill, the feeble elderly, and members of minority racialized groups.

One of the most extreme and blatant expressions of eugenics was the Holocaust, occurring between 1939 and 1945, when under the totalitarian leadership of Adolf Hitler in Nazi Germany, an estimated 6 million Jewish men, women, and children were killed; in addition, another estimated 300 000 non-Jewish were killed for being homosexuals or for being physically, mentally, or emotionally disabled. This was done in an effort to produce a "pure master race" (Evans, 2004). Consequently, after World War II, the field of eugenics lost much support. How is it, then, that the field has regained momentum? Again, the answers are multi-faceted.

In the late 1960s, former Prime Minister Pierre Elliot Trudeau famously said, "The State has no business in the bedrooms of the nation," thereby easing laws on abortion, contraception, and homosexuality. Such a public statement by the country's prime minister ignited several decades of public debate prior to the Supreme Court rulings of the late 1980s and early 1990s.

Annually, at birth, approximately 1 in 25 infants is diagnosed with one or more congenital anomalies such as Down syndrome, neural tube defects, congenital heart defects, orofacial clefts, limb deficiency defects, and gastroschis (Taylor, 2013). Genetic screening can now determine whether or not a child has the potential for particular diseases or conditions, providing choices that were unavailable prior to 1988, the year that abortions were decriminalized in Canada, (although strict professional guidelines exist for pregnancies over 24 weeks' gestation). Today there are approximately 31 abortions per 100 live births, half of which are performed in hospitals and half in clinics (University of Ottawa, 2015).

CRISPR is a genetic editing tool that enables researchers to generate permanent genetic mutations and in the process offset genetically transmitted diseases (New England Biolabs, 2016). However, Dr. Peter Bretscher of the Department of Microbiology and Immunology at the University of Saskatchewan, cautions, "Genes that are detrimental in one context would be weeded out by natural selection if they were only detrimental; they are likely advantageous in another context, and hence their presence is maintained" (Bretscher, 2016). Responding to a proposal put forward by the Francis Crick Institute of London, the United Kingdom is the first country to approve DNA-altering techniques in embryos, so that research will gain a deeper understanding of how a healthy embryo develops. Implanting edited embryos, however, remains illegal; nevertheless, the United Kingdom's policy change sparked controversy and opened the door to genetically-modified (GM) babies (Gallager, 2016).

The possibility of creating "designer" babies is as real as the potential of genetic manipulation to address life-threatening diseases. Will we use our knowledge of genetics to control disease or to create a superior human, or perhaps both? Eugenics aims to find ways to incorporate the interplay of physiologic factors and our genes. This is what the field of eugenics is all about, and this very controversial area of research will shape future legislation and social policy. How will our social policies grapple with scientific advances?

The Human Genome Project

The Human Genome Project involves international efforts to map the human genome—the complete set of developmental instructions for creating proteins that initiate the making of a human organism (Brooker, 2015; Cummings, 2014). The term *genome* is a combination of the words *gene* and *chromosome*. The Human Genome Project is as enormous as it is complex. The enormity and complexities of the project are reflected in Dr. Hsein-Hsein Lei's description: "If the genome were a book, it would be as large as 800 dictionaries. Further, it would take a person typing 60 words a minute, 8 hours a day, about 50 years to type it" (Genome Canada, 2012).

One of the big surprises of the Human Genome Project was an early report indicating that humans have only about 30 000 genes (Human Genome Project Information, 2001). More recent analysis proposes that humans may actually have less than 20 000 protein-producing genes (Ezkurdia et al., 2014). Rather than being a group of independent genes, the human genome consists of many genes that collaborate both with each other and with non-genetic factors inside and outside the body (Moore, 2013). The collaboration operates at many points. For example, the cellular machinery mixes, matches, and links small pieces of DNA to reproduce the genes—and that machinery is influenced by what is going on around it.

Whether a gene is "turned on"—working to assemble proteins—is also a matter of collaboration. The activity of genes (*genetic expression*) is affected by their environment (Gottlieb, 2007; Moore, 2013). For example, hormones that circulate in the blood make their way into the cell where they can turn genes "on" and "off." And the flow of hormones can be affected by environmental conditions, such as light, day length, nutrition, and behaviour. Numerous studies have shown that external events outside of the original cell and the person, as well as events inside the cell, can excite or inhibit gene expression (Gottlieb, Wahlsten, & Lickliter, 2006). Factors such as stress, radiation, and temperature can influence gene expression (Craft et al., 2014; Dedon & Begley, 2014). For example, one study revealed that an increase in the concentration of stress hormones such as cortisol produces a fivefold increase in DNA damage (Flint et al., 2007). Another study found that exposure to radiation changes the rate of DNA synthesis in cells (Lee et al., 2011).

With funding from Genome Canada, physicians are finding ways to diagnose and treat diseases. Under the leadership of Dr. Tony Pawson of the Simon Lunenfeld Research Institute at Mount Sinai Hospital in Toronto, a team is discovering drugs that may halt the division of cancerous cells and lead to recovery. Dr. Stephen Scherer of Sick Kids Hospital in Toronto is the lead researcher of the Autism Genome Project, an unprecedented international initiative involving 10 countries (Genome Canada, 2012). Developments such as these will greatly influence both health care and social policy.

To this point, we have explored a number of ideas about genetic foundations. For a review, see the Reach Your Learning Outcomes section at the end of this chapter.

Reproduction Challenges and Choices

LO3 Identify some important reproductive challenges and choices.

- **Prenatal Diagnostic Tests**
- **Infertility and Reproductive Technology**
- **Adoption**

The facts and principles we have discussed regarding mitosis, meiosis, fertilization, and genetics are a small part of the current explosion of knowledge and research about human biology. This research will not only help us understand human development, but will also open up many new choices for prospective parents—choices that can also raise ethical questions.

Prenatal Diagnostic Tests

A number of tests can indicate whether a fetus is developing normally, including amniocentesis, fetal MRI, maternal blood screening, ultrasound sonography, chorionic villus sampling, and non-invasive prenatal diagnosis.

Amniocentesis is a prenatal medical procedure in which a sample of amniotic fluid is withdrawn by syringe and tested to discover if the fetus is suffering from any chromosomal or metabolic disorders (Menon et al., 2014). Amniocentesis is performed between the 15th and 18th weeks of pregnancy. The later amniocentesis is performed, the better its diagnostic potential. After the amniotic fluid is withdrawn, it may take two weeks for enough cells to grow and amniocentesis test results to be obtained (see Figure 3.8).

Chorionic villus sampling (CVS) may be used between the 10th and 12th weeks of pregnancy to detect genetic defects and chromosomal abnormalities such as those discussed in the previous section. CVS is a prenatal medical procedure in which a small sample of the placenta (the vascular organ that links the fetus to the mother's uterus) is removed (Gimovsky et al., 2014). Diagnosis takes about 10 days. There is a small risk of limb deformity when CVS is used (see Figure 3.8).

Both amniocentesis and chorionic villus sampling provide valuable information about the presence of birth defects, but they also raise difficult issues for parents about whether an abortion should be obtained if birth defects are present (Zhang et al., 2010). Chorionic villus sampling allows a decision to be made earlier, near the end of the first 12 weeks of pregnancy, when abortion is safer and less traumatic.

Ultrasonography or *ultrasound test*, often conducted seven weeks into a pregnancy and again at various times later, is a risk-free prenatal medical procedure in which high-frequency sound waves are directed into the pregnant woman's uterus. The echo from the sounds is transformed into a visual representation of the fetus's inner structures. This technique has been able to detect such disorders as microencephaly, a form of developmental disability involving an unusually small brain. Ultrasonography is often used in conjunction with amniocentesis to determine the precise location of the fetus and the number of fetuses in the mother's uterus. It can also give clues to the baby's sex (Gerards et al., 2008).

Figure 3.8

Amniocentesis and Chorionic Villi Sampling

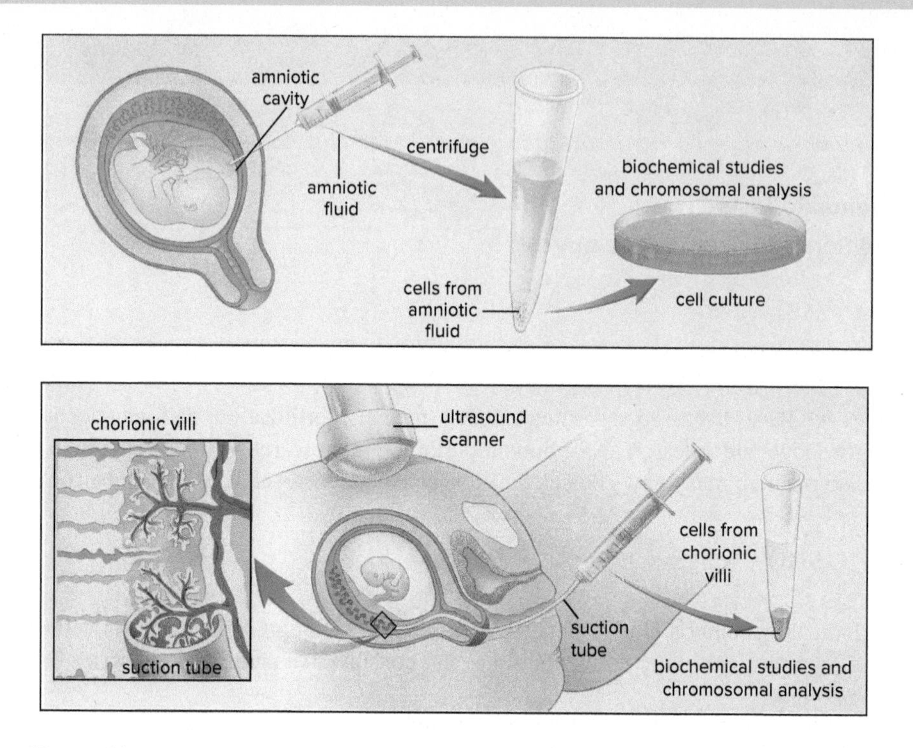

From *Biology*, 6/e by Mader, S. Copyright © 1998 by The McGraw-Hill Companies. Reproduced with permission of The McGraw-Hill Companies.

Fetal MRI is a brain-imaging technique used to diagnose fetal malformations (Daltro et al., 2010; Duczkowska et al., 2010) (see Figure 3.9). MRI stands for magnetic resonance imaging and uses a powerful magnet and radio images to generate detailed images of the body's organs and structures. Currently, ultrasound is still the first choice in fetal screening, but fetal MRI can provide more detailed images than ultrasound. In many instances, ultrasound will indicate a possible abnormality and then fetal MRI will be used to obtain a clearer, more detailed image (Obenauer & Maestre, 2008). Among the fetal malformations that fetal MRI may be able to detect better than ultrasound sonography are certain central nervous system, chest, gastrointestinal, genital/urinary, and placental abnormalities (Baysinger, 2010; Panigrahy, Borzage, & Blümi, 2010; Weston, 2010).

Figure 3.9

A fetal MRI, which is increasingly being used in prenatal diagnosis of fetal malformations.

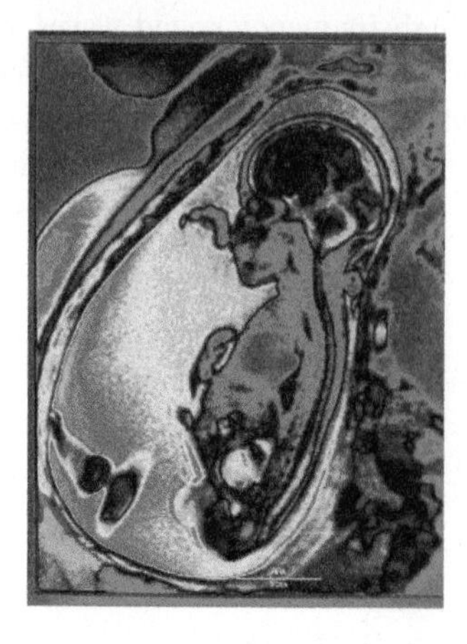

Larry Berman

Maternal blood screening may be performed during the 16th to 18th weeks of pregnancy. This process identifies pregnancies that have an elevated risk for birth defects such as spina bifida (a defect in the spinal cord) and Down syndrome (Bernard et al., 2013). The current blood test is called the triple screen because it measures three substances in the mother's blood. After an abnormal triple screen result, the next step is usually an ultrasound examination. If an ultrasound does not explain the abnormal triple screen results, amniocentesis is typically used.

Non-invasive prenatal diagnosis (NIPD) is increasingly being explored as an alternative to such procedures as chorionic villus sampling and amniocentesis (Kantak et al., 2014; Li et al., 2014). Researchers have used NIPD to successfully test for genes inherited from a father that cause cystic fibrosis and Huntington disease. They also are exploring the potential for using NIPD to diagnose a baby's sex, as well as Down syndrome as early as five weeks after conception (Lim, Park, & Ryu, 2013).

FETAL SEX DETERMINATION

Chorionic villus sampling has often been used to determine the sex of the fetus at some point between 11 and 13 weeks of gestation. Recently, though, some non-invasive techniques have been able to detect the sex of the fetus at an earlier point (Moise et al., 2013). Being able to detect an offspring's sex as well as the presence of various diseases and defects at such an early stage raises concerns about couples' motivation to terminate a pregnancy (Dickens, 2014).

Infertility and Reproductive Technology

Canada's fertility rate is reported to be 1.6 births per woman (Statistics Canada, 2016). This represents a drop from 1.65 in 2007 (CIA World Factbook, 2012). The "replacement rate"—that is, the number of births that sustain a population—is 2.1 children per woman, so birthrates below that trigger a number of social and economic concerns. Women are waiting longer to have a baby; for example, the fertility rate of women between ages 30 and 34 is now higher than that of women between 25 and 29. Both nationally and internationally, more women over 40 are having children.

Infertility is defined as the inability to conceive a child after 12 months of regular intercourse without contraception for women under 35 and 6 months for women over 35 years of age. Roughly one in six Canadian couples experience infertility (Government of Canada, 2013). The cause of infertility can rest with the woman or the man (Reindollar & Goldman, 2012). The woman may not be ovulating; she may be producing abnormal ova; her fallopian tubes may be blocked; or, she may have a disease that prevents implantation of the ova. The man may have a seminal problem, either too few sperm (a condition called *oligospermia*), or no sperm (a condition called *azoospermia*); the sperm may lack motility (the ability to move adequately); or the man may have a blocked passageway (see Figure 3.10). In some cases of infertility, surgery may correct the cause. The Royal Commission on New Reproductive Technologies examined three forms of infertility treatment: fertility drugs, assisted insemination (AI), and in vitro fertilization (IVF). The most common form of fertility treatment in Canada is the use of fertility drugs. The Commission found that many of the drugs in use do not have research that clearly supports their effectiveness.

Figure 3.10
Fertility Problems, Possible Causes, and Treatments

	MEN	
Problem	**Possible Causes**	**Treatment**
Low sperm count	Hormone imbalance, varicose vein in scrotum, possibly environmental pollutants	Hormone therapy, surgery, avoiding excessive heat
	Drugs (cocaine, marijuana, lead, arsenic, some steroids and antibiotics)	
	Y chromosome gene deletions	

Immobile sperm	Abnormal sperm shape	None
	Infection	Antibiotics
	Malfunctioning prostate	Hormones
Antibodies against sperm	Problem in immune system	Drugs
	WOMEN	
Ovulation problems	Pituitary or ovarian tumour	Surgery
	Underactive thyroid	Drugs
Antisperm secretions	Unknown	Acid or alkaline douche, estrogen therapy
Blocked fallopian tubes	Infection caused by IUD or abortion or by sexually transmitted disease	Surgical incision, cells removed from ovary and placed in uterus
Endometriosis (tissue buildup in uterus)	Delayed parenthood until the thirties	Hormones, surgical incision

The oldest form of assisting a woman to become pregnant when she or her partner are subfertile, or infertile, or she wishes to have a baby without a male partner, is assisted insemination (AI). In this procedure, the sperm of either the woman's partner or of a donor is placed in the vagina, near the cervix, or in the uterus. AI is the most common fertility procedure available in Canada. The Commission found AI to have "the potential to be a safe, inexpensive, and relatively low-tech" method to treat infertility. Yet, they raised concerns for the storage and handling of sperm, the definition of success, and the variations in procedural technique employed across the country.

The third form of infertility treatment studied by the Commission is the widely publicized use of high-tech IVF procedures, in which the woman's eggs are retrieved from the ovaries and fertilized by the man's sperm in a laboratory dish. If any eggs are successfully fertilized, one or more of the resulting zygotes is transferred into the woman's uterus. The Canadian Fertility and Andrology Society (CFAS, 2012) reported that 9,904 live births resulted from in vitro treatment cycles at Canada's 28 IVF centres.

critical thinking

According to Dr. Robert Glossop, former executive director of programs and research at the Vanier Institute of the Family, "what is personal is political and what is political is personal." Private decisions are very much linked with public policies. With that in mind, how affordable is in vitro fertilization (IVF)? IVF may cost anywhere from $4500 to $9500, plus medications and other fees (Haaf, 2015). Quebec was the first province to cover IVF treatment in its provincial health plan, but in November 2015 that province ended the publicly-funded IVF program and replaced it with tax credits for one IVF cycle. A similar tax credit is offered in Manitoba. Ontario now covers the cost of one cycle for qualifying individuals, and New Brunswick offers a one-time grant of up to $5,000 for IVF. To qualify for coverage, these provinces have individual sets of qualifiers such as age, residency and citizenship, and so on (Haaf, 2015; CFAS, 2012; Fertility Matters Canada, 2016). Should all provinces follow the examples set by Ontario, Quebec, Manitoba, and New Brunswick and cover or offset all or a limited number of the health care costs? What limitations might be reasonable to impose? Suppose that you learn you are infertile; what steps would you take? What considerations would affect your decision?

One consequence of fertility treatments is an increase in multiple births. Twenty-five to 30 percent of pregnancies achieved by fertility treatments—including in vitro fertilization—now result in multiple births. A meta-analysis (a statistical technique that combines the results of multiple studies to determine the strength of the effect) revealed that in vitro fertilization twins have a slightly increased risk of low birth weight (McDonald et al., 2010), and another meta-analysis found that in vitro fertilization singletons have a significant risk of low birth weight (McDonald et al., 2009).

Adoption

Another possible response to infertility problems is adoption (Grotevant & McDermott, 2014). Adoption is a social and legal process by which a parent–child relationship is established between persons unrelated by birth. Citizenship and Immigration Canada reports that in 2010, there were 1968 international adoptions, down from 2130 in 2009. By contrast, international adoption in the United States dropped from 22 991 in 2004 to 9320 in 2011. Changes in laws and costs involved have impacted adoption rates (Pearce, 2012). China has been the most popular country for adopting children, particularly girls. On the other hand, although international adoptions are declining, Ontario's Ministry of Children and Youth Services reported that Ontario increased domestic adoptions by 21 percent between 2008 and 2012, and is making efforts to make adoption a smoother process (Pearce, 2012).

Wanting to be a parent and choosing to adopt, or conversely, deciding to place an infant up for adoption, are both riddled with emotion. According to Origins Canada (2010), mothers who have given their baby up for adoption have a higher than average likelihood of suffering from a variety of mental disorders including complex post-traumatic stress disorder, postpartum depression following the birth of a subsequent child, anxiety disorders, grief lasting a lifetime, depression, stress-related ailments (including fibromyalgia, migraines, etc.), plus difficulty developing and maintaining intimate relationships.

Generally, adopted children fare considerably better than their biological mothers. A study of internationally adopted Chinese girls reported the children to be relatively well-adjusted and to demonstrate resilience and characteristics of love, creativity, humour, curiosity, and kindness. As they entered their teens, traits such as teamwork and gratitude are added (Loker et al., 2012). At the same time, persons who have been adopted identified issues related to problems with attachment, identity, abandonment, and parenting of their own children (Origins Canada, 2012). The amount of time a child spends in an orphanage is linked to adjustment; hence the earlier the adoption, the better the outcomes (Bernard & Dozier, 2008; Julian, 2013). Children adopted from an orphanage in the first six months of their lives showed no lasting negative effects of their early experience at age 6 years. However, children from the orphanage who were adopted after 6 months of age had abnormally high levels of cortisol, indicating that their stress regulation had not developed adequately (Ambert, 2003). Those adopted after 12 months of age had a three to four times higher risk of delinquent behaviour than their non-adopted counterparts.

York University professor Anne-Marie Ambert (2003) reported that adoptive parents are usually equally attached to their adopted children and their biological children, if they have them; however, another issue is whether there should be any contact with children's biological parents. Open adoption involves sharing identifying information and having contact with the biological parents; in contrast, closed adoption involves not having such sharing and contact. Most adoption agencies today offer adoptive parents the opportunity for both. A longitudinal study found that when adopted children reach adulthood, adoptive parents describe open adoption positively and see it as serving the child's best interests (Siegel, 2013). Another longitudinal study found that birth mothers, adoptive parents, and adopted children who have contact are more satisfied with their arrangements than those who did not (Grotevant et al., 2013). Also, in this study, contact was linked to more optimal adjustment for adolescents and emerging adults (Grotevant et al., 2013). Further, birth mothers who are more satisfied with their contact arrangements have less unresolved grief 12 to 20 years after placement.

To this point, we have discussed a number of ideas about reproduction challenges and choices. For a review, see the Reach Your Learning Outcomes section at the end of this chapter.

Heredity–Environment Interaction: The Nature–Nurture Debate

LO4 Explain some of the ways that heredity and environment interact to produce individual differences in development.

- **Behaviour Genetics**
- **Heredity–Environment Correlations**
- **Shared and Non-shared Environmental Experiences**
- **The Epigenetic View**
- **Conclusions about Heredity–Environment Interaction**

Is it possible to untangle the influence of heredity from that of environment and discover the role each plays in producing individual differences in development? When heredity and environment interact, how does heredity influence the environment and vice versa?

Behaviour Genetics

Behaviour genetics is the field that seeks to discover the influence of heredity and environment on individual differences in human traits and development (Krushkal et al., 2014; Maxson, 2013). Note that behaviour genetics does not determine the extent to which genetics or the environment affects an individual's traits. Instead, what behaviour geneticists try to do is to figure out what is responsible for the differences among people—that is, to what extent do people differ because of differences in genes, environment, or a combination of these (Carlson, Mendle, & Harden, 2014; Chen et al., 2014). To study the influence of heredity on behaviour, behaviour geneticists often use either twins or adoption situations (Goldsmith, 2011). Most experts today agree that the environment plays an important role in intelligence. This means that improving children's environments can raise their intelligence.

CONNECTING through research

Ethical Considerations of Stem Cell Research and Genetic Screening: An Overview

When scientific inquiry collides with chance, the future may be irrevocably transformed. Such is the story behind stem cell research. In 1961, two men, who some now refer to as the founding fathers of stem cell research, physicist James Till and biologist Ernest McCulloch, were experimenting with bone marrow and mice. Much to their surprise, they observed a startling phenomenon: cells were renewing themselves! From these beginnings in a modest Toronto lab to today's activity in multi-million-dollar facilities around the world, stem cell research has created a furor of activity and spawned heated debate.

The tension between research possibilities and ethical concerns ignited passionate debates about when and how life begins; who, if anyone, can create life; and how evolution will be determined. In 1997, the first mammal, Dolly the sheep, was cloned by Scottish scientists at the Roslin Institute of the University of Edinburgh (Human Genome Project Information, 2009). This event triggered speculation about human cloning. Little more than a decade later, Dr. Zavos, often referred to as the father of andrology, working out of a secret lab in the Middle East, where no laws prohibiting human cloning exist, became the first to inseminate women with cloned embryos (Connor, 2009; Human Cloning Foundation, 2012).

© epa european pressphoto agency b.v. / Alamy Stock Photo

Drs. Till and McCulloch's incisive and award-willing findings have paved the way for life-saving bone marrow transplants that have not only increased the longevity of leukemia patients, but also sparked a plethora of research for more effective treatments of life-threatening conditions such as cancer, heart disease, and spinal cord and neurological disorders (Smith, 2005; UHN, 2006). They were inducted into the Canadian Medical Hall of Fame in 2004 (NET, 2006).

In 2007, Dr. Andras Nagy and his research team at the Samuel Lunenfeld Research Institute of Mount Sinai Hospital in Toronto, building on research conducted in Japan and the United States, made another major breakthrough. They were able to use skin cells to grow embryonic stem cells without the use of unpredictable virus cells. Because cloned organs can be used not only for transplants but also to test new medical therapies, research continues worldwide. In fact, in 2012, British researcher Sir John Gurdon and Shinya Yamanaka of Japan won the Nobel Prize in medicine for their innovative work on stem cell reprogramming.

A new breakthrough is a gene-editing technique called CRISPR, an acronym for clustered regularly interspaced short palindromic repeats. This technique facilitates moving genes around in anything from bacteria to people. With this technique, researchers have reversed mutations that cause blindness, stopped cancer cells from multiplying, and made cells impervious to the virus that causes AIDS. Like all revolutionary breakthroughs, the CRISPR technique raises ethical concerns, such as: Should we clone humans? and Will we produce "designer" babies? (Maxmen, 2015). In fact, in China, CRISPR is presently being used to edit non-viable human embryos.

As the controversy and debate continue to capture worldwide media attention, public expectation and speculation escalates. On the one hand, some embrace the possibility of cures and treatments that will ease the lives of many; on the other hand, some are horrified by the notion of growing human organs in a laboratory and are infuriated by the possibility of human cloning. Recognizing that Canadian researchers have been pioneers in the area of stem cell research and the tension generated between the potential to provide treatment for many debilitating diseases and the ethical, social, and legal issues, the Canadian Institutes of Health Research worked to establish guidelines. To receive federal or provincial funding, research must adhere to these guidelines, which, according to Alan Bernstein, chair of the board of directors of the Canadian Stem Cell Foundation, have become the gold standard for other countries (Bernstein, 2012; CIHR, 2012b). Even so, engineered humans may be part of the future—researchers know they are no longer science fiction (Maxmen, 2015).

Heredity–Environment Correlations

Heredity–environment correlations involve the interpretation of the complexities of heredity–environment interactions. An individual's genes may influence the types of environments to which they are exposed (Klahr & Burt, 2014). In a sense, individuals inherit environments that may be related or linked to genetic tendencies (Plomin et al., 2003). Behaviour geneticist Sandra Scarr (1993) described three ways that heredity and environment are correlated: passively, evocatively, and actively.

Passive genotype–environment correlations occur when biological parents, who are genetically related to the child, provide a rearing environment for the child. For example, the parents might have a genetic predisposition to be intelligent and read skillfully. Because they read well and enjoy reading, they provide their children with books to read. The likely outcome is that their children, given their own inherited predispositions, will become skilled readers.

Evocative genotype–environment correlations occur because a child's genotype elicits certain types of physical and social environments. For example, active, smiling children receive more social stimulation than passive, quiet children. Similarly, athletically-inclined children tend to elicit encouragement to engage in school sports. As a consequence, these adolescents tend to be the ones who try out for sport teams and go on to participate in athletically-oriented environments.

Twin studies compare identical twins with fraternal twins. Identical twins develop from a single fertilized egg that splits into two genetically identical organisms. Fraternal twins develop from separate eggs, making them genetically no more similar than non-twin siblings. *What is the nature of the twin study method?*

Active (niche-picking) genotype–environment correlations occur when children and adolescents seek out environments they find compatible and stimulating. Niche-picking refers to finding a niche or setting that is suited to one's abilities. Adolescents select from their surrounding environment some aspect that they respond to, learn about, or ignore. Their active selections of environments are related to their particular genotype.

Scarr believes that the relative importance of the three genotype–environment correlations changes as children develop from infancy through adolescence. In infancy, much of the environment that children experience is provided by adults. Thus, passive genotype–environment correlations are more common in the lives of infants and young children than they are for older children and adolescents, who can extend their experiences beyond the family's influence and create their environments to a greater degree.

Shared and Non-shared Environmental Experiences

Behaviour geneticists have argued that to understand the environment's role in differences between people, we should distinguish between shared and non-shared environments. That is, we should consider experiences that children share in common with other children living in the same home, and experiences that are not shared (Burt, 2014; White et al., 2014).

Shared environmental experiences are children's common experiences, such as their parents' personalities and intellectual orientation, the family's social class, and the neighbourhood in which they live. By contrast, **non-shared environmental experiences** are a child's unique experiences, both within the family and outside the family, that are not shared with another sibling. Thus, experiences occurring within the family can also be part of the "non-shared environment."

Behaviour geneticist Robert Plomin (2004) has found that common rearing, or shared environment, accounts for little of the variation in children's personality or interests. In other words, even though two children live under the same roof with the same parents, their personalities often are very different. Heredity influences the non-shared environments of siblings through the heredity–environment correlations described earlier. For example, a child who has inherited a genetic tendency to be athletic is likely to spend more time in environments related to sports, while the child who has inherited a tendency to be musically inclined may spend more time in environments related to music.

Recall Erikson's psycho-social theory of development described in Chapter 2. The primary challenge of adolescence is resolving of "identity versus identity confusion." Lynn Perlman (2008), herself a twin, a psychologist who works with twins and author of *Am I an "I" or a "We"?*, identifies the struggle twins have in developing a sense of being an individual, as peers, neighbours, teachers, and other social contacts often mistake one for the other. Of course, triplets have the same issue, possibly even more strongly so. On a humorous note, Perlman describes an event in which one set of triplets entered a beauty contest as one person and won the contest! The need to separate from "we" to "I" often accelerates in adolescence, and if not, separation in early adulthood can be emotionally quite painful (Pearlman, 2013).

In their book *Hold On to Your Kids: Why Parents Matter*, Canadian psychologist Gordon Neufeld and physician Gabor Maté (2004) find that some parents distance themselves from their children during the early years, allowing the children to spend most of their time with other children. Neufeld and Maté say this results in a stronger attachment with peers than with parents for these children. The results are often rejection of parental authority, influence, and connection during adolescence, a time when parental attachment might prevent, or at least soften, some of the problems teenagers can encounter. Thus, Neufeld and Maté believe a strong and nurturing attachment with parents is critical for adolescents' positive experience of life. Perhaps it is in our nature to be nurtured.

The Epigenetic View

Darwin believed that genetic changes evolve over generations as a result of natural selection; in other words, choices that parents make would not influence the genetic makeup of their children. More recently, however, scientific investigation suggests that environmental factors, including choices such as whether or not to smoke, may in fact trigger changes in inherited characteristics for generations to come. How and why this occurs is the focus of **epigenetics**, the study of ongoing, bidirectional interchange of biological and environmental factors that result in heritable modifications, but which do not alter DNA, our genetic code.

A baby inherits genes from both parents at conception. During prenatal development, toxins, nutrition, and stress can influence some genes to stop functioning while others become stronger or weaker. In the epigenetic view, environmental factors, both imposed (such as famine, poverty, or war) or chosen (such as nutrition or smoking), can change ways that genes interact and collaborate. In other words, heredity and environment operate together—or collaborate—to produce a person's intelligence, temperament, height, weight, ability to pitch a baseball, ability to read, and so on (Gottlieb, 2007; Meaney, 2010). During infancy, environmental experiences such as toxins, nutrition, stress, learning, and encouragement continue to modify genetic activity and the activity of the nervous system that directly underlies behaviour. This also helps to explain why identical twins can be quite different.

Dr. Michael Meaney and Dr. Moshe Szyf, working with rat models at the Michael Meaney Lab at McGill University (2004), reported that the gene expression in rat pups could be affected by maternal care in infancy. Excited by this finding, Patrick McGowan, who had previously studied with Meaney, wanted to expand this research to humans; he wondered if there is a link between child abuse and adult suicide. McGowan analyzed brain tissue from the Quebec Suicide Brain Bank, where brain tissue from dozens of people who committed suicide is stored in Pyrex containers, and conducted validating interviews with family members of those whose brain tissue was stored. Having both the brains and the histories, McGowan, in collaboration with scientists at the newly formed Sackler Program for Epigenetics and Psychobiology at McGill University, discovered a biological link to some male suicides. Although the connection between childhood abuse and suicide was known, this study demonstrated, at least to some extent, the biological factors, representing another step forward for the field of epigentics. Dr. Gustavo Turecki, director of the McGill Group for Suicide Studies, notes that his study represents advancements in understanding of epigenetics, but cautions that conclusions are tentative. Further, he notes that "Abuse and its severity is subjective; however, impact is important" (Reynolds, 2012).

CONNECTING development to life

Segun's Life Journey

Rarely do our lives travel along straight highways. More often than not, they zig-zag along divergent paths as we grow and develop. Family, media, friends, and circumstances sometimes bring us to life-altering crossroads. The issues and approaches introduced in these first three chapters offer some insights and explanations about how growth and development occur. With these in mind, consider the journey of 28-year-old Oluwasegun (Segun for short) Olufemi Akinsanya, then consider the questions asked at the end.

When he was 3 years of age, Segun's family immigrated from Nigeria and settled in a small town in rural Quebec. His father, a chemist, was proud of the math awards his bright, joyful son won in school and hoped that one day he would become a doctor. His three older sisters were also excellent students. Then, when Segun was 8 years old, tragedy struck. His mother, a nurse, was killed in an automobile accident and Segun's life began to zig-zag. A few years later, another adjustment: his father remarried and the family moved to Toronto.

Frequently in trouble with school and the law, Segun gained street status when he served a 30-day prison sentence for violating probation. Upon release, he found an eviction notice on the door when he arrived home. He later learned that his father had been quite ill with complications related to diabetes and was unable to work. These factors catapulted Segun to the street, where his entrepreneurial spirit and ability to adapt to just about any situation enabled him not only to fit in, but to assume leadership.

Then, at age 18, Segun hit a sharp curve in the road. While defending himself in a violent knife attack, his attacker was killed. Segun pleaded guilty to manslaughter and was incarcerated. His sisters and father visited him regularly. A poignant memory was the time his father spoke to him, "man-to-man" rather than "father-to-wayward son," saying that he would help, but that Segun would have to want to change. Feeling the support of his family, he reflected on his life and concluded that change was vital. To that end, while in prison, he wrote a manual designed to help troubled teens find a more constructive path.

Since his release, Segun has not only finished high school, but is working on a B.A. in human geography. His leadership skills and entrepreneurial spirit made it possible for him to become the founder of Currant Group, an organization devoted to helping youth and building community. Segun presents workshops in schools, and is actively engaged in initiatives designed to build community. He says, "I'm alive today so I can share my story and heal... Now I'm part of something important and productive. I'm defined by something good."

In Chapter 1, you read about three issues in psychology: *interactional model, continuity* and *discontinuity, and stability and change*. In Chapter 2, several approaches to the field were introduced, namely *psychoanalytic, cognitive, humanist, bio-ecological, and the contemporary approach of positive psychology.* And in Chapter 3, you have read a more in-depth discussion about *nature versus nurture*. Now, consider:

1. How might each of the issues in Chapter 1 help explain Segun's journey?
2. What insights might *hereditary-environment correlations, passive-genotype-environment, evocative genotype-environment, and active (niche-picking genotype) environment* offer to explain Segun's profile as outlined here?
3. Which theoretical approaches might provide some insights into Segun's life journey?
4. Perhaps you yourself, or someone you know, have come to major crossroads that redirected life's journey. How might the issues and the approaches discussed here provide some insights?

Conclusions about Heredity–Environment Interaction

Both genes and environment are necessary for a person even to exist. Because environmental influences depend on genetically-endowed characteristics, the two factors interact. Humans are driven to match their internal neurological structures to the external environment (Wexler, 2006).

The relative contributions of heredity and environment are not formulaic, one part genes, one part environment; nor does full genetic expression occur at any one time such as at conception or birth. Genes produce proteins throughout the life span, in many different environments, or they don't produce these proteins, depending in part on how harsh or nourishing those environments are.

The emerging view is that complex behaviours have some genetic loading that gives people a propensity for a particular developmental trajectory (Asbury & Plomin, 2014). Environment is as complex as the mixture of genes we inherit (Cicchetti & Toth, 2015; Bronfenbrenner & Morris 2006). Environmental influences range from the things we lump together under "nurture" (such as parenting, family dynamics, schooling, and neighbourhood quality) to biological encounters (such as viruses, birth complications, and even biological events in cells).

Growing up with many of the "advantages" of life does not guarantee success any more than growing up with many disadvantages guarantees failure. People who grew up in privileged families might take opportunities for granted and fail to develop the motivation to succeed. By the same token, people who grow up in impoverished conditions may make the best of the opportunities available to them and learn to seek out advantages that can help them improve their lives.

To this point, we have discussed heredity–environment interaction and the nature–nurture debate. For a review, see the Reach Your Learning Outcomes section at the end of this chapter.

Reach Your **Learning Outcomes**

The Evolutionary Perspective

LO1 Discuss the evolutionary perspective on life-span development.

Natural Selection and Adaptive Behaviour	▪ Natural selection, originally proposed by Charles Darwin in 1859, is the process that favours individuals of a species that are best adapted to survive and reproduce. ▪ In evolutionary theory, adaptive behaviour promotes the organism's survival in a natural habitat. ▪ Biological evolution shaped human beings into a culture-making species. ▪ In this view, adaptation, reproduction, and "survival of the fittest" are important in explaining behaviour.

Evolutionary Psychology	▪ Emphasizes that behaviour is a function of mechanisms, requires input for activation, and is ultimately related to survival and reproduction. ▪ Developmentalists propose that behaviour may evolve. ▪ According to Baltes, the benefits of evolutionary selection decrease with age mainly because of a decline in reproductive fitness. ▪ While evolutionary selection benefits decrease with age, cultural and social support needs increase. ▪ Social cognitive theorist Albert Bandura acknowledges evolution's important role in human adaptation and change, but argues for a bi-directional view that enables organisms to alter and construct new environmental conditions. ▪ Biology allows for a broad range of cultural possibilities.

Genetic Foundations

LO2 Describe what genes are and how they influence human development.

The Collaborative Gene	▪ Genes are short segments of DNA, and each gene has its own location. ▪ Various technologies, such as linkage analysis and next generation analysis, enable researchers to examine the role of heredity in diseases such as cancers and Alzheimer's disease. ▪ Hereditary information that directs cells to reproduce and manufacture proteins is contained in genes. ▪ The nucleus of each human cell contains 46 chromosomes, which are composed of DNA. ▪ Genes act collaboratively, not independently. ▪ Each of us, even identical twins, have a unique human genome sequence.
Genes, Chromosomes	▪ Reproduction takes place when a female gamete (ovum) is fertilized by male gamete (sperm) to create a zygote. ▪ Mitosis is the process of cell division.
Genetic Principles	▪ Genes are transmitted from parents to offspring by gametes, or sex cells. ▪ Gametes are formed by the splitting of cells, a process called meiosis. ▪ Genetic principles include those involving dominant-recessive genes, sex-linked genes, and polygenically inherited characteristics.
Chromosome and Gene-Linked Variations	▪ Occasionally chromosomes are harmful or they do not divide evenly, causing variations. ▪ Sex-linked chromosomal abnormalities include Klinefelter syndrome, fragile X syndrome, Turner syndrome, and XYY syndrome. ▪ Gene-linked disorders include phenylketonuria (PKU) and sickle-cell anemia.
The Human Genome Project	▪ The Human Genome Project has made stunning progress in mapping the human genome. ▪ Current research is aimed at finding ways to diagnose and treat diseases, as well as to shape health care policies.

Reproduction Challenges and Choices

LO3 **Identify some important reproductive challenges and choices.**

Prenatal Diagnostic Tests	▪ Amniocentesis, ultrasonography, chorionic villi sampling, and the maternal blood test are used to determine the presence of defects once pregnancy has begun.
Infertility and Reproductive Technology	▪ Genetic counselling has increased in popularity because couples want information about their risk of having a child with defective characteristics. ▪ Some infertility problems can be corrected through surgery or fertility drugs. ▪ Methods include in vitro fertilization and other more recently developed techniques.
Adoption	▪ Adopted children and adolescents are relatively well-adjusted, but report difficulties with issues related to attachment, identity, abandonment, and parenting their own children. ▪ When adoption occurs very early in development, the outcomes for the child are improved.

Heredity–Environment Interaction: The Nature–Nurture Debate

LO4 **Explain some of the ways that heredity and environment interact to produce individual differences in development.**

Behaviour Genetics	▪ The nature–nurture debate: Heredity and environment interact to produce individual differences in development. ▪ Behaviour genetics is the field concerned with the influence of heredity and environment on individual differences in human traits and development. Methods used by behavioural geneticists include twin studies and adoption studies.
Heredity–Environment Correlations	▪ Sandra Scarr argues that the environments parents select for their children depend on the parents' genotypes. ▪ Passive genotype–environment, evocative genotype–environment, and active (niche-picking) genotype–environment are three correlations. ▪ Scarr believes the relative importance of these three genotype–environment correlations changes as children develop.
Shared and Non-shared Environmental Experiences	▪ Shared environmental experiences refer to siblings' common experiences such as parents' personalities, the family's socio-economic status, and the neighbourhood in which they live. ▪ Non-shared environmental experiences refer to the child's unique experiences, such as those both within and outside of the family environment.
The Epigenetic View	▪ Development is the result of ongoing, bi-directional interaction between environment and heredity. ▪ Environmental factors, both imposed and chosen, can change the ways that genes interact and collaborate.
Conclusions about Heredity–	▪ Many complex behaviours have some genetic loading that gives people a propensity for a particular developmental trajectory.

Environment Interaction	▪ Actual development also requires an environment, and that environment is complex. ▪ The interaction of heredity and environment is extensive.

review → connect → reflect

review

1. How would you describe the evolutionary perspective? LO1
2. What are genes and why are they considered collaborative? LO2
3. How do mitosis and meiosis differ? LO2
4. What is the Human Genome Project about? LO2
5. What happens when chromosomes do not divide evenly? LO2
6. What strategies are people using to address reproductive challenges? LO3
7. What are some of the ethical considerations of stem cell research and genetic screening? LO3
8. What is the epigenetic view? LO4

connect

When you consider all the members of your family, including those you may not have met but of whom you have heard, what are the commonalities? With one of your family members in mind, describe how you think the interaction of genetics and heredity may have affected personality and development.

reflect

Your Own Personal Journey of Life

How much of your behaviour and personality development reflect your home environment, and how much might be genetic? Consider the possibility that you or a friend you know fairly well were adopted. What questions might you have about your genetic make-up? How might environmental factors have played a role in your personality development?

CHAPTER 4

Prenatal Development and Birth

CHAPTER OUTLINE

Prenatal Development

LO1 Examine prenatal development.

- **The Course of Prenatal Development**
- **Teratology and Hazards to Prenatal Development**
- **Prenatal Care**
- **Positive Prenatal Development**

Birth

LO2 Outline the birth process.

- **The Birth Process**
- **Special Neonatal Considerations**
- **Measures of Neonatal Health and Responsiveness**

The Postpartum Period

LO3 List the changes that take place in the postpartum period.

- **What Is the Postpartum Period?**
- **Physical Adjustments**
- **Emotional and Psychological Adjustments**

"Each time you look at your child you see something mysterious and contradictory—bits and pieces of other people—grandparents, your mate, yourself, all captured in a certain stance, a shape of the head, a look in the eye, combined with something very precious—a new human soul rich in individuality and possibility. That's immortality."

—JOAN SUTTON, CANADIAN AUTHOR

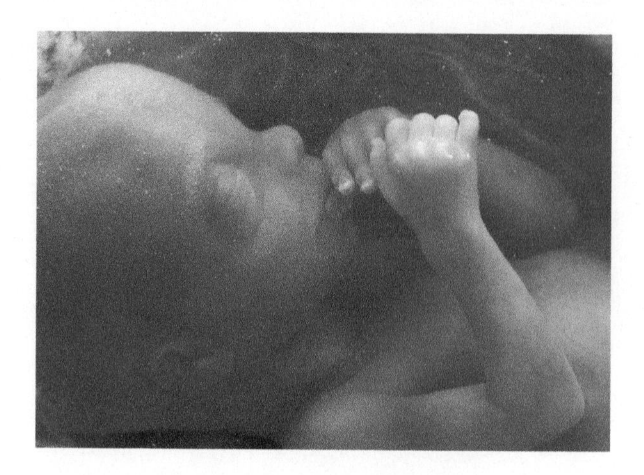

© Steve Allen/The Image Bank/Getty Images

Birth: Yesterday, Today, and Tomorrow

Anticipating or witnessing the birth of an individual in another species or our own inspires a sense of awe at the wonders of nature. From the first news of conception, the biological beginnings (discussed in Chapter 3), through prenatal development, to birth, we are reminded of the vast complexities of life. Seeing a newborn's tiny features, hearing her first cry, or touching his silken skin moves us deeply. Such is the wonder of birth. To appreciate fully the successive stages of pregnancy, the Society of Obstetricians and Gynaecologists of Canada (SOGC) has developed an essential resource called "Healthy Beginnings." This valuable guide helps mothers-to-be and caregivers to understand more completely not only how a body prepares itself for birth, but also what the growing baby requires during pregnancy (Schuurmans, Senikas, & Lalonde, 2009).

When a child is born in the developed world today, whether in the hospital under the care of a physician or at home under the care of a midwife, the child and mother have all the resources of the medical world. This includes neonatal intensive care units, ready or on standby to assist them. Compare the births of today with the birth of the Dionne quintuplets in 1934. The "quints" were born to Oliva and Elzire Dionne, a French-Canadian couple from a small town in Northern Ontario. Assisted into the world by two midwives and one physician, they were the first medically recorded quintuplets. Their combined weight at birth was less than 6500 grams. Against all odds, they survived.

Although today multiple births are not uncommon, the rarity of such an event in 1934 created quite a media stir. The news of the Dionne quintuplets' birth spread like wildfire. Media and public response afforded the family virtually no privacy. Two months after their births, the five babies—Yvonne, Emilie, Annette, Cécile, and Marie—were made wards of the state. The Ontario government appointed a board of guardians to protect the health and interests of the girls, thereby effectively stripping control from the parents. The parents, Oliva and Elzire, along with the quints' seven sisters and brothers, were allowed to visit the quints, but the parents were completely excluded from any decisions about how their daughters were to be raised.

The miracle of their births was a magnet for human-interest news stories; the quints immediately became celebrities and a major tourist attraction. People travelled for hundreds of kilometres to view them in their sheltered environment. Stories of their birthdays, Christmases, vacations, hobbies, education, and even family arguments were popular news items. "Quintland" became an instant money-maker for the provincial government. The five identical sisters' lives were displayed in glass bubbles, for all the world to see. In 1998, the three surviving quints, Cécile, Yvonne, and Annette, received a $4 million settlement from the government in response to their request for an inquiry into the management of the funds and for compensation.

Major advances have occurred in the sciences of fertility and neonatal medicine. Where medical resources are in place, delivery is now much safer for both mother and infant. The use of hormone-based fertility treatments or in vitro fertilization has given rise to more multiple and premature births. Parents today have the opportunity to make choices and decisions that were not available to parents 20 years ago. Some decisions may be influenced by spiritual beliefs. In addition, contemporary scientists investigate the possibilities of DNA manipulation and cloning. Possibilities unimagined in 1934 are reality today, just as possibilities unimagined today will be tomorrow's reality. These advances raise a number of interesting and ethical questions about how life is defined and sustained.

Let us now explore the development of a fetus from the time of conception through the moment of birth.

Toronto Star/CP Photo/The Canadian Press

The birth and lives of the Dionne quints became an international event that captured the hearts and interests of the world. Their story contrasts remarkably with the births and lives of multiples today. *What are some of the major changes in hospital care available today that were unavailable in 1934? In media and public response? How would the Canadian federal or provincial governmental responses be different? What are some of the ethical questions posed by the treatment of the Dionne quintuplets? What are some of the ethical questions posed by fertility treatments?*

Prenatal Development

LO1 Examine prenatal development.

- **The Course of Prenatal Development**
- **Teratology and Hazards to Prenatal Development**
- **Prenatal Care**
- **Positive Prenatal Development**

Imagine how a baby comes to be. Out of thousands of eggs and millions of sperm, one egg and one sperm unite to produce a baby. If the union of sperm and egg come a day or even an hour earlier or later, the results may be very different. Remember from Chapter 3 that conception occurs when a single sperm cell from the male unites with an ovum (egg) in the female's fallopian tube in a process called fertilization, and that the fertilized egg is called a zygote. By the time the zygote ends its three-to-four-day journey through the fallopian tube and reaches the uterus, it has divided into approximately 12 to 16 cells. About 266 to 280 days (38 to 40 weeks) after fertilization, a fully formed baby makes its way from the womb to the outside world, prepared to breathe, take nourishment, and interact with the new environment. Prenatal development concerns the incredible story of the journey from fertilization through transition to the outside world.

The Course of Prenatal Development

Prenatal development is divided into three periods: germinal, embryonic, and fetal.

The Germinal Period

The **germinal period** is the period of prenatal development that takes place in the first two weeks after conception. It includes the creation of the zygote, continued cell division, and the attachment of the zygote to the uterine wall. By approximately one week after conception, the zygote is composed of 100 to 150 cells. The differentiation of cells has already begun, as inner and outer layers of the organism are formed. The **blastocyst** is the inner mass of cells that develops during the germinal period. These cells later develop into the embryo. The **trophoblast** is the outer layer of cells that develops during the germinal period. It later provides nutrition and support for the embryo. Implantation, the attachment of the zygote to the uterine wall, takes place 11 to 15 days after conception. Figure 4.1 illustrates some of the most significant developments during the germinal period.

Figure 4.1

Significant Developments in the Germinal Period

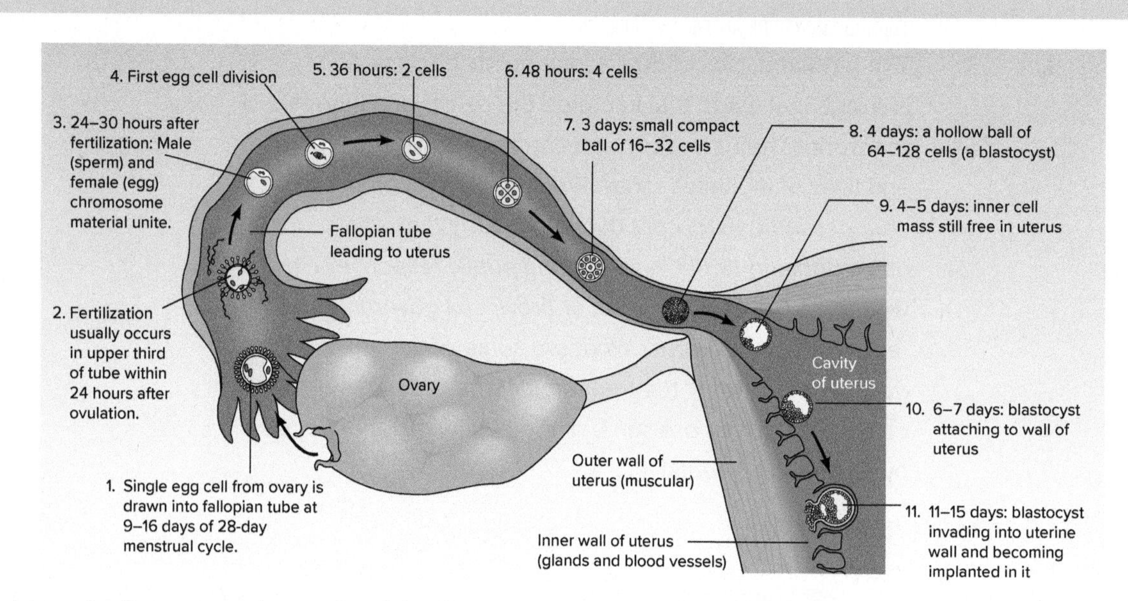

Just one week after conception, cells of the blastocyst have already begun specializing. The germination period ends when the blastocyst attaches to the uterine wall. *Which of the steps shown in the drawing occur in the laboratory when IVF (described in Chapter 3) is used?*

The Embryonic Period

The **embryonic period** is the period of prenatal development that occurs from two to eight weeks after conception. During the embryonic period, the rate of cell differentiation intensifies, support systems for the cells form, and organs appear. As the zygote attaches to the uterine wall, its cells form two layers. At this time, the name of the mass of cells changes from zygote to embryo. The embryo's endoderm is the inner mass of cells, which will develop into the digestive and respiratory systems. The outer layer of cells is divided into two parts. The ectoderm is the outermost layer, which will become the nervous system, sensory receptors (ears, nose, and eyes, for example), and skin parts (hair and nails, for example). The mesoderm is the middle layer, which will become the circulatory system, bones, muscles, excretory system, and reproductive system. Every body part eventually develops from these three layers. The endoderm primarily produces internal body parts, the mesoderm primarily produces parts that surround the internal areas, and the ectoderm primarily produces surface parts.

As the embryo's three layers form, life-support systems for the embryo mature and develop rapidly. These life-support systems include the amnion, the placenta, and the umbilical cord. The **amnion** is like a bag or an envelope that contains a clear fluid in which the developing embryo floats. The amniotic fluid provides an environment that is temperature- and humidity-controlled, as well as shockproof. The **placenta** consists of a disc-shaped group of tissues in which small blood vessels from the mother and the offspring intertwine but do not join. The **umbilical cord** contains two arteries and one vein, and connects the fetus to the placenta.

Figure 4.2 provides an illustration of the placenta, the umbilical cord, and the blood flow in the expectant mother and developing fetus in the uterus. Very small molecules—oxygen, water, salt, food from the mother's blood, as well as carbon dioxide and digestive wastes from the embryo's blood—pass back and forth between mother and fetus.

Figure 4.2

The Placenta and the Umbilical Cord

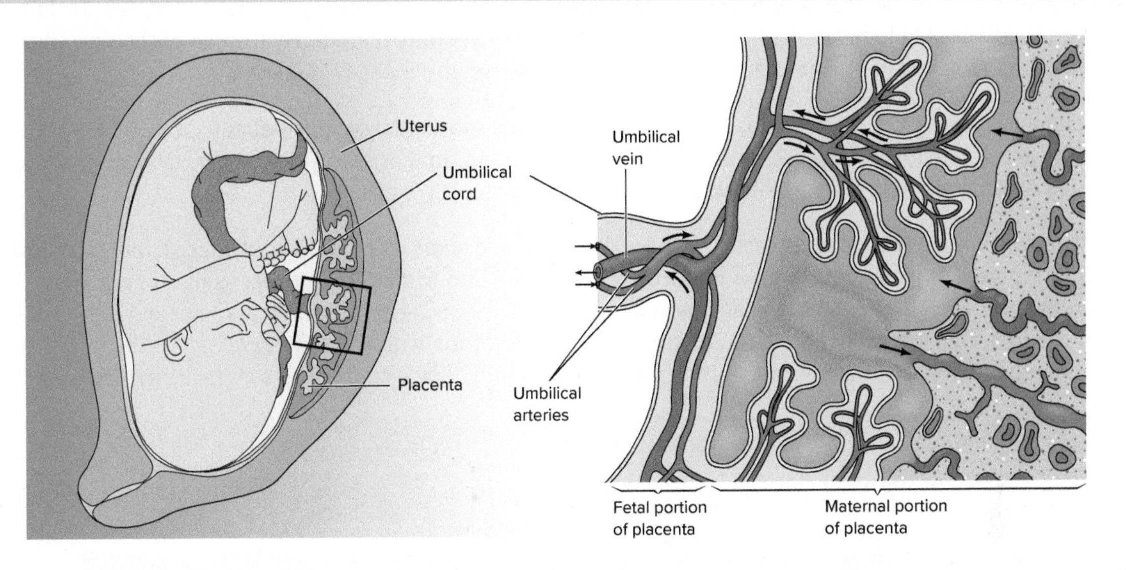

Maternal blood flows through the uterine arteries to the spaces housing the placenta, and it returns through the uterine veins to the maternal circulation. Fetal blood flows through the umbilical arteries into the capillaries of the placenta and returns through the umbilical veins to the fetal circulation. The exchange of materials takes place across the layer separating the maternal and fetal blood supplies, and so the bloods never come into contact. *Note:* The area bound by the square is enlarged in the right half of the illustration. Arrows indicate the direction of blood flow.

Large molecules cannot pass through the placental wall; these include red blood cells and harmful substances, such as most bacteria, maternal wastes, and hormones. The mechanisms that govern the transfer of substances across the placental barrier are complex and still not entirely understood (Klieger, Pollex, & Koren, 2008; Nanovskaya et al., 2008). At approximately 16 weeks, the kidneys of the fetus begin to produce urine. This fetal urine remains the main source of the amniotic fluid until the third trimester, when some of the fluid is excreted from the lungs of the growing fetus. Although the amniotic fluid increases in volume tenfold from the 12th to the 40th week of pregnancy, it is also removed in various ways. Some of it is swallowed by the fetus and some is absorbed through the umbilical cord and the membranes covering the placenta.

Organogenesis is the process of organ formation that takes place during the first two months of prenatal development. While organs are being formed, they are especially vulnerable to environmental changes (Mullis & Tonella, 2008). In the third week, the neural tube that eventually becomes the spinal cord forms. At about 21 days, eyes begin to appear, and at 24 days, the cells for the heart begin to differentiate. During the fourth week, the first appearance of the urogenital system is apparent, and arm and leg buds emerge. The four chambers of the heart take shape, as do blood vessels. From the fifth to the eighth week, arms and legs differentiate further; at this time, the face starts to form but still is not very recognizable. The intestinal tract develops, and the facial structures fuse. At eight weeks, the developing organism weighs about 1 gram and is just over 1.27 cm long.

The Fetal Period

The **fetal period** is the prenatal period of development that begins two months after conception and lasts for seven months, on average. Growth and development continue their dramatic course during this time. Three months after conception, the fetus is about 7.62 cm long and weighs about 28 grams. It has become active, moving its arms and legs, opening and closing its mouth, and moving its head. The face, forehead, eyelids, nose, and chin are distinguishable, as are the upper arms, lower arms, hands, and lower limbs. In most cases, the genitals can be identified as male or female. By the end of the fourth month, the fetus has grown to 15.2 cm in length and weighs 112 to 196 grams. At this time, a growth spurt occurs in the body's lower parts. Prenatal reflexes are stronger; arm and leg movements can be felt for the first time by the mother.

By the end of the fifth month, the fetus is about 30 cm long and weighs close to 454 grams. Structures of the skin have formed—toenails and fingernails, for example. The fetus is more active, showing a preference for a particular position in the womb. By the end of the sixth month, the fetus is about 35.6 cm long and already has gained another 225 to 450 grams. The eyes and eyelids are completely formed, and a fine layer of hair covers the head. A grasping reflex is present, and irregular breathing movements occur.

By the sixth month of pregnancy (about 24 to 25 weeks after conception), the fetus for the first time has a chance of surviving outside of the womb—that is, it is viable (Hernandez-Reif, 2007). Infants born early, or between 24 and 37 weeks of pregnancy, usually need help breathing because their lungs are not yet fully mature. By the end of the seventh month, the fetus is about 40 cm long and has gained another 450 grams; it now weighs about 1.4 kg.

During the eighth and ninth months, the fetus grows longer and gains substantial weight—about another 1.8 kg. At birth, the average North American baby weighs 3.2 kg and is about 50.8 cm long. In these last two months, fatty tissues develop, and the functioning of various organ systems—heart and kidneys, for example—steps up.

An overview of some of the main developments we have discussed and some more specific changes in prenatal development is presented in Figure 4.3. Note that we have divided these changes into trimesters, or three equal time periods. The three trimesters are not the same as the three prenatal periods we have discussed—germinal, embryonic, and fetal. An important point is that the first time a fetus has a chance of surviving outside of the womb is the beginning of the third trimester (at about seven months). Even when infants are born in the seventh month, they usually need assistance in breathing.

Figure 4.3

The Three Trimesters of Prenatal Development

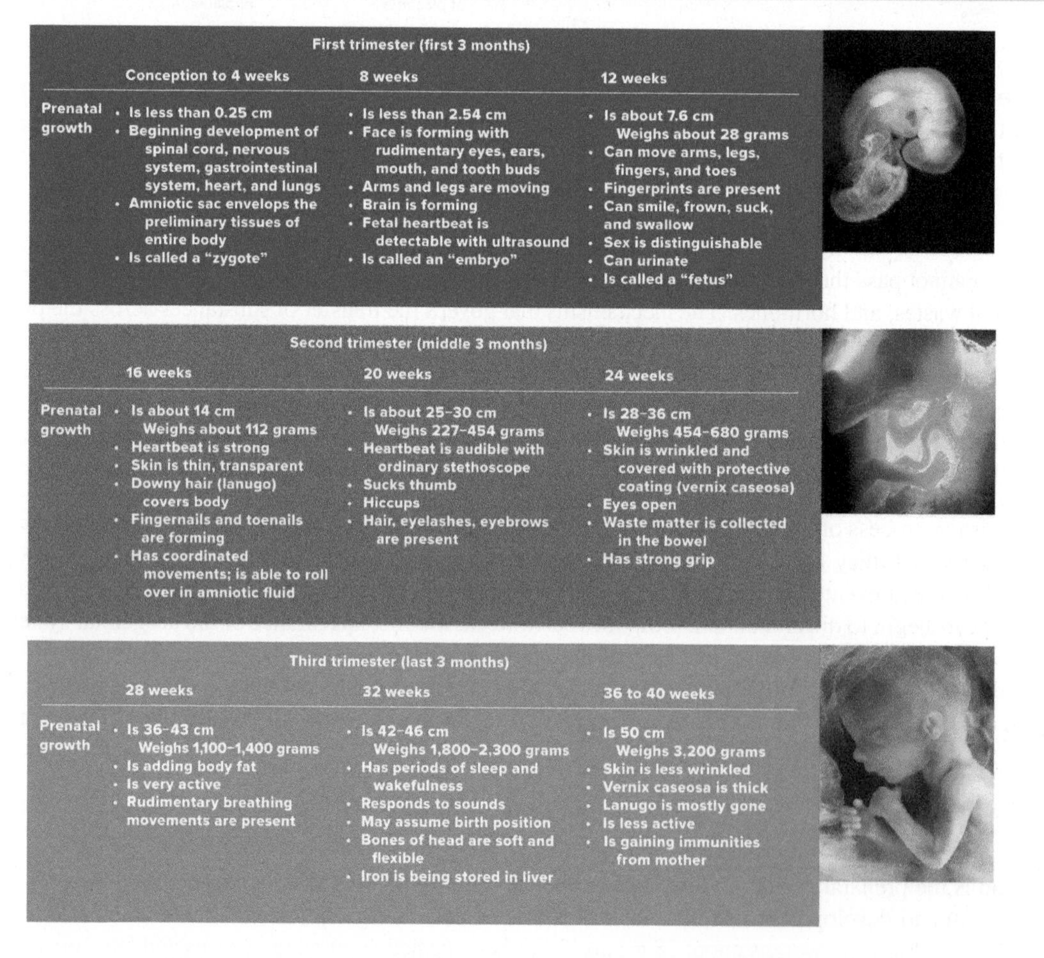

First trimester (first 3 months)	Conception to 4 weeks	8 weeks	12 weeks
Prenatal growth	• Is less than 0.25 cm • Beginning development of spinal cord, nervous system, gastrointestinal system, heart, and lungs • Amniotic sac envelops the preliminary tissues of entire body • Is called a "zygote"	• Is less than 2.54 cm • Face is forming with rudimentary eyes, ears, mouth, and tooth buds • Arms and legs are moving • Brain is forming • Fetal heartbeat is detectable with ultrasound • Is called an "embryo"	• Is about 7.6 cm Weighs about 28 grams • Can move arms, legs, fingers, and toes • Fingerprints are present • Can smile, frown, suck, and swallow • Sex is distinguishable • Can urinate • Is called a "fetus"

Second trimester (middle 3 months)	16 weeks	20 weeks	24 weeks
Prenatal growth	• Is about 14 cm Weighs about 112 grams • Heartbeat is strong • Skin is thin, transparent • Downy hair (lanugo) covers body • Fingernails and toenails are forming • Has coordinated movements; is able to roll over in amniotic fluid	• Is about 25–30 cm Weighs 227–454 grams • Heartbeat is audible with ordinary stethoscope • Sucks thumb • Hiccups • Hair, eyelashes, eyebrows are present	• Is 28–36 cm Weighs 454–680 grams • Skin is wrinkled and covered with protective coating (vernix caseosa) • Eyes open • Waste matter is collected in the bowel • Has strong grip

Third trimester (last 3 months)	28 weeks	32 weeks	36 to 40 weeks
Prenatal growth	• Is 36–43 cm Weighs 1,100–1,400 grams • Is adding body fat • Is very active • Rudimentary breathing movements are present	• Is 42–46 cm Weighs 1,800–2,300 grams • Has periods of sleep and wakefulness • Responds to sounds • May assume birth position • Bones of head are soft and flexible • Iron is being stored in liver	• Is 50 cm Weighs 3,200 grams • Skin is less wrinkled • Vernix caseosa is thick • Lanugo is mostly gone • Is less active • Is gaining immunities from mother

THE BRAIN

One of the most remarkable aspects of the prenatal period is the development of the brain (Fair & Schlaggar, 2008; Nelson, 2009). By the time babies are born, they have approximately 100 billion *neurons*, or nerve cells, which handle information processing at the cellular level in the brain. During prenatal development, neurons spend time moving to the right locations and start to become connected. The basic architecture of the human brain is assembled during the first two trimesters of prenatal development. In typical development, the third trimester of prenatal development and the first two years of postnatal life are characterized by connectivity and functioning of neurons (Moulson & Nelson, 2008).

As the human embryo develops inside its mother's womb, the nervous system begins forming as a long, hollow tube located on the embryo's back. This pear-shaped *neural tube*, which forms at about 18 to 24 days after conception, develops out of the ectoderm. The tube closes at the top and bottom ends at about 24 days after conception. Figure 4.4 shows that the nervous system still has a tubular appearance six weeks after conception.

Figure 4.4
Development of the Nervous System

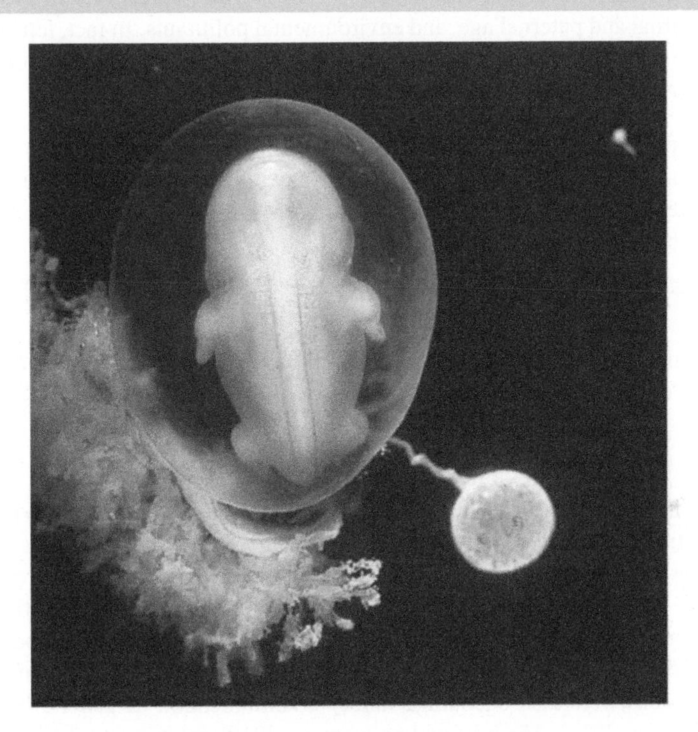

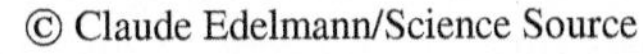

This photograph shows the primitive, tubular appearance of the nervous system at six weeks in the human embryo.

Two birth defects related to a failure of the neural tube to close are anencephaly and spina bifida. The highest regions of the brain fail to develop when fetuses have anencephaly or when the head end of the neural tube fails to close, and they die in the womb, during childbirth, or shortly after birth (Kuntz, Stansbury, & Wilson, 2015). Spina bifida results in varying degrees of paralysis of the lower limbs. Individuals with spina bifida usually need assistive devices such as crutches, braces, or wheelchairs. A strategy that can help to prevent neural tube defects is for women to take adequate amounts of the B vitamin folic acid, a topic we will further discuss later in the chapter (Johnston, 2008; Ryan-Harshman, & Aldoori, 2008).

In a normal pregnancy, once the neural tube has closed a massive proliferation of new immature neurons begins to take place at about the fifth prenatal week, and continues throughout the remainder of the prenatal period. The generation of new neurons is called *neurogenesis*. At approximately 6 to 24 weeks after conception, *neuronal migration* occurs (Nelson, 2009). This involves cells moving outward from their point of origin to their appropriate locations and creating the different levels, structures, and regions of the brain (Hepper, 2007). Once a cell has migrated to its target destination, it must mature and develop a more complex structure.

At about the 23rd prenatal week, connections between neurons begin to occur, a process that continues post-natally (Moulson & Nelson, 2008). We will have much more to say about the structure of neurons, their connectivity, and the development of the infant brain in Chapter 5.

Teratology and Hazards to Prenatal Development

Some expectant mothers carefully tiptoe about in the belief that everything they do and feel has a direct effect on their unborn child. Others behave casually, assuming that their experiences will have little effect. The truth lies somewhere between these two extremes. A mother's womb can provide a protective environment or affect the fetus adversely in many well-documented ways.

General Principles

A **teratogen** is any agent that can potentially cause a birth defect or negatively alter cognitive and behavioural outcomes (the word comes from the Greek word *tera*, meaning "monster"). The field of study that investigates the causes of birth variations is called *teratology*. Teratogens include drugs, incompatible blood types, infectious diseases, nutritional deficiencies, maternal stress, advanced maternal and paternal age, and environmental pollutants. In fact, fetuses can sometimes be affected by events that occurred in the mother's life as early as one or two months before conception. Additionally, some factors related to the health of the sperm can influence prenatal development.

So many teratogens exist that practically every fetus is exposed to some degree. For this reason, it can be difficult to determine which teratogen causes which problem. In addition, it may take a long time for the effects of a teratogen to show up. Only about half of all potential effects appear at birth. The dose, genetic susceptibility, and the time of exposure to a particular teratogen influence both the type and severity of effect.

DOSE–RESPONSE RELATIONSHIP

The dose effect is rather obvious—the greater the dose of an agent, such as a drug, the greater the effect. That is, there should be a relationship between the "dose" or the amount of exposure and the outcome (Holmes, 2011).

GENETIC SUSCEPTIBILITY

Genetic testing and screening is a patient-centred approach to learning whether or not an individual's genes or chromosomes are linked to a genetic condition such as Down syndrome (Government of Canada, 2013). Prenatal screening is offered routinely to pregnant women at any age. In higher risk pregnancies, more invasive and risky procedures are used. Meanwhile, genetic counselling is used to assess a patient's family history, and discuss the risks, benefits, and limitations of genetic testing. The genetic counsellor can provide the patient and family with support so that a personal decision can be made regarding the management of the individual's health, the child's health, or the pregnancy (Canadian Association of Genetic Counsellors, 2016). Genetic counsellors also encourage family communication of genetic information that might benefit family members (Gaff & Hodgson, 2014). Mackoff and colleagues (2010) explain that future research is expected to focus on better understanding the concerns of genetic counsellors surrounding genetic susceptibility in children.

TIME OF EXPOSURE

Teratogens have greater effect when they occur at some points in development rather than at others (Nava-Ocampo & Koren, 2007; Rifas-Shiman et al., 2006). During the germinal period they may even prevent implantation. In general, the embryonic period is the most vulnerable (Tanner, Warren, & Bellack, 2015).

Figure 4.5 summarizes additional information about the effects of time of exposure to a teratogen. The probability of a structural defect is greatest early in the embryonic period, when organs are being formed (Hill, 2007). Each body structure has its own critical period of formation. Recall from Chapter 2 that a *critical period* is a fixed time period very early in development during which certain experiences or events can have a long-lasting effect on development. The critical period for the nervous system (week 3) is earlier than for arms and legs (weeks 4 and 5). After organogenesis is complete, teratogens are less likely to cause anatomical defects. Instead, exposure during the fetal period is more likely to stunt growth or to create problems in the way organs function. To examine some key terotogens and their effects, let's begin with drugs.

Figure 4.5
Teratogens and the Timing of Their Effects on Prenatal Development

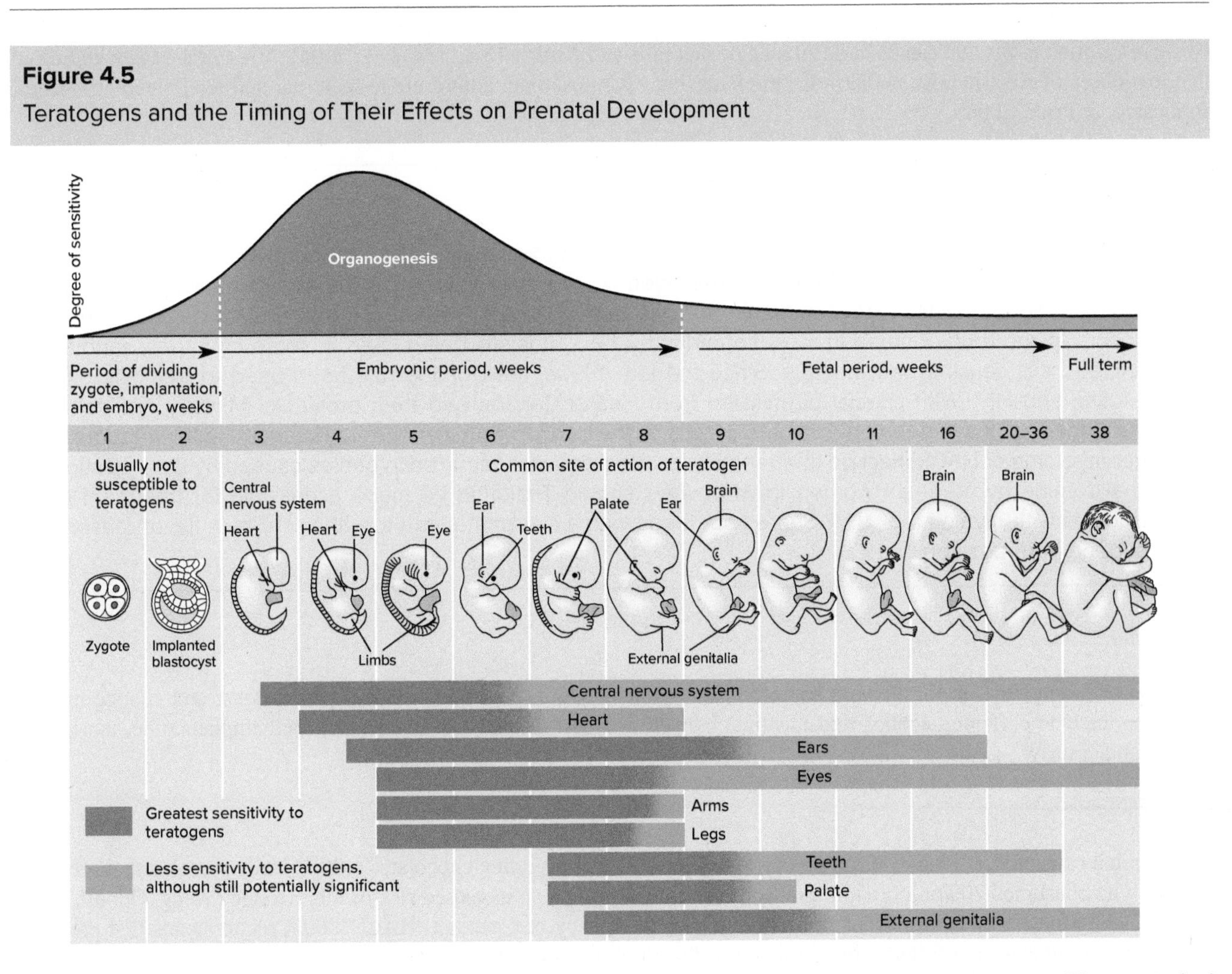

The danger of structural defects caused by teratogens is greatest early in embryonic development. This period of organogenesis (red colour) lasts for about six weeks. Later assaults by teratogens (blue colour) typically occur in the fetal period and, instead of structural damage, are more likely to inhibit growth or cause problems of organ function.

Prescription and Non-Prescription Drugs

The Society of Obstetricians and Gynaecologists of Canada advises women to consult with a health care professional before and during pregnancy prior to taking any prescription or non-prescription medication, herbal remedy, or drug (SOGC, 2011b). Failure to consider pregnancy, as well the underuse of pregnancy testing, may lead to overuse of teratogenic medications, which would have adverse effects on the fetus and cause emotional distress to the mother (Goyal et al., 2015).

It should be stressed that prescription as well as over-the-counter medications, herbal products, topical creams, inhalers, and megadoses of vitamins can all cross the placenta into the fetal bloodstream. Prescription drugs that can function as teratogens include certain antidepressants and some hormones, such as progestin and synthetic estrogen (Garcia-Bournissen et al., 2008). Interestingly, an antimicrobial, such as tetracycline, can cause tooth enamel discoloration of deciduous teeth in the second and third trimesters (Healthy Canada, 2011). Between 1957 and 1962, thalidomide was prescribed to women to offset morning sickness during the early stages of pregnancy. The drug was withdrawn from the Canadian market in 1962 after over 100 children were born with limb defects and other organ anomalies (Greener, 2011). According to SOGC, the only prescription medication approved by Health Canada for the treatment of nausea and vomiting in pregnancy is Diclectin (SOGC, 2011b).

Although clinical studies have indicated that a small number of medications are safe for use during pregnancy, the effects of many other drugs are not known. The safe use of all medication is essential to optimize the health of both a pregnant woman and her unborn child. The Motherrisk Program at the Hospital for Sick Children in Toronto is a recognized leader in providing valuable information about medications during pregnancy as well as breastfeeding. The toll-free number is 1-877-439-2744, or visit www.motherrisk.org.

Non-prescription drugs that can be harmful include diet pills and Aspirin (Nørgård et al., 2006). A research review indicated that low doses of Aspirin pose no harm for the fetus, but high doses can contribute to maternal and fetal bleeding (James, Brancazio, & Price, 2008).

critical thinking

As noted above, thalidomide was used as a treatment for morning sickness in Canada and resulted in over 100 children being born with shortened arms, cleft lip or palate, missing limbs and/or heart, and kidney and genital abnormalities (Greener, 2011). Worldwide, over 10 000 people were born with defects due to exposure to the drug. Banned in most countries by 1962, it is still being used in some countries, such as Brazil, and still causing birth defects. Since the late 1990s, thalidomide has been used to treat leprosy, myeloma, and HIV. With special permission from Health Canada and their provincial Ministry of Health, some Canadians have been able to gain access to the banned drug (its current name is Thalomid) to treat either myeloma or HIV. Reflect on the genetic abnormalities that occurred in babies caused by the ingestion of thalidomide by pregnant women. In what ways should Thalomid be made accessible for treatment to individuals with myeloma or HIV? Share your ideas with a classmate, and together create a list of reasons to support your position.

PSYCHOACTIVE DRUGS

Psychoactive drugs act on the nervous system to alter states of consciousness, modify perceptions, and change moods. Examples include caffeine, alcohol, and nicotine, as well as illicit drugs such as cocaine, methamphetamine, marijuana, heroin, and ecstasy.

CAFFEINE

People often consume caffeine by drinking coffee, tea, or colas, or by eating chocolate. A 2008 study revealed that pregnant women who consumed 200 or more milligrams of caffeine a day had an increased risk of miscarriage (Weng, Odouli, & Li, 2008). Taking these results into account, the Public Health Agency of Canada (PHAC, 2009a) recommends that pregnant women either not consume caffeine, or consume less than 300 mg of caffeine per day.

ALCOHOL

Heavy drinking can be devastating to the fetus (Duncan & Forbes-McKay, 2012). No one knows with certainty the extent to which drinking causes fetal alcohol spectrum disorders (described below). In essence, there is no safe amount of alcohol that pregnant mothers can consume (PHAC, 2011g). Alcohol use, mostly heavy drinking, affects estrogen and progesterone levels in women and increases the risk of infertility in both men and women (Anderson, Nisenbblat, & Norman, 2011). Furthermore, at least one study has indicated reduced sperm count in male offspring with moderate prenatal exposure to alcohol (Ramlau-Hansen et al., 2010).

Fetal alcohol spectrum disorders (FASD) are a cluster of abnormalities and problems that appear in the offspring of mothers who drink alcohol heavily during pregnancy (Olson, King, & Jirikowic, 2008). The abnormalities include facial deformities and defective limbs, face, and heart (see Figure 4.6). Most children with FASD have learning problems and many are below average in intelligence, while some are intellectually disabled (Casey et al., 2008; Cuzon et al., 2008). Although many mothers of FASD infants are heavy drinkers, heavy drinking does not always result in a child being born with FASD.

Figure 4.6
Fetal Alcohol Spectrum Disorder

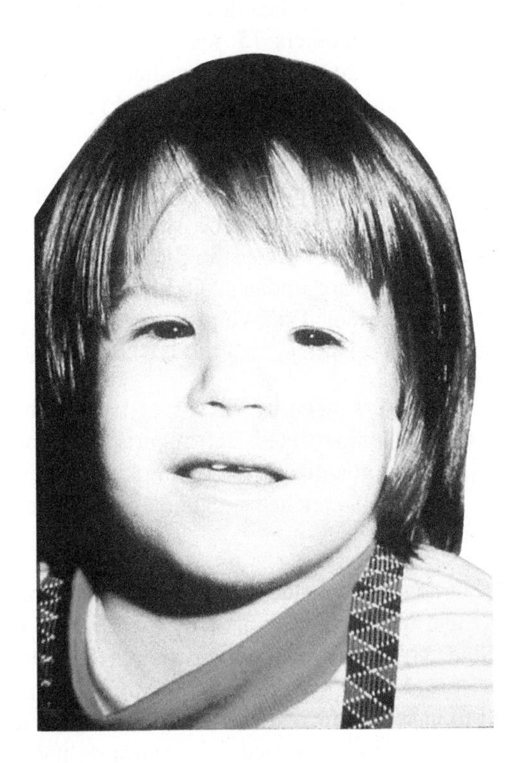

Streissguth, AP, Landesman-Dwyer S, Martin, JC, & Smith, DW (1980). Teratogenic effects of alcohol in humans and laboratory animals. *Science*, 209, 353-361

Fetal alcohol spectrum disorders (FASD) are characterized by a number of physical abnormalities and learning problems. Notice the wide-set eyes, flat cheekbones, and thin upper lip in this child with FASD.

Consuming alcohol during pregnancy can result in serious effects in offspring even when they are not afflicted with FASD (Duncan & Forbes-McKay, 2012). For example, birth defects related to prenatal alcohol consumption and exposure, known as alcohol-related birth defects (ARBD), include abnormalities in the heart, kidneys, bones, and/or hearing (Gallicano, 2010; Khalil & O'Brien, 2010).

Researchers from Canada, the United Kingdom, and France have found that, in a population-based sample of 19 months of age toddlers, low level exposure to alcohol throughout pregnancy was associated with disrupted cortisol secretion. Furthermore, the findings suggest that low levels of prenatal alcohol exposure (PAE) might be associated with disrupted patterns of limbic-hypothalamic-pituitary-adrenal (LHPA) axis activity, and that males seem to be at a higher risk (Ouellet-Morin et al., 2011).

FASD is often viewed as an issue that primarily affects families of low socio-economic status, Aboriginal communities, and mothers who seem not to care about their children. However, such views tend to create harmful assumptions and stigmatization associated with this disability (Healthy Child Manitoba, 2012). FASD is a nation-wide health concern. It does not discriminate on the basis of race, socio-economic status, or sex (Health Canada, 2012). In fact, national prevalence data demonstrate that women from all financial and ethnic backgrounds tend to consume some alcohol during pregnancy. The Public Health Agency of Canada provided a grant (2011–2012) to the province of Manitoba to lead the development of a national prevalence plan (Healthy Child Manitoba, 2012). The focus of this plan is to collect, analyze, and distribute information in a timely fashion to direct policy, create evidence-based programs, implement prevention and intervention strategies, and inform public awareness on this issue.

What are some guidelines for alcohol use during pregnancy? Even drinking just one or two servings of beer or wine or one serving of hard liquor a few days a week can have negative effects on the fetus, although it is generally agreed that this level of alcohol use will not cause FASD. Health Canada recommends that if a woman is pregnant or is trying to become pregnant, she should not drink any alcohol.

NICOTINE

The Public Health Agency of Canada (PHAC, 2009e) conducted the Canadian Maternity Experiences Survey (MES) to facilitate understanding, and to promote and improve the health of new mothers across Canada. The sample of women to whom the survey was administered comprised mothers 15 years of age or older who had given birth to a single child in Canada during a three-month period prior to the 2006 Canadian Census. The MES included women who had smoked before, during, and following their pregnancy. The sample excluded First Nations women living on the reserve and institutionalized women.

Overall, the proportions of women who smoked during pregnancy showed variations between provinces and territories, from 9 percent in British Columbia and Ontario to 25 percent in the Northwest Territories and 64 percent in Nunavut. The proportion of women who smoked during pregnancy was highest in the younger age group (15–24 years). During the last trimester of their pregnancy, 90 percent of women did not smoke at all. It is interesting to note that those women who did not smoke during the third trimester of pregnancy had resumed smoking either daily or occasionally by the time of the interview. This rate indicates a high proportion of postpartum relapse among those who quit smoking during pregnancy.

These smoking rates are based solely on self-reports made by the survey participants. Actually, this finding is somewhat problematic because, as research studies have demonstrated, self-reports of smoking tend to underestimate smoking prevalence. Other studies have concluded that the non-disclosure of smoking ranges from 23 to 28 percent (Dietz et al., 2010). According to Al-Sahab and colleagues (2010), conclusive data on the prevalence and predictors of smoking among Canadian women during pregnancy are limited.

Cigarette smoking by pregnant women can adversely influence prenatal development, birth, and postnatal development (Cooper & Moley, 2008). Preterm births and low birth weights (see Figure 4.7), fetal and neonatal deaths, respiratory problems, and sudden infant death syndrome (SIDS, also known as crib death) are all more common among the offspring of mothers who smoked during pregnancy (Henderson, 2008; Landau, 2008; Finnegan, 2013). Prenatal exposure to cigarette smoking during pregnancy is also related to increased incidence of attention deficit hyperactivity disorder at 5 to 16 years of age (Wang, Ordean, & Kahan, 2013). Another study revealed that environmental tobacco smoke or second-hand smoke is linked to increased risk of low birth weight in offspring (Leonardi-Bee et al., 2008). Evidence also exists that lower income groups have a higher prevalence of smoking during pregnancy and of offspring who are of shorter height and are underweight as compared with those in higher income brackets (Hayward et al., 2012).

Figure 4.7

The Effects of Smoking by Expectant Mothers on Fetal Weight

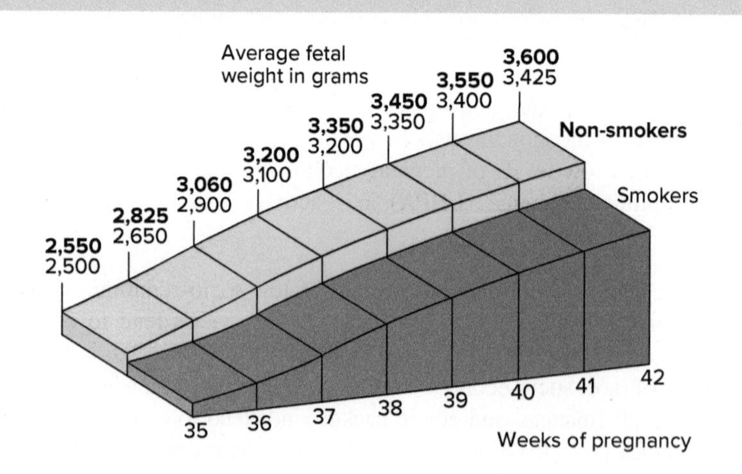

Throughout prenatal development, the fetuses of expectant mothers who smoke weigh less than the fetuses of expectant mothers who do not smoke.

Intervention programs designed to help pregnant women stop smoking can reduce some of smoking's negative effects, especially by raising birth weights (Barron et al., 2007). A recent study revealed that women who quit smoking during pregnancy had offspring with higher birth weights than their counterparts who continued smoking (Jaddoe et al., 2008). Another intervention is nicotine replacement therapy (NRT), which has been widely developed as a pharmacotherapy of smoking cessation. It is considered to be a safer alternative for women to smoking during pregnancy (Bruin, Gerstein, & Holloway, 2010).

COCAINE

Prenatal cocaine exposure has been linked to impaired motor development at 2 years of age and to a slower rate of growth through to 10 years of age (Richardson, Goldschmidt, & Willford, 2008). One particularly harmful result of cocaine use is the depletion of dopamine, which with chronic use, can result in decreased attention, movement disorder, psychosis, and panic disorder (Goldstein et al., 2009). In addition, lower birth weight, length, and reduced head circumference (dose dependent), as well as congenital anomalies and genitourinary malformations, have been also found (Wong, Ordean, & Kahan, 2011). Increased frequency of crack cocaine use is associated with poorer perceived physical, social, and mental health (Minnes et al., 2012).

Some researchers argue that the findings from cocaine studies should be interpreted cautiously. Reports of fetal cocaine effects have been controversial, as the interpretation of results is hampered by the fact that cocaine use is often accompanied by other confounding maternal factors. These factors include cigarette smoking, other drug use (heroin, marijuana, alcohol, and others), as well as lower socio-economic status and lack of adequate prenatal care, all of which may combine to contribute to poor pregnancy outcome (Gouin et al., 2011). Cocaine use by pregnant women is never recommended.

METHAMPHETAMINE

Methamphetamine is a neurotoxic parasympathetic stimulant whose use is associated with a host of negative consequences for the user (Berman et al., 2008). Although the negative consequences of methamphetamine are experienced by the majority of the users, pregnant women in particular represent an important subpopulation. In fact, research has confirmed wide-ranging negative effects of prenatal methamphetamine exposure (PME) on the developmental outcomes of the child (Abar et al., 2012). Several studies have clearly documented that prenatal exposure to illicit drugs, including methamphetamine, places children at risk for developmental, medical, psychological, and behavioural problems (Lester & Lagasse, 2010). It is clearly established that fetal intra-uterine growth retardation is a problem (van Dyk et al., 2014). Specifically, one study revealed that methamphetamine exposure during prenatal development is linked to decreased arousal, increased stress, and poor movement in newborns (Smith et al., 2008).

MARIJUANA

Cannabis, referred to as marijuana, is not only the most widely used illicit drug in Canada, but it is the most frequently used illicit drug consumed during pregnancy (Porath-Walker, 2015). An increasing body of evidence suggests that marijuana use may negatively impact several aspects of people's lives, including mental and physical health, cognitive functioning, ability to drive a motor vehicle, and pre- and postnatal development among children (Porath-Walker, 2015). When marijuana is consumed during pregnancy, the main psychoactive ingredient, delta-9-tetrahydrocannabinol (THC), enters the mother's blood stream and crosses the placenta. The THC interacts with the cannabinoid receptors in the endogenous cannabinoid system (ECS) and affects brain development, putting the child at significant risk for problems with emotional regulation, memory, and depression (Jutras-Aswald et al., 2009). Researchers found that prenatal marijuana exposure (PME) is associated with subsequent use by offspring in young adulthood after controlling for significant excoriates, such as race, gender, and age (Sonon et al., 2015). These findings have alarming implications for public health given the recent trend toward the legitimization of marijuana use. Day and colleagues (2015) propose that not only is it likely that prenatal marijuana use will increase in the future, but the dose per joint will also be greater.

Regarding marijuana, the Canadian government has promised to legalize, regulate, and restrict access to marijuana by creating a federal/provincial/territorial task force. This task force will receive input from experts in public health, substance abuse, and law enforcement to design a new system of strict marijuana sales and distribution, with appropriate federal, provincial, and territorial excise taxes being applied (Liberal Party of Canada, 2016).

OPIOID DEPENDENCY

Although opioids can reduce pain and improve function, regular use of large quantities of opioids during pregnancy increases the risk of premature delivery and withdrawal in the infant (Canadian Centre on Substance Abuse, 2015). Infants born to chronic opioid users are frequently born with dependency to such drugs, and they tend to experience withdrawal after the opioids cease to be administered following birth. The resulting effects are known as neonatal abstinence syndrome (NAS). This syndrome is characterized by respiratory, gastrointestinal, central nervous symptom, and autonomic responses (Wong, Ordean, & Kahan, 2011). In other words, NAS has a negative impact on vital bodily functions such as feeding, elimination, and sleeping (Finnigan, 2013).

As Ontario has Canada's highest rate of narcotic use, physicians are seeing more NAS cases and longer lengths of hospital stay among these babies. In 2003–2004, 171 infants had been diagnosed with NAS; in 2010–2011, there were 654 cases (CIHI, 2016). Heroin-exposed infants sometimes demonstrate symptoms within 24 hours of birth (Wong, Ordean, & Kahan, 2011). When a woman with opioid dependence becomes pregnant, adequate management of the addiction is of critical importance for the well-being of both the mother and the child (Jumah, Graves, & Kahan, 2015). Suspected opioid addiction is managed with structured opioid therapy, methadone or buprenorphine treatment, or abstinence-based treatment (Kahan et al., 2011). Currently, methadone maintenance treatment is the standard of care for opioid dependence during pregnancy (Wong, Ordean, & Kahan, 2011). Even though methadone has definite treatment advantages for the mother, there is mounting evidence of adverse effects upon developing cortical function in the unborn child (Mactier, 2011).

ECSTASY

Ecstasy, referred to as MDMA, is one of the most widely used illicit recreational drugs among young adults. Singer and colleagues (2012) conducted a study to examine the neurobehavioural outcomes of infants (at age 1 to 4 months) exposed to ecstasy and other recreational drugs taken by mothers during pregnancy. The results indicated a difference in sex ratio; that is, a greater number of male births was associated with ecstasy use. The mechanisms by which such alterations in sex ratio occur are not known. Another finding indicated that the ecstasy-associated infants also had lower quality of motor functioning and, at 4 months, lower milestone attainment, such as the ability to sit up without support, or to roll from their back to their side. These findings suggest risk to the developing infant following MDMA exposure, and that continued research studies are warranted to determine whether early motor delays persist or become resolved (Singer et al., 2012).

Incompatible Blood Types

Incompatibility between the blood types of the mother and father poses another risk to prenatal development. Blood types are created by differences in the surface antigens (proteins) of red blood cells. There are two major blood group systems in the human body. The ABO blood group system determines blood type as either A, B, AB, or O. The Rhezius, or RH factor, blood group system determines whether or not an individual is RH positive (Rh+) or Rh negative (Rh–) (Canadian Blood Services, 2012).

There are two different alleles for the Rh factor known as Rh+ and Rh–. The Rh factor assumes a special importance in maternal–fetal interactions. A mother who is Rh– can bear an Rh+ child if the father is Rh+ (and homozygous for the Rh factor). In this case, all the offspring will be Rh positive. Since there are no natural anti-Rh antibodies, there is no special risk for the first pregnancy. At the time of birth, tissue damage resulting from separation of the placenta from the uterine wall can result in a significant amount of fetal blood entering the maternal circulation. Such a result could stimulate a strong IgG anti-Rh response in the mother. If the same mother (RH–) then bears a second Rh+ child, the existing anti-Rh antibodies can cross the placenta during pregnancy and destroy red blood cells. Possible damage to various organs can result in the potentially dangerous condition called Erythroblastosis Fetalis (Copstead & Banasik, 2013; Li et al., 2010).

However, the production of anti-Rh antibodies in an Rh– mother can often be prevented by administering anti-Rh immune globulin (i.e., RhoGAM) into the mother, typically at around 28 weeks of gestation and again within 72 hours of the birth of her Rh+ baby (Copstead & Banasik, 2013).

Environmental Hazards

Many aspects of our industrial world can endanger the embryo or fetus (O'Connor & Roy, 2008). An embryo or fetus may be harmed if the mother's diet includes toxins such as mercury, or if the father's exposure to certain chemicals caused changes in his sperm. Some specific hazards to the embryo or fetus that are worth a closer look include radiation, toxic wastes, and other chemical pollutants (Orecchia, Lucignani, & Tosi, 2008; Raabe & Muller, 2008). Environmental challenges during the prenatal period can result in behavioural abnormalities and cognitive deficits later in life, such as autism. Prenatal exposure to valproic acid, ethanol, thalidomide, or misoprostol has also been associated with an increased incidence of autism (Dufour-Rainfray et al., 2011).

RADIATION

Prior to the time when a woman is aware of her pregnancy, she is at risk from exposure to non-ionizing and ionizing radiation. Such risks can arise from necessary medical procedures, workplace exposure, and therapeutic or diagnostic interventions during pregnancy (Williams & Fletcher, 2010). In utero exposure to non-ionizing radiation, such as microwaves or electromagnetic waves, is not associated with significant risks. However, in utero exposure to ionizing radiation, such as gamma rays and X-rays, can have a negative impact on the fetus (Groen, Bae, & Lim, 2012). In fact, the effects of such exposures are directly related not only to the level of exposure, but also to the stage of fetal development. The fetus is most susceptible to radiation during organogenesis (2 to 7 weeks after conception), and in the early fetal period (8 to 15 weeks after conception). It is important for pregnant women and their physician to weigh the risk of exposure to radiation from an X-ray when an actual, or potential, pregnancy is involved (Menias et al., 2007).

ENVIRONMENTAL POLLUTANTS

Environmental pollutants and toxic wastes are also sources of danger to the fetus. An extensive review of the literature by University of Ottawa's Donald T. Wigle and colleagues (2008) noted that the timing of the exposure in the life of either parent and/or during prenatal development influences the impact of the environmental chemical contaminant. Among the dangerous pollutants and wastes are carbon monoxide, mercury, and lead. During pregnancy, lead can cross the placenta and affect the unborn child; no "safe" level of exposure to lead has been identified (Health Canada, 2011b). Several epidemiological studies have reported an association between early-life lead exposure and adverse developmental effects (Health Canada, 2011a). Wigle and colleagues (2008) also found evidence that any exposure is dangerous and impacts the cognitive functioning of the infant. They urged that health policies should strive to eliminate all lead exposure in "housing (paint, plumbing), ambient air, consumer products, such as artist's supplies, and drinking water" (p. 486).

In Canada, lead was eliminated from all paints in 1991; however, homes built and painted between 1960 and 1990 frequently reveal small amounts of lead in some of the painted indoor surfaces. Highest amounts of lead were used in exterior paints (Health Canada, 2011b). In the United States, the risk of lead exposure is higher among poor, urban, and immigrant populations than among other groups (Cleveland et al., 2008).

critical thinking

You are aware that the spraying of pesticides to control mosquitoes is occurring in some cities. Compare and contrast the responsibilities of the individual relative to those of the provincial and federal government toward environmental teratogens. In what ways do social determinants, such as family income and education, play a role in people's lives regarding their health and safety in the environment? What policies could be developed to promote health in society? What would be required to enact these policies? Analyze and make comparisons regarding the severity of environmental teratogens on the health of individuals, first in rural and then in urban communities.

Maternal Factors

RUBELLA

Maternal diseases and infections can produce defects in offspring by crossing the placental barrier, or they can cause damage during birth. Rubella (German measles) is one disease that can cause prenatal defects. Women who plan to have children should have a blood test before they become pregnant to determine if they are immune to the disease (Dontigny et al., 2008). Vaccinations such as rubella and varicella can only be administered prior to pregnancy as they are live vaccines (Shannon et al., 2014).

SYPHILIS

The spectrum of perinatal syphilis is similar to that of other infections in which the infecting organism spreads hematogenously from the mother to involve the placenta and infect the fetus. Damage to the fetus depends presumably on the stage of development at which infection takes place and, secondly, the time that has elapsed before treatment. It is interesting to note that primary, secondary, early latent, and in some cases late latent stage maternal syphilis can lead to a haematogenous spread to the fetus resulting in a systematic inflammatory response (Valentini, 2013).

GENITAL HERPES

Another infection that has received widespread attention recently is genital herpes. Newborns contract this virus when they are delivered through the birth canal of a mother with genital herpes (Hollier & Wendel, 2008). About one-third of babies delivered through an infected birth canal die; another one-quarter become brain damaged. If an active case of genital herpes is detected in a pregnant woman close to her delivery date, a Caesarean section can be performed (in which the infant is delivered through an incision in the mother's abdomen) to keep the virus from infecting the newborn (Wilson, Bruening, & Lowdermilk 2015).

HPV

Human papillomavirus (HPV) is very common among reproductive-age women. HPV, known as anogenital warts, is one of the most frequently diagnosed sexually transmitted infections (Porterfield, 2011). A critical clinical consequence of HPV infection is increased risk of cervical cancer (Garolla, Pizzol, & Foresta, 2011). Generally, the acquisition of HPV is attributed to sexual transmission, or by skin-to-skin contact (Porterfield, 2011).

HPV occurrence during pregnancy has not been well studied. Although indications are that the infection has been linked with spontaneous abortion, this finding yet has to be confirmed (Narducci, Einarson, & Bozzo, 2012). On the other hand, the fact that this infection can be transmitted from mother to infant has been demonstrated (LaCour & Trimble, 2012). Given the prevalence of HPV in the population, it is now essential to research the manner in which this virus is actually transmitted to the newborn and to substantiate such findings with clinical relevance (LaCour & Trimble, 2012).

HIV AND AIDS

AIDS is a sexually transmitted infection that is caused by the human immunodeficiency virus (HIV). The demographic profile of HIV-infected women varies widely across Canada and may reflect the distribution of different racial groups as well as immigrant populations (Forbes et al., 2011). As a result of HIV infection among women of childbearing age, fetal exposure to HIV during pregnancy has been on the rise in Canada (PHAC, 2011d). Mother-to-child transmission can occur in three ways: (1) during gestation (in utero transmission), (2) during delivery as the newborn comes into contact with maternal blood and cervical–vaginal secretions, and (3) postpartum (after birth) through breastfeeding (PHAC, 2011d). Antiretroviral therapy is effective in reducing mother-to-child transmission of HIV, and yet several infants prenatally exposed to HIV are confirmed infected each year in Canada (PHAC, 2011d). Prenatal HIV testing is offered to all pregnant women in Canada; however, the approach to testing varies by province and territory (PHAC, 2011d).

A significant knowledge gap remains regarding issues related to HIV and its implications for the pregnant woman and her infant (Dorval, Ritchie, & Gruslin, 2007). Whenever possible, it is essential for health care professionals to provide HIV-infected women with information required to make an informed choice about pregnancy, contraception, and reduction of vertical transmission. In this manner, the health of women and their partners, as well as the protection of future children, is maximized (Loutfy et al., 2012; McCall & Vicol, 2011).

DIABETES

Diabetes mellitus is a frequently occurring gestational complication which affects pregnancies. In fact, women with diabetes in pregnancy have high rates of pregnancy complications (Feig et al., 2014). Diabetes in pregnancy has been associated with a number of adverse neonatal outcomes including congenital anomalies, preterm birth, macrosomia, neonatal hyperglycemia, and neonatal death (Rosenn, 2008). Canadian researchers conducted a population-based cohort study of women who delivered in Ontario between 1996 and 2010. They categorized women as gestational diabetes (GDM), pregestational diabetes (pre-GDM), or no diabetes. It was concluded that the incidence of both GDN and pre-GDM had doubled over the previous 14 years. Although congenital anomaly rates have declined in women with diabetes, perinatal mortality rates remain unchanged, and the risk of both remains significantly elevated compared with non-diabetic women (Feig et al., 2014). The overall burden of diabetes in pregnancy is growing.

Figure 4.8 summarizes some of the maternal diseases that can affect the fetus.

Figure 4.8

Maternal Diseases Impacting Perinatal Development

Diseases	Effects
Rubella (German measles)	▪ Rubella contracted in the third or fourth week of pregnancy as well as in the second month may cause intellectual disability, blindness, deafness, and heart problems. Preventive vaccines are routinely administered.
Sexually transmitted infections: ▪ Syphilis	▪ Syphilis damages organs in the fourth month after conception. Eye lesions that may cause blindness, skin lesions, and damage to the central nervous system and the gastrointestinal tract are also linked to syphilis.
▪ Genital herpes can be contracted through the birth canal	▪ About one-third of babies delivered through a birth canal infected with genital herpes die; another one-quarter become brain damaged. Caesarean section can prevent the virus from infecting the newborn.
▪ AIDS (caused by HIV), damages the body's immune system through the placenta, through fluid exchange between baby and mother, and through breastfeeding	▪ The transmission of HIV has been reduced due to counselling, voluntary testing, and the use of Atripla. Prenatal screening can lead to antiretroviral therapy, use of formula feeding, and elective Caesarean section births (Burdge et al., 2003a, b; Loutfy et al., 2012).
▪ HPV is common among reproductive-age women	▪ HPV can be transmitted from mother to infant and may be linked with spontaneous abortion.

MATERNAL AGE

When the mother's age is considered in terms of possible harmful effects on the fetus and infant, two maternal ages are of special interest: adolescence and women aged 35 or older (Chen et al., 2007; Maconochie et al., 2007). The mortality rate of infants born to adolescent mothers is double that of infants born to mothers in their twenties. Although this high rate probably reflects the immaturity of the mother's reproductive system, poor nutrition, lack of prenatal care, and low socio-economic status may also play a role (Smith Battle, 2007). Adequate prenatal care decreases the probability that a child born to an adolescent girl will have physical problems. However, adolescents are the least likely of women in all age groups to obtain prenatal assistance from clinics, pediatricians, and health services.

The birth rate among teenage mothers has decreased constantly over the last three decades, from about 30 births per 1000 in 1974, to 12 births per 1000 in 2009 (HRSDC, 2012b). Despite the evidence of a birth rate decrease, teenage motherhood is still an important public health issue due to various adverse maternal and health outcomes (PHAC, 2008). Health problems during teenage pregnancies include poor maternal weight gain and anemia. Many factors contribute to the poor outcomes associated with teenage childbearing, including disadvantaged social environment, biological immaturity, inadequate antenatal care, physical and sexual abuse, smoking, and drug use (PHAC, 2008).

Young parents under 20 years of age and their children are considered particularly vulnerable when associated with socio-economic disadvantage. Mills and colleagues (2012) conducted a study to identify young parents' perceptions and their experiences with a parenting support program. This study demonstrated not only the importance for young parents to participate in all forms of interaction—whether one-on-one, in a group, or social networking—but most importantly, it showed the benefits of having someone to talk to (Mills et al., 2012). It is likely that the declining trends in teen pregnancy rates could reflect several of the following: increasing levels of effective contraceptive use, exposure to higher quality sexual health education, and/or shifting social norms in a direction that provides greater support for the capacity of young women to exercise reproductive choice (SIECCAN, 2012). It should also be noted that the decline in teen pregnancy rates in Canada between 1996 and 2006 was greater than in other countries, including the United States and England, where teen pregnancy rates did decline but to a lesser extent (McKay, 2006).

In 2009, the average age of mothers at birth in Nunavut was significantly younger (25.1 years) compared to the national average (29.4 years) (HRSDC, 2012b). In addition, the rate of births to teens in Nunavut was almost eight times the Canadian average. In contrast, Ontario and British Columbia had the highest number of mothers aged 30 years and over, as well as the highest percentage of births to mothers aged 30 and over (HRSDC, 2012b).

The chances of having a baby with Down syndrome, a form of developmental disability, increases relative to the mother's age (Feldman & Landry, 2014). A baby with Down syndrome is rarely born to a mother under the age of 35, but the risk increases after the mother reaches 30. By age 40, the probability is slightly over 1 in 100, and by age 50 it is almost 1 in 10.

One of the most important changes in reproductive behaviour during recent decades has been the rising proportions of births among mothers at advanced ages (Billari et al., 2011). The average age of childbearing mothers in Canada is increasing, and older mothers tend to be married, highly educated, and affluent (Joseph et al., 2005). Many Canadian women stay in school longer and seek to establish their careers before beginning a family (Vézina & Turcotte, 2009). Policy decision makers must be cognizant of the need for additional high-risk obstetric and neonatal health services when societal norms especially encourage women to delay childbearing in favour of education and career objectives (Feldman & Landry, 2014).

Crompton and Keown (2009) found Canadian women might also be forestalling having children until they have access to maternal benefits. In combination with the existing maternity leave benefit of 15 weeks, an amendment to Canada's *Employment Insurance Act* in 2000 increased prenatal leave benefits from 10 to 35 weeks. The total employment-protected (not necessarily paid) maternity and parental leave period increased from six months to one year (PHAC, 2009e).

What are some of the risks for infants born to adolescent mothers?

When mothers are 35 years and older, risks also increase for low birth weight, preterm delivery, and fetal death (Fretts, Zera, & Heffner, 2008). In one study, fetal death was low for women 30 to 34 years of age, but increased progressively for women 35 to 39 and 40 to 44 years of age (Canterino et al., 2004). Carolan and Nelson (2007) found that concern over the expected risk of a pregnancy after age 35 created stress for pregnant women in this age group. However, if women remain active, exercise regularly, and are careful about their nutrition, their reproductive systems may remain healthier at older ages than was thought possible in the past.

DIET, NUTRITION, AND EXERCISE

A developing embryo or fetus depends completely on the mother for nutrition, which comes from the mother's blood (Derbyshire, 2007a, b). The nutritional status of the embryo or fetus is determined by the mother's total caloric intake and her intake of proteins, vitamins, and minerals. Children born to malnourished mothers are more likely than other children to have physical disabilities.

Being overweight before and during pregnancy can also put the embryo or fetus at risk (Reece, 2008). Recent studies indicate that maternal obesity doubles the risk of stillbirth and neonatal death, and is linked with problems in the central nervous system, including spina bifida (Frederick et al., 2008; Guelinckx, Devlieger, & Vansant, 2008; Kriebs, 2009). Further, a recent analysis proposed that overeating by pregnant women results in a series of neuroendocrine changes in the fetus that in turn program the development of fat cells and appetite regulation system (McMillen et al., 2008). In this analysis, it was predicted that such early fetal programming is likely linked to being overweight in childhood and adolescence. Health Canada's recommended weight gain for pregnant women, based on pre-pregnancy body mass index (BMI), is given in Figure 4.9.

Figure 4.9

Health Canada Suggested Weight Gain during Pregnancy based on Pre-Pregnancy BMI (weight in kg divided by height in metres squared)

Pre-Pregnancy BMI Category	Recommended Range of Total Weight Gain
BMI < 18.5 underweight	12.5 to 18 kg
BMI 18.5 to 24.9 normal weight	11.5 to 16 kg
BMI 25.0 to 29.9 overweight	7.0 to 11.5 kg
BMI ≥ 30 obese	5.0 to 9.0 kg

One aspect of maternal nutrition that is important for normal prenatal development is folic acid, a B-complex vitamin (Shannon et al., 2014; Goh & Koren, 2008). As noted earlier in the chapter, a lack of folic acid is linked with neural tube defects in offspring, such as spina bifida, a typically fatal defect in the spinal cord (Ryan-Harshman & Aldoori, 2008). Health officials recommend that pregnant women consume a minimum of 0.4 mg of folic acid per day (about twice the amount the average woman gets in one day). Orange juice and spinach and broccoli are examples of foods rich in folic acid (Health Canada, 2007a).

Fish is often recommended as part of a healthy diet, but increased pollution has made many fish a risky choice for pregnant women. Some fish contain high levels of mercury, which is released into the air both naturally and by industrial pollution. When mercury falls into the water, it can become toxic and accumulate in large fish, such as shark, swordfish, king mackerel, and some species of large tuna. Mercury is easily transferred across the placenta, and the embryo's developing brain and nervous system are highly sensitive to the metal (Greener, 2011). In "Eating Well with Canada's Food Guide," Health Canada (2007a) recommends eating cooked fish and shellfish.

PCBs (polychlorinated biphenyls) are chemicals that were used in manufacturing until they were banned in the 1970s, but they are still present in landfills, sediments, and wildlife. One concern focuses on pregnant women eating PCB-polluted fish (Hertz-Picciotto et al., 2008). A research review concluded that PCB-polluted fish pose a potential risk to prenatal neurodevelopment (Korrick & Sagiv, 2008). Inuit infants in Nunavut currently have much higher levels of PCBs in their umbilical cord blood than other children, presumably due to the large amounts of fish and marine animals eaten by their mothers.

Proper exercise during pregnancy is an important activity to ensure appropriate weight gain, to promote better sleep, to relax and reduce stress, and to offset the risk of gestational diabetes. Health Canada recommends that drinking water during exercise is important to avoid overheating and dehydration. Before undertaking a new exercise program, the pregnant woman should consult with her doctor or nurse (PHAC, 2011g).

Inuit infants in Nunavik have higher levels of PCBs in their umbilical cord blood than other children due to the large amounts of fish and marine animals eaten by their mothers (Korrick & Saguin, 2008).

EMOTIONAL STATES AND STRESS

When a pregnant woman experiences intense fears, anxieties, and other emotions or negative mood states, physiological changes occur that may affect her fetus (Taige et al., 2007). Maternal stress may increase the level of corticotropin-releasing hormone (CRH), a precursor of the stress hormone cortisol, early in pregnancy (Nakamura, Sheps, & Arck, 2008). Elevated levels of CRH and cortisol in the fetus have been linked to premature delivery in infants (Field, 2007). A study also revealed that a decline in stress during pregnancy is linked to a lower incidence of preterm birth (Glynn et al., 2008). A mother's stress may influence the fetus indirectly by increasing the likelihood that the mother will engage in unhealthy behaviours, such as taking drugs and engaging in poor prenatal care.

The mother's emotional state during pregnancy can influence the birth process, too. An emotionally distraught mother might have irregular contractions and a more difficult labour, which can cause irregularities in the supply of oxygen to the fetus or other problems after birth. Babies born after extended labour also may adjust more slowly to their world and be more irritable.

High maternal anxiety and stress during pregnancy can have long-term consequences for the offspring (Bowen, Bowen, Maslany, & Muhajarine, 2008; Davis et al., 2007). A recent research review indicated that pregnant women with high levels of stress are at increased risk for having a child with emotional or cognitive problems, attention deficit hyperactivity disorder (ADHD), and language delay (Taige et al., 2007).

Paternal Factors

Some paternal factors such as age and exposure to environmental hazards, including exposing the mother and fetus to secondhand smoke, may also influence prenatal and child development. Men's exposure to lead, radiation, certain pesticides, and petrochemicals may cause abnormalities in sperm that lead to miscarriage or diseases such as childhood cancer (Cordier, 2008). It is known that rapidly dividing and differentiating cells, such as those of the embryo, have increased radiation sensitivity. As with other teratogens, the type of effect produced is highly correlated with the stage of development at which the radiation exposure occurs (Wilson & Wilson, 2015).

The father's age also makes a difference (Bennett, 2015). About 5 percent of children with Down syndrome have older fathers. The offspring of older fathers also face increased risk for other birth defects, including dwarfism and Marfan syndrome, which involves head and limb deformities.

Prenatal Care

Prenatal care varies enormously, but usually involves a package of medical care services in a defined schedule of visits. In addition to medical care, prenatal care programs often include comprehensive educational, social, and nutritional services (Moos, 2006).

Prenatal care usually includes screening that can reveal manageable conditions and/or treatable diseases that can affect the baby or the mother (Lu & Lu, 2008). The education an expectant woman receives about pregnancy, labour and delivery, and caring for the newborn can be extremely valuable, especially for first-time mothers (Massey, Rising, & Ickovics, 2006; Moos, 2006).

Inadequate prenatal care can occur for a variety of reasons. These include shortcomings in the health care system, provider practices, and individual and social characteristics (Bravo & Naya, 2014). According to the College of Family Physicians of Canada, approximately one-third of Canadian women who live in rural areas (80 or more kilometres from an urban centre) find accessing advanced maternity care difficult. Lack of transportation and child care, as well as financial difficulties, are commonly cited as barriers to getting prenatal care. Women who have unplanned or unwanted pregnancies, or who have negative attitudes about being pregnant, are more likely to delay prenatal care or to miss appointments.

Because a healthy pregnancy and infancy are key to optimal child development, the Canadian Perinatal Surveillance System (CPSS) of Health Canada (PHAC, 2012b) monitors care provided and outcomes.

Positive Prenatal Development

Bravo and Noya (2014) state that positive feelings and expectations are associated with prenatal care, adequate nutrition, and the avoidance of substance use. In turn, such positive activities help build social support and good interdependent relationships that promote maternal and infant health in the context of protective cultural norms.

To this point, we have discussed a number of ideas about prenatal development. For a review, see the Reach Your Learning Outcomes section at the end of this chapter.

Birth

LO2 Outline the birth process.

- **The Birth Process**
- **Special Neonatal Considerations**
- **Measures of Neonatal Health and Responsiveness**

As we saw in the opening vignette, many changes have taken place in giving birth since 1934, when the Dionne quintuplets were born. Today, there are more multiple births, fewer home births, and more extensive medical care.

The Birth Process

To learn more about the birth process, we will examine the stages of birth, the transition from fetus to newborn, childbirth strategies, special neonatal (newborn) considerations, and measures of neonatal health and responsiveness.

Stages of Birth

The birth process occurs in three stages. For a woman having her first child, the first stage lasts an average of 12 to 24 hours; it is the longest of the three stages. In the first stage, uterine contractions are 15 to 20 minutes apart at the beginning and last up to a minute. These contractions cause the woman's cervix to stretch and open. As the first stage progresses, the contractions come closer together, appearing every two to five minutes. Their intensity increases, too. By the end of the first birth stage, contractions dilate the cervix to an opening of about 10 cm so that the baby can move from the uterus to the birth canal.

The second birth stage begins when the baby's head starts to move through the cervix and the birth canal. It terminates when the baby completely emerges from the mother's body. This stage lasts approximately 1.5 hours. With each contraction, the mother bears down hard to push the baby out of her body. By the time the baby's head is out of the mother's body, the contractions come almost every minute and last for about a minute. **Afterbirth** is the third stage, when the placenta, umbilical cord, and other membranes get detached and expelled. This final stage is the shortest of the three birth stages, lasting only minutes.

The Transition from Fetus to Newborn

Being born involves considerable stress for the baby. During each contraction, when the placenta and umbilical cord are compressed as the uterine muscles draw together, the supply of oxygen to the fetus is decreased. If the delivery takes too long, the baby can develop *anoxia*, a condition in which the fetus or newborn has an insufficient supply of oxygen. Anoxia can cause brain damage (Smith, 2008).

The baby has considerable capacity to withstand the stress of birth. Large quantities of adrenaline and noradrenalin, hormones that help protect the fetus in the event of oxygen deficiency, are secreted in stressful circumstances. These hormones increase the heart's pumping activity, speed up heart rate, channel blood flow to the brain, and raise blood-sugar levels. This circumstance underscores how stressful it is to be born, but also how prepared and adapted the fetus is for birth (Von Beveren, 2008).

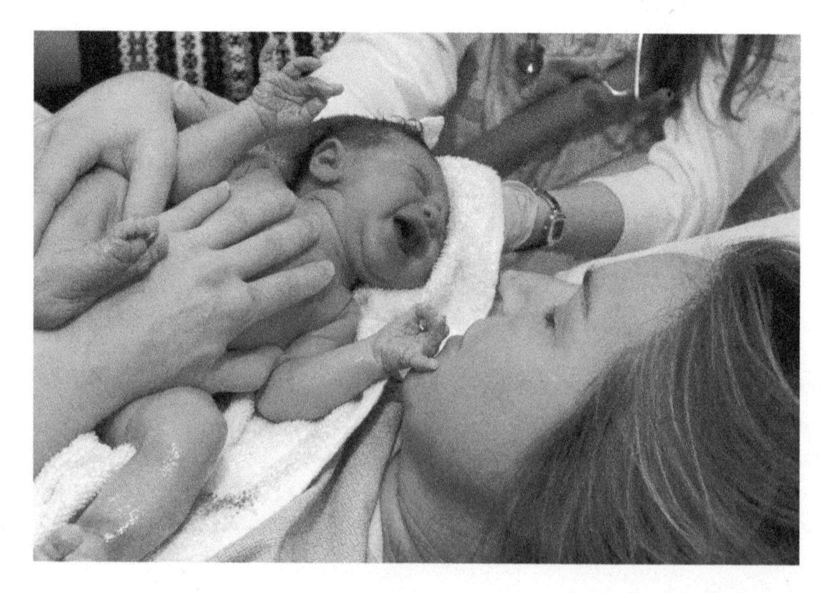

After the long journey of prenatal development, birth takes place. During birth, the baby is on a threshold between two worlds. *What is the fetus-to-newborn transition like?*

At the time of birth, the baby is covered with what is called *vernix caseosa*, a protective skin grease. This vernix consists of fatty secretions and dead cells, thought to protect the baby's skin against heat loss before and during birth.

The umbilical cord is cut immediately after birth, and the baby is on its own; 25 million little air sacs in the lungs must be filled with air. Until now, oxygen came from the mother via the umbilical cord, but now the baby has to be self-sufficient and breathe on its own. The newborn's bloodstream is redirected through the lungs and to all parts of the body. These first breaths may be the hardest ones at any point in the life span (Wheeler, 2015).

CHILDBIRTH SETTING AND ATTENDANTS

Although an increasing number of home births occur, as evidenced by the increased number of midwifery programs to train midwives, most births still take place in hospitals and are attended by physicians. Many hospitals now have birthing centres, where fathers or birth coaches may be with the mother during labour and delivery. Some people believe these so-called alternative birthing centres offer a good compromise between a technological, depersonalized hospital birth (which cannot offer the emotional experience of a home birth) and a birth at home (which cannot offer the immediate medical backup of a hospital). The birthing room allows for a full range of birth experiences, from a totally unmedicated, natural birth to the most complex, medically intensive care.

Although midwifery is relatively new to many parts of Canada, education and training for midwifery is now offered at many universities. Knowing that reliable studies have attested to the safety of home births and that midwives are highly trained to deliver the newborn and assist the mother, a woman can make the decision with her family with considerable confidence. *What decision would you make regarding the birth of your child?*

Midwifery in Canada is an autonomous self-regulating profession that has undergone tremendous growth since 2010. In all regulated provinces and territories, midwives must be registered with the regulatory authority in order to legally call themselves a midwife and to practise their profession. As such, the **midwife** is recognized as a responsible and accountable professional who works in partnership with women to give the necessary support, care, and advice during pregnancy, labour, and the postpartum period. Midwives conduct births on their own and provide care for the newborn and the infant (ICM, 2011). Midwifery care is associated with a decrease in regional anaesthesia, instrumental birth, and episiotomy. Mothers are more likely to have spontaneous birth, initiate breastfeeding, and feel in control when giving birth with a midwife (Sandell et al., 2010).

Midwifery education in Canada is offered at a university baccalaureate level (Canadian Midwifery Regulators Consortium, 2012). The Society of Obstetricians and Gynaecologists of Canada (SOGC) continues its support of ongoing evaluation and accreditation of midwifery education and supports the integration of midwifery into the obstetrical interprofessional health care team to foster excellence in maternity care for women living in Canada. Where midwifery is provided within an obstetrical health care team, women then have a familiar caregiver with them during labour and birth, and for their postpartum care (SOGC, 2009). Registered midwives remain current on maternity-related research. The evidence, available in journals and research studies, allows them to provide comprehensive information so that women and their families can make informed choices about all aspects of their care (Canadian Midwifery Regulators Consortium, 2012). On May 5, 2011, the National Aboriginal Health Organization (NAHO) joined midwives and their supporters from across Canada to mark the International Day of the Midwife (NAHO, 2012).

CONNECTING through Social Policy

Home or Hospital: Where Would You Like to Give Birth?

"There's no place like home!" "Home is where the heart is!" We have all heard these refrains; but is home the best place to give birth? In preparing for the birth of a baby, parents consider the health and well-being of both mother and newborn, as well as the role of a midwife. Should a woman choose to give birth in a hospital, she will have immediate care and reassurance from healthcare providers intent on making her comfortable. Full healthcare services are ready should they be required. Should she choose to give birth at home, she will be surrounded by her family and have all the comforts of home, including food to her liking, available to her.

Canadian research indicates that home births and hospital births are equally safe for both mothers and infants (Janssen et al., 2009). To qualify for a home birth, the woman must be in good health and be assessed in the low-risk category. A low-risk pregnancy is one without complications for the mother or the infant. Generally, the mother is in good health, seeks prenatal care as soon as she believes she is pregnant, and continues seeing her healthcare provider. Women with low-risk pregnancies require minimum medical attention.

In many countries, a doula attends a childbearing woman. Doula is a Greek word that means "a woman who helps." A **doula** is a caregiver who provides continuous physical, emotional, and educational support for the mother before, during, and after childbirth. Doulas remain with the mother throughout labour, assessing and responding to her needs. Researchers have found positive effects when a doula is present at the birth of a child (Vonderheid et al., 2011). Gilliland (2010) states that doula support during labour is considered one of the more positive interventions in childbirth.

BIRTH PLANS

Canadian women deserve quality maternity care whether they live in an urban, rural, or remote community (Miller et al., 2012). Childbirth is a natural event and, coupled with the advent of family-centred care, childbearing families and health care providers now realize the advantage of a birth plan. A birth plan informs the health care provider about the following: the type of delivery the mother-to-be wants; the choice of birth companion (usually the father or partner); the choice of medication management to be implemented or not during labour; and the care of the baby postpartum (SOGC, 2011a).

In hospital settings that provide obstetrical care and birthing units, a specialized interprofessional health care team is on hand. Analgesics can be used to reduce the discomfort of labour. An *epidural block* is regional anaesthesia that numbs the woman's body from the waist down. *Oxytocics* are synthetic hormones that are used to stimulate contractions; pitocin is the most commonly used oxytocic. The benefits and risks of oxytocin as a part of childbirth continue to be debated (Vasdev, 2008). Predicting how a particular drug will affect an individual pregnant woman and the fetus is difficult (Funai, Evans, &

Lockwood, 2008). It is important for the mother to assess her level of pain and be an important voice in the decision of whether she should receive medication.

The emphasis today is on broadly educating the pregnant woman so that she can be reassured and confident in her birthing experience. This objective is most relevant in light of the Canadian Maternity Experiences Survey (PHAC, 2009e). Chalmers and colleagues (2012), in examining the results of the survey, found that women need to be better informed about the advantages and disadvantages of different birthing procedures and technologies to make informed decisions. Though the trend at one time was toward natural childbirth without any medication, today the emphasis is on using some medication, but keeping it to a minimum when possible.

Debate regarding the safety implications of home births is still prevalent in the literature. The results of one study conducted by Janssen and her colleagues (2009) revealed that planned home births attended by a registered midwife were associated not only with very low rates of perinatal death, but also with reduced rates of obstetric interventions and adverse maternal outcomes, compared to planned hospital birth attended by a midwife or physician.

Natural childbirth was developed in 1914 by an English obstetrician, Grantley Dick-Read. It attempts to reduce the mother's pain by decreasing her fear through education about childbirth and by teaching her to use breathing methods and relaxation techniques during delivery. Dick-Read also believed that the doctor's relationship with the mother is an important factor in reducing her pain. He said the doctor should be present during her active labour prior to delivery and should provide reassurance.

Prepared childbirth was developed by French obstetrician Fernand Lamaze. This childbirth strategy is similar to natural childbirth but includes a special breathing technique to control pushing in the final stages of labour and a more detailed anatomy and physiology course. The Lamaze method has become very popular in the United States. The pregnant woman's partner or a friend usually serves as a coach, and attends childbirth classes with her and helps with her breathing and relaxation during delivery.

Many other prepared childbirth techniques have also been developed (Davidson, London, & Ladewig, 2008). They usually include elements of Dick-Read's natural childbirth or Lamaze's method, plus one or more new components. French obstetrician Frederick Leboyer opposed the standard techniques of childbirth and advocated "birth without violence." In the Leboyer method, soft lights are used in the delivery room, and the newborn is placed on the mother's abdomen immediately after birth to foster bonding and then immersed in lukewarm water to relax. The umbilical cord is not cut until the newborn is able to breathe on his or her own. Virtually all of the prepared childbirth methods emphasize some degree of education, relaxation, and breathing exercises and support. In recent years, new ways of teaching relaxation have been offered, including guided mental imagery, massage, and meditation. In sum, the current belief in prepared childbirth is that when information and support are provided, women *know* how to give birth.

In a **Caesarean delivery**, the baby is removed from the mother's uterus through an incision made in her abdomen. This is sometimes called a Caesarean section, or C-section. A Caesarean section is usually performed if the baby is in a **breech position**, which causes the baby's buttocks to be the first part to emerge from the vagina.

The benefits and risks of Caesarean section continue to be debated (Declercq et al., 2008; Vendittelli et al., 2008). In fact, the current rapid increase in the rate of Caesarean section births in Canada has received growing attention (CIHI, 2012). After examining the Caesarean section rates in Canada using the Robson Classification system, Canadian researchers concluded that all hospitals and health authorities should use this standardized classification system as part of a quality improvement initiative to monitor Caesarean section rates. Furthermore, this classification system helps to identify relevant areas for interventions and resources to reduce rates of Caesarean sections (Kelly et al., 2013). One such obstetrical intervention includes non-pharmacological pain control methods, such as continuous support during childbirth (Rossignol et al., 2013). The Society of Obstetricians and Gynaecologists of Canada promote normal childbirth, without technological interventions, when possible (SOGC, 2008).

Caesarean deliveries are safer than breech deliveries, but they involve a higher infection rate, a longer hospital stay, and the greater expense and stress that accompany any surgery. Liston and colleagues (2008) conducted a study to determine the impact of Caesarean delivery on the incidence of neonatal outcome. They found that Caesarean delivery in labour, compared with vaginal delivery, is more likely to be associated with an increased risk for respiratory conditions and depression at birth than is the case with Caesarean delivery without labour.

It is interesting to note that Caesarean delivery appears to be somewhat protective against neonatal birth trauma, especially when performed without labour. Further, client-initiated elective Caesarean delivery is emerging as an urgent issue for practitioners, hospitals, and policy makers, as well as for pregnant women. For many childbearing mothers, the persuasive influence of positive Caesarean stories and negative vaginal stories must be considered by healthcare professionals. Care providers need to become familiar with the social influences impacting women's decisions for mode of delivery so that realistic informed discussions can be pursued with the childbearing woman (Munro, Kornelson, & Hutton, 2009).

critical thinking

From 1993 to 2006, Canada's C-section rate increased from 18 to 26 percent. For Canada, one of the safest places in the world to give birth, this increasing rate presents a concerning trend for the future. Design a plan for women to facilitate the decision-making process between a vaginal birth or a Caesarean birth. Compare and contrast complications between vaginal and Caesarean births.

Currently, women who rarely have witnessed a live birth are using technological interventions, such as Caesarean section, because they believe it will reduce the pain, stress, and uncertainty of labour (Romano & Lothian, 2008). Some obstetricians, wanting to be safe rather than sorry, opt for Caesarean births. Some healthcare providers argue that women should have the right to choose either vaginal delivery or Caesarean section; others who oppose this choice note that Caesarean section should not be used unless absolutely necessary. They argue that postpartum depression, risk of infection, and hospital costs all increase with Caesarean section (Simpson, 2010).

Special Neonatal Considerations

Some newborns present special situations that require additional consideration. For example, how can we distinguish between a preterm infant and a low-birth-weight infant? How do children with special needs gain access to all aspects of life available to the able-bodied child?

Preterm and Low-Birth-Weight Infants

The birth rate of babies born in Canadian hospitals has been declining gradually over the last several years. In 2013–2014, the rate was 106 per 10 000 population, down from 112 per 10 000 population in 2009 (CIHI, 2014a). Although the changes in the number of births are influenced by many factors, the two key factors are fertility rates and the number of women in the childbearing years (age 20 to 39) (CIHI, 2012b).

Three related conditions pose threats to many newborns: having a low birth weight, being preterm, and being small for date. **Low-birth-weight infants** weigh less than 2.5 kilograms (5.5 pounds) at birth. *Very-low-birth-weight* newborns weigh under 1.6 kilograms (3.5 pounds), and *extremely-low-birth-weight* newborns weigh under 0.9 kilograms (2 pounds). **Preterm infants** are those born three weeks or more before the pregnancy has reached its full term—in other words, prior to 37 weeks after conception. **Small-for-date infants** (also called *small-for-gestational-age infants*) are those whose birth weight is below normal when the length of the pregnancy is considered. They weigh less than 90 percent of all babies of the same gestational age. Small-for-date infants may be preterm or full-term. An infant is full term when it has grown in the womb for a full 37 to 42 weeks between conception and delivery.

In 2013–2014, the rate of preterm babies (born before 37 weeks of gestation) in Canadian hospitals was 8 percent. The percentage rate of single babies born who were small for gestational age (SGA; smaller than 90 percent of the babies with the same gestational age and sex) was 8.9 percent (CIHI, 2014a). These rates have remained unchanged since 2006 (CIHI, 2014a). The main factors leading to preterm babies include the following (CIHI, 2014c):

- Mother behaviours such as smoking, alcohol, or drug use and lack of prenatal care
- Factors related to social determinants of health such as stress, lack of social support, poverty, and ethnicity
- Medical conditions such as infections, hypertension, diabetes, clotting disorders, under or over weight, multiple pregnancy, history of preterm birth and uterine/cervical disorders
- Demographic factors such as age (i.e., mother over 35 or under 17)

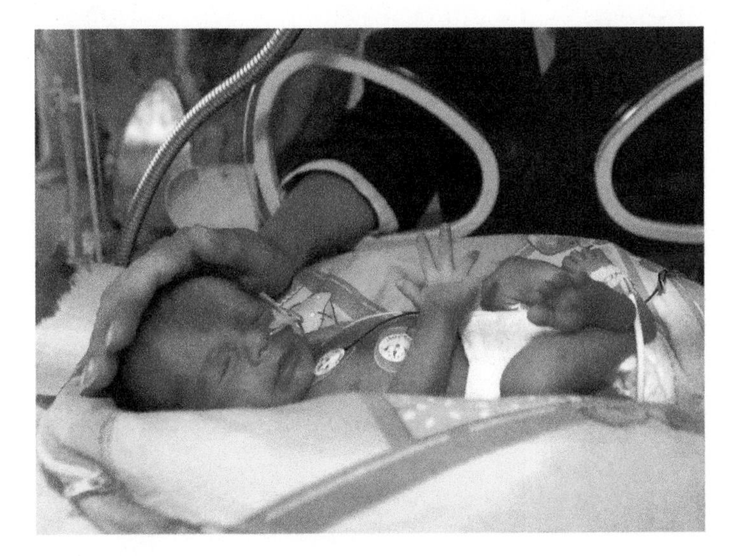

A "kilogram kid," weighing 1 kilogram (2.2 pounds) or less at birth. *What are some long-term potential consequences from weighing so little at birth?*

The causes of low birth weight vary from country to country. One study compared the mortality and morbidity of very low birth weight infants between Canada and Japan. Interestingly, very low birth weight infants in the Canadian Neonatal Network had higher rates of maternal diabetes, maternal hypertension, and prenatal steroid administration compared to the infants from the Neonatal Research Network in Japan (Isayama et al., 2012).

Long-Term Outcomes for Low-Birth-Weight Infants

Although most preterm and low-birth-weight infants are healthy, as a group they have more health and developmental problems than normal-birth-weight infants (Minde & Zelkowitz, 2008; van de Weijer-Bergsma, Wijnroks, & Jongmans, 2008). For preterm birth, the terms *extremely preterm* and *very preterm* are increasingly being used (Smith, 2008). Extremely preterm infants are those born less than 28 weeks preterm, and very preterm infants are those born less than 33 weeks of gestational age.

Figure 4.10 shows the results of a Norwegian study indicating that the earlier preterm infants are born, the more likely they will drop out of school (Swamy, Ostbye, & Skjaerven, 2008). Another recent study found that extremely preterm infants are more likely to show pervasive delays in early language development (such as vocabulary size and quality of word use) than very preterm infants, who in turn show more early language delays than full-term infants (Foster-Cohen et al., 2007). One predominantly Canadian study found that male sex and low birth weight are significant predictors of developmental coordination disorder (DCD). This disorder is a motor disorder of unknown origin that significantly interferes with a child's ability to perform daily tasks (e.g., tying shoes, riding a bicycle, and printing) (Zwicker et al., 2013).

Figure 4.10

Percentage of Preterm and Full-term Birth Infants Who Dropped Out of School

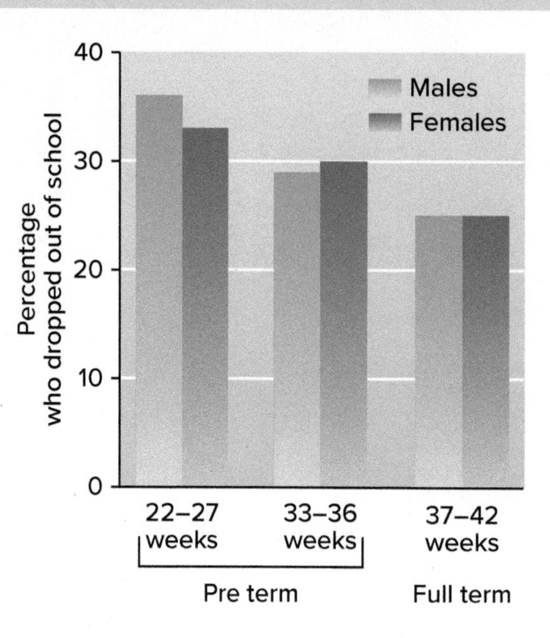

Survival rates for infants who are born very early and very small have risen, but with this improved survival rate has come increases in rates of severe brain damage (Allen, 2008; Casey, 2008). A recent MRI study revealed that adolescents who experienced very preterm birth are more likely to show reduced prefrontal lobe and corpus callosum functioning than full-term adolescents (Narberhaus et al., 2007).

At school age, children who were born low in birth weight are more likely than their normal-birth-weight counterparts to have a learning disability, attention deficit disorder, or breathing problems such as asthma (Greenough, 2007; Joshi & Kotecha, 2007). Some of the devastating effects of being born low in birth weight can be reversed. Intensive enrichment programs that provide medical and educational services for both the parents and the child have been shown to improve short-term developmental outcomes for low-birth-weight children.

Kangaroo Care and Massage Therapy

Beginning life as a preterm or low-birth-weight baby in a neonatal intensive-care unit (NICU) means living in an incubator attached to monitoring equipment and trying to sleep in an often very noisy environment. Kangaroo care is a way of holding a preterm infant so that there is skin-to-skin contact. The baby, wearing only a diaper, is held upright against the parent's bare chest, much as a baby kangaroo is carried by its mother. Many studies find that newborns exposed to kangaroo care sleep more deeply, gain weight more quickly, and spend more time alert than do infants with standard care (Ludinton-Hoe, 2011). Canadian researchers also found kangaroo care helps to diminish pain responses in infants undergoing procedures involving a heel lance (Johnston et al., 2008). Increasingly, kangaroo care is being recommended for full-term infants as well (Ferber & Makhoul, 2008; Walters et al., 2007).

Many preterm infants experience less touch than full-term infants because they are isolated in temperature-controlled incubators. Tiffany Field's (2007) research has led to a surge of interest in the role that massage might play in improving the developmental outcomes of low-birth-weight infants. In one study, preterm infants in an NICU were randomly assigned to a massage therapy group or a control group. Behaviour indicators of stress such as crying, grimacing, leg movements, and startles were recorded. The therapy group then received three 15-minute massage sessions per day for five days, while the control group did not. At the end of the five days, the preterm infants in the massage therapy group showed a significantly lower stress response rating than the control group (Hernandez-Reif & Field, 2007).

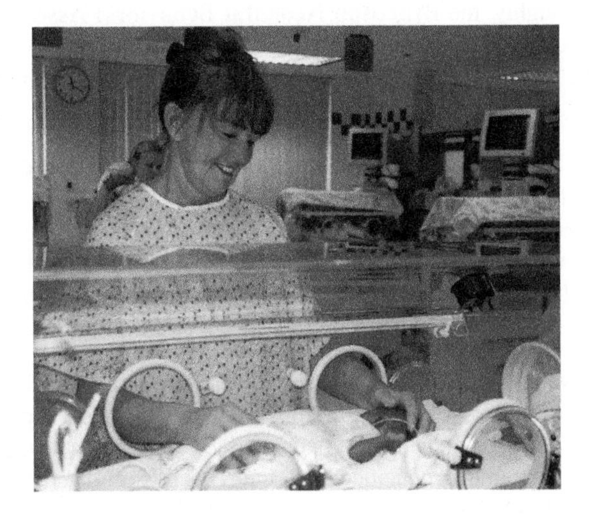

Courtesy of Dr. Tiffany Field

Shown here is Tiffany Field massaging a newborn infant. *What types of infants has massage therapy been shown to help?*

Measures of Neonatal Health and Responsiveness

The **Apgar scale** is widely used to assess the health of newborns at one and five minutes after birth by evaluating the infant's heart rate, respiratory effort, muscle tone, body colour, and reflex irritability. An obstetrician or a nurse does the evaluation and gives the newborn a score, or reading, of 0, 1, or 2 on each of these five health signs (see Figure 4.11). A total score of 7 to 10 indicates that the newborn's condition is good. A score of 5 indicates there may be developmental difficulties. A score of 3 or below signals an emergency and indicates that the baby might not survive. The Apgar scale also identifies high-risk infants who need resuscitation.

Figure 4.11

The Apgar Scale

SCORE	0	1	2
Respiratory effort	No breathing for more than one minute	Irregular and slow	Good breathing with normal crying
Body colour	Blue and pale	Body pink, but extremities blue	Entire body pink
Heart rate	Absent	Slow—less than 100 beats per minute	Fast—100 to 140 beats per minute
Muscle tone	Limp and flaccid	Weak, inactive, but some flexion of extremities	Strong, active motion
Reflex irritability	No response	Grimace	Coughing, sneezing, and crying

From Virginia A. Apgar, 1975, "A Proposal for a New Method of Evaluation of a Newborn Infant," in *Anesthesia and Analgesia*, Vol. 32, pp. 260-267. Reprinted by permission.

To evaluate the newborn more thoroughly, the **Brazelton Neonatal Behavioral Assessment Scale (NBAS)** is performed within 24 to 36 hours after birth to evaluate the newborn's neurological development, reflexes, and reactions to people and objects. It is also used as a sensitive index of neurological competence up to one month after birth for typical infants, and as a measure in many studies of infant development (Mamtani, Patel, & Kulkarni, 2008).

An "offspring" of the NBAS, the **Neonatal Intensive Care Unit Network Neurobehavioral Scale (NNNS)**, provides a more comprehensive analysis of the newborn's behaviour, neurological and stress responses, and regulatory capacities (Brazelton, 2004; Lester, Tronick, & Brazelton, 2004). Whereas the NBAS was developed to assess normal, healthy term infants, T. Berry Brazelton, along with Barry Lester and Edward Tronick, developed the NNNS to assess the "at-risk" infant. It is especially useful for evaluating preterm infants (although it may not be appropriate for those less than 30 weeks' gestational age) and substance-exposed infants (Boukydis & Lester, 2008; Smith et al., 2008).

Gestational age (GA) assessment is an important part of early neonatal examination. The most widely accepted scoring system for postnatal estimation of GA is the New Ballard Score (NBS). It assigns a score to various criteria across twelve categories in order to ascertain the gestational age of the baby. These categories cover physical and neurological criteria, including posture, skin and genitals. Researchers concluded that the NBS is a valid and reliable tool for GA assessment until day 7 (Sasidharan, Dutta, & Narang, 2009).

To this point, we have studied a number of ideas about birth. For a review, see the Reach Your Learning Outcomes section at the end of this chapter.

The Postpartum Period

LO3 List the changes that take place in the postpartum period.

- **What Is the Postpartum Period?**
- **Physical Adjustments**
- **Emotional and Psychological Adjustments**

What Is the Postpartum Period?

The **postpartum period** is the period after childbirth or delivery. It is a time when the woman's body adjusts, both physically and psychologically, to the process of childbirth. It lasts for about six weeks or until the body has completed its adjustment and has returned to a near pre-pregnant state. Some health professionals refer to the postpartum period as the "fourth trimester." Though the time span of the postpartum period does not necessarily cover three months, the terminology of fourth trimester demonstrates the idea of continuity and the importance of the first several months after birth for the mother.

Parenting during the early postpartum period is a time of maternal learning and adaptation. Mothers are called upon to learn new behaviours to be able to care effectively for their infants and to achieve maximum satisfaction with parenting (Leahy-Warren & McCarthy, 2011). During this period, families may receive home visits from a public health nurse. Postpartum care by the nurse in the home usually includes monitoring the physical and emotional well-being of all family members; identifying potential or developing complications for the mother and newborn; and acting as an advocate between mother and other healthcare providers such as a lactation consultant. While providing effective care, it is essential to understand the postpartum health needs of the new mother and to teach her to care for her infant, her family, and herself. Doing so will help the mother respond to physical and emotional postpartum changes, and to the transition to parenthood (PHAC, 2009e).

Physical Adjustments

The woman's body makes numerous physical adjustments in the first days and weeks after childbirth (London et al., 2007). A concern is the loss of sleep that the primary caregiver experiences in the postpartum period (Gunderson et al., 2008; Signal et al., 2007). A 2008 analysis indicated that the primary caregiver loses as much as 700 hours of sleep in the first year following the baby's birth (Maas, 2008). The loss of sleep can contribute to stress, marital conflict, and impaired decision making (Meerlo, Sgoifo, & Suchecki, 2008). Even after their newborn begins to sleep better through the night by the middle of the baby's first year, many mothers report waking up several times a night even when their baby is asleep. Sleep experts say it takes several weeks to several months for parents' internal sleep clocks to adjust.

Women navigate themselves through many social changes when they become a mother. One such change is in the area of sexual and intimate relationships. Most women having a first birth do not resume vaginal sex until later than six weeks postpartum. Women who have an operative vaginal birth, Caesarean section, perineal tear, or an episiotomy appear to delay sexual activity longer (McDonald & Brown, 2013). Woolhouse and colleagues (2014) found that a considerable decrease in both emotional satisfaction and physical pleasure in intimate relationships occurs after birth. Emotional satisfaction continued to decrease until 4.5 years postpartum. The women also reported insufficient opportunities provided by health professionals for them to discuss changes affecting their sexual and intimate relationships. The researchers recommend that more information about sexual and intimate relationships be made available to women postpartum (Woolhouse, McDonald, & Brown, 2014).

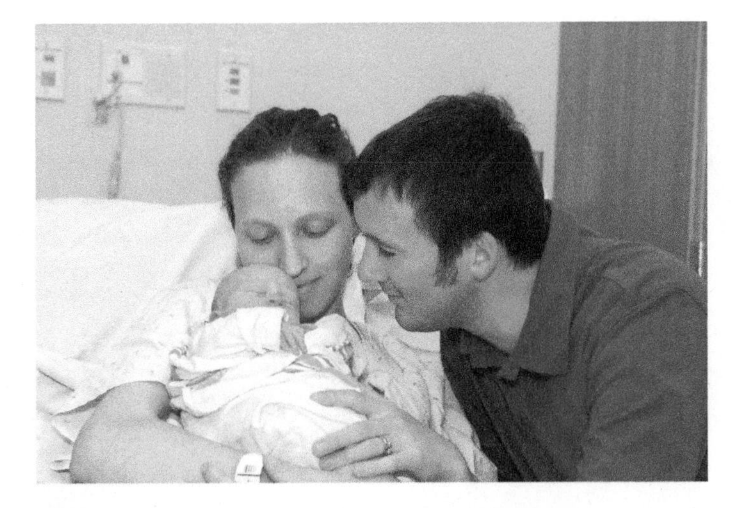

The weeks following childbirth are likely to present many challenges to new parents and their offspring. Many health professionals believe that the best postpartum care is family centred, using the family's resources to support an early and smooth adjustment to the newborn by all family members.

Pregnancy and delivery-related factors seem to be the main risk factors for the development of urinary incontinence. Pelvic floor muscle exercises are quite effective for urinary incontinence during pregnancy and the postpartum period (Dine, Kizilkaya Beji, & Yalcin, 2009).

Postnatal women often wish to resume abdominal exercise shortly after delivery to restore their abdominal figure and level of fitness. A group of international researchers gave a group of 84 first-time mothers two exercises, the abdominal crunch and the drawing-in exercise (Mota et al., 2015). They discovered that overall, the abdominal crunch was the most effective exercise. This result was consistent with another previous study performed with a sample of postpartum women (Pascoal et al., 2014).

Relaxation techniques are also helpful during the postpartum period. Five minutes of slow breathing on a stressful day in the postpartum period can relax and refresh the new mother, as well as the new baby.

Emotional and Psychological Adjustments

Emotional fluctuations are common for mothers in the postpartum period. Mothers, whose feelings of depression last more than a few weeks, even when they are getting adequate rest, may benefit from professional help in dealing with their problems. The term "postpartum mood disorders" generally refers to the baby blues and can affect 30–70 percent of women shortly after childbirth. Accompanying symptoms often include mood liability, tearfulness, insomnia, anxiety, and irritability (Sharma & Sharma, 2012).

Postpartum depression (PPD) involves a major depressive episode that typically occurs about four weeks after delivery. Women with postpartum depression have such strong feelings of sadness, anxiety, or despair that for at least a two-week period they have trouble coping with their daily tasks. Postpartum depression is a relatively common mental disorder estimated to affect 13–19 percent of women in the first year following childbirth (O'Hara & McCabe, 2013). Without treatment, postpartum depression may become worse and last for many months (Gjerdingen, Katon, & Rich, 2008). Canadian researchers noted that anxiety during pregnancy is correlated with postpartum depression (Bowen et al., 2008). Thus, identifying pregnant women experiencing clinical levels of anxiety and treating the anxiety would be one possible method of preventing or reducing their experience of postpartum depression. These researchers also noted that younger pregnant women tend to be more anxious than older women. Other findings indicate that postpartum depressed mothers tend to have lower levels of education in comparison to mothers that have not experienced postpartum depression (Vliegen & Luyten, 2009).

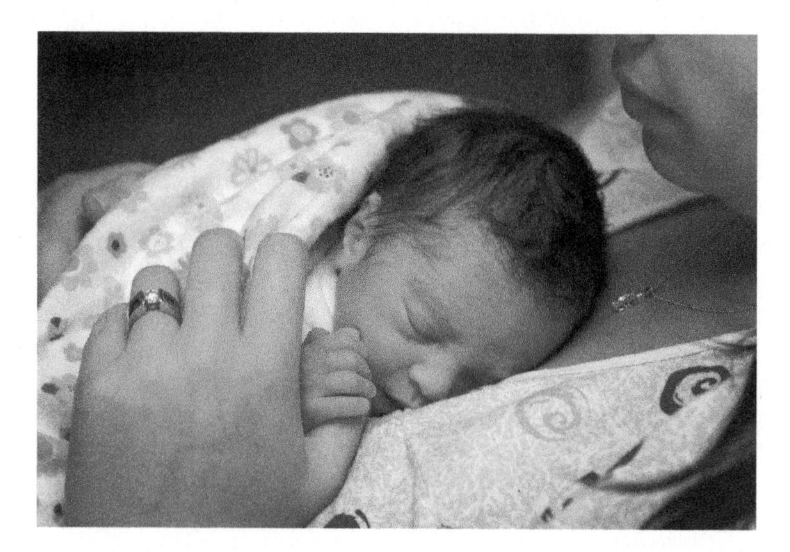

A mother bonds with her infant moments after it is born. *How critical is bonding for the development of social competence later in childhood?*

The exact cause of postpartum depression remains unknown. Changing hormone levels was once thought to be one of the major determinants. Current research demonstrates that PPD may be a compilation of numerous stressors encountered by the family, including biochemical, genetic, psychosocial factors, and everyday life stressors (Murray, McKinney, & Murray, 2010). Canadian researchers investigated the perception of men and women regarding the causes of women's PPD symptoms. The participants identified nine possible causes of PPD, including societal expectations and pressures on women, physical health problems, and transition to parenthood. It is interesting to note that only men mentioned societal pressure on women (Habel et al., 2015).

Maternal postpartum depression in rural areas is a particularly critical issue. One of the main factors in decreasing the likelihood that a rural mother will seek treatment is the lack of available resources (Brannen et al., 2012).

critical thinking

Postpartum depression is a very serious and potentially dangerous state for a new mother to experience. Based on information in this chapter, construct a set of "helpful tips" that you could provide to an expectant mother and father to decrease the likelihood of postpartum depression developing. The list ought to include both information and activities in which the parents-to-be could engage. How would you interact with a mother who is experiencing postpartum depression? What support would you give to the mother and father, as well as the baby?

One concern about postpartum depression is that breastfeeding is less common among postpartum-depressed women. They may not breastfeed because of their concern about potentially negative effects of antidepressants that can be transmitted to their young infant through breast milk (Einarson & Ito, 2007). Currently, little research has been conducted on whether the positive effects of breastfeeding might outweigh the positive effects of antidepressants for both the mother and the infant (Field, 2008). Can a mother's postpartum depression affect her child? Researchers have found that depressed mothers interact less with their infants and are less likely to respond to their infant's efforts to get attention (Teti & Towe-Goodman, 2008).

Education and early identification seem to be the key to treating PPD. First-time mothers and families need to be aware of this problem and understand that it is a serious medical condition that should not be ignored. As part of the regular prenatal appointments, mothers should be taught about possible causes PPD, what to look for, and where to obtain help. Numerous informational websites and support groups can be accessed for more information (Camp, 2013).

A Father's Adjustment

A study conducted by Yu and colleagues (2012) assessed expectant fathers' support network, marital intimacy, and health status during the third trimester of their partner's pregnancy. The results indicated that fathers who perceived more marital intimacy and support from their partners were actually more attached to their infants. The researchers concluded that marital intimacy and partner support are important predictors for father–infant attachment. It is interesting to note that a longitudinal study examined perceptions of fatherhood over the first 18 months after the birth of a first child. The results suggested that when couples become parents, the reciprocal interaction of new mothers and fathers influences their perspective perceptions relative to fatherhood (Tremblay & Pierce, 2011).

With the support of the Public Health Agency of Canada, the Father Involvement Initiative–Ontario Network (FII-ON) has produced a website that serves as an online booklet for new and expecting fathers. The website provides detailed information using a combination of articles and videos to provide answers to the most common new-dad questions using a father-friendly approach (FIRA, 2012).

To help the father adjust, parents should set aside some special time to be together with each other. The father's postpartum reaction also likely will be improved if he has taken childbirth classes with the mother and is an active participant in caring for the baby.

CONNECTING development to life

Global Responses to Pregnancy and Attachment after Birth

All cultures have beliefs and rituals that surround life's major events, including pregnancy and birth.

Pregnancy: Some cultures view pregnancy and infancy as a natural occurrence; others see it as a medical condition (Walsh, 2006). How expectant mothers behave during pregnancy may depend in part on the prevalence of traditional homecare remedies and folk beliefs, the importance of indigenous healers, and the influence of health care professionals in their culture (Walsh, 2006). In various cultures, pregnant women may turn to herbalists, faith healers, root doctors, or spiritualists for help (Mbonye, Neema, & Magnussen, 2006). In fact, in developing countries, encouraging male partners to accompany women to prenatal care is an important first step in engaging men on maternal and newborn health (Aguiar & Jennings, 2015).

Chinese expectant mothers commonly listen to classical music during pregnancy because they believe it will help the offspring develop patience, wisdom, and artistic sensitivity. Many Chinese people also think that a child's moral disposition is at least partially developed in the womb. As a consequence, expectant Chinese mothers may avoid contact with people they perceive to be dishonest, may engage in charitable deeds, and try to avoid having negative thoughts or feelings. In some Asian countries, such as the Philippines, many expectant mothers will not take any medication during pregnancy. Also, some immigrant Asian women return to their parents' home in their native country to deliver their baby, especially if it is their firstborn child (American Public Health, 2006).

Mexican and other Hispanic immigrants frequently live in low socio-economic neighbourhoods and attend fewer medical visits prenatally. These factors can compromise their gestational and birth outcomes (Bravo & Noya, 2014). Most pregnant women living in European countries, Canada, and Australia report barriers in obtaining prenatal care, similar to those reported by U.S. minority women (Boerleider et al., 2013). Certain factors such as accurate recognition and readiness, sensitive providers, inter-dependent relationships, and social support can enhance prenatal attitudes and behaviours in minority mothers (Wheatley et al., 2008). In fact, communalism, described as a lifestyle underscoring the benefits of interdependent relationships, may improve the emotional and physical health of pregnant women, irrespective of ethnicity or socio-economic status (Abdou et al., 2010).

Infancy: A special component of the parent–infant relationship is **bonding**, the occurrence of close contact, especially physical, between parents and newborn in the period shortly after birth. During the period immediately following birth, the parents "fall in love" with the child they have and that newborn elicits protection and loving responses from caregivers. Whether humans have a critical period for bonding is inconclusive and debatable, but varying levels of attachment emerge as a result of caregiver and child interaction during the first months of the child's life (Kennell, 2006).

The degree of security of attachment is related to the level of sensitivity caregivers provide newborns, as evidenced by responsive behaviours to distress, vocalization, and gazing, as well as proximity, holding, and carrying behaviours (Whaley et al., 2002; Tulviste & Ahtonen, 2007). Infant security is not related to gender, economic status, or who the primary caregiver is (Tulviste & Ahtonen, 2007).

Secure attachment is linked to desirable childhood and adulthood behaviours, whether the cultural values favour individualism or collectivism. Considerable variation exists in the extent to which behaviours, particularly self-directed behaviours, are valued and how behaviours associated with security are defined and interpreted (Rothbaum et al., 2007; Tulviste & Ahtonen, 2007; Whaley et al., 2002). Cultural contexts shape caregiver responses (Rothbaum et al., 2007). To North Americans (economically secure mothers who spent most of their lives in Canada or the United States), secure attachment is the balance between closeness and exploration and leads to the development of autonomy, self-esteem, and self-reliance. In contrast, Puerto Ricans view secure attachment as the balance between emotional connectedness and proper demeanour and leads to respect, obedience, and calmness. In Japan, secure attachment leads to the development of empathy, accommodation, and interdependence. Whereas North American parents associate insecure attachment with anger and aggression in adulthood, Japanese mothers attribute inappropriate behaviours as security-seeking behaviours (Rothbaum et al., 2007).

How women behave toward their newly born children is also related to cultural norms and interpretation. In North America, mutual gazing and vocal maternal behaviours are thought to be predictors of optimal development. In Kenya, however, maternal vocalization and gazing are comparatively absent. Patterns of shared caregiving by multiple family and community members exist in several countries, such as Botswana, India, Kenya, and Zaire. In these countries, older siblings frequently care for infants and younger siblings, a practice for which a North American parent would be deemed irresponsible. At all ages, Kenyan caregivers hold or carry infants more than North American mothers, who decrease the amount of carrying and holding time as infants age. Kenyan mothers spend less time engaged in vocalization and gazing than their North American counterparts, but when multiple caregiver responses are factored in, the amount of such behaviours doubled in Kenya while increasing by only 2 percent in North America (Whaley et al., 2002). It is interesting to note that in Kenya, women with spouses who attended the antenatal care program had significantly (by a factor of 2.17) greater odds of giving birth with a doctor or nurse/midwife compared to women with non-present spouses (Mangeni et al., 2013).

Findings such as these are based on naturalistic observation by trained experts, which was discussed in Chapter 1. You can conduct your own mini–field research by observing and questioning practices in your own family. For example, are multiple caregivers from family and/or community involved in responding to a newborn in your family? How much gazing and vocalization does the mother engage in compared to other family members? What are the benefits or drawbacks to having greater or less involvement of extended family in child rearing? How might this change in different social contexts?

To this point, we have discussed the postpartum period. For a review, see the Reach Your Learning Outcomes section at the end of this chapter.

Reach Your **Learning Outcomes**

Prenatal Development

LO1 Examine prenatal development.

The Course of Prenatal Development	Germinal Period: ▪ From conception until 10 to 14 days later. ▪ A fertilized egg is called a zygote. ▪ This period ends when the zygote attaches to the uterine wall. Embryonic Period: ▪ Approximately two to eight weeks after conception. ▪ The embryo differentiates into three layers, life-support systems develop, and organ systems form (organogenesis). Fetal Period: ▪ Lasts from about two months after conception until nine months, or when the baby is born. ▪ Growth and development continue their dramatic course, and organ systems mature to the point at which life can be sustained outside of the womb. The Brain: ▪ The nervous system begins as a hollow tube in the embryo's neck, closing at both ends about day 24. ▪ The nearly 100 billion neurons are formed over the remainder of the prenatal period. ▪ The neurons migrate to their appropriate location in the brain and begin to build interconnections and form the various brain structures. ▪ Brain growth and development continues after delivery.
Teratology and Hazards to Prenatal Development	▪ Teratology investigates the causes of congenital (birth) disabilities. ▪ Any agent that causes disability in the offspring by the time of birth is called a teratogen. ▪ The dose, genetic susceptibility, and the time of exposure influence the type and severity of the effect.

Prenatal Care	▪ Prenatal care varies considerably, but usually involves medical care services with a defined schedule of visits.
Positive Prenatal Development	▪ Most pregnancies and prenatal development go well, although it is important to avoid the vulnerabilities that teratogens produce.

Birth

LO2 Outline the birth process.

The Birth Process	▪ The first stage of labour lasts about 12 to 24 hours for a woman having her first child. The cervix dilates to about 10 cm. ▪ The second stage begins when the baby's head moves through the cervix and ends with the baby's complete emergence. ▪ The third stage is the delivery of the placenta and membranes, commonly called the afterbirth.
Special Neonatal Considerations	▪ Preterm infants are those born after an abnormally short time in the womb. ▪ Infants who are born after a regular gestation period of 38 to 42 weeks but who weigh less than 2,500 grams are called low-birth-weight infants. ▪ Although most low-birth-weight infants are normal and healthy, as a group, they have more health and developmental problems than normal-birth-weight infants.
Measures of Neonatal Health and Responsiveness	▪ The Apgar scale is used to assess the newborn's health. ▪ The Brazelton Neonatal Behavioral Assessment Scale, a more recently developed scale, is used for long-term neurological assessment and social responsiveness. ▪ The Neonatal Intensive Care Unit Neurobehavioral Scale provides a more comprehensive analysis of the newborn's behaviour, neurological and stress responses, and regulatory capacities. ▪ The New Ballard Score is the most widely accepted scoring system for postnatal estimation of gestational age (GA).

The Postpartum Period

LO3 List the changes that take place in the postpartum period.

What Is the Postpartum Period?	▪ This is the period after childbirth or delivery. ▪ The woman's body adjusts physically and psychologically to the process of childbearing. ▪ It lasts for about six weeks or until the body has completed its adjustment.
Physical Adjustments	▪ These include fatigue, involution (the process by which the uterus returns to its pre-pregnant size five or six weeks after birth), hormonal changes, when to resume sexual intercourse, and exercises to recover body contour and strength.
Emotional and Psychological Adjustments	▪ Emotional fluctuations on the part of the mother are common in this period, and they can vary a great deal from one mother to the next. ▪ Postpartum depression can occur in some women. ▪ The father also goes through a postpartum adjustment.

review → connect → reflect

review

1. Why is it important to take a positive approach to prenatal development? LO1
2. What is meant by the term *teratology*? What are the significant hazards to prenatal development? LO1
3. What is the course of the birth process? LO2
4. What are a few measures of neonatal health and assessment? LO2
5. What physical and emotional adjustments characterize the postpartum period? LO3
6. What role does the father play during pregnancy? LO3

connect

You are asked to design a health teaching program for pregnant mothers who smoke. What will you include in this plan?

reflect

Your Own Personal Journey of Life

If you are a female, which birthing process would you prefer? Explain. If you are a male, how involved would you want to be in helping your partner through the birth of your baby? Explain.

SECTION 3

Infancy

CHAPTER 5

Physical and Cognitive Development in Infancy

CHAPTER OUTLINE

Physical Development and Health

LO1 Outline steps involved in physical growth and development in infancy.

- **Physical Growth**
- **Brain**
- **Sleep**
- **Health**

Motor, Sensory, and Perceptual Development

LO2 Examine infant motor development and summarize the course of sensory and perceptual development in infancy.

- **Motor Development**
- **Sensory and Perceptual Development**

Cognitive Development

LO3 Determine how infants learn, remember, and conceptualize.

- **Piaget's Sensorimotor Stage**
- **Information Processing**
- **Infant Intelligence**

Language Development

LO4 Explain the nature of language and how it develops in infancy.

- **Language Acquisition**
- **Biological Foundations of Language**
- **Behavioural and Environmental Influences**

"A baby is an angel whose wings decrease as his legs increase."

—FRENCH PROVERB

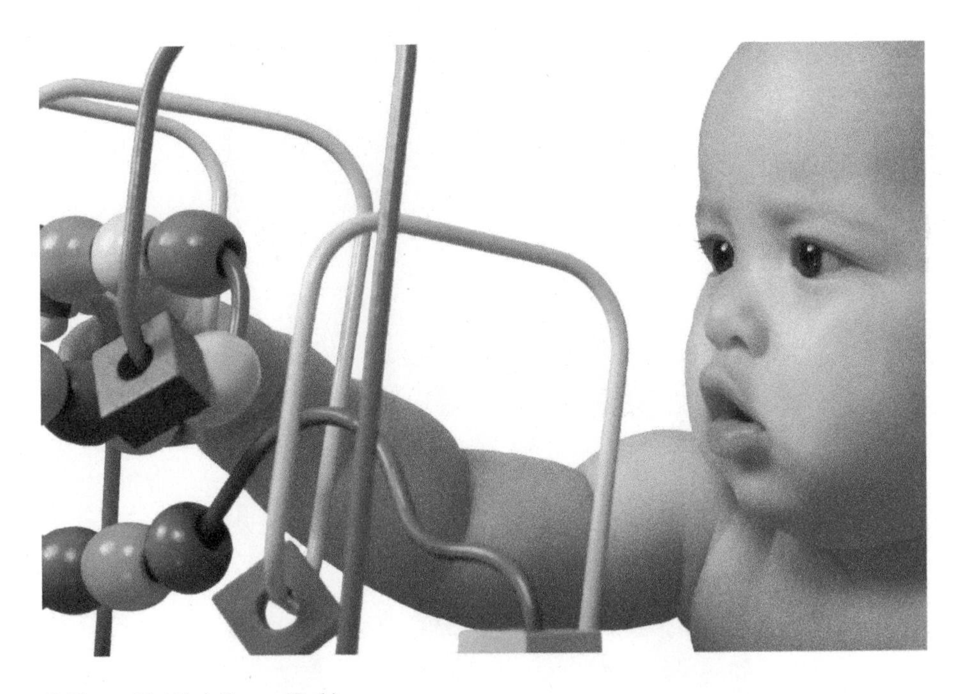

© Marcus Mok/Asia Images/Corbis

Bottle- and Breastfeeding in Africa and Canada

Latonya is a newborn baby in the African country of Ghana. The culture of the area in which she was born discourages breastfeeding. She has been kept apart from her mother and bottle-fed in her first days of infancy. Manufacturers of infant formula provide the hospital where she was born with free or subsidized milk powder. Her mother has been persuaded to bottle-feed her, rather than breastfeed. When her mother bottle-feeds Latonya, she overdilutes the milk formula with unclean water. Latonya's feeding bottles also have not been sterilized. She starts to get sick—very sick. She dies before her first birthday.

By contrast, Ramona lives in nearby Nigeria. Her mother is breastfeeding her. Ramona was born at a Nigerian hospital where a "baby-friendly" program has been initiated. In this program, babies are not separated from their mothers when they are born, and the mothers are encouraged to breastfeed. The mothers are told of the perils that bottle-feeding can bring because of unsafe water and unsterilized bottles. They also are informed about the advantages of breast milk, such as its nutritious and hygienic qualities, its ability to immunize babies against common illnesses, and its role in reducing the mother's risk of breast and ovarian cancers. At 1 year of age, Ramona is very healthy.

The World Health Organization (WHO) and UNICEF have been trying to reverse the trend toward bottle-feeding of infants in many impoverished countries. They have instituted the baby-friendly initiative program in many of them. In fact, the Baby-Friendly Hospital Initiative was launched by the WHO and UNICEF in 1989 to promote, protect, and support breastfeeding worldwide (Chalmers et al., 2009).

The advantages of breastfeeding in impoverished countries are substantial. However, these advantages must be balanced against the risk of passing the human immunodeficiency virus (HIV) to the babies through breast milk if the mothers have the virus; the majority of mothers don't know that they are infected (Dube et al., 2008). In some areas of Africa, more than 30 percent of mothers have HIV.

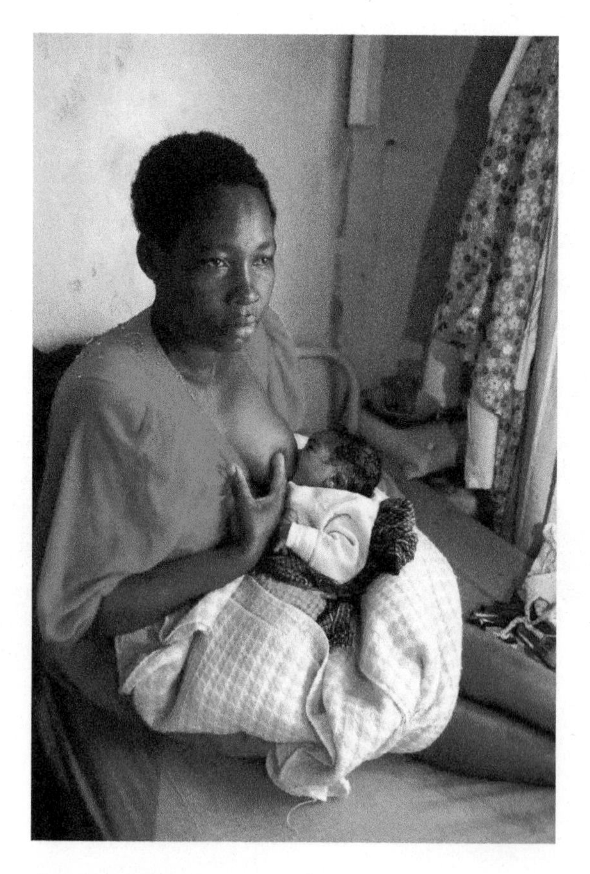

An HIV-infected mother breastfeeding her baby in Nairobi, Kenya.

According to Canadian researchers Levitt and colleagues (2011), the Baby-Friendly Hospital Initiative (BFHI) promotes both the World Health Organization International Code of Marketing of Breast-Milk Substitutes (WHO Code) and the WHO/UNICEF's Ten Steps to Successful Breastfeeding (Ten Steps). Between 1993 and 2007, Levitt and her team of researchers surveyed all Canadian maternity hospitals on routine maternity practices and policies, including infant feeding. They concluded that in the 14 years between the two surveys, Canadian maternity hospitals substantially improved their implementation of the WHO Code and their adherence to the WHO/UNICEF Ten Steps (Levitt et al., 2011). Among other benefits, breastfeeding has been shown to be related to a lower risk of obesity (Cope & Allison, 2008).

A Rwandan mother bottle-feeding her baby. *What are some concerns about bottle- versus breastfeeding in impoverished African countries?*

Physical Development and Health

LO1 Outline steps involved in physical growth and development in infancy.

- **Physical Growth**
- **Brain**
- **Sleep**
- **Health**

Infants' physical development in the first two years after birth is extensive (Caulfield, 2001). Their bodies and brains experience rapid growth. Two important elements that promote this growth are sleep and health.

Physical Growth

Typically, the full-term newborn is 48 to 53 cm, and weighs 2500 to 4000 grams. In the first several days the newborn typically loses approximately 10 percent of its initial birth weight due to the loss of meconium (the first feces of a newborn) and extracellular fluid, as well as limited food intake (Chow et al., 2013). It is expected that this newborn weight loss will be regained within 10 to 14 days. Weight loss of more than 10 percent requires close monitoring (Burns et al., 2013).

Once an infant has adjusted to sucking, swallowing, and digesting, it grows rapidly, gaining 150 to 210 grams weekly until 5 to 6 months, by which time birth weight has typically doubled. By 1 year of age, the infant's birth weight has tripled. Infants who are breastfed beyond 4 to 6 months of age typically gain less weight than those who are bottle-fed. Infants grow about 2.5 cm per month during the first six months of life; growth slows during the second six months (Hockenberry & Wilson, 2013).

The growth rate of infants is considerably slower in the second year of life. By 2 years of age, infants weigh approximately 12 kg. The birth weight is quadrupled by 2.5 years of age. At 2 years of age, the average height is 86.6 cm, which is nearly one-half of their adult height (Hockenberry & Wilson, 2013).

Physical development tends to follow two patterns. The **cephalocaudal pattern** is the sequence in which the greatest growth in size, weight, and feature differentiation gradually works down from top to bottom. This same pattern occurs in the head area: the top parts of the head—the eyes and brain—grow faster than the lower parts, such as the jaw. A large proportion of the total body is occupied by the head during prenatal development and early infancy (see Figure 5.1).

Figure 5.1

Changes in Proportions of the Human Body during Growth

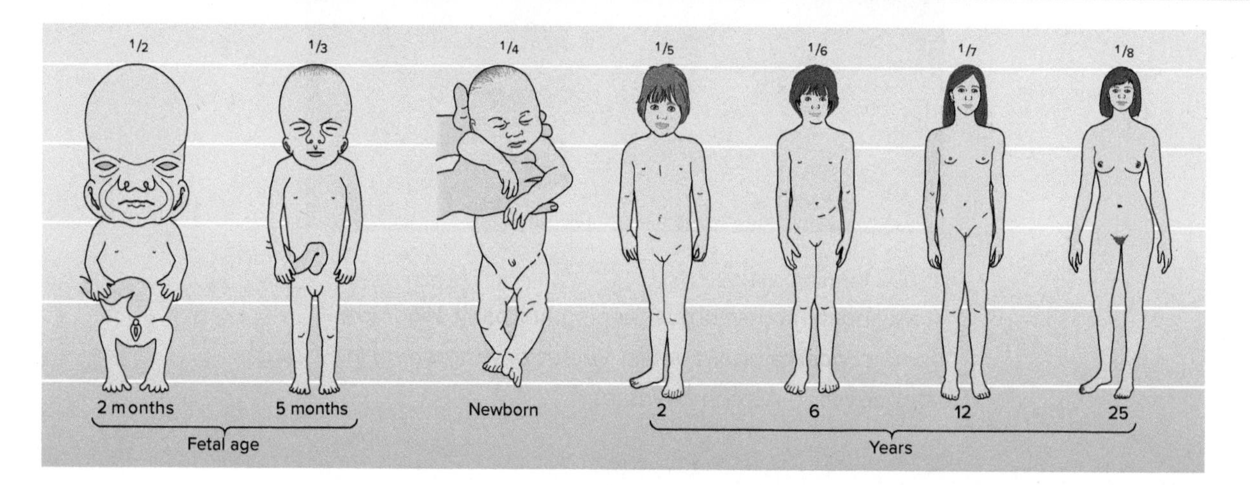

From Santrock, *Children*, 9/e, Figure 6.1. Copyright © 2007 The McGraw-Hill Companies.

Reproduced by permission of The McGraw-Hill Companies.

As individuals develop from infancy through adulthood, one of the most noticeable physical changes is that the head becomes smaller in relation to the rest of the body. The fractions listed refer to head size as a proportion of total body length at different ages.

Later in the chapter, you will see that sensory development and motor development also proceed according to the cephalocaudal principle. For example, infants can use their hands long before they can crawl or walk.

The **proximodistal pattern** is the sequence in which growth starts at the centre of the body and moves toward the extremities. An example of this is the early maturation of muscular control of the trunk and arms, as compared with that of the hands and fingers. Furthermore, infants use their whole hand as a unit before they can control several fingers.

Brain

At birth, the infant that began as a single cell is estimated to have a brain that contains approximately 100 billion nerve cells, or neurons. Extensive brain development continues after birth, through infancy and later (de Haan & Martinos, 2008; Nelson,

2011). Because the brain is still developing so rapidly in infancy, the infant's head should be protected from falls or other injuries and the baby should never be shaken. *Shaken baby syndrome*, which includes brain swelling and hemorrhaging, affects hundreds of babies in North America each year (Altimer, 2008; Squire, 2008).

Goulet and colleagues (2009) conducted a study in Canada to evaluate the opinions of parents and nurses regarding the benefit of a program on shaken baby syndrome: the Perinatal Shaken Baby Syndrome Prevention Program (PSBSPP). The researchers found that the program achieved two important goals. First, it increased parents' knowledge about infant crying, anger, and shaken baby syndrome. Secondly, the program helped parents to identify coping strategies. The study concluded that introducing the PSBSPP in all birthing institutions is highly relevant.

Health Canada, together with a diverse group of professionals and advocacy associations, has developed the Joint Statement on Shaken Baby Syndrome (SBS) as an essential step to stimulate action across Canada to address this problem. The statement was developed to create a common understanding of the definition, causes, outcomes, and consequences of SBS and to encourage effective strategies to prevent SBS (PHAC, 2011b).

Brain Development

At birth, the newborn's brain is about 25 percent of its adult weight. By the second birthday, the brain is about 75 percent of its adult weight. However, areas of the brain do not mature uniformly. Some areas, such as the primary motor areas, develop earlier than others, such as the primary sensory areas.

It is amazing that the infant began life as a single cell and nine months later is born with a brain and nervous system that contain approximately 100 billion nerve cells, or neurons. A **neuron** is a nerve cell that handles information processing at the cellular level. Among the most dramatic changes in the brain in the first two years of life are the spreading connections of dendrites. Figure 5.2 illustrates these changes.

Figure 5.2
The Development of Dendritic Spreading

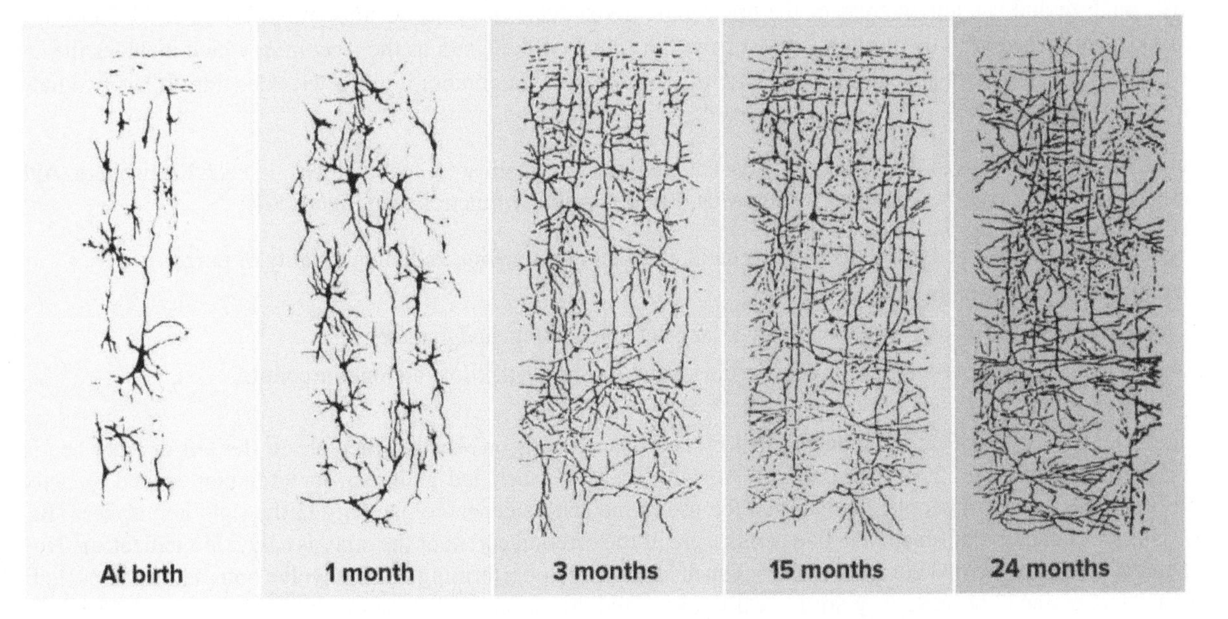

From *The Postnatal Development of the Human Cerebral Cortex*, Vol. I-VIII by Jesse LeRoy Conel, Cambridge, MA: Harvard University Press, Copyright © 1939-1975 by the President and Fellows of Harvard College. Reprinted with permission from Kolb, Bryan. *Development of the Child's Brain and Behavior*. Copyright 1997 © Springer Science+Business Media.

Note the increase in connectedness between neurons over the course of the first two years of life.

A neuron is made of several parts: the cell body, many dendrites, and an axon. The dendrites are short fibres that extend from the cell body and receive information from other neurons and carry it into the cell body. The neuron's axon carries the message (an electrical signal) from the cell body to the point where it is passed to the next neuron. This point is at the end of the axon, which splits into multiple finger-like filaments that end with a structure called the terminal button. Here the electrical signal triggers the release of one or more of the many neurotransmitters (chemical substances, such as serotonin) that cross a very small gap (called the synaptic gap) between the terminal button on the axon to a dendrite of another neuron. When the neurotransmitter bonds with the next dendrite, it serves to trigger that neuron.

A myelin sheath, which is a layer of fat cells, encases most axons. Not only does the myelin sheath insulate nerve cells, it also helps nerve impulses travel faster (Silk & Wood, 2011). Myelination, the process of encasing axons with fat cells, begins prenatally and continues after birth. Myelination for visual pathways occurs rapidly after birth and is completed in the first six months. Auditory myelination is not completed until 4 or 5 years of age. Some aspects of myelination continue even into adolescence (Fair & Schlaggar, 2008). However, during infancy, dendrite formation, synapse production, and myelination are most prominent (Hadders-Algra, 2011).

The connections that are used become strengthened and survive, while the unused ones are replaced by other pathways or disappear. In the language of neuroscience, these connections will be "pruned" (Giedd, 2008). For example, the more babies engage in physical activity or use language, the more those pathways will be strengthened.

The notion of the development of new neurons in the brains of mammals has received considerable research attention, and related investigations are ongoing. Baringa (2003) claims that certain brain regions are at least replenished with the development of new neurons. Researchers are not certain, however, what exactly is the contribution of these "newcomer" neurons and what they contribute to the behaviours controlled by certain brain regions, such as singing, smelling, and learning. Some of the most persuasive research has been conducted on songbirds. It has been posited that newly generated neurons have been found in the high vocal centre (HVC) of canaries, a brain area that helps produce their characteristic song. For example, during breeding season, male canaries seem to learn new song elements believed to be due to the HVC enlargement caused by the addition of new neurons (Baringa, 2003). Based on this rather interesting evidence regarding songbirds, what assumptions can you hypothesize regarding these findings to the behaviour of infants that just might be caused by the development of new neurons in the infant's brain?

MAPPING THE BRAIN

Scientists analyze and categorize areas of the brain in numerous ways (Fischer & Immordino-Yang, 2008; Nelson, 2011). We are most concerned with the portion farthest from the spinal cord, known as the *forebrain*, which includes the cerebral cortex and several structures beneath it. The *cerebral cortex* covers the forebrain like a wrinkled cap. It has two halves, or hemispheres (see Figure 5.3).

Based on ridges and valleys in the cortex, scientists distinguish four main areas, called lobes, in each hemisphere. Although the lobes usually work together, each has a somewhat different primary function (see Figure 5.4):

- Frontal lobes are involved in voluntary movement, thinking, personality, and intentionality or purpose.
- Occipital lobes function in vision.
- Temporal lobes have an active role in hearing, language processing, and memory.
- Parietal lobes play important roles in registering spatial location, attention, and motor control.

To some extent, the type of information handled by neurons depends on whether they are in the left or right hemisphere of the cortex (Bianco et al., 2008; Spironelli & Angrilli, 2008). Speech and grammar, for example, depend on activity in the left hemisphere in most people; humour and the use of metaphors depend on activity in the right hemisphere (Banasik, 2013). This specialization of function in one hemisphere of the cerebral cortex or the other is called **lateralization**. However, most neuroscientists agree that complex functions such as reading or performing music involve both hemispheres. Labelling people as "left-brained" because they are logical thinkers and "right-brained" because they are creative thinkers does not correspond to the way the brain's hemispheres work. Complex thinking in normal people is the outcome of communication between both hemispheres of the brain (Liégeois et al., 2008).

At birth, the hemispheres of the cerebral cortex already have started to specialize: newborns show greater electrical brain activity in the left hemisphere than the right hemisphere when they are listening to speech sounds (Hahn, 1987). How are the areas of the brain different in the newborn and the infant from those in an adult, and why do the differences matter? Important differences have been documented at both the cellular and the structural level.

Figure 5.3
The Human Brain's Hemispheres

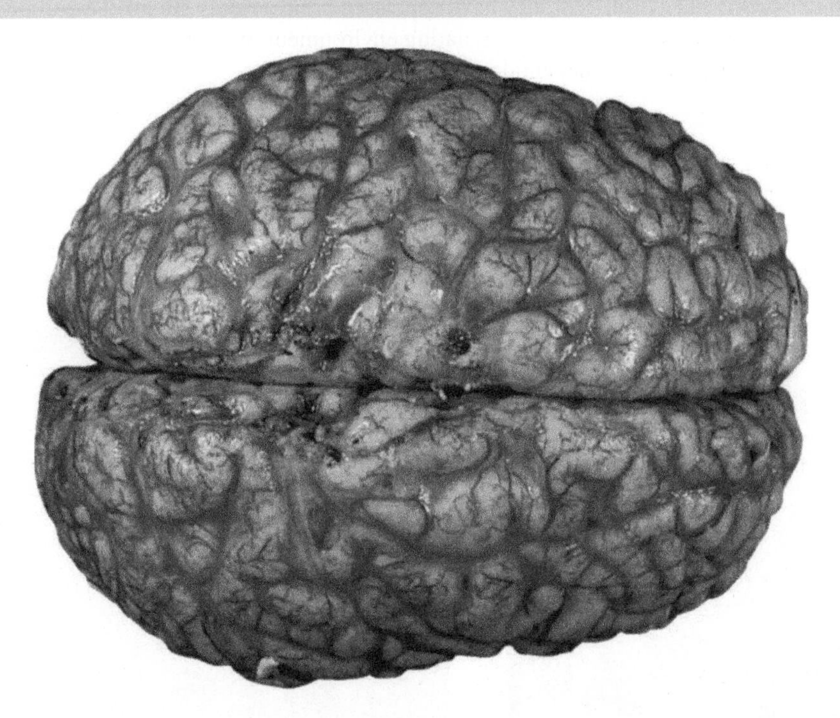

The two hemispheres of the human brain are clearly seen in this photograph. It is a myth that the left hemisphere is the exclusive location of language and logical thinking or that the right hemisphere is the exclusive location of emotion and creative thinking.

Figure 5.4
The Brain's Four Lobes

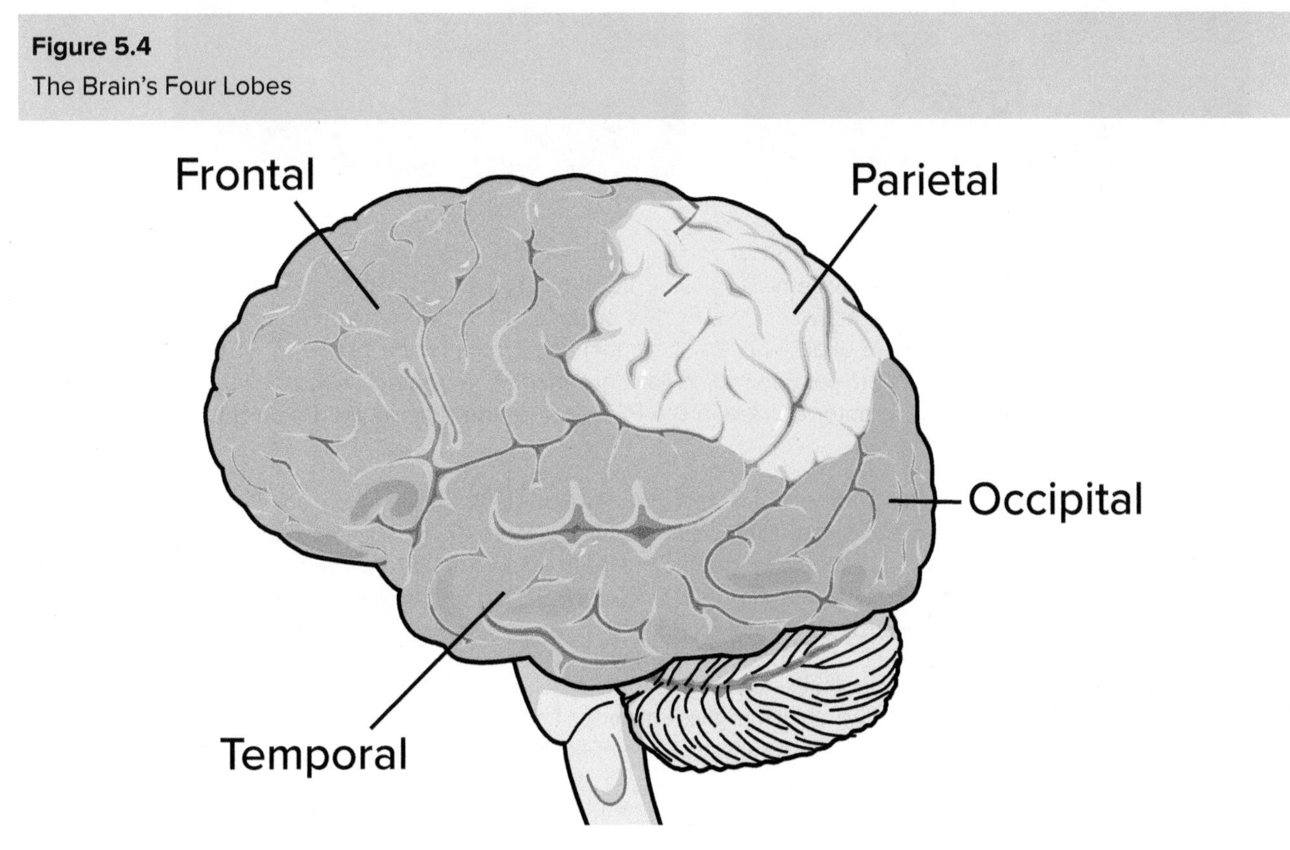

Shown here are the locations of the brain's four lobes: frontal, occipital, temporal, and parietal.

Early Experience and the Brain

Children who grow up in a deprived environment may have depressed brain activity (Reeb et al., 2008). As shown in Figure 5.5, a child who grew up in the unresponsive and unstimulating environment of a Romanian orphanage shows considerably depressed brain activity compared with a normal child.

Figure 5.5

Early Deprivation and Brain Activity

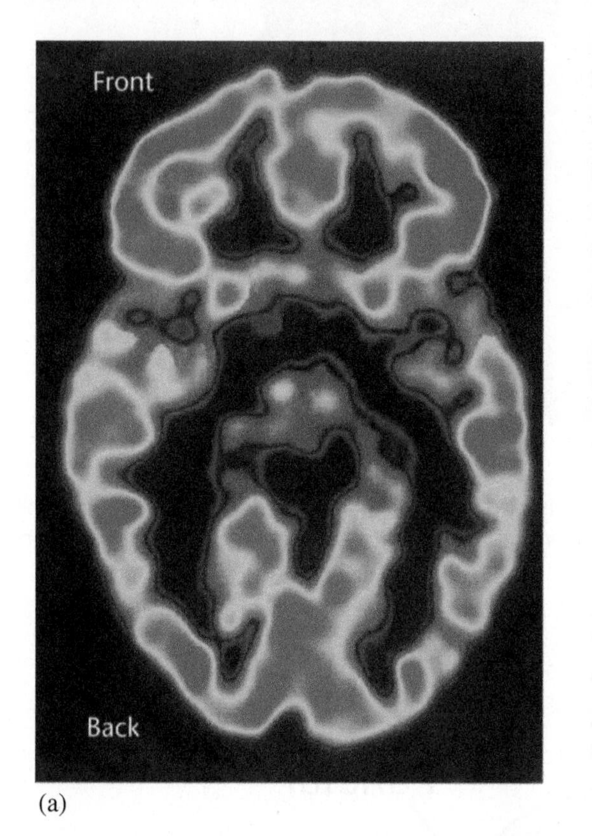

(a)

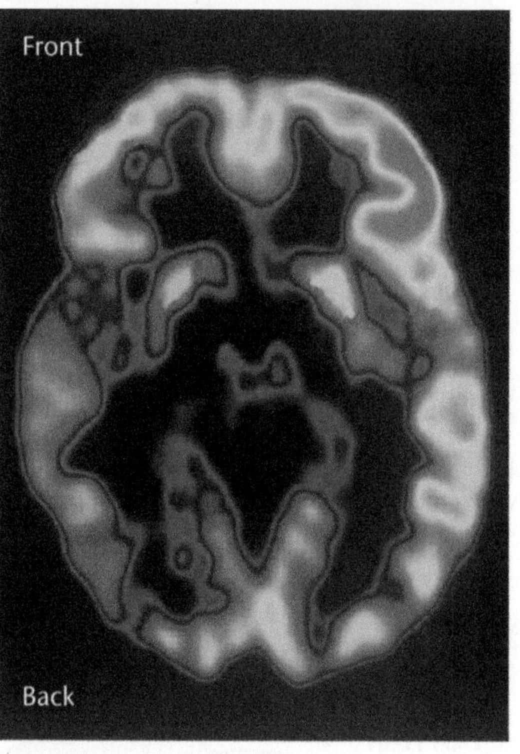

(b)

Courtesy of Dr. Harry T. Chugani, Children's Hospital of Michigan

These two photographs are PET (positron emission tomography) scans (which use radioactive tracers to image and analyze blood flow and metabolic activity in the body's organs) of the brains of (a) a normal child, and (b) an institutionalized Romanian orphan who experienced substantial deprivation since birth. In PET scans, the highest to lowest brain activity is reflected in the colours red, yellow, green, blue, and black, respectively. As can be seen, red and yellow show up to a much greater degree in the PET scan of the normal child than that of the deprived Romanian orphan.

Are the effects of deprived environments irreversible? There is reason to think the answer is no. The brain demonstrates both flexibility and resilience. Consider 14-year-old Michael Rehbein. At age 7, he began to experience uncontrollable seizures—as many as 400 a day. Doctors said the only solution was to remove the left hemisphere of his brain where the seizures were occurring. Recovery was slow, but his right hemisphere began to reorganize and take over functions that normally occur in the brain's left hemisphere, including speech.

Neuroscientists believe that what wires the brain—or rewires it, in the case of Michael Rehbein—is repeated experience. Each time a baby tries to touch an attractive object or gazes intently at a face, tiny bursts of electricity shoot through the brain, knitting together neurons into circuits. The results are some of the behavioural milestones we discuss in this chapter.

In sum, the infant's brain depends on experiences to determine how connections are made. Before birth, it appears that genes mainly direct basic wiring patterns. Neurons grow and travel to distant places awaiting further instructions (Sheridan & Nelson, 2008). After birth, the inflowing stream of sights, sounds, smells, touches, language, and eye contact help shape the brain's neural connections (Nelson, 2011).

Researchers evaluated interventions for 3- to 6-month-old infants at high biological risk of developmental disorders (Hadders-Algra, 2011). Results indicated in particular that the coaching received by parents was associated with improved developmental outcomes at the age of 18 months (Hadders-Algra, 2011). The researchers defined coaching as professional guidance aiming to empower caregivers so parents and caregivers make their own choices during daily care activities.

Sleep

As a means of supporting their rapid growth and development, sleep is as vital to infants as good nutrition. Here, we look at sleep patterns of newborns and infants, different sleeping arrangements, and risk factors for sudden infant death syndrome.

Sleep Patterns and Arrangements

When we were infants, sleep consumed more of our time than it does now (Sadeh, 2008; Taveras et al., 2008). Newborns sleep 16 to 17 hours a day, although some sleep more and others less. The range is from a low of about 10 hours to a high of about 21 hours. Infants' sleep during the day does not always follow a rhythmic pattern. An infant might change from sleeping several long bouts of seven or eight hours to three or four shorter sessions only a few hours in duration. Researchers reported a twofold higher prevalence of obesity among infants and toddlers who slept less than 12 hours per day, compared with those who slept more. These researchers observed a distinct dose response relationship between reduced sleep duration and obesity (Taveras et al., 2008).

Figure 5.6
Sleep across the Human Life Span

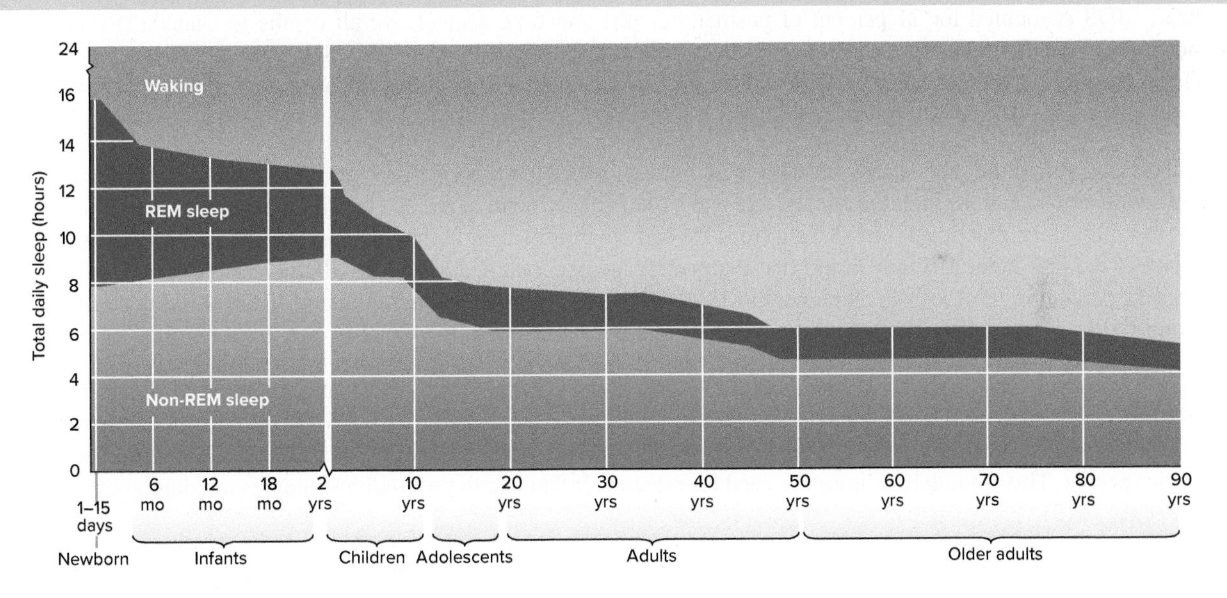

Reprinted with permission from H.P. Roffwarg, J.N. Muzio and W.C. Dement, 1966, "Ontogenetic Development of the Human Dream Sleep Cycle," *Science*, Vol. 152, no. 3722, pp. 604-609. Copyright © 1966, American Association for the Advancement of Science.

Considerable variation exists across cultures in newborns' sleeping arrangements (Burns, 2008). For example, sharing a bed with a mother is a common practice in many cultures, such as Guatemala and China, whereas in others, such as Canada and Great Britain, newborns sleep in a crib, either in the same room as the parents or in a separate room. In some cultures, infants sleep with the mother until they are weaned, after which they sleep with siblings until middle and late childhood (Sobralske & Gruber, 2009).

Cultural variations exist in infant sleeping patterns. Mindell and colleagues (2010) examined cross-cultural sleep patterns and sleep problems in a large sample of children from birth to 36 months of age in countries with predominantly Asian and Caucasian cultures. This study concluded that, overall, children from predominantly Asian countries have significantly shorter total sleep times, later bedtimes, and high parentally-perceived sleep problems. Asian children are also more likely to room-share than are children from predominantly Caucasian countries/ regions. These researchers report substantial differences in sleep patterns among young children across culturally diverse countries/regions. Further research will seek to understand the bases for, and impact of, these interesting differences.

Researchers are intrigued by the various forms of infant sleep. They are especially interested in **REM (rapid eye movement) sleep**, a recurring sleep stage during which vivid dreams commonly occur. Most adults spend about one-fifth of their night in REM sleep, and REM sleep usually appears about one hour after non-REM sleep. However, about one-half of an infant's sleep is REM sleep, and infants often begin their sleep cycle with REM sleep, rather than non-REM sleep. By the time infants reach 3 months of age, the percentage of time they spend in REM sleep falls to about 40 percent, and their sleep cycle no longer begins with REM sleep. The large amount of REM sleep may provide infants with added self-stimulation since they spend less time awake than do older children, and might also promote the brain's development (Graver, 2006). Figure 5.6 illustrates the amount of time spent in REM sleep across the human life span.

Some child experts believe there are benefits to shared sleeping, such as promoting breastfeeding, responding more quickly to the baby's cries, and detecting breathing pauses in the baby that might be dangerous. In a review prepared for the Public Health Agency of Canada, Wendy Trifunov (2009) noted that no studies of bed sharing in Canada had appeared in the academic literature. In Canada and the United States, there is great concern over the relationship between bed sharing and the incidence of sudden infant death syndrome (discussed below) (Ruys et al., 2007). Furthermore, shared sleeping is likely to place the infant at greater risk if the caregivers are impaired by alcohol, smoking, or tend to be overtired (Ostfield et al., 2010).

SIDS

In Canada, infant mortality rates due to of **sudden infant death syndrome (SIDS)** have fallen in recent decades. SIDS is defined as the sudden death of an infant less than one year of age, without apparent cause (PHAC, 2014). Between 2003 and 2007, SIDS accounted for 21 percent of postnatal deaths and 6 percent of overall deaths in Canada (PHAC, 2008). The incidence of SIDS among First Nations and Inuit populations is significantly higher than among non-Aboriginal groups (McShane, Smylie, & Adomako, 2009). Risk factors for SIDS include sleeping prone (on the abdomen), maternal smoking during pregnancy, and the lack of breastfeeding (PHAC, 2011).

Researchers also found that bed sharing is associated with an increased risk of SIDS, and that the risk is higher for infants of parents who smoke and for infants less than 12 weeks old (Vennermann et al., 2011). Trifunov (2009) notes that it is very difficult to separate the practice of bed sharing from the bed environment and other factors that might contribute to SIDS. In her review of the literature, Trifunov found that the percentage of infant deaths due to SIDS while sleeping "with a parent rose from 12 percent in the 1980s to 50 percent in 1999–2003" (p. 7). In addition, the rate of SIDS while in a crib has been cut by one-sixth, as opposed to SIDS deaths while sharing a bed with a parent, which has only been halved.

Canadian researchers investigated differences and time trends in neonatal, postnatal, and SIDS mortality across neighbourhood income quintiles related to live births in Canada from 1991 to 2005. They concluded that despite a decrease in both infant mortality and SIDS across all neighbourhood income quintiles over time in Canada, socio-economic inequalities persist. This finding highlights the need for effective infant health promotion strategies in vulnerable populations (Gilbert et al., 2013).

There is no definitive way to predict which infants will become victims of SIDS. However, researchers have found the following:

- Low-birth-weight infants are more at risk to die of SIDS than are their normal-weight counterparts (Blair et al., 2006).
- Subsequent siblings of an infant who has died of SIDS have a higher risk of also dying from SIDS (Strehle et al., 2011).
- SIDS is more common in infants who are passively exposed to cigarette smoke (Shea & Steiner, 2008).
- SIDS is more common in lower socio-economic groups (Gilbert et al., 2013).

The Public Health Agency of Canada recognizes SIDS, and other infant deaths, as a major public health concern that occurs during sleep. The *Joint Statement on Safe Sleep: Preventing Sudden Infant Deaths in Canada* (PHAC, 2012) is part of the Canadian government's commitment to raise awareness of sudden infant deaths and sleeping environments. Recommendations include placing infants to sleep on their backs, ensuring the environment is smoke-free, and not placing infants on soft chairs, sofas, waterbeds, or cushions whether sleeping with another person or not (Trifunov, 2009). PHAC, (2014) suggests that firm flat bedding is best for normal healthy infants, with sheets and light blankets as required, and recommends the avoidance of products to maintain the sleeping position.

Since the onset of risk-reduction education the incidence of SIDS has declined, although it remains the leading cause of infant mortality from the age of 1 month to 1 year (Ostfeld et al., 2010).

Health

Infants' physical growth depends on appropriate intake of nutrients. Here we examine their nutritional needs, breastfeeding, and malnutrition.

Nutritional Needs

The importance of adequate energy and nutrient intake consumed in a loving and supportive environment during the infant years cannot be overstated. From birth to 1 year of age, infants' weight triples and their length increases by 50 percent. Individual differences among infants in terms of their nutrient reserves, body composition, growth rates, and activity patterns make defining actual nutrient needs difficult. However, nutritionists recommend that infants consume approximately 242 joules per day for each kilogram they weigh—more than twice an adult's requirement per kilogram. High-calorie, high-energy foods are part of a balanced diet for infants. In addition, parents should know that fat is also very important to an infant's health. It is recommended that children under the age of 2 years should not consume skim milk.

Children in Canada are at risk of vitamin D deficiency. Sunlight stimulates vitamin D production in the skin. Because of the long winters in Canada, there can be little exposure of the skin to the sun. Therefore, the Public Health Agency of Canada (2009) recommends vitamin D supplements, either in the form of fortified infant formula milk or other sources.

Crocker and other Canadian researchers (2011) conducted a survey of breastfeeding mothers of healthy infants to determine whether or not parents and caregivers follow the advice of Health Canada, which urges that all breastfed infants receive a daily supplement of 400 IU of vitamin D. It was found that although 90 percent of infants received breast milk at 2 months of age, the vitamin supplementation rate was only 80 percent. One of the conclusions was that subsequent studies should monitor breastfeeding duration and vitamin D supplementation rates as children get older.

A mother's weight gain during pregnancy and a mother's own high weight before pregnancy may result in the newborn being overweight and staying overweight through infancy (Hockenberry & Wilson, 2015; Wardlaw & Smith, 2009). One likely important factor is whether an infant is breastfed or bottle-fed. Breastfed infants have lower rates of weight gain than bottle-fed infants by school age, and it is estimated that breastfeeding reduces the risk of obesity by approximately 20 percent (Rossiter et al., 2015).

critical thinking

What three pieces of advice about the infant's physical development and health would you want to give a friend who has just had a baby? Why those three? Compare and contrast breastfeeding and bottle-feeding as each applies to the infant's health. How would you explain to a group of mothers how cultural forces and geographic locations, such as rural areas, influence breastfeeding?

Twells and Newhook (2010) conducted a study to examine the prevalence of overweight and obesity in a Canadian preschool population located in eastern Canada and the relationship between exclusive breastfeeding and preschool obesity. Their results indicated that exclusive breastfeeding appears to be a protective factor for obesity in preschoolers.

Crucial to the proper intake of nutrients is oral health. One issue is how soon children should be seen by a dentist. While many parents are told 3 years is the ideal earliest age, University of Toronto's Dr. Lynn Poranganel and her colleagues' answer is "within six months of the eruption of the first teeth and no later than 1 year of age" (Poranganel, Titley, & Kulkarni, 2006, p. 11). These researchers have developed a video to help parents and expectant parents anticipate and handle their baby's oral health. You can find out more on Connect at www.mcgrawhillconnect.ca.

Breastfeeding

For years, debate has focused on the benefits of breastfeeding versus those of bottle-feeding. The growing consensus is that breastfeeding is better for the baby's health (Wheeler, 2015) and the mother's health. The Public Health Agency of Canada (2014) recommends that women breastfeed their babies for the first six months of life as breast milk is the best food for optimal growth of the infant. Breastfeeding has been associated with improved health outcomes for mother and infant. If possible, breastfeeding (along with the introduction of solid foods) is recommended to continue through age 2 years and beyond (Health Canada, 2015).

Breastfeeding results in benefits in many areas during the first two years of life and later:

- *Gastrointestinal infections:* Breastfed infants have fewer gastrointestinal infections (Newburg & Walker, 2007).
- *Lower respiratory tract infections:* Breastfed infants have fewer lower respiratory tract infections (Yamakawa et al., 2015).
- *Asthma:* A research review by the American Academy of Pediatrics concluded that exclusive breastfeeding for three months protects against wheezing in babies, but whether it prevents asthma in older children is unclear (Greer et al., 2008).
- *Otitis media:* Breastfed infants are less likely to develop this middle ear infection (Bowatte et al., 2015).
- *Atopic dermatitis:* Breastfed babies are less likely to have this chronic inflammation of the skin (Snijders et al., 2007). A research review by the American Academy of Pediatrics also concluded that for infants with a family history of allergies, breastfeeding exclusively for at least four months is linked to a lower risk of skin rashes (Greer et al., 2008).
- *Overweight and obesity:* Consistent evidence indicates that breastfed infants are less likely to become overweight or obese in childhood, adolescence, and adulthood (Moschonis, Grammatikaki, & Manios, 2008).
- *Diabetes:* Breastfed infants are less likely to develop Type 1 diabetes in childhood (Ping & Hagopian, 2006) and Type 2 diabetes in adulthood (Villegas et al., 2008).
- *SIDS:* Breastfed infants are less likely to experience SIDS (Alm, Lagercrantz, & Wennergren, 2006).

In 2011–2012, 89 percent of mothers in Canada breastfed their babies. This rate reflects a slight increase from 85 percent in 2003. During the same years, more mothers who were breastfeeding exclusively for six months (or more) tended to be in their thirties or older, and to have post-secondary education. Furthermore, in 2011–2012, the most common reasons cited for stopping breastfeeding before six months were "not enough breast milk" and "difficulty with breastfeeding technique" (Gionet, 2015).

A mother's decision to breastfeed, and her ability to do so, can be a complex personal decision influenced by families and social factors. A supportive household and social environment, as well as policy-based interventions, can contribute to sustained breastfeeding (Rossiter et al., 2015). Mothers who are encouraged to breastfeed within minutes of giving birth and those who receive information and guidance about breastfeeding maintain breastfeeding longer than mothers who wait several hours to breastfeed or who receive little or no support (Kramer et al., 2008). As for mothers who return to work in the infant's first year of life, they can extract breast milk by using a breast pump, and store the milk for later use.

Benefits of breastfeeding for the mother are observed in the following areas:

- *Breast cancer:* Consistent evidence indicates a lower incidence of breast cancer in women who breastfeed their infants (Shema et al., 2007).
- *Ovarian cancer:* Evidence also reveals a reduction in ovarian cancer in women who breastfeed their infants (Jordan et al., 2008).
- *Type 2 diabetes:* Some evidence suggests a small reduction in Type 2 diabetes in women who breastfeed their infants (Ip et al., 2007).

Are there circumstances when mothers should not breastfeed? A mother should not breastfeed (1) if she is infected with HIV or some other infectious disease that can be transmitted through her milk, (2) if she has active tuberculosis, or (3) if she is taking any drug that may not be safe for the infant (Dube et al., 2008).

Some women cannot breastfeed their infants because of physical difficulties; others feel guilty if they terminate breastfeeding early. Mothers may also worry that they are depriving their infants of important emotional and psychological benefits if they bottle-feed rather than breastfeed. For women who cannot or choose not to breastfeed, Health Canada (2012b) recommends using powdered infant formula (PIF). They caution that proper preparation, handling, and storage is necessary to avoid contamination with harmful bacteria (such as *Enterobacter sakazakii* and *Salmonella enterica*). For pre-term, low-birth-weight, or infants with compromised immune systems, they advise consultation with a physician, who will likely recommend using commercially-produced liquid infant formulas.

In either breastfeeding or infant formula use, the Public Health Agency of Canada (2012) suggests starting to introduce solid foods at 6 months of age. Foods should be introduced one at a time for a week or so to test the infant's response, looking for any allergenic response. Foods rich in iron should be introduced first (single grains or iron-fortified infant cereal), followed by meats and well-cooked legumes. Salt, sugar, and spices should be avoided. By 1 year of age, the infant should be consuming a variety of foods based on *Eating Well with Canada's Food Guide* (Health Canada, 2007a).

Malnutrition in Infancy

Malnutrition can result in serious health problems in infants. Two of these problems are marasmus and kwashiorkor. **Marasmus** is a wasting away of body tissues in the infant's first year, caused by severe protein-calorie deficiency. The infant becomes grossly underweight, and the muscles atrophy. **Kwashiorkor** is a condition caused by a deficiency in protein, in which the child's abdomen and feet swell with water. This disease usually appears between 1 and 3 years of age. Kwashiorkor sometimes makes children appear well-fed, even though they are not. It causes a child's vital organs to collect the nutrients that are present and deprive other parts of the body of them. The child's hair becomes thin, brittle, and colourless, and the child's behaviour often becomes listless. The main cause of marasmus and kwashiorkor is early weaning from breast milk to inadequate nutrients, such as unsuitable and unsanitary cow's milk formula.

Growth failure, or *failure to thrive* (FTT), is a sign of inadequate growth resulting from the inability to obtain or use the calories required for proper growth. FTT has no universal definition. One criterion that has been used, however, considers weight and sometimes height that falls below the fifth percentile for the child's age (Hockenberry & Wilson, 2013). At the Hospital for Sick Children (Sick Kids) in Toronto, several special-interest clinics form part of the Paediatric Consultation Clinic (PCC). One such clinic is the Infant and Toddler Growth and Feeding Program (for children under 3 years showing failure to thrive). Dr. Emma Cory is a director of the PCC. One of Dr. Cory's clinical interests includes failure to thrive in infants and toddlers (Sick Kids, 2012).

As a final note for this section, it is important to keep in mind that nutrition is not the only factor for infants' growth. Other environmental factors such as a safe environment and immunization are also important.

To this point, we have studied a number of ideas about infants' physical development and health. For a review, see the Reach Your Learning Outcomes section at the end of this chapter.

Motor, Sensory, and Perceptual Development

LO2 Examine infant motor development and summarize the course of sensory and perceptual development in infancy.

- **Motor Development**
- **Sensory and Perceptual Development**

Along with the development of the brain, infants also experience rapid progress in their motor, sensory, and perceptual skills. In this section, we explore these advances.

Motor Development

As a newborn, Ramona could suck, fling her arms, and tightly grip a finger placed in her tiny hand. Within just two years, she is toddling around on her own, opening doors and jars as she explores her little world. Are her accomplishments inevitable? How do infants develop their motor skills, and which skills do they develop when?

Dynamic Systems Theory

According to **dynamic systems theory**, infants assemble motor skills for perceiving and acting (Smith & Breazeal, 2007; Thelen & Smith, 2006). In this theory, "assembly" means the coordination or convergence of a number of factors, such as the development of the nervous system, the body's physical properties and movement possibilities, the goal the infant is motivated to reach, and the environmental support for the skill. This theory also emphasizes that perception and action work together in the infant's mastery of a skill. In their development of motor skills, infants must perceive something in their environment that motivates them to act and to use their perceptions to fine-tune their movements. Clearfield and colleagues (2008) claim that many studies show that the transition from crawling to independent walking changes the way in which infants experience the environment to the point that infants must learn skills as walkers in a similar manner to those skills mastered as crawlers.

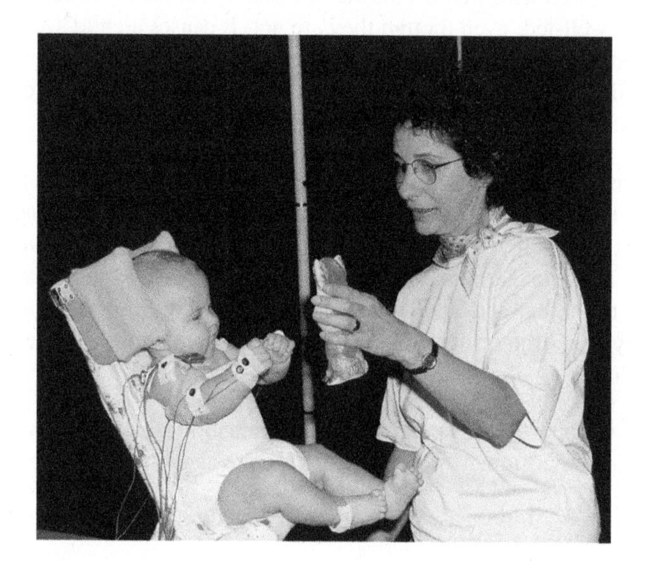

Courtesy of Esther Thelen

Esther Thelen is shown conducting an experiment to discover how infants learn to control their arms to reach and grasp for objects. A computer device monitors the infant's arm movements and tracks muscle patterns. Thelen's research is conducted from a dynamic systems perspective. *What is the nature of this perspective?*

The dynamic systems view contrasts with the traditional maturational view by proposing that even the universal milestones, such as crawling, reaching, and walking, are learned through a process of adaptation (Adolph & Joh, 2008). It emphasizes exploration and selection in finding solutions to new task demands. In other words, infants modify their movement patterns to fit a new task by using social information, and by exploring and selecting possible configurations (Adolph, Karasik, & Tamis-LeMonda, 2010; Karasik, Tamis-LeMonda, & Adolph, 2011). The assumption is that the infant is motivated by a new challenge—desire to get a new toy into his or her mouth, or to cross the room to join other family members. In fact, an infant's locomotor status might actually have profound implications for maternal responsiveness (Karasik, Tamis-LeMonda, & Adolph, 2014). It is the new task—the challenge of the context, not a genetic program—that represents the driving force for change. Karasik and colleagues (2015) examined infants and their mothers from six cultural groups in regards to sitting proficiency. They concluded that naturalistic contexts of everyday life actually determine the opportunities infants have to practise specific motor skills, which in turn have implications for the emergence and proficiency of infants' skills.

Reflexes

The newborn is not completely helpless. Among other things, it has some basic reflexes, which are genetically carried survival mechanisms. For example, the newborn has no fear of water, naturally holding its breath and contracting its throat to keep water out. Reflexes can serve as important building blocks for subsequent purposeful motor activity.

Reflexes are built-in reactions to stimuli; they govern the newborn's movements, which are automatic and beyond the newborn's control. The **sucking reflex** occurs when the newborn automatically sucks an object placed in its mouth. The sucking reflex enables the newborn to get nourishment before it has associated a nipple with food. The **rooting reflex** occurs when the infant's cheek is stroked or the side of the mouth is touched. In response, the infant turns its head toward the side that was touched in an apparent effort to find something to suck. The sucking and rooting reflexes disappear when the infant is 3 to 4 months old. They are replaced by the infant's voluntary eating. The sucking and rooting reflexes have survival value for newborn mammals, which must find the mother's breast to obtain nourishment. The **Moro reflex** is a neonatal startle response that occurs in response to a sudden, intense noise or movement. When startled, the newborn arches its back, throws back its head, and flings out its arms and legs. Then, the newborn rapidly draws its arms and legs close to the centre of its body.

Some reflexes present in the newborn—coughing, blinking, and yawning, for example—persist throughout life. Other reflexes disappear or eventually become incorporated into complex, voluntary actions. One example is the **grasping reflex**, which occurs when something touches the infant's palm; the infant responds by grasping tightly. By the end of the third month, the grasping reflex diminishes, and the infant shows a voluntary grasp, which is often produced by visual stimuli (Hockenberry & Wilson, 2013).

Figure 5.7 provides an overview of some of the main reflexes.

Figure 5.7
Infant Reflexes

Reflex	Stimulation	Infant's Response	Developmental Pattern
Babinski	Sole of foot stroked	Fans out toes, twists foot in	Disappears after 9 months to 1 year
Blinking	Flash of light, puff of air	Closes both eyes	Permanent
Grasping	Palms touched	Grasps tightly	Weakens after 2 months, disappears after 1 year
Moro (startle)	Sudden stimulation, such as hearing loud noise or being dropped	Startles, arches back, throws head back, flings out arms and legs and then rapidly closes them to centre of body	Disappears after 3 to 4 months
Rooting	Cheek stroked or side of mouth touched	Turns head, opens mouth, begins sucking	Disappears after 3 to 4 months
Stepping	Infant held above surface and feet lowered to touch surface	Moves feet as if to walk	Disappears after 3 to 4 months
Sucking	Object touching mouth	Sucks automatically	Disappears after 3 to 4 months
Swimming	Infant put face down in water	Makes coordinated swimming movements	Disappears after 6 to 7 months
Tonic neck	Infant placed on back	Forms fists with both hands and usually turns head to the right (sometimes called the "fencer's pose" because the infant looks like it is assuming a fencer's position)	Disappears after 2 months

Gross Motor Skills

Gross motor skills involve large muscle activities, such as moving one's arms and walking. New motor skills are the most dramatic and observable changes in the infant's first year. These motor progressions transform babies from being unable even to lift their heads, to being able to grab things off the grocery store shelf, to chase the cat, and to participate actively in the family's social life. How do gross motor skills develop? As a foundation, these skills require postural control. Posture is more than just holding still and straight. Posture is a dynamic process that is linked with sensory information in the skin, joints, and muscles, which tell us where we are in space; in vestibular organs in the inner ear that regulate balance and equilibrium; and in vision and hearing (Thelen & Smith, 2006).

A summary of the accomplishments in gross motor skills is shown in Figure 5.8. The actual month at which the milestones occur varies, especially among older infants. What remains fairly uniform, however, is the sequence of accomplishments. An important implication of these motor accomplishments is the increasing degree of independence they bring.

Figure 5.8
Milestones in Gross Motor Development

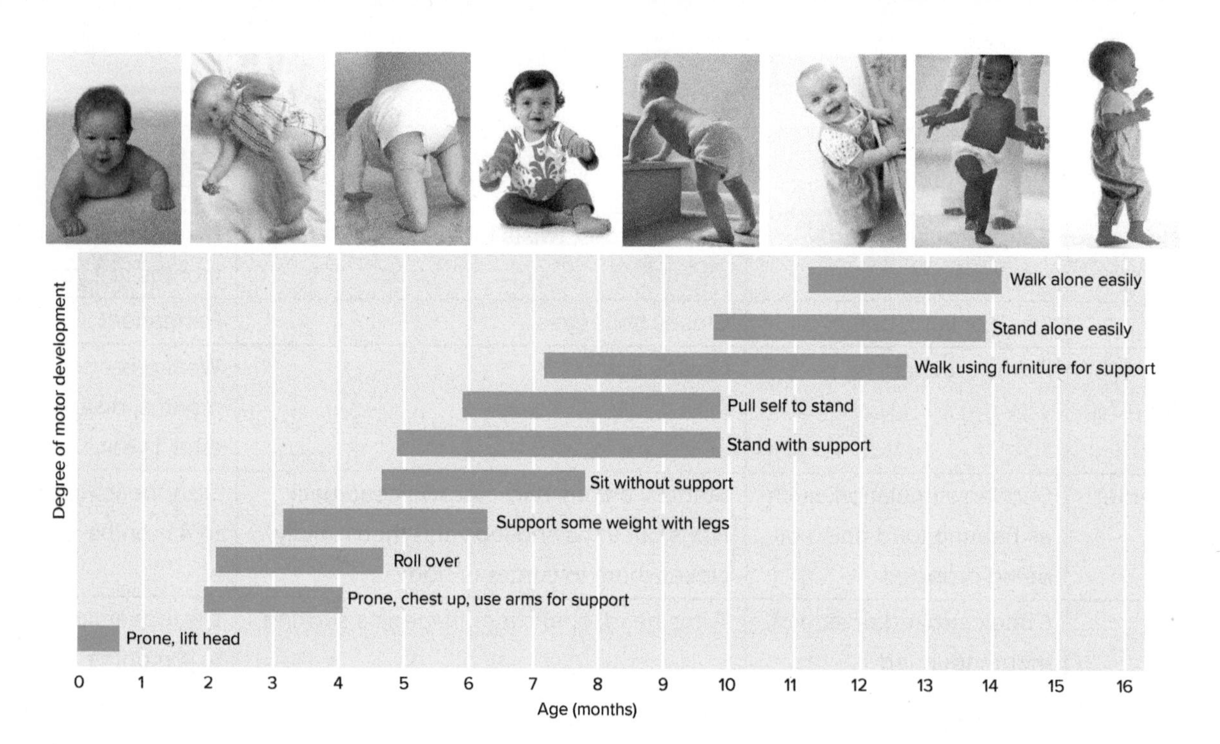

Reprinted from *Journal of Pediatric*, Vo. 71W.K. Frankenburg and J.B. Dobbs, "The Denver Develoment Screening Test," pp. 181-191. Copyright ©1967 with permission from Elsevier. Photos l to r: (left to right) © Barbara Penoyar/Getty Images; © Digital Vision/Getty Images; © Image Source/Alamy; Titus/Getty Images; © Digital Vision; Banana Stock/PictureQuest; Corbis/PictureQuest; © BrandXPictures/PunchStock

critical thinking

Many parents worry that their infants are behind other babies when it comes to motor performance. On the basis of what you have learned in the milestone charts in this section, how would you respond to their concern? A mother informs you that she would like to take her infant, Robbie, to exercise class with her. She wants to involve Robbie in some stretches and movement to accelerate his physical growth. How would you respond to the mother? Differentiate between the palmer grasp and the pincer grasp.

If infants can produce forward-stepping movements so early in their first year of life, why does it take them so long to learn to walk? The key skills in learning to walk appear to be stabilizing balance on one leg long enough to swing the other forward and shifting the weight without falling. This is a difficult biomechanical problem to solve, and it takes infants about a year to do it.

After their first birthday, toddlers become more motorically skilled and mobile. By 13 to 18 months, toddlers can pull a toy attached to a string, use their hands and legs to climb up a number of steps, and ride four-wheel wagons. By 18 to 24 months, toddlers can walk quickly or run stiffly for a short distance, walk backward without losing their balance, stand and throw a ball, and jump in place.

With the increased interest in fitness today, some parents have tried to give their infants a head start on becoming physically fit and physically talented. However, it may not be good to give structured exercise classes for babies. When an adult is stretching and moving an infant's limbs, it is easy to go beyond the infant's physical limits without realizing it.

It is interesting to note the functional outcomes in children regarding motor development, especially those who are born prematurely (Kelly, 2012). Miller and colleagues (2009) found that small-for-gestational age (SGA), medical pre-term, and neurological pre-term groups showed significantly lower motor scores on the Bruininks-Oseretsky Test of Motor Proficiency compared to full-term newborns. That is, motor scores for premature children are lower than those born at-term. This finding is especially significant as Canadian researchers have found that pre-term birth rates between 32 and 36 weeks of gestation are significantly higher in Canada when compared to similar scores from other countries such as England, Wales, and Northern Ireland. This upward temporal trend could be due to changes in obstetrical practice such as the recent increases in Caesarean sections (Lisonkova et al., 2012).

Fine Motor Skills

Fine motor skills involve more finely tuned movements, such as finger dexterity. Infants have hardly any control over fine motor skills at birth, although they have many components of what later become finely coordinated arm, hand, and finger movements. The onset of reaching and grasping marks a significant achievement in infants' functional interaction with their surroundings (van Hof et al., 2008).

Although infants usually learn to walk around the time of their first birthday, the neural pathways that control the leg alteration component of walking are in place from a very early age, possibly even at birth or before. The clue for this belief is that when 1- to 2-month-olds are given support with their feet in contact with a motorized treadmill, they show well-coordinated, alternating steps.

The development of reaching and grasping becomes more and more refined during the first two years of life. Initially, infants show only crude shoulder and elbow movements; later, they show wrist movements, hand rotation, and coordination of the thumb and forefinger. For example, 4-month-old infants rely greatly on touch to determine how they will grip an object; 8-month-olds are more likely to use vision as a guide (Newell et al., 1989). The maturation of hand–eye coordination is reflected in the improvement of fine motor skills. Figure 5.9 provides an overview of the development of fine motor skills during the first two years.

Figure 5.9
The Development of Fine Motor Skills in Infancy

Birth to 6 Months	Fine Motor Skill
2 months	Holds rattle briefly
2½ months	Glances from one object to another
3–4 months	Plays in simple way with rattle; inspects fingers; reaches for dangling ring; visually follows ball across table
4 months	Carries object to mouth

Birth to 6 Months	Fine Motor Skill
4–5 months	Recovers rattle from chest; holds two objects
5 months	Transfers object from hand to hand
5–6 months	Bangs in play; looks for object while sitting
6 months	Secures cube on sight; follows adult's movements across room; immediately fixates on small objects and stretches out to grasp them; retains rattle
6½ months	Manipulates and examines an object; reaches for, grabs, and retains rattle
7 months	Pulls string to obtain an object
6–12 Months	
7½–8½ months	Grasps with thumb and finger
8–9 months	Persists in reaching for toy out of reach on table; shows hand preference; bangs spoon; searches in correct place for toys dropped within reach of hands; may find toy hidden under cup
10 months	Hits cup with spoon; crude release of object
10½–11 months	Picks up raisin with thumb and forefinger; pincer grasp; pushes car along
11–12 months	Puts three or more objects in a container
12–18 Months	
	Places one 5-cm block on top of another 5-cm block (in imitation); scribbles with a large crayon on large piece of paper
	Turns two to three pages in a large book with cardboard pages while sitting in an adult's lap
	Places three 2.5-cm cube blocks in a 15-cm diameter cup (in imitation)
	Holds a pencil and makes a mark on a sheet of paper
	Builds a four-block tower with 5-cm cube blocks (in imitation)
18–24 Months	
	Draws an arc on piece of unlined paper with a pencil after being shown how
	Turns a doorknob that is within reach, using both hands
	Unscrews a lid put loosely on a small jar after being shown how
	Places large pegs in a pegboard
	Connects and takes apart a pop bead string of five beads
	Zips and unzips a large zipper after being shown how

CONNECTING development to life

The Effect of Maternal Mental Health and Childbearing Context on the Development of Children

© John Carter/Science Source

Lung and colleagues (2010) found that 12 factors, including breastfeeding, a low-income environment, and the mother's mental health, affected children's development at 6 months; but the impact of some factors dissipated with the child's growth. Of all of these factors, maternal education had the most enduring effect on different domains of child development and this effect intensified as the child grew older. Children who grew up in a family with multiple siblings showed a delay in language development at 6 months, and delays in motor and social development were evident at 18 and 36 months. Further, maternal mental health affects children's fine motor development at 6 months. Fortunately, this effect disappeared at 18 months, but influenced children's social development at 36 months. Maternal mental health has frequently been found to be a major risk factor in child development (Tough et al., 2008). The research concludes that changes in maternal conditions, and family and environmental factors, are vital to understand how these early infantile factors affect each other and influence the developmental trajectories of children into early childhood.

Just as infants need to exercise their gross motor skills, they also need to exercise their fine motor skills (Needham, 2008). Especially when they can manage a pincer grip, infants delight in picking up small objects. Many develop the pincer grip and begin to crawl at about the same time, and infants at this time pick up virtually everything in sight, especially on the floor, and put the objects in their mouth. Thus, parents need to be vigilant in regularly monitoring what objects are within the infant's reach (Karasik et al., 2012).

Sensory and Perceptual Development

How does a newborn know that her mother's skin is soft rather than rough? How does a 5-year-old know what colour his hair is? Infants and children "know" these things as a result of information that comes through the senses. Without vision, hearing, touch, taste, and smell, we would be isolated from the world; we would live in dark silence, a tasteless, and colourless void, feelingless void.

Sensation and Perception

All information comes to the infant through the senses. **Sensation** occurs when a stimulus reaches sensory receptors—the eyes, ears, tongue, nostrils, and skin. The sensation of hearing occurs when waves of pulsating air are collected by the outer ear and transmitted through the bones of the inner ear to the auditory nerve. The sensation of vision occurs as rays of light contact the eyes and become focused on the retina. **Perception** is the interpretation of what is sensed. The information about physical events that contacts the ears may be interpreted as musical sounds, for example. The physical energy transmitted to the retina may be interpreted as a particular colour, pattern, or shape.

Visual Perception

Can newborns see? How does visual perception develop in infancy?

ACUITY AND COLOUR

Just how well can infants see? At birth, the nerves and muscles and lens of the eye are still developing. As a result, newborns cannot see small things that are far away. The newborn's vision is estimated to be 20/240 on the well-known Snellen chart used for eye examinations, which means that a newborn can see at 20 feet what a normal adult can see at 240 feet (Aslin & Lathrop, 2008). In other words, an object 20 feet (6 metres) away is only as clear to the newborn as it would be if it were 240 feet (73 metres) away from an adult with normal vision (20/20). By 6 months of age, though, on average the infant's vision is 20/40 (Aslin & Lathrop, 2008). Figure 5.10 shows a computer estimation of what a picture of a face looks like to an infant at different points in development from a distance of about 15 cm.

Figure 5.10

Visual Acuity during the First Months of Life

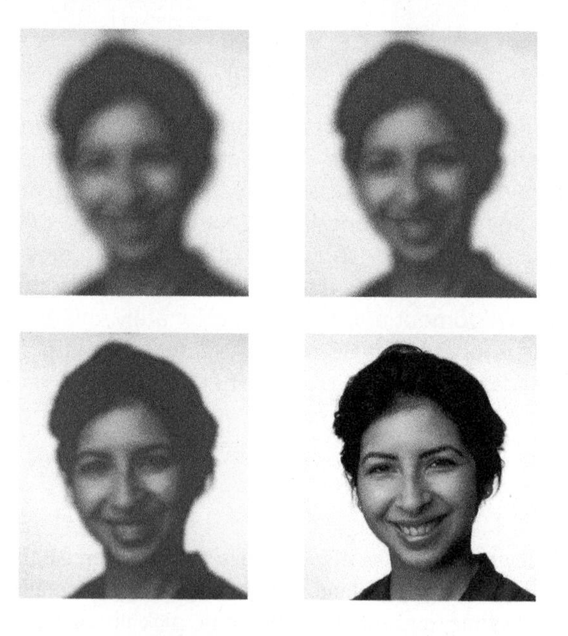

The four photographs represent a computer estimation of what a picture of a face looks like to a 1-month-old, 2-month-old, 3-month-old, and 1-year-old (which approximates that of an adult).

Young infants can perceive certain patterns. With the help of his "looking chamber" (see Figure 5.11), Robert Fantz (1963) revealed that even 2- to 3-week-old infants prefer to look at patterned displays rather than non-patterned displays. For example, they prefer to look at a normal human face rather than one with scrambled features, and prefer to look at a bull's-eye target or black-and-white stripes rather than a plain circle.

Figure 5.11

Fantz's Experiment on Infants' Visual Perception

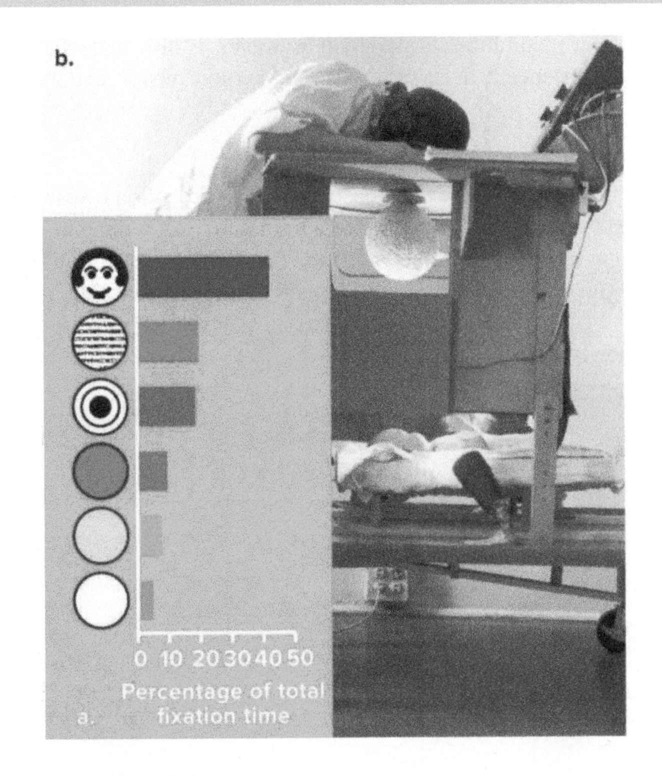

David Linton

(*a*) Infants 2 to 3 weeks old preferred to look at some stimuli more than others. In Fantz's experiment, infants preferred to look at patterns, rather than at colour or brightness. (*b*) Fantz used a "looking chamber" to study infants' perception of stimuli.

According to Lewis and Maurer (2009), visual capabilities continue to improve after early infancy, but the age at which the vision of children is as good as that of adults varies widely with the particular aspect of vision under study. For example, by 6 to 7 years of age, children are as accurate as adults on the measures of acuity, and holistic and featural face processing, but at age 6 children are not as accurate as adults on sensitivity to global form (the ability to integrate individual dots forming a swirl among randomly positioned dots).

Lewis and Maurer (2009) studied children treated for dense cataracts in one or both eyes. The cataracts were so dense that they prevented patterned vision from reaching the retina until the cataracts were removed surgically, replacing the natural lens with a contact lens of a suitable refractive power. It was found in studying the visual outcomes of such children that visual deprivation has different effects on various aspects of vision, and at different times, during development.

The infant's colour vision also improves over time (Kellman & Arterberry, 2006). Both behavioural and electrophysiological experiments indicate that human colour vision appears in a very immature rate at birth. Fortunately, the skill develops quite rapidly over the first few months of life (Teller, Pereverzeva, & Zemach, 2006). It is well established that young infants can make chromatic discriminations (Zemach, Chang, & Teller, 2007). For instance, by 3 months of age, infants can make a variety of chromatic discriminations. This fact suggests that infants possess functional short-, mid-, and long-wavelength sensitive cone systems in the retina and the requisite neural opponent channels within the developing central nervous system (Mercer et al., 2014).

Using a forced choice preferential looking procedure, Canadian researchers tested over 200 infants between 3 and 23 months of age, using pseudoisochromatic targets (colour plates that appear to those with colour-abnormalities to be of a single colour) that fell on either a red/green or a blue/yellow dichromatic fusion axis. They also tested colour-normal and colour-defective adults using the same targets, for comparison. Their observations showed that all babies and adults passed the blue/yellow target, but many of the younger infants failed the red/green target, likely due to the interaction of the lingering immaturities within the visual system. However, older infants (17–23 months), colour-normal adults, and colour-defective adults all performed as would be expected. An interesting observation was that performance on the red/green plate was better among female infants, higher than the expected rate of genetic differences between genders. The researchers concluded that the test used in this study serves as a promising tool for the detection of early colour vision anomalies among young children (Mercer et al., 2014).

In part, these changes in vision reflect maturation. Experience, however, is also necessary for vision to develop normally. For example, one study found that experience is necessary for normal colour vision to develop (Sugita, 2004).

DEPTH PERCEPTION

How early can infants perceive depth? To investigate this question, infant perception researchers Eleanor Gibson and Richard Walk (1960) conducted a classic experiment. They constructed a miniature cliff with a drop-off covered by glass. Then, they placed infants on the edge of a visual cliff and had their mothers coax them to crawl onto the glass (see Figure 5.12). Most infants would not crawl out on the glass, choosing instead to remain on the shallow side, indicating that they could perceive depth. However, because the 6- to 14-month-old infants had extensive visual experience, this research did not answer the question of whether depth perception is innate.

Figure 5.12

Examining Infants' Depth Perception on the Visual Cliff

Eleanor Gibson and Richard Walk (1960) found that most infants would not crawl out on the glass, which indicated that they had depth perception.

What about younger infants? Research with 2- to 4-month-old infants showed differences in heart rate when they were placed directly on the deep side of the visual cliff instead of on the shallow side (Campos, Langer, & Krowitz, 1970). However, an alternative interpretation is that young infants respond to differences in some visual characteristics of the deep and shallow cliffs with no actual knowledge of depth.

VISUAL EXPECTATIONS

Recent evidence suggests that infants can generate expectations about future events from a sample of probabilistic data (Lawson & Rakison, 2013). For example, in a study by Xu and Garcia (2008), 8 month-olds were familiarized to a large box that contained 70 balls of one colour (red) and 5 balls of a different colour (white). The contents of the box were then concealed and an experimenter "randomly" selected a sample of five balls from the population. On some test trials, the sample contained a distribution of balls consistent with the distribution in the population (e.g., four red balls and one white ball), and on other trials, the sample included a distribution that was inconsistent with the population (e.g., four white balls and one red ball). Eight-month-olds looked longer when the inconsistent sample was drawn from the population. Presumably, this event occurred because the sample violated their expectation that the chosen sample would have the same distribution as the population from which it was selected. Interestingly Denison and colleagues (2013) presented similar results with 6-month-old infants.

Lawson and Rakison (2013) conducted three experiments concerning the ability of infants, within the first year of life, to use samples of probabilistic evidence to generate expectations about single future events. These researchers concluded that the ability to generate expectations about future events undergoes development in the first year of life and that these changes may be due to the development of information-processing capacities. Clearly, further investigation is warranted in such an exciting behavioural development.

Hearing

During the last two months of pregnancy, as the fetus nestles in the mother's womb, it can hear sounds such as the mother's voice, music, and so on (Kisilevsky et al., 2004; Saffran, Werker, & Werner, 2006). Two psychologists wanted to find out if a fetus that heard Dr. Seuss's classic story *The Cat in the Hat* while still in the mother's womb would prefer hearing the story after birth (DeCasper & Spence, 1986) (Figure 5.13). During the last months of pregnancy, 16 women read the story to their fetuses. Then shortly after they were born, the mothers read either *The Cat in the Hat* or a story with a different rhyme and pace, *The King, the Mice and the Cheese.* The infants sucked on a nipple in a different way when the mothers read the two stories, suggesting that the infants recognized the pattern and tone of *The Cat in the Hat.* This study illustrates not only that fetuses can hear, but also that we have a remarkable ability to learn even in the mother's womb.

Figure 5.13
Mom Reading to Fetus

A pregnant mom reading to her fetus.

What kinds of changes in hearing take place from infancy on? It seems that these changes involve perceptual changes in the loudness, pitch, and localization of the sound (Saffran, Werker, & Werner, 2006). Newborns can determine the general direction of the source of the sound. By the age of 6 months, however, they are significantly more proficient at localizing sounds, and detecting their origins. The ability to localize sounds continues to improve during the second year (Saffran, Werker, & Werner, 2006).

It is likely that melodic aspects of the mother's speech, perhaps involving signature tunes that are individually distinctive pitch patterns, contribute to the preference of the mother's voice. Bergeson and Trehub (2007) state that signature tunes, and other recurring maternal vocalizations, may together facilitate the infant's ability to process speech. The purpose of a study conducted by Hannon and Trehub (2005) was to demonstrate that 12-month-old infants show an adult-like culture-specific pattern of responding to musical rhythms. This is in contrast to the culture-general responding that is evident at 6 months of age. The researchers found that brief exposures to foreign music enables 12-month-olds, but not adults, to perceive rhythmic distinctions in foreign music contexts (Hannon & Trehub, 2005). These results may possibly indicate a sensitive period early in life for the acquisition of rhythm.

Other Senses

In addition to vision and hearing, the senses of touch and pain, smell, and taste also experience changes in infancy.

Newborns respond readily to touch. This might suggest that touch is the most well-developed sense at that age. A touch to the cheek produces a turning of the head, whereas a touch to the lips produces sucking movements. Increasing documentation suggests that touch and motion are essential to normal growth and development (Hockenberry & Wilson, 2015). Newborns, it seems, can also feel pain (Field & Hernandez-Reif, 2008). Newborns cry in protest when pricked with a needle by a technician drawing blood for a laboratory test. Similar adaptation to the social world occurs for the sense of smell and taste, even though these senses have been studied less extensively.

Newborns are also able to differentiate odours (Doty & Shah, 2008). As babies learn to recognize the smell and handling procedure of each adult, they relax when cradled by that familiar caregiver, and they even close their eyes (Berger, 2011). The newborn has the ability to distinguish among tastes. A tasteless solution elicits no facial expression. On the other hand, a sweet solution elicits an eager suck, a sour solution causes the usual puckering of the lips, and a bitter solution produces an angry expression (Wheeler, 2015).

Intermodal Perception

When mature observers look and listen to an event, they experience a unitary episode. But can very young infants, with little practice at perceiving, put vision and sound together as precisely as adults do?

Intermodal perception is the ability to relate and integrate information from two or more sensory modalities such as vision and hearing (Jeschonedk, Pauen, & Babocsai, 2013; Walker et al., 2010). Early, exploratory forms of intermodal perception exist even in newborns (Bahrick & Hollich, 2008; Sann & Streri, 2007).

For example, Trehub and colleagues (2009), from the University of Toronto, demonstrated that 6- to 8-month-old infants will watch the silent video of a stranger speaking whose voice soundtrack they had previously been exposed to, rather than a stranger whose voice soundtrack they had not heard. Infants' intermodal skills develop quickly from combining single sounds with the features of a familiar face that accompany the sound, to matching spoken statements with the numerous facial features that a stranger's face makes during the production of the sentence.

Perceptual-Motor Coupling

As we come to the end of this section, we return to the important theme of perceptual-motor coupling. Babies continually coordinate their movements with perceptual information to learn how to maintain balance, reach for objects in space, and move across various surfaces and terrains (Adolph & Joh, 2007, 2008; Thelen & Smith, 2006). They are motivated to move by what they perceive. Consider the sight of an attractive toy across the room. In this situation, infants must perceive the current state of their bodies and learn how to use their limbs to reach the toy. Although their movements at first are awkward and uncoordinated, babies soon learn to select patterns that are appropriate for reaching their goals.

Equally important is the other part of the perception-action coupling. That is, action educates perception (Adolph & Joh, 2007, 2008; Smith & Breazeal, 2007; Thelen & Smith, 2006). Only by moving the eyes, heads, hands, and arms, and by moving from one location to another, can individuals fully experience their environment and learn how to adapt to it. Perception and action are coupled (Corbetta & Snapp-Childs, 2009; Adolph & Joh, 2007: 2008; Thelen & Smith, 2006).

To this point, we have discussed a number of ideas about infants' motor, sensory, and perceptual development. For a review, see the Reach Your Learning Outcomes section at the end of this chapter.

Cognitive Development

LO3 Determine how infants learn, remember, and conceptualize.

- **Piaget's Sensorimotor Stage**
- **Information Processing**
- **Infant Intelligence**

Piaget's Sensorimotor Stage

Recall from Chapter 2 that Piaget proposed a theory that emphasized the qualitative changes in cognitive development from infancy to adolescence. Because thinking is qualitatively different in each stage, progression can be seen in stages, with each later one being more advanced in terms of the way people understand the world. For example, an infant may understand an object only by seeing and touching it, while an adolescent can think about the same object in terms of its possible uses in various situations without the object being present.

Piaget introduced the concept of **scheme**, a cognitive structure that helps individuals organize and understand their experiences. Schemes change over time, and the changes involve two processes you learned in Chapter 2: assimilation (incorporating new information into existing knowledge) and accommodation (changing the existing knowledge to fit the new information). Infants assimilate all sorts of objects into their sucking scheme. Over a short time, they learn that some items such as fingers and mother's breast can be sucked, but others such as fuzzy blankets should not be; thus, they accommodate their sucking scheme.

To make sense out of their world, said Piaget, children cognitively organize their experiences. **Organization** in Piaget's theory is the grouping of isolated behaviours and thoughts into a higher-order system. Continual refinement of this organization is an inherent part of development. For example, a girl who has only a vague idea about how to use a hammer may also have a vague idea about how to use other tools. After learning how to use each one, she relates these uses, organizing her knowledge.

Assimilation and accommodation always take the child to a higher ground, according to Piaget. In trying to understand the world, the child inevitably experiences cognitive conflict, or disequilibrium. That is, the child is constantly faced with counterexamples to his existing schemes and with inconsistencies. For example, if a child believes that pouring water from a short and wide container into a tall and narrow container changes the amount of water, then the child might be puzzled by where the "extra" water came from and whether there is actually more water to drink. The puzzle creates disequilibrium; for Piaget, an internal search for equilibrium creates motivation for change. The child assimilates and accommodates, adjusting old schemes, developing new schemes, and organizing and reorganizing the old and new schemes. Eventually, the organization is fundamentally different from the old organization; it is a new way of thinking. **Equilibration** is the name Piaget gave to this mechanism by which children shift from one stage of thought to the next.

According to Piaget, mental development in this early age is characterized by the infant's ability to organize and coordinate sensations with physical movements and actions. He termed this period in cognitive development the sensorimotor stage. Piaget divided the sensorimotor stage into six substages, as shown in Figure 5.14):

1. **simple reflexes**
2. **first habits and primary circular reactions**
3. **secondary circular reactions**
4. **coordination of secondary circular reactions**
5. **tertiary circular reactions, novelty, and curiosity**
6. **internalization of schemes**

Figure 5.14

Piaget's Six Substages of Sensorimotor Development

Substage	Name	Age Range	Description and Examples
1	Simple Reflexes	1st month	Reflexive behaviour determines the coordination of sensation and action; e.g., a newborn will suck a nipple or bottle when it is placed directly in the baby's mouth or touched to the lips
2	First Habits and Primary Circular Reactions	1 to 4 months	Reflexes evolve into more refined and coordinated adaptive schemes. The infant develops schemes to reproduce an interesting or pleasurable event that initially occurred by chance; e.g., infant might suck on anything he/she brings to mouth
3	Secondary Circular Reactions	4 to 8 months	The infant becomes more object-oriented, or focused on the world, moving beyond a preoccupation with the self in sensorimotor interactions; e.g., by chance infant might shake a rattle, and will repeat the action for the sake of fascination
4	Coordination of Secondary Circular Reactions	8 to 12 months	Several significant changes take place that involve the coordination of schemes and intentionality; e.g., infants might look at an object and grasp it simultaneously, or they might visually inspect a toy and finger it simultaneously, exploring it tactilely
5	Tertiary Circular Reactions, Novelty, and Curiosity	12 to 18 months	The infant becomes intrigued by the variety of properties that objects possess and the multiplicity of things it can make happen to objects; e.g., infant explores new possibilities with new objects, doing new things to them and exploring the results, a trial-and-error exploration
6	Internalization of Schemes	18 to 24 months	The infant's mental functioning shifts from a purely sensorimotor plane to a symbolic plane, and the infant develops the ability to use primitive symbols; e.g., infant develops the use of symbols to represent objects or events. Symbols allow the infant to manipulate and transform the represented events in simple ways.

Object Permanence

Object permanence is the Piagetian term for one of an infant's most important accomplishments: understanding that objects and events continue to exist even when they cannot directly be seen, heard, or touched. The principal way that object permanence is studied is by watching an infant's reaction when an interesting object or event disappears (see Figure 5.15). If infants show no reaction, it is assumed they believe the object no longer exists. By contrast, if infants are surprised at the disappearance and search for the object, it is assumed they believe it continues to exist.

Figure 5.15

Object Permanence

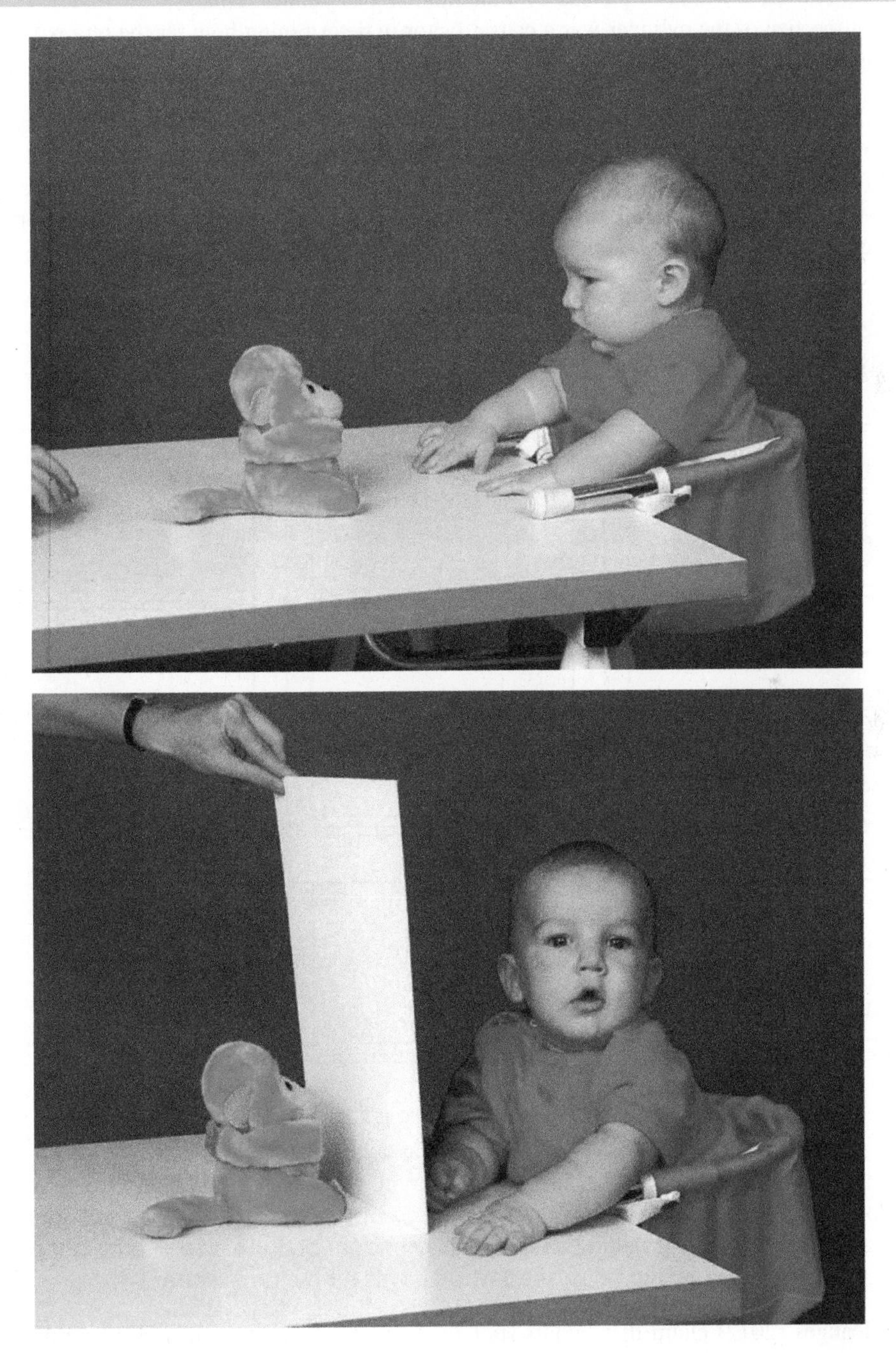

Piaget thought that object permanence is one of infancy's landmark cognitive accomplishments. For this 5-month-old boy, "out-of-sight" is literally out of mind. The infant looks at the toy monkey (*top*), but when his view of the toy is blocked (*bottom*), he does not search for it. Several months later, he will search for the hidden toy monkey, reflecting the presence of object permanence.

Causality

Piaget was very interested in infants' knowledge of cause and effect. His conclusions about infants' understanding of causality were based mainly on his observations of the extent to which infants acted to produce a desired outcome, such as pushing aside an obstacle to reach a goal.

One study on infants' understanding of causality found that even young infants comprehend that the size of a moving object determines how far it will move a stationary object if it collides with it (Kotovsky & Baillargeon, 1994). In this research, a cylinder was rolled down a ramp and hit a toy bug that was located at the bottom of the ramp. By 5½ to 6½ months of age, infants understand that the bug would roll farther if it was hit by a large cylinder than if it was hit by a small cylinder, after they had observed how far it would be pushed by a medium-sized cylinder. Thus, by the middle of the first year, these infants understood that the size of the cylinder was a causal factor in determining how far the bug would move when it was hit by the cylinder. Figure 5.16 outlines this main characteristic of sensorimotor thought.

As expressed by Baillargeon (2008), infants have a pre-adapted innate view, called the *principle of persistence,* which explains their assumption that objects do not change their properties—including such factors as how solid they are and their location colour, and form—unless some external factor (a person moves an object, for example) obviously intervenes. The research findings obtained by Kotovsky and Baillargeon (1994) indicate that infants develop object permanence and causal reasoning much earlier than Piaget proposed (Luo, Kaufman, & Baillargeon, 2009; Luo & Baillargeon, 2010).

Figure 5.16

Infants' Understanding of Causality

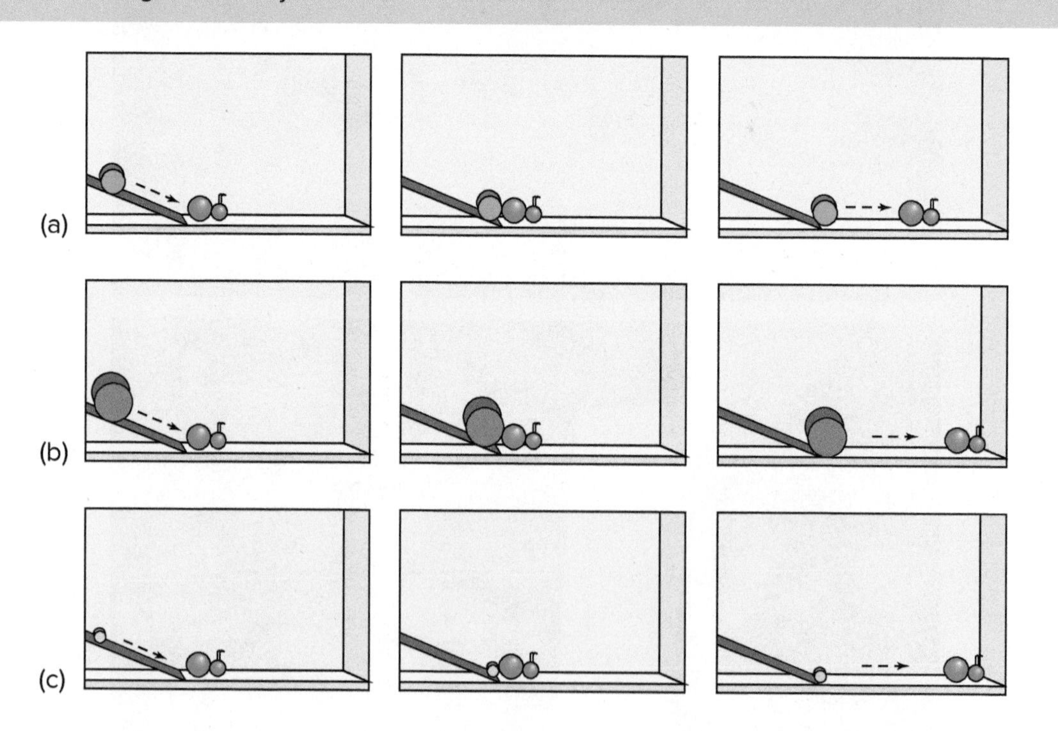

After young infants saw how far the medium-sized cylinder (*a*) pushed a toy bug, they showed more surprise at the event in (*c*) that showed a very small cylinder pushing the toy bug as far as the large cylinder (*b*). Their surprise, indicated by looking at (*c*) longer than (*b*), indicated that they understood the size of a cylinder was a causal factor in determining how far the toy bug would be pushed when it was hit by the cylinder.

Hohenberger and colleauges (2012) claim that infants start to develop an understanding of dynamic events in the world. These understandings are of two kinds: (1) human actions and (2) physical events. A characteristic of the former is that they are goal-directed, whereas the physical events are not. Koyotsky and Baillargeon's (1994) collision event was adapted as a test for understanding physical causality. Importantly, they contrasted infants' performance in this non-social event-related task with their performance in a social action-related task such as the BoH (Back of Hand—touching an object with the back of one's hand), or goal directed. While both tasks share major parameters such as the presence of objects, contact, movement, causality, and action events, they differ in the social dimension. In the physical causality task, neither a human agent nor any goal is involved, whereas in the BoH task a human agent's hand is present, which may induce the representation of an action goal. The results indicated that for the BoH, 6-month-old infants did not distinguish between goal-directed vs non-goal-directed human action, but 10-month-old infants did (Hohenberger et al., 2012). This finding is well in line with the general finding that sensitivity to goal-directed human actions is observed at 6 months of age at the earliest (Hofer et al., 2008). However, such sensitivity to goal-directed behaviour becomes more reliably observed in somewhat older infants of 8 and 10 months of age.

Critiques

Piaget opened up a whole new way of looking at the development of infants' understanding of the world. However, he constructed his view of infancy mainly by observing the development of his own three children. Few laboratory techniques were available at the time, and much of the new research suggests that Piaget's view of sensorimotor development needs to be modified (Carlson & Zelazo, 2008; Meltzoff, 2007).

An ongoing debate is occurring in developmental psychology regarding whether or not the stage models are valid. Stages are problematic and discontinuous over different domains of development. Alternative conceptions of development contend that development is quantitative, continuous, modular, and gradual, implying that development can be understood without recourse to stage models. For example, neo-Piagetian models have been constructed to allow for the construct of individual differences in cognitive development (Young, 2011).

Theorists such as Eleanor Gibson (2001) and Elizabeth Spelke (1991; Spelke & Kinzler, 2007a, b) believe that infants' perceptual abilities are highly developed very early in development, challenging the slow progress toward object permanence understood by Piaget.

The violation-of-expectation (VOE) method has been used to investigate the fact that young infants can represent and reason about hidden objects. The apparent success of young infants in the VOE method reflects novelty and familiarity preferences brought about by habituation or familiarization trials in the tasks. To challenge some of the controversy regarding the VOE method, Wang and colleagues (2004) concluded from their study that young infants can succeed at VOE tasks involving hidden objects even when given no habituation or familiarization. Krist and Krüger (2012) explain that amazing cognitive competencies have been demonstrated on VOE paradigms in young infants; but such competencies could not be shown either in toddlers or older infants. However, this particular divergence might be caused by different research methods as much as by discontinuities in development.

It is further believed that the cognitive abilities of young infants may be richer and more continuous than previously believed by Piaget. Unfortunately, Piaget did not have access to the sophisticated new methods available to researchers today. Consequently, his conclusions tended to underestimate the physical knowledge and reasoning abilities of infants (Baillargeon, 2004).

Many researchers have concluded that Piaget wasn't specific enough about how infants learn about their world, and that infants are more competent than Piaget thought (Bremner, 2007; Spelke & Kinzler, 2007a, b). As they have examined the specific ways that infants learn, the field of infant cognition has become very specialized. If there is a unifying theme, it is that investigators in infant development seek to understand more precisely how developmental changes in cognition take place, and the big issue of nature and nurture (Spelke & Kinzler, 2007b).

Information Processing

In this section, we will explore aspects of how infants learn, remember, and sort information. The approaches we look at here do not describe infant development in terms of stages, but adopt a continuous view of development.

Conditioning

In Chapter 2, we described Pavlov's classical conditioning (in which, as a result of pairing, a new stimulus comes to elicit a response previously given to another stimulus) and Skinner's operant conditioning (in which the consequences of behaviour produce changes in the probability of the behaviour's occurrence). Infants can learn through both types of conditioning. For example, if an infant's behaviour is followed by a rewarding stimulus, the behaviour is likely to recur.

Carolyn Rovee-Collier (1987) demonstrated that infants can retain information from the experience of being conditioned. In one study, she placed a 2½-month-old baby in a crib under an elaborate mobile (see Figure 5.17). She then tied one end of a ribbon to the baby's ankle and the other end to the mobile. Subsequently, she observed that the baby kicked and made the mobile move. The movement of the mobile was the reinforcing stimulus (which increased the baby's kicking behaviour). Weeks later, the baby was returned to the crib, but its foot was not tied to the mobile. The baby kicked, indicating retention of the information that kicking moved the mobile.

Figure 5.17

The Technique Used in Rovee-Collier's Investigation of Infant Memory

Courtesy of Dr. Carolyn Rovee-Collier

In Rovee-Collier's experiment, operant conditioning was used to demonstrate that infants as young as 2½ months of age can retain information from the experience of being conditioned.

In addition, Campanella and Rovee-Collier (2005) found that 3-month-old infants can make associations between objects and their physical surroundings. The concept of association is fundamental and is invoked to explain a variety of both simple and complex cognitive phenomena. The researchers concluded that latent learning by very young infants is both extensive and enduring, and that their knowledge base begins to form early in life. In fact, such learning can occur long before infants are able to express what they know. For example, Giles and Rovee-Collier (2011) conducted an experiment with 6- and 9-month-old infants to discover how long an association between events remains latent before being forgotten, and also what exposure conditions affect their persistence. The two groups were pre-exposed to two puppets for one hour per day for two days, one hour on one day or one hour on one day in two sessions: 1–27 days later, target actions were modelled on one puppet, and infants were tested with the other puppet one day later. The data revealed that the pre-exposure regimen determined retention. Regardless of exposure time, both ages remembered the association longer after two sessions, and younger infants remembered longer than older infants.

Cuevas and colleagues (2006) found that infants as young as 6 months can not only form new associations between objects, but also can form new associations with memories of objects. These results provide evidence that what infants merely see "brings to mind" what they saw before, and that events and memories can combine in new ways. These results go far to highlight the important role that early experiences, combined with enriching environments, have upon cognitive development.

Sadly, Carolyn Rovee-Collier died in 2014 at the age of 72 after a prolonged struggle with breast cancer (Cuevas, 2015).

Attention

Attention, the focusing of mental resources on select information, improves cognitive processing on many tasks. Even newborns can detect a contour and fix their attention on it. Older infants scan patterns more thoroughly. By 4 months of age, infants can selectively attend to an object. Attention in the first year of life is dominated by an *orienting/investigative process* (Posner & Rothbart, 2007). This process involves directing attention to potentially important locations in the environment (i.e., *where*) and recognizing objects and their features, such as colour and form (i.e., *what*) (Courage & Richards, 2008). From 3 to 9 months of age, infants can deploy their attention more flexibly and quickly. Another important type of attention is *sustained attention*, also referred to as *focused attention* (Courage & Richards, 2008).

New stimuli typically elicit an orienting response followed by sustained attention. This sustained attention allows infants to learn about and remember characteristics of a stimulus as it becomes familiar. Researchers have found that infants as young as 3 months of age engage in five to ten seconds of sustained attention. From this age through the second year, the length of sustained attention increases (Courage & Richards, 2008). Memorial University's Mary Courage and associates (2006) found infants nearing 1 year of age held sustained attention for longer time periods when attending to more complex rather than simple stimuli (faces and *Sesame Street* material versus achromatic patterns, respectively) than did younger infants, who showed no preference.

Habituation and Dishabituation

If a stimulus—a sight or sound—is presented to infants several times in a row, they usually pay less attention to it each time. This is the process of **habituation**—decreased responsiveness to a stimulus after repeated presentations of the stimulus. **Dishabituation** is the increase in responsiveness after a change in stimulation. As explained by Colombo and Mitchell (2009), although nearly 800 reports were published between 1962 and 2008 using habituation or infant-controlled habituation procedures, only 25 percent of these papers reported the actual process of habituation. Perhaps the infant-controlled habituation procedure has for too long incorporated a 50 percent criterion (i.e., when the infant has reduced her initial or longest looking time at a stimulus by 50 percent), with the assumption that this criterion is well-suited for infants of different ages. As a result, Flom and Pick (2012) indicated that the criterion used to define habituation at one age may not be appropriate for defining habituation at another age. Such conclusions highlight the fact that one should not conclude infants "cannot do something" when they fail to show discrimination.

In another study, Brez and colleagues (2012) studied the integration of non-numerical (featural) and numerical information in the performance of infants at 9, 11, and 13 months of age on a number discrimination task. The infants were habituated to pictures of objects (e.g., bowl, shoe) in groups of two or three. Infants saw both new and old objects in both groups. Distinct differences in levels of discrimination appeared among the infants at different ages. The researchers concluded that "early number representations are dissociated from featural information, and the integration of these stimulus properties is a developmental process that occurs across the first year" (Brez, Columbo, & Cohen, 2012). In other words, as infants develop, their ability to discriminate in terms of the number and features of an object improves.

Infants' attention is strongly governed by novelty and habituation (Courage & Richards, 2008; Snyder & Torrence, 2008). Knowing about habituation and dishabituation can help parents interact effectively with infants. Infants respond to changes in stimulation. Wise parents sense when an infant shows an interest and realize that they may have to repeat something many times for the infant to process information. But if the stimulation is repeated often, the infant stops responding to the parent. In parent–infant interaction, it is important for parents to do novel things and to repeat them often until the infant stops responding.

Imitation and Memory

Can infants imitate someone else's facial expressions? If an adult opens her mouth, widens her eyes, and raises her eyebrows, will the baby follow suit?

Infant development researcher Andrew Meltzoff (2007; Meltzoff & Williamson, 2008; Meltzoff et al., 2009) believes infants' imitative abilities are biologically based because infants can imitate a facial expression within the first few days after birth. Meltzoff also emphasizes that the infant's imitative abilities are not like what ethologists conceptualize as a hardwired, reflexive, innate releasing mechanism, but rather involve flexibility, adaptability, and intermodal perception. In Meltzoff's observations of infants in the first 72 hours after birth, the infants gradually displayed a full imitative response of an adult's facial expression, such as protruding the tongue or opening the mouth wide. Meltzoff and colleagues (2012) state that observational causal learning is a powerful mechanism for inducing rapid learning of causal relations.

Meltzoff (2005) also has studied **deferred imitation,** which occurs after a time delay of hours or days. In one study, Meltzoff (1988) demonstrated that 9-month-old infants could imitate actions that they had seen performed 24 hours earlier. Each action consisted of an unusual gesture—such as pushing a recessed button in a box (which produced a beeping sound). Piaget believed that deferred imitation does not occur until about 18 months of age. Meltzoff's research suggests that it occurs much earlier.

Can young infants remember? Some infant researchers, such as Carolyn Rovee-Collier, argue that infants as young as 2 to 6 months of age can remember some experiences through to the age of 1½ to 2 years (Rovee-Collier, 2008). However, critics such as Jean Mandler (2004), a leading expert on infant cognition, argue that Rovee-Collier failed to distinguish between retention of a perceptual motor activity that is involved in conditioning tasks (such as that involved in kicking a mobile), often referred to as *implicit memory*, and the ability to consciously recall the past, often referred to as *explicit memory*.

When people talk about memory, they are usually referring to explicit memory. Most researchers find that babies do not show explicit memory until the second half of the first year (Bauer, 2007, 2008; Bauer et al., 2003). Then, explicit memory improves substantially during the second year of life (Bauer, 2007, 2008; Carver & Bauer, 2001). In one longitudinal study, 1-year-old infants were assessed several times (Bauer et al., 2000). These infants showed more accurate memory and required fewer prompts to demonstrate their memory than infants under the age of 1 year.

What changes in the brain are linked to infants' memory development? From about 6 to 12 months of age, the maturation of the hippocampus and the surrounding cerebral cortex, especially the frontal lobes, make the emergence of explicit memory possible (Nelson, Thomas, & de Haan, 2006). Explicit memory continues to improve in the second year, as these brain structures further mature and connections between them increase. Less is known about the areas of the brain involved in implicit memory in infancy.

Most adults cannot remember anything from the first three years of their life: this is referred to as *infantile amnesia*. The few reported adult memories of life at age 2 or 3 yers are at best very sketchy (Newcombe, 2008). Elementary school children also do not remember much of their early childhood years (Lie & Newcombe, 1999). One reason older children and adults have difficulty recalling events from their infant and early child years is that during these early years the prefrontal lobes of the brain are immature; this area of the brain is believed to play an important role in storing memories for events (Boyer & Diamond, 1992). After reviewing recent research, Canadian researchers Mark Howe and Mary Courage (2004) concluded that "memory... begins well after our entrance into this world." An alternative description is that memory formed in infancy cannot be expressed by the representational tools—like words—we learn later (Richardson & Hayne, 2007).

Regarding the effect on children of the electronic world such as television, very young infants do not absorb content from television, but do become engaged by its formal features. As they approach the end of their second year, they appear to grasp the content of television provided it corresponds to their cognitive level and their interest. However, such children prefer to connect with humans and they learn more effectively from other people (Courage & Howe, 2010). The important point is that infants are "inherently social beings, and much of their cognitive development emerges in a social context" (Courage & Setliff, 2010).

Concept Formation and Categorization

Concepts are cognitive groupings of similar objects, events, people, or ideas. The brain organizes concepts about the world, and then classifies them into categories based on shared similarities (Schacter et al., 2014). Concepts are fundamental to a person's ability to think and make sense of the world.

Research reported over the last several decades has made clear that infants live a rich conceptual life. Indeed, their interpretation of the objects and events they experience lays the foundation for adult conceptual functioning (Mandler, 2012). Infants begin with a spatial conceptual system and then wait for other kinds of information to be added (Mandler, 2012). Actual experiences in handling objects and moving around in the world will bring about a stronger impression in the child.

Skider and Fleer (2014) provide evidence that infants and toddlers aged 10 to 36 months experience scientific concepts through everyday activities and play. For example, understanding small science concepts (e.g., push/pull/motion) begins the process of maturing their understanding toward future comprehension of science concepts (i.e., force) at school age (Sikder, 2015). In addition, the purposeful actions of parents in relation to science concepts create the conditions for individual-toddler development (Bozhuvich, 2009). In summary, small science concepts can be learned by children in the infant-toddler stage with the support of conscious collaboration of parents in the family context (Skider & Fleer, 2014).

critical thinking

If a 1-year-old infant does well on a developmental scale, how confident should the parents be that this baby is going to be a genius later in life? Determine the importance of concepts in cognitive development in infants. Provide a few examples.

Infant Intelligence

So far, we have made general statements about how the cognitive development of infants progresses. We have emphasized what is typical of the largest number of infants or the average infant, but the results obtained for most infants do not apply to all infants. Individual differences in infant cognitive development have been studied primarily through the use of developmental scales, or infant intelligence tests.

The **Bayley Scales of Infant Development**, developed by Nancy Bayley (1969) to assess infant behaviour and predict later development, is widely used in the assessment of infant development. The current version, Bayley-III, has five scales: cognitive, language, motor, socio-emotional, and adaptive (Bayley, 2005). The first three scales are administered directly to the infant, while the latter two are questionnaires given to the caregiver. The Bayley-III also is more appropriate for use in clinical settings than the two previous editions (Lennon et al., 2008).

How well should a 6-month-old perform on the Bayley mental scale? The 6-month-old infant should be able to vocalize pleasure and displeasure, persistently search for objects that are just out of immediate reach, and approach a mirror that is placed in front of the infant by the examiner. By 12 months of age, an infant should be able to inhibit behaviour when commanded to do so, imitate words the examiner says (such as "Mama"), and respond to simple requests (such as "Take a drink").

Another assessment tool, the Fagan Test of Infant Intelligence (Fagan, 1992), focuses on the infant's ability to process information, including encoding the attributes of objects, detecting similarities and differences between objects, forming mental representations, and retrieving these representations. The Fagan test estimates babies' intelligence by comparing the amount of time they look at a new object with the amount of time they spend looking at a familiar object. This test elicits similar results from infants in different cultures and is correlated with measures of intelligence in older children. A recent longitudinal study found that when administered to 6- and 12-month-old infants, the Fagan test was moderately predictable of the infants' IQ and academic achievement at 21 years of age (Fagan, Holland, & Wheeler, 2007).

It is important, however, not to go too far and think that the connections between early infant cognitive development and later childhood cognitive development are so strong that no discontinuity takes place. Rather, we should be examining the ways in which cognitive development is both continuous and discontinuous. We will describe these changes in cognitive development in subsequent chapters.

To this point, we have studied a number of ideas about infants' cognitive development. For a review, see the Reach Your Learning Outcomes section at the end of this chapter.

Language Development

LO4 Explain the nature of language and how it develops in infancy.

- **Language Acquisition**
- **Biological Foundations of Language**
- **Behavioural and Environmental Influences**

What is language? **Language** is a form of communication, whether spoken, written, or signed, that is based on a system of symbols. All human languages have some common characteristics. These include infinite generativity and organizational rules. **Infinite generativity** is the ability to produce a seemingly endless number of meaningful sentences using a finite set of words and rules. This quality makes language a highly creative enterprise.

Language Acquisition

As infants develop, they reach a number of language milestones. At birth they communicate by crying, but by about 2 years of age, most can say approximately 200 words in the language their parents use. How does this remarkable ability develop?

Babbling and Other Vocalizations

Babies actively produce sounds and try to communicate with the outside world from birth onward. In the first year, the infant's effort to communicate is characterized by the following:

- *Crying:* This is present at birth, and, as you will discover in Chapter 6, different types of crying can signal different things.
- *Cooing:* This first occurs at about 1 to 2 months of age. These are */oo/* sounds such as */cool* or */goo/* that usually occur during interaction with the caregiver.
- *Babbling:* This first occurs in the middle of the first year and includes strings of consonant–vowel combinations.
- *Gestures:* Infants use gestures, such as showing and pointing, at about 7 to 15 months of age. Some examples are waving bye-bye, nodding the head to mean "yes," and pointing to a pet to draw attention to it.

Many deaf children and infants gain access to speech through cochlear implantations (Housten & Bergeson, 2014). However, the benefits of learning sign language remains of great importance. For parents and families who are willing and able, sign language seems clearly preferable to an approach that focuses solely on oral communication (Mellon et al., 2015).

Recognizing Language Sounds

Long before infants learn words, they can make fine distinctions among the sounds of the language (Sebastian-Galles, 2007; Werker & Hensch, 2015). Kuhl, (2007, 2009, 2011a, 2011b) argues that from birth to about 6 months of age, infants are "universal linguists"; they recognize when sounds change most of the time, no matter what language syllables come from. This ability to distinguish sounds and gestures in the language (or languages) of caregivers improves over the first year (Narayan, Werker, & Beddor, 2010). In fact, Moon and colleagues (2009) state that the category organization of sounds begins in utero. Furthermore, over their first six months, infants become even better at perceiving changes in sounds in their "own" language—the one their parents speak—and they gradually lose the ability to recognize differences that are not important in their own language (Kuhl, 2011a).

Not only do they notice human speech sounds, infants as young as 2½ months of age actually prefer human speech sounds to similar non-speech sounds, as a team at the University of British Columbia has discovered (Vouloumanos & Werker, 2004). Curtin (2010), a Canadian researcher, states that over the course of the first year of life, infants become proficient word learners. Newborns can discriminate the phonemes, or basic speech sounds that carry linguistic meaning and that are present in all human languages. They can even remember acoustical patterns and rhythms of speech (Gervain & Mehler, 2010). Infants also appear to prefer certain specific categories of words to others. In English, lexical words such as nouns and verbs tend to carry greater meaning and have different acoustic characteristics (i.e., longer vowel durations) when compared to grammatical words such as prepositions.

First Words

Spoken vocabulary begins when the infant utters its first word. As early as 5 months of age, infants recognize their name when someone says it. Thus, in infancy *receptive vocabulary* (words the child understands) considerably exceeds *spoken vocabulary* (words the child uses).

A child's first words include those that name important people (*dada*), familiar animals (*kitty*), vehicles (*car*), toys (*ball*), food (*milk*), body parts (*eye*), clothes (*hat*), household items (*clock*), and greeting terms (*bye*). These were the first words of babies 50 years ago, and they are the first words of babies today.

The infant's spoken vocabulary rapidly increases once the first word is spoken (Pan & Uccelli, 2009). The average 18-month-old can speak about 50 words, but by the age of 2 years the child can speak about 200 words. Like the timing of a child's first word, the timing of the vocabulary spurt varies (Lieven, 2008). Children sometimes overextend or underextend the meanings of the words they use. *Overextension* is the tendency to apply a word to objects that are inappropriate for the word's meaning. For example, children at first may say "*dada*" not only for "father" but also for other men, strangers, or boys. With time, overextensions decrease and eventually disappear. *Underextension* is the tendency to apply a word too narrowly; it occurs when children fail to use a word to name a relevant event or object. For example, a child might use the word *boy* to describe a 5-year-old neighbour, but not apply the word to a male infant or to a 9-year-old male. Figure 5.18 shows some of the language milestones in infancy.

Figure 5.18

Some Language Milestones in Infancy

Typical Age	Language Milestones
Birth	Crying
2 to 4 months	Cooing begins
5 months	Understands first word
6 months	Babbling begins
7 to 11 months	Change from universal linguist to language-specific listener
8 to 12 months	Use gestures, such as showing and pointing Comprehension of words appears
13 months	First word spoken
18 months	Vocabulary spurt starts
18 to 24 months	Uses two-word utterances Rapid expansion of understanding of words

Despite great variations in the language input received by infants, around the world they follow a similar path in learning to speak.

Two-Word Utterances

By the time children are 18 to 24 months of age, they usually can utter two-word statements. During this two-word stage, they quickly grasp the importance of expressing concepts and of the role that language plays in communicating with others. To convey meaning with two-word utterances, the child relies heavily on gesture, tone, and context.

Although two-word sentences omit many parts of speech, they are remarkably succinct in conveying many messages. In fact, in every language, a child's first combinations of words have this economical quality: **telegraphic speech,** the use of short and precise words to communicate. In a telegram, articles, auxiliary verbs, and other connectives usually are omitted, and young children's two- and three-word utterances are characteristically telegraphic.

Young children learn to speak in two-word utterances, in most cases, at about 18 to 24 months of age. *What are some examples of these two-word utterances?*

Biological Foundations of Language

The strongest evidence for the biological basis of language is that children all over the world reach language milestones at about the same time developmentally and in about the same order. This occurs despite the vast variation in the language input they receive. For example, in some cultures, adults do not talk to children under 1 year of age, yet these infants still acquire language. There is no other convincing way to explain how quickly children learn language than through biological foundations.

The last decade has produced a research explosion in neuroscience research examining language development (Kuhl, 2011a). Brain imaging of various kinds is one recent addition to the infant researcher's toolkit. Although the precise meaning of brain activation patterns is not yet well established, the notion holds definite promise in the future (Vivona, 2012).

There is evidence that particular regions of the brain are predisposed to be used for language (Opitz & Friederici, 2007; Skipper et al., 2007). Two regions involved in language were first discovered in studies of brain-damaged individuals: **Broca's area**, an area in the left frontal lobe of the brain involved in producing words, and **Wernicke's area**, a region of the brain's left hemisphere involved in language comprehension (see Figure 5.19). Individuals with damage to Broca's area have difficulty producing words correctly; individuals with damage to Wernicke's area have poor comprehension and often produce fluent but incomprehensible speech.

Figure 5.19
Broca's Area and Wernicke's Area

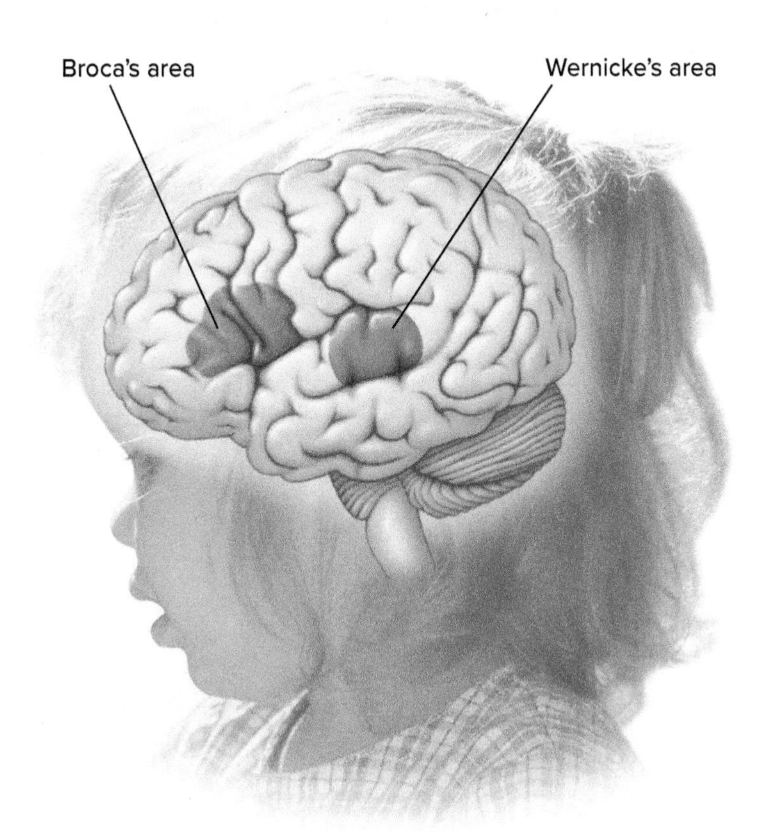

Broca's area is located in the frontal lobe of the brain's left hemisphere, and it is involved in the control of speech. Wernicke's area is a portion of the left hemisphere's temporal lobe that is involved in understanding language. *How does the role of these areas of the brain relate to lateralization?*

McMaster University researchers have established that 4-month-old infants have developed an automated skill, located in their auditory cortex, to monitor repeating sound input for any change (He, Hotson, & Trainor, 2009). This automated function is absent in 2-month-old infants. The 4-month-old infant's skill mirrors the stimulus change detection ability noted in adults. This ability is an essential element in infants' early language development, and appears to be located in the right frontal hemisphere. This type of research helps to understand the areas of the brain where language acquisition begins.

Linguist Noam Chomsky (1957) believes humans are biologically prewired to learn language at a certain time and in a certain way. He believes children are born into the world with a **language acquisition device (LAD)**, a biological endowment that enables the child to detect certain language categories, such as phonology, syntax, and semantics. Phenomena such as the uniformity of language milestones across languages and cultures, biological substrates for language, and evidence that children create language even in the absence of well-formed input suggest the existence of an LAD. Neural and behavioural research studies indicate that exposure to language in the first year of life influences the circuitry of the brain even before infants have spoken their first words (Kuhl, 2010). A few neuroimaging studies have indicated that neural circuitry supporting phonetic discrimination is less mature in bilingual than in same-aged monolingual infants (Garcia-Sierra et al., 2009). However, Petitto and colleagues (2012) argue that phonetic discrimination may be equally mature but involves different circuitry, specifically with greater connectivity to prefrontal areas. More research is required in this area. However, this current decade might represent the dawn of a golden age regarding the development of neuroscience of language in humans (Kuhl, 2010).

Behavioural and Environmental Influences

Behaviourists view language as just another behaviour. They argue that language represents chains of responses (Skinner, 1957) or imitation (Bandura, 1977). However, many of the sentences we produce are novel; we have not heard them or spoken them before. For example, a child hears the sentence "The plate fell on the floor," and then says, "My mirror fell on the blanket," after dropping the mirror on the blanket. The behavioural mechanisms of reinforcement and imitation cannot completely explain this.

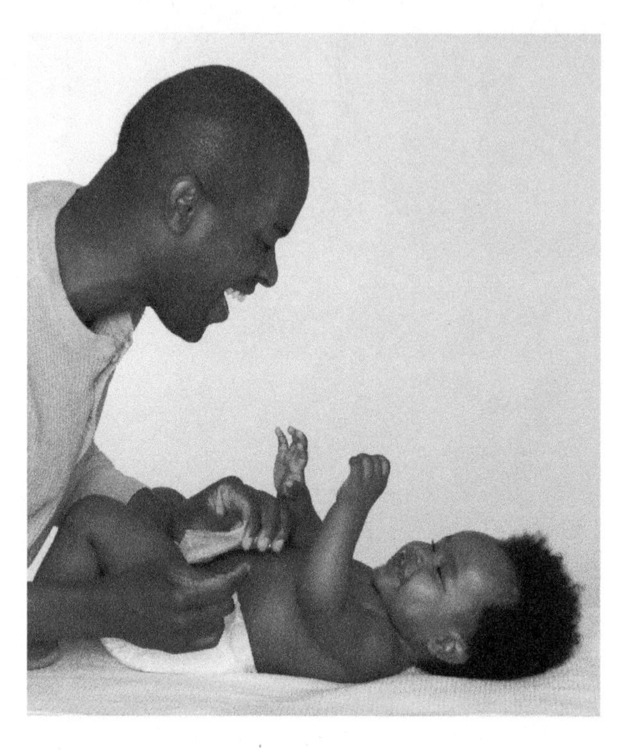

Blend Images/Getty Images

It is a good idea for parents to begin talking to their babies from the start. The best language teaching occurs when the talking is begun before the infant becomes capable of intelligible speech. *What are some other guidelines for parents to follow in helping their infants and toddlers develop their language? What are some characteristics of infant-directed speech?*

Another criticism of the behavioural view is that it fails to explain the extensive orderliness of language. The behavioural view predicts that vast individual differences should appear in children's speech development because of each child's unique learning history. However, as we have seen, all infants coo before they babble; all toddlers produce one-word utterances before two-word utterances; and all state sentences in the active form before they state them in the passive form.

Nevertheless, people do not learn language in a social vacuum. Most children are bathed in language from a very early age (Bornstein, 2014; Kuhl, 2011a; Tomasello, 2006). In contrast, the Wild Boy of Aveyron, who never learned to communicate effectively, had lived in social isolation for years. The support and involvement of caregivers and teachers greatly facilitate a child's language learning (Narayan, Werker, & Beddor, 2010). A study investigating the relationship between mother–child interactions, conducted by Licata and colleagues (2014), found that emotionally available caregiving certainly promotes social-cognitive development in preverbal infants.

An intriguing aspect of the environment in the young child's acquisition of language is called **infant-directed speech**. This type of speech has a higher-than-normal pitch and involves the use of simple words and sentences. Parents and even other children make use of this speech pattern, often without conscious awareness. Infant-directed speech has the important functions of capturing the infant's attention and maintaining communication.

It appears that mothers have a "signature tune" in their speech patterns for their infants. In a series of audio recorded interactions between mother and infant, identifiable tunes with unique pitch contours were detected for each mother when speaking to their baby (Bergeson & Trehub, 2007). Nakata and Trehub (2004; 2010) and Trehub and Hannin (2009) found that mothers singing to their infants created a stronger visual fixation along with movement reduction (indicating greater attention) than when mothers spoke to their infants. While we all might use child-directed speech, mothers' speech and singing are unique to their infants. Whether the father's voice arouses the same attention and has the same unique character remains to be discovered.

While infant-directed speech helps maintain infants' interest in oral interactions, adults sometimes use specific strategies to enhance children's acquisition of language. Four such techniques are recasting, echoing, expanding, and labelling. *Recasting* is rephrasing something the child has said in a different way, perhaps turning it into a question. For example, if the child says, "The dog was barking," the adult can respond by asking, "When was the dog barking?" Recasting fits with the idea that letting a child initially indicate an interest and then proceeding to elaborate that interest—commenting, demonstrating, and explaining—improves communication and helps language acquisition. *Echoing* is repeating what a child says, especially if it is an incomplete phrase or sentence. *Expanding* is restating, in a linguistically sophisticated form, what a child has said. *Labelling* is identifying the names of objects. When adults ask young children to identify the names of objects, the youngsters acquire vocabulary.

critical thinking

Should infants be exposed to numerous languages because they can easily acquire languages at an early age? Would this kind of language learning be harmful to a baby? Develop a research question to determine the effects on an infant's visual fixation caused by the mothers' singing and talking to them. In what ways can you assist adolescent mothers from a low socio-economic class in increase language development over the first two years of the child's life?

Each of the techniques mentioned above and child-directed speech indicate that we should make special effort to speak to and teach language to children. Melanie Soderstrom (2007) reminds us, however, that children also learn about language as adults engage in conversation with other adults in the presence of the child. What we say and how we say it can be easily observed and learned by the child to whom we are not directly speaking.

An interactionist view emphasizes that both biology and experience contribute to language development. How much of language is biologically determined, and how much depends on interaction with others, is a subject of debate among linguists and psychologists. However, all agree that both biological capacity and relevant experience are necessary (Gathercole & Hoff, 2007; Tomasello, Carpenter, & Liszkowski, 2007).

To this point, we have discussed a number of ideas about infants' language development. For a review, see the Reach Your Learning Outcomes section at the end of this chapter.

Reach Your **Learning Outcomes**

Physical Development and Health

LO1 Outline steps involved in physical growth and development in infancy.

Physical Growth	▪ The average full-term newborn is 48 to 53 centimetres long and weighs 2500 to 4000 grams. ▪ Infants grow about 2.5 centimetres per month in the first 6 months of life, but growth slows during the second 6 months. ▪ The cephalocaudal pattern refers to growth that occurs from top down. ▪ The proximodistal pattern refers to growth that occurs from centre out.
Brain	▪ Dendritic formation and synapse production are most prominent. ▪ Myelination continues to develop in infancy and childhood. ▪ Connections between neurons increase. ▪ Lateralization refers to specialization of function in one hemisphere or the other. ▪ Early experience is important for the development of the brain.
Sleep	▪ Newborns usually sleep 16 to 17 hours a day. By 4 months of age, many Canadian infants' sleeping patterns approach adult patterns. ▪ REM sleep, which might promote brain development, is present more in early infancy than in childhood or adulthood. ▪ There is no foolproof method to predict the occurrence of sudden infant death syndrome. Some risk factors include low birth weight and exposure to cigarette smoke.
Health	▪ High-calorie, high-energy foods are part of a balanced diet for infants. ▪ Deficiencies in vitamin D are a health concern in infancy. ▪ Infants should be taken to the dentist for the first time within six months of the eruption of the first teeth. ▪ Breastfeeding is superior to bottle-feeding. ▪ One cause of malnutrition in infancy is early weaning from breast milk to inadequate nutrients.

Motor, Sensory, and Perceptual Development

LO2 Examine infant motor development and summarize the course of sensory and perceptual development in infancy

Motor Development	▪ Reflexes are automatic movements that govern the newborn's behaviour. ▪ Gross motor skills involve large muscle activities, such as moving one's arms and walking. ▪ Fine motor skills involve movements that are fine tuned, such as using fingers to grasp an object. ▪ Bruininks-Oseretsky Test of motor performance measures motor skills and yields a gross motor, fine motor and total battery score. ▪ A number of milestones in these motor skills are achieved in infancy.

Sensory and Perceptual Development	▪ Sensation occurs when a stimulus reaches sensory receptors, such as the eyes and skin. ▪ Perception is the interpretation of what is sensed. ▪ Gibson and Walk's visual cliff study showed that babies as young as six months have depth perception. ▪ The fetus can hear sounds such as the mother's voice and music in the last two months of pregnancy. Both fetuses and newborns prefer the mother's voice. ▪ Newborns can feel touch and pain and prefer certain odours and tastes. ▪ Intermodal perception of matches between silent videos and recognizable strangers voices occurs as early as two months of age. ▪ Babies are constantly coordinating their motor movements with concurrent perceptual information.

Cognitive Development

LO3 **Determine how infants learn, remember, and conceptualize.**

Piaget's Sensorimotor Stage	▪ A scheme is a cognitive structure that helps a person organize experience and changes with age. ▪ This stage lasts from birth to about 2 years of age. ▪ The infant is able to organize and coordinate sensations with physical movements. ▪ The infant's understanding of the physical world is shown by the attainment of object permanence and a sense of causality. ▪ Object permanence refers to the ability to understand that objects continue to exist, even though the infant is no longer observing them. ▪ Research suggests that children acquire perceptual and conceptual skills earlier than Piaget thought.
Information Processing	▪ Habituation is the repeated presentation of the same stimulus, causing reduced attention to the stimulus. It has been used to demonstrate infants' perception. ▪ Explicit memory—that is, the ability to recall the past consciously—does not emerge until the second half of the first year after birth. ▪ Concepts and categories help simplify and summarize information. Research has shown that infants can form concepts.
Infant Intelligence	▪ The Bayley-III has five scales: cognitive, language, motor, socio-emotional, and adaptive. The first three scales are administered directly to the infant, while the latter two are questionnaires given to the caregiver. ▪ The Fagan test of infant intelligence focuses on the infant's ability to process information. ▪ Development of cognitive skills from infancy to childhood shows both continuity and discontinuity.

Language Development

LO4 **Explain the nature of language and how it develops in infancy.**

Language Acquisition	▪ In the first year, infants use crying, cooing, then babbling as well as gestures to communicate. ▪ As early as 5 months of age, infants recognize their name Their vocabulary spurt begins at around 18 months, when infants can speak about 50 words; six months later, they have a vocabulary of about 200 words. ▪ In the so-called two-word stage, infant speech is "telegraphic." ▪ In infancy, receptive vocabulary exceeds spoken vocabulary.
Biological Foundations of Language	▪ Broca's area is involved in producing words. Wernicke's area is involved in language comprehension. An automated skill is located in the right hemisphere to monitor sound input. ▪ Chomsky's notion of a language acquisition device is one example to show how a biological endowment allows children to detect language categories.
Behavioural and Environmental Influences	▪ Behaviourists view language as just another behaviour. They argue that language represents chains of responses or imitation. ▪ Among the ways that adults teach language to children are infant-directed speech, recasting, echoing, expanding, and labelling. ▪ An interactionist view emphasizes that both biology and experience contribute to language development.

review → connect → reflect

review

1. What are some key features of the brain and its development in infancy? LO1
2. What are the infant's nutritional needs? LO1
3. How do gross motor skills develop in infancy? LO2
4. How do fine motor skills develop in infancy? LO2
5. How is imitation involved in infant learning? LO3
6. What is intermodal perception? LO3
7. What are some biological and environmental influences on language? LO4

connect

What are the main differences between the grasping reflex present at birth and the fine motor grasping skills an infant develops between 4 and 12 months of age?

reflect

Your Own Personal Journey of Life

What types of sensory stimulation would you provide to your own baby on a daily basis? Is it possible for you to overstimulate your baby? Explain.

CHAPTER 6

Socio-Emotional Development in Infancy

CHAPTER OUTLINE

Emotional Development

LO1 Outline the development of emotions in infancy.

- **Defining Emotion**
- **Biological and Environmental Influences**
- **Early Emotions**
- **Emotion Expression and Social Relationships**
- **Emotion Regulation and Coping**

Temperament and Personality Development

LO2 Summarize the development of temperament and personality during infancy.

- **Temperament**
- **Personality Development**

Social Orientation/Understanding and Attachment

LO3 Analyze social orientation/understanding and the development of attachment in infancy.

- **Social Orientation/Understanding**
- **Attachment and Its Development**
- **Individual Differences in Attachment**
- **Caregiving Styles and Attachment Classifications**
- **Attachment, Temperament, and the Wider Social World**

Social Contexts

LO4 Determine how social contexts influence the infant's development.

- **The Family**
- **Child Care**
- **Infants with Special Needs**

"When you heal a child, you heal a family.
When you heal a family, you heal a community.
When you heal a community, you heal a nation."

—SHAWN ATLEO, NATIONAL CHIEF OF THE ASSEMBLY OF THE FIRST NATIONS

Meg Takamura/Getty Images

Tom and His Father

Tom is a 1-year-old infant who is being reared by his father during the day. His mother works full-time at her job away from home, and his father is a writer who works at home; they prefer this arrangement over putting Tom in daycare. Tom's father is doing a great job of caring for him. Tom's father keeps Tom nearby while he is writing and spends lots of time talking to him and playing with him. From their interaction, it is clear that they genuinely enjoy each other.

Tom's father looks to the future and imagines the hockey and soccer games Tom will play in and the many other activities he can enjoy with Tom. Remembering how little time his own father spent with him, he is dedicated to making sure that Tom has an involved, nurturing experience with his father.

When Tom's mother comes home in the evening, she spends considerable time with him. Tom shows a positive attachment to both his mother and his father. His parents have cooperated and successfully juggled their careers and work schedules to provide 1-year-old Tom with excellent child care.

Tom's experience highlights some developmental issues related to a child's future outcomes: child care arrangements, parenting style, paternal caregiving, and attachment. These issues concern many researchers and families and will be discussed in this chapter.

Nancy R. Cohen/Getty Images

Many fathers are spending more time with their infants today than in the past.

Emotional Development

LO1 Outline the development of emotions in infancy.

- **Defining Emotion**
- **Biological and Environmental Influences**
- **Early Emotions**
- **Emotion Expression and Social Relationships**
- **Emotion Regulation and Coping**

Infants can express a number of emotions. We will explore what these are and how they develop, but first we need to define *emotion*.

Consistent with this data, Hart and colleagues have reported that infants as young as 6 months of age respond to a loss of maternal attention with negative affectivity along with approach-type behaviours, including higher levels of maternal-directed gaze proximity, touch, negative affect, as well as protest vocalizations (Hart & Carrington, 2002; Hart 2010).

Figure 6.2

Research Setting for Sybil Hart's Attempt to Assess the Early Development of Jealousy

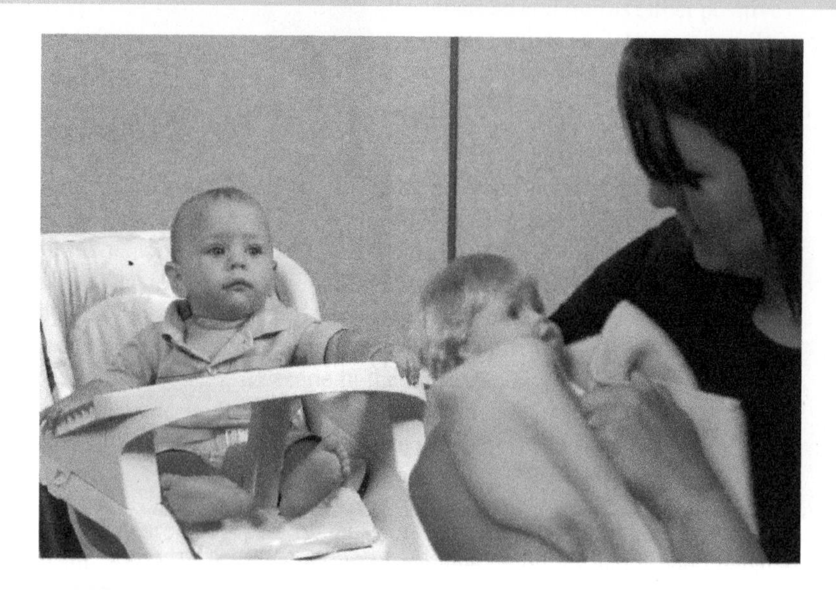

An infant becomes distressed when his mother gives attention to a lifelike baby doll. *What are some possible interpretations of the infant's distress?*

Emotion Expression and Social Relationships

Emotional expressions are involved in infants' first relationships. The ability of infants to communicate emotions permits coordinated interactions with their caregivers and the beginning of an emotional bond between them (Thomann & Carter, 2008; Thompson, 2009b). Not only do parents change their emotional expressions in response to infants' emotional expressions, but infants also modify their emotional expressions in response to their parents' emotional expressions. In other words, these interactions are mutually regulated. Because of this coordination, the interactions are described as *reciprocal*, or *synchronous*, when all is going well. Sensitive, responsive parents help their infants grow emotionally, whether the infants respond in distressed or happy ways (Thompson & Newton, 2009).

Cries and smiles are two emotional expressions that infants display when interacting with parents. These are babies' first forms of emotional communication.

Crying

Crying is the most important mechanism newborns have for communicating with others. This is true for the first cry, which tells the mother and doctor the baby's lungs have filled with air. Cries also may tell physicians and researchers something about the central nervous system. One recent study revealed that newborns of depressed mothers showed less vocal distress when another infant cried, reflecting emotional and physiological dysregulation (Jones, 2012).

Babies do not have just one type of cry; they have at least three. The **basic cry** is a rhythmic pattern that usually consists of a cry, followed by a briefer silence, then a shorter inspiratory whistle that is somewhat higher in pitch than the main cry, then another brief rest before the next cry. Some infancy experts believe that hunger is one of the conditions that incite the basic cry. The **anger cry** is a variation of the basic cry. However, in the anger cry, more excess air is forced through the vocal cords. The **pain cry**, which is stimulated by high-intensity stimuli, differs from other types of cries. A sudden appearance of loud crying without preliminary moaning and a long initial cry followed by an extended period of breath holding characterize the pain cry.

What are some developmental changes in emotion during infancy?
What are some different types of crying that infants display?

Most adults can determine whether an infant's cries signify anger or pain (Zeskind, 2009). Parents also can distinguish the cries of their own baby better than those of another baby. There is little consistent evidence to support the idea that mothers and other females, but not fathers and other males, are innately programmed to respond in a comforting way to an infant's crying.

To soothe or not to soothe—should a crying baby be given attention and soothed, or does this spoil the infant? Many years ago, famous behaviourist John Watson (1928) argued that parents spent too much time responding to infant crying. As a consequence, he said, parents were actually rewarding infant crying and increasing its incidence. In contrast, infancy experts Mary Ainsworth (1979) and John Bowlby (1989) considered the caregiver's quick, comforting response to the infant's cries an important ingredient in the development of secure attachment. Overall, developmentalists increasingly argue that an infant cannot be spoiled in the first year of life, which suggests that parents should soothe a crying infant rather than be unresponsive; in this manner, infants likely will develop a sense of trust and secure attachment to the caregiver in the first year of life. Other researchers have found that a tactile stimulus (touch) can be useful for ending an infant's crying behaviour (Feldman & Eidelman, 2003; Feldman et al., 2003).

Evolutionary psychologists look to nature—that is, the inborn biological forces that have evolved to promote survival—to explain why individuals act in certain ways. According to them, such individuals cannot be changed by modifying the reinforcers. These reactions are based on the human genetic code that we all share. However, evolutionary psychologists alert us to the fact that we do need to pay close attention to basic human needs (Belsky, 2010).

Nakayama (2010) examined the development of infant crying behaviour after 6 months of age. Two female infants were observed twice a month for six months when the infants were between 7 and 14 months of age. It appeared that the crying behaviour of the infants became more sophisticated and communicative with increasing age. This behaviour suggests a proactive stance by the infant in interacting with the mother. The findings seem to indicate that at 11–12 months of age, it is possible to observe "fake crying" during naturalistic interaction with the mother. Fake crying is the behaviour used by an infant to convey attention to the mother so that the mother comes nearer and provides attention to the infant. This study indicates that normal infants might be capable of deceptive behaviour such as "fake crying" by the end of the first year. The results also provide strong evidence that infants communicate proactively with the mother by using crying behaviour. Fake crying has come to be regarded as a favourable sign of a normal infant's social development.

In summary, primary health care professionals have a responsibility to provide parents with information and strategies to help them understand and manage both the infant's crying as well as their own frustration with crying (Evanoo, 2007).

Smiling

Smiling is another important communicative affective behaviour of the infant. Two types of smiling can be distinguished in infants—one reflexive, the other social. A **reflexive smile** does not occur in response to external stimuli. It appears during the first month after birth, usually during irregular patterns of sleep. By contrast, a **social smile** occurs in response to an external stimulus, which, early in development, typically is a face. The power of an infant's smiles was appropriately captured by British attachment theorist John Bowlby (1969): "Can we doubt that the more and better an infant smiles, the better he is loved and cared for? It is fortunate for their survival that babies are so designed by nature that they beguile and enslave mothers."

Daniel Messinger (2008) recently described the developmental course of infant smiling. From two to six months after birth, infants' social smiling increases considerably, both in self-initiated smiles and smiles in response to others' smiles. At the age of 6 to 12 months, smiles that couple what is called the Duchenne marker (eye constriction) and mouth opening occur in the midst of highly enjoyable interactions and play with parents. In the second year, smiling continues to occur in such positive circumstances with parents, and in many cases an increase in smiling occurs when interacting with peers. Also in the second year, toddlers become increasingly aware of the social meaning of smiles, especially in their relationship with parents.

Fear

Expressions of fear become increasingly observable between 6 and 12 months of age (Brooker et al., 2013). The link between maternal depressive symptoms and changes in infant fear is potentially an important key to gaining greater understanding into developmental processes related to fearfulness. At the physiological level, underlying mechanisms have been suggested for the process whereby infants of depressed mothers become increasingly negative and fearful (Gartstein et al., 2016). Researchers have found that infant fear is linked to guilt, empathy, and low aggression at 6 to 7 years of age (Rothbart, 2007).

The most frequent expression of an infant's fear involves **stranger anxiety**, in which an infant shows fear and wariness of strangers. This reaction starts to appear in the second half of the first year. There are individual variations in stranger anxiety, and not all infants show distress when they encounter a stranger. Stranger anxiety usually emerges gradually, first appearing at about 6 months of age in the form of wary reactions. By age 9 months, the fear of strangers is often more intense, reaching a peak toward the end of the first year of life, then decreasing thereafter (Scher & Harel, 2008).

In addition to stranger anxiety, infants often experience fear of being separated from their caregivers. The result is **separation protest**—crying when the caregiver leaves. Separation protest is initially displayed by infants at approximately 7 to 8 months and peaks at about 15 months (Kagan, 2008).

Emotion Regulation and Coping

Emotion regulation consists of effectively managing arousal to adapt to and reach a goal (Thompson, 2011). Arousal involves a state of alertness or activation, which can reach levels that are too high for effective functioning.

During the first year after birth, the infant gradually develops an ability to inhibit or minimize the intensity and duration of emotional reactions (Calkins, 2007; Kopp, 2008). From early in infancy, many babies put their thumbs in their mouths to soothe themselves. They also depend on caregivers to help them soothe their emotions by rocking them to sleep, singing lullabies to them, gently stroking them, and so on. As a result, the caregivers' actions influence the infant's neurobiological regulation of emotions (Thompson, Meyer, & Jochem, 2008). By soothing the infant, caregivers help infants to modulate their emotion and reduce the level of stress hormones (Gunnar & Quevedo, 2007). Many developmentalists stress that it is a good strategy for a caregiver to soothe an infant before the infant gets into an intense, agitated, uncontrolled state.

Contexts can influence emotional regulation (Thompson & Goodvin, 2007; Thompson, 2011). Infants are often affected by such factors as fatigue, hunger, time of day, and the people around them. Infants must learn to adapt to different contexts that require emotional regulation. Further, new context demands appear as the infant becomes older and parents modify their expectations. For example, a parent may not expect a 1½-year-old to scream loudly in a restaurant, but may not have been as bothered by this when the child was 6 months old.

By 2 years of age, toddlers can use language to define their feeling states and the context that is upsetting them (Kopp, 2008). A toddler might say, "Feel bad. Dog scare." The communication of this type of information about feeling states and context may help caregivers to assist the child in regulating emotion. Toddlers can also be very good at using physically aggressive behaviour to express feeling states, such as anxiety, fear, and jealousy, instead of using their language abilities. In a study following a group of children in Quebec from ages 4 months through 7 years, Barker and colleagues (2008) found that children who showed a higher level of aggressive behaviour (biting, kicking, hitting, etc.) by age 17 months were more likely to be subject to peer victimization by the time they entered grade 2. Their inappropriate interpersonal skills made them liable to bullying. This finding underlines the importance of teaching toddlers to verbally express and resolve negative emotional states.

To this point, we have studied a number of ideas about emotional development in infancy. For a review, see the Reach Your Learning Outcomes section at the end of this chapter.

Temperament and Personality Development

LO2 Summarize the development of temperament and personality during infancy.

- **Temperament**
- **Personality Development**

Infants show different emotional responses. One infant might be cheerful and happy much of the time; another baby might cry constantly. These behaviours reflect differences in temperament (Casalin et al., 2012).

Temperament

Temperament is an individual's behavioural style and characteristic way of emotionally responding. Developmentalists are especially interested in the temperament of infants.

Defining and Classifying Temperaments

Given the uniqueness of infants' temperamental responses, many developmentalists have attempted to classify temperament into different styles.

CHESS AND THOMAS'S CLASSIFICATION

Psychiatrists Alexander Chess and Stella Thomas (Chess & Thomas, 1977; Thomas & Chess, 1991) believe there are three basic types, or clusters, of temperament—easy, difficult, and slow to warm up.

- An **easy child** is generally in a positive mood, quickly establishes regular routines in infancy, and adapts easily to new experiences.
- A **difficult child** tends to react negatively and cry frequently, engages in irregular daily routines, and is slow to accept new experiences.
- A **slow-to-warm-up** child has a low activity level, is somewhat negative, shows low adaptability, and displays a low intensity of mood.

Various dimensions make up these three basic clusters of temperament. Chess and Thomas found that 40 percent of the children they studied could be classified as easy, 10 percent as difficult, and 15 percent as slow-to-warm-up (35 percent did not fit any of the three patterns). These three basic clusters of temperament are moderately stable across the childhood years.

KAGAN'S BEHAVIOURAL INHIBITION

Another way of classifying temperament focuses on the differences between a shy, subdued, timid child and a sociable, extraverted, bold child (Asendorph, 2008). Jerome Kagan (Kagan et al., 2007; Kagan, 2010, 2012) regards shyness with strangers (peers or adults) as one feature of a broad temperament category called *inhibition to the unfamiliar*. Inhibited children react to many aspects of unfamiliarity with initial avoidance, distress, or subdued affect, beginning at about 7 to 9 months of age. Kagan has found that inhibition shows considerable stability from infancy through early childhood. One study classified toddlers into extremely inhibited, extremely uninhibited, and intermediate groups (Pfeifer et al., 2002). Follow-up assessments occurred at 4 and 7 years of age. Continuity was demonstrated for both inhibition and lack of inhibition, although a substantial number of the inhibited children moved into the intermediate groups at 7 years of age. Another study revealed that behavioural inhibition at 3 years of age is linked to shyness four years later (Volbrecht & Goldsmith, 2010). And in yet another study, 24-month-olds who were fearful in situations relatively low in threat were likely to experience higher than average levels of anxiety in kindergarten (Buss, 2011). In fact, researchers have found that shyness or inhibition in infancy and childhood are linked to social anxiety at 21 years of age (Bohlin & Hagekull, 2009).

ROTHBART AND BATES'S CLASSIFICATION

Mary Rothbart and John Bates (2006) argue that three broad dimensions best represent what researchers have found to characterize the structure of temperament: extraversion/ surgency, negative affectivity, and effortful control (self-regulation):

- *Extraversion/surgency* includes "positive anticipation, impulsivity, activity level, and sensation seeking" (Rothbart, 2004, p. 495). Kagan's uninhibited children fit into this category.
- *Negative affectivity* includes "fear, frustration, sadness, and discomfort" (Rothbart, 2004, p. 495). These children are easily distressed; they may fret and cry often. Kagan's inhibited children fit this category.
- *Effortful control (self-regulation)* includes "attentional focusing and shifting, inhibitory control, perceptual sensitivity, and low-intensity pleasure" (Rothbart, 2004, p. 495). Infants who are high on effortful control show an ability to keep their arousal from getting too high and have strategies for soothing themselves. By contrast, children low on effortful control often are unable to control their arousal; they become easily agitated and intensely emotional.

In Rothbart's view, "early theoretical models of temperament stressed the way we are moved by our positive and negative emotions or level of arousal, with our actions driven by these tendencies" (2004, p. 497). The more recent emphasis on effortful control, however, advocates that individuals can engage in a more cognitive, flexible approach to stressful circumstances.

critical thinking

How would you describe your temperament now and in childhood? Are they the same? Is your present temperament similar to what your parents remember about your temperament in your early years? What is temperament in an infant? Compare and contrast infant gender differences of temperament.

Rothbart and Maria Gartstein (2008) describe the following developmental changes in temperament during infancy. During early infancy, smiling and laughter emerge as part of the positive affectivity dimension of temperament. Also, by 2 months of age, infants show anger and frustration when their actions don't produce an interesting outcome. During this time, infants often are susceptible to distress and overstimulation. From 4 to 12 months of age, fear and irritability become more differentiated, with inhibition (fear) increasingly linked to new and unpredictable experiences. Not all temperament characteristics are in place by the first birthday. Positive emotionality becomes more stable later in infancy, and the characteristics of extraversion/surgency can be determined in the toddler period. Improved attention skills in the toddler and preschool years are related to an increase in effortful control, which serves as a foundation for improved self-regulation.

Biological Foundations and Experience

How does a child acquire a certain temperament? Kagan (2002; 2010) argues that children inherit a physiology that biases them to have a particular type of temperament. However, through experience they may learn to modify their temperament to some degree. For example, children may inherit a physiology that biases them to be fearful and inhibited, but they learn to reduce their fear and inhibition to some degree.

BIOLOGICAL INFLUENCES

Physiological characteristics have been linked with different temperaments (Mize & Jones, 2012). In particular, an inhibited temperament is associated with a unique physiological pattern that includes high and stable heart rate, high level of the hormone cortisol, and high activity in the right frontal lobe of the brain (Kagan, 2008). This pattern may be tied to the excitability of the amygdala, a structure of the brain that plays an important role in fear and inhibition. Canadian researchers Louis Schmidt and colleagues (2009) reported evidence for a gene–environment interaction in predicting child temperament. Children who exhibited left frontal EEG asymmetry at 9 months and who possessed the DRD4 long allele were significantly more soothable at 48 months than other children who exhibited right EEG asymmetry and possessed the DRD4 long allele. The researchers conclude that a gene involved in the regulation of dopamine moderates the relation between frontal brain activity and two basic components of early temperament, one cognitive and the other affective. Furthermore, their data serve as a starting point for considering the impact of genetic factors and other environmental factors on gene expression to explain the complexities of temperament and other complex traits.

What is the role of heredity in the biological foundations of temperament? Twin and adoption studies suggest that heredity has a moderate influence on differences in temperament within a group of people (Plomin et al., 2009). Temperament changes throughout childhood because of developmental changes that occur in the central nervous system, and because of changes in other processes that underlie the child's ability to moderate emotional responses. Recently, greater acknowledgement has been given to environmental influences that might have important implications for the development of temperament (Rothbart & Bates, 2006; Blandon et al., 2010). The fact that the environment interacts with developmental influences is not surprising—development is complex and is rarely guided by only one, or a few, primary influences.

GENDER, CULTURE, AND TEMPERAMENT

Gender may be an important factor in shaping the context that influences the fate of temperament. For example, parents might react differently to an infant's temperament depending on whether the baby is a boy or a girl.

Similarly, the reaction to an infant's temperament may depend in part on culture (Perez & Gauvain, 2007). For example, an active temperament might be valued in some cultures (such as Canada), but not in other cultures (such as China). Indeed, children's temperament can vary across cultures (Chen, 2011). Behavioural inhibition is more highly valued in China than in North America, and researchers have found that Chinese children are more inhibited than Canadian infants (Chen et al., 1998). These cultural differences in temperament are linked to parent attitude and behaviours: Canadian mothers of inhibited 2-year-olds are less accepting of their infants' inhibited temperament, whereas Chinese mothers are more accepting.

In short, many aspects of a child's environment can encourage or discourage the persistence of temperament characteristics (Bates & Pettit, 2007; Rothbart & Sheese, 2007). One useful way of thinking about these relationships applies the concept of goodness of fit, which we examine next.

Tom Merton /Getty Images

What are some ways that developmentalists have classified infants' temperaments? Which classification makes the most sense to you, on the basis of your observations of infants?

Goodness of Fit and Parenting

Goodness of fit refers to the match between a child's temperament and the environmental demands the child must cope with (Thompson, Meyer, & Jochem, 2008). Goodness of fit can be important to the child's adjustment. For example, consider an active child who is made to sit still for long periods of time or lives in a small apartment. Consider also a slow-to-warm-up child who is abruptly pushed into new situations on a regular basis. Such a lack of fit between the child's temperament and environmental demands can produce adjustment problems for the child (Rothbart, 2011).

As a result, adults, especially parents, should be aware of children's temperament. Interestingly, many parents do not realize temperament's importance until the birth of their second child; instead, they view the first child's behaviour as being solely a result of how they socialized the child. However, they soon find that management strategies that worked with the first child might not be as effective with the second child. Problems experienced with the first child (such as those involved in feeding, sleeping, and coping with strangers) might not exist with the second child, but new problems might arise. Such experiences strongly suggest that nature as well as nurture influence child development, that children differ from each other very early on in life, and that these differences have important implications for parent–child interaction (Mortensen & Mastergeorge, 2014).

What are the implications of temperamental variations for parenting? Some experts have reached the following conclusions (Putnam, Sanson, & Rothbart, 2002):

- *Attention to and respect for individuality:* An important implication of taking children's individuality seriously is that it becomes difficult to generate prescriptions for "good parenting," other than possibly specifying that parents need to be sensitive and flexible. Parents need to be sensitive to the infant's signals and needs. A goal of parenting might be accomplished in one way with one child and in another way with another child, depending on the child's temperament (Putnam, Sanson, & Rothbart, 2002)
- *Structuring the child's environment:* Crowded, noisy environments can pose greater problems for a "difficult" child than an "easygoing" child. Similarly, a fearful, withdrawing child could benefit from slower entry into new contexts.
- *The "difficult child" and packaged parenting programs:* Some books and programs for parents focus on temperament, and usually on *difficult* temperaments. Acknowledgement that some children are harder to parent is often helpful, and advice on how to handle particular difficult temperament characteristics can also be useful. However, the label *difficult* should be used with care because whether a particular characteristic of a child is difficult, by and large, depends on its fit with the environment.

What are some good strategies for parents to adopt when responding to their infant's temperament?

Costa and Figueiredo (2011) conducted a study to analyze differences in infant temperament at 3 and 12 months according to the infant's psychophysiological profile (withdrawn, extroverted, or underaroused). They also explored changes in infant temperament from 3 to 12 months according to the infant psychophysiological profile and the quality of mother–infant interaction. These researchers concluded that significant differences in mothers' perception of infant temperament are found at both 3 and 12 months in infants with distinct psychophysiological profiles. For example, mothers of withdrawn infants perceive them as more difficult. These difficulties then predispose to difficulties in the relational level between mother and infant, which may lead to an increased probability of developmental problems in the infant. However, it becomes apparent that when a good mother–infant interaction is established, an increased positive emotionality is possible to develop, which may act as a protective factor in infant development.

A U.S. study examined the contributions of infant temperament, marital functioning, and the division of parenting on the quality of the co-parenting relationship for couples parenting 6-month-old infants. The researchers found that mothers who perceive their infants as more reactive report more negative co-parenting only if their infants are also not easily soothed, or if mothers are dissatisfied with how parenting tasks are divided and performed given their prior expectations. Meanwhile, fathers report more negative co-parenting when faced with a more reactive infant and when they report a low-quality marital relationship (Burney & Leerkes, 2010).

Personality Development

We have explored some important aspects of emotional development and temperament. What about personality development?

Trust

According to Erik Erikson (1968), the trust-versus-mistrust stage of development characterizes the first year after birth. Following a life of regularity, warmth, and protection in the mother's womb, the infant faces a world that is less secure. Erikson believes that infants learn trust when they are cared for in a consistent, warm manner. If the infant is not well-fed and kept warm on a consistent basis, a sense of mistrust is likely to develop.

Trust versus mistrust is not resolved once and for all in the first year of life. It arises again at each successive stage of development. There is hope as well as danger in this. Children who enter school with a sense of mistrust may regain a sense of trust because of a responsive teacher. By contrast, children who leave infancy with a sense of trust can still have their sense of mistrust activated at a later stage, perhaps if their parents separate or divorce under acrimonious circumstances.

Self

Individuals carry with them a sense of who they are and what makes them different from everyone else. Real or imagined, this sense of self is a strong motivating force in life. When does the individual begin to sense a separate existence from others? Infants are not "given" a self by their parents or the culture. Rather, they find and construct selves. Studying the self in infancy is difficult, mainly because infants are unable to use language to describe their experiences of themselves (Thompson, 2007).

To determine whether infants can recognize themselves, psychologists have used mirrors. First, the mother puts a dot of rouge on her infant's nose. The observer watches to see how often the infant touches its nose. Next, the infant is placed in front of a mirror, and observers detect whether nose touching increases. In two independent investigations, it was discovered that not until the second half of the second year of life did infants recognize their own image and coordinate the image they saw with the actions of touching their own body (Lewis & Brooks-Gunn, 1979). Mirrors are not familiar to infants in all cultures. Physical self-recognition may be a more important marker of self-recognition in Western than non-Western cultures (Thompson & Virmani, 2010). Signs of self-recognition begin to appear among some infants when they are 15 to 18 months old. By the time they are 2 years old, most children recognize themselves in the mirror. In sum, infants begin to develop a self-understanding called self-recognition at approximately 18 months of age (Lewis, 2005). Figure 6.3 shows the findings of these studies. Late in the second year and early in the third year, toddlers show other emerging forms of self-awareness that reflect a sense of "me" (Laible & Thompson, 2007).

Figure 6.3

The Development of Self-Recognition in Infancy

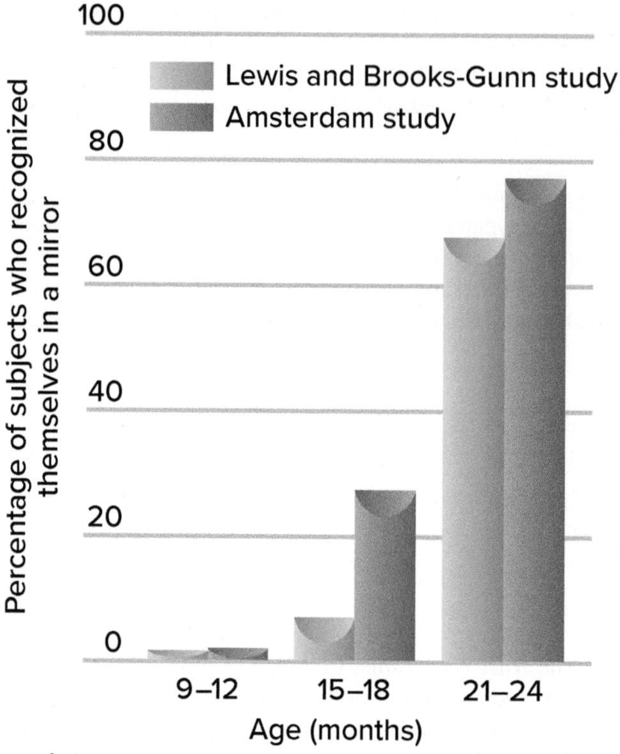

The graph shows the findings of the two studies in which infants less than 1 year of age did not recognize themselves in the mirror. A slight increase in the percentage of infant self-recognition occurred around 15 to 18 months of age. By 2 years of age, a majority of children recognized themselves. *Why do researchers study whether infants recognize themselves in a mirror?*

Independence

Independence is an important theme in the infant's life. The theories of Margaret Mahler and Erik Erikson have implications for both self-development and independence. Mahler (1979) believed that the child goes through a separation and then an individuation process. Separation involves the infant's movement away from the mother. Individuation involves the development of self.

Erikson (1968), like Mahler, believed that independence is an important issue in the second year of life. Erikson described the second stage of development as the stage of autonomy versus shame and doubt. Autonomy builds on the infant's developing mental and motor abilities. At this point in development, infants can not only walk, but also climb, open and close, drop, push and pull, and hold and let go. Infants feel pride in these new accomplishments and want to do everything themselves, whether it is flushing a toilet, pulling the wrapping off a package, or deciding what to eat. It is important for parents to recognize the motivation of toddlers to do what they are capable of doing at their own pace. Then the infants can learn to control their muscles and their impulses themselves. But when caregivers are impatient and do for toddlers what they are capable of doing themselves, shame and doubt develop. Every parent has rushed a child from time to time. It is only when parents consistently overprotect toddlers or criticize accidents (wetting, soiling, or breaking, for example) that children develop an excessive sense of shame and doubt about their ability to control themselves and their world.

Erikson also believed that the stage of autonomy versus shame and doubt has important implications for the development of independence and identity during adolescence. The development of autonomy during the toddler years gives adolescents the courage to be independent individuals who can choose and guide their own future.

To this point, we have studied a number of ideas about the infant's temperament and personality development. For a review, see the Reach Your Learning Outcomes section at the end of this chapter.

Social Orientation/Understanding and Attachment

LO3 Analyze social orientation/understanding and the development of attachment in infancy.

- **Social Orientation/Understanding**
- **Attachment and Its Development**
- **Individual Differences in Attachment**
- **Caregiving Styles and Attachment Classifications**
- **Attachment, Temperament, and the Wider Social World**

So far, we have discussed how emotions and emotional competence change as children develop. We have also examined the role of emotional style; in effect, we have seen how emotions set the tone of our experiences in life. But emotions also write the lyrics, because they are at the core of our relationships with others.

Social Orientation/Understanding

As socio-emotional beings, infants show a strong interest in the social world and are motivated to orient to it and understand it. In earlier chapters, we described many of the biological and cognitive foundations that contribute to the infant's development of social orientation and understanding. We will call attention to relevant biological and cognitive factors as we explore social orientation; locomotion; intention, goal-directed behaviour, and cooperation; and social referencing. Discussing biological, cognitive, and social processes together reminds us of an important aspect of development that was pointed out in Chapter 1: These processes are intricately intertwined (Diamond, 2007).

Social Orientation

From early in their development, infants are captivated by the social world. As we discussed in our coverage of infant perception in Chapter 4, young infants stare intently at faces and are attuned to the sounds of human voices, especially their caregivers' (Ramsey-Rennels & Langlois, 2007). Later, they become adept at interpreting the meaning of facial expressions.

Face-to-face play often begins to characterize caregiver–infant interactions when the infant is about 2 to 3 months of age. The focused social interaction of face-to-face play may include vocalizations, touch, and gestures (Leppanen et al., 2007). Such play is part of many mothers' motivation to create a positive emotional state in their infants (Laible & Thompson, 2007; Thompson, 2009a). However, infants also learn about the social world through contexts other than face-to-face play with their caregivers (Thompson, 2009b; Thompson & Newton, 2009; Lowe et al., 2012; Sugden, Mohamed-Ali, & Moulson, 2014).

Even though infants as young as 6 months of age show an interest in each other, their interaction with peers increases considerably in the last half of the second year. One recent study involved presenting 1- and 2-year-olds with a simple cooperative task that consisted of pulling a lever to get an attractive toy (Brownell, Ramani, & Zerwas, 2006) (see Figure 6.4). Any coordinated actions of the 1-year-olds appeared to be more coincidental than cooperative, whereas the 2-year-olds' behaviour was characterized as more active cooperation to reach a goal. As increasing numbers of North American infants experience child care outside the home, they are spending more time in social play with other peers (Field, 2007). Later in the chapter, we will further discuss child care.

Figure 6.4
The Cooperation Task

Courtesy of Celia A. Brownell, University of Pittsburgh

The cooperation task consisted of two handles on a box, atop of which was an animal musical toy, surreptitiously activated by remote control when both handles were pulled. The handles were placed far enough apart that one child could not pull both handles. The experimenter demonstrated the task, saying, "Watch! If you pull the handles, the doggie will sing" (Brownell, Ramani, & Zerwas, 2006).

Locomotion

Recall from earlier in the chapter how important independence is for infants, especially in the second year of life. As infants develop the ability to crawl, walk, and run, they are able to explore and expand their social world. These newly developed self-produced locomotor skills allow the infant to independently initiate social interchanges on a more frequent basis (Laible & Thompson, 2007; Thompson, 2006). Remember also from Chapter 4 that the development of these gross motor skills is the result of a number of factors, including the development of the nervous system, the goal the infant is motivated to reach, and environmental support for the skill (Adolph, 2010; Adolph, Kretch, & LoBue, 2014).

Locomotion is also important for its motivational implications (Thompson, 2008). Once infants have the ability to move in goal-directed pursuits, the reward from these pursuits leads to further efforts to explore and develop skills.

Intention, Goal-Directed Behaviour, and Cooperation

Perceiving people as engaging in intentional and goal-directed behaviour is an important social cognitive accomplishment, and this initially occurs toward the end of the first year (Laible & Thompson, 2007). Joint attention and gaze following help the infant to understand that other people have intentions (Deák et al., 2014). Joint attention is defined as a state during which both social partners are actively focused on a particular object, event, or topic, and both are aware of each other's active participation and focus (Nowakowski, 2009). According to Racine and Carpendale (2007), pointing during joint attention is often thought to be the clearest indicator of early social understanding. More specifically, Gaffan and colleagues (2010) found that maternal teaching behaviours (i.e., pointing or demonstrating) at 6 months of age predicted active joint attention with the mother at 9 months of age.

Interestingly, one recent study by Meins and colleagues (2011) investigated relations between infant–mother attachment security and infants' previous (age 8 months) and concurrent (age 15 months) joint attention abilities. These researchers reported security-related differences specifically in infant initiations with the experimenter and mother. Infants with insecure-avoidant attachments initiated more joint attention with an experimenter and less joint attention with their mothers than did their counterparts in the secure and insecure-resistant attachment groups. However, these differences were apparent only at a later age, when the attachment relationships were fully formed. The researchers concluded that insecure-avoidant infants who show a heightened tendency to initiate joint attention with a new social partner actually might be doing so as a strategy to compensate for their own avoidance of social contact with their mother (Meins et al., 2011).

Further, another study revealed that initiating and responding to joint attention at 12 months of age are linked to being socially competent (for example, not aggressive or defiant, showing empathy, and engaging in sustained attention) at 30 months of age (Vaughan et al., 2007).

Social Referencing

One important accomplishment during infancy is that the infant develops the ability to "read" the emotions of other people (Cornew et al., 2012). *Social referencing* involves the "reading" of emotional cues in others to help determine how the infant is to act in a particular circumstance. The development of social referencing helps infants to more accurately interpret ambiguous situations. One example occurs when the infant encounters a stranger and needs to know whether or not to fear or trust that person (Pelaez, Virrues-Ortega, & Gewirta, 2012). By the end of the infant's first year, a mother's facial expression—either smiling or fearful—influences whether or not an infant will explore or avoid an unfamiliar environment.

The development of face processing abilities appears to start very early in infancy (Dobkins & Harms, 2014). In habituation studies, it has been shown that infants can discriminate between different faces (Kelly et al., 2008; Slater et al., 2010). Recently, using a familiarization paradigm, Turati and colleagues (2011) explored the role of positive emotional expressions on the identity recognition of 3-month-old infants. Results indicated that, as in adults, infants' face recognition is enhanced when faces display a happy emotional expression. This finding suggests the presence of a mutual interaction between face identity and emotion recognition at as early as 3 months of age. Another group of researchers investigated the extent to which and in what ways the presence of an emotional expression may affect identity recognition at 3 months of age. The results support the presence of a mutual interaction between face identity and emotion recognition (Brenna et al., 2012).

Finally, Dobkins and Harms (2014) measured inversion effects for faces in infants. The results indicated that infants have preferences for upright faces. The findings indicate that infants, similar to adults, may find it difficult to process emotional expressions in inverted faces, irrespective of age.

Infants' Social Sophistication and Insight

In sum, researchers are discovering that infants are more socially sophisticated and insightful at younger ages than previously envisioned (Hamlin, Hallinan, & Woodward, 2008; Thompson, 2008, 2009a, b; Thompson, 2015). This sophistication and insight is reflected in infants' perceptions of others' actions as intentionally motivated and goal-directed (Brune & Woodward, 2007), and their motivation by their first birthday to share and participate in that intentionality (Tomasello & Carpenter, 2007). The more advanced social cognitive skills of infants could be expected to influence their understanding and awareness of attachment to a caregiver.

Attachment and Its Development

In everyday language, attachment is a relationship between two individuals who feel strongly about each other and do a number of things to continue the relationship. In the language of developmental psychology, though, **attachment** is a close emotional bond between two people. During infancy, the infant's attachment is usually with one or more adult caregivers, and the phenomenon is a close emotional bond (Bowlby, 1969, 1989).

There is no shortage of theories about infant attachment. Freud believed that infants become attached to the person or object that provides oral satisfaction. For most infants this is the mother, because she is most likely to feed the infant.

Is feeding as important as Freud thought? A classic study by Harry Harlow (1958) reveals that the answer is no (see Figure 6.5). Harlow evaluated whether feeding or contact comfort was more important to infant attachment. Infant monkeys were removed from their mothers at birth and reared for six months by surrogate "mothers." One of the mothers was made of wire, the other of cloth. Half the infant monkeys were fed by the wire mother, half by the cloth mother. Periodically, the amount of time the infant monkeys spent with either the wire or the cloth mother was computed. Regardless of whether they were fed by the wire or the cloth mother, the infant monkeys spent far more time with the cloth mother. This study clearly demonstrated that feeding is not the crucial element in the attachment process, and that contact comfort is important.

Figure 6.5

Harlow's Classic "Contact Comfort" Study

Regardless of whether they were fed by a wire mother or by a cloth mother, the infant monkeys overwhelmingly preferred to be in contact with the cloth mother, demonstrating the importance of contact comfort in attachment.

Erik Erikson (1968) believed that the trust versus mistrust stage in the first year of infancy is the key time frame for the development of attachment. A sense of trust requires a feeling of physical comfort and a minimal amount of fear and apprehension about the future. Trust in infancy sets the stage for a lifelong expectation that the world will be a good and pleasant place.

The ethological perspective of British psychiatrist John Bowlby (1969, 1989) also stresses the importance of attachment and the responsiveness of the caregiver early in life. Bowlby believed that an infant and the primary caregiver form an attachment. The baby cries, clings, coos, and smiles. Later, the infant crawls, walks, and follows the mother. The immediate result is to keep the primary caregiver nearby; the long-term effect is to increase the infant's chances of survival (Raikes & Thompson, 2008).

Attachment does not emerge suddenly but rather develops in a series of phases, moving from a baby's general preference for human beings to a partnership with primary caregivers. The following are four such phases based on Bowlby's (1969) conceptualization of attachment:

Phase 1:	Birth to 2 months	Infants instinctively direct their attachment to human figures. Strangers, siblings, and parents are equally likely to elicit smiling or crying from the infant.
Phase 2:	2 to 7 months	Attachment becomes focused on one figure, usually the primary caregiver, as the baby gradually learns to distinguish familiar people from unfamiliar ones.

Phase 3:	7 to 24 months	Specific attachments develop. With increased locomotor skills, babies actively seek contact with regular caregivers, such as the mother or father.
Phase 4:	24 months on	A goal-directed partnership is formed in which children become aware of others' feelings, goals, and plans and begin to take these into account in forming their own actions.

As the phases above indicate, attachment focuses on specific individuals and is reflected by infants' behaviour in the second half of the first year after birth. You may recall in an earlier discussion that stranger anxiety also emerges at around the same time. This suggests that stressful situations may provoke attempts to seek comfort from a trusted individual. The occurrence of these phenomena at approximately the same time also indicates that infants visually recognize the differences between the caregiver and the stranger, have some knowledge of causality of their own action (e.g., crawling toward the caregiver in the hope of getting comforted), and use locomotor skills to achieve goals. Together, these phenomena serve to remind us that physical, cognitive, and social developments are interrelated.

Individual Differences in Attachment

Although attachment to a caregiver intensifies midway through the first year, isn't it likely that some babies have a more positive attachment experience than others? Mary Ainsworth (1979) thought so. Ainsworth created the **Strange Situation**, an observational measure of infant attachment that requires the infant to move through a series of introductions, separations, and reunions with the caregiver and an adult stranger in a prescribed order (see Figure 6.6). The goal of using the Strange Situation is to obtain information about the infant's motivation to be near the caregiver and the degree to which the caregiver's presence provides the infant with security and confidence. Based on how babies respond in the Strange Situation, they are described as being securely attached or insecurely attached (in one of three ways) to the caregiver.

Figure 6.6
The Ainsworth Strange Situation

Episode	Participants	Duration of Episode	Description of Setting
1	Caregiver, baby, and observer	30 seconds	Observer introduces caregiver and baby to experimental room, then leaves. (Room contains many appealing toys scattered about.)
2	Caregiver and baby	3 minutes	Caregiver is non-participant while baby explores; if necessary, play is stimulated after 2 minutes.
3	Stranger, caregiver, and baby	3 minutes	Stranger enters. First minute: stranger is silent. Second minute: stranger converses with caregiver. Third minute: stranger approaches baby. After 3 minutes caregiver leaves unobtrusively.
4	Stranger and baby	3 minutes or less	First separation episode. Stranger's behaviour is geared to that of baby.
5	Caregiver and baby	3 minutes or more	First reunion episode. Caregiver greets and/or comforts baby, then tries to settle the baby again in play. Caregiver then leaves, saying "bye-bye."

Episode	Participants	Duration of Episode	Description of Setting
6	Baby alone	3 minutes or less	Second separation episode.
7	Stranger and baby	3 minutes or less	Continuation of second separation. Stranger enters and gears behaviour to that of baby.
8	Caregiver and baby	3 minutes	Second reunion episode. Caregiver enters, greets baby, then picks baby up. Meanwhile stranger leaves unobtrusively.

Adapted from M.D.S. Ainsworth & S.M. Bell, 1971, "Attachment, Exploration, and Separation: Illustrated by the Behavior of One-Year-Olds in a Strange Situation," Child Development, Vol. 41, (1), pp. 49-67. Reprinted by permission of Society for Research in Child Development.N/A

Mary Ainsworth developed the Strange Situation to assess whether infants are securely or insecurely attached to their caregiver. The episodes involved in the Ainsworth Strange Situation are described above.

Securely attached babies use the caregiver as a secure base from which to explore the environment. When in the presence of their caregiver, securely attached infants explore the room and examine toys that have been placed in it. When the caregiver departs, securely attached infants might mildly protest, and when the caregiver returns these infants re-establish positive interaction with her, perhaps by smiling or climbing on her lap. Subsequently, they often resume playing with the toys in the room.

Insecure avoidant babies show insecurity by avoiding the caregiver. In the Strange Situation, these babies engage in little interaction with the caregiver, often display distress by crying when the adult leaves the room, usually do not re-establish contact upon reunion, and may even turn their back on the caregiver at this point. If contact is established, the infants usually lean away or look away.

Insecure resistant babies often cling to the caregiver and then resist the caregiver by fighting against the closeness, perhaps by kicking or pushing away. In the Strange Situation, these babies often cling anxiously to the caregiver and do not explore the playroom. When the caregiver leaves, they often cry loudly and push away if the caregiver tries to comfort them on their return.

Insecure disorganized babies show insecurity by being disorganized and disoriented. In the Strange Situation, these babies might appear dazed, confused, and fearful. To be classified as disorganized, strong patterns of avoidance and resistance must be shown or certain select behaviours, such as extreme fearfulness around the caregiver, must be present.

Although the Strange Situation has been used in a large number of studies of infant attachment, some critics believe that the isolated, controlled events of the setting might not necessarily reflect what would happen if infants were observed with their caregiver in a natural environment. Even though cultural variations exist in attachment classification, the most frequent classification in every culture so far is secure attachment (Thompson, 2006).

Whipple and colleagues (2009), of the University of Montreal, suggest that self-determination theory could add to our understanding of how attachment occurs. Self-determination theory holds that children are active agents, naturally inclined to explore their world through interaction with its various elements. This inclination does not assure exploration, however, as the social forces (e.g., parents) influence the child's exploration activity. Since secure attachment strikes a balance between attachment and exploration, examination of how mothers (and fathers) promote or limit self-determined exploratory behaviour could add much to our understanding of attachment.

Caregiving Styles and Attachment Classifications

Is the caregiving style of the parent linked to this close emotional bond called attachment? Securely attached babies tend to have caregivers who are sensitive to their signals and are consistently available to the needs of the infant (Powell et al., 2014). Such caregivers often let their babies assume an active part in determining the onset and pacing of interaction during first year of life. One study revealed that maternal sensitive responding is linked to infant attachment security (Finger et al.,

2009). Another study found that maternal sensitivity—but not infant temperament—when infants are 6 months old is linked to subsequent attachment security (Leerkes, Parade, & Gudmundson, 2011).

How, then, do caregivers of insecurely attached babies interact with them? Caregivers of avoidant babies tend to be insensitive, hostile, or rejecting (Madigan, Moran, & Pederson, 2006). In general, such caretakers tend not to be very affectionate with their babies, and they tend to show little synchrony when interacting with them. Caregivers of disorganized babies often neglect or even physically abuse their babies (Benoit, 2009; Toth, 2009; Bernard et al., 2012). In some cases, these caregivers actually show depression (Thompson, 2008). A mother's behaviours are reflective of her state of mind regarding her attachment with her baby. Studies of toddlers' attachments to mothers and fathers show that some infants are securely attached to one parent, but are insecurely attached to the other (Minzi, 2010).

Camille Tokerud/Getty Images

What is the nature of secure and insecure attachments?

critical thinking

What character strengths of fathers would promote secure attachments? What other factors, besides the child's environment and family history, should be taken into account in assessing attachment behaviours?

Attachment, Temperament, and the Wider Social World

If early attachment to a caregiver is important, it should relate to a child's social behaviour later in development. For some children, early attachments seem to foreshadow later functioning (Cassidy, 2009; Egeland, 2009). Indeed, researchers have found that early secure attachment *and* subsequent experiences, especially maternal care and life stresses, are linked with children's later behaviour and adjustment (Thompson, 2006).

Some developmentalists conclude that too much emphasis has been placed on the attachment bond in infancy (Newcombe, 2007). Jerome Kagan (1987, 2002), for example, points out that infants are highly resilient and adaptive; he argues that they are evolutionarily equipped to stay on a positive developmental course, even in the face of wide variations in parenting. Kagan and colleagues stress that genetic characteristics and temperament play more important roles in a child's social competence than the attachment theorists, such as Bowlby and Ainsworth, are willing to acknowledge

(Bakermans-Kranenburg et al., 2007). For example, if some infants inherit a low tolerance for stress, this, rather than an insecure attachment bond, may be responsible for an inability to get along with peers.

Another criticism of attachment theory is that it ignores the diversity of socializing agents and contexts that exist in an infant's world. A culture's value system can influence the nature of attachment (Grossman & Grossman, 2009; van Ijzendoorn & Sagi-Schwartz, 2009). Figure 6.7 shows a cross-cultural comparison of attachment among the United States, Germany, and Japan.

Figure 6.7

Cross-Cultural Comparison of Attachment

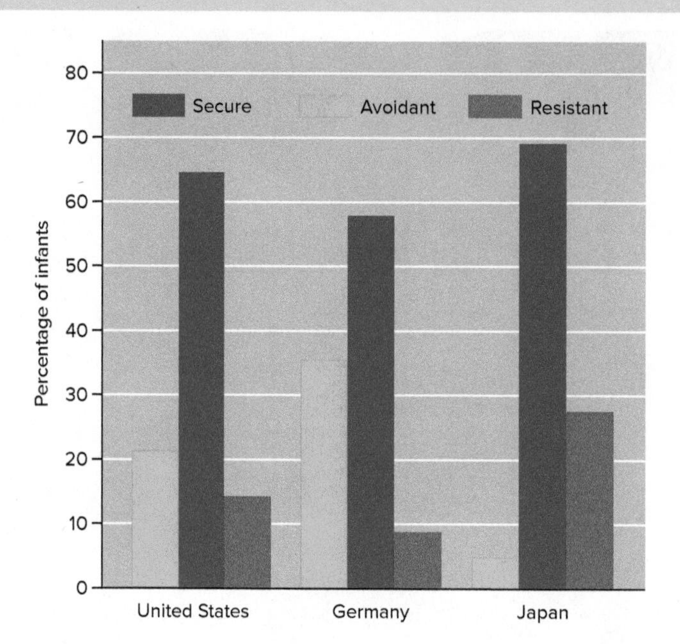

From van Ijzendoorn & Kroonenberg, 1988, "Cross Cultural Patterns of Attachment," *Child Development*, 59, 147-156. Adapted by permission of the Society for Research in Child Development.

In one study, infant attachment in three countries—the United States, Germany, and Japan—was measured in the Ainsworth Strange Situation (van Ijzendoorn & Kroonenberg, 1988). The dominant attachment pattern in all three countries was secure attachment. However, German infants were more avoidant and Japanese infants were less avoidant and more resistant than American infants.

When reviewing cross-cultural research, there emerges a theme that the dynamics described in attachment theory reflect Western ways of thinking and styles of relatedness. Attachment goals from a Western perspective move the individual from reliance on a safe base to personal exploration encompassing a wider periphery, with the goal being autonomy. However, in a collectivist culture, for example, such as the Mennonites and Hutterites in Canada, the goal of the caretaker would more likely be to encourage mutual effort, rather than one of reliance on self (Brown et al., 2008).

There is ample evidence that security of attachment is important to development (Posada, 2008; Thompson, 2009b). Secure attachment in infancy is important because it reflects a positive parent–infant relationship and provides the foundation that supports healthy socio-emotional development in the years that follow. The importance of secure attachment has led to the suggestion that attachment theory–based interventions be developed for dealing with abusive family situations (Tarabulsy et al., 2008). In this approach, the parents' attachment to the child, their sensitivity to the child's needs, and the child's own level of attachment are all assessed. A treatment plan to move everyone in the family to a more secure attachment pattern is established and implemented.

To this point, we have discussed a number of ideas about the infant's social orientation/understanding and attachment. For a review, see the Reach Your Learning Outcomes section at the end of this chapter.

Social Contexts

LO4 Determine how social contexts influence the infant's development.

- **The Family**
- **Child Care**
- **Infants with Special Needs**

The Family

The family can be thought of as a constellation of subsystems—a complex whole made up of interrelated, interacting parts—defined in terms of generation, gender, and role. Each family member participates in several subsystems (Fiese & Winter, 2008; Parke et al., 2008). The father and child represent one subsystem, the mother and father another, the mother-father-child yet another, and so on. At the same time, the family is but one unit nested in larger suprasystems, such as neighbourhoods, organizations, and church communities. The hierarchy of systems and the boundaries that create systems are useful concepts to apply when working with, and attempting to conceptualize, the uniqueness of each particular family (Wright & Leahey, 2013).

These subsystems have reciprocal influences on each other (Belsky, 2009), as Figure 6.8 highlights. For example, Jay Belsky (1981) emphasizes that marital relations, parenting, and infant behaviour and development can have both direct and indirect effects on each other. An example of a direct effect is the influence of the parents' behaviour on the child. An indirect effect is how the relationship between the spouses mediates the way a parent acts toward the child (Hsu, 2004).

Figure 6.8

Interaction between Children and Their Parents: Direct and Indirect Effects

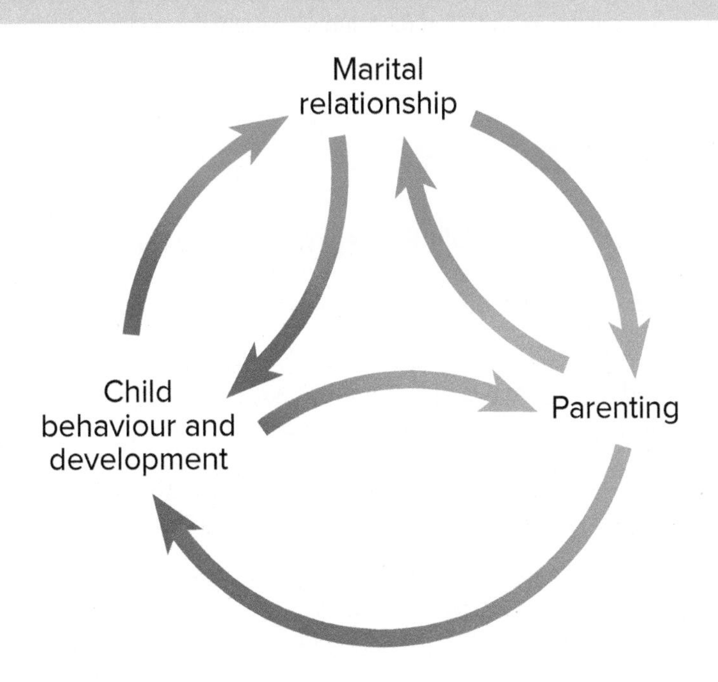

From Jay Belsky, " Early Human Experiences: A Family Perspective: in *Developmental Psychology*, Vol. 17, pp. 3-23.

The Transition to Parenthood

When people become parents through pregnancy, adoption, or step-parenting, they face disequilibrium and must adapt. Parents want to develop a strong attachment to their infant, but they still want to maintain strong attachments to each other and to friends, and possibly continue their careers. Parents ask themselves how this new being will change their lives. A baby places new restrictions on parents; no longer will they be able to rush out to a movie on a moment's notice, and money may not be as readily available for vacations and other luxuries. Dual-career parents ask themselves if it will harm the baby to place her in daycare, and wonder if they will be able to find responsible babysitters.

At some point during the early years of the child's life, parents face the difficult task of juggling their roles as parents and as self-actualizing adults. Until recently, nurturing children and having a career were thought to be incompatible. In fact, a study with female health care workers in Ontario—a group highly vulnerable to sleep difficulty—showed that positive family relationships actually helped the subjects deal with work-related stress and improved the sleep quality of this sample of women, most of whom were parents (Williams et al., 2006).

Reciprocal Socialization

For many years, socialization between parents and children was viewed as a one-way process: children were considered to be the products of their parents' socialization techniques. However, parent–child interaction is reciprocal (Fiese & Winter, 2008; Thompson & Newton, 2009). **Reciprocal socialization** is socialization that is bi-directional. That is, children socialize parents just as parents socialize children.

When reciprocal socialization has been studied in infancy, mutual gaze, or eye contact, has been found to play an important role in early social interaction. One study revealed that *parent–infant synchrony*—the temporal coordination of social behaviour—plays an important role in children's development (Feldman, 2007). In this study, parent–infant synchrony at 3 and 9 months of age were positively linked to children's self-regulation from 2 to 6 years of age. In sum, the behaviours of mothers and infants involve substantial interconnection, mutual regulation, and synchronization (Moreno, Posada, & Goldyn, 2006).

An important form of reciprocal socialization is **scaffolding**, in which parents time interactions in such a way that the infant experiences turn-taking with the parents. Scaffolding involves parental behaviour that supports children's efforts, allowing them to be more skillful than they would be if they were to rely only on their own abilities (Field, 2007). In using scaffolding, caregivers provide a positive, reciprocal framework in which they and their children interact. For example, in the game peek-a-boo, the mother initially covers the baby. Then she removes the cover and registers "surprise" at the infant's reappearance. As infants become more skilled at peek-a-boo, pat-a-cake, and so on, other caregiver games exemplify scaffolding and turn-taking sequences.

CONNECTING through Research

Singing in the Crib: Sandra Trehub's Research on Maternal Singing

Sandra Trehub has conducted extensive research on maternal singing—which, like motherease, helps to regulate a child's attention and emotions.

The purpose of one such study (Bergeson & Trehub, 2007) was to determine whether or not mothers use discernible tunes (i.e., specific interval sequences) in their speech to infants, and whether or not such tunes are individually distinctive. The findings confirm the prominence of tunes and the presence of signature tunes in maternal speech. Signature tunes are believed to facilitate infants' recognition of their mother's voice. Such experience is thought to enhance reciprocal emotional ties between the infant and mother.

Caregivers, as well as parents, can provide a positive, reciprocal framework in which they and their children interact. One study examined the links between mother and child synchrony, shared affect, and the aggressive behaviour of young children. The results revealed that non-aggressive dyads exhibit more interactional synchrony and shared positive affect, and fewer instances of shared negative affect, than do aggressive dyads (Pasiak & Menna, 2015).

Maternal and Paternal Caregiving

Over the last three decades, the need for child care in Canada has grown steadily, with the rise of employment rates among women and the corresponding increase in dual-income earner families (Sinha, 2014). Beyond need, the demand for quality child care has also increased because of the potential benefits on peer socialization, school readiness, and numeracy and language skills (Nores & Barnett, 2010). Finding the most appropriate child care arrangement can at times be extremely challenging. Most parents need to balance overall quality with the convenience, availability, and cost of child care. The rates of paid child care are generally highest among dual-income earner families. Child care rates are also high for lone parent families, while the lowest rates paid are within couple households where only one parent works for pay (Sinha, 2014).

Developmental perspectives posit that parental behaviour during the first years of life is critical for optimal development (Edwards, Sheridan, & Koche, 2010). Infancy is a time during which fathers tend to influence, in a unique way, their children's rapidly developing social, cognitive, and language skills. These influences will last beyond the earliest years. When fathers engage with their children in ways that support their healthy development, they also increase their own enjoyment and commitment to their infants. Such a result can lead to long-term involvement (Cabrera, Fagan, & Farrie, 2008).

A recent study suggests that early father–infant engagement in various activities, including taking care of the baby's basic needs, engaging in play, and reading or telling stories, is not only associated with later father involvement, but definitely promotes cognitive development. It may also reduce the likelihood of infant cognitive delay (Pancsofar & Vernon-Feagans, 2010). In another recent study, findings indicated that fathers engage with their infants in high levels of caregiving and physical play, but less so in verbal stimulating activities. However, predictors of father engagement depend on the *type* of father engagement. For example, fathers' human capital (college education) is most predictive of father engaging with their infants in verbal stimulating activities (Cabrera, Hofferth, & Chae, 2011).

Studies on immigrant Chinese-Canadian and mainland Chinese families with 1 year olds indicated that Chinese fathers in both communities demonstrate an egalitarian and child-centred framework in their parenting approach. When fathers were asked what their roles and responsibilities were in their families, both Chinese-Canadian and Chinese fathers stated that their roles are multi-dimensional: economic provider, caregiver, playmate, educator, and household chore performer (Chuang, 2013; Chuang & Su, 2008).

Another recent study indicates that fathers who take on a stay-at-home role made a deliberate choice by assuming a caregiving role while mothers pursue employment outside the home (Karmer, Kelly, & McCulloch, 2015). Although the number of stay-at-home-father households has increased dramatically over time, most fathers still report that they are at home because they are not employed and/or are unable to work.

Significant changes in societal attitudes and a diminishing gender income gap for women working in high-skilled professions increase the likelihood that the number of caregiving stay-at-home-father households will continue to rise. Such a possibility merits future study (Kramer, Kelly, & McCulloch, 2015). At the same time, many social service organizations have developed programs for current and prospective fathers. For example, in Ontario, Catholic Community Services of York Region's Focus on Fathers teaches fathering skills and, to accommodate immigrant communities, the program has instructional materials in nine languages (FIRA, 2016).

In summary, according to Lamb (2010), it is a well-established fact that both men and women have the capacity to be good parents. The quality of parent–child relationships is determined by the degree to which parents offer love, affection, emotional commitment, reliability, and consistency (Lamb, 2012). Another relevant factor is the extent to which parents can effectively "read" their children or adolescents and provide the appropriate guidance, stimulation, and limit setting that is important (Lamb & Lewis, 2011).

Parental Leaves

Regardless of differing parental styles, taking care of children, especially newborns, requires a substantial amount of time. In Canada, both the federal and provincial/territorial governments have parental leave policies. Federal programs, such as Employment Insurance (EI), also help parents during their leave. Under the current *Employment Insurance Act,* a couple can split up to 37 weeks of parental leave, in addition to 17 weeks of maternity leave after the birth or adoption of a child (Canada Labour Code, 2013). However, the total duration of the maternity and parental leaves must not exceed 52 weeks. Individuals who are entitled to maternal or parental leaves must have completed six consecutive months of continuous employment (Canada Labour Code, 2013). Under the *Employment Insurance Act*, self-employed Canadian residents and permanent residents—those who work for themselves—are able to apply for EI special benefits.

The provincial government of Quebec introduced its own *Parental Insurance Plan* in 2006, with 18 weeks of maternity leave and 5 weeks of paternity leave, up to 70 percent of wages, with no waiting period. This plan also applies to the inclusion of self-employed individuals. Quebec offers 32 weeks of parental leave to birth parents and 37 weeks to adoptive parents (Quebec Parental Insurance Plan, 2015).

Moreover, Canadian fathers outside of Quebec are very unlikely to take advantage of the parental leave benefits. Still, the number of men taking parental leave rose between the years 2000 and 2006 to the point where one in five dads elected to take some or all of the parental leave available to them (Marshall, 2008). Decisions to claim are very complex, involving the incomes of both parents, job type, and values toward parental leave both in their work environment and the larger community.

critical thinking

In addition to parental leaves, what other arrangements in the workplace can allow parents to spend more time with their children? Can you come up with some suggestions for employers? What are some advantages and disadvantages of parental leave? What are the policies for parental leave in your province or territory? Discuss them with your peers.

Child Care

The types of child care into which infants are placed can have major impact on their development. Mustard (2009) draws attention to the fact that "brain development is highly sensitive to external influences" (p. 689). Unfortunately, children are more likely to experience poor quality of child care if they come from families with relatively few resources (psychological, social, and economic) (McCartney, 2009). However, it has been found that attending a high-quality care program can serve as a powerful lifeline when a child's home environment is poor (Philips & Lowenstein, 2011). Canadian researchers conducted a study regarding parent's knowledge and satisfaction regarding their child's care experience. The study concluded that the parents' knowledge about their child's daycare experience may be incomplete at times. More frequent and informative parent-educator communication is required, particularly about the children's learning and development (How et al., 2013). Crosnoe and colleagues (2010) argue that what matters most for child development is consistent positive stimulation at the centres and at home.

In 2011, almost half (46 percent) of parents reported using some type of child care for their children aged 14 years and younger in the past year. Child care was more often used for children aged 4 years and younger (54 percent) than for children over the age of 4 years (39 percent) (Sinha, 2014). Different options for non-parental care exist: care can be provided in daycare centres (33 percent); home daycares (31 percent), and private arrangements (28 percent). The uses of these arrangements vary widely by province. Figure 6.9 illustrates the type of child care arrangements available by region in Canada (Sinha, 2014).

Figure 6.9

Type of Child Care Arrangement Among Parents Using Child Care, by Region

Type of Child Care Arrangement for Children Aged 4 and Under			
	Home daycare	Daycare centre	Private care
	percent		
Atlantic provinces	16	36	44
Quebec	50	38	10

Type of Child Care Arrangement for Children Aged 4 and Under			
	Home daycare	**Daycare centre**	**Private care**
	percent		
Ontario	19	36	32
Prairie provinces	31	23	43
British Columbia	25	20	40
Canada	**31**	**33**	**28**
Note: Responses of preschool and other child care arrangements are included in the calculation of percentages, but are not shown in the table. Therefore, the totals will not add up to 100%.			

Source: From *Child Care in Canada* by Maire Sinha, Chart 1. Statistics Canada, General Social Survey, 2011.

CONNECTING development to life

Comparing Child Care Policies In The Canadian Provinces (Pasoli, 2015)

The ten Canadian provinces offer rich sites for comparative analyses of child care policies. A special framework was constructed that used comparative measures to assess the variation in child care arrangements across the ten provinces. The findings suggest that provincial care variation is multi-dimensional and often involves trade-offs or compromises. For example, in Prince Edward Island, staff wages and availability of service are relatively high, but levels of non-profit delivery and parental subsidies are low. More in-depth research is required to identify new concepts and divergence in child care policy arrangements across the country (Pasoli, 2015).

critical thinking

What are the characteristics of competent caregivers? Would you have different criteria for caregivers in a family (e.g., parents and grandparents) and for caregivers in an institution (e.g., nurses and daycare workers)? What criteria are essential for the safety of children in a regulated child care facility? You are thinking of becoming an unregulated child care provider; what steps would you take to get started?

Early Childhood Education and Care (ECEC) has become a policy priority in many countries. A number of countries have established monitoring systems to ensure quality and accountability in ECEC programs. Starting Strong IV explores how countries can develop and use these systems to enhance service and staff quality for the benefits of child development (OECD, 2016). In Canada, the previous Conservative government implemented a national Universal Child Care Benefit program that issued a taxable $100 monthly payment to families for each child under the age of 6 to help cover the cost of child care (Amoroso, 2010). The new Liberal federal government has proposed to invest $500 million in 2017–18 to support the establishment of a National Framework on Early Learning and Child Care (Child Care Canada, 2016).

The Parent Quality Information Project is a Canadian undertaking intended to provide resources for Canadian parents to help them understand and access high-quality care to meet not only their children's needs, but their own needs as well. A website was developed jointly by the Childcare Research and Resource Unit (CRRU) and the Canadian Union of Postal Workers (CUPW) (Early Childhood Education and Care, 2016). Figure 6.10 outlines the characteristics of high-quality daycare.

Figure 6.10
What Is High-Quality Daycare?

STANDARDS TO CONSIDER IN A CHILD CARE SITUATION

Health and safety:

- In a regulated setting, the licence is posted in a visible place
- Centre is kept clean
- Toys are disinfected on a regular basis
- Menus are posted, food is nutritious and appealing
- Number of children in home/group/room (at a minimum) meets the provincial/territorial standard

Staff/caregiver:

- Have education or training related to working with children
- Provide references
- Encourage co-operation, problem-solving, and independence in children
- Plan for staff/caregiver replacement in the event of illness or other absence

Overall program

- Policy manual is available to parents
- Goals and objectives for children are available and articulated
- Parents are involved or consulted about the program

Other information

- Fee schedule
- Board of directors with parent involvement
- Hours of operation

The shift to a new paradigm is occurring across Canada. Quebec is ahead of the rest of Canada in establishing the universality of child care, although creating a high standard of quality care is still a concern (Hertzman, 2009). Prince Edward Island has shifted responsibility for child care programs to the Department of Education, as has Saskatchewan (Beach & Bertrand, 2009). Most provinces are moving to initiate education programs that link early childhood development with the schooling that begins at age 4. Ontario, as we will see in the following chapter, initiated an extensive pilot project in full-day kindergarten (for 4- and 5-year-olds) in 2011, and full implementation across the province was achieved in 2016. While these initiatives may cost taxpayers more money, Daniel Trefler (2009) suggests the benefits arising from a better-educated and healthier population will offset the initial investment in a "high-quality, universal early child development program" (p. 684).

Infants with Special Needs

The organization of health and other community services in ways that enhance their access and coordination can substantially benefit children and families with special needs (Perrin et al., 2007). Historically, hospital-based institution care has been the only option for most children with complex medical conditions, technology dependence, and significant emotional and behavioural needs (Murphy, Carbone, & Council on Children with Disabilities, 2011). In fact, social policy has promoted community-based programs that provide care for children with disabilities in their homes and communities (McPherson et al., 2004).

Patient and family-centred care is an innovative approach that is grounded in a mutually beneficial partnership with participation among patients, families, and healthcare providers. According to the Committee on Hospital Care and the Institute for Patient and Family-Centred Care (2012), patient and family-centred care can significantly improve patient and family outcomes. In one study, conducted by Woodgate and colleagues (2012), parents' conceptualizations of participation were examined, including their perspectives of participation involving themselves, their children, and their family unit. The findings revealed that parents describe participation as a dynamic and reciprocal social process of involvement in being with others. For participation in everyday life to be meaningful, according to parents, the attributes of choice, safety, acceptance, accessibility, and accommodation have to be present. In fact, participation is valued highly by parents because it results in positive outcomes.

One developmental disorder that has gained considerable attention in our society over the past few decades is that of autistic spectrum disorder (ASD). According to Canadian researchers, ASD is characterized by persistent deficits in communication abilities and social reciprocity, as well as restricted, repetitive, or stereotyped behaviours (Bennett et al., 2015). A 2012 report from the now-defunct National Epidemiological Database for the Study of Autism in Canada (NEDSAC) reported that increased rates of ASD have been diagnosed among children in Prince Edward Island, Newfoundland and Labrador, and Southeastern Ontario (NEDSAC, 2012).

The two signs for ASD are: (1) problems in social interactions including the social use of language, and (2) restricted repetitive patterns of behaviour. Support for early intervention for children (younger than age 3 years) with ASD has begun to emerge in the literature (Webb et al., 2014). In fact, two studies have reported positive effects of even brief interventions during this time period (Rogers et al., 2012; Landa & Kalb, 2012). A randomized clinical trial for young toddlers (18–30 months) with autism was conducted by a group of researchers (Dawson et al., 2010). The trial was based on the Early Start Denver Model (ESDM), a developmental model that integrates play-based behaviour analysis. The researchers concluded that children who received ESDM for two years exhibited significantly greater gains in IQ, language, and adaptive and social behaviour compared to children who received standard treatment in the community (Dawson et al., 2010). Researchers who conducted a pilot study on the treatment of autism in the first year of life concluded that it appears feasible to identify and enrol symptomatic infants in parent-implemented interventions before 12 months (Rogers et al., 2014).

To this point, we have studied how social contexts influence the infant's development. For a review, see the Reach Your Learning Outcomes section at the end of this chapter.

Reach Your **Learning Outcomes**

Emotional Development

LO1 Outline the development of emotions in infancy.

Defining Emotion	▪ Emotion can involve physiological arousal, conscious experience, and behavioural expression.
Biological and Environmental Influences	▪ Brain areas such as the brain stem, hippocampus, and amygdala are involved in emotions. ▪ Social relationships provide the setting for the development of a rich variety of emotions.
Early Emotions	▪ Primary emotions are present in humans and other animals and emerge early in life; examples are joy, anger, sadness, fear, and disgust. ▪ Self-conscious emotions require self-awareness, especially consciousness and a sense of "me"; examples include jealousy, empathy, and embarrassment.

Emotion Expression and Social Relationships	▪ The basic cry, the anger cry, and the pain cry are observed in babies. ▪ The reflexive smile occurs at birth and the social smile comes around two to three months of age. ▪ The most frequent expression of an infant's fear is stranger anxiety. ▪ Stranger anxiety emerges gradually, starting at about age six months and escalating through the first birthday.
Emotion Regulation and Coping	▪ Emotion regulation consists of managing arousal to adapt to and reach a goal. ▪ One example of emotion regulation is when infants suck their thumbs to soothe themselves. ▪ In early infancy, babies mainly depend on caregivers for soothing. ▪ Factors such as parental expectation can influence an infant's emotion regulation. ▪ The use of language helps toddlers to communicate their feelings.

Temperament and Personality Development

LO2 Summarize the development of temperament and personality during infancy.

Temperament	▪ Temperament is an individual's behavioural style and characteristic way of emotional responding. Developmentalists are especially interested in the temperament of infants. ▪ Chess and Thomas classified infants as (1) easy, (2) difficult, or (3) slow to warm up. ▪ Kagan proposed the temperament category of inhibition to the unfamiliar. ▪ According to Rothbart and Bates, the structure of temperament consists of (1) extraversion/surgency, (2) negative affectivity, and (3) effortful control. ▪ Goodness of fit refers to the match between a child's temperament and the environmental demands the child must cope with. ▪ Although research evidence is sketchy at this point in time, some general recommendations are that caregivers should (1) be sensitive to the individual characteristics of the child, (2) be flexible in responding to these characteristics, and (3) avoid negative labelling of the child.
Personality Development	▪ Erikson argued that the first year is characterized by the crisis of trust versus mistrust. ▪ At some point in the second half of the second year of life, the infant develops a sense of self. ▪ Independence becomes a central theme in the second year of life. Mahler argued that the infant separates itself from the mother and then develops individuation. Erikson stressed that the second year of life is characterized by the stage of autonomy versus shame and doubt.

Social Orientation/Understanding and Attachment

LO3 Analyze social orientation/understanding and the development of attachment in infancy.

Social Orientation/ Understanding	▪ Social orientation is infants' captivation with the social world around them made up of parents and other children. ▪ Locomotion allows infants to initiate social interaction on their own through exploration. ▪ Development of intention, goal-directed behaviour, and cooperation facilitate social interactions. ▪ Social referencing involves "reading" emotional cues in others, such as the mother, to learn how to act in a situation. ▪ Infants' perceptions of others' actions reveal an earlier development of social sophistication and insight than previously imagined.
Attachment and Its Development	▪ Attachment is a close emotional bond between the infant and caregiver. ▪ Contact comfort and trust are important for attachment. ▪ Bowlby's ethological theory stresses that the caregiver and the infant instinctively trigger attachment. ▪ Attachment develops in four phases.
Individual Differences in Attachment	▪ Securely attached babies use the caregiver, usually the mother, as a secure base from which to explore the environment. ▪ Three types of insecure attachment are avoidant, resistant, and disorganized. ▪ Mary Ainsworth created the Strange Situation, an observational measure of attachment.
Caregiving Styles and Attachment Classifications	▪ Caregivers of secure babies are sensitive to the babies' signals and are consistently available to meet their needs. ▪ Caregivers of avoidant babies tend to be unavailable or rejecting. ▪ Caregivers of resistant babies tend to be inconsistently available to their babies and are usually not very affectionate. ▪ Caregivers of disorganized babies often neglect or physically abuse their babies. ▪ Changes in the caregiving relationship over time may affect the stability of attachment patterns.
Attachment, Temperament, and the Wider Social World	▪ Early attachment relationships and subsequent experiences with the caregiver are linked with later behaviour and adjustment. ▪ Some critics argue that attachment theorists have not given adequate attention to genetics and temperament. ▪ Other critics stress that they have not adequately taken into account the diversity of social agents and contexts. ▪ Cultural variations in attachment have been found, but in all cultures studied to date, secure attachment is the most common classification. ▪ Attachment theory has a western influence; attachment behaviours may be different in other cultures.

Social Contexts

LO4 Determine how social contexts influence the infant's development.

The Family	▪ The transition to parenthood requires considerable adaptation and adjustment on the part of parents. ▪ Children socialize parents just as parents socialize children. ▪ Belsky's model describes direct and indirect effects. ▪ Mothers tend to be the primary caregiver to children, and children prefer their mothers to fathers during stressful times. ▪ Many fathers perform both instrumental and expressive functions in their children's lives, but parenting publications tend to ignore their role.
Child Care	▪ Child care has become a basic need of the Canadian family. ▪ Early daycare experiences are related to later social adjustment. ▪ The Canadian Child Care Federation values children and is an excellent resource.
Infants with Special Needs	▪ Patient and family-centred health care is important, especially for autistic children.

review → connect → reflect

review

1. What is the nature of an infant's emotions? In what ways do they change? LO1
2. What is temperament? How does it develop in infancy? LO2
3. How is secure attachment developed in infancy? LO3
4. What are some individual variations in attachment? LO3
5. What are some important family processes in infant development? LO4

connect

According to Bowlby, attachment is important to the infant. Explain the importance of an internal working model of attachment as the infant grows and develops.

reflect

Your Own Personal Journey of Life

If you had an opportunity to design a child care facility for infants, what type of play activity would you suggest for infants as they progress from the age of 1 month to 1 year?

SECTION 4

Early Childhood

CHAPTER 7

Physical and Cognitive Development in Early Childhood

CHAPTER OUTLINE

Physical Development

LO1 Identify physical changes in early childhood.

- **Body Growth**
- **The Brain**
- **Motor and Perceptual Development**

Health and Wellness

LO2 Identify the factors involved in determining the health and wellness of children in Canada and in other countries.

- **Sleep**
- **Nutrition and Exercise**
- **Wellness in Canada**
- **Wellness in Other Countries**

Cognitive Development

LO3 Describe three views of the cognitive changes that occur in early childhood.

- **Piaget's Preoperational Stage**
- **Vygotsky's Theory**
- **Information Processing**

Language Development

LO4 Summarize how language develops in early childhood.

Early Childhood Education

LO5 Identify different approaches to early childhood education.

- **Variations in Early Childhood Education**
- **Developmentally Appropriate Practices**
- **Young Children's Literacy and Numeracy**
- **Education for Children Who Are Disadvantaged**

"I used to draw like Raphael but it has taken me a lifetime to draw like young children."

PABLO PICASSO

© Ariel Skelley/Blend Images/Getty Images

The Reggio Emilia Approach

The Reggio Emilia approach is an educational program for young children that was developed in the northern Italian city of Reggio Emilia. Children of single parents and children with disabilities are given priority for admission; other children are admitted according to a scale of needs. Parents pay on a sliding scale based on income.

The children are encouraged to learn by investigating and exploring topics that interest them. A wide range of stimulating media and materials is available for children to use as they learn music, movement, drawing, painting, sculpting, collages, puppets and disguises, and photography, for example (Freeman, 2011).

In this program, children often explore topics in a group, which fosters a sense of community, respect for diversity, and a collaborative approach to problem solving. Two co-teachers serve as guides for the children. The Reggio Emilia teachers consider a project as an adventure, which can start from an adult's suggestion, from a child's idea, or from an event, such as a snowfall or something else unexpected. The teachers allow children enough time to think about a topic and craft a project.

At the core of the Reggio Emilia approach is the image of children who are competent and have rights, especially the right to receive outstanding care and education. Parent participation is considered essential, and cooperation is a major theme in the schools. Many early childhood education experts believe the Reggio Emilia approach provides a supportive, stimulating context in which children are motivated to explore their world in a competent and confident manner (Martin & Evaldsson, 2012).

© Ruby Washington/The New York Times/Redux Pictures

In this chapter, we will discuss the physical and cognitive development of children between the ages of 2 and 5 years, examining such questions as: How does the body grow and develop? What are young children's motor skills like? What are the theories and findings pertaining to children's cognitive abilities? We will also talk about health and wellness and early childhood education in Canada. As you are reading, you might be able to envision young children running, playing, thinking, and talking.

As you may recall, Chapter 5 described the rapid and dramatic growth of infants in the first year, and that growth follows cephalocaudal and proximodistal patterns. The growth rate slows down in early childhood. (Otherwise, we would be a species of giants!) Continued myelination in early childhood provides children with much better hand–eye coordination, and improved fine motor skills. While infants make amazing progress in their attentional, memory, concept formation, and language skills, in this chapter you will discover that these information-processing skills continue to show remarkable advances in early childhood.

Physical Development

LO1 Identify physical changes in early childhood.

- **Body Growth**
- **The Brain**
- **Motor and Perceptual Development**

Body Growth

Growth in height and weight is the obvious physical change that characterizes early childhood. Unseen changes in the brain and nervous system are no less significant in preparing children for advances in cognition and language.

Height and Weight

The average child grows about 6.4 cm in height and gains between 2.2 and 3.2 kg a year during early childhood. As the preschool child grows older, the percentage of increase in height and weight decreases with each additional year (Wilson & Hockenberry, 2012). Girls are slightly smaller and lighter than boys during these years, a difference that continues until puberty. During the preschool years, both boys and girls slim down as the trunks of their bodies lengthen. Although their heads are still somewhat large for their bodies, by the end of the preschool years most children have lost their top-heavy look. Body fat also shows a slow, steady decline during the preschool years. Growth patterns vary individually (Burns et al., 2013). Much of the variation is due to heredity, but environmental experiences, such as nutrition, are also involved.

The Brain

One of the most important physical developments during early childhood is the continuing development of the brain and nervous system (Bell & Cuevas, 2014; Markant & Thomas, 2013). The changes that occur during this period enable children to plan their actions, react to stimuli more effectively, and make considerable strides in language development.

Brain Size and Growth

Brain growth continues during early childhood, but at a slower pace. By the time children reach 3 years of age, the brain is three-quarters of its adult size. By age 6, the brain has reached about 95 percent of its adult volume (Lenroot & Giedd, 2006). Thus, the brain of a 6-year-old is nearly the size it will be when the child reaches adulthood, but as we will see in later chapters, the development that occurs inside the brain continues through the remaining childhood and adolescent years (Raznahan et al., 2014). Figure 7.1 reveals how the growth curve for the head and brain advances more rapidly than the growth curve for height and weight.

Some of the brain's interior changes involve increases in dendritic connections as well as **myelination,** in which nerve cells are covered and insulated with a layer of fat cells. This has the effect of increasing the speed of information travelling through the nervous system. Myelination is important in the maturation of a number of children's abilities such as hand–eye coordination, and focusing attention, which continue to develop throughout childhood (Diamond, 2013; Yates, 2014).

The more rapid growth of the brain and head can easily be seen. Height and weight advance more gradually over the first two decades of life.

Figure 7.1

Growth Curves for the Head and Brain and for Height and Weight

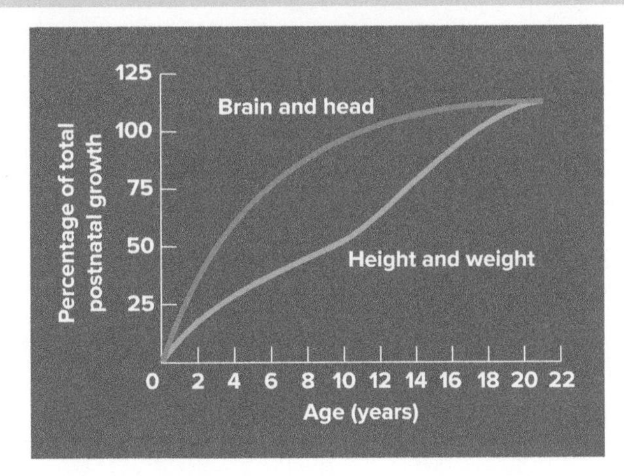

Reprinted from *Human Biology and Ecology*, by Albert Damon, with the permission of W.W. Norton & Company, Inc. Copyright © 1977 by W.W. Norton and Company, Inc.

The Brain and Cognitive Development

The increasing maturation of the brain, combined with opportunities to experience a widening world, contribute to children's emerging cognitive abilities. Consider a child who is learning to read aloud. Input from the child's eyes is transmitted to the child's brain, then passes through many brain systems that translate (process) the patterns of black and white into codes for letters, words, and associations. The output occurs in the form of messages to the child's lips and tongue. The child's own gift of speech is possible because brain systems are organized in ways that permit language processing.

The brain is organized in many neural circuits, which consist of neurons with certain functions. One neural circuit has an important function in attention and working memory (a type of memory similar to short-term memory that is like a mental workbench in performing many cognitive tasks) (Krimer & Goldman-Rakic, 2001). This neural circuit involves the prefrontal cortex and the neurotransmitter dopamine (Diamond, 2001) (see Figure 7.2).

Flashon Studio/Shutterstock

Physical changes in early childhood are most obvious. Note how the 5-year-old not only is taller and weighs more, but also has a longer trunk and longer legs than the 2-year-old. *What might be some other physical differences between 2- and 5-year-olds?*

Figure 7.2

The Prefrontal Cortex

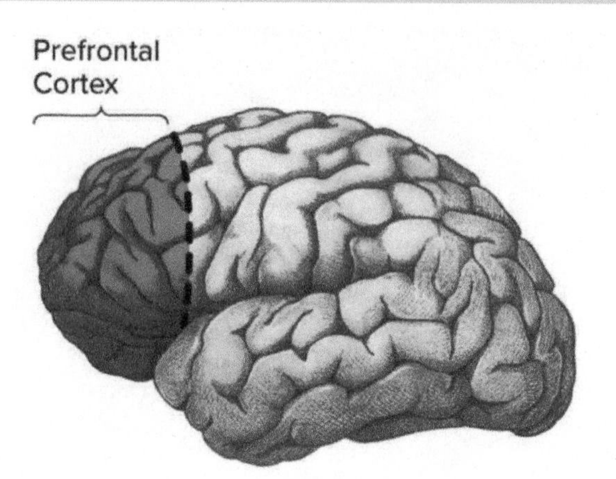

This evolutionary advanced portion (shaded in purple) of the brain shows extensive development from 3 to 6 years of age and is believed to play important roles in attention and working memory.

By repeatedly obtaining brain scans of the same children for up to four years, researchers have discovered that children's brains undergo dramatic anatomical changes, including rapid growth spurts and local brain patterns, between the ages of 3 and 15 years (Gogtay & Thompson, 2010; Steinberg, 2011, 2015a, b). The amount of brain material in some areas can nearly double within a year, followed by a drastic loss of tissue as unneeded cells are purged and the brain continues to reorganize itself. Researchers have found that in children from 3 to 6 years of age, the most rapid growth takes place in the frontal lobe areas involved in planning and organizing new actions, and in maintaining attention to tasks (Carlson, Zelazo, & Faja, 2013; Gogtay & Thompson, 2010).

Parents and educators know intuitively that reading books to and with children is vital to cognitive development. Is there scientific evidence to support this intuitive knowledge? Martha Farer of the University of Pennsylvania tracked children from lower socio-economic homes, many of them single-parent homes, for a 20-year period. Basically, she and her colleagues walked around the homes noting the number of books and educational toys available to the children. When the children were 18 or 19 years of age, brain scans revealed a high correlation between the amount of stimulation children had at age 4 and the development of the brain dedicated to language and cognition. In other words, stimulation, particularly at age 4, is critical to cortex development (Jha, 2012). Referring to the tremendous difficulty people of lower socio-economic means have in trying to break the cycle of poverty, Farer says, "It is a tragic irony that they so often face this challenge with diminished capabilities as a result of the hardships experienced early in life" (Farer, 2011).

As advances in technology allow scientists to "look inside" the brain and observe its activity, we will likely understand more precisely how the brain functions in cognitive development.

Motor and Perceptual Development

Most preschool children are as active as they will ever be—running as fast as they can, falling down, getting up, running again. Let's explore what this activity involves in young children's lives.

Gross Motor Skills

As children move their legs with more confidence and carry themselves more purposefully, moving around in the environment becomes more automatic (Burns et al., 2013). However, there are large individual differences in young children's gross motor skills (Ball, Bindler, & Cowan, 2014).

At 3 years of age, children enjoy simple movements, such as hopping, jumping, and running back and forth, just for the sheer delight of performing these activities. They enjoy showing how they can run across a room and jump all of 15 cm. Running and jumping for the 3-year-old is a source of considerable pride and accomplishment.

At 4 years of age, children still enjoy the same kind of activities, but they have become more adventurous. They scramble over low jungle gyms to display their athletic prowess.

At 5 years of age, children are even more adventuresome. It is not unusual for self-assured 5-year-olds to perform hair-raising stunts on practically any climbing object. A summary of development in gross motor skills during early childhood is shown in Figure 7.3.

Figure 7.3
The Development of Gross Motor Skills in Early Childhood

37–48 Months	49–60 Months	61–72 Months
Throws ball underhand (1.2 m)	Bounces and catches ball	Throws ball (13.4 m boys; 7.6 m girls)
Pedals tricycle 3 m	Runs 3 m and stops	Carries a 7-kg object
Catches large ball	Pushes/pulls a wagon/doll buggy	Kicks rolling ball
Completes forward somersault (aided)	Kicks 0.25 m ball toward target	Skips alternating feet
Jumps to floor from 0.3 m	Carries 5.4 kg object	Roller skates
Hops three hops with both feet	Catches ball	Skips rope
Steps on footprint pattern	Bounces ball under control	Rolls ball to hit object
Catches bounced ball	Hops on one foot four hops	Rides two-wheel bike with training wheels

From G.J . Schirmer (Ed) Performance Objectives for Preschool children, Adapt Press, Sioux Falls, SD 1974.

You probably have arrived at one important conclusion about preschool children: They are very, very active. Indeed, 3-year-old children have the highest activity level of any age in the entire human life span. They fidget when they watch television. They fidget when they sit at the dinner table. Even when they sleep, they move around quite a bit. Because of their activity level and the development of large muscles, especially in the arms and legs, preschool children need daily exercise.

Fine Motor Skills

At 3 years of age, children are still emerging from the infant ability to place and handle things. Although they have had the ability to pick up the tiniest objects between their thumb and forefinger for some time, they are still somewhat clumsy at it. Three-year-olds can build surprisingly high block towers, each block placed with intense concentration but often not in a completely straight line. When they play with a form board or a simple jigsaw puzzle, they are rather rough in placing the pieces. Even when they recognize the hole a piece fits into, they are not very precise at positioning the piece. They often try to force the piece in the hole or pat it vigorously.

By 4 years of age, children's fine motor coordination has improved and become much more precise. Sometimes, 4-year-old children have trouble building high towers with blocks because in their desire to place each of the blocks perfectly, they may upset those already stacked. Hand, arm, and body all move together under better command of the eye. Rather than building a simple tower, the 5-year-old will build a house or building. A summary of the development of fine motor skills in early childhood is shown in Figure 7.4.

Figure 7.4

The Development of Fine Motor Skills in Early Childhood

37–48 Months	49–60 Months	61–72 Months
Approximates circle	Strings and laces shoelace	Folds paper into halves and quarters
Cuts paper	Cuts following line	Traces around hand
Pastes using pointer finger	Strings 10 beads	Draws rectangle, circle, square, and triangle
Builds three-block bridge	Copies figure X	Cuts interior piece from paper
Builds eight-block tower	Opens and places clothespins (one-handed)	Uses crayons appropriately
Draws 0 and 1	Builds a five-block bridge	Makes clay object with two small parts
Dresses and undresses doll	Pours from various containers	Reproduces letters
Pours from pitcher without spilling	Prints first name	Copies two short words

Note: The skills are listed in the approximate order of difficulty within each age period.

From G.J . Schirmer (Ed) Performance Objectives for Preschool children, Adapt Press, Sioux Falls, SD 1974.

Perceptual Development

Changes in children's perceptual development continue in childhood (Atkinson & Braddick, 2013; Lee et al., 2013). Children become increasingly efficient at detecting the boundaries between colours (such as red and orange) at 3 to 4 years of age (Gibson, 1969). When children are about 4 or 5 years old, their eye muscles usually are developed enough that they can move their eyes efficiently across a series of letters. Many preschool children are farsighted, unable to see close up as well as they can see far away. By the time they enter grade 1, however, most children can focus their eyes and sustain their attention effectively on close-up objects.

What are the signs of vision problems in children? They include rubbing the eyes, blinking or squinting excessively, appearing irritable when playing games that require good distance vision, shutting or covering one eye, and tilting the head or thrusting it forward when looking at something. A child who shows any of these behaviours should be examined by an ophthalmologist.

After infancy, children's visual expectations about the physical world continue to develop.

To this point, we have studied many ideas about physical development in early childhood. For a review, see the Reach Your Learning Outcomes section at the end of this chapter.

Health and Wellness

LO2 Identify factors involved in determining the health and wellness of children in Canada and in other countries.

- **Sleep**
- **Nutrition and Exercise**
- **Wellness in Canada**
- **Wellness in Other Countries**

What are a preschool child's energy needs? What are preschoolers' sleep patterns and eating behaviours like? How do habits formed in early childhood affect growth and development?

Sleep

Getting a good night's sleep is important for children's development. Experts recommend that young children get 11 to 13 hours of sleep each night. However, it is sometimes difficult to get young children to go to sleep as they often drag out their bedtime routine; in fact, sleep problems during infancy and early childhood are among the most frequent complaints that parents present to healthcare professionals (Weiss & Corkum, 2012).

Behavioural insomnia is defined as "repeated difficulty with sleep initiation, duration, consolidation, or quality that occurs despite age appropriate time and opportunity for sleep, which results in some form of daytime functional impairment for the child and/or family" in children over the age of 6 months. Insomnia may be a symptom of many physical and mental health disorders such as eczema, gastrointestinal reflux, anxiety, depression, and ADHD (Weiss & Corkum, 2012).

To improve children's sleep, Mona El-Sheikh (2013) recommends making sure that the bedroom is cool, dark, and comfortable; maintaining consistent bed times and wake times; and building positive family relationships. Also, helping the child slow down before bedtime often contributes to less resistance in going to bed. Reading the child a story, playing quietly with the child in the bath, and letting the child sit on the caregiver's lap while listening to music are quieting activities.

Nutrition and Exercise

Eating habits are critical to development during early childhood (Schiff, 2015; Sorte, Daeschel, & Amador, 2014). What children eat affects their skeletal growth, body shape, and susceptibility to disease. Equally important are exercise and physical activity (Graham, Holt/Hale, & Parker, 2013).

According to the World Health Organization (WHO), childhood obesity is a global problem and one of the most serious threats of the twenty-first century, putting children at serious risk for Type 2 diabetes, asthma, and heart failure. Today, Canada is facing an obesity epidemic (Public Health Agency, 2016). Research conducted in 2008 indicated that 15.2 percent of children between ages 2 and 5 years were overweight and that 6.3 percent were obese. According to Statistics Canada, by 2012–2013, that figure had doubled. Thirty-one percent of children and youth ages 5 to 17 are overweight and obese based on BMI (Weiss & Corkum, 2012; Statistics Canada, 2015; World Health Organization, 2016).

Body Mass Index (BMI), a measure of weight in relation to height, is used to indicate if a person has the expected weight or is overweight or obese. Figure 7.5 shows the Body Mass Index score indicating that a child is overweight or obese for ages 2 through 5 years.

Figure 7.5

Body Mass Index (BMI) Cut-Off Points for Overweight and Obese Children Ages 2 to 5 Years*

	Overweight		**Obese**	
	BMI greater than or equal to:**		**BMI greater than or equal to:**	
Age (years)	**Boys**	**Girls**	**Boys**	**Girls**
2	18.41	18.02	20.09	19.81
3	17.89	17.56	19.57	19.36
4	17.55	17.28	19.29	19.15
5	17.42	17.15	19.30	19.17

* Figure adapted from Table E.1 in Chief Public Health Officer (2009) p. 95.

** BMI is calculated by dividing the person's body weight (in kilograms) by their height (in metres) squared.

Energy requirements for individual children are determined by the **basal metabolism rate (BMR),** which is the minimum amount of energy a person uses in a resting state. Energy needs of individual children of the same age, sex, and size vary. Reasons for these differences remain unexplained. Differences in physical activity, basal metabolism, and the efficiency with which children use energy are possible explanations. Most children gain weight prior to a growth spurt, then thin out as they grow taller—and all need routine physical activity.

In addition to health problems noted above, childhood obesity contributes to a number of social and psychological problems. For example, from as early as 5 years of age, being overweight is linked with lower self-esteem, negative self-image, a pervading sense of sadness, loneliness, and an increase in high-risk behaviours (Chief Public Health Officer, 2009).

The risk that overweight children will continue to be overweight when they are older was documented in a recent U.S. study of nearly 8000 children (Cunningham et al., 2014). In this study, overweight 5-year-olds were four times more likely to be obese at 14 years of age than their 5-year-old counterparts who began kindergarten at a normal weight. Also, another study, which found that obesity rates were decreasing among preschool children, reported that preschool children who were obese were five times more likely to be overweight or obese as adults (Ogden et al., 2014).

The food children eat affects brain development. A study of 7000 children who were tracked at ages 15 months, 2 years, and 8 years reported that IQ could be affected by as much as two points depending on the children's diets. Dr. Lisa Smithers of the University of Adelaide in South Australia led the study and found that children who were breastfed at 6 months and who had a healthy diet regularly including foods such as legumes, cheese, fruit, and vegetables at 15 and 24 months had an IQ up to 2 points higher by age 8 years. While the difference is small, it does reinforce the importance of nutrition for young children (Smithers, 2012).

A healthy diet includes various nutrients. To help Canadians achieve healthy eating habits, Health Canada published the first food guide in 1942 and has revised it periodically (Garriguet, 2007). The first food guide for First Nations, Inuit, and Métis, which takes into account the content of their traditional meals, was published in 2007. Similarly, the latest edition of Canada's Food Guide includes guidelines based on the dietary practices of various cultures. Visit http://www.hc-sc.gc.ca for more information.

Wellness in Canada

In recent decades, vaccines have nearly eradicated disabling bacterial meningitis and are available to prevent measles, rubella, mumps, and chicken pox. The disorders still most likely to be fatal during early childhood today are birth defects, cancer, and diseases of the nervous system. Although the dangers of many diseases for children have been greatly diminished, it still is important for parents to keep young children on an immunization schedule. Children's safety is a major concern in schools, communities, and homes. Accidental deaths include motor vehicle accidents, drownings, poisoning, falls, and burns (Theurer & Bhavsar, 2013; Zielinski, Rochette, & Smith, 2012).

Another concern about children's health is exposure to parental smoking. A number of studies have concluded that children are at risk for health problems when they live in homes in which a parent smokes (Carlsson et al., 2013; Jarosinska et al., 2014). Children exposed to tobacco smoke in the home are more likely to have weakened immune systems, pneumonia, or pulmonary bronchitis, and to develop wheezing symptoms and asthma than children in non-smoking homes (Gonzales-Barcala et al., 2013; Hur, Liang, & Lin, 2014). One study found that parental smoking is a risk factor for higher blood pressure in children (Simonetti et al., 2011). And another study revealed that maternal cigarette smoking and alcohol consumption when children were 5 years of age are linked to onset of smoking in early adolescence (Hayatbakhsh et al., 2013). Further, another study revealed that children living in low-income families are more likely to be exposed to environmental tobacco smoke than their counterparts in middle-income families (Kit et al., 2013). In a review of Canadian research, Gupta and associates (2007) found that children under 5 years of age living in a low-income family had higher rates of asthma and injuries (both lethal and non-lethal), were more likely to be overweight or obese, had poorer mental health ratings, and had a lower level of readiness for school and functional health than children in middle- or high-income families.

Canada has no official definition of poverty, as there are several approaches to determining it; most are based on gross or net income filings. No matter what criteria is used, certain trends can be noted: Poverty rates are higher among marginalized peoples, lone (usually female) parents, people with disabilities, indigenous peoples, racialized persons, and recent immigrants. Campaign 2000 reports that in 2013, approximately 19 percent of children were living in poverty, down slightly from 22.3 percent in 2000. Of special concern is the poor health status of many young children from low-income families. In addition, malnutrition and food insecurity affect 62 percent of children living in the North. For example, in Nunavut, where child poverty is highest (37.7 percent), food costs twice as much as anywhere else in Canada (Canada Without Poverty, 2016; Campaign 2000, 2015). Living in poverty has a negative impact on physical and emotional health, as well as on cognitive development (Canadian Nurses Association, 2009; Gupta, de Wit, & McKeown, 2007). Food Banks Canada (2015) reported that 852 137 people, one-third of whom are children, access food banks monthly. Food bank usage across Canada in 2016 was 26 percent higher than it was in 2008 (Canada Without Poverty, 2016).

Poverty rates for Inuit and First Nations children are considerably higher than average and are correlated with poorer health. The number of Aboriginal children who are obese or overweight has also become a major concern in Aboriginal communities (Ferris, 2010). In 2004, 58 percent of Aboriginal children living on reserve, between 2 and 11 years of age, were overweight or obese (Chief Public Health Officer, 2009). Type 2 diabetes is on the increase among obese and overweight children, bringing with it significant health issues. Another concern for Aboriginal people is the tuberculosis rate, which in 2004 was 4.8 times higher than that of the general population (Public Health Agency of Canada, 2008). When foreign-born Canadians are removed from the comparison, the rate for Aboriginal people is actually 26.4 times higher compared with Canadian-born non-Aboriginals (the rate for foreign-born Canadians is 18.4 times higher than Canadian born non-Aboriginals). Health issues for many Aboriginal Canadians are further complicated by the fact that they live in isolated communities beyond the easy reach of food banks and health care providers, factors which impact nutrition as well as diagnosis and timely treatment.

critical thinking

More than two decades have passed since the House of Commons' unanimous resolution "to seek to achieve the goal of eliminating poverty among Canadian children by the year 2000." Today, 19 percent, or nearly 1 in 5 non-indigenous children, and 40 percent, or 2 in 5 indigenous children, are affected by poverty (Campaign 2000, 2015). Food insecurity and malnutrition, as well as readiness for education, go hand-in-hand with poverty. Canada Without Poverty (2016) argues that poverty is a violation of human rights. Do you agree? If so, how? What are the short- and long-term effects of child poverty for the individual? For schools? For the community? For the country? What steps can schools and communities take to address the impacts of poverty? Canada Without Poverty notes that it is estimated that $1 invested in the early years of a child's life can save up to $9 in future health care costs. Do you think this is reasonable? If so, how might this be done? How might we make food in Nunavut, for example, more affordable?

Wellness in Other Countries

The link between poverty and children's health is an issue not only in Canada, but also in the rest of the world. The poor of the world often experience lives of hunger, malnutrition, unsafe water, and inadequate access to health care (UNICEF, 2006). In almost every country, more children live in poverty than adults, and the lifelong consequences are devastating for their physical, cognitive, and socio-emotional growth and development (Campaign 2000, 2015).

The vast majority of the 7.6 million deaths of children under 5 years of age reported by UNICEF in 2010 occurred in Africa and South Asia. Silent killers, such as poverty, hunger, and illnesses, account for much of that total; however, war and natural catastrophes are major contributors. For example, in 2013, in Syria alone, 11 000 children were killed in war, most by explosives (Taylor, 2013; Shah, 2011). On a positive note, death to children under 15 years of age due to HIV/AIDS has decreased. In 2013, 31 percent fewer children younger than 15 years died from HIV compared with 2009, and 40 percent fewer died compared with 2005 (World Health Organization, 2015). Pneumonia and dehydration from diarrhoea are the two leading causes of childhood death in 15 countries of the world (WHO, 2008a). Giving children plenty of water and liquids usually prevents dehydration, but the source of the water must be uncontaminated. Many of the deaths of young children around the world can be prevented by a reduction in poverty and improvements in nutrition, sanitation, education, and health services (UNICEF, 2006, 2012).

To this point, we have studied a number of ideas about health and wellness in early childhood. For a review, see the Reach Your Learning Outcomes section at the end of this chapter.

Cognitive Development

LO3 Describe three views of the cognitive changes that occur in early childhood.

- **Piaget's Preoperational Stage**
- **Vygotsky's Theory**
- **Information Processing**

The cognitive world of the preschool child is creative, free, and fanciful. Preschool children's imaginations work overtime, and their mental grasp of the world improves. Our coverage of cognitive development in early childhood focuses on three theories: Piaget's, Vygotsky's, and information processing.

Piaget's Preoperational Stage

Recall from Chapter 5 that during Piaget's sensorimotor stage of development, infants progress in their ability to organize and coordinate sensations and perceptions with physical movements and actions. The second stage, Piaget's **preoperational stage,** lasts from approximately 2 to 7 years of age. Piaget used the label *preoperational* to emphasize that children at this stage do not yet think in an operational way; in other words, children can add and subtract when they are able to move objects physically, but they are unable to perform these functions mentally. Piaget believed that the ability to perform functions such as these mentally comes in the third stage, which he labelled the concrete operational stage. **Operations** are internalized and reversible sets of actions that allow children to do mentally what before they could do physically.

Preoperational thought is the beginning of the ability to reconstruct in thought what has been established in behaviour. Language is a hallmark of this stage; as well, children form stable concepts and begin to reason and to represent the world with words, images, drawings, and imaginary play. For example, the child may develop an imaginary friend, build a fort from blankets and pillows, or pretend that a broom is a horse. At the same time, the young child's cognitive world is dominated by egocentrism and magical beliefs.

The preoperational stage can be divided into two substages: the symbolic function substage and the intuitive thought substage.

Symbolic Function Substage

In the **symbolic function substage,** roughly between the ages of 2 and 4 years, the young child gains the ability to mentally represent an object that is not present. The ability to engage in such symbolic thought is called symbolic function, and it vastly expands the child's mental world (Mandler & DeLoache, 2012). Young children use scribbled designs to represent people, houses, cars, clouds, and so on. Other examples of symbolism in early childhood are language and pretend play. However, although young children make distinct progress during this substage, their thinking still has several important limitations, two of which are egocentrism and animism.

Egocentrism is the inability to distinguish between one's own perspective and that of someone else. Piaget and Barbel Inhelder (1969) initially studied young children's egocentrism by devising the three mountains task (see Figure 7.6). The child walks around the model of the mountains and becomes familiar with what the mountains look like from different perspectives. The child is then seated on one side of the table. The experimenter moves a doll to different locations around the table, at each location asking the child to select, from a series of photos, the one photo that most accurately reflects the view the doll is seeing. Children in the preoperational stage often pick the view from where they are sitting, rather than the doll's view.

Figure 7.6

The Three Mountains Task

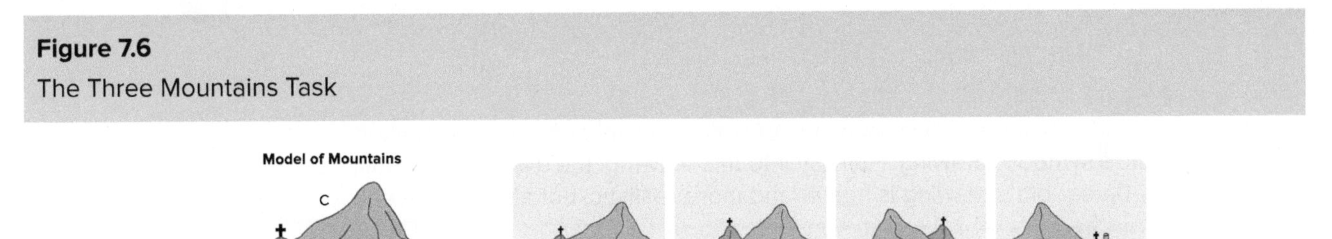

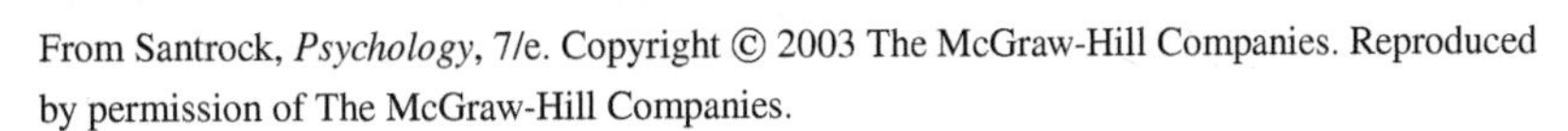

View 1 shows the child's perspective from where he or she is sitting. View 2 is an example of one of the photographs the child would be shown, along with other photographs taken from different perspectives. It shows what the mountains look like to a person sitting at spot B. When asked what a view of the mountains looks like from position B, the preoperational child selects a photograph taken from location A, the child's view at the time. A child who thinks in a preoperational way cannot take the perspective of a person sitting at another spot.

Animism, another limitation within preoperational thought, is the belief that inanimate objects have "lifelike" qualities and are capable of action. A young child might show animism by saying, "The sidewalk made me mad; it made me fall down" (Gelman & Opfer, 2011).

Possibly because young children are not very concerned about reality, their drawings are fanciful and inventive. One 3½-year-old looked at a scribble he had just drawn and described it as a pelican kissing a seal (see Figure 7.7a). In the elementary school years, a child's drawings become more realistic, neat, and precise (see Figure 7.7b).

Figure 7.7

The Symbolic Drawings of Young Children

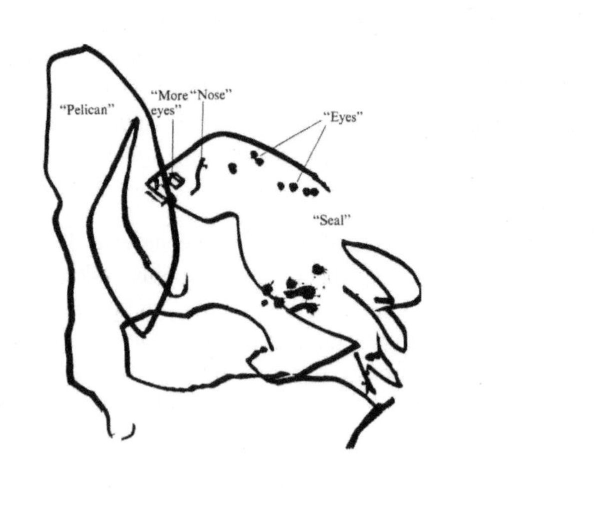

(a)

(b)

"The Symbolic Drawings of Young Children," reprinted courtesy of D. Wolf and J. Nove.

(a) A 3½-year-old's symbolic drawing. Halfway into this drawing, the 3½-year-old artist said it was "a pelican kissing a seal." *(b)* This 11-year-old's drawing is neater and more realistic, but also less inventive.

Intuitive Thought Substage

The **intuitive thought substage** occurs between approximately 4 and 7 years of age. In this substage, children begin to use primitive reasoning and want to know the answers to all sorts of questions. Piaget called this time period intuitive because young children seem quite sure about their knowledge and understanding, yet are unaware of how they know what they know. That is, they say they know something but know it without the use of rational thinking.

In this substage, children begin to use primitive reasoning and want to know the answers to all sorts of questions. Consider 4-year-old Ryan, who is at the beginning of the intuitive thought substage. Although he is starting to develop his own ideas about the world he lives in, his ideas are still simple, and he is not very good at thinking things out. He has difficulty understanding events that he knows are taking place but that he cannot see. His fantasized thoughts bear little resemblance to reality. He cannot yet answer the question "What if?" in any reliable way. For example, he may have difficulty negotiating traffic because he cannot do the mental calculations necessary to estimate whether an approaching car will hit him when he crosses the road.

By the age of 5, children have just about exhausted the adults around them with "why" questions. The child's questions signal the emergence of interest in reasoning and in figuring out why things are the way they are. Following are some examples of the questions children ask during the questioning period of 4 to 6 years of age (Elkind, 1976): "What makes you grow up?" "Who was the mother when everybody was a baby?" "Why do leaves fall?" "Why does the sun shine?"

Centration and the Limits of Preoperational Thought

One characteristic of preoperational thought is **centration**—the focusing, or centring, of attention on one characteristic to the exclusion of all others. Centration is most clearly evidenced in young children's lack of **conservation**—awareness that altering an object's or a substance's appearance does not change its basic properties. In the conservation task, a child is presented with two identical beakers, each filled to the same level with liquid (see Figure 7.8). The child is asked if these beakers have the same amount of liquid, and the child usually replies yes. Then, the liquid from one beaker is poured into a third beaker, which is taller and thinner than the first two. The child is then asked if the amount of liquid in the tall, thin beaker is equal to that which remains in one of the original beakers. Children younger than 7 or 8 years old usually say no and justify their answers in terms of the differing height or width of the beakers. This kind of justification shows centration in that children are focusing on just one aspect of the event. In contrast, older children usually answer yes and justify their answers appropriately ("If you poured the milk back, the amount would still be the same").

Figure 7.8

Piaget's Conservation Task

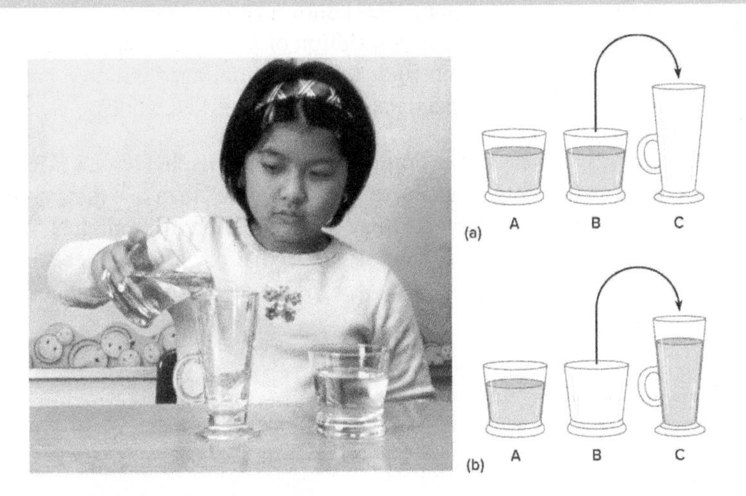

© Tony Freeman/PhotoEdit

The beaker test is a well-known Piagetian test to determine whether a child can think operationally.

In Piaget's theory, failing the conservation-of-liquid task is a sign that children are at the preoperational stage of cognitive development. The failure demonstrates not only centration, but also an inability to mentally reverse actions. For example, in the conservation of matter example shown in Figure 7.9, preoperational children say that the longer shape has more clay because they assume that "longer is more." Preoperational children cannot mentally reverse the clay-rolling process to see that the amount of clay is the same in both the shorter ball shape and the longer stick shape.

Figure 7.9

Some Dimensions of Conservation: Number, Matter, and Length

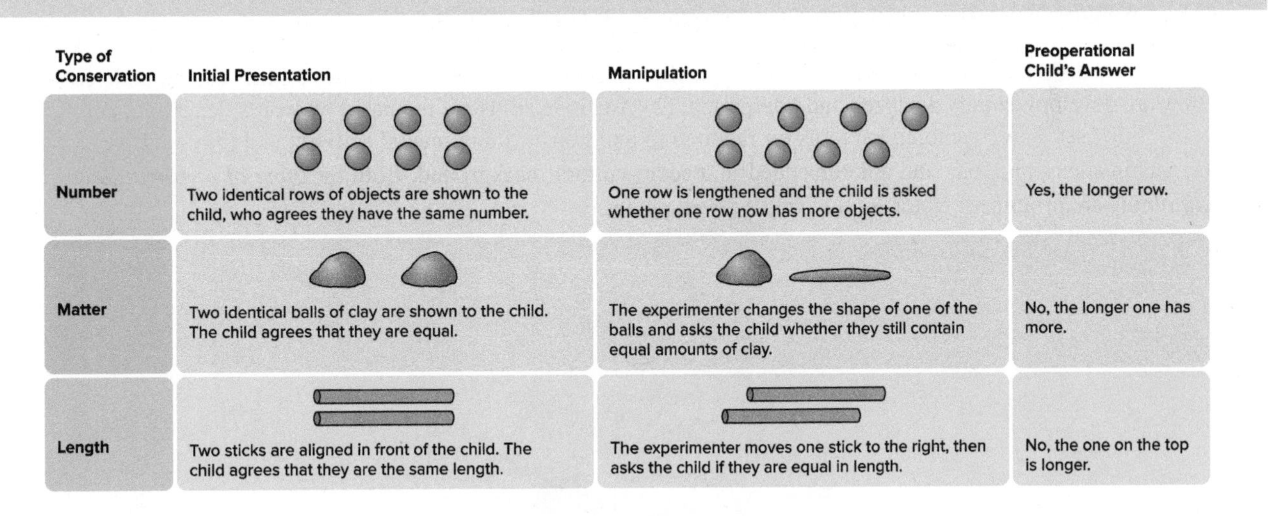

In addition to failing to conserve volume, preoperational children also fail to conserve number, matter, length, and area. However, children often vary in their performance on different conservation tasks. Thus, a child might be able to conserve volume but not number. A recent MRI brain-imaging study of conservation of number revealed that advances in a network in the parietal and frontal lobes were linked to 9- and 10-year-olds' conservation success in comparison with non-conserving 5- and 6-year-olds (Houde et al., 2011).

Some developmentalists believe Piaget was not entirely correct in his estimate of when children's conservation skills emerge. For example, Rochel Gelman (1969) showed that when the child's attention to relevant aspects of the conservation task is improved, the child is more likely to conserve. Gelman also believes that conservation appears earlier than Piaget thought, and that attention is especially important in explaining conservation.

Some other aspects of the preoperational stage have also been called into question. For example, due to egocentrism, children should not realize that they need to provide an audience with information concerning the time and location, not just the action, of their past experiences if the audience were not present at the same events. However, Carole Peterson of Memorial University of Newfoundland (e.g., Peterson & McCabe, 1994) showed that children as young as 26 to 31 months could actually provide the when and where information in their description of past experiences, suggesting children may not be as egocentric as Piaget suggested. Further, recent research finds that preschool-aged children are able to make up stories and tell falsehoods indicates some awareness of differing perspectives (Talwar & Lee, 2006).

As for the notion of animism, Quebec researchers Diane Poulin-Dubois and Gisèle Héroux (1994) found that both adults and children (5- to 9-year-olds) considered an object that can move as "more alive" than one that cannot, indicating that children's cognitive structure regarding the "aliveness" of objects may not be different from that of adults. The animism that preoperational children sometimes show may reflect a lack of knowledge of certain objects, rather than the presence of a qualitatively different cognitive structure. Figure 7.10 summarizes the characteristics of preoperational thought.

Figure 7.10

Characteristics of Preoperational Thought

More symbolic than sensorimotor thought

Inability to engage in operations; cannot mentally reverse actions; lacks conservation skills

Egocentric (inability to distinguish between own perspective and someone else's)

Intuitive, rather than logical

Vygotsky's Theory

Like Piaget, Vygotsky (1962) emphasized that children actively construct their knowledge and understanding; however, Vygotsky's theory describes children as social creatures who develop their way of thinking and understanding primarily through social interaction. Children's cognitive development is linked to the tools provided by society, and their minds are shaped by the cultural context in which they live (Gauvain, 2013; Gredler, 2012).

In Chapter 2, we described the basic principles of Vygotsky's theory: (1) the child's cognitive skills can be understood only when they are developmentally analyzed and interpreted; (2) cognitive skills are mediated by words, language, and forms of discourse, which serve as psychological tools for facilitating and transforming mental activity; and (3) cognitive skills have their origins in social relations and are embedded in a socio-cultural background. Both the *zone of proximal development* and *scaffolding* are prominent factors in the child's development.

© Lee Lorenz The New Yorker Collection/The Cartoon Bank

"I still don't have all the answers, but I'm beginning to ask the right questions."

The Zone of Proximal Development

The **zone of proximal development (ZPD)** refers to the range of tasks too difficult for a child to master alone but that can be learned with the guidance and assistance of adults or more-skilled children. ZPD reflects Vygotsky's belief in the importance of social influences, especially instruction on children's cognitive development. As shown in Figure 7.11, the lower limit of the ZPD is the level of problem solving reached by the child working independently. The upper limit is the level of additional responsibility the child can accept with the assistance of an able instructor. An example of the ZPD is an adult helping a child put together a jigsaw puzzle.

Figure 7.11

Vygotsky's Zone of Proximal Development

Vygotsky's zone of proximal development has a lower limit and an upper limit. Tasks in the ZPD are too difficult for the child to perform alone. They require assistance from an adult or a skilled child. As children experience the verbal instruction or demonstration, they organize the information in their existing mental structures so that they can eventually perform the skill or task alone.

The ZPD captures the child's cognitive skills that are in the process of maturing and can be accomplished only with the assistance of a more-skilled person (Mahn & John-Steiner, 2013; Petrick-Steward, 2012). Vygotsky (1962) called these the "buds" or "flowers" of development, to distinguish them from the "fruits" of development, which the child already can accomplish independently.

Researchers have found that the following factors can enhance the ZPD's effectiveness (Gauvain, 2013): better emotion regulation, secure attachment, absence of maternal depression, and child compliance.

Scaffolding

Closely linked to the idea of zone of proximal development is the concept of scaffolding. **Scaffolding** means changing the level of support. Over the course of a teaching session, a more-skilled person (perhaps a teacher or a more advanced peer) adjusts the amount of guidance to fit the child's current performance (Daniels, 2011). When the child is learning a new skill, the more-skilled person may use direct instruction. As the child's competence increases, less guidance is given.

A recent study found that scaffolding techniques that heighten engagement, direct exploration, and facilitate "sense-making," such as guided play, improved 4- to 5-year-old children's acquisition of geometric knowledge (Fisher et al., 2013).

Language and Thought

The use of dialogue as a tool for scaffolding is only one example of the important role of language in a child's development. According to Vygotsky, children use speech not only to communicate socially but also to help them solve tasks. Vygotsky (1962) further believed that young children use language to plan, guide, and monitor their behaviour. This use of language for self-regulation is called private speech. For Piaget, private speech is egocentric and immature, but for Vygotsky it is an important tool of thought during the early childhood years (John-Steiner, 2007).

Eyewire Collection/Getty Images

In Vygotsky's theory, an important point is that children need to learn the skills that will help them do well in their culture. Vygotsky believed that this should be accomplished through interaction with more-skilled members of the culture, such as this boy learning to read with the guidance of his father. *What are some other ways that skilled members of a society can interact with young children?*

Dialogue is an important tool of scaffolding in the zone of proximal development (Tappan, 1998). Vygotsky viewed children as having rich but unsystematic, disorganized, and spontaneous concepts. In a dialogue, these concepts meet with the skilled helper's more systematic, logical, and rational concepts. As a result, the child's concepts become more systematic, logical, and rational. For example, a dialogue might take place between a teacher and a child when the teacher uses scaffolding to help a child understand a concept like "transportation."

Vygotsky believed that language and thought initially develop independently of each other and then merge. He said that all mental functions have external, or social, origins. Children must use language to communicate with others before they can focus inward on their own thoughts. Children also must communicate externally and use language for a long period of time before the transition from external to internal speech takes place. This transition period occurs between the ages of 3 and 7 years of age and involves talking to oneself. After a while, the self-talk becomes second nature to children, and they can act without verbalizing. When this occurs, children have internalized their egocentric speech in the form of inner speech, which becomes their thoughts.

Vygotsky reasoned that children who use a lot of private speech are more socially competent than those who do not. He argued that private speech represents an early transition to becoming more socially communicative. Piaget maintained that self-talk is egocentric and reflects immaturity. However, researchers have found support for Vygotsky's view that private speech plays a positive role in children's development (Winsler, Carlton, & Barry, 2000). Researchers have found that children use private speech more when tasks are difficult, following errors, and when they are not sure how to proceed. They also have revealed that children who use private speech are more attentive and improve their performance more than children who do not use private speech (Berk & Spuhl, 1995).

Teaching Strategies

Vygotsky's theory has been embraced by many teachers and has been successfully applied to education. Here are some ways Vygotsky's theory can be incorporated in classrooms:

1. *Assess the child's ZPD.* Like Piaget, Vygotsky did not recommend formal, standardized tests as the best way to assess children's learning. Rather, Vygotsky argued that assessment should focus on determining the child's zone of proximal development. The skilled helper presents the child with tasks of varying difficulty to determine the best level at which to begin instruction.
2. *Use the child's ZPD in teaching.* Teaching should begin toward the zone's upper limit, so that the child can reach the goal with help and move to a higher level of skill and knowledge. Offer just enough assistance. You might ask, "What can I do to help you?" Or simply observe the child's intentions and attempts and provide support when it is needed. When the child hesitates, offer encouragement. And encourage the child to practise the skill. You may watch and appreciate the child's practice or offer support when the child forgets what to do.
3. *Use more-skilled peers as teachers.* Remember that it is not just adults who are important in helping children learn. Children also benefit from the support and guidance of more-skilled children.
4. *Place instruction in a meaningful context.* Educators today are moving away from abstract presentations of material; instead, they provide students with opportunities to experience learning in real-world settings. For example, rather than just memorizing math formulas, students work on math problems with real-world implications.
5. *Transform the classroom with Vygotskian ideas.* What does a Vygotskian classroom look like? The Kamehameha Elementary Education Program (KEEP) in Hawaii is based on Vygotsky's theory (Tharp, 1994). The ZPD is the key element of instruction in this program. Children might read a story and then interpret its meaning. Many of the learning activities take place in small groups. All children spend at least 20 minutes each morning in a setting called "Center One." In this context, scaffolding is used to improve children's literary skills. The instructor asks questions, responds to students' queries, and builds on the ideas that students generate.

Unlike Piaget, for Vygotsky the conceptual shift is one from the individual to collaboration, social interaction, and sociocultural activity (Gauvain, 2013). The endpoint of cognitive development for Piaget is formal operational thought. For Vygotsky, the endpoint can differ depending on which skills are considered to be the most important in a particular culture. For Piaget, children construct knowledge by transforming, organizing, and reorganizing previous knowledge. The implication of Piaget's theory for teaching is that children need support to explore their world and discover knowledge. The main implication of Vygotsky's theory for teaching is that students need many opportunities to learn with the teacher and more-skilled peers. In both Piaget's and Vygotsky's theories, teachers serve as facilitators and guides, rather than as directors of learning. Figure 7.12 compares Vygotsky's and Piaget's theories.

Figure 7.12
Comparison of Vygotsky's and Piaget's Theories

	Vygotsky A.R. Lauria/Dr. Michael Cole, Laboratory of Human Cognition, University of California, San Diego	**Piaget** © Bettmann/CORBIS
Constructivism	**Social Constructivist**	**Cognitive Constructivist**
Stages	No general stages of development proposed	Strong emphasis on stages (sensorimotor, preoperational, concrete operational, and formal operational)
Key processes	Zone of proximal development, language, dialogue, tools of the culture	Schema, assimilation, accommodation, operations, conservation, classification, hypothetical-deductive reasoning
Role of language	A major role; language plays a powerful role in shaping thought	Language has a minimal role; cognition primarily directs language
View on education	Education plays a central role, helping children learn the tools of the culture	Education merely refines the child's cognitive skills that already have emerged
Teaching implications	Teacher is a facilitator and guide, not a director; establish many opportunities for children to learn with the teacher and more-skilled peers	Also views teacher as a facilitator and guide, not a director; provide support for children to explore their world and discover knowledge

Evaluating Vygotsky's Theory

Even though Vygotsky's work was not translated into English until the 1960s, and thus has not been evaluated as thoroughly as Piaget's ideas, both theorists were actually contemporaries. Moreover, their theories are both constructivist and state that children actively construct knowledge and understanding, rather than being passive receptacles. However, Vygotsky's **social constructivist approach** emphasizes that both learning and the construction of knowledge occur in social contexts. On the other hand, Piaget's theory does not have this social emphasis. Moving from Piaget to Vygotsky, the conceptual shift is from the individual to collaboration, social interaction, and socio-cultural activity (Holzman, 2009).

Some critics point out that Vygotsky was not specific enough about age-related changes (Gauvain, 2008; Gauvain & Parke, 2010). Another criticism suggests that Vygotsky did not adequately describe how changes in socio-emotional capabilities contribute to cognitive development. Yet another criticism is that he overemphasized the role of language in thinking. Additionally, his emphasis on collaboration and guidance has potential pitfalls. Might facilitators be too helpful in some cases, as when a parent becomes too overbearing and controlling? Further, some children might become lazy and expect help when they might have done something on their own.

Information Processing

Piaget's and Vygotsky's theories provided important ideas about how young children think and how their thinking changes. More recently, the information-processing approach has generated research that illuminates how children process information during the preschool years (Bjorklund, 2013; Feldman, 2013). What are the limitations and advances in the young child's ability to pay attention to the environment, to remember, to develop strategies and solve problems, and to understand their own mental processes and those of others?

Attention

In Chapter 5, we defined attention as the focusing of mental resources on select information. The child's ability to pay attention improves significantly during the preschool years (Bell & Cuevas, 2013; Rothbart, 2011). The toddler wanders around, shifts attention from one activity to another, and seems to spend little time focused on any one object or event. By comparison, the preschool child might be observed building a fort for half an hour. A recent study revealed that watching television and playing video games were both linked to attention problems in children (Swing et al., 2010).

Young children especially make advances in two aspects of attention—executive attention and sustained attention (Bell & Cuevas, 2013; Rothbart, 2011). **Executive attention** involves action planning, allocating attention to goals, error detection and compensation, monitoring progress on tasks, and dealing with novel or difficult circumstances. **Sustained attention** is focused and extended engagement with an object, task, event, or other aspect of the environment.

Mary Rothbart and Maria Gartstein (2008) explained why advances in executive and sustained attention are so important in early childhood:

The development of the . . . executive attention system supports the rapid increases in effortful control in the toddler and preschool years. Increases in attention are due, in part, to advances in comprehension and language development. As children are better able to understand their environment, this increased appreciation of their surroundings helps them to sustain attention for longer periods of time. (p. 332)

In at least two ways, however, the preschool child's control of attention is still deficient:

- *Salient versus relevant dimensions:* Preschool children are likely to pay attention to stimuli that stand out, or are salient, even when those stimuli are not relevant to solving a problem or performing a task. For example, if a flashy, attractive clown presents the directions for solving a problem, preschool children are likely to pay more attention to the clown than to the directions. After the age of 6 or 7, children attend more efficiently to the dimensions of the task that are relevant, such as the directions for solving a problem. This change reflects a shift to cognitive control of attention, so that children act less impulsively and reflect more.
- *Planfulness:* When experimenters ask children to judge whether two complex pictures are the same, preschool children tend to use a haphazard comparison strategy, not examining all of the details before making a judgment. By comparison, elementary school age children are more likely to systematically compare the details across the pictures, one detail at a time (Vurpillot, 1968) (see Figure 7.13).

Figure 7.13

The Planfulness of Attention

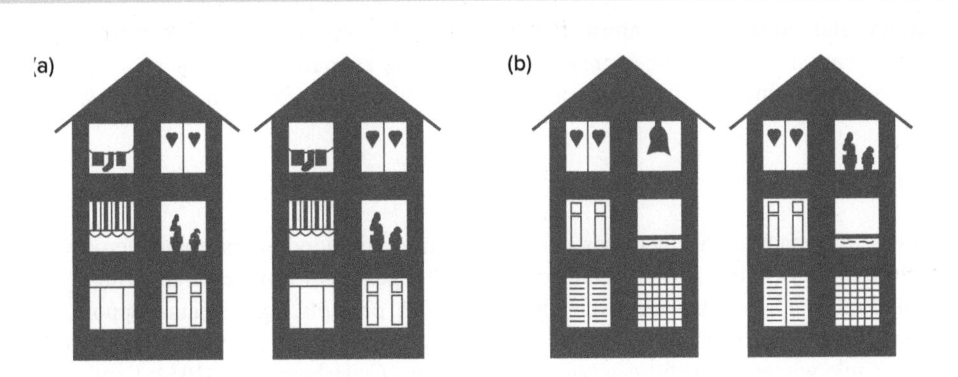

In one study, children were given pairs of houses to examine, like the ones shown here (Vurpillot, 1968). For three pairs of houses, what was in the windows was identical *(a)*.For the other three pairs, the windows had different items in them *(b)*. By filming the reflection in the children's eyes, it could be determined what they were looking at, how long they looked, and the sequence of their eye movements. Children under 6 years of age examined only a fragmentary portion of each display and made their judgments on the basis of insufficient information. By contrast, older children scanned the windows in more detailed ways and were more accurate in their judgments of which windows were identical.

In Central European countries such as Hungary, kindergarten children participate in exercises designed to improve their attention (Mills & Mills, 2000; Posner & Rothbart, 2007). For example, in one eye-contact exercise the teacher sits in the centre of a circle of children and each child is required to catch the teacher's eye before being permitted to leave the group. In other exercises created to improve attention, teachers have children participate in stop-go activities during which they have to listen for a specific signal, such as a drumbeat or an exact number of rhythmic beats, before stopping the activity.

Computer exercises recently have been developed to improve children's attention (Jaeggi, Berman, & Jonides, 2009; Rueda & Posner, 2013; Stevens & Bavelier, 2012; Tang & Posner, 2009). For example, one study revealed that five days of computer exercises that involved learning how to use a joystick, working memory, and the resolution of conflict improved the attention of 4- to 6-year-old children (Rueda et al., 2005).

Preschool children's ability to control and sustain their attention is related to their school readiness (Posner & Rothbart, 2007). For example, one study of more than 1000 children found that the ability to sustain attention at 54 months (4½ years) of age is linked to school readiness, which includes achievement and language skills (NICHD Early Child Care Research Network, 2005). In another study, children whose parents and teachers rated them higher on a scale of having attention problems at 54 months of age, had a lower level of social skills in peer relations in grades 1 and 3 than their counterparts who were rated lower on the attention problems scale at 54 months of age (NICHD Early Child Care Research Network, 2009). In yet another study, the ability to focus attention better at age 5 was linked to a higher level of school achievement at age 9 (Razza, Martin, & Brooks-Gunn, 2012).

Memory

Memory is a central process in children's cognitive development that involves the retention of information over time. In Chapter 5, we saw that most of a young infant's memories are fragile and, for the most part, short-lived—except for the memory of perceptual-motor actions, which can be substantial (Bauer, 2013; Bauer & Fivush, 2014). A study conducted by Dr. Peterson and colleagues at Memorial University of Newfoundland found that memory retrieval by children under 8 years of age, especially by those under 6 years of age, was less stable than for children over 8 years. A child's social interactions, acquisition of more complex language and narrative skills, as well as development of self-concept all play a role in memory.

Childhood amnesia refers to the inability to remember childhood experiences from before 3 or 4 years of age. Events embedded with personal meaning are more memorable (Peterson, Warren, & Short, 2011). Trauma events have a higher level of chronological coherence (Peterson et al., 2013).

To understand the child's capacity to remember, we need to distinguish implicit memory, the ability to repeat certain tasks without conscious awareness, from explicit memory, the ability to consciously recall events. Explicit memory itself, however, comes in many forms. One distinction occurs between relatively permanent or long-term memory and short-term memory.

SHORT-TERM MEMORY

In **short-term memory**, individuals retain information for up to 30 seconds, assuming there is no rehearsal. Using rehearsal (repeating information after it has been presented), people can keep information in short-term memory for a much longer period. Rehearsal and chronology play a role in memory survivability (Peterson, Warren, & Short, 2011; Peterson et al., 2013).

LONG-TERM MEMORY

While toddlers' short-term memory span increases during the early childhood years, their memory also becomes more accurate. In **long-term memory**, information is retained for a longer period of time, even indefinitely. Young children can remember a great deal of information if they are given appropriate cues, prompts, and rehearsal opportunities (Bruck & Ceci, 2012, 2014; Schneider, 2011; Peterson et al., 2013). Increasingly, young children are even being allowed to testify in court, especially if they are the sole witnesses to abuse, a crime, and so forth (Cederborg et al., 2014; Lamb et al., 2015).

Several factors can influence the accuracy of a young child's memory:

- *Age differences exist in children's susceptibility to suggestion.* Preschoolers are the most suggestible age group in comparison with older children and adults (Lehman et al., 2010; Pipe, 2008). For example, preschool children are more susceptible to believing misleading or incorrect information given after an event (Ghetti & Alexander, 2004). Despite these age differences, there is still concern about the reaction of older children when they are subjected to suggestive interviews (Ahern & Lamb, 2014; Bruck & Ceci, 2012).

- *Individual differences exist in susceptibility.* Some preschoolers are highly resistant to interviewers' suggestions, whereas others immediately succumb to the slightest suggestion Ceci & Klemfuss, 2010; Sim & Lamb, 2014. One study revealed that preschool children's ability to produce a high-quality narrative was linked to their resistance to suggestion (Kulkofsky & Klemfuss, 2008).

In sum, whether a young child's eyewitness testimony is accurate or not may depend on a number of factors such as the type, number, and intensity of the suggestive techniques the child has experienced (Lamb et al., 2015). It appears that the reliability of young children's reports has as much to do with the skills and motivation of the interviewer as with any natural limitations on young children's memory (Bruck & Ceci, 2012, 2014). Preschool aged children are impressionable, as was demonstrated by a case in Martensville, Saskatchewan. In the early 1990s, nine adults were found guilty of performing Satanic rituals against children based on the false memories of children. After over a decade of living with the pain and the angry suspicions of others, all were cleared of any wrong-doing. Recent studies related to child witness issues—namely childhood amnesia and children's eyewitness memory for stressful events, including emergency hospital treatment—revealed that children can have excellent memory for highly salient events over long periods of time; however, they may be vulnerable to suggestion, coercion, and response manipulation through reinforcement. Children should be interviewed carefully to minimize interviewer contamination (Peterson, 2012).

critical thinking

Would you, as a juror, believe a child's testimony of past abuses? What evidence would you need to make a decision beyond reasonable doubt—the criminal record of the accused? The testimonies of a teacher or neighbour? Have you ever been surprised by a young child's memory? If so, how accurate was the memory? How might your interactions with young children affect your ability as a juror to believe a child's testimony? What other factors might influence you?

AUTOBIOGRAPHICAL MEMORY

Another aspect of long-term memory that has been extensively studied in research on children's development is autobiographical memory (Pathman & St. Jacques, 2014; Peterson, 2012). Autobiographical memory involves memory of significant events and experiences in one's life. During the preschool years, young children's memories increasingly take on more autobiographical characteristics (Bauer, 2013; Bauer & Fivush, 2014; Miller, 2014; Peterson, 2011). In some areas, such as remembering a story, a movie, a song, or an interesting event or experience, young children have been shown to have reasonably good memories. From 3 to 5 years of age, they (1) increasingly remember events as occurring at a specific time and location, such as "on my birthday last year" and (2) include more elements that are rich in detail in their narratives (Bauer, 2013). Events described with emotion were two and a half times more likely to be remembered two years later than events described without emotion (Peterson et al., 2011). Children demonstrate excellent long-term recall for injuries requiring emergency room treatment; however, their recall of the specific details of what happened in the hospital, for example, are not as coherent (Peterson, 2012).

EXECUTIVE FUNCTION

Recently, increasing attention has been given to the development of children's **executive function**, an umbrella-like concept that consists of a number of higher-level cognitive processes linked to the development of the brain's prefrontal cortex. Executive function involves managing one's thoughts to engage in goal-directed behaviour and self-control.

In early childhood, executive function especially involves developmental advances in cognitive inhibition (such as inhibiting a strong tendency that is incorrect), cognitive flexibility (such as shifting attention to another item or topic), goal-setting (such as sharing a toy or mastering a skill like catching a ball), and delay of gratification (waiting longer to get a more attractive reward, for example) (Carlson, Zelazo, & Faja, 2013; Zelazo & Muller, 2011). During early childhood, the relatively stimulus-driven toddler is transformed into a child capable of flexible, goal-directed problem solving that characterizes executive function (Zelazo & Muller, 2011). Researchers have found that advances in executive function during the preschool years are linked with school readiness (Bierman et al., 2008).

Walter Mischel and colleagues (Berman et al., 2013; Mischel, Cantor, & Feldman, 1996; Mischel & Moore, 1980; Mischel et al., 2011; Schlam et al., 2013) have conducted a number of studies of delay of gratification with young children. One way in which they have assessed delay of gratification is to place a young child alone in a room with an alluring marshmallow that is within reach. The child can ring a bell at any time and eat the marshmallow, or the child can wait until the experimenter returns and will then get two marshmallows. Young children who waited for the experimenter to return engaged in a number of strategies to distract their attention from the marshmallows, including singing songs, picking their noses, or doing other things to keep from looking at the marshmallows. Mischel and colleagues labelled these strategies "cool thoughts" (that is, doing non-marshmallow-related thoughts and activities). In contrast, young children who looked at the marshmallow were engaging in "hot thoughts." The young children who engaged in cool thoughts were more likely to eat the marshmallow later or wait until the experimenter returned to the room. In one study using the delay of gratification task just described, longer delay of gratification at 4 years of age was linked to a lower body mass index (BMI) three decades later (Schlam et al., 2013).

Stephanie Carlson and colleagues (2010, 2011; Carlson, Claxton, & Moses, 2014; Carlson & White, 2013; Carlson, White, & Davis-Unger, 2014) have conducted a number of research studies on young children's executive function. In one study, young children listened as an adult read aloud either *Planet Opposite*—a fantasy book in which everything is turned upside down—or *Fun Town*—a reality-oriented fiction book (Carlson & White, 2011). After hearing the adult read one of the books, the young children completed the Less Is More Task, in which they were shown two trays of candy—one with five pieces, the other with two—and were told that the tray they pick will be given to the stuffed animal seated at the table. This task was difficult for the 3-year-olds, who tended to pick the tray that they themselves wanted (and so ended up losing the tray to the stuffed animal). Sixty percent of the 3-year-olds who heard the Planet Opposite story selected the smaller number of candies (hence keeping the five pieces of candy) compared with only 20 percent of their counterparts who heard the more straightforward story. The results indicated that learning about a topsy-turvy imaginary world likely helped the young children become more flexible in their thinking.

Parenting practices are linked to children's development of executive function (Carlson, Zelazo, & Faja, 2013; Cuevas et al., 2014). For example, several studies have linked greater use of verbal scaffolding by parents (providing age-appropriate support during cognitive tasks) to children's more advanced executive function (Bernier, Carlson, & Whipple, 2010; Bibok, Carpendale, & Muller, 2009; Hammond et al., 2012; Hughes & Ensor, 2009). Another study found that preschool children who were securely attached to their mothers had a higher level of executive function than their insecurely attached counterparts (Bernier et al., 2011).

Other predictors of better executive function in children include higher socio-economic status (Obradovic, 2010); some aspects of language, including vocabulary size, verbal labelling, and bilingualism (Bell, Wolfe, & Adkins, 2007; Bialystok, 2010; Muller et al., 2008); imagination (generating novel ideas, for example) (Carlson & White, 2013); cultural background (for example, Asian children, especially urban Chinese and Korean children, show better executive function than U.S. children) (Lan et al., 2011; Sabbagh et al., 2006); and fewer sleep problems (Friedman et al., 2009).

Strategies and Problem Solving

Strategies consist of using deliberate mental activities to improve the processing of information (Bjorklund, 2008; Pressley, 2007). For example, rehearsing information and organizing it are two typical strategies for remembering. The relatively stimulus-driven toddler may become transformed into a child capable of flexible, goal-directed problem solving (Zelazo & Müller, 2004). Consider a problem in which children must sort stimuli using the rule of colour. In the course of the colour sorting, a child may describe a red rabbit as "a red one" to solve the problem. However, in a subsequent task, the child may need to discover a rule that describes the rabbit as just "a rabbit" to solve the problem. If 3- to 4-year-olds fail to understand that it is possible to provide multiple descriptions of the same stimulus, they persist in describing the stimulus as "a red rabbit." Researchers have found that at about 4 years of age, children acquire the concept of perspectives, which allows them to appreciate that a single stimulus can be described in two different ways (Frye, 1999).

Zhe Chen and Robert Siegler (2000) placed young children at a table at which an attractive toy was placed too far away for the child to reach it. On the table, between the child and the toy, were six potential tools (see Figure 7.14). Only one of them was likely to be useful in obtaining the toy. After initially assessing the young children's attempts to obtain the toy on their own, the experimenters either modelled how to obtain the toy (using the appropriate tool) or gave the child a hint (telling the child to use the particular tool). These 2-year-olds learned the strategy and subsequently mapped it onto new problems. This study shows that children as young as 2 years of age can learn a strategy.

Figure 7.14
The Toy-Retrieval Task in the Study of Young Children's Problem-Solving Strategies

The child needs to choose the target tool (in this illustration, the toy rake) to pull in the toy (in this case, the turtle).

Theory of Mind

Theory of mind refers to the awareness of one's own mental processes and the mental processes of others. Even young children are curious about the nature of the human mind, and developmentalists have shown a flurry of interest in children's thoughts about what the human mind is like (Wellman et al., 2008). Studies of theory of mind view the child as "a thinker who is trying to explain, predict, and understand people's thoughts, feelings, and utterances" (Harris, 2006, p. 847).

Children's theory of mind changes as they develop through childhood (Gelman, 2013; Lillard & Kavanaugh, 2014; Wellman, 2011). From 18 months through age 3, children begin to understand three mental states:

- *Perceptions:* Children realize that other people see what is in front of their eyes and not necessarily what is in front of the child's eyes.
- *Desires:* Children understand that if people want something, they will try to get it.
- *Emotions:* Children can distinguish between positive (for example, happy) and negative (sad, for example) emotions.

One of the landmark developments in understanding others' desires is recognizing that someone else may have different desires from one's own (Doherty, 2008). Eighteen-month-olds understand that their own food preferences may not match the preferences of others—they will give an adult the food to which she says "Yummy!" even if the food is something that the infants detest (Repacholi & Gopnik, 1997). As they get older, they can verbalize that they themselves do not like something but an adult might (Flavell et al., 1992).

Between 3 and 5 years of age, children come to understand that the mind can represent objects and events accurately or inaccurately (Low & Simpson, 2012). This realization can be seen in two phenomena: false beliefs and preference of information source. The knowledge that people can have false beliefs—beliefs that are not true—develops in a majority of children by the time they are 5 years old (Wellman, Cross, & Watson, 2001). This point is often described as a pivotal one in understanding the mind—recognizing that beliefs are not just mapped directly into the mind from the surrounding world, but that different people can also have different, and sometimes incorrect, beliefs (Gelman, 2009). While age-related memory and conceptual deficits may explain young children's problems with false beliefs, as Susan Birch (2005) from the University of British Columbia points out, the "curse" of knowledge—people who are knowledgeable about an issue assume others to have the same information—may be the reason here. The younger we are, the less we are able to resist making this assumption.

Children who perform better at such executive function tasks show a better understanding of theory of mind (Astington & Hughes, 2013; Sabbagh et al., 2006). In a recent study, 3½-year-old children who showed poor performance on false-belief tasks were given training to improve their executive function (Benson et al., 2014). Improvements in children's executive function as a result of the training were linked to improvements in theory of mind. The researchers concluded that executive function skills promote advances in theory of mind by facilitating children's ability to reflect on and learn from relevant experience.

University of Waterloo researchers Daniela O'Neill, Rebecca Main, and Renata Ziemski (2009) examined peer-to-peer conversations of preschoolers. They found the children overwhelmingly initiated conversation to express a particular personal desire or need, or to direct the listener to do something. The subject matter of the conversations led the researchers to surmise that children may have used their developing sense of theory of mind to establish mutual understanding with their listener. Further, around 4 to 5 years of age, children develop a sense of audience. For example, even 4-year-old children speak differently to a 2-year-old than to a same-aged peer; they use shorter sentences with the 2-year-old. They also speak differently to an adult than to a same-aged peer, using more polite and formal language with the adult.

Young Children's Literacy

Early precursors of literacy and academic success include language skills, phonological and syntactic knowledge, letter identification, and conceptual knowledge about print and its conventions and functions (Christie et al., 2014; Jalongo, 2014). Children should be active participants and be immersed in a wide range of interesting listening, talking, writing, and reading experiences (Senechal & LeFevre, 2014). One study revealed that children whose mothers had more education had more advanced emergent literacy levels than children whose mothers had less education (Korat, 2009). Another study found that literacy experiences (such as how often the child was read to), the quality of the mother's engagement with her child (such as attempts to cognitively stimulate the child), and provision of learning materials (such as age-appropriate activities and books) were important home literacy experiences in low-income families that were positively linked to the children's language development (Rodriguez et al., 2009). Building instruction on what children already know about oral language, reading, and writing is effective. The following three longitudinal studies indicate the importance of early language skills and children's school readiness:

- Phonological awareness, letter name and sound knowledge, and naming speed in kindergarten were linked to reading success in grades 1 and 2 (Schattschneider et al., 2004).
- Children's early home environment influenced their early language skills, which in turn predicted their readiness for school (Forget-Dubois et al., 2009).
- The number of letters children knew in kindergarten was highly correlated (.52) with their reading achievement in high school (Stevenson & Newman, 1986).

Children's speech during preschool years shows another characteristic: questions. Children's earliest questions appear around the age of 3, and by the age of 5 they have just about exhausted the adults around them with "why" questions. Children's questions yield clues about their mental development and reflect intellectual curiosity, signalling the emergence of an interest in verbal reasoning and figuring out why things are the way they are.

To this point, we have discussed language development in early childhood. For a review, see the Reach Your Learning Outcomes section at the end of this chapter.

Early Childhood Education

LO5 Identify different approaches to early childhood education.

- **Variations in Early Childhood Education**
- **Developmentally Appropriate Practices**
- **Young Children's Literacy and Numeracy**
- **Education for Children Who Are Disadvantaged**

To the teachers in a Reggio Emilia program (described in the chapter opener), preschool children are active learners who are engaged in exploring the world with their peers, constructing their knowledge of the world in collaboration with their community, and aided but not directed by their teachers. In many ways, the Reggio Emilia approach applies ideas consistent with the views of Piaget and Vygotsky that were discussed earlier in this chapter. Our exploration of early childhood education focuses on variations in programs, education for young children who are disadvantaged, and some controversial aspects.

Variations in Early Childhood Education

Both parents work in almost 70 percent of Canadian homes; consequently, for many all-day kindergarten seemed to be a panacea. However, because the all-day program hours usually end at 2:30 or 3:00, and most parents work beyond that, after-school programs also are part of the scene. Quite often children go to daycare, then to kindergarten, then back to daycare. In each scenario, the curriculum is set to assist the child's social, emotional, and academic development.

In the **child-centred kindergarten**, education involves the whole child and includes concern for the child's physical, cognitive, and social development (Morrison, 2014, 2015). Instruction is organized around the child's needs, interests, and learning styles. Emphasis is on the process of learning, rather than on what is learned (Kostelnik et al., 2015; Weissman & Hendrick, 2014). Each child follows a unique developmental pattern, and young children learn through first-hand experience with people and materials. Moreover, play is considered extremely important in the child's total development. These programs emphasize experimenting, exploring, discovering, trying out, restructuring, speaking, and listening.

Education is a provincial responsibility and is only mandatory in New Brunswick. The curriculum varies across Canada. Newfoundland and Labrador started full-day kindergarten in 2016, joining other provinces such as British Columbia (2010), Ontario (2014), Quebec (1999), Prince Edward Island (2010), Nova Scotia (1995), and the Northwest Territories (2014). Other provinces offer half-day, or a blend of half-day/full-day programs or a specified number of hours. Most schools in Alberta offer kindergarten, but it is not mandatory (McCuaig, 2014). According to a study conducted by McMaster University and Ontario Ministry of Education, attending kindergarten enhances children's readiness for grade 1 in every area: physical health and well-being, social competence, emotional maturity, language, cognition, communication skills, and general knowledge (Janus, Duku, & Schell, 2012).

Most kindergarten programs have targeted achievement goals in such areas as language arts, social sciences, art, physical education, and math. Manitoba uses an "activity-based approach," Saskatchewan uses "learning through play," while New Brunswick employs a "student-centred" focus. In Nunavut, the Elders Advisory Committee works with teachers to develop an Inuit perspective to the curriculum, focusing on knowledge, skills, and values.

The Montessori Approach

Montessori schools are patterned after the educational philosophy of Maria Montessori (1870–1952), an Italian physician-turned-educator who crafted a revolutionary approach to young children's education at the beginning of the twentieth century. The **Montessori approach** is a philosophy of education in which children are given considerable freedom and spontaneity in choosing activities. They are allowed to move from one activity to another as they desire. The teacher acts as a facilitator, rather than a director of learning. The teacher shows the child how to perform intellectual activities, demonstrates interesting ways to explore curriculum materials, and offers help when the child requests it. "By encouraging children to make decisions from an early age, Montessori programs seek to develop self-regulated problem solvers who can make choices and manage their time effectively" (Hyson, Copple, & Jones, 2006, p. 14).

Some developmentalists favour the Montessori approach, but others believe that it neglects children's social development. For example, although Montessori fosters independence and the development of cognitive skills, it de-emphasizes verbal interaction between the teacher and child and peer interaction. Montessori's critics also argue that it restricts imaginative play.

critical thinking

Put yourself in the shoes of a single parent with a kindergarten-aged child. Your job demands that you be onsite from 9 to 5:30; your child attends an all-day kindergarten from 9 to 2:30. Because you live in an urban setting, you are able to manage this by enrolling your child in a daycare. The daycare provides lunch, walks the children to school, and meets them after school to walk them back to the daycare facility. What criteria would you use in choosing a daycare for your child? What adjustments would both you and the child have to make? How much energy at the end of the day would you and your child have? What additional stresses may you encounter?

Developmentally Appropriate Practices

A number of educators and psychologists believe that preschool and young elementary school children learn best through active, hands-on teaching methods such as games and dramatic play. They recognize that children develop at varying rates and that schools need to allow for these individual differences (Miranda, 2004). They also believe that schools should focus on improving children's social development, as well as their cognitive development (Bredekamp, 2011; Kostelnik, Soderman, & Whiren, 2011). Educators refer to this type of schooling as **developmentally appropriate practice**, which is based on knowledge of the typical development of children within an age span (age appropriateness) and the uniqueness of the child (individual appropriateness). Developmentally appropriate practice emphasizes the importance of creating settings that encourage children to be active learners and reflect children's interests and capabilities (Bredekamp, 2011; Kostelnik, Soderman, & Whiren, 2011). Desired outcomes for developmentally appropriate practice include thinking critically, working cooperatively, solving problems, developing self-regulatory skills, and enjoying learning. The emphasis in developmentally appropriate practice is on the process of learning rather than its content (Barbarin & Miller, 2009; Ritchie, Maxwell, & Bredekamp, 2009).

Young Children's Literacy and Numeracy

Activities that stimulate experimentation with talking, listening, writing, and reading engage students because they become active participants in the learning process, rather than passive recipients (Hardman & Taylor, 2006). Where reading problems are suspected, Vellutino and colleagues (2006) suggest that one-on-one reading remedial assistance be offered throughout kindergarten and into grade 1.

Numeracy is just as important as literacy. Most children at 2 years of age begin to learn a few number words, and by age 5 will be able to count backwards from 10 and work at counting up from pre-designated numbers (e.g., "start counting from 7") (Canadian Child Care Federation, 2009). They can use the concept of ordinal place to order such things as the sequence of events, winners of a race, or their top five favourite toys. In the next year they will expand their counting range to 100, use units of ten, and do simple multiplication and fractions. Like literacy, numeracy skills need to be addressed and fostered through interactive activity with adults.

Challenges for School Readiness

A risk factor for children's readiness for formal education is the education approach of another culture. In one longitudinal study in Montreal (Pagani et al., 2006), children with foreign-born parents who did not speak French at home lagged behind children with Canadian-born French-speaking parents in number and receptive vocabulary skills at the beginning of kindergarten. The deficit in numeracy was due to the children's difficulty with French. Hence, language knowledge appears to be the key for the academic success of children in a linguistic minority. Teachers certainly can help children in this situation. As the study by Pagani and colleagues showed, linguistic-minority children who achieved better progress in verbal skills over time tended to have teachers who were willing to switch away from child-driven methods popular in Canadian schools to adult-driven techniques that many immigrant families feel comfortable with.

For deaf children, school readiness appears to involve learning sign language at home as their native language, along with a familiarity with oral language (Meristo et al., 2007). Children with a background in both forms of language (with sign language as their native language) developed a better ability to express a theory of mind promoting the understanding of the emotional states of others when compared to deaf children who did not develop sign language within the home from infancy. Bailes and associates (2009) stress the importance of parents (especially hearing parents) of deaf children using American Sign Language as early as possible in interactions with their infant.

Education for Children Who Are Disadvantaged

Another risk factor for school readiness is low income. Children from poor families tend to fare worse in their readiness to learn. In one study, Canadian children from lower-income families were more likely to have delays in cognitive and language development in the preschool years and were more likely to repeat a grade in elementary schools than their peers. Similarly, in an analysis of 5-year-olds (Thomas, 2006), household income, children's activities (the likelihood of being read to daily and participation in organized sports and other physical activities), and school readiness variables (vocabulary and number skills) were found to be interrelated. These results suggest that children in low-income families may be disadvantaged in the area of school preparedness because of adults' lack of time and resources for activities that may promote such readiness.

What can be done to solve this problem? A comprehensive child care approach may be an answer. In Canada, one of the programs that follows this approach is Aboriginal Head Start. Launched in 1995 and funded by Health Canada, this program mirrors Project Head Start in the United States, which was started in the 1960s. The U.S. program was based on a belief that compensatory intervention to help low-income children to succeed in school should involve both academic and non-academic aspects of their lives, such as health and the local community.

Aboriginal Head Start is offered in 133 sites across the country, serving almost 5000 children up to age 6 and their families. The program provides structured half-day preschool experiences for Aboriginal children between 3 and 5 years of age. The program's six components include Aboriginal culture and language, education and school readiness, health promotion, nutrition, social support, and parent involvement (Public Health Agency Canada, 2015). Elders and parents in each locale also participate in developing projects appropriate for the community (Public Health Agency of Canada, 2013). The program has had a positive effect on school readiness, specifically in improving children's language, social, motor, and academic skills. Experts in the field would like to expand the program to reach more children (Public Health Agency of Canada, 2012).

To this point, we have studied a number of ideas about early childhood education. For a review, see the Reach Your Learning Outcomes section at the end of this chapter.

Reach Your **Learning Outcomes**

Physical Development

LO1 **Identify physical changes in early childhood.**

Body Growth	• The average child grows in height and gains between 2.2 and 3.2 kg a year during early childhood. Growth patterns vary individually. • Some children are unusually short because of congenital problems, a physical or emotional problem that develops in childhood, or growth hormone deficiency.
The Brain	• Some of the brain's increase in size is due to increases in the number and size of nerve endings, while some is due to myelination. • From ages 3 to 15, local patterns of the brain experience major changes. The frontal lobe areas involving planning and organizing functions show rapid growth between ages 3 and 6, while temporal and parietal lobe areas responsible for language and spatial functions develop quickly from age 6 to puberty. • Increasing brain maturation contributes to improved cognitive abilities.
Motor and Perceptual Development	• Gross motor skills increase dramatically during early childhood. • Children become increasingly adventuresome as their gross motor skills improve. • Fine motor skills also improve substantially during early childhood.

Health and Wellness

LO2 Identify the factors involved in determining the health and wellness of children in Canada and in other countries.

Sleep Nutrition and Exercise	▪ Sleep is the number one complaint parents have of their young children. Experts recommend children get 11 to 13 hours of sleep nightly; however, children often drag out their bedtime. Sleep deprivation may be a symptom of many physical and mental health disorders such as eczema, gastrointestinal reflux, anxiety, depression, and ADHD. A calm routine that slows a child's activity is a helpful parental strategy to get children ready for bed. ▪ Energy requirements vary according to basal metabolism, rate of growth, and level of activity. ▪ A special concern is that too many young children are being raised on diets that are too high in fat. Eating habits formed in early childhood are critical to healthy eating habits and good health as the child matures. ▪ Body Mass Index, a measure of weight in relation to height, is of concern because of the increasing rate of obesity.
Wellness in Canada	▪ Factors of well- being include sleep, exercise, and nutrition. ▪ Congenital anomalies, cancer, diseases of the nervous system, unintentional injuries, and exposure to parental smoking are major health concerns for children in early childhood.
Wellness in Other Countries	▪ Poor countries around the world have higher mortality rates for children under age 5 than do Western industrialized nations. ▪ Pneumonia, dehydration from diarrheal diseases, and preventable injuries are the main causes of death among the world's children. ▪ Child deaths due to the transmission of HIV/AIDS from parents have decreased in poor countries. ▪ Many childhood diseases and deaths can be prevented by a reduction in poverty and improvements in nutrition, sanitation, education, and health services.

Cognitive Development

LO3 Describe three views of the cognitive changes that occur in early childhood.

Piaget's Preoperational Stage	▪ This stage marks the beginning of the ability to reconstruct at the level of thought what has been established in behaviour. ▪ The two substages are the symbolic function substage and the intuitive thought substage. ▪ Preoperational thinking is characterized by egocentrism, animism, and centration, the last of which can be shown in the lack of conservation.
Vygotsky's Theory	▪ The zone of proximal development refers to a range of tasks too difficult for children to master alone, but that can be learned with the guidance and assistance of people with greater expertise. ▪ Scaffolding involves changing support over the course of a teaching session to fit a learner's current performance level. ▪ Language plays a key role in guiding cognition. ▪ Teaching strategies may be based on Vygotsky's theory.

Information Processing	▪ Preschool children's attention is strongly influenced by the salient features of a task. ▪ Short-term memory increases during early childhood. ▪ Appropriate cues can improve young children's long-term memory. At the same time, children can be led into developing false memories. ▪ Preschool children are capable of learning simple problem-solving strategies. ▪ Theory of mind refers to thoughts about how mental processes work. Children's theory of mind changes during the early childhood years. By age 5, children have some understanding of false beliefs and use past accuracy to judge sources of information.

Language Development

LO4 Summarize how language develops in early childhood

- Children's grasp of the morphological rules improves during early childhood, as Jean Berko's (1958) study and overregularization errors show.
- At age 6, the size of a child's speaking vocabulary is about 14 000 words.
- Children have some understanding of the parts of speech.
- Early childhood also witnesses improved performance in pragmatics.
- Children's questions indicate not only language skills, but also intellectual curiosity at this age.

Phonology and Morphology

- Children's understanding of phonology and morphology improves as children age; in other words, they demonstrate a better understanding of how sounds are organized and used as well as the structure and form of words, including inflection, suffixes and prefixes, and compound words.

Syntax and Semantics

- Children's grasp of syntax and semantics improves as evidenced by their mastery of grammatically correct sentence structure.

Pragmatics

- Children become increasingly more adept in pragmatics as they are increasingly able to understand the social context, have a sense of audience, and become more capable of conversation.

Young Children's Literacy

- Studies indicate that exposure to reading materials is important to the child's development of language skills.
- Studies also indicated that early development of language skills is highly linked to the child's readiness for school.

Early Childhood Education

LO5 Identify different approaches to early childhood education.

Variations in Early Childhood Education	▪ The child-centred kindergarten emphasizes the whole child's physical, cognitive, and social development. ▪ There is a very wide range of kindergarten programs across Canada. ▪ In a Montessori school, children are given considerable freedom and spontaneity in choosing activities.

Developmentally Appropriate Practices	▪ Developmentally appropriate practice focuses on the typical patterns of children and the uniqueness of each child. ▪ Literacy skills in early childhood are related to reading performance in elementary and secondary schools. ▪ Development of numeracy skills between the ages of 2 and 5 are critical to later number learning.
Young Children's Literacy and Numeracy	▪ Literacy is important for school achievement. ▪ Early literacy programs should include: instruction built on what children already know; reading integrated into the communication process; a wide variety of reading materials; adults as models for using language appropriately; individualized attention; and children as active participants in the learning process. ▪ Numeracy is just as important as literacy in early childhood. ▪ Numeracy skills should be addressed and fostered through interactive activity with adults.
Education for Children Who Are Disadvantaged	▪ Child-driven teaching may not help linguistic-minority children achieve progress in verbal skills. ▪ Comprehensive preschool programs that provide academic and non-academic support, such as Head Start, including Aboriginal Head Start, may have positive effects on children from disadvantaged economic backgrounds.

review → connect → reflect

review

1. Describe the development of gross and fine motor skills in early childhood.LO1
2. What role do nutrition and exercise play in early childhood? LO2
3. Compare and contrast Piaget's and Vygotsky's theories of cognitive development. LO3
4. What is theory of mind and how does this change in the early childhood years? LO3
5. Describe the primary changes in language development in early childhood. LO4
6. What is meant by a child-centred kindergarten?LO5
7. How is a child's physical and cognitive development affected by poverty? (LO1, LO2, LO3, LO4, LO5)

connect

In this chapter you read about children and lying. In your interaction with young children, have you been able to tell when they are telling the truth and when they might be lying? What are some of the signals that might be tell-tale? How does language development play a role in a child's ability to tell a lie successfully?

reflect

Your Own Personal Journey of Life

What were your eating habits like as a young child? In what ways are they similar to or different from your current eating habits? Were your early eating habits a forerunner of whether or not you have weight problems today? If you are a parent, have your eating habits changed? If you are not a parent, do you think your eating habits may change when and if you decide to become a parent? Why or why not?

CHAPTER 8

Socio-Emotional Development in Early Childhood

CHAPTER OUTLINE

The Self and Emotional Development

LO1 Discuss the emergence of the self and emotional development in early childhood.

- **The Self**
- **Emotional Development**

Moral Development and Gender

LO2 Summarize moral development and gender in early childhood.

- **Moral Development**
- **Gender**

The Changing Family in a Changing Society

LO3 Explain how families can influence young children's development.

- **Parenting**
- **Divorce**
- **Sibling Relationships and Birth Order**

Peer Relations, Play, and Social Media

LO4 Describe the roles of peers, play, and social media in young children's development.

- **Peer Relations**
- **Play**
- **Media/Screen Time**

"What are little boys made of? Frogs and snails and puppy dogs' tails. What are little girls made of? Sugar and spice and all that's nice."

—J.O. HALLIWELL, NINETEENTH-CENTURY ENGLISH AUTHOR

©Robert Churchill/iStockphoto

Is the Sky the Limit for a Parent's Love?

How often does a mother write a song for her children? And how often does such a song draw tears from strangers outside the family? For Canadian songwriter and singer Amy Sky, the answers would have been "one for each child" and "all the time."

Although autobiographical—talking about the milestones of her own life—the song for her first child, "I Will Take Care of You," shows an unconditional commitment to raising her daughter. She promised that:

I will take care of you
The very best that I can
With all of the love here in my heart
And all of the strength in my hands
Your every joy I'll share
For every tear I'll be there
My whole life through
I will take care of you

Amy Sky's motherly love did not subside with the arrival of her second-born. To her, seeing him grow was like witnessing "Ordinary Miracles" every day, something that she would cherish even when her boy became a grown-up.

This chapter will discuss significant developmental tasks for children in early childhood—like an emergent understanding of the self, an awareness of one's own biological sex, moral reasoning and action, and relationships with siblings and peers. To students, researchers, and policymakers, these make interesting research topics and policy issues. To parents, however, each of these pieces in the child's early childhood—like every one before this time and every one after—is truly an "ordinary miracle."

The Self and Emotional Development

LO1 Discuss the emergence of the self and emotional development in early childhood.

- **The Self**
- **Emotional Development**

Between the ages of 2 and 3 years, children's social worlds expand and they start to take independent initiatives. They learn more and more about themselves, their peers, and people other than their parents. We will begin our discussion of socio-emotional development with a look at the child's understanding of the self and emotions.

The Self

We learned in Chapter 6 that toward the end of the second year of life, children develop a sense of self. During early childhood, some important developments in the self take place.

Initiative versus Guilt

Erik Erikson (1968) identified the psychosocial stage that characterizes early childhood as *initiative versus guilt.* By now, children use their perceptual, motor, cognitive, and language skills to make things happen, and become convinced that they are their own persons. They have a surplus of energy that permits them to approach new areas—even if they seem dangerous—with undiminished zest and increased sense of direction. On their own initiative at this stage, children move out exuberantly into a wider social world. The great governor of initiative is *conscience.* The initiative and enthusiasm of young children may not only bring them rewards, but sometimes guilt, which lowers the child's self-esteem.

Self-Understanding and Understanding Others

Erikson believed that the young child has begun to develop **self-understanding**, which is the representation of self, the substance and content of self-conceptions (Harter, 2012). Though not the whole of personal identity, self-understanding provides its rational underpinnings. Recent research, conducted mainly through interviews, has revealed that young children are more psychologically aware—of themselves and others—than was once thought (Easterbrooks et al., 2013). This awareness reflects expanding psychological sophistication.

Early self-understanding involves self-recognition. Recall that recognizing one's body parts in a mirror takes place by approximately 18 months of age (see Chapter 6). A sense of "me" emerges later in the second year and early in the third year. Young children distinguish themselves from others through many physical and material attributes. Says 4-year-old Sandra, "I'm different from Jennifer because I have brown hair and she has blond hair." Says 4-year-old Ralph, I am different from my sister because I have a bicycle." Although young children primarily describe themselves in terms of concrete, observable features and action tendencies, at about 4 to 5 years of age, as they hear others use psychological traits and emotion terms, they begin to include these in their own self-descriptions (Marsh, Ellis, & Craven, 2002). Thus, in a self-description, a 4-year-old might say, "I'm not scared. I'm always happy." Young children's self-descriptions are typically unrealistically positive, as reflected in the comment of the 4-year-old who says he is always happy, which he is not (Harter, 2012). Children express optimism because they don't yet distinguish between their desired competence and their actual competence, tend to confuse ability and effort (thinking that differences in ability can be changed as easily as can differences in effort), don't engage in spontaneous social comparison of their abilities with those of others, and tend to compare their present abilities with what they could do at an earlier age (by which they usually look quite good). Perhaps as adults we should all be so optimistic about our abilities (Thompson, 2011).

However, as in virtually all areas of human development, there are individual variations in young children's self-conceptions. There is increasing evidence that some children are vulnerable to negative self-attributions (Thompson, 2011). For example, one study revealed that insecurely attached preschool children whose mothers reported a high level of parenting stress and depressive symptoms had a lower self-concept than other young children in more positive family circumstances (Goodvin et al., 2008). This research indicates that young children's generally optimistic self-ascriptions do not buffer them from adverse, stressful family conditions (Thompson, 2011).

Understanding Others

Studies indicate that young children's ability to understand their own and others' emotions precede advances in their theory of mind and is characterized by individual differences (Nelson et al, 2013a; O'Brien et al., 2011; Laible & Thompson, 2007). A better basic understanding of emotions in early childhood enables children to develop a more advanced understanding of others' perspectives (Harter, 2012; Mills, 2013; Thompson, 2014a, 2015). At about 4 to 5 years of age, children not only start describing themselves in terms of psychological traits, but also begin to perceive others in terms of psychological traits. Thus, a 4-year-old might say, "My teacher is nice."

Some preschoolers are better than others at understanding what people are feeling and what they desire, To some degree, these individual differences are linked to conversations caregivers have with young children about other people's feelings and desires, and children's opportunities to observe others talking about people's feelings and desires. For example, a mother might say to her 3-year-old, "Before you hit him next time, think about Ralph's feelings. How would you feel if Ralph hit you?"

As young children mature, they need to develop an understanding that people don't always give accurate reports of their beliefs (Landrum, Mills, & Johnston, 2013; Mills, 2013; Mills, Elashi, & Archacki, 2011; Mills & Landrum, 2012). Researchers have found that even 4-year-olds understand that people may make statements that aren't true to obtain what they want or to avoid trouble (Lee et al., 2002). For example, one study revealed that 4- and 5-year-olds were increasingly skeptical of another child's claim to be sick when the children were informed that the child wanted to avoid going to camp (Gee & Heyman, 2007). Another study compared preschool children's trust in an expert's comments under different conditions (Landrum, Mills, & Johnston, 2013). In this study, in one condition, 5-year-olds trusted the expert's claim more than 3-year-olds did. However, in other conditions, preschoolers tended to trust a nice non-expert more than a mean expert, indicating that young children often are likely to believe someone who is nice to them rather than someone who is an expert.

Another important aspect of understanding others involves understanding joint commitments. As children approach their third birthday, their collaborative interactions with others increasingly involve obligations to the partner (Tomasello & Hamann, 2012). A study revealed that 3-year-olds, but not 2-year-olds, recognized when an adult is committed and when they themselves are committed to joint activity that involves obligation to a partner (Grafenhain et al., 2009).

Piaget's concept of egocentrism has become so ingrained in people's thinking about young children that too often the current research on social awareness in infancy and early childhood has been overlooked. Research increasingly shows that young children are more socially sensitive and perceptive than was previously imagined, suggesting that parents and teachers can help them to better understand and interact in the social world by modelling the desired behaviour (Thompson, 2014a). If young children are seeking to better understand various mental and emotional states (intentions, goals, feelings, desires) that underlie people's actions, then talking with them about these internal states can improve young children's understanding (Thompson, 2011, 2014a, 2015). However, debate continues to surround the question of whether young children are socially sensitive or basically egocentric.

Emotional Development

Children develop an increased understanding of emotions in early childhood because of greater cognitive and language skills, knowledge of the self, and social interactions in this age than in infancy.

Self-Conscious Emotions

As noted in Chapter 6, even young infants experience emotions such as joy and fear. But to experience *self-conscious emotions,* children must be able to refer to themselves and be aware of themselves as distinct from others (Lewis, 2007). Pride, shame, embarrassment, and guilt are examples of self-conscious emotions. Self-conscious emotions do not seem to develop until self-awareness appears in the last half of the second year of life.

During early childhood, emotions such as pride and guilt become more common. A recent study revealed that young children's emotional expression was linked to their parents' own expressive behaviour (Nelson et al., 2012). For example, a young child may experience shame when a parent says, "You should feel bad about biting your sister."

Emotion Language and Understanding of Emotion

Among the most important changes in emotional development in early childhood are the increased use of language and the better understanding of emotion (Denham et al., 2012; Easterbrooks et al., 2013; Goodvin, Winer, & Thompson, 2014). Young children increasingly understand that certain situations are likely to evoke particular emotions, that facial expressions indicate specific emotions; that emotions affect behaviour; and that emotions can be used to influence others (Cole et al., 2009). Researchers have found that young children's understanding of emotions is linked to their prosocial behaviour (Ensor, Spencer, & Hughes, 2011).

Between 2 and 4 years of age, children considerably increase the number of terms they use to describe emotions. As well, they are learning about the causes and consequences of feelings (Denham et al., 2011). When they are 4- to 5-years-of-age, children show an increased ability to reflect on emotions. They also begin to understand that the same event can elicit different feelings in different people. Moreover, they show a growing awareness that they need to manage their emotions to meet social standards.

Shyness

Most of us—in fact, according to research, 90 percent of us—have felt shy at one time or another (Rubin & Barstead, 2015). According to Robert Coplan of Carleton University, shyness is a temperament trait characterized by fear of novel social situations and self-consciousness in situations of perceived social evaluation. When shy children enter a daycare situation for the first time, they may be overcome with an internal conflict: wanting to engage with other children, but at the same time feeling anxious, embarrassed, and stressed about these social interactions (Coplan et al., 2004).

It has been suggested that shyness is less socially acceptable for boys than girls because it violates gender-stereotypes about male assertiveness and dominance. Perhaps as a result, parents and peers tend to respond more negatively to shy behaviours in young boys compared to girls. Consequently, shyness can lead to a higher risk of maladjustment for boys than for girls (Coplan & Armer, 2005). Hyperactivity, more prevalent in preschool boys than girls, combined with high levels of shyness, are associated with lower levels of peer acceptance (Rubin & Barstead, 2015).

Multiple factors such as gender, physiology, family makeup, peers, social cognition, culture, and context, all play a role in the development of temperament; consequently, studies of behaviour are complex, multifaceted, and often inconclusive (Rubin & Barstead, 2015). However, research does indicate that from early childhood through adolescence, shyness is associated with a host of negative outcomes including poor peer relationships (e.g., exclusion, victimization), internalizing problems (e.g., anxiety, depression), and school adjustment difficulties (e.g., lack of academic success, school avoidance) (Doey, Coplan, & Kingsbury, 2014).

Positive relations with parents, teachers, siblings, and others are buffers to negative outcomes in early education experiences (Coplan & Graham, 2012).

critical thinking

Internalizing and externalizing behaviours differ. Internalizing behaviours are behaviours that result from negative feelings about oneself. Social withdrawal and self-blame with thoughts such as "I'm no good" and "It's all my fault" are examples of internalizing behaviours. Externalizing behaviours are negative behaviours taken out on others. Bullying and damaging property are two examples of externalizing behaviours. Both are linked to low self-esteem, and some children as young as 2 or 3 years may demonstrate one or the other of these behaviours. Review your experiences in your family, school, and community. Describe a time when you observed these behaviours. What behaviours might a child venture into as he or she matures? For example, what damaging internalizing and externalizing behaviours might a child exhibit in his or her teens? What interventions might help the child avoid the most negative outcomes of these behaviours?

Regulating Emotions

As we saw in Chapter 6, emotion regulation is an important aspect of development and plays a key role in children's ability to manage the demands and conflicts they face in interacting with others (Lewis, 2013; Thompson, 2011, 2013c, d). Recall from Chapter 7 that executive function is increasingly thought to be a key concept in describing the young child's higher-level cognitive functioning (Carlson, White, & Davis-Unger, 2014; Carlson, Zelazo, & Faja, 2013). Many researchers consider the growth of emotion regulation in children as fundamental to becoming socially competent (Cole & Hall, 2012; Perry et al., 2012; Thompson, 2014a, 2015).

Children start to regulate their emotions in infancy. As early as 6 months of age, boys demonstrate more difficulty than girls. Two-year-old boys are more likely to initiate conflicts with other children than girls. By ages 3 and 4 years, girls tend to outperform boys at tasks that require inhibition and theory of mind (Rubin & Barstead 2015).

Emotion-Coaching and Emotion-Dismissing Parents

Parents play an important role in helping young children regulate their emotions (Dunsmore, Booker, & Ollendick, 2013). Depending on how they talk with their children about emotion, parents can be described as taking an emotion-coaching or an emotion-dismissing approach (Gottman, 2013). The distinction between these approaches is most evident in the way the parent deals with the child's negative emotions (anger, frustration, sadness, and so on). *Emotion-coaching* parents monitor their children's emotions, view their children's negative emotions as opportunities for teaching, assist them in labelling emotions, and coach them in how to behave more effectively. In contrast, *emotion-dismissing parents* deny, ignore, or change negative emotions. The children of emotion-coaching parents are better at soothing themselves when they get upset, more effective in regulating their negative affect, focus their attention better, and have fewer behaviour problems than the children of emotion-dismissing parents (Gottman, 2014). Further studies have found that fathers' emotion coaching was related to children's social competence (Baker, Fenning, & Crnic, 2011), and that mothers' emotion coaching was linked to less oppositional behaviour (Dunsmore, Booker, & Ollendick, 2013).

Parents' knowledge of their children's emotional world can help them guide their children's emotional development and teach them how to cope effectively with problems. One study found that mothers' knowledge about what distresses and comforts their children predicted the children's coping, empathy, and prosocial behaviour (Vinik, Almas, & Grusec, 2011).

A challenge parents face is that young children typically don't want to talk about difficult emotional topics, such as being distressed or engaging in negative behaviours. Among the strategies young children use to avoid these conversations are to not talk at all, change the topic, or run away. In one study, Ross Thompson and colleagues (2009) found that young children were more likely to openly discuss difficult emotional circumstances when they were securely attached to their mother and when their mother conversed with them in a way that validated and accepted the child's views.

©LWA-Dann Tardif/zefa/Corbis

A young child expressing the emotion of shame, which occurs when a child evaluates his or her actions as not living up to standards. A child experiencing shame wishes to hide or disappear. *Why is shame called a self-conscious emotion?*

Emotion Regulation and Peer Relations

Emotions play a strong role in determining the success of a child's peer relationships (Denham et al., 2011). Specifically, the ability to modulate one's emotions is an important skill that benefits children's relationships with peers. Emotionally negative children are more likely to experience rejection, whereas emotionally positive children get along more easily. One study revealed that 4-year-olds recognized and generated strategies for controlling their anger more than 3-year-olds (Cole et al., 2009). Another recent study found that children who regulated their frustration and distress at an earlier age during preschool years (3 years), had a more rapid decline in externalizing problem behaviour, such as blaming others, when interacting with peers across the early childhood period (3 to 5 years of age) (Perry et al., 2013). Emotion regulation at ages 4 and 5 did not reduce the problem behaviour to the same extent that it did at 3 years of age, suggesting that earlier emotion regulation puts children on a more adaptive trajectory in interacting with peers.

To this point, we have discussed a number of ideas about the self and emotional development. For a review, see the Reach Your Learning Outcomes section at the end of this chapter.

Moral Development and Gender

LO2 Summarize moral development and gender in early childhood.

- **Moral Development**
- **Gender**

What Is Gender?

Sex refers to the biological dimension of being male or female, and gender refers to the social and psychological dimensions of being male or female. **Gender identity** involves a sense of one's own gender, including knowledge, understanding, and acceptance of being male or female (Egan & Perry, 2001; Perry, 2012). One aspect of gender identity involves knowing whether you are a girl or boy, an awareness that most children develop by about 2½ years of age (Blakemore, Berenbaum, & Liben, 2009).

Gender role is a set of expectations that prescribe how females or males should think, act, and feel. During the preschool years, most children increasingly act in ways that match their culture's gender roles. **Gender typing** refers to the acquisition of a traditional masculine or feminine role. For example, fighting is more characteristic of a traditional masculine role and crying is more characteristic of a traditional feminine role. A study revealed that sex-typed behaviour (boys playing with cars and girls with jewellery, for example) increased during the preschool years and that children engaging in the most sex-typed behaviour during the preschool years still did so at 8 years of age (Golombok et al., 2008).

Biological Influences

Biology clearly plays a role in sex development (Arnold, 2012; Hines, 2013). Among the possible biological influences are chromosomes, hormones, and evolution.

CHROMOSOMES AND HORMONES

Recall that humans normally have 46 chromosomes arranged in pairs (see Chapter 3). The 23rd pair consists of a combination of X and Y chromosomes, usually two X chromosomes in a female and an X and a Y in a male. In the first few weeks of gestation, however, female and male embryos look alike.

Males start to differ from females when genes on the Y chromosome in the male embryo trigger the development of testes rather than ovaries; the testes secrete copious amounts of the class of hormones known as androgens, which leads to the development of male sex organs. Low levels of androgens in the female embryo allow the normal development of female sex organs. Thus, hormones play a critical role in the development of sex differences (Hines, 2013). The two main classes of sex hormones are estrogens and androgens, which are secreted by the *gonads* (ovaries in females, testes in males). *Estrogens*, such as estradiol, influence the development of female physical sex characteristics. *Androgens*, such as testosterone, promote the development of male physical sex characteristics. Chromosomes and hormones also influence children's socio-emotional development.

CONNECTING through development

Gender Identity – Variations

Although many of us fit quite easily into the gender designated for us at birth, others do not; nonetheless, each of us develops uniquely (Children's Hospital of Eastern Ontario, 2016). Both our physiologic make up and societal stereotypes shape our growth development.

By the age of 2 or 3 years, many children start behaving in a way that expresses the idea that dolls are for girls and trucks are for boys. By this age, children are often able to declare themselves as a boy or a girl, or sometimes, something in between, and other times as neither (CHEO, 2016; Aina & Cameron, 2011). Between ages of 3 and 5 years, children begin to understand what it means to be male or female and by 4 years of age, most children have a stable sense of gender identity (American Academy of Paediatrics, 2016; CHEO, 2016; Aina & Cameron, 2011).

Children absorb and process information from their surroundings. Vygotsky's concepts of scaffolding and the zone of proximal development rely on role models assisting with challenging tasks and intentionally or unintentionally passing along cultural meanings. Kohlberg's thinking about moral development was influenced by Piaget, who portrayed children as active learners who use interactions with their environment to construct knowledge of the world around them. Kohlberg believed that children's cognitive understanding of gender developed this way and influenced behaviour (Kohlberg, 1981; Aina & Cameron, 2011).

Early gender bias and the absorption of stereotypes contribute to a culture of prejudice that children experience; this shapes children's attitudes and beliefs as well as ideas of their grown-up selves. Societal pressures to conform are strongly felt and internalized in such a way that non-conforming children may come to believe that something is wrong with them, that they don't "fit in." Such experiences may stifle a child's developmental well-being, particularly if the child and the child's family are coming to terms with variations or differences in the child's physiologic makeup (Aina & Cameron, 2011).

In 2006, The American Academy of Pediatrics proposed the term "disorders of sex development" (DSD) to refer to congenital conditions in which development of chromosomal, gonadal, and anatomic sex is atypical (Collier, 2015). Estimates are that annually in North America, 1 of every 1500 to 2000 children is born with noticeably atypical genitalia (Intersex Society of North America, 2008). Physician examinations determine the type of DSD, with parents determining the most appropriate sex to assign at birth. Not all DSDs are evident at birth; some, such as Klinefelder and Turner Syndromes, are more likely to show up in puberty.

Some gender non-conforming children in early childhood may grow up to become transgender adults (persistently identifying with a gender that is different from their birth sex). Others identify with a gay, lesbian, or bisexual orientation (i.e., attracted to the same or both genders as opposed to feeling they are a different gender), and others grow up to be heterosexual (i.e., attracted to the opposite gender) (American Academy of Paediatrics, 2016; American Psychological Association (APA) Task Force, 2006).

When the gender identity assigned at birth doesn't fit, many children hide their gender non-conforming identity as well their feelings about themselves, often feeling confused and fearing rejection. DSD conditions, whether discovered at birth or later in life, can be very challenging for the individual and for their families. Shame, isolation, anger, depression, and even suicide are not uncommon responses (APA Task Force2006; Aina & Cameron, 2011; CHEO, 2016).

critical thinking

Many people have taken exception to the term "disorders of sex development" proposed by The American Academy of Pediatrics, arguing that either "differences" or "variations" would be more appropriate terms. The AAP has defended its terminology, arguing that DSDs are a disorder. What is your view?

THE EVOLUTIONARY PSYCHOLOGY VIEW

How might physical differences between the sexes give rise to psychological differences? According to evolutionary psychology, adaptation during human evolution has produced psychological differences between males and females (Brooker et al., 2015; Buss, 2012). Because of their differing roles in reproduction, males and females faced differing pressures when the human species was evolving. In particular, because having multiple sexual liaisons improves the likelihood that males will pass on their genes, natural selection favours males who adopt short-term mating strategies. These strategies allow a male to win the competition with other males for sexual access to females. Therefore, say evolutionary psychologists, males have evolved dispositions that favour violence, competition, and risk taking.

In contrast, according to evolutionary psychologists, females' contributions to the gene pool are improved when they secure resources that ensure the survival of their offspring; this outcome is promoted by obtaining long-term mates who can support a family. As a consequence, natural selection favours females who devote effort to parenting and choose successful, ambitious mates who can provide their offspring with resources and protection.

Critics of evolutionary psychology argue that its hypotheses are backed by speculations about prehistory, not evidence, and that in any event people are not locked into behaviour that was adaptive in the evolutionary past. Critics also claim that the evolutionary view pays little attention to cultural and individual variations in gender differences (Hyde & Else-Quest, 2013).

Social Influences

Many social scientists argue that gender differences are due to social experiences.

SOCIAL THEORIES OF GENDER

Three main social theories of gender have been proposed—social role theory, psychoanalytic theory, and social cognitive theory. Alice Eagky (2001, 2010, 2012) proposed the **social role theory**, which states that gender differences result from the contrasting roles of women and men. In most cultures, women have less power and status and control fewer resources than men (UNICEF, 2011). Consequently, as women adapted to roles with less power and less status, they showed more cooperative and less dominant profiles than men. Thus, the social hierarchy and division of labour may be important causes of gender differences in power, assertiveness, and nurture.

The **psychoanalytic theory of gender** stems from Freud's view that the preschool child develops a sexual attraction to the opposite-sex parent, a process known as the Oedipus (for boys) or Electra (for girls) complex. At 5 or 6 years of age, the child renounces this attraction because of anxious feelings. Subsequently, the child identifies with the same-sex parent, unconsciously adopting the same-sex parent's characteristics. However, some developmentalists have observed that gender development does not proceed as Freud proposed. For example, children become gender-typed much earlier than 5 or 6 years of age, and they become masculine or feminine even when the same-sex parent is not present in the family.

The **social cognitive theory of gender** explains that children's gender development occurs through observing and imitating what other people say and do, and through being rewarded and punished for gender-appropriate and gender-inappropriate behaviour (Bussey & Bandura, 1999). From birth onward, males and females are treated differently. When infants and toddlers show gender differences, parents tend to reward them. In addition to parents, environmental factors such as culture, schools, peers, the media, and other family members also provide gender role models (Smith, 2007). Let's take a closer look at the influence of parents and peers.

PARENTAL INFLUENCES

Parents, by action and by example, influence their children's gender development (Liben, Bigler, & Hilliard, 2014; Leaper, 2013). Both mothers and fathers are psychologically important to their children's gender development (Hyde & Else-Quest, 2013; Leaper, 2013; Tenenbaum & May, 2014). Cultures around the world tend to give mothers and fathers different roles (Chen et al., 2011). A recent research review provided these conclusions (Bronstein, 2006):

- *Mothers' socialization strategies:* In many cultures, mothers socialize their daughters to be more obedient and responsible than their sons. They also place more restrictions on daughters' autonomy.
- *Fathers' socialization strategies:* Fathers show more attention to sons than daughters, engage in more activities with sons, and put forth more effort to promote sons' intellectual development.

Thus, according to Bronstein (2006, pp. 269–270), "Despite an increased awareness in Western cultures of the detrimental effects of gender stereotyping, many parents continue to foster behaviours and perceptions that are consonant with traditional gender role norms."

PEER INFLUENCES

Parents provide the earliest influence on gender roles, but before long peers join the process of responding to and modelling masculine and feminine behaviour. Peers extensively reward and punish gender-appropriate behaviour and often reject children who act in a manner that is considered more characteristic of the other gender (Leaper, 2013; Leaper & Bigler, 2011). A little girl who brings a doll to the park may find herself surrounded by new friends; a little boy might be jeered.

Pressure for boys to conform to a traditional male role is greater than for girls to conform to a traditional female role (Fagot, Rogers, & Leinbach, 2000). For example, a preschool girl who wants to wear boys' clothing receives considerably more approval than a boy who wants to wear a dress. The very term "tomboy" implies broad social acceptance of girls' adopting traditional male behaviours.

Gender moulds important aspects of peer relations (Field & others, 2012; Zozuls et al., 2012). For example, gender influences the following factors:

- *Gender composition of children's groups:* Around the age of 3 years, children already show a preference to spend time with same-sex playmates. From 4 to 12 years of age, this preference for playing in same-sex groups increases, and during the elementary school years children spend a large majority of their free time with children of their own sex.
- *Group size:* Research by Joyce Benenson at McGill University shows that from about 5 years of age onward, boys are more likely to associate together in larger clusters than girls (Benenson & Heath, 2006). Moreover, girls are more likely than boys to play in dyads or triads, while boys are more likely to interact in larger groups and seek to attain a group goal (Benenson, Apostoleris, & Parnass, 1997).
- *Interaction in same-sex groups:* Boys are more likely than girls to engage in rough-and-tumble play, competition, conflict, ego displays, risk taking, and seeking dominance. By contrast, girls are more likely to engage in "collaborative discourse," in which they talk and act in a more reciprocal manner.

Cognitive Influences

One influential cognitive theory is **gender schema theory**, which states that gender-typing emerges as children gradually develop gender schemas of what is gender-appropriate and gender-inappropriate in their culture (Blakemore, Berenbaum, & Liben, 2009; Miller et al., 2013). A *schema* is a cognitive structure, a network of associations that guide an individual's perceptions. A *gender schema* organizes the world in terms of female and male. Bit by bit, children pick up what is gender-appropriate and gender-inappropriate in their culture, and develop gender schemas that shape how they perceive the world, and act in accordance with their developing schemas (Conry-Murray, Kim, & Turiel, 2012). Because children are motivated to act in ways that conform with these gender schemas, they fuel gender-typing.

altrendo images/Getty Images

© Cindy Charles/PhotoEdit

As reflected in this tug-of-war battle between boys and girls, the playground is like going to "gender school." By elementary school, children show a clear preference for being with and liking same-sex peers. *Think back to your earliest memories of play. Did your play reflect gender schema?*

To this point, we have studied a number of ideas about moral development and gender. For a review, see the Reach Your Learning Outcomes section at the end of this chapter.

The Changing Family in a Changing Society

LO3 Explain how families influence young children's development.

- **Parenting**
- **Divorce**
- **Sibling Relationships and Birth Order**

Families everywhere reflect the wider social, economic, and cultural environment; for example, families living in urban areas such as Vancouver, Montreal, Ottawa, and Toronto are accustomed to city density, pavement, and relatively easy access to facilities. By contrast, families living in rural settings such as Nunavut, Bonnyville, or Notre-Dame-de-Ham experience life very differently—quieter, more farmland, and much less access to facilities such as health care and education. This section will explore parenting styles, sibling relationships, and family cohesion as they interact reciprocally within the environment and reflect the wider national cultural and economic shifts.

Everywhere, family structures are changing. The number of single parent, step-, blended, or childless families has increased, and the role of parents and grandparents has changed. First we will take a look at how parental roles are changing, then consider the structure of the family.

Parenting

Shifting Parental Roles

Given the economic burdens facing families, more women are working outside the home, and their incomes are essential to the financial security of most households. Eighty-two percent of women between ages 25 and 54 are active participants in the workforce. While the number of women has increased, the same is not true for men, whose participation has declined slightly (Vanier Institute, 2010). In 2009, women who were single mothers were less likely to be employed than mothers in two parent families; and women were more likely to work part-time than were men (Statistics Canada, 2015).

The Vanier Institute (2012) indicated that 75 percent of fathers report being actively engaged with their children, spending an average of 3.1 hours daily caring for them. Not only are more fathers taking parental leave—an increase from 3 percent to 27 percent between 2001 and 2007—but 10 percent of all stay-at-home parents in 2008 were men. A greater proportion of working men in dual-income families spend more time doing housework daily than their own fathers did. Nevertheless, women still assume double the amount of household work and childcare than men (Statistics Canada, 2015). In addition, working mothers are more likely to feel stressed about time and less likely to be happy with their work–life balance than working fathers (Marshall, 2006).

Good parenting takes time and effort (Grusec et al., 2013). The quantity of time parents spend with children is not as important for children's development as the quality of the time (Clarke-Stewart & Parke, 2014). For example, a recent study found that maternal scaffolding, sensitivity, and support for autonomy were linked to better executive function in preschool children (Blair, Raver, & Berry, 2014). To understand variations in parenting, let's consider the styles parents use when they interact with their children, how they discipline their children, and co-parenting.

Baumrind's Parenting Styles

Diana Baumrind (1971) argued that parents should be neither punitive nor aloof. Rather, they should develop rules for their children and be affectionate with them. She described four types of parenting styles: authoritarian, authoritative, neglectful, and indulgent.

Authoritarian parenting is a restrictive, punitive style in which parents exhort the child to follow their directions and to respect work and effort. The authoritarian parent places firm limits and controls on the child and allows little verbal exchange. For example, a parent might say, "You do it my way or else." Authoritarian parents also might enforce rules rigidly but not explain them, and show rage toward the child. Children of authoritarian parents are often unhappy, fearful, and anxious about comparing themselves with others, fail to initiate activity, and have weak communication skills.

Authoritative parenting encourages children to be independent but still places limits and controls on their actions. Extensive verbal give-and-take is allowed, and parents are warm and nurturing toward the child. An authoritative parent might put his arm around the child in a comforting way and say, "You know you should not have done that. Let's talk about how you can handle the situation better next time." Authoritative parents show pleasure in and support of children's constructive behaviour. They also expect mature, independent, and age-appropriate behaviour of children. Children whose parents are authoritative are often cheerful, self-controlled and self-reliant, and achievement-oriented. They also maintain friendly relations with peers, cooperate with adults, and cope well with stress.

Neglectful parenting is a style in which the parent is very uninvolved in the child's life. The well-known psychoanalyst, Karen Horney, argued that neglect is the single most damaging factor in a child's development because the child has no way to rail against neglect. Children whose parents are neglectful develop the sense that other aspects of the parents' lives are more important than they are. Many have poor self-control and do not handle independence well. They frequently have low self-esteem, are immature, and may be alienated from the family. In adolescence, they may show patterns of truancy and delinquency.

Indulgent parenting is a style of parenting in which parents are highly involved with their children but place few demands or controls on them. Such parents let their children do what they want. The result is that the children never learn to control their own behaviour and always expect to get their way. Some parents deliberately rear their children in this way because they believe the combination of warm involvement and few restraints will produce a creative, confident child. However, children whose parents are indulgent rarely learn respect for others and have difficulty controlling their behaviour. They might be aggressive, domineering, and non-compliant.

These four classifications of parenting involve combinations of acceptance and responsiveness on the one hand, and demand and control on the other (Maccoby & Martin, 1983). How these dimensions combine to produce authoritarian, authoritative, neglectful, and indulgent parenting is shown in Figure 8.1.

Figure 8.1

Classification of Parenting Styles

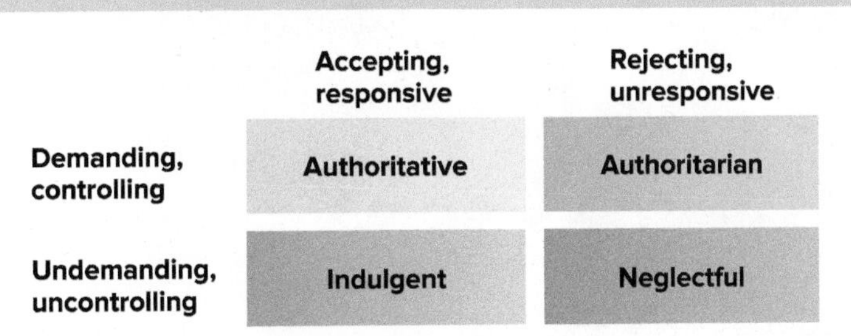

The four types of parenting styles (authoritative, authoritarian, neglectful, and indulgent) involve the dimensions of acceptance and responsiveness on the one hand, and demand and control on the other. For example, authoritative parenting involves being both accepting/responsive and demanding/controlling.

Parenting Styles in Context

Recall from Bronfenbrenner's ecological theory (Chapter 2) that culture, ethnicity, and socio-economic status are classified as part of the macrosystem because they represent broader societal contexts that influence the individual. Researchers have found that in some ethnic groups, aspects of the authoritarian style may be associated with more positive child outcomes than Baumrind predicts; for example, context is an important aspect of meaning (Parke & Clarke-Stewart, 2011). In a study examining the use of authoritative or authoritarian styles by Chinese parents in Canada and China, Chuang and Su (2009) found that parents in China were more apt to be authoritarian, while Chinese-Canadian parents were more authoritative. They suggested that cultural socialization accounted for the difference in parenting style.

Diversity

Canada prides itself on its diversity. In 2011, Canada's foreign-born population represented 20.6 percent of the total population, with most immigrants settling in urban areas such as Montreal or Toronto (Statistics Canada, 2015). Chinese languages are most common among new Canadians, followed by Tagalog (Philippines), Spanish, and Punjabi (Statistics Canada, 2015). Limited knowledge of English or French is a major challenge and has an enormous ripple effect, as the consequences range from poor diagnosis of health and learning problems to confusion, anxiety, withdrawal, and depression (Chang, 2010).

For many immigrant families, parenting can also be affected by how individual family members adjust to the mainstream culture. Less assimilated and more assimilated family members may have different views on discipline and the child's freedom, resulting in conflicts and confusion. Not only can this diaspora influence parenting behaviour, it can also affect parent–child interactions in general. One parenting model that has stood the test of time—and backed by five decades of research—is Baumrind's authoritative parenting, which combines qualities of responsiveness and demandingness (Divecha, 2015).

Immigrant and refugee families are frequently separated, with one or both parents immigrating to or seeking asylum in Canada, then working and sending support to the family in the home country. In such cases, the children may live with their grandparents, occasionally connecting with the parent or parents through social media. Once the adult is able, he or she may initiate the long process of family reunification. In the case of refugee claimants, such reunion of parents and children may take several years, exponentially heightening the complexities of adjustment (Canadian Council for Refugees, 2012).

Keep in mind that research on parenting styles and children's development is correlational, not causal, in nature. Thus, if a study reveals that authoritarian parenting is linked to higher levels of children's aggression, it may be that aggressive children elicited authoritarian parenting just as much as authoritarian parenting produced aggressive children (Bush & Peterson, 2013). Also recall from Chapter 1 that, in correlational studies, a third factor may influence the correlation between two factors. Thus, in the example of the correlation between authoritarian parenting and children's aggression, possibly authoritarian parents (first factor) and aggressive children (second factor) share genes (third factor) that predispose them to behave in ways that produced the correlation.

What are some characteristics of families within different ethnic groups?

Working Parents

According to Statistics Canada (2015), in 2014, 69 percent of two-parent families with children ages 16 or younger were dual income families. This is almost double the percentage in 1976 when only 36 percent of families were dual income. Both parents work full-time in nearly three-quarters of dual-income families (Statistics Canada, 2015). As a result, children are spending more time in daycare facilities or with grandparents.

critical thinking

What parenting style or styles did your parents use in raising you? Did they model one parenting style, or was there a mix of styles? What do you understand about your parents' upbringing that may have contributed to their parenting practices? What effects do you think their parenting styles had on your development? What parenting practices might you keep? What might you change? Why?

Punishment

Discipline is the process of teaching a child what types of behaviours are acceptable and those that are not. Positive reinforcement, modelling, and loving responses are effective, of course, but what about when the child misbehaves? Canada's National Longitudinal Survey of Children and Youth (2006), supported by subsequent studies, found a link between punitive parenting and increased aggressive behaviour, more anxiety, and lower prosocial behaviour in children under 5 years of age (Mulvaney & Mebert, 2007). The research suggests changing from punitive to non-punitive parenting styles can produce positive results in the child's behaviour and self-esteem.

Early in 2004, the Supreme Court of Canada upheld the provision in the *Criminal Code* allowing parents or a person who has taken all of the obligations of parenthood, to use force to "correct" a child. The Court ruled that spanking by hand with non-excessive force is lawful; however, it could be used only on children between the ages of 2 and 12 years (Justice for Children and Youth, 2012).

The UN Committee on the Rights of the Child defines corporal punishment as "any punishment in which physical force is used and intended to cause some degree of pain or discomfort, however slight," and adds that physical punishment is "invariably degrading" (Fitzgerald, 2015). How does Canada compare with countries across the world? In 1979, Sweden became the first country to ban corporal punishment and, in November 2015, Ireland became the 47th country, protecting about 10 percent of the world's children (Fitzgerald, 2014). Pointing out that children are the only group in society on which we inflict corporal punishment, children's rights advocates across the country continue to fight for the Supreme Court ruling to be repealed (Coghlan, 2015). A Global News poll with over 14 000 responses indicated that just under 60 percent (58.79 percent) of those polled believe that spanking should be illegal, and that 41.21 percent believed that it should be legal (Wilson, 2016).

Experts recommend several disciplinary techniques other than spanking, all designed to reinforce the behaviour the parent is seeking. Fundamental to these techniques are being respectful and consistent, in addition to setting well-communicated limits, rewards, and punishments.

Toddlers respond well to an organized structure, with recognizable routines, such as a bedtime routine. Because toddlers have very short attention spans, distraction is an effective technique; however, lectures are not. Toddlers are naturally curious and don't understand punishment, so a soft and firm "No" or "Stop," with or without an explanation such as "You might get hurt," is all that is usually required. Other tips include praising good behaviour, using punishment that reflects logical and natural consequences of misbehaviour, removing privileges, and using time outs.

Like older children, when young children misbehave or become cranky, there may be an underlying reason, perhaps something as simple as being tired or hungry. Understanding children's reasons for acting badly is helpful in coaching them about how to control the behaviour in order to obtain what they really want, such as a nap or something to eat. Setting limits and teaching children how to calm down when they are upset is essential. For example, when children are upset, perhaps a deep breath, or a calming toy, blanket, or thumb, may help them calm down, feel better, and use their words (WebMed, 2016).

Causes for concern such as ongoing disrespectful or destructive behaviours, prolonged sadness, or threatening suicide may require the professional help of a doctor or psychologist (WebMed, 2016).

Child Maltreatment

Although widely condemned, child maltreatment is a worldwide social problem. Unfortunately and frequently, discipline leads to maltreatment, the term used increasingly by developmentalists, or child abuse, the term used by many professionals and the public. Maltreatment can be physical, emotional, sexual, or neglect, and often occurs in combinations of these (Cicchetti & Toth, 2015; McCoy & Keen, 2014).

Statistics of child maltreatment in Canada are controversial for a number of reasons, including definitions, recognition, and reporting, as well as investigations that are substantiated or unsubstantiated (Volpe, 2014). However, in the five years between 1998 and and 2003, the rate of child maltreatment investigations nearly doubled, and remained at approximately 38.33 per 1000 children through to 2008. Reports of maltreatment of children under the age of 1 year were the most likely to be investigated, with a rate of 51.81 investigations per 1000 children. Rates of investigations decreased with age: 43.14 investigations per 1000 children ages 1 to 3 years, and 41.73 investigations per 1000 children ages 4 to 7 years (Trocmé et al., 2012). Social and economic impoverishment are major contributing factors for child maltreatment (Volpe, 2014).

CONNECTING development to life

Parental Attitudes of the Sami

To many, Norway may seem an ethnically homogeneous country with beautiful mountains and fjords. However, just like Canada, Norway has a sizeable minority group, the Sami, who, live in the circumpolar area. The Sami are a traditionally nomadic people. Yet despite their assimilation with mainstream Norwegian culture, researchers wonder if the childrearing values among the Sami remain different from the Western values dominant in the country. In a study of both Norwegian and Sami parents of preschoolers, researchers asked the parents about their attitudes toward child behaviour in everyday situations, such as mealtime and bedtime, and found some interesting differences—and similarities—between the two groups (Javo, Rønning, & Heyerdahl, 2004).

Overall, there is greater emphasis on child autonomy among the Sami (Javo et al., 2004). In contrast to Norwegian mothers, Sami mothers are less comfortable with their children's clingy behaviour, but are more flexible with mealtime and bedtime rules. For example, Sami mothers did not find children's talking while eating and their desire to stay up late as annoying as did Norwegian mothers. At the same time, Sami mothers are less tolerant of children's temper tantrums and expressions of jealousy, and are more willing to slap or threaten their misbehaving children than Norwegian mothers. This highlights the importance of self-control and communal harmony in the pursuit of independence.

Despite these differences, both groups have similar parental attitudes in several areas, one of which is the expectations parents have for their daughters (Javo et al., 2004). Girls are expected to take care of simple everyday tasks, such as dressing and undressing, earlier than boys. Such similarities may be the result of assimilation, or simply result from longstanding beliefs held independently by each group.

In sum, the Sami parents are more likely to expect and encourage child autonomy than Norwegian parents. Interestingly, the Sami's attitudes are similar to those of the Inuit in Canada (Javo et al., 2004). Maybe the unforgiving conditions of the North have developed a strong desire to foster their children's independence in both Sami and Inuit parents.

critical thinking

Some argue that the line between corporal punishment and child maltreatment is a very fine one that can easily be crossed. Is corporal punishment of a preschooler a valid parenting strategy? What other strategies might be used? Were you spanked as a child? What other punishments did your parents administer? What did you learn from them? Should Canada join the 47 countries that have outlawed corporal punishment? If so, how can such a law be enforced?

Divorce

Approximately 35 percent to 40 percent of marriages or common-law relationships in Canada end in divorce, dissolving the family unit (Sinha, 2015; Government of Canada, 2016). Most common-law relationships that fail do so before the couple are 30 years of age, and in 70 percent of the cases no children are involved (Beaupré & Cloutier, 2006). Where there are children, they are usually under 6 years of age. Divorces in a marriage relationship usually occur a bit later and the children are usually older.

Should parents stay together in an unhappy or conflicted marriage for the sake of the children? If the stresses and disruptions in family relationships associated with an unhappy, conflictual marriage that erode the well-being of children are reduced by the move to a divorced, single-parent family, divorce can be advantageous. However, if the diminished resources and increased risks associated with divorce are accompanied by inept parenting and sustained or increased conflict, the best choice for the children would be that an unhappy marriage is retained (Hetherington & Stanley-Hagan, 2002). It is difficult to determine how these "ifs" will play out when parents either remain together in an acrimonious marriage or become divorced.

Co-Parenting

Parenting is an interactive process, a reciprocal engagement between people acting in various ways (Burton, Phipps, & Curtis, 2005). Co-parenting, therefore, involves both the parents and the children. In highly charged emotional situations, such as divorce or separation, not only are routines upended, but living arrangements, support agreements, and co-parenting plans must be negotiated.

Arrangements are made in the best interest of the child. While most agreements are made by the parents, many turn to the courts to settle disputes. When this is the case, joint custody is awarded in 47 percent of the cases (Vanier Institute, 2010). Although caught in the middle of these stressful negotiations, the majority of children from broken homes do not experience clinical problems or serious developmental difficulties. However, the negative effects of parental breakup are quite real and children may feel the impact both emotionally and physically. Research on whether different types of custodial arrangements are better for children in divorced families has been inconsistent as multiple factors are involved in determining how divorce influences a child's development (Spruijt & Duindam, 2010; Amato & Dorius, 2010).

Parental breakup is usually a gradual process; hence, the stress level is already high prior to the final break-up. In this context, children often display symptoms of confusion, anger, anxiety, depression, social-relational problems, and other psycho-affective disorders such as oppositional behaviour. The problems are not exclusively emotional. When compared to children from intact families, those whose parents have broken up are more likely to experience physical health problems (Desrosiers, Cordin, & Belleau, 2013; Amato, 2010). Children who have experienced multiple divorces are at greater risk. However, one study found that 20 years after their parents had divorced when they were children, approximately 80 percent of adults concluded that their parents' decision to divorce was a wise one (Ahrons, 2004).

Children in Divorced Families

The majority of children in divorced families do not have significant adjustment problems in coping with their parents' divorce. A common assumption has been that children from single-parent families do not fare as well as those from two-parent families; however, a study conducted by Avison and Seabrook, of the Western University (2015), found evidence to the contrary. Data collected over a 25-year period from single- and two-parent families living in London, Ontario, indicated that the mother's educational attainment, whether single or married, not the family structure per se, is the primary factor driving children's success. Based on their research, they concluded that growing up in a "stable" two-parent family in London, Ontario, was not more advantageous for children than growing up in a "stable" single-parent family or in a family that transitioned from one parent to two parents.

Avison and Seabrook's findings have implications for social policy as they imply that greater attention should be paid to addressing disparities in education and family income than to concerns about the kinds of families in which children grow up. Programs to help divorced parents are available across Canada. For example, the six-hour For the Sake of the Children program in Manitoba is designed to help parents learn about children's adjustment, financial issues, legal options, and so on, after a divorce or separation (Government of Manitoba, 2016). A study of 10 such programs across the country indicated that participants have a high level of satisfaction with the programs immediately following participation (McKenzie & Bacon, 2002).

DAJ/Getty Images

In Japan, only 6 percent of children live in lone-parent families, compared with 15.9 percent in Canada and 27 percent in the United States (Martin & Kats, 2003; Vanier Institute, 2010). *What might explain this difference?*

Socio-Economic Status

Poverty is a significant factor in growth and development, and plays a role in the lives of children in lone-parent families. Lone-parent families account for 15.9 percent of families and, although some men are lone parents, most—80 percent—are headed by single moms (Vanier Institute, 2010). Custodial mothers experience the loss of about one-fourth to one-half of their pre-divorce income, in comparison with a loss of only one-tenth by custodial fathers. This income loss for divorced mothers is accompanied by increased workloads, high rates of job instability, and residential moves to less desirable neighbourhoods with inferior schools (Sayer, 2006). According to a UNICEF report released in 2012, 14 percent of Canadian children live in poverty; this high rate puts Canada in the bottom third of the countries measured. Poverty poses additional major challenges for racialized minority and immigrant families.

Step- or Blended Families

The Step and Blended Family Institute of Canada (2016) distinguishes between step- and blended families: a *stepfamily* is any committed relationship where at least one of the partners has a child, or children from a previous relationship; a *blended family* is a union where in addition to one or both partners bringing children into the family, the new couple have had a least one child together. Blended families account for most of the newly-formed families and are considerably more complex, as the children of each parent must adjust to a new sibling.

No-fault divorce, implemented in Canada in 1987, along with the increase of common-law unions, have resulted in higher numbers of separations, particularly of couples with children. In 2011, nearly half a million families were step- or blended families. As well, the number of lone fathers entering complex blended families has increased. While no significant difference between family income of intact families and blended families was noted, Statistics Canada reported that 85 percent of blended family parents work full-time compared with 77 percent of parents in intact families (Vézina, 2015).

Step- and blended families function differently from the traditional intact or biological family. Both parents and children are adjusting to a complicated new situation. In-laws shift; as one youngster told his daycare teacher, "I have six grandparents." In an effort to define their place, children often compete with their stepparent and siblings to be first in the eyes of their biological parent. Boundaries and discipline strategies are being worked out at the same time as day-to-day management of meals, household chores, school, and work are making demands on everyone's time and, perhaps, patience. Into this conundrum parents and children must factor in visitation schedules and rights of the other biological parent and grandparents, who may affect the child's adjustment through conflict and competition. Time is vital and may help soothe many of the initial problems.

Children from step- or blended families are more susceptible to peer pressure and may misbehave more than children from happily intact first families. On the other hand, research indicates that children from step- or blended families are better adjusted than children from unhappy, but intact, first families (Stepfamilies Canada, 2012).

How does living in a stepfamily influence a child's development?

Gay and Lesbian Parents

Like heterosexual couples, gay and lesbian parents vary greatly. Many lesbian mothers and gay fathers are non-custodial parents because they lost custody of their children to heterosexual spouses after a divorce. In addition, gays and lesbians are increasingly choosing parenthood through donor insemination or adoption. Researchers have found that the children conceived through new reproductive technologies—such as in vitro fertilization—are as well adjusted as their counterparts conceived by natural means (Golombok, 2011a, b; Golombok & Tasker, 2010).

Researchers have found few differences between children growing up with lesbian mothers or gay fathers and children growing up with heterosexual parents (Golombok & Tasker, 2010; Patterson, 2013a, b; Patterson & Farr, 2014). For example, children growing up in gay or lesbian families are just as popular with their peers, and no differences are found in the adjustment and mental health of children living in these families when they are compared with children in heterosexual families (Hyde & DeLamater, 2014). Further, a recent study revealed more positive parenting in adoptive gay father families and fewer child externalizing behaviours (directing negative behaviours such as bullying others) than in heterosexual families (Golombok et al., 2014). Contrary to the once-popular expectation that being raised by a gay or lesbian parent would result in the child growing up to be gay or lesbian, in fact the overwhelming majority of children from gay or lesbian families have a heterosexual orientation (Golombok & Tasker, 2010).

Another study compared the incidence of co-parenting in adoptive heterosexual, lesbian, and gay couples with preschool-aged children (Farr & Patterson, 2013). Both self-reports and observations confirmed that lesbian and gay couples share child care more than heterosexual couples, with lesbian couples being the most supportive.

critical thinking

Considering the challenges that both divorce and entry into a step- or blended family can have for a child, what are some of the factors that could help to ease the difficulties for each situation? What are some of the possible positive outcomes of divorce? How might co-parenting arrangements be helpful? What are some of the complications that would arise in a blended family? How might parents facilitate adjustment?

Sibling Relationships and Birth Order

The average size of Canadian households in 2006 was 2.5 people. Due to the diversity of family structures, the number of children per family is now 1.1, down from 1.4 in 1981 (Government of Canada, 2016). Nevertheless, not everyone is an only child; many have siblings. What are sibling relationships like?

Sibling Relationships

For many, sibling relationships are the longest relationships they have with any individual in life. Curiously, siblings' impact on development was largely overlooked by researchers until recently (Dunn, 2005; Kramer & Bank, 2005). Siblings very likely have rich memories of aggressive, hostile interchanges. In home observations of 2- and 4-year-old siblings, University of Toronto's Michal Perlman and University of Waterloo's Hildy Ross found that verbal and physical aggression to resolve a dispute tended to lead to disruptive reactions like unwillingness to comply in the older sibling and crying in the younger sibling. In contrast, there was some indication of both parties' willingness to reason if the other one used reasoning first (Perlman & Ross, 2005).

Judy Dunn (2007), a leading expert on sibling relationships, has described three important characteristics of sibling relationships:

- *Emotional quality of the relationship:* Both intensive positive and negative emotions are often expressed by siblings toward each other. Many have mixed feelings toward their siblings.
- *Familiarity and intimacy of the relationship:* Siblings typically know each other very well, and this intimacy suggests that they can either provide support or tease and undermine each other, depending on the situation.
- *Variation in sibling relationships:* Some siblings describe their relationships more positively than others. Thus, there is considerable variation in sibling relationships. While many siblings have mixed feelings about each other, some children mainly describe their sibling in warm, affectionate ways, whereas others primarily talk about how irritating and mean a sibling is.

Birth Order

Alfred Adler, who you read about in Chapter 2, was the first to suggest that birth order is a significant factor in growth and development. He suggested two firstborn possibilities: actual birth order (ABO) and psychological birth order (PBO), the first being the actual numerical rank, and the second being the perceived position in the family (Whitbourne, 2013). The PBO child may assume a mature care-taking nature with his or her siblings.

Compared with later-born children, firstborn children have been described as more conscientious, adult-oriented, helpful, conforming, and self-controlled. The middle child may have a more sociable, flexible, and rebellious nature, while the baby of the family may be the spoiled, more pampered member of the family. The only child, while receiving all the attention, may feel constantly scrutinized (Paulhus, 2008; Whitbourne, 2013). However, when such birth-order differences are reported, they often are small; in fact, family variations are so complex that analysis of traits associated with birth order are difficult to ascertain. Gender, time gaps between births, blended family structures, as well as definitions of terms add to the complexity of studies (Whitbourne, 2013). A more recent study concluded that the relation between birth order and intelligence and performance declines slightly from the first to the last born; but it also found no birth-order effects on traits such as extraversion, emotional stability, agreeableness, conscientiousness, or imagination (Rohrer, Egloff, & Schmikle, 2015).

To this point, we have studied many aspects of families. For a review, see the Reach Your Learning Outcomes section at the end of this chapter.

Peer Relations, Play, and Social Media

LO4 Describe the roles of peers, play, and social media in young children's development.

- **Peer Relations**
- **Play**
- **Media/Screen Time**

The family is an important social context for children's development. However, children's development is also strongly influenced by peer relations and play.

Peer Relations

One of the most important functions of the peer group is to provide a source of information and comparison about the world outside the family. Children receive feedback about their abilities from their peers. Children evaluate what they do in terms of whether it is better than, as good as, or worse than what other children do. It is hard to do this at home because siblings are usually older or younger.

Ariel Skelley/Getty Images

How is play essential to young children's development?

Good peer relations can be necessary for normal socio-emotional development (Howes, 2008; Prinstein & Dodge, 2008). Special concerns focus on children who are withdrawn or aggressive (Bukowski, Brendgen, & Vitaro, 2007). Withdrawn children who are rejected by peers or are victimized and feel lonely are at risk for depression. Children who are aggressive with their peers are at risk for developing a number of problems, including delinquency and dropping out of school (Dishion, Piehler, & Myers, 2008; Dodge, Coie, & Lynam, 2006; Tremblay, Gervais, & Petitclerc, 2008).

Just like parenting, peer relations are influenced by cultural values. In Canada, reticent, quiet behaviour signals lack of social competence in children, while in mainland China the same type of behaviour shows maturity. A recent study with 4-year-olds in both countries found that Canadian children who displayed this behaviour were more likely to be rejected and less likely to receive positive affect and compliance from peers when they did initiate peer interaction than Chinese children in the same situation. These young children reacted to one another according to their culture's views of reticent behaviour (Chen et al., 2006).

Play

Play is essential to the young child's development and encompasses an extensive amount of peer interaction. Play is a pleasurable activity that is engaged in for its own sake, and its functions and forms vary (Hirsh-Pasek & Golinkoff, 2014).

Play's Functions

Play increases affiliation with peers, releases tension, advances cognitive development, increases exploration, and provides a safe haven in which to engage in potentially dangerous behaviour.

According to Freud and Erikson, play is a useful form of adjustment that helps children master anxieties and conflicts. Because tensions are relieved in play, children learn to cope with life's problems by playing, permitting the child to work off excess physical energy and release pent-up tensions. Through *play therapy*, the therapist can analyze the child's conflicts and ways of coping. Children may feel less threatened and be more likely to express their true feelings in the context of play (Yanof, 2013).

Piaget (1962) believed that play advances children's cognitive development, yet at the same time, children's cognitive development constrains the way they play. Piaget thought that cognitive structures need to be exercised, and play provides the perfect setting for this exercise. For example, children who have just learned to add or multiply begin to play with numbers in different ways as they perfect these operations, laughing as they do so.

Vygotsky (1962) also believed that play is an excellent setting for cognitive development. He was especially interested in the symbolic and make-believe aspects of play, such as when a child substitutes a stick for a horse and rides the stick as if it were a horse. For young children, the imaginary situation is real. By encouraging imaginary play, parents advance the child's creative thought and cognitive development.

More recently, play has been described as an important context for the development of language and communication skills (Harris, Golinkoff, & Hirsh-Pasek, 2011; Hirsh-Pasek & Golinkoff, 2013). Language and communication skills may be enhanced through discussions and negotiations regarding roles and rules in play as young children practise various words and phrases. These types of social interactions can benefit young children's literacy skills (Gunning, 2013). And, as we saw in Chapter 7, play is a central focus of the child-centred kindergarten and is thought to be an essential aspect of early childhood education (Feeney, Moravcik, & Nolte, 2013; Henninger, 2013).

Types of Play

The contemporary perspective on play emphasizes both the cognitive and the social aspects (Hirsh-Pasek & Golinkoff, 2013; Vong, 2012). Among the most widely studied types of children's play today are sensorimotor and practice play, pretense/symbolic play, social play, constructive play, and games (Bergen, 1988).

Sensorimotor and Practice Play

Sensorimotor play is behaviour by infants that lets them derive pleasure from exercising their sensorimotor schemes. The development of sensorimotor play follows Piaget's description of sensorimotor thought, which we discussed in Chapter 5. Infants initially engage in exploratory and playful visual and motor transactions at about 9 months of age. At this time, infants begin to select novel objects for exploration and play, especially responsive objects such as toys that make noise or bounce.

Practice play involves the repetition of behaviour when new skills are being learned or when physical or mental mastery and coordination of skills are required for games or sports. Sensorimotor play, which often involves practice play, is primarily confined to infancy, whereas practice play can be engaged in throughout life. During the preschool years, children often engage in practice play.

Pretense/Symbolic Play

Pretense/symbolic play occurs when the child transforms the physical environment into a symbol. Between 9 and 30 months of age, children increase their use of objects in symbolic play. They learn to transform objects—substituting them for other objects and acting toward them as if they were those other objects. For example, a preschool child treats a table as if it were a car and says, "I'm fixing the car," as he grabs a leg of the table.

Many experts on play consider the preschool years the "golden age" of symbolic/pretense play that is dramatic or socio-dramatic in nature. This type of make-believe play often appears at about 18 months of age and reaches a peak at 4 to 5 years of age, then gradually declines.

Some child psychologists conclude that pretend play is an important aspect of young children's development and often reflects advances in their cognitive development, especially as an indication of symbolic understanding. For example, Catherine Garvey (2000) and Angeline Lillard (2006) emphasize that hidden in young children's pretend play narratives are remarkable capacities for role-taking, balancing of social roles, metacognition (thinking about thinking), testing of the reality–pretense distinction, and numerous non-egocentric capacities that reveal the remarkable cognitive skills of young children. An analysis found that a major accomplishment in early childhood is the development of children's ability to share their pretend play with peers (Coplan & Arbeau, 2009). Researchers have found that pretend play contributes to young children's self-regulation, mainly because of the self-monitoring and social sensitivity that is required in creating and enacting a socio-dramatic narrative in cooperation with other children (Diamond et al., 2007).

Social Play

Social play involves interaction with peers. Social play increases dramatically during the preschool years. For many children, social play is the main context for young children's social interactions with peers (Power, 2011).

Constructive Play

Constructive play combines sensorimotor/practice play with symbolic representation. It occurs when children engage in the self-regulated creation of a product or a solution. Constructive play increases in the preschool years as symbolic play increases and sensorimotor play decreases. It also becomes a frequent form of play in the elementary school years, both in and out of the classroom.

Games

Games are activities that children engage in for pleasure and that have rules. Often they involve competition. Preschool children may begin to participate in social games that involve simple rules of reciprocity and turn taking. However, games take on a much stronger role in the lives of elementary school children. In one study, the highest incidence of game playing occurred between 10 and 12 years of age (Eiferman, 1971). After age 12, games decline in popularity (Bergen, 1988).

Trends in Play

Researchers Kathy Hirsh-Pasek, Roberta Golinkoff, and Dorothy Singer (Hirsh-Pasek et al., 2009; Singer, Golinkoff, & Hirsh-Pasek, 2006) are concerned about the small amount of time for free play that young children have, reporting that it has declined considerably in recent decades. They underscore that learning in playful contexts captivates children's minds in ways that enhance their cognitive and socio-emotional development. Singer and colleagues (2006) cite the cognitive benefits of play including creativity, abstract thinking, imagination, attention, concentration, and persistence. Problem-solving, social cognition, empathy, and perspective taking, language, and mastery of new concepts are also enhanced by play. Among the socio-emotional experiences and development they believe play promotes are enjoyment, relaxation, and self-expression; cooperation, sharing, and turn-taking; anxiety reduction; and self-confidence. With so many positive cognitive and socio-emotional outcomes, play is clearly an important aspect in young children's lives.

Media/Screen Time

Few developments in society in the second half of the twentieth century have had a greater impact than television and technology (Maloy et al., 2014). Television continues to have a strong influence on children's development, but children's use of other media and information/communication devices has recently led to the use of the term "screen time," or how much time individuals spend with television, DVDs, computers, video games, tablets, and mobile media such as iPhones (Sterin, 2014). A recent recommendation for children ages 2 to 4 years of age is to limit screen time to no more than one hour per day (Tremblay et al., 2012).

Many children spend more time with various screen media than they do interacting with their parents and peers. Statistics Canada reports that self-reported screen time for Canadian youth is approximately 6 hours daily on weekdays, and more than 7 hours a day on weekends (Colley et al., 2015). Television can have a negative influence on children by making them passive learners, distracting them from doing homework, teaching them stereotypes, providing them with violent models of aggression, and presenting them with unrealistic views of the world (Murray, 2007). However, television can have a positive influence by presenting motivating educational programs, increasing children's information about the world beyond their immediate environment, and providing models of prosocial behaviour (Bryant, 2007; Wilson, 2008).

Effects of Screen Time on Children's Prosocial Behaviour

Social media can teach children that it is better to behave in positive, prosocial ways than in negative, antisocial ways as well as facilitate learning. For example, LeapFrog offers a range of learning activities for children to enhance numeracy and literacy competence. Many of the cartoons on TVO or Treehouse, for instance, illustrate creative exploration of nature, constructive conflict resolution, problem solving-skills, and attitudes toward others (Mares & Pan, 2013).

To this point, we have discussed a number of ideas about peer relations, play, and social media. For a review, see the Reach Your Learning Outcomes section at the end of this chapter.

Reach Your **Learning Outcomes**

The Self and Emotional Development

LO1 Discuss the emergence of the self and emotional development in early childhood.

The Self	▪ Erikson believed that early childhood is a period when development involves resolving the conflict of initiative versus guilt. ▪ In early childhood, the self is understood in terms of physical or material attributes.
Emotional Development	▪ Self-conscious emotions like pride and shame develop later than basic emotions like joy and fear. ▪ Preschoolers become more and more adept at talking about their own and others' emotions. ▪ Two- and 3-year-olds can use a large number of terms to describe emotion. ▪ At 4 to 5 years of age, children show an increased ability to reflect on emotions. They also show a growing awareness of the need to control and manage emotions to meet social standards. ▪ Shy boys may be at more risk for maladjustment than shy girls. ▪ Emotion-coaching and emotion-dismissing parents act differently toward their children's expressions of emotions. ▪ Ability to control one's emotions is related to children's peer relationships.

Moral Development and Gender

LO2 Summarize moral development and gender in early childhood.

Moral Development	▪ Moral development refers to the development of thoughts, feelings, and behaviours regarding standards of right and wrong. ▪ Piaget distinguished between the heteronomous morality of younger children and the autonomous morality of older children. ▪ There is considerable situational variability in moral behaviour. ▪ According to Freud's psychoanalytic theory, the superego, the moral branch of personality, develops through the Oedipus conflict and identification with the same-gender parent. In Freud's view, children conform to societal standards to avoid guilt.
Gender	▪ Gender is the social dimension of being male or female. ▪ For most children, gender identity is acquired by 3 years of age. ▪ A gender role is a set of expectations that prescribes how females or males should think, act, and feel. ▪ The 23rd pair of chromosomes may have two X chromosomes to produce a female or one X and one Y chromosome to produce a male. ▪ The two main classes of sex hormones are estrogens, which are dominant in females, and androgens, which are dominant in males. ▪ Evolutionary psychology explains behavioural differences in males and females in terms of adapting to their different roles in reproduction. ▪ The social role theory, the psychoanalytic theory, and the social cognitive approach explain how people acquire gender-appropriate behaviour through interaction with the environment. ▪ Gender schema theory emphasizes the role of cognition in gender development.

The Changing Family in a Changing Society

LO3 Explain how families can influence young children's development.

Parenting	▪ Parental roles have shifted; economic pressures require dual incomes and fathers are more engaged with child raising. ▪ Baumrind's four parenting styles are authoritarian, authoritative, neglectful, and indulgent. ▪ Parenting styles in context: Cultural and economic factors shape parenting styles. ▪ Diversity: Immigrant and refugee families face challenges of language and separation in addition to cultural adjustment. ▪ Culture and ethnicity are influential factors and include multifaceted challenges facing immigrant and refugee families such as language, poverty, and family reunification. ▪ Co-parenting refers to the support that parents provide each other in jointly raising a child. ▪ Punishment: In 2004, the Supreme Court ruled that spanking is legal so long as excessive force is not used. Research links harsh punitive punishment to aggressive behaviour.

Divorce	▪ Four in 10 marriages end in divorce. Children adjust more readily when parents maintain a relatively harmonious relationship and engage in authoritative parenting styles. ▪ Like heterosexual couples, gay and lesbian parents vary greatly, but observations and self-reports confirm that child care is shared evenly, with lesbian couples being the most supportive. ▪ Step- or blended families pose many challenges for both children and parents.
Sibling Relationships and Birth Order	▪ Families are smaller and more diverse. ▪ Siblings interact with each other in positive and negative ways. ▪ Birth order has not been found to affect personality traits such as agreeableness, extroversion, conscientiousness, imagination, and emotional stability.

Peer Relations, Play, and Social Media

LO4 **Describe the roles of peers, play, and social media in young children's development.**

Peer Relations	▪ Peers are children who are of about the same age or maturity level. ▪ Peers are powerful socialization agents. ▪ Peers provide a source of information and comparison about the world outside the family.
Play	▪ Play's functions include affiliation with peers, tension release, advances in cognitive development, exploration, and provision of a safe haven. ▪ Freud and Erikson saw play as a way to help children deal with anxiety. ▪ Piaget and Vygotsky suggested that play is important for cognitive development.
Media/ Screen Time	▪ Viewing television and playing some computer games can negatively influence later learning ability and encourage the expression of violence. ▪ Social media can also increase prosocial behaviour and assist children with early literacy milestones.

review → connect → reflect

review

1. How might Erikson's fourth stage, initiative versus guilt, be resolved? LO1
2. How do self-esteem and self-concept differ? Give an example of each. LO1
3. How do heteronomous and autonomous morality differ? LO2
4. What is meant by the term *gender?* LO2
5. How do the definition and assumptions of family today differ from the definition and assumptions about family a generation ago? LO3
6. What are the long-term effects of child maltreatment? LO3
7. What are some of the positive and negative impacts of social media? LO4

connect

You read in this chapter that research has linked harsh punishment to aggressive behaviour. You also read that the Supreme Court of Canada has determined that spanking is legal as long as it does not include excessive force. How might you define the terms *harsh punishment, spanking*, and *excessive force*?

reflect

Your Own Personal Journey of Life

Did your parents monitor your use of television and the Internet? If so, what strategies did they use? If not, why? What might be some of the challenges facing parents in terms of television and social media? What guidelines might you develop or recommend to monitor children's use of television and other forms of social media? What safety net could be offered to a child who is the victim of cyberspace bullying?

SECTION 5

Middle and Late Childhood

CHAPTER 9

Physical and Cognitive Development in Middle and Late Childhood

CHAPTER OUTLINE

Physical Changes and Health

LO1 Describe physical changes and health in middle and late childhood.

- **Body Growth and Change**
- **The Brain**
- **Motor Development**
- **Exercise**
- **Health, Illness, and Disease**

Cognitive Development

LO2 Explain cognitive changes in middle and late childhood.

- **Piaget's Concrete Operational Stage**
- **Information Processing**
- **Intelligence**

Language Development

LO3 Discuss language development in middle and late childhood.

- **Vocabulary, Grammar, and Metalinguistic Awareness**
- **Reading**
- **Bilingualism**

Educational Approaches and Issues

LO4 Discuss approaches and issues related to education.

- **Approaches to Student Learning**
- **Educational Issues**
- **International Comparisons**
- **Private Schools and Home Education**

Children with Disabilities

LO5 Identify children with different types of disabilities and discuss issues related to their education.

- **Learning Disabilities**
- **Attention Deficit Hyperactivity Disorder (ADHD)**
- **Autism Spectrum Disorders**
- **Physical Disabilities**
- **Children's Disabilities and the Family**
- **Educational Issues**

"I have never let my schooling interfere with my education."

—MARK TWAIN, NINETEENTH-CENTURY AMERICAN WRITER

Courtesy of World Literacy Canada

Gandhi's Glasses

Do we see the world differently when we put on glasses? What if those glasses were ones that had been worn by the famous peace advocate Mahatma Gandhi, the man who said, "Be the change you want to see in the world"? Inspired by the project The Gandhi Way: Engaging Youth in Global Citizenship, 15 teachers in 15 different schools guided 300 elementary school children from Toronto's Model School for Inner Cities program to write and illustrate a children's book. The book, *Gandhi's Glasses*, addresses social justice and equity issues that the children identified—issues such as recycling, violence, poverty, and gender discrimination.

The young authors decided the hero would be a little girl named Asha and that she would be confronted by all these concerns in one school day. At first, Asha thought she was "too busy" to help the boy who did not have enough bus fare, or to do anything about the backpacks blocking the wheelchair access ramp or all the litter on the playground. She thought she was "too little" to do anything about the way boys were not including girls in basketball games. Certainly she was "too little" to do anything about the bulldozing of the local park.

Then, she found a pair of Gandhi's glasses and she saw the world differently. She realized that indeed, in a peaceful way, she could make a difference. As the young authors say, "Whatever you do will be insignificant, but it's important that you do it. Seeing ourselves as citizens of the globe, we have to always be fair." Another author reminded that "In a gentle way, you can change the world," to which two more added, "An eye for an eye will lead to blindness."

The Canadian International Development Agency (CIDA), World Literacy Canada (WLC), and the Toronto District School Board (TDSB) partnered to engage children to write and illustrate ways that global citizenship could be achieved in their own lives. Please refer to the World Literacy Canada website http://www.worldlit.ca/programs-history/gandhi-way-2/ for more information.

Imagine for a moment that you were engaged in writing and illustrating this book. What might you have written? The collaborative efforts and dedication of those who guided the making of *Gandhi's Glasses* illustrate many of the concepts, theories, and approaches about cognitive development, intelligence, and education that you will be reading about in this chapter.

Physical Changes and Health

LO1 Describe physical changes and health in middle and late childhood

- **Body Growth and Change**
- **The Brain**
- **Motor Development**
- **Exercise**
- **Health, Illness, and Disease**

Body Growth and Change

Physical growth during the elementary school years is relatively slow, but consistent; children grow 5 to 7.5 cm a year and gain about 2.3 to 3.2 kg annually. The weight increase is due mainly to increases in the size of the skeletal and muscular systems and the size of some body organs. Muscle mass and strength gradually increase as "baby fat" decreases. Proportional changes are among the most pronounced physical changes in middle and late childhood. Head circumference and waist circumference decrease in relation to body height (Kliegman et al., 2012). A less noticeable physical change is that bones continue to ossify during middle and late childhood but yield to pressure and pull more than mature bones.

Young children's information-processing skills also improve considerably—executive and sustained attention advance, short-term memory gets better, executive function increases, and understanding of the human mind makes considerable progress. Young children also increase their knowledge of language's rule systems, and their literacy benefits from being active participants in a wide range of language experiences. Both gross and fine motor skills become smoother and more coordinated. As well, many have attended an early childhood education program prior to elementary school, and may also attend before- and after-school programs until their parents come home from work.

The Brain

The development of brain-imaging techniques such as magnetic resonance imaging (MRI) has led to an increase in research on the changes in the brain during middle and late childhood, and how these brain changes are linked to improvements in cognitive development (Diamond, 2009; Diamond, Casey, & Munakata, 2011). The total brain volume stabilizes by the end of middle and late childhood, but significant changes in various structures and regions of the brain continue to occur. In particular, the brain pathways and circuitry involving the prefrontal cortex, the highest level in the brain, continue to increase (Durston & Casey, 2006) (see Figure 9.1). These advances in the prefrontal cortex are linked to children's improved attention, reasoning, and cognitive control (Markant & Thomas, 2013).

Figure 9.1
The Prefrontal Cortex

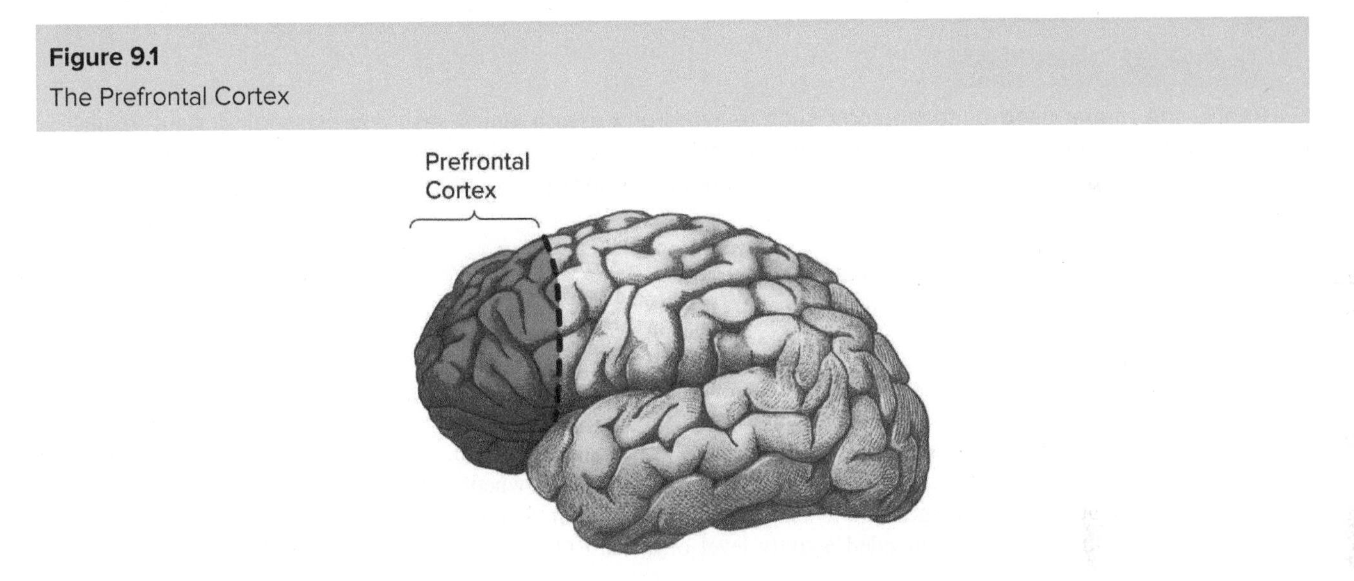

The brain pathways and circuitry involving the prefrontal cortex (shaded in purple) show significant advances in development during middle and late childhood. *What cognitive processes are these changes in the prefrontal cortex linked to?*

Leading developmental neuroscientist Mark Johnson and his colleagues (2009) proposed that the prefrontal cortex likely orchestrates the functions of many other brain regions during development. As part of this neural leadership and organizational role, the prefrontal cortex may provide an advantage to neural networks and connections that include the prefrontal cortex. Consequently, the prefrontal cortex coordinates the best neural connections for solving a problem at hand.

Changes also occur in the thickness of the cerebral cortex (cortical thickness) in middle and late childhood (Thomason & Thompson, 2011). One study used brain scans to assess cortical thickness in 5- to 11-year-old children (Sowell et al., 2004). Cortical thickening across a two-year time period was observed in the temporal and frontal lobe areas that function in language, which may reflect improvements in language abilities such as reading.

As children develop, activation of some brain areas increase while others decrease (Diamond, 2013; Nelson, 2013; Raznahan et al., 2014). One shift in activation that occurs is from diffuse larger areas to more focal smaller areas (Turkeltaub et al., 2003). This shift is characterized by synaptic pruning, in which areas of the brain not being used lose synaptic connections and those being used show an increase in connections. In one study, researchers found less diffusion and more focal activation in the prefrontal cortex from 7 to 30 years of age (Durston et al., 2006). The activation change was accompanied by increased efficiency in cognitive performance, especially in cognitive control, which involves flexible and effective controlling attention, reducing interfering thoughts, inhibiting motor actions, and being flexible in switching between competing choices (Diamond, Casey, & Munakata, 2011).

Motor Development

During middle and late childhood, children's gross motor skills become much smoother and more coordinated. For example, only one child in a thousand can hit a tennis ball over the net at 3 years of age, yet most children can learn to play tennis by age 10 or 11. Running, riding a bike, swimming, skating, and playing sports such as hockey and soccer are just a few of the many physical skills elementary children can master. In gross motor skills, boys usually outperform girls.

Increased myelination of the central nervous system is reflected in the improvement of fine motor skills during middle and late childhood. Children can use their hands as tools more adroitly. Six-year-olds can hammer, paste, tie shoes, and fasten clothes. By 7 years of age, children's hands become steadier. At this age, children prefer a pencil to a crayon for printing, and reversal of letters is less common. Printing becomes smaller. Between 8 and 10 years of age, children can use their hands independently with more ease and precision. Fine motor coordination develops to the point that children can write rather than print words. Cursive letter size becomes smaller and more even. At 10 to 12 years of age, children begin to show manipulative skills similar to the abilities of adults. The complex, intricate, and rapid movements needed to produce fine-quality crafts or to play a difficult piece on a musical instrument can be mastered. Girls usually outperform boys in fine motor skills.

critical thinking

Print is the format used by technology, such as word processing, email, and text messaging. As a result, many wonder whether cursive writing is becoming obsolete. How often do you use cursive writing? As a student, are you able to submit your work using cursive writing? Do you think it is becoming obsolete? If so, should it be dropped from the curriculum?

Exercise

According to Active Healthy Kids Canada, physical activity is linked positively to physical, socio-emotional, and cognitive development. Not only is physical activity associated with better health and physical skills, but it also fosters creativity, problem solving, executive brain functioning, academic performance, self-esteem, and social skills such as sharing, turn taking, and negotiation. So much positive gain is linked to physical activity, whether structured or unstructured, that there is cause for concern that between the ages of 6 to 11 years, only 11 percent of boys and 2 percent of girls meet the Canadian Physical Activity Guidelines' recommended activity level of at least 60 minutes of moderate to vigorous activity a day (Statistics Canada, 2015).

Children who have access to unsupervised outdoor play have better-developed physical skills, social behaviour, independence, and conflict resolution skills (Participaction Report Card, 2015); however, instead of physical activities, children are spending an average of 8 hours daily in sedentary screen activities such as watching television or playing video games (Statistics Canada, 2015). This is far in excess of the Canadian Paediatric Society's recommendation that children's television viewing be limited to one or two hours daily (Active Healthy Kids Canada, 2012). Active play has been replaced by sedentary play, which, in the words of Dr. Tremblay, "...is seductive, it's convenient, and it's cheaper than a babysitter, but it's really bad for their health" (Picard, 2012).

Like their children, most Canadian adults fail to meet the guideline of 150 minutes of physical activity per week. Busy work schedules and safety concerns are the two primary reasons for the lack of physical activity. Parents report that as children, their physical activity levels were considerably higher than those of their children. A generation ago, children ran loose and were freer to explore the world around them.

Does playing on a team guarantee vigorous physical activity?

Parents and schools play important roles in determining children's exercise levels (Participaction Report Card, 2015; Gilbertson & Graves, 2014; Meyer et al., 2014). Growing up with parents who exercise regularly provides positive models of exercise for children (Crawford et al., 2010). One study revealed that mothers are more likely than fathers to limit sedentary behaviour in boys and girls (Edwardson & Gorely, 2010). In this study, fathers did have an influence on their sons' physical activity, but primarily through explicit modelling of physical activity, such as showing their sons how to handle a hockey stick. A research review found that school-based physical activity is successful at improving children's fitness and lowering their fat levels (Kriemler et al., 2011).

In light of the problem of child inactivity, many organizations are promoting an active lifestyle among Canada's young people. Among these groups are Right to Play and Active Healthy Kids Canada. Canadian Olympian Silken Laumann has been an active advocate in the formation of these organizations.

critical thinking

Mothers report having more than twice as much daily outdoor play when they were children than their children do now. What are some of the factors that might account for this decline? What are some strategies for increasing children's physical activity? Do you engage in the recommended 150 minutes of physical activity a week? If not, what changes might you make to improve your level of physical activity?

Health, Illness, and Disease

Do Canadian children maintain a healthy diet? Is obesity really a problem? For the most part, middle and late childhood is a time of excellent health.

Balanced or Unbalanced Diet?

A healthy diet promotes normal growth and development and contributes to overall health. Canada's Food Guide recommends that children eat four to five servings of vegetables and fruits, three to four grain products, two glasses of milk or its equivalent, and one meat or meat alternative daily (Canada's Food Guide, 2007; Canadian Cancer Society, 2016).

Surveys conducted by Health Canada, the Canada Food Guide, and other associations provide an assessment of our diets. Findings from Health Canada (2012) indicated that many children are not eating the balanced diet suggested by Canada's Food Guide; in fact, fewer than 40 percent of 9- to 13-year-olds are getting enough vegetables and fruit daily. Moreover, 61 percent of boys and 83 percent of girls aged 10 to 16 are not taking in enough milk products daily. Health Canada (2012) reported that the diet of children between 1 and 8 years of age provides adequate amounts of most vitamins and minerals. However, the survey found that one in five children take in more energy than they expend, and that 75 percent of children take in more sodium than recommended.

Obesity

Childhood obesity rates have tripled over the past thirty years (Government of Canada, 2015). One in four children is overweight, and one in ten is obese. An international study of obesity ranked Canada 11th highest of the 40 countries studied. The good news is that the trend toward obesity has slowed down (Government of Canada, 2015; Organization for Economic Cooperation and Development (OECD), 2014; Obesity Network, 2014). Sadly, the UNICEF Report Card reported that when compared with 29 other rich countries, Canada ranks second from the bottom in childhood obesity rates (Adamson, 2013).

Not only do obesity rates increase as children move into their teens, but they also predict obesity in adulthood. Health risks include high blood pressure or heart disease, type 2 diabetes, sleep apnea, and mental health concerns such as low self-esteem, depression, or feeling judged, teased, or bullied (Government of Canada, 2015).

Parents play an important role by modelling a good example of healthy eating and activity. Following Canada's Food Guide, keeping the refrigerator full of fruits and vegetables to nibble on between meals, and teaching children about the importance of being healthy and fit are important aspects in cultivating healthy lifestyles for children.

critical thinking

Research indicates that parents are important role models for their children. What advice would you give to parents who want to ensure that their children get enough exercise and eat a nutritious diet? How do you incorporate healthy nutrition and exercise into your lifestyle?

Obese children who are embarrassed by their peers or parents may choose to lose weight to the extent of becoming anorexic (Johnston, 2004). One study found that a significant proportion of girls as young as 5 years of age associate a diet with food restriction, weight loss, and thinness. Such ideas about dieting are predicted by the girls' mothers' dieting behaviours. Further, the ratio of girls to boys diagnosed with anorexia or bulimia is 5 to 1; in adolescence the ratio doubles to 10 to 1 (National Eating Disorder Information Centre, 2014). As well, research indicates a link between disordered eating and girls who have been subjected to violence. Research reveals that for over 90 percent of girls who have survived sexual abuse, the onset of eating disorders occurs after their first abuse. The research concludes that eating disorders may be a form of resistance to further violation for some, and for others it may be a way to purge feelings of shame and guilt. The context for each individual girl or woman shapes the meaning and significance of their particular experience. Further, thinness in itself may become a goal as it is often perceived as a sign of interpersonal and economic success (Moore et al., 2009).

Striving for Thinness

A child's desire for thinness is as important a health issue as obesity (Johnston, 2004). In fact, Chapter 11 will show you how an obsession with dieting and anorexia nervosa is affecting many Canadian teens. However, as noted earlier, the trend often starts in the pre-teen years.

A longitudinal study in Australia reported that over 40 percent of girls as young as 5 to 8 years of age want to be thinner (Dohnt & Tiggemann, 2006). This desire for thinness foreshadowed the lowered self-esteem experienced by young girls a year later, highlighting the relationship of body weight and psychological well-being. The Public Health Agency of Canada (2011) reported that 33 percent of girls and 22 percent of boys between grades 6 and 10 think they are too fat. Boys more often reported being too thin. As both boys and girls age, their satisfaction with their body image declines; importantly, unrealistic perceptions of body size may carry significant short- and long-term health risks.

An obsession with thinness among school-age children may lead to disordered eating behaviour, such as unnecessary fasting. Parental awareness of their children's desire to be thin and the underlying reasons for this desire is vital. In some instances, such as those involving abuse, finding the underlying cause may be difficult and outside counselling may be helpful. Promoting a sense of competence in their children, listening to youngsters' concerns about not being as good as their peers, and explaining the unrealistic and unhealthy aspects of the media's portrayal of thinness may help children develop a positive body image.

Accidents and Injuries

Unintentional injuries and accidents, particularly falls, are the leading cause of hospitalization, death, and disability during middle and late childhood; as well, they rank fourth among causes of death for all ages (Yanchar et al., 2012). The most common cause of injury and death is motor vehicle accidents, either as a pedestrian or as a passenger (Wilson & Hocken-Berry, 2008). Other serious injuries involve bicycles, skateboards, roller skates, falls, and drowning (Birkin et al., 2006). Research also indicates that a higher level of injury-related mortality occurs in urban neighbourhoods of lower socio-economic status, indicating that an injury prevention strategy is needed (Birkin et al., 2006).

Many children suffer injuries and even death in preventable accidents. Most accidents occur at or near the child's home or school. One reason for these accidents is unnecessary risk taking. A study at the University of Guelph in Ontario showed that boys are more willing to take risks in everyday activities than girls (Morrongiello & Dawber, 2004). Another Canadian study found that boys are more likely to play sports and have played for more years by the ages of 11 to 14 years (Bowker, 2006). Together, these findings partly explain why boys are more likely than girls to experience injuries.

The most effective prevention strategy is to educate children about the proper use of equipment and the hazards of risk taking (Beta & Sowden, 2008). Safety helmets, protective eye and mouth shields, and protective padding are recommended for children who engage in active sports (Briem et al., 2004).

Cancer

Although childhood cancers account for less than 1 percent of all cancers diagnosed in Canada, cancer is the second leading cause of death in children between 1 and 14 years of age (PHAC, 2012). Cancers are characterized by an uncontrolled proliferation of abnormal cells. Adult cancers are typically carcinomas that primarily attack glands and tissues that line organs such as lungs, colon, breast, prostate, and pancreas. Carcinomas are rare in children; childhood cancers are more likely to be rapid-growing tumours that primarily attack white blood and lymphatic systems. Leukemia, which accounts for one-third of all childhood cancers, is a disease in which the bone marrow makes an abundance of white blood cells that do not function properly. They invade the bone marrow and crowd out normal cells, making the child susceptible to bruising and infection. Brain and spinal tumours account for 20 percent of childhood cancers, and 12 percent are either Hodgkin (cancer of the lymph nodes) or non-Hodgkin lymphoma (cancer of the fighting cells) (PHAC, 2012).

To this point, we have studied physical changes and health in middle and late childhood. For a review, see the Reach Your Learning Outcomes section at the end of this chapter.

Cognitive Development

LO2 Explain cognitive changes in middle and late childhood.

- **Piaget's Concrete Operational Stage**
- **Information Processing**
- **Intelligence**

Piaget's Concrete Operational Stage

According to Piaget (1952), the preschool child's thought is preoperational. Preschool children can form stable concepts and they have begun to reason, but their thinking is flawed by egocentrism and magical belief systems. As we discussed in Chapter 7, however, Piaget may have underestimated children's abilities; in fact, some researchers argue that, under the right conditions, young children may display abilities characteristic of concrete operational thought, Piaget's next stage. First we will cover the characteristics of concrete operational thought and evaluate Piaget's portrait of this stage, then we will do a critical analysis to evaluate Piaget's theory.

Piaget with his wife and three children; he often used his observations of his children to provide examples of his theory.

Information Processing

If instead of analyzing the type of thinking children in middle and late childhood display we examine how they process information, what would we find? During these years, most children dramatically improve their ability to sustain and control attention (Siegler, 2012). As discussed in Chapter 7, they pay more attention to task-relevant stimuli than to salient stimuli. Other changes in information processing during middle and late childhood are those involving memory, thinking, metacognition, and executive function (Bauer & Zelazo, 2013; Cowan, 2014; Friedman, 2014).

Memory

In Chapter 7, we concluded that short-term memory increases considerably during early childhood, but does not show as much increase after the age of 7. On the other hand, long-term memory is a relatively permanent and unlimited type of memory that increases with age during middle and late childhood. In part, improvements in memory reflect children's increased knowledge and their increased use of strategies. Keep in mind that it is important not to view memory in terms of how children add something to it but rather to underscore how children actively construct their memory (Bjorklund, 2013; Cohen, 2012; Willoughby et al., 2012).

WORKING MEMORY

Short-term memory is like a passive storehouse with shelves to store information until it is moved to long-term memory. Alan Baddeley (1990, 2001, 2007, 2010, 2012) defines **working memory** as a kind of mental "workbench" where individuals manipulate and assemble information when they make decisions, solve problems, and comprehend written and spoken language (see Figure 9.4). Working memory is described as more active and powerful in modifying information than short-term memory. Working memory involves bringing information to mind and mentally working with or updating it, as when you link one idea to another and relate what you are reading now to something you read earlier.

Figure 9.4
Working Memory

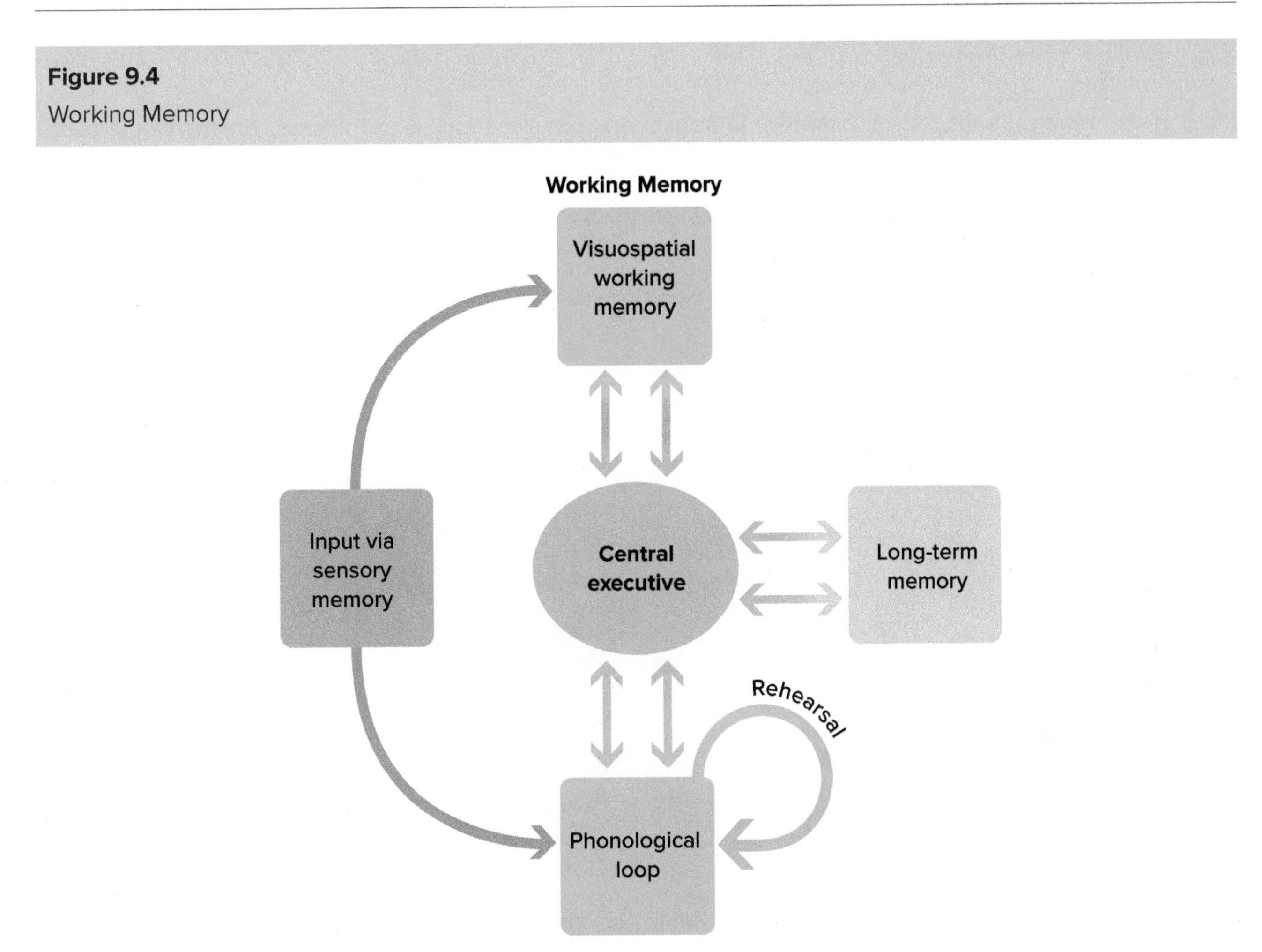

A key component of working memory is the central executive, which supervises and controls the flow of information. The central executive is especially important in selective attention and inhibition, planning and decision making, and trouble shooting. Recall from Chapter 7 our description of executive function as an umbrella-like concept that encompasses a number of higher-level cognitive processes. One of those cognitive processes is working memory, especially its central executive dimension.

In Baddeley's model, working memory consists of three main components, with the phonological loop and visuospatial working memory helping the central executive to do its work. Input from sensory memory goes to the phonological loop, where information about speech is stored and rehearsal takes place, and visuospatial working memory, where visual and spatial information, including imagery, are stored. Working memory is a limited-capacity system, and information is stored there for only a brief time. Working memory interacts with long-term memory, using information from long-term memory in its work and transmitting information to long-term memory for longer storage.

Working memory is linked to many aspects of children's development (Cowan, 2014; Myatchin & Lagae, 2013; Reznick, 2014). The following studies illustrate the importance of working memory to children's cognitive and language development:

- A recent research review concluded that children with learning difficulties in reading and math have working memory deficits (Peng & Fuchs, 2014).
- Working memory capacity at 9 to 10 years of age predicted foreign language comprehension two years later at 11 to 12 years of age (Andersson, 2010).
- Working memory capacity predicted how many items on a to-be-remembered list grade 4 children forgot (Aslan, Zellner, & Bauml, 2010).

Knowledge and Expertise

Much of the research on the role of knowledge in memory has compared experts and novices. *Experts* have acquired extensive knowledge about a particular content area; this knowledge influences what they notice and how they organize, represent, and interpret information (Siegler, 2013). When individuals have expertise about a particular subject, their memory also tends to be good regarding material related to that subject (Martinez, 2010).

For example, one study found that 10- and 11-year-olds who were experienced chess players ("experts") were able to remember more information about chess pieces than university students who were not chess players ("novices") (Chi, 1978) (see Figure 9.5). In contrast, when presented with other stimuli, university students were able to remember them better than the children were. Thus, the children's expertise in chess gave them superior memories, but only in chess.

Figure 9.5

The Role of Expertise in Memory

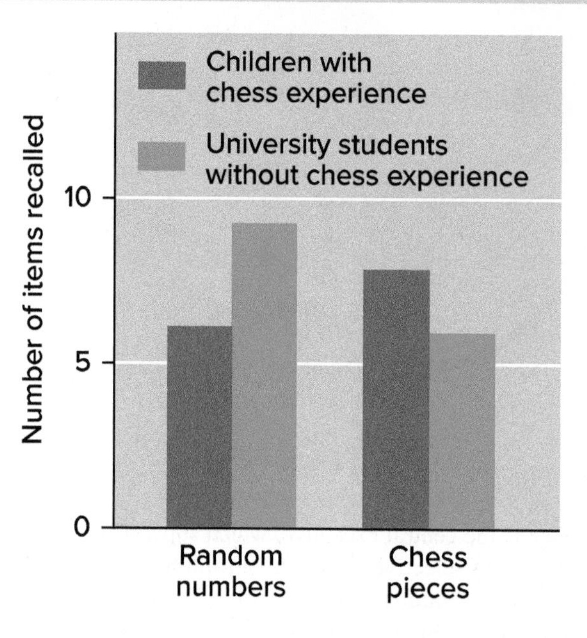

When 10- to 11-year-old children and university students were asked to remember a string of random numbers that had been presented to them, the university students fared better. However, the children who were chess "experts" had better memory for the location of chess pieces on a chess board than university students with no chess experience ("novices") (Chi, 1978).

There are developmental changes in expertise (Blair & Somerville, 2009; Ericsson, 2014). Older children usually have more expertise about a subject than younger children do, which can contribute to their better memory for the subject.

AUTOBIOGRAPHICAL MEMORY

Recall that autobiographical memory involves memory of significant events and experiences in one's life. You are engaging in autobiographical memory when you answer questions such as: Who was your grade 1 teacher and what was she or he like? What is the most traumatic event that happened to you as a child?

Autobiographical memory involves both episodic and semantic memory. **Episodic memory** is memory of events—the where and when of life's happenings. **Semantic memory** involves an understanding of the world around us—including one's fields of expertise, general academic knowledge of the sort learned in school, and "everyday knowledge." As children develop through middle and late childhood, and through adolescence, their autobiographical narratives broaden and become more elaborated (Bauer, 2013; Bauer & Fivush, 2014; DeMarie & Lopez, 2014; Pathman & St. Jacques, 2014). Researchers have found that children develop more detailed, coherent, and evaluative autobiographical memories when their mothers reminisce with them in elaborated and evaluative ways (Fivush, 2010).

Using the newly developed Children's Autobiographical Interview (CAI) described in Chapter 7, researchers from Sick Kids Hospital in Toronto found that both episodic and semantic memory improve between the ages of 8 and 16 years, and that girls recall more episodic memories, especially with the use of probing questions. Older children and girls exhibited better episodic autobiographical memory as well as memory for everyday activities (Willoughby et al., 2012).

Strategies

If we know anything at all about long-term memory, it is that long-term memory depends on the learning activities individuals engage in when they are learning and remembering information (Friedman, 2014). A key learning activity involves **strategies**, which consist of deliberate mental activities to improve the processing of information. For example, organizing is a strategy that older children, adolescents, and adults use to remember more effectively. Strategies do not occur automatically; they require effort and work.

Some effective strategies for adults to use when attempting to improve children's memory skills include the following:

- *Advise children to elaborate on what is to be remembered.* **Elaboration** is an important strategy that involves engaging in more extensive processing of information. When individuals engage in elaboration, their memory benefits (Schneider, 2011). Thinking of examples and relating information to one's own self and experiences are good ways to elaborate information. Forming personal associations with information makes the information more meaningful and helps children to remember it. For example, if the word "win" is on a list of words a child is asked to remember, the child might think of the last time he "won" a bicycle race with a friend.
- *Encourage children to engage in mental imagery.* Mental imagery can help even young schoolchildren to remember pictures. However, for remembering verbal information, mental imagery works better for older children than for younger children (Schneider, 2011).
- *Motivate children to remember material by understanding it rather than by memorizing it.* Children will remember information better over the long term if they understand the information rather than just rehearse and memorize it. Rehearsal works well for encoding information into short-term memory, but when children need to retrieve the information from long-term memory, it is much less efficient. For most information, encourage children to understand it, give it meaning, elaborate on it, and personalize it. Give children concepts and ideas to remember and then ask them how they can relate the concepts and ideas to their own personal experiences and meanings. Give them practice on elaborating a concept so they will process the information more deeply.
- *Repeat with variation on the instructional information and link early and often.* These are memory development research expert Patricia Bauer's (2009) recommendations to improve children's consolidation and reconsolidation of the information they are learning. Variations on a lesson theme increase the number of associations in memory storage, and linking expands the network of associations in memory storage; both strategies expand the routes for retrieving information from storage.
- *Embed memory-relevant language when instructing children.* Teachers vary considerably in how much they use memory-relevant language that encourages students to remember information. In research that involved extensive observations of a number of grade 1 teachers in the classroom, Peter Ornstein and his colleagues (Ornstein, Coffman, & Grammer, 2009; Ornstein et al., 2007, 2010) found that for the time segments observed, the teachers rarely used strategy suggestions or metacognitive (thinking about thinking) questions. In this research, when lower-achieving students were placed in classrooms in which teachers were categorized as "high-mnemonic teachers" who frequently embedded memory-relevant information in their teaching, their achievement increased (Ornstein, Coffman, & Grammer, 2007).

Fuzzy Trace Theory

Might something other than knowledge and strategies be responsible for the improvement in memory during the elementary school years? Charles Brainerd and Valerie Reyna (1993; Reyna, 2004) argue that fuzzy traces account for much of this improvement. Their **fuzzy trace theory** states that memory is best understood by considering two types of memory representations: (1) verbatim memory trace, and (2) gist. The verbatim memory trace consists of the precise details of the information, whereas gist refers to the central idea of the information. When gist is used, fuzzy traces are built up. Although individuals of all ages extract gist, young children tend to store and retrieve verbatim traces. At some point during the early elementary school years, children begin to use gist more. and according to the theory, gist contributes to improved memory, reasoning, and decision making of older children because fuzzy traces are more enduring and less likely to be forgotten than verbatim traces.

Thinking

Four important aspects of thinking are executive function, thinking critically, thinking creatively, and thinking scientifically.

"For God's sake, think! Why is he being so nice to you?"

EXECUTIVE FUNCTION

In Chapter 7, you read about executive function and its characteristics in early childhood (Carlson, Claxton, & Moses, 2014; Carlson, White, & Davis-Unger, 2014; Carlson, Zelazo, & Faja, 2013). Some important cognitive topics—working memory, critical thinking, creative thinking, and metacognition—can be considered under the umbrella of executive function and linked to the development of the brain's prefrontal cortex. Also, earlier in the chapter in the coverage of brain development in middle and late childhood, you read about the increase in cognitive control, which involves flexible and effective control in a number of areas such as focusing attention, reducing interfering thoughts, inhibiting motor actions, and exercising flexibility in deciding between competing choices.

Adele Diamond and Kathleen Lee (2011) highlighted the following dimensions of executive function that they conclude are the most important for 4- to 11-year-old children's cognitive development and school success:

- *Self-control/inhibition:* Children need to develop self-control that will allow them to concentrate and persist on learning tasks, to inhibit their tendencies to repeat incorrect responses, and to resist the impulse to do something now that they later would regret.
- *Working memory:* Children need an effective working memory to mentally work with the masses of information they will encounter as they go through school and beyond.
- *Flexibility:* Children need to be flexible in their thinking to consider different strategies and perspectives.

Executive function and good parenting skills are related. Masten says,"When we see kids with good executive function, we often see adults around them that are good self-regulators... Parents model, they support, and they scaffold these skills" (Masten, 2012, p. 11). Further, researchers have found that executive function is a better predictor of school readiness than general IQ (Blair & Razza, 2007). Some types of school curricula, such as the Montessori curriculum, as well as exercise and play, also increase executive function (Diamond, 2013; Diamond & Lee, 2011).

CRITICAL THINKING

Psychologists and educators are currently very interested in critical thinking (Barnett & Francis, 2012). **Critical thinking** involves thinking reflectively and productively, and evaluating evidence. In this book, the Critical Thinking questions challenge you to think critically about a topic or an issue related to the discussion.

According to Ellen Langer (2005), mindfulness—being alert, mentally present, and cognitively flexible while going through life's everyday activities and tasks—is an important aspect of thinking critically. Mindful children and adults maintain an active awareness of the circumstances in their life and are motivated to find the best solutions to tasks. Mindful individuals create new ideas, are open to new information, and operate from a single perspective. By contrast, mindless individuals are entrapped in old ideas, engage in automatic behaviour, and operate from a single perspective.

CREATIVE THINKING

Cognitively competent children think not only critically, but also creatively (Kaufman & Sternberg, 2013. **Creative thinking** is the ability to think in novel and unusual ways and to come up with unique solutions to problems. Thus, intelligence and creativity are not the same thing. This difference was recognized by J. P. Guilford (1967), who distinguished between **convergent thinking**, which produces one correct answer and characterizes the kind of thinking required on conventional tests of intelligence, and **divergent thinking**, which produces many different answers to the same question and characterizes creativity. For example, a typical item on a conventional intelligence test is "How many quarters will you get in return for 60 dimes?" In contrast, the following question has many possible answers: "What image comes to mind when you hear the phrase 'sitting alone in a dark room' or 'some unique uses for a paper clip'?"

Adults can contribute to a child's creative thinking by allowing children to select their own interests and supporting their inclinations, as this is less likely to destroy their natural curiosity than dictating which activities children should engage in (Csikszentmihalyi, 2000).

CONNECTING development to life

Strategies for Increasing Children's Creative Thinking

The following are some strategies for increasing children's creative thinking.

Brainstorming

Brainstorming is a technique that encourages participants to come up with creative ideas in a group, play off each other's ideas, and say practically whatever comes to mind that seems relevant to a particular issue. Facilitators usually tell participants to hold off from criticizing others' ideas.

Stimulating Environments

Some environments nourish creativity, while others inhibit it. Using children's natural curiosity, parents and teachers can provide exercises and activities that stimulate children to find insightful solutions to problems, rather than ask a lot of questions that require rote answers (Baer & Kaufman, 2013). Trips to science centres, museums, art galleries, and zoos offer rich opportunities to stimulate creativity.

Exploration Opportunities

Teresa Amabile (1993) says that telling children exactly how to do things leaves them feeling that originality is a mistake and exploration is a waste of time. Instead of dictating which activities they should engage in, teachers and parents who let children select their interests and who support their inclinations are less likely to destroy their natural curiosity (Hennessey, 2011).

Internal Motivation

Excessive use of prizes, such as gold stars, money, or toys can stifle creativity by undermining the intrinsic pleasure students derive from creative activities (Hennessey, 2011). Creative children's motivation is the satisfaction generated by the work itself.

Confidence Builders

Encouraging children to believe in their own ability to create something innovative and worthwhile expands creativity and builds confidence in their creative skills. This approach aligns with Bandura's (2008, 2009b, 2010) concept of self-efficacy, the belief that one can master a situation and produce positive outcomes.

knowledge about one's own memory, such as a student's ability to monitor whether she has studied enough for a test that is coming up next week or a child's confidence in eyewitness judgments (Buratti, Allwood, & Johansson, 2014).

Young children do have some general knowledge about memory (Lukowski & Bauer, 2014). By 5 or 6 years of age, children usually already know that unfamiliar items are harder to learn than familiar ones, that short lists are easier than long ones, that recognition is easier than recall, and that forgetting is more likely to occur over time (Lyon & Flavell, 1993). However, in other ways, young children's metamemory is limited. They don't understand that related items are easier to remember than unrelated ones, and that remembering the gist of a story is easier than remembering the piece verbatim (Kreutzer, Leonard, & Flavell, 1975). Not until about grade 5 do students understand that gist recall is easier than verbatim recall.

Young children have only limited knowledge about their own memory abilities. For example, in one study, a majority of young children predicted that they would be able to recall all 10 items on a list, but none of them managed this feat when tested (Flavell, Friedrichs, & Hoyt, 1970). Throughout the elementary school years, children gain more realistic evaluations of their memory skills (Schneider, 2011).

In addition to metamemory, metacognition includes knowledge about strategies, the focus of a number of microgenetic studies (McCormick, Dimmitt, & Sullivan, 2013; Sperling et al., 2012; Kuhn, 2013). Recall from Chapter 1 that the microgenetic method involves obtaining detailed information about processing mechanisms as they are occurring moment to moment (Siegler, 2013). Using the microgenetic approach, researchers have shown that developing effective strategies occurs gradually. This research has found considerable variability in children's use of strategies, even revealing that they may use an incorrect strategy in solving a math problem for which they had used a correct strategy several trials earlier (Siegler et al., 2013).

Pressley and his colleagues (Pressley 2003, 2007; Pressley et al., 2001, 2004) have spent considerable time observing strategy instruction by teachers and strategy use by students in elementary and secondary school classrooms. In Pressley's view, the key to education is helping students learn a rich repertoire of strategies that produce solutions to problems. Good thinkers routinely use strategies and effective planning to solve problems. Good thinkers also know when and where to use strategies. Understanding when and where to use strategies often results from monitoring the learning situation (Serra & Metcalfe, 2010). Pressley and his colleagues conclude that strategy instruction is far less complete and intense than what students need in order to learn how to use strategies effectively. They argue that education needs to be restructured so that students are provided with more opportunities to become competent, strategic learners.

Intelligence

The word "intelligence" conjures up many notions ranging from brilliant physicists to the counterintelligence spies depicted in *The Bridge of Spies*. Indeed, defining and understanding intelligence is both engaging and controversial. Government, industries, and educational systems use various methods of assessment to determine an individual's abilities and needs. Here we define **intelligence** as problem-solving skills and the ability to learn from and adapt to life's everyday experiences and **individual differences** as the stable, consistent ways in which people differ from each other. But even this broad definition doesn't satisfy everyone.

More than any other, the domain of intelligence has been directed at individual differences (Kehle & Bray, 2014). For example, an intelligence test purports to inform us about whether a student can reason better than others who have taken the test. Intelligence tests generally attempt to measure capabilities in a five areas: verbal skills, visual-spatial reasoning, quantitative skills, memory, and processing speed. Let's go back in history and see what the first intelligence test was like.

The Stanford-Binet Tests

Over a century ago, public education became mandated in most of North America and Europe. Creating a system that could accommodate the large number of students was, and still is, a major challenge. In 1904, psychologist Alfred Binet was asked by the French Ministry of Education to design a test that would help distinguish those children who could benefit from public education from those who needed special education. School officials wanted to reduce crowding by placing students who did not benefit from regular classroom teaching in special schools. Binet and his student Theophile Simon developed the first intelligence test to meet this request, the 1905 Scale. It consisted of 30 questions on topics ranging from the ability to touch one's ear to the ability to draw designs from memory and define abstract concepts.

Binet also developed the concept of **mental age (MA)**, an individual's level of mental development relative to others. Not much later, in 1912, William Stern created the concept of **intelligence quotient (IQ)**, a person's mental age divided by chronological age (CA), multiplied by 100. That is: $IQ = MA/CA \times 100$.

The Binet test has been revised many times to incorporate advances in the understanding of intelligence and intelligence tests. These revisions are called the Stanford-Binet tests (Stanford University is where the revisions have been done). In 2004, the test—now called the Stanford-Binet Intelligence Scales, Fifth Edition (SB-5)—was revised to analyze an individual's response in five content areas: fluid reasoning, knowledge, quantitative reasoning, visual-spatial reasoning, and working memory. A general composite score also is still obtained.

By administering the test to large numbers of people of different ages (from preschool through late adulthood) from different backgrounds, researchers have found that scores on the Stanford-Binet approximate a normal distribution. A **normal distribution** is symmetrical, with a majority of the scores falling in the middle of the possible range of scores and few scores appearing toward the extremes of the range (see Figure 9.6).

Figure 9.6

The Normal Curve and Stanford-Binet IQ Scores

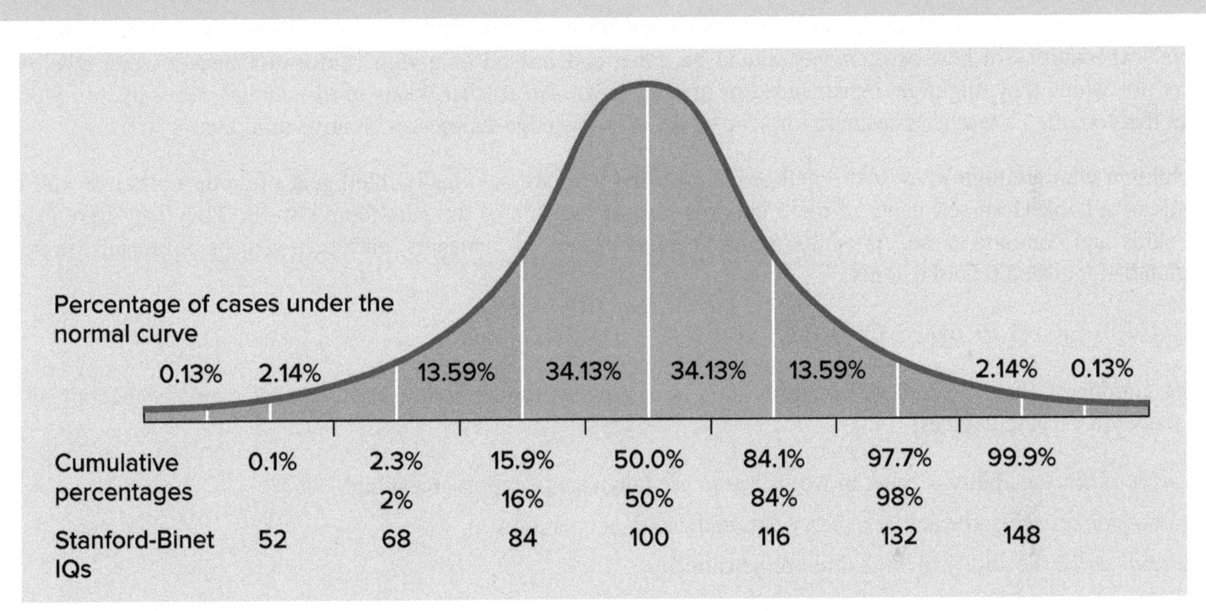

The distribution of IQ scores approximates a normal curve. Most scores fall in the middle range. Extremely high and extremely low scores are very rare. Slightly more than two-thirds of the scores fall between 84 and 115. Only about 1 in 50 individuals has an IQ of more than 130, and only about 1 in 50 individuals has an IQ of less than 70.

The Wechsler Scales

Another set of widely-used tests to assess intelligence is the Wechsler scales developed by David Wechsler, who defined intelligence as "the global capacity of the individual to act purposefully, think rationally, and deal effectively with his environment." (Solovey & Mayer, 1990). The tests include the Wechsler Preschool and Primary Scale of Intelligence—Fourth Edition (WPPSI-IV) to test children from 2.5 years to 7.25 years of age; the Wechsler Intelligence Scale for Children—Fifth Edition (WISC-V) for children and adolescents 6 to 16 years of age; and the Wechsler Adult Intelligence Scale—Fourth Edition (WAIS-IV).

The Wechsler scales provide an overall IQ as well as verbal and performance IQs. Verbal IQ is based on six verbal subscales, ranging from vocabulary to comprehension, word reasoning, general knowledge or information, and word similarities. Performance IQ is based on five performance subscales including block design, picture coding, object assembly, picture arrangement, and picture completion; this allows the examiner to see patterns of strengths and weaknesses in different areas of intelligence.

Types of Intelligence

Is intelligence a general ability or a number of specific abilities? Sternberg and Gardner, and Mayer, Salovey, and Caruso, have proposed influential theories oriented toward answering this question.

STERNBERG'S TRIARCHIC THEORY

Robert J. Sternberg (1986, 2004, 2010b, 2011, 2013, 2014a,b, c) developed the **triarchic theory of intelligence**, which states that intelligence comes in three forms: (1) analytical intelligence—the ability to analyze, judge, evaluate, compare, and contrast; (2) creative intelligence—the ability to create, design, invent, originate, and imagine; and (3) practical intelligence—the ability to use, apply, implement, and put ideas into practice.

Sternberg (2013, 2014a, b) says that children with different triarchic patterns perform differently in school. Students with high analytic ability tend to be favoured in conventional schooling. They often do well under direct instruction, in which the teacher lectures and gives objective tests. They often are considered "smart" students who get good grades, show up on high-level tracks, do well on traditional tests of intelligence, and get admitted into competitive programs in colleges and universities.

In contrast, children who are high in creative intelligence often are not "top students." They may not conform to their teachers' expectations of how assignments should be done, and instead of giving conformist answers, they give unique answers, for which they might get reprimanded or marked down. No teacher wants to discourage creativity, but Sternberg stresses that too often a teacher's desire to improve students' knowledge suppresses creative thinking.

Like children who are high in creative intelligence, children who are practically intelligent often do not relate well to the demands of school. However, many of these children do well outside of the classroom's walls. They may have excellent social skills and common sense. As adults, some become successful managers, entrepreneurs, or politicians, in spite of having undistinguished school records.

GARDNER'S EIGHT FRAMES OF MIND

Howard Gardner (1983, 1993, 2002) believes there are eight types of intelligence and that everyone has all of these intelligences to varying degrees:

- *Verbal skills*: the ability to think in words and to use language to express meaning
- *Mathematical skills*: the ability to carry out mathematical operations
- *Spatial skills*: the ability to think three-dimensionally
- *Bodily-kinesthetic skills*: the ability to manipulate objects and be physically skilled
- *Musical skills*: sensitivity to pitch, melody, rhythm, and tone
- *Interpersonal skills*: the ability to understand and effectively interact with others
- *Intrapersonal skills*: the ability to understand oneself and effectively direct one's life
- *Naturalist skills*: the ability to observe patterns in nature and understand natural and human-made systems

We all prefer to learn and process information in different ways. People learn best when they can do so in a way that uses their stronger intelligences.

Courtesy of Dr. Howard Gardner and Jay Gardner

Howard Gardner, shown here working with a young child, developed the view that intelligence comes in the forms of these eight kinds of skills: verbal, mathematical, spatial, bodily-kinesthetic, musical, intrapersonal, interpersonal, and naturalist.

MAYER-SALOVEY-CARUSO EMOTIONAL INTELLIGENCE (EI)

Professors John D. Mayer, Peter Salovey, and David R. Caruso propose that emotional intelligence represents an ability to validly reason with emotions and to use emotions to enhance thought. EI includes the abilities to (1) accurately perceive emotions; (2) reason with emotions, that is to access and generate emotions in order to assist thought—to ask "what if?"; (3) to understand emotions and emotional knowledge; and (4) to reflectively regulate and manage emotions to promote emotional and intellectual growth (Cherry, 2012; Mayer, 2004).

Because emotions are one of the primary forms of information that we process, EI is important. People who score high on emotional intelligence tests find establishing relationships and avoiding conflict relatively easy. Emotionally intelligent people are more likely to have positive interactions with others, enjoy strong social support, and be particularly good at understanding the ingredients of psychologically healthy living (Mayer, 2004).

EVALUATING THE MULTIPLE INTELLIGENCE APPROACHES

The Sternberg, Gardner, and Mayer-Salovey-Caruso approaches have much to offer. They have stimulated educators to think more broadly about what makes up children's competencies and to develop programs that instruct students in multiple domains. In addition, they have contributed to interest in assessing intelligence and learning in innovative ways, such as by evaluating student portfolios (Moran & Gardner, 2006, 2007). One innovative program in Canada is Learning Through the Arts™ (LTTA). In this program, artists work with students and teachers receive training in arts education. In a sequential study (see Chapter 2), Queen's University researchers found that grade 6 students with three years of LTTA participation did better in mathematics than their peers in other schools (Upitis et al., 2003). The children also showed more positive attitudes toward their schools. Because students in schools with or without LTTA started out with similar academic performance and attitudes, the improvements might have come from the greater commitment, motivation, and discipline that arts fostered in LTTA schools.

Still, doubts about multiple-intelligence approaches persist. A number of psychologists think that the multiple-intelligence approaches have taken the concept of specific intelligences too far (Reeve & Charles, 2008). Some argue that a research base to support the three intelligences of Sternberg, the eight intelligences of Gardner, or the emotional intelligence proposed by Mayer, Salovey, and Caruso has not yet emerged. One expert on intelligence, Nathan Brody (2007), observes that people who excel at one type of intellectual task are likely to excel in others. Thus, individuals who do well at memorizing lists of digits are also likely to be good at solving verbal problems and spatial layout problems. If musical skill reflects a distinct type of intelligence, ask other critics, why not label the skills of outstanding chess players, prizefighters, painters, and poets as types of intelligence?

The argument between those who support the concept of general intelligence and those who advocate the multiple-intelligence view is ongoing (Gardner, 2014; Irwing et al., 2012; Traskowski et al., 2013). Sternberg (2013, 2014a,b) actually accepts that there is a general intelligence for the kinds of analytical tasks that traditional IQ tests assess, but thinks that the range of tasks those tests measure is far too narrow.

INTERPRETING DIFFERENCES IN IQ SCORES

The IQ scores that result from tests such as the Stanford-Binet and Wechsler scales provide information about children's mental abilities. However, interpreting what performance on an intelligence test means is a subject of debate among researchers.

Music and Intelligence

Can music affect intelligence? Research on this question has followed two lines of approach, one dealing with the impact of taking music lessons and the other focusing on the effects of listening to music (Schellenberg, 2004).

In one study on the former, Glenn Schellenberg of the University of Toronto randomly assigned 6-year-olds to either voice lessons, music keyboard lessons, drama lessons, or no lessons—the last two groups being the control groups—for 36 weeks. The IQs for children in all four groups rose at the end of the study, but the changes were slightly higher in the music groups than in the control groups in almost every subtest of the Wechsler scale used, suggesting improvement in general intelligence due to music training. In a subsequent study, Schellenberg (2006) found that a rise of two IQ points for school-age children was related to one year of music training, but for university students the same two-point increase was associated with six years of playing music regularly in their younger years.

How can the causal link between taking music lessons and improved IQ performance be explained? One possibility is the similarity between skills developed in learning music and skills promoting cognitive development such as memorization of long pieces, persistent practice, and understanding visual symbols (Schellenberg, 2006).

Another approach to examining music and intelligence is to see if listening to music changes people's performance in cognitive tasks. This approach tackles the so-called Mozart effect—a short-term improvement on performance of spatial tasks after listening to Mozart's music (Jones, West, & Estell, 2006; Schellenberg, 2006). Research suggests that the ability to complete spatial tasks (such as imagining what a piece of paper would look like after cutting and folding) is probably not enhanced by the characteristics of Mozart's music per se; instead, any improvement is likely a result of arousal or a happy mood in an individual because of exposure to a favourite audio stimulus (Jones et al., 2006; Schellenberg, 2006), whether it be Mozart or Lady Gaga.

The short-term effects of music instruction on cognitive abilities is consistent among researchers; the long-term cognitive benefits of music instruction are associated with the importance of practice (Costa-Glomi, 2015).

The Influence of Genetics

How strong is the effect of genetics on intelligence? This question is difficult to answer because (as we discussed in Chapter 2) making clear-cut distinctions between the influences of heredity and environment is virtually impossible. Also, most research on heredity and environment does not include environments that differ radically. Thus, it is not surprising that many genetic studies show environment to be a fairly weak influence on intelligence.

Have scientists been able to pinpoint specific genes that are linked to intelligence? A recent research review concluded that there may be more than 1000 genes that affect intelligence, each possibly having a small influence on an individual's intelligence (Davies et al., 2011). However, researchers have not been able to identify the specific genes that contribute to intelligence (Deary, 2012; Zhao, Kong, & Qu, 2014).

Why? A number of environmental factors may be at play. First, healthier diets may have improved children's attention and intellectual functioning. Improvements in prenatal environments resulting from the reduction or abstinence from tobacco and alcohol during pregnancy may be another contributing factor, along with improved parenting skills and access to information through social media and the Internet (Trahan et al., 2014). Growing exposure to computers and the like may also have stimulated children's cognitive skills. Also, smaller family sizes, coupled with higher parental income, likely provides children with more resources in learning. Moreover, longer schooling in later generations may also have enhanced children's intellectual skills.

Speculation about our heritability has also emerged; however, the heritability index has several flaws. It is only as good as the data entered into its analysis and the interpretation made from them (Trahan et al., 2014; Sternberg, Kaufman, & Grigorenko, 2008). The data are virtually all from traditional IQ tests, which some experts think are not always the best indicator of intelligence (Sternberg, 2008a, b). Also, the heritability index assumes that we can treat genetic and environmental influences as factors that can be separated, with each part contributing a distinct amount of influence. As we discussed in Chapter 2, genes always exist in an environment and the environment shapes their activity.

Today, most researchers agree that genetics and environment interact to influence intelligence. For most people, this means that modifications in environment can change their IQ scores considerably, as illustrated in Schellenberg's research about music and intelligence. Although genetic endowment may always influence a person's intellectual ability, the environmental influences and opportunities we provide children and adults do make a difference (Campbell, 2007; Sternberg, 2009a, c).

Environmental Influences

The *nature vs. nurture* debate is nowhere more evident than in discussions about intelligence. For example, one of the first very heated arguments a young couple may have upon learning that their newborn child is learning delayed may be about whose family had the genetic liability. Susan Cain (2012) suggests that rather than asking which part is nature, which is nurture, and which is free will, we might ask how these factors are intertwined. Schooling clearly influences intelligence (Gustafsson, 2007). The biggest effects have been found when large groups of children have been deprived of formal education for an extended period, resulting in lower intelligence (Ceci & Gilstrap, 2000).

Another possible effect of education can be seen in rapidly increasing IQ test scores around the world (Flynn, 1999, 2007, 2011, 2013). IQ scores have been increasing so fast that a high percentage of people regarded as having average intelligence at the turn of the century would now be considered below average in intelligence. If a representative sample of people today took the Stanford-Binet test version used in 1932, about 25 percent would be defined as having very superior intelligence, a label usually accorded to fewer than 3 percent of the population. Because the increase has taken place in a relatively short time, it can't be due to heredity. Rather, it may be due to increasing levels of education attained by a much greater percentage of the world's population, or to other environmental factors such as the explosion of information, including information about nutrition, to which people are exposed.

The worldwide increase in intelligence test scores that has occurred over a short time frame has been called the *Flynn effect* after the researcher who discovered it, James Flynn. The Flynn effect begs the question: Are we getting smarter or just thinking differently? (Flynn, 2013). To hear more about the Flynn effect, tune into Flynn's talk at TED.com: https://www.ted.com/talks/james_flynn_why_our_iq_levels_are_higher_than_our_grandparents.

CONNECTING development to life

The "Flynn Effect": Are We Smarter than Our Grandparents?

If intelligence or IQ scores are determined by both nature and nurture, do the variations in the environment, such as improvements in nutrition and increases in family income, change the IQ across generations? The answer is a clear yes. The "Flynn effect" refers to the observed rise of intelligence over time as measured by standardized test scores. Dr. James Flynn, political scientist, researcher, and philosopher from New Zealand, conducted a landmark study which revealed a rise in intelligence of 2.80 points per decade (Trahan et al., 2014).

Researchers are increasingly concerned about improving the early environment of children who are at risk for impoverished intelligence (Love et al., 2013; Maholmes, 2014). For various reasons, many low-income parents have difficulty providing an intellectually stimulating environment for their children. Programs that educate parents to be more sensitive caregivers and better teachers, as well as support services such as quality child care programs, can make a difference in a child's intellectual development (Bredekamp, 2014; Follari, 2015; Morrison, 2015). Thus, the efforts to counteract a deprived early environment's effect on intelligence emphasize prevention rather than remediation.

A review of the research on early interventions concluded that (1) high-quality child care centre–based interventions are associated with increases in children's intelligence and school achievement; (2) the interventions are most successful with poor children and children whose parents have little education; (3) the positive benefits continue through adolescence, but are not as strong as in early childhood or the beginning of elementary school; and (4) the programs that continue into middle and late childhood have the best long-term results (Brooks-Gunn, 2003).

In sum, there is a consensus among psychologists that both heredity and environment influence intelligence (Grigorenko & Takanishi, 2012). This consensus reflects the nature-nurture issue that was highlighted in Chapter 1. Recall that the nature–nurture issue focuses on the extent to which development is influenced by nature (heredity) and nurture (environment). Although psychologists agree that intelligence is the product of both nature and nurture, there is still disagreement about how strongly each influences intelligence.

CULTURE AND INTELLIGENCE

Differences in conceptions of intelligence occur not only among psychologists, but also among cultures (Zhang & Sternberg, 2011). What is viewed as intelligent in one culture may not be thought of as intelligent in another. For example, people in Western cultures tend to view intelligence in terms of reasoning and thinking skills, whereas people in Eastern cultures see intelligence as a way for members of a community to engage successfully in social roles (Nisbett, 2003).

CREATING CULTURE-FAIR TESTS

Culture-fair tests are tests of intelligence that are intended to be free of cultural bias. Two types of culture-fair tests have been devised. The first includes items that are familiar to children from all socio-economic and ethnic backgrounds, or items that at least are familiar to the children taking the test. For example, a child might be asked how a bird and a dog are different, on the assumption that all children have been exposed to birds and dogs.

The second type of culture-fair test has no verbal questions. The test-taker may need to identify and replace the missing piece in a pattern, for example. Even though non-verbal tests are designed to be culture-fair, people with more education still score higher on them than do those with less education.

Why is it so hard to create culture-fair tests? Most tests tend to reflect what the dominant culture thinks is important. The language and context used favour one group over another. If tests have time limits, that will bias the test against groups not concerned with time. If languages differ, the same words might have different meanings for different language groups. Even pictures can produce bias because some cultures have less experience with drawings and photographs. Because of such difficulties in creating culture-fair tests, Robert Sternberg concludes that there are no culture-fair tests, only culture-reduced tests.

Within the same culture, different subgroups could have different attitudes, values, and motivation, and this could affect their performance on intelligence tests. For example, a study indicated that Aboriginal children in New Brunswick had lower performance in science, reading, and writing tests than other children in grade 6 (Ma & Klinger, 2000). The researchers speculated that Native students' weaker performance was due to their lack of assimilation into the mainstream culture. Given the ethnic diversity, educational levels, and standards of living within a country, heredity-based arguments cannot explain this difference in intelligence. This emphasis on environmental influence is consistent with other research findings.

THE USE AND MISUSE OF INTELLIGENCE TESTS

Like any psychological test, intelligence tests are tools, and their effectiveness depends on the knowledge, skill, and integrity of the user. The following are some cautions on the use of information from IQ tests.

- *Avoid stereotyping and expectations.* A special concern is that the scores on an IQ test easily can lead to stereotypes and expectations. Sweeping generalizations are too often made on the basis of an IQ score. An IQ test should always be considered a measure of current performance. It is not a measure of fixed potential. Maturational changes and enriched environmental experiences can advance a student's intelligence.

- *Know that IQ is not a sole indicator of competence.* Another concern about IQ tests occurs when they are used as the main or sole assessment of competence. A high IQ is not the ultimate human value. As we have seen in this chapter, an individual's creative and practical skills are important, yet not measured, areas of competence.
- *Use caution in interpreting an overall IQ score.* Intelligence consists of a number of domains such as those described by Sternberg, Gardner, and Mayer, Salovey, and Caruso. By considering the different domains of intelligence, it is clear that every child has at least one area of strength.

The Extremes of Intelligence

Intelligence tests have been used to discover indications of intellectual disability or intellectual giftedness, the extremes of intelligence. At times, intelligence tests have been misused for this purpose. Keeping in mind the idea that an intelligence test should not be used as the sole indicator of intellectual disability or giftedness, we will explore the nature of these intellectual extremes.

INTELLECTUAL DISABILITY

The most distinctive feature of intellectual disability (formerly called mental retardation) is inadequate intellectual functioning. Long before formal tests were developed to assess intelligence, individuals with an intellectual disability were identified by a lack of age-appropriate skills in learning and caring for themselves. Once intelligence tests were developed, they were used to identify the degree of intellectual disability. But of two individuals with an intellectual disability who have the same low IQ, one might be married, employed, and involved in the community and the other might require constant supervision in an institution. Such differences in social competence led psychologists to include deficits in adaptive behaviour in their definition of intellectual disability.

Intellectual disability is a condition of limited mental ability in which an individual (1) has a low IQ, usually below 70 on a traditional intelligence test; (2) has difficulty adapting to everyday life; and (3) first exhibits these characteristics by age 18 (Hodapp et al., 2011). The age limit is included in the definition of intellectual disability because, for example, we don't usually think of a college student who suffers massive brain damage in a car accident, resulting in an IQ of 60, as having an intellectual disability. The low IQ and low adaptiveness should be evident in childhood, not after normal functioning is interrupted by damage of some form. According to Statistics Canada (2015), 1–3 percent of Canadians have an intellectual disability ranging from mild, to moderate, to severe.

About 90 percent of people diagnosed with developmental delay fall into the mild category, with IQs of 55 to 70. About 6 percent are classified as moderately disabled, with IQs of 40 to 54. People in this category can attain skills at a grade 2 level and may be able to support themselves as adults through some types of labour. About 3.5 percent are in the severe category, with IQs of 25 to 39; these individuals learn to talk and engage in very simple tasks, but require extensive supervision. Fewer than 1 percent have IQs below 25; they are profoundly disabled and need constant supervision. More boys than girls are reported to have either intellectual or developmental delay conditions; of those, over 60 percent have more than one disability and 10 percent have six or more disabilities (Statistics Canada, 2015).

Some cases of intellectual disability have an organic cause. **Organic intellectual disability** describes a genetic disorder or a lower level of intellectual functioning caused by brain damage. Down syndrome, which accounts for 700 to 900 births annually, is one form of organic intellectual disability. It occurs when an extra chromosome is present (Government of Canada, 2015). Other causes of organic intellectual disability include Fragile X syndrome (an abnormality in the X chromosome that was discussed in Chapter 2, "Biological Beginnings"); prenatal malformation; metabolic disorders; and diseases that affect the brain. Most people who suffer from organic intellectual disability have IQs between 0 and 50.

When no evidence of organic brain damage can be found, cases are labelled **cultural-familial intellectual disability**. Individuals with this type of disability have IQs between 55 and 70. Psychologists suspect that this type of disability often results from growing up in a below-average intellectual environment. Children with this type of disability can be identified in schools, where they often fail, need tangible rewards (candy rather than praise), and are highly sensitive to what others expect of them. However, as adults, they are usually not noticeable, possibly because they increase their intelligence as they move toward adulthood.

A child with Down syndrome. *What causes a child to develop Down syndrome? In which major classification of intellectual disability does the condition fall?*

critical thinking

Patrick Lenon of L'Arche Lethbridge, Alberta, spoke at the Second Annual International Conference on Intellectual Disabilities/Mental Retardation in Bangkok, Thailand (2007), and made two prominent points: (1) disability is a way of life, not a medical condition, and all of us at times in our lives have special needs; and (2) we need to move from seeing that we are service providers to recognizing that persons with an intellectual disability have gifts that the world needs—gifts of the heart that draw us into vulnerability and relationships. Would you agree with Mr. Lenon that disability is a way of life? If so, why; if not, why not? What are some of the special needs all of us may have at times in our lives? What "gifts of the heart" might persons with intellectual disabilities give us?

GIFTEDNESS

There have always been people whose abilities and accomplishments outshine those of others—the whiz kid in class, the star athlete, the natural musician. People who are **gifted** have above-average intelligence (an IQ of 130 or higher) and/or superior talent for something. When it comes to programs for the gifted, most school systems select children who have intellectual superiority and academic aptitude, whereas children who are talented in the visual and performing arts (art, drama, dance), who demonstrate skill in athletics, or who have other special aptitudes tend to be overlooked (Olszewski-Kubilius & Thomson, 2013). Gifted children are identified as children who, according to tests, have a mental age considerably higher than their chronological age.

Dr. Joan Freeman, founding president of the European Council for High Ability, has studied gifted and non-gifted children, noting their similarities and differences. She conducted the only longitudinal study of 20 people who were identified as gifted, tracking their lives over a period of 35 years. Dr. Freeman identified four characteristics of gifted children: a lively mind, a keen sense of awareness, the ability to learn, and independence. However, Dr. Freeman also points out that, "Success in school did not predict success outside of it." Most of the world's highest achievers, she points out, were never identified as gifted children. A gifted child is just one who has advanced beyond his or her peers; it takes drive, application, perseverance, and insight to turn that potential into exceptional adult success (Freeman, 2009). Despite speculation that giftedness is linked with having a mental disorder, no relation has been found. Studies support the conclusion that gifted people tend to be more mature than others, have fewer emotional problems than others, and grow up in a positive family climate (Davidson, 2000).

critical thinking

Internationally recognized educator Sir Ken Robinson argues that schools can do more to foster creativity if they transform the curriculum dramatically by eliminating the existing hierarchy of subjects. By that, Robinson argues that all fields of study be given equal importance; that is, the arts—for example, dance—should be given as much academic weight as the sciences—for example, physics. Each has an equal and central contribution to make to enabling students with diverse talents. Further, he argues that all subjects have much in common, so dividing learning into subjects undermines their fluid and dynamic interdisciplinary nature. Robinson also makes the point that learning is a personal process that happens in the minds and hearts of individuals, not in results on standardized or multiple-choice tests (Robinson, 2009). What do you think of Robinson's ideas? What changes would you recommend for the education system, if any, and why? If none, why not? What worked for you in school, and why? What did you learn outside the classroom, and how has this learning shaped your life?

DOMAIN-SPECIFIC GIFTEDNESS AND DEVELOPMENT

As you have read, various researchers have proposed that there are many types of intelligence. This being the case, it follows logically that there would be many types of giftedness and that being gifted would pose challenges as well as opportunities. Individuals who are highly gifted are typically not gifted in many domains, and research on giftedness is increasingly focused on domain-specific developmental trajectories (Kell & Lubinski, 2014; Sternberg & Bridges, 2014; Thagard, 2014; Winner, 2009, 2014). During the childhood years, the domain(s) in which individuals are gifted usually emerges. Thus, at some point in the childhood years the child who is to become a gifted artist or the child who is to become a gifted mathematician begins to show expertise in that domain. Regarding domain-specific giftedness, software genius Bill Gates (1998), the founder of Microsoft and one of the world's richest persons, commented that sometimes you have to be careful when you are good at something and resist the urge to think that you will be good at everything. Gates says that because he has been so successful at software development, people expect him to be brilliant about other domains in which he is far from being a genius.

Identifying an individual's domain-specific talent and providing individually appropriate and optional educational opportunities need to be accomplished at the very latest by adolescence (Keating, 2009). During adolescence, individuals who are talented become less reliant on parental support and increasingly pursue their own interests.

An increasing number of experts argue that the education of children who are gifted requires a significant overhaul (Ambrose, Sternberg, & Sriraman, 2012; Reis & Renzulli, 2014). Ellen Winner (1996, 2006) argues that too often children who are gifted are socially isolated, called "nerds" or "geeks" by their classmates, and under-challenged in the classroom. In fact, according to educationalist Sir Ken Robinson (2009) and Dr. Freeman (2009), the school system, an industrial-age concept, cannot possibly address the needs of every child and often is unable to nurture the creative minds of students. Some especially precocious middle school students may benefit from taking university or college classes in their area of expertise. For example, Bill Gates took college math classes at age 13, and Yo-Yo Ma, a famous cellist, graduated from high school at age 15 and attended Julliard School of Music in New York City.

© Koichi Kamoshida/Newsmakers/Getty Images

At 2 years of age, art prodigy Alexandra Nechita coloured in colouring books for hours and also took up pen and ink. She had no interest in dolls or friends. By age 5 she was using watercolours. Once she started school, she would start painting as soon as she got home. At the age of 8, in 1994, she saw the first public exhibit of her work. In succeeding years, working quickly and impulsively on canvases as large as 5 feet by 9 feet, she has completed hundreds of paintings, some of which sell for close to $100 000 apiece. She continues to paint relentlessly and passionately. It is, she says, what she loves to do. *What are some characteristics of children who are gifted?*

Luc Novovitch / Alamy Stock Photo

A young Bill Gates, founder of Microsoft and box centernow one of the world's richest people. Like many highly gifted students, Gates was not especially fond of school. He hacked a computer security system when he was 13, and as a high school student he was allowed to take some college math classes. He dropped out of Harvard University and began developing a plan for what was to become Microsoft Corporation. *What are some ways that schools can enrich the education of such highly-talented students as Gates to make it a more challenging, interesting, and meaningful experience?*

To this point, we have examined a number of ideas about cognitive development in middle and late childhood. For a review, see the Reach Your Learning Outcomes section at the end of this chapter.

Language Development

LO3 Discuss language development in middle and late childhood.

- **Vocabulary, Grammar, and Metalinguistic Awareness**
- **Reading**
- **Writing**
- **Bilingualism**

Language skills continue to develop during middle and late childhood, so that by the time children enter elementary school, learning to read and write is possible. They are able to use language about things that are not physically present, learn what a word is, and know how to recognize and talk about sounds. They also learn the *alphabetic principle*, that the letters of the alphabet represent sounds of the language. Here we examine the changes in vocabulary, grammar, and reading, as well as the issue of bilingualism.

Vocabulary, Grammar, and Metalinguistic Awareness

During middle and late childhood, a change occurs in the way children think about words. When asked to say the first word that comes to mind when they hear a word, young children typically provide one that often follows the word in a sentence. For example, when asked to respond to "dog," the young child may say "barks." At about 7 years of age, children begin to respond with a word that is the same part of speech as the stimulus word. For example, a child may now respond to the word "dog" with "cat" or "horse." This is evidence that children now have begun to categorize their vocabulary by parts of speech. The process of categorizing becomes easier as children increase their vocabulary (Clark, 2012). Children's vocabulary increases from an average of about 14 000 words at age 6 to an average of about 40 000 words by age 11.

Children make similar advances in grammar (Behrens, 2012). During the elementary school years, children's improvement in logical reasoning and analytical skills helps them to understand such constructions as the appropriate use of comparatives (*shorter, deeper*) and subjectives ("If you were Prime Minister..."). As well, children become increasingly able to understand and use complex grammar, such in "The boy who kissed his mother wore a hat." They also learn to use language in a more connected way, producing connected discourse. They become able to relate sentences to one another to produce descriptions, definitions, and narratives that make sense. Children must be able to do these things orally before they can be expected to deal with them in written assignments.

These advances in vocabulary and grammar during the elementary school years are accompanied by the development of **metalinguistic awareness**, which is knowledge about language, such as knowing what a preposition is or the ability to discuss the sounds of a language (Tong, Deacon, & Cain, 2014). This understanding improves considerably between grades 1 and 6 (Pan & Uccelli, 2009). Defining words becomes a regular part of classroom discourse, and children increase their knowledge of syntax as they study and talk about the components of sentences such as subjects and verbs (Crain, 2012).

Children also make progress in understanding how to use language in culturally appropriate ways, called *pragmatics* (Bryant, 2012). By the time they enter adolescence, most children know the rules for the use of language in everyday contexts—that is, what is appropriate and inappropriate to say.

Reading

Before learning to read, children learn to use language to talk about things that are not present; they learn what a word is, and they learn how to recognize sounds and talk about them. Children who begin elementary school with a robust vocabulary have an advantage when it comes to learning.

How should children be taught to read? Debate currently focuses on the whole-language approach versus the basic skills and phonics approach.

The **whole-language approach** stresses that reading instruction should parallel children's natural language learning. In some whole-language classes, beginning readers are taught to recognize whole words or even entire sentences, and to use the context of what they are reading to guess at the meaning of words. Reading materials that support the whole-language approach are whole and meaningful; that is, children are given material in its complete form, such as stories and poems. In this way, say whole-language advocates, children learn to understand language's communicative function. Reading is connected to writing skills. Although there are variations in whole-language programs, most share the premise that reading should be integrated with other skills and subjects, such as science and social studies, and that it should focus on real-world material. Thus, a class might read newspapers, magazines, or books, and then write about and discuss them.

By contrast, the **basic-skills-and-phonetics approach** emphasizes that reading instruction should teach phonetics and its basic rules for translating written symbols into sounds. Early phonics-centred reading instruction should involve simplified materials. Only after children have learned correspondence rules that relate spoken phonemes to the letters of the alphabet that represent them should children be given complex reading materials, such as books and poems. Advocates of this approach often point to low reading achievement scores occurring as an outgrowth of the recent emphasis on holistic, literature-based instruction and the consequent lack of attention to basic skills and phonetics (Cunningham & Hall 2009; Mayer, 2008).

Which approach is better? Research suggests that children can benefit from both approaches, but instruction in phonics needs to be emphasized (Tompkins, 2013). An increasing number of experts in the field of reading now conclude that direct instruction in phonics is a key aspect of learning to read (Cunningham, 2013; Fox, 2014).

© Richard Howard Photography

Children's reading is a complex process. *What kinds of information-processing skills are involved?*

Writing

As they begin to write, children often invent spellings. Corrections of spelling and printing made in positive ways are more effective than criticisms and do not discourage the child's writing and spontaneity.

Like becoming a good reader, becoming a good writer takes time and practice (Tompkins, 2015). As children's language and cognitive skills improve, so will their writing skills. For example, developing a more sophisticated understanding of syntax and grammar serves as an underpinning for better writing. So do such cognitive skills as organization and logical reasoning. Through the course of the school years, students develop increasingly sophisticated methods of organizing their ideas.

The metacognitive strategies needed to be a competent writer are linked with those required to be a competent reader because the writing process involves competent reading and rereading during composition and revision (McCormick, Dimmitt, & Sullivan, 2013). Further, researchers have found that strategy instruction involving planning, drafting, revising, and editing improves older elementary school children's metacognitive awareness and writing competence (Harris et al., 2009).

Bilingualism

Canada has been officially bilingual since the *Constitution Act* in 1867; however, French immersion programs in schools were first introduced in St. Lambert, outside Montreal, in 1965, and since then have become increasingly popular throughout Canada (Genesee & Jared, 2008; Statistics Canada, 2008). Language acquisition is the greatest predictor of a child's success in school and in later life (Canadian Paediatric Society, 2016).

A survey of research on French as a second language education in Canada suggests that French immersion students enjoy significant linguistic, academic, and cognitive benefits. As well, immersive instruction enables students to develop high levels of proficiency in both languages. Further, heightened mental flexibility, creative thinking skills, enhanced metalinguistic awareness, and greater communicative sensitivity are cognitive benefits of French immersion programs (Lazaruk, 2013). Children enrolled in bilingual programs are more likely to be bilingual as adults. According to Statistics Canada, 57 percent of all youth report being able to converse in French, and 70 percent report their French language skills as very good to excellent (Allen, 2013). Children in immersion programs also seem to have greater acceptance of people from other language backgrounds.

Parents who model their first language in the home provide the best models for their children because having a solid base in their first language enables learning a second language. In other words, parents from Poland or Nigeria who model Polish or Yoruba at home make it easier for their children to learn English. Learning a second language can happen at any age (Canadian Paediatric Society, 2016). When benchmarked against 16 other countries with similar approaches to education, Canada ranked second to Australia in the performance of immigrant children who did not speak the test language (either English or French) in their homes (Conference Board of Canada, 2016).

Can some of the bilingual children's advantages in non-linguistic tasks be attributed to the characteristics of either of the languages they know? For example, research has shown superior mathematical performances in Chinese-speaking children, including counting skills in preschoolers, compared to English-speaking American children, prompting some to wonder if the numbering structure in Chinese helped these children. A team from the University of Alberta studied this matter and found that Chinese–English bilingual preschoolers counted better in their dominant language, whether it was English or Chinese. Therefore, it is the everyday practice of the language users, not the peculiarities of a language, that affects children's counting. At the same time, because a language encompasses many different characteristics, research is needed to test if any of these characteristics helps the speaker in specific cognitive tasks (Rasmussen et al., 2006).

Second language acquisition can be exciting—and useful.

To this point, we have discussed a number of ideas about language development in middle and late childhood. For a review, see the Reach Your Learning Outcomes section at the end of this chapter.

Educational Approaches and Issues

LO4 Discuss approaches and issues related to education.

- **Approaches to Student Learning**
- **Educational Issues**
- **Private Schools and Home Education**

Approaches to Student Learning

The Conference Board of Canada (2016) reports that although not perfect, Canada earns an A in delivering high-quality education with comparative modest spending for students between ages 5 and 19 years. Of the 16 countries ranked, Finland ranked first, Canada second, Japan third, and Australia fourth.

Certainly school exerts more influence on children than the transfer of knowledge. Controversy swirls about the best way to teach children and how to hold schools and teachers accountable (Johnson et al., 2011; Parkay & Stanford, 2010). Two prominent approaches, the constructivist approach and the direct instruction approach, are at the centre of this controversy.

The **constructivist approach** is a learner-centred approach that emphasizes the importance of individuals actively constructing their knowledge and understanding. This view, introduced by Piaget, fosters opportunities for children to explore, discover, collaborate, reflect, and think critically about the world around them (HLWIKI International, 2014). The intention of the constructivist approach is to enable children to grasp deeper meaning of ideas with an open mind to different approaches and perspectives. In this type of classroom, desks are often arranged in a circle so that students can see each other when they share ideas and initiate activities. Shelly Wright's high school class in Moosejaw, Saskatchewan illustrates this approach. Under her guidance, students decided they wanted to help war-orphaned children in Uganda. After doing some research, they developed plans, set goals, and initiated fundraising activities. With the help of social media, students surpassed their goals; not only did they raise over $22 000 for aid, but they also launched a multi-media campaign against modern day slavery and created a Holocaust museum (Wright, 2013).

By contrast, the **direct instruction approach** is characterized by teacher direction and control, maximum time spent by students on academic tasks, and efforts by the teacher to keep negative affect to a minimum. An important goal in this approach is maximizing student learning time. In the traditional classroom where the directive approach dominates, desks may be set up in rows and the teacher sets the pace and explains the subject in ways that will capture student attention and motivate learning usually from the front of the classroom. Students may ask questions and seek guidance. Most university lecture halls illustrate this approach.

Which approach is better? Advocates of the constructivist approach argue that the direct instruction approach turns children into passive learners and does not adequately challenge them to think critically and creatively (Abruscato & DeRosa, 2010; Eby, Herrell, & Jordan, 2011). The direct instruction enthusiasts say that the constructivist approaches are too relativistic and vague, and do not give sufficient attention to disciplines such as history and science. Author Susan Cain (2012) argues that the focus on collaboration often disadvantages the introverted child who prefers to learn independently. She contends that one or two usually more extroverted children may dominate; consequently, the contributions of the shy or the introverted child may be overlooked (Cain, 2012).

Some experts in educational psychology believe that many effective teachers use both approaches, depending on the circumstances (Bransford et al., 2006). Some aspects of the curriculum may call more for a constructivist approach while others, such as teaching students who have a reading or writing disability, may lend themselves more to a direct instruction approach (Berninger, 2006).

critical thinking

Some of us are naturally more extraverted or introverted than others. Introverted children tend to become inspired when working independently; on the other hand, extraverted children excel when working in groups and often assume leadership roles in group activities. Because the introverted child is reluctant to speak up, his or her ideas often go unsaid, and when voiced, are often voiced quietly and therefore ignored. Whether using the constructivist approach or the direct instruction approach, how can teachers accommodate different learning styles of students? Would you define yourself as an introvert or an extravert? What behaviours lead you to define yourself? In what classroom situations are you most comfortable, and why?

Educational Issues

We have discussed some of the challenges facing educators in developing curriculum and classroom approaches that would improve critical thinking, creativity, as well as address the different learning styles and aptitudes of students. Social issues such as poverty, ethnicity, and international comparisons further complicate these critical issues.

CONNECTING through social policy

How Inclusive Is Canada's Education?

Inclusive education is an approach that strives to make public education accessible to all by removing barriers associated with economic status, gender, race, religion, or abilities. Canada has one of the world's most inclusive systems and is fully aligned with international legislation, such as the United Nations Declaration of the Rights of Persons with Disabilities, which protects the rights of children with disabilities to education (Bennett, 2012; Towle, 2015). Every child with special needs, whether emotional, behavioural, visual, intellectual, language, speech, sight, or hearing, has the right to free public education. Further, by law, all publicly-funded schools must have a special education program (Towle, 2015).

Canada's inclusive approach to education is ripe with debate as definitions, practices, and policies vary from jurisdiction to jurisdiction. This variance is illustrated by how children with "special needs" are defined, how educational access is implemented, and even how "inclusion" is defined. For example, can the words "disability," "special needs," "exceptionality," "intensive needs," and "giftedness" be used interchangeably?

An increasing number of children are being diagnosed with various behavioural challenges such as ADHD, autism spectrum disorder, or giftedness (Towle, 2015). How is "normal" defined, and is it changing?

Are separate schools for the deaf and blind an example of segregation or inclusion? How are additional costs of residence, counselling, and transportation absorbed by families who are already financially burdened?

As each jurisdiction strives to provide inclusive education, children with "special needs," no matter how the needs are defined, are often separated in special classes rather than mainstreamed (Towle, 2015). **Mainstreaming** means educating a child with special education needs in a regular classroom. Advocates of mainstreaming argue that children with disabilities must be given opportunities to learn in a welcoming environment, one which will more likely foster a more dignified adult life. Studies also suggest that inclusive welcoming classrooms benefit all learners (Bennett, 2012; Towle, 2015).

Research indicates that adults with disabilities have lower levels of education, higher rates of unemployment, and lower economic status (Towle, 2015). These studies raise questions about how Canadian public education can help prevent children with disabilities and special needs from falling into these same pitfalls when they become adults.

A number of social policy questions are being raised and debated by educators and parents: (1) Do we need a federal policy to unify and guide provincial and territorial practices in order to ensure equality of access to education? (2) What are the advantages and disadvantages of mainstreaming children with disabilities? (3) Can we improve our educational approaches so today's students with disabilities will attain higher levels of education, employment, and income? And if so, how?

Poverty

Canada has no clear-cut definition of poverty; however, according to UNICEF's report card, Canada ranked 21 out of 29 rich countries in child poverty rates (Adamson, 2013). Further, the National Food Bank reports that although children and youth make up 21 percent of the population, they comprise 38 percent of those helped by food banks (Food Banks Canada, 2012). When a child pretends he or she has forgotten lunch, doesn't have shoes for gym, or can't go on school trips, poverty may be at the root. According to the Canadian Teachers' Federation (CTF) (2009), children with disabilities as well as children from families that are racialized, Aboriginal, or new to Canada are at a greater risk of living in poverty. Because parents are unable to pay the rent, children from poor families are more likely to move, changing schools frequently. Academic performance is diminished considerably as children are hungry, ashamed, and suffer from lowered self-esteem. Not only is academic performance adversely affected, so is student behaviour and school retention (CTF, 2009; Ferguson, 2009).

An overview of the homes in impoverished neighbourhoods reported that such neighbourhoods lacked positive activities for children, suffered from food insecurity, and provided predominantly low wage jobs. As a result, parents struggled to provide fundamental health supports, such as dental check-ups, eye exams, glasses, or appropriate sleeping arrangements. Additionally, in the environment of toxic stress that accompanies poverty-stricken households, children see what it looks and feels like to be parenting on low hope. Poverty limits the futures of children in many respects: diminishing health, education, and opportunities on the one hand, while on the other increasing the child's vulnerability to medical and health conditions (Ford-Jones, 2014; Adamson, 2013).

Many schools in rural areas, especially in First Nations communities, are in disrepair and lack educational facilities such as gyms and libraries. The dropout rate among First Nations youth is close to 60 percent (Mendleson, 2008). Frequently portables rather than proper buildings serve as schools. To quote the Hon. Jim Prentice, former Minister of Indian and Northern Affairs Canada, in his speech to the House of Commons upon introduction of the First Nations Jurisdiction Over Education in British Columbia Act: "First Nation children, frankly, have been the only children in Canada who have lacked an education system" (Mendelson, 2008).

John Woods/The Canadian Press

The local school in Pikangikum.

critical thinking

Recall that the microsystem in Bronfenbrenner's bio-ecological approach includes the neighbourhood in which we live. As you just read, Dr. Elizabeth Lee Ford-Jones' (2014) observations of impoverished neighbourhoods led her to conclude that growing up in such neighbourhoods leads to an increased risk of medical and health-related diseases that arise as a direct result of living conditions. How might Bronfenbrenner's bio-ecological approach help to explain this?

Ethnicity in Schools

Children from immigrant or Aboriginal backgrounds have the additional stress of trying to adjust to the mainstream culture and conflicting values, and learning either of Canada's official languages.

IMMIGRANT CHILDREN

Immigrant children face a multitude of challenges in addition to the obvious ones such as adjustment to Canadian climate, food, and social norms. Language poses a challenge that affects many dimensions of adjustment. Possibly neither the child nor the parents speak either one of Canada's two national languages, and health and ability issues may go undetected as the behaviour or the learning delay may be assumed to be related exclusively to language. Further, in addition to financial hardship, children may face discrimination, racism, and adverse peer relations such as bullying (Chang, 2010). Despite various challenges, children of recent immigrants fare better than children in general in psychological well-being and are less likely to experience situations that lead to poor school performance—hyperactivity, conduct disorder, emotional disorder, family dysfunction, and hostile parenting behaviour. Furthermore, even though immigrant children whose first language is not English or French have poorer mathematics, reading, and writing skills in the early elementary school years, their performance catches up with that of the rest of the class by age 10 or 11 (Statistics Canada, 2008). The reasons for these achievements range from cultural values for education to the motivating experience of having to start from zero in a new country.

ABORIGINAL CHILDREN

The chronological history of Canadian Residential Schools spans more than century. The *Civilization Act* of 1857 sought to assimilate Aboriginal peoples into Canadian culture. To accomplish this, children were removed from their home, forced into labour, and denied the right to speak their language or practise their religion. Many other abuses occurred, and gradually the schools were closed, the last one as late as 1996. However, according to Aboriginal Affairs and Northern Development Canada (2010), the consequences of this policy has had a damaging negative impact on Aboriginal culture, heritage, and language. In July 2008, then-Prime Minister Steven Harper made a formal apology on behalf of Canada to the students, their families, and communities (Truth and Reconciliation Commission of Canada, 2012). Approximately 80 000 former students are living today and are able to share their experiences (AANDC, 2010).

According to the Chiefs Assembly on Education (2012), First Nations youth are the fastest growing demographic, yet only 22 percent of these children have access to early childhood programs. Consequently, the implications are long-term; in fact, only 36 percent of First Nations youth finish high school, compared to 72 percent of non-Aboriginal children. Another contributing factor is the high rate of poverty. One in four children in First Nations' communities lives in poverty. The report also documented high rates of suicide and youth imprisonment for children as young as 8, 9, or 10 years of age. Further, the report notes that more young people end up in jail than graduate from high schools.

In response to the needs of Aboriginal children, some educators advocate the use of their native languages and Aboriginal teachers. The establishment of the Eva Bereti Cree Leadership Academy at Our Lady of Peace Elementary School in Edmonton illustrates this approach. Named after Elder Eva Bereti, who had to hide her language from teachers when she was young and who worked with the Edmonton Catholic School District for 22 years as a counsellor, coordinator, and classroom teacher for native studies and arts, the centre offers a Cree bilingual program from kindergarten to grade 2 (Gauri, 2007). As for preparing Aboriginal teachers, a number of training initiatives, such as Saskatchewan's Urban Native Teacher Education Program, have been established to enrich awareness of cultural differences.

Private Schools and Home Education

A large number of Canadian children are receiving private school education and home schooling. According to Statistics Canada (2001c), private school enrolment jumped by almost 24 percent throughout the 1990s. In contrast, the student population in public schools increased by 3.2 percent in the same period. Approximately 2 percent of children are home schooled (HSLDA, 2016) Home-schooling families share many characteristics with private-school families in that they are concerned about class sizes, differing values, and inadequate parental input. Additionally, some parents are disillusioned by the sometimes antagonistic relationships between school boards and teachers' unions.

Wilfred Laurier University's Bruce Arai (2000) has noted that family income and parental education vary greatly among home-schooling parents. These parents have to make sacrifices, such as giving up paid employment, finding appropriate instructional materials, and enduring the stigma of being antisocial (Brown, 2003). Still, many parents choose home schooling for their children because of religion, the need for a tailored curriculum for a gifted child, and fear of undesirable socialization in schools (Arai, 2000). Many home-schooling parents do not dislike public education; they just find home schooling more suited to their needs. Research in Canada and the United States justifies their efforts: Home-schooled children have higher-than-average performances (Basham, 2001).

Recognizing parents' sacrifice, some schools or organizations offer financial support to families with children in private schools. For example, Children First: School Choice Trust provides need-based bursaries to children in private elementary schools in Calgary and Ontario. Information about this organization can be found at http://www.childrenfirstgrants.ca.

critical thinking

Have you or someone you know experienced home schooling or private schooling? What are the advantages and disadvantages of each to a child's development? What approach to education would you choose for your own children? Why?

To this point, we have reviewed a number of ideas about educational approaches and issues in middle and late childhood. For a review, see the Reach Your Learning Outcomes section at the end of this chapter.

Children with Disabilities

LO5 Identify children with different types of disabilities and discuss issues relating to their education.

- **Learning Disabilities**
- **Attention Deficit Hyperactivity Disorder (ADHD)**
- **Autism Spectrum Disorders**
- **Physical Disabilities**
- **Children's Disabilities and the Family**
- **Educational Issues**

Children with disabilities, whether they be physical, cognitive, or emotional in nature, have difficulty functioning as the condition limits the amount and/or kind of activity they can perform. The condition, once diagnosed by a health professional, is expected to last at least six months, and may last a lifetime. Physical disabilities include difficulty with hearing, seeing, speaking, or being understood, walking and dexterity. Chronic conditions include asthma, heart conditions, cancer, epilepsy, spina bifida, and muscular dystrophy. Cognitive/emotional disabilities include attention problems, dyslexia, cognitive limitations due to disorders such as Down syndrome or autism, and emotional, psychological, or behavioural conditions. Learning disabilities and chronic health conditions are the two most frequently reported disabilities. Some sort of reported disability affects approximately 4 percent of children between the ages of 5 and 14 (Kohen et al., 2008). The presence of a child with a disability often impacts the employment and stress level of the parents. As well, peer relations, daily routines, and interaction in the community and school are also impacted; and the more severe the disability, the greater the impact (Government of Canada, 2012).

Learning Disabilities

The World Health Organization (WHO) defines learning disabilities as "a state of arrested or incomplete development of mind," and emphasizes that they are not diseases, nor are they mental or physical illnesses. They are lifelong and are characterized by difficulty with relatively specific skills such as language, attention, coordination, and self-control. Children with learning disabilities have average to above-average intelligence; in other words, they are not intellectually impaired (Fiedorowicz et al., 2015). Intellectual impairment is diagnosed when performance on intelligence tests by qualified professionals is a measured IQ of 70 or below (Fiedorowicz et al., 2015). The distinction is important in assessing the type of support and interventions that best suit the child. Children with a **learning disability** (1) are of normal intelligence or above, (2) have difficulties in at least one academic area and usually several, and (3) have a difficulty that is not attributable to any other diagnosed problem or disorder. The global concept of learning disabilities includes problems in listening, concentrating, speaking, and thinking. A comprehensive definition of learning disabilities is available on Connect at http://www.mcgrawhillconnect.ca.

According to Statistics Canada, more than half (59 percent) of the children with a disability have a learning disability. Most children with a learning disability have a reading problem (Kohen et al., 2008). **Dyslexia** is a category that is reserved for individuals who have a severe impairment in their ability to read and spell (Harley, 2009; Reid et al., 2009).

Diagnosing whether a child has a learning disability is often a difficult task (Bender, 2008; Fritschmann & Solari, 2008). Unlike in the United States, where national guidelines are established, in Canada each province and territory sets its own educational policies, including guidelines for responding to needs of children with learning disabilities. Saskatchewan has the most comprehensive policy, and is one of only three provinces (along with Ontario and Quebec) to refer to learning disabilities in its educational policies (Kozey & Siegel, 2008). As a result, the same child may be diagnosed as having a learning disability in one province, but not in another. Although school-aged children with learning disabilities are relatively well-served, diagnostic practices and services vary within provinces as well as between provinces. Canada has two official languages (French and English), as well as large Aboriginal and multi-cultural populations. Where special needs arise, poverty has an impact on the education and services that children with learning disabilities can access (Wiener & Siegel, 2010).

The precise causes of learning disabilities have not yet been determined (Friend, 2014; Vaughn & Bos, 2015). Researchers use brain imaging techniques, such as magnetic resonance imaging, to reveal any regions of the brain that might be involved in learning disabilities (Shaywitz, Lyon, & Shaywitz, 2006) (see Figure 9.7). These techniques indicate it is unlikely that learning disabilities reside in a single specific brain location. Learning disabilities are more likely due to problems with integrating information from multiple brain regions or subtle difficulties in brain structures and functions.

behaviour of children with ADHD better than medical or behaviour management alone, although this is not true in every case (Statistics Canada, 2015). Recently, mindfulness training has been given to children and adolescents and the results have been positive. Another possible treatment under investigation is neurofeedback, a type of training that enables children to become more aware of their physiologic responses to they can exercise more control of their brain's prefrontal cortex where executive control primarily occurs (Statistics Canada, 2015).

Studies have also focused on the possibility that exercise might reduce ADHD (Tantillo et al., 2002). Some mental health experts now recommend that children with ADHD exercise several times a day, and speculate that the increased rates of ADHD have coincided with the decline in children's activity levels (Ratey, 2006).

Autism Spectrum Disorder

Autism spectrum disorder (ASD) is a general term for a group of complex disorders of brain development. Such disorders are characterized by varying degrees of deficits in communicating appropriately for social interaction, as well as difficulties in following conversations, leading to functional limitations in effective communication, social participation, academic or occupational performance, as well as restricted, repetitive patterns of behaviour, interests, or activities (Autistic Speaks, 2016). Each individual condition is unique as the degree of impairment varies along the spectrum. Severity is based on social communication impairments and restricted, repetitive patterns of behaviour. The most severe form, autistic disorder, is life-long and usually has its onset during the first three years of life, (Autism Speaks, 2016; Statistics Canada, 2015;). ASD may occur with or without accompanying intellectual or physical impairment; in other words, intellectual disability may be evident in some children, while others show average or above-average intelligence. Some persons with ASD may excel in music, math, or art (Autism Speaks, 2016).

Although privacy issues limit data collection from schools and hospitals in Canada, data collected by the National Epidemiologic Database for the Study of Autism in Canada (NEDSAC) indicates that the prevalence of autism spectrum disorders is increasing in every province where studies were conducted (Newfoundland and Labrador, Prince Edward Island, and Southeastern Ontario) (Oullette-Kuntz et al., 2012). The preliminary findings of an epidemiological study conducted a decade ago at Montreal Children's Hospital found the rate of children with autistic disorder to be one in 147; rates are four to five times greater for boys than girls (Statistics Canada, 2015; Norris, Paré, & Starkey, 2006).

What causes the autism spectrum disorders? Just as there is no one type of ASD, there is no single cause. Research has identified a number of rare gene-changes, or mutations to be associated with autism; however, most cases appear to be caused by a combination of autism risk genes and environmental factors that influence early brain development both before and during birth. Parental age, maternal illness during pregnancy, and certain difficulties during birth, particularly those that involve periods of oxygen deprivation to the baby's brain, are risk factors that may modestly increase the risk when combined with genetic predisposition to autism (Autism Speaks, 2016). The current consensus is that autism is a brain dysfunction with abnormalities in brain structure and neurotransmitters (Catarino et al., 2013; Doll & Broadie, 2014). There is no evidence that family socialization causes autism. Recent interest has focused on a lack of connectivity between brain regions as a key factor in autism (Just et al., 2012; Verly et al., 2014).

Although children diagnosed with ASD may have average or above-average intelligence, they are often socially isolated and frequently the victims of bullying as their peers may view them as odd (Statistics Canada, 2015). Children with autism benefit from a well-structured classroom, individualized instruction, and small-group instruction (Simmons, Lanter, & Lyons, 2014). As with children who are intellectually disabled, behaviour modification techniques are sometimes effective in helping autistic children learn (Odom et al., 2014).

Physical Disabilities

Physical disabilities tend to be visible and often are a risk factor for academic as well as psychological problems. Children's activities may be limited in various ways such as sight or hearing, or by a physical handicap or epilepsy. Children with disabilities face barriers in school and, particularly in rural communities, are frequently barred from participating in activities due to inaccessibility and lack of transportation (Hanvey, 2015).

Children's Disabilities and the Family

A child's disabilities can cause much stress in parents. According to a research team from Dalhousie University, factors such as finding time and money to meet the needs of the child and fulfilling one's own and society's expectations of taking care of a sick child can place a heavy burden on parents of children with chronic medical problems (Burton, Lethbridge, & Phipps, 2006).

Article 23 of the *UN Convention on the Rights of the Child* recognizes that children with disabilities have the right to enjoy full and decent lives. However, this report indicates that this opportunity is not fully enjoyed by all children with special needs (Hanvey, 2015). Parents have the power to advocate for their children, and some exert that power to create change. Advocacy can be exhilarating when the outcome is positive, as it was for parents who successfully appealed to the Supreme Court of Canada, asserting that British Columbia's failure to provide treatment to their four autistic children was a violation of their rights to equality (Tiedemann, 2008). But the day-to-day advocacy that parents assume in their communities, in schools, and even within their nuclear and extended families can be a source of chronic stress. The Dalhousie research team found that caring for a child with a chronic condition was associated with maternal depression. Significantly, a mother with a chronically ill child had a lower probability of good health than one who smoked but did not have such a child (Burton, Lethbridge, & Phipps, 2006).

Educational Issues

The provision of special education in Canada has gone through significant changes. Before the early 1900s, the education system did not accept people with disabilities. Then, public schools began to accept exceptional students, but segregated them from ordinary students. Children with more severe disabilities, however, were institutionalized. For decades the movement toward inclusion has been challenging Canadian schools (Lupart, 1998). The 1970s saw parents' efforts to open the public school system to all children with disabilities. Subsequent provincial legislation promising access to public education for all children demonstrates the success of parents' efforts.

Despite all the changes, some wonder whether mainstreaming is, indeed, the best approach to teaching students with disabilities. Some experts believe that separate programs may be more effective and appropriate for children with disabilities because segregated classrooms can provide individualized instructions to meet students' special needs.

Even when the merits of mainstreaming are accepted, other issues can arise. As a survey with teachers in Nova Scotia shows, schools and the government sometimes do not provide enough personnel, time, and training for teachers to handle the diverse needs of special-education students in the mainstreamed classroom (Macmillan & Meyer, 2006). This has led to a sense of guilt among teachers who find themselves unable to meet the professional standard they set for themselves.

Some experts suggest that mainstreaming children with disabilities is important. *What do you think?*

In addition, students who need special support do not always get it. In a national survey of parents with children with special needs, 31 percent reported problems accessing appropriate help, with parents of boys more likely to report this difficulty than those of girls (Uppal, Kohen, & Khan, 2006). The parents noted problems such as inadequate staff and learning aids, lack of services in the local area, and difficulty in communicating with the school and in getting an assessment.

In sum, mainstreaming or not, appropriate support and training for teachers is essential, and schools should have enough learning materials (such as talking books) to accommodate students with special needs. The Canadian Centre for Policy Alternatives (2015) proposes that such policies implemented by provinces need to be updated and renewed (Towle, 2015).

To this point, we have discussed children with disabilities in middle and late childhood. For a review, see the Reach Your Learning Outcomes section at the end of this chapter.

Reach Your **Learning Outcomes**

Physical Changes and Health

LO1 Describe physical changes and health in middle and late childhood.

Body Growth and Change	▪ During middle and late childhood, children grow an average of 5 to 7.5 cm a year. Muscle mass and strength gradually increase. ▪ Among the most pronounced changes are decreases in head circumference, waist circumference, and leg length in relation to body height.
The Brain	▪ Advances in the prefrontal cortex are linked to children's improved attention, reasoning, and cognitive control. ▪ Temporal and frontal lobe development in childhood are reflected by improved language abilities such as reading.
Motor Development	▪ Motor development becomes much smoother and more coordinated. ▪ Boys tend to develop gross motor skills earlier than girls; girls tend to develop fine motor skills earlier than boys. ▪ Increased myelination of the central nervous system is reflected in improved motor skills.
Exercise	▪ Exercise plays an important role in children's growth and development. ▪ The sedentary lifestyle of children is a cause of concern for educators and policy makers in many parts of the world. ▪ Higher incidence of screen time, (television, computer games, texting, etc.) has been linked with being overweight and less physically fit, as well as with health issues such as diabetes and higher levels of cholesterol. Mothers report that when they were children, they experienced much higher levels of outdoor play activity than their children.
Health, Illness, and Disease	▪ Nearly one of every three children (31.5 percent) are overweight. More boys than girls are obese and 36.2 percent of First Nations children living on reserves are obese. ▪ Children's low activity level and high-fat diets are the main reasons for the rise in obesity. ▪ Treatment of obesity focuses mainly on diet, exercise, and behaviour modification. ▪ An obsession with thinness among young girls can affect their psychological well-being. ▪ Unintentional accidents are the primary cause of hospitalization and death in middle and late childhood. ▪ Childhood cancers have a different profile from adult cancers and are the second leading cause of death in children between 1 and 14 years of age.

Cognitive Development

LO2 Explain cognitive changes in middle and late childhood.

Piaget's Concrete Operational Stage	▪ Concrete operational thought involves operations, conservation, classification, seriation, and transitivity. ▪ Critics question Piaget's estimates of competence at different developmental levels, his stage concept, and other ideas.
Information Processing	▪ Changes in information processing during middle and late childhood involve the following: **1.** Increased short- and long-term memory, which reflects increased knowledge and expertise. **2.** Increased application of strategies, including creative, critical, and scientific thinking skills. **3.** Increased metacognition (cognition about cognition), which further enhances a child's ability to process information.
Intelligence	▪ Intelligence is defined as problem-solving skills and the ability to learn from and adapt to life's everyday experiences. ▪ The Stanford-Binet test and the Wechsler scales are widely used IQ tests. ▪ Sternberg proposed a triarchic theory of intelligence: analytical, creative, and practical. ▪ Gardner's eight types of intelligence include verbal, mathematical, spatial, movement, self-insight, insight about others, musical skills, and naturalist skills. ▪ Mayer-Salovey-Caruso propose that emotional intelligence has four primary elements: perceiving, using, understanding, and managing emotions. ▪ Music training is related to small increases in IQ. ▪ Most researchers agree that genetics, environment, and free will interact to influence intelligence. ▪ The Flynn effect refers to the worldwide increase in intelligence scores that has occurred over a short time. This increase is thought to be the result of improved educational opportunities. ▪ Culture-fair tests are those that are free of cultural bias. ▪ Several levels of intellectual disability or developmental delay exist, and may be organic or cultural-familial in nature. ▪ Giftedness refers to people who have higher than average intelligence and/or superior talent for something. ▪ Caution and care must be taken when using intelligence tests scores, as they do not measure different domains of intelligence.

Language Development

LO3 **Discuss language development in middle and late childhood.**

Vocabulary, Grammar, and Metalinguistic Awareness	▪ Children become more analytical in their approach to words and grammar. ▪ Metalinguistic awareness, knowledge about language and the ability to discuss language, accompanies advances in vocabulary and grammar.
Reading	▪ Current debate focuses on the whole-language approach versus the basic skills and phonetics approach. ▪ Metalinguistic awareness, knowledge about language and the ability to discuss language, accompanies advances in vocabulary and grammar. ▪ Effective reading instruction involves a balance of the two approaches and a positive classroom atmosphere. ▪ Many children weak in reading make good progress throughout the elementary school years even without remedial instruction.
Writing	▪ Children often invent spellings as they begin to write. ▪ It takes time and practice to become a good writer. ▪ The metacognitive strategies needed to be a good writer are linked to those required to be a good reader.
Bilingualism	▪ Many positive outcomes have been associated with knowledge of a second language. ▪ Success in learning a second language may be related to age.

Educational Approaches And Issues

LO4 **Discuss approaches and issues related to education.**

Approaches to Student Learning	▪ Debate exists between which is more effective in teaching children: the constructivist approach or the direct instruction approach.
Educational Issues	▪ Poverty is a major factor in school performance: children from low-income families tend to fare poorer academically and behaviourally. ▪ Ethnicity also influences school performance; children from immigrant or Aboriginal backgrounds are faced with additional challenges including poverty, bullying, value differences, and language. ▪ Immigrant children catch up with their classmates by age 10 or 11. ▪ Aboriginal children may experience a feeling of alienation due to the school's lack of understanding and respect for the world-views, spirituality, and other aspects of their culture.
Private Schools and Home Education	▪ Many Canadian children are being educated in private schools or through home schooling. ▪ Not all private-school children come from wealthy families. ▪ The reasons for enrolling children in these forms of education include family values and parents' discomfort with specific aspects of public schools.

Children with Disabilities

LO5 Identify different types of disabilities and discuss issues relating to their education.

Learning Disabilities	▪ Children with a learning disability are of normal intelligence or above, have difficulties in at least one academic area and usually several, and have a difficulty that is not attributable to another diagnosed problem or disorder. ▪ The most common learning disability in children involves reading. Dyslexia is a severe impairment in the ability to read and spell. ▪ Diagnosis of a learning disability is often a difficult task, as diagnostic practices and services vary within and between provinces. ▪ The precise causes of learning disabilities have yet to be determined; however, they tend to run in families. Both genetics and environmental factors come into play. ▪ Children with learning disabilities show more anxiety and aggression and less altruism than other children.
Attention Deficit Hyperactivity Disorder (ADHD)	▪ ADHD is a condition in which children consistently show problems in one or more of inattention, hyperactivity, and impulsivity. ▪ Considerable controversy surrounds the diagnosis and treatment of ADHD.
Autism Spectrum Disorders	▪ Autism spectrum disorders range from severe developmental autism spectrum disorder to the relatively milder Asperger syndrome.
Physical Disabilities	▪ Physical disabilities are often visible and pose a risk factor for academic performance, particularly when the disability is "activity-limiting."
Children's Disabilities and the Family	▪ Issues such as finding appropriate treatments for the child and fulfilling expectations to take care of a sick child add stress to parents' lives.
Educational Issues	▪ The old approach to educating children with disabilities was to segregate them from ordinary classrooms. Since the 1960s, some professionals have been promoting mainstreaming of those children. ▪ Lack of training and support for teachers and lack of learning aids are concerns in the education of special needs children.

review → connect → reflect

review

1. Characterize the changes that occur in the brain's development during middle and late childhood. LO1
2. How does Piaget's stage of concrete operational thought differ from the earlier preoperational stage? LO2
3. What are some of the different types of intelligence? LO2
4. What is metalinguistic awareness? LO3
5. What are some of the major issues in education that affect academic performance? LO4

connect

In this chapter, you read about the role of exercise and nutrition on children's health. With this information in mind, design a child's day that would optimize his or her health and development. What would the child have for meals and snacks? In addition to school, in what activities would you engage the child?

reflect

Your Own Personal Journey of Life

Consider Gardner's eight frames of mind. Create an ordered list of your strengths and weaknesses, putting your major strength first and your major weakness last. What activities do you enjoy the most? How do these activities compare with your list of strengths and weaknesses?

CHAPTER 10

Socio-Emotional Development in Middle and Late Childhood

CHAPTER OUTLINE

Emotional and Personality Development

LO1 Discuss emotional and personality development in middle and late childhood.

- **The Self**
- **Emotional Development**

Moral Development and Gender

LO2 Describe moral development and gender.

- **Moral Development**
- **Gender**

Families

LO3 Describe developmental changes in parent–child relationships and child maltreatment.

- **Developmental Changes in Parent–Child Relationships**
- **Child Maltreatment: Prevalence and Consequences**

Peers, Bullying, and Social Media

LO4 Identify changes in peer relationships, the roles in bullying and its impact, and the influence of social media on growth and development in middle and late childhood.

- **Friends**
- **Peer Statuses**
- **Social Cognition**
- **Bullying**
- **Social Media**

"Children need models rather than critics."

—JOSEPH JOUBERT, NINETEENTH-CENTURY FRENCH ESSAYIST

© Juice Images/ Corbis RF

Meeting my Dad

It's funny to remember the day I came to Canada. It was four years ago. When I first came to Canada I didn't know what my dad looked like. I had a picture of him, but he was not looking to the picture I had, because he got older. I hadn't met my dad for eight years. He used to call me every Sunday, so I had a feeling of what he sounded like. He left Eritrea when I was 6 months old, not because he wanted to, but his job put him in danger.

He was editor-in-chief and co-founder of the largest newspaper in Eritrea. He had written many things against the government. So, the government didn't like his work and shut down his newspaper. Then when they came to arrest him, my dad left right away. So that was the reason my dad left me when I was 6 months old.

After eight years of separation, my mom, my brother, my sister, and I came to Canada to live with my dad. Some people were waiting for us in the airport. I didn't know who my dad was. Two guys came towards us. I knew one of them because that was my uncle, but I wasn't sure who was the guy coming with him. Then they both got there and the guy that came with my uncle started to hug my sister, my brother, and my mom. When he finished hugging my mom, he came to me. I started to run toward my uncle, I was hiding behind his back. Then the guy came and hugged me, and asked me if I knew him. I didn't say a single word back to him, until my mom whispered and told me that was my dad. I asked the guy if he was my dad, he said he was but I didn't trust him so I told him to speak to me on the phone. He pulled out his cell phone and called to my uncle's cell phone. So, my uncle gave it to me so as to speak with my dad. When he finished talking I was SHOCKED! I stared at him for a while. Then I ran toward him and hugged him really hard. I was really happy to see my dad for the first time after eight years. I was also tired because I had jet lag from the plane, so then we all went to my dad's house and slept there.

The next morning my dad took my family and I to shopping. We bought lots of awesome clothes. Then we went to an amazing restaurant. It was delicious. I ate like I have never eaten before. After we had a really fun and exhausting day we went to bed. But my dad was still up and writing on his computer. At 12:30 a.m. I woke up to use the washroom and I saw my dad on the computer. I asked him what he was doing. He said he was working. I was confused because I thought work was only done in the office during the day. He told me about his work. A journalist has to finish his story before the deadline. He showed me his newspaper and told me that he would print his newspaper tomorrow. I told him he had an amazing job and went to bed.

The next day my dad took me to Baycrest School to be registered. When my dad registered me in a school, I was happy to go because I wanted to make friends badly. I thought I had to wait till tomorrow to go. But the principal said I could go to my class right now. I was excited to see my teacher and classmates of grade 3. When the principal introduced me to the class, the students ran up to me and took my bag off for me. In that exact moment I knew I was going to have an amazing year.

After eight years of separation, Eivan Berhane finally got to meet his father.

But I was wrong. The next day of school at recess time, some students started to say something to me. I didn't say anything because I didn't know what they were saying. They started shoving me and pushing me around. I didn't want to get in trouble so I just ignored them. But this one mean kid came up to me and slapped me. I was mad. I punched the kid and kicked him hard. I hurt the kid badly. So the supervisor at recess told the kid and I to go to the office. I didn't understand what she was saying so she took both of us to the office. When we got there at the office, the principal asked the kid what happened.

The kid told him his side of the story. Then the principal asked me for my side of the story. I didn't understand but I started talking to the principal in my language. He didn't understand me. He asked me to speak in English. But I didn't know English so I just kept on talking in my language to the principal. Then the principal called my dad and told him what I did.

My dad came from work and picked me up and told me never to fight ever again. I told him that he started the fighting. My dad said, "it doesn't matter who started it, but you don't beat anyone because you are stronger than him. You have to tell your teachers what he did." He also told me to respect the rule of this country. I tried to respect the rule, but some students kept fighting me and what could I do, I beat them back. I got into trouble. My dad got a call and he came to warn me. That's how I got used to my school in a week.

There are four things that I have learned from this.

1. If you're bothered by some mean students, tell your teacher immediately.
2. Respect your teachers, because they are here to look after us.
3. Try to be friendly with everyone, especially the new students. They need our help.
4. And never bother your parents while they are at work, because they will get cranky. Especially if you do something wrong in school and they get a call about it.

Eivan's essay, written when he was 10 years old, reflects some of the challenges children have when their families immigrate or seek asylum in Canada. His essay also reflects the all-encompassing social and emotional changes that children experience in middle and late childhood. Transformations in their relationships with parents and peers occur and schooling takes on a more academic flavour. Significant development of self-conception, moral reasoning, and moral behaviour also occur.

Emotional and Personality Development

LO1 Discuss emotional and personality development in middle and late childhood.

- **The Self**
- **Emotional Development**

In this section we will explore how the self continues to develop during middle and late childhood and the emotional changes that occur during these years. We will also explore the child's moral development and the role of gender during these years.

The Self

What is the nature of the child's self-understanding and self-esteem in the elementary school years? What role do self-efficacy and self-regulation play in children's achievement?

The Development of Self-Understanding

In middle and late childhood, especially between ages 8 and 11, children increasingly define themselves through psychological traits and characteristics in contrast to the more concrete descriptions of younger children. Elementary school children also are more likely to define themselves in terms of social characteristics and social comparisons, such as smart, popular, or dumb (Harter, 2006, p. 526).

critical thinking

Eivan Berhane describes his move to Canada. How might Urie Bronfenbrenner's bio-ecological theory of development, outlined in Chapter 2, be helpful in understanding some of the challenges Eivan may have faced? Imagine that you relocate to another country anywhere in the world. What expectations and challenges might you have?

In addition to the increase in psychological characteristics in self-definition, children become more likely to recognize the social aspects of the self (Harter, 2012, 2013). In one investigation, elementary school children often included references to social groups in their self-descriptions. For example, some children referred to themselves as part of a sports team or member of a science group.

Diane Ruble (2010) investigates children's acquisition of a sense of self and noted the use of social comparison in their self-evaluations. Children were given a difficult task and then offered feedback on their performance, as well as information about the performances of other children their age. The children were then asked for self-evaluations. Children younger than age 7 made virtually no reference to the information about other children's performances. However, many children older than 7 included socially comparative information in their self-descriptions.

Children's self-understanding in the elementary school years also includes increasing reference to social comparison (Harter, 2012, 2013). At this point in development, children are more likely to distinguish themselves from others in comparative rather than in absolute terms. That is, elementary-school-age children are no longer as likely to think about what they do or do not do, but are more likely to think about what they can do in comparison with others.

Between 8 and 12 years of age, children become increasingly aware of race, religion, authority roles, gender, and other social categories. They often evaluate themselves, sometimes quite harshly, based on what they think others may think of them. For example, a child might say, "No one will like me with this stupid haircut" (Kennedy-Moore, 2012). In sum, in middle and late childhood self-description increasingly involves psychological and social characteristics, including social comparison.

UNDERSTANDING OTHERS

In middle and late childhood, children show an increase in **perspective taking**, the ability to assume other people's perspectives and understand their thoughts and feelings. Perspective taking is thought to be important in whether children develop prosocial or antisocial attitudes and behaviour (Davis-Kean, Jager, & Collins, 2009). Executive function, discussed in Chapters 7 and 8, is at work in perspective taking. Among the executive functions called on when children engage in perspective taking are cognitive inhibition (controlling one's own thoughts to consider the perspective of others) and cognitive flexibility (seeing situations in different ways).

In Chapter 8, we indicated that 4-year-old children show some skepticism of others' claims. In middle and late childhood, children become increasingly skeptical of some sources of information about psychological traits. (Heyman, Fu, & Lee, 2013; Mills, Elashi, & Archacki, 2011). For example, in one study, 10- to 11-year-olds were more likely to reject other children's self-reports that they were *smart* and *honest* than were 6- to 7-year-olds (Heyman & Legare, 2005).

In terms of prosocial behaviour, taking another's perspective improves children's likelihood of understanding and sympathizing with others when they are distressed or in need. A recent study revealed that in children characterized as being emotionally reactive, good perspective-taking skills were linked to being able to regain a neutral emotional state after being emotionally aroused (Bengtsson & Arvidsson, 2011). In this study, children who made gains in perspective-taking skills reduced their emotional reactivity over a two-year period.

Self-Esteem and Self-Concept

High self-esteem and a positive self-concept are important for children's well-being (Marsh, Martin, & Xu, 2012). **Self-esteem** refers to global evaluations of the self; it is also referred to as self-worth or self-image. For example, a child may perceive that she is not merely a person but a good person. Of course, not all children have an overall positive image of themselves. **Self-concept** refers to domain-specific evaluations of the self. Children can make self-evaluations in many domains of their lives—academic, athletic, appearance, and so on. In sum, self-esteem refers to global self-evaluations, and self-concept to more domain-specific evaluations.

The foundations of self-esteem and self-concept emerge from the quality of parent–child interaction in infancy and early childhood. Thus, if children have low self-esteem in middle and late childhood, they may have experienced neglect or abuse in relationships with their parents earlier in development. Children with high self-esteem are more likely to be securely attached to parents and have parents who engage in sensitive caregiving (Thompson, 2011, 2013a, b, c, d).

Self-esteem reflects perceptions that do not always match reality (Baumeister et al., 2003; Jordan & Zeigler-Hill, 2013). A child's self-esteem might reflect a belief about whether he or she is intelligent and attractive, for example, but that belief is not necessarily accurate. Thus, high self-esteem may refer to accurate, justified perceptions of one's worth as a person and one's successes and accomplishments, but it can also refer to an unwarranted sense of superiority over others (Gerstenberg et al., 2014). In the same manner, low self-esteem may reflect either an accurate perception of one's shortcomings, or a distorted—even pathological—insecurity and inferiority.

critical thinking

What are some of the traits that shape your self-concept? How did you come to understand these strengths and weaknesses? How have your strengths and weaknesses shaped your overall self-esteem? Do you think parents and educators are overly concerned with children's self-esteem?

Variations in self-esteem have been linked with many aspects of children's development. However, much of the research is *correlational* rather than *experimental*. Recall from Chapter 1 that correlation does not equal causation. Thus, if a correlational study finds an association between children's low self-esteem and low academic achievement, low academic achievement could cause the low self-esteem as much as low self-esteem causes low academic achievement. In fact, there are only moderate correlations between school performance and self-esteem, and these correlations do not suggest that high self-esteem produces better school performance (Baumeister et al., 2003).

Children with high self-esteem have greater initiative, but this can produce positive or negative outcomes (Baumeister et al., 2003). These children are prone to both prosocial and antisocial actions (Krueger, Vohs, & Baumeister, 2008). One study revealed that over time, aggressive children with high self-esteem increasingly valued the rewards that aggression can bring and belittled their victims (Menon et al., 2007).

Children have the highest self-esteem when they perform competently in domains that are important to them. These areas might include academic skills, sports, social acceptance, and physical attractiveness. Anne Bowker, of Carleton University in Ottawa, studied how self-esteem and physical competence/appearance might be related in late childhood and early adolescence (2006). Noticeable physical changes and society's emphasis on fitness may cause children in this age period to be rather sensitive to their appearance. While both physical skills and appearance are important components of self-esteem, Bowker found that girls who are not athletic placed less importance on physical competence and treated appearance as an important criterion in determining their self-esteem.

A current concern is that too many of today's children grow up receiving praise for mediocre or even poor performance and as a consequence have inflated self-esteem (Graham, 2005; Stipek, 2005). These children may have difficulty handling competition and criticism. In a series of studies, researchers found that inflated praise, although well intended, may cause children with low self-esteem to avoid important learning experiences, such as tackling challenging tasks (Brummelman et al., 2014).

What are the consequences of low self-esteem? Low self-esteem has been implicated in overweightness and obesity, anxiety, depression, suicide, and delinquency (Blanco et al., 2014; O'Brien, Bartoletti, & Leitzel, 2013; Ziegler-Hill, 2013). One study revealed that youths with low self-esteem had lower life satisfaction at 30 years of age (Birkeland et al., 2012). Another study found that low and decreasing self-esteem in adolescence was linked to adult depression two decades later (Steiger et al., 2014).

Emotional support and social approval from others can also influence children's self-esteem. Some children with low self-esteem come from conflicted families or conditions in which they experience abuse or neglect—situations in which support was unavailable. In some cases, alternative sources of support can be implemented either informally through the encouragement of a teacher, a coach, or another significant adult, or more formally through such programs as Big Brothers and Big Sisters.

What are some good strategies for effectively increasing children's self-esteem? See Connecting Development to Life for some answers to this question.

CONNECTING development to life

Increasing Children's Self-Esteem

Ways to improve children's self-esteem include identifying the causes of low self-esteem, providing emotional support and social approval, helping children achieve, and helping children cope (Bednar, Wells, & Peterson, 1995; Harter, 2006, 2012).

- Identify the causes of low self-esteem. Intervention should target the causes of low self-esteem.
- Provide emotional support and social approval. Some children with low self-esteem come from conflicted families or conditions in which they experienced abuse or neglect—situations in which support was not available.
- Help children achieve. Achievement also can improve children's self-esteem. For example, the straightforward teaching of real skills to children often results in increased achievement and, thus, in enhanced self-esteem.
- Help children cope. Self-esteem often increases when children face a problem and try to cope with it, rather than avoid it. If coping rather than avoidance prevails, children face problems realistically, honestly, and non-defensively. This produces favourable self-evaluative thoughts, which lead to the self-generated approval that raises self-esteem.

critical thinking

Recall Baumrind's parenting styles from Chapter 8: authoritarian parenting, authoritative parenting, neglectful parenting, and indulgent parenting. Which parenting approach might help accomplish the last goal mentioned in the Connecting Development to Life feature? How? How can parents help children develop higher self-esteem?

Self-Efficacy

Self-efficacy is the belief that one can master a situation and produce favourable outcomes. Albert Bandura (2001, 2008, 2009a, b; 2010), whose social cognitive theory we described in Chapter 2, states that self-efficacy is a critical factor in whether or not students achieve. Self-efficacy is the belief that "I can"; helplessness is the belief that "I cannot." Students with high self-efficacy endorse such statements as, "I know that I will be able to learn the material in this class" and "if others can do this, so can I."

Dale Schunk (2012) has applied the concept of self-efficacy to many aspects of students' achievement. In his view, self-efficacy influences a student's choice of activities. Students with low self-efficacy for learning may avoid many learning tasks, especially those that are challenging. By contrast, high-self-efficacy counterparts eagerly work at learning tasks (Schunk, 2011). Students with high self-efficacy are more likely to expend effort and persist longer at a learning task than are students with low self-efficacy.

Self-Regulation

One of the most important aspects of the self in middle and late childhood is the increased capacity for self-regulation (Carlson, Zelazo, & Faja, 2013; Flouri, Midouhas, & Joshi, 2014). This increased capacity is characterized by deliberate efforts to manage one's behaviour, emotions, and thoughts, leading to increased social competence and achievement (Schunk & Zimmerman, 2013; Thompson, 2014c, 2015). A study found that self-control increased from 4 years of age to 10 years of age and that high self-control was linked to lower levels of deviant behaviour (Vazsonyi & Huang, 2010). In this study, parenting characterized by warmth and positive affect predicted the developmental increase in self-control. Another study of almost 17 000 3- to 7-year-old children revealed that self-regulation was a protective factor for children growing up in low socio-economic (SES) conditions (Flouri, Midouhas, & Joshi, 2014). In this study, 7-year-old children with low self-regulation living in low-SES conditions had more emotional problems than their 3-year-old counterparts with higher self-regulation. Thus, low self-regulation was linked to a widening gap in low-SES children's emotional problems over time. Another study revealed that children from low-income families who had a higher level of self-regulation earned better grades in school than their counterparts who had a lower level of self-regulation (Buckner, Mezzacappa, & Beardslee, 2009).

The increased capacity for self-regulation is linked to developmental advances in the brain's prefrontal cortex, as discussed in Chapter 9, "Physical and Cognitive Development in Middle and Late Childhood" (Markant & Thomas, 2013). Increased focal activation in the prefrontal cortex is linked to improved cognitive control, which includes self-regulation (Diamond, 2013).

Industry versus Inferiority

In Chapter 2, we described Erik Erikson's (1968) eight stages of human development. His fourth stage, *industry versus inferiority*, occurs during middle and late childhood. The term "industry" expresses a dominant theme of this period: children become interested in how things are made and how they work. When children are encouraged to make, build, and work—whether building a model airplane, constructing a tree house, fixing a bicycle, solving an addition problem, or making pancakes—their sense of industry increases. However, parents who see their children's efforts at making things as "making a mess" may contribute to children's development of a sense of inferiority.

Children's social worlds beyond their families also contribute to a sense of industry. School becomes especially important in this regard. Consider children who are slightly below average in intelligence. They are too bright to be in special classes but not bright enough to be in gifted classes. They fail frequently in their academic efforts, developing a sense of inferiority. By contrast, consider children whose sense of industry is derogated at home. A series of sensitive and committed teachers may revitalize their sense of industry (Elkind, 1970).

What characterizes Erikson's stage of industry versus inferiority?

Alfred Adler (1927) believed that realization of the ideal and behaviour toward that goal were likely formed in the first few months of life. During this time, the infant senses and responds to joy and sorrow. Upon this foundation, the child develops a primitive sense of well-being. Multiple factors influence the child's development—family, peers, television, community, schools, teachers—all of which set up boundaries intended to help the child regulate his or her behaviour. Like adults, children learn to wriggle their way around these boundaries in an attempt to attain a particular goal, be it a feeling of dominance or of achievement. In so doing, the child's sense of the ideal directs this activity and often leads to a sense of inferiority, as we cannot always achieve our ideal. Adler believed that much behaviour, prosocial or otherwise, is compensating for feelings of inferiority.

Emotional Development

In Chapter 8, we saw that preschoolers become more and more adept at talking about their own and others' emotions. They also show a growing awareness about controlling and managing emotions to meet social standards. In middle and late childhood, children further develop their understanding and self-regulation of emotion (McRae et al., 2012; Thompson, 2013c, d).

Developmental Changes

The following important developmental changes in emotions occur during the elementary school years (Denham, Bassett, & Wyatt, 2007; Denham et al., 2011; Kuebli, 1994; Thompson, 2014c, 2015). Some of these changes are illustrated by Eivan's composition that you read in the chapter-opening vignette.

- *Increased ability to understand complex emotions such as pride and shame:* These emotions become less tied to the reactions of other people and more internalized and integrated with a sense of personal responsibility.
- *Increased understanding that more than one emotion can be experienced in a particular situation:* A grade 3 child, for example, may realize that achieving something might involve both anxiety and joy.
- *Increased tendency to take into account the events leading to emotional reactions:* A grade 4 child may become aware that her sadness today is influenced by her friend moving to another town last week.
- *Marked improvement in the ability to suppress or conceal negative emotional reactions:* A grade 5 child learns to tone down his anger better than he used to when one of his classmates irritates him.
- *Increased use of self-initiated strategies for redirecting feelings:* In the elementary school years, children become more reflective about their emotional lives and increasingly use strategies to control their emotions. They become more effective at cognitively managing their emotions, such as soothing oneself after an upset.
- *Increased capacity for genuine empathy:* For example, a grade 4 child feels sympathy for a distressed person and experiences vicariously the sadness the distressed person is feeling.

Emotional Intelligence (EI)

As you read in Chapter 9, **emotional intelligence** is a form of social intelligence that involves the ability to monitor one's own and others' feelings and emotions, to discriminate among them, and to use this information to guide one's thinking and action (Cherry, 2012; Mayer, 2004).

Many schools have introduced social and emotional learning so that children can learn to recognize and manage emotions, care about others, make good decisions, behave ethically and responsibly, develop positive relationships, and avoid negative behaviours (Zins, 2004). For example, one elementary school in a Toronto suburb organized a series of 13 workshops dealing with feeling-related issues, such as empathy, friendship, and anger management (Griffin, 2001).

Other schools in North America have implemented a class called "self science." The contents for self science match up with many of the components of emotional intelligence and include developing self-awareness (in the sense of recognizing feelings and building a vocabulary for them); seeing the links among thoughts, feelings, decisions, and reactions; managing emotions and realizing what is behind a feeling (such as the hurt that triggers anger); and learning how to listen, cooperate, and negotiate. Names for these classes vary, but their common goal is to raise every child's emotional competence through regular education. In 2006, the Faculty of Education at the University of British Columbia launched the first Social and Emotional Learning Practicum for graduate students so that educators can integrate social-emotional learning concepts and strategies into the curriculum (UBC, 2010). Research reported in *Education Canada* shows that fostering students' emotional skills is highly linked to their success in schools, both academically and socially (Schonert-Reichl & Hymel, 2007).

E. Audras / PhotoAlto

What are some changes in emotion during the middle and late childhood years?

Coping with Stress

An important aspect of children's emotional lives is learning how to cope with stress (Masten, 2013, 2014a, b; Morris, Thompson, & Morris, 2013. As children get older, they more accurately appraise a stressful situation and determine how much control they have over it. Older children generate more coping alternatives to stressful conditions and use more cognitive coping strategies (Saarni et al., 2006). They are better than younger children at intentionally shifting their thoughts to something that is less stressful, seeing another perspective and reframing, or changing their perception of a stressful situation. For example, a younger child may be very disappointed that a teacher did not say hello when the child arrived in the classroom. An older child may reframe the situation and think, "My teacher may have been busy with other things and just forgot to say hello." However, in families characterized by turmoil or trauma, children may be so overwhelmed by stress that they do not use such strategies.

Disasters such as earthquakes or wars can harm children's development and produce adjustment problems (Scheerings, Cobham, & McDermott, 2014). Among the outcomes for children who experience disasters are acute stress reactions, depression, panic disorder, and post-traumatic stress disorder (Pfefferbaum, Newman, & Nelson, 2014). The likelihood that a child will face these problems following a disaster depends on factors such as the nature and severity of the disaster and the type of support available to the child.

In research on disasters/trauma, the term "dose-response effects" is often used. Research findings indicate that the more severe the disaster/trauma (dose), the worse the adaptation and adjustment (response) following the disaster/trauma (Masten, 2013; Masten & Narayan, 2012). For example, educators on "The Agenda with Steve Paikin" (TVO, April 28, 2016) shared experiences and advice about integrating Syrian refugee children in their schools and classes. They reported that sounds from airplanes or sirens often trigger fear responses from the children.

Researchers have offered the following recommendations for parents, teachers, and other adults caring for children after a disaster (Gurwitch et al., 2001):

- Reassure children (numerous times, if necessary) of their safety and security.
- Allow children to retell events and be patient when listening to them.
- Encourage children to talk about any disturbing or confusing feelings, reassuring them that such feelings are normal after a stressful event.
- Protect children from re-exposure to frightening situations and reminders of the trauma—for example, by limiting discussion of the event in front of the children.

- Help children make sense of what happened, keeping in mind that children may misunderstand what took place. For example, young children "may blame themselves, believe things happened that did not happen, believe that terrorists are in the school, etc. Gently help children develop a realistic understanding of the event" (p. 10).

CONNECTING through social policy

Challenges Facing Immigrants and Refugees

Canada reports that Syria is the most dangerous place for a child to be and estimates that six million Syrian children are in need (Kilkenny, 2016). Canada has taken in more than 25 000 Syrian refugees, 50 percent of whom are children. In spite of all the supports being offered by churches, community groups, and the government, like other new arrivals to Canada, Syrian refugees may find themselves confronted with unexpected parenting challenges (Bornstein & Bohr, 2011).

If you have ever moved, you know that moving is challenging as each location has its unique atmospheric adaptation of the overall country's culture, whether the move is across town, from one region to another, or across the country. The cultural diaspora of moving to a new country altogether, either as an immigrant or as a refugee, is exponentially more challenging. Among the changes one might expect are those in climate, diet, language, employment, dress, and societal infrastructure such as education, government regulations, and supports. All this requires adjustment, openness, and resilience.

According to Statistics Canada, in 2011 22 percent of the total population was born outside of Canada. Of this 22 percent, most arrived as immigrants; 4.9 percent, or one quarter, as refugees; and some as citizens by birth who were born in another country (for example, a child born to Canadians parents who are living outside of Canada at the time of the child's birth). This diverse group arrived from 200 different countries (Statistics Canada, 2015). Toronto, Vancouver, and Montreal are popular home destinations for almost half, (47.1 percent) of the newcomers. As well, Statistics Canada reports that the median age is nearly ten years younger than in the general population—31.9 years of age versus 40.1 years of age—and 29.8 percent are visible minorities (Dobson, Maheux, & Chui, 2015).

Families moving to Canada know life will be different and are looking forward to change; however, they often have absolutely no idea how drastic that change may be. Parents may find their credentials are not recognized, so they take whatever jobs they can just to survive. A geologist or physician may find work in a convenience store or as a taxi cab driver. Political and economic hurdles may overwhelm and exhaust parents, taxing their time and patience. For their children adjusting to new neighbourhoods, friends, and schools, and facing academic and social, challenges can be daunting, placing even more pressure on their parents as they strive to make a new life for themselves and their families.

Parenting practices differ from family to family, and are drawn from the social culture in which they live. As a result, traditions and values for immigrant families may vary considerably from mainstream Canadian values. For example, in many parts of the world, overt strictness is a parental practice and this often becomes a major cause of dissonance in immigrant families (D'Souza, 2011). Gender roles differ and men may become disenfranchised when their wives become an important economic provider. (Jimeno et al., 2010). In many countries boys and girls do not go to the same school, so finding your child in a class with both genders can be disarming for the parent. Parents may fear losing control over their children as their children become "Canadianized." The power balance between parent and child may shift as the child may be better able to communicate, may be the translator, and may have access to more information than the parents. This gap may undermine the parents' abilities to manage the family. Immigration presents one of the most difficult challenges to parent–child relations and to family stability (Jimeno et al., 2010).

Children of refugee claimants have additional hurdles to overcome as they may have been traumatized or separated from their parents for a prolonged period of time. For example, Eivan, whose story you read in the opening vignette, was separated from his father for eight years.

Immigration requires cultural and psychological changes. Customs, language, values, and internalized life-scripts such as gender roles become challenged and dissected. Peers and schools exert major socializing influences on children who then become more acculturated than their parents. Immigration and resulting acculturation are major transformative processes, that in most cases require enormous economic, physical, and psychological sacrifice. Immigrants and refugees must negotiate a balance between the practices, traditions, and values of two cultures (Bornstein & Bohr, 2011).

To this point, we have discussed a number of ideas about emotional and personality development in middle and late childhood. For a review, see the Reach Your Learning Outcomes section at the end of this chapter.

Moral Development and Gender

LO2 Describe moral development and gender.

- **Moral Development**
- **Gender**

Recall that Piaget proposed that younger children are characterized by *heteronomous* morality—but that, by 10 years of age, they have moved into a higher stage called *autonomous* morality. According to Piaget, older children consider the intentions of the individual, believe that rules are subject to change, and are aware that punishment does not always follow wrongdoing.

A second major perspective on moral development was proposed by Lawrence Kohlberg (1958, 1986). Piaget's cognitive stages of development serve as the underpinnings for Kohlberg's theory, but Kohlberg suggested there are six stages of moral development. These stages, he argued, are universal. Development from one stage to another, said Kohlberg, is fostered by opportunities to take the perspective of others and to experience conflict between one's current stage of moral thinking and the reasoning of someone at a higher stage.

Moral Development

Kohlberg arrived at his view after 20 years of using a unique interview technique with children. In the interview, children were presented with a series of stories in which characters face moral dilemmas. The following is the most well-known Kohlberg dilemma:

> *In Europe, a woman was near death from a special kind of cancer. There was one drug that the doctors thought might save her. It was a form of radium that a druggist in the same town had recently discovered. The drug was expensive to make, but the druggist was charging ten times what the drug cost him to make. He paid $200 for the radium and charged $2000 for a small dose of the drug. The sick woman's husband, Heinz, went to everyone he knew to borrow the money, but he could only get together $1000, which is half of what it cost. He told the druggist that his wife was dying and asked him to sell it cheaper or let him pay later. But the druggist said, "No, I discovered the drug, and I am going to make money from it." So, Heinz got desperate and broke into the man's store to steal the drug for his wife (Kohlberg, 1969, p. 379).*

This story is one of eleven that Kohlberg devised to investigate the nature of moral thought. After reading the story, the interviewee answers a series of questions about the moral dilemma. Should Heinz have stolen the drug? Is it a husband's duty to steal the drug for his wife if he can get it no other way? Did the druggist have the right to charge that much when there was no law setting a limit on the price? Why, or why not? It is important to note that whether the individual says to steal the drug or not is not important in identifying the person's moral stage. What is important is the individual's moral reasoning behind the decision.

Harvard University Archives, UAV 605.295.8, Box 7, Kohlberg

Lawrence Kohlberg, the architect of a provocative cognitive developmental theory of moral development. *What is the nature of his theory?*

From the answers interviewees gave for this and other moral dilemmas, Kohlberg proposed three levels of moral development, each of which is characterized by two stages. A key concept in understanding moral development in his proposal is **internalization**, the developmental change from behaviour that is externally controlled to behaviour that is controlled by internal standards and principles. As children and adolescents develop, their moral thoughts become more internalized.

Kohlberg's Level 1: Preconventional Reasoning

Preconventional reasoning is the lowest level in moral development. At this level, the individual shows no internalization of moral values—moral reasoning is controlled by external rewards and punishments.

- Stage 1: *Heteronomous morality.* At this stage, moral thinking is often tied to punishment.
- Stage 2: *Individualism, instrumental purpose, and exchange.* At this stage, individuals pursue their own interests but also let others do the same. Thus, what is right involves an equal exchange. People are nice to others so that others will be nice to them in return.

Kohlberg's Level 2: Conventional Reasoning

At the **conventional reasoning** level, internalization is intermediate. Individuals abide by certain standards (internal), but they are the standards of others (external), such as parents or society.

- Stage 3: *Mutual interpersonal expectations, relationships, and interpersonal conformity.* At this stage, individuals value trust, caring, and loyalty to others as the basis of moral judgments. Children and adolescents often adopt their parents' moral standards at this stage, seeking to be thought of by their parents as a "good girl" or a "good boy."
- Stage 4: *Social systems morality.* At this stage, moral judgments are based on understanding the social order, law, justice, and duty. For example, adolescents may say that for a community to work effectively, it needs to be protected by laws that are adhered to by its members.

Kohlberg's Level 3: Postconventional Reasoning

Postconventional reasoning is the highest level in Kohlberg's theory of moral development. At this level, morality is completely internalized and is not based on others' standards. The individual recognizes alternative moral courses, explores the options, and then decides on a personal moral code.

- Stage 5: *Social contract or utility and individual rights.* At this stage, individuals reason that values, rights, and principles transcend the law. Laws and social systems can be examined in terms of the degree to which they preserve and protect fundamental human rights and values.
- Stage 6: *Universal ethical principles.* At this stage, the person has developed a moral standard based on universal human rights. When faced with a conflict between law and conscience, the person will follow conscience even though the decision might involve personal risk.

Kohlberg maintained that these levels and stages occur in a sequence and are age-related: before age 9, most children use level 1, preconventional reasoning based on external rewards and punishments, when they consider moral choices. By early adolescence, their moral reasoning is increasingly based on the application of standards set by others. Most adolescents reason at stage 3, with some signs of stages 2 and 4. By early adulthood, a small number of individuals reason in postconventional ways.

In support of this description of development, a 20-year longitudinal investigation found that use of stages 1 and 2 decreases with age (Colby et al., 1983) (see Figure 10.1). Stage 4, which did not appear at all in the moral reasoning of 10-year-olds, was reflected in the moral thinking of 62 percent of the 36-year-olds. Stage 5 did not appear until age 20 to 22 and never characterized more than 10 percent of the individuals.

Figure 10.1

Kohlberg's Three Levels and Six Stages of Moral Development

LEVEL 1 Preconventional Level No Internalization		LEVEL 2 Conventional Level Intermediate Internalization		LEVEL 3 Postconventional Level Full Internalization	
Stage 1 Heteronomous Morality	Stage 2 Individualism, Purpose, and Exchange	Stage 3 Mutual Interpersonal Expectations, Relationships, and Interpersonal Conformity	Stage 4 Social System Morality	Stage 5 Social Contract or Utility and Individual Rights	Stage 6 Universal Ethical Principles
Children obey because adults tell them to obey. People base their moral decisions on fear of punishment.	Individuals pursue their own interests but let others do the same. What is right involves equal exchange.	Individuals value trust, caring, and loyalty to others as a basis for moral judgments.	Moral judgments are based on understanding the social order, law, justice, and duty.	Individuals reason that values, rights, and principles undergird or transcend the law.	The person has developed moral judgments that are based on universal human rights. When faced with a dilemma between law and conscience, a personal, individualized conscience is followed.

Thus, the moral stages appeared somewhat later than Kohlberg initially envisioned, and reasoning at the higher stages, especially stage 6, was rare. Although stage 6 has been removed from the Kohlberg moral judgment scoring manual, it still is considered to be theoretically important in the Kohlberg scheme of moral development.

Influences on the Kohlberg Stages

What factors influence movement through Kohlberg's stages? Although moral reasoning at each stage presupposes a certain level of cognitive development, Kohlberg argued that advances in children's cognitive development do not ensure development of moral reasoning. Instead, moral reasoning also reflects children's experiences in dealing with moral questions and moral conflict.

Several investigators have tried to advance individuals' levels of moral development by having a model present arguments that reflect moral thinking one stage above the individuals' established levels. This approach applies the concepts of equilibrium and conflict that Piaget used to explain cognitive development. By presenting arguments slightly beyond the children's level of moral reasoning, the researchers created a disequilibrium that motivated the children to restructure their moral thought. The upshot of studies using this approach is that virtually any plus-stage discussion, for any length of time, seems to promote more advanced moral reasoning.

Kohlberg emphasized that peer interaction and perspective taking are critical aspects of the social stimulation that challenges children to change their moral reasoning. Whereas adults characteristically impose rules and regulations on children, the give-and-take among peers gives children an opportunity to take the perspective of another person and to generate rules democratically. Kohlberg stressed that in principle, encounters with any peers can produce perspective-taking opportunities that may advance a child's moral reasoning. A research review of cross-cultural studies involving Kohlberg's theory revealed strong support for a link between perspective-taking skills and more advanced moral judgments (Gibbs et al., 2007).

Kohlberg's Critics

Kohlberg's theory of moral development has not gone unchallenged (Gibbs, 2014; Killen & Smetana, 2014; Lapsley & Yeager, 2013; Narváez, 2014). Some key criticisms involve the link between moral thought and moral behaviour, inadequate consideration of the role of culture and the family, and the significance of concern for others.

critical thinking

Frequently, someone on the Internet circulates something that may be considered offensive because of its racist, sexist, political, or religious/anti-religious nature. Is there a line between being funny and being offensive? Have you received emails that cross that line? How do you handle emails you find offensive? Do you alert the sender? If so, what do you say? If not, why not?

MORAL THOUGHT AND MORAL BEHAVIOUR

Kohlberg's theory has been criticized for placing too much emphasis on moral thought and not enough emphasis on moral behaviour (Walker, 2004). Moral reasons can sometimes be a shelter for immoral behaviour. Corrupt CEOs and politicians endorse the loftiest of moral virtues in public before their own behaviour is exposed. Whatever the latest public scandal, you will probably find that the culprits displayed virtuous thoughts but engaged in immoral behaviour. No one wants a nation of cheaters and thieves who can reason at the postconventional level. Heinous actions can be cloaked in a mantle of moral virtue.

Social cognitive theorist Albert Bandura (1998, 2002) argues that people usually do not engage in harmful conduct until they have justified the morality of their actions to themselves. Immoral conduct is made personally and socially acceptable by portraying it as serving socially worthy or moral purposes, or even as doing God's or Allah's will.

One area of research on moral behaviour of children often studied is **altruism**, an unselfish interest in helping someone else. Three examples of altruism are those of Ryan Hreljac, Hannah Taylor, and the Kielburger brothers:

- When he was 6-years-old Ryan Hreliac heard about the lack of drinkable water in parts of Africa. Aware that building a well in Africa would cost $70, he told his parents he would do household chores to raise the money. This began a fundraising campaign that would eventually become Ryan's Well Foundation, which finances the construction of wells in Africa.
- After seeing a homeless man eating from a garbage bin, 5-year-old Hannah, helped by her father, started collecting donations in ladybug jars to launch the Big Boss Lunches campaign to raise money for the homeless. At 9 years of age, in a speech to the business community, she described homeless people as "great people, wrapped in old clothes with sad hearts." Over the past few years, the Ladybug Foundation has raised over $1 million (Perkins, 2006).

- At age 12, the younger Kielberger brother, Craig, learned about the murder of a 12-year-old boy from Pakistan because the boy had spoken out for human rights. He convinced his grade 7 classmates to start a fund to Free the Children. With his older brother, Marc, and their humanitarian efforts to change ME to WE, their Free the Children organization has had a large international impact.

To learn more about Ryan, Hannah, and the Kielbergers, visit their websites: http://www.ryanswell.ca/; http://www.ladybugfoundation.ca/; and http://www.we.org.

What role does religion plan in children's altruistic behaviour? Eighty-four percent of families around the world identify with a religion. In an effort to understand the role religion might play, a study of over 1000 children from Canada, China, Jordan, South Africa, Turkey, and the United States was undertaken. The study reported that children whose families hold religious beliefs express more empathy and sensitivity for justice in everyday life than children whose parents are non-religious. At the same time, children from religious families demonstrate harsher punitive measures than those from non-religious families. This study challenges the view that religiosity facilitates altruism (Decety et al., 2015).

CULTURE AND MORAL DEVELOPMENT

Kohlberg emphasized that his stages of moral reasoning are universal, but some critics argue that his theory is culturally biased (Gibbs, 2014; Miller & Bland, 2014). Both Kohlberg and his critics may be partially correct. One review of 45 studies in 27 cultures around the world, mostly non-European, provided support for the universality and sequence of Kohlberg's first four stages. Stages 5 and 6, however, were not found in all cultures (Gibbs et al., 2007; Snarey, 1987). In sum, although Kohlberg's approach does capture much of the moral reasoning voiced in various cultures around the world, critics point out that his approach misses or misconstrues some important moral concepts in particular cultures (Gibbs, 2009).

The Connecting through Research feature describes a Canadian researcher's findings on cultural differences and their effect on children's moral judgments.

CONNECTING through Research

Morality and Modesty

Kang Lee of the University of Toronto has extensively studied cultural differences in child behaviour. In one study, school-age children in Canada and China were asked to rate a hypothetical character's prosocial or antisocial behaviour and subsequent admission or denial of the behaviour (Lee et al., 1997). Although children in both countries believed it was good to admit one's guilt and a bad to deny wrongdoing, there was a difference in the prosocial situations. Not admitting a good deed was rated positively by Chinese children, but not by Canadian children. Because modesty is highly valued in the Chinese culture, these findings show that children's moral judgment may be strongly related to culture.

Similarly, a more recent study (Fu et al., 2007) found that Canadian children aged 9 and 11 were more willing to lie to help a friend or themselves than to lie to help a group, while Chinese children showed the opposite pattern. In fact, the older Chinese children were more willing to lie for a group than their younger peers, indicating increasing internalization of cultural values in their moral understanding in this age group.

While the description and explanation of cultural differences are interesting, a practical issue here is what to do with the information. Perhaps more awareness, particularly among educators, may foster understanding helpful to immigrant children trying to learn social mainstream expectations.

FAMILY AND MORAL DEVELOPMENT

Kohlberg believed that family processes are essentially unimportant in children's moral development. He argued that parent–child relationships are usually power-oriented and provide children with little opportunity for mutual give-and-take or perspective taking. Kohlberg said that such opportunities are more likely to be provided by children's peer relations. However, most experts on children's moral development conclude that parents' moral values and actions influence children's development of moral reasoning (Grusec et al., 2014; Thompson, 2014a). Nonetheless, most developmentalists agree with Kohlberg and Piaget that peers play an important role in the development of moral reasoning.

GENDER AND THE CARE PERSPECTIVE

The most publicized criticism of Kohlberg's theory has come from Carol Gilligan (1982, 1992, 1996), who argues that Kohlberg's theory reflects a gender bias. According to Gilligan, Kohlberg's theory is based on a male norm that puts abstract principles above relationships and concern for others. Kohlberg's **justice perspective** puts justice at the heart of morality by positioning the individual as standing alone and independently making moral decisions. In contrast to Kohlberg's view, Gilligan proposes a **care perspective**, which is a moral perspective that views people in terms of their connectedness with others and emphasizes interpersonal communication, relationships with others, and concern for others. According to Gilligan, Kohlberg greatly underplayed the care perspective, perhaps because he was a male, because most of his research was with males rather than females, and because he used male responses as a model for his theory.

In extensive interviews with girls from 6 to 18 years of age, Gilligan and her colleagues found that girls consistently interpret moral dilemmas in terms of human relationships and base these interpretations on listening to and watching other people (Gilligan, 1992; Gilligan et al., 2003). However, questions have also been raised about Gilligan's gender conclusions (Walker & Frimer, 2009). For example, a meta-analysis (a statistical analysis that combines the results of many different studies) casts doubt on Gilligan's claim of substantial gender differences in moral judgment (Jaffee & Hyde, 2000). Another review concluded that girls' moral orientations are "somewhat more likely to focus on care for others than on abstract principles of justice, but they can use both moral orientations when needed (as can boys ...)" (Blakemore, Berenbaum, & Liben, 2009, p. 132).

Other research, though, has revealed differences in how boys and girls tend to interpret some aspects of moral situations (Eisenberg, Fabes, & Spinrad, 2006). In support of this idea, one study found that females rated prosocial dilemmas (those emphasizing altruism and helping) as more significant than males did (Wark & Krebs, 2000). Another study revealed that young adolescent girls used more care-based reasoning about dating dilemmas than boys (Weisz & Black, 2002).

SOCIAL CONVENTIONAL REASONING

Some theorists and researchers argue that Kohlberg did not adequately distinguish between moral reasoning and social conventional reasoning (Smetana, 2011a, b, 2013; Turiel, 2014). **Social conventional reasoning** focuses on conventional rules that have been established by social consensus to control behaviour and maintain the social system. The rules themselves are arbitrary, such as raising your hand in class before speaking, or not cutting in line when at the grocery store.

In contrast, **moral reasoning** focuses on ethical issues and rules of morality. Unlike conventional rules, moral rules are not arbitrary. They are obligatory, widely accepted, and somewhat impersonal (Helwig & Turiel, 2011). Rules pertaining to lying, cheating, stealing, and physically harming another person are moral rules because violation of these rules affronts ethical standards that exist apart from social consensus and convention. Moral judgments involve concepts of justice, whereas social conventional judgments are concepts of social organization. Violating moral rules is considered more serious than violating conventional rules.

The social conventional approach is a serious challenge to Kohlberg's approach because Kohlberg argued that social conventions are a stopover on the road to higher moral sophistication. For social conventional reasoning advocates, social conventional reasoning is not lower than postconventional reasoning, but rather something that needs to be disentangled from the moral thread (Smetana, 2013; Smetana, Jambon, & Ball, 2014).

Recently, a distinction has also been made between moral and conventional issues, which are viewed as legitimately subject to adult social regulation, and personal issues, which are more likely subject to the child's or adolescent's independent decision making and personal discretion (Smetana, 2011a, b, 2013). Personal issues include control over one's body, privacy, and choice of friends and activities. Thus, some actions belong to a personal domain and are not governed by moral reasoning or social norms.

Prosocial Behaviour

Whereas Kohlberg's and Gilligan's theories focus primarily on the development of moral reasoning, the study of prosocial behaviour places more emphasis on the behavioural aspects of moral development. Children engage in both immoral antisocial acts, such as lying and cheating, and prosocial moral behaviour, such as showing empathy or acting altruistically (Eisenberg, Spinrad, & Morris, 2013; Padilla-Walker & Carlo, 2014). Even during the preschool years, children may care for others or comfort others in distress (Laible & Karahuta, 2014). In addition, children's sympathetic responses in the preschool years predict future prosocial behaviour (Malti, Dys, & Zuffianò, 2015).

Children's sharing becomes a more complex sense of what is just and right during middle and late childhood. By the start of the elementary school years, children begin to express objective ideas about fairness (Eisenberg, Fabes, & Spinrad, 2006). For example, most 4-year-olds are not selfless saints, and adult encouragement produces a sense of obligation to share. However, use of the word "fair" as synonymous with equal or same is common among 6-year-olds. By the mid- to late-elementary school years, children believe that equity sometimes means people with special merit or special needs deserve special treatment.

Moral Personality

Beyond the development of moral reasoning and specific moral feelings and prosocial behaviours, do children also develop a pattern of moral characteristics that is distinctively their own? In other words, do children develop a moral personality, and if so, what are its components? Researchers have focused attention on three possible components: (1) moral identity, (2) moral character, and (3) moral exemplars (Walker & Frimer, 2009b, 2011; Walker, Frimer, & Dunlop, 2010).

- *Moral identity:* Individuals have a moral identity when moral notions and moral commitments are central to their lives. They construct the self with reference to moral categories. Violating their moral commitment would place the integrity of their self at risk.
- *Moral character:* A person with moral character has the willpower, desires, and integrity to stand up to pressure, overcome distractions and disappointments, and behave morally. A person of good moral character displays moral virtues such as "honesty, truthfulness, and trustworthiness, as well as those of care, compassion, thoughtfulness, and considerateness. Other salient traits revolve around virtues of dependability, loyalty, and conscientiousness" (Walker, 2002, p. 74).
- *Moral exemplars:* Moral exemplars are people who have lived exemplary moral lives. Their moral personality, identity, character, and set of virtues reflect moral excellence and commitment.

In sum, moral development is a multifaceted, complex concept. Included in this complexity are thoughts, feelings, behaviours, and personality.

Gender

As we discussed in Chapter 8, preschool children display a gender identity and gender-typed behaviour that reflects biological, cognitive, and social influences. Here we will examine the pervasive influence of gender stereotypes, gender similarities and differences, and gender-role classification.

Gender Stereotypes

According to the old ditty, boys are made of "frogs and snails and puppy dog tails" and girls are made of "sugar and spice and all that is nice." In the past, a well-adjusted boy was supposed to be independent, aggressive, and powerful. A well-adjusted girl was supposed to be dependent, nurturing, and uninterested in power. These notions reflect **gender stereotypes**, which are broad categories that reflect general impressions and beliefs about females and males.

Contemporary research has found that gender stereotypes are, to a great extent, still present in today's world, both in the lives of children and adults (Hyde, 2014; Leaper, 2013; Liben, Bigler, & Hilliard, 2014). Gender stereotyping continues to change during middle and late childhood and adolescence (Blakemore, Berenbaum, & Liben, 2009). By the time children enter elementary school, they have considerable knowledge about which activities are linked with being male or female. By 5 years of age, both boys and girls stereotype boys as powerful and in more negative terms, such as mean, and girls in more positive terms, such as nice (Martin & Ruble, 2010). Across the elementary school years, children become more flexible in their gender attitudes (Trautner et al., 2005).

A recent study of children from 3 to 10 years of age revealed that girls and older children use a higher percentage of gender stereotypes (Miller et al., 2009). In this study, appearance stereotypes were more prevalent on the part of girls, while activity (sports, for example) and trait (aggressive, for example) stereotyping was more commonly engaged in by boys. Researchers also have found that boys' gender stereotypes are more rigid than girls' (Blakemore, Berenbaum, & Liben, 2009).

Gender Similarities and Differences

Let us now examine some of the similarities and differences between the sexes, keeping in mind that (a) the differences are averages—not all females versus all males; (b) even when differences are reported, there is considerable overlap between the sexes; and (c) the differences may be due primarily to biological factors, socio-cultural factors, or both. First, we will examine physical similarities and differences, including brain structure, and then we will turn to cognitive and socio-emotional similarities and differences.

PHYSICAL DEVELOPMENT

Women have about twice the body fat of men, most of it concentrated around their breasts and hips. In males, fat is more likely to go to the abdomen. On the average, males grow to be 10 percent taller than females. Other physical differences are less obvious. From conception on, females have a longer life expectancy than males, and females are less likely than males to develop physical or mental disorders. Males have twice the risk of coronary disease as females.

BRAIN STRUCTURE

Does gender matter when it comes to brain structure and function? Human brains are much alike, whether the brain belongs to a male or a female (Halpern et al., 2007). However, researchers have found some differences in the brains of males and females (Hofer et al., 2007). Female brains are approximately 10 percent smaller than male brains (Giedd, 2012; Giedd et al., 2012). However, female brains have more folds; the larger folds (called convolutions) allow more surface brain tissue within the skulls of females than males (Luders et al., 2004). An area of the parietal lobe that functions in visuospatial skills is larger in males than females (Frederikse et al., 2000).

However, many of these differences are either small or the research is inconsistent. Also, when sex differences in the brain have been revealed, in many cases they have not been directly linked to psychological differences (Blakemore, Berenbaum, & Liben, 2009). Although research on sex differences in the brain is still in its infancy, it is likely that there are far more similarities than differences in the brains of females and males. A further point is worth noting: anatomical sex differences in the brain may be due to the biological origins of these differences, behavioural experiences (which underscores the brain's continuing plasticity), or a combination of these factors.

Figure 10.2

Visuospatial Ability of Males and Females

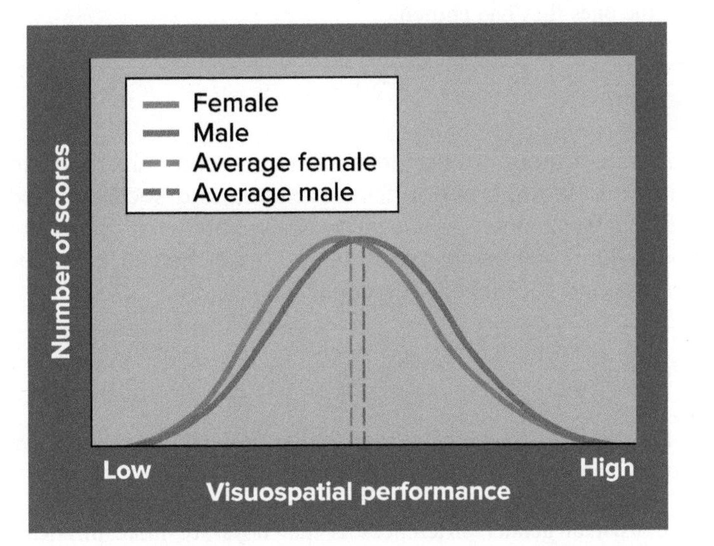

From John Santrock, *A Topical Approach to Life-Span Development*, 3/e, Figure 12-4. Copyright © 2007 The McGraw-Hill Companies. Used with permission.

Note that although the average male's visuospatial ability is higher than the average female's, the overlap between the sexes is substantial. Not all males have better visuospatial ability than all females—the substantial overlap indicates that although the average score of males is higher, many females outperform many males on such tasks.

Research in this area fuels the nature versus nurture debate: Are anatomical sex differences in the brain due to the biological origins of these differences? Do our brains reflect the traditional roles we have played? For example, are women more attuned to social situations than men because they give birth and nurture their babies? Have men developed more visuospatial skills because of their roles in providing for and protecting their family? What role is played by behavioural experiences, which underscores the brain's continuing plasticity? For example, will focused practice enhance ability? Or are our brains shaped by a combination of these factors? Figure 10.2 illustrates differences in visuospatial performance in males and females.

COGNITIVE DEVELOPMENT

No gender differences in general intelligence have been revealed, but some gender differences have been found in some cognitive areas (Halpern, 2012). Research has shown that in general, girls and women have slightly better verbal skills than boys and men, although in some verbal skill areas the differences are substantial (Blakemore, Berenbaum, & Liben, 2009). One area of math that has been examined for possible gender differences is visuospatial skills, which include being able to rotate objects mentally and to determine what they would look like when rotated (Halpern, 2012). Although boys generally exhibit better visuospatial skills than girls, the differences are small (Hyde, 2014; Hyde & Else-Quest, 2013) (see Figure 10.2). A meta-analysis found no gender differences in math for adolescents (Lindberg et al., 2010). A recent research review concluded that girls have more negative math attitudes and that parents' and teachers' expectancies for children's math competence are often gender-biased in favour of boys (Gunderson et al., 2012).

On the other hand, there is strong evidence that females outperform males in reading and writing. In national studies, girls have higher reading achievement than boys. An international study in 65 countries found that girls had higher reading achievement than did boys in every country (Reilly, 2012). In this study, the gender difference in reading was stronger in countries with less gender equity and lower economic prosperity. Although most children do not fall behind, a Quebec study reported that more boys than girls repeat a grade in elementary school, and the gap increases considerably in secondary school (Pellitier, 2004). In addition to gender differences, *State of Learning in Canada: No Time for Complacency* (Canadian Council on Learning, 2007) further reports that economically disadvantaged children, be they boys or girls, have more difficulty with learning (Booth et al., 2009).

One interesting area of gender differences in cognition is risk taking. In her study of elementary school children, Barbara Morrongiello of the University of Guelph found that boys were more likely than girls to select riskier options in everyday recreational activities (Morrongiello & Dawber, 2004). Girls' decision making was largely determined by concerns for safety, while boys' was influenced by fun, competence, and convenience, as well as safety. This difference in thinking may reflect different environmental influences on the cognitive development of girls and boys. Girls tended to believe their choices were the same as the ones their parents would want them to select; on the other hand, most boys said their parents would want them to pick a safer option than the ones they had chosen.

critical thinking

What do you think? Are women more attuned to social situations? Are men more likely to take risks? If so, are these traits hardwired in the brain or have evolution and social context influenced the brain's development? The research is as complex as it is inconclusive, but what do you think? What role has your gender played in your behaviour? Academic performance? Your choices, including career choices? Have your choices been consistent with societal expectations?

SOCIO-EMOTIONAL DEVELOPMENT

Three areas of socio-emotional development in which gender similarities and differences have been studied extensively are aggression, emotion, and prosocial behaviour.

Aggression One of the most consistent gender differences is that boys are more physically aggressive than girls. The difference occurs in all cultures and appears very early in children's development (White, 2001). The aggression difference is especially pronounced when children are provoked. Once again, both biological and environmental factors may account for these differences. Biological factors include heredity and hormones. Environmental factors include cultural expectations, adult and peer models, and social agents who reward aggression in boys and punish aggression in girls.

Emotion Girls are more likely to express their emotions openly and intensely than are boys, especially in displaying sadness and fear (Blakemore, Berenbaum, & Liben, 2009). Girls also are better at reading others' emotions and more likely to show empathy than are boys (Blakemore, Berenbaum, & Liben, 2009). Males usually show less self-regulation of emotion than females, and this low self-control can translate into behavioural problems (Eisenberg, Spinrad, & Smith, 2004).

Prosocial Behaviour Females view themselves as more prosocial and empathic (Eisenberg & Morris, 2004). Across childhood and adolescence, females engage in more prosocial behaviour (Hastings, Utendale, & Sullivan, 2007). The biggest gender difference occurs for kind and considerate behaviour, with a smaller difference in sharing.

Emotional development is multifaceted in that a variety of factors influence growth. In addition to gender, other factors include the cutoff dates to enter school or sports programs, which were originally established so that children in classes or on playing fields would be about the same age. However, when a child must be 5 years old by January 1 to enter kindergarten or to play a sport, that child may be almost a year older or younger than other children in the same group. Researchers have identified **relative age** as the differences among children of the same age group, and **relative age effect (RAE)** as the consequence of relative age (Musch & Grodin, 2001). Because a child's physical, socio-emotional, and cognitive abilities differ, the older children are advantaged. Consequently, they perform much better both academically and athletically and are, in fact, even less likely to be classified as learning disabled (Musch & Grodin, 2001).

Through effort and hard work, the academic differences tend to level off. However, the same is not true of sports. The older children are often recipients of special supports such as better coaching because they are on the "rep" teams, easier access to ice time for hockey, and so on. As a result, they continue to outperform the younger members of the cohort right into adulthood, as measured by the birth dates of professional hockey, soccer, football, and baseball players in Europe and North America. Both physical and psychological factors are at work (Gladwell, 2008; Musch & Grodin, 2001).

critical thinking

Were you surprised to read about relative age and relative age effect (RAE)? Do you think RAE may be a factor in your development or the development of people you know? If so, how? If you have found RAE to be a factor in development, what effect do you think RAE may have on an individual's self-esteem and self-concept? Why do you think the RAE levels off academically but not athletically?

Gender-Role Classification

As both men and women became dissatisfied with the burdens imposed by stereotypical roles, researchers in the 1970s proposed alternatives to femininity and masculinity, and suggested that individuals could have both masculine and feminine traits. This thinking led to the development of the concept of **androgyny**, the presence of masculine and feminine characteristics in the same person (Bem, 1977; Spence & Helmreich, 1978).

Gender experts such as Sandra Bem argue that androgynous individuals are more flexible, competent, and mentally healthy than their masculine or feminine counterparts. To some degree, though, which gender-role classification is best depends on the context involved. For example, in close relationships, feminine and androgynous orientations might be more desirable. One study found that girls and individuals high in femininity showed a stronger interest in caring than did boys and individuals high in masculinity (Karniol, Grosz, & Schorr, 2003). However, masculine and androgynous orientations might be more desirable in traditional academic and work settings because of the achievement demands in these contexts.

Despite talk about the "sensitive male," William Pollack (1999) argues that little has been done to change traditional ways of raising boys. He says that the "boy code" tells boys that "big boys don't cry." Boys learn the boy code in many contexts—sandboxes, playgrounds, schoolrooms, camps, and hangouts. Pollack and others suggest that boys would benefit from being socialized to express their anxieties and concerns and to better regulate their aggression.

Measures have been developed to assess androgyny. One of the most widely used is the Bem Sex-Role Inventory. To check whether your gender-role classification is masculine, feminine, or androgynous, see Figure 10.3.

increased probability of physical health issues in adulthood. The most recent study conducted by Statistics Canada concluded that "From a public health perspective, it is increasingly recognized that prevention of child abuse has major implications for reduction in mental health problems, but it is also possible that reducing child abuse may lead to better physical health outcomes" (Afifi et al., 2016).

To this point we have discussed a number of ideas about families in middle and late childhood. For a review, see the Reach Your Learning Outcomes section at the end of this chapter.

Peers, Bullying, and Social Media

LO4 Identify changes in peer relationships, the roles in bullying and its impact, and the influence of social media on growth and development in middle and late childhood.

- **Friends**
- **Peer Statuses**
- **Social Cognition**
- **Bullying**
- **Social Media**

During middle and late childhood, children spend an increasing amount of time in peer interaction. As you will see in this section, friends are important for many reasons. You may also see your own experience with friends in the descriptions here.

Friends

Friendship is an important aspect of children's development (Neal, Neal, & Cappella, 2014; Rose et al., 2012). Like adult friendships, children's friendships are typically characterized by similarity (Brechwald & Prinstein, 2011). Throughout childhood, friends are more similar than dissimilar in terms of age, sex, race, and many other factors. Friends often have similar attitudes toward school, similar educational aspirations, and closely aligned achievement orientations.

Engaging in positive interactions, resolving conflicts in non-aggressive ways, and having quality friendships in middle and late childhood not only have positive outcomes, but also are linked to more positive relationship outcomes in adolescence and adulthood (Huston & Ripke, 2006).

According to Willard Hartup (1983, 1996, 2009), who has studied peer relations and friendship for more than three decades, friends can be cognitive and emotional resources from childhood through old age. Friends can foster self-esteem and a sense of well-being.

More specifically, children's friendships can serve six functions (Gottman & Parker, 1987):

- *Companionship:* Friendship provides children with a familiar partner and playmate, someone who is willing to spend time with them and join in collaborative activities.
- *Stimulation:* Friendship provides children with interesting information, excitement, and amusement.
- *Physical support:* Friendship provides time, resources, and assistance.
- *Ego support:* Friendship provides the expectation of support, encouragement, and feedback, which helps children maintain an impression of themselves as competent, attractive, and worthwhile individuals.
- *Social comparison:* Friendship provides information about where the child stands vis-à-vis others, and whether the child is doing okay.

- *Intimacy and affection:* Friendship provides children with a warm, close, trusting relationship with another individual in which self-disclosure takes place.

Friends also seem to have similar risk-taking tendencies. At the University of Guelph, Barbara Morrongiello's work shows that 53 percent of the dyads of best friends in her elementary school sample "fairly frequently" did risky things—"meaning that someone could get hurt"—together (Morrongiello & Dawber, 2004). In fact, the two children in each dyad expected their best friends to choose the same risky/safe action as they did in various situations. If both of them could not agree on an action, the success of persuading the other to follow along depended on the quality of the friendship.

Similarity happens in terms of age and sex, as well as race. For example, a study in Montreal (Aboud, Mendelson, & Purdy, 2003) showed that throughout the elementary school years, same-race friendships become more prevalent and cross-race friendships become rarer. Although children still socialize with peers of other races in school and some maintain a strong friendship with each other, "the shift away from cross-race friendships is observable" (p. 171). The researchers suggest that this shift may be a result of the older children's search for an identity, for which one's own race is an important issue.

Intimacy in friendships is self-disclosure and the sharing of private thoughts. Research reveals that intimate friendships may not appear until early adolescence (Berndt & Perry, 1990). By spending time with one another, finding common interests, and developing and showing trust, children can start the path of building friendships that will allow them to share their deep thoughts and feelings.

While face-to-face interactions are important for intimacy in friendships, researchers have come to wonder if online communication may reduce the intimacy levels with friends. According to a recent survey reported by Media Awareness Network, "over one quarter of students in grade 4 now have their own cell phones" (Steeves, 2014). This high level of online communication is increasing annually and may change the nature of modern friendships.

Although having friends can be a developmental advantage, not all friendships are alike (Vitaro, Boivin, & Bukowski, 2009; Wentzel, 2013). People differ in the company they keep—that is, who their friends are. Developmental advantages occur when children have friends who are socially skilled and supportive. However, it is not developmentally advantageous to have coercive and conflict-ridden friendships (Laursen & Pursell, 2009). A recent study found that students who engage in classroom aggressive-disruptive behaviour are more likely to have aggressive friends (Powers & Bierman, 2013).

Friendship also plays an important role in children's emotional well-being and academic success. Students with friends who are academically oriented are more likely to achieve success in school themselves (Wentzel, 2013). In one study, grade 6 students who did not have a friend engaged in less prosocial behaviour (cooperation, sharing, helping others), had lower grades, and were more emotionally distressed (depression, lower levels of well-being) than their counterparts who had one or more friends (Wentzel, Barry, & Caldwell, 2004). In this study, two years later, in grade 8, the students who did not have a friend in grade 6 continued to be more emotionally distressed.

Peer Statuses

Which children are likely to be popular with their peers? Developmentalists address this and similar questions by examining *sociometric status,* a term that describes the extent to which children are liked or disliked by their peer group (Cillessen & van den Berg, 2012). Sociometric status is typically assessed by asking children to rate how much they like or dislike each of their classmates. It can also be assessed by asking children to nominate the children they like the most and those they like the least.

Developmentalists have distinguished five peer statuses (Wentzel & Asher, 1995):

- *Popular children* are frequently nominated as a best friend and are rarely disliked by their peers.
- *Average children* receive an average number of both positive and negative nominations from their peers.
- *Neglected children* are infrequently nominated as a best friend but are not disliked by their peers.
- *Rejected children* are infrequently nominated as someone's best friend and are actively disliked by their peers.
- *Controversial children* are frequently nominated both as someone's best friend and as being disliked.

Popular children have the social skills that contribute to their being well-liked. They give out reinforcements, listen carefully, maintain open lines of communication with peers, are happy, control their negative emotions, act like themselves, show enthusiasm and concern for others, and are self-confident without being conceited.

Neglected children engage in low rates of interaction with their peers, who often describe them as shy. Rather than shy, however, they may be introverted, or perhaps a combination of introversion and shyness. The goal of many training programs for neglected children is to help them attract attention from their peers in positive ways and to hold that attention by asking questions, by listening in a warm and friendly way, and by saying things about themselves that relate to the peers' interests. They also are taught to enter groups more effectively.

Rejected children often have more serious adjustment problems later in life than do neglected children (Rubin et al., 2013). John Coie (2004, pp. 252–253) provides three reasons why aggressive peer-rejected boys have problems in social relationships:

> *First, the rejected, aggressive boys are more impulsive and have problems sustaining attention. As a result, they are more likely to be disruptive of ongoing activities in the classroom and in focused group play.*
>
> *Second, rejected, aggressive boys are more emotionally reactive. They are aroused to anger more easily and probably have more difficulty calming down once aroused. Because of this they are more prone to become angry at peers and attack them verbally and physically....*
>
> *Third, rejected children have fewer social skills in making friends and maintaining positive relationships with peers.*

Not all rejected children are aggressive (Rubin et al., 2013). Although aggression and its related characteristics of impulsiveness and disruptiveness underlie rejection about half the time, approximately 10 to 20 percent of rejected children are shy.

How can rejected children be trained to interact more effectively with their peers? Rejected children may be taught to more accurately assess whether the intentions of their peers are negative (Bierman & Powers, 2009). They may be asked to engage in role playing or to discuss hypothetical situations involving negative encounters with peers, such as when a peer cuts into a line ahead of them. In some programs, children are shown videotapes of appropriate peer interaction and asked to draw lessons from what they have seen (Ladd, Buhs, & Troop, 2004).

Social Cognition

A boy accidentally trips and knocks another boy's soft drink out of his hand. That boy misinterprets the encounter as hostile, which leads him to retaliate aggressively against the boy who tripped. Through repeated encounters of this kind, the aggressive boy's classmates come to perceive him as habitually acting in inappropriate ways.

This encounter demonstrates the importance of social cognition—thoughts about social matters, such as the aggressive boy's interpretation of an encounter as hostile and his classmates' perception of his behaviour as inappropriate (Crone & Dahl, 2012; Vetter et al., 2014). Children's social cognition about their peers becomes increasingly important for understanding peer relationships in middle and late childhood. Of special interest are the ways in which children process information about peer relations and their social knowledge (Dodge, 2011a, b).

Kenneth Dodge (1983, 2011a, b) argues that children go through five steps in processing information about their social world. They decode social cues, interpret, search for a response, select an optimal response, and then act. Dodge found that aggressive boys are more likely to perceive another child's actions as hostile when the child's intention is ambiguous. When aggressive boys search for cues to determine a peer's intention, they respond more rapidly, less efficiently, and less reflectively than do non-aggressive children. These are among the social cognitive factors believed to be involved in the nature of children's conflicts.

Social knowledge is also involved in children's ability to get along with peers. Children need to know what scripts to follow to get other children to be their friends. For example, as part of the script for getting friends, it helps to know that saying nice things, regardless of what the peer does or says, will make the peer like the child more.

Bullying

Once upon a time, children got into fights, called each other names, and could run home, perhaps crying, to escape. But today, the nature of bullying has changed dramatically and the implications are much more serious due to cyber-bullying and the possibility of YouTube videos going viral. There is no safe place.

Bullying is the use of strength to intimidate or coerce another and is often repeated, even habitual, and may have devastating consequences for both the bully and the bullied.

WHAT IS BULLYING?

By definition, **bullying** is the use of strength to intimidate or coerce another and is often repeated, even habitual. The bully will use his or her physical strength, popularity, or access to embarrassing information to control or harm others. Making threats, spreading rumours, attacking physically and/or verbally, and purposely excluding someone from a group are examples of bullying behaviours. According to Dr. Debra Pepler of York University and Dr. Wendy Craig of Queen's University, bullying is a relationship problem in which the bully learns to appreciate his or her power, the victim becomes increasingly powerless, and the bystander often aligns himself or herself with the aggressor (Pepler, 2009). Boys tend to be more likely to bully and be bullied physically, whereas girls tend to be more prone to indirect bullying such as social exclusion and gossiping (Public Safety Canada, 2016). Three roles are involved: *the bully, the bullied,* and *the bystander.* A fourth role, identified by Shelagh Dunn of the University of Alberta, is the *upstander*. The upstander refers to children whose empathy with the victimized child leads them to employ intervention strategies.

HOW PREVALENT IS BULLYING?

Among adults, 38 percent of men and 30 percent of women report having experienced occasional or frequent bullying during their childhood (Canadian Institutes of Health Research, 2012; PREVNet, 2015). Children are either the bully, the bullied, or the bystander. Few have the confidence to be the upstander. In most playground bullying incidents, peers are drawn in and become captive audiences, thereby increasing the bully's status (PREVNet, 2015). Should a peer have the confidence to intervene, the majority of the time, the bullying stops. In fact, according to the RCMP (2015), 60 percent of the time when a peer intervenes, the bullying stops. The children who intervene model Gandhi's famous quote, "Be the change you want to see" (Dunn, 2009).

WHAT IS THE IMPACT OF BULLYING?

The ramifications of bullying are serious for all. Bullying can be a traumatic experience and have devastating consequences for both the bully and the bullied. Children who bully others often engage in unlawful activities in their teens, including substance abuse, dropping out of school, sexual harassment and dating aggression, gang involvement, and criminal activity. Many boys who bully in school will have criminal records by the time they reach their twenties (PREVNet, 2012; Royal Canadian Mounted Police (RCMP), 2015). In other words, the idea that individuals will outgrow bullying is a myth. The impact on the bullied child ranges from depression to low self-esteem, social anxiety, loneliness, stress-related health problems, and suicidal thoughts (RCMP 2015).

A disturbing number of Canadian children have committed suicide as a result of prolonged victimization by peers (Pepler et al., 2011). One of the tragic cases was the suicide of Mitchell Wilson, a boy with muscular dystrophy, brutally beaten by a boy who wanted his iPhone. Wilson took his life at age 11 when he learned he would have to face the boy who had victimized him in court (Mayer, 2011). In the opening vignette, you read about Eivan's experience with bullying. Fortunately, with the support of his family, he was able to manage this situation quite well. As we have read or heard in the news, this isn't always the case. You may have read or heard about the suicides of teenage girls such as Amanda Todd and Rheteah Parsons who were victims of bullying. Their stories were complex and heart-breaking.

WHAT CAN BE DONE?

Relationship solutions are needed to stop bullying. Each participant in the relationship needs help: the child who bullies, the one who is bullied, and the ones who stand by. All three need to build confidence in their social skills and the supports need to be tailored to the individual situation. The overriding principle is that children depend on adults to help them in the development of relationship capacity (Pepler, 2009). Author Barbara Coloroso (CBC, 2012) recommends employing the "three R's":

- *Restitution:* The person who acted as a bully and the one(s) who acted as bystander(s) admit to the wrongdoing and recognize the harm they have caused.
- *Resolution:* In an effort to mitigate the harm inflicted, those who assumed the roles of bully and bystander(s) identify what they will and won't do.
- *Reconciliation:* The persons who inflicted harm directly through bullying behaviour or indirectly as a bystander attempt to talk to the person who was targeted, who may or may not be ready to accept an apology. If the targeted person chooses not to be friends, he or she can request that the behaviour stop. Once verbal confirmation is given, the targeted person can agree to move on and not hold a grudge. It may take a while, even a lifetime, for the targeted person to forgive and forget, let alone become friends with those who have inflicted physical and/or emotional pain.

The Royal Canadian Mounted Police recommend that the victim of bullying walk away or leave the online conversation, keep track of the occurrences, tell a trusted adult or report to the school administrator, and report criminal offences such as threats, assaults, or sexual exploitation to the local police department. If you know of someone who is being bullied, tell the bully to stop if you feel safe doing so, find someone to help, befriend the victim, and report it to a teacher, even anonymously (RCMP 2015). For more information, go to http://www.rcmp-grc.gc.ca/cycp-cpcj/bull-inti/index-eng.htm.

Many schools have initiated a variety of educational approaches to combat bullying. Dr. Pepler of York University and Dr. Craig of Queen's University launched PREVNet, a national network to bring together researchers, strategies, and information to address bullying. After a bullying incident in a high school in British Columbia, a teacher, Trevor Knowlton, launched STOP A BULLY, a national charity that allows victims, bystanders, and bullies to report incidents, thereby increasing awareness and accountability, as well as prevention strategies. For more information, go to http://www.prevnet.ca/research/bullying-statistics/bullying-the-facts or http://www.stopabully.ca/bullying-information.html.

Social Media

For some children, screen time spent watching TV or playing computer games has become their best friend, replacing school or neighbourhood friendships. Educators, parents, and researchers are all concerned about the negative effect that television, social media, and computer games may have on children. As Figure 10.4 illustrates, children spend a considerable amount of time online. The more-rapid-than-life action of television and of computer games triggers the release of dopamine, the neurotransmitter in the brain associated with pleasure. This creates a desire for more and faster action, and ultimately can lead to addiction (Doidge, 2007). Is there a link between violence and aggression in children and the violence and aggression illustrated on television and in video games?

Figure 10.4

How Wired Are Canadian Children?

▪ In grades 4 and 5, 24 percent of children have their own cell phones. By grade 11, this number rises to 85 percent.
▪ 20 percent of grade 4 students and over half of grade 11 students sleep with their phones in case they get a message in the night.
▪ YouTube, Facebook, Twitter, and games are the most popular Internet sites used by young people.
▪ Almost one-third of students in grades 4–6 have a Facebook account (even though the terms of use bar children from having one before the age of 13).
▪ Sites promoting learning and creativity rank in the top 50 sites.
▪ One-third of students worry that they spend too much time online, though only half of them think they would be upset if they had to unplug for a week.

Highlights from *Young Canadians in a Wired World Phase III*: Trends and Recommendations and Life Online: Executive Summary (MediaSmarts, 2014)

Another concern is whether children internalize the images on advertisements and in games. For example, does the media portrayal of young girls as sexual creatures influence the way young girls see themselves, or the way young boys see them? Are these media contributing to obesity? Does schoolwork suffer because of these media? Is targeting advertisements to children effective?

critical thinking

In her memoir, *My Life on the Road,* Gloria Steinem observes that "...people in the same room understand and empathize with each other in a way that is impossible on page or screen." Do you agree with her? Is the wired world of our children diminishing for them the very experience of being human?

Students see talking to strangers online as safe and believe they have the skills needed to protect themselves from online risks such as bullying and sexting if necessary. (Reassuringly, 97 percent report rarely or never having had a problem with online threats.) Boys are more likely to report having been mean or cruel and are far more likely to have been harassed than girls. In addition, racism and homophobia may put some children at a higher risk for bullying.

Students report that network technologies are used to keep in touch with families and friends and that trust between themselves and their parents is important. Online privacy is important to children and becomes increasingly important in the pre-teen and teenage years, and young people feel that teachers and parents may overreact to some online communications which is intended to be humorous, not harmful.

Although there are positive applications and outcomes from both computer games and television, research supports that there are also causes for concern. Researchers are recommending that digital literacy instruction, including its emotional and ethical aspects, be integrated across the curriculum. Such instruction includes searching for information, using privacy settings, understanding how companies collect personal information online, and learning how to know what is legal and illegal online (Steeves, 2014). The digital world is accelerating at a blistering speed, one that most find very difficult to keep up with. For more information, including recommendations, the Media Smarts 2105 report, "Young Canadians in a Wired World, Phase III: Trends and Recommendations" may be accessed online at http://mediasmarts.ca/ycww.

Reach Your **Learning Outcomes**

Emotional and Personality Development

LO1 Discuss emotional and personality development in middle and late childhood.

The Self	▪ The internal self, the social self, and the socially comparative self become more prominent in middle and late childhood. ▪ Self-esteem refers to global evaluations of the self; self-esteem is also referred to as self-worth or self-image. Self-concept refers to domain-specific self-evaluations. ▪ Self-efficacy is the belief that one can master a situation and produce favourable outcomes. ▪ Erikson's fourth stage, industry versus inferiority, occurs in the elementary school years. ▪ Adler believed that a multitude of factors lead to varying degrees of inferiority and that the goal of behaviour, prosocial and otherwise, is to reduce or eliminate feelings of inferiority.
Emotional Development	▪ Increased understanding, reasoning, and controlling of emotions occur in middle and late childhood. ▪ Emotional intelligence is a form of social intelligence that involves the ability to monitor one's own and others' feelings and emotions, to discriminate among them, and to use this information to guide one's own thinking and action. ▪ A child's ability to assess and cope with stress becomes more competent as the child matures.

Moral Development and Gender

LO2 Describe moral development and gender.

Moral Development	▪ Kohlberg developed a theory of moral reasoning with three levels—preconventional, conventional, and postconventional—and six stages (two at each level). Increased internalization characterizes movement to levels 2 and 3. ▪ Criticisms of Kohlberg's theory include the claims that Kohlberg overemphasized cognition and underemphasized behaviour, underestimated culture's role as well as the family's role, inadequately considered the significance of concern for others and the universality of the stages (e.g., stages 5 and 6 may not be found in all cultures). ▪ A moral personality has three possible components: moral identity, moral character, and moral exemplars.
Gender	▪ Using stereotypes, including gender stereotypes, helps people simplify the complexity of everyday life. ▪ Some differences in brain structure exist between boys and girls, but the link to behaviour is complex and inconclusive. ▪ Some experts, such as Hyde, argue that cognitive differences between females and males have been exaggerated. ▪ Current research reports that boys have more difficulty learning, particularly reading, than girls, and are more likely to repeat a grade than girls. ▪ In terms of socio-emotional differences, boys are more physically aggressive and active, while girls are more likely to better regulate their emotions and show more

	relational aggression. Prosocial behaviour, although linked to stereotyped behaviours, is contextual. ▪ Androgyny means having both masculine and feminine characteristics. ▪ Context plays an important role in gender classification and roles.

Families

LO3 **Describe developmental changes in parent–child relationships and child maltreatment.**

Developmental Changes in Parent–Child Relationships	▪ New parent–child issues emerge in middle and late childhood years. Parents spend less time with their children in this stage, though parents continue to be extremely important in their children's lives. Some control is transferred from parent to child and becomes more coregulatory. ▪ Parents take on a role of manager, monitoring their children's behaviour and organizing their environment. ▪ Stepfamilies or blended families are common. ▪ Children who have parents with mental disorders may experience confusion and fear about the situation.
Child Maltreatment: Prevalence and Consequences	▪ Child maltreatment has serious health, justice, educational, and educational ramifications. Forms of child maltreatment include neglect, physical abuse, emotional abuse, sexual abuse, and exposure to family violence. ▪ Emotional abuse is linked with most other kinds of abuse. ▪ Neglect is the most common form of abuse. ▪ Most cases of maltreatment are thought to go unreported. ▪ Child maltreatment has long-term effects that impair an individual's functioning in adolescence and adulthood.

Peers, Bullying, and Social Media

LO4 **Identify changes in peer relationships, the roles in bullying and its impact, and the influence of social media on growth and development in middle and late childhood.**

Friends	▪ Children's friendships serve six functions: companionship, stimulation, physical support, ego support, social comparison, and intimacy/affection. ▪ Intimacy and similarity are common characteristics of friendships.
Peer Statuses	▪ Five peer statuses have been identified: popular, average, neglected, rejected, and controversial.
Social Cognition	▪ Social information-processing skills and social knowledge are two important dimensions of social cognition in peer relations.
Bullying	▪ Bullying can result in short-term and long-term negative effects, including suicide, for the victim. ▪ Children who bully often engage in risk-taking behaviours in adolescence such as excessive alcohol and substance use. ▪ Most children who bully have excellent social skills and use these skills in relational bullying, such as isolating a victim, gossiping, or texting.

	▪ Children may engage in one or more of these four categories: bully, bullied, bystander, or upstander. ▪ There is some overlap between offenders and victims of traditional bullying and cyberbullying. ▪ Parents and educators are engaging in strategies to address bullying.
Social Media	▪ Although screen time—television, social media, online activities and computer games—may offer interesting and educational content, the nature of friendship may change and researchers recommend that digital literacy instruction be integrated across the curriculum.

review → connect → reflect

review

1. What impact does socio-economic status, ethnicity, and culture have in contributing to the development of Erikson's fourth stage of development, *industry versus inferiority?* LO1
2. How does Kohlberg's theory of moral development differ from Gilligan's? LO2
3. What are some of the factors that contribute to gender identity? LO2
4. How do parent–child relationships change in middle and late childhood? LO3
5. Describe child maltreatment and identify some of the long-term consequences to socio-emotional development. LO3
6. What are the roles and long-term impacts of bullying? LO4

connect

More children are using food banks than ever before, and of the children using food banks many have disabilities and/or come from backgrounds that are racialized, Aboriginal, or new to Canada. What is the impact of poverty on identity, self-esteem, self-concept, and learning?

reflect

Your Own Personal Journey of Life

Nearly half—47 percent—of Canadian parents report having a child who is a victim of bullying. Such a high percentage would indicate that most, if not all, of us have in some way been involved, either as the bully, the victim, the bystander, or perhaps the upstander. How is bullying defined, and what strategies could be put in place to encourage more children to be the upstander?

SECTION 6

Adolescence

CHAPTER 11

Physical and Cognitive Development in Adolescence

CHAPTER OUTLINE

The Nature of Adolescence

LO1 Analyze the life stage of adolescence.

Physical Changes during Puberty

LO2 Describe the physical changes that occur during puberty.

- **Sexual Maturation, Height, and Weight**
- **Hormonal Changes**
- **Body Image**
- **Teen Perspectives on Maturity**
- **The Brain**

Adolescent Sexuality

LO3 Describe adolescent sexuality, sexual identity, and risk factors related to intimate sexual behaviour.

- **Developing a Sexual Identity**
- **The Timing of Adolescent Sexual Behaviours**
- **Risk Factors and Sexual Problems**
- **Adolescent Pregnancy and Health**

Adolescent Health Problems and Wellness

LO4 Compare and contrast adolescent health issues related to eating disorders, substance use, and depression.

- **Nutrition, Exercise, and Sleep**
- **Eating Disorders**
- **Risk and Vulnerability**
- **Substance Use and Addiction**
- **Teen Depression**

Adolescent Cognition

LO5 Explain cognitive development in adolescence and the influence of schools on adolescent cognition.

- **Piaget's Theory**
- **Adolescent Egocentrism**
- **Information Processing**
- **Education**

"In youth, we clothe ourselves with rainbows, and go brave as the zodiac."

—RALPH WALDO EMERSON, NINETEENTH-CENTURY AMERICAN POET AND ESSAYIST

Adolescence: A Time of Firsts

Childhood is often romanticized as a relatively carefree period, free from adult responsibilities. Adolescence, on the other hand, is often characterized as a period of moodiness, temptation, and rebellion, during which we move away from the shelter of our family to the companionship of our friends.

The adolescent's world is filled with possibilities inconceivable 30 years ago. Thirty years ago very few families had computers, and even fewer were connected to the Internet. Facebook, Twitter, blogs, avatars, virtual communities, text-messaging, and smartphones are relatively recent developments, altering communication patterns for all. New technologies or applications appear daily. Growing up with these communication tools, adolescents are highly adept at using them for entertainment, retrieving information, and socializing with friends (either two time zones or two houses away), and often spend considerable time doing so.

Like toddlerhood, adolescence is a period of "firsts"; however, instead of first steps and first words cheered on by delighted parents, teenagers often experience their first dance, first unchaperoned party, first kiss, first wet dream, and first menstrual period, often without the same degree of parental guidance. Unlike toddlerhood, our teenage "firsts" are (1) remembered, (2) often accomplished away from parents, and (3) usually shared with peers, rather than parents.

New responsibilities accompany a teen's developing sense of independence. Demands related to homework, part-time jobs, household chores, and other extracurricular activities are made even more complicated by demands such as choosing a career direction, getting good grades, keeping up with friends, and dating. Adolescence is a time of evaluation, independent decision making, commitment, and carving a place in the world.

Bodily changes converge with a heightened concern for body image. The desire to belong and to fit in fashions the teen's taste in a range of things, such as musical preferences, friendships, hairstyle, and even language. "Fitting in" is a must, for as one 12-year-old boy exclaimed, "If you're a guy and you don't fit in, you'll get pounded!" For many youngsters, "fitting in" may jeopardize health; for example, 12- and 13-year-old girls may share information about diet pills, rather than nutrition. Planning for the future, challenging authority, identifying hypocrisy, and breaking curfews are aspects of behaviour and thinking that may leave parents scratching their heads in puzzlement, or pulling out their hair in frustration. Most parents realize their child's desire for independence and strive for an appropriate balance between being overly protective and not protective enough.

Teens whose childhoods were riddled with various kinds of abuse and neglect will find the teenage years particularly painful. Coming to terms with these experiences, dealing with continued abuse, and possibly having fewer social supports may lead to risky behaviour and feelings of isolation, which jeopardize the transition to adulthood. Media bombardments of sex and violence, plus the availability of alcohol, pornography, illicit drugs, and gambling, offer some teens permanent avenues for escape, rather than temporary detours for adventure and experimentation. For most, parental pressures and adolescent adventures may collide frequently as teens seek identity and independence.

This chapter focuses on the physical and cognitive development of adolescents, including puberty, adolescent sexuality, health challenges, risks and wellness, cognition, and education.

The Nature of Adolescence

LO1 Analyze the life stage of adolescence.

As in childhood development, genetic, biological, environmental, and social factors influence adolescent development (Berger, 2011). During their childhood years of development, adolescents experienced thousands of hours of interactions with parents, peers, and teachers. However, now they face dramatic biological changes, new experiences, and new developmental tasks. Relationships with parents take a different form, moments with peers become more intimate, and dating occurs for the first time, as do sexual exploration and possibly intercourse. The adolescent's thoughts are more abstract and idealistic. Biological changes trigger a heightened interest in body image (Polan & Taylor, 2011).

The issue of social change is relevant in the conceptualization of youth mainly because of the direct effect upon youth of changes in social institutions, and changes in the youth's relations (White, Wyn, & Albanese, 2011). Widespread agreement exists among social scientists that the last quarter-century has witnessed significant social changes that affect the experience of adolescence. Crosnoe and Johnson (2011) conclude that the experiences of young people developing in a contemporary world are quite different from those encountered by the youth of previous generations. That is, current adolescents construct different meanings, and they make sense of the social conditions in ways that adolescents from previous generations did not (Johnson, Crosnoe, & Elder, 2011). Many researchers have designed studies that they hope will guide effective social policy-making efforts in society, especially for the adolescent (Little et al., 2009).

critical thinking

According to the research, teens who have secure attachments and good relationships with their parents are more likely to make a smoother transition from childhood to adolescence. Think of your high school years. What was your transition to adolescence like? Compare and contrast your own transition to adolescence to that of two of your peers. Outline particularly relevant influences that affected your transition to adolescence. Observe a few adolescents in a movie theatre or a shopping mall. What specific behaviours do you observe to suggest these adolescents might be struggling with their identity?

An adolescent's enthusiasm for trying on new identities and enjoying moderate amounts of outrageous behaviour does not equate with hostility toward parental and societal standards. Acting out and boundary testing are time-honoured ways in which adolescents move toward integrating, rather than rejecting, parental values. However, in matters of taste and manners, the young people of every generation have seemed unnervingly radical and different from adults—different in how they look, in how they behave, in the music they enjoy, in their hairstyles, and in the clothing they choose. Although most adolescents negotiate the lengthy path to adult maturity successfully, too many do not (Lerner, Boyd, & Du, 2008). Ethnic, cultural, gender, socio-economic, age, and lifestyle differences influence the actual life trajectory of every adolescent (Patterson & Hastings, 2007). Different portrayals of adolescence emerge, depending on the particular group of adolescents being described (Balsano et al., 2008). Today's adolescents are exposed to a complex menu of lifestyle options, and the rate of adolescent drug use in Canada remains higher than a generation ago.

Too many adolescents are not provided with adequate opportunities and support to become competent adults (Eccles, Brown, & Templeton, 2008). In many ways, today's adolescents are presented with a less stable environment than adolescents of a decade or two ago. The explosion of technology and the war on terrorism, combined with economic pressures, higher divorce rates, youth crime, teen pregnancy, and increased geographic mobility of families, contribute to this lack of stability.

To this point, we have discussed a number of ideas about the nature of adolescence. For a review, see the Reach Your Learning Outcomes section at the end of this chapter.

Physical Changes during Puberty

LO2 Describe the physical changes that occur during puberty.

- **Sexual Maturation, Height, and Weight**
- **Hormonal Changes**
- **Body Image**
- **Teen Perspectives on Maturity**
- **The Brain**

One father remarked that the problem with his teenage son was not that he grew, but that he did not know when to stop growing. As we will see, there is considerable variation in the timing of the adolescent growth spurt.

Puberty is the most important marker of the beginning of adolescence, but it is not the same as adolescence. Great variations among individuals occur in the timing of puberty. Strong evidence argues for environmental and physiological effects and at the same time supports secular trends. One example is the earlier onset of menstruation. Considerable progress has been made in identifying genes that regulate the timing of puberty onset (Gajdos, Hirschhorn, & Palmert, 2009). Furthermore, estrogen-like endocrine disrupting chemicals (EEDC), found in various plastic products needed for daily use as well as pesticides, have exerted the greatest effects on puberty (Roy, Chakraborty, & Chakraborty, 2009). For most, puberty ends long before adolescence does; the average age for puberty is between 8 and 15, and may take on average from 1.5 to 6 years for completion. What is puberty? **Puberty** is not a single, sudden event, but rather a period of rapid physical maturation involving hormonal and bodily changes that occur primarily during early adolescence. Pinpointing the beginning and the end is difficult; but the most notable changes are signs of sexual maturation, height, and weight (Polan & Taylor, 2011).

Sexual Maturation, Height, and Weight

Think back to the onset of puberty. Of the striking changes that were taking place in your body, what was the first to occur? Researchers have found that male pubertal characteristics typically develop in this order: increase in penis and testicle size, appearance of straight pubic hair, minor voice change, first ejaculation (which usually occurs through masturbation or a wet dream), appearance of kinky pubic hair, onset of maximum growth in height and weight, growth of hair in armpits, more detectable voice changes, and, finally, growth of facial hair.

What is the order of appearance of physical changes in females? First, either the breasts enlarge or pubic hair appears. Later, hair appears in the armpits. As these changes occur, the female grows in height and her hips become wider than her shoulders. **Menarche**—a girl's first menstruation—comes rather late in the pubertal cycle. Initially, her menstrual cycles may be highly irregular (Belsky, 2013). For the first several years, she may not ovulate every menstrual cycle; some girls do not ovulate at all until a year or two after menstruation begins. No voice changes comparable to those in pubertal males occur in pubertal females. By the end of puberty, the female's breasts have become more fully rounded. Figure 11.1 illustrates a comparison of the median ages at menarche in different countries.

Figure 11.1

Median Ages at Menarche in Selected Northern European Countries and North America from 1845 to 1969

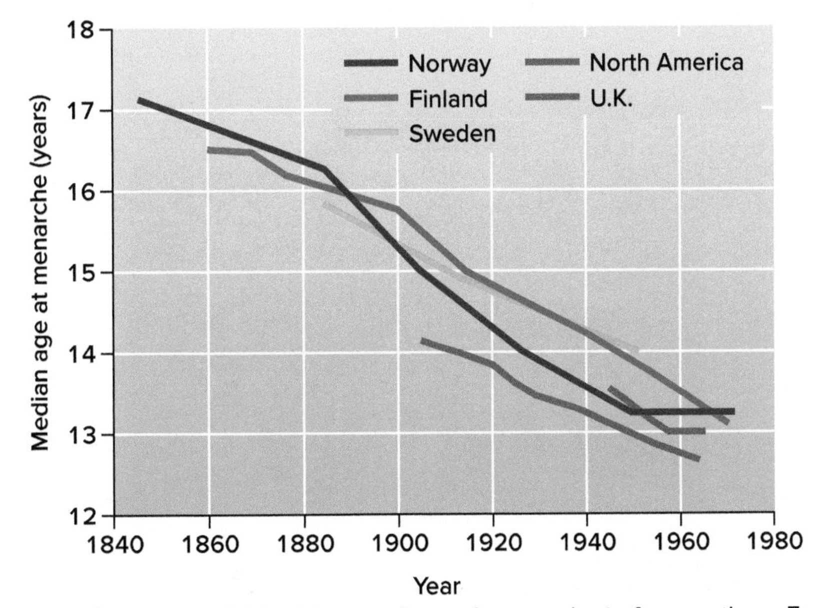

Notice the steep decline in the age at which girls experienced menarche in four northern European countries and North America from 1845 to 1969. Recently, the age at which girls experience menarche has been levelling off.

Marked weight gains coincide with the onset of puberty (Jasik & Lustig, 2008). During early adolescence, girls tend to outweigh boys, but by about age 14 boys begin to surpass girls. Similarly, at the beginning of the adolescent period, girls tend to be as tall as or taller than boys of their age, but by the end of the middle school years most boys have caught up or, in many cases, surpassed girls in height.

As indicated in Figure 11.2, the growth spurt occurs earlier in girls than it does in boys. Boys grow 10 to 30 cm while girls grow 5 to 20 cm during this period. Increases in weight follow increases in height, both of which are related to increases in fat, bone, and muscle tissue (Polan & Taylor, 2011).

Figure 11.2

Pubertal Growth Spurt

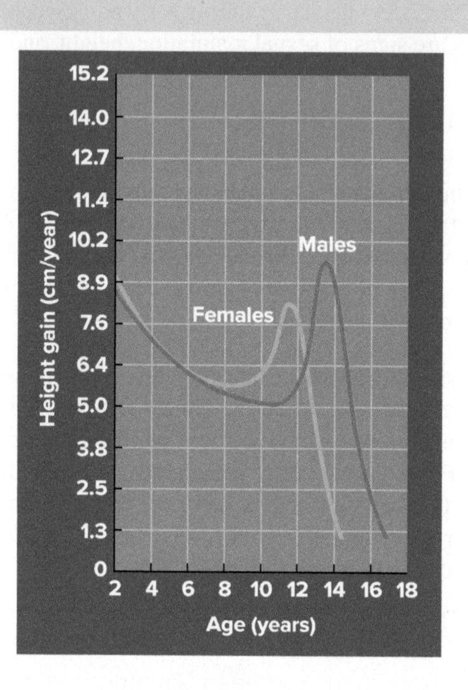

On average, the growth spurt that characterizes pubertal change occurs two years earlier for girls (10½) than for boys (12½).

Value RF/Corbis

What are some of the differences in the ways girls and boys experience pubertal growth?

Hormonal Changes

Behind the first whisker in boys and the widening of hips in girls is a flood of **hormones**, powerful chemical substances secreted by the endocrine glands and carried through the body by the bloodstream. The endocrine system's role in puberty involves the interaction of the hypothalamus, the pituitary gland, and the gonads (sex glands). The **hypothalamus** is a structure in the higher portion of the brain that monitors eating, drinking, and sex. The **pituitary gland** is an important endocrine gland that controls growth and regulates other glands. The **gonads** are the sex glands—the testes in males, the ovaries in females.

How do the gonads, or sex glands, work? The pituitary sends a signal via *gonadotropins* (hormones that stimulate the testes or ovaries) to the appropriate gland to manufacture the hormone. Then, the pituitary gland, through interaction with the hypothalamus, detects when the optimal level of hormones is reached and responds by maintaining gonadotropin secretion (Banasik, 2013).

The concentrations of certain hormones increase dramatically during adolescence (Herbison et al., 2008). *Testosterone* is a hormone associated in boys with the development of genitals, an increase in height, and a change in voice. *Estradiol* is a hormone associated in girls with breast, uterine, and skeletal development. Note that both testosterone and estradiol are present in the hormonal makeup of both boys and girls, but testosterone dominates in male pubertal development and estradiol dominates in female pubertal development (Richmond & Rogol, 2007).

The same influx of hormones that puts hair on a male's chest and imparts curvature to a female's breast may contribute to psychological development (DeRose & Brooks-Gunn, 2008; Vermeersch et al., 2008; Holder & Blaustein, 2014). However, hormonal effects by themselves do not account for adolescent development (Graber, 2008). Behaviour and moods also can affect hormones (DeRose & Brooks-Gunn, 2008). Stress, eating patterns, exercise, sexual activity, tension, and depression can activate or suppress various aspects of the hormonal system (Foster & Brooks-Gunn, 2008; Sontag et al., 2008; Marceau, Dorn, & Susman, 2012). In sum, the hormone–behaviour link is complex.

Timing and Variations in Puberty

In North America—where children mature up to a year earlier than children in European countries—the average age of menarche has declined significantly since the mid-nineteenth century (refer to Figure 11.1). Fortunately, however, we are unlikely to see pubescent toddlers, since what has happened in the past century is likely the result of improved nutrition and health.

Why do the changes of puberty occur when they do, and how can variations in their timing be explained? The basic genetic program for puberty is wired into the species (Dvornyk & Waqar-u-Haq, 2012). Experiences that are linked to earlier pubertal onset include an urban environment, adoption, father absence, low socioeconomic status, family conflict, maternal harshness, child maltreatment, and early substance use (Ji & Chen, 2008; Ellis et al. 2011). In many cases, puberty occurs months earlier in such situations, and this earlier onset is often accompanied by high rates of conflict and stress. A recent cross-cultural study representing 34 countries found that childhood obesity was linked to early puberty in girls (Currie et al., 2012).

Evolutionary psychologists argue that harmonious relationships with parents, particularly the quality of fathers' investment in the family, are associated with later pubertal timing of the daughter. Conversely, dysfunctional and harsh family relations have been linked with early onset of puberty.

For most boys, the pubertal sequence may begin as early as age 10 or as late as 13, and may end as early as age 13 or as late as 17. Thus the normal range is wide enough that, given two boys of the same chronological age, one might complete the pubertal sequence before the other one has begun it. For girls, menarche is considered within the normal range if it appears between the ages of 8 and 15.

Body Image

One psychological aspect of physical change in puberty is certain: adolescents are preoccupied with their bodies and develop individual images of what their bodies are like (Allen et al., 2008; Jones, Bain, & King, 2008). Perhaps you looked in the mirror on a daily—and sometimes even on an hourly basis—to see if you could detect anything different about your changing body. Preoccupation with one's body image is strong throughout adolescence, but it is especially acute during puberty, a time when adolescents are more dissatisfied with their bodies than in late adolescence.

Gender Differences in Body Image

In general, girls are less happy with their bodies and have more negative body images than boys throughout puberty (Bearman et al., 2006). As pubertal change proceeds, girls often become more dissatisfied with their bodies. This dissatisfaction may be due to media portrayals of the attractiveness of being thin and the increase of body fat during puberty (Benowitz-Fredricks et al., 2012). In addition, early- and late-maturing girls have different perceptions of body image, depending on their age. Early maturers are more likely to have a positive body image when they are young, and late maturers are more likely to have a positive body image when they are older.

Increasingly, researchers have found that early maturation in girls tends to increase their vulnerability to a number of problems (Graber, 2013; Hamilton et al., 2014). For example, early maturing girls are more likely to smoke, drink, be depressed, have an eating disorder, engage in delinquency, struggle for earlier independence from their parents, and have older friends. In addition, their bodies are more likely to elicit responses from males that lead to earlier dating and earlier sexual experiences (Baker et al., 2012; Hamilton et al., 2014). Early maturing girls tend to have sexual intercourse earlier and have more unstable sexual relationships (Moore, Harden, & Mendle, 2014). In their study of undergraduate women, Brenner-Shumann and Warren (2013) found that early maturing girls are less likely to become science, technology, engineering, and math (STEM) majors.

A recent study found that in early high school years, late-maturing boys tend to have a more negative body image than early maturing boys (deGuzman & Nishina, 2014). However, another study found that early maturing boys are less physically active compared to late maturing boys aged 10 to 14 (Latt et al., 2015). Different studies have shown that early maturing boys have a higher Body Mass Index (BMI) (Zitouni & Guinhouya, 2012). Early maturing boys have been characterized as more overweight or obese, compared to average or late maturing boys, a characteristic that might affect the extent of physical activity engaged in by early maturing boys (Rangul et al., 2011). However, boys become more satisfied as they move through puberty, probably because their muscle mass increases (Bearman et al., 2006).

A recent study found that both boys' and girls' body image becomes more positive as they move from the beginning to the end of adolescence (Holsen et al., 2012).

Teen Perspectives on Maturity

Canadian researchers Barker and Galambos (2005) explored conceptions of maturity held by 170 adolescents in grades 7 and 10. These adolescents were asked at what age they expected to reach adulthood, experience the greatest freedom, and have the most fun. The results specified that adolescents expect to have fun at an earlier age than they expect freedom or adulthood. Further, the adolescents cited the gaining of independence as critical to their expectations for the ages of adulthood (71 percent) and freedom (74 percent). Meanwhile, certain chronological transitions, such as reaching driving age (41 percent) and acquiring independence (41 percent), were associated with the expected age for fun. Adolescents who felt older than their age and who admitted to engaging in more problem behaviours, but were low on psychological maturity, were more likely than other adolescents to cite chronological transitions as indicative of freedom. These findings suggest that establishing independence or autonomy—a key developmental task of adolescence—is especially important to all adolescents. The finding also indicates that adolescents hold the widespread conception that independence is a positive feature of growing up (Arnett & Galambos, 2003).

Another study by Galambos and her colleagues (2005) examined the relationships between cognitive performance and psychosocial maturity among 48 adolescents in grades 9 and 12. These findings suggest that cognitive abilities are in fact related to psychosocial maturity. The concept of psychosocial maturity encompasses attainments in several domains, including independent functioning, effective interpersonal communication and interaction, and social responsibility (Galambos, Barker, & Tilton-Weaver, 2003). Many teens effectively balance their work and play activities and get along easily with others. Teens who are maturity-focused tend to prefer the presence of others who are similarly focused (Galambos et al., 2003).

critical thinking

Think back to your own experience of entering puberty. Compare photos of yourself from elementary school and high school. Illustrate a few incredible changes that occurred for you during puberty. What are some of some of the beliefs regarding pubertal changes held by the adolescent in the Western culture as compared to the non-Western cultures?

Body Art

Tattooing and other forms of body art are usually referred to either as body art or body modification, Body art has become increasingly popular among school-age children and adolescents (Mayers & Chiffriller, 2008; Tielsch-Goddard, 2007). One study has revealed that having multiple body piercings is especially noted as a marker for risk-taking behaviour (Suris et al., 2007). The Association of Professional Piercers provides suggested aftercare guidelines for body piercings that can be confidently recommended to an adolescent with either body piercing or tattooing (Association of Professional Piercers, nd).

The Brain

Along with the rest of the body, the brain continues to change during adolescence; but the study of adolescent brain development is in its infancy. As advances in technology take place, significant strides will also likely be made in charting developmental changes in the adolescent brain (Giedd, 2008; McAnarney, 2008; Steinberg, 2009). What do we know now?

Using functional magnetic resonance imaging (fMRI) brain scans, scientists have discovered that adolescents' brains undergo significant structural changes (Casey, Getz, & Galvan, 2008; Raznahan et al., 2014). The *corpus callosum*, where fibres connect the brain's left and right hemispheres, thickens in adolescence, and this improves adolescents' ability to process information (Gilliametal, 2011). We described advances in the development of the *prefrontal cortex*—the highest level of the frontal lobes involved in reasoning, decision making, and self-control—in Chapters 8 and 10. The prefrontal cortex doesn't finish maturing until the emerging adult years, approximately 18 to 25 years of age or later, but the *amygdala*—the seat of emotions such as anger—matures earlier than the prefrontal cortex. Figure 11.3 shows the locations of the corpus callosum, prefrontal cortex, and amygdala.

Figure 11.3
Developmental Changes in the Adolescent Brain

Prefrontal cortex
This "judgment" region reins in intense emotions but doesn't finish developing until at least emerging adulthood.

Corpus callosum
These nerve fibres connect the brain's two hemispheres; they thicken in adolescence to process information more effectively.

Amygdala
The seat of emotions such as anger; this area develops quickly before other regions that help to control it.

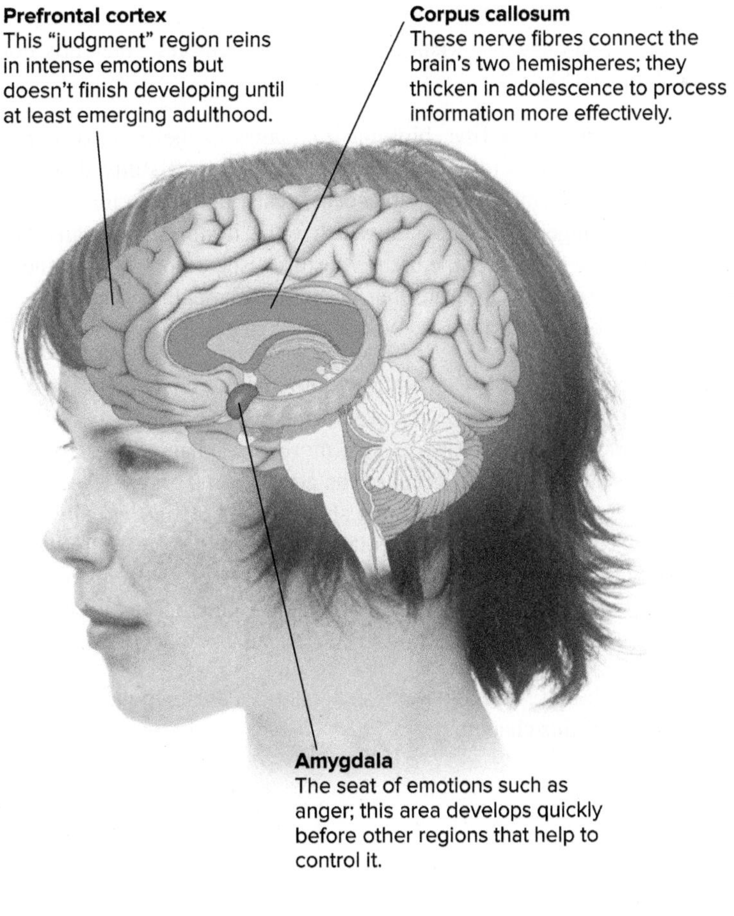

Dr. Bruce D. Perry (2004) is an internationally recognized authority on both child trauma and the effects of child maltreatment. He continues to serve as senior consultant to the Ministry of Children's Services in Alberta. He contends that traumatic experiences from early childhood affect long-term behaviour. In fact, traumatic events in childhood actually increase the risk for a host of social problems, including teenage pregnancy, adolescent drug use, and certain medical problems (Perry, 2003). Perry's ideas are supported by neurological studies indicating that severe maltreatment during childhood is related to molecular and neurobiological damage in the emotional and memory parts of the brain that are still growing (Child Welfare Information Gateway, 2009). Perry's research is supported by Dr. Ruth Lanius of Western University. Using functional magnetic resonance imaging studies, she has investigated whether individuals who experience traumatic events use different regions of the brain when they recall events (Lanius et al., 2004). It has been established that different brain areas are, in fact, used by those who have experienced post-traumatic stress disorder (PTSD) compared to those who do not have PTSD.

Other researchers have found that both the amygdala and hippocampus increase in volume during adolescence. Both structures are involved in emotion and are part of the group of structures called the limbic system. However, because of the relatively slow development of the prefrontal cortex, which is still maturing during adolescence, adolescents may lack the cognitive skills to effectively control their pleasure seeking (Toga, Thompson, & Sowell, 2006). This developmental disjunction between the limbic system and prefrontal cortex may account for an increase in risk taking and other problems in adolescence.

Leading researcher Charles Nelson (2003) points out that although adolescents are capable of very strong emotions, their prefrontal cortex hasn't adequately developed to the point where they can control these passions. It is as if their brain doesn't have the brakes to slow down their emotions. Or consider this interpretation of the development of emotion and cognition in adolescents: "early activation of strong 'turbo-charged' feelings with a relatively un-skilled set of 'driving skills' or cognitive abilities to modulate strong emotions and motivations" (Dahl, 2004, p. 18). Evidence supports the notion that emotional control during adolescence, revealed by MRI studies, is not fully developed until adulthood (Luna, Padmanablan & O'Hearn, 2010). In fact, when comparisons are made between 8 to 23 year olds and 14 to 15 year olds, the younger ones indicated heightened arousal reward centres in the brain, allowing them to seek greater excitement and pleasure (van Leijenhorst et al., 2010). However, Canadian researchers state that evidence from their research indicates that young adults at university level report greater frequency of risk taking behaviours, such as alcohol use, relative to younger high school students. These researchers highlight the role of social context on the engagement of risk-taking behaviours in young adults (Willoughby et al., 2013). Laurence Steinberg, one of the world's leading experts on adolescence, states that many adolescents are driven primarily by the urges to pursue novel and new experiences—and at the same time blatantly not heeding to parental advice (Steinberg, 2008; Steinbreg & Chein, 2015).

Of course, a major issue involves which comes first, biological changes in the brain or experiences that stimulate these changes (Lerner, Boyd, & Du, 2008). For example, consider the findings of a study that indicated the prefrontal cortex thickens and more brain connections are formed when adolescents resist peer pressure (Paus et al., 2008). Scientists have yet to determine whether the brain changes come first or whether the brain changes are the result of experiences with peers, parents, and others. Once again we encounter the nature/nurture issue that is so prominent in examining development throughout the life span. Evidence continues to indicate that both environmental experience and genetics make important contributions to brain development (Johnson, Dariotis, & Wang, 2012; Berardi, Sale, & Maffei, 2015).

Are there implications for drug use as a result of what we now know about changes in the adolescent's brain? According to leading expert Jay Giedd (2007, pp. D1–2), "Biology doesn't make teens rebellious or have purple hair or take drugs. It does not mean you are going to do drugs, but it gives you more of a chance to do that." Also, can the recent brain research we have just discussed be used to argue that because the adolescent's brain—especially the higher-level prefrontal cortex—is still developing, adolescents who commit crimes should not be tried as adults? Maroney (2009) states that "developmental neuroscience can play a small role in juvenile justice going forward" (p. 89). However, the courts must remember that neuroscience is only one source, among many, on which to base decisions. Other sources indicate critical legal and environmental factors that are important to consider. Expert Elizabeth Sowell (2004) says that scientists can't just do brain scans on adolescents and make decisions regarding legal age.

To this point, we have discussed a number of ideas about physical changes during puberty. For a review, see the Reach Your Learning Outcomes section at the end of this chapter.

Adolescent Sexuality

LO3 Describe adolescent sexuality, sexual identity, and risk factors related to intimate sexual behaviour.

- **Developing a Sexual Identity**
- **The Timing of Adolescent Sexual Behaviours**
- **Risk Factors and Sexual Problems**
- **Adolescent Pregnancy and Health**

Adolescence is not only characterized by substantial changes in physical growth and the development of the brain, but it is also a bridge between the asexual child and the sexual adult (Kelly, 2008; Strong et al., 2008). Every society gives some attention to adolescent sexuality. In some societies, adults clamp down and protect adolescent females from males by chaperoning them. Other societies promote very early marriage. Yet other societies allow some sexual experimentation, such as many parts of Europe and North America, where sexual culture is widely available through television, videos, magazines, lyrics of popular music, computer games, and websites. However, considerable controversy exists about just how far sexual experimentation should be allowed to go.

Evidence indicates that social and entertainment media such as television, videos, song lyrics, and the Internet all contribute to adolescent knowledge about sex (Herdt & Polen-Petict, 2014; King & Regan, 2014; Steinberg & Monahan, 2010). Smaller-scale studies have indicated that adolescent exposure to sexual imagery is more common in music lyrics than it is in television programs, but such imagery is comparable in film and television (Roberts, Henriksen, & Foehr, 2009). Moreover, other factors such as parental permissiveness, parent–adolescent conflict, and developing friendships with sexually active friends are well-established risk factors for early sexual encounters (Steinberg & Monahan, 2010).

The *Canadian Youth, Sexual Health and HIV/AIDS Study: Factors Influencing Knowledge, Attitudes and Behaviours* is a comprehensive study undertaken by the Council of Ministers of Education, Canada (CMEC, 2003) to increase understanding of the factors contributing to adolescent sexual knowledge, attitudes, and behaviour. The study uses the World Health Organization's definition of sexual health: "the integration of the physical, emotional, intellectual, and social aspects of sexual being, in ways that are positively enriching and that enhance personality, communication, and love."

Researchers from four Canadian universities (Acadia, Alberta, Laval, and Queen's) surveyed over 11 000 students in grades 7, 9, and 11 from each province and territory with the exception of Nunavut (Boyce et al., 2006). The findings indicated that compared to the last such national study conducted in 1988, some interesting differences are evident. For example, males but not females are less likely to engage in sexual intercourse, and all students are significantly more likely to believe they can protect themselves adequately from HIV/AIDS (Boyce et al., 2006).

Healthy sexual development in adolescence is the outgrowth of healthy development from infancy through childhood. Many behaviour patterns, including values related to gender roles and power, are formed well before adolescence. Positive childhood experiences help develop the self-confidence, trust, and autonomy a young person needs to handle peer pressure and navigate the sensual and sexual feelings natural to the teenage years. Conversely, healthy growth may be inhibited by destructive sexual attitudes, media images, and physical, emotional, and sexual abuse or neglect that may occur at this age.

Behaviour patterns influence choices and affect the risk of pregnancy and sexually transmitted infections (STIs) and HIV/AIDS. The *Canadian Guidelines for Sexual Health Education* focus on the importance of providing youth with the knowledge, motivation, and behavioural skills they need to make informed as well as responsible sexual decisions to enhance their sexual health. These guidelines, which are sensitive to diverse the needs of youth, are intended to equip them with current and accurate information on reducing specific-risk taking behaviours including the proper use of contraceptives (PHAC, 2008a).

Developing a Sexual Identity

Sexual identity can be broadly defined as the recognition, acceptance, and expression of numerous aspects of one's sexuality. It includes aspects such as individual sexual values, behaviours, and desires, as well as sexual orientation. Actually defining and identifying one's sexual identity can be particularly challenging (Morgan, 2012). It has been found that some adolescents are strongly sexually aroused, while others are less aroused. Further, some adolescents are very active sexually, and others do not indicate such behaviour (Hyde & DeLamater, 2014). Specifically, sexual orientation refers to one's sexual attraction and/or behavioural predispositions toward one or both sexes (Morgan, 2012). In fact, achieving sexual identity can be a life-long task because, in part, societal standards keep on changing (Berger, 2011). Several researchers have proposed that most heterosexual individuals do not think about their sexual identity. In fact, heterosexuality is frequently understood as a silent and unmarked identity (Konik & Stewart, 2004). Actually, the invisibility of sexuality is especially prominent for men whose heterosexuality has been mandated from a young age through rigid masculine roles (Frankel, 2005).

Even though some adolescents who are attracted to individuals of the same sex fall in love with these individuals, others claim that their same-sex attractions are purely physical (Savin-Williams, 2006, 2008). A commonly held belief is that most gay males and lesbians quietly struggle with same-sex attractions in childhood, do not engage in heterosexual dating, and gradually recognize that they are a gay male or a lesbian in mid to late adolescence (Savin-Williams & Diamond, 2004). Many youth do follow this developmental pathway, but others do not (Bos et al., 2008; Diamond, 2008). For example, many youth have no recollection of early same-sex attractions and experience a more abrupt sense of their same-sex attraction in late adolescence. The majority of adolescents with same sex attraction also experience other-sex attraction to some degree (Hock, 2012). However, according to Diamond (2008), bisexuality has remained under-investigated.

Getty/Photodisc RF

One important aspect of developing a sexual identity involves sexual orientation. These two individuals have a lesbian orientation. *What are some of the stigmas that adolescents who are homosexual face?*

Gay male and lesbian youth have diverse patterns of initial attraction, often have bisexual attractions, and may have physical or emotional attraction to same-sex individuals but do not always fall in love with them (Diamond, 2008; Savin-Williams, & Cohen, 2007; Savin-Williams & Ream, 2007). In Canada, the literature reveals that exclusion, isolation, and fear remain realities for Canadian lesbian, gay, bisexual, transgendered, intersexed, and questioning queer (LGBTIQ) adolescents. They face greater risks related to their health and well-being than their heterosexual age-mates (Dysart-Gale, 2010). Mayer, Garofalo, and Makadon (2014) state that because of societal discomfort with atypical expressions of sexual orientation and gender identity, lesbian, gay, bisexual, and transgender (LGBT) youth tend to experience enhanced developmental challenges, compared to their heterosexual peers. In fact, the social stigma has resulted in a wide range of health disparities, ranging from an increased likelihood of depression and substance use to an increased risk of cancer and cardiovascular disease. It becomes extremely important that all involved with LGBT youth become comfortable in speaking openly about their sexual orientation and gender identity, and to connect these youths with positive role models and beneficial social opportunities.

The McGill University Sexual Identity Centre (MUSIC) provides specialized mental health care to all individuals. Couples and families with sexual orientation issues are particularly welcome (Sexual Identity Centre, 2012). In Chapter 13, "Physical and Cognitive Development in Early Adulthood," we will further explore same-sex and heterosexual attraction.

The Timing of Adolescent Sexual Behaviours

Sexual behaviour is a major determinant of sexual and reproductive health. In fact, early sexual intercourse, unprotected sex, and having multiple sexual partners put youth at risk of sexually transmitted infections (STIs) (Rotermann, 2012). Most Canadian youth have their first experience of sexual intercourse during their teenage years (SIECCAN, 2012). In fact, 9 percent of 15- to 24-year-olds reported in 2009/2010 that they had their first sexual intercourse when they were younger than age 15, and about 25 percent had had intercourse for the first time at age 15 or 16. Interestingly, in 2003 similar percentages of males and females reported having had sexual intercourse before age 15, but in 2009/2010 this was less common among females (8 percent) than males (10 percent) (Rotermann, 2012). Figure 11.4 shows the reported rates among youth ages 15 to 19.

Figure 11.4
Percentage of Canadian Youth Aged 15–17, 18–19 Reporting Ever Having Sexual Intercourse

Age Group	1996/1997	2003	2005	2009/2010
15–17	32%	30%	29%	30%
18–19	70%	68%	65%	68%

Sources: Rotermann, M. (2008). Trends in teen sexual behaviour and condom use. *Health Reports, 19*(3), 1-5; Rotermann, M. (2012). Sexual behaviours and condom use of 15- to 24-year-olds in 2003 and 2009/2010. *Health Reports, 23*(1), 1-5.

Many adolescents are not emotionally prepared to handle sexual experiences, especially in early adolescence (Coley et al., 2013). Early sexual activity is linked with risky behaviours such as drug use, delinquency, and school-related problems (Chan et al., 2015). A recent study confirmed that early engagement in sexual intercourse is associated with high-risk sexual factors (having multiple partners last month, forced sex, using drugs/alcohol last sex, not using a condom last sex, and becoming pregnant or causing a pregnancy, as well as experiencing dating violence) (Kaplan et al., 2013). Other risk factors for sexual problems in adolescence include socioeconomic status (SES) and poverty, family/parenting, and peer factors (Van Ryzin et al., 2011).

A recent research review found that earlier onset of sexual intercourse was linked to living with other than two biological parents and a lower level of parental monitoring (Zimmer-Gembeck & Helfand, 2008). Having an absent father has also been linked to early sexual activity among girls.

Risk Factors and Sexual Problems

Dating Violence

According to the National Clearinghouse on Family Violence (2015), dating violence is a significant and widespread social problem. Dating violence is expressed in a range of harmful behaviours—from threats, to emotional maltreatment, to physical and sexual aggression. It is difficult to determine how many adolescents are affected by dating violence because many incidents of such violence go unreported. However, it is estimated from several studies that up to one-third of all adolescents may experience this type of abuse during an intimate partner relationship (Wolfe et al., 2009). Prevention is key to eliminating dating violence and promoting health, and so the process of well-being among adolescents can move forward (Runciman, 2012; Wekerle & Tanaka, 2010). Research on dating violence is of special importance because violence during adolescent dating relationships is often the catalyst for a pattern of abuse in later adult relationships (Marquart et al., 2007).

Contraceptive Use

Sexual activity carries with it considerable risks if appropriate safeguards are not taken (Carroll, 2007; Strong et al., 2008). Young people encounter two kinds of risks: unintended unwanted pregnancy and sexually transmitted infections. Both of these risks can be reduced significantly if contraception is used. Although contraceptive use is increasing, many sexually active adolescents still do not use contraceptives consistently (Finer & Philbin, 2013). A recent study found that greater age difference between sexual partners in adolescence is associated with less condom use (Volpe et al., 2013).

Gay and lesbian youth who do not experiment with heterosexual intercourse are spared the risk of pregnancy, but like their heterosexual peers they still face the risk of sexually transmitted diseases.

Sexually Transmitted Infections (STIs)

Sexually transmitted infection (STIs) are contracted primarily through sexual contact, which is not limited to sexual intercourse. Oral–genital and anal–genital contact can also transmit STIs and STDs.

Sexually active adolescents are at greater risk than non–sexually active adolescents to contract sexually transmitted infections. Physiologically speaking, the cervix of an adolescent girl is composed of columnar epithelial cells that are more susceptible to STIs, especially human papillomavirus (HPV) and chlamydia infection. The immune systems of the adolescents tend to contribute to the increased risk because adolescents have not had the opportunity to develop sufficient resistance to these organisms (Kollar, Jordan, & Wilson, 2013).

According to Boyce and colleagues (2006), the key findings of the 2003 *Canadian Youth, Sexual Health and HIV/AIDS Study* revealed that 75–80 percent of grade 9 students and 64–75 percent of grade 11 students reported being protected from STIs by condom use at last intercourse. According to the Canadian Council on Learning (CCL, 2009), the reported rates of chlamydia among adolescents ages 15 to 19 and 20 to 24 increased, with females having higher increases (PHAC, 2011e). Geographic variations were observed, with the highest chlamydia rates being reported in Nunavut, the Northwest Territories, and Yukon (PHAC, 2012a). Regarding gonorrhea, females between the ages of 14 to 24 and males between the ages of 20 and 24 accounted for the highest rates (PHAC, 2012a).

Human Papillomavirus (HPV)

HPV, a virus that can infect many different parts of the body, is thought to be one of the most commonly transmitted STIs. Over 100 types of HPV have been identified, and they can cause anogenital warts and cancer. HPV causes 70 percent of all cervical cancers and is linked to other cancers in both men and women. The virus is transmitted by oral, vaginal, and anal sex, as well as by intimate skin-to-skin contact with an infected individual. Fortunately, since 2006, a vaccine, Gardasil, has been approved for immunization for females and males between 9 and 26 years of age. The vaccine provides protection against four HPV types: two that cause approximately 70 percent of all cervical cancers (HPV-16 and HPV-18), and two others that cause approximately 90 percent of all anogenital warts in males and females (HPV-6 and HPV-11). A second vaccine, Cervarix, has been approved for use in females aged 10 to 25. This vaccine provides protection against the two HPV types that cause approximately 70 percent of all cervical cancer (HPV-16 and HPV-18) (PHAC, 2011f).

The vaccine protects against some high-risk types of HPV, but will not have an impact on an existing infection or existing pre-cancerous conditions. Nor does the vaccine protect against all types of HPV. Side effects related to pregnancy and breastfeeding are unknown.

Adolescent Pregnancy and Health

Although the social stigma once attached to pregnancy out of wedlock has diminished, the health problems associated with adolescent pregnancies are not only serious, but they affect both the mother and baby (Kaeppeler & Farb, 2014). Pregnant adolescents run the risk of experiencing a series of obstetrical complications. Examples of such complications are anemia, toxaemia, eclampsia, and hypertension (Chen et al., 2007). Adolescent mothers, in addition, also are more likely than their peers to be depressed and to drop out of school (Siegel & Brandon, 2014). Infants born to adolescent mothers are more likely to have low birth weights—a prominent factor in infant mortality—as well as neurological problems and childhood illness (Khashan, Baker, & Kenny, 2010).

critical thinking

Urie Bronfenbrenner viewed each individual at the centre of an expanding circle of environmental influences. Discuss whether it is the early maturity of girls, or their environmental influences, that is the prime factor in teenage pregnancy. How might environmental influences be factors in teenage pregnancy? Design an adolescent-oriented sex-education program for your province or territory to focus on providing information on contraception.

Rates of Adolescent Pregnancy in Canada

Pregnancy rates among Canadian adolescents have been decreasing in recent decades (Leslie, 2006, 2016). In 2009, the live birth rate for Canadian adolescent girls under age 20 was 15 638, while in 2012, the live birth rate was 12 922 (Statistics Canada, 2016). This three-year decline represents a drop of about 47 percent. The pregnancy rate is highest among 18- to 19-year-olds, but many of these are planned pregnancies. On the other hand, pregnancies among girls younger than 15 years represent only a small proportion of overall pregnancies in the adolescent population (Leslie, 2006, 2016).

The live birth rates vary among provinces and territories. For example, Nunavut and the Northern Territories have the highest proportions (24.0 percent and 10.6 percent respectively), followed by Saskatchewan (10.1 percent). The lowest teenage birth rates are reported in Quebec (2.7 percent), Ontario (3.3 percent) and British Columbia (3.5 percent) (Al-Sahab, 2011). It is important, however, that health care workers and others remain vigilant to prevent unplanned and unwanted pregnancies. Such pregnancies are generally expected to have negative consequences on a teenager's health and future. For example, pediatricians must be able to provide adequate and acceptable birth control and resources (Yen & Martin, 2013).

Adolescent Pregnancy: Global Comparisons

There has been a decrease in birth rates among adolescent girls since 1990. The 2014 World Health Statistics indicate that the average global birth rate among 15- to 19-year-olds is 49 per 1000 girls. Rates by country range from 1 to 299 births per 1000 girls. The highest rate of births is in sub-Saharan Africa (WHO, 2014). In the United States, adolescent births rates have declined in general, but they remain relatively high in certain groups, especially among black and Hispanic teens, and in the southern states, compared to those in other developed countries (CDC, 2011).

Figure 11.5 illustrates socio-economic deprivation, both a cause and consequence of adolescent pregnancy (World Development Report, 2006; World Bank, 2006).

Figure 11.5
Socio-Economic Deprivation

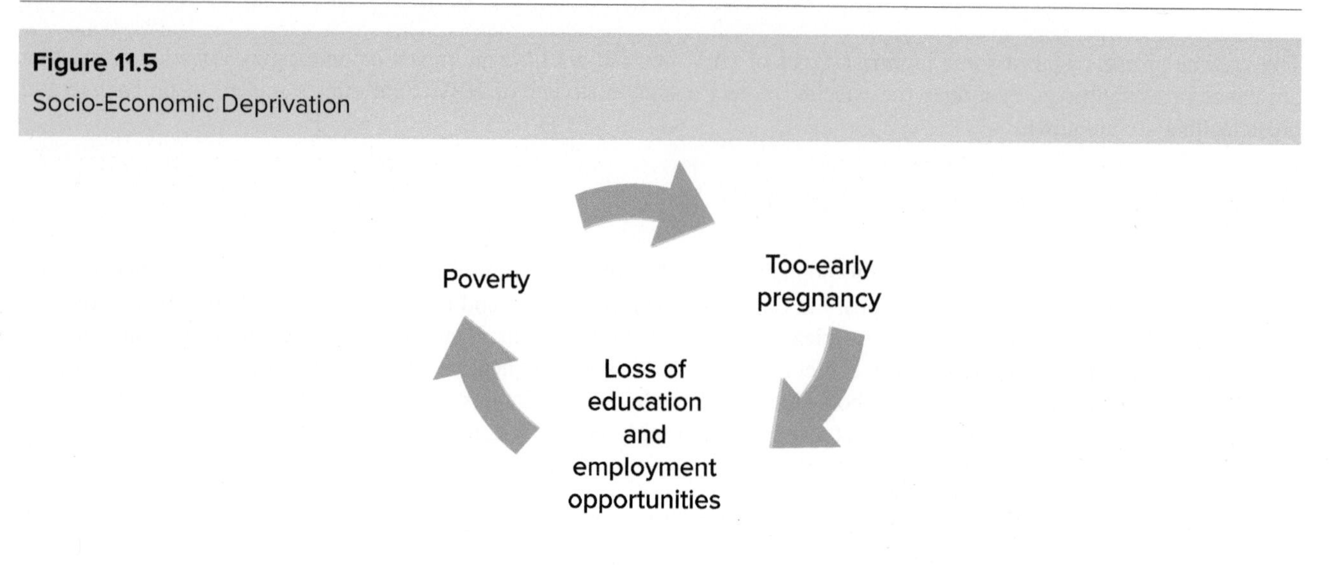

Reprinted from *Preventing early & unwanted pregnancy & pregnancy related mortality and morbidity in adolescents: Training Course in Sexual and Reproductive Health Research*, p. 9. Geneva 2012, World Health Organization.

Consequences of Adolescent Pregnancy

The consequences of adolescent pregnancy are of great concern. Many mothers are more likely to come from low SES backgrounds (Molina et al., 2010). A recent study revealed that adolescent mothers spent more time negatively interacting and less time in play and positive interactions than did adult mothers (Riva Crugnola et al., 2014). However, on a positive note, teen mothers were more likely to attend prenatal classes than average-aged mothers (Al-Sahab, 2012). Although adolescent pregnancy is a high-risk circumstance, some adolescent mothers do well in school and have positive outcomes (Schaffer et al., 2012).

Reducing Adolescent Pregnancy

The Canadian Paediatric and Adolescent Gynaecology and Obstetricians (CPAGO) committee has prepared adolescent pregnancy guidelines, which have been approved by the Executive and Board of the Society of Obstetricians and Gynaecologists of Canada (SOGC, 2015). A few of these guidelines are as follows: health care practitioners should be sensitive to the health care needs of the adolescent; fathers and partners should be included, as much as possible, in pregnancy preparation and prenatal/infant care education; and routine and repeated screening procedures should be conducted for substance abuse and violence in pregnancy, as well as for mood disorders. For reviews of additional guidelines, go to http://www.sogc.org/clinical-practice-guidelines/.

According to the Canadian Paediatric Society (2016), teens most as risk are those who:

- are experiencing family problems
- were born to adolescent mothers
- undergo early puberty
- have been sexually abused
- have frequent absenteeism and/or lack vocational goals
- have siblings who were pregnant during adolescence
- use alcohol, drugs, and tobacco
- live in group homes, detention centres, or on the street

The Canadian Paediatric Society (2016) believes that physicians, especially primary-care physicians, should discuss decision making with their young patients from an early age. The role of abstinence, the level of sexual activity, and the increased use of contraceptives all play a role in the rate of teenage pregnancy. Education also plays a vital role (Langille, 2007).

To this point, we have discussed a number of ideas about adolescent sexuality. For a review, see the Reach Your Learning Outcomes section at the end of this chapter.

Adolescent Health Problems and Wellness

LO4 Compare and contrast adolescent health issues related to eating disorders, substance use, and depression.

- **Nutrition, Exercise, and Sleep**
- **Eating Disorders**
- **Risk and Vulnerability**
- **Substance Use and Addiction**
- **Teen Depression**

Adolescence is a critical juncture in the adoption of health-related behaviours (Park et al., 2008; Sirard & Barr-Anderson, 2008). Good nutrition, exercise, and adequate sleep are the foundations of good health. Many of the behaviours linked to poor health habits and early death in adults begin during adolescence. Conversely, the early formation of healthy behaviour patterns, such as regular exercise and a preference for foods low in fat and cholesterol, not only have immediate health benefits, but also help in adulthood to delay or prevent disability and mortality from heart disease, stroke, diabetes, and cancer (Schiff, 2009).

Nutrition, Exercise, and Sleep

Nutrition and Exercise

Exercise and good nutrition are proven ingredients for health and intellectual performance. This fact is supported by studies within Canada and across the globe linking fitness and active living to positive academic performance. According to the Active Healthy Kids Canada *Report Card on Physical Activity for Children and Youth* (2012), comprehensive approaches to fitness are linked to improved brain activity and memory, along with increased self-esteem, self-confidence, and self-image. In addition, young people who are engaged in physical fitness activities have reduced behavioural problems and feel more connected to their schools.

Evident disparities in access to organized sports and activities are a cause of concern. Young people from lower socio-economic backgrounds and those with disabilities are disadvantaged either by the costs of sports programs or access to them. These young people are missing out on the benefits (Active Healthy Kids Canada, 2012).

According to a report released by federal, provincial, and territorial ministers concerned with sport and physical activity (CFLRI, 2005) and Human Resources and Skills Development Canada (HRDC) (2010), approximately 50 percent of teenagers are at least moderately active. However, only about one in five are active enough to meet international guidelines for optimal growth and development. In this group, teenage boys are twice as likely to be active than girls (CFLRI, 2005). The 24 hour Movement Guidelines for children and youth provide a recommendation for the amount of physical activity, sleep, and sedentary behaviour that is needed in a 24 hour period for a child's optimal health (www.participaction.com, 2016).

Although peers are a factor in the amount of exercise in which a teen engages, parents may be the most effective role models for children and teens in terms of participating in healthy amounts of exercise.

Nutrition is essential to good health at all ages, but the adolescent body is undergoing so many changes that nutrition is particularly important. Canada's food guide offers guidelines for healthy eating. Snack foods often contain high levels of trans fats, which are unhealthy and may lead to cholesterol and heart problems later in adulthood. A good breakfast fuels the brain and body so that performance in school can be optimized, yet many teens skip breakfast.

As a pioneer in the field of adolescent medicine, Tonkin extended the range of health services to youth. For example, he founded REACH Centre, a multidisciplinary community health centre that provides specialized service to a large number of transient youth. To promote a healthier lifestyle and encourage normal levels of activity and eating habits for young people, he conceived, built, and ran Camp Elsewhere on Gabriola Island. His unique approach to treating eating disorders has gained international attention and has served as a model for other countries.

In 1977, Tonkin founded the McCreary Centre Society, a small, non-profit agency concerned with the health of young people in British Columbia. The McCreary Centre Society's mission is to foster wider understanding of the importance of youth health, increase knowledge about youth health needs and issues, advocate for continuing commitment to youth issues, and initiate and implement innovative projects that directly address unmet health needs of young people.

Dr. Tonkin's work did not go unnoticed. In 1998, he received the Order of British Columbia. In June 2010, the Canadian Paediatric Society awarded Dr. Tonkin the prestigious Ross Award. Both awards were given in recognition of his life-long work that has influenced health care standards for adolescents, both nationally and internationally (SPA, 2010).

Sadly, Dr. Tonkin died peacefully at the age of 79, in Nanaimo, British Columbia, on December 23, 2015. His incomparable contributions to individual lives, to community, and to society will be remembered and cherished for years to come (*Vancouver Sun*, January 9, 2016).

Courtesy of Roger Tonkin

Anorexia Nervosa

Anorexia nervosa (AN) is a life-threatening disorder that involves the relentless pursuit of thinness through starvation. AN is one of the most common psychiatric conditions in young women. Rice and LaMarre (2014), at the University of Guelph, point out that statistics regarding anorexia nervosa represent only those cases of individuals who seek out medical intervention. That means that the actual incidence of AN could be much higher than the numbers suggest (Pinhas et al., 2011). Men and boys, members of ethnic and visible minority groups, and members of sexual and gender minority groups, might be less likely to seek treatment due to fear of the possibility of stigma and shame (Rice & LaMarre, 2014).

Four main characteristics apply to people suffering from anorexia nervosa: (1) they weigh less than 85 percent of what is considered normal for their age and height; (2) they have an intense fear of gaining weight that does not decrease with weight loss; (3) they have a distorted image of their body shape (Stewart et al, 2012); and (4) they suffer from amenorrhea (lack of menstruation) in girls who have reached puberty (Langlois et al., 2012).

Even when those suffering from AN are extremely thin, they see themselves as too fat. They never think they are thin enough, especially in the abdomen, buttocks, and thighs. They usually weigh themselves frequently, often take their body measurements, and gaze critically at themselves in mirrors.

Anorexia nervosa typically begins in the early to middle teenage years, but is increasingly recognized in pre-pubertal children, often following an episode of dieting and the occurrence of some type of life stress. Most people with anorexia are white adolescent or young adult females from well-educated, middle- and upper-income families; further, they are usually competitive and high-achieving. They set high standards, become stressed about not being able to reach these standards, and are intensely concerned about how others perceive them. Unable to meet these high expectations, they turn to something they can control: their weight. Offspring of mothers with anorexia nervosa are at higher risk for becoming anorexic themselves (Striegel-Moore & Bulik, 2007).

Problems in family functioning are increasingly found to be linked to the appearance of anorexia nervosa in adolescent girls (Stiles-Shield et al., 2012). One research review indicated that family therapy is often the most effective treatment for adolescent girls with anorexia nervosa (Bulik et al., 2007). Parents are considered to be an extremely vital part of the treatment process. Self-directedness (having a clear sense of one's self and one's goals) is also associated with better outcomes in individuals with anorexia nervosa.

The fashion image in North American culture that emphasizes "thin is beautiful" contributes to the incidence of anorexia nervosa (Striegel-Moore & Bulik, 2007). The media portray thin as beautiful in their choice of fashion models, whom many adolescent girls want to emulate. A recent study of adolescent girls revealed that friends often share similar body image and eating problems (Hutchinson & Rapee, 2007). In this study, an individual girl's dieting and extreme weight-loss behaviour could be predicted from her friends' dieting and extreme weight-loss behaviour.

Anorexia nervosa has become an increasing problem for adolescent girls and young adult women, and is becoming more common in boys and men. *What are some possible causes of anorexia nervosa? How does Urie Bronfenbrenner's theory that we are intensified by our environment factor in? Where on Maslow's hierarchy of needs would a person with anorexia nervosa fit? Why?*

Bulimia Nervosa

People with anorexia control their eating by restricting it. Most people with bulimia do not. **Bulimia nervosa (BN)** is an eating disorder in which the individual consistently follows a binge-and-purge eating pattern. The bulimic individual goes on an eating binge and then purges by self-induced vomiting or by using laxatives. Although many people binge and purge occasionally, and some experiment with it, a person is considered to have a serious bulimic disorder only if the episodes occur at least twice a week for three months (Cuzzolaro, 2014; Uher & Rutter, 2012).

Most adolescents with bulimia are preoccupied with food. They have a strong fear of becoming overweight, are depressed or anxious, and have a distorted body image (Langlois et al., 2012). One recent study indicated that adolescents with bulimia have difficulty controlling their emotions (Lavender et al., 2014). Similar to adolescents who are anorexic, those with bulimia are highly perfectionistic (Lampard et al., 2012). Unlike the adolescent with anorexia, individuals who binge and purge typically fall within a normal weight range. This situation makes bulimia difficult to detect. Treatment of bulimia nervosa usually involves a combination of individual and family therapy, behaviour modification, and nutritional rehabilitation (Langlois et al., 2012).

Obesity

Obesity is having too much fatty tissue as measured by the ratio of weight and height, which is called the body mass index (BMI). Obesity affects health, life expectancy, and quality of life. The World Health Organization defines obesity as having a BMI of 30 or more. A healthy BMI is between 18 and 24; a BMI between 25 and 29 indicates the individual is overweight. A BMI under 18 (anorexia nervosa) and over 30 are causes for serious concern. According to measured height and weight data from 2007 to 2009, more than one in four Canadian adults are obese. Regarding children and youth aged 6 to 17 years, 8.6 percent are obese (PHAC & CIHI, 2011). Between 1981 and 2007/2009, measured obesity doubled unevenly among males and females in most age groups in the adult and youth categories. In 2014, 306 895 males between the ages 12 to 17 were obese. Meanwhile, 161 075 females in this age range were obese (Statistics Canada, 2015). Even though obesity rates are increasing across all age groups, the rise in childhood and adolescence remains particularly alarming (Hwang & Kim, 2013). It is most interesting that, not only has the prevalence of obesity increased over time, but obesity is becoming increasingly more severe; and fitness levels are decreasing as well (PHAC & CIHI, 2011). Canadian data indicate that one-third of normal-weight 20-year-olds will become overweight within 10 years (Warshawski, 2010).

Risk and Vulnerability

For generations, adolescents have taken risks; in fact, risk taking is one of the ways in which teens challenge themselves and define their identity. Each individual has a unique definition of "risky" behaviour. To one teen, risk may be trying out for the math team, while for another it's flying over ravines on a mountain bike. Whatever the definition, taking some risks is normal and healthy, according to psychiatrist Lynn Ponton, author of *The Romance of Risk* (1997).

Unfortunately, some risk taking is harmful and can lead to permanent problems and even death. The leading cause of death for teenagers is automobile accidents. Nearly half of all deaths in adolescents are due to accidents, and most of those, especially among older adolescents, involve motor vehicles. Mothers Against Drunk Driving (MADD) (2012) estimates that over 5 percent of 16- to 17-year-olds and 15 percent of 18- to 20-year-olds were reported to be driving under the influence of alcohol in the previous year. Risky driving habits, such as speeding, tailgating, and driving under the influence of alcohol or other drugs, may be more important contributors to those accidents than is the lack of driving experience (Marcotte et al., 2012).

Suicide is the second leading cause of teenage death. Suicide has increased five-fold for adolescent boys and three-fold for girls (Statistics Canada, 2010c). Gay and lesbian adolescents are more likely to think about and attempt suicide, and suicide rates are five to eight times higher among First Nations and Inuit teens.

Self-injury is any attempt to alter one's mood by inflicting pain sufficient to cause tissue damage on one's self. Cutting has become a more common method of deliberate self-injury. Other injurious behaviours include burning, biting, and scratching. Such behaviours are deliberate, usually done in private and covered up. Self-injury is considered not to be self-destructive, but rather is seen as a way of coping, mostly with personal difficulties (Duffy, 2009). Results from a study suggest that self-injury is primarily associated with reductions in negative affect as opposed to increases in positive affect, and is more probably to be a negatively- rather than a positively-reinforced behaviour (Klonsky, 2009).

Muehlenkamp and Brausch (2012) found that body image may represent a necessary, but not sufficient, risk factor for non-suicidal self-injury (NSSI) in adolescents. Furthermore, the treatment for NSSI should consider targeting body-related pathology in addition to emotional regulation. A self-harm questionnaire has been designed to improve identification of self-harm (Ougrin & Boege, 2013). This questionnaire is an important tool that can be used effectively in the assessment process with adolescents to identify the risk of self-harm. Hooley and colleagues (2010) reported that community-based adolescents with NSSI histories have significantly higher pain tolerance thresholds.

A special concern involves teens who begin using drugs early in adolescence or even in childhood (King & Chassin, 2007). Scientists at the Mount Sinai School of Medicine and Columbia University have discovered that people who start using illicit substances in their early teen years are more likely to experience psychiatric disorders, especially depression, in their late twenties. For some adolescents, risky behaviours can escalate and become serious problems. In fact, early experimentation with alcohol, drugs, and substance misuse might coexist with emotional and behavioural problems, which have been found to affect emotional well-being (Langille et al., 2009). Another major risk factor in the use of illicit substances is that it has been known to increase the potential for criminal activity in the user (PHAC, 2012).

Substance Use and Addiction

In 2007, the police-reported rate of drug offences in Canada had reached its highest point in 30 years. Part of the increase in this overall rate is attributed to an increase in the rate of youths being accused of drug offences, which, in fact, doubled over the past decade. In recent years, however, most youths accused of drug offences have been cleared by means other than by formal charges by police. Examples include police discretion or referral to a diversion program (Canada Statistics, 2009).

Substance use by young people is a constantly evolving phenomenon. Canadian surveys indicate that tobacco, alcohol, and cannabis are the substances most frequently used by youth (Canada Centre on Substance Use, 2007). According to the *Cross-Canada Report on Student Alcohol and Drug Use* (CCSA, 2011), among students in grades 7 to 12 (approximately 11 to 18 years of age), alcohol use was twice as prevalent as cannabis use (46 to 62 percent of students reported alcohol use and 17 to 32 percent reported cannabis use in the past year). Aside from alcohol and cannabis, ecstasy was the most prevalent drug used (CCSA, 2011).

According to the report *Substance Abuse in Canada: Youth in Focus* (CCSA, 2007), "Early substance use has consistently been linked to negative consequences, including regular heavy use, dependence, and physical and social problems during young adulthood."

Cigarette Smoking

The prevalence of current smokers in grades 6 to 9 significantly decreased between 2008 and 2009 (3 percent) and 2010 and 2011 (2 percent). No difference was detected in the prevalence of current smokers between male and female. However, among youth in grades 10 to 12, 10 percent reported that they were current smokers, which is a significant decrease from 2008/09 (13 percent). At the same time there was a significantly greater proportion of male current smokers (11 percent) than female current smokers (9 percent) within this age group (Health Canada, 2012c).

Woodgate and Busolo (2015) conducted a qualitative study on perspectives held by Canadian youth about their peers who smoke. The results indicated that youth who smoke are considered by their peers to be less popular and less socially acceptable. The researchers concluded that Canadian youth view smoking as unhealthy and "uncool." Non-smoking youth are endeavouring to influence their friends who smoke to quit smoking. Another study by Woodgate and Kreklewetz (2012) investigated the perceptions held by youth regarding the smoking habits of their family members. The findings indicated that youth struggle to understand and make sense of the grounds on which parents smoke around their children. These youth perceive smoking by parents as an unjust act.

Prescription and Non-Prescription Drugs

An alarming trend is the use of prescription painkillers and over-the-counter drugs by adolescents. A study conducted at the Ontario Institute for Studies in Education (OISE) in Toronto reported that women with eating disorders also abuse sleeping pills, diet pills, and prescription medications.

Williams-Wheeler, 2004). Another study also revealed that adolescents who averaged fewer than two family dinners a week were more likely to drink alcohol, smoke cigarettes, and abuse prescription drugs than their adolescent counterparts who averaged five or more family dinners a week (CASA, 2007). Another study of more than 5000 middle school students revealed that having friends in their school's social network and having fewer friends who use substances were related to a lower level of substance use (Ennett et al., 2006). Researchers have also recently found that educational success—getting good grades, not dropping out of school, being connected to their school—has a protective role in reducing adolescents' drug use (Bachman et al., 2008).

What is the pattern of alcohol consumption among adolescents?

critical thinking

Statistically, Aboriginal Canadians have suicide rates that are six times the national average for adolescents. As an example, in Attawapiskat First Nation in Northern Ontario, a community of 2000 people, there were 101 suicide attempts between September 2015 and April 2016, causing the Chief and Council to declare a state of emergency. Consider the social contexts of Aboriginal youth, on reserves, in small towns, and in urban areas. What factors do you think account for this alarmingly high rate? In what ways can the government provide educational plans for the prevention of suicide? What steps of suicidal prevention would you include in an educational program?

Teen Depression

What is the nature of depression in adolescence? What causes an adolescent to commit suicide? Do depression and suicide run in families? Is depression genetically caused or a product of environment? According to the World Health Organization (WHO, 2009), depression is the leading cause of disability in developed nations, and the second most cited reason for visits to family doctors in Canada. Adolescence represents a time of heightened risk for the onset of depressive disorders (Vijayakumar et al., 2016). Depression is more likely to occur in adolescence than in childhood, but causes and treatments remain undefined.

Whether some people are more prone to depression by virtue of genetic makeup or whether environmental conditions play a determining role is not fully understood. What is known is that just as a young person undergoes pubescence and a tremendous physiological growth spurt, his or her brain undergoes massive reconstruction, or exuberance, which, combined with socio-cultural factors, sets the stage for mood swings and depression. Researchers suggest that early puberty in girls may increase the risk of depression (Galvao et al., 2014). Further, adolescence is a period of significant development in cognitive control (Luna, 2009). That is, the adolescent is able to engage in goal-directed behaviour, such as control of impulses, suppression of unwanted thoughts, and the intention of regulating personal emotions (Hofmann, Schmeicchel, & Baddeley, 2012). Presently, it is widely-acknowledged that cognitive control deficits are an important aspect of depression. In such cases, individuals tend to experience difficulties in attending behaviour and in concentration (Vijayakumar et al., 2016).

In 2004, Nancy Galambos and Erin T. Barker of the University of Alberta and Bonnie J. Leadbeater of the University of Victoria conducted a longitudinal study of 1322 teenagers between 12 and 19 years of age to investigate gender differences in and risk factors for depressive symptoms. For this study, **depression** was defined as experiencing over a prolonged period of time, a range of symptoms, including fatigue, irritability, inability to make decisions, sleeping problems, lack of interest in daily activities, and suicidal thoughts. They found that boys were half as likely as girls to experience depression; in fact, in Galambos's words, the study revealed "a startling number of young women (25 percent) who should be identified as depressed and treated."

The study investigated four predictors of depressive symptoms: social support, body image, smoking, and physical activity. Although the results are inconclusive, no link was found between physical activity and depression among the teens; however, the study reported a link between smoking, social relationships, and body image with depression, although the link is not necessarily causal. Adolescents from families with a depressed parent may be at risk for both depression and smoking.

Reasons given for the higher rate of depression among adolescent girls include the following:

- Females tend to internalize emotions.
- Females tend to ruminate in their depressed mood and amplify it.
- Females' self-images, especially their body images, are more negative than those of males.
- Females face more discrimination than do males.

Some specific factors may make an adolescent more prone to depression than others. Parents who divorce or have high marital conflict while their children are teens, and parents who are depressed or emotionally unavailable or who are experiencing financial problems, place adolescents at risk for developing depression. Poor peer relationships are also associated with adolescent depression. Not having a close relationship with a best friend, having less contact with friends, and experiencing peer rejection all increase depressive tendencies in adolescents. A cognitive explanation has been proposed to account for gender differences in depression. That is, rumination—repeatedly thinking and talking about past experiences—is more common among girls than boys (Ayduk & Kross, 2008).

Woodgate (2006), an internationally-renowned Canadian researcher, conducted a phenomenological study to gain an understanding of what it is like to be an adolescent living with depression. Thematic statements representative of the adolescent's lived experience were identified based upon interviews and field notes. The statement "living in the shadow" emerged as the essence of the adolescents' lived experiences. These experiences ultimately came to define what it was like to live with depression. The shadow of fear was associated not only with the fear of the return of "bad" feelings related to depression, but fear of not being able to receive help to manage those feelings. On top of that was the fear of having to do all the "hard work" in overcoming the bad feelings. Woodgate (2006) advocates that adolescents with depression need adequate resources and support throughout the illness trajectory, including those periods when their depression is under control.

Just as genetic factors are associated with depression, they are also associated with suicide. The closer a person's genetic relationship to someone who has committed suicide, the more likely that person will also commit suicide.

CONNECTING development to life

Suicide

According to Kollar, Jordan, and Wilson (2013), suicide is defined as the deliberate act of self-injury with the intent that the injury results in death. In 2012, 227 Canadian teenagers aged 15–19 committed suicide. In the same year, suicide was rated as the second leading cause of death among teenagers in that age group, preceded only by accidents (Statistics Canada, 2012d). Each year, nearly 300 Canadian youths complete suicide. Many more attempt suicide. Suicide rates are five to seven times more prevalent among Aboriginal youth than for non-Aboriginal youth. Inuit youth suicide rates are among the highest in the world, at 11 times the national average (CIHR, 2012a). Suicide rates vary widely, however, among Aboriginal communities, and the maintenance of cultural continuity and support systems might be influential in offsetting the suicide rates (Chandler & LaLonde, 2008; Harder et al., 2012).

While youth complete suicide at a lower rate than any other age group, the dramatic increase in the youth suicide rate over the past 40 years has made this group a special concern to health professionals (Roher & Casement, 2011). A retrospective analysis of standardized suicide rates using Statistics Canada mortality data for the period from 1980 to 2008 was conducted by Skinner and McFaull (2012). They analyzed the data by sex and by suicide method, over time for two age groups: 10- to 14-year-olds (children) and 15- to 19-year-olds (adolescents). The findings revealed a gradual increase in suicide by suffocation among female children and adolescents. In addition, the researchers found a decrease in suicides involving poisoning and firearms during the study period. The investigators conclude that suicide rates in Canada are increasing among female children and adolescents and decreasing among male children and adolescents.

Among adolescents, cyberbullying has become an increasing reality. Research indicates that youth who have been bullied are at a higher risk, notably not only for suicide ideation and thoughts, but also for suicide attempts and completed suicides (Centre for Suicide Prevention, 2012). Due to the pervasive nature of social media sites, it has become more difficult than ever for victims to escape from their tormentors. It can happen anywhere—at home, at school, or at any time of the day or night (Brown, Cassidy, & Jackson, 2006). Victims, in extreme cases, become aggressive and fight back, or they become depressed and attempt suicide. Youth who have experienced cyberbullying are almost twice as likely to attempt suicide compared to those who were not subjected to cyberbullying (Patchin & Hinduja, 2010).

Regarding suicide in rural and urban areas, Rhodes and colleagues (2008) noted that in many countries, including Canada, suicide rates tend to be higher in rural areas than in urban areas. It is well known that suicide rates in British Columbia's rural areas are much higher generally for Aboriginal compared to non-Aboriginal groups (Chandler & LaLonde, 2008).

White, Wyn, and Albanese (2011) argue that the reason for the rising rates of suicide in the Western world might be that society is failing young people. Even though many opportunities are available to them, youth feel adrift once they leave home and try to be successful in the world. It becomes important to acknowledge that the demise of traditional belief systems and narratives of meaning has made their journey more difficult. Such a result inevitably may leave some youth without a clear sense of connection.

Risk Factors. Suicide is a complex process. The causal basis for suicides can seldom be attributed to one single factor, such as a family breakup or homelessness (Centre for Suicide Prevention, 2012). It may be a routine incident or an overwhelming event that overloads a youth's coping mechanism (CMHA, 2013). Mental disorders seem to be the most important risk factor for adolescent suicide. Other common precursors to suicide include the presence of addictions, mood disorders, interpersonal problems with parents, conduct disorders, or a previous suicide attempt (Friedman, 2006). Substance abuse, for example, can impair judgment and exacerbate impulsivity. An impulsive teen might act speedily on suicidal thoughts (Kostenuik & Ratnapalan, 2010). For certain teens, suicide becomes the final pathway for release from their psychiatric and social problems (Kollar, Jordan, & Wilson, 2013). One other factor includes contagion or copycat suicide, terms that refer to the spread of suicidal activity. An increase in youth suicide is at times found after the suicide of one teenager is publicized in the community (Olson, 2013; Insel & Gould, 2008). Gay, lesbian, and bisexual adolescents are at particularly high risk for suicide attempts. These attempts seem to occur especially among those who have been raised in an environment devoid of adequate support systems (Saewyc et al., 2007).

Interventions. Strategies for suicide prevention frequently focus on risk factors. Public education campaigns, for example, are aimed at the improvement of the recognition of suicide risk and increasing the understanding of causes and risk factors for suicidal behaviour, especially mental disorders (CASP, 2016). Other specific education strategies aimed at youth in particular include school and community programs (Calear et al., 2016). Promising school-based programs emphasize the process of screening students for mental health problems, and to referring them to health care professionals (Kutcher & Szumilas, 2008). Other strategies include providing teachers with "gatekeeper" training to recognize depression; learning procedures for referral to mental health services; and developing peer-helper programs and crisis debriefing interventions aimed at youth (Kutcher & Szumilas, 2008). Appropriate emotional and psychological supports from friends and families appear to safeguard against suicide (Kostenuik & Ratnapalan, 2010). The media can help suicide prevention efforts by being a path for public education; on the other hand, media can hinder certain preventive efforts by glamourizing suicide, or by promoting it as a solution for life problems (Christensen, Betterham, & O'Dea, 2014).

© BananaStock/PunchStock

To this point, we have discussed many ideas about adolescent health problems and wellness. For a review, see the Reach Your Learning Outcomes section at the end of this chapter.

Adolescent Cognition

LO5 Explain cognitive development in adolescence and the influence of schools on adolescent cognition.

- **Piaget's Theory**
- **Adolescent Egocentrism**
- **Information Processing**
- **Education**

Adolescents' developing power of thought opens up new cognitive and social horizons.

Piaget's Theory

Recall from Chapter 9 that Piaget proposed children enter the *concrete operational stage* of cognitive development at about 7 years of age. At this stage they can reason logically about events and objects, categorizing them and identifying relationships. This stage lasts until about 11 years of age, when, according to Piaget, the fourth and final stage of cognitive development begins.

The Formal Operational Stage

How does formal operational thought differ from concrete operational thought? One major difference is that formal operational thought is more abstract than concrete operational thought. Adolescents are no longer limited to thinking about concrete experiences; they can imagine hypothetical possibilities or abstract propositions. Further, they can reason logically about them.

The abstract quality of the adolescent's thought at the formal operational level is evident in the adolescent's verbal problem-solving ability. Whereas the concrete operational thinker needs to see the concrete elements A, B, and C to be able to make the logical inference that if A = B and B = C, then A = C, the formal operational thinker can solve this problem merely through verbal presentation.

Accompanying the abstract nature of formal operational thought in adolescence are thoughts full of idealism and possibilities. While children frequently think in concrete ways, or in terms of what is real and limited, adolescents begin to engage in extended speculation about ideal characteristics—qualities they desire in themselves and in others. Such thoughts often lead adolescents to compare themselves with others in regard to such ideal standards. During adolescence, the thoughts of individuals are often fantasy flights into future possibilities.

At the same time that adolescents have increased ability to think more logically, they are less likely to use trial and error to figure out problems. Adolescents begin to think more scientifically, devising plans to solve problems and systematically testing solutions. This type of problem solving requires **hypothetical-deductive reasoning**, in which an individual creates a hypothesis, deduces implications, and tests implications. Thus, formal operational thinkers develop hypotheses, or best guesses, about ways to solve problems, then they systematically figure out and determine the best path to follow in solving the problem.

For adolescents who become formal operational thinkers, *assimilation* (incorporating new information into existing knowledge) dominates the initial development of formal operational thought, and the world is perceived subjectively and idealistically. Later in adolescence, as intellectual balance is restored, these individuals *accommodate* (adjust to new information) to the cognitive upheaval that has occurred. Figure 11.7 summarizes the characteristics of formal operational thought.

Figure 11.7

Characteristics of Formal Operational Thought

Abstract	Idealistic	Logical
Adolescents think more abstractly than children. Formal operational thinkers can solve abstract algebraic equations, for example.	Adolescents often think about what is possible. They think about ideal characteristics of themselves, others, and the world.	Adolescents begin to think more like scientists, devising plans to solve problems and systematically testing solutions. Piaget called this type of logical thinking "hypothetical-deductive reasoning."

Adolescents begin to think in more abstract, idealistic, and logical ways than when they were children.

Evaluating Piaget's Theory

Some of Piaget's ideas on formal operational thought have been challenged (Byrnes, 2008). Those who have challenged Piaget's ideas argue that individual variation is greater than Piaget envisioned. Only about one in three young adolescents is a formal operational thinker, and many adults never think in this way. Furthermore, education in science and mathematics employs the scientific method and thereby fosters articulation of the types of responses that are thought to be evidence of formal operational thought.

Culture and education exert stronger influences on cognitive development than Piaget believed (Rogoff et al., 2007). Most contemporary developmentalists agree that cognitive development is not as stage-like as Piaget thought (Siegler et al., 2013; Kellman & Arterberry, 2006). Furthermore, children can be trained to reason at a higher cognitive stage, and some abilities emerge earlier than Piaget thought (Scholnick, 2008).

Ethologists are scientists who research the connections between animal and human behaviours, as described in Chapter 2. Ethologists distinguish between biologically primary and secondary abilities, defining the biologically primary abilities as those that are learned universally, at approximately the same age. Biologically secondary abilities, or higher-level abilities, are those that are not learned easily and require effort. Ethologists suggest that Piaget's early stages—sensorimotor, preoperational, and concrete operational—rely on biologically primary abilities because they are learned universally at approximately the same age. Walking, conservation, and seriation are learned whether a child is in a classroom environment or not. Secondary abilities are those abilities that are not universal and take more effort to obtain. Examples include participation in complex oral traditions such as storytelling, piano-playing, or agricultural skills. Within a singular culture, greater variation of achievement exists. Children who grow up in Eastern Ontario may become bilingual as a matter of course. Adults who move into the region may have to expend considerable effort and time learning French or English. Ethologists cite the lack of universality of biologically secondary abilities as a major flaw in Piaget's formal operational stage.

Despite these critiques, Piaget can still be credited with the current field of cognitive development as he developed a long list of comprehensive and useful concepts of enduring influence. These include his theories of assimilation, accommodation, object permanence, egocentrism, conservation, and others. The current paradigm of children as active, constructive thinkers rather than passive receptacles of knowledge is attributed to him.

Many adolescent girls spend long hours in front of the mirror, depleting cans of hairspray, tubes of lipstick, and jars of cosmetics. *How might this behaviour be related to changes in adolescent cognitive and physical development?*

Piaget's theoretical ability was complemented by his adept skills of observation. His careful observations demonstrated inventive ways to discover how children act on and adapt to their world. He showed us that children simultaneously conceptualize their experiences in a way that fits their schematic view of the world while they adjust their world-view to account for new information and experiences. Piaget also revealed how cognitive change is likely to occur if the context is structured to allow gradual movement to the next level. Mature concepts do not emerge suddenly, but instead develop through a series of partial accomplishments that lead to increasingly comprehensive understandings.

In addition to thinking more logically, abstractly, and idealistically, characteristics of Piaget's formal operational thought stage, adolescent egocentrism plays an important role in adolescent thinking.

Adolescent Egocentrism

Recall from Chapter 7 that egocentrism in preschoolers is the child's belief that everyone can see the same things that the child sees. **Adolescent egocentrism** shifts to a heightened self-awareness and self-consciousness. David Elkind (1976) believed that adolescent egocentrism has two key components: the imaginary audience and personal fable.

Imaginary audience involves adolescents' belief that others are as interested in them as they themselves are. It may include the belief that everyone notices them as well as behaviours intended to attract attention, or exaggerated attempts not to be noticed. Adolescents, especially young adolescents, sense that they are "on stage," believing they are the main actors and all others are the audience.

According to Elkind, the **personal fable** is the part of adolescent egocentrism that involves a sense of uniqueness and invincibility. Adolescents' sense of personal uniqueness gives them the sense that no one else, especially parents, can understand how they really feel. As part of their effort to retain a sense of personal uniqueness, adolescents might craft a story about the self that is filled with fantasy, immersing themselves in a world that is far removed from reality. Personal fables frequently show up in adolescent diaries or in the names they use in computer games. Some teens create *avatars*, virtual representatives or caricatures of themselves, for use on the Internet. Avatars appeal greatly to the adolescent's personal fable because they can remain anonymous yet experience aspects of life, or alter-life, in the virtual world not available to them in the real world. They can attend lectures, art galleries, cafés, parties, etc. They can meet friends and carry on friendships in the virtual world.

Adolescents also often show a sense of invincibility, believing that nothing horrible can happen to them. Life is new, and they are young, so being in an automobile accident, getting caught shoplifting, becoming pregnant, or developing diseases caused by smoking happen to someone else. A sense of invincibility or invulnerability has been linked to engaging in risky behaviours, such as smoking cigarettes, drinking alcohol, and delinquency, whereas a sense of personal uniqueness is related to depression and suicidal thoughts (Albert, Elkind, & Ginsberg, 2007). A growing number of studies suggest that, rather than perceiving themselves to be invulnerable, adolescents tend to perceive themselves as vulnerable to experiencing death (Reyna & Rivers, 2008). In a recent study of the perceived risk of dying of adolescents, the results indicated that adolescents significantly overestimated their chance of dying (Fischhoff et al., 2010). In a more recent study, researchers concluded that nearly one in four youth (23 percent) expressed a perceived risk of a premature death occurring at some point in their lives (Duke et al., 2011).

Information Processing

According to Deanna Kuhn (2009), the most important cognitive change in adolescence is improvement in *executive functioning,* which involves higher-order cognitive activities such as reasoning, making decisions, monitoring critical thinking, and monitoring one's cognitive progress. Improvements in executive functioning permit more effective learning and an improved ability to determine how attention will be allocated, to make decisions, and to engage in critical thinking.

Decision Making

Adolescence is a time of increased decision making—career choices, education, dating, and so on (Rivers, Reyna, & Mills, 2008; Sunstein, 2008; Rena & Zayas, 2014). Adolescents are increasingly more likely to set realistic goals, anticipate consequences, and determine strategies for reaching their goals as they age. Compared with children, young adolescents are more likely to generate different options, examine a situation from a variety of perspectives, anticipate the consequences of decisions, and consider the credibility of sources.

For older adolescents and adults, the ability to make competent decisions does not guarantee that they will be made in everyday life, where breadth of experience often comes into play. For example, driver-training courses improve adolescents' cognitive and motor skills to levels equal to, or sometimes superior to, those of adults. However, driver training has not been effective in reducing adolescents' high rate of traffic accidents, although recently researchers have found that implementing a graduated driver licensing (GDL) program can reduce crash and fatality rates for adolescent drivers (Keating, 2007). GDL components include a learner's holding period, practice driving certification, night driving restriction, and passenger restriction.

Interestingly, some personality traits, such as introversion, extraversion, conscientiousness, and agreeableness, may influence decision making. Most people make better decisions when they are calm rather than emotionally aroused. That may be especially true for adolescents, who have a tendency to be emotionally intense. The same adolescent who makes a wise decision when calm may make an unwise decision when emotionally aroused (Giedd, 2008; Steinberg, 2009). In the heat of the moment, emotions may overwhelm decision-making ability.

The social context plays a key role in adolescent decision making (Smith Cheine & Steinberg, 2014). For example, adolescents' willingness to make risky decisions is more likely to occur in contexts where substances and other temptations are readily available (Gerrard et al., 2008; Reyna & Rivers, 2008). Recent research reveals that the presence of peers in risk-taking situations increases the likelihood that adolescents will make risky decisions (Steinberg, 2008). One view is that the presence of peers activates the brain's reward system, especially dopamine pathways (Steinberg, 2008).

Critical Thinking

The development of critical-thinking skills is essential when adolescents enter formal education (Marin & Halpern, 2011). The ability to think critically for the adolescent is essential for success in the contemporary world where the rate of creation of new knowledge is accelerating rapidly each day (Gainer, 2012). Instruction that compels critical thought in the adolescent can be accomplished either by threading critical thinking skills into the content matter, or through explicit instruction specifically designed to provide guidance in the essentials of critical thinking skills (Marin & Halpern, 2011). For example, Brookfield (2011) has designed assignments to develop critical thinkers. These assignments encourage adolescents to reason in a reflective manner and process information more efficiently.

If fundamental skills (such as literacy and math skills) are not developed during childhood, critical-thinking skills are unlikely to mature in adolescence. For the subset of adolescents who lack such fundamental skills, potential gains in adolescent thinking are unlikely. For other adolescents, however, cognitive changes that allow improved critical thinking in adolescence include the following: (1) increased speed, automaticity, and capacity of information processing, which free cognitive resources for other purposes; (2) more breadth of content knowledge in a variety of domains; (3) increased ability to construct new combinations of knowledge; and (4) a greater range and more spontaneous use of strategies or procedures for applying or obtaining knowledge, such as planning, considering alternatives, and cognitive monitoring.

The Brain

Neuroscientist Jay Giedd and his collaborators from UCLA, Harvard, the Montreal Neurological Institute, and other institutions found that of all parts of the brain, the frontal lobe undergoes the most complex change during adolescence (Giedd et al., 1999). Sometimes called the CEO, or chief executive officer, the frontal lobe is our head office, monitoring our decisions. It helps us plan ahead, resist impulses, understand consequences, focus attention, set priorities, and engage in other decision-making activities. Giedd's longitudinal study found the frontal lobe to be the last section of the brain to develop. During puberty, as the brain produces more neural connections it starts to specialize, pruning back to the essentials. This allows the brain to function more efficiently, but what gets pruned away is largely determined by the choices the teen makes. According to Giedd (2008), because the frontal lobe of the brain is still under construction, "it's sort of unfair to expect them to have adult levels of organizational skills or decision making before their brain is finished being built."

Education

Nowhere is the convergence of the three processes of life-span development more evident than in high school. Changing hormones, restructuring of the brain, worrying about body image, developing emotional control, and managing time and money as well as relationships are very much a part of the teen's world. As anyone who has ever been in junior high or high school knows, the classroom and homework frequently play a secondary role to other life situations.

A great many of today's high school students have grown up with the social spaces created by technology. They are tweeting and chatting on blogs, on Facebook, and in other virtual spaces. Many teachers and school administrators may be just learning these technologies in an effort to keep up with their students. Knowing how to use technology and manage information in itself transforms the classroom; no longer is the teacher the only or primary source of knowledge and skill. A major challenge facing education today is preparing students to manage all the information that is available to them (Silverslides, 2012).

critical thinking

Three girls in Indiana were expelled from their school for making jokes on Facebook about fellow students they would like to kill. Many students in both high school and university use Facebook and other social media sites. Write three policy statements that you think students should be required to follow in using social media. How do you suggest these policies be regulated? Should there be different policies depending on which social media site one is considering?

Service-Learning

Service-learning is a form of education intended to promote social responsibility and service to the community. In service-learning, students engage in activities such as tutoring, helping older adults, working in a hospital, assisting at a child-care centre, or cleaning up a vacant lot to make a play area. Thus, service-learning takes education out into the community. One important goal of service learning is that adolescents become less self-centered and more strongly motivated to help others (Davidson et al., 2010).

Researchers have found that service-learning effectively assists adolescents in a number of ways (Gonsalves, 2011; Kielsmeier, 2011), such as obtaining higher grades, increased self-esteem, heightened belief in their ability to influence others, and developing problem solving skills. A recent study indicated that the volunteer activities of adolescents also provide opportunities for them to explore and to reason about moral issues (van Goethem et al., 2012).

Katimavik, the Inuit word for "meeting place," is the name for a government program organized in 1977. Since its implementation, Katimavik has enabled over 30 000 youth between 17 and 21 years of age to work, live, and learn together in 2000 communities across Canada. The primary goal of Katimavik is to enhance personal development by enabling young people to meet, live with, work with, and learn from each other (Katimavik, 2010).

Effective Schools

Schools that are most effective in responding to adolescent needs do far more than teach basic skills of reading, writing, and math. They offer an environment that is accountable and responsive to public scrutiny. While some schools buckle under increasing public criticism and dwindling resources, others form collaborative relationships within the community. Effective leadership, clear academic goals, a safe and orderly climate, expectation of minimum mastery of skills by all students, testing for program evaluation and redirection, parental involvement, and collegiality are the trademarks of effective schools (Bonell et al., 2013).

The Manitoba School Improvement Program (MSIP) cites strong community ties as essential to better schools (MSIP, 2011). Schools with open and respectful communication and an environment that builds confidence and academic enthusiasm among students foster effective learning. Additionally, shared vision and academic focus, combined with an ethic of caring, enables students to make a successful transition from elementary school to middle or junior high school to high school. These ingredients contribute to the **hidden curriculum**, the moral atmosphere that is communicated through the school's rules, regulations, deportment, and moral orientation. In this way, every school and classroom within a school infuses a value system. When students make the transition from one school to the next, and from one classroom to the next, they must figure out and adjust to this often unspoken curriculum.

As discussed throughout the chapter, the transition to middle or junior high school takes place at a time when many changes—in the individual, in the family, and in school—are occurring simultaneously. When students make the transition to middle or junior high school they experience the *top-dog phenomenon*, moving from being the oldest, biggest, and most powerful students in the elementary school to being the youngest, smallest, and least powerful students in the middle or junior high school.

There can also be positive aspects to the transition to middle or junior high school. Students are more likely to feel grown up, have more subjects from which to select, have more opportunities to spend time with peers and locate compatible friends, and enjoy increased independence from direct parental monitoring. They also may be more challenged intellectually by academic work.

Ministries of education across Canada have introduced innovative curriculum to prepare students for further education and work. Recall that Piaget and Kohlberg suggested that a child's moral development moves steadily from being externally controlled by the rewards associated with pleasing parents, teachers, and other adults to being internally controlled by the intrinsic rewards associated with making decisions that serve the common good of the community. On the basis of these theories, much curriculum, such as service-learning, prejudice reduction, and emotional intelligence (EI), has been developed to address various moral concerns.

Technology has brought about another radical transformation to our concept of education. Computers and high-speed Internet access have been altering the nature of learning ever since their introduction. Rather than simply absorbing information, the technologies allow students to access original-source materials and discover truths for themselves. The classroom has become globalized as well, linking communities with Internet access across the world. This may help expand Canadian students' multicultural experiences to international frontiers.

Dropping Out of High School

In Canada, high school dropout rates fell in all provinces from the early 1990s to 2010 (Figure 11.8).

The Atlantic provinces had the most significant change. For example, rates fell from a range of 15–20 percent in the early 1990s to 11 percent a decade later. In 1990/1993, Newfoundland and Labrador had the highest provincial dropout rate in Canada (19.9 percent). By 2007/2010, it had one of the lowest (7.4 percent). In 2007/2010, dropout rates were lowest in British Columbia at 6.2 percent, and highest in Quebec, at 11 percent, followed closely by the three prairie provinces. In the three territories, dropout rates were persistently higher than those of the provinces. Nunavut had the highest dropout rate of all, at 50 percent. (Gilmore, 2010).

Figure 11.8
Dropout Rate in Canada from 1990 to 2010

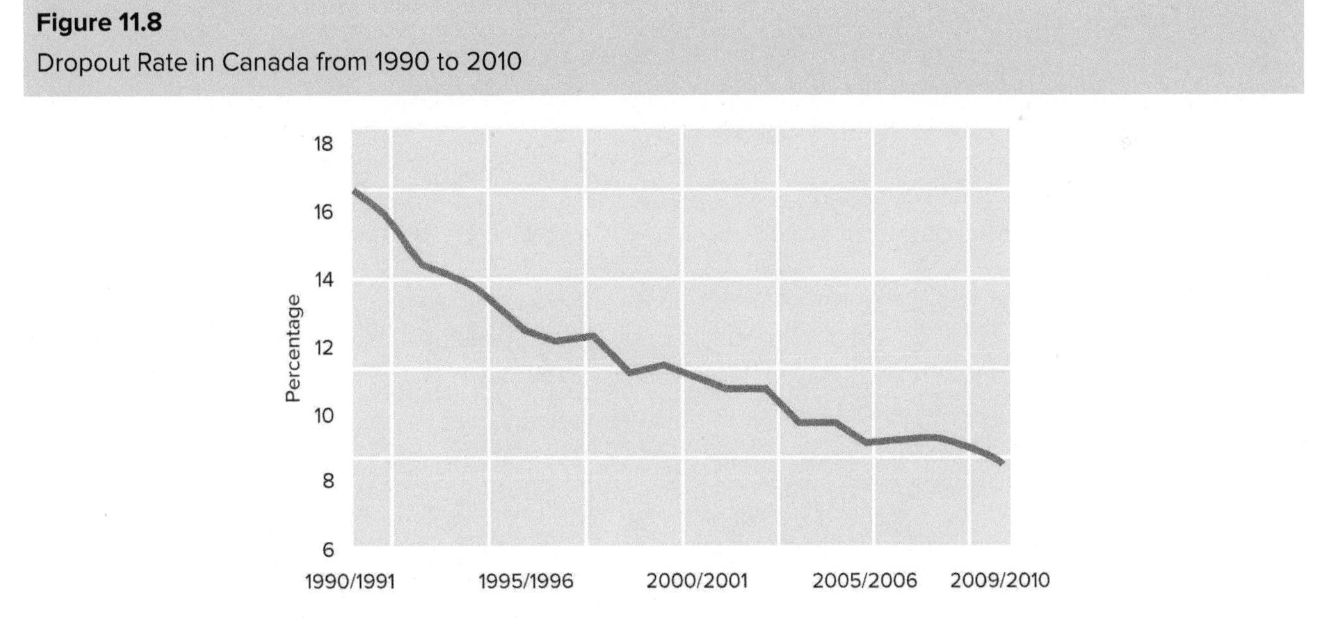

Source: Statistics Canada, Labour Force Survey

Earlier studies have provided a few examples of the various reasons that young men and women decide to drop out before completing high school. Young men tend to state that they dropped out mainly because they were not sufficiently involved in school and/or that they wanted to work and earn money. Meanwhile, young women were more likely to drop out because of personal or family issues, such as pregnancy or having a young child at home (Raymond, 2008).

Statistics indicate that dropout rates for Aboriginal people in 2007 to 2010 were much higher (22.6 percent) compared to 8.5 percent for non-Aboriginal people (Gilmore, 2010). Immigrant dropout rates of 6.2 percent in 2009/2010 were lower than those of their Canadian-born counterparts.

To this point, we have discussed a number of ideas about adolescent cognition. For a review, see the Reach Your Learning Outcomes section at the end of this chapter.

Reach Your **Learning Outcomes**

The Nature of Adolescence

LO1 Analyze the life stage of adolescence.

- Biological, emotional, and environmental factors influence adolescent development.
- Adolescence is a period of idealistic and abstract thinking.
- Risks and temptations are more numerous than in previous generations.
- Although adolescence is a vulnerable period, most, especially those who report good family relationships, make the transition fairly smoothly.
- Although risk-taking is part of identity formation, for some the experimentation with sex, alcohol, drugs, and gambling lead to permanent problems in adulthood.
- Adolescents today have a less stable environment than they did a decade ago.

Physical Changes during Puberty

LO2 Describe the physical changes that occur during puberty.

Sexual Maturation, Height, and Weight	▪ Puberty is a rapid change to physical maturation involving hormonal and bodily changes that occur primarily during early adolescence. ▪ The onset of puberty can occur anytime between the ages of 8 and 15 and last from 1.5 to 6 years. ▪ Menarche, the female menstrual cycle, occurs toward the end of the puberty period. ▪ Growth spurts occur about two years earlier in girls than boys.
Hormonal Changes	▪ Hormones are powerful chemical substances secreted by the endocrine glands and carried throughout the body in the bloodstream. ▪ The concentration of testosterone in boys and estradiol in girls dominate pubertal development. ▪ Individual variation is puberty is extensive.
Body Image	▪ Adolescents show considerable interest in their body image. ▪ Young adolescents are more preoccupied and less satisfied with their body image than are late adolescents. ▪ Girls have more negative body images throughout puberty due to increase of body fat. ▪ Early maturing boys have been characterized as more overweight compared to late maturing boys, however there is widespread individual variation. ▪ A recent study found that both boys' and girls' body image become more positive as they move from the beginning to end of puberty.

Teen Perspectives on Maturity	▪ Research indicates that establishing independence or autonomy is a key developmental task of adolescence. ▪ In adolescence, cognitive abilities are related to psychosocial maturity.
The Brain	▪ During adolescence, the brain undergoes a rapid transformation called exuberance. ▪ The frontal lobe, or executive branch of the brain, is last to develop, making individuals more prone to respond with "gut" reactions to emotional stimuli. ▪ Because the frontal lobe is last to develop, adolescents are more likely to take risks than are adults.

Adolescent Sexuality

LO3 **Describe adolescent sexuality, sexual identity, and risk factors related to intimate sexual behaviour.**

Developing a Sexual Identity	▪ Mastering emerging emotions and forming a sense of sexual identity are multifaceted. ▪ An adolescent's sexual identity involves sexual orientation, activities, interests, and styles of behaviour. ▪ LGBT youth have enhanced developmental challenges.
The Timing of Adolescent Sexual Behaviours	▪ The percentage of teens who report they have had intercourse has declined; however, age, gender, and jurisdiction are factors. ▪ Those who decide to engage in sexual activity do so because they are in a serious relationship; however, peer pressure, alcohol, and drugs also play a role in their decision. ▪ Findings revealed that 75–80 percent of grade 9 students and 64–75 percent of grade 11 students reported being protected from STI by condom use.
Risk Factors and Sexual Problems	▪ Use of contraceptives has increased. ▪ Human papillomavirus (HPV) is thought to be the most commonly transmitted STI. Two types of vaccine are now available in Canada for protection against HPV. ▪ Rates of pregnancy vary by country; international comparisons can be variable. ▪ Adolescent pregnancy increases health risks for both the mother and the offspring. ▪ Adolescent mothers have difficulty breaking the cycle of poverty as they are more likely to drop out of school and have lower-paying jobs as adults than adolescent girls who do not bear children.
Adolescent Pregnancy and Health	▪ Canadian pregnancy guidelines are available that include sex education and family planning, access to contraception, life options, community involvement and support, and abstinence. ▪ Aboriginal community policy initiatives provide emotional support, safe-sex guidelines, and family planning goals.

- Effective schools are characterized by their academic focus and open environment conducive to learning.
- Innovative curriculum is developed and reviewed in partnership with parents, police, community members, and students, and is responsive to social needs and technology.
- The hidden curriculum is the moral atmosphere infused by the school through its policies and deportment.
- Fewer Canadians are leaving high school before completion than a generation ago.
- Francophone and Aboriginal youth have the lowest high school completion rates and face unique challenges.
- Nunavut has the highest school dropout rate.

review → connect → reflect

review

1. What characterizes adolescent development? LO1
2. What are several key aspects of puberty? LO2
3. What factors affect the timing of puberty? LO2
4. What are some important aspects of adolescent sexuality? LO3
5. How effective are the *Canadian Guidelines for Sexual Health Education* for adolescents? LO3
6. What are the key aspects of eating disorders? LO4
7. What are a few important aspects of information processing in adolescence? LO5

connect

Peers exert both positive and negative pressure. How do they exert negative pressure in our society today?

reflect

Your Own Personal Journey of Life

Reflect on your adolescence. Was it a time of stress and storm or a time of transition into young adulthood? Explain.

CHAPTER 12

Socio-Emotional Development in Adolescence

CHAPTER OUTLINE

Self-Esteem and Identity Development

LO1 Describe self-esteem, the changes in the self and identity, and several of the prominent theories.

- **Self-Esteem**
- **Identity**

Identity: Family, Religion, Race, Ethnicity, Culture, and Sexual Orientation

LO2 Compare and contrast how family, religion, race, ethnicity, culture, and sexual orientation influence adolescent development.

- **Families**
- **Religion**
- **Racial, Ethnic, and Cultural Identity**
- **Traditions and Changes in Adolescence around the World**
- **Sexual Orientation and Identity**

Friendship

LO3 Outline the changes that occur in peer relations and dating during adolescence.

- **Adolescent Groups versus Children's Groups**
- **Peer Groups**
- **Dating and Romantic Relationships**

Adolescent Problems

LO4 Analyze adolescent problems in socio-emotional development, and the causes of the problems.

- **Young Offenders**
- **Causes of Delinquency**

Successful Prevention and Intervention Programs

LO5 Design strategies for helping adolescents with problems.

"We are not just our future . . . we are also our present."

—HARINI SHIVALINGAM, CANADIAN YOUTH REPRESENTATIVE TO THE UNITED NATIONS WORLD CONFERENCE AGAINST RACISM, RACIAL DISCRIMINATION, XENOPHOBIA, AND RELATED INTOLERANCE (WCAR)

© Huntstock, Inc./Alamy Stock Photo

The Challenges of Being an Adolescent

As we discussed in Chapter 11, no two people are alike. However, the transition from childhood to adulthood encompasses similar milestones in both physical and cognitive development. The same applies to socio-emotional development, where significant changes occur during adolescence. The mainstay of the changes includes increased efforts for self-understanding and increased searching for an identity. Changes also occur in the social contexts of adolescents' lives, with transformations occurring in relationships with families and peers and other cultural contexts, such as schools, health care facilities, communities, and even countries. Some adolescents may develop socio-emotional problems, such as delinquency and depression. The scenarios below are a snapshot of some of the variations and unique contexts shaping an individual's choices and decisions.

THIRTEEN: *Amelia* worries that something is wrong with her because all her friends wear bras, have begun to menstruate, and are interested in boys. She wonders if these events will ever happen to her. *Spencer* and his friends attend a private school where laptops for each student are part of the tuition. They create a re-enactment of Louis Riel for their history project. Virtual world avatars are used as actors because their school has created a "controlled" account for all students.

FOURTEEN: When *Renée* isn't riding horses, she is studying. Ever since she can remember, she has wanted to be a veterinarian. She has a small circle of friends and isn't too interested in boys, although she does "swoon" whenever she sees Cal. *Joe* avoids everyone. He is attracted to other boys and is afraid if he shows this side of him, he will be beaten up. He knows that he is the subject of gossip and rumours.

FIFTEEN: *Carl* played on the football team last year in another high school and tried out for the team this year in his new high school. When he checks the board to see who had made the team, he sees that he has been cut. He loses his temper, kicks his locker, shouts profanities, and stomps out of the school angrily. On Tuesdays, Thursdays, and Sunday afternoons, *Samantha* babysits her neighbour's 3-year-old daughter, Lisa, a child with Down syndrome. Samantha loves Lisa, and has learned so much from her that she thinks she'd like to become a teacher of children with special needs.

SIXTEEN: As soon as she got her licence, *Michelle* borrowed her father's car. With great pride, she picked up her best friend and they went for a ride. Michelle was very careful not to speed and to return the car on time because she doesn't want to jeopardize her father's trust. With a fake passport in his hand, *Sallieu* left Sierra Leone, landing at Toronto's Pearson International Airport. He learns that he is in Canada when he sees the signs that read, "Welcome to Canada." He has no money and nowhere to stay. Sallieu is one of hundreds of thousands of adolescents who flee their war-torn country of origin to seek what they hope will be a healthier and more peaceful environment.

SEVENTEEN: Because she was failing all her courses, *Jessica,* who has attention deficit disorder, dropped out of school, much to her parents' dismay. She got a job at Tim Hortons. Three months later she quit, and hasn't worked since. She moved out of the family home because she "can't put up with their nagging anymore." *Philip* sends his university application in to three universities. He really isn't sure what he wants to study, and keeps changing his mind between medicine, international law, and child psychology.

EIGHTEEN: *Lynne* was referred to a nutritional counsellor after her hospitalization for anorexia nervosa. Her first appointment is after school at 4:30, and she is dreading it. She knows what the counsellor will say; after all, she has been through this before. She snorts a line of coke to brace herself for her counselling appointment. *Jason's* avatar, Jake, meets Jude, another avatar, at a virtual café where they share anecdotes about their parents, classmates, and teachers. They leave the café and go to a bar. Although you are supposed to be 18 to have an Avatar account, Jason and a friend opened accounts a couple of years ago and created macho body images of themselves that they thought would appeal to the girls.

NINETEEN: *Evan* is excited about his first year at Carleton University in Ottawa. Although he has been looking forward to the freedom of living away from home, now that the time has come, he is worried about who his roommates will be. *Janice* has applied to participate in Katimavik because she isn't sure what she wants to do now that she has finished high school. She is tired of working in retail stores and wants to learn more about Canada.

Each scenario illustrates some of the milestones, challenges, and problems facing adolescents. Like the teens in this vignette, during adolescence each individual grapples with identity in a manner very different from childhood. As you can see from these snapshots, and as you may remember from your own adolescent years, the integrative physical, cognitive, and socio-emotional processes of development are strongly at play in the search for identity and the development of self-esteem.

Self-Esteem and Identity Development

LO1 Describe self-esteem, the changes in the self and identity, and several of the prominent theories.

- **Self-Esteem**
- **Identity**

Recall from Chapter 10 that *self-esteem* is the overall way we evaluate ourselves, and it is also referred to as self-image or self-worth. Controversy characterizes the extent to which self-esteem changes during adolescence and whether there are gender differences in adolescents' self-esteem (Harter, 2006, 2012). Self-esteem and other personality traits are not entirely stable constructs: they are subject to change across the life span, especially during adolescence (Steinberg, 2008). That is, the relations between self-concept facets and self-esteem might change and shift as students age, due to the importance students allocate to different life domains (Arens & Hasselhorn, 2014).

Self-Esteem

Does self-esteem in adolescence foreshadow adjustment and competence in adulthood? A New Zealand longitudinal study assessed self-esteem at 11, 13, and 15 years of age, and adjustment and competence of the same individuals when they were 26 years old (Trzesniewski et al., 2006). The results revealed that adults characterized by poorer mental and physical health, worse economic prospects, and higher levels of criminal behaviour were more likely to have had low self-esteem in adolescence than their better-adjusted, more competent adult counterparts.

Recent research also indicates that self-esteem is often implicated in the development of adolescent behaviour, with high self-esteem serving as a role of positive adaptation (Boden, Fergusson, & Horwood, 2008). Conversely, low self-esteem has been considered an important factor in relation to manifestations of depression, both in adolescents and in adult samples (Bos et al., 2010).

Self-esteem is a large part of adolescents' self-understanding; it is likely to be a fluctuating and dynamic construct, susceptible to internal and external influences during adolescence (Erol & Orth, 2011). One study found that gender differences in self-esteem narrow between grade 9 and grade 12 because self-esteem increases at a faster rate among girls than boys during high school (Falci, 2011). For example, girls with high self-esteem are more likely to than boys to establish positive peer relationships (Doumen et al., 2012). However, in a study by Erol and Orth (2011), no significant gender difference in the level of self-esteem was discovered. These findings also indicate that self-esteem increases and continues to increase slowly during the adolescent years. Actually, adolescent self-esteem changes more strongly than in young adulthood (Erol & Orth, 2011). According to the maturity principle, through adolescence and particularly young adulthood, young people adapt more completely to social roles in society. This development enables them to become more emotionally stable, conscientious, confident, and capable, all of which helps to lead to an increase in self-esteem (Trzesniewski, Donnellan, & Robins, 2013).

Identity

Who am I? What am I all about? What am I going to do with my life? What is different about me? How can I make it on my own? These questions, captured in the snapshot scenarios in the opening vignette, reflect the search for an identity. **Identity** refers to our self-portraits that develop over our lifetime and are made up of many components, including negations and affirmations of various roles and characteristics. By far the most comprehensive and provocative theory of identity development is Erik Erikson's. In this section, we examine his views on identity. We also discuss contemporary research on how identity develops and how social contexts influence that development.

Identity is a self-portrait composed of many pieces. These pieces include the following:

- The career and work path a person wants to follow (vocational/career identity)
- Whether a person is conservative, liberal, or a centrist (political identity)
- A person's spiritual beliefs (religious identity)
- Whether a person is single, married, divorced, and so on (relationship identity)
- The extent to which the person is motivated to achieve and is intellectual (achievement, intellectual identity)
- Whether a person is heterosexual, homosexual, or bisexual (sexual identity)
- The part of the world or country a person is from and how intensely the person identifies with his or her cultural heritage (cultural/ethnic identity)
- The kinds of things a person likes to do, which may include sports, music, hobbies, and so on (interests)
- The individual's personality characteristics, such as being introverted or extroverted, anxious or calm, friendly or hostile, and so on (personality)
- The individual's body image (physical identity)

Synthesizing the identity components can be a long and drawn-out process, with many negations and affirmations of various roles and characteristics. Identity development gets done in bits and pieces. Decisions are not made once and for all, but have to be made again and again. Identity development does not happen neatly, and it does not happen cataclysmically (Kroger, 2007; Orbe, 2008; Phinney, 2008).

Erik Erikson

By far the most comprehensive and provocative theory of identity development is Erik Erikson's. Erikson's psychosocial development theory is epigenetic, suggesting a synchrony between individual growth and social expectations. At each of eight chronological periods in the life span, physical changes occur to which one's social environment responds with particular expectations and supports in the form of cultural practices and institutions (Marcia & Josselson, 2013).

It was Erikson who first understood how central questions about identity are to understanding adolescent development. As you may remember from Chapter 2, identity versus identity confusion, the fifth of Erikson's eight stages, occurs at about the same time as adolescence. Erikson believed adolescence to be a time when individuals are interested in finding out who they are, what they are all about, and where they are headed in life. In fact, according to Erikson (1968), developing a coherent and synthesized sense of identity is one of the primary developmental tasks of the transition to adulthood.

The search for an identity during adolescence is aided by a **psychosocial moratorium**, which is Erikson's term for the gap between childhood security and adult autonomy. During this period, society leaves adolescents relatively free of responsibilities and free to try out different identities. Adolescents in effect search their culture's identity files, experimenting with different roles and personalities. They may want to pursue one career one month (lawyer, for example) and another career the next month (doctor, actor, teacher, social worker, or astronaut, for example). They may change their handwriting or signature daily. This experimentation is a deliberate effort on the part of adolescents to find out where they fit in the world.

Youth who successfully cope with conflicting identities emerge with a new sense of self that is both refreshing and acceptable. Adolescents who do not successfully resolve this identity crisis suffer what Erikson calls identity confusion. The confusion takes one of two courses: individuals withdraw, isolating themselves from peers and family, or they immerse themselves in the world of peers and lose their identity in the crowd.

Identity Development

Contemporary views of identity development suggest several important considerations. First, identity development is a lengthy process; in many instances, it is a more gradual, less cataclysmic transition than Erikson's term "crisis" implies. Second, identity development is extraordinarily complex.

Identity formation neither begins nor ends with adolescence; rather, it is a life-long process. Identity formation begins with the appearance of attachment, the development of a sense of self, and the emergence of independence in infancy, and it reaches its final phase with a life review and integration in old age. What is important about identity in adolescence, especially late adolescence, is that for the first time, physical development, cognitive development, and social development advance to the point at which the individual can sort through and integrate childhood identities and identifications to construct a reasonable pathway toward adult maturity. Resolution of the identity issue at adolescence does not mean that identity will be stable throughout the remainder of one's life. A person who develops a healthy identity is flexible, adaptive, and open to changes in society, in relationships, and in careers. This openness assures numerous reorganizations of identity features throughout the life of the person who has achieved identity.

Identity formation does not happen neatly, and it usually does not happen suddenly; in addition, identities are developed in bits and pieces. At the bare minimum, identity involves commitment to a vocational direction, an ideological stance, and a sexual orientation. Decisions are not made once and for all, but have to be made again and again. The number of decisions may seem overwhelming at times: whom to date, whether or not to break up, whether or not to have intercourse, whether or not to take drugs, whether to go to college or university after high school or get a job, which major to choose, whether to study or whether to play, whether or not to be politically active, and so on. Over the years of adolescence, identity is a critical development task during the transition to adulthood in Western societies (Schwartz et al., 2011).

James Marcia's Identity Statuses and Development

How do individual adolescents go about the process of forming an identity? Eriksonian researcher James Marcia (1980, 1994, 2013) reasons that Erikson's theory of identity development contains four statuses of identity, or ways of resolving the identity crisis: identity diffusion, identity foreclosure, identity moratorium, and identity achievement. What determines an individual's identity status? Marcia classifies individuals based on the existence or extent of their crisis or commitment (see Figure 12.1). **Crisis** is defined as a period of identity development during which the individual is exploring alternatives. Most researchers use the term *exploration* rather than crisis. **Commitment** is personal investment in identity. Marcia viewed exploration as the process underlying identity development and viewed commitment as the outcome of the process. Newer models now view both exploration and commitment as processes. These newer models have also been used empirically to extract identity statuses that strongly resemble and extend those proposed by Marcia (Crocetti et al., 2008). Interestingly, in demonstrating that identity statuses can be empirically derived from continuous measures of identity processes, strong evidence is provided that the status model does indeed capture the process of identity development (Schwartz et al., 2011).

Figure 12.1

Marcia's Four Statuses of Identity

Position on Occupation and Ideology	Identity Status			
	Identity diffusion	Identity foreclosure	Identity moratorium	Identity achievement
Crisis	Absent	Absent	Present	Present
Commitment	Absent	Present	Absent	Present

The four statuses of identity are described as the following:

- **Identity diffusion** occurs when individuals have not yet experienced a crisis (that is, they have not yet explored meaningful alternatives) or made any commitments. Not only are they undecided about occupational and ideological choices, but they are also likely to show little interest in such matters.
- **Identity foreclosure** occurs when individuals have made a commitment but have not yet experienced a crisis. This occurs most often when parents hand down commitments to their adolescents, usually in an authoritarian manner. In these circumstances, adolescents have not had adequate opportunities to explore different approaches, ideologies, and vocations on their own.
- **Identity moratorium** occurs when individuals are in the midst of a crisis but their commitments are either absent or only vaguely defined.
- **Identity achievement** occurs when individuals have undergone a crisis, and have made a commitment.

critical thinking

Think about your development and the development of one or two close friends from high school in the following areas: vocational/career, political, religious, sexual, ethnic/ cultural, and physical/sport. Compare and contrast ways in which Marcia's identity statuses (diffused, foreclosed, moratorium, or achieved) relate to you and friends in each of these areas. In what ways have you or someone you know shifted from one identity status to one another? What suggestions would you make to a friend who seems stuck in either a moratorium or foreclosed status, to assist him or her to shift to an achievement identity status? How would you apply Marcia's identity statuses to the teens portrayed in the opening vignette? What suggestions do you have for them to progress to an identity achievement status?

Emerging Adulthood and Beyond

A consensus is developing that the key changes in identity are more likely to take place in emerging adulthood (18 to 25 years of age) or later than in adolescence (Kroger, 2007; Luyckx et al., 2008a; Cote, 2009).

One of emerging adulthood's themes is not having many social commitments, which gives individuals considerable independence in developing a life path. James Cote (2009) argues that because of this freedom, developing a positive identity in emerging adulthood requires considerable self-discipline and planning. Without this self-discipline and planning, emerging adults are likely to drift and not follow any particular direction. Cote also stresses that emerging adults who obtain a higher education are more likely to be on a positive identity path. Those who don't obtain a higher education, he says, tend to experience frequent job changes, not because they are searching for an identity, but rather because they are just trying to eke out a living in a society that rewards higher education. Phinney (2008) states that the increased complexity in the reasoning skills of post-secondary students, combined with a wide range of new experiences that highlight contrast between home and post-secondary schools, and between themselves and others, stimulates students to reach a higher level of ability to integrate various dimensions of their identity.

Resolution of the identity issue during adolescence and emerging adulthood does not mean that identity will be stable through the remainder of life. Many individuals who develop positive identities follow what are called **MAMA cycles**; that is, their identity status changes from moratorium to achievement to moratorium to achievement (Marcia, 1994). These cycles may be repeated throughout life (Francis, Fraser, & Marcia, 1989). Marcia (2002, 2013) points out that the first identity is just that—it is not, and should not be expected to be, the final product.

In short, questions about identity come up throughout life. An individual who develops a healthy identity is flexible and adaptive, and open to changes in society, in relationships, and in careers. This openness assures numerous reorganizations of identity throughout the individual's life.

Elkind's Age Dynamisms

As adolescents reconcile their sense of self, they often employ what Elkind calls "age dynamisms"; that is, they wish to put as much distance between their more sophisticated teenage self and their childish or juvenile self of the past. Yet, in doing so, individuals recognize a certain level of continuity about themselves—they still have the same birthmark or eye colouring, for example. Research indicates that as children move through Piaget's stages of cognitive development, they become more sophisticated in understanding the persistence or continuity of their personal identities and the identities of others. This understanding is strongly influenced by cultural background. When individuals belong to a cultural group that realizes that their heritage has been ravaged by war, disruption, dislocation, and its future is dismal, they may fail to see their own personal continuity and feel a loss of identity. For example, suicidal behaviours are among the most profound mental-health related issues found in youth. Suicide behaviours are even more significant among the youngest generations of First Nations communities across Canada (Walls, Hautala, & Hurley, 2014). Although there are common factors between Aboriginal and non-Aboriginal suicides, these aspects are not sufficient to explain the increased Aboriginal suicide rates (MacNeil, 2008). Many believe that Aboriginal youth run higher risks of suicide primarily because of their quest for personal identity. Their past and present narratives reflect not only the typical struggle, but the loss of a culture, that has been scorned and devalued (Walls, Hautala, & Hurley, 2014).

CONNECTING development to life

Child or Adult? The Case of Omar Khadr

Adolescence is the transition from childhood to adulthood, marked by dramatic changes in all three processes: biological changes occur as the young person goes through puberty; cognitive changes occur as the adolescent develops more abstract and hypothetical thinking patterns and is better equipped to think logically; and socio-emotional changes occur as the young person moves further and further from his or her family and begins navigating social systems such as friends, school, jobs, and community more independently. Just when is this transition complete? When is an individual considered an adult? This is more than a philosophical question—it is also a question of law. When should a person be tried in a juvenile court? When should a person be tried in an adult court, where sentencing is much farther-reaching?

This question was at the heart of the debate surrounding a Canadian citizen, Omar Khadr. In 2002, 15-year-old Omar Khadr was arrested by the U.S. government and imprisoned in Guantanamo Bay (Steinberg, 2009). He was accused of killing a U.S. soldier in Afghanistan, war crimes, and supporting terrorism. His defence attorney argued that he was a boy soldier, a minor at the time of his crime, and therefore should not be tried in an adult court. They pointed out that he is the first child-soldier ever tried by the United States for war crimes (Steinberg, 2009).

Omar's family background further exacerbated his situation. His older brother was incarcerated in Toronto for several years on charges related to terrorism, and another brother was also arrested on charges related to ties with the terrorist group Al-Qaeda. Omar's father was believed to be a friend and major financer of Osama Bin Laden, the man who masterminded the 9/11 attacks on the United States. The family's travels between Egypt, Afghanistan, Pakistan, and Canada since 1980 attracted the attention of national security agencies in both Canada and the United States (CBC News, April 29, 2010). In October 2010, Khadr pleaded guilty to the charges as part of a plea bargain with the U.S. government. He was sentenced to 40 years in prison, but due to the pretrial plea deal would have to serve only eight years (CBC News, November 1, 2010). On September 29, 2012, at the hands of the American government, Omar Khadr was flown off the U.S. naval base from Guantanamo Bay, Cuba, to a maximum-security prison in Eastern Ontario with little chance of rehabilitation or parole for at least two years.

Khadr was transferred to a maximum security facility in Edmonton in May 2013 to serve the remainder of his sentence. In February, 2014, he was again transferred to the medium-security Bowden Institution in Innisfail, Alberta. In April 2015, an Alberta judge granted him bail pending the outcome of his appeal in the United States for his war crime conviction. He was released on bail on May 7, 2015. As part of his initial bail conditions, Khadr has to continue to see a psychologist and live with his lawyer, Dennis Edney, under a curfew from 10 p.m. to 7 a.m. In October of 2015, Justice June Ross of the Alberta Court of Queen's Bench ruled Khadr could remove his electronic monitoring bracelet and visit his grandparents in Toronto (CBC. News February 18, 2016). An announcement came on May 5, 2016 that Khadr celebrated the first anniversary of his release by having several bail conditions removed and relaxed. In the same year, Khadr became engaged to activist Muna Abougoush, who remained a faithful friend after his repatriation to Canada (Free Omar, 2016).

Neuroscientists who study the brain and the nervous system have shown through magnetic resonance imaging (MRI) that the adolescent brain is undergoing rapid changes, and that the prefrontal cortex, the executive branch that factors in consequences when making decisions and determining goals, is the last part of the brain to develop (Steinberg, 2009). This finding is important because it verifies what many already knew: adolescents tend to respond to situations with emotion, or with their gut feelings, whereas, adults, whose prefrontal cortex has developed, tend to use more logic and less emotion when making decisions. This finding could have been useful in mounting Khadr's defence.

Consider some of the theories you have learned about so far: Bronfenbrenner, Erikson, Freud, Kohlberg, Marcia, Maslow, Piaget, Vygotsky. How might each theorist explain Omar Khadr's behaviour? What are some of the many pieces that may be part of Khadr's identity resolution? What arguments would you make if you were the prosecuting attorney for the U.S. government? What arguments would you make if you were Khadr's defence attorney? What concepts and theories would you use to support your position?

To this point, we have studied a number of ideas about self-esteem and identity development in adolescence. For a review, see the Reach Your Learning Outcomes section at the end of this chapter.

Identity: Family, Religion, Race, Ethnicity, Culture, and Sexual Orientation

LO2 Compare and contrast how family, religion, race, ethnicity, culture, and sexual orientation influence adolescent development.

- **Families**
- **Religion**
- **Racial, Ethnic, and Cultural Identity**
- **Traditions and Changes in Adolescence around the World**
- **Sexual Orientation and Identity**

As indicated earlier, identity is very complex. Family, cultural and ethnic heritage, and sexual orientation all affect the development of an adolescent's identity (Youngblade et al., 2007). Another major contributory factor is socio-economic status, which underpins opportunities and access to resources and further shapes identity. This section will discuss areas where socio-economic status comes into play.

Families

Like people, families come in all sizes and shapes. Some families are lone-parent, while others, extended families, may have three or more generations under the same roof. Some families live in the same communities, while continents separate others. Some families are rich, others are middle-class, and many are poor. No matter the configuration, families provide the first source of information about the world. The family into which the adolescent was born shapes his or her sense of humour, understanding of right and wrong, notions of common sense, and sense of self. Families provide models that the emerging adult considers, accepts, or rejects. Attachment, autonomy, and conflict are typical as adolescents assert their independence from their families.

Family Influences

In addition to studying parenting styles, researchers have also examined the roles of individuality and connectedness in the development of identity. **Individuality** consists of self-assertion, the ability to have and communicate a point of view, and separateness, the use of communication patterns to express how one is different from others. **Connectedness** consists of two dimensions: mutuality, sensitivity to and respect for others' views, and permeability, openness to others' views. Parents are important figures in the adolescent's development of identity (Beyers & Goossens, 2008; Cooper, Behrens, & Trinh, 2008; Luyckx et al., 2007, 2008b; Schacter & Ventura, 2008). Relationships between parents and adolescents affect every aspect of adolescent development.

In general, research findings reveal that identity formation is enhanced by family relationships that are both individuated, which encourage adolescents to develop their own point of view, and connected, which provide a secure base from which to explore the widening social worlds of adolescence. When connectedness is strong and individuation weak, adolescents often have an identity foreclosure status. When connectedness is weak, adolescents often reveal identity confusion.

Research has demonstrated that parental behaviours and the quality of parent–child relationships related to empathy and prosocial behaviour are important correlates of youth development. Yoo, Feng, and Day (2013) found that parental behaviours, parental solicitation, and parental psychological control are particularly associated with empathy and prosocial behaviour in adolescents. Such influences are brought about through the degree of balanced connectedness (the balanced state of closeness and autonomy) in the parent–adolescent relationships. Another research study used an observational coding scheme to identify parenting behaviour that reflected psychological control and the granting of autonomy. The study examined relations between these parenting dimensions and certain indices of child and family functioning. The findings identified particular patterns of psychological control and autonomy that undermine youth adjustment (Hauser Kunz & Grych, 2013). In fact, these findings suggest that the way in which parents respond to bids for greater independence by their children have implications for the child's psychological health in early adolescence. Parkin and Kuczynski (2012) examined 32 adolescents regarding their perspectives on parental expectations and on their own strategies for expressing resistance. It was found that adolescents described their strategies for expressing resistance as multifaceted, consisting of overt behavioural strategies and covert cognitive strategies that reflect autonomous and relational motives. In essence, adolescents thrive when they have superior executive functioning and can thoughtfully direct their own lives (Urban, Lewin-Bizan, & Lerner, 2010).

One emerging field of study focuses on the adolescent as thriving, especially in supportive relationships with parents. In fact, the facilitation of high levels of student engagement in their schooling has been suggested to be an important outcome in their development. Further, thriving adolescents flourish when they succeed academically and, at the same time, are connected to school (Lewis et al., 2011). Extracurricular activities provide a key context for youth development, and the interest and participation of thriving adolescents has been linked with positive developmental outcomes. For example, the effect of having an interest in music, arts, or even sports is deemed vital and each interest can be enhanced if nurtured by caring adults (Scales, Benson, & Roehlkepartain, 2011). These ideas coincide with Diana Baumrind's (1971, 1991) authoritative parenting style, which was discussed in Chapter 8, "Socio-Emotional Development in Early Childhood."

With most adolescents, parents are likely to find themselves engaged in a delicate balancing act, weighing competing needs for autonomy and control, for self-assertion and commitment.

Autonomy and Attachment

Recall from Chapter 6 that one of the most widely discussed aspects of socio-emotional development in infancy is secure attachment to caregivers. In the past decade, researchers have explored whether secure attachment also might be an important concept in adolescents' relationships with their parents (Collins & Steinberg, 2006). Normative changes in thoughts, feelings, and behaviours do occur during adolescence; such changes can serve to "activate" the attachment system in ways that parallel the physical separation from caregivers during infancy. This activation can serve as a signal to parents and adolescents, as well, that adjustments need to be made within the parent–adolescent relationship to accommodate adolescent needs. Both the parental sensitivity that typically accompanies secure attachment and the level of openness and flexibility between parents and adolescents with regard to evaluating and re-evaluating the attachment relationship can increase the probability that securely attached teens and their parents can successfully recognize and adapt to the ongoing developmental changes. In fact, a secure parent–adolescent relationship should first acknowledge the teen's efforts as she or he strives for autonomy and, secondly, provide support the adolescent needs while maintaining the relationship.

A secure attachment goes far toward enabling the adolescent to develop that important safe haven in which he or she can cope as successfully as possible with stressful events. A secure attachment helps the adolescent to create a firm base upon which the normal exploration of life can occur (Mikulincer & Shaver, 2007). Therefore, the critical role of the attachment figures (such as parents) is to supply both safety and support in times of discomfort and to provide opportunities and the necessary guidance to explore the environment in a safe manner and with a self-confident and autonomous approach (Van Petegem et al., 2013; deVries et al., 2016). Attachment security is thought to provide adolescents with capacities to function well in close relationships and to maintain positive images of themselves and others, even when under stress (Allen, 2008). Some studies have suggested that adolescent associations with antisocial or deviant peers are connected to various problematic outcomes during adolescence such as relatively high levels of aggression (Benson & Buchler, 2012).

Clearly, secure attachment with parents can be an asset for the adolescent, fostering the trust to engage in close relationships with others and laying the foundation for skills in close relationships. But a significant minority of adolescents from strong, supportive families nonetheless struggle in peer relations for a variety of reasons, such as being outside the norms of physical attractiveness, maturing late, and experiencing cultural and socio-economic status (SES) discrepancies. On the other hand, some adolescents from troubled families find a positive, fresh start with peer relations that can compensate for their problematic family backgrounds (Berger, 2011).

The adolescent's push for autonomy and responsibility may puzzle many parents. Parents who see their teenager slipping from their grasp may have an urge to take stronger control as the adolescent seeks autonomy and responsibility. Heated emotional exchanges may ensue, with either side calling names, making threats, and doing whatever seems necessary to gain control. Parents may feel frustrated because they expect their teenager to heed their advice, to want to spend time with the family, and to grow up to do what is right. The ability to attain autonomy and gain control over one's behaviour in adolescence is acquired through appropriate adult reactions to the adolescent's desire for control (Soenens et al., 2007; Al-Yagon et al., 2016).

At the onset of adolescence, the average individual does not have the knowledge to make appropriate or mature decisions in all areas of life. As the adolescent pushes for autonomy, the wise adult relinquishes control in those areas in which the adolescent can make reasonable decisions, but continues to guide the adolescent to make reasonable decisions in areas in which the adolescent's knowledge is more limited. Gradually, adolescents acquire the ability to make mature decisions on their own. The expectations about the appropriate timing of adolescents' autonomy often varies across cultures, parents, and adolescents (Roma et al., 2014; Laursen & Collins, 2009).

Research in many countries has found that teens who remain closely attached to their parents are more likely to be academically successful and enjoy good peer relations (Mayseless & Scharf, 2007). Even while teens are becoming more autonomous, they need their parents to provide a safe psychological base.

Balancing Freedom and Control

We have seen that parents play very important roles in adolescent development (Collins & Steinberg, 2006). Although adolescents are moving toward independence, they still need to stay connected with families (Schwartz, Stutz, & Ledermann, 2012). In adolescence, parental and peer relationships are important sources of support and self-evaluation. These relationships are influential even though they change considerably as the adolescent matures, becomes increasingly independent, and comes to rely on parents and friends in different ways than before. Parental and peer relationships are shaped, as well, by broad cultural values that serve to define family relationships and their importance to the development of self. Whereas many youth in Western societies perceive peer relationships as increasingly important for establishing independence from the family, parents in many non-Western societies remain important sources of adolescent self-evaluations and may even surpass peer influence (Song, Thompson, & Ferrer, 2009).

Cultural studies of close relationships and their impact on adolescent psychological development, particularly those encountered in non-Western societies, can contribute to understanding more closely how social values help to define the significance to the developing person of these relationships. Researchers Song, Thompson, and Ferrer (2009) examined age and gender differences related to the quality of attachment with mothers, fathers, and peers. The associations of attachment were coupled with measures of self-evaluation among 584 Chinese adolescents in junior high, high school, and university. The findings revealed that in a context of considerable consistency of findings with Western studies, parent–child attachment in adolescents is also influenced by culture-specific practices that influence parent–youth relationships and their meaning to the child.

One philosophical variation among cultures is **locus of control**, or the perceived extent to which individuals believe they have control over the events that affect them. Some cultures favour an **external locus of control**, wherein events that affect individuals are considered to be the result of fate or higher powers. The community exerts considerable influence such that decisions are made that are for the common good of the family and the community. Those cultures, such as North American, with an **internal locus of control**, believe that the individual can control life events. This orientation holds that individuals can control outcomes and should be self-reliant.

The range from a strong external to a strong internal locus of control falls on a broad continuum and shapes behaviour and decisions (Ahlin & Antunes, 2015). For example, in a culture where the locus of control is external, individuals may believe that an illness is the result of fate and must be surrendered to honourably. In another culture, where the orientation is more toward an internal locus of control, individuals may believe they have control over and can cure the disease. Their optimism affects their health in many ways (Geers et al., 2007). Such orientations influence parenting styles as well as the communication patterns between parents and their children.

Parent–Adolescent Conflict

The classical Greek philosopher Socrates (469 BCE to 399 BCE) said, "Children today are tyrants" who "contradict their parents, gobble their food, and terrorize their teachers" (Bibby, 2010). This stereotype of teen behaviour and parent–adolescent conflict has a long history and abounds today. Rarely, however, do the conflicts involve major dilemmas such as drugs or delinquency. Project Canada (2008) reported that 80 percent of the teens surveyed rate trust and honesty as extremely important. Sixty percent rate politeness and concern for others as very important to them. Most (80 percent) report that they try to stay out of trouble and that they have never been in trouble with the police (Bibby, 2010). So the stereotype really does not fit most teens, in spite of appearances, media reports, and fashion trends such as piercing and body art.

Conflict exists, and much of it involves the everyday events of family life, such as keeping a bedroom clean, dressing neatly, getting home by a certain time, not accumulating huge cell phone bills, or spending too much time staring at screens. Such conflict with parents often escalates during early adolescence, remains somewhat stable during the high school years, and then lessens as the adolescent reaches 17 to 20 years of age (Berger, 2011).

The everyday conflicts that characterize parent–adolescent relationships may actually serve a positive developmental function. These minor disputes and negotiations facilitate the adolescent's transition from being dependent on parents to becoming an autonomous individual. For example, one of the more consistent findings in the adolescent attachment literature is that when adolescents hold secure attachment states of mind, their interactions with their parents are characterized by healthy autonomy support. That is, the adolescents engage in productive problem-solving discussions that allow divergent opinions to be expressed while remaining engaged in the discussions. Meanwhile, those who are insecure tend to withdraw and disengage from parents when faced with the challenge of adapting to new demands of autonomy. It is interesting to note that the socialization field has moved from parent-centred deterministic models to models that assign children an agentic role to direct their own socialization. Children are coming to be viewed as acting in purposeful ways that reflect their ability to interpret and evaluate parental messages and consequently evade intrusions into their personal lives (Parkin & Kuczynski, 2012).

Parent–adolescent conflict may serve a positive developmental function in the adolescent's transition to adulthood.

However, no developmentalist would dispute that the roles of communication and support are helpful, even essential, in parent–child relationships. The complexity is that some adolescents happily tell their parents about their activities, while others are secretive (Vieno et al., 2009). Meanwhile, most adolescents remain selectively non-communicative in sharing aspects of their lives of which their parents probably would not approve (Brown & Bakken, 2011). Does the question of secure attachment prevail in these instances?

The old model of parent–adolescent relationships suggested that as adolescents mature, they detach themselves from parents and move into a world of autonomy apart from parents. The old model also suggested that parent–adolescent conflict is intense and stressful throughout adolescence. The new model emphasizes that parents serve as important attachment figures and support systems while adolescents explore a wider, more complex social world. The new model also emphasizes that, in most families, parent–adolescent conflict is moderate rather than severe, and that the everyday negotiations and minor disputes not only are normal, but can also serve the positive developmental function of helping the adolescent make the transition from childhood dependency to adult independence (see Figure 12.2).

When families move to another country, adolescents typically acculturate quickly to the norms and values of their new host country (Fuligni, 2012). These norms and values tend to be different than the norms of their parents, especially in the areas of autonomy and romantic relationships. Such divergences frequently escalate to parent–adolescent conflict in some immigrant families. Many times these conflicts are not expressed openly, but are commonly present in internal feelings (Fuligni, 2012). Often too, the adolescent feels that their parents want them to give up their personal interests, which feels unfair. Such acculturation-based disparity can seriously disrupt the quality of parent–adolescent relationships in immigrant families (Tardif & Geva, 2006; Juang & Umana-Taylor, 2012).

critical thinking

Currently, ease with technology characterizes the differences between many parents and their children. Parents may not be familiar with the social media their teenaged son or daughter visits regularly. On the other hand, some parents are equally savvy. For example, one mother uncovered her son's "anonymous" name and signed into Facebook to carry on a discussion with him and his peers. She believed she was able to understand her son better. When her son learned of her activity, he was furious and accused her of invading his privacy. Did the mother invade her son's privacy, or is Facebook a public space? What can she do to resolve the conflict? In what ways would a family meeting be helpful?

Figure 12.2
Old and New Models of Parent–Adolescent Relationships

© BananaStock/PunchStock

Peers

Peers play powerful roles in the lives of adolescents (Allen & Antonishak, 2008; Brown et al., 2008). When you think back to your own adolescent years, you probably recall many of your most enjoyable moments as experiences shared with peers. Peer relations undergo important changes in adolescence, including changes in friendships and in peer groups and the beginning of romantic relationships. In middle and late childhood, as we discussed in Chapter 10, the focus of peer relations is on being liked by classmates and being included in games or lunchroom conversations. Being overlooked or, worse yet, being rejected can have damaging effects on children's development that sometimes is carried forward to adolescence (Bukowski, Velasquez, & Brendgen, 2008). Prinstein (2007) conducted a study that found adolescents who feel unsure about their social identity, possibly evident in low self-esteem and high social anxiety, are most likely to conform to peers. These "unsure" feelings in the adolescent increase during times of transition, such as changing circumstances in school and family life.

In this present age, online social networking sites have become a popular mode of communication among adolescents. Results from a Huang and colleagues (2014) study indicated that adolescents who are exposed to friends' risky online displays are more likely to smoke and use alcohol. The researchers suggest to continue to examine online peer influence mechanisms to effectively educate adolescents about these risks (Huang et al., 2014).

We will take a closer look at the role peers play a bit later in the chapter.

Religion

critical thinking

Religion—whether Buddhism, Christianity, Islam, Judaism, Hinduism, or other—is a core factor of how we identify ourselves. Quite often religion shapes a number of very important aspects of family life as well as life decisions, including whom we may or may not marry. During adolescence, an individual might question the beliefs and traditions of his or her family, and may choose not to participate or to visit other places of worship. How might Marcia's identity statuses be applied to religious identity in adolescence? How might the MAMA effect be applied to religious identity during one's life? What effects would the adolescent's behaviour have upon the family? Suggest strategies the family can implement to accept such behaviours from the adolescent.

Religious and Spiritual Development

In Chapter 11, we described the many positive benefits of service-learning. A number of studies have found that adolescents who are involved in religious institutions are more likely to engage in service-learning than their counterparts who don't participate in religious institutions. Let's explore adolescents' concepts of religion and spirituality, as well as their religious and spiritual experiences.

It is interesting to note that Canadian sociologist and pollster Reginald Bibby states that the decline of religion is not nearly as dramatic as once believed. The big boost in the numbers of religious adherents comes from abroad. Among those born outside of Canada, almost 40 percent are inclined to embrace religion, while less than a quarter reject it. In considering the Canadian born population, the figures are levelling out: 29 percent embrace religion, while 27 percent reject it (Hutchins, 2015). According to the National Household Survey (NHS), the largest religion in Canada is Christianity. However, consistent with the changing immigration patterns, growing proportions of the population report religious affiliations other than Christian, including include Islam, Hinduism, Sikhism, and Buddhism (NHS, 2011).

According to Project Teen Canada, teenagers today are less likely to identify as religious compared to teenagers a decade ago. In 2008, Project Teen Canada findings indicated that 32 percent of teens identified themselves as atheist. Fewer teens identified themselves as Christian, but more identified themselves as Muslim, Buddhist, or Hindu (Li, 2013). For many churches, temples, and mosques, increasing youth engagement is a key priority. Youth groups have been established whereby teenagers and young adults meet weekly to participate in activities and learn about their faith (Li, 2013).

Religion and Identity Development

As we saw earlier in this chapter, identity development becomes a central focus of adolescence and emerging adulthood (Kroger, 2007). As part of their search for identity, adolescents and emerging adults begin to grapple in more sophisticated, logical ways with such questions such as, "Is there really a God or higher spiritual being, or have I just been believing what my parents and the church imprinted in my mind?" and "What really are my religious views?" In Bibby's words, teens are "post-religious and pre-spiritual" (Bibby, 2010). A recent analysis of the link between identity and spirituality concluded that adolescence and adulthood can serve as gateways to a spiritual identity that "transcends, but not necessarily excludes, the assigned religious identity in childhood" (Templeton & Eccles, 2006, p. 261).

The Positive Role of Religion in Adolescents' Lives

Researchers have found that various aspects of religion are linked with positive outcomes for adolescents (Benson, Roehlkepartain, & Hong, 2008; Good & Willoughby, 2008; Lerner, Roeser, & Phelps, 2008). Religion also plays a role in adolescents' health and whether they engage in problem behaviours (Benson & Scales, 2009). For example, in a national random sample of more than 2000 11- to 18-year-olds, those who were higher in religiosity were less likely to smoke, drink alcohol, use marijuana, skip school, participate in delinquent activities, and be depressed than their low-religiosity counterparts (Sinha, Cnaan, & Gelles, 2007). A study of Indonesian Muslim 13-year-olds revealed that their religious involvement was linked to their social competence, including positive peer relations, academic achievement, emotional regulation, prosocial behaviour, and self-esteem (French et al., 2008). One of the findings of another recent study that explored Muslim adolescents in non-Western settings indicated that religiosity was the most significant factor of prosocial behaviour (Krauss et al., 2014).

MORAL DEVELOPMENT

Moral judgments are influenced both indirectly and directly by parents. Moral development is especially fostered by the openness and emphatic responses of parents to the adolescents (Polan & Taylor, 2011). Adolescents, using learned standards as a guide, learn to form decisions on which to direct their behaviour. During early adolescence, teens are usually at the conventional level of moral development (Polan & Taylor, 2011). They become more rule-oriented, and they begin to care about others. Following this stage of development, adolescents begin to question everything and everyone, which often places them in direct conflict with persons of authority. However, one of the benefits of this transition is that adolescents begin to try out their own values in relationships. By the time they reach adolescence, young people can reason at a higher plane if they have reached Piaget's stage of formal operations (Feldman & Landry, 2014).

Racial, Ethnic, and Cultural Identity

Each family's socio-economic status, priorities, educational levels, religious beliefs, and even ideas of what is humorous, what is common sense, and what constitutes acceptable behaviour for males and females—these are some of the ingredients of the family's shared understanding of the world around them. Recall from Chapter 1 that context is the setting in which development occurs. This setting is influenced by historical, political, economic, geographic, social, and cultural factors. All of these aspects of socio-cultural contexts influence identity. Not only is each family unique, but individuals within the family unit are also unique. Personal contexts such as genetics, health, interests, talents, perspective, and position within the family are part of the factors that make one sibling different from another. For individuals of differing races, ethnicities, and cultures, adolescence and emerging adulthood are often special junctures in their development (Phinney, 2008; Syed & Azmitia, 2008; Umana-Taylor et al., 2008; Way et al., 2008). Although children are aware of some differences, most individuals consciously confront these aspects of their identities for the first time in adolescence (Statistics Canada, 2012i).

Erikson was especially sensitive to the role of culture in identity development. He pointed out that throughout the world, ethnic groups have struggled to maintain their cultural identities while blending into the dominant culture (Erikson, 1968). Erikson said that this struggle for an inclusive identity, or identity within the larger culture, has been the driving force in the founding of churches, empires, and revolutions throughout history.

Adolescence is more than a stage of development; it represents a unique culture with common values, challenges, and characteristics. For example, adolescents share specific behavioural aspects associated with culture including their shared language, music, and rituals (Nelson & Nelson, 2010).

As you may recall from Chapter 1, ethnicity and cultural have very different meanings, as does race. **Race** refers to physical features such a skeletal structure, the shape of the skull, the texture of the hair, and the colour of the skin. The Canadian census uses the term **visible minority** for people to identify themselves as neither Aboriginal nor Caucasian. A person who identifies as a member of a visible minority may be of Asian, African, or Irish decent, and may be Muslim, Christian, or Buddhist. **Ethnicity** is based on cultural heritage, nationality characteristics, race, religion, and language. An individual who identifies as Native Canadian or Aboriginal may be Iroquois, Métis, or Inuit. **Culture** refers to the behaviour patterns, beliefs, transmitted values, norms, and life practices of a particular group. These patterns of behaviours guide decision making and are passed on from generation to generation (Kozier et al., 2010). For example, although both are Canadian, people from the East Coast have a shared history and understanding of the world that differs from people who live in the Prairie provinces of Alberta, Manitoba, and Saskatchewan. Location, employment histories, and settlement issues are among the factors unique to each area.

Like a very complex symphony, Canada is composed of people from all racial groups and hundreds of ethnic and cultural groups who were either born here or immigrated here. Toronto, one of the most multicultural cities in the world, boasts over 200 distinct ethnic groups and over 140 languages and dialects are spoken (City of Toronto, 1998–2010). As people interact with each other, their personal world-views and their personal identities are challenged. Such integration can be overwhelming at times and may lead to confusion and conflict. Many adolescents resolve this choice by developing a **bicultural identity**: they identify in some ways with their cultural group and in other ways with the mainstream culture (Knight et al., 2014; Agbakwu et al., 2016).

There is growing evidence today that bicultural individuals who are able to form, strong positive multi-ethnic identities have better self-esteem, fewer mental health problems, and higher academic achievement than their peers with less developed singular (monoculture) ethnic identities (Smokowski & Bacallao, 2007). In fact, developing ethnic and racial identities, whether with mixed ethnic and racial ancestry or across multiple cultural contexts (home and school), is a dynamic life-long process (Marks, Patton, & Garcia Coll, 2011).

Social Exclusion, Assimilation, and Multiculturalism

One of the more important social determinants of health is social exclusion (Mikkonen & Raphael, 2010). Social exclusion refers to situations in which specific groups are denied participation in Canadian life. Social exclusion practices exerted upon recent immigrants are well documented. It creates undesirable living conditions and personal experiences that endanger health. Social exclusion creates in the victims a sense of powerlessness, hopelessness, and depression, all of which further diminish the possibility of inclusion and assimilation into a given society (Mikkonen & Raphael, 2010).

According to Macionis and Gerber (2011), *assimilation* is a process through which minorities adapt patterns of the dominant culture in a gradual way thus becoming increasingly more similar to the dominant group. Assimilation involves changing modes of dress, values, religion, language, and even friends. Assimilation involves changes in ethnicity—not race.

Fortunately, Canada embraces the ideal of **multiculturalism**, recognition of cultural heterogeneity, and mutual respect among culturally diverse groups (Macionis & Gerber, 2011). Canada's policy of multiculturalism preserves the right of choice, leading to what many identify as the Canadian mosaic. In other words, individuals can choose the aspects of their heritage they wish to leave behind and those they wish to preserve. The kind of controversy that can arise is illustrated by the cultural practice of some Islamic women who choose to wear *burqas*, outer garments that cover the entire body except for the eyes and hands. Those who support assimilation might argue that the burqa should not be worn, whereas those who hold a multiculturalist viewpoint are more likely to argue that wearing a burqa is a matter of personal choice. Whether we are talking about patterns of location, intermarriage, youth conflict, or employment equity, issues of race, ethnicity, and culture are in the forefront (Kozier et al., 2010).

People who identify as a visible minority cite racism, discrimination, and bigotry as substantial problems influencing their relationships with authority figures, such as police, and their ability to find employment. Often these problems lead to feelings of alienation and health problems. For example, Aboriginal youth suicide has become a normalized response to a hopeless existence. Young immigrants voice the belief that Canada's tolerance lessens the problems of racism, but feel that efforts to promote tolerance and understanding should focus on schools and be aimed at staff, administrators, and teachers, as well as students.

The indicators of identity change often differ for each succeeding generation (Phinney & Ong, 2007). First-generation immigrants are likely to be secure in their identities and unlikely to change much; they may or may not develop a new identity. The degree to which they begin to feel "Canadian" appears to be related to whether or not they learn English or French, develop social networks beyond their ethnic group, and become culturally competent in their new country. Second-generation immigrants are more likely to think of themselves as "Canadians," possibly because citizenship is granted at birth. Their ethnic identity is likely to be linked to retention of their language of origin and social networks. In the third and later generations, the issues become more complex. Historical, contextual, and political factors that are unrelated to acculturation may affect the extent to which members of later generations retain their ethnic identities. Racism and discrimination may further influence how ethnic identity is retained.

Researchers are increasingly finding that a positive ethnic identity is linked to positive outcomes for adolescents (Umana-Taylor et al., 2014; Gonzales-Backen, 2013). In one study, Navajo adolescents' affirmation and belonging to their ethnic heritage is linked to higher self-esteem, school connectedness, and social functioning (Jones & Galliher, 2007). Another study found that exploration is an important part of establishing a secure sense of one's ethnic identity, which in turn is linked to a positive attitude toward one's own group and other groups (Whitehead et al., 2009). Researchers found that

Asian-American adolescents' ethnic identity is associated with high self-esteem, positive relationships, academic motivation, and decreased levels of depression (Kiang, Witkow, & Champagne, 2013).

Ethnicity, Race, and Socio-Economic Status

Much of the research related to ethnicity and socio-economic status has shown a levelling out of economic well-being among ethnic groups, especially those of English and European heritage. What does stand out, however, is that visible minorities and immigrant groups are overrepresented in the lower socio-economic levels of society (Healey, 2009; Rowley, Kurtz-Costes, & Cooper, 2009). Not all visible minority or immigrant families are poor, however poverty contributes to the stressful life experiences of many (Leon-Guerrero, 2009). Thus, many adolescents experience multiple disadvantages: (1) prejudice, discrimination, and bias; and (2) the stressful effects of poverty.

Although some visible minority youth have middle-income backgrounds, economic advantage does not entirely enable them to escape the prejudice, discrimination, and bias associated with being a member of a minority group (Banks, 2008; Harris & Graham, 2007). Many visible minority youth report incidents of racial profiling while shopping or in interactions with the police.

Kwan Ho

Part of the development of a sense of self is the acquisition of an ethnic identity. Some adolescents achieve this by learning the customs of their heritage.

critical thinking

Immigration from one country to another is a complex and challenging endeavour. Not only do individuals and families have to make considerable adjustments, so too do our urban and rural communities. What are some of the adjustments immigrants must make? How have communities responded to the needs of newcomers? Outline a welcoming program for immigrant families in a rural community. What resources would you be able to offer such families?

Rites of Passage

Culture plays an important role in identity. Many cultures signal the transition from childhood to adulthood by a **rite of passage**, a ceremony or ritual that marks an individual's transition from one status to another. Glozah and Lawani (2014) compared and contrasted the "Dipo" rite of the Krobo in Ghana and the "Russ" rite in Norway, with specific references to social change and modernity. They found that a noticeable distinction in both rites of passage was the observance of processes, procedures, and stages through which adolescents pass. For example, both rites involve participation in a procession characterized by a special symbolic outfit of clothes to herald the celebration of the rite. Adolescents in both cultures believe they are parting from the adolescent stage and preparing to assume young adult roles. It is interesting to note that while adults participate, or supervise, the Dipo, the Russ has no adults involved in either supervision or participation. In addition, if an adolescent fails to participate in the Dipo, he or she is not recognized by his or her family and is deemed not fit for marriage. In contrast, adolescents are not governed by this treatment should they decide not to participate in the Russ. The authors claim that both rites have undergone several positive and/or negative transformations and adjustments due to social change and modernity (Glozah & Lawani, 2014).

Most rites of passage focus on the transition to adult status. To a Canadian youth, such a rite of passage might be a religious celebration, such as the Jewish bar or bat mitzvah, or Catholic confirmation. Such events as obtaining a driver's licence, being of legal age to drink alcohol, being of legal age to vote, or getting married are fairly universal indicators of the increasing responsibility associated with the transition to adulthood. Graduations from high school, college, or university are other culture-wide celebrations of maturity.

In some cultures, rites of passage are the avenue through which adolescents gain access to sacred adult practices, knowledge, and sexuality. These rites often involve dramatic practices intended to facilitate the adolescent's separation from the immediate family, especially the mother. The transformation is usually characterized by some form of ritual death and rebirth, or by means of contact with the spiritual world. In some cases, bonds are forged between the adolescent and the adult instructors through shared rituals, hazards, and secrets that allow the adolescent to enter the adult world. This kind of ritual provides a forceful and discontinuous entry into the adult world at a time when the adolescent is perceived to be ready for the change.

An especially rich tradition of rites of passage for adolescents has prevailed in African cultures, especially sub-Saharan Africa. Recall Sallieu, the adolescent in the opening vignette. Although well-educated, part of his decision to leave Sierra Leone was related to the rite of passage his father insisted on to prove the youth's transition from boyhood to manhood. In Sallieu's particular ethnic tribe, part of the rite of passage included the cutting of the backs of young men with knives (Dainkeh, 2010, interview). Under the influence of Western industrialized culture, many of these rites are disappearing today, although they are still prevalent, especially in locations where formal education is not readily available.

Traditions and Changes in Adolescence around the World

Today, countless variations of expectations of adolescent behaviour are evident around the world. For example, North American culture encourages individuals to accentuate the positive (Kim, Schimmack, & Oishi, 2012). However, we can observe many similar cultural practices around the world—walking on the streets of Seoul, South Korea, Kuala Lumpur, Malaysia, or Cairo, Egypt, we see young people wearing jeans, listening to familiar pop music, and reading ads for many of the same products used in Canada (Macionis & Gerber, 2011). English is rapidly emerging as the preferred second language around the world. Satellite-based communication enables individuals to experience sights and sounds of events taking place tens of thousands of kilometres away—often they happen at home, too (Macionis & Gerber, 2011). Are similar happenings occurring to adolescents as well? It is important to note that whether it is text-messaging, using Facebook, or tweeting, adolescents are always on the cutting edge of technology (Nelson & Nelson, 2010).

Thus, depending on the culture being observed, adolescence may involve many different experiences (Strohmeier & Schmitt-Rodermund, 2008). Some cultures have retained their traditions regarding adolescence, but rapid global change is altering the experience of adolescence in many places, presenting new opportunities and challenges to young people's health and well-being. Around the world, adolescents' experiences differ.

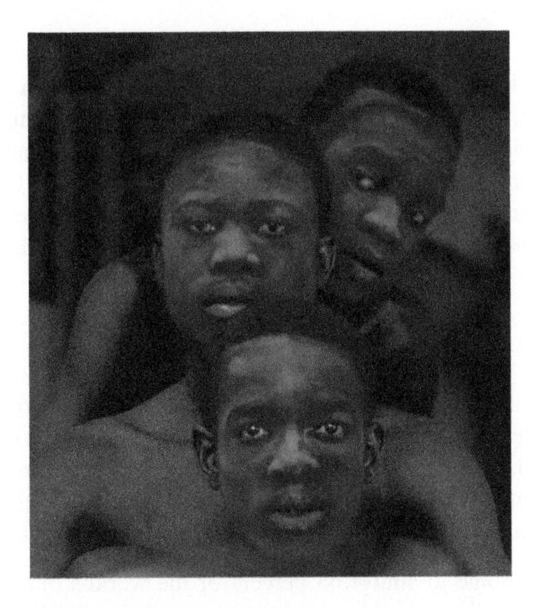

These Congolese Kota boys painted their faces as part of a rite of passage to adulthood. *What kinds of rites of passage do Canadian adolescents have?*

Health

Adolescent health, as well as adolescent well-being, has improved in some areas and not in others (UNICEF, 2014). For example, in countries such as Burundi and Zimbabwe, 88 percent of adolescents ages 15–19 years correctly identified two major ways of preventing sexual transmission of HIV. One way was using condoms and the second, limiting sexual intercourse to one faithful unprotected partner. In other countries, such as Malaysia and Saint Lucia, adolescents had no knowledge of HIV prevention (UNICEF, 2014). However, the *State of the World's Children 2015 Report* claims that young people are discovering new ways of solving problems in various countries and communities around the world using innovative means. Such problem solving practices present many of these innovators with valuable experiences and insights. This report contains the first fully digital platform that allows the user to browse through categories and engages them with the most meaningful content (UNICEF, 2014).

Gender

Around the world, the experiences of male and female adolescents continue to be quite different (Larson, Wilson, & Reitman, 2009). Except for a few regions, such as Japan, the Philippines, and Western countries, males have far greater access to educational opportunities than females (UNICEF, 2014). In many countries, adolescent females have less freedom than males to pursue a variety of careers and engage in various leisure activities. Gender differences in sexual expression are widespread, especially in India, Southeast Asia, Latin America, and Arab countries, where there are far more restrictions on the sexual activity of adolescent females than on males. These gender differences do appear to be narrowing over time. Contemporary adolescents often have friends of the other sex who are not their lovers (Berger, 2010). More recently, a large Dutch study of high school students found that 1 in 12 teens stated that they are attracted to individuals of the same sex as themselves (Bos et al., 2008).

In some countries, educational and career opportunities for women are expanding, and control over adolescent girls' romantic and sexual relationships is weakening. As well, the laws that exist in Canada today that are intended to protect women from spousal abuse and rape do not exist in many parts of the world.

Family

Several researchers have focused specifically on the parent–child differences between young people in Hong Kong and the United States or Australia. In every culture, adolescents seem to benefit from increasing autonomy, but parents in the United States allow more independence than do parents in Hong Kong (Qin, Pomerantz, & Wang, 2009). By age 18, many teenagers appreciate their parents, who have learned to allow more independence (Masche, 2010). Furthermore, in the United States, Hong Kong, and Australia alike, parent–adolescent communication and encouragement benefit the youth, insulating them somewhat from depression, suicide, and low self-esteem and helping them to have high achievements and aspirations (Kwok & Shek, 2010).

Education

The ratio of school enrolment attendance for both girls and boys in primary and secondary schools has rising dramatically in recent years. As might be expected, greater enrolment rates are found among girls. The enrolment gap between boys and girls is actually narrowing around the world. Considering secondary school enrolment in Greece and Hungary, the percentage gap between male and female net enrolment is virtually eliminated. However, in other countries, such as Antigua and Barbados, the percentage of net enrolment of females is higher (UNICEF, 2014).

Unfortunately, Sub-Saharan Africa is home to almost 43 percent of the world's out-of-school children. Of those who do attend school, more are transitioning from primary school to secondary education (UNESCO, 2011). The demand for higher education has risen abruptly, reflected by the fact that the number of tertiary students has increased six-fold in the last 40 years. Internationally, the number of mobile students is expected to multiply by about 12 percent annually (UNESCO, 2011).

Work

There is a trend for youth to stay longer in school. From age 16 it now takes students 8 years to complete the transition from high school to regular employment (Franke, 2003). Global economic work depends upon highly-educated workers. Partly because political leaders recognize that educated adults advance national wealth and health, every nation is increasing the number of students in secondary schools (Berger, 2014).

There are certain stipulations in Canada regarding the number of hours adolescents can work. For example, in Alberta, an adolescent (defined as someone who is 12, 13, or 14 years old) may not work more than 2 hours on a school day, not more than 8 hours on a non-school day, and not between 9:00 p.m. and 6:00 a.m. (Government of Alberta, 2014). If teens work too many hours, grades tend to fall because work hours interfere with academic achievements. Further, if adolescents work more than 20 hours a week during the school year, they are more likely to quit school, have conflicts with their parents, smoke cigarettes, and hate their jobs—in adulthood as well as in adolescence (Staff & Schulenberg, 2010).

Peers

Some cultures give peers a stronger role in adolescence than others (Brown et al., 2008). In most Western nations, peers figure prominently in adolescents' lives, in some cases taking on roles that are otherwise assumed by parents. For example, among street youth in South America, the peer network serves as a surrogate family that supports survival in dangerous and stressful settings. In other regions of the world, such as in Arab countries, peer relations are restricted, especially for girls (Booth, 2002).

Time Allocation to Different Activities

Larson and his colleagues (Larson & Angus, 2011; Larson & Dawes, 2014) have examined the time adolescents spend in work, play, and developmental activities, such as school. U.S. adolescents have greater quantities of discretionary time than adolescents in other industrialized countries (Larson, Wilson, & Rickman, 2009). Canadian researchers found that male adolescents spend less time in personal care and domestic activities, compared to female adolescents (Hillbrecht, Zuzanek, & Mannell, 2008). This gender gap in leisure activities narrows with increasing age as teens tend to take on more employment as well as academic responsibilities compared to their younger counterparts (Hillbrecht, Zuzanek, & Mannell, 2008).

Although relaxation and social interaction are important aspects of life, spending large numbers of hours per week in unchallenging activities is unlikely to foster cognitive and socio-emotional development. Structured voluntary activities may provide more promise for adolescent development than unstructured time, especially if adults give responsibility to adolescents, challenge them, and provide competent guidance in these activities (Larson et al., 2007; Watkins, Larson, & Sullivan, 2008; Sharp et al., 2015).

In sum, adolescents' lives are characterized by a combination of change and tradition. Researchers have found both similarities and differences in the experiences of adolescents in different countries (Larson & Wilson, 2004).

Sexual Orientation and Identity

Freud and Erikson believed that during adolescence, individuals make the transition from sexual latency to mature sexual behaviour. For heterosexuals, social and educational supports are in place. Role models, course materials, peer validation, and media portrayals mirror and support the heterosexual, non-transgendered, and non-intersexed young person's emerging sexual identity. For the homosexual, intersexual, or transsexual youth, the supports are quite different, or in many rural areas, non-existent. Additionally, the young person may feel that the act of accessing whatever supports may be available would pose great personal risk.

Sexual identity is the individual's inner conviction about his or her male or femaleness. **Sexual orientation** is related to the individual's sexual interests. That is, no accepted explanation currently exists why some adolescents develop a heterosexual orientation. Most experts believe that sexual orientation develops out of a complex interplay of genetic, physiological, and environmental factors. **Gender identity** refers to the individual's sense of belonging to a particular sexual category (male, female, lesbian, gay, and so on). Gender roles or scripts refer to behaviours that meet widely-shared expectations about how members of a particular sexual category are supposed to behave (Brym et al., 2013).

Sexual identity development is a central developmental task of adolescence and young adulthood. This task can be especially challenging for sexual minority youth (Bregman et al., 2013). Many gay youth either hide or deny their orientation by dating members of the opposite sex. In addition, binge drinking, drug addiction, and suicidal thoughts are more common among bisexual youth and among youth who are confused about their sexuality (Reiger & Savin Williams, 2012). Canadian researchers have shown that transgendered youth bear a higher rate of discrimination and harassment. Very few statistically significant findings surface about the LGBTQ (lesbian, gay, bisexual, transgendered, questioning) (Taylor & Peter, 2011).

Parental responses to the status of sexual minority youth have been found to vary extensively. Ryan and her colleagues (2009, 2010) have established a notable line of research that documents parental rejection and parental support as predictors of a variety of mental health and physical outcomes in LGB youth. For example, family rejection was found to be associated with an increased likelihood of experiencing depression, using illicit drug, and indications of suicidal ideation (Ryan et al., 2009). Meanwhile, family acceptance generates higher self-esteem and social support, and promotes good general health status (Ryan et al., 2010). Furthermore, pediatricians are aware that some youth in their care may have serious concerns about their sexual orientation. Such sexually-related questions should be answered with factual, current, and non-judgmental information, in a confidential manner (Levine, 2013).

To this point, we have explored a number of ideas about family, religion, race, ethnicity, culture, and sexual orientation in adolescence. For a review, see the Reach Your Learning Outcomes section at the end of this chapter.

Friendship

LO3 Outline the changes that occur in peer relations and dating during adolescence.

- **Adolescent Groups versus Children's Groups**
- **Peer Groups**
- **Dating and Romantic Relationships**

In Chapter 10, we discussed the fact that children spend more time with their peers in middle and late childhood than in early childhood. Friendships become increasingly important in middle and late childhood, and relationships with peers are a strong motivation for most children. Advances in cognitive development during middle and late childhood also enable children to take the perspective of their peers and friends more readily, and their social skills increase.

Remember leaving elementary school full of confidence and self-assurance, only to enter junior high school full of trepidation? This reflects the "top-dog" phenomenon discussed in Chapter 11. The swing from feeling great to feeling just plain terrible can occur within seconds, depending on the interactions that may influence the individual. Peers play an important role by helping each other to fit in, not be alone, and negotiate their way through high school. Positive friendship interactions in adolescence are associated with many positive outcomes, including lower rates of delinquency, substance abuse, and bullying, and a higher rate of academic achievement (Yu et al., 2013).

As you just read, for adolescents whose sexual orientation is homosexual, lesbian, or bisexual, and for those whose sexual identity is transsexual or intersexed, the socialization process and the pressure to fit in may be quite painful due to homophobic behaviours and feelings that heterosexual youth, sorting out their sexual identities, may have.

Adolescent Groups versus Children's Groups

Children's groups differ from adolescent groups in several important ways. The members of children's groups often are friends or neighbourhood acquaintances, and their groups usually are not as formalized as many adolescent groups. During the adolescent years, groups tend to include a broader array of members. In other words, adolescents other than friends or neighbourhood acquaintances often are members of adolescent groups. New friendships emerge.

Harry Stack Sullivan (1953) was the most influential theorist to discuss the importance of adolescent friendship. He believed that friends are important in shaping development. Everyone has basic social needs, such as the need for tenderness (secure attachment), playful companionship, social acceptance, intimacy, and sexual relations. Whether or not these needs are fulfilled largely determines our emotional well-being. For example, if the need for playful companionship goes unmet, then we become bored and depressed; if the need for social acceptance is not met, we suffer a lowered sense of self-worth (Sullivan, 1953; Buhrmester, 2005).

Many of Sullivan's ideas have withstood the test of time (Buhrmester, 2005). Adolescents say they depend more on friends than on parents to satisfy their needs for companionship, reassurance of worth, and intimacy. The ups and downs of experiences with friends have profound effects on the shaping of adolescents' well-being (Cook, Buchler, & Blair, 2013). Adolescent girls are more likely to disclose information about pertinent issues than are adolescent boys (Rose et al., 2012; Landoll et al., 2011).

The characteristics of friends have an important influence on adolescent development (Crosnoe et al., 2008; Rubin, Fredstrom, & Bowker, 2008). A study revealed that friends' grade-point averages were important positive attributes (Cook, Deng, & Morgano, 2007). Friends' grade-point averages were a consistent predictor of positive school achievement and also were linked to a lower level of negative behaviour in areas such as drug abuse and acting out.

Although most adolescents develop friendships with individuals who are close to their own age, some adolescents become best friends with younger or older individuals. Do older friends encourage adolescents to engage in delinquent behaviour or early sexual behaviour? A study also revealed that over time, from grade 6 through grade 10, girls were more likely to have older male friends, which places some girls on a developmental trajectory for engaging in problem behaviour (Poulin & Pedersen, 2007). Many aspects of the search for identity have become more arduous than when Erikson first described them. Developmentalists still believe that teens struggle through the identity crisis, but it now seems that attaining autonomy and achieving identity before the age of 18 is somewhat unlikely (Kroger, Martinussen, & Marcia, 2010).

Adolescents have embraced online social networking. Many teens make themselves vulnerable to embarrassment and damage their credibility or even become victims because of unwise online postings (Patchin & Hinduja, 2010). However, on a positive note, emerging identity is an important aspect of every adolescent's development. Using social networking sites allows adolescents to assert their identity in a unique way, checking out what their friends think of their creative endeavours (Clarke, 2009).

Peer Groups

Peers exert both positive and negative pressure. On the one hand, teens join school clubs, community organizations, and teams in which they work toward a common goal, perhaps raising money for a charitable organization or putting on a school play. On the other hand, young girls may want to be thin and young boys may want to be muscular. Some may fear being bullied or may become bullies.

According to PHAC (2012d), bullying is a relationship problem. Bullying is a form of repeated aggression in which a young person is intentionally harassed or harmed. Bullying can impact the physical, emotional, and social health of a young person (Lemstra et al., 2012). Numerous cases have been reported in the media in which suicide, or attempted suicide, has been attributed to bullying (Klomek, Sourander, & Gould, 2010). Many categories of bullying exist, such as physical, relational, verbal, and electronic (CCL, 2008). Electronic or "cyber" bullying is similar to relational and verbal bullying, but it occurs online. The Internet has become the new playground, and there are no limits. Victimization on the Internet through cyber-bullying is increasing in frequency and scope; electronic bullies can remain "virtually" anonymous (Enough-Is-Enough, 2009–2013). On an international scale, of 35 countries, Canada had the ninth highest rate of bullying among 13-year-olds (CCL, 2008). More recently, reports indicate that at least one in three adolescent students report being bullied (CIHR, 2012a).

BullyingCanada.ca is Canada's first youth-created anti-bullying website and is presently Canada's only national anti-bullying charity. It has a toll free line that can be called 24/7. It offers information, support, and help to anyone involved in bullying. The website and toll free line both rely solely on donations from the public and businesses (Bullying Canada, 2016). Jones and Augustine (2015) list six characteristics that should be included in attempting to design an effective anti-bullying program. They are: "community involvement, an assessment of the school climate, a consensus of the definition of bullying, student and parental engagement, professional development for faculty and staff, and ongoing program evaluation" (p. 73). These characteristics appear to incorporate all members and elements involved in an effort to design a program that will be as effective as possible.

Peer Pressure

Peers can be more helpful than harmful, especially in early and middle adolescence. During that time the biological and social stresses can be overwhelming (Nelson & DeBecker, 2008). A study revealed that 14 to 18 years of age is an especially important time for developing the ability to stand up for what one believes in and resist peer pressure to do otherwise (Steinberg & Monahan, 2007). Results of a study by Sumter and colleagues (2009) indicated that general resistance to peer influence increases during the adolescence period. Furthermore, gender differences are more noticeable during mid-adolescence, when girls are more resistant to peer influence than boys are. It is likely that resistance can be seen to some degree in almost any interaction. However, resistance is more obvious when it is directed toward "other" groups of peers rather than toward friends of those with whom the adolescents identify (Bell & Baron, 2015).

Dumas, Ellis, and Wolfe (2012) conducted a study to examine identity development as a moderator of the relation between peer group pressure and control, and adolescents' engagement in risk behaviours. These investigators concluded that in more controlling peer groups, adolescents with greater identity commitment engaged in fewer risk behaviours than adolescents with lower identity commitment. Therefore, identity development may be an appropriate agent to discourage the negative effects of peer pressure in high-risk adolescents. The importance of identity development for adolescents cannot be overestimated. In fact, Oyserman and Destin (2010) have demonstrated that the identity construction of adolescents can be modified through short term in-class and after-school intervention programs.

Cliques and Crowds

Cliques exist in schools, creating tension between the adolescent's desire to belong and his or her desire to be an individual. The conflict between conformity and individualism is demonstrated in tastes in fashion, music, language, and behaviour, and often is dictated by the clique (Brown, 2011). The focus of the clique may be sports, popularity, drugs, rowdy behaviour, academics, or friendship emerging from childhood. Pressures to diet, smoke, drink, have sex, drive recklessly, join a club, or go to a particular movie or concert are all part of the powerful influence of cliques.

A *crowd* is a larger group of adolescents who share common interests. Cliques and crowds provide social control and social support via comments, admiration, and isolation. For instance, one study in the Midwest United States found that "tough" and "alternative" crowds felt that teenagers should behave as they want to, whereas the "prep" crowd thought that parental authority carried most weight (Daddis, 2010).

Dating and Romantic Relationships

Adolescents spend considerable time either dating or thinking about dating (Furman & Simon, 2008). Dating can be a form of recreation, a source of status, a setting for learning about close relationships, as well as a way of finding a mate. Regardless of racial, cultural, or ethnic backgrounds or gender, romantic relationships in adolescence form the initial steps toward the development of intimacy and commitments that characterize adult relationships (Connolly & McIsaac, 2009).

Developmental Changes in Dating

Can you remember confiding to a friend in middle school or junior high that you "liked" someone? Or what it was like when you first had an exclusive relationship with someone, "going out" with that person and only that person? Around grade 10, half of adolescents have had a romantic relationship that lasted two months or longer. By grade 12, a quarter of adolescents still have not had a romantic relationship that lasted two months or longer (see Figure 12.3).

Figure 12.3

Age of Onset of Romantic Activity

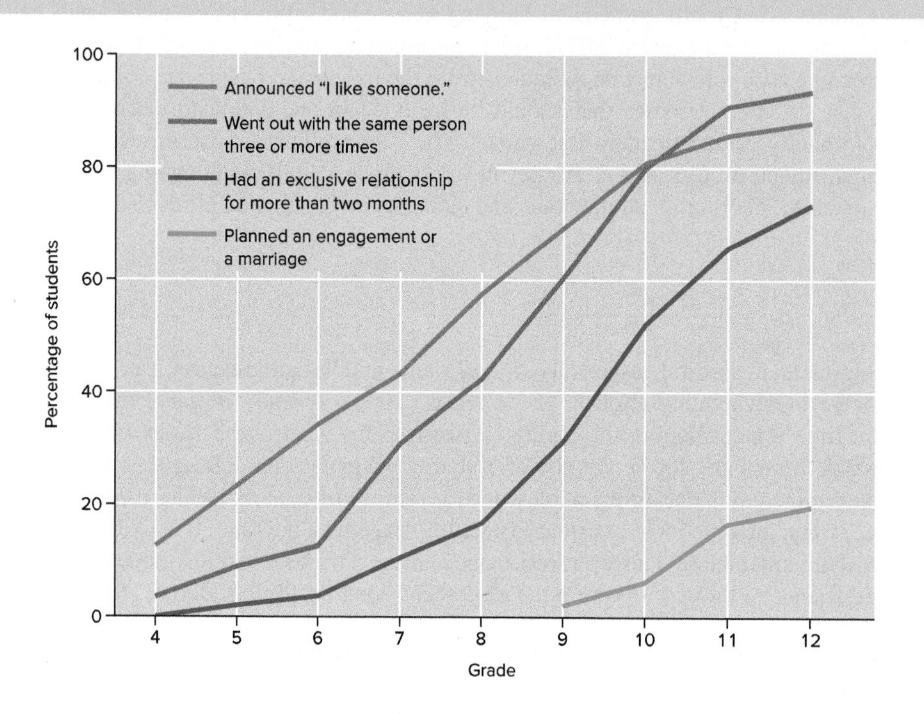

From "Romantic Development: Does Age at Which Romantic Involvement Starts Matter?" by Duane Buhrmester, April 2001, paper presented at the meeting of the Society for Research in Child Development, Minneapolis, MN. Reprinted with permission from the author.

In this study, announcing that "I like someone" occurred earliest, followed by going out with the same person three or more times, having an exclusive relationship for over two months, and finally planning an engagement or marriage (which characterized only a very small percentage of participants by grade 12) (Buhrmester, 2001).

The functions of dating and romantic relationships also tend to change over the course of adolescence. Young adolescents are likely to see romantic relationships not as a way of fulfilling attachment or sexual needs, but as a context for exploring how attractive they are, how they should romantically interact with someone, and how all of this looks to the peer group. In fact, romantic relationships form an integral part of adolescent development. Awakening sexuality and passionate attraction are experienced for the first time in adolescence, and are markers of the healthy transition from childhood to adulthood (Connolly & McIsaac, 2009).

Cyberdating

In their early exploration of romantic relationships, today's adolescents often find comfort in numbers and begin hanging out together in mixed-sex groups (O'Sullivan et al., 2007). Sometimes they just hang out at someone's house or get organized enough to get someone to drive them to a mall or a movie. Or they may try *cyberdating*—"dating" over the Internet—as another alternative to traditional dating. Cyberdating is popular especially among middle school students. Of course, cyberdating can be dangerous, since one does not really know who is at the other end of the computer link. By the time they reach high school and are able to drive, most adolescents are more interested in real-life dating.

The term "sexting" refers to a combination of sex and texting (SIECCAN Newsletter, 2011). Many young people choose to display information about their sexuality and sexual lives by indicating their sexual orientation on their social networking profile. They post stories and poems about sexual desires and experiences on blogs. In addition, some share nude or semi-nude images of themselves. They use either social networking sites or mobile phones ("sexting") (Brown, Keller, & Stern, 2009). Certain forms of sexting may violate Canadian child pornography laws when it involves nude images of individuals under the age of 18 (SIECCAN Newsletter, 2011). More worrisome is the possibility that the display of sexual content online can lead to an increased probability of teens being victimized online. However, despite the high level of public concerns about sexting, very little research has been conducted into the contexts in which sexting actually occurs (Albury & Crawford, 2012).

Socio-Cultural Contexts and Dating

The socio-cultural context exerts a powerful influence on adolescents' dating patterns. Values and religious beliefs of people of various cultures often dictate the age at which dating begins, how much freedom is allowed in dating, whether dates must be chaperoned by adults or parents, and the roles of males and females in dating. For example, parents of Indian and Islamic cultures have more conservative standards regarding adolescent dating than parents in Canadian culture. Dating may be a source of cultural conflict for many immigrants and their families who have come from cultures in which dating is non-existent, begins at a later age, requires a chaperone, or is otherwise restricted.

Dating and Adjustment

Researchers have linked dating and romantic relationships with various measures of how well-adjusted adolescents are (Collins, Welsh, & Furman, 2009). Not surprisingly, one study of grade 10 adolescents found that those who date are more likely than those who do not date to be accepted by their peers and to be perceived as more physically attractive (Furman, Low, & Ho, 2009). Another study of 14- to 19-year-olds found that adolescents who are not involved in a romantic relationship have more social anxiety than their counterparts who are dating or romantically involved (La Greca & Harrison, 2005).

Dating and romantic relationships at an unusually early age have been linked with several problems. Early dating and "going with" someone is associated with adolescent pregnancy and problems at home and school (Connelly & McIsaac, 2009). However, grade 10 adolescents who date also have more externalized problems, such as delinquency, and engage in substance use (as well as genital sexual behaviour) more than their counterparts who do not date (Furman, Low, & Ho, 2009). A study of adolescent girls revealed that a higher frequency of dating is linked to having depressive symptoms and emotionally unavailable parents (Steinberg & Davila, 2008; Starr et al., 2012). Another study of adolescent girls found that those who engage in co-rumination (excessive discussion of problems with friends) are more likely to be involved in a romantic relationship, and together co-rumination and romantic involvement predict an increase in depressive symptoms (Starr & Davila, 2008).

To this point, we have discussed a number of ideas about friendship in adolescence. For a review, see the Reach Your Learning Outcomes section at the end of this chapter.

Adolescent Problems

LO4 Analyze adolescent problems in socio-emotional development, and the causes of the problems.

- **Young Offenders**
- **Causes of Delinquency**

In Chapter 11, we described adolescent problems: substance abuse, sexually transmitted infections and diseases, and eating disorders. Here, we will examine the problems of youth violence and gangs, as well as some of the causes and some of the solutions. First, however, we will examine the recent research on brain development in adolescence, as it may help explain why most teens do a few stupid things, while only a few get into serious trouble.

Young Offenders

Images from American newspaper accounts and movies have strongly influenced the way the phenomenon of youth violence and gangs is defined in Canada. However, the youth gang problem in the United States bears little resemblance to what is going on in most Canadian communities. The *Youth Criminal Justice Act*, which replaced the *Young Offenders Act* in 2003, is a key part of Canada's Youth Justice Renewal Initiative. The principles of the youth criminal justice system are to prevent crime, to rehabilitate and reintegrate offenders into society, and to ensure meaningful consequences for offences committed by young people. These principles underline the values, rights, and responsibilities of both society and young people in relation to youth crime.

Young offenders are those young people between the ages of 12 and 18 who commit criminal acts. The *Youth Criminal Justice Act* defines a youth as an individual who, in the absence of evidence to the contrary, appears to be between 12 and 18 years of age. A child is defined as any person who, in the absence of evidence to the contrary, appears to be under 12. If the Crown successfully applies to the court, children between the ages of 10 and 12 who commit criminal acts may be dealt with as young criminals and be sentenced under this Act; as well, young people 14 years of age or more who are convicted of offences punishable by more than two years in jail may receive adult sentences. Violent crimes that fall into this category include murder, attempted murder, manslaughter, and aggravated sexual assault (*Youth Criminal Justice Act*, 2012). The range of crimes is extensive, including harassment, threatening, theft, "swarming" (which involves groups of young people victimizing individuals, often stealing items of clothing, such as shoes or jackets), and "wilding" (which involves indiscriminate acts of violence perpetrated by groups of young people). Date rape, sexual assault, and hate/bias crimes can range from verbal or psychological to physical threats or a combination of all three.

Youth Violence

Youth violence is a special concern. Gangs exist in every Canadian city, with the average age of gang members being 17 to 18 years. Gangs often engage in violent and criminal activities and use these activities as an indication of gang identity and loyalty. A distinction is made between early-onset (before age 11) and late-onset (after age 11) antisocial behaviour. Early-onset antisocial behaviour is associated with more negative developmental outcomes than late-onset antisocial behaviour (Lochman et al., 2010). Early-onset antisocial behaviour is also more likely to persist into emerging adulthood and is associated with more mental health and relationship problems (Loeber et al., 2007).

Street Youth

Street youth are young people who have left home and live "on the street," in shelters or abandoned buildings ("squats"), primarily because the street seems a safer place than the home. Many migrate to cities from smaller communities. Not all are homeless; some live with their families at least part of the time. According to the McCreary Centre Society, most street youth in Vancouver have, at some time, experienced physical or sexual abuse, and most either have run away or been kicked out of the home. About half the youth have addiction problems, and about 25 percent are involved in the sex trade. The problems that lead youth to the street begin long before adolescence.

Key findings of the McCreary Centre Society's report (2015) *Our Communities, Our Youth: The Health of Homeless and Street Involved Youth in BC* include the following:

- Almost half of street youth (42 percent) have seriously thought about suicide and almost 1/3 have attempted suicide.
- Over half (51 percent) have been in government care, including foster care or group homes.
- More than 21 percent of males and 14 percent of females have stayed in a custody centre at some point.
- Two-thirds say they are currently attending school, although most street youth have been expelled or suspended from school at some time.

Despite their apparent alienation from school and family, many street youth continue to have hope for a better life and reach out to adults for guidance.

Immigrant and refugee youth may face a double challenge in the transition from adolescence to adulthood. Not only are they confronted with the adjustment to adulthood, but they also must deal with the complexities of adapting to a new culture, one which may have been harsh to their self-esteem. Some of these young people may choose to join gangs to satisfy their unmet emotional, psychological, or social needs. Gangs often target those who are, or are thought to be, homosexual or lesbian.

Causes of Delinquency

Researchers have proposed many causes of delinquency, including heredity, identity problems, community influences, and family experiences. Erik Erikson (1968), for example, points out that adolescents whose development has restricted them from acceptable social roles or made them feel that they cannot measure up to the demands placed on them may choose a negative identity. Adolescents with a negative identity may find support for their delinquent image among peers, reinforcing the negative identity. For Erikson, delinquency is an attempt to establish an identity, although a negative one.

Economic realities may play a part in antisocial behaviours. Canada has a growing number of working-poor families where the parent or parents are working several part-time jobs to make ends meet, leaving little time and energy left for their family (Dodge, Coie, & Lynam, 2006). Among the risk factors that increase the likelihood an adolescent will become a gang member are disorganized neighbourhoods characterized by economic hardship, having other family members in a gang, drug use, lack of family support, and peer pressure (Ambert, 2007). Furthermore, adolescents in communities with high crime rates observe many models who engage in criminal activities (Loeber et al., 2007). These communities may be characterized by poverty, unemployment, and feelings of alienation toward the rest of society (Byrnes et al., 2007). Quality schooling, educational funding, and organized neighbourhood activities may also be lacking in these communities (Molnar et al., 2007).

Certain characteristics of family support systems are also associated with delinquency (Connell, Dishion, & Klostermann, 2012; Feinberg et al., 2007). Parents of delinquents are less skilled in discouraging anti-social behaviour and in encouraging skilled behaviour than are parents of non-delinquents. Parental monitoring of adolescents is especially important in determining whether an adolescent becomes a delinquent (Foscoe, Stormshak, & Dishion, 2012). Family discord and inconsistent and inappropriate discipline are also associated with delinquency (Bor, McGee, & Fagan, 2004). A recent study revealed that being physically abused in the first five years of life was linked to a greater risk of delinquency in adolescence (Lansford et al., 2007). One study found that low rates of delinquency from 14 to 23 years of age were associated with a higher rate of maternal authoritative parenting style (Murphy et al., 2012).

An increasing number of studies have found that siblings can have a strong influence on delinquency (Bank, Burraston, & Snyder, 2004). Finally, having delinquent peers greatly increases the risk of becoming delinquent (Foscoe, Frank, & Dishion, 2012). For example, a study found that peer rejection and having deviant friends at 7 to 13 years of age were linked with increased delinquency at 14 to 15 years of age (Vitaro, Pedersen, & Brendgen, 2007). Also, another study revealed that association with deviant peers was linked to a higher incidence of delinquency in male African American adolescents (Bowman, Prelow, & Weaver, 2007).

Other causes of problematic and delinquent behaviour are thought to include the swift rise in visual media, including violent computer games, materialism, and consumerism (Ambert, 2007). Changing perceptions of male and female personality traits, increased divorce, and a reduction of interest in religion are thought to be contributing factors (Ambert, 2007).

Cognitive factors, such as low self-control, low intelligence, and lack of sustained attention, also are implicated in delinquency. For example, a study revealed that low-IQ serious delinquents were characterized by low self-control (Koolhof et al., 2007). Another study found that at age 16, non-delinquents were more likely to have a higher verbal IQ and engage in sustained attention than delinquents (Loeber et al., 2007).

critical thinking

Recall Bandura's social cognitive theory from Chapter 2. How might personal cognitive factors, behaviour, and environment interact and contribute to the delinquency of a younger sibling? In what ways is role modelling involved in developing delinquent behaviour? In what ways can the delinquent adolescent build a strong sense of socially acceptable self-efficacy?

Attitudes surrounding youth and their involvement in Canada's justice system have transformed and evolved over many years. Under the Youth Criminal Justice Act, emphasis is placed on diverting youth (ages 12 to 17) accused of minor, non-violent offences from the formal court system using diversionary and extrajudicial measures. In 2010/2011, the number of cases completed in youth court declined for the second year in a row. Interestingly, the majority of cases completed in 2010/2011 involved non-violent cases (73 percent) in youth court. Violent cases accounted for the remaining 27 percent of youth court cases (Statistics Canada, 2012). Figure 12.4 discusses some antecedents of becoming a young offender.

Figure 12.4
The Antecedents of Becoming a Young Offender

Antecedent	Association with Delinquency	Description
Identity	Negative identity	Erikson believes delinquency occurs because the adolescent fails to resolve a role identity. This failure is connected to a variety of factors in the person's life, not the least of which is relationship with family.
Self-control	Low degree	Some children and adolescents fail to acquire the essential controls that others have acquired during the process of growing up.
Age	Early initiation	Early appearance of antisocial behaviour is associated with serious offences later in adolescence. However, not every child who acts out becomes a delinquent.
Sex	Males	Boys engage in more antisocial behaviour than girls, although girls' involvement in gangs has increased.
Expectations for education and school grades	Low expectations and low grades	Adolescents who become delinquents often have low educational expectations and low grades. Their verbal abilities are often weak. Due to a variety of circumstances such as poverty, for example, the teen may not see a bright future for him or herself.
Parental influences	Monitoring (low), support (low), discipline (ineffective)	Young offenders often come from families in which parents rarely monitor their adolescents, provide them with little support, and discipline them ineffectively.
Peer influences	Heavy influence, low resistance	Having peers who break the law greatly increases the risk of breaking the law.
Socio-economic status	Low	Serious offences are committed more frequently by lower-class males who, because of the stress of poverty, may not see a bright future for themselves.
Neighbourhood quality	Urban, high crime, high mobility	Communities often breed crime. Living in a high-crime area, which also is characterized by poverty and dense living conditions, increases the probability that a child will become a young offender. These communities often have grossly inadequate schools.

To this point, we have studied a number of ideas about adolescent problems. For a review, see the Reach Your Learning Outcomes section at the end of this chapter.

Successful Prevention and Intervention Programs

LO5 Design strategies for helping adolescents with problems.

We have described some of the major adolescent problems in this chapter as well as in Chapter 11: substance abuse; juvenile delinquency; school-related problems, such as dropping out of school; adolescent pregnancy; and sexually transmitted diseases.

The most at-risk adolescents have more than one problem. Researchers are increasingly finding that problem behaviours in adolescence are interrelated (Passini, 2012). For example, heavy substance abuse is related to early sexual activity, lower grades, dropping out of school, and delinquency. Delinquency is related to early sexual activity, early pregnancy, substance abuse, and dropping out of school (Grigsby et al., 2014). Repeated pregnancies are associated with intimate violence. People with anorexia nervosa frequently take illicit drugs. Many, but not all, of these very high-risk youth "do it all."

In addition to understanding that many adolescents engage in multiple problem behaviours, it also is important to understand that all behaviour is motivated by something. Maslow and Rogers would say that individuals who commit antisocial acts are trying to improve themselves in some way. Until the multidimensional causes are understood, developing programs that reduce adolescent problems is difficult. An all-out effort by youth, parents, communities, police, and governments is essential; understanding the causes can be helpful in finding solutions.

critical thinking

Suicide has often been thought of as an attention-getting behaviour; however, nothing could be farther from the truth. A suicide attempt is a "cry for help" from an individual who feels surrounded by hopelessness and has been unable to obtain relief from his or her impossible situation. This person may well be a successful repeater. In what ways can you help an adolescent who is contemplating suicide? What community resources would you use for references?

Effective Interventions

Provincial and municipal governments across Canada have mounted successful campaigns and interventions, all of which include a broad range of partnerships within their jurisdictions. The campaign against bullying is an example of one recent large-scale campaign mounted in both Canada and the United States. There are many other interesting and effective interventions, including the following:

- *British Columbia:* The British Columbia Integrated Youth Services Initiative is a provincial movement of community agencies, government, donors, young people, and families working together to empower young people by bringing together core services and supports for those aged 12–24.
- *Calgary:* YARD (Youth at Risk Development) programming involves partnerships between police, schools, and community agencies to support youth between the ages of 10 and 17 who are at risk for gang involvement.
- *Edmonton:* The Step Up and Step In program focuses on youth engagement, leadership, and empowerment and aims to reduce and prevent youth violence and criminal involvement.
- *Winnipeg*: Project OASIS (New Directions for Children, Youth, Adults and Families) supports youth and their families who come from countries of political strife. Refugee youth are considered at risk of youth gang involvement.
- *Toronto:* The Breaking the Cycle: Youth Gang Exit and Ambassador Leadership program focuses on reducing the effects of traumatic histories by providing various support for participants with the expected outcomes of reducing gang membership, limiting risk factors, increasing labour force participation, and prosocial community participation.

The Minister of Justice and Attorney General of Canada, of the former Conservative federal government, announced that the Government of Canada will continue to provide funding to support youth justice services in the provinces and territories. Effective April 1, 2013 to 2018, the Youth Justice Service Funding program will be funded at a level of $141.7 million annually (Department of Justice Canada, 2013).

Other strategies to reduce youth violence include training parents in authoritative parenting strategies. Some of the techniques suggested include:

- *Use one-word signals.* Because teens have short attention spans and tune out adult nagging or perceived nagging quickly, one-word reminders are more effective than lectures.
- *Use reflective questioning strategies.* Ask questions that help adolescents understand what they stand to lose, what they stand to gain, and what action plan might be useful in obtaining the goal they want. The follow-up question is to determine how the parent can assist the teen in obtaining the goal.
- *Choose your arguments carefully.* As one parent said, "Because I only have so many 'no's' they better be ones I can enforce and that will make a difference; this rules out tattooing, body piercing, and fashion whims, but rules in respect for property, integrity, and accountability." Arguing with a teenager is an invitation for disaster, as their increased critical thinking skills and sense of invincibility will give them responses for every point an adult makes.
- *Listen. Listen. Listen.* Keep your mouth shut and listen. Use questions to help teens answer their own moral dilemmas.
- *Praise when earned.* Provide praise at every opportunity at which achievement can be acknowledged. Remember, it takes at least seven positive interactions to overcome the barriers of one negative interaction!

To this point, we have studied a number of ideas about successful prevention and intervention programs in adolescence. For a review, see the Reach Your Learning Outcomes section at the end of this chapter.

Reach Your **Learning Outcomes**

Self-Esteem and Identity Development

LO1 Describe self-esteem, the changes in the self and identity, and several of the prominent theories.

Self-Esteem	▪ Self-esteem is an individual's self-evaluation of his/her overall sense of self-worth.
Identity	▪ Identity is a self-portrait composed of many pieces. ▪ Identity formation is extraordinarily complex. ▪ Erikson's theory is the most comprehensive view of identity development. Identity versus identity confusion is the stage in which the individual comes to terms with many aspects of his/her identity central to his/her being. Aspects of identity include career, political, religious, vocational, and sexual orientation. ▪ Marcia proposed four statuses of identity: diffusion, foreclosure, moratorium, and achievement. Achievement is attained when thought and commitment are present. ▪ Recent research indicates no significant gender differences in level of self-esteem. ▪ According to Elkind, age dynamism is the desire of adolescents to distance themselves from a childish or juvenile self in past.

Identity: Family, Religion, Race, Ethnicity, Culture, and Sexual Orientation

LO2 Compare and contrast how family, religion, race, ethnicity, culture, and sexual orientation influence adolescent development.

Families	▪ Parental responses and behaviour influence adolescent development. ▪ The internal struggle for autonomy and the restraining tug of attachment may vary according to gender and cultural influences. ▪ Parental conflicts emerge as the struggle for autonomy competes with attachment needs. ▪ A new model emphasizes that parent–adolescent conflict is more moderate than severe. **Religion** ▪ Religion is important to adolescent identity. ▪ Findings in Canada are that adolescents are identifying themselves as Muslim, Buddhist, or Hindu more than Christian.
Racial, Ethnic, and Cultural Identity	▪ Erikson believed that ethnic groups struggle to maintain their heritage, while at the same time blend into the dominant culture. ▪ During adolescence, individuals interpret their racial, ethnic, and cultural backgrounds for the first time. ▪ Racial, ethnic, and cultural aspects of identity are enduring, basic factors of the self that include a sense of membership in a group or groups and the attitudes and feelings related to that membership. ▪ Immigrant youth in Canada may have a bicultural identity because they identify with both the land of their birth and with Canada. ▪ Socio-economic status (SES), particularly poverty, may adversely affect identity development. ▪ Rites of passage are ceremonies that mark an individual's transition from one status to another, especially to adulthood.
Traditions and Changes in Adolescence around the World	▪ As in other periods of development, culture influences adolescents' development. ▪ Cultural traditions around the world affect health, gender, family, peers, school, and work. ▪ Rapid global change is altering the experience of the adolescent.
Sexual Orientation and Identity	▪ Erikson and Freud both believed adolescence to be a critical period in understanding sexual orientation and identity. ▪ Sexual identity is an individual's innermost understanding of his/her maleness or femaleness. ▪ Sexual orientation is related to an individual's sexual interests. ▪ Gender identity refers to an individual belonging to a particular sexual category. ▪ Transgender or intersexed individuals can either adjust in society or risk problems. ▪ Homophobia is the intense fear, prejudice, and willingness to cause harm to anyone not heterosexual. ▪ Symbols related to sexual orientation and identity are internalized at an early age and may jeopardize an individual's self-esteem.

Friendship

LO3 **Outline the changes that occur in peer relations and dating during adolescence.**

Adolescent Groups versus Children's Groups	▪ Children's groups are less formal, less heterogeneous, and less heterosexual than adolescent groups. ▪ During adolescence, groups tend to include a broader array of members. New friendships emerge. ▪ Harry Stack Sullivan was the most influential theorist to discuss the importance of friendship. He argued that there is a dramatic increase in the psychological importance and intimacy of close friends in early adolescence.
Peer Groups	▪ The nature of groups broadens in adolescence. ▪ The pressure to conform to peers is strong during adolescence, especially during grades 8 and 9. ▪ Findings indicate general resistance to peer influence increases during adolescence.
Dating and Romantic Relationships	▪ Dating takes on added importance in adolescence, and it can have many functions. Younger adolescents often begin to "hang out" together in heterosexual groups. ▪ Emotions are heavily involved in adolescent dating and romantic relationships. ▪ Culture can exert a powerful influence on adolescent dating. ▪ Dating and romantic relationships are linked to how well-adjusted adolescents are. Those who date are more accepted by their peers. ▪ Social networking, which includes cyberdating and sexting, has increased among adolescents in society.

Adolescent Problems

LO4 **Analyze adolescent problems in socio-emotional development, and the causes of the problems.**

Young Offenders	▪ A young offender is an adolescent who breaks the law or engages in conduct that is considered illegal.
Causes of Delinquency	▪ Multiple factors contribute to delinquency, including heredity, identity problems, family experiences, economic realities, and the swift rise in visual media including violent computer games. ▪ Researchers are increasingly finding that problem behaviours in adolescence are interrelated.

Successful Prevention and Intervention Programs

LO5 **Design strategies for helping adolescents with problems.**

	▪ Researchers have found a number of common components in successful programs designed to prevent or reduce adolescent problems. Broad-based partnerships, a specific program focus, training, and educational curricula and resources are the keys to effective interventions.

review → connect → reflect

review

1. What are several changes in self-esteem that occur during adolescence? LO1
2. How does identity develop in adolescence? LO1
3. What characterizes religious and spiritual development in adolescence? LO2
4. How does ethnicity influence adolescent development? LO2
5. What is the nature of adolescent dating and romantic relationships? LO3
6. What features of peer groups are important for the adolescent? LO3
7. What is juvenile delinquency? Identify several contributing factors to juvenile delinquency. LO4
8. What are a few components of successful prevention/intervention programs for adolescents? LO5

connect

Adolescence is identified as the second time in the life of an individual when seeking independence is especially strong. From your own memories, when do you think that first time occurred? What characterized it?

reflect

Your Own Personal Journey of Life

Reflect on your adolescence and your relationships with your parents. What was a source of conflict with your parents? How intense was your conflict? Would you behave differently toward your own adolescent than your parents did with you? If so, in what ways?

SECTION 7

Early Adulthood

CHAPTER 13

Physical and Cognitive Development in Early Adulthood

CHAPTER OUTLINE

The Transition from Adolescence to Adulthood

LO1 Outline the transition from adolescence to early adulthood.

- **The Criteria for Becoming an Adult**
- **The Transition from High School to College, University, or Work**

Physical Development, Health, and Wellness

LO2 Describe physical changes and health considerations for emerging adults.

- **Health**
- **Eating and Weight**
- **Regular Exercise**
- **Substance Abuse**

Sexuality

LO3 Examine the concept of sexuality in young adults.

- **Sexual Activity in Emerging Adulthood**
- **Sexually Transmitted Infections**
- **Violence against Women**

Cognitive Development

LO4 Analyze the cognitive changes that occur in early adulthood.

- **Piaget's View**
- **Creativity**

Careers and Work

LO5 Explain the key dimensions of careers and work in early adulthood.

- **Developmental Changes**
- **Values and Careers**
- **The Occupational Outlook**
- **The Impact of Work**

"Or perhaps you have spent too long in the chalkfield of education, filling in the blanks. Memorize this or mark that. The poem is writing a multiple choice exam. Which of the above."

—FROM "DRIVING IN THE BLIZZARD" IN *HARM'S WAY,* BY MAUREEN HYNES, CANADIAN POET

"Whatever you can do, or dream you can, begin it. Boldness has genius, power, and magic."

—JOHANN WOLFGANG VON GOETHE, NINETEENTH-CENTURY GERMAN PLAYWRIGHT AND NOVELIST

Winning Gold: Canada's Women's Hockey Team, Olympics 2010–2014

Early adulthood is an exciting time for work, dreams, play, and love. Finding our place in adult society and committing to the work required to attain our goals can take longer and be more difficult than we imagined. At times, we may doubt ourselves and wonder if we're on the right path, or if it isn't enough to just be. Sex and love are powerful passions—at times angels of light, and at other times fiends of torment. But at some point, the challenges of our goals force us to become realistic and more pragmatic. In this way, through our efforts and perseverance, the dreams of our childhood weave their way into the texture of our adult lives. The women of Canada's 2010 and 2014 Olympic hockey team illustrate this transition.

In 2014, Team Canada defended their Olympic gold, won in 2010, by defeating their arch competitors, Team USA. The team's dramatic overtime win made Sochi their fourth consecutive Olympic gold performance. This Olympic moment was especially celebrated for the intensity and drama that unfolded during the game. In contrast, their 2010 win was overshadowed by an exuberant post-win celebration that happened on the ice with champagne, beer, cigars, and a youthful sense of fun. That 2010 celebration was captured by the media and raised considerable controversy when the IOC (International Olympic Committee) made inquiries. The women apologized for any embarrassment that may have been caused for the IOC, the COC (Canadian Olympic Committee), or the Canadian nation. To quote one player after the 2014 epic gold medal win, "It's the best feeling ever, It's like a dream come true" (Maki, February 21, 2014). Unlike their previous win, the focus was on the battle of the game, unmarred by any post-game celebration caught on camera.

The team illustrates many aspects of early adulthood: peak physical strength and the ability to make a commitment, set goals, and plan ahead. And last, but not least, the players demonstrated a youthful spontaneity, captured by the eye of the media in 2010, but most definitely also present in 2014 in a more private realm. This gold, maybe even more so than golds of past Olympics, marked a proud and joyful moment for women's hockey in Canada.

Jonathan Hayward/The Canadian Press

The Transition from Adolescence to Adulthood

LO1 Outline the transition from adolescence to early adulthood.

- **The Criteria for Becoming an Adult**
- **The Transition from High School to College, University, or Work**

For most individuals, becoming an adult involves a lengthy transition period. Recently, the transition from adolescence to adulthood has been referred to as *emerging adulthood*, which occurs from approximately 18 to 25 years of age (Arnett, 2006, 2007, 2012). Experimentation and exploration characterize the emerging adult. Choosing a career path, deciding where to live, and determining a lifestyle (for example, single, cohabiting, or married) are among the wide-ranging choices the young person makes. These decisions are connected to the type of life the individual has had.

Consider the changing life of Michael Maddaus (Broderick, 2003; Masten, Obradovic, & Burt, 2006). Growing up as a child and adolescent, Michael's mother drank heavily and his stepfather abused him. He coped by spending an increasing amount of time on the streets. He was arrested more than 20 times for his delinquency, frequently placed in detention centres, and rarely went to school. At 17, he joined the Navy and the experience helped him to gain self-discipline and hope. After his brief stint in the Navy, he completed high school through an adult learning centre, and began taking community college classes. However, he continued to have some setbacks with drugs and alcohol. A defining moment came when he delivered furniture to a surgeon's home. The surgeon became interested in helping Michael, and his mentorship led to Michael volunteering at a rehabilitation centre, then to a job with a neurosurgeon. Eventually, he obtained his undergraduate degree, went to medical school, got married, and started a family. Today, Michael Maddaus is a successful surgeon. One of his most gratifying volunteer activities is telling his story to troubled youth.

critical thinking

Reflect on your life as an adolescent. What are a few positive life experiences that you encountered that had an impact on your life today?

The Criteria for Becoming an Adult

Around the world, youth are increasingly delaying their entry into adulthood, largely because contemporary society requires more education and skills than earlier generations (Clark, 2009). Thus, the transition is likely to be longer than previous generations. In addition to staying in school longer, economic factors contribute to the delay, including the increase in part-time employment and the rising costs of housing (Clark, 2009). How is adulthood determined? Statistics Canada identifies five markers of the transition to adulthood (Clark, 2009):

- Has left school
- Has left parental home
- Has full-time full-year work
- Is in a conjugal union
- Has children who live with them

Jeffrey Arnett (2006) has labelled the age range from 18 to 25 as **emerging adulthood**. He says that during this time frame, individuals have left the dependency of childhood, but have not yet entered the enduring responsibilities of adulthood. They are at a point when they are exploring a variety of possible directions in what they want to do with their lives, especially in the areas of work and love.

Arnett (2006) describes five features of emerging adulthood:

- *Identity exploration, especially in love and work:* As we saw in Chapter 12, emerging adulthood is the time during which key changes in identity take place for many individuals (Cote, 2006; Kroger, 2007).
- *Instability:* Residential changes peak during early adulthood, a time during which there also is often instability in love, work, and education.
- *Self-focused:* According to Arnett (2006, p. 10), emerging adults "are self-focused in the sense that they have little in the way of social obligations, little in the way of duties and commitments to others, which leaves them with a great deal of autonomy in running their own lives."
- *Feeling in-between:* Many emerging adults don't consider themselves adolescents or full-fledged adults.
- *The age of possibilities, a time when individuals have an opportunity to transform their lives:* Arnett (2006) describes two ways in which emerging adulthood is the age of possibilities: (1) many emerging adults are optimistic about their future; and (2) for emerging adults who have experienced difficult times while growing up, emerging adulthood presents an opportunity to direct their lives in a more positive direction (Schulenberg & Zarett, 2006).

critical thinking

What are some of the criteria being considered to qualify as an adult? Which criterion do you think is the most important? State why you think so. Do adolescents suddenly become adults at 19, or does the term "emerging adulthood," which suggests that individuals become adults over a period of years, make more sense to you? What makes you think so? Reflect on your own life. What events contributed to your "emerging adulthood"?

Taking responsibility for oneself is an important marker of adult status. In a study, both parents and university/college students agreed that taking responsibility for one's actions and developing emotional control are important aspects of becoming an adult (Nelson et al., 2007). However, parents and students didn't always agree on other aspects of what it takes to become an adult.

In many countries, marriage is often a significant marker for entry into adulthood; however, getting married and starting a family is becoming less common. More couples cohabit and many young people return home in between relationships (Arnett, 2004; Clark, 2009). For example, in 1971, 65 percent of men and 80 percent of women were in or had been in a conjugal relationship by age 25; by 2001, these percentages had dropped by almost half to 34 percent and 49 percent, respectively (Clark, 2009).

Not only is life satisfaction a global evaluation of one's quality of life, it is also an important component of personal well-being and a marker of self-perceived success (Pavol & Deiner, 2008). Both endeavours of exploring and preparing for meaningful work are central to identity development throughout the twenties. In fact, finding satisfying and stable work, as well as identifying one's work as a "career" are all important markers in the successful transition to adulthood (Mortmer et al., 2008). However, Pavot and Deiner (2008) claim that in addition to career satisfaction being a dominant specific indicator, it is distinct from life satisfaction.

Canadian researchers conducted a study to explore ways in which trajectories of depressive symptoms and expressed anger from age 18 to 25, along with important life transitions, predict life and career satisfaction at age 32. They found that higher depressive symptoms at age 18 predict lower life satisfaction in both men and women, and lower career satisfaction in women. Meanwhile in emerging adulthood, slower declines in women's depressive symptoms predict lower life satisfaction, but slower declines in women's expressed anger predict higher career satisfaction. Given the absence of effects related to mental health trajectories among men, it could be that their self-perceived success, as young adults, relies heavily on marriage and work combined, overshadowing depression and anger (Howard, Galambos, & Krahn, 2010).

The Transition from High School to College, University, or Work

Just as the transition from elementary school to middle or junior high school involves change and possible stress, so does the transition from high school to college or university, or the transition from school to work. In many instances, there are parallel changes in the transitions. For many individuals, graduating from high school and going to college or university is an important aspect of the transition to adulthood (Bowman, 2010). Going from being a senior in high school to being a first-year student in college or university or the youngest person in the work group replays the "top-dog" phenomenon that occurred at the start of high school.

The transition from high school to college or university involves movement to a larger, more impersonal school structure. Interactions with peers and new friends tend to include students from a broader range of geographical and cultural backgrounds. Another difference is the increased focus on achievement and assessment. Students are more likely to feel grown up, and have more subjects from which to select, more time to spend with peers, and more opportunities to explore different lifestyles and values. In addition, students have greater independence from parental guidance and monitoring. Challenges in academic work tend to be greater than those experienced before this point (Halonen & Santrock, 2013).

The same holds true of those who enter the work force full-time. They, too, are likely to feel more grown up and explore different lifestyles and values. Plus, they also experience greater independence from parental guidance and monitoring.

Stress

Each year, more than 100 000 students enter college and university. Some live at home, and others live in residence (McIntyre, 2009). The advantage of living at home is that changes in behaviour that signal depression may be noticed by someone in the family. The same signals may not be noticed in students living away from home. For example, in a survey of students at Simon Fraser University in British Columbia, 18 percent reported that their academic performance is compromised by feelings of hopelessness, depression, anxiety, and seasonal affective disorder (Whiting, 2007). This study echoes a U.S. study of more than 300 000 freshmen at more than 500 colleges and universities, which found that post-secondary students experience more stress and are more depressed than in the past (Pryor et al., 2007). In 2005, 27 percent (up from 16 percent in 1985) said they frequently "felt overwhelmed with what I have to do." College/university females were twice as likely as their male counterparts to feel overwhelmed. The pressure to succeed in college or university, get a great job, and make lots of money were pervasive concerns of these students. The personal circumstances that caused the most stress for students were intimate relationships, finances, parental conflicts and expectations, and roommate conflicts.

Stress can be dealt with both negatively and positively. Negative ways to cope with stress include such things as repressing your feelings, projecting your frustration and anger on others, keeping your feelings bottled up inside, denying your feelings, and eating and/or drinking more.

Fortunately, there are positive ways to help cope with stress. Baghurst and Kelley (2014) conducted a study to verify whether differing stress reduction strategies could change stress levels experienced by female and male college/university students from the beginning to the end of a semester. Components of stress included overall perceived stress, test anxiety, and perceived burnout. The 16-week course focused specifically on cognitive-behavioural stress management, cardiovascular fitness, generalized physical activity, or a control with no intervention. Findings indicated that in addition to gender differences, both the stress management and physical activity groups had significantly lower levels of perceived stress, test anxiety, and personal burnout at the end of the semester. The researchers conclude that it is evident that stress reduction strategies do have an impact on reducing stress variables in students over the course of a semester. Cardinal, Sorensen, and Cardinal (2012) advocate that colleges and universities should not streamline physical activity requirements for students in undergraduate programs while students are taking a degree. This cutback could be detrimental to the students' health.

Marcos Townsend, The Gazette (Montreal)

The transition from high school to college or university often involves positive as well as negative features. Loneliness, academic and work pressures, children, and other family members are all factors affecting the transition from high school to college or university. *What was your transition like?*

The Canadian Mental Health Association (2010) recommends these tips:

- Keep things in perspective. Try not to get flustered by one bad mark or one period when things aren't going well.
- Talk to someone about what's bothering you.
- Identify what helps you relax and practise doing it.
- Take a break from what is causing you stress and try meditation, tai chi, or yoga.
- Get enough sleep by going to bed at a reasonable time every night.
- Exercise regularly and make time for fun in your life.
- Watch your diet, especially your intake of caffeine and sugar.

As we learn more about healthy lifestyles and how they contribute to a longer life span, emerging and young adults are increasingly interested in learning about physical performance, health, nutrition, exercise, and addiction.

To this point, we have studied a number of ideas about the transition from adolescence to adulthood. For a review, see the Reach Your Learning Outcomes section at the end of this chapter.

Physical Development, Health, and Wellness

LO2 Describe physical changes and health considerations for emerging adults.

- **Health**
- **Eating and Weight**
- **Regular Exercise**
- **Substance Abuse**

Most of us reach our peak physical performance under the age of 30, often between the ages of 19 and 26. This peak of physical performance occurs not only for the average young adult, but for outstanding athletes as well (Feldman & Landry, 2014). Different types of athletes, however, reach their peak performances at different ages. Most swimmers and gymnasts reach their peak performance in their late teens. Golfers and marathon runners tend to peak in their late twenties. In other areas of athletics, peak performance is often in the early to mid-twenties.

Not only do we reach our peak in physical performance during early adulthood, but it is also during this age period that we begin to decline in physical performance. Muscle tone and strength usually begin to show signs of decline around the age of 30. Sagging chins and protruding abdomens also may begin to appear for the first time. The lessening of physical abilities is a common complaint among the just-turned thirties. Sensory systems show little change in early adulthood, but the lens of the eye loses some of its elasticity and becomes less able to change shape and focus on near objects. Hearing peaks in adolescence, remains constant in the first part of early adulthood, and then begins to decline in the last part of early adulthood. And in the mid- to late-twenties, the body's fatty tissue increases.

The health profile of emerging and young adults can be improved by decreasing the incidence of certain health-impairing lifestyles, such as overeating, and alternatively, by engaging in health-improving practices that include healthy eating habits and regular exercise patterns, and by not abusing drugs (Waldron & Dieser, 2010). For example, the Canadian Society for Exercise Physiology indicates that to achieve health benefits, adults should be required to accumulate at least 150 minutes of moderate- to vigorous-intensity aerobic physical activity per week, in bouts of 10 minutes or more (CSEP, 2012).

Health

Emerging adults have more than twice the mortality rate of adolescents (Park et al., 2006). Although emerging adults have a higher death rate than adolescents, emerging adults have few chronic health problems, and they have fewer colds and respiratory problems than when they were children (Rimsza & Kirk, 2005). Although most college and university students know what it takes to prevent illness and promote health, they don't fare very well when it comes to applying this information to themselves. In many cases, emerging adults are not as healthy as they seem (Fatusi & Hindin, 2010). A recent study revealed that college/university students from low-SES backgrounds engaged in lower levels of physical activity, consumed more fast food and less fibre (fruits and vegetables), and used more unhealthy weight control methods than did their higher-SES counterparts (VanKim & Laska, 2012).

Many post-secondary students, it seems, have the same sense of invincibility they had in adolescence, and have overly optimistic beliefs about their future health status. As emerging adults, many individuals develop patterns of not eating breakfast, not eating regular meals, and relying on snacks as the main food source during the day; overeating to a point that exceeds the normal weight for their age; smoking and drinking moderately or excessively; failing to exercise; and getting by with only a few hours of sleep per night (Cousineau, Goldstein, & Franco, 2005). These lifestyles are associated with poor health, which tends to diminish life satisfaction (Luo et al., 2015).

One study explored links between health behaviour and life satisfaction in more than 17 000 individuals, aged 17 to 30, in 21 countries (Grant, Wardle, & Steptoe, 2009). The life satisfaction of young adults was positively related to not smoking, exercising regularly, using sun protection, eating fruit, and limiting fat intake, but was not related to alcohol consumption and fibre intake.

The health profile of emerging young adults can be improved by reducing the incidence of certain health-impairing lifestyles. These lifestyle practices include engaging in health-improving lifestyles, exercising regularly, eating well, abstaining from drugs, and getting adequate sleep (Blake, Munoz, & Volpe, 2014; Sussman & Arnett, 2014; Robbins, Powers, & Burgess, 2008; Teague et al., 2009). As an example, one recent study of college/university students found that regularly engaging in moderate or vigorous physical activity is linked to consuming an adequate amount of fruits and vegetables daily, having a healthy body mass index, not smoking, being less depressed, having a lower incidence of binge drinking, being less likely to have multiple sex partners, and getting adequate sleep (Dinger, Brittain, & Hutchinson, 2014). In addition, another recent study found a bidirectional link between sleep quality/duration and adjustment (Tavernier & Willoughby, 2014). Yet another recent study examined the delivery of preventative health services to emerging adults 18 to 26 year of age. Lau and colleagues (2013) found rates of preventative services used by emerging adults are generally low. In addition, females are more likely to receive health care services than are males.

Eating and Weight

In earlier chapters, we explored obesity in childhood (Chapters 7 and 9) and examined the eating disorders of anorexia nervosa and bulimia nervosa in adolescence (Chapter 11). Now, we turn our attention to obesity in the adult years and the extensive preoccupation that many adults have with dieting.

Obesity

Obesity is a serious and pervasive health problem for many individuals (Corbin et al., 2008; Hahn, Payne, & Lucas, 2009). Information about weight and obesity is based on self-reporting, a practice that tends to underestimate the prevalence of obesity. As you may recall from Chapter 11, obesity is becoming increasingly more severe, and at the same time fitness levels are decreasing (PHAC & CIHI, 2011). Canadian data indicate that one-third of normal weight 20-year-olds will become overweight within 10 years (Warshawski, 2010). Although rates of obesity are rising in men, a higher percentage of women are morbidly obese (a body mass index (BMI) of 40 or more). Figure 13.1 demonstrates how BMI is calculated.

Figure 13.1

Figuring Your Body Mass Index

Weight (pounds)

Height	120	130	140	150	160	170	180	190	200	210	220	230	240	250
4'6"	29	31	34	36	39	41	43	46	48	51	53	56	58	60
4'8"	27	29	31	34	36	38	40	43	45	47	49	52	54	56
4'10"	25	27	29	31	34	36	38	40	42	44	46	48	50	52
5'0"	23	25	27	29	31	33	35	37	39	41	43	45	47	49
5'2"	22	24	26	27	29	31	33	35	37	38	40	42	44	46
5'4"	21	22	24	26	28	29	31	33	34	36	38	40	41	43
5'6"	19	21	23	24	26	27	29	31	32	34	36	37	39	40
5'8"	18	20	21	23	24	26	27	29	30	32	34	35	37	38
5'10"	17	19	20	22	23	24	26	27	29	30	32	33	35	36
6'0"	16	18	19	20	22	23	24	26	27	28	30	31	33	34
6'2"	15	17	18	19	21	22	23	24	26	27	28	30	31	32
6'4"	15	16	17	18	20	21	22	23	24	26	27	28	29	30
6'6"	14	15	16	17	19	20	21	22	23	24	25	27	28	29
6'8"	13	14	15	17	18	19	20	21	22	23	24	25	26	28

Underweight | Healthy weight | Overweight | Obese

From National Institutes of Health (US)

Body mass index is a measure of weight in relation to height. Anyone with a BMI of 25 or more is considered overweight. People who have a body mass index of 30 or more (a BMI of 30 is roughly 30 pounds over a healthy weight) are considered obese (Kirk et al., 2012). BMI has some limitations: it can overestimate body fat in people who are very muscular, and it can underestimate body fat in people who have lost muscle mass, such as the elderly.

Obesity is linked to increased risk of hypertension, diabetes, and cardiovascular disease (Hahn, Payne, & Lucas, 2009). As indicated in Chapter 11, obesity is overtaking tobacco as the leading cause of death. For individuals who are 30 percent overweight, the probability of dying in middle adulthood increases by about 40 percent. What factors are involved in obesity? The possible culprits include heredity, leptin, set point, metabolism and environmental factors, and gender.

HEREDITY

Until recently, the genetic component of obesity was underestimated by scientists. It is now understood that some individuals inherit a tendency to be overweight (Heath, 2014). Researchers have documented that animals can be inbred to have a propensity for obesity (Brown et al., 2011). Further, identical twins have similar weights, even when they are reared apart (Collaku et al., 2004).

LEPTIN

Leptin (from the Greek word *leptos,* which means "thin") is a protein that is involved in satiety (the condition of being full to satisfaction) and released by fat cells, resulting in decreased food intake and increased energy expenditure. Leptin acts as an anti-obesity hormone. In humans, leptin concentrations have been linked with weight, percentage of body fat, weight loss in a single diet episode, and cumulative percentage of weight loss (de Luis et al., 2007). Some scientists are interested in the possibility that leptin might help obese individuals lose weight.

SET POINT

The amount of stored fat in your body is an important factor in your set point, the weight you maintain when you make no effort to gain or lose weight. Fat is stored in what are called adipose cells. When these cells are filled, you do not get hungry. When people gain weight—because of genetic predisposition, childhood eating patterns, or adult overeating—their number of fat cells increases, and they might not be able to get rid of them. A normal-weight individual has 30 to 40 billion fat cells. An obese individual has 80 to 120 billion fat cells. Some scientists have proposed that these fat cells can shrink but might not go away.

ENVIRONMENTAL FACTORS

Environmental factors play an important role in obesity (Thompson & Manore, 2015). The human genome has not changed markedly in the last century, yet obesity has noticeably increased (Li et al., 2007). The dramatic increase in obesity is likely due to greater availability of food (especially food high in fat), energy-saving devices, and declining physical activity.

Socio-cultural factors are also involved in obesity, which is six times more prevalent among women with low incomes than among women with high incomes. Americans also are more obese than Europeans and people in many other areas of the world (OECD, 2010).

A Word about Dietary Fats

Dietary fats are both a necessary and unavoidable part of our diets. Some fats, such as those found in avocados and other such vegetables, are healthy; but the fats found in french fries, doughnuts, and fast foods are dangerous to health because they contain high levels of trans fats. Canadians spend about one-third of their food budgets on restaurant foods, which is where the trans fat levels are the highest. Called the *silent killer* by nutritionists, trans fats wreak havoc with the body's ability to regulate cholesterol and increase the risk of heart disease exponentially. A number of food manufacturers are currently taking steps to remove trans fats from their products, and soon legislation will require accurate labelling of fats for both store-bought and restaurant foods.

Dieting

Ironically, while obesity is on the rise, dieting has become an obsession with many (Schiff, 2009). Although many people regularly embark on a diet, few are successful in keeping weight off long-term (Bombak, 2014). A research review of the long-term outcomes of calorie-restricting diets revealed that overall, one-third to two-thirds of dieters eventually regain more weight than they lost on their diets (Mann et al., 2007).

Many divergent interests are involved in the topic of dieting. These include the public, health professionals, policy makers, the media, and the powerful diet and food industries. On one side are the societal norms that promote a very lean, aesthetic body. This ideal is supported by billions of dollars spent annually on diet books, programs, videos, foods, and pills. On the other side are health professionals and a growing minority of the press. Although they recognize the alarmingly high rate of obesity, they are frustrated by high relapse rates and the obsession with excessive thinness that can lead to chronic dieting and serious health risks. However, some individuals do lose weight and maintain the loss (Applebaum, 2008; Herman, van Strien, & Polivy, 2008). How often this occurs and whether some diet programs work better than others are still open questions.

What we do know about losing weight is that the most effective programs include exercise (Fahey, Insel, & Roth, 2009; Wardlaw & Hampl, 2007). Exercise not only burns up calories, but continues to elevate the person's metabolic rate for several hours *after* exercising. A recent study found that exercising 30 minutes a day, planning meals, and weighing themselves daily were the main strategies used by successful dieters compared with unsuccessful dieters (Kruger, Blanck, & Gillespie, 2006) (see Figure 13.2). A research review concluded that that adults who engaged in a diet-plus-exercise program lost more weight than those who relied on diet-only programs (Wu et al., 2009).

Figure 13.2

Comparison of Strategies in Successful and Unsuccessful Dieters

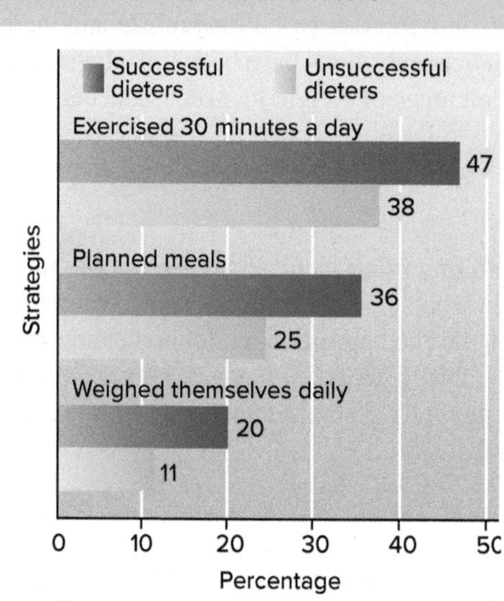

From J. Kruger, H.M. Blank, and G. Gillespie, Comparisons of Strategies in Successful and Unsuccessful Dieters in "Dietary and Physical Activity Behaviors Among Adults Successful at Weight Loss Management," in *International Journal of Behavioral Nutrition and Physical Activity*, v. 3, p. 17, 2006. Bio Medical Central.

Even when diets do produce weight loss, they can place the dieter at risk for other health problems (Cunningham & Hyson, 2006). One main concern focuses on weight cycling—yo-yo dieting—in which the person is in a recurring cycle of weight loss and weight gain (Janacek et al., 2005). Also, liquid diets and other very low-calorie strategies are linked with gallbladder damage. With these problems in mind, when overweight people diet and maintain their weight loss, they become less depressed and reduce their risk for a number of health-impairing disorders (Daubenmier et al., 2007; Mensah & Brown, 2007).

Restrained Eating

One area related to dieting that psychologists have studied is restrained eating. Too many people live their lives as one big long diet, interrupted by occasional hot fudge sundaes or chocolate chip cookies. **Restrained eaters** are individuals who chronically restrict their food intake to control their weight. Restrained eaters often are on diets, are very conscious of what they eat, and tend to feel guilty after splurging on sweets (de Lauzon-Guillain et al., 2006). An interesting characteristic of restrained eaters is that when they stop dieting, they tend to binge eat—that is, eat large quantities of food in a short time. Also, when under stress, restrained eaters tend to increase their food intake, while unrestrained eaters tend to decrease their food intake (Lowe & Kral, 2006).

Regular Exercise

One of the main reasons why health experts want people to exercise is that it helps to prevent heart disease, diabetes, and other diseases (Anspaugh, Hamrick, & Rosato, 2009; Hoeger & Hoeger, 2008; Thompson & Manore, 2015). Although exercise designed to strengthen muscles and bones or to improve flexibility is important to fitness, many health experts stress aerobic exercise. **Aerobic exercise** is sustained exercise—jogging, swimming, or cycling, for example—that stimulates heart and lung activity.

According to the Public Health Agency of Canada (PHAC) (2012), as little as 2½ hours of light-to-moderate activity weekly—equivalent to a brisk walk—can improve health. This time can be broken into parts; that is, short bouts of as little as 10 minutes of activity can produce wanted health benefits. Physical activity is an important part of a healthy lifestyle. Research on the benefits of exercise suggest that both moderate and intense activity produce important physical and psychological gains. In particular, exercise improves self-concept and tends to reduce both anxiety and depression (Behrman & Ebemeier, 2014; Henchoz et al., 2014). As this suggests, researchers have found that exercise benefits not only physical health, but mental health as well. A recent daily diary study found that on days when emerging adults (18 to 25 years of age) who were post-secondary students engaged in more physical activity, they also reported greater satisfaction with life (Maher et al., 2013; Centre for Disease Control and Prevention, 2015).

Some people enjoy rigorous, intense exercise. Others enjoy more moderate exercise routines (see Figure 13.3).

Figure 13.3

Moderate and Vigorous Physical Activities

Moderate	Vigorous
Walking, briskly (7 to 9 kph)	Walking, briskly uphill or with a load
Cycling, for pleasure or transportation (≤22 km)	Cycling, fast or racing (>16 km)
Swimming, moderate effort	Swimming, fast treading crawl
Conditioning exercise, general calisthenics	Conditioning exercise, stair ergometer or ski machine
Racquet sports, table tennis	Racquet sports, singles tennis or racquetball
Golf, pulling cart or carrying clubs	Golf, practise at driving range
Canoeing, leisurely (~5 kph)	Canoeing, rapidly (≥7 kph)
Home care, general cleaning	Moving furniture
Mowing lawn, with power mower	Mowing lawn, with hand mower
Home repair, painting	Home repair, fix-up projects

Adapted from Pate, et al., *Journal of the American Medical Association*, 273, 404.

Substance Abuse

In Chapter 11, we explored substance abuse in adolescence. Fortunately, by the time individuals reach their mid-twenties, many have reduced their use of alcohol and drugs. In 2012, a total of 2.8 million Canadians aged 15 and older, or 10.1 percent of the population, reported symptoms consistent with at least one of the following mental or substance use disorders: a major depressive episode; bipolar disorder; generalized anxiety disorder; and abuse of and/or dependence on alcohol, cannabis, or other drugs (Statistics Canada, 2015). Recent national studies in the United States indicate that individuals who don't go to college/university are more likely to take drugs than college/university students and college/university-educated adults except for one substance —alcohol—which college/university students are more likely to use (Miech et al., 2016). Also, as in adolescence, male students attending post-secondary and young adults are more likely to take drugs than their female counterparts (Johnston et al., 2014). One study revealed that only 20 percent of college/university students reported abstaining from alcohol (Huang et al., 2009).

Let's take a closer look at the use of alcohol and nicotine by young adults and at the nature of *addiction.*

Alcohol

Alcohol is widely consumed around the world and frequently linked to injuries, impaired driving, unprotected sexual activity, sexually transmitted infections (STIs), and HIV (Mundt et al., 2009). The World Health Organization noted another interesting co-relation: the rate of deaths from alcohol and HIV in the regions that were studied (African Region; Region of the Americas, Eastern Mediterranean Region; European Region; Southeast Asia Region; and Western Pacific Region) were very close, with the highest incidence occurring in the European Region (WHO, 2014). Approximately one-third of Canadian undergraduates report a pattern of heavy drinking, and 36 percent report drinking excessively more than four times a week (CCSA, 2014).

According to the WHO (2005), there are five patterns linking alcohol use and sexual behaviour:

1. construction of maleness in terms of alcohol use
2. denial and neglect of risk as a way of coping with life
3. use of alcohol-serving venues as contact places for sexual encounters
4. use of alcohol at/during sexual encounters
5. promotion of alcohol use in pornographic materials

BINGE DRINKING

Heavy binge drinking often increases in college and university, and it can take its toll on students (Kinney, 2012). Students reported that they drink to get drunk, to celebrate, to forget their worries, and to feel good. One study assessed college students' mood, or affect, and heavy drinking over a period of seven semesters. The researchers found that the longer students were in college and tended to associate a positive affect with heavy drinking, the more likely they were to engage in heavy drinking on both weekdays and weekends, compared to earlier in college (Howard, Patrick, & Maggs, 2014). However, binge drinking is a particularly dangerous form of alcohol consumption. Men who consume five drinks (50 g) or more, and women who consume four drinks (40 g) or more in one sitting are considered binge drinkers (Flage, MacDonald, & Hebert, 2011). Reports suggest that the percentage of young women binge drinking is on the rise and encompasses nearly one in four Canadian women between the ages of 20 and 34 (Davison, 2015). Binge drinking is reported to be twice as likely as daily heavy drinking to cause myocardial infarction or death (Ruidavets et al., 2010).

Drinking games, catalysts for binge drinking, are popular in colleges and universities; however, student associations oppose restrictions to reduce drinking, such as raising the legal age of drinking or increasing the cost of alcohol at campus pubs. Many colleges and universities across Canada have initiated strategies to educate and help students who have problems with alcohol and drugs. Researchers also want to raise awareness of the hazards associated with alcohol abuse and to educate pub staff to recognize problem drinking and stop selling drinks to those who are overindulging. A longitudinal study revealed that binge drinking peaks at about 21 to 22 years of age and then declines through the remainder of the twenties (CCSA, 2014).

ALCOHOLISM

Alcoholism is a disorder that involves long-term, repeated, uncontrolled, compulsive, and excessive use of alcoholic beverages. Further, this pattern impairs the drinker's health, work, and social relationships. One in nine individuals who drink continues the path to alcoholism (Gordith, Brkic, & Soderpalm, 2011). Family studies consistently reveal a high frequency of alcoholism in the first-degree relatives of alcoholics (Lee et al., 2013). Indeed, researchers have found that heredity likely plays a role in alcoholism, although the precise hereditary mechanism has not been found (Miles & Williams, 2007). An estimated 50 to 60 percent of individuals who become alcoholics are believed to have a genetic predisposition for it.

Although studies reveal a genetic influence on alcoholism, they also show that environmental factors play a role (Ksir, Hart, & Ray, 2008; O'Malley, 2014). The large cultural variations in alcohol use mentioned earlier also underscore the environment's role in alcoholism.

The prolonged sense of invincibility in young adults may lead them to believe that they would never become alcoholics, but this may be naive. Social norms on campuses support binge drinking, and many students who drink frequently and excessively may find they have a chemical or psychological dependency by the time they leave school.

Cigarette Smoking

Converging evidence from a number of studies underscores the dangers of smoking or being around those who smoke (Canadian Cancer Society, 2016). Between 1950 and 2011, the prevalence of cigarette smoking (including both daily and non-daily) among adults aged 20 years and older decreased steadily in men from 68.9 percent to 18.6 percent, but in women increased slightly from 38.2 percent to 39.1 percent before declining to 15.4 percent in 2011. Rates of smoking by both women and men were higher in the Atlantic Provinces and Quebec, although in men these differences have declined since the 1990s. In a subset of data from 1999 to 2011, those with lower levels of education had higher levels of smoking initiation and lower levels of cessation (Corsi et al., 2014).

Fewer people smoke today than in the past, and according to the *Report on the State of Public Health in Canada,* people in middle age are the heaviest smokers (PHAC, 2011c). However, Canadians are starting to smoke at a slightly younger age, and more young smokers are females. The earlier an individual starts smoking, the greater the health risks are for that individual. The effects of smoking are both long-term, as noted above, and short-term. In the short term, smokers develop more colds and infections such as bronchitis and pneumonia. Smokers also consume more alcohol, develop a smoker's cough (related to chronic lung irritation), and suffer more after-effects such as headaches and hangovers than non-smokers. Second hand smoke is implicated in over 800 Canadian deaths each year. Children of smokers are at special risk for respiratory and middle-ear diseases (Canadian Cancer Society, 2016).

Electronic cigarettes (e-cigarettes) have gained popularity in recent years, both globally and within Canada. E-cigarettes are products that heat liquid components to deliver a vapour (Reid et al., 2015). They are typically composed of propylene glycol and/or glycerin, additives such as flavouring, and sometimes nicotine (Hajek et al., 2014). Recent surveys suggest that approximately one in six younger adults (aged 16–30 years) have tried e-cigarettes (Czoli, Hammond, & White, 2014).

Most adult smokers would like to quit. However, their addiction often makes quitting an insurmountable challenge (Mennecke et al., 2014). Nicotine, the active drug in cigarettes, is a stimulant that increases the smoker's energy and alertness, a pleasurable and reinforcing experience. Nicotine also stimulates neurotransmitters that have a calming or pain-reducing effect. A recent search of databases revealed that the cessation of smoking is the most effective way for smokers to reduce the risk of premature death and disability (Zeng et al., 2015).

Four main methods are used to help smokers overcome their addiction to nicotine: (1) using a substitute source of nicotine, such as nicotine gum and the nicotine patch; (2) taking an antidepressant such as Zyban; (3) controlling stimuli associated with smoking—for example, sensitizing the smoker to social cues that are linked to smoking, such as a social drink; and (4) going "cold turkey," that is, simply stopping smoking without making any major changes in their lifestyle. Lighter smokers usually have more success with going "cold turkey" than heavy smokers.

The province of Ontario is increasing its efforts to reduce smoking. The provincial government is proposing regulatory changes to prohibit the sale of flavoured tobacco products and is seeking increased penalties for selling tobacco to youth. There are also laws in place to ban smoking on playgrounds, sports fields, restaurant patios, and in bars . In general, public health interventions, such as the promotion of indoor and outdoor smoke-free policies, the enforcement of policies limiting tobacco availability, and increased prevention programs are central to efforts directed towards smoking cessation (Hanusik et al., 2012).

Studies indicate that when people do stop smoking, their risk of cancer is reduced. For example, a study revealed a decrease in lung cancer deaths after smoking cessation (Wakai et al., 2007). In this study, earlier cessation of smoking resulted in a lower rate of lung cancer.

Addiction

Addiction is a physical and/or psychological dependence on a drug. Experts on drug abuse use the term *addiction* to describe either physical and/or psychological dependence on the drug (CAMH, 2011). Like drug and alcohol abusers, gamblers become completely preoccupied with gambling and pursue it compulsively despite adverse consequences. Run-ins with the law often accompany drug and alcohol addiction. Although gambling is a legally sanctioned government-run activity, individuals who gamble compulsively often experience financial ruin and exhibit antisocial behaviours. In 2014, almost 32 000 Canadians made helpline calls regarding gambling concerns. Almost 100 government-funded treatment agencies/entities and some 183 full-time-equivalent problem gambling counsellors were available to treat almost 7000 clients—and these clients sought help mainly for their own problem, rather than for someone else's gambling problem (Canadian Gambling Council, 2015). In an effort to provide supports for people with dependence on gambling, responsible gambling (RG) information terminals and on-site support centres are available across Canada.

According to Holden (2012), addiction is a maladaptive response to an underlying condition such as the non-specific inability to cope with the world. Addiction does not meet the criteria specified for a core disease entity, such as the presence of a primary measurable deviation from an anatomical or physiological norm. In fact, medicalizing addiction has not led to any management advances at the individual level. The requirement for facilitating help with addiction is but a social problem that requires social intervention (Holden, 2012).

Alcohol consumption is responsible for substantial increases in morbidity, mortality, and social problems in both developing and developed countries (Rehm et al., 2010). For Canada, the mortality burden attributable to alcohol consumption is large, as well as unnecessary. This mortality burden could be substantially reduced in a short period of time if effective public health policies were implemented (Shield et al., 2012). Because of the considerable harm caused by alcohol consumption, during the 63rd World Health Assembly held in May 2010, the World Health Organization agreed to a global strategy for reducing the harmful use of alcohol. The strategy focuses on strengthening reliable information about alcohol consumption and recognizing alcohol-related harms, and on effectively disseminating this information. Each member country, such as Canada, has the responsibility to monitor its own alcohol consumption. The progress of the strategy was assessed at the 66th World Health Assembly in 2013, where it was reported that "[a]n increasing number of countries are developing or reformulating national alcohol policies and progress has been made in the collection and use of national data" (WHO, 2013).

Addiction affects many people. One such group that has not received much attention is the affected family members (AFM) who are at a high risk of ill health (Orford et al., 2013). It is evident that AFMs bear substantial personal and household family costs. A study of more than 25 000 AFMs in the United States found that these people contributed to significantly higher health care costs over a two-year period compared to family members of individuals who had illnesses such as asthma or diabetes (Ray, Mertens, & Weisner, 2009).

Recovery from alcohol addiction is often unpredictable. Terrion (2013), a Canadian researcher at the University of Ottawa, explored aspects of the academic experience of post-secondary students in recovery. The researcher explored several variables, including the identity formation process, the development of relationships, and the use of support services. The researcher concluded that social and personal relationships are important to both abstinence and academic success for students in recovery. For example, positive and supportive relationships—with peers in school, with peers and family members outside of school, with professors, and with members of support groups such as Alcoholics Anonymous (AA)—appeared to be central to the experience of both recovery and post-secondary education for the participants in this study (Terrion, 2013).

One of the main treatment modalities is Alcoholics Anonymous (AA), a movement that has experienced unmeasured success. AA is a fellowship of men and women who share their experiences, strengths, and hopes with each other so that each may help others to solve their common problems and help others to recover from alcoholism (Alcoholics Anonymous, 2013).

Relapse, or a return to heavy drinking following a period of abstinence, occurs in many drinkers who have undergone alcoholism treatment. Preventing relapse, or at least minimizing its extent, is a prerequisite for any attempt to facilitate successful, long term changes in addictive behaviours (Hendershot et al., 2011). Three decades after its introduction, the Relapse Prevention (RP) Model remains an influential cognitive-behavioural approach in the treatment and study of addiction (Marlatt, 1996). The model suggests that immediate determinants such as high-risk situations and covert antecedents, including urges and cravings, can contribute to relapse. The RP model combines numerous client-centred intervention strategies, specific and global, that allow the therapist and client to address carefully each step of the relapse process (Larimer, Palmer, & Marlatt, 1999). A study conducted by Hibbert and Best (2011) involved a group of 53 recovering problem drinkers. The results indicated that those in recovery can expect to experience significant improvements in many aspects of their lives as abstinence duration increases. This result goes far toward establishing much needed hope in the client.

critical thinking

Do you abuse drugs? Respond yes or no to the following items:

Yes	No	
_____	_____	I have gotten into problems because of using drugs.
_____	_____	Using alcohol or other drugs has made my college or university life unhappy at times.
_____	_____	Drinking alcohol or taking other drugs has been a factor in my losing a job.
_____	_____	Drinking alcohol or taking other drugs has interfered with my studying for exams.
_____	_____	Drinking alcohol or taking drugs has jeopardized my academic performance.
_____	_____	My ambition is not as strong since I've been drinking a lot or taking drugs.
_____	_____	Drinking or taking drugs has caused me to have difficulty sleeping.
_____	_____	I have felt remorse after drinking or taking drugs.
_____	_____	I crave a drink or other drugs at a definite time of the day.
_____	_____	I want a drink or another drug the next morning.
_____	_____	I have had a complete or partial loss of memory as a result of drinking or using other drugs.
_____	_____	Drinking or using other drugs is affecting my reputation.
_____	_____	I have been in the hospital or another institution because of my drinking or taking drugs.

College and university students who responded yes to items similar to these on the Rutgers Collegiate Abuse Screening test were more likely to be substance abusers than those who answered no. If you responded yes to just one of the 13 items on this screening test, consider going to your health or counselling centre for further screening.

To this point, we have studied a number of ideas about physical development, health, and wellness in early adulthood. For a review, see the Reach Your Learning Outcomes section at the end of this chapter.

Sexuality

LO3 Examine the concept of sexuality in young adults.

- **Sexual Activity in Emerging Adulthood**
- **Sexually Transmitted Infections**
- **Violence against Women**

Sexual awareness, feelings, and expressions—as fundamental to health as rest, nutrition, and exercise—develop over the life span. This is true for all of us, regardless of age, gender, sexual orientation, culture, career choices, or any other components that form our identities. Intimacy, commitments, marriage, and children are primary concerns for young adults.

In earlier chapters, we explored elements of childhood cognition. We learned that children develop self-esteem, learn to think critically, and make decisions. Positive early childhood development has a profound impact on healthy adult sexuality, attitudes, and activity. Freedom from harmful physical, emotional, and sexual abuse, combined with good nurturing and positive social interaction, contribute to the child's ability to make a successful transition from childhood to adolescence.

Similarly, a healthy transition from adolescence to adulthood is fostered by positive social interactions (Polan & Taylor, 2011). Media gender-role stereotyping, the linkage of violence and sex, unrealistic body images, combined with the prevalence of homophobia, complicate the adolescent transition to adulthood by creating a climate of fear, fascination, excitement, and temptation. Developmental milestones in cognition, including the ability to see other perspectives, reason abstractly, communicate effectively, and develop relationships with peers and adults, occur against a backdrop of mixed messages (Polan & Taylor, 2011). In addition, the young adult faces challenging realities, such as sexual orientation, unwanted pregnancies, miscarriages, addictions, infertility, poverty, violence (including sexual violence), artificial insemination and other reproductive technologies, infertility, and reproductive diseases (including cancer and endometriosis), which are rudely added to the experience of young adults as they are launched from the family home (Berger, 2014).

Sexual Activity in Emerging Adulthood

At the beginning of emerging adulthood (age 18), surveys indicate that slightly more than 60 percent of individuals have experienced sexual intercourse; by the end of emerging adulthood (age 25), most (80 percent) individuals have had sexual intercourse (Lefkowitz & Gillen, 2006).

Emerging adulthood, therefore, is a time frame during which individuals are both sexually active and unmarried (Lefkowitz & Gillen, 2006). Several large scale studies have provided data on the percentage of Canadian teens who have experienced sexual intercourse at least once (SOGC, 2012). According to self-reports in the 2009/2010 Canadian Community Health Survey (CCHS), two-thirds of 15- to 24-year-olds reported having sexual intercourse at least once. A third of the age group not only had initial sexual intercourse when they were younger than 17, but also had more than one partner in the past year (Rotermann, 2012). A larger percentage of sexually active males than females reported having sexual intercourse with more than one partner. Condom use increased between 2003 and 2009/2010, particularly among those reporting just one sexual partner. Despite this particular increase, more than three in ten young adults did not use condoms the last time they had intercourse (Rotermann, 2012).

Sexual Orientation

Until the end of the nineteenth century, it was generally believed that people were either heterosexual or homosexual. Today, it is more accepted to view sexual orientation not as an either/or dichotomy, but as a continuum from exclusive male–female relations to exclusive same-sex relations (Strong et al., 2008) (see Figure 13.4). Some individuals are also *bisexual;* that is, sexually attracted to people of both sexes.

Attitudes and laws related to homosexuality today reflect a history of controversy and struggle. In 1948, Canada ruled that homosexual activity was illegal. In the mid-1950s, homosexuality was considered to be a psychological disorder; that designation was discontinued in the 1970s. In 1968, former Prime Minister Pierre Elliott Trudeau decriminalized homosexual intimacy when he decreed, "The government has no business in the bedrooms of the nation." In the early 1990s, gay activists fought hard to obtain legal status for their unions, and in 2006, the Canadian government proclaimed same-sex marriages to be legal (Macionis & Gerber, 2014). A 2009 Angus Reid poll revealed that 66 percent of Canadians believe that sexual relations between two people of the same sex is morally acceptable (Angus Reid, 2009). Toronto's Pride Parade has a 35-year history and continues to grow and renew each year. The organizers welcome all Canadians to celebrate their victories, to honour their history, and to continue to fight for justice (Pride Toronto, 2016).

Figure 13.4

The Continuum of Sexual Orientation

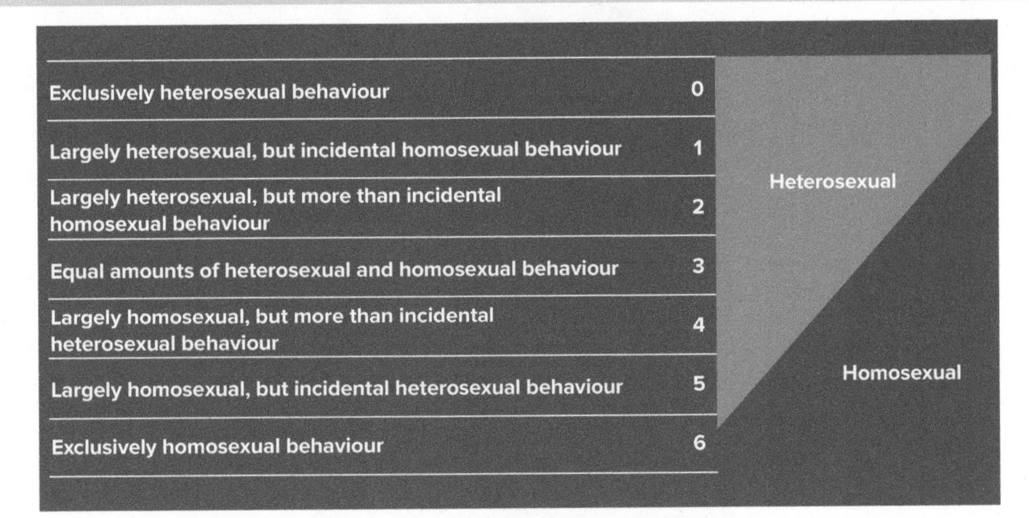

The continuum of sexual orientation ranges from exclusive heterosexuality, which Kinsey and associates (1948) rated as 0, to exclusive homosexuality (6). People who are about equally attracted to both sexes (ratings 2 to 4) are bisexual.

All people, regardless of their sexual orientation, have similar physiological responses during sexual arousal and seem to be aroused by the same types of tactile stimulation. Investigators typically find no differences among lesbian, gay, and bisexual individuals and heterosexuals in a wide range of attitudes, behaviours, and adjustments (Fingerhut & Peplau, 2013). Previous studies have reported that sexual minorities, compared to heterosexual individuals, are more likely to experience mental health problems (Ueno, 2010). In fact, sexual minority adults report significantly higher levels of depressive symptoms and drug use compared to heterosexual youth (Hatzenbuehler, McLaughlin, & Nolen-Hocksema, 2008). A community sample of 246 LGBT youth (aged 16 to 20 years) was studied. Findings revealed that a history of attempted suicide, impulsivity, prospective LGBT victimization, and low social support were all associated with an increased risk of suicidal ideation (Liu & Mustanski, 2011). A special concern involving sexual minority individuals is the hate crimes and stigma-related experiences they encounter (Clark, 2014). In one study, approximately 20 percent of sexual minority adults stated they had experienced a person or property crime related to their sexual orientation, and about 50 percent stated that they had experienced verbal harassment (Herek, 2009).

Researchers have explored the possible biological basis of same-sex relations (James, 2005). The results of hormone studies have been inconsistent. If gay males are given male sex hormones (androgens), their sexual orientation doesn't change; their sexual desire merely increases. A very early prenatal critical period might influence sexual orientation (Hines, 2013). If this critical-period hypothesis turns out to be correct, it would explain why clinicians have found that sexual orientation is difficult, if not impossible, to modify.

An individual's sexual orientation—same-sex, heterosexual, or bisexual—is most likely determined by a combination of genetic, hormonal, cognitive, and environmental factors (Berger, 2014). Most experts on same-sex relations believe that no one factor alone causes sexual orientation, and the relative weight of each factor can vary from one individual to the next.

In effect, no one knows exactly why some individuals are lesbian, gay, or bisexual. Nevertheless, scientists have discounted some of the myths. For example, children raised by gay or lesbian parents or couples are no more likely to be lesbian, gay, or bisexual than are children raised by heterosexual parents. There also is no evidence that being a gay male is caused by a dominant mother or a weak father, or that being a lesbian is caused by girls choosing male role models.

What likely determines an individual's sexual preference?

Attitudes and Behaviour of Lesbians and Gay Males

Many gender differences that appear in heterosexual relationships occur in same-sex relationships (Savin-Williams, 2015; Savin-Williams & Ream, 2007). For example, like heterosexual women, lesbians have fewer sexual partners than gay men, and lesbians have less permissive attitudes about casual sex outside a primary relationship than gay men (Fingerhut & Peplau, 2013). In a study that compared same-sex couples with opposite-sex dating, engaged, and married dyads, no differences were found in attachment security (Roisman et al., 2008). In this study, one difference between dyads was that lesbians were the most effective at working together in positive ways during laboratory observations.

Sexually Transmitted Infections

Sexually transmitted infections (STIs) are diseases and infections that are contracted primarily through sexual contact. This contact is not limited to vaginal intercourse, but includes oral–genital and anal–genital contact as well. STIs are an increasing health problem. Among the main STIs individuals can get are bacterial infections (such as gonorrhea and syphilis), chlamydia, and two STIs caused by viruses—genital herpes and AIDS (acquired immune deficiency syndrome). Some infections are asymptomatic, especially in the early stages.

Human Papillomavirus (HPV)

Recall from Chapter 11 that **HPV** is thought to be the most common sexually transmitted disease. Many types have been identified, some leading to cancer, others to anogenital warts. Fortunately, there are two vaccines now available and recommended for use in Canada. The first is Gardasil which has been approved for use by males and females between the ages of 9 to 26. The second is Cervarix, which has been approved for females only between the ages of 10 and 25 years (PHAC, 2011; PHAC 2012).

These vaccines offer protection against the type of HPV responsible for 70 percent of cervical cancers. More than 70 percent of Canadians will have at least one HPV infection in their lifetime (PHAC, 2012). HPV is thought of as the silent infection, as the symptoms may go unnoticed and there are no obvious signs of infection, which may be either active or inactive. Consultation with a physician is important for treating anogenital warts. Having routine Pap (Papanicolaou) tests, practising safer sex, reducing the number of partners, and receiving vaccinations are important in screening for and reducing the risk of HPV (Health Canada, 2007c). HPV, even when treated, is generally thought not to go away.

Gonorrhea

Gonorrhea, commonly called the "drip" or the "clap," is the second most commonly reported STI (PHAC, 2013a; PHAC, 2015b). Like HPV, most men and women do not experience symptoms. Gonorrhea is caused by a bacterium from the *Gonococcus* family, which thrives in the moist mucous membranes lining the mouth, throat, vagina, cervix, urethra, and anal tract. The bacterium is spread by contact between the infected moist membranes of one individual and the membranes of another (PHAC, 2015b).

Gonorrhea can be successfully treated in its early stages with penicillin or other antibiotics. Reported rates between 2003 and 2012 have increased by 38.9 percent from 26.0 to 36.2 per 100 000 (PHAC, 2015a).

Syphilis

Syphilis is a sexually transmitted disease caused by the bacterium *Treponema pallidum,* a member of the spirochete family. Like other STIs, it too has increased in incidence, up 101.0 percent from 2003 to 2012, with a jump from 2.9 to 5.8 per 100 000 (PHAC, 2015a). The spirochete needs a warm, moist environment to survive, and it is transmitted by penile–vaginal, oral–genital, or anal contact. It can also be transmitted from a pregnant woman to her fetus after the fourth month of pregnancy. If the mother is treated before this time with penicillin, the syphilis will not be transmitted to the fetus.

In its early stages, syphilis can be effectively treated with penicillin. In its advanced stages, syphilis can cause paralysis or even death.

Chlamydia

Chlamydia, one of the most common of all sexually transmitted diseases, is named for *Chlamydia trachomatis,* an organism that spreads by sexual contact and infects the genital organs of both sexes. The number of reported cases of chlamydia increased 57.6 percent from 2003 to 2012, a rise of 189.6 to 298.7 per 100 000 (PHAC, 2015a). Both males and females are at risk of contracting chlamydia, with those aged 20 to 24 showing the highest rates of contraction (PHAC, 2015a). The greatest number of infections is found in individuals 15 to 24 years old (SOGC, 2011).

Males with chlamydia often get treatment early because of noticeable symptoms in the genital region. However, females are more often asymptomatic in the early stages, increasing the risk of the disease being unknowingly spread (PHAC, 2013a). Also, when females go untreated, the chlamydia spreads to the upper reproductive tract where it can cause pelvic inflammatory disease (PID). The resultant scarring of tissue in the fallopian tubes can result in infertility or ectopic pregnancies (tubal pregnancies, or a pregnancy in which the fertilized egg is implanted outside the uterus). Some researchers suggest it is the number one preventable cause of female infertility. Chlamydia can also be passed from mother to infant in childbirth (SOGC, 2011; PHAC, 2013b).

Genital Herpes

Genital herpes is a highly contagious sexually transmitted disease caused by a large family of viruses with many different strains. The actual number of cases is not known, but the risk factors include unprotected oral, genital, and anal intercourse (Li et al., 2008; PHAC, 2013a). These strains produce other, non–sexually transmitted diseases, such as chicken pox and mononucleosis. Herpes is the single most prevalent STI, affecting one in five Canadians (Branswell, 2013). Three to five days after contact, itching and tingling can occur, followed by an eruption of sores and blisters. The attacks can last up to three weeks and may recur in a few weeks or a few years.

Although such drugs as acyclovir can be used to alleviate symptoms, there is no known cure for herpes. Therefore, people infected with herpes often experience severe emotional distress in addition to considerable physical discomfort. The virus can be transmitted through non-latex condoms and foams, making infected individuals reluctant to engage in sex, angry about the unpredictability of their lives, and fearful that they will not be able to cope with the pain of the next attack. For these reasons, support groups for victims of herpes have been established.

critical thinking

Caroline contracted genital herpes from her boyfriend, whom she had been dating for the past three years. After breaking off that relationship and spending some time on her own, Caroline began dating Charles. Before becoming sexually involved with him, Caroline told Charles about her herpes infection, thinking that it was the right thing to do. Charles seemed accepting of the news, but soon after the discussion began treating Caroline differently. He became distant and cold toward her and eventually broke off their relationship saying that it "just wasn't working." Caroline firmly believed it was because she had told him about the herpes.

Caroline later met Jeff, whom she really liked and wanted to start dating. As they became closer to developing a sexual relationship, Caroline felt that she should tell Jeff about the herpes, but she was afraid that he also would abandon her. She thought that if she arranged it so that they never had sexual contact when she had herpes blisters (the time when infecting someone else is most likely to occur), she could protect him. She also thought that if they used latex condoms for protection, he would be safe, even though condoms can break.

Is Caroline making the right decision? If Caroline came to you for advice, what advice would you give? What should Caroline say, if anything, to Jeff? If Caroline did tell Jeff, and he did end their relationship, would telling him have been a mistake? Does Jeff have a right to know? Does Caroline have a right to privacy?

HIV and AIDS

No single STI has had a greater impact on sexual behaviour, or created more public fear in the last several decades, than infection with the human immunodeficiency virus (HIV) (Strong et al., 2008). HIV is a sexually transmitted infection that destroys the body's immune system. Once infected with HIV, the virus breaks down and overpowers the immune system, which leads to **AIDS** (acquired immune deficiency syndrome). HIV is transmitted through unprotected sexual intercourse and needle-sharing, and through pregnancy, delivery, and from an infected mother to her breast-fed child. An individual sick with AIDS has such a weakened immune system that a common cold can be life threatening. Medications can enhance the quality of life for patients with AIDS, but if left untreated, AIDS is fatal (PHAC, 2015a).

By the end of 2014, an estimated 75 000 Canadians were living with HIV infection, including AIDS. Of these, about 28 percent were not aware of their infection (CATIE, 2016; PHAC, 2014). The incidence of HIV and AIDS has generally decreased in Canada. However, the rates of infection in First Nations and Inuit populations, where injection drug use continues to be a key mode of HIV transmission, are steadily increasing. As well, Aboriginal people are being infected at younger age than the general population. Although the number of women contracting the disease is increasing, street youth, especially those men who have sex with men and those who inject drugs, are most vulnerable (PHAC, 2014).

Globally, the total number of individuals who have contracted HIV reached 71 million in 2014; of those, 36.9 million remain alive (WHO, 2016). The greatest concern about AIDS is in sub-Saharan Africa, where it has reached epidemic proportions (Stephen Lewis, 2006: WHO, 2016).

Because of education and the development of more-effective drug treatments, deaths due to AIDS in North America have begun to decline. Contrast the figures in Canada, where an estimated 3175 new infections occurred in 2011, with figures in Africa, where about 1.5 million people contracted the disease in 2013 (AVERT, 2015). According to Statistics Canada, the national population is estimated to be 36 155 487 as of April 2016. Should the AIDS plague be of the same magnitude in Canada as in Africa, whole cities would be wiped out. For example, Montreal, the second largest city in Canada, has a population of a little over 1.6 million people. Contrast this with the number of people who died of AIDS in sub-Saharan Africa in 2013—1.1 million (AVERT, 2015).

Protecting against STIs

Just asking a potential partner about his or her prior sexual experience or their sex-related behaviour does not guarantee protection from HIV and other sexually transmitted diseases. For example, in one investigation, 181 participants (79 percent women, and 21 percent men) were asked questions about their interpersonal relationships, including inquiries about the content of their sexual partner's discussions about sexual history (Mullinax, 2013). The study showed that while 52 percent reported talking to their partners about STIs, over 32 percent did not have this discussion with their partners before having sex. In terms of the content of these discussions, only half of the participants clarified for what types of STIs they had been tested. The majority of participants did not ask for proof of STI testing nor request that STI testing be done. Actually, 4.4 percent of participants knowingly lied about their STI status to their partners, while 34.6 percent reported having no STIs, although they had never been tested (Mullinax, 2013).

The following are some good strategies for protecting against HIV and other sexually transmitted infections:

- *Know your and your partner's risk status.* Anyone who has had previous sexual activity with another person might have contracted an STI without being aware of it. Spend time getting to know a prospective partner before you have sex. Use this time to inform the other person of your STI status and inquire about your partner's. Remember that many people lie about their STI status.
- *Obtain medical examinations.* Many experts recommend that couples who want to begin a sexual relationship should have a medical checkup to rule out STIs before they engage in sex. Contact your family doctor, campus health service, or a public health clinic.
- *Have protected, not unprotected, sex.* When correctly used, latex condoms help to prevent many STIs from being transmitted. Condoms are most effective in preventing gonorrhea, syphilis, chlamydia, and HIV. They are less effective against the spread of herpes (Norton et al., 2012).
- *Do not have sex with multiple partners.* One of the best predictors of getting an STI is having sex with multiple partners. Having more than one sex partner elevates the likelihood that you will encounter an infected partner.

Violence against Women

Presently, at the federal level, the main source of information regarding violence against women is the Statistics Canada's omnibus Crime Victimization Survey. According to this 2014 survey, women recorded a higher rate of violent victimization (85 incidents per 1000 women) than men (67 per 1000 men) (Perrault, 2015). However, it should be noted that the overall rates of violent victimization between 2004 and 2014 declined for both women (from 102 to 85 incidents per 1000 women) and men (from 111 to 67 incidents per 1000 men) (Perrault, 2015). The territories have consistently recorded the highest rate in the country of police-reported violence against women.

Sexual Assault

The term sexual assault refers to all incidents of unwanted sexual activity including sexual attacks and sexual touching. Too often, sex involves the exercise of power (Clark & Carroll, 2008). According to Sinha (2013), the rate of police-reported sexual assaults against women increased in 2010 and remained stable in 2011. Family-related physical and sexual assaults have declined modestly in recent years (Canada Statistics, 2015). However, of every 100 sexual assault incidents, only 6 are reported to the police (Sexual Assault and Rape Statistics, Canada, 2014). It is noteworthy that a significant proportion of sexual assaults are never brought to the attention of the police even though legislative changes have been introduced to address the specific types of crimes where women are predominantly the victims (Sinha, 2013).

The estimates of sexual violence rates among young women are generated primarily from university and college campuses. The Canadian Federation of Students (2015) claims that sexual assaults occur most frequently during the first eight weeks of classes. Most rapes are committed by someone known to the victim, and half of these assaults occur on dates. The high level of under-reporting of assaults leads one to believe that the occurrence of sexual violence is underestimated (Canadian Federation of Students, 2015).

Sexual assault rates among Aboriginal females are high. A rate of 115 incidents of sexual assault per 1000 population were recorded, much higher than the rate of 35 per 1000 recorded by their non-Aboriginal counterparts (Perrault, 2015).

critical thinking

Has violence, particularly dating violence, become so prevalent that it is considered the norm? What would you do if you or someone you know experienced violence or rape? What strategies could be put in place in your school to address violence against women and sexual harassment? What role does the Internet play in this? Outline a campaign against dating violence that could be implemented in a high school. What benefits and drawbacks might be encountered in such a program?

Why is violence in a dating relationship so prevalent? The Nova Scotia Advisory Council on the Status of Women (2013) cites four contributing factors:

- *Patriarchal theory:* Men are socialized to exhibit dominance in relationships. Despite changing gender values, there are still some men who feel it is their right to punish, control, or batter their partners.
- *Peer pressure:* Boys often feel pressure from their peers to be sexually aggressive, which can contribute to sexually abusive behaviour and date rape.
- *Intergenerational violence:* Children who are victims of family violence or who witness abuse in the home often repeat abusive patterns in adolescence and adulthood. These young people often believe violence is an acceptable, or at least tolerable, means of resolving conflict.
- *Social learning theory:* The media bombard today's youth with violent and sexist images that convey the notion that violence is acceptable.

Sexual Harassment

Sexual harassment takes many forms—from sexist remarks and covert physical contact (patting, brushing against the body) to blatant propositions, stalking, and sexual assaults (Leaper & Brown, 2008; Mitchell, Koien, & Crow, 2008). It is a manifestation of power and the domination of one person by another, and millions of women experience such harassment each year in work and educational settings. The elimination of such exploitation requires the creation of work and academic environments that provide equal opportunities to develop a career and obtain an education in a climate free of sexual harassment (Das, 2008; Rospenda, Richman, & Shannon, 2008). Although sexual harassment of men by women occurs less frequently than the sexual harassment of women by men, it has equally devastating consequences.

CONNECTING development to life

Violence against Aboriginal Women—A Continuing Outrage

The scale and severity of violence faced by Indigenous women and girls in Canada—including First Nations, Inuit and Metis—constitutes a national human crisis (Amnesty International, 2014). A 2014 report by the RCMP concluded that 1017 aboriginal women had been murdered between 1980 and 2012, and another 164 were missing across Canada (The Canadian Press, 2016). On December 8, 2015, the new federal Liberal government announced the launch of a National Inquiry to address the high number of missing and murdered indigenous women and girls. Prime Minister Justin Trudeau aims to establish a new "nation to nation" relationship with indigenous people. The government began by engaging survivors, family members, and loved ones of victims, as well as the National Aboriginal provincial and territorial representatives, to seek their views on the design and scope of the proposed inquiry. These meetings were spearheaded by the Honourable Carolyn Bennett, Minister of Ingenious and Northern Affairs, the Honourable Jody Wilson-Raybould, Minister of Justice and Attorney General of Canada, and the Honourable Patty Hajdu, Minister of Status of Women. Meetings were initiated across Canada. Such measures are being taken because the government of Canada believes that a proper inquiry can be designed only after hearing from those directly affected (Government of Canada News Release, 2015). The Trudeau Liberal government will complete its consultations after seeking input from all concerned on what a national inquiry should look like and what it should attempt to accomplish (The Canadian Press, 2016).

Generally speaking, Aboriginal women, in contrast to the rest of the Canadian female population, have an extremely high likelihood of being victimized (Sinha, 2013). The Aboriginal female population grew by 20 percent between 2006 and 2011, more than four times the growth of the non-Aboriginal female population at 4.8 percent (Milan, 2015). A serious danger to the well-being of many Aboriginal women is the violence they experience in their own homes, their communities, and in Canadian society. The high rates of violence that Aboriginal women experience are related not only to lower levels of socio-economic status, but to exposure to the residential school system where many experienced sexual, physical, and emotional abuse (Halseth, 2013). Furthermore, Aboriginal women face the disadvantages of intergenerational legacies of racism, sexual violence, intimate partner violence, and physical violence (Johnson & Colpitts, 2013). Some Aboriginal women reported having experienced multiple incidents of violence (Brennan, 2011). For many of these women, the legacy of these abuses include damaged self-esteem and an increase in alcohol and drug abuse. Prolonged exposure to abuse and neglect has been associated with a wide range of many complex mental issues. A few such disorders include post-traumatic stress disorder, psychiatric ailments, and chronic self-destructive behaviours (Halseath, 2013).

The disproportionally high number of Aboriginal women in Canada who have either gone missing or been murdered has been identified as a most serious issue (Sinha, 2013). It is clear that the National Inquiry must concentrate heavily upon support services for these women. Improving the health of Aboriginal women is critical, not only for the women themselves, but for the revitalization of their families and communities.

To this point, we have discussed a number of ideas about sexuality in early adulthood. For a review, see the Reach Your Learning Outcomes section at the end of this chapter.

Cognitive Development

LO4 Analyze the cognitive changes that occur in early adulthood.

- **Piaget's View**
- **Creativity**

Are young adults more advanced in their thinking than adolescents are? Let's examine what Piaget and others have said about this intriguing question.

Piaget's View

Piaget believed that an adolescent and an adult think *qualitatively* in the same way. That is, Piaget argued that formal operational thought (more logical, abstract, and idealistic than the concrete operational thinking of 7- to 11-year-olds) is entered into in early adolescence at approximately 11 to 15 years of age. Piaget believed that young adults are more *quantitatively* advanced in their thinking in the sense that they have more knowledge than adolescents. He also believed, as do information-processing psychologists, that adults especially increase their knowledge in a specific area, such as a physicist's understanding of physics or a financial analyst's knowledge of finance.

Some developmentalists believe many individuals do not consolidate their formal operational thinking until adulthood. That is, they may begin to plan and hypothesize about intellectual problems in adolescence, but they become more systematic and sophisticated at this as young adults. Nonetheless, many adults do not think in formal operational ways at all (Keating, 2004).

Realistic and Pragmatic Thinking

Other developmentalists believe that the idealism that Piaget described as part of formal operational thinking decreases in early adulthood. This occurs especially as young adults move into the world of work and face the constraints of reality (Labouvie-Vief, 1986).

K. Warner Schaie and Sherry Willis (2000) proposed a related perspective of adult cognitive change. They concluded that it is unlikely that adults go beyond the powerful methods of scientific thinking characteristic of the formal operational stage.

However, Schaie argued that adults do progress beyond adolescents in their use of intellect. For example, he said that in early adulthood, individuals often switch from acquiring knowledge to applying knowledge. This occurs especially as individuals pursue long-term career goals and attempt to achieve success in their work.

Reflective and Relativistic Thinking

William Perry (1999) also described some changes in cognition that take place in early adulthood. He said that adolescents often view the world in terms of polarities—right/wrong, we/they, good/bad. As youth move into adulthood, they gradually move away from this type of absolute thinking as they become aware of the diverse opinions and multiple perspectives of others. Thus, in Perry's view, the absolute, dualistic thinking (either/or) of adolescence gives way to the reflective, relativistic thinking of adulthood. Other developmentalists also observe that reflective thinking is an important indicator of cognitive change in young adults (Fischer & Bidell, 2006).

Expanding on Perry's view, Gisela Labouvie-Vief (2006, 2008) proposed that the increasing complexity of cultures in the past century has generated a greater need for reflective, more complex thinking that takes into account the changing nature of knowledge and challenges. She also emphasizes that key aspects of cognitive development in emerging adulthood include deciding on a particular world-view, recognizing that the world-view is subjective, and understanding that diverse world-views should be acknowledged. In her perspective, considerable individual variation characterizes the thinking of emerging adults, with the highest level of thinking attained only by some. She argues that the level of education emerging adults achieve especially influences the likelihood that they will maximize their thinking potential. Labouvie-Vief and Studer (2010) argue that reflective thinking continues to increase and becomes more internal and less contextual in middle ages.

As we see next, some theorists have pieced together some of these different aspects of thinking and proposed a new qualitative stage of cognitive development.

Is There a Fifth, Post-formal Stage?

Post-formal thought is qualitatively different from Piaget's formal operational thought (Moshman, 2006). **Post-formal thought** involves understanding that the correct answer to a problem requires reflective thinking and can vary from one situation to another, and that the search for truth is often an ongoing, never-ending process (Kitchener, King, & DeLuca, 2006). Also part of post-formal thought is the belief that solutions to problems need to be realistic and that emotion and subjective factors can influence thinking.

What is post-formal thought like in practice? As young adults engage in more reflective judgment when solving problems, they might think deeply about many aspects of politics, their career and work, relationships, and other areas of life (Labouvie-Vief & Diehl, 1999). They might understand that what might be the best solution to a problem at work (with a co-worker or boss) might not be the best solution at home (with a romantic partner). Many young adults also become more skeptical about the existence of a single truth, and often are not willing to accept an answer as final. They also often recognize that thinking can't just be abstract, but rather has to be realistic and pragmatic. And many young adults understand that emotions can play a role in thinking—for example, that they are likely to think more clearly when they are in a calm and collected state than when they are angry and highly aroused.

How strong is the research evidence for a fifth, post-formal stage of cognitive development? Researchers have found that young adults are more likely to engage in this post-formal thinking than adolescents are (Commons & Bresette, 2006). The fifth stage is controversial, however, and some critics argue that the research evidence has yet to be provided to document it as a qualitatively more advanced stage than formal operational thought. Another criticism is that rather than a discrete way of thinking, post-formal thought may be a collection of attitudes about knowledge.

Creativity

Young adulthood is a time of great creativity for some people. At the age of 30, Thomas Edison invented the phonograph, Hans Christian Anderson wrote his first volume of fairy tales, and Mozart composed *The Marriage of Figaro.*

More recently, researchers have found that creativity peaks in adulthood and then declines, but that the peak often occurs in the forties. However, qualifying any conclusion about age and creative accomplishments are (1) the magnitude of the decline in productivity, (2) contrasts across creative domains, and (3) individual differences in lifetime output (Simonton, 1996).

Even though a decline in creative contributions is often found in the fifties and later, the decline is not as great as commonly thought. An impressive array of creative accomplishments occurs in late adulthood. One of the most remarkable examples of creative accomplishment in late adulthood can be found in the life of Henri Chevreul. After a distinguished career as a physicist, Chevreul switched fields in his nineties to become a pioneer in gerontological research. He published his last research paper just a year prior to his death—at the age of 103!

Pictured below are three notables whose creative talents have made an impact on three diverse fields: Dr. Susan Tighe (engineering), Sarah Polley (film), and Nikki Yanofsky (music).

Courtesy of Susan Tighe

In 2006, Dr. Susan Tighe, Ph.D., P.Eng., a professor of civil and environmental engineering at the University of Waterloo, was recognized as one of the top 40 under 40 in Canada for her creative work in civil engineering. Then, in 2007, she was awarded one of the Top 40 under 40 Awards for Vision and Leadership. In 2008, Tighe was identified as one of Canada's 80 Women to Watch by *Chatelaine* magazine. And in 2009, Tighe was selected as one of the Region of Waterloo's inaugural Top 40 under 40. She won the Ontario Premier's Excellence award for her research in infrastructure management, pavement, and transportation. Safety and environment concerns frame her work; for example, she is working to develop environmentally quiet pavements from recycled tires. She has written many scholarly articles and is currently affiliated with many professional boards and committees at the University of Waterloo.

Moviestore collection Ltd / Alamy Stock Photo

Sarah Polley played the lead in *Road to Avonlea* when she was a child, won a Gemini Award for her performance in the TV series *Straight Up* in 1996, and has starred in many films, including *The Sweet Hereafter.* She has shunned Hollywood, choosing to participate in non-commercial, independent projects. She received critical acclaim for her debut direction of *Away from Her,* based on a short story written by Alice Munro. *Away from Her* won best director and best feature film of 2006 at the Directors Guild of Canada Awards. In between directing *Take this Waltz,* a romantic drama, Polly starred in the science fiction movie *Splice,* about gene-combining experiments. Of her varied choices, Polly says, "I think my only criteria for choosing a role is if it's in a film I would want to go see." She is now an acclaimed director and committed political activist.

VALENTIN FLAURAUD / POOL/EPA/Newscom

Nikki Yanofsky, a musical prodigy, debuted at the Montreal International Jazz Festival in 2006, at the age of 16. Both a jazz-pop singer and a composer, she sang “I Believe” in the closing ceremonies of the 2010 Olympics and the opening ceremony of the Paralympics. In addition to her music career, Nikki is an ambassador for the Montreal Children’s Hospital, the Children’s Wish Foundation, and Music Counts. She has raised money for Haiti and to assist organizations such as War Child and World Vision Canada. September 2013 saw the release of her single and video “Something New” produced by Quincy Jones. What is evident to the listener, whether to her music or an interview, is her engaging enthusiasm.

Any consideration of decline in creativity with age requires consideration of the domain involved. In such fields as philosophy and history, older adults often show as much creativity as when they were in their thirties and forties. By contrast, in such fields as lyric poetry, abstract math, and theoretical physics, the peak of creativity is often reached in the twenties or thirties.

There also is extensive individual variation in the lifetime output of creative individuals. Typically, as illustrated by the three examples above, the most productive creators in any field are far more prolific than their least productive counterparts. However, those whom society recognizes or who become icons of their generation are as much a product of social and political factors as of talent. For example, the great writers of the Harlem Renaissance, all of whom were black, were not widely read by mainstream Americans until the middle or late 1970s. Now, no course in contemporary literature would exclude the writings of Langston Hughes and Zora Neale Hurston. As well, women authors and artists traditionally have not received the same recognition as their male counterparts. Pop icons such as Céline Dion, Justin Bieber, and Drake are very much the products of aggressive marketing strategies.

To this point, we have studied a number of ideas on cognitive development in early adulthood. For a review, see the Reach Your Learning Outcomes section at the end of this chapter.

Careers and Work

LO5 Explain the key dimensions of careers and work in early adulthood.

- **Developmental Changes**
- **Values and Careers**
- **The Occupational Outlook**
- **The Impact of Work**

At age 23, Joel graduated from university and accepted a job as a teacher at a Montreal high school. At 35, Marianne graduated from a community college and took a job as a computer programmer. At 25, Al and Shaohua graduated from nursing school and took part-time jobs in hospitals in Nova Scotia and Saskatoon. At 36, Anna has been contracted to teach English in both colleges and universities for each semester for the past six years; she would like a permanent job. Earning a living, choosing an occupation, establishing a career, and developing a career are important themes of early adulthood.

Developmental Changes

Children have idealistic fantasies about what they want to be when they grow up. For example, young children might want to be a superhero, a sports star, or a movie star. In the high school years, they often have begun to think about careers on a somewhat less idealistic basis. In their late teens and early twenties, career decision making usually turns more serious and practical as they explore different career possibilities and settle on the career they want to enter. Going to college or university often means choosing a major or specialization that is designed to lead to work in a particular field. From the mid-twenties through the remainder of early adulthood, individuals often seek to establish their emerging career in a particular field. They may work hard to move up the career ladder and improve their financial standing.

critical thinking

Take a few minutes and think about the career you want to pursue. What do you think the profile of an ideal job candidate in this career field would be? What would be the profile of a co-worker with whom you would like to work? How have your career decisions evolved? If you had an opportunity would you make any career changes?

Values and Careers

An important aspect of choosing a career is that it matches up with your values. When people know what they value most—what is important to them in life—they can refine their career choice more effectively. For example, one person values working in a career that involves helping others, and another prefers a career in which creativity is essential. Among the values that some individuals think are important in choosing a career are working with people they like, working in a career with prestige, making a lot of money, being happy, not having to work long hours, being mentally stimulated, having plenty of time for leisure pursuits, working in the right geographical location, and working where physical and mental health are important.

Other values that some individuals think are important when they make choices about their work life are related to the contribution they may make to society at large. They may join Doctors, Engineers, or Teachers Without Borders, or other organizations dedicated to improving the lives of others. Dr. Samatha Nutt's passion for the welfare of children in war-torn countries led her not only to visit countries and experience first-hand the devastation caused by war, but also to bring her awareness to the public arena by organizing her professional life in Canada in ways that engage others. This chapter's

Connecting through Social Policy features Dr. Nutt and the organization she founded, War Child. Her book *Damned Nations: Greed, Guns, Armies, and Aid* was released in 2011 (Nutt, 2016).

CONNECTING through Social Policy

Dr. Samantha Nutt

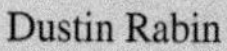

Dustin Rabin

Nothing affects policies, particularly economic policies, like disasters and war. To North Americans war brings about changes in economies and erosion of civil liberties, but to people who experience warfare in their homelands, such as the people of Syria, Iraq, Israel, Nigeria, and Darfur, war cripples economies, causes or contributes to famine, and contaminates resources. Further, war causes widespread psychological trauma. According to Dr. Samantha Nutt, war has "horrific implications for millions of people," and she wishes people could see military action through the eyes of a child (Hass, 2001; Nutt, 2007).

Can one Canadian influence change? Dr. Nutt believes that collectively we can make a difference to the lives of people affected by wars. To increase awareness of what happens to these women, children, and their families, Dr. Nutt tells their stories because she believes the "lessons of peace are best told through the stories of war" (Nutt, 2007). She tells the heart-wrenching story of how pre-adolescent boys find acquiring guns easier than obtaining water, or of a mother shot down in a pool of blood before her family and neighbours.

Dr. Nutt is a medical doctor with over a decade's experience working in war zones. Her work has always been aimed at improving the lives of women and children devastated by war. She believes that youth can effect change, and encourages students who want to do humanitarian work to get experience by working with or volunteering with international causes because, "once you have been in a war zone, your life changes, your perspective changes. It is impossible not to acknowledge that your life has been fundamentally altered." She is founder and executive-director of War Child, an educational and fundraising forum. When in Canada, she practises medicine with new immigrants, refugees, the poor, and young women (Hass, 2001). She has been awarded many prestigious designations, from being named one of Ten Great Canadian Women to Know by *Homemaker* magazine to National Trailblazer by Global TV. She was chosen as Personnalité de la Semaine by *La Presse* and CBC Radio Canada, and one of 200 Young Global Leaders in the World by the *World Economic Forum.*

Dr. Nutt concludes her essay "The Lessons of Peace" by saying, "War has taught me to place my trust in peace, and I believe that all citizens of the world deserve the right, and the opportunity, to live without violence. I believe it will be possible, some day, for war—and all the death, destruction, and unfathomable hardship that war brings—to be a footnote in the history of humankind. At the very least, I believe, it is incumbent upon us to try" (2007).

More information about Dr. Nutt's work is available at warchild.org and warchild.ca.

By dedicating every day to raising awareness and providing relief and support for women and children harmed by the atrocities of war in the world, University of Toronto professor and family physician Samantha Nutt aligns her values with her work-life.

critical thinking

Every dream and vision you might develop about your future can be broken down into specific goals and time frames. Keeping your career dreams in focus, write some of the specific educational and career goals you have for the next 20, 10, and 5 years. Be as concrete and specific as possible. In making up goals, start from the farthest point—20 years—and work backward. If you go the other way, you run the risk of adopting goals that are not precisely and clearly related to your dream. Compare and contrast your educational career goals after you have completed your work.

The Occupational Outlook

As you explore the type of work you are likely to enjoy and in which you can succeed, it is important to be knowledgeable about different fields and companies. Occupations may have many job openings one year but few in another year as economic conditions change. Thus, it is critical to keep up with the occupational outlook in various fields. On the way, you can monitor your future by keeping up with the occupational outlook in various fields and enhancing your skill sets accordingly.

What characteristics are employers looking for? According to a survey conducted by the Conference Board of Canada, employers are looking for people who possess a combination of academic experience, personal management, and teamwork skills to form the foundation of a high-quality Canadian workforce. Academic skills include the ability to communicate effectively, think critically, and engage in lifelong learning. Personal management skills include positive attitudes and behaviours, such as confidence, honesty, ethics, willingness to learn, as well as initiative, energy, and persistence. Teamwork skills include the ability to work with others, make cooperative decisions, and respect the thoughts and opinions of others in the group. Happily, the Conference Board of Canada (2016) reports that Canada's relatively high position on the employment indicator reflects that the country emerged from the 2008–2009 recession with minimal job loss.

The combination of the above skills, attitudes, and behaviours provides the foundation to get, keep, and progress in a job and to achieve the best results.

The Impact of Work

Work plays a powerful role in our lives. It defines people in fundamental ways (Blustein, 2008; Fouad & Bynner, 2008). As Dr. Samantha Nutt illustrates, people identify with their work, and that work shapes their identity and self-concept. In many ways, the relationship between a person and his or her work is quite reciprocal in that as the worker shapes the workplace, at the same time he or she is shaped by that working environment. In Canada, almost two-thirds of individuals are working more than 45 hours a week—50 percent more than two decades ago. Work weeks are now more rigid. Flex time arrangements have decreased by a third in the past 10 years (O'Kane, 2012).

Being able to work is critical to everyone. Work is an economic issue, and it contributes importantly to one's self esteem. People work to establish their self-identity and social status, and to engage in interactions. Work is a way to structure one's time in their day, and to contribute to community and to society as a whole (Mayer, 2009). The pleasure of doing a job well is universal, as is the good feeling one experiences from having supportive supervisors and friendly co-workers. Job satisfaction correlates more with challenge, productivity, and creativity and with relationships among employees than it does with high pay or easy work (Pfeffer, 2007). The power of intrinsic rewards suggests the reason that older employees display, on average, less absenteeism, more punctuality, and more job commitment than do younger workers (Landy & Conte, 2007). Satisfaction at work spills over to satisfaction at home and vice versa. For example, family members who are supportive of other family members regarding employment and job status benefit from that person's sense of satisfaction and mental health (Berger & Chuang, 2014).

Many adults have changing expectations about work, yet employers often are not meeting these expectations (Moen, 2007; Orrange, 2007). For example, current policies and practices were designed for a single breadwinner, a traditionally male workforce, and an industrial economy, making these policies and practices out of step with a workforce of women and men, and of single parents and dual earners. Many workers today want flexibility and greater control over the time and timing of their work, and yet most employers offer little flexibility even though policies like flextime and job-sharing may be "on the books."

Work After Post-secondary Education

We know that past demographic trends and changes in post-secondary participation rates have had a tremendous impact on post-secondary enrolments over the past half century. There is a longstanding debate over the value of specific post-secondary programs in facilitating employment after graduation (Fenesi & Sana, 2015). In fact, higher education is one of the most important investments that individuals choose to make (Schneider, 2013). In the "New Knowledge Economy," guaranteeing access to post-secondary education (PSE) is of fundamental importance to every nation for several reasons: for future economic prosperity; for the broader development of its population; and for fair and equal opportunity among all its citizens (Finnie, 2012).

Over 2 million students were enrolled in Canadian post-secondary institutions during the academic year 2012–2013 (Statistics Canada, 2014). Women accounted for 56.3 percent of total enrolment compared with 43.7 percent for men. Interestingly, these proportions have remained stable over the past decade. International student enrolment increased 6.9 percent in 2012/2013 to 199 836 (Statistics Canada, 2014). Aboriginal women and men (aged 25–44) have made significant gains in education, employment, and income (Gerber, 2014).

Unemployment

Unemployment produces stress, regardless of whether the job loss is temporary, cyclical, or permanent (Kalousoua & Burgard, 2014). Researchers have found that unemployment is related to physical problems (such as heart attack and stroke), mental problems (such as depression and anxiety), marital difficulties, and homicide (Backhaus & Hemmingsson, 2012; Freyer-Adam et al., 2013). A study also revealed that immune system functioning declined with unemployment and increased with new employment (Cohen et al., 2007). A recent study revealed that 90 or more days of unemployment was associated with subsequent cardiovascular disease across an eight-year follow-up period (Lundis et al., 2014).

Stress comes not only from a loss of income and the resulting financial hardships, but also from decreased self-esteem. Individuals who cope best with unemployment have financial resources to rely on, often savings or the earnings of other family members. The support of understanding, adaptable family members also helps individuals cope with unemployment. Job counselling and self-help groups can provide practical advice on job searching, creating resumés, and developing interviewing skills, as well as giving emotional support (van Hooft, 2014).

Dual-Career Couples

Dual-earner couples may have particular problems finding a balance between work and the rest of life (Shimazu et al., 2014). Balancing family life, work, and leisure is a challenge for many young dual-career couples. When both partners are working, the tasks of managing home and family can tax the relationship. An additional complication arises when one or both of the people are working from home.

In heterosexual unions, men are taking increased responsibility for maintaining the home and caring for children, and women are taking increased responsibility for providing economic support. In same-sex unions, individuals divide the labour outside of the prescribed and internalized gender roles.

In spite of shifting roles, women in heterosexual unions perform a far greater proportion of household tasks than their husbands, even when they earn more money or their husband is unemployed (Budworth, Enns, & Rowbotham, 2007). Women continue to do traditionally ascribed work such as cooking, laundry, and housecleaning, and men still do yard work, take out the garbage, and do auto maintenance. Thus, an important issue for many young relationships is juggling career and family work (Dunn & O'Brien, 2013).

Another issue that dual-career couples face focuses on compatible job schedules and/or locations. One individual might work primarily during the day, the other in the evening or at night, in which case they rarely see each other. If one spouse receives a job offer in another geographical location, the issues of whose career takes priority or whether the couple should consider a long-distance relationship are raised. Fluid boundaries are important to achieve in these families (Minnotte, Minotte, & Pedersen, 2013).

To this point, we have studied a number of ideas about careers and work in early adulthood. For a review, see the Reach Your Learning Outcomes section at the end of this chapter.

Reach Your **Learning Outcomes**

The Transition from Adolescence to Adulthood

LO1 **Outline the transition from adolescence to early adulthood.**

The Criteria for Becoming an Adult	▪ Statistics Canada (2009) identifies five criteria of adulthood: – Has left parental home – Has left school – Has full-time full-year work – Is in a conjugal union – Has children who live with them ▪ An emerging adult is one between ages 18 and 25 who has not yet assumed all the responsibilities of adulthood.
The Transition from High School to College, University, or Work	▪ The challenges of emerging adulthood are many and may cause stress as well as bring happiness. ▪ Finding positive ways to deal with stress is important to successful transitioning.

Physical Development, Health, and Wellness

LO2 **Describe physical changes and health considerations for emerging adults**

Health	▪ Peak physical status is often reached between 18 and 30 years of age. There is a hidden hazard in this time period as this is when bad health habits are often formed. ▪ Toward the latter part of early adulthood, a detectable slowdown in physical development is apparent for most individuals.
Eating and Weight	▪ Obesity is a serious problem, associated with heart disease, diabetes, and hypertension. ▪ Heredity, leptin, set point, and basal metabolism are biological factors involved in obesity. Environmental factors and culture also influence obesity. ▪ Many divergent interests are involved in the topic of dieting. ▪ For those who diet, exercise is usually an important component. Depending on the diet, dieting can be harmful; however, when overweight people diet and exercise, they can maintain their weight loss.
Regular Exercise	▪ Both moderate and intense exercise produce important physical and psychological gains, such as lowered risk of heart disease and lowered anxiety. ▪ Only 15 percent of Canadians over age 18 years of age are active enough to gain health benefits.

Substance Abuse	▪ Although some reduction in alcohol use has occurred among college and university first-year students, binge drinking is still a major concern. By the mid-twenties a reduction in both alcohol and drug use often occurs. ▪ E-cigarettes have gained popularity, both globally and in Canada. ▪ A number of strategies, such as nicotine substitutes, have shown some success in getting smokers to quit, but quitting is difficult because of the addictive properties of nicotine. ▪ Addiction is a maladaptive response to an underlying condition such as a non-specific inability to cope with the world. Alcohol consumption is responsible for substantial increase in morbidity, mortality, and social problems.

Sexuality

LO3 **Examine the concept of sexuality in young adults.**

Sexual Activity in Emerging Adulthood	▪ Sexual awareness, attitudes, and expressions develop over the life span and are critical to healthy adult life. ▪ Media influence, which is often negative toward women and links sex and violence, is powerful. ▪ Although homophobia is still prevalent today, most Canadians take a live-and-let live attitude and believe that homosexuals should have the right to marry. This attitude is reflected in current legislation. ▪ Pride Parade has gained momentum across Canada. ▪ Reproductive disease and manipulations are challenges faced by today's young adults.
Sexually Transmitted Infections	▪ Sexually transmitted infections, or STIs are contracted primarily through sexual contact. ▪ Gonorrhea, syphilis, chlamydia, genital herpes, and HPV are among the most common STIs. ▪ Many STIs may be asymptomatic. ▪ AIDS (acquired immune deficiency syndrome), is caused by HIV, a virus that destroys the body's immune system. ▪ Some good strategies for protecting against AIDS and other STIs are to (1) know your own and your partner's risk status, (2) obtain medical examinations, (3) have only protected sex, and (4) not have sex with multiple partners.
Violence against Women	▪ Sexual assault is a term referring to all incidents of unwanted sexual activity, including sexual attacks and sexual touching. ▪ A significant proportion of sexual assaults do not come to the attention of police.

Cognitive Development

LO4 **Analyze the cognitive changes that occur in early adulthood.**

Piaget's View	▪ Formal operational thought, entered into at age 11 to 15, is Piaget's final cognitive stage. ▪ Piaget said that adults are quantitatively more knowledgeable than adolescents, but that adults do not enter a new, qualitatively different stage. ▪ Some experts argue that the idealism of Piaget's formal operational stage declines in young adults and is replaced by more realistic, pragmatic thinking. ▪ Perry said that adolescents often engage in dualistic, absolute thinking, while young adults are more likely to engage in reflective, relativistic thinking.

	▪ Post-formal thought involves understanding that the correct answer might require reflective thinking and might vary from one situation to another, and that the search for truth is often never-ending. ▪ The post-formal stage includes the understanding that solutions to problems often need to be realistic and that emotion and subjective factors can be involved in thinking.
Creativity	▪ Creativity peaks in adulthood, often in the forties, and then declines. However, (a) the magnitude of the decline is often slight, (b) the creativity–age link varies by domain, and (c) there is extensive individual variation in lifetime creative output.

Careers and Work

LO5 Explain the key dimensions of careers and work in early adulthood.

Developmental Changes	▪ Many young children have idealistic fantasies about a career. By the late teens and early twenties, their career thinking has usually turned more serious. ▪ By their early to mid-twenties, many individuals have completed their education or training and started in a career. In the remainder of early adulthood, they seek to establish their emerging career and start moving up the career ladder.
Values and Careers	▪ It is important to match up a career to your values. There are many different values, ranging from the importance of money to working in a preferred geographical location. ▪ Service-producing industries will account for the most jobs in the next decade. Employment in the computer industry is projected to grow rapidly. ▪ Jobs that require a post-secondary education will be the fastest growing and highest paying.
The Occupational Outlook	▪ The Conference Board of Canada reports that employers want a combination of academic, personal management, and teamwork skills. ▪ Canadian employers seek employees who have excellent generic skills, including computer and communication skills, plus the ability to work effectively on teams.
The Impact of Work	▪ Work defines people in fundamental ways and is a key aspect of their identity. Most individuals spend about one-third of their adult life at work. ▪ The relationship between the workplace and the individual is reciprocal in that the worker shapes the workplace and the workplace shapes the individual's identity. ▪ Many workers would like more flexibility through policies such as flex-time and job-sharing.
	▪ Unemployment creates stress and is related to health, mental health, and marital problems. ▪ Dual-career couples find balancing work and the rest of their lives challenging. ▪ Fluid boundaries need to be created in these families.

review → connect → reflect

review

1. What are two main criteria for becoming an adult? LO1
2. What causes physical performance to peak and then slow down in early adulthood? LO2
3. What are some benefits of exercise? LO2
4. What characterizes the sexual activity of emerging adults? LO3
5. What are sexually transmitted infections? LO3
6. What changes in the cognitive development of young adults have been identified? LO4
7. What are some developmental changes in careers and work? LO5

connect

How does one's gender affect work opportunities and work environment for the young adult?

reflect

Your Own Personal Journey of Life

If you are an emerging young adult, what career do you want to pursue? How many years of education will your career of choice require? If you have a young family and reside in a rural area, what resources are available for you, as a woman, if you wish to work?

CHAPTER 14

Socio-Emotional Development in Early Adulthood

CHAPTER OUTLINE

Stability and Change from Childhood to Adulthood

LO1 Examine stability and change in temperament, and summarize adult attachment styles.

- **Temperament**
- **Attachment**

Attraction, Love, and Close Relationships

LO2 Identify three key aspects of attraction, love, and close relationships.

- **Attraction**
- **The Faces of Love**
- **Falling Out of Love**
- **Friendship**
- **Loneliness**

Intimate Relationships: Marriage and the Family Life Cycle

LO3 Describe intimate relationships such as marriage, the family life cycle, and cultural influences on family life.

- **Marital Trends in Canada**
- **Social Contexts**
- **Making Marriage Work**
- **Benefits of a Good Marriage**
- **The Family Life Cycle**
- **Parenting Myths and Realities**

The Diversity of Adult Lifestyles

LO4 Compare and contrast the diversity of adult lifestyles.

- **Single Adults**
- **Cohabiting Adults**
- **Divorced Adults**
- **Remarried Adults**
- **Parenting Adults**
- **Lone-Parent Adults**
- **Gay and Lesbian Adults**

Gender, Relationships, and Moral Development

LO5 Summarize moral development and gender development.

- **Moral Development**
- **Women's Development**
- **Men's Development**

"...love is only possible between two equals."

Guy Vanderhaeghe, Canadian author

GUY VANDERHAEGHE, CANADIAN AUTHOR

© Lumi Images / Alamy Stock Photo

Variations: Do Any of These Scenarios Resemble Someone You Know?

As in Chapter 12, these snapshots are tiny glimpses into some of the challenges and milestones facing young adults.

THE SINGLE: Remaining single is a life choice for many young adults, such as Jerry. He is beginning to understand that many advantages exist in living the single lifestyle. For example, one such advantage is freedom to make autonomous decisions and pursue his own schedule and interests, which he really likes to do. A disadvantage of the single life is confronting his loneliness. But Jerry is active. He has many friends, and does not see loneliness as being an issue for him. What must become a concern for Jerry is pressure from society, around the age of 30, to settle down and get married. However, Jerry knows that at that time he can make a conscious decision to either marry or remain single.

THE ARRANGED MARRIAGE: Mehri is proud and happy that her father was able to arrange her marriage before he died of terminal cancer. She says the husband her father chose for her when she was 14 is perfect. He is kind, generous, and a good father to their two sons, who are now 8 and 10 years old.

LIVING APART: Dawit, a refugee to Canada, fled his homeland leaving behind a wife and child. He looks forward to the time when his family can be reunited. In the meantime, he sends as much money as he can to the wife and child he loves and misses.

SPOUSAL ABUSE: Jen had hoped that having a baby would bring them closer together and that Emanuel would soften. Emanuel, exhausted from working two part-time jobs and stressed with financial worries, took out his frustrations yet again, verbally abusing and threatening Jen. Fearful for her safety, Jen moved into a shelter with her 4-month-old son. She is determined not to subject herself or her son to further abuse.

SAME-SEX MARRIAGE: Since their marriage, Sandra and Barb have been busy renovating their new house in addition to working full time. They also are the parents of an 11-year-old girl and an 8-year-old boy from Barb's first marriage, which ended in divorce once she came to terms with her lesbian status.

COHABITATING UNION: Melanie and James have lived together for 12 years. They enjoy their home and a wide circle of friends. James has a bipolar condition, which limits his ability to work. Melanie enjoys travelling, although James can rarely join her. Every year they privately renew their commitment to each other, and part of their commitment to each other is to value each other's freedom and autonomy.

POLYGAMOUS MARRIAGE: Sasha and Merianna pass themselves off as sisters to those who do not know them well. As far as the government is concerned, that is the status which allowed their husband, Ahmed, to bring them to Canada. To those they know well and trust, Sasha and Merianna are Ahmed's polygamous wives.

FEAR OF COMMITMENT: After a six-month period during which Gwenna gave Greg the emotional space he needed to sort out his ambivalence and doubt about their relationship, Greg requested more time to make up his mind. At this time, Gwenna took the painful—but ultimately empowering—step of ending the relationship.

EQUALITY IN MARRIAGE: Once their first child was born, traditional fixed gender roles seeped into George and Noreen's marriage, although they had consciously vowed to reject these well-indoctrinated scripts. George, feeling the pressure to provide for his family's economic future, thought Noreen should take over the responsibility for household chores. Needless to say, Noreen, who had a career of her own, did not agree.

EARLY ENDING OF A MARRIAGE: At 38 years of age, Jason finds himself the widowed father of two young children, Mary, age 10, and Bobby, age 8. His wife succumbed to breast cancer after a two-year battle. He feels alone and lost and has no idea where to begin.

Psychologist and philosopher Erich Fromm equates love to art, pointing out that love takes patience and practice (Fromm, 1956). Certainly, most would agree that love is central to our lives. As a result, finding a way to fit patience and practice into our busy schedules is sometimes overlooked until we find ourselves alone, like Jason in the above scenario. As these scenarios illustrate, relationships are complex and unique. Into each relationship, people carry their personal contexts and their unique factors of identity: family traditions, social and political attitudes, religious beliefs, and their ambitions for the future. Social contexts of class, ethnicity, gender, and race add further complexities, as no two individuals, no matter how superficially similar they are, share the same values and attitudes.

How do you think the individuals described above will negotiate their present or future relationships?

Stability and Change from Childhood to Adulthood

LO1 Examine stability and change in temperament, and summarize adult attachment styles.

- **Temperament**
- **Attachment**

For adults, socio-emotional development revolves around adaptively integrating our emotional experiences into enjoyable relationships with others on a daily basis. Young adults face choices and challenges in adopting lifestyles that will be emotionally satisfying, predictable, and manageable for them. They do not come to these tasks as blank slates, but do their decisions and actions simply reflect the person they had already become when they were 5 years old or 10 years old or 20 years old? Young adults around the world face challenges; however, many overcome them and continue their personal growth.

Current research shows that the first 20 years of life are not meaningless in predicting an adult's socio-emotional life (Cicchetti & Toth, 2015; Thompson, 2015). And there is every reason to believe that experiences in the early adult years are important in determining what the individual will be like later in adulthood. A common finding is that the smaller the time intervals over which we measure socio-emotional characteristics, the more similar an individual will look from one measurement to the next. Thus, if we measure an individual's self-concept at the age of 20 and then again at the age of 30, we will probably find more stability than if we measured the individual's self-concept at the age of 10 and then again at the age of 30.

In trying to understand the young adult's socio-emotional development, looking at an adult's life only in the present tense, ignoring the unfolding of social relationships and emotions, would be misleading. It would also be a mistake to only search through a 30-year-old's first 5 to 10 years of life when trying to understand why he or she is having difficulty in a close relationship.

Temperament

How stable is temperament? Recall that *temperament* is an individual's behavioural style and characteristic emotional responses. In early adulthood, most individuals assume greater responsibilities, foresee consequences, plan ahead, and are more even-keeled than in adolescence, and they become more responsible and engage in less risk-taking behaviour (Charles & Luong, 2011). Along with these signs of general change in temperament, researchers also find links between some dimensions of childhood temperament and adult personality (Shiner & DeYoung, 2013).

Is temperament in childhood linked with adjustment in adulthood? Here is what we know on the basis of the few longitudinal studies that have been conducted on this topic.

Recall from Chapter 6 the distinction between an *easy* and a *difficult* temperament. In one longitudinal study, children who had an easy temperament at 3 to 5 years of age were likely to be well adjusted as young adults (Chess & Thomas, 1987). In contrast, many children who had a difficult temperament at 3 to 5 years of age were not well-adjusted as young adults.

Inhibition is a temperament characteristic that has been studied extensively by Jerome Kagan (2000, 2002, 2008, 2010, 2013) and his associates (Fox et al., 2015). Kagan concluded that individuals with an inhibited temperament in childhood are less likely as adults to be assertive or to experience social support and more likely to delay entering a stable job track. A longitudinal study revealed that the 15 percent most inhibited girls and boys at 4 to 6 years of age were rated by their parents as inhibited, and they were actually delayed in establishing a stable partnership and in finding their first full-time job by 23 years of age (Asendorph, Denissen, & van Aken, 2008). Further, in the Uppsala (Sweden) Longitudinal Study, shyness/inhibition in infancy and childhood was linked to social anxiety at 21 years of age (Bohlin & Hagekull, 2009). These researchers found unexpected gender differences as well. Williams and colleagues (2010) found that formerly inhibited boys were more likely than the average adolescent to use drugs. Conversely, inhibited girls were less likely to use drugs.

Ability to control one's emotions (a dimension in Mary Rothbart's and John Bates's analysis of temperament) has also been studied. In one longitudinal study, when 3-year-old children showed good control of their emotions and were resilient in the face of stress, they were likely to continue to handle emotions effectively as adults (Block, 1993). By contrast, when 3-year-olds had low emotional control and were not very resilient, they were likely to show problems in these areas as young adults.

In sum, a small number of studies reveal some continuity between certain aspects of temperament in childhood and adjustment in early adulthood (Rothbart, 2011). More research is needed to verify these linkages. Indeed, Theodore Wachs (1994, 2000) recently proposed ways that linkages between temperament in childhood and personality in adulthood might vary depending on the intervening contexts in individuals' experience (see Figure 14.1). Many aspects of the environment—including gender, culture, parenting, and general goodness of fit—may influence the persistence of aspects of a child's temperament through life. Previous studies indicate that temperament is also genetically influenced from childhood through adolescence. For example, new genes may be activated with puberty, causing changes in reactions and behaviours (Ganiban et al., 2008).

Figure 14.1

Temperament in Childhood, Personality in Adulthood, and Intervening Contexts

Initial Temperament Trait: Inhibition		
	Child A	**Child B**
	Intervening Context	
Caregivers	Caregivers (parents) who are sensitive and accepting, and let the child set his or her own pace.	Caregivers who use inappropriate "low level control" and attempt to force the child into new situations.
School Environment	Presence of "stimulus shelters" or "defensible spaces" that the child can retreat to when there is too much stimulation.	Child continually encounters noisy, chaotic environments that allow no escape from stimulation.
Peers	Peer groups consist of other inhibited children with common interests, so the child feels accepted.	Peer groups consist of athletic extroverts, so the child feels rejected.
Schools	School is macro-managed so inhibited children are more likely to be tolerated and feel they can make a contribution.	School is micro-managed so inhibited children are less likely to be tolerated and more likely to feel undervalued.
	Personality Outcomes	
	As an adult, individual is closer to extroversion (outgoing, sociable) and is emotionally stable.	As an adult, individual is closer to introversion and has more emotional problems.

From Wachs, T.D. "Fit, Context, and the Transition Between Temperament and Personality," in C. Halverson, G. Kohnstamm & R. Martin (Eds.) *The Developing Structure of Personality from Infancy to Adulthood.* Copyright © 1994 Lawrence Erlbaum Associates, Reprinted by permission.

Varying experiences with caregivers, the physical environment, peers, and schools can modify links between temperament in childhood and personality in adulthood. The example given above is for inhibition.

Attachment

Like temperament, attachment appears during infancy and plays an important part in socio-emotional development (Cassidy, 2009; Weinfield et al., 2009; Thompson, 2015). We discussed its role in infancy, childhood, and adolescence. Attachment continues to shape development in early adulthood (Feeney & Thrush, 2010). The Connecting through Research box illustrates how Susan Johnson has applied attachment theory to counselling couples.

CONNECTING through Research

Dr. Susan Johnson, Psychologist, Counsellor, Researcher, and Co-Developer of Emotionally Focused Therapy

Courtesy of Susan Johnson

Visit Dr. Susan Johnson's Emotionally Focused Therapy website at http://www.iceeft.com.

Married couples normally experience stressful periods that threaten the stability of their relationship. When this happens, couples may seek professional guidance, most of which is based on behavioural theories that use communication strategies to modify behaviour and seek solutions to problems.

Dr. Susan Johnson, believing many counselling strategies provided short-term relief from marital stress, partnered with Dr. Les Greenberg in the early 1980s to originate Emotionally Focused Couple Therapy (EFT). Based on John Bowlby's attachment theory, EFT "depathologizes dependency" by telling couples they are emotionally dependent on each other. Breaches of attachment, called "attachment injuries," between partners occur when one partner is experiencing insecurity because the other is either unsupportive or emotionally unavailable. EFT legitimizes vulnerability and encourages couples to listen for and respond to the childlike dependencies in our spouses and ourselves.

This novel and uniquely Canadian approach has an unprecedented track record of success: 70 to 75 percent of marriages stabilize once couples go through EFT counselling. The *Journal of Marital and Family Therapy* calls EFT ". . .one of the major advances in marital and family therapy of the last decade."

Dr. Johnson is the founding Director of the International Centre for Excellence in Emotionally Focused Therapy where training in EFT occurs, and Director of the Ottawa Couple and Family Institute. As well, she is a Distinguished Research Professor at Alliant University in San Diego, California, and Professor Emerita, Clinical Psychology at the University of Ottawa. Johnson's interest with couples and relationships began as a child as she observed people in an English pub. "I grew up in an English pub," she says, and observing people sparked a fascination about how couples connect, disconnect, and communicate in general. What better place than a pub to observe all that?

Not only is she the author of numerous books, articles, and much research on couples therapy, she delivers EFT workshops all over the world. In 2003 she received an Excellence in Education Award from the University of Ottawa and in 2005 an Award for Research in Family Therapy bestowed by the American Family Therapy Academy. More recently, in 2009 she received a Lifetime Achievement Award from the Belgium Association for Couple and Family Therapy and in 2013, a Training Award presented to her by the American Association of Marital and Family Therapy. Her recent book, *Love Sense: The Evolutionary New Science of Romantic Relationships* outlines the new logical understanding of why and how we love—based on new scientific evidence and cutting-edge research (Dr. Sue Johnson, 2016).

Although relationships with romantic partners differ from those with parents, romantic partners fulfill some of the same needs for adults as parents do for their children (Mikulincer & Shaver, 2007, 2009; Mikulincer et al., 2010). Recall from Chapter 6 that *securely attached* infants are defined as those who use the caregiver as a secure base from which to explore the environment. Similarly, adults may count on their romantic partners to be a secure base to which they can return and obtain comfort and security in stressful times (Feeney, 2009; Shaver & Mikulineer, 2013; Zayas & Hazan, 2014).

Hazan and Shaver (1987, p. 515) measured attachment styles using the following brief assessment, where individuals are asked to read each paragraph and then place a check mark next to the description that best describes them:

1. I find it relatively easy to get close to others and I am comfortable depending on them and having them depend on me. I don't worry about being abandoned or about someone getting too close to me.
2. I am somewhat uncomfortable being close to others. I find it difficult to trust them completely and to allow myself to depend on them. I get nervous when anyone gets too close to me and it bothers me when someone tries to be more intimate with me than I feel comfortable with.
3. I find that others are reluctant to get as close as I would like. I often worry that my partner doesn't really love me or won't want to stay with me. I want to get very close to my partner, and this sometimes scares people away.

These items correspond to three attachment styles—secure attachment (option 1) and two insecure attachment styles (avoidant—option 2, and anxious—option 3):

- *Secure attachment style:* Securely attached adults have positive views of relationships, find it easy to get close to others, and are not overly concerned with or stressed out about their romantic relationships. These adults tend to enjoy sexuality in the context of a committed relationship and are less likely than others to have one-night stands.
- *Avoidant attachment style:* Avoidant individuals are hesitant about getting involved in romantic relationships, and once in a relationship, they tend to distance themselves from their partner.
- *Anxious attachment style:* These individuals demand closeness, are less trusting, and are more emotional, jealous, and possessive.

However, the majority of adults (about 60 to 80 percent) describe themselves as securely attached, and not surprisingly adults prefer having a securely attached partner (Shaver & Mikulincer, 2007; Zeifman & Hazan, 2009).

Researchers are studying links between adults' current attachment styles and many aspects of their lives (Craparo et al. 2014; Zayas & Hazan, 2014). For example, securely attached adults are more satisfied with their close relationships than insecurely attached adults, and the relationships of securely attached adults are more likely to be characterized by trust, commitment, and longevity (Feeney, 2009). Securely attached individuals are fully open to love. They are able to allow their partners to have space in their relationship and yet are firmly committed. They become animated when talking about their partner. The joy that is in their love for the other is well demonstrated. Decades of studies exploring different attachment styles indicate that insecurely attached adults have difficulty with their relationships. Meanwhile, securely attached individuals are more successful in the world of love (Belsky, 2013). A recent study of 18- to 20-year-olds revealed that recent secure attachment to parents is linked to ease in forming friendships in college/university (Parade, Leerkes, & Blankson, 2010).

A research review of 10 000 adult attachment interviews revealed that attachment insecurity is linked to depression (Bakermans-Kranenburg & van Lizendoorn, 2009). In regards to anxiety and depression, one study found that attachment-anxious and attachment-avoidant adults had higher levels of depressive and anxious symptoms than attachment-secure adults (Jinyao et al., 2012). Another study found that adults with avoidant and anxious attachment styles have a lower level of sexual satisfaction than their counterparts with a secure attachment pattern (Brassard et al., 2012). And a study of young women revealed a link between having an avoidant attachment pattern and a lower incidence of female orgasm (Cohen & Belsky, 2008).

Recent interest in adult attachment has focused on ways that genes can affect ways in which adults can experience the environment (Diamond, 2009). Another study examined the link between the serotonin transporter gene (5-HTTLPR) and adult unresolved attachment (Caspers et al., 2009). In an attachment interview, unresolved attachment was assessed by listening to certain specific speech patterns giving excessive detail about the death of a parent, indicating that the deceased parent continued to play a major role in the adult's life. In this study, parental loss in early childhood was more likely to result in unresolved attachment in adulthood, especially for individuals who had the shorter version of the gene. The long version of the gene apparently provided some protection from the negative psychological effects of parental loss.

Susan Johnson, of the University of Ottawa, and Les Greenberg, of York University, have developed a successful approach to therapy for couples called Emotionally Focused Therapy, or EFT, based on the findings of British psychiatrist John Bowlby, whom many acclaim as the "father of attachment theory." Bowlby, who was commissioned by the World Health Organization to study the psychological adjustment of babies and children orphaned during World War II, concluded that children have attachment needs of trust and security that must be met by at least one caregiver. Bowlby believed that adults transfer these needs to a romantic partner. Applying Bowlby's theories to intimate adult relationships, Greenberg and Johnson's EFT is based on the premise that romantic partners must meet each other's innate needs for attachment for the relationship to succeed. Greenberg and Johnson believe that we should treat our partners as adults, but in so doing we must tap into and respond to our partner's needs with the same care and concern we would give to a child. They claim that "attachment injuries" result when our innate needs are not met, and intimate partners can respond to each other in such a way that old "injuries" are healed and new ones averted (Makinen & Johnson, 2006).

A study conducted by Halchuk, Makinen, and Johnson (2010) indicated that EFT was effective at helping couples heal through the trauma of infidelity with sustained forgiveness and trust. Greenman and Johnson (2012) conclude that EFT appears to be successful in the treatment of post-traumatic stress disorder (PTSD). That is, EFT is applicable to numerous aspects of the clinical presentation of PTSD, including isolation, flashbacks, difficulties with affect regulation, and dissociation. The perception of the supportiveness from a significant other within the context of a safe and loving relationship appears to create a vital contribution toward the reestablishment of interpersonal connections that are critical to overcoming this disorder (Greenman & Johnson, 2012).

A research review and conceptualization of attachment by leading experts Mario Mikulincer and Phillip Shaver (2007, 2013) concluded that individuals who are securely attached have a well-integrated sense of self-acceptance, self-esteem, and self-efficacy. They have the ability to control their emotions, are optimistic, and are resilient. Facing stress and adversity, they activate cognitive representations of security, are mindful of what is happening around them, and mobilize effective coping strategies.

Mikulincer and Shaver's (2007, 2013) review also concluded that attachment insecurity places couples at risk for relationship problems. For example, when an anxious individual is paired with an avoidant individual, the anxious partner's needs and demands frustrate the avoidant partner's preference for distance in the relationship; the avoidant partner's need for distance causes stress for the anxious partner's need for closeness. The result: both partners are unhappy in the relationship and the anxious–avoidant pairing can produce abuse or violence when a partner criticizes or tries to change the other's behaviour.

Researchers also have found that when both partners have an anxious attachment pattern, the pairing usually produces dissatisfaction with the marriage and can lead to a mutual attack and retreat in the relationship (Feeney, 2009). When both partners have an anxious attachment style, they feel misunderstood and rejected, excessively dwell on their own insecurities, and seek to control the other's behaviour (Mikulincer & Shaver, 2007, 2009, 2013). It also is important to note that although attachment insecurities are linked to relationship problems, attachment style makes only a moderate-size contribution to relationship functioning, and other factors contribute to relationship satisfaction and success (Mikulincer & Shaver, 2007, 2009, 2013). Later in the chapter, we will discuss such factors in our coverage of marital relationships.

©RF/CORBIS

What are some key dimensions of attachment in adulthood? How are they related to relationship patterns and well-being?

To this point, we have discussed stability and change from childhood to adulthood. For a review, see the Reach Your Learning Outcomes section at the end of this chapter.

Attraction, Love, and Close Relationships

LO2 Identify three key aspects of attraction, love, and close relationships.

- **Attraction**
- **The Faces of Love**
- **Falling Out of Love**
- **Friendship**
- **Loneliness**

One question has intrigued philosophers, poets, and songwriters for centuries: What is love? Is it lustful and passionate? According to Erich Fromm, "The affirmation of one's own life, happiness, growth, freedom is rooted in one's capacity to love, i.e., in care, respect, responsibility and knowledge. If an individual is able to love productively, he loves himself too; if he can love only others, he cannot love at all" (Fromm, 1956, p. 60).

Attraction

What attracts us to others and motivates us to spend more time with them? Does just being around someone increase the likelihood a relationship will develop? Are we more likely to associate with those who are similar to us? How important is physical attraction in a relationship?

Familiarity and Similarity

Social psychologists have found that familiarity is a necessary condition for a close relationship to develop. According to Berscheid and Regan (2011), the most basic principle of attraction is familiarity. In fact, the core concept of interpersonal attraction is the principle of familiarity. For the most part, friends and lovers are individuals who have been around each other for a long time. For example, they may have grown up together, gone to high school or college or university together, worked together, or gone to the same social events.

The saying "birds of a feather do, indeed, flock together" helps to somewhat explain attraction. Guerrero, Anderson, and Afifi (2011) state that, overall, friends and lovers tend to be more alike than not alike. They appear to have the same attitudes, lifestyles, and physical attractions. Why are people attracted to others who have similar attitudes, values, and lifestyles? **Consensual validation**, which provides an explanation of people's attraction to others who are similar to them, is one reason. Our own attitudes and behaviour are supported when someone else's attitudes and behaviour are similar to ours—their attitudes, tastes, and values validate ours. People tend to shy away from the unknown. Instead, they tend to prefer people whose attitudes and behaviour they can predict. Similarity implies that we will enjoy doing things with the other person, which often requires a partner who likes the same things and has similar attitudes.

Recently, it has come to the forefront that attractions occur not only in person, but also over the Internet (Bateson et al., 2012; Park, 2010). Some critics argue that online romantic relationships never gain the interpersonal connection, while others state that the Internet may actually benefit anxious or shy individuals who find it difficult to meet potential partners in person (Rosenfeld & Thomas, 2012). Although online dating has become a popular strategy in finding a romantic partner, academic research into the antecedents of online dating are scarce. Valkenburg and Peter (2007) conducted a study using participants who were between 18 and 60 years of age. They found that respondents between 30 and 50 years of age were the most active online daters. Researchers have actually found that marriages resulting from online matchmaking service have significantly higher scores for marital adjustment than marriages between partners who met through unfettered choice (Carter & Buckwalter, 2009).

Physical Attraction

As important as familiarity and similarity may be, they do not explain the spark that often ignites a romantic relationship: physical attractiveness. How important is physical attractiveness in relationships? Psychologists do not consider the link between physical beauty and attraction to be as clear-cut as advertisers would like us to believe. For example, heterosexual men and women across many cultures differ on the importance they place on good looks when they seek an intimate partner. Women tend to rate as most important such traits as considerateness, honesty, dependability, kindness, and understanding; in contrast, men prefer good looks, cooking skills, and frugality (Eastwick & Finkel, 2008). A recent study found that partner physical attractiveness played a larger role in predicting husbands' marital satisfaction than in predicting wives' marital satisfaction (Meltzer, McNulty Jackson, & Karney, 2014).

Although physical attractiveness may contribute to the early formation of relationships, physical attraction probably assumes less importance as they endure. David Roche, keynote speaker, humorist, and performer, pictured with his wife Marlena Blavin, is a case in point. He describes his face as a gift that makes him unique and has helped him learn that every person has feelings of being disfigured, or different, or unacceptable. David had to understand his own inner strength to face the difficulties of peer relations during childhood and adolescence.

Credit Lois Tema; http://www.davidroche.com
David Roche, keynote speaker, humorist, and performer, is pictured here with his wife, Marlena Blavin. *Have you ever been shocked by someone's appearance at first but come to appreciate his or her inner strength and beauty?*

The Faces of Love

Once we are initially attracted to another person, other opportunities exist that may deepen the relationship to love. Love refers to a vast and complex territory of human behaviour, spanning a range of relationships that includes friendship, romantic love, affectionate love, and consummate love (Berscheid, 2010). In most of these types of love, one recurring theme is intimacy (Weis & Sternberg, 2008).

Intimacy

Self-disclosure and the sharing of private thoughts are the hallmarks of intimacy. As we discussed in Chapter 12, adolescents have an increased capacity and need for intimacy. At the same time, they are engaged in the essential tasks of developing an identity and establishing their independence from their parents. Juggling the competing demands of intimacy, identity, and independence also becomes a central task of adulthood.

ERIKSON'S STAGE: INTIMACY VERSUS ISOLATION

Recall from our discussion in Chapter 12 that Erik Erikson (1968) believes *identity versus identity confusion*—pursuing who we are, what we are all about, and where we are going in life—is the most important issue to be negotiated in adolescence. According to Erikson, in early adulthood, after individuals are well on their way to establishing stable and cohesive identities, they enter the sixth developmental stage, *intimacy versus isolation.* Erikson describes intimacy as finding oneself, yet losing oneself in another person, and it requires a commitment to another person. If young adults form healthy friendships and an intimate relationship with another individual, intimacy will be achieved. If not, isolation will result. A study confirmed Erikson's theory that identity development in adolescence is a precursor to intimacy in romantic relationships during emerging adulthood (Beyers & Seiffge-Krenke, 2010). A meta-analysis revealed a positive link between identity development and intimacy with the connection being stronger for men than for women (Arseth et al., 2009).

An inability to develop meaningful relationships with others can harm an individual's personality. It may lead individuals to repudiate, ignore, or attack those who frustrate them. Such circumstances account for the shallow attempts of youth to merge themselves with a leader. Many youth want to be apprentices or disciples of leaders and adults who will shelter them from the harm of the "out-group" world. If this fails, and Erikson believes that it must, sooner or later the individuals recoil into a self-search to discover where they went wrong. This introspection sometimes leads to painful depression and isolation. It also may contribute to a mistrust of others.

Contemporary psychologists who have investigated the development of girls and women point out that a relationship can be only as strong as its weakest link. Relationships formed on equality will be much stronger than those where one partner is deemed stronger or more powerful than the other. Love, sexuality, and the desire for intimacy are important features from birth until death (Hatfield, Rapson, & Martel, 2007). The experience of love is centrally important to close relationships (Graham, 2011).

INTIMACY AND INDEPENDENCE

Development in early adulthood often involves balancing intimacy and commitment on the one hand, and independence and freedom on the other. At the same time as individuals are trying to establish an identity, they face the difficulty of having to cope with increasing their independence from their parents, developing an intimate relationship with another individual, and increasing their friendship commitments. They also face the task of being able to think for themselves and do things without always relying on what others say or do.

The extent to which young adults develop autonomy has important implications. Young adults who have not sufficiently moved away from parental ties may have difficulty in both interpersonal relationships and career development. Consider a son or daughter who is overprotected by his or her parents and continues to depend on them for financial support in early adulthood. He or she may have difficulty developing mature intimate relationships and a career. When an opportunity comes up that involves more responsibility and possibly more stress, he or she may turn it down. When things do not go well in his or her relationship, he or she may respond inappropriately.

The balance between intimacy and commitment, on the one hand, and independence and freedom, on the other, is delicate. Some individuals are able to experience a healthy independence and freedom along with an intimate relationship. Keep in mind that intimacy and commitment, and independence and freedom, are not just concerns of early adulthood. They are important themes of development that are worked and reworked throughout the adult years.

Romantic Love

Romantic love, also called passionate love or eros, has strong components of sexuality and infatuation, and often predominates in the early part of a love relationship (Berscheid, 2010). Poets, playwrights, and musicians through the ages have lauded the fiery passion of romantic love—and lamented the searing pain when it fails.

A complex intermingling of different emotions goes into romantic love—including such emotions as passion fear, anger, sexual desire, joy, and jealousy (Del Giudice, 2011; Regan, 2008). A recent study revealed that a heightened state of romantic love in young adults was linked to stronger depression and anxiety symptoms but better sleep quality (Bajoghli et al., 2014).

Affectionate Love

Love is more than just passion (Berscheid, 2010). **Affectionate love**, also called companionate love, is the type of love that occurs when individuals desire to have the other person near and have a deep, caring affection for the person. The early stages of love have more romantic love ingredients; but as love matures, passion tends to give way to affection (Sternberg & Sternberg, 2013).

Consummate Love

So far, we have discussed two types of love: romantic (or passionate) and affectionate (or companionate). According to Dr. Robert J. Sternberg (1986, 1988, 2004), these are not the only forms of love. Sternberg proposed a **triangular theory of love** in which love can be thought of as having three main dimensions: passion, intimacy, and commitment. Intimacy relates to the emotional feelings of warmth, closeness, and sharing in a relationship. Commitment is the cognitive appraisal of the relationship and the intent to maintain the relationship, even in the face of problems.

In Sternberg's theory, the strongest, fullest form of love is *consummate love,* which involves all three dimensions (see Figure 14.2). If passion is the only ingredient in a relationship (with intimacy and commitment low or absent), we are merely *infatuated.* However, a fraction of couples (1 in 10 people) manage to stay passionate for years (Acevedo & Aron, 2009). An affair or a fling, or a teenage "crush" in which there is little intimacy, knowledge, and even less commitment, is an example. A relationship marked by intimacy and commitment but low or lacking in passion is called *affectionate love,* a pattern often found among couples who have been married for many years. If passion and commitment are present but intimacy is not, Sternberg calls the relationship *fatuous love,* as when one person worships another from a distance. But if couples share all three dimensions—passion, intimacy, and commitment—they experience consummate love (Sternberg & Sternberg, 2013).

Figure 14.2
Sternberg's Triangle of Love

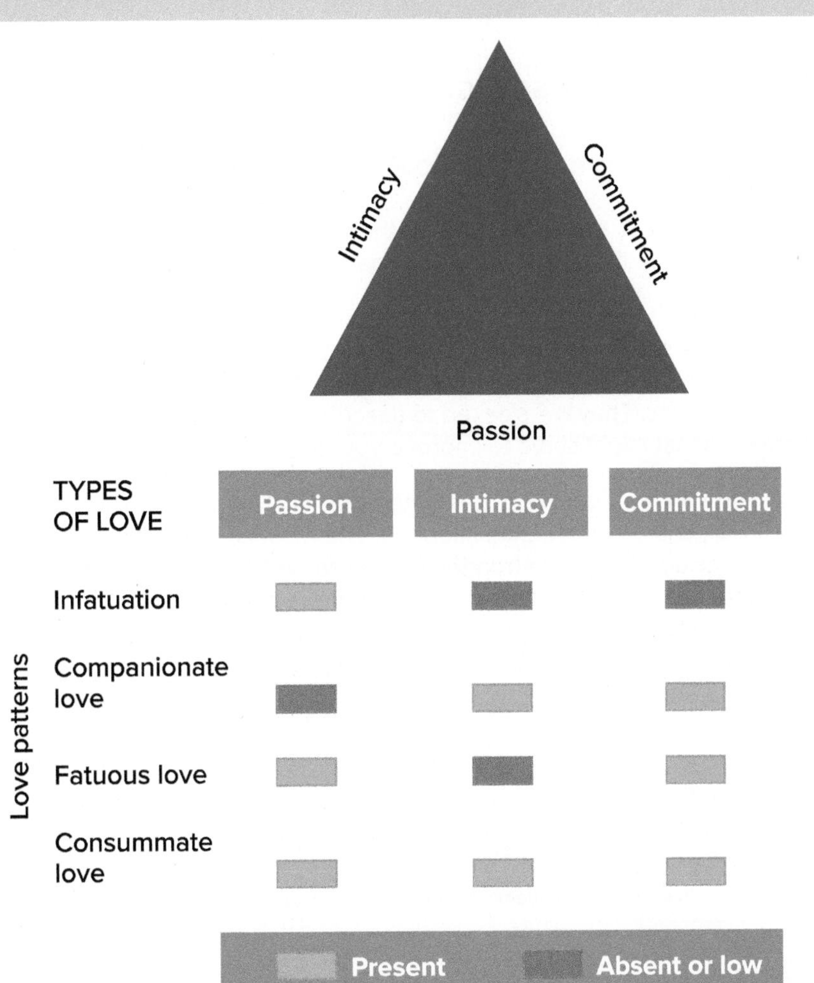

Sternberg identified three types of love: passion, intimacy, and commitment. Various combinations of these types of love result in these patterns of love: infatuation, affectionate love, fatuous love, and consummate love.

The readiness for love is not global across cultures. In many diverse cultures, passionate romantic love is a foreign concept. Marriages are frequently arranged on the basis of economic and status considerations. The concept of "love" was invented during the Middle Ages, when a few social philosophers first suggested that love ought to be a requirement for marriage (Feldman & Landry, 2014).

Falling Out of Love

The collapse of a close relationship may feel tragic. In the long run, however, our happiness and personal development may benefit from getting over being in love and ending a close relationship.

In particular, falling out of love may be wise if you are obsessed with a person who repeatedly betrays your trust; if you are involved with someone who is draining you emotionally or financially; or if you are desperately in love with someone who does not return your feelings. Being in love when love is not returned can lead to depression, obsessive thoughts, sexual dysfunction, inability to work effectively, difficulty in making new friends, and self-condemnation (Sbarra, 2012). Thinking clearly in such relationships is often difficult, because our thoughts are so coloured by arousing emotions (Guerro, Andersen, & Afifi, 2011). A study of unmarried relationship dissolution in 18- to 35-year-olds revealed that experiencing a breakup was linked to an increase in psychological stress and decrease in life satisfaction (Rhoades et al., 2011).

Some people get taken advantage of in relationships (Metts & Cupach, 2007; Tafoya & Spitzberg, 2007). For example, without either person realizing it, a relationship can evolve in a way that creates dominant and submissive roles. Detecting this pattern is an important step toward learning either to reconstruct the relationship or to end it if the problems cannot be worked out. To read further about breakups of romantic relationships, see Connecting through Research.

CONNECTING through Research

Personal Growth Following a Romantic Relationship Breakup

Studies of romantic breakups have mainly focused on their negative aspects (Kato, 2005; Moreau et al., 2011; Simon & Barrett, 2010). Few studies have examined the possibility that a romantic breakup might lead to positive changes.

One study assessed the personal growth that can follow the breakup of a romantic relationship (Tashiro & Frazier, 2003). The participants were 92 undergraduate students who had experienced a relationship breakup in the past nine months. They were asked to describe "what positive changes, if any, have happened as a result of your breakup that might serve to improve your future romantic relationships" (p. 118).

Self-reported positive growth was common following a romantic breakup. Changes were categorized in terms of person, relational, and environmental changes. The most commonly reported types of growth were person changes, which included feeling stronger and more self-confident, more independent, and better off emotionally. Relational positive changes included gaining relational wisdom, and environmental positive changes included having better friendships because of the breakup. Figure 14.3 provides examples of these positive changes. Women reported more positive growth than did men.

Figure 14.3

Examples of Positive Changes in the Aftermath of a Romantic Breakup

Change category	Exemplars of frequently mentioned responses
Person positives	1. "I am more self-confident." 2. "Through breaking up I found I could handle more on my own." 3. "I didn't always have to be the strong one, it's okay to cry or be upset without having to take care of him."
Relational positives	1. "Better communication." 2. "I learned many relationship skills that I can apply in the future (for example, the importance of saying you're sorry)." 3. "I know not to jump into a relationship too quickly."
Environmental positives	1. "I rely on my friends more. I forgot how important friends are when I was with him." 2. "Concentrate on school more: I can put so much more time and effort toward school." 3. "I believe friends' and family's opinions count—will seek them out in future relationships."

Friendship

Increasingly researchers are finding that friendship plays an important role in development throughout the human life span (Blieszner & Roberto, 2012; Rawlins, 2009). As we saw in Chapter 8, friendship can serve many functions—companionship, intimacy/affection, support, and a source of self-esteem. In some cases, friends can provide a better buffer from stress and be a better source of emotional support than family members. This might be because friends choose each other, whereas family ties are obligatory. Individuals often select a friend in terms of such criteria as loyalty, trustworthiness, and support. Thus, it is not surprising that in times of stress, individuals turn to their friends for emotional support (Rawlins, 2009).

As with children, adult friends usually come from the same age group. For many individuals, friendships formed in their twenties often continue through the twenties and into the thirties, although some new friends may be made in the thirties and some may be lost because of moving or other circumstances. Adulthood brings opportunities for new friendships as individuals relocate and may establish new friends in their neighbourhood or place of work (Blieszner, 2009).

Although it is unlikely that the phenomenon of "friends with benefits" relationships (FWBRs) is new, research on this type of relationship has emerged primarily within the last decade. FWBRs involve ongoing sexual activity occurring between partners who do not identify the relationships as romantic (Owen & Fincham, 2011). These relationships appear to be more common among today's youth and young adults than in previous generations (Bisson & Levine, 2009). In fact, Bogle (2008) argues that a shift has occurred from the predominant dating script to the hook-up script, which comprises many forms of casual dating relationships including FWBRs. One positive aspect of FWBRs is easy access to sex; a negative aspect is that of ruining the friendship (MacDonald, MacKeigan, & Weaver, 2011).

Gender Differences in Friendships

As in the childhood years, there are gender differences in adult friendships (Blieszner & Roberto, 2012). Compared with men, women have more close friends and their friendships involve more self-disclosure and exchange of mutual support (Dow & Wood, 2006). Women are more likely to listen at length to what a friend has to say and be sympathetic, and women have been labelled as "talking companions" because talk is so central to their relationship (Dow & Wood, 2006). Women's friendships tend to be characterized not only by depth, but also by breadth: Women share many aspects of their experiences, thoughts, and feelings (Helgeson, 2012).

When female friends get together, they like to talk, but male friends are more likely to engage in activities, especially outdoors. Thus, the adult male pattern of friendship often involves keeping one's distance while sharing useful information. Men are less likely than women to talk about their weaknesses with their friends, and men want practical solutions to their problems rather than sympathy. Also, adult male friendships are more competitive than those of women. For example, male friends disagree with each other more often than women friends do (Felmlee, Sweet, & Sinclair, 2012).

critical thinking

Gender roles are clearly defined throughout our lives—so well-defined that men and women have been indoctrinated and may follow them unconsciously, even when, like Noreen and George in the opening vignette, they consciously refute them. Traditionally, men earned the money and, therefore, made many or most of the decisions and women "obeyed" their husband's wishes. Obedience was tied to dependency on spousal economic support. Although the word "obey" has been removed from most marriage ceremonies, these traditional roles are well-ingrained. What are the traditional gender roles and how do they define our most intimate relationships? Do they still hold true? Why or why not? In your culture what are the traditional gender roles? In what ways do they not hold true?

Friendships between Women and Men

Cross-gender friendships can provide both opportunities and problems (Rawlins, 2009). The opportunities involve learning more about common feelings and interests and shared characteristics, as well as acquiring knowledge and understanding of beliefs and activities that historically have been typical of one gender.

Problems can arise in cross-gender friendships because of different expectations. Females appear to hold higher expectations for same-sex friends than for males (Helgeson, 2012).

©Fancy Collections/Superstock © Laurence Mouton/PhotoAlto ©Sigrid Olsson/PhotoAlto

How is adult friendship different among female friends, male friends, and cross-gender friends?

Loneliness

Recall that Erik Erikson (1968) believed that intimacy versus isolation is the key developmental issue for young adults to resolve. Social isolation can result in loneliness.

Each of us has times in our lives when we feel lonely, but for some people loneliness is a chronic condition. More than just an unwelcome social situation, chronic loneliness is linked with impaired physical and mental health. Chronic loneliness can even lead to an early death.

Weiss (1973) was one of the first researchers to conceptualize loneliness in a multidimensional way. He differentiated emotional and social loneliness as distinct states with different provisions. For example, emotional loneliness is due to an absence of an attachment and close intimate relationships. On the other hand, social loneliness is one result of a lack of social reassurance, and it acts as a response to social deficiencies. Marshall (2010) states that emotional loneliness arises as a lifelong disposition coming from poor quality childhood attachments. Secure attachment styles seem to be consistently associated with lower levels of loneliness, whereas a positive relationship was found between insecure attachment and feelings of loneliness (Wiseman, Mayseless, & Sharabany, 2006).

critical thinking

What are the factors that contribute to loneliness in individuals? To what extent do the gender differences described here reflect your own observations of loneliness? To what extent is social media a factor in promoting loneliness? What are four strategies that you could use with a colleague who confides in you that he/she is lonely?

To this point, we have discussed many ideas about attraction, love, and close relationships. For a review, see the Reach Your Learning Outcomes section at the end of this chapter.

Intimate Relationships: Marriage and the Family Life Cycle

LO3 Describe intimate relationships such as marriage, the family life cycle, and cultural influences on family life.

- **Marital Trends in Canada**
- **Social Contexts**
- **Making Marriage Work**
- **Benefits of a Good Marriage**
- **The Family Life Cycle**
- **Parenting Myths and Realities**

Until about 1950, a stable marriage was widely accepted as the endpoint of adult development. In the last 75 years, however, personal fulfillment both inside and outside marriage has emerged as a goal that competes with marital stability (Skolnick, 2007). The changing norm of male–female equality in marriage has produced marital relationships that are more fragile and intense than they were earlier in the twentieth century.

Marital Trends in Canada

The nuclear family is no longer the norm in Canada. In fact, the nuclear family that typified Canadian households of 50 years ago has changed into a complex and diverse web of family ties involving living alone, re-marriage, stepchildren, empty-nesters, and multiple generations living together and sharing a home (Census Shows, 2012). What is interesting is that for the first time in 2011, Statistics Canada (2011b) measured the number of stepfamilies in the country, indicating that 1 in 10 children lives in some sort of reconstituted arrangement.

Despite a growing population, the number of married couples declined by 132 715 over the previous decade (Statistics Canada, 2011b). Lone-parent families and multiple-family households, on the other hand, were on the rise. Same-sex couples were also on the steep incline, up 42.4 percent between 2006 and 2011. In Canada's first-ever national count of foster children, the agency indicated that there were 29 590 of them under the age of 14 in 2011, with the highest rate in the province of Manitoba, where there is a high First Nations population (Census Shows, 2012).

As elsewhere in the world, the face of the Canadian family continues to evolve in terms of age, size and configuration, and longevity. Canadian men and women are waiting until their late twenties to marry, and are not starting their families until they are well into their thirties and even early forties. One constant, however, is the level of stress people report. For example, married people report lower levels of extreme stress than singles. A recent study indicated that there is a protective effect associated with marriage that provides benefits to both physical and mental health, and in particular lowers rates of stress and depressive symptoms (Avertt, Argys, & Sorkin, 2013).

Social Contexts

A substantial body of evidence indicates that finding a partner and establishing a satisfying romantic relationship are central goals across many cultures (Fletcher et al., 2015). The traits that people look for in a marriage partner vary around the world.

Domesticity is also valued in some cultures, but not in others. In one study, adults from the Zulu culture in South Africa, Estonia, and Colombia placed a high value on housekeeping skills in their marital preference. By contrast, adults in the United States, Canada, and all Western European countries except Spain said that housekeeping skill was not an important trait in their partner.

Religion plays an important role in marriage in many cultures. However, several longitudinal studies have reported mixed findings concerning the relationship between religiosity and marital satisfaction (David & Stafford, 2015). In a longitudinal study with a community sample of couples, religion and spirituality were found to contribute directly to marriage satisfaction, especially if religious communication was high between partners (David & Stafford, 2015). For example, Islam stresses the honour of the male and the purity of the female. It also emphasizes the woman's role in childbearing, childrearing, educating children, and instilling the Islamic faith in their children. Interfaith relationships can be very difficult; further, parental and family pressures may prohibit an interfaith relationship. In India, more than 70 percent of marriages continue to be arranged. However, as more women enter the workforce in India and move from rural areas to cities, these Indian women are increasingly resisting arranged marriage (Purnell, 2013).

In Scandinavian countries, cohabitation is popular among young adults; however, most Scandinavians eventually marry (Popenoe, 2007). In Sweden, on average women delay marriage until they are 31 years of age, while men delay marriage until they are 33. Some countries, such as Hungary, encourage early marriage and childbearing to offset declines in the population. Like Scandinavian countries, Japan has a high proportion of unmarried young people. However, rather than cohabiting as the Scandinavians do, unmarried Japanese young adults live at home longer with their parents before marrying. In 2008, the average age for Canadian women to marry was 29.6 and for men the average age was 31 (Milan, 2015).

Making Marriage Work

John Gottman (1994, 2006, 2011; Gottman & Gottman, 2009; Gottman, Gottman, & Declaire, 2006) has been studying married couples' lives since the early 1970s. He uses extensive methods to study what makes marriages work. Gottman interviews couples about the history of their marriage, their philosophy about marriage, and how they view their parents' marriages. He videotapes them talking to each other about how their day went, and evaluates what they say about the good and bad times of their marriages. Gottman also uses physiological methods to measure their heart rate, blood flow, blood pressure, and immune functioning moment by moment. He checks back in with the couples every year to see how their marriages are faring. Gottman's research represents the most extensive assessment of marital relationships available. Currently, he and his colleagues are following up with 700 couples in seven different studies.

In his research, Gottman has found that seven main principles determine whether a marriage will work or not:

- *Establishing love maps:* Individuals in successful marriages have personal insights and detailed maps of each other's life and world. They are not psychological strangers. In good marriages, partners are willing to share their feelings with each other. They use these "love maps" to express not only their understanding of each other, but also their fondness and admiration.
- *Nurturing fondness and admiration:* In successful marriages, partners sing each other's praises. More than 90 percent of the time, when couples put a positive spin on their marriage's history, the marriage is likely to have a positive future.
- *Turning toward each other instead of away:* In good marriages, spouses are adept at turning toward each other regularly. They see each other as friends, and this friendship acts as a powerful shield against conflict. The friendship does not keep arguments from occurring, but it can prevent differences of opinion from overwhelming a relationship. In these good marriages, spouses respect each other and appreciate each other's point of view, even though they might not agree with it.
- *Letting your partner influence you:* Bad marriages often involve one spouse who is unwilling to share power with the other or be influenced by his or her ideas or desires. Although power mongering is more common in husbands, some wives also show this problem. A willingness to share power and to respect the other person's view is a prerequisite to compromising. One study revealed that equality in decision-making was one of the main factors that predicted positive marriage quality (Amato, 2007).
- *Solving solvable conflicts:* Gottman has found two types of problems that occur in marriage, perpetual and solvable. Perpetual problems include spouses differing on whether to have children, one spouse wanting sex far more frequently than the other, or differing political or religious views. Solvable problems can be worked out and may include such things as not helping each other reduce daily stresses, and not being verbally affectionate. Work, stress, in-laws, money, sex, housework, a new baby—these are among the typical areas of marital conflict, even in happy marriages. When there is conflict in these areas, it usually means that a husband and wife have different ideas about the tasks involved, their importance, or how they should be accomplished. If the conflict is perpetual, no amount of problem-solving expertise will fix it. The tension will decrease only when both partners feel comfortable living with the ongoing difference. However, when the issue is solvable, the challenge is to find the right strategy for dealing with it. Unfortunately, more than two-thirds of marital problems fall into the perpetual category. Fortunately, marital therapists have found that

couples often don't have to solve their perpetual problems for the marriage to work. Couples may decide to respect each other's autonomy rather than try to convince each other to change.

- *Overcoming gridlock:* One partner wants the other to attend church, and the other is an atheist. One partner is a homebody, while the other wants to go out and socialize a lot. Such problems often produce gridlock. Gottman believes the key to ending gridlock is not to try to solve the problem, but to move from gridlock to dialogue and to be patient.
- *Creating shared meaning:* The more the partners can speak candidly and respectfully with each other, the more likely it is that they will create shared meaning in their marriage. This also includes sharing goals with one's spouse and working together to achieve each other's goals.

In his research, Gottman has found that to resolve conflicts, couples should start out with a soft rather than a harsh approach, try to make and receive "repair attempts," regulate their emotions, compromise, and be tolerant of each other's faults. Conflict resolution is not about one person making changes; it is about negotiating and accommodating each other.

In addition to Gottman's view, other experts on marriage argue that such factors as forgiveness and commitment are important aspects of a successful marriage (Fincham, Stanley, & Beach, 2007). These factors function as self-repair processes in healthy relationships. For example, spouses may have a heated argument that has the potential to harm their relationship (Amato, 2007). After calming down, they may forgive each other and repair the damage. Also, spouses who have a strong commitment to each other may sacrifice their personal self-interest in times of conflict for the benefit of the marriage. Commitment especially becomes important when a couple is not happily married and can help them get through hard times with the hope that the future will involve more positive changes in the relationship.

"Marriages start to crack early," says Gottman's colleague, Robert Levenson, "and they are very hard to repair." Disagreements and arguments occur with regularity over money, raising children, work, and so forth. The major indicators that a marriage is "cracking" include contempt, aggression, stonewalling, avoiding, and anticipating the worst. Gottman's research indicates, "It's not the fight that does the damage—even the healthiest couples argue and disagree, and often never resolve perpetual problems—but what counts is the way the fight goes, and how well the couple succeeds at 'managing the conflict.'"

critical thinking

According to experts on marriage and family life, not every problem or conflict has a solution. One such problem may be views on church and religion. What are other possible perpetual problems? How do you think successful couples deal with conflicts such as these? What would be the consequences of conflict if it did not get resolved? What may happen to the couple?

Benefits of a Good Marriage

Now that you know the early signs of a marriage "cracking" and what makes a marriage work, what are the benefits to having a good marriage? Individuals who are happily married live longer, healthier lives than either divorced individuals or those who are unhappily married (Miller et al., 2013; Shor et al., 2012; Proulx & Synder-Rivas, 2013). A study assessed 94 000 Japanese, 40 to 79 years of age, on two occasions: at the beginning of the study and approximately 10 years later (Ikeda et al., 2007). Compared with never-married individuals, those who were married had a lower risk of dying in the 10-year period. Similarly, a study of U.S. adults 50 years and older revealed that a lower portion of adult life spent in marriage was linked to an increased likelihood of dying at an earlier age (Henretta, 2010). A large-scale analysis of data from a number of studies indicated that being married benefits the longevity of men more than women (Rendall et al., 2011). And another study indicated that the longer women are married, the less likely they are to develop a chronic health condition, and the longer that men are married, the lower their risk is of developing a disease (Dupre & Meadows, 2007).

What are the reasons for these benefits of a happy marriage? People in happy marriages likely feel less physically and emotionally stressed, which puts less wear and tear on a person's body. Such wear and tear can lead to numerous physical ailments, such as high blood pressure and heart disease, as well as psychological problems such as anxiety, depression, and substance abuse.

For some couples, an active choice is made not to have children (Blackstone & Stewart, 2012). Childfree adults do not universally reach the decision to remain so at the same stage of life or in the same way. When examining why some adults remain voluntarily childless, explanations may range from the impact of macro-level forces such as women's increasing labour force participation, to micro-level motivations such as autonomy and freedom (Agrillo & Netini, 2008).

Image Source Plus / Alamy Stock Photo

What makes marriages work? What are the benefits of having a good marriage?

The Family Life Cycle

Intimacy, as Erikson points out, is the major crisis of young adulthood. The process of forming intimate relationships, leaving the parental home, and establishing a new home poses many challenges and many moments of tremendous joy. Although young people are staying single longer, cohabiting much more commonly, and forming same-sex unions more openly, the ebb and flow of the family life cycle permeates the activities and decisions. Whatever lifestyle young adults choose, challenges posed by family life will emerge. As we go through life, we are at different points in the family life cycle.

Figure 14.4 shows a summary of these stages in the family life, along with key aspects of emotional processes involved in the transition from one stage to the next, and changes in family status required for developmental change to take place (McGoldrick, Carter, & Garcia-Preto, 2011).

Leaving Home and Becoming a Single Adult

Leaving home and becoming a single adult is the first stage in the family life cycle and involves launching. **Launching** is the process by which youths move into adulthood and exit their family of origin. Adequate completion of launching requires that the young adult separate from the family of origin without cutting off ties completely or reactively fleeing to find some form of substitute emotional refuge. The launching period is a time for youth and young adults to formulate personal life goals, to develop an identity, and to become more independent before joining with another person to form a new family. This is a time for young people to sort out emotionally what they will take along from the family of origin, what they will leave behind, and what they will create for themselves.

The shift to adult-to-adult status between parents and children requires a mutually respectful and personal form of relating in which young adults can appreciate parents as they are, needing neither to make them into what they are not nor to blame them for what they could not be. In addition, young adults do not need to comply with parental expectations and wishes at their own expense.

Figure 14.4
The Family Life Cycle

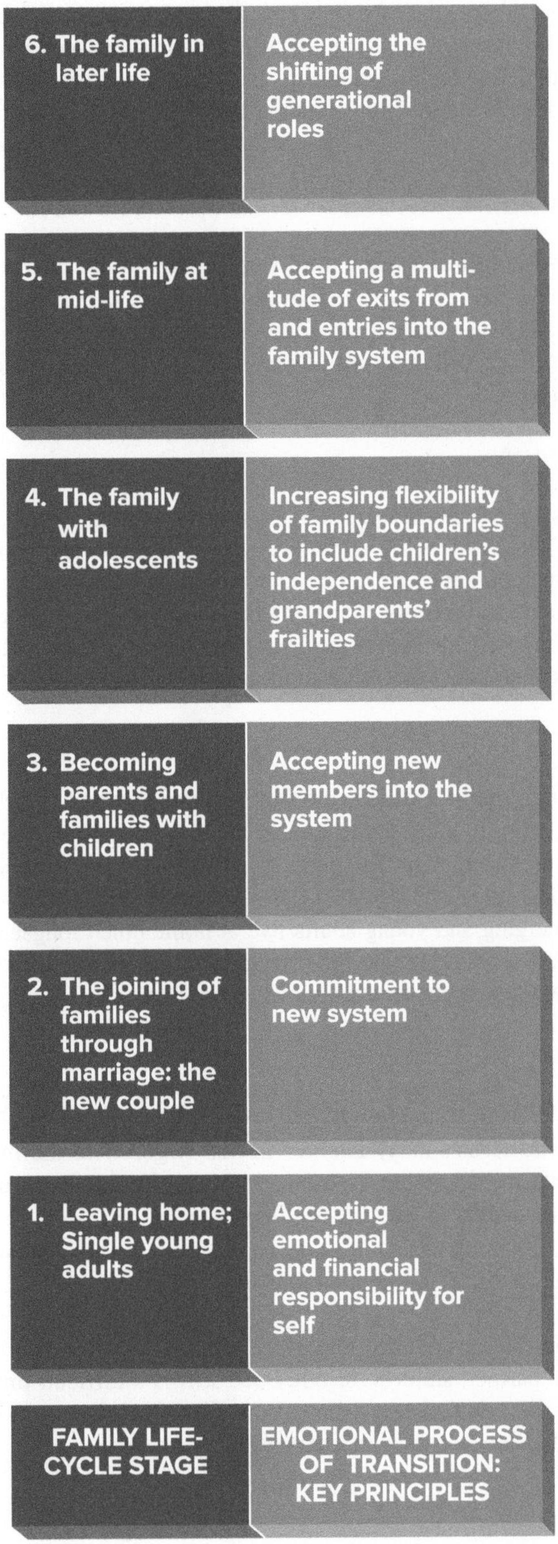

FAMILY LIFE-CYCLE STAGE	EMOTIONAL PROCESS OF TRANSITION: KEY PRINCIPLES
6. The family in later life	Accepting the shifting of generational roles
5. The family at mid-life	Accepting a multitude of exits from and entries into the family system
4. The family with adolescents	Increasing flexibility of family boundaries to include children's independence and grandparents' frailties
3. Becoming parents and families with children	Accepting new members into the system
2. The joining of families through marriage: the new couple	Commitment to new system
1. Leaving home; Single young adults	Accepting emotional and financial responsibility for self

The Joining of Families through Marriage: The New Couple

The **new couple** is the second stage in the family life cycle, in which two individuals from separate families of origin unite to form a new family system. This stage involves not only the development of a new marital system, but also an often complex realignment with extended families and friends. Women's changing roles, the increasingly frequent marriage of partners from divergent cultural backgrounds, and the increasing physical distances between family members are currently placing a much greater burden on couples to define their relationships for themselves than was true in the past. Marriage is usually described as the union of two individuals, but in reality, it is the union of two entire family systems and the development of a new, third system.

Becoming Parents and a Family with Children

Becoming parents and a family with children is the third stage in the family life cycle that requires adults to move up a generation and become caregivers to the younger generation. For many young adults, parental roles are well planned, coordinated with other roles in life, and developed with the individual's economic situation in mind. For others, the discovery that they are about to become parents is a startling surprise. In either event, the prospective parents may have mixed emotions and romantic illusions about having a child.

The Family with Adolescents

The **family with adolescents** represents the fourth stage of the family life cycle, in which adolescents push for autonomy and seek to develop their own identity. This involves a lengthy process of self-discovery, which transpires over at least 10 to 15 years. During this period, parents and their adolescent children may find themselves at a crossroads of sorts as the adolescent struggles to develop a mature autonomy and identity. Managing time and resources may cause family disagreements as teens take their first jobs, determine how to spend the money they earn, choose how much time to spend on homework, and so on. We discussed adolescent development and the family with adolescents in Chapter 12.

Launching Children and Moving On

Launching children and moving on is the fifth stage in the family cycle, a time of launching children, playing an important role in linking generations, and adapting to mid-life changes in development. Until about a generation ago, most families were involved in raising their children for much of their adult lives until old age. Because of the lower birth rate and longer life of most adults, parents now launch their children about 20 years before retirement, which frees many mid-life parents to pursue other activities. Many emerging and young adults live at home much longer than a generation ago, so the final launching may be delayed by several years. Planning for retirement and menopause are two challenges for the family in mid-life. We will discuss mid-life families in greater detail in Chapter 16.

The Families in Later Life

The **family in later life** is the sixth stage in the family life cycle, when retirement alters a couple's lifestyle, requiring adaptation. Grandparenting also characterizes many families in this stage. With the increase in dual family earners and divorce, more and more grandparents are helping to raise grandchildren. Health concerns become more challenging to the family in later life. We will discuss the family in later life in Chapter 18.

Families Nearing the End of Life

The **family nearing the end of life** is the seventh and final stage of the family life cycle. At this time death is near and the spouse must deal with the loss of a partner, siblings, or other peers. It is a difficult time when preparation for death and legacy must be made. The caregiver role takes on a new dimension, with altering support from family members. Family loss, bereavement, and preparation for death are discussed in Chapter 19.

Parenting Myths and Realities

The needs and expectations of parents have stimulated many myths about parenting (Williams, Sawyer, & Wahlstrom, 2012), including the following:

- The birth of a child will save a failing marriage.
- As a possession or extension of the parent, the child will think, feel, and behave like the parents did in their childhood.
- Having a child gives the parents a "second chance" to achieve what they should have achieved.
- Parenting is an instinct and requires no training.

Parenting requires a number of interpersonal skills and imposes emotional demands, yet there is little in the way of formal education for this task. Most parents learn parenting practices from their own parents—some they accept, some they discard. Unfortunately, when methods of parents are passed on from one generation to the next, both desirable and undesirable practices are perpetuated. Adding to reality of the task of parenting, husbands and wives may bring different parenting practices to the marriage. The parents, then, may struggle with each other about which is a better practice to interact with a child. The task or challenge facing new parents is to form a united leadership style for their new family.

Moving successfully through this lengthy stage requires a commitment of time as a parent, understanding the roles of parents, and adapting to developmental changes in children. Problems that emerge when a couple first assumes the parental role include struggles with each other about taking responsibility, as well as a refusal or inability to function as competent parents to children. We extensively discussed this stage of the family life cycle in Chapters 6, 8, and 9.

To this point, we have discussed a number of ideas about intimate relationships: marriage and the family life cycle. For a review, see the Reach Your Learning Outcomes section at the end of this chapter.

The Diversity of Adult Lifestyles

LO4 Compare and contrast the diversity of adult lifestyles.

- **Single Adults**
- **Cohabiting Adults**
- **Divorced Adults**
- **Remarried Adults**
- **Parenting Adults**
- **Lone-Parent Adults**
- **Gay and Lesbian Adults**

Today's adult lifestyles are increasingly being reshaped. Adults may choose from many lifestyle options and form different types of families (Benokraitis, 2008). One of the most striking social changes in recent decades is the decreased stigma attached to people who do not maintain what were long considered conventional families. They may choose to live alone, cohabit, marry, divorce, remarry, or live with someone of the same sex. Let's explore each of these lifestyles and how they affect adults.

Single Adults

The extraordinary increase in the number of people living alone is among the most significant social changes of the modern world (Klinenberg, 2016). Recent decades have seen a dramatic rise in the percentage of single (unmarried) adults. In Canada in 2011 there was a large increase in the proportions of the population who never married in their twenties and thirties compared to 2008. For young adults aged 25 to 29, the proportion who had never married rose from about one-quarter of this population (26.0 percent) in 1981 to close to three-quarters (73.1 percent) in 2011 (Milan, 2013). Even among individuals in their early thirties, the proportion of women who had never married increased from 10.5 percent in 1981 to 43.4 percent in 2011. For men, the increase was 15.0 percent in 1981 to 54.0 percent in 2011(Milan, 2013). Men, it seems are more likely than women to be single. It appears that men have their own reasons for delaying marriage or not marrying at all (Macionis & Gerber, 2014).

Even when singles enjoy their lifestyles and are highly competent, they often are stereotyped (Schwartz & Scott, 2012). Stereotypes associated with being single range from the "swinging single" to the "desperately lonely, suicidal" single. Of course, most single adults fall somewhere between these extremes. The stigma associated with singlehood stems from the social status in society of being a couple (Cobb, 2011). Single adults who have newly transitioned out of their university/college undergraduate years face increasingly insurmountable pressure about the necessity of becoming part of a couple (Klinenberg, 2012). In fact, single people who are actively trying to depart from being single into couplehood are less stigmatized (McKeown, 2015).

Some advantages of being single include having time to make decisions about one's life course, time to develop personal resources to meet goals, and freedom to make autonomous decisions and pursue one's own schedule and interests. Compared with married couples, single adults are more likely to spend time with friends and neighbours, dine in restaurants, and attend art classes and lectures (Klinenberg, 2012).

Common problems of single adults may include forming intimate relationships with other adults, confronting loneliness, and finding a niche in a society that is marriage-oriented. Bella DePaulo (2006, 2011) argues that society has a widespread bias against unmarried adults that is evident in missed employment perks to deep and financial prejudices.

Cohabiting Adults

Cohabitation refers to living together in an emotional and sexual relationship without being married. Cohabitation is perceived as being a freer lifestyle (Casper & Bianchi, 2007; Cherlin, 2007; Popenoe, 2008). Cohabiting couples make up a growing proportion of all families in Canada. Since the Canadian census started to collect data on cohabitation in 1981, the rate more than tripled from 5.6 percent to 16.7 percent of all families in 2011 (Statistics Canada, 2012). Within Quebec, common-law couple families represent more than one third (37.8 percent) of all couples in the province. That is much higher than the average for the rest of Canada (14.5 percent) (Institute of Marriage and Family Canada, 2013). Growing rates of cohabitation in Canada mirror what is happening in other high-income countries, although with some variation. Cohabitation is the norm in Sweden and Denmark but remains rare (although the rate is on the increase) in Italy, Greece, and Poland (Perrelli-Harris et al., 2012).

Today, most Canadians between the ages 20 and 29 experience a common-law relationship as their first union (Guzzo, 2014). However, relationships starting with cohabitation are nearly twice as likely to dissolve as those which began with marriage, regardless of whether or not they marry (Institute of Marriage and Family Canada, 2013). Much of the research on cohabitation indicates that couples who cohabitate before being engaged or married are more likely to experience marital instability and divorce (Anita, O'Leary, & Moyer, 2010). It is interesting to note that most marriages are preceded by cohabitation (Kennedy & Bumpass, 2008) even as less cohabitation started with marital intentions (Vespa, 2014).

Cohabitation is now an acceptable union for young adults, in part because of delays in first marriage and the prolongation of having children (Settersten & Ray, 2010). Several researchers have examined reasons for cohabitation (Johnson, Anderson, & Aducci, 2011; Willoughby, Carrol, & Busby, 2011). Rhoades and colleagues (2009) found that a few of the reasons for cohabitation are that the couples wanted to spend more time together to test the relationship, and because it was simply convenient for them to cohabitate.

Divorced Adults

Divorce rates are increasing, but the statistics reported are often confusing and misleading. To interpret the statistics, we need to know both how they are derived and their context. Are they based on total population, including children and singles, or are they based on the number of marriages? If they are based on the number of marriages, are these marriages new marriages or all marriages? Marriages for the sole purpose of citizenship usually end in divorce and become part of the statistics. Additionally, the population is aging, which means that there are not as many people in the vulnerable first five years of marriage, the peak time for divorce unless the individuals were previously married. As well, an unknown number of couples separate but never legally divorce. There were 70 226 divorces in Canada in 2008, or a crude divorce rate of 21.1 divorces per 10 000 population (Milan, 2013).

If a divorce is going to occur, it usually takes place early in a marriage, peaking between the fifth and tenth year of marriage (Ambert, 1998) (see Figure 14.5). Although divorce has increased for all socio-economic groups, those in some groups have a higher incidence of divorce. Youthful marriage, low educational level, low income, not having a religious affiliation, having parents who are divorced, and having a baby before marriage are factors that are associated with increases in divorce (Hoelter, 2009).

Figure 14.5

The Divorce Rate in Relation to Number of Years Married

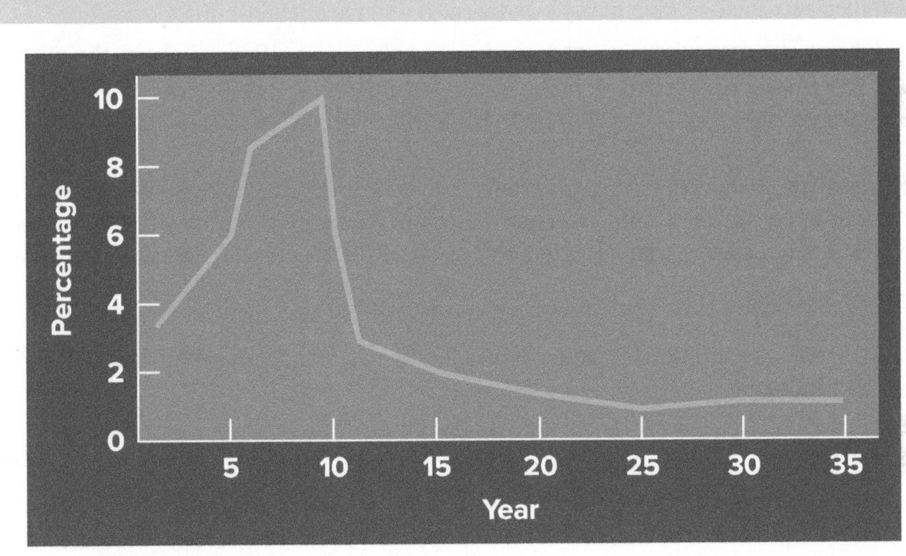

National Center for Health Statistics, 2000 (US)

Shown here is the percentage of divorces as a function of how long couples have been married. Note that most divorces occur in the early years of marriage, peaking between the fifth and tenth year of marriage.

Dealing with Divorce

Both partners experience challenges after a marriage dissolves (Feeney & Monin, 2009). Both divorced women and divorced men complain of loneliness, diminished self-esteem, anxiety about the unknowns in their lives, and difficulty in forming satisfactory new intimate relationships (Hetherington, 2006). A study revealed that following marital dissolution, both men and women were more likely to experience an episode of depression than individuals who remained with a spouse over a two-year period (Rotermann, 2007). The challenges of divorce differ somewhat for custodial and non-custodial parents and for men and women (Rotermann, 2007). Research shows this to be one of the most stressful aspects of divorce. Custodial parents have concerns about childrearing and overload in their lives. Non-custodial parents register complaints about alienation from or lack of time with their children. However, both partners experience challenges after a marriage dissolves (Breslau et al., 2011). Divorced adults have higher rates of depression, anxiety, physical illness, suicide, motor vehicle accidents, alcoholism, and mortality (Braver & Lamb, 2013).

If a marriage doesn't work, what happens after divorce? Psychologically, one of the most common characteristics of divorced adults is difficulty in trusting someone else in a romantic relationship. Following a divorce, though, people's lives can take diverse turns (Tashiro, Frazier, & Berman, 2006). In E. Mavis Hetherington's research, men and women took six common pathways in exiting divorce (Hetherington & Kelly, 2002, pp. 98–108):

- *The enhancers:* Accounting for 20 percent of the divorced group, most were females who "grew more competent, well adjusted, and self-fulfilled" following their divorce (p. 98). They were competent in multiple areas of life, showing a remarkable ability to bounce back from stressful circumstances and create something meaningful out of problems.
- *The good-enoughs:* The largest group of divorced individuals was described as average people coping with divorce. They showed some strengths and some weaknesses, some successes and some failures. When they experienced a problem, they tried to solve it. Many of them attended night classes, found new friends, developed active social lives, and were motivated to get higher-paying jobs. However, they were not as good at planning and were less persistent than the enhancers. Good-enough women usually married men who educationally and economically were similar to their first husbands, often going into a new marriage that was not much of an improvement over the first one.
- *The seekers:* These individuals were motivated to find new mates as soon as possible. "At one year post-divorce, 40 percent of the men and 38 percent of women had been classified as seekers. But as people found new partners or remarried, or became more secure or satisfied in their single life, this category shrank and came to be predominated by men" (p. 102).
- *The libertines:* People in this category often spent more time in singles bars and had more casual sex than their counterparts in the other divorce categories. However, by the end of the first year post-divorce, they often grew disillusioned with their sensation-seeking lifestyle and wanted a stable relationship.
- *The competent loners:* These individuals, who made up only about 10 percent of the divorced group, were "well-adjusted, self-sufficient, and socially skilled." They had a successful career, an active social life, and a wide range of interests. However, "unlike enhancers, competent loners had little interest in sharing their lives with anyone else" (p. 105).
- *The defeated:* Some of these individuals had problems before their divorce, and these problems increased after the breakup when "the added stress of a failed marriage was more than they could handle. Others had difficulty coping because divorce cost them a spouse who had supported them, or in the case of a drinking problem, restricted them" (p. 106).

Wright and Leahey (2013) state that the developmental issues for divorced family members include adapting to living apart and dealing with the extended family.

Remarried Adults

Remarriage occurs sooner for partners who initiate a divorce (especially in the first several years after divorce and for older women) than those who do not initiate a divorce (Sweeney, 2009, 2010). Remarried families are more likely to be unstable than first marriages, with divorce more likely to occur, especially in the first several years of the remarried family, than in the first marriages (Waite, 2009). However, researchers have found that remarried adults' marital relationship is more egalitarian and more likely to be characterized by shared decision-making than first marriages (Waite, 2009). Remarried wives report that they have more influence on financial matters in their new family than do wives in first marriages (Waite, 2009).

Why do remarried adults with families find it so difficult to stay married? For one thing, many remarry not for love but for financial reasons, for help in rearing children, and to reduce loneliness. They also might carry into the blended family negative relationship patterns that resulted in the failure of an earlier marriage. Remarried couples also experience more stress in rearing children than do parents in never-divorced families (Ganong, Coleman, & Hans, 2006). A recent study concluded that a positive attitude toward divorce, when combined with low marital quality, tended to make remarried individuals more likely to seek divorce than those in first marriages (Whitton et al., 2013).

critical thinking

What are some of the variations in family structure with which you are familiar? What might be some of the unique tasks for each? What challenges must blended or reconstituted families overcome to ensure a successful adjustment? How do the tasks differ for each member; for example, how are the tasks of the custodial parent different from that of stepparent–stepchild? What are some of the adjustment tasks for siblings? for extended family members such as grandparents, cousins, aunts, and uncles? A lone-parent family may be headed by a single, separated, divorced, or widowed adult. What challenges and tasks face the lone-parent family? How does the context influence each scenario?

Parenting Adults

Family life in Canada will continue to change. The family where the father is the provider and mother is homemaker is now the minority. Contemporary families are more diverse, more complex, and smaller than they used to be. As birth control has become common practice, many individuals consciously choose when they will have children and how many children they will rear; as well, the number of one-child families is increasing. In addition, children are increasingly expensive to raise (Brym et al., 2016). Several new trends are becoming apparent (Sinha, 2015):

- By giving birth to fewer children and reducing the demands of child care, women free up a significant portion of their life spans for other endeavours.
- Men are apt to invest a greater amount of time in fathering.
- Parental care is often supplemented by institutional care (child care, for example).

As more women show an increased interest in developing a career, they are not only marrying later, but also having fewer children and having them later in life. Some of the advantages of having children early (in their twenties) are that the parents are likely to have more physical energy (for example, they can cope better with such matters as getting up in the middle of the night with infants and waiting up until adolescents come home at night). As well, the mother is likely to have fewer medical problems with pregnancy and childbirth, and the parents may be less likely to build up expectations for their children, as do many couples who have waited many years to have children. There are also advantages to having children later (in their thirties): the parents will have had more time to consider their goals in life, such as what they want from their family and career roles; the parents will be more mature and will be able to benefit from their life experiences to engage in more competent parenting; and the parents will be better established in their careers and have more income for childrearing expenses (Brym et al., 2016).

Despite the changes and controversies that have taken place in the family, most individuals still report being happy as partners, as parents, and, it seems, as children. ((Macionis & Gerber, 2014).

critical thinking

Dual-income families are an economic reality as well as an indicator of the changing roles for both men and women. What are some of the challenges dual-income parents face as they shape the emotional climate of the home? What strategies would you suggest a couple put in place to deal with these challenges?

Lone-Parent Adults

Lone-parent families are those families usually headed by adults who are either separated, divorced, or widowed. Another route to lone parenthood involves single, never married mothers who give birth to children on their own. The biological father may or may not be in the picture but does not live with the child (Brym et al., 2016).

In 2011, 16 percent of Canadian families were headed by a lone parent, with more than eight in ten lone parent families headed by women (Statistics Canada, 2012). Meanwhile in 2014, 69 percent of lone mothers were employed, mostly on a full-time basis. This represented an increase from the 48 percent of lone mothers who were employed in 1976 (Statistics Canada, 2015). Ravanera (2008) states that almost two-thirds (63 percent) of lone fathers—defined as men living with at least one child aged 24 years or younger who are not living with a marital spouse or a partner in common law union—became lone fathers through separation or divorce. About 26 percent of lone fathers have never been married, meaning their children were born in a cohabiting union or outside a union. Eight percent of lone fathers are widowers.

Who are lone parents? As an example, Marion, a 43-year-old teacher, found herself on her own with three teenagers, aged 15, 17, and 19, all in high school and all wanting to go to university. Her ex-husband provided no financial support; consequently, both she and her children incurred debt and delays while the children finished their education. On the other hand, Alicia, with two teenagers, was working part-time at the time of her divorce, and the children's father agreed to support the children financially until they finish their undergraduate work. Tina fits the profile of adolescent single parents described in Chapter 12. She had her first baby when she was 16, and her second at 19. In both cases, the child's father was older and abusive. Now, at 22, Tina has entered a community college to get the training she needs to, in her words, ". . . get off welfare and support myself and my children." Tina struggles to balance daycare, a part-time job, her studies, and her social life.

Another interesting phenomenon is the number of women in their mid-thirties who have decided to have and raise children as lone parents. They may have in vitro fertilization or adopt, but in either case, these women, who often have successful careers, decide to have and raise children on their own.

Gay and Lesbian Adults

Same-sex couples are also on a steep increase, however, they only made up 0.8 percent of all couples in 2011 (The Canadian Press, 2012). Researchers have found that gay and lesbian relationships are similar—in their satisfactions, loves, joys, and conflicts—to heterosexual relationships (Mohr, 2009; Fingerhut & Peplau, 2013). For example, like heterosexual couples, gay and lesbian couples need to find a balance in their relationships that is acceptable to both partners in terms of romantic love, affection, how much autonomy is acceptable, and how egalitarian the relationship will be (Kurdek, 2006).

There are a number of misconceptions about homosexual couples (Kurdek, 2007; Fingerhut & Peplau, 2013). Contrary to stereotypes, one partner rarely takes the "masculine" counterpart to the other partner's "feminine" function. Only a small segment of the gay male population have a large number of sexual partners, and multiple partners is uncommon among lesbians as well. Researchers have found that lesbian and gay men prefer long-term, committed relationships (Fingerhut & Peplau, 2013). Although same-sex marriages are lawful in Canada, laws surrounding divorce of same-sex couples remain unclear (Green & Mitchell, 2009; Weston, 2007).

Digital Vision/Getty Images/Punchstock

What are the research findings regarding the development and psychological well-being of children raised by gay and lesbian couples?

Increasingly, gay and lesbian couples are creating families that include children (Bos, van Balen, & van den Boom, 2008). An increasing number of same-sex couples are adopting children (Farr & Patterson, 2013). Researchers have found that children growing up in gay or lesbian families are just as well-liked as their peers, and there are no differences in the adjustment and mental health of children living in these families compared to children in heterosexual families. Same-sex couples tend to be more egalitarian than heterosexual couples; that is, they share most decision-making and household duties equally (Goldberg, Smith, & Perry-Jenkins, 2012).

To this point, we have discussed the diversity of adult lifestyles. For a review, see the Reach Your Learning Outcomes section at the end of this chapter.

Gender, Relationships, and Moral Development

LO5 Summarize moral development and gender development.

- **Moral Development**
- **Women's Development**
- **Men's Development**

In Chapter 10, we discussed Kohlberg and Gilligan's theories on moral development. In this section, we will look at another theory of moral development put forward by Urie Bronfenbrenner, whose bio-ecological theory was outlined in Chapter 2. Building on the discussion of gender roles in Chapters 8, 10, and 12, an overview of women and men's development also follows.

Moral Development

Urie Bronfenbrenner, whose bio-ecological theory of development you read about in Chapter 2, proposed five moral orientations based on an individual's context rather than on individual's passing through stages (see Figure 14.6). Individuals may move forward and backward in these orientations depending on the culture, an individual's exposure to differing values, the situation, and personal contexts.

Figure 14.6
Bronfenbrenner's Five Moral Orientations

Orientation	Description
1. Self-oriented morality	An individual's personal needs take precedence over everyone else's needs. Others are considered only insofar as they can assist or hinder the individual.
2. Authority-oriented morality	Compliance to those who have authority or power, such as parents, teachers, police, and religious and political leaders.
3. Peer-oriented morality	Making choices about what is right and what is wrong based on what one's peers think, say, and do.
4. Collective-oriented morality	Making moral choices based on duty or obligation to family, country, etc.
5. Objectively-oriented morality	Belief that universal principles have a morality of their own.

As outlined by Dr. George Boeree, http://webspace.ship.edu/cgboer/genpsymoraldev.html.

Movement between orientations 2, 3, and 4 (authority, peer, and collective orientations) are related to the role religion, obedience to an authority, and peers play in an individual's culture. For example, an individual whose religious views are fundamentalist Christian may make decisions based on his or her understanding of religious beliefs. These moral choices would differ from those made by an individual who does not adhere to any faith group, or one who adheres to the Muslim faith, for example. Another example would be voicing political dissent. Speaking against a government may be far more difficult, perhaps dangerous, in a country where compliance to authority means agreeing with the present government. And, another example would be the number of children a couple may decide to have. In one country such a decision is a matter of choice, whereas in another it's a matter of law.

Movement among orientations 3, 4, or 5 (peer, collective, and objective orientations) occurs when an individual is exposed to values that conflict, at least in part, with his or her own. For example, moving to Canada where women are not circumcised may cause parents to rethink their views. Moving from Canada to a country where women do not show their arms and legs in public may cause a woman to rethink her wardrobe.

Movement within the first four orientations involves situations where concern for others takes precedence over concern for self. For example, the service education adopted by Ontario schools is based on the notion that students who do volunteer work will develop a lasting concern for others. Through participation with others, an individual learns differing perspectives and develops empathy and altruism.

At any time in a person's life, adverse events may cause the individual to move to self-oriented morality as a matter of self-preservation. For example, an individual or family member who, because of economic upheaval, is thrust into poverty may experience the potential threat of losing his or her home. This person may make decisions and behave in ways he or she would not in other circumstances. Once economic stability is regained, the individual's decision making and behaviour may change again. In any case, the person's understanding of the world is influenced by these experiences.

Bronfenbrenner believed that very few people sustain objectively-oriented morality. He thought that the hectic pace of modern life poses a threat second only to poverty and unemployment. The hectic pace of life may result in parents making hasty decisions that adversely affect the children and the harmony of the home. This deprives children of what he believed to be the development of their birthright virtues, such as honesty, responsibility, compassion, and integrity.

Women's Development

Jean Baker Miller's (1986) writings have been important in stimulating the examination of psychological issues from a female perspective. She believed that the study of women's psychological development opens up paths to a better understanding of all psychological development, male or female. She also concluded that when researchers examine what women have been doing in life, a large part of it is active participation in the development of others. According to Miller, women often try to interact with others in ways that will foster the other person's development along many dimensions—emotional, intellectual, and social.

Most experts believe it is important for women not only to maintain their competency in relationships, but to be self-motivated as well (Hyde, 2007; Matlin, 2008). Miller believed that through increased self-determination, coupled with already-developed relationship skills, many women would gain greater power in the North American culture. And, as Harriet Lerner (1989) concludes in her book *The Dance of Intimacy,* it is important for women to bring to their relationships nothing less than a strong, assertive, independent, and authentic self. She believes competent relationships are those in which the separate "I-ness" of both persons can be appreciated and enhanced while still staying emotionally connected to each other.

In sum, Miller, Lerner, Gilligan, and other gender experts believe that women are more relationship-oriented than men—and that this relationship orientation should be prized as a skill in our culture more than it currently is. Critics of this view of gender differences in relationships contend that it is too stereotypical (Hyde, 2005, 2007). They argue that there is greater individual variation in the relationship styles of men and women than this view acknowledges (Hyde, 2007). However, the newest aspect in women's development theory consists of "post-feminists," young women who take their equality with men for granted (Everingham, Stevenson, & Warner-Smith, 2007). They make their own choices as to what they want to do with their life.

Men's Development

In taking a father's role, men often experience a shift away from their individual concerns and toward family and broader social relationships (Settersten & Cancel-Tirado, 2010). Fatherhood can enhance their development by allowing them to become less self-centred and more giving, and to achieve a greater sense of responsibility and direction in life. It can also direct men to take fewer risks and temper their lifestyle (Olmstead, Futris, & Pasley, 2009).

Men as fathers focus more on their family and social relationships; they become more aware of the needs of their children and others. This transformation can increase their attachment to communities and social networks (Settersten & Cancel-Tirado, 2010). Institutions and policies can play important roles in transforming attitudes toward men and fatherhood (O'Brien, 2009).

It is important to note that male aggression against women still exists and is associated with levels of gender inequality in the family. It is more common in families where men believe that male dominance is justified (Franklin & Kercher, 2012). Daily patterns of gender domination are built into courtship, sexual, family, and work norms (Stewart, McMillan, & Wathen, 2013).

What are some changes in men's roles in home and family matters in the last 40 years?

To this point, we have discussed a number of ideas about gender, relationships, and moral development. For a review, see the Reach Your Learning Objectives section at the end of this chapter.

Reach Your **Learning Outcomes**

Stability and Change from Childhood to Adulthood

LO1 Examine stability and change in temperament, and summarize adult attachment styles.

Temperament	▪ The issue of stability versus change is a factor in both temperament and attachment. ▪ The first 20 years are important in predicting an adult's personality, but so, too, are continuing experiences in the adult years; the question is whether or not our core temperament changes as a result of our experiences. ▪ Previous studies indicate that temperament is genetically influenced from childhood to adolescence. ▪ In early adulthood, most individuals assume greater responsibilities, foresee consequences, plan ahead, and are more even-keeled than in adolescence.
Attachment	▪ Attachment patterns in young adults are linked to their attachment history, although attachment styles can change in adulthood as adults experience relationships.

Attraction, Love, and Close Relationships

LO2 Identify three key aspects of attraction, love, and close relationships.

Attraction	▪ Familiarity precedes a close relationship. We like to associate with people who are similar to us. The principles of consensual validation and matching can explain this. ▪ Physical attraction is usually more important in the early part of a relationship; criteria of physical attractiveness vary across cultures and historical time.
The Faces of Love	▪ Erikson theorized that intimacy versus isolation is the key developmental issue in early adulthood. There is a delicate balance between intimacy and commitment on the one hand, and independence and freedom on the other. ▪ Romantic love, also called passionate love, is involved when we say we are "in love." It includes passion, sexuality, and a mixture of emotions, not all of which are positive. ▪ Affectionate love, also called companionate love, usually becomes more important as relationships mature. ▪ Sternberg's triangular theory of love includes passion, intimacy, and commitment. When all three are present, Sternberg called this consummate love.
Falling Out of Love	▪ In the long run, the collapse of a relationship may be beneficial to one's health and future happiness. ▪ Dysfunctional relationships are those in which one person exploits another emotionally, financially, and/or physically. ▪ Women report more positive growth after a relational breakup than men.
Friendship	▪ Friendship plays an important role in adult development, especially in terms of emotional support. ▪ Female, male, and female–male friendships often have different characteristics. For example, self-disclosure and support is more common in female friendships. ▪ Friends with benefits relationships have emerged primarily within the last decade.

Loneliness	▪ Loneliness often emerges when people make life transitions, and so it is not surprising that loneliness is common among first-year college and university students. ▪ Social loneliness results from an unsatisfying network of friends, whereas emotional loneliness is the product of unsatisfactory romantic or family relationships. Social loneliness is strongly linked to mental and physical health. ▪ Secure attachment experiences in childhood enable young adults to initiate and sustain relationships, resolve conflicts, and overcome loneliness.

Intimate Relationships: Marriage and the Family Life Cycle

LO3 **Describe intimate relationships such as marriage, the family life cycle, and cultural influences on family life.**

Marital Trends in Canada	▪ Even though adults are remaining single longer and the divorce rate is high, we still show a strong predilection for marriage. ▪ The age at which individuals marry, expectations about what the marriage will be like, and the developmental course of marriage may vary not only across historical time within a culture, but also across cultures.
Social Contexts	▪ Cultural and religious backgrounds influence the characteristics desired in a partner. ▪ The average age for marriage in Canada is early thirties.
Making Marriage Work	▪ Gottman has conducted the most extensive research on what makes marriages work. ▪ In his research, these principles characterize good marriages: establishing love maps, nurturing fondness and admiration, turning toward each other instead of away, letting your partner influence you, solving solvable conflicts, overcoming gridlock, and creating shared meaning.
Benefits of a Good Marriage	▪ Better mental and physical health and a longer life are benefits of marriage.
The Family Life Cycle	▪ There are seven stages in the family life cycle: leaving home and becoming a single adult; the joining of families through marriage—the new couple; becoming parents and a family with children; the family with adolescents; launching children and moving on; the family in later life; and families nearing the end of life.
Parenting Myths and Realities	▪ For some, the parental role is well planned and coordinated. For others, it is a surprise and sometimes chaotic. ▪ Some of the many myths about parenting include the following: the birth of a child will save a failing marriage; having a child gives the parents a "second chance" to achieve what they should have achieved; parenting is an instinct and requires no training.

The Diversity of Adult Lifestyles

LO4 **Compare and contrast the diversity of adult lifestyles.**

Single Adults	▪ The economy, increased levels of education, and fear of divorce are some of the reasons young adults are waiting longer to marry.
Cohabiting Adults	▪ Most young people who cohabit intend to marry. ▪ Cohabiting relationships are not as stable as married relationships. ▪ Although cohabitation is more prevalent today than a generation ago, no evidence supports that it is beneficial to marriage.
Divorced Adults	▪ One in four marriages end in divorce by 30 years of marriage, with the greater number of divorces occurring within the first 5 to 10 years of marriage. ▪ Divorce brings unique challenges, including custodial arrangements.
Remarried Adults	▪ On average, divorced adults remarry within four years. ▪ Blended or reconstituted families present unique challenges.
Parenting Adults	▪ The advantages and disadvantages of adults becoming a parent in their twenties differ from those in their thirties. ▪ Managing time for child care, along with busy work schedules, is a priority for most parenting adults. ▪ Fathers are taking a greater role in parenting.
Lone-Parent Adults	▪ Lone-parent families are headed by single, separated, divorced, and widowed adults. ▪ Poverty is the primary challenge to lone-parent families headed by young single women. ▪ More single women in their thirties and older who have completed their education and have stable jobs are deciding to become parents through in vitro fertilization or adoption.
Gay and Lesbian Adults	▪ Gay and lesbian unions face the same challenges as heterosexual unions. ▪ The stereotypes of one partner taking the masculine role and the other taking the female role are erroneous.

Gender, Relationships, and Moral Development

LO5 Summarize moral development and gender development.

Moral Development	▪ Urie Bronfenbrenner proposed five moral orientations that may vary according to the individual's context.
Women's Development	▪ Many experts believe that it is important for females to retain their competence and interest in relationships, but also to direct more effort to self-development.
Men's Development	▪ Fatherhood can enhance men's development. ▪ Male aggression against women still exists

review → connect → reflect

review

1. How stable is temperament from childhood to adulthood? LO1
2. Which styles of attachment characterize adults? How are these styles of attachment linked to relationship outcomes? LO1
3. What are the three types of love? LO2
4. What makes a marriage work? LO3
5. Which stage in the family life cycle pertains to early adulthood? LO3
6. What similarities can be seen between homosexual and heterosexual relationships? LO4
7. What are several differences in the ways in which men and women communicate? LO5

connect

What may be several effects that divorce and remarriage can have on the children in those families?

reflect

Your Own Personal Journey of Life

Which type of lifestyle are you living today? What, for you, are the advantages and disadvantages of this lifestyle? If you could have a different lifestyle, would you change it? Why?

SECTION 8

Middle Adulthood

CHAPTER 15

Physical and Cognitive Development in Middle Adulthood

CHAPTER OUTLINE

The Nature of Middle Adulthood

LO1 Explain how midlife is changing, and define middle adulthood.

- **Changing Midlife**

Physical Development

LO2 Discuss physical changes in middle adulthood.

- **Physical Changes**
- **Health Concerns and Wellness Strategies**
- **Culture, Relationships, and Health**
- **Mortality Rates**
- **Sexuality**

Cognitive Development

LO3 Identify cognitive changes in middle adulthood.

- **Intelligence**
- **Information Processing**

Careers, Work, and Leisure

LO4 Characterize career development, work, and leisure in middle adulthood.

- **Work in Midlife**
- **Career Challenges and Changes**
- **Leisure**

Meaning in Life

LO5 Explain the roles of meditation, religion, and spirituality in understanding meaning in life during middle adulthood.

- **Meditation, Religion, and Spirituality**
- **Meaning in Life**
- **Health and Well-Being**

"The event of creation did not take place many aeons ago. Astronomically or biologically speaking, creation is taking place every moment of our lives."

—DAVID SUZUKI, CONTEMPORARY CANADIAN SCIENTIST, ENVIRONMENTALIST, AND BROADCASTER

Image Source/Getty Images

Middle Age

Social determinants of health include income and social status; social support networks; education; employment/working conditions; social environments; physical environments; personal health practices and coping skills; healthy child development; gender; and culture. These determinants are highly influential on both life expectancy and the overall quality of life in any country (PHAC, 2016; Central Intelligence Agency, 2016). Fortunately, in Canada, access to the majority of these social determinants—particularly education, health care, social networks, and government supports—all make for generally good living conditions. As a result, life expectancy for a child born in 2015 in Canada is projected to be 81.76 years: 79.15 for men and 84.52 for women (Statistics Canada, 2016).

The National Collaborating Centre for Aboriginal Health (NCCAH) (2013) points out that heath determinants are indirectly associated to social, economic, cultural, and political factors. Further, NCCAH notes that significant disparities in social determinants of health exist between Aboriginal and non-Aboriginal Canadians, particularly those living in rural areas or on reserves where water, education, and health supports are not as accessible. Consequently, Aboriginal Canadians, in addition to having higher suicide rates, experience a considerably shorter life expectancy than non-Aboriginal Canadians. For example, life expectancy for Inuit peoples is 64 for men and 73 for women (Statistics Canada, 2015; Health Canada, 2016; NCCAH, 2014). By comparison, life expectancy for a child born in Chad or Afghanistan is 50 years of age (Central Intelligence Agency, 2016). Considering these variations of life expectancy, middle adulthood might occur as early as 18 or 20 in Chad or Afghanistan and between 32 and 37 for Inuit Canadians. For a cross-section of both Aboriginal and non-Aboriginal Canadians, middle age would be just under 40 years of age.

So, given all these complexities, how is middle age defined and what does it mean? As you have read in the previous chapters, early adulthood is vastly different today than a generation ago. The milestones that were once associated with the twenties—completing education, procuring secure employment, getting married, starting a family, purchasing a home—are now milestones associated with the thirties, if they occur at all. Such a shift of milestones for early adulthood creates a definite paradigm shift for middle adulthood, with an obvious shift in the age that Canadians first become grandparents.

Young adults often postpone starting a family usually until their late twenties or later. As a result, there are fewer grandparents in middle adulthood than in previous generations. In 1985, for example, almost 60 per cent of women between the ages of 50 and 54 were grandmothers; however, in 2011, less than 30 percent of women in this age group had grandchildren, illustrating that the Canadian grandparent population is aging (Margolis & Iciaszczyk, 2015). Fortunately, in spite of being older than their counterparts of a generation or two earlier, many of today's grandparents are in better health and have attained higher levels of education (Margolis & Iciaszczyk, 2015). More people lead healthier lifestyles, plus medical discoveries help to stave off the aging process.

Although people in middle adulthood are healthier than in previous generations, they are constantly reminded that they are aging. All those outward signs—wrinkles, greying hair, declining strength, receding hairlines, declining vision, diminishing hearing—are constant reminders. The unwelcome onset of chronic diseases, many of which are associated with stress (e.g., hypertension and cardiovascular disease), as well as hormonal changes, also accompany and complicate middle adulthood. Thus, although people in middle adulthood are generally healthier and abler to help raise their grandchildren, care for their elderly parents, and work full- or part-time, all this activity requires considerable juggling and problem solving. In the words of David Suzuki, people in middle adulthood are in the midst of the complicated process of creation: building a future for the next generation.

The Nature of Middle Adulthood

LO1 Explain how midlife is changing, and define middle adulthood.

- **Changing Midlife**

As the opening vignette illustrates, midlife today is much different from a generation ago. How can middle adulthood be defined, and what are some of its main characteristics?

Changing Midlife

As a much greater percentage of the population lives to an older age, the midpoint of life and what constitutes middle age or middle adulthood are getting harder to pin down (Cohen, 2012). When Carl Jung studied midlife transitions early in the twentieth century, he referred to midlife as the "afternoon of life" (Jung, 1933). Midlife serves as an important preparation for late adulthood, the "evening of life" (Lachman, 2004, p. 306). But "midlife" came much earlier in Jung's time.

As noted above, life expectancy in Canada is 80 for men and 84 for women, and by 2031 Statistics Canada projects that life expectancy will rise to 81.9 for men and 86 for women. On average, Canadians can expect to enjoy 70 to 80 years of good health (Statistics Canada, 2015). Healthier lifestyles, including reduced tobacco intake, and medical discoveries are two reasons for the increasing life expectancy.

Defining Middle Adulthood

The median age in Canada is 39.8 years, which means that half the population is older and the other half younger (Statistics Canada, 2015). In 1966, the median age was only 25.4 years. The rising median age is one of the many indicators that the nation's population is aging, and has many implications for the labour force, economy, social services, and health care. So just how is middle adulthood defined today? As you read in the opening vignette, the age boundaries are not set in stone; however, we will consider **middle adulthood** as the developmental period that begins at approximately 40 to 45 years of age and extends to about 60 to 65 years of age. For many healthy adults, middle age is lasting longer.

The concept of gains (growth) and losses (decline) is an important one in life-span development (Dixon et al., 2013). Middle adulthood is the age period in which gains and losses as well as biological and socio-cultural factors balance each other (Baltes, Lindenberger, & Staudinger, 2006). Compared with earlier midlife, milestones in late midlife are more likely to be characterized by "the death of a parent, the last child leaving the parental home, becoming a grandparent, the preparation for retirement, and in most cases actual retirement. Many people in this age range experience their first confrontation with health problems" (Deeg, 2005, p. 211). Overall, then, although gains and losses may balance each other in early midlife, losses may begin to dominate gains for many individuals in late midlife (Baltes, Lindenberger, & Staudinger, 2006). Remember, though, that midlife is characterized by individual variations (Ailshire & Burgard, 2012; Schaie, 2013). As life-span expert Gilbert Brim (1992) commented, middle adulthood is full of changes, twists, and turns; the path is not fixed. People move in and out of states of success and failure.

To this point, we have discussed the nature of middle adulthood. For a review, see the Reach Your Learning Outcomes section at the end of this chapter.

Physical Development

LO2 Discuss physical changes in middle adulthood.

- **Physical Changes**
- **Health Concerns and Wellness Strategies**
- **Culture, Relationships, and Health**
- **Mortality Rates**
- **Sexuality**

What physical changes characterize middle adulthood? How healthy are middle-aged adults? What are the main causes of death in middle age? How sexually active are individuals in middle adulthood?

Physical Changes

Unlike the rather dramatic physical changes that occur in early adolescence and the sometimes abrupt decline in late adulthood, physical changes in midlife are usually gradual. Although everyone experiences some physical change due to aging, the rates of this aging vary considerably from one individual to another. Genetic makeup and lifestyle factors play important roles in whether chronic disease will appear and when. Middle age is a window through which we can glimpse later life while there is still time to engage in prevention and to influence some of the course of aging (Bertrand et al., 2013; Lachman, 2004).

Turning 50 is a milestone for many, as is turning 30 or 40 or 60. As we leave one decade, we lose a small part of our youth. Amusing hints of aging are that our children are older than we ever thought they would be, and strangers start to address us more respectfully, calling us "sir" or "ma'am." Although many may laugh at these subtle indicators that life is marching on, many may spend considerable time, effort, and money trying to hide aging's visible signs.

Visible Signs

Appearance is one of the most visible signs of middle adulthood. The skin begins to wrinkle and sag because of a loss of fat and collagen in underlying tissues (Pageon et al., 2014). Small, localized areas of pigmentation in the skin produce aging spots, especially in areas that are exposed to sunlight, such as the hands and face. Hair becomes thinner and greyer due to a lower replacement rate and a decline in melanin production. Fingernails and toenails develop ridges and become thicker and more brittle. A recent twin study found that twins who had been smoking longer were more likely to have sagging facial skin and wrinkles, especially in the middle and lower portion of the face, than their non-smoking sibling (Okada et al., 2013).

Since a youthful appearance is stressed in our culture, many individuals whose hair is greying, whose skin is wrinkling, whose bodies are sagging, and whose teeth are yellowing strive to make themselves look younger. Undergoing cosmetic surgery, dyeing hair, purchasing wigs, enrolling in weight reduction programs, participating in exercise regimens, and taking heavy doses of vitamins are common in middle age. As well, middle-aged adults have shown a strong interest in plastic surgery and Botox, which may reflect their desire to take control of the aging process (Chen & Dashtipour, 2013; Jiang et al., 2014).

Boris Spremo/Toronto Star via Getty Images

THE CANADIAN PRESS/Jeff McIntosh

Prime Minister Justin Trudeau, in 1986 and 2016. *What are some of the most noticeable signs of aging?*

Height and Weight

Individuals lose height in middle age, and many gain weight (Paoli et al., 2014; Winett et al., 2014). On average, from 30 to 50 years of age, men lose about an inch (2.5 cm) in height, then may lose another inch from 50 to 70 years of age (Hoyer & Roodin, 2003). The height loss for women can be as much as two inches (5 cm) from 25 to 75 years of age. Note that there are large variations in the extent to which individuals become shorter with aging. The decrease in height is due to bone loss in the vertebrae. On average, body fat accounts for about 10 percent of body weight in adolescence but makes up 20 percent or more in middle age.

According to Statistics Canada, 52 percent of adults between 35 and 45 reported themselves to be overweight or obese in 2011. As adults age, the rate increased to 59.6 percent between ages 45 and 65 in 2012 (Statistics Canada, 2012a). Obesity is on the rise globally and here in Canada. The probability that an individual will suffer a number of chronic conditions, including type 2 diabetes, cardiovascular diseases, hypertension, gallbladder disease, digestive disorders and certain types of cancer, is increased if the individual is obese (Navaneelan & Janz, 2015). As well, for individuals who are 30 percent or more overweight, the probability of death in middle adulthood increases by about 40 percent (Bazzane, et al., 2010; Bloomgarden, 2010). Although we have highlighted the health risks of being overweight or obese in middle adulthood, severe weight loss also can pose a risk in the case of acute diseases.

Strength, Joints, and Bones

As we saw in Chapter 13, maximum physical strength and functioning is usually attained in the twenties. Age-related loss of muscle mass and strength, called *sarcopenia*, occurs in the back and legs. Researchers are seeking to identify genes linked to the development of sarcopenia (Marcell, 2013; Tan et al., 2012). Obesity is a risk factor for sarcopenia (Parr, Coffey, & Hawley, 2013). Recently, researchers have increasingly used the term "sarcopenic obesity" to describe individuals who have sarcopenia and are obese (Scott et al., 2014). One study found that sarcopenic obesity was linked to hypertension (Park et al., 2013). A research review concluded that weight management and resistance training are the best strategies to slow down the decline of muscle mass and muscle strength (Rolland et al., 2011).

Peak functioning of the body's joints also usually occurs in the twenties. The cushions for the movement of bones (such as tendons and ligaments) become less efficient in middle adulthood, a time when many individuals experience joint stiffness and more difficulty in movement.

Maximum bone density occurs by the mid- to late-thirties, after which there is a progressive loss of bone. The rate of this bone loss begins slowly but accelerates with further aging (Baron, 2012). Women lose bone mass twice as fast as men do. By the end of midlife, bones break more easily and heal more slowly (Rachner, Khosia, & Hofbauer, 2011).

Vision and Hearing

Accommodation of the eye—the ability to focus and maintain an image on the retina—experiences its sharpest decline between 40 and 59 years of age. In particular, middle-aged individuals begin to have difficulty viewing close objects, which means that many individuals wear glasses with bifocal lenses. The eye's blood supply also diminishes, although usually not until the fifties or sixties. The reduced blood supply may decrease the visual field's size and accounts for an increase in the eye's blind spot. At 60 years of age, the retina receives only one-third as much light as it did at 20 years of age, much of which is due to a decrease in the size of the pupil (Scialfa & Kline, 2007).

Hearing also can start to decline by the age of 40. Auditory assessments indicate that hearing loss occurs in as many as 50 percent of individuals 50 years and older (Fowler & Leigh-Paffenroth, 2007). Sensitivity to high pitches usually declines first, though the ability to hear low-pitched sounds does not seem to decline much in middle adulthood. Men usually lose their sensitivity to high-pitched sounds sooner than women do. However, this gender difference might be due to men's greater exposure to noise in occupations such as mining, automobile work, and so on.

Researchers are identifying new possibilities for improving the vision and hearing of people as they age. One way this is being carried out is through better control of glare or background noise (Natalizia et al., 2010). Laser surgery and implantation of intraocular lenses have become routine procedures for correcting vision in middle-aged adults (Fang, Wang, & He, 2013). Further, recent advances in hearing aids have dramatically improved hearing for many individuals (Banerjee, 2011).

Cardiovascular System

Heart disease and stroke combined are second to cancer as the leading cause of death in Canada, and are a major cause of illness and disability (Statistics Canada, 2012). In fact, the Heart and Stroke Foundation (2016) reported that in 2012, one person died of heart disease or stroke every 7 minutes. As we age, fatty deposits and scar tissue slowly accumulate in the linings of blood vessels, gradually reducing blood flow to various organs, including the heart and brain. Fatty deposits can begin in childhood, and thus eating food high in fat content and being overweight as a child may have serious health consequences later in life (Masoro, 2006).

Midlife is the time when high cholesterol levels increase and begin to accumulate on the artery walls, increasing the risk of cardiovascular disease (Emery et al., 2013). The type of cholesterol in the blood, however, influences its effect (Chan et al., 2013; Wang et al., 2014). Cholesterol comes in two forms: LDL (low-density lipoprotein) and HDL (high-density lipoprotein). LDL is often referred to as "bad" cholesterol because when the level of LDL is too high, it sticks to the lining of blood vessels, which can lead to atherosclerosis (hardening of the arteries) (Wenger, 2014). HDL is often referred to as "good" cholesterol because when it is high and LDL is low, the risk of cardiovascular disease is lower (Karavia et al., 2014; Li et al., 2013).

Blood pressure (hypertension) also usually rises in the forties and fifties (Roberie & Elliott, 2012; Tzourio, Laurent, & Debette, 2014). At menopause, a woman's blood pressure rises sharply and usually remains above that of a man through life's later years (Taler, 2009). A study found that uncontrolled hypertension can damage the brain's structure and function as early as the late thirties and early forties (Maillard et al., 2012). In this study, structural damage to the brain's white matter (axons) and decreased volume of grey matter (cell bodies and dendrites) occurred for individuals who had hypertension (top number above 140 and bottom number above 90). And a recent study revealed that hypertension in middle age is linked to risk of cognitive impairment in late adulthood (23 years later) (Virta et al., 2013).

An increasing problem in middle and late adulthood is *metabolic syndrome,* a condition characterized by hypertension, obesity, and insulin resistance (Samson & Garber, 2014). Metabolic syndrome often leads to the development of diabetes and cardiovascular disease (Landsberg et al., 2013; Scuteri et al., 2014). Several studies have provided information about risk factors for metabolic syndrome:

- A meta-analysis revealed that metabolic syndrome is an important risk factor for any cause of death (Wu, Liu, & Ho, 2010).
- Of four indices of obesity (body mass index, waist circumference, waist hip ratio, and waist height ratio), waist circumference is the best predictor of metabolic syndrome (Bener et al., 2013).
- Individuals with metabolic syndrome who are physically active reduce their risk of developing cardiovascular disease (Broekhuizen et al., 2011).

Weight loss and exercise are strongly recommended as part of the treatment (Samson & Garber, 2014; Vissers et al., 2013). A diet rich in fruits, vegetables, and whole grains can often help to stave off many cardiovascular problems in middle age (Cuenca-Garcia et al., 2014; Santilli et al., 2013). For example, cholesterol levels are influenced by heredity, but LDL can be reduced and HDL increased by eating food that is low in saturated fat and cholesterol and by exercising regularly (Logan, 2011). One study of post-menopausal women revealed that 12 weeks of aerobic exercise training improved cardiovascular functioning (O'Donnell, Kirwan, & Goodman, 2009).

Sleep

The average North American adult gets just under seven hours of sleep a night. How much sleep do adults need to function optimally the next day? An increasing number of experts note that eight hours of sleep or more per night are necessary for optimal performance the next day. These experts argue that many adults have become sleep deprived (McKenna et al., 2013). Work pressures, school pressures, family obligations, and social obligations often lead to long hours of wakefulness and irregular sleep/wake schedules (Soderstrom et al., 2012). Habitual sleep deprivation is linked to morbidity, especially among people with cardiovascular disease (Grandner et al., 2013).

Some aspects of sleep, such as sleep-disordered breathing and restless legs syndrome, become more problematic in middle age (Green et al., 2012; Polo-Kantola, 2011). The total number of hours slept usually remains the same as in early adulthood, but beginning in the forties, wakeful periods are more frequent and there is less of the deepest type of sleep (stage 4). The amount of time spent lying awake in bed at night begins to increase in middle age, and this can produce a feeling of being less rested in the morning. One study found that middle-aged adults who sleep less than six hours a night on average have an increased risk of developing stroke symptoms (Ruiter et al., 2012). Another study revealed that sleep deprivation is associated with less effective immune system functioning (Wilder-Smith et al., 2013). A research review concluded that sleep deprivation is linked to problems in long-term memory consolidation (Abel et al., 2013). Also, sleep problems in midlife are more common among individuals who use a higher number of prescription and non-prescription drugs, are obese, have cardiovascular disease, or are depressed (Loponen et al., 2010).

Sleep apnea is a serious sleep disorder that prevents a person from sleeping. Specifically, apnea is a temporary cessation of breathing caused when the airways become blocked, which occurs repeatedly during sleep. Men, women, and children who suffer from sleep apnea literally stop breathing when they sleep. In self-reported surveys, 3 percent of adults 18 years and over reported experiencing sleep apnea. The rate increased to 5 percent in adults over 45 years of age. Among adults reporting sleep apnea, 75 percent were over 45 years of age, with nearly twice as many men reporting the condition as women (PHAC, 2010e). Canadians reporting sleep apnea are more vulnerable to having diabetes, hypertension, heart disease, and mood disorders such as depression, bipolar disorder, mania, or dysthymia (PHAC, 2010e).

Getting adequate sleep is essential to good health. Good sleep is not necessarily measured in hours, although consistency is recommended by health practitioners. However, the busy lifestyles of middle-aged adults may mean that that sleep patterns may be interrupted for a variety of reasons, such as waiting for teenagers to come home, financial worries, and so on. Approximately 40 percent of adults report experiencing *insomnia,* the inability to get to sleep or fall back to sleep once awakened, at some point in their lives (Fallows, 2011). Jet lag, room temperature, or resolving short-term problems may result in occasional insomnia; however, illness, depression, pain, and stress may cause chronic insomnia, a serious condition that results in irritability, depression, loss of concentration, and inability to work (Fallows, 2011).

Lungs

Research also has found that low cognitive ability in early adulthood is linked to reduced lung functioning in middle age (Carroll et al., 2011). And reduced lung functioning is related to lower cognitive ability later in development (Shipley et al., 2007). Such links between reduced lung functioning and cognitive ability are likely related to the influence of pulmonary functioning on brain structure and function which affects cognitive ability.

Lung capacity shows little change through middle age for individuals who have not smoked. However, smoking is linked with a precipitous drop in lung capacity in middle-aged and older adults. When individuals stop smoking, their lung capacity becomes greater than those who continue to smoke, but not as great as the lung capacity of individuals who have never smoked (see Figure 15.1). Even for lifetime non-smokers, at about the age of 55, the proteins in lung tissue become less elastic. This change, combined with a gradual stiffening of the chest wall, decreases the capacity of the lungs to shuttle oxygen from the air people breathe to the blood in their veins.

Figure 15.1

The Relation of Lung Capacity to Age and Cigarette Smoking

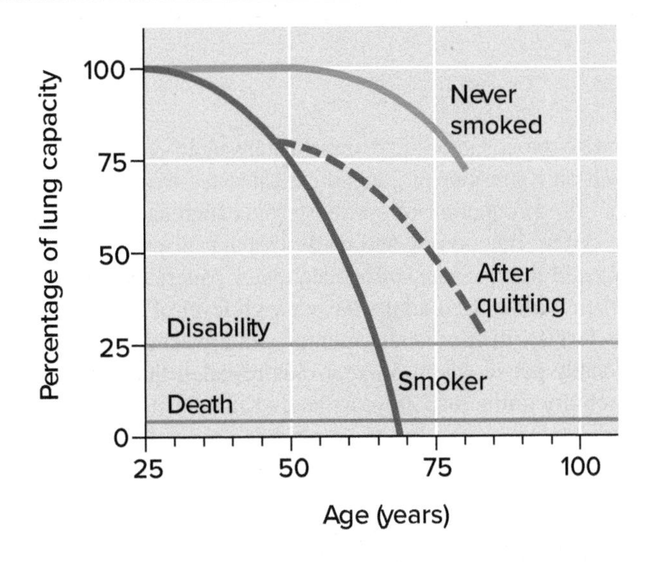

Adapted from *Newsweek*, Health for Life, special section, Fall/Winter 2001.

Health Concerns and Wellness Strategies

Health

Those born between 1945 and 1964 belong to the first generations of Canadians to receive the benefits of access to education, health care, employment, and welfare services. As a result, they are healthier in middle adulthood than previous generations (Canadian Public Health Association (CPHA), 2015). As well, the frequency of accidents declines in middle age, and individuals are less susceptible to colds and allergies than they were when younger. Indeed, many individuals live through middle adulthood without having a disease or persistent health problem. However, for other individuals, disease and persistent health problems become more common in middle adulthood.

Chronic disorders are characterized by a slow onset and long duration (Hoyt & Stanton, 2012; Ory et al., 2013). Chronic disorders are rare in early adulthood, increase in middle adulthood, and become common in late adulthood. Overall, arthritis is the leading chronic disorder in middle age, followed by hypertension. The most common chronic disorders in middle age vary by gender (see Figure 15.2). Men have a higher incidence of fatal chronic conditions (such as coronary heart disease, cancer, and stroke); women have a higher incidence of non-fatal conditions (such as arthritis, varicose veins, and bursitis).

Figure 15.2

Leading Chronic Disorders for Women and Men in Middle Age

Women	Men
1. Arthritis	1. Hypertension
2. Hypertension	2. Arthritis
3. Sinus problems	3. Hearing impairments

Stress and Disease

Stress is increasingly being found to be a factor in disease (Schwarzer & Luszczynska, 2013). David Almeida and colleagues (2011) concluded that chronic stress or prolonged exposure to stressors can have damaging effects on physical functioning, including an unhealthy overproduction of corticosteroids such as cortisol. Chronic stress is linked to disease through interference with immune system functioning and cardiovascular diseases (Emery et al., 2013; Stowell, Robles, & Kane, 2013). A recent study discovered that chronic stress accelerates pancreatic cancer growth (Kim-Fuchs et al., 2014). Additionally, a study found that when middle aged adults have a high level of allostatic load (wearing down of the body's systems in response to high stress levels), their episodic memory and executive function is harmed (Karlamangia et al., 2014). Another study of occupationally active 44- to 58-year-olds revealed that perceived stress symptoms in midlife are linked to self-care disability and mobility limitations 28 years later (Kulmala et al., 2013).

THE IMMUNE SYSTEM AND STRESS

The immune system keeps us healthy by recognizing foreign materials such as bacteria, viruses, and tumours, and then destroying them (Stowell, Robles, & Kane, 2013). The immune system's machinery consists of billions of white blood cells located in the circulatory system. The number of white blood cells and their effectiveness in killing foreign viruses or bacteria are related to stress levels. When a person is under stress, viruses and bacteria are more likely to multiply and cause disease. Natural killer (NK) cells are a type of white blood cell, more present in low-stress-stress circumstances; lower levels of NK cells in stressful situations indicate a weakened immune system. One study of young and middle-aged adults revealed that persistently unemployed individuals had lower NK cell levels than their previously unemployed counterparts who became reemployed (Cohen et al., 2007). Chronic stress is an impediment to immune system functioning.

Immune system functioning becomes less effective with normal aging (Dougall et al., 2013; Evers et al., 2014). Sheldon Cohen and colleagues have conducted a number of studies on immunity and susceptibility to infectious disease (Cohen & Janicki-Deverts, 2012; Cohen et al., 2012, 2013; Cohen & Shachar, 2012). They have found that factors such as stress, emotion, and lack of social support compromise people's immune system functioning in ways that alter their bodies' ability to fight off disease. Worries about immigrating and settling in a new country, failures in close relationships (divorce, separation, and marital distress), depression, loneliness, and burdensome caregiving for a family member with progressive illness are some poignant stressors (Fagundes, Glaser, & Kiecolt-Glaser, 2013; Fagundes et al., 2013; Jaremka et al., 2013a, b; Jaremka et al., 2014a).

STRESS AND THE CARDIOVASCULAR SYSTEM

Stress and negative emotions can affect the development and course of cardiovascular disease by altering underlying physiological processes (Emery et al., 2013; Lamy et al., 2014). Sometimes the link between stress and cardiovascular disease is indirect. For example, people who live in a chronically stressed condition are more likely to take up smoking, start overeating, and avoid exercising (Sowah, Busse, & Amoroso, 2013). All of these stress-related behaviours are linked with the development of cardiovascular disease (Sultan-Taieb et al., 2013)

Control

Although many diseases increase in middle age, having a sense of control is linked to many aspects of health and well-being (Bertrand, Kranz Graham, & Lachman, 2013). Researchers have found that having a sense of control peaks in midlife and then declines in late adulthood (Lachman, 2006; Lachman, Rosnick, & Rocke, 2009). However, in any adult age period, there is a wide range of individual differences in beliefs about control. Margie Lachman and colleagues (2011) argue that having a sense of control in middle age is one of the most important modifiable factors in delaying the onset of diseases in middle adulthood and reducing the frequency of diseases in late adulthood.

Poverty and Health

As noted in the opening vignette, income is one of the determinants of health. Further, longer durations of poverty result in more serious health consequences. Canadians most vulnerable to poverty, and therefore more vulnerable to poor health, are lone mothers, Aboriginal peoples, new Canadians, and racialized individuals. These groups have consistently poorer health than the general population. For further information, read Connecting Development to Life, "The Thin Door."

Health Canada website and Media Photo Gallery, Health Canada, http://www.hc-xc.gc.ca Reproduced with permission of the Minister of Public Works and Government Services Canada 2008.

These Inuit people are attending a course on nutrition and heart health. *Why are Aboriginal people more susceptible to disease?*

CONNECTING development to life

The Thin Door

"Today continuing poverty and distress are a deeper and more important cause of international tensions, of the conditions that can produce war, than previously." Lester B. Pearson, Former Prime Minister of Canada (April 1963–1968), winner of the 1957 Nobel Peace Prize.

According to the United Nations Office of High Commission for Human Rights, the debilitating global issue of poverty involves not only the deprivation of economic and material resources, but also a violation of human dignity (United Nations, 2016). As noted in Chapter 9, Canada has no official definition of poverty; however, an estimated one in seven Canadians struggle to make ends meet (Canada Without Poverty, 2016). Cash-strapped individuals struggling with vital decisions such as which bill to pay or how to afford school supplies for their children suffer greater depths of stress and have an increased risk of poor mental and physical health. As well, they are most at risk of losing the roof over their heads, be that a mortgaged or rental home.

Those most susceptive to poverty are Aboriginal Canadians, recent immigrants, refugees, people with mental and physical disabilities, the elderly, lone parents (particularly single mothers), and racialized groups. For racialized groups, the rate of poverty is reportedly twice that of non-racialized Canadians; and within impoverished racialized group, 66 percent are immigrants (Canada Without Poverty, 2016; Picot & Hou, 2014; National Council of Welfare Reports, 2013; Murphy, 2012). Statistics Canada reports that those whose earnings were at the bottom of the distribution spectrum experienced greater income decline after the economic downturn of 2008 than those at the top; consequently, immigrants and Aboriginal Canadians were more significantly affected because they are more concentrated at the bottom of the earning distribution tables (Canada Without Poverty, 2016; Picot & Hou, 2014).

What are the implications of monthly struggles to ensure that you and your family do not end up homeless, on the wrong side of your home's thin door? Chronic stress caused by this type of worry impedes immune system functioning, thereby increasing the risk of illness. A study conducted at McMaster University found a staggering 21-year difference in life expectancies between the poorest and wealthiest members living in Hamilton, Ontario (Hwang et al., 2009; Canada Without Poverty, 2016).

Immigration to Canada is a life-changing event (Qamar, 2015). Most people who move to Canada wish to provide a better future for their children or to escape war and trauma in their country of origin. However, due to the stress of financial demands, loneliness, and possible post-traumatic stress disorder, on top of uncertainties of cultural diaspora, new Canadians often experience depression. In fact, clinical depression is the most common mental health issue for new immigrants (Qamar, 2015).

The costs of chronic poverty are high, and may include those beyond the immediately obvious. Pat Capponi, who drew from personal battles with poverty and mental health when she wrote *Dispatches from the Poverty Line* in 1997, noted, "The hardest thing is keeping your sense of self...I fear the loss of self" (Capponi, 1997, p. 40). A sense of self is core to self-esteem and self-concept. For many who are struggling, a very thin door separates them from homelessness, posing an enormous risk to their sense of self. The cycle of poverty is easier to fall into than to climb out of.

critical thinking

As you have read, poverty plays an important role in health. Consider the life map for an infant born into and growing up in poverty. Visualize the place of birth, the parent or parents, and the living accommodations. Visualize the individual going to public school, to high school, entering adulthood, and so on. What are the factors affecting the individual's health throughout the life span, and how does poverty play a role? What specific data should be gathered and resources developed to provide assistance to those who live in poverty? Must individuals change their economic situation to improve their health? How would the life map you have created differ in a rural and in an urban setting?

In 1997, Jeff Reading, head of the Institute of Aboriginal Peoples' Health, said, "Raising the standard of living is the single most important factor to improve health status." Although improvements have been made in recent years, the gap between health among Aboriginal Canadians when compared to non-Aboriginal Canadians remains a significant challenge (NCCAH, 2013; Health Canada, 2012). While poverty is a major contributor, the reasons are more complex than poverty alone. The British Columbia Ministry of Aboriginal Health cites multi-generational experiences of racism, colonialism, residential schools, loss of culture, and loss of political institutions as contributing factors.

Mental Health

In Chapter 10, you read about the challenges of being a child whose parent has a mental health illness. One of the issues for both the child and the adult is the stigma and fear attached to mental illness. Yet all of us either have suffered, are suffering, or know someone—perhaps a family member, a friend, or a colleague—who is suffering from a mental health illness. According to the Mental Health Commission of Canada and the Centre for Addiction and Mental Health (CAMH), in any given year one in five Canadians experience mental health problems or illness. In fact, mental illness is the second leading cause of disability and premature death in Canada (CAMH, 2013).

The onset of 70 percent of mental health problems and illnesses occurs in childhood or adolescence. CAMH reports that at least half a million people are unable to work due to mental illness and that much worker absenteeism is related to mental health issues; consequently, those in the lowest income group are three to four times more likely to report fair to poor mental health (CAMH, 2013).

The prevalence of mental illness and the impact on the workplace led to the introduction of the Psychological Health and Safety in the Workplace standard in February, 2013. The standard was developed by the Mental Health Commission of Canada in collaboration with the Bureau de Normalisation du Quebec and the non-profit Canada Standards Association Group (CSA). The purpose of this initiative is to reduce the stigma associated with mental health issues, to promote mental health in the workplace, and to provide support for employees dealing with mental health issues (Bradley, 2012).

Culture, Relationships, and Health

Emotional stability and a support network of family, friends, neighbours, and colleagues are related to health in middle adulthood. In 2016, Canada planned to welcome between 280 000 and 305 000 new permanent residents. For immigrants, many of these factors are missing. Research shows that immigrants from the Philippines, China, and India, the three countries from which most immigrants come, are over-represented in the prevalence of chronic disease. Language and cultural adjustment, as well as overcoming or coping with feelings of isolation, are perhaps the biggest barriers to health. Studies indicate that Chinese Canadians have higher rates of cancer and lower rates of cardiovascular disease than the general population, and that the longer South Asians live in Canada, the more prone they are to factors, such as obesity, that lead to heart disease (Taylor, 2012).

critical thinking

In addition to other groups of immigrants and asylum seekers, Canada welcomed 25 000 Syrians in 2015/early 2016, and pledged to resettle another 10 000 Syrians by the end of 2016. Identify some challenges that Syrian families may experience. What strategies might be helpful to alleviate stress and enhance resettlement?

Mortality Rates

Cancer is the leading cause of death in Canada for men and women over the age of 35, followed by heart disease and strokes. Prior to that age, unintentional injuries are the leading cause of death (Statistics Canada, 2015; Public Health Agency Canada (PHAC), 2016). With every decade of age, the mortality rates increase; for example, the rate of death from cancer for those between the ages of 35 to 44 years is 28.1 per 100 000 people, compared with 106.8 per 100 000 for those between 45 and 55 years of age, and 309.2 per 100 000 people for those between 55 and 65 years of age. After 65, the rate quadruples to 1322.8 per 100 000 persons. A similar incremental rate of increase is true of circulatory system diseases (PHAC, 2016).

Sexuality

What kinds of changes characterize the sexuality of women and men as they go through middle age? **Climacteric** is a term that is used to describe the midlife transition in which fertility declines. Let us explore the substantial differences in the climacteric of women and men.

Menopause

Menopause is the time in middle age, usually in the late forties or early fifties, when a woman's menstrual periods completely cease. The average age of menopause is 51, however there is large variation in the age, and menopause occurs anywhere from 39 to 59 years of age. Virtually all women are post-menopausal by 60 years of age. Later menopause is linked with increased risk for breast cancer (Mishra et al., 2009).

Perimenopause is the transitional period from normal menstrual periods to no menstrual periods at all, which often takes up to 10 years (Martins et al., 2014). Perimenopause is most common in the forties, but can occur in the thirties. A study of 30- to 50-year-old women found that depressed feelings, headaches, moodiness, and palpitations were the symptoms that women in perimenopause most frequently discussed with health care providers (Lyndaker & Hulton, 2004). Lifestyle factors such as whether women are overweight, smoke, drink heavily, or exercise regularly during perimenopause influence aspects of their future health, such as whether they develop cardiovascular disease or chronic illnesses (ESHRE Capri Workshop Group, 2011; Kagitani et al., 2014).

Not only the timing but also the side effects of menopause vary greatly. In menopause, production of estrogen by the ovaries declines dramatically, and this decline produces uncomfortable symptoms in some women: hot flashes, nausea, fatigue, and rapid heartbeat, for example (Brockie et al., 2014). Cross-cultural studies reveal wide variations in the menopause experience (Lerner-Geva et al., 2010; Sievert & Obermeyer, 2012). For example, hot flashes are uncommon in Mayan women (Beyene, 1986). Asian women also report fewer hot flashes than women in Western societies. It is difficult to determine the extent to which these cross-cultural variations are due to genetic, dietary, reproductive, or cultural factors.

Menopause overall is not the negative experience for most women that it was reputed to be (Henderson, 2011). Most women do not have severe physical or psychological problems related to menopause. For example, a research review concluded that there is no clear evidence that depressive disorders occur more often during menopause than at other times in a woman's reproductive life (Judd, Hickey, & Bryant, 2012). However, the loss of fertility is an important marker for women. Women in their thirties who have never had children sometimes speak about being "up against the biological clock" because they cannot postpone choices about having children much longer.

HORMONE REPLACEMENT THERAPIES

One common treatment for menopausal discomforts approved by Health Canada has been hormone replacement therapy (HRT). Hormone replacement therapy (HRT) augments the declining levels of reproductive hormone production by the ovaries (Terry & Tehranifar, 2013; Canadian Cancer Society, 2016). Although a research review found increased evidence that effective use of menopausal hormone replacement therapy is not linked to cardiovascular disease problems during perimenopause, the Canadian Cancer Society notes that there are various forms of HRTs and recommends that women consult with their family doctor as the risks may sometimes outweigh the advantages. Factors influencing the decision to use HRTs include family history, the length of time an individual will be taking HRT, as well as the severity of menopausal symptoms (Canadian Cancer Society, 2016; Valdiviezo, Lawson, & Ouyang, 2013).

Many middle-aged women are seeking alternatives to HRT such as regular exercise, dietary supplements, herbal remedies, relaxation therapy, acupuncture, and non-steroidal medications (Al-Safi & Santoro, 2014; Buhling et al., 2014; Velders & Diel, 2013; Ward-Ritacco et al., 2014). One study revealed that in sedentary women, aerobic training for 6 months decreased menopausal symptoms, especially night sweats, mood swings, and irritability (Moilanen et al., 2012). Another study found that yoga improved the quality of life of menopausal women (Reed et al., 2014).

Researchers have found that almost 50 percent of Canadian and American women have occasional hot flashes, but Taiwanese women report no significant effect of menopause. *What factors might account for these variations?*

Hormonal Changes in Middle-Aged Men

Is there a male menopause? Men experience hormonal changes in their fifties and sixties, and a modest decline in their sexual hormonal level and activity, but nothing like the dramatic drop in estrogen that women experience (Blumel et al., 2014). Testosterone production begins to decline about 1 percent a year during middle adulthood and sperm count usually shows a slow decline, but men do not lose their fertility in middle age. The term male hypogonadism is used to describe a condition in which the body does not produce enough testosterone (Mayo Clinic, 2013).

Recently, there has been a surge of interest in testosterone replacement therapy (TRT) (Kaplan & Hu, 2013; Rahnema et al., 2014; Ullah, Riche, & Koch, 2014). For many decades, it was thought that TRT increased the risk of prostate cancer, but recent research reviews indicate that is not the case, at least when taken for one year or less (Cui et al., 2014; Khera et al., 2014). It is now accepted that TRT can improve sexual functioning, muscle strength, and bone health (Isidori et al., 2014; Mayo Clinic, 2013). Two recent studies found that TRT improves older men's sexual function as well as their mood (Miner et al., 2013; Okada et al., 2014). Further, a recent study found that a higher testosterone level is linked to better episodic memory in middle-aged males (Panizzon et al., 2014).

However, a recent research review concluded that the benefit-risk ratio for older adult men is uncertain (Isidori et al., 2014). Men who have prostate cancer or breast cancer should not take TRT (Osterberg, Bernie, & Ramasamy, 2014). Health Canada reports the potential for cardiovascular risks, strokes, blood clots in the legs or lungs, and irregular heart rate (Health Canada, 2014).

A common development in middle-aged men is **erectile dysfunction**, the inability to adequately achieve and maintain an erection that results in satisfactory sexual performance (Berookhim & Bar-Charma, 2011). According to a recent Canadian study, approximately 49.4 percent of men between the ages of 40 and 88 experience erectile dysfunction (ED). Knowledge and management have improved, and physicians now recognize erectile dysfunction as an indicator of vascular health and a marker for cardiovascular risk (Elliot, 2011). Low testosterone levels can contribute to erectile dysfunction. Smoking, diabetes, hypertension, elevated cholesterol levels, obesity, and lack of exercise also are associated with erectile problems in middle-aged men (Asian et al., 2014; Tanik et al., 2014; Weinberg et al., 2013). The main treatment for men with erectile dysfunction has not focused on TRT but on Viagra and similar drugs such as Levitra and Cialis (Kim et al., 2014; Kirby, Creanga, & Stecher, 2013; McMahon, 2014). These drugs work by allowing increased blood flow into the penis, which produces an erection. Their success rate is in the 60 to 85 percent range (Claes et al., 2010).

Lifestyle also plays a role in erectile dysfunction. Obesity, a sedentary lifestyle, and misuse of alcohol and drugs significantly increase the risk of erectile dysfunction (Heidelbaugh, 2010). In one study, middle-aged men were randomly assigned to one of two treatment groups: (1) An experimental group that was given detailed, individualized information about the importance of reducing body weight, improved quality of diet, and increased physical activity in reducing erectile dysfunction; and (2) a control group that was provided general information about healthy food choices and increasing physical activity (Esposito et al., 2009). After two years of intervention, the men in the experimental group were more successful in improving their lifestyles and had a greater reduction in erectile dysfunction.

The male brain contains estrogen receptors as well, so the interplay between hormones and the brain is the subject of further study. What has been referred to as "male menopause" probably has less to do with hormonal change than with the psychological adjustment men must make when they are faced with declining physical energy and with family and work pressures. Testosterone therapy has not been found to relieve such symptoms, suggesting that they may not be induced by hormonal change (Harman, 2007).

Sexual Attitudes and Behaviour

People vary tremendously in their sexual desire, and our sex lives are a complex and intricate combination of factors: desire, time, energy, opportunity, stress, privacy or lack of it, along with our feelings about our partners, about ourselves, and about our bodies. Although the ability of men and women to function sexually shows little biological decline in middle adulthood, sexual activity usually occurs less frequently than in early adulthood (Waite, Das, & Laumann, 2009). Career interests, family matters, energy level, and routine may contribute to this decline.

In a survey of 10 000 people across 15 countries conducted by Durex, a condom manufacturer, four dimensions of sexual intimacy were ranked: partner's satisfaction, safer sex (condom always used with a casual partner), frequency of sex ranking, and average per year (Durex, 2006). Canadian participants ranked number one in placing their partner's satisfaction above their own. In a Canadian study of 40- to 64-year-olds, only 30 percent reported that their sexual life was less satisfying than it had been when they were in their twenties (Wright, 2006).

Sexually Transmitted Infections (STIs)

Improved health care benefits and access to drug treatments such as Viagra have elevated the level of sexual activity in both middle- and late-adulthood. This increased activity, combined with reduced immunity for individuals as they age, has led to higher levels of STIs such as chlamydia, genital herpes, genital warts, gonorrhoea, syphilis, and HIV/AIDS. The fact that STI symptoms may be delayed for a considerable period of time increases the likelihood that infections could be spread (Abeykoon & Lucyk, 2015). Consequently, the risk is the same several weeks into the relationship as it is on the first night. Mary is a typical example. After 15 years of marriage, Mary separated from her husband and started to date. She had not been intimate with any other man for 17 years. After a few drinks, Mary had intercourse with her date. Just as a teenaged girl would be astonished to find she was pregnant, Mary was astonished to find she had contracted chlamydia. No age group is invincible.

To this point, we have discussed a number of ideas about physical development in middle adulthood. For a review, see the Reach Your Learning Outcomes section at the end of this chapter.

Cognitive Development

LO3 Identify cognitive changes in middle adulthood.

- **Intelligence**
- **Information Processing**

In Chapter 13, we saw that cognitive abilities are very strong in early adulthood. Do they decline as we enter and move through middle adulthood? To answer this question, we will explore the possibility of cognitive changes in intelligence and information processing.

Intelligence

Our exploration of possible changes in intelligence in middle adulthood focuses on the concepts of fluid and crystallized intelligence, the Seattle Longitudinal Study, and cohort effects.

Fluid and Crystallized Intelligence

Cognitive psychologist John Horn believes that some abilities begin to decline in middle age while others increase (Horn & Donaldson, 1980). Horn maintains that **crystallized intelligence**, an individual's accumulated information and verbal skills, continue to increase in the middle adulthood years, whereas **fluid intelligence**, one's ability to reason abstractly, begins to decline in the middle adulthood years (see Figure 15.3).

Figure 15.3
Fluid and Crystallized Intellectual Development across the Life Span

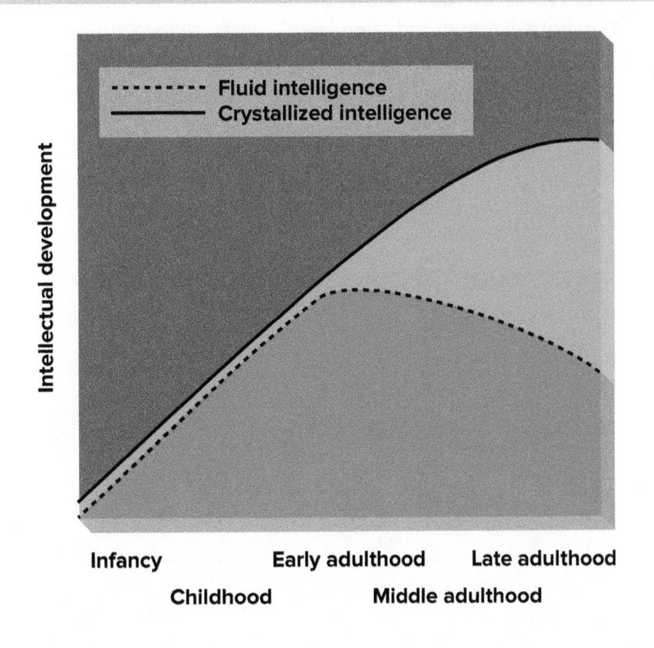

According to Horn, crystallized intelligence (based on cumulative learning experiences) increases throughout the life span, but fluid intelligence (the ability to perceive and manipulate information) steadily declines from middle adulthood.

Horn's data were collected in a cross-sectional manner. Recall from Chapter 1 that this involves assessing individuals of different ages at the same point in time. For example, a cross-sectional study might assess the intelligence of different groups of 40-, 50-, and 60-year-olds in a single evaluation. The average 40-year-old and the average 60-year-old were born in different decades, which produced different economic and educational opportunities. For example, people born in the 1950s had no cell phones or Internet access until they were 45 or 50. However, those born in the 1970s likely had cell phones and Internet access by the time they were age 25. Thus, if we find differences between 40- and 60-year-olds on intelligence tests when they are assessed cross-sectionally, these differences might be due to cohort effects related to technological differences rather than to age.

As we see next, whether data on intelligence are collected cross-sectionally or longitudinally can make a difference in the conclusions drawn about intellectual decline (Abrams, 2009; Schaie, 2011a, b, 2013).

The Seattle Longitudinal Study

For over half a century, since 1956, Dr. K. Warner Schaie, along with Dr. Sherry L. Willis who joined him as a principal co-investigator in 1983, has conducted the most extensive evaluative study of human intellectual activities during adulthood (1994, 1996, 2005, 2010, 2011a, b, 2013). Over 5600 people have participated in this study; the oldest participant in the 2011 wave was 103, and the youngest was 36. New waves of participants have been added periodically, however 26 of the original 500 individuals tested in 1956 are still participating (University of Washington Medicine, 2011). The main focus of this study is to understand change and stability in intellectual activities and abilities during adulthood. To do this, a psychometric, measurement-based approach such as the one described in Chapter 9 has been used to test individuals at seven-year intervals (1956, 1963, 1970, etc.).

The main mental abilities tested include:

- Vocabulary (ability to understand ideas expressed in words)
- Verbal memory (ability to encode and recall meaningful language units, such as a list of words)
- Number (ability to perform simple mathematical computations, such as addition, subtraction, and multiplication)
- Spatial orientation (ability to visualize and mentally rotate stimuli in two- and three-dimensional space)
- Inductive reasoning (ability to recognize and understand patterns and relationships in a problem and use this understanding to solve other instances of the problem)
- Perceptual speed (ability to quickly and accurately make simple discriminations in visual stimuli)

As shown in Figure 15.4, the highest level of functioning for four of the six intellectual abilities occurs in the middle adulthood years (Schaie, 2013). For both women and men, peak performance on vocabulary, verbal memory, inductive reasoning, and spatial orientation is attained in middle age. There are declines in middle age for only two of the six abilities: numerical ability and perceptual speed. Perceptual speed shows the earliest decline, beginning in early adulthood.

Figure 15.4

Longitudinal Changes in Six Intellectual Abilities from Age 25 to Age 67

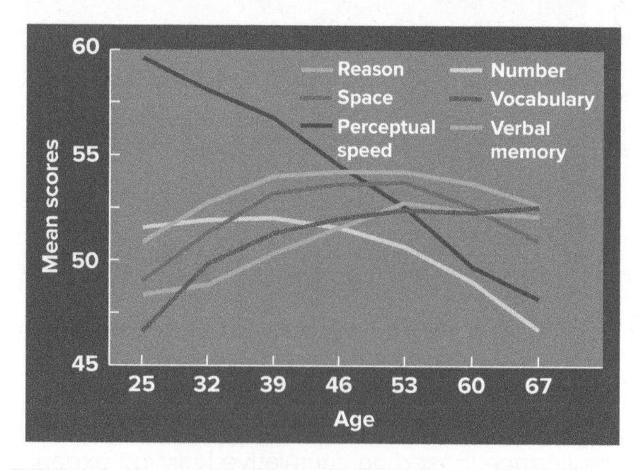

Source: Adapted from K.W. Schaie: "Longitudinal Changes in Six Intellectual Abilities from Age 25 to Age 95" Figure 5.7a, in *Developmental Influences on Intelligence: The Seattle Longitudinal Study*, (2nd rev edit.) 2013, p. 162.

Interestingly, for the participants in the Seattle Longitudinal Study, middle age was a time of peak performance for some aspects of both crystallized intelligence (verbal ability) and fluid intelligence (spatial orientation and inductive reasoning).

Notice, too, in Figure 15.5 that decline in functioning for most cognitive abilities began to steepen in the sixties, although the decline in verbal ability did not steepen until the mid-seventies. From the mid-seventies through the late eighties, all cognitive abilities showed considerable decline.

Figure 15.5

Cross-Sectional and Longitudinal Comparisons of Intellectual Change in Middle Adulthood

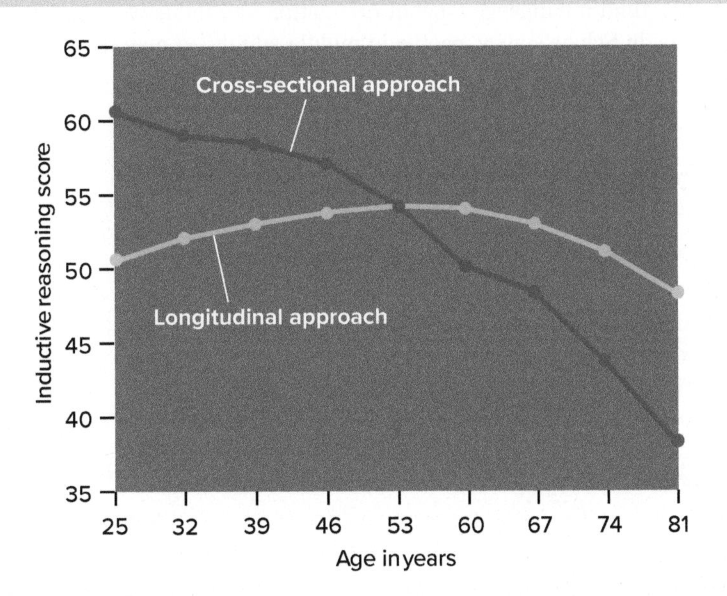

Adapted from "Developmental Influences on Intelligence: *The Seattle Longitudinal Study*," (2nd rev ed), 2013, p. 162.

When Schaie and Willis (1994) assessed intellectual abilities both cross-sectionally and longitudinally, they found decline more likely in the cross-sectional than in the longitudinal assessments. For example, as shown in Figure 15.5, when assessed crosssectionally inductive reasoning shows a consistent decline in the middle adulthood years. In contrast, when assessed longitudinally, inductive reasoning increases until toward the end of middle adulthood, when it begins to show a slight decline. In Schaie's (2008, 2009, 2010, 2011a, b, 2013) view, it is in middle adulthood, not early adulthood, that people reach a peak in their cognitive functioning for many intellectual skills.

In further analysis, Schaie (2007) examined generational differences in parents and their children over a seven-year time frame from 60 to 67 years of age. That is, parents were assessed when they were 60 to 67 years of age, and when their children reached 60 to 67 years of age, they also were assessed. Higher levels of cognitive functioning occurred for the second generation in inductive reasoning, verbal memory, and spatial orientation, whereas the first generation scored higher on numeric ability. Noteworthy was the finding that the parent generation showed cognitive decline from 60 to 67 years of age, but their offspring showed stability or modest increases in cognitive functioning across the same age range.

Such differences across generations involve cohort effects. In one analysis, Schaie (2011b) concluded that the advances in cognitive functioning in middle age that have occurred in recent decades are likely due to factors such as educational attainment, occupational structures (increases of workers in professional occupations and work complexity), health care and lifestyles, immigration, and social interventions in poverty. The impressive gains in cognitive functioning in recent cohorts have been documented more clearly for fluid intelligence than for crystallized intelligence (Schaie, 2011b).

The results from Schaie's study that have been described so far focus on average cognitive stability or change for all participants across the middle adulthood years. Schaie and Sherry Willis (Schaie, 2005; Willis & Schaie, 2005) examined individual differences for the participants in the Seattle study and found substantial individual variations. They classified participants as "decliners," "stable," or "gainers" for three categories—number ability, delayed recall (a verbal memory task), and word fluency—from 46 to 60 years of age. The largest percentage of decline (31 percent) or gain (16 percent) occurred for delayed recall; the largest percentage with stable scores (79 percent) occurred for numerical ability. Word fluency declined for 20 percent of the individuals from 46 to 60 years of age.

Might the individual variations in cognitive trajectories in midlife be linked to cognitive impairment in late adulthood? In Willis and Schaie's analysis, cognitively normal and impaired older adults did not differ on measures of vocabulary, spatial orientation, and numerical ability in middle adulthood. However, declines in memory (immediate recall and delayed recall), word fluency, and perceptual speed in middle adulthood were linked to neuropsychologists' ratings of the individuals' cognitive impairment in late adulthood.

Interestingly, in terms of John Horn's ideas, middle age is a time of peak performance, both for some aspects of crystallized intelligence (vocabulary) and for fluid intelligence (spatial orientation and inductive reasoning) for the participants in the Seattle Longitudinal Study. Thus, in Schaie's view, people in middle adulthood may reach their peak functioning for many cognitive skills.

CONNECTING through Research

K. Warner Schaie, Professor of Human Development

K. Warner Schaie is a professor of human development and psychology at Pennsylvania State University, where he teaches and conducts research on adult development and aging. He also directs the Gerontology Center there. He is one of the pioneering psychologists who helped create the life-span perspective. He is the author or editor of more than 25 books and more than 250 journal articles and book chapters on adult development and aging. Dr. Schaie conducted the Seattle Longitudinal Study of Intellectual Development, a major research investigation that revealed that many intellectual skills are maintained or even increase during the years of middle age.

Courtesy of K. Warner Shaie

Life-span developmentalist K. Warner Schaie (right) with two older adults who are actively using their cognitive skills.

Evaluating Schaie and Willis

Some researchers disagree with Schaie and Willis's theory that middle adulthood is the time when the level of functioning in a number of cognitive domains is maintained or even increases. For example, psychologist Timothy Salthouse (2009, 2012), who has specialized in cognitive aging, concluded that cross-sectional research on aging and cognitive functioning should not be dismissed and that this research indicates reasoning, memory, spatial visualization, and processing speed begin declining in early adulthood and show further decline in the fifties. Salthouse (2009, 2012) does agree that cognitive functioning involving accumulated knowledge, such as vocabulary and general information, does not show early age-related decline and increases at least until 60 years of age.

Salthouse (2009, 2012) argued that a lower level of cognitive functioning in early and middle adulthood is likely due to age-related neurobiological decline. Cross-sectional studies have shown that these neurobiological factors decline in the twenties and thirties: regional brain volume, cortical thickness, synaptic density, some aspects of myelination, the functioning of some aspects of neurotransmitters such as dopamine and serotonin, blood flow in the cerebral cortex, and the accumulation of tangles in neurons (Del Tredici & Braak, 2008; Erixon-Lindroth et al., 2005; Finch, 2009; Hsu et al., 2008; Pieperhoff et al., 2008; Salat et al., 2004).

Schaie (2009, 2010 2011, 2013) continues to emphasize that longitudinal studies hold the key to determining age-related changes in cognitive functioning and that middle age is the time during which many cognitive skills actually peak. In the next decade, expanding research on age-related neurobiological changes and their possible links to cognitive skills should further refine our knowledge about age-related cognitive functioning in the adult years (Finch, 2009).

Information Processing

In our discussion of theories of development in Chapter 2 and in a number of child development and adolescence (Chapters 7, 9, and 11), we examined the information-processing approach to cognition. Among the information-processing changes that take place in middle adulthood are those involved in the speed of processing information, memory, expertise, and practical problem-solving skills.

Speed of Information Processing

As we saw in Schaie's Seattle Longitudinal Study, perceptual speed begins declining in early adulthood and continues to decline in middle adulthood. A common way to assess speed of information is through a reaction-time task, in which individuals simply press a button as soon as they see a light. Middle-aged adults are slower to push the button when the light appears than are young adults. However, the decline is not dramatic—under one second in most investigations.

A current interest focuses on possible causes for the decline in speed of processing information in adults (Salthouse, 2009, 2012). The causes may occur at different levels of analysis, such as cognitive ("maintaining goals, switching between tasks, or preserving internal representations despite distraction"), neuroanatomical ("changes in specific brain regions, such as the prefrontal cortex"), and neurochemical ("changes in neurotransmitter systems") such as dopamine (Hartley, 2006, p. 201).

Memory

According to the Seattle Longitudinal Study (Schaie, 1994, 1996), verbal memory peaks in one's fifties. However, in some other studies, verbal memory shows a decline in middle age, especially when assessed in cross-sectional studies (Salthouse, 2009, 2012). For example, in several studies, when asked to remember lists of words, numbers, or meaningful prose, younger adults outperformed middle-aged adults (Salthouse & Skovronek, 1992). Although there is still some controversy about whether memory declines in the middle adulthood years, most experts conclude that it does at some point during this period of adult development (Lundervold, Wollschlager, & Wehling, 2014; McCabe & Loaiza, 2012; Salthouse, 2012). However, some experts argue that studies that have concluded there is a decline in memory during middle age often have compared young adults in their twenties with adults in their late fifties and sixties (Schaie, 2000). In this latter view, memory decline in the early part of middle age is either non-existent or minimal and does not occur until the latter part of middle age or late adulthood (Backman, Small, & Wahlin, 2001).

Cognitive aging expert Denise Park (2001) argues that starting in late middle age, more time is needed to learn new information. The slowdown in learning new information has been linked to changes in **working memory**, the mental "workbench" where individuals manipulate and assemble information when making decisions, solving problems, and comprehending written and spoken language (Baddeley, 2007, 2012). In this view, in late middle age working memory capacity—the amount of information that can be immediately retrieved and used—becomes more limited. Think of this situation as an overcrowded desk with many items in disarray. As a result of the overcrowding and disarray, long-term memory becomes less reliable, more time is needed to enter new information into long-term storage, and more time is required to retrieve the information. Thus, Park believes that much of the blame for declining memory in late middle age is a result of information overload that builds up as we go through the adult years.

Memory decline is more likely to occur when individuals don't use effective memory strategies, such as organization and imagery (Small et al., 2012). By organizing lists of phone numbers into different categories, or imagining the phone numbers as representing different objects around the house, many individuals can improve their memory in middle adulthood. Although evidence suggests that the brains of older adults show less neuroplasticity than younger people, the aging brain is malleable, and has the capacity to develop neural scaffolding. Cognitive functioning can be facilitated through training, or engagement in demanding tasks (Parks & Bischof, 2013).

critical thinking

Design a working memory workbench. What might you include? Expertise, problem solving, and creativity are generally at their strongest in middle adulthood. Why is that? What role might technology play? What challenges might technology present to people in middle adulthood?

Expertise

Because it takes so long to attain, expertise often shows up more in middle adulthood than in the early adulthood years (Charness & Krampe, 2008). Recall from Chapter 9 that **expertise** involves having an extensive, highly organized knowledge and understanding of a particular domain. Developing expertise and becoming an "expert" in a field usually is the result of many years of experience, learning, and effort.

Strategies that distinguish experts from novices include the following:

- Experts are more likely to rely on their accumulated experience to solve problems.
- Experts often process information automatically and analyze it more efficiently when solving a problem in their domain.
- Experts have better strategies and shortcuts to solving problems in their domain.
- Experts are more creative and flexible in solving problems in their domain.

Practical Problem Solving

Everyday problem solving is another important aspect of cognition (Margrett & Deshpande-Kamat, 2009). An analysis of research found no evidence for significant changes in everyday cognition from 20 to 75 years of age (Salthouse, 2012). One possible explanation for the lack of any decline in everyday cognition is the increase in accumulated knowledge individuals possess as they grow older (Allaire, 2012).

Creativity

Creativity is the process of divergent thinking that requires encounters with the world and a degree of intensity and absorption. Through encounters with the world, the individual gains a heightened consciousness of possibilities and limitations; in this manner, creative contributions become realistic, constructive, and achievable. Recall from Chapter 13 that creativity peaks along some domains in early adulthood, while others are more likely to peak in middle adulthood. The contemporary guru of creativity, Mihaly Csikszentmihalyi, believes everyone is capable of it (see Connecting through Research).

Any consideration of decline in creativity with age requires attention to the field involved (Jones, Reedy, & Weinberg, 2014; Kozbelt, 2014; McKay & Kaufman, 2014). For example, in such fields as philosophy and history, older adults often show as much creativity as they did when they were in their thirties and forties. By contrast, in other fields as lyric poetry, abstract math, and theoretical physics, the peak of creativity is often reached in the twenties or thirties.

Existential psychologist Rollo May wrote, "Creativity is the process of bringing something new into being." He noted further that creativity requires passion, commitment, and courage. Creativity brings to our awareness what was previously hidden and points to new life. The experience is one of heightened consciousness—ecstasy." In his book *The Courage to Create* (1975), May argued that the ultimate betrayal is not to listen to our own original ideas. Listening to and acting upon our own ideas requires commitment and courage, both vital to finding innovative patterns on which society can be built.

Dr. Walter De Brouwer illustrates both Csikszentmihalyi's and May's theories as he became passionately absorbed in a challenge, then listened and acted upon his convictions. His 5-year-old son's fall and subsequent months in intensive care heightened De Brouwer's consciousness of possibilities and limitations. He wondered why most homes, like his, had only a thermometer when access to more information would be so much more helpful and vital in emergencies (De Brouwer, 2012). This encounter led to the foundation in 2011 of Scanadu, a company that develops medical technology applications for consumers, and the launch in 2012 of Scout, a device that when held to a person's temple for 10 seconds can wirelessly monitor five different vital signs (temperature, heart rate, blood oxygenation level, pulse, respiratory rate) and transmit results to the person's smartphone. ScoExpertiseut is currently being used in the United States for investigational purposes only, as part of a medical research study. Meanwhile, Scanadu is seeking FDA clearance for a related consumer product, Scanadu Vitals. Vitals, along with existing and future social networking sites for patients, will be key factors in revolutionizing the health care field, as patients will have access to more information and be abler to monitor their health. To listen to De Brouwer discuss how health care may be revolutionized, follow this link: http://www.youtube.com/watch?v=BSZJjN7o8Ck.

Notably, there also is extensive individual variation in the lifetime output of creative individuals. Typically, the most productive creators in any field are far more prolific than their least productive counterparts. The contrast is so extreme that the top 10 percent of creative producers frequently account for 50 percent of the creative output in a particular field. For instance, only 16 composers account for half of the music regularly performed in the classical repertoire.

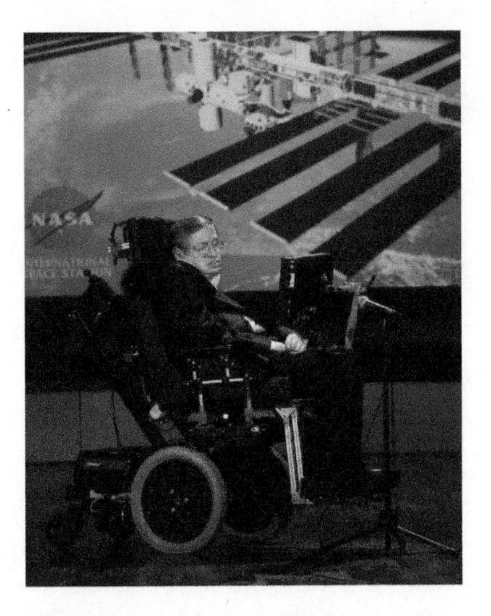

Paul E. Alers/ZUMA Press/Newscom

"There should be no boundaries to human endeavour. We are all different. However bad life may seem, there is always something you can do, and succeed at. While there's life, there is hope." These are the words of Stephen Hawking, a world renown physicist who was diagnosed with a crippling neurological disease at the age of 21. *How might his words reflect some of the concepts in this chapter such as expertise, problem solving, creativity, meaning in life, and others?*

CONNECTING through Research

Mihaly Csikszentmihalyi

Courtesy Mihaly Csikszentmihalyi

Mihaly Csikszentmihalyi, in the setting where he gets his most creative ideas. *When and where do you get your most creative thoughts?*

Mihaly Csikszentmihalyi is Director of the Quality of Life Research Center (QLRC), a non-profit institute that studies "positive psychology," the study of happiness, optimism, creativity, intrinsic motivation, and responsibility. He is one of the main architects of changing psychology's focus from the negative to the positive, believing that for too long the field has studied the dark side of life and that it is high time psychologists started focusing more on the good aspects of people. Often described as the guru of creativity, Csikszentmihalyi, who has studied the nature of creativity for a number of decades, is best known for his concept of "flow," the mental state of joy or effortlessness individuals feel when they are "in the zone." Flow is characterized by having clear attainable goals and feedback.

Based on his interviews with some of the most creative people in the world, Csikszentmihalyi notes that the first step toward a more creative life is cultivating your curiosity and interest. He found that certain settings are more likely to stimulate creativity than others. Csikszentmihalyi (1997, 2000) believes everyone is capable of achieving flow. This being the case, how can each of us do this? His tips involve a daily change of behaviour. Here are some of them:

- Try to be surprised by something every day. Maybe it is something you see, hear, or read about. Become absorbed in a lecture or a book. Be open to what the world is telling you. Life is a stream of experiences. Swim widely and deeply in it, and your life will be richer.
- Try to surprise at least one person every day. In a lot of things you do, you have to be predictable and patterned. Do something different for a change. Ask a question you normally would not ask. Invite someone to go to a show or a museum you never have visited.
- Write down each day what surprised you and how you surprised others. Most creative people keep a diary, notes, or lab records to ensure that their experience is not fleeting or forgotten. Each evening record the most surprising event that occurred that day and your most surprising action. After a few days,

reread your notes and reflect on your past experiences. After a few weeks, you might see a pattern of interest emerging in your notes, one that might suggest an area you can explore in greater depth.

- When something sparks your interest, follow it. Usually when something captures your attention, it is short-lived—an idea, a song, a flower. Too often we are too busy to explore the idea, song, or flower further. Or we think these areas are none of our business because we are not experts about them. Yet the world is our business. We can't know which part of it is best suited to our interests until we make a serious effort to learn as much about as many aspects of it as possible.
- Wake up in the morning with a specific goal to look forward to. Creative people wake up eager to start the day. Why? Not necessarily because they are cheerful, enthusiastic types, but because they know that there is something meaningful to accomplish each day, and they can't wait to get started.
- Spend time in settings that stimulate your creativity.

In Csikszentmihalyi's (1995) research, he gave people an electronic pager and beeped them randomly at different times of the day. When he asked them how they felt, they reported the highest levels of creativity when walking, driving, or jogging. One of your authors does her most creative thinking when swimming or listening to classical music. (She loves other music, but it makes her sing, dance, and laugh, whereas classical music puts her closer to "flow.") These activities are semiautomatic in that they take a certain amount of attention while leaving some time free to make connections among ideas.

In 2000, the Dana Alliance, a non-profit organization of neuroscientists, awarded its first Thinker of the Year Award to Mihaly Csikszentmihalyi, in recognition of his life-long contribution to the field of positive psychology (Needle, 2001). Through his research methods, his dedication, and his own creative courage, Csikszentmihalyi has contributed an innovative pattern for understanding human motivation.

To this point, we have studied a number of ideas about cognitive development in middle adulthood. For a review, see the Reach Your Learning Outcomes section at the end of this chapter.

Careers, Work, and Leisure

LO4 Characterize career development, work, and leisure in middle adulthood.

- **Work in Midlife**
- **Career Challenges and Changes**
- **Leisure**

Are middle-aged workers as satisfied with their jobs as young adult workers? What are some of the issues workers face in midlife? What role does leisure play in the lives of middle-aged adults?

Work in Midlife

The role of work—whether one works in a full-time career or a part-time job, as a volunteer, or as a homemaker—is central during the middle years. Middle-aged adults may reach their peak in position and earnings. They may also be saddled with multiple financial burdens such as rent or mortgage, child care, home repairs, college or university tuition, loans to family members, or caregiving expenses.

Leading Finnish researcher Clas-Hakan Nygard (2013) concluded from his longitudinal research that the ability to work effectively peaks during middle age because of increased motivation, work experience, and employer loyalty, and better strategic thinking. Nygard also has found that the quality of work done by employees in middle age is linked to how much their work is appreciated and how well they get along with their immediate supervisors (von Bonsdorff et al., 2011, 2012). Age-related declines occur in some occupations, such as air traffic controllers and professional athletes, but for most jobs, no differences have been found in the work performance of young adults and middle-aged adults (Sturman, 2003; Salthouse, 2012).

The proportion of dual-earner families in Canada has increased steadily since 1976 from approximately one-third to three-quarters. Sixty-eight percent of men and 54 percent of women work more than 45 hours a week; as well, many are bringing work home at the end of the day, adding another few hours to their work day. Reconciling work and family responsibilities, obligations, and commitments is challenging. To accommodate the demands, many employers are responding by providing more flexibility with respect to work hours and location (Spinks & Battams, 2016).

Historically, retirement has been a male transition, but today far more couples are planning two retirements—his and hers. Many Canadians (59 percent) say they expect to work past 65 (32 percent full-time, and 27 percent part-time) (Spinks & Battams, 2016). The recent economic downturn and recession has forced some middle-aged individuals into premature retirement because of job loss (Cahill, Giandrea, & Quinn, 2014). Such premature retirement also may result in insufficient financial resources to cover an increasingly long retirement period (de Wind et al., 2014; Lusardi, Mitchell, & Curto, 2012).

Important considerations when examining the role of work are job satisfaction and the quality of employment. An International Task Force headed by Canada, with participation from the United Nations (UN) and the International Labour Organization (ILO), identified the following factors as key to employment quality: job safety, both financial and non-financial remuneration, working hours, work–life balance, job stability, social dialogue, skills development, and job satisfaction. An analysis of the Canadian labour force indicated that immigrant workers, particularly those newest to Canada, ranked lower on each of these dimensions than non-immigrant workers. As noted by the International Task Force, when an individual's values and job security are aligned with his or her work, satisfaction increases notably (see Figure 15.6) (Gilmore, 2009).

Figure 15.6

Age and Job Satisfaction

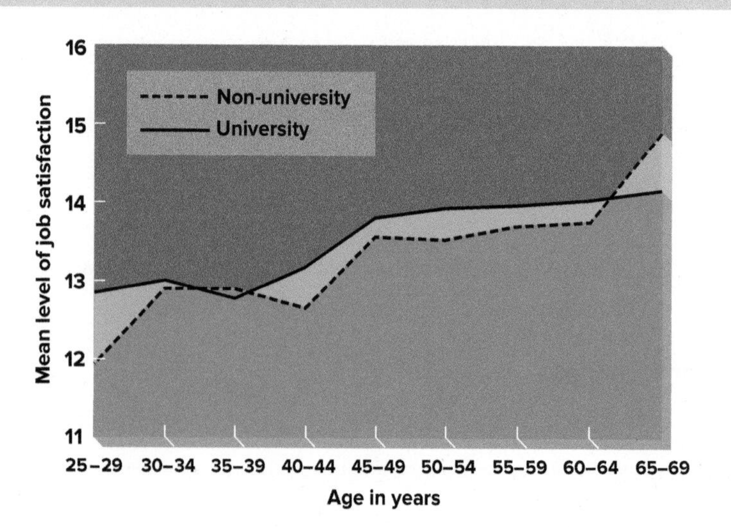

From *Men in Their Forties: The Transition to Middle Age*, by Lois M. Tamir, 1982. Used by permission of Springer Publishing Company, New York 10012.

Job satisfaction increases with age for both college/university and non–college/university-educated adults. Among the reasons for increased satisfaction are more income, higher-status jobs, greater job security, and stronger job commitment.

According to Statistics Canada, the economic downturn that began in 2008 adversely affected both Aboriginal workers and new Canadians the hardest and the longest (Gilmore, 2009; Usalcas, 2011). Creating an inclusive working environment and engaging in non-discriminatory practices, often systemic in nature, continues to be a challenge for employers (Human Resources and Skills Development Canada, 2012a).

Career Challenges and Changes

The current middle-aged worker faces several important challenges (Brand, 2014). These include the globalization of work, rapid developments in information technologies, restructuring, downsizing, and privatization of organizations, as well as early retirement and concerns about pensions. Some midlife career changes are self-motivated; others are the consequence of these challenges which may result in losing one's job (Brand, 2014). Some individuals decide that they don't want to do the same work they have been doing for the rest of their lives (Hoyer & Roodin, 2009). Reconciling the dreams they may have had in their youth with the challenges of providing for their families and their future is often a critical source of stress. If individuals perceive that they are behind schedule, if their goals are unrealistic, if they don't like the work they are doing, or if their job has become too stressful, they could become motivated to change jobs.

Photodisc/Getty Images

Sigmund Freud once commented that the two things adults need to do well to adapt to society's demands are to work and to love. To his list we add "to play and laugh." In our fast-paced society, it is all too easy to get caught up in the frenzied, hectic pace and ignore leisure and play. *Imagine your life as a middle-aged adult. What would be the ideal mix of work and leisure? What leisure activities do you want to enjoy as a middle-aged adult? Why do you think laughter is important?*

HAGGAR © 1987 by King Features Syndicate, Inc. World rights reserved. Used with permission.

Approximately two-thirds (66.8 percent) of women with children under 6 years of age are employed outside the home (Human Resources and Skills Development Canada, 2012a). Finding suitable and affordable daycare and before- and after-school care programs can be challenging. Women may also find that parental leaves have interrupted their skill levels and networking aspects of career development. Further, women remain the primary caregivers of needy family members such as a sister who has been diagnosed with breast cancer or a parent suffering from congestive heart failure. As a result, workers often experience intense conflict between work and family responsibilities (Human Resources and Skills Development Canada, 2012c).

More than a quarter-million of those seeking work are men and women between the ages of 45 and 64. Most older workers who lose their jobs because of globalization or restructuring want to find another full-time job; however, most jobs available are contract positions that do not offer benefits or vacation pay. Human Resources and Skills Development Canada (HRSDC) reports that this group of employment-seekers face four major barriers: (1) lower educational levels; (2) outdated skills; (3) lack of job-seeking know-how; and (4) negative stereotyping by employers about their abilities, ambitions, and productivity. When laid-off workers are able to return to work, they do so at disproportionately lower wages. Many feel a sense of failure, become discouraged, give up looking for work, and are no longer included in the statistical count.

critical thinking

Globalization strategies are shifting the work from expensive, unionized North American labour sources to cheaper sources elsewhere in the world. Particularly hard hit have been textile workers; in fact, finding products made in Canada is more challenging today than a decade ago, as more and more garments are made outside of Canada. How might the impact differ in urban and rural settings? What might be the impact of job loss on an individual? On his or her family? What steps can a person take to help prepare for unexpected job loss in the future?

Leisure

Not only must adults learn how to work well, but they also need to learn how to relax and enjoy leisure (Eriksson Sorman et al., 2014). **Leisure** refers to the pleasant times after work when individuals are free to pursue activities and interests of their own choosing—hobbies, sports, or reading, for example. Leisure can be an especially important aspect of middle adulthood (Nicolaisen, Thorsen, & Eriksen, 2012). By middle adulthood, more money is available to many individuals, and there may be more free time and paid vacations. In short, midlife changes may produce expanded opportunities for leisure.

Vacations are important. In one study, 12 338 men aged 35 to 57 years were assessed each year for five years regarding whether they took vacations or not (Gump & Matthews, 2000). Then, the researchers examined the medical and death records over nine years for men who lived for at least a year after the last vacation survey. Compared with those who never took vacations, men who went on annual vacations were 21 percent less likely to die over the nine years and 32 percent less likely to die of coronary heart disease.

Adults at midlife need to begin preparing psychologically for retirement. Constructive and fulfilling leisure activities, including hobbies, are an important part of this preparation. If an adult develops leisure activities that can be continued into retirement, the transition from work to retirement can be less stressful.

To this point, we have studied a number of ideas about careers, work, and leisure in middle adulthood. For a review, see the Reach Your Learning Objectives section at the end of this chapter.

Meaning in Life

LO5 Explain the roles of meditation, religion, and spirituality in understanding meaning in life during middle adulthood.

- **Meditation, Religion, and Spirituality**
- **Meaning in Life**
- **Health and Well-Being**

What role do meditation, religion, and spirituality play in our development as adults? Is meaning in life an important theme for many middle-aged adults?

Meditation, Religion, and Spirituality

Recall that Piaget believed that people engage in the *formal operation stage* starting in adolescence, and that in this stage we are more capable of abstract thought that is both idealistic and logical. As well, recall that in Kohlberg's highest stage of moral reasoning, the *post-conventional stage,* morality becomes completely internalized and is not based on the ideas of others. Core to these concepts is human nature's quest to try to understand and explain the origin of the universe, our purpose in life, as well as gain confidence to cope with life's ups and downs. Many turn to meditation or religion for understanding, while others turn to spirituality. In many ways these approaches may be similar and even overlapping, but they do differ. Each one is defined differently depending on determinants such as culture, gender, age, and general well-being. The following definitions are intended to provide a brief overview.

Meditation

"To meditate" means to think about something. In this context, **meditation** refers to a variety of practices intended to foster clarity of thought, well-being, and relief from stress by focusing attention with calmness and concentration. Once understood, practitioners can apply this stylized mental technique and meditate anyplace for as much time as they have. It is both restful and silent. Religions, particularly Eastern religions, have used meditation widely and have reported profound changes in how an individual perceives him- or herself, and thus alters his or her world-view (Shapiro & Walsh, 2008).

Religion

Religion is an organized set of beliefs about how the universe originated, as well as the nature and the purpose of the universe. Religions also provide rituals, rites of passage, celebratory festivals, and a code of conduct that governs behaviour. The largest religious groups in Canada are Christianity, Buddhism, Hinduism, Islam, Judaism, and Sikh (Statistic Canada, 2016). Within each large group are many sub-groups as well as many interpretations related to the nature of the universe and our roles. Indeed, within a family one may find as many views or interpretations as there are members of the family.

Statistics Canada combines four dimensions of religion—affiliation, attendance, personal practices, and importance of religion—to arrive at a *religiosity index,* which determines how religious a person is. Using these criteria, 40 percent of Canadians have a low degree of religiosity, 31 percent are moderately religious, and 29 percent are highly religious. Those in the highly religious group tend to be those in older age groups. Immigrants, especially those from South East Asia (e.g., the Philippines) and the Caribbean and Central America, as well as women, tend to have higher religiosity (Clark & Schellenberg, 2006). Within Canada, people in the Atlantic provinces are more likely to participate in religious practices than those in British Columbia.

Godong / Alamy Stock Photo

What roles do meditation, religion, and spirituality play in the lives of middle-aged adults?

Overall, 44 percent report that religion is important to their lives. In 2004, 48 percent of Canadians between the ages of 15 and 59 reported either no religious affiliation or not attending religious services. However, 53 percent engage in private religious practices such as prayer or meditation at least once monthly (Clark & Schellenberg, 2006). According to the Canadian Encyclopedia (2015), there is no single "Aboriginal religion and contemporary and spiritual practices vary widely and consist of complex social and cultural customs for addressing the sacred and the supernatural."

Spirituality

Spirituality refers to efforts to find meaning in life. Three characteristics of spirituality are an emotional response to the world, a cognitive context or set of beliefs about oneself and the world, and a spiritual practice. Spiritual practices vary considerably and may include prayer, observance of silence, reciting mantras, and acts of charity toward humans and animals (Jain et al., 2013).

A growing number of people self-identify either as **atheist**, a person who does not believe in the existence of any higher power, or as **agnostic**, a person who isn't sure whether or not a higher power exists. Atheists and agnostics are more likely than not to look for scientific evidence in support of the existence a higher power. Over 7 million people in Canada report no religious affiliation (Statistics Canada, 2016). Internationally, Canada ranks number 10 of the top 20 countries surveyed for the number of people who identify as either agnostic or atheist (Zukerman, 2005). However, determining the number of atheists is difficult as Census Canada does not request that information. As a result, we rely on estimates, which range from 19 percent to 23 percent (Zukerman, 2005; Trottier, 2010).

critical thinking

In his book, provocatively titled *The God Delusion,* atheist and biologist Richard Dawkins articulates the view that clashes of religion are responsible for a great deal of conflict the world over. He argues that religious claims should be subject to the same burden of proof to which other claims (such as scientific theories) are subject (Dawkins, 2006). Some might argue that faith, intuition, or sensing something without empirical evidence is an important aspect of religion, while others support Dawkins's assertions. What do you think? Is God or some kind of higher power a delusion? Can or should the existence of a higher power be subjected to the burden of scientific proof? What role does religion play in clashes and wars that exist today? What are some, if any, other contributing factors?

Meaning in Life

Austrian psychiatrist Victor Frankl's mother, father, brother, and wife died in the concentration camps and gas chambers in Auschwitz. Frankl survived the concentration camp and went on to write about meaning in life. In his book *Man's Search for Meaning* (1984), Frankl emphasized each person's uniqueness and the finiteness of life. He believes that examining the finiteness of our existence and the certainty of death adds meaning to life. If life were not finite, says Frankl, we might spend our life doing just about whatever we please because time would continue forever.

Frankl said that the three most distinct human qualities are spirituality, freedom, and responsibility. Spirituality, in his view, does not have a religious underpinning. Rather, it refers to a human being's uniqueness—to spirit, philosophy, and mind. Frankl proposed that people need to ask themselves such questions as why they exist, what they want from life, and what the meaning of their life is.

In middle adulthood, individuals begin to be faced with death, perhaps for the first time. They may experience the deaths of parents, older relatives, and friends. Also, faced with the prospect of their own mortality in a more immediate way than early adulthood, and recognizing changes in their own aging bodies, many individuals in middle age begin to ask and evaluate the questions that Frankl proposed.

Roy Baumeister and Kathleen Vohs (2002, pp. 610–611) argue that the quest for a meaningful life can be understood in terms of four main needs for meaning that guide how people try to make sense of their lives:

- *Need for purpose:* Present events draw meaning from their connection with future events. Purposes can be divided into (1) goals, and (2) fulfillments. Life can be oriented toward a future anticipated state, such as living happily ever after or being in love.

- *Need for values:* This can lend a sense of goodness or positive characterization of life and justify certain courses of action. Values help people to determine whether certain acts are right or wrong. Frankl's (1984) view of meaning in life emphasized value as the main form of meaning that people need.
- *Need for a sense of efficacy:* This involves the belief that one can make a difference. A life with purposes and values but no efficacy might consist of a person knowing what is desirable but who is unable to do anything with that knowledge. With a sense of efficacy, people believe that they can control their environment, which has positive physical and mental health benefits (Bandura, 2001).
- *Need for self-worth.* Most individuals want to be good, worthy persons. Self-worth can be pursued individually, such as finding out that one is very good at doing something, or collectively, as when people find self-esteem from belonging to a group or category of people.

Intelligent Design

One contemporary debate is that of intelligent design versus the theory of *natural selection* and evolution as proposed by Darwin. Those who believe in **intelligent design** postulate that the origin and existence of life and all the wondrous miracles of nature, including natural processes, are the plan of a supreme intelligence or creator, who is external to the world in which we live. Specifically, this external creator is the God of Christianity. Many biologists, physicists, philosophers, and others argue that the origin of the universe is uncertain; furthermore, in time, rigorous scientific investigation may provide explanations for the wondrous mysteries.

Health and Well-Being

The World Health Organization (WHO) defines health as more than the absence of disease. WHO includes positive physical, social, psychological, mental, and spiritual aspects as ingredients to overall well-being (Jain et al., 2013). This definition is used not only by WHO, but also by neuroscientists who are examining the impact of prayer and meditation on the brain. Isabelle Raynauld's documentary *Mystical Brain,* put out by the National Film Board of Canada, reports the findings of neuroscientists from the University of Montreal and from the University of Wisconsin–Madison. Doctors viewed and recorded brain activity (theta waves) of people skilled in prayer and meditation—Carmelite nuns in Montreal and monks in Wisconsin—during prayer or meditation. In both studies, researchers report a robust impact of prayer or meditation on the brain. Further, they also observed positive physical and psychological responses in new practitioners within three months of practice (Raynauld, 2013).

Do spirituality, religion, and meditation contribute to our overall well-being? Scientists who are expanding the field of neuroscience to explore areas of spirituality and theology would emphatically agree that prayer and meditation do contribute to peace of mind. In addition, today's technology enables us to gain an appreciation for how the brain influences our overall health and well-being.

While it is true that some cults and religious sects encourage behaviours that are damaging to health, such as ignoring sound medical advice, for individuals in the religious mainstream there is generally either no link between religion and physical health or a positive effect (Koenig, 2007; Williams & Sternthal, 2007). Researchers have found that religious commitment helps to moderate blood pressure and reduce hypertension, and that religious attendance is linked to a reduction in hypertension (Gillum & Ingram, 2007). One analysis of a number of studies revealed that a high level of spirituality/religion had a stronger link to longevity than 60 percent of 25 other health interventions (such as eating fruits and vegetables and taking medications for cardiovascular disease) (Lucchetti, Lucchetti, & Koenig, 2011).

Meditation is successful as a therapy for treating psychiatric disorders as well as hypertension (Shapiro & Walsh, 2008). A common thread or goal of spirituality is to restore the brain and bodily imbalances caused by a host of internal and external factors. Researchers have found that those who define themselves as spiritual have experienced favourable responses to illness, including cardiovascular diseases. Many also have attributed their recovery from illness to their belief in spirituality (Jain et al., 2013).

To this point, we have discussed a number of ideas about meaning in life in middle adulthood. For a review, see the Reach Your Learning Outcomes section at the end of this chapter.

Reach Your **Learning Outcomes**

The Nature of Middle Adulthood

LO1 Explain how midlife is changing, and define middle adulthood.

Changing Midlife	▪ Middle age is generally between the ages of 40 and 60; however, the age boundaries of middle age are not set in stone. ▪ As more people live to an older age, what we think of as middle age seems to be occurring later. ▪ Developmentalists are beginning to study middle age more in response to the number of people in middle adulthood.

Physical Development

LO2 Discuss physical changes in middle adulthood.

Physical Changes	▪ Physical changes in midlife are gradual. Genetic and lifestyle factors play important roles in whether chronic diseases will appear and when. ▪ Among the physical changes are outwardly noticeable changes in appearance (wrinkles, age spots); decreases in height; increases in weight; decreases in strength; deterioration of joints and bones; and changes in vision, hearing, cardiovascular system, and sleep.
Health Concerns and Wellness Strategies	▪ Major health and wellness concerns include arthritis, hypertension, and obesity. ▪ Men have more fatal chronic disorders and women more non-fatal disorders in middle age. ▪ Accidents, colds, and allergies decline in number. ▪ Mental illness is the second leading cause of disability and premature death.
Culture, Relationships, and Health	▪ Culture plays an important role in incidence of coronary disease. ▪ Poverty plays a critical role in health. Aboriginal people are poorer and have proportionately more health problems than any other group. ▪ Language is a primary health barrier for new Canadians. ▪ Health in middle age is linked to the current quality of social relationships.
Mortality Rates	▪ Obesity is the silent killer, contributing to an increasing number of deaths and health concerns. ▪ Cancer has overtaken heart and cerebrovascular diseases as the number one cause of death in Canada.
Sexuality	▪ Climacteric is the midlife transition in which fertility declines. ▪ Menopause is a natural part of aging for women and signals the end of childbearing. ▪ Hormone replacement therapy (HRT) has more risks than benefits if taken for over five years, causing cancer, heart disease, blood clots, and dementia. ▪ Although men may continue to father children in middle age, they experience physiological changes resulting in lower testosterone levels. ▪ Sex occurs less frequently, primarily due a variety of constraints. ▪ Middle-aged adults, particularly those who are sexually active, are vulnerable to STIs.

Cognitive Development

LO3 Identify cognitive changes in middle adulthood.

Intelligence	▪ Horn argued that crystallized intelligence (accumulated information and verbal skills) continues to increase in middle adulthood, whereas fluid intelligence (ability to reason abstractly) declines. ▪ The Seattle Longitudinal Study, initiated by K. Warner Schaie over half a century ago and now conducted by Schaie and his partner Sherry L. Willis, found that intellectual abilities are less likely to be found to decline and more likely to be found to improve when assessed longitudinally than when assessed cross-sectionally in middle adulthood. ▪ The highest levels of four intellectual abilities (vocabulary, verbal memory, inductive reasoning, and spatial ability) occur in middle age.
Information Processing	▪ Speed of information processing, often assessed through reaction time, declines in middle adulthood. ▪ Problem-solving skills remain relatively stable in early and middle adulthood, and then decline in late adulthood. ▪ Although Schaie found that verbal memory increased in middle age, some researchers have obtained results that contradict this. ▪ Memory is more likely to decline in middle age when individuals do not use effective strategies. ▪ Expertise involves having extensive, highly organized knowledge and understanding of a domain. Expertise often increases in the middle adulthood years. ▪ On the basis of interviews with leading experts in different domains, Csikszentmihalyi charted the way creative people go about living a creative life, such as waking up every morning with a mission and spending time in settings that stimulate their creativity.

Careers, Work, and Leisure

LO4 Characterize career development, work, and leisure in middle adulthood.

Work in Midlife	▪ Work is central to identity in midlife. ▪ Individuals may reevaluate the type of work they are doing in midlife and make changes. ▪ Balancing work and family life is a major challenge of work in midlife.
Career Challenges and Changes	▪ The current middle-aged worker faces such challenges as the globalization of work, rapid developments in information technologies, downsizing of organizations, economic downturn, and early retirement. ▪ People who are laid off realize both psychological and economic setbacks, from which recovery may be difficult or impossible. ▪ Career development for women is often interrupted by parental leave and the need to provide care for aging parents. ▪ Midlife job or career changes can be self-motivated or forced on individuals.
Leisure	▪ Leisure refers to the pleasant times after work when individuals are free to pursue activities and interests of their own choosing—hobbies, sports, or reading, for example. ▪ Vacations and preparation for retirement are important in midlife.

Meaning in Life

LO5 Explain the roles of meditation, religion, and spirituality in understanding meaning in life during middle adulthood.

Meditation, Religion and Spirituality	▪ Meditation, religion, and spirituality are approaches to understanding the meaning and purpose of life. ▪ The religiosity index is comprised of affiliation, practice, attendance, and importance. ▪ Many sub-groups exist within religious groups and offer different interpretations. ▪ Many people self-identify as either agnostic or atheist.
Meaning in Life	▪ Frankl believes that examining the finiteness of our existence leads to exploration of meaning in life. ▪ Faced with the death of older relatives and less time to live themselves, many middle-aged individuals increasingly examine life's meaning. ▪ To make sense of their lives, individuals have four needs: purpose, values, efficacy, and self-worth. ▪ Intelligent design is the belief that a higher power is responsible for the creation of the universe.
Health and Well-Being	▪ The World Health Organization's definition of health includes positive physical, social, psychological, mental, and spiritual aspects as ingredients to overall well-being. ▪ In mainstream religions, religion usually shows either a positive association or no association with physical health; however, those who engage in meditation, religion, or spirituality report improved well-being.

review → connect → reflect

review

1. Identify key physical and cognitive changes in middle adulthood. LO1, LO2
2. What role do poverty and culture play in the health concerns of middle age? LO1, LO2, LO3
3. What are some of the key factors of procession information in middle adulthood? LO2
4. What are some approaches to understanding meaning in life? LO3
5. The International Task Force identified several factors key to the quality of employment. What are these factors and what are the major challenges facing workers today? LO4
6. How do meditation, religion, and spirituality contribute to an individual's sense of well-being? LO5

connect

In this chapter, you read about career challenges and changes. What are some of the challenges you might face? How might you prepare for these challenges?

reflect

Your Own Personal Journey of Life

One of the signs of aging is the vulnerability of the body to illness. What strategies might you put in place to maintain overall health?

CHAPTER 16

Socio-Emotional Development in Middle Adulthood

CHAPTER OUTLINE

Personality Theories and Development in Middle Adulthood

LO1 Describe personality theories and development in middle adulthood.

- **Stages of Adulthood**
- **The Life-Events Approach**
- **Stress and Personal Control in Midlife**
- **Contexts of Midlife Development**

Stability and Change

LO2 Discuss stability and change in development during middle adulthood, including longitudinal studies.

- **Longitudinal Studies**
- **Conclusions**

Close Relationships

LO3 Identify some important aspects of close relationships in middle adulthood.

- **Love and Marriage at Midlife**
- **The Empty Nest and Its Refilling**
- **Sibling Relationships and Friendships**
- **Grandparenting**
- **Intergenerational Relationships**

"I remember when I was a boy, I watched my grandfather carve for me a whistle from the red willow. Blowing that whistle was not that amusing to me at the time. What was amusing was the way he worked with his hands. My grandfather had such sure hands. To me, he was a great creator and his hands were like his little helpers . . . I feel so happy that I was able to watch and learn from this man, my "Grandfather," because he taught me the meaning of 'Creating.'"

—DALE AUGER, CREE ARTIST, 1991

Chantal Petitclerc

PA Images / Alamy Stock Photo

In middle adulthood, Erikson believed we resolve the conflict of *generativity versus stagnation*. When the conflict is resolved in middle adulthood, individuals gain the virtue of care and are more able to shift concerns from themselves to others, thereby building a constructive legacy through family, work, and community activities. Chantal Petitclerc has faced enormous challenges and now, in early middle adulthood, she has already created a very inspirational legacy.

As you read in Chapter 12, Erikson theorized that adolescents resolve the conflict of *identity versus role confusion*. At this time, teenagers come to terms with, or at least gain a deeper understanding of their capabilities, goals, race, gender, and ability to get along with others. Teens often test the limits of rules and regulations in an effort to understand the world around them. Maybe you did some things like that too. Imagine for a moment an accident occurs that changes your life irrevocably. Were this to happen, resolving this conflict may prove even more challenging.

In a public presentation, Senator Chantal Petitclerc shared that when she was 12, her parents warned her not to go close to an old barn near their home in the small rural town of Saint-Marc-des-Carrières in Quebec, because it was falling apart and could be dangerous. Well, she and a couple of friends did exactly what their parents warned them not to do: They decided to remove the door from that old barn so they could build a bike ramp. But catastrophe struck—the very heavy barn door fell on top of Chantal, breaking her spine. Chantal became a paraplegic, and had to rethink her identity.

Fortunately for Chantal, her family and community responded with care. The school was made wheelchair-accessible; the home-economics teacher even located a special sewing machine that Chantal could use; and, last, but not least, the physical education teacher taught her to swim, whetting her appetite for competition and sport. Swimming triggered her passion for sports and competition so much that later, when she took up wheelchair racing, she dreamed of becoming the best in the world—a dream that came true.

Determined to compete, Chantal needed a really good racing wheelchair, which, in 1987, cost about $4000. Coming from a modest family, her father gave her $400. With this gift, she put her ingenuity and determination to task. She created a racing chair from second-hand parts and entered her first wheelchair race, coming in last. Did this deter her? Certainly not! Later, in 2011, when interviewed about the event, she said, "Everyone needs to start at the base and fight their way up step-by-step … If you put the time and training in, you can make it happen, if you choose to." Clearly, Chantal chose to do just that.

Since that first race, Chantal has participated in five Paralympic Games and won 21 medals, 14 of which are gold. In addition to being a participant, she has become a dedicated advocate for athletes and the Paralympic Games. In her final Paralympic Games (Beijing, 2008), she won five gold medals and set three world records. She was the first Paralympic athlete to serve as Canada's *chef de mission* at the 2014 Commonwealth Games, and later assumed the role in the Rio Olympics of 2016. Advocating for and inspiring people with disabilities has brought her many accolades and awards. She was voted Female Athlete of the Year by The Canadian Press; was awarded both the Queen's Golden Jubilee and Diamond Jubilee Medals; and was named Companion of the Order of Canada (2009).

In addition to these accomplishments, Chantal is married to James Duhamel, electro-acoustic music composer, and gave birth to their son, Elliot, in 2013. Although Chantal is not a member of any political party, Prime Minister Justin Trudeau appointed her to Canada's Senate in 2016. Chantal talks about how helpful gestures, whether they be small or large, resonate deeply with her, enriching her understanding of herself and others, enabling her to reach her potential, and help others reach theirs, as well as providing her with the fortitude to turn self-doubt into focus (Canadian Enclyclopedia, 2015; Petitclerc, May 12, 2016). Clearly, from adversity Chantal Petitclerc has created an impressive legacy and, at the same time, has become an inspiration to others.

Personality Theories and Development in Middle Adulthood

LO1 Describe personality theories and development in middle adulthood.

- **Stages of Adulthood**
- **The Life-Events Approach**
- **Stress and Personal Control in Midlife**
- **Contexts of Midlife Development**

What is the best way to conceptualize middle age? Is it a stage or a crisis? How pervasive are midlife crises? How extensively is middle age influenced by life events? Is personality linked with the contexts, such as the point in history at which individuals go through midlife, their culture, and their gender?

Stages of Adulthood

Adult stage theories have been plentiful, and they have contributed to the view that midlife is a crisis in development. Two prominent adult stage theories are Erik Erikson's life-span view and Daniel Levinson's seasons of a man's life.

Erikson's Stage of Generativity versus Stagnation

Erikson (1968) proposed that middle-aged adults face a significant issue in the seventh stage of the life span, *generativity versus stagnation*. Generativity encompasses adults' desires to leave legacies to the next generation (Busch & Hofer, 2012; Tabuchi et al., 2014). Through these legacies, adults achieve a kind of immortality. By contrast, *stagnation* (sometimes called self-absorption) develops when individuals sense they have done nothing for the next generation. A sense of boredom and apathy characterize the feeling of having lived an unfulfilled life.

By middle adulthood, the individual may have resolved the conflicts of earlier stages. With the successful resolution of the identity crisis, the virtue of *fidelity* emerges, enabling the person to sustain loyalties freely pledged in spite of value differences and contradictions. To resolve the crisis of early adulthood, intimacy versus isolation, young adults confront affiliations with partners, friends, gender, competition, and cooperation. Love is the virtue that can emerge from this stage. In middle age, as the conflict of *generativity versus stagnation* is resolved, the virtue of care emerges. According to Erikson, care is "the widening concern for what has been generated by love, necessity, or accident; it overcomes the ambivalence adhering to irreversible obligation" (Tonks, 1992). With the emergence of care, the individual is able to shift his or her perspective away from self and toward others. Erikson believed that generativity is the link between generations by which adults find renewal and concern for the following generation, especially their own children.

Middle-aged adults can develop generativity in a number of ways. Through biological generativity, adults have offspring. Through parental generativity, adults nurture and guide children. Through work generativity, adults develop skills that are passed down to others. And through cultural generativity, adults create, renovate, or conserve some aspect of culture that ultimately survives. Chantal Petitclerc, who you read about in the opening vignette, is in the process of developing generativity in each of these four ways.

Adults promote and guide the next generation by parenting, teaching, leading, and doing things that benefit the community. In George Vaillant's (2002) longitudinal studies of aging in middle age, generativity (defined in this study as "taking care of the next generation") was more strongly related than intimacy to whether individuals would have an enduring and happy marriage at 75 to 80 years of age. One of the participants in Vaillant's studies said, "From 20 to 30, I learned how to get along with my wife. From 30 to 40, I learned how to be a success at my job, and at 40 to 50, I worried less about myself and more about the children" (Vaillant, 2002, p. 114).

Generative adults commit themselves to the continuation and improvement of society as a whole through their connection to the next generation. Generative adults develop a positive legacy of the self and then offer it as a gift to the next generation.

More contemporary research supports Erikson's (1968) view on the importance of generativity (Newton & Stewart, 2012). A longitudinal study of individuals from their college years through age 43 revealed that Erikson's stage of generativity versus stagnation shows a pattern of slow but steady increase in becoming more generative (Whitbourne, Sneed, & Sayer, 2009). In another longitudinal study of Smith College women, generativity increased from the thirties through the fifties (Stewart, Ostrove, & Helson, 2001) (see Figure 16.1).

Figure 16.1

Changes in Generativity from the Thirties through the Fifties

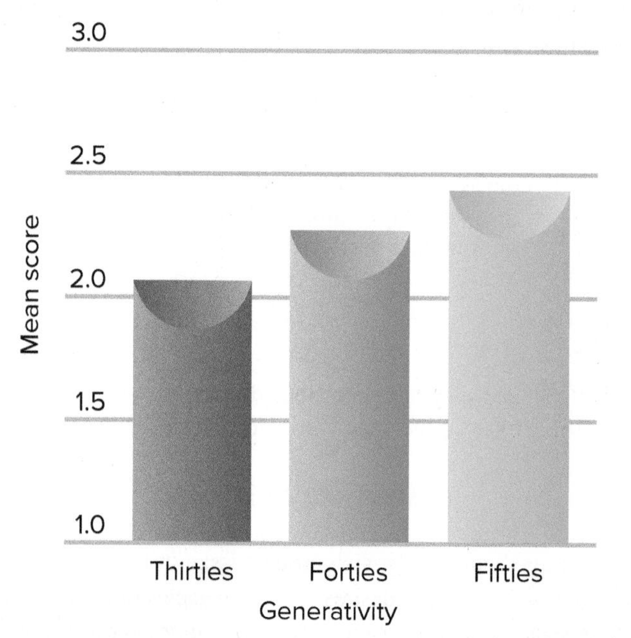

Generativity increased in Smith College women as they aged from their thirties through their fifties (Stewart, Ostrove, & Helson, 2001). The women rated themselves on a three-point scale indicating the extent to which they thought the statements about generativity were descriptive of their lives. Higher scores reflect greater generativity.

critical thinking

Erik Erikson believed that if the crisis of generativity versus stagnation is successfully resolved, the middle-aged adult develops the virtue of care; if unresolved, the middle-aged adult develops a lack of caring for others, sometimes called self-absorption. How do you think the resolution of earlier stages contributes to the successful or unsuccessful completion of Erikson's seventh stage? Consider people you know, perhaps your parents or grandparents. In what ways have they developed generativity or stagnation? Do men and women develop generativity differently? If so, how and why? What tips or words of advice would you give to someone you thought was stagnating?

Levinson's Seasons of a Man's Life

In *The Seasons of a Man's Life* (1978), clinical psychologist Daniel Levinson reported the results of extensive interviews with 40 middle-aged men who worked as hourly workers, business executives, academics, and novelists. Levinson bolstered his conclusions with information from the biographies of famous men and the development of memorable literary characters. Although Levinson's major interest focused on midlife change, he described a number of stages and transitions during the period from 17 to 65 years of age, as shown in Figure 16.2. Levinson emphasized that developmental tasks must be mastered at each stage.

According to Levinson, adulthood for men has three main stages that are surrounded by transition periods. Specific tasks and challenges are associated with each stage. From about the ages of 28 to 33, the man goes through a transition period in which he must face the more serious question of determining his goals. During his thirties, he usually focuses on family and career development. In the later years of this period, he enters a phase of becoming one's own man (or BOOM, as Levinson calls it). By age 40, he has reached a stable location in his career, has outgrown his earlier, more tenuous attempts at learning to become an adult, and now must look forward to the kind of life he will lead as a middle-aged adult.

Levinson believed that the transition to middle adulthood lasts about five years (ages 40 to 45) and requires the adult male to come to grips with four major conflicts that have existed in his life since adolescence: (1) being young versus being old, (2) being destructive versus being constructive, (3) being masculine versus being feminine, and (4) being attached to others versus being separated from them. Seventy to 80 percent of the men Levinson interviewed found the midlife transition tumultuous and psychologically painful, as many aspects of their lives came into question. According to Levinson, the success of the midlife transition rests on how effectively the individual reduces the polarities and accepts each of them as an integral part of his being.

Because Levinson interviewed middle-aged males, the data about middle adulthood is considered more reliable than the data about early adulthood. When individuals are asked to remember information about earlier parts of their lives, they may distort and forget things. The original Levinson data included no females, although Levinson (1996) reported that his stages, transitions, and the crisis of middle age hold for females as well as males. Levinson's work did not include statistical analysis. The quality and quantity of the Levinson biographies make them outstanding examples of the clinical tradition.

critical thinking

Levinson's study was conducted in 1978. Since then, young adults have been staying in school longer and living at home longer. How might this change affect Levinson's theory? Levinson focused his study on men in middle adulthood; however, he believed that the stages, transitions, and crisis of middle age apply to women as well. What are the four conflicts Levinson believed men had to come to terms with? Are these conflicts as true today as Levinson thought in 1978? Is Levinson's theory equally true for men and for women? Are Levinson's transitions in line with your experience and observations?

Figure 16.2

Levinson's Periods of Adult Development

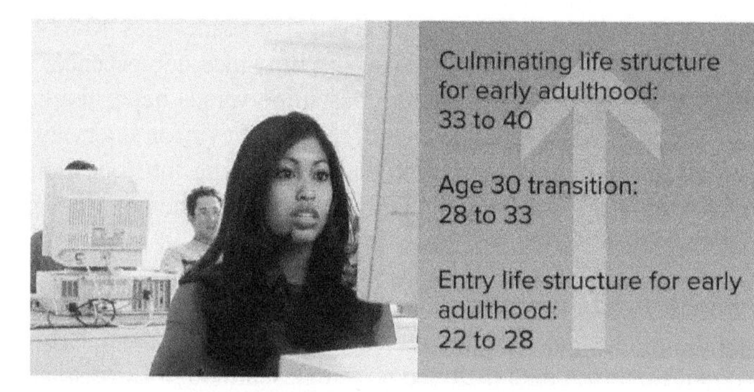

Amos Morgan/Getty Images; SelectStock/Getty Images; Image100 Ltd.

At the end of one's teens, according to Levinson, a transition from dependence to independence should occur. This transition is marked by the formation of a dream—an image of the kind of life the youth wants to have, especially in terms of a career and marriage. Levinson sees the twenties as a novice phase of adult development. It is a time of reasonably free experimentation and of testing the dream in the real world. In early adulthood, the two major tasks to be mastered are exploring the possibilities for adult living and developing a stable life structure.

How Pervasive Are Midlife Crises?

Levinson (1978) views midlife as a crisis, arguing that the middle-aged adult is suspended between the past and the future, trying to cope with this gap that threatens life's continuity. George Vaillant (1977) has a different view. Vaillant's study—called the "Grant Study"—involved Harvard University men in their early thirties and in their late forties who initially had been interviewed as undergraduates. He concluded that just as adolescence is a time for detecting parental flaws and discovering the truth about childhood, the forties are a decade of reassessing and recording the truth about the adolescent and adulthood years. However, whereas Levinson sees midlife as a crisis, Vaillant believes that only a minority of adults experience a midlife crisis.

During middle adulthood, the significance of our lives is made even more complicated as we experience a heightened awareness of our mortality when we witness the death of friends, acquaintances, and our parents. The death of our parents is a clear signal that we are approaching old age and that our own mortality is approaching. We experience loss of youth, youthful strength, and healing capacities. Introspective appraisals of our values, behaviours, successes, as well as our failures, may contrast sharply with youthful dreams. The successful resolution of our midlife period is related to the legacy we may leave behind, the contribution we have made to our spouses, our children, our workplace, and our communities. The nature of our reflection helps us define the path we will take in our late adult years.

A number of research studies have documented that midlife is not characterized by pervasive crises:

- One study found that 26 percent of middle-aged U.S. adults said they had experienced a midlife crisis, but most attributed the crisis to negative life events rather than aging (Wethington, Kessler, & Pixley, 2004).
- A longitudinal study of more than 2000 individuals found few midlife crises (McCrae & Costa, 1990; Siegler & Costa, 1999). In this study, the emotional instability of individuals did not significantly increase during their middle-aged years (see Figure 16.3).
- A study of individuals described as young adults (average age 19), middle-aged adults (average age 46), and older adults (average age 73) found that their ability to master their environment, autonomy, and personal relations improved during middle age (Keyes & Ryff, 1998) (see Figure 16.4).

Adult development experts are virtually unanimous in their belief that midlife crises have been exaggerated (Brim, Ryff, & Kessler, 2004; Lachman, 2004; Wethington, Kessler, & Pixley, 2004). For most people, midlife is not a crisis (Pudrovska, 2009). On the contrary, a study found that adults experience a peak of personal control and power in middle age. A study of individuals described as young (average age 19), middle-aged (average age 46), and older (average age 73) adults found that their ability to master their environment, autonomy, and personal relations improved during middle age (Keyes & Ryff, 1998) (see Figure 16.4). As we saw in Chapter 15, many cognitive skills such as vocabulary, verbal memory, and inductive reasoning peak in midlife, and many individuals reach the height of their career success in midlife. Further, reports of general well-being and life satisfaction tend to be high in midlife (Martin, Grünendahl, & Martin, 2001).

Figure 16.3

Emotional Instability and Age

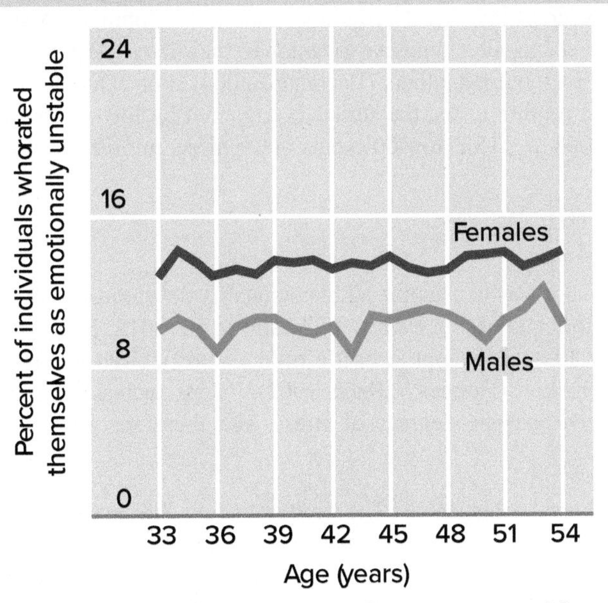

In one longitudinal study, the emotional instability of individuals was assessed from age 33 to age 54 (McCrae & Costa, 1990). No significant increase in emotional instability occurred during the middle-aged years.

Figure 16.4
Age and Well-Being

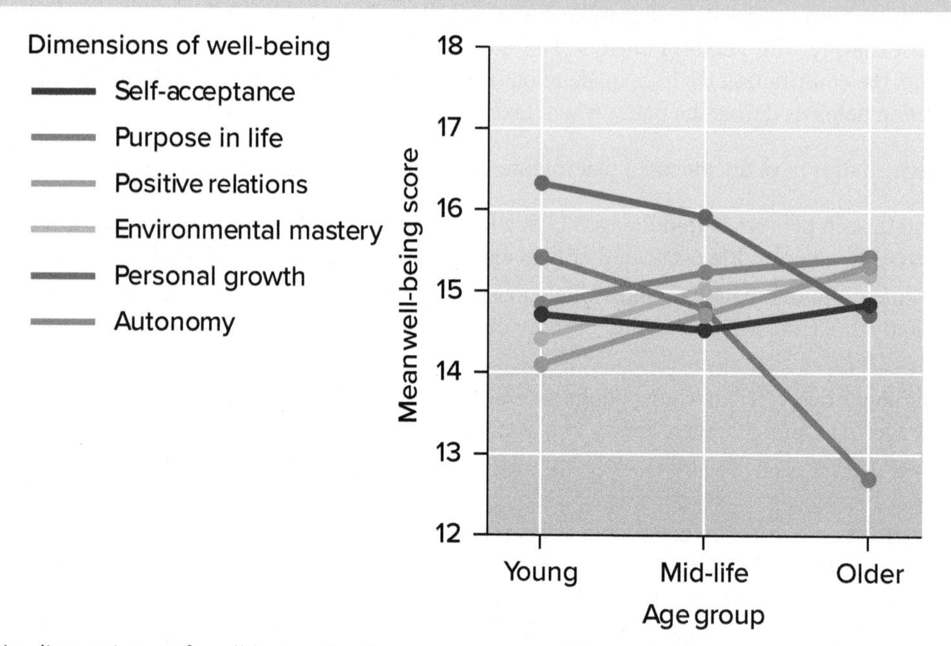

In one study, six dimensions of well-being (self-acceptance, positive relations, personal growth, purpose in life, environmental mastery, and autonomy) were assessed in three different age groups of individuals (young adults, middle-aged adults, and older adults) (Keyes & Ryff, 1998). An increase or little change in most of the dimensions of well-being occurred during middle adulthood.

Individual Variations

Stage theories focus on the universals of adult personality development as they try to pin down stages that typify adult lives. These theories do not adequately address individual variations in adult development. According to the individual variations view, middle-aged adults interpret, shape, alter, and give meaning to their lives (Arpanantikul, 2004). Some may experience a crisis in some aspects of their lives but not others (Lachman, 2004). For example, in one-third of the cases in which individuals have reported having a midlife crisis, the "crisis is triggered by life events such as divorce, job loss, financial problems, or illness" (Lachman, 2004, p. 315). How do events in life affect midlife development?

The Life-Events Approach

Age-related stages represent one major way to examine adult personality development. A second major way to conceptualize adult personality development is to focus on life events (Luhmann et al., 2012; Schwarzer & Luszezynska, 2013; Serido, 2009). In the early version of the life-events approach, life events were viewed as taxing circumstances for individuals, forcing them to change their personalities (Holmes & Rahe, 1967). Events such as the death of a spouse, divorce, marriage, and so on were believed to involve varying degrees of stress, and therefore were likely to influence the individual's development.

Today's life-events approach is more sophisticated. The **contemporary life-events approach** emphasizes that how life events influence the individual's development depends not only on the life event, but also on mediating factors (physical health, family supports), the individual's adaptation to the life event (appraisal of the threat, coping strategies), the life-stage context, and the socio-historical context (see Figure 16.5). If individuals are in poor health, for example, and have little family support, life events are likely to be more stressful. A divorce may be more stressful after many years of marriage, when adults are in their fifties, than when they have been married only a few years and are in their twenties, indicating that the life-stage context of an event makes a difference. The socio-historical context, as Bronfenbrenner's bio-ecological theory suggests, also makes a difference. For example, adults may be able to cope more effectively with being a single parent today than in the 1950s because this family type is more common and accepted in today's society. Whatever the context or mediating variables, however, one individual may perceive a life event as highly stressful, whereas another individual may perceive the same event as a challenge.

Figure 16.5

A Contemporary Life-Events Framework for Interpreting Adult Development Change

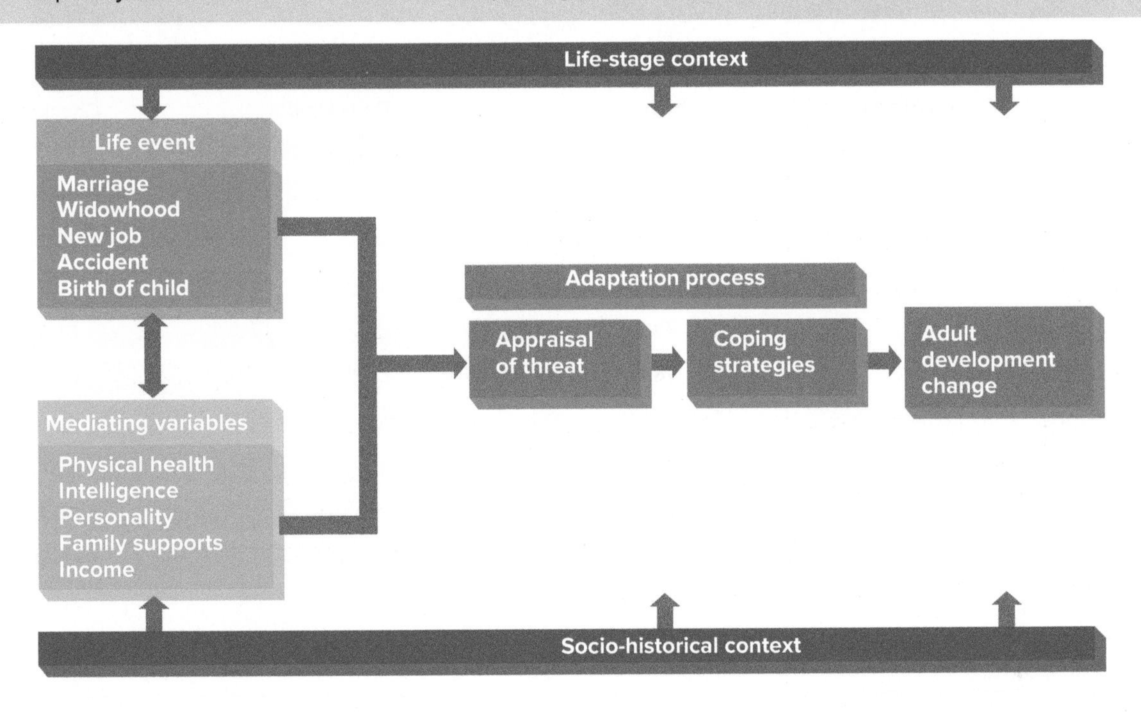

Although the life-events approach is a valuable addition to understanding adult development, like other approaches, it has its drawbacks. One of the most significant drawbacks is that the life-events approach places too much emphasis on change. It does not adequately recognize the stability that, at least to some degree, characterizes adult development.

Another drawback of the life-events approach is that it may not be life's major events that are the primary sources of stress, but rather our daily experiences (Almeida et al., 2011; Hamilton & Julian, 2014; Jacob et al., 2014; O'Connor et al., 2009). Enduring a boring but tense job or marriage and living in poverty do not show up on scales of major life events. Yet the everyday pounding we take from these living conditions can add up to a highly stressful life and eventually illness.

Research has also linked greater emotional reactivity to daily stressors to increased risk of reporting a chronic physical health condition and anxiety/mood disorders 10 years later (Charles et al., 2013; Piazza et al., 2013). Further, another study found that daily stressors were linked to cortisol secretion (cortisol is the body's primary stress hormone) in older adults who were experiencing depression and anxiety (Vasiliadis, Forget, & Preville, 2013). And another study of adults (mean age of 57 years) revealed that higher levels of daily stressors were associated with increased cortisol output, especially if the stressors included arguments and other problems at home (Stawski et al., 2013).

Some psychologists conclude that we can gain greater insight into the source of life's stresses by focusing less on major events and more on daily hassles and daily uplifts (McIntosh, Gillanders, & Rodgers, 2010). In one study, the most frequent daily hassles of middle-aged adults were concerns about weight and the health of a family member, while their most frequent daily uplifts involved relating well with a spouse or lover, or a friend (see Figure 16.6). Middle-aged adults were more likely than college/university students to report that their daily hassles involved economic concerns (rising prices and taxes, for example). Critics of the daily hassles approach argue that some of the same problems involved with life-events scales occur when daily hassles are assessed. For example, knowing about an adult's daily hassles tells us nothing about physical changes, about how the individual copes with hassles, or about how the individual perceives hassles.

Figure 16.6

The Ten Most Frequent Daily Hassles and Uplifts of Middle-Aged Adults over a Nine-Month Period

Daily Hassles	Percentage of Times Checked	Daily Uplifts	Percentage of Times Checked
Concerns about weight	52.4	Relating well with your spouse or lover	76.3
Health of family member	48.1	Relating well with friends	74.4
Rising prices of common goods	43.7	Completing a task	73.3
Home maintenance	42.8	Feeling healthy	72.7
Too many things to do	38.6	Getting enough sleep	69.7
Misplacing or losing things	38.1	Eating out	68.4
Yardwork/outside home maintenance	38.1	Meeting your responsibilities	68.1
Property, investment, or taxes	37.6	Visiting, phoning, or writing someone	67.7
Crime	37.1	Spending time with family	66.7
Physical appearance	35.9	Home (inside) pleasing to you	65.5

How do these hassles and uplifts compare with your own?

critical thinking

Identify some of the daily hassles and uplifts that face adolescents and young adults. How might these hassles be similar and how might they differ from those faced in middle adulthood? What is the major stressor in your life right now? How might that differ from the major stressor in your parents' lives?

Stress and Personal Control in Midlife

Canadian psychologist Hans Selye, the "father of modern stress theory," defined **stress** as "the non-specific response of the body to any demand made upon it" and advanced the theory that stress plays a role in every disease (Pomfrey, 2012; Selye, 2013). Stress can be episodic or chronic, and positive or negative in nature. **Episodic stress** is related to an event which, once coped with, is over. Such stress can be positive because it is motivational. One such stress would be final exams; another might be competing in a sporting event. **Chronic stress** is negative, persistent, and as such can be crippling. Selye believed that if stress continues unabated, the body will eventually shut down and not be able to rebound. Stress affects the immune system, making an individual vulnerable to illness and disease.

In addition to daily hassles, many immigrants report that language is a chief, but not the only, source of stress. First- and second-generation individuals reported different responses to daily hassles in a study of South Asian people. Second-generation individuals from South Asia reported significantly more hassles with members of their own ethnic group and marginally lower self-esteem than first-generation immigrants. For first-generation individuals, hassles with members of their own ethnic groups predicted lower self-esteem, and hassles with people outside their own groups predicted greater depression (Abouguendia & Noels, 2001).

Racialized individuals report experiencing racism and discrimination. One study of the Chinese community in Toronto found that perceived discrimination correlated with various psychological symptoms, such as nervousness, sleep problems, headaches, moodiness, and worry (Health Canada, 2002). Profiling on the basis of race by police and officials at border crossings serve as documented and public examples of the type of stress related to racism and discrimination.

As noted in Chapter 15, single-parent families, especially those headed by women, and Aboriginal families have persistently low incomes and experience more than double the national rate of poverty. Consequently, they are subject to more daily stresses.

Do middle-aged adults experience stress differently than young adults and older adults? One study using daily diaries over a one-week period found that both young and middle-aged adults had more stressful days "and more days with multiple stresses than older adults" (Almeida & Horn, 2004). The study further reported that, although young adults experienced daily stressors more frequently than middle-aged adults, middle-aged adults experienced more "overload" stressors that involve juggling too many activities at once (Almeida & Horn, 2004). Another study also revealed that middle-aged and older adults show a smaller increase in psychological distress to interpersonal stressors than younger adults, and middle-aged adults are less physically reactive to work stressors than are younger adults (Neupert, Almeida, & Charles, 2007).

To what extent do middle-aged adults perceive that they can control what happens to them? Researchers have found that, on average, a sense of personal control decreases as adults become older (Lachman, 2006). In one study, approximately 80 percent of the young adults (25 to 39 years of age), 71 percent of the middle-aged adults (40 to 59 years of age), and 62 percent of the older adults (60 to 75 years of age) reported that they are often in control of their lives (Lachman & Firth, 2004). However, some aspects of personal control increase with age while others decrease (Lachman, 2006). For example, middle-aged adults feel they have a greater sense of control over their finances, work, and marriage than younger adults, but less control over their sex life and their children (Lachman & Firth, 2004).

critical thinking

Discrimination and harassment on the basis of race, creed, ethnic origin, gender, sexual orientation, age, or physical or mental ability are in violation of the Canadian Human Rights Code. Nevertheless, Canadians experience harassment almost daily, either directly or indirectly in the form of racist or sexist slurs or e-mail jokes, etc. In addition to feeling isolated and devalued, demeaning behaviours, intended or unintended, may be internalized, affecting the individual's self-concept and confidence. A hostile or poisoned environment not only affects the quality of work, but also people's personal lives. Who might be most vulnerable to experiencing the behaviours associated with a poisoned environment? Why? What behaviours might the victim have to experience? What steps could a bystander or an individual subjected to discrimination or harassment take to address this situation? What have you experienced or observed, both inside and outside of work settings?

Stress and Gender

Women and men differ in the way they experience and respond to stressors (Almeida et al., 2011). When men experience stress, they are more likely to respond in a fight-or-flight manner—to become aggressive, withdraw from social contact, or drink alcohol. By contrast, according to Shelley Taylor and her colleagues (2011a, b, c; Taylor et al., 2000), when women experience stress, they are more likely to engage in a tend-and-befriend pattern, seeking social alliances with others, especially friends. Taylor argues that when women experience stress an influx of the hormone oxytocin, which is linked to nurturing in animals, is released.

A study of more than 2800 adults 50 years and older in Taiwan also found that women are more susceptible to depressive symptoms when they feel constant stress from finances, increasing stress from jobs, and fluctuating stress in family relationships (Lin et al., 2011).

Contexts of Midlife Development

People live through middle age in a variety of contexts, and each is unique. Bronfenbrenner's bio-ecological theory described in Chapter 2 provides an overview of how such things as historical contexts (cohort effects), gender, and culture influence the individual. Like Bronfenbrenner's theory, the contemporary life-events approach highlights the importance of the complex settings of our lives—of everything from our income and family supports to our socio-historical circumstances.

Historical Contexts (Cohort Effects)

Some developmentalists argue that changing historical times and different social expectations influence how different cohorts—groups of individuals born in the same year or time period—move through the life span. Bernice Neugarten (1986) argues that our values, attitudes, expectations, and behaviours are influenced by the period in which we live. For example, people born before 1985 grew up without smartphones, iPods, virtual social spaces, Twitter, and Facebook. In vitro fertilization (IVF) was not an option to people who wanted but were unable to have children, nor was same-sex marriage possible. Science and social change enable more choices.

Neugarten (1986) holds that the social environment of a particular age group can alter its **social clock**—the timetable according to which individuals are expected to accomplish life's tasks, such as getting married, having children, or establishing themselves in a career and retiring. Social clocks provide guides for our lives, and individuals whose lives are not synchronized with these social clocks find life to be more stressful than those who are on schedule, says Neugarten. She argues that today there is much less agreement than in the past on the right age or sequence for the occurrence of major life events. One study found that between the late 1950s and the late 1970s, there was a dramatic decline in adult's beliefs in a "right age" for major life events and achievements (Passuth, Maines, & Neugarten, 1984) (see Figure 16.7).

Figure 16.7

Individuals' Conceptions of the Right Age for Major Life Events and Achievements: Late 1950s and Late 1970s

Activity/event	Appropriate age range	Percent who agree (late '50s study)		Percent who agree (late '70s study)	
		Men	Women	Men	Women
Best age for a man to marry	20–25	80	90	42	42
Best age for a woman to marry	19–24	85	90	44	36
When most people should become grandparents	45–50	84	79	64	57
Best age for most people to finish school and go to work	20–22	86	82	36	38
When most men should be settled on a career	24–26	74	64	24	26
When most men hold their top jobs	45–50	71	58	38	31
When most people should be ready to retire	60–65	83	86	66	41
When a man has the most responsibilities	35–50	79	75	49	50
When a man accomplishes most	40–50	82	71	46	41
The prime of life for a man	35–50	86	80	59	66
When a woman has the most responsibilities	25–40	93	91	59	53
When a woman accomplishes the most	30–45	94	92	57	48

Adapted from "Individuals' Conceptions of the Right Age for Major Life Events and Achievements: Late 1950s and Late 1970s," from D.F. Hultsch and J.k. Plemons, *Life Events and Life Span Development and Behavior*, Vol. 2, by P.B. Baltes and O.G. Brun (eds). Photos: Corbis; © H. Armstrong Roberts/Retrofile/Getty Images.

How have these conceptions for the "right" age changed? Do the ages indicated match your views, and what role does culture play?

critical thinking

Review the dates in Figure 16.7. How do the appropriate age ranges of the late 1950s and the late 1970s compare with those of today? If you were to survey your friends and classmates, what differences might you find? How do you account for the changes? What additional changes might occur in the next decade? How are economics and technology factors in creating change?

Gender Contexts

Critics say that the stage theories of adult development have a male bias. For example, the central focus of stage theories is on career choice and work achievement, which historically have dominated men's life choices and life changes more than women's. The stage theories do not adequately address women's concerns about relationships, interdependence, and caring

(Gilligan, 1982). The adult stage theories also have placed little importance on childbearing and childrearing. Women's roles are often more complex, as the balance of career and family life usually is not experienced as intensely by men.

Conditions that distinguish the lives of women in their early fifties from those of women in other age periods include more "empty nests," better health, higher income, and more concern for parents. Women in their early fifties show confidence, involvement, security, and breadth of personality. Basic social attitudes about workforce participation and distribution of household chores have broadened the experience for both men and women. For example, today parental leave has replaced maternity leave, and many men enjoy the opportunity of being home with their newborn child.

In sum, midlife is a diversified, heterogeneous period for women, just as it is for men.

The stage theories assume a normative sequence of development, but as women's roles have become more varied and complex, determining what is normative is difficult. *What kinds of changes have taken place in middle-aged women's lives in recent years? What changes might you anticipate in the future?*

Cultural Contexts

In many cultures, especially non-industrialized cultures, the concept of middle age is not very clear, or in some cases is absent. Non-industrialized societies commonly describe individuals as young or old, but not as middle-aged (Grambs, 1989). Some cultures have no words for "adolescent," "young adult," or "middle-aged adult." In countries where life expectancy is in the mid-fifties, or where girls are promised in marriage by age 12, an age of 35 is considered old. The life course for men and women in developing countries differs considerably from that of North Americans. For example, the chart below illustrates how the African Gusii culture, located south of the equator in Kenya, divides the life course for females and males (LeVine, 1979):

Females	**Males**
1. Infant	1. Infant
2. Uncircumcised girl	2. Uncircumcised boy
3. Circumcised girl	3. Circumcised boy warrior
4. Married woman	4. Male elder
5. Female elder	

Thus, in the Gusii culture, movement from one status to the next is due primarily to life events, not age. Although the Gusii do not have a clearly labelled midlife transition, some of the Gusii adults do reassess their lives around the age of 40. At this time, these Gusii adults examine their current status and the limited time they have remaining in their lives. Their physical strength is decreasing, and they know they cannot farm their land forever, so they seek spiritual powers by becoming ritual practitioners or healers. As in North American culture, however, a midlife crisis in the Gusii culture is the exception, rather than the rule.

Middle-aged women in many countries find themselves raising their grandchildren because their own children succumbed to the AIDS pandemic. In addition, women may join advocacy groups such as Women Against Rape (WAR), or in Botswana, retired nurses may join the retired nurses society, BORNUS, which advocates for and provides assistance and care to women, men, vulnerable youth, and children struggling with HIV/AIDS, TB, malaria, or emotional disturbances. Women in these cultures experience not only the stress of the loss of a loved one and increased responsibilities, including child care, but their rights may also be challenged and undermined by restraining social conventions.

CONNECTING development to life

Immigrants Define Canada: "The Land of the Second Chance"— Nellie McClung (1873–1951)

In 1915, Nellie McClung, pioneer of women's rights in Canada, described her vision of Canada's future in "The Land of the Second Chance" as

> a land of the Fair Deal, where every race, colour, and creed will be given exactly the same chance; where no person can 'exert influence' to bring about his personal ends; where no man or woman's past can ever rise up to defeat them; where no crime goes unpunished; where every debt is paid; where no prejudice is allowed to masquerade as reason; where honest toil will insure an honest living; where the man who works receives the reward of his labour. (Morton & Weinfeld, 1998)

A bountiful landscape, plentiful water supply, peaceful elections and accessible education, health care, social supports, as well as guaranteed personal freedoms make Canada an enticing destination. Newcomers arrive with a spirit of adventure and optimism, sprinkled with a bit of anxiety. Expectations collide with stark realities. Where else can one meet such a diverse population, hear so many different languages, taste such diverse cuisines, and experience such changeable weather? Treatment of pets, superstitions, sports, fashion, and even the national anthem are wrought with cognitive dissonance. Language schools, social policies, and settlement programs are all designed to facilitate integration into Canadian life. McClung's vision has often been tarnished by our policies and practices.

Immigration policies and practices are constantly under review in an effort to be fair and to provide alternate routes for immigrants, refugees, and investors. The process not only takes considerable time, but is also expensive, financially, socially, and emotionally. For refugees, leaving their homeland often means leaving in desperation, without family, possessions, or sometimes even identification documents. For all newcomers, maintaining a sense of self and personal values while grappling with and adapting to a new cultural context and a new language entails an extraordinarily complex set of skills and experiences.

Statistics indicate that economic settlement into Canadian life takes approximately 10 years. Members of racialized groups are the most vulnerable to economic fluctuation and prejudice, and may require considerably more time (Lye, 1995; Pendakur, 2000). An individual's way of understanding the world around him or her is complicated by Canadian norms, family life, work, health, and leisure, in addition to the day-to-day challenges of tending to a family, finding a home, a job, and making new friends. Hard work, exhaustion, nostalgia, painful searches for an orderly sense of self, intergenerational and marital conflicts, embarrassing or damaging misunderstandings of the new culture, racism, rejection, and humiliation are all on the list of the newcomer's varied experiences.

Challenging decisions have to be made about which traditions to hold on to and which to leave behind. "Do we arrange our child's marriage?" "Do I wear my traditional clothes?" "How can I practise my religion?" "How safe am I? Will those from whom I escaped when I sought asylum be able to find and harm me here?" Skills and training are frequently not recognized or are underused. The doctor from China works as a security guard in Vancouver, while the lawyer from Sri Lanka goes back to school to study nursing in Toronto. With both hope and hardship, immigrants have built Canada's bridges, roads, churches, and institutions, whether they arrived 5 years ago or 305 years ago. Fleeing wars, persecution, and poverty, people come to Canada to build a better way of life for their families and, in so doing, they have irrevocably altered the country's cultural landscape.

According to writer Oscar Handlin: "The history of immigration is the history of alienation and its consequences . . . For every freedom won, a tradition lost. For every second generation assimilated, a first generation in one way or another spurned. For the gains of goods and services, an identity lost, and uncertainty found" (Lye, 1995). While not perfect, multiculturalism in Canada works because newcomers integrate by the generosity, benevolence and sincerity of the national character. Newcomers of all backgrounds settle very nicely in this easygoing country (Hussain, 2013).

To this point, we have studied a number of ideas about personality theories and development in middle adulthood. For a review, see the Reach Your Learning Outcomes section at the end of this chapter.

Stability and Change

LO2 Discuss stability and change in development during middle adulthood, including longitudinal studies.

- **Longitudinal Studies**
- **Conclusions**

Recall from Chapter 1 that an important issue in life-span development is the extent to which individuals show stability in their development versus the extent to which they change. A number of longitudinal studies have addressed the stability–change issue as they assess individuals at different points in their adult lives. In other words, are traits such as extraversion and conscientiousness consistent over time? Can an individual be conscientious during childhood, for example, and disorganized in young adulthood? Introverted in adolescence and outgoing in middle age?

Longitudinal Studies

We will examine four longitudinal studies to help understand the extent to which there is stability or change in adult development: Costa and McCrae's Baltimore Study, the Berkeley Longitudinal Studies, Helson's Mills College Study, and George Vaillant's Grant Study.

Costa and McCrae's Baltimore Study

A major study of adult personality development continues to be conducted by Paul Costa and Robert McCrae (McCrae & Costa, 2003, 2006; McCrae et al., 1998). They focus on what are called the **big five factors of personality**, which consist of openness to experience, conscientiousness, extroversion, agreeableness, and neuroticism (emotional stability). They are described in Figure 16.8. (Note that an acronym for these factors is OCEAN.) A number of research studies point toward these factors as important dimensions of personality (McCrae & Costa, 2003, 2006; McCrae et al., 1998).

Figure 16.8

The Big Five Factors of Personality

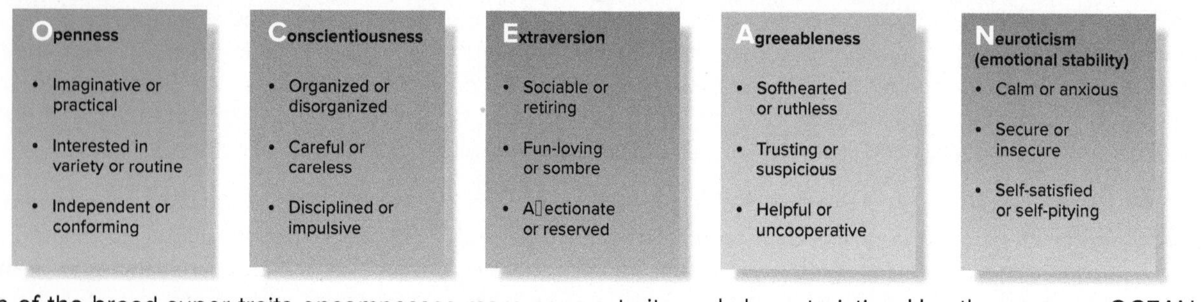

Each of the broad super traits encompasses more narrow traits and characteristics. Use the acronym OCEAN to remember the big five personality factors (openness, conscientiousness, extroversion, agreeableness, neuroticism).

Using their five-factor personality test, Costa and McCrae (1995, 2000) studied approximately 1000 university-educated men and women aged 20 to 96, assessing the same individuals over a period of many years. Data collection began in the 1950s to the mid-1960s and is ongoing. Costa and McCrae concluded that considerable stability occurs in the five personality factors—openness, conscientiousness, extroversion, agreeableness, and neuroticism (emotional stability). However, more contemporary research indicates greater developmental changes in the five personality factors in adulthood (Kranz Graham & Lachman, 2013; Lucas & Donnellan, 2011; Soto et al., 2011). For example, one study found that emotional stability, extroversion, openness, and agreeableness were lower in early adulthood, peaked between 40 and 60 years of age, and decreased in late adulthood, while conscientiousness showed a continuous increase from early adulthood to late adulthood (Specht, Egloff, & Schukle, 2011). Most research studies indicate that the greatest change occurs in early adulthood (Hill, Allemand, & Roberts, 2014: Lucas & Donnellan, 2011; Roberts, Donnellan, & Hill, 2013).

Further evidence for the importance of the big five factors indicates that they are related to such important aspects of a person's life as health, intelligence, achievement and work, relationships, and happiness (Quoidbach, Gilbert, & Wilson, 2013; McCrae, Gaines, & Wellington, 2013; Soto, 2014). Researchers also have found that personality stability or changes in a positive direction (lower neuroticism, for example) are associated with better health and more competent cognitive functioning (Kranz Graham & Lachman, 2013; Turiano et al., 2012). The following research reflects such connections of personality traits to other aspects of people's lives:

- Across a 10-year period, four of the five factors (the exception being openness) predicted outcomes involving physical health, blood pressure, and number of days limited at work or home due to physical health problems (Turiano et al., 2012). Individuals high on neuroticism report more health complaints (Carver & Connor-Smith, 2010).
- A study found that conscientiousness is related to college/university students' grade point-averages (Noftle & Robins, 2007).
- A meta-analysis revealed that openness is linked to pursuing entrepreneurial goals such as starting a new business, and to success in those pursuits (Zhao, Seibert, & Lumpkin, 2010).
- Individuals high on agreeableness are more likely to have satisfying romantic relationships (Donnellan, Larsen-Rife, & Conger, 2005).

Further studies to understand the big-five framework are being conducted in an effort to investigate various aspects. Professor Daniel Paulhus of British Columbia, for example, has conducted studies to determine the reliability of self-reported traits to actual behaviour, as well as the universality of these traits. One study reported that cultural contexts influence self-reporting; for example, people from East Asia are more ambivalent and dialectical in their self-description than North Americans, hence a person from East Asia is more likely to describe him- or herself as being "outgoing but shy" (Hamamura, Heine, & Paulhus, 2008). In another study, the test was translated into 29 languages and administered to over 17 000 participants in 57 countries. The study noted ambivalence in both East Asian and African respondents, but nevertheless reported significant replication of the big five personality traits (Schmitt et al., 2007). Analysis of the big-five framework is also being investigated to determine how much of an individual's personality may be revealed in Facebook posts or in tweets.

critical thinking

How would you describe yourself on Costa and McCrae's big five personality factors? According to research findings, personality traits can change over the life span with the greatest changes occurring in early adulthood. Is this true of you? If so, how? Have you observed some of the other changes indicated by the studies?

Berkeley Longitudinal Studies

By far the longest-running longitudinal inquiry is the series of analyses called the Berkeley Longitudinal Studies. Initially, more than 500 children and their parents were studied in the late 1920s and early 1930s. The book *Present and Past in Middle Life* (Eichorn et al., 1981) profiled these individuals as they became middle-aged. The results from early adolescence through a portion of midlife did not support either extreme in the debate over whether personality is characterized by stability or change. Some characteristics were more stable than others, however. The most stable characteristics were the degree to which individuals are intellectually oriented, self-confident, and open to new experiences. The characteristics that changed the most include the extent to which the individuals are nurturing or hostile, and whether they have good self-control or not.

John Clausen (1993), one of the researchers in the Berkeley Longitudinal Studies, believes that too much attention has been given to discontinuities as exemplified in the adult stage theories. Rather, he believes that some people experience recurrent crises and change a great deal over the life course, while others have more stable, continuous lives and change far less.

Helson's Mills College Study

Another longitudinal investigation of adult personality development was conducted by Ravenna Helson and her colleagues (George, Helson, & John, 2011; Helson, 1997; Helson & Wink, 1992; Stewart, Ostrove, & Helson, 2001). They initially studied 132 women who were seniors at Mills College in California in the late 1950s. In 1981, when the women were 42 to 45 years old, they were studied again. Helson and her colleagues distinguished three main groups among the Mills women: family-oriented, career-oriented (whether or not they also wanted families), and those who followed neither path (women without children who pursued only low-level work).

During their early forties, many of the women shared the concerns that stage theorists, such as Levinson, found in men: concern for young and old, introspectiveness, interest in roots, and awareness of limitations and death. However, the researchers in the Mills College Study concluded that rather than being in a midlife crisis, what was being experienced was *midlife consciousness.* They also indicated that commitment to the tasks of early adulthood—whether to a career or family (or both)—helped women learn to control their impulses, develop interpersonal skills, become independent, and work hard to achieve goals. Women who did not commit themselves to one of these lifestyle patterns faced fewer challenges and did not develop as fully as the other women (Rosenfeld & Stark, 1987).

In the Mills study, some women moved toward becoming "pillars of society" in their early forties to early fifties. Menopause, caring for elderly parents, and an empty nest were not associated with an increase in responsibility and self-control (Helson & Wink, 1992). The identity certainty and awareness of aging of the Mills College women increased from their thirties through their fifties (Stewart, Ostrove, & Helson, 2001). And as you read earlier, in a study that assessed the Mills College women from their twenties to their seventies, the big five factors were linked to changing historical circumstances in the women's lives (George, Helson, & John, 2011).

George Vaillant's Studies

Longitudinal studies by George Vaillant help us examine a somewhat different question than the studies described so far: Does personality at middle age predict what a person's life will be like in late adulthood? Vaillant (2002) conducted three longitudinal studies of adult development and aging: (1) a sample of 268 socially advantaged Harvard graduates born about 1920 (called the Grant Study); (2) a sample of 456 socially disadvantaged inner-city men born about 1930; and (3) a sample of 90 middle-SES, intellectually-gifted women born about 1910. These individuals have been assessed numerous times (in most cases, every two years), beginning in the 1920s to 1940s and continuing today for those still living. The main assessments involve extensive interviews with the participants, their parents, and teachers.

Vaillant categorized 75- to 80-year-olds as "happy–well," "sad–sick," and "dead" (see Figure 16.9). He used data collected from these individuals when they were 50 years of age to predict which categories they were likely to end up in at 75 to 80 years of age. Alcohol abuse and smoking at age 50 were the best predictors of which individuals would be dead at 75 to 80 years of age. Other factors at age 50 were linked with being in the "happy–well" category at 75 to 80 years of age: getting regular exercise, avoiding being overweight, being well-educated, having a stable marriage, being future-oriented, being thankful and forgiving, empathizing with others, being active with other people, and having good coping skills.

Figure 16.9

Links between Characteristics at Age 50 and Health and Happiness at Age 75 to 80

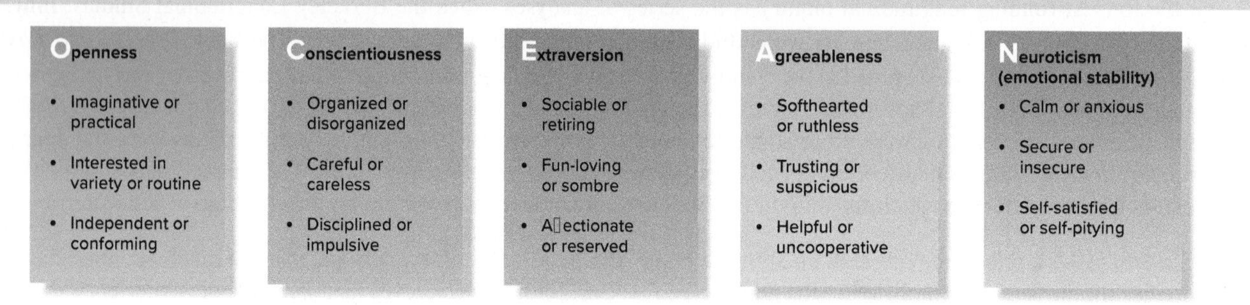

In a longitudinal study, the characteristics shown above at age 50 were related to whether individuals were happy–well, sad–sick, or dead at age 75 to 80 (Vaillant, 2002). Note that when individuals at 50 years of age were not heavy smokers, did not abuse alcohol, had a stable marriage, exercised, maintained a normal weight, and had good coping skills, they were more likely to be alive and happy at 75 to 80 years of age.

Wealth and income at age 50 were not linked with being in the "happy–well" category at 75 to 80 years of age. Generativity in middle age (defined as "taking care of the next generation") was more strongly related than intimacy to whether individuals would have an enduring and happy marriage at 75 to 80 years of age (Vaillant, 2002). Further, when individuals at 50 years of age were not heavy smokers, did not abuse alcohol, had a stable marriage, exercised, maintained a normal weight, and had good coping skills, they were more likely to be alive and happy at 75 to 80 years of age.

Conclusions

What can we conclude about stability and change in personality development during the middle adult years?

According to a research review by leading researchers Brent Roberts and Daniel Mroczek (2008), there is increasing evidence that personality traits continue to change during the adult years, even into late adulthood. However, in the meta-analysis of 92 longitudinal studies described earlier, the greatest change in personality traits occurs in early adulthood—from about 20 to 40 years of age (Roberts, Walton, & Viechtbauer, 2006). Thus, people show greater stability in their personality when they reach midlife than when they were younger adults (Roberts, Donnellan, & Hill, 2013). These findings support what is called a *cumulative personality model* of personality development, which states that with time and age, people become more adept at interacting with their environment in ways that promote the stability of personality (Caspi & Roberts, 2001).

However, this does not mean that change is absent throughout midlife. Ample evidence shows that social contexts, new experiences, and socio-historical changes can affect personality development, but the changes in middle and late adulthood are usually not as great as those in early adulthood (Mroczek, Spiro, & Griffin, 2006; Quoidbach, Gilbert, & Wilson, 2013). In general, changes in personality traits across adulthood occur in a positive direction. Over time, "people become more confident, warm, responsible, and calm" (Roberts & Mroczek, 2008, p. 33). Such positive changes equate with becoming more socially mature.

In sum, recent research contradicts the old view that stability in personality begins to set in at about 30 years of age (Bertrand, Kranz Graham, & Lachman, 2013; Donnellan, Hill, & Roberts, 2014; Quoidbach, Gilbert, & Wilson, 2013; Shanahan et al., 2014). Although there are some consistent developmental changes in the personality traits of large numbers of people, at the individual level people can show unique patterns of personality traits—and these patterns often reflect life experiences related to themes of their particular developmental period (Roberts & Mroczek, 2008). For example, researchers have found that individuals who are in a stable marriage and have a solid career track become more socially dominant, conscientious, and emotionally stable as they go through early adulthood (Roberts & Wood, 2006). And for some of these individuals, there is greater change in their personality traits than for other individuals (McAdams & Olson, 2010; Roberts & Mroczek, 2008; Roberts et al., 2009).

To this point, we have discussed a number of ideas about stability and change in middle adulthood. For a review, see the Reach Your Learning Outcomes section at the end of this chapter.

Close Relationships

LO3 Identify some important aspects of close relationships in middle adulthood.

- **Love and Marriage at Midlife**
- **The Empty Nest and Its Refilling**
- **Sibling Relationships and Friendships**
- **Grandparenting**
- **Intergenerational Relationships**

There is a consensus among middle-aged people that a major component of well-being involves positive relationships with others, especially parents, spouse, and offspring (Blieszner & Roberto, 2012; Markus et al., 2004). To begin our examination of midlife relationships, let's explore love and marriage in middle-aged adults.

Love and Marriage at Midlife

Recall from Chapter 14 that two major forms of love are romantic love and affectionate love. The fires of romantic love are strong in early adulthood. Affectionate or companionate love increases during middle adulthood. That is, physical attraction, romance, and passion are more important in new relationships, especially in early adulthood. Security, loyalty, and mutual emotional interest become more important as relationships mature, especially in middle adulthood (see Figure 16.10).

Marital Trends

According to Statistics Canada (2011), the portrait of marriage and the family is undergoing dramatic shifts. Married couples remained the predominant family structure (67.0 percent) in 2011, but the share has decreased over time. This portrait includes the following trends:

- Between 2006 and 2011, the number of common-law couples rose 13.9 percent, more than four times the 3.1 percent increase for married couples.
- For the first time, in 2011 the number of common-law couple families (16.7 percent) surpassed, by a narrow margin, the number of lone-parent families (16. 3 percent).
- Lone-parent families increased 8.0 percent over the same period. Growth was higher for male lone-parent families (16.2 percent) than for female lone-parent families (6.0 percent); however, 8 of 10 lone parent families were headed by women.
- The number of same-sex married couples nearly tripled between 2006 and 2011.

Figure 16.10

The Development of Relationships

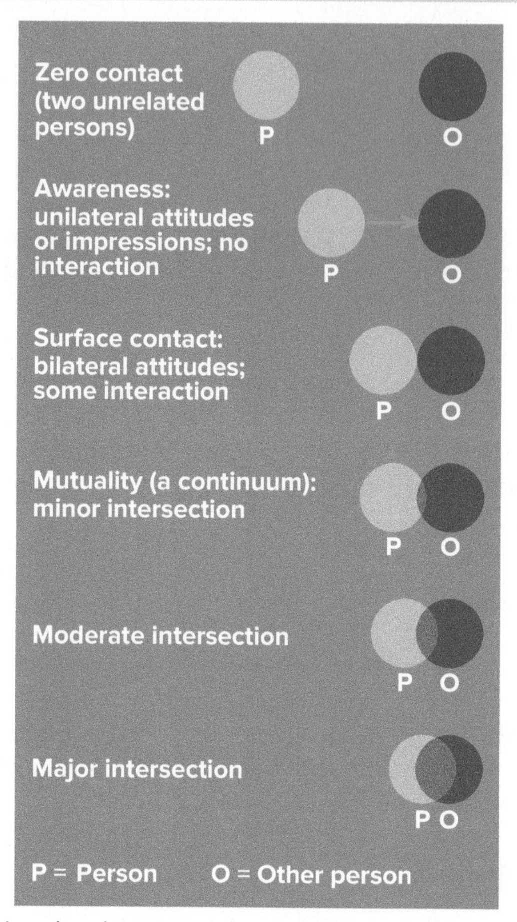

One view of how close relationships develop states that we begin a relationship with someone at a zero point of contact (*top*), and then gradually move from a surface relationship into more intense, mutual interaction, sharing ourselves more and more with the other person as the relationship develops. At the final stage, a major intersection, we are probably experiencing affectionate or companionate love (*bottom*).

For the first time, Statistics Canada counted stepfamilies and found that 87.4 percent of those counted in 2011 were intact families—that is, they were comprised of two parents and their biological or adopted children—and 12.6 percent were stepfamilies. The findings indicated that 7.4 percent of couples with children were simple stepfamilies, in which all children were the biological or adopted children of one and only one married spouse or common-law partner. An additional 5.2 percent of couples with children were complex stepfamilies, most of which were comprised of at least one child of both parents as well as at least one child of one parent only.

In 2011, about one-fifth (20.5 percent) of people aged 15 and over did not live in a census family (defined as "a married couple and the children, if any, of either or both spouses; a couple living common law and the children, if any, of either or both partners; or a lone parent of any marital status with at least one child living in the same dwelling and that child or those children"), including those who lived alone (13.5 percent), with non-relatives only (4.5 percent), or with other relatives (2.5 percent).

Numerous factors have contributed to these changes. Not only are people waiting longer to marry, but those considering marriage may also have experienced the divorce of their own parents. This experience may create additional caution. Those who have divorced may choose more informal arrangements than marriage. Further, as economic self-sufficiency for both women and men has taken on greater importance, marriage may no longer be viewed as the primary rite of passage into adulthood.

A recent study revealed that marital satisfaction increased in middle age (Gorchoff, John, & Helson, 2008). Even some marriages that were difficult and rocky during early adulthood turn out to be better adjusted during middle adulthood.

Although the partners may have lived through a great deal of turmoil, they eventually discover a deep and solid foundation on which to anchor their relationship. Possibly by middle age, many of the worst marriages already have dissolved. However, a study revealed that married and partnered middle-aged adults are more likely to view their relationships with ambivalence or indifference than their late adulthood counterparts (Windsor & Butterworth, 2010).

Marriage and Divorce

As noted, some marriages that were difficult and rocky during early adulthood turn out to be better adjusted during middle adulthood. Partners who engage in mutually pleasing activities usually view their marriage as more positive at this time. In 2010/2011, the national divorce rate declined by 2 percent in every province except British Columbia, where the rate increased by 4 percent. The decline in divorce rate since 2006 was 22 percent in Nova Scotia, where a couple's chances of reaching their thirtieth wedding anniversary are great. The rate of divorce declines with each additional year of marriage (Kelly, 2013). In Quebec, where the rate of divorce is highest, about 50 percent of those who marry can anticipate sharing their thirtieth wedding anniversary. The risk of divorce prior to the thirtieth wedding anniversary for Canadian couples is 38 percent, and for U.S. couples, the rate is 44 percent (Ambert, 2005).

Are there any differences in the factors that predict whether couples will divorce in midlife rather than as younger adults? John Gottman has conducted extensive research on the factors that make a successful marriage. In a 14-year longitudinal study, Gottman and Robert Levenson (2000) found that couples who divorce in midlife tend to have a relationship characterized as cool and distant, with suppressed emotions. The midlife divorcing couples are alienated and avoidant; it is a distant relationship with little or no laughter, love, or interest in each other. One of the divorcing midlife partners often feels that his or her life is "empty." The researchers found that when divorce occurs among younger adults (often in the first five years of a marriage), it is characterized by heated emotions that tend to burn out the marriage early. The young divorcing couples frequently are volatile and expressive, full of disappointment that they let each other know about.

Divorce in middle adulthood may be more positive in some ways and more negative in others than divorce in early adulthood. For mature individuals, who may have more resources at their disposal, the perils of divorce can be fewer and less intense than for younger individuals. Their children are adults and may be able to cope better with their parents' divorce. The partners may have attained a better understanding of themselves, and may be searching for changes that could include ending a poor marriage.

In contrast, the emotional and time commitment to a marriage that has existed for so many years may not be lightly given up. Many midlife individuals perceive divorce as a failure in what they had hoped would be the best years of their lives. The divorcer might see the situation as an escape from an untenable relationship, but the divorced partner frequently sees it as a betrayal, the ending of a relationship that had been built up over many years and that involved a great investment of commitment and trust.

Studies reported by Anne-Marie Ambert (2005) indicate that the top three socio-cultural and demographic factors that put marriages at risk are:

- Youthful marriages (defined as those who marry before their personalities have stabilized)
- Low income and poverty
- Cohabitation prior to marriage—particularly cohabiting couples with children

According to Ambert, the reasons people give for relationship breakdown (alcoholism, adultery, violence, fell out of love) are related to North American cultural values such as individualism. She argues that some of the reasons given for divorce would be considered frivolous in some cultures where family solidarity is more deeply ingrained in the cultural values. In many countries, the only acceptable causes for marital dissolution are abandonment and abuse (Ambert, 2005).

A recent study found that women who initiate a divorce in midlife are characterized more by self-focused growth and optimism than women whose husbands initiate the divorce (Sakraida, 2005). Financial stress infiltrates relationships. Today, 85 percent of Canadian couples with children are dual income, and most are carrying a debt load equal to more than their combined incomes (Sauvé, 2005). The busyness of their lives, combined with financial burden, exact additional stress on relationships. Paul Gottman of the Gottman Institute (U.S.) who uses rigorous scientific observations to understand relationships, reports that the magic ratio of positivity (empathy, asking questions, showing affection, etc.) and negativity (criticism, blame, showing disdain or contempt) is an indicator of stability or instability in a relationship. For couples whose relationships are likely to succeed, there are more positive than negative interactions. In fact, he found the ratio is five to one;

that is, there are five times as many positive than negative interactions in relationships that succeed. For couples heading for divorce the ratio is reversed—that is, there is more negativity than positivity (Gottman, 2007).

critical thinking

Divorce rates in Canada, although considerably lower than those in the United States, are the third highest in the world. Approximately 30 percent of Canadians divorce; the most vulnerable period for a marriage is the fifth year, when the rate is highest. On the basis of what you have read in Chapter 14 and this chapter, your observations, and your experience, what are the factors that contribute to a lasting relationship? What factors do you believe can potentially destroy a relationship? What, if any, societal factors may influence decisions to marry? to remain in a marriage? to divorce? If you were a marriage counsellor, what advice would you give to a couple who came to you?

The Empty Nest and Its Refilling

Recall from Chapter 14 that the family at midlife, the fifth stage in Carter and McGoldrick's family life cycle, is characterized by multiple entries and exits. An important event in a family is the launching of a child into adult life, to a career, or to family independent of the family of origin. Parents face new adjustments as disequilibrium is created by a child's absence. In the **empty nest syndrome**, marital satisfaction decreases because parents derive considerable satisfaction from their children, and the children's departure leaves parents with empty feelings. For most parents, marital satisfaction does not decline; on the contrary, it increases during the years after childrearing (Fingerman & Baker, 2006). With their children gone, marital partners have time to pursue career interests and to spend with each other. A recent study revealed that the transition to an empty nest increased marital satisfaction and this increase was linked to an increase in the quality of time—but not the quantity of time—spent with partners (Gorchoff, John, & Helson, 2008).

With the recent economic downturn, the refilling of the empty nest is becoming a common occurrence, as adult children return to live with their parents after several years of college or university, after graduating, after a relationship breakdown, or to save money after finding work (Merrill, 2009). Some do not leave home until their late twenties or early thirties because they are unable to support themselves, they are completing their education, or they are launching their careers. Numerous labels have been applied to these young adults who return to their parents' homes to live, including "boomerang kids," and "B2B" (or back-to-bedroom) (Furman, 2005).

The middle generation has always provided support for the younger generation, even after the nest is bare. Through loans and monetary gifts for education and through emotional support, the middle generation continues to help the younger generation. Adult children appreciate the financial and emotional support their parents provide them at a time when they often feel considerable stress about their career, work, and lifestyle. And parents feel good that they can provide this support. Another study of 40- to 60-year-old parents revealed that they provide financial, practical, and emotional support on average every few weeks to each of their children over 18 years of age (Fingerman et al., 2009).

Some families are skillful at handling the multiple entries and exits, while others experience disequilibrium. When young adults remain at home, they need to be treated more like adults than children. A common complaint voiced by both adult children and their parents is a loss of privacy. The adult children complain that their parents restrict their independence, cramp their sex lives, reduce their music listening, and treat them as children rather than adults. Parents often complain that their quiet home has become noisy and messier, that they stay up late worrying when their adult children will come home, that meals are difficult to plan because of conflicting schedules, that their relationship as a married couple has been invaded, and that they have to shoulder too much responsibility for their adult children. In sum, when adult children return home to live, there is a disequilibrium in family life that requires considerable adaptation by parents and their adult children.

Sibling Relationships and Friendships

Sibling relationships persist over the entire life span for most adults (Whiteman, McHale, & Soli, 2011). Eighty-five percent of today's adults have at least one living sibling. Sibling relationships in adulthood may be extremely close, apathetic, or highly competitive (Bedford, 2009). The advent of technology has made it easier for siblings to remain in contact. The majority of sibling relationships in adulthood have been found to be close (Cicirelli, 1991). Those siblings who are psychologically close to each other in adulthood tend to have been that way in childhood. It is rare for sibling closeness to develop for the first time in adulthood (Dunn, 1984, 2007). A study revealed that adult siblings often provide practical and emotional support to each other (Voorpostel & Blieszner, 2008). Another study revealed that men who had poor sibling relationships in childhood are more likely to develop depression by age 50 than men who had more positive sibling relationships as children (Waldinger, Vaillant, & Orav, 2007).

Friendships and social networks continue to be important in middle adulthood, just as they were in early adulthood (Blieszner & Roberto, 2012). It takes time to develop intimate friendships, and so friendships that have endured over the adult years are often deeper than those that have just been formed in middle adulthood. Nevertheless, friendships provide a support system when problems arise.

Grandparenting

Becoming a grandparent in a major milestone of middle adulthood, and, like everything else, this role is changing. For example, as you have read, young adults are becoming parents at an older age than previous generations, so, naturally, grandparents are older. Statistics Canada (2015) reports that in 2011, over 600 000 grandparents were over 45 years of age, and have an average of 4.2 grandchildren each (Milan, Laflamme, & Wong, 2015). Due to longevity and improved health, the relationship between children and grandparents lasts for 20 years, frequently more. In a survey, university students reported feeling close to their grandparents, exchanging visits, phone calls, and emails on a regular basis (B.C. Council for Families, 2007).

For some, being a grandparent is a source of biological reward and continuity. For others, being a grandparent is a source of emotional self-fulfillment, generating feelings of companionship and satisfaction that may have been missing in earlier adult–child relationships. And for yet others, being a grandparent is a remote role, especially when the children and grandchildren have relocated. Fortunately, technology is enabling people to stay more connected. Because the grandparent role links three generations—grandparents, parents, and grandchildren—the grandparent role is often mediated by parents at least until grandchildren become adults (Szinovacz, 2009). Researchers have consistently found that grandmothers have more contact with grandchildren than grandfathers (Watson, Randolph, & Lyons, 2005). Perhaps women tend to define their role as grandmothers as part of their responsibility for maintaining ties between family members across generations. Men may have fewer expectations about the grandfather role and see it as more voluntary.

Grandparent Roles and Styles

Although the Internet offers a plethora of parenting information, today's grandparents continue to be a major family resource, providing babysitting, financial support, as well as passing on family folklore, history, traditions, recipes, and social values. Additionally, grandparents often serve as confidants and role models (B.C. Council for Families, 2007).

Although grandparents continue to serve these roles, as families have changed, so too has grandparenting. Dual-earning families, increased divorce rates of the child's parents as well as of the grandparents themselves, custody arrangements, plus the divergent health and interests of individuals who become grandparents are some of the situations that can make grandparenting more challenging today than in the past. In some cases, grandparents may be step-grandparents; for example, one child explained to his class that he was very lucky because he had six grandparents who loved him.

An early study identified three styles of grandparent interaction with their grandchildren: dominant-formal, fun-seeking, and distant (Neugarten & Weinstein, 1964). In the formal style, the grandparent performed what was considered to be a proper and prescribed role. These grandparents showed a strong interest in their grandchildren, but were careful not to give childrearing advice. In the fun-seeking style, the grandparent was informal and playful. Grandchildren were a source of leisure activity and mutual satisfaction was emphasized. A substantial portion of grandparents were distant figures. In the distant-figure style, the grandparent was benevolent but interaction was infrequent. Grandparents who were over the age of 65 were more likely to display a formal style of interaction, while those under 65 were more likely to display a fun-seeking style (Szinovacz, 2009).

According to tradition among Aboriginal peoples, "children are gifts from the spirit world and they have to be treated gently lest they become disillusioned. . . ." Elders play an important role in helping their children and grandchildren understand the interconnectedness and harmony or imbalance of aspects or elements within the universe. These things include the individual, the family, the community, the nation, as well as the natural and spiritual phenomena of the universe. A recent study revealed that grandparenting can provide a sense of purpose and a feeling of being valued during middle and late adulthood, when generative needs are strong (Thiele & Whelan, 2008). Read more about Elders in Connecting Development to Life.

CONNECTING development to life

Elders—The Glue That Binds

When asked what an Elder is, Nellie Makokis Carlson, from Saddle Lake Amiskwachly Academy, thought a moment before saying, "It's a lifetime of experience. What you have lived through, good and bad. Also, it's an experience where Elders have this wisdom which they can pass on to the young people" (Carlson, 2007). As we have discussed, the extended family is considerably more diverse than it once was. Young people relocate to urban areas, sometimes "getting into trouble" according to Elder Margaret Bear of Ochapowace First Nation (Interviews with Saskatchewan Elders, 2007). Consequently, family gatherings become less frequent and more complicated because people may have to travel considerable distances to attend.

Health, cultural dissonance, poverty, and emotional burdens further exacerbate problems. Too often, Elders report that their grandchildren would rather play video games than learn about their heritage. Some community leaders discredit the Elders, accusing them of living in the past. Others revere the Elders, agreeing with Elder Maggie Auger that, "Elders are the glue that holds us all together. They hold what little tradition we have left" (Meili, 1994). Further, they argue that one of the most effective ways to mend family circles is to rekindle relationships with Elders who can offer much in the way of physical, mental, and spiritual healing, and who can serve to remind their families of spiritual beliefs, traditions, and history (Meili, 1994).

CP Photo/Kevin Frayer

"My grandmother taught me everything I do has a consequence. Even if I break a twig or step on a flower, the world will never be the same again. I learned to think about everything I did," said Francis Tootoosis, a Cree grandfather (Meili, 1994). Grandparents have often faced trials and hardships in the past, and now have the time and patience to share and teach their grandchildren about their culture and traditions. Their stories are interesting and insightful. Elders may share their stories about survival through winter. For example, Elder Nancy Bitternose talks about melting snow and ice in the winter to wash her family's clothes (Interviews with Saskatchewan Elders, 2007).

Elders initiated the Aboriginal healing movement of the 1970s, which seeks a restoration of spiritual values and balance. Previously, many of the healing practices and ceremonies of Aboriginal people were made illegal by the newcomers to North America. According to one Native healer, "In order to preserve the culture and the old ways, sacred traditional 'bundles,' teachings and rituals were passed on behind closed doors and brought back to the surface near the start of the seventies. As the Euro-western world began to not only accept but also express an interest in Aboriginal views on life, acceptance became more widespread, even among the native culture" (Criger, interview, 2007).

As divorce and remarriage have become more common, a special concern of grandparents is visitation privileges with their grandchildren. In the last 10 to 15 years, more laws have been passed giving grandparents the right to petition a court for visitation privileges with their grandchildren, even if a parent objects. Whether such forced visitation rights for grandparents are in the child's best interest is still being debated.

The Changing Profile of Grandparents

As the Canadian population ages and ethnicity increases, living arrangements and family structures also change. Understanding the changes in family structure and the changing role of grandparents is important since it has implications for the provision of care, support, and housing. Although most grandparents reside in private homes, the number of multigenerational home and "skip generation" households—that is, those with grandparents and children but no parents—has increased. For example, according to the census of 2011, 7 percent of the 8 million children aged 24 and under live with their grandparents. The census further reported that approximately 8 percent of grandparents live with their grandchildren, and one-third of these homes are technically "lone" parent households. Grandparents 45 years of age and over, of Aboriginal identity (24 percent across the country; 32 percent in Nunavut), or recent immigrants (20 percent) are more likely to co-reside with their children and grandchildren (Milan, Laflamme, & Wong, 2015).

Immigrants account for 26 percent of the population over 45 years of age, and for more than half of the co-residing grandparents. These living arrangements may be the result of a shortage of affordable housing as well as custom and tradition. The Family Reunification Program, which falls under the *Immigration and Refugee Protection Act*, is another factor shaping co-residing grandparents. Under this program, the sponsor financially supports the parent or grandparent who is immigrating to Canada for ten years, during which time the sponsored person is not eligible for government income assistance. Nearly all (95 percent) of immigrants who arrived in Canada prior to 2006 lived in multi-generational households. Shared living arrangements can make it easier to share caregiving, housekeeping, and financial responsibilities (The Vanier Institute, 2016; Milan, Laflamme, & Wong, 2015).

The number of Canadian grandparents who have full custodial care of their grandchildren who are under 18 years of age rose by 20 percent between 1991 and 2001. Divorce, adolescent pregnancies, and drug use by parents are the main reasons that grandparents are thrust back into the "parenting" role they thought they had shed. Suicide and depression also factor into grandparents assuming custodial care. Among the Aboriginal population, one-third of the grandparents have full custodial care. As you have read, suicide rates among Aboriginal populations are 6 to 11 times greater than elsewhere in Canada, and tragically, in Nunavut, 27 percent of all deaths since 1999 have been attributed to suicide (PHAC, 2012). Consequently, grandparents are stepping up to the plate to raise their grandchildren, many of whom have suffered, or are suffering, from a variety of conditions including depression and fetal alcohol syndrome.

Adding to the responsibility of assuming custodial care for their grandchildren, many are also caring for seniors. Physical, emotional, and financial stress put these grandparents at an elevated risk for developing health problems, especially depression (Hadfield, 2014; Silverstein, 2009).

Intergenerational Relationships

Family is important to most people. When 21 000 adults aged 40 to 79 in 21 countries were asked, "When you think of who you are, you think mainly of _____," 63 percent said "family," 9 percent said "religion," and 8 percent said "work" (HSBC Insurance, 2007). In this study, in all 21 countries, middle-aged and older adults expressed a strong feeling of responsibility between generations in their family, with the strongest intergenerational ties indicated in Saudi Arabia, India, and Turkey. More than 80 percent of the middle-aged and older adults reported that adults have a duty to care for their parents (and parents-in-law) in time of need later in life.

Some researchers have found that relationships between aging parents and their children are usually characterized by ambivalence (Birditt, Fingerman, & Zarit, 2010; Birditt & Wardjiman, 2012; Fingerman & Birditt, 2011; Fingerman et al., 2011a; Fingerman, Sechrist, & Birditt, 2013; Pitzer, Fingerman, & Lefkowitz, 2014). Perceptions include love, reciprocal help, and shared values on the positive side, and isolation, family conflicts and problems, abuse, neglect, and caregiver stress on the negative side. A study found that middle-aged adults positively support family responsibility to emerging adult children but are more ambivalent about providing care for aging parents, viewing it as both a joy and a burden (Igarashi et al., 2013).

A dark side exists in some families. Statistics Canada reports that adult children are the biggest perpetrators of violence against seniors, which can take one or more of several forms including neglect, physical abuse, psychological/emotional abuse, and economic/financial abuse (RCMP, 2012; Statistics Canada, 2012k). On the other hand, a study in the Netherlands revealed that affection and support, reflecting solidarity, are more prevalent than ambivalence in intergenerational relationships (Hogerbrugge & Komter, 2012).

With each new generation, personality characteristics, attitudes, and values are replicated or changed. As older family members die, their biological, intellectual, emotional, and personal legacies are carried on in the next generation. Their children become the oldest generation and their grandchildren the second generation. As we continue to stay connected with our parents and our children as we age, both similarity and dissimilarity across generations are found. For example, similarity between parents and an adult child is most noticeable in religion and politics; it is least noticeable in gender roles, lifestyle, and work orientation.

The following studies provide further evidence of the importance of intergenerational relationships in development.

- The motivation of adult children to provide social support to their older parents is linked with earlier family experiences (Silverstein et al., 2002). Children who spent more time in shared activities with their parents and were given more financial support by them earlier in their lives provide more support to their parents when they become older.
- Adult children of divorce who are classified as securely attached are less likely to divorce in the early years of their marriage than their insecurely attached counterparts (Crowell, Treboux, & Brockmeyer, 2009).
- Children of divorced parents are disproportionately likely to end their own marriage than are children from intact, never-divorced families, although the transmission of divorce across generations has declined in recent years (Wolfinger, 2011).
- Divorce in the grandparent generation is linked to less education and marital conflict in the grandchild generation (Amato & Cheadle, 2005). These links are mediated by these characteristics of the middle generation: less education, increased marital conflict, and more tension in early parent–child relationships.
- Parents who smoke early and often, and persist in becoming regular smokers, are more likely to have adolescents who become smokers (Chassin et al., 2008).
- Safe, stable, and supportive/trusting relationships with intimate partners and between mothers and children are linked to breaking the intergenerational cycle of abuse in families (Jaffee et al., 2013).

Gender differences also characterize intergenerational relationships (Etaugh & Bridges, 2010). Women's relationships across generations are thought to be closer than other family bonds (Merrill, 2009). Also in this study, married men are more involved with their wife's kin than with their own. And maternal grandmothers and maternal aunts are cited twice as often as their counterparts on the paternal side of the family as the most important or loved relative. Another study revealed that mothers' intergenerational ties are more influential for grandparent–grandchild relationships than fathers' are (Monserud, 2008). Although researchers have documented that mothers and daughters in adulthood generally have frequent contact and mutually positive feelings, little is known about what mothers and daughters like about their relationship. For instance, how do mothers' and daughters' descriptions of enjoyable visits differ at different points in adult development?

When adults immigrate into another country, intergenerational stress may increase (Lin et al., 2014). The pattern of immigration usually involves separation from the extended family (Parra-Cardona et al., 2006). It may also involve separation of immediate family members, with the husband coming first and then later bringing his wife and children. Those who were initially isolated, especially the wife, experience considerable stress due to relocation and the absence of family and friends. Within several years, a social network is usually established in the ethnic neighbourhood. As soon as some stability in their lives is achieved, families may sponsor the immigration of extended family members, such as a maternal or paternal sister or mother who provides child care and enables the mother to go to work. In some cases, the older generation remains behind and joins their grown children in old age.

The discrepancies between acculturation levels can give rise to conflicting expectations within immigrant families (Sarkisian, Gerena, & Gerstel, 2006; Simpkins, Vest, & Price, 2011). The immigrant parents' model of child rearing may be out of phase with the dominant culture's model, which may cause reverberations through the family's generations, as discussed in earlier chapters. For example, parents and grandparents may be especially resistant to the demands for autonomy and dating made by adolescent daughters (Wilkinson-Lee et al., 2006).

What is the nature of intergenerational relationships?

Family Caregiving

Adults in midlife play important roles in the lives of the young and the old (Birditt & Wardjiman, 2012; Fingerman et al., 2014; Fingerman & Birditt, 2011; Fingerman, Sechrist, & Birditt, 2013). Middle-aged adults share their experience and transmit values to the younger generation. They may be launching children and experiencing the empty nest, adjusting to their grown children returning home, or becoming grandparents. While middle-aged adults are guiding and financially supporting their children through adolescence and early adulthood, they may also be providing emotional and financial support to elderly parents (Etaugh & Bridges, 2010; Pudrovska, 2009). These simultaneous pressures from adolescents or young adult children and aging parents may contribute to stress in middle adulthood. On the other hand, family caregiving may heighten the warmth and intimacy of relationships. Consequently, middle-aged adults have been described as the "sandwich" generation, and their situation has been labelled the "generation squeeze" or "generational overload" because of the responsibilities they have for their adolescent and young adult children as well as their aging parents (Etaugh & Bridges, 2010; Pudrovska, 2009). However, an alternative view is that a "sandwich" generation occurs less often than a "pivot" generation, in which the middle generation alternates attention between the demands of grown children and aging parents (Birditt & Wardjiman, 2012; Fingerman & Birditt, 2011; Fingerman, Sechrist, & Birditt, 2013).

A valuable service that adult children can perform is to coordinate and monitor services for an aging parent who becomes disabled mentally, emotionally, physically, or in combination thereof. Support for their parents might involve locating a nursing home and monitoring its quality, procuring medical services, arranging public service assistance, and handling finances. In some cases, adult children provide direct assistance with daily living, including such activities as eating, bathing, and dressing. Even less severely impaired older adults may need help with shopping, housework, transportation, home maintenance, and bill paying.

One of Canada's leading workplace health researchers, Dr. Linda Duxbury, reports that approximately 47 percent, or almost one in two adult Canadians, spend an average of two hours per week in caregiving-related activities. The essential care for family members who are chronically ill, physically or mentally challenged, or frail or elderly is often demanding and exhausting. The Canadian Caregiver Coalition describes the cost to informal caregivers in terms of " . . . lost time at work, reduced productivity, high stress levels, increased health problems, lack of free time, financial pressures, and . . . negative impact on relationships." Two studies revealed that middle-aged parents are more likely to provide support to their grown children than to their parents (Fingerman et al., 2011b).

In response to this stressful challenge, provincial groups are calling attention to the needs of the caregiver as well as the needs of those in need of care. The Family Caregivers Association of Nova Scotia (FCgANS), organized in the early 1990s, was the first organization of its kind to respond to the needs of caregivers by offering a toll-free information line, a newsletter, and a database of services and products. In conjunction with the Canadian Caregiver Coalition, FCgANS attempts to raise awareness of caregiving issues and to influence policy.

To this point, we have discussed a number of ideas about close relationships in middle adulthood. For a review, see the Reach Your Learning Outcomes section at the end of this chapter.

Reach Your **Learning Outcomes**

Personality Theories and Development in Middle Adulthood

LO1 **Describe personality theories and development in middle adulthood.**

Stages of Adulthood	Erikson's theory: ▪ The seventh stage of the human life span, generativity versus stagnation, occurs in middle adulthood. ▪ Care is the virtue that emerges when the crisis of generativity versus stagnation is successfully resolved. ▪ Four types of generativity are biologial, parental, work, and cultural. Levinson's theory: ▪ Developmental tasks should be mastered at different points in development. ▪ Changes in middle age focus on four conflicts: being young versus being old, being destructive versus being constructive, being masculine versus being feminine, and being attached to others versus being separated from them. Other research findings: ▪ For the most part, midlife crises have been exaggerated. Most adults feel a greater sense of autonomy and mastery in middle adulthood. ▪ Many who experience a crisis attribute it to a negative life event rather than age. ▪ There is considerable individual variation in development during the middle adulthood years.
The Life-Events Approach	▪ Life events influence the individual's development. ▪ How life events influence the individual's development depends not only on the life event, but also on mediating factors, adaptation to the event, the life-stage context, and the socio-historical context.
Stress and Personal Control in Midlife	▪ Stress can be positive or negative, episodic or chronic. ▪ Chronic stress can affect an individual's immune system, causing distress and disease. ▪ Poverty, discrimination, or family conflict may produce chronic stress. ▪ Immigrants, Aboriginal people, lone parents, and seniors are more likely to experience daily hassles and stress related to racialized discrimination and/or poverty.
Contexts of Midlife Development	▪ Historical, gender, and cultural are three midlife contexts. ▪ Neugarten believed that the social environment of a particular cohort can alter its social clock, the timetable according to which individuals are expected to accomplish life's tasks, such as getting married, having children, and establishing a career. She noted a diminished agreement between the late 1950s and 1970s in the "right" time for events to occur. ▪ Critics say that the adult stage theories are male-biased because they place too much emphasis on achievement and careers. The stage theories do not adequately address women's concerns about relationships. ▪ Midlife is a heterogeneous period for women, as it is for men. For some women, midlife is the prime of their lives. ▪ In many non-industrialized societies, a woman's status often improves in middle age. ▪ In many cultures, where life expectancy is lower than in North America and social roles are prescribed at earlier ages, the concept of middle age is not clear. ▪ Most cultures distinguish between young adults and old adults.

Stability and Change

LO2 Discuss stability and change in development during middle adulthood, including longitudinal studies.

Longitudinal Studies	Costa and McCrae's Baltimore study: ▪ The big five personality factors are openness to experience, conscientiousness, extroversion, agreeableness, and neuroticism. ▪ These factors show considerable stability; however, early adulthood is when most change occurs. Berkeley Longitudinal Studies: ▪ The extremes in the stability–change argument are not supported. ▪ The most stable characteristics are intellectual orientation, self-confidence, and openness to new experiences. ▪ The characteristics that change the most are nurturance, hostility, and self-control. Helson's Mills College Study: ▪ In this study of women, there was a shift toward less traditional feminine characteristics from age 27 to the early forties, but this might have been due to societal changes. ▪ In their early forties, women experience many of the concerns that Levinson described for men. However, rather than a midlife crisis, this is best called midlife consciousness. George Vaillant's Grant Study: ▪ This study investigated whether or not personality in middle adulthood is a predictor of what the individual's life is like in late adulthood. ▪ Individuals who do not abuse tobacco or alcohol, who have stable marriages, exercise, and maintain a normal weight, and who have good coping skills are more likely to be alive and happy at ages 75 to 80 years.
Conclusions	▪ Amid change, there is still some underlying coherence and stability. ▪ Social context, experiences, socio-historical changes can influence personality development.

Close Relationships

LO3 Identify some important aspects of close relationships in middle adulthood.

Love and Marriage at Midlife	▪ Affectionate love increases in midlife, especially in marriages that have endured many years. ▪ A majority of middle-aged adults who are married say that their marriage is good or excellent. ▪ Researchers recently have found that couples who divorce in midlife are more likely to have a cool, distant, emotionally suppressed relationship, whereas divorcing young adults are more likely to have an emotionally volatile and expressive relationship. ▪ Divorce is a special concern. In one study, divorce in middle age had more positive emotional effects for women than for men, while marriage had more positive emotional effects for men than for women.
The Empty Nest and Its Refilling	▪ Rather than decreasing satisfaction as once thought, the empty nest increases it. ▪ An increasing number of young adults are returning home to live with their parents.

Sibling Relationships and Friendships	▪ Sibling relationships continue throughout life. Some are close, some are distant, and others are competitive. ▪ Friendships continue to be important in middle age.
Grandparenting	▪ Becoming a grandparent is a major milestone of middle adulthood. ▪ Due to increasing divorce rates and the career and work life of parents, the role of grandparents is undergoing considerable change. ▪ Two contemporary trends are the role of grandparents raising their grandchildren and the visitation rights of grandparents in the event of parental divorce.
Intergenerational Relationships	▪ Continuing contact across generations in families usually occurs. ▪ Mothers and daughters have the closest relationships. ▪ The middle-aged generation plays an important role in linking generations. ▪ The middle-aged generation has been called the "sandwich" or "squeezed generation" because it is caught between obligations to children and obligations to parents. ▪ The demands of family caregiving have both positive and negative implications for individual life-course development and for the family systems to which they belong.

review → connect → reflect

review

1. What activities in middle adulthood illustrate Erikson's stage of generativity versus stagnation? LO1
2. How have cohort effects influenced changes in the social clock? LO2
3. What are Costa and McCrae's big five factors of personality? LO2
4. How can love and marriage at midlife be characterized? LO3
5. How has the profile of grandparents changed? LO3
6. Explain how close relationships have an impact on aspects of personality development in middle adulthood. LO3

connect

What are the different kinds of stress and what role does stress play in our lives?

reflect

Your Own Personal Journey of Life

What is the nature of your relationship with your grandparents? What legacy have they left? What are the intergenerational relationships like in your family?

SECTION 9

Late Adulthood

CHAPTER 17

Physical and Cognitive Development in Late Adulthood

CHAPTER OUTLINE

Longevity and Biological Theories of Aging

LO1 Describe longevity and the biological theories of aging.

- **Life Expectancy and Life Span**
- **The Young Old, the Old Old, and the Oldest Old**
- **The Robust Oldest Old**
- **Biological Theories of Aging**

The Course of Physical Development in Late Adulthood

LO2 Describe and give examples of how a person's brain and body change in late adulthood.

- **The Aging Brain**
- **Sleep**
- **The Immune System**
- **Physical Appearance and Movement**
- **Sensory Development**
- **The Circulatory System and Lungs**
- **Sexuality**

Physical and Mental Health and Wellness

LO3 Identify factors of health and wellness in late adulthood.

- **Health Problems**
- **Exercise, Nutrition, and Weight**
- **The Nature of Mental Health in Late Adulthood**
- **Dementia, Alzheimer's Disease, and Related Disorders**
- **Health Promotion**

Cognitive Functioning in Older Adults

LO4 Describe the cognitive functioning of older adults.

- **The Multi-Dimensional, Multi-Directional Nature of Cognition**
- **Education, Work, and Health: Links to Cognitive Functioning**
- **Promoting Cognitive Skills in Later Life: Use It or Lose It**
- **Cognitive Neuroscience and Aging**

Meditation, Prayer, and Spirituality in Late Adulthood

LO5 Explain the role of meditation, prayer, and spirituality in late adulthood.

"What continues to perplex me is that all these years of existence taught me so little. I had hoped for wisdom, but I don't even know what wisdom is. I hope it has something to do with putting the top of my car up when it rains hard, because I almost always do that."

—JUNE CALLWOOD, CANADIAN JOURNALIST, AUTHOR, AND SOCIAL ACTIVIST, IN 2001 WHEN SHE WAS 75

Seniors Making a Difference

Here are brief descriptions of three prominent Canadians who continue to make a difference to our lives.

Dr. Arthur B. McDonald

THE CANADIAN PRESS/Fred Chartrand

Arthur B. McDonald, professor emeritus at Queen's University in Kingston, Ontario, is the co-winner, with Takaaki Kajita of the University of Tokyo, of the 2015 Nobel Peace Prize in Physics. Shortly after winning this prestigious prize, Professor McDonald was one of five winners (three in Japan, one in China, and this one in Canada) of the prestigious Fundamental Physics prize for breakthrough experiments in neutrino oscillation (the changes produced by decay of radioactive elements in subatomic particles). Physicists study these subatomic particles to learn more about the events and processes that gave birth to them and to learn about energy, matter, the galaxy, and the cosmos.

Buffy Sainte-Marie

THE CANADIAN PRESS/Jonathan Hayward

Buffy Sainte-Marie, an internationally renowned singer, songwriter, educator, and political activist, brought First Nations issues to the fore in the 1960s and 1970s with songs like "My Country 'Tis of Thy People You're Dying." During her rise to stardom while playing in Greenwich Village coffeehouses and appearing on children's television, including "Sesame Street," she completed her Ph. D. in Fine Art. In 2015, she won the Polaris Music Prize for her album, "Power in the Blood." Presently, she is working with NASA and calling for a think-tank of experts in environmental studies, sustainable resources, science, and cultural studies for her initiative, "Green Indians," a project to address the housing crisis faced by many First Nations peoples.

Dr. Roberta Lynn Bondar

HEINZ RUCKEMANN/UPI/Newscom

Dr. Roberta Bondar is a neurologist and a clinical and basic science researcher of the nervous system. She is one of six Canadian astronauts selected in 1983, and in 1985, she was named the chairperson on the Canadian Life Sciences Subcommittee. She is a Civil Aviation medical examiner and is conducting research into blood flow in the brain during microgravity, lower body negative pressure, and various pathological states. She left the Canadian Space Agency in 1992. She has received many honours, including the Order of Canada, the NASA Space Medal, and an induction into the Canadian Medical Hall of Fame.

Longevity and Biological Theories of Aging

LO1 Describe longevity and the biological theories of aging.

- **Life Expectancy and Life Span**
- **The Young Old, the Old Old, and the Oldest Old**
- **The Robust Oldest Old**
- **Biological Theories of Aging**

Each of the three people pictured in the opening vignette was born before 1945, which means they are in well into their seventies. Without a doubt, a 70-year-old body does not work as well as it once did; however, this is not preventing many from living very full and active lives or from contributing to their communities. For example, a 90-plus man or woman might enjoy a game of golf, even if he or she can't hit the ball as far as when he or she was 70. Seniors today are healthier and more active than a generation ago, changing the stereotypical image of late adulthood.

Life Expectancy and Life Span

Recall from Chapter 1 that life span and life expectancy are two different concepts. *Life span* is the upper boundary of life, the maximum number of years an individual can live, whereas *life expectancy* is the number of years that probably will be lived by the average person born in a particular year. We are no longer a youthful society. Did you know that life expectancy for people who lived during the Roman Empire was only 25? At the turn of the twentieth century, it was 50 (Conference Board of Canada, 2016). In fact, the concept of a period called "late adulthood" is a relatively recent one.

Today, according to the World Health Organization (2016), global life expectancy for children born in 2015 is 71.4 years. In fact, in the 29 high income countries, the average life expectancy is 80 or more. Between 2000 and 2015, life expectancy increased five years globally, the fastest increase since the 1960s. Life expectancy in Canada reflects this increase. As you read in Chapter 15, Canada, being one of the world's richest countries, reported life expectancy for a child born in 2015 to be 79.15 for men and 84.52 for women (Statistics Canada, 2016).

Globally and at home, economics plays a critical role in life expectancy. People in high income countries live as many as 19 years longer than people in low income countries. Within a country, areas with higher levels of income, education, and occupation generally enjoy better health, housing, and supportive environments; consequently they have longer life expectancy. For example, due to poor socio-economic conditions, life expectancy for Aboriginal populations is five or more years less than those of the total Canadian population (Conference Board of Canada, 2016).

In virtually all species, females outlive males. Why is this? One reason is that physiologically, women have more resistance to infections and degenerative diseases (Pan & Chang, 2012). Female estrogen production helps protect women from arteriosclerosis (hardening of the arteries). Plus, the additional X chromosome that women carry in comparison with men may be associated with the production of more antibodies to fight off disease.

Social factors such as health attitudes, habits, lifestyles, and occupation are also important factors contributing to longevity (Saint Onge, 2009). Men are heavier smokers and drinkers than women, therefore they are more likely than women to die from cancer of the respiratory system, cirrhosis of the liver, emphysema, and coronary heart disease (Robine, 2011). As well, men are more likely than women to take risks such as driving fast, and to work in dangerous occupations, such as construction, where they are more prone to accidents. The sex difference in mortality is still present but less pronounced than in the past.

Improvements in medicine, nutrition, exercise, and overall lifestyle, along with a reduction in intake of tobacco, are some of the factors that contribute to longevity. Another contributing factor is a substantial reduction in infant deaths in recent decades. What about the quality of life? Rather than *quantity* of life, the health-adjusted life expectancy, or HALE indicator, measures the *quality* of life. HALE is obtained by subtracting the average years of severe ill-heath from life-expectancy, which differs from country to country, or from region to region within a country. For Canadians, the quality of life according to HALE is 86.9 percent of the life-expectancy, Using this measurement, HALE estimates that the quality of life would be 68.81 for men and 73.44 for women.

Centenarians

According to Statistics Canada (2015), 5825 people self-identified as being over the age of 100 in the 2011 census, 1490 more people than in 2006. This represents nearly an 8 percent increase in five years. Projections are that the number will escalate to 17 000 by 2031, and will be close to 80 000 by 2061 (Statistics Canada, 2015). The chances of reaching 100 years of age remain higher for women than men.

These projections have stimulated research into aging and researchers around the world are finding that the view "the older you get, the sicker you get" could be a myth as older people are healthier and more active than a generation ago. In fact, the New England Centenarian Study (NECS), which was initiated in 1994, refers to the people between the ages of 100 and 119 who have participated in their study as supercentenarians (Andersen et al., 2012). Thomas Perls, the director of the NECS, refers to the staving off of chronic disease, cardiovascular disease, and functional decline until the end of their lives as the compression of morbidity (Perls, 2007, 2009; Sebastiani et al., 2012, 2013; Sebastiani & Perls, 2012; Terry et al., 2008).

A Quebec study showed that siblings of centenarians, who share half of their genes and a common childhood environment, live three to four years longer than their birth cohort (Jarry, Gagnon, & Bourbeau, 2012). Researchers of NECS also have discovered a strong genetic component of living to be 100 that consists of many genetic links that individually have modest effects, but which in combination can have a strong influence (Sebastiani & Perls, 2012). A meta-analysis of five studies conducted in Europe, Japan, and the United States concluded that when the influence of approximately 130 genes is combined, they "do a relatively good job" of differentiating centenarians from non-centenarians. These genes play roles in Alzheimer's disease, diabetes, cardiovascular disease, cancer, and various biological processes (Sebastiani et al., 2013).

The ability to cope with stress is another factor that NECS found to be associated with becoming a centenarian. Lifestyle also factors into longevity. The NECS found that few centenarians are obese, habitual smoking is rare, and only a small percentage (less than 15 percent) have had significant changes in their thinking skills (disproving the belief that most centenarians likely would develop Alzheimer's disease). According to estimates of the Canadian government, 6–15 percent of Canadians age 65 years and older suffer from Alzheimer disease and other forms of dementia. Women are twice as likely as men to suffer from dementia, and are two and a half times as likely as men to be the caregivers for someone suffering from the disease (Government of Canada, 2014).

Another study out of Japan investigated the possibility of a link between longevity and the big five personality traits that you read about in Chapter 15. Results from this study suggest that high scores on three specific personality traits—openness, conscientiousness, and extroversion—are associated with longevity (Masui et al., 2006).

Although a disproportionate number of centenarians are women, men are more likely to be healthier than women (Terry et al., 2008). One explanation for this gender difference in centenarians' health is that to reach this exceptional age, men may need to be in excellent health (Perls, 2007). By contrast, women may be more adaptive to living with illnesses when they are older, and thus can reach an exceptional old age in spite of having a chronic disability.

What about you? What chance do you have of living to be 100? To find out, several life-expectancy calculators are available online. Search for life-expectancy calculators, compare their differences and similarities, and find your life-expectancy. You will note that most of the calculator questions are about lifestyle, including height and weight, education, economic status, and family history.

The rapid growth in the 85- and 100-year-old age categories suggests that some potentially important changes might lie ahead:

- Even if it is still an option, retiring at 65 might be too young for many of tomorrow's older adults.
- Increasing health and longer productivity of the elderly might offset some of the economic burden that planners have long assumed will exist for a greying North America.
- Society's dismal view of old age might get a needed push toward a more positive image.

THE CANADIAN PRESS/Paul Chiasson

Following the 2010 earthquake in Haiti, Cecilia Laurent immigrated to Quebec. At that time, she was 114 years of age. Surrounded by family, friends, and neighbours, she celebrated her 120th birthday in her home. Once her birth date is validated by Guinness Book of Records, she will be identified as the oldest person alive. Cecilia attributes here longevity to the will of God. Her great-grandson, 28-year-old Cory, says that daily news and contemporary films upset her. He believes her preference for natural food and cartoons play a role as well.

critical thinking

Close your eyes for a moment and picture a 75-year-old man or woman in each of these four situations: (1) seeking health care; (2) driving a car; (3) engaged with family; and (4) participating in a community or social activity. Write down the first three or four descriptors that come to your mind about this person in each scenario. Do any of the words you wrote or the images you visualized reflect stereotypical views of seniors? If so, which ones? Would your words be the same for both men and women? If they differ, how so? Why? Do any of the words you wrote match how you might see yourself in late adulthood? What might you change?

The Young Old, the Old Old, and the Oldest Old

Late adulthood, which begins in the sixties and can extend to 120 to 125 years of age, is potentially the longest span of any period of human development—lasting 50 to 60 years. Increasingly, developmentalists distinguish between the young old (65 to 84 years of age) and the old old or old age (85 years and older). An increased interest in successful aging is producing a portrayal of the oldest-old that is more optimistic than stereotypes of the past (Andersen et al., 2012; Jeste et al., 2013). Interventions such as cataract surgery and a variety of rehabilitation strategies are improving the functioning of the oldest-old. More people in late adulthood are participating in regiments of prevention and intervention, such as engaging in nutritious eating and regular exercise (Buchman et al., 2012; Haltiwanger, 2013).

Many experts differentiate aging categories in terms of function rather than age. In Chapter 1, we described age not only in terms of chronological age, but also in terms of biological age, psychological age, mental age, and social age. Thus, in terms of functional age—the person's actual ability to function—an 85-year-old might well be more biologically and psychologically fit than a 65-year-old. Another concept to factor in is the HALE indicator introduced at the beginning of this chapter. Still, significant differences exist between adults in their sixties and seventies and those over 85.

As discussed in Chapter 1, Paul Baltes and his colleagues (Baltes, 2003; Scheibe, Freund, & Baltes, 2007) argue that the oldest-olds (85 and over) face a number of problems, including sizable losses in cognitive potential and learning ability. Other factors include an increase in chronic stress; a sizable prevalence of physical and mental disabilities; high levels of frailty; increased loneliness; and the difficulty of dying with dignity at older ages. According to Baltes (2003; Scheibe, Freund, & Baltes, 2007), when compared with the oldest old, the young old have a substantial potential for physical and cognitive fitness, higher levels of emotional well-being, and more effective strategies for mastering the gains and losses of old age.

As noted earlier, the oldest old are much more likely to be female, and the majority are widowed and live alone if they are not institutionalized. Their needs, capacities, and resources are often different from those in their sixties and seventies (Scheibe, Freund, & Baltes, 2007).

The Robust Oldest Old

A substantial portion of the oldest old function effectively. Society's preoccupation with the disability and mortality of the oldest old has concealed the fact that the majority of adults aged 80 and over continue to live in the community. Sixty-five percent of women over the age of 85 live outside institutions, while 77 percent of men in this age group live outside institutions. Twenty-two percent of seniors over the age of 85 live alone. Sixty-three percent rate their general health as good, 43 percent say they are independent in their daily living activities, and 95 percent rate their mental health as good (Shields & Martel, 2005). Shields and Martel found that exercise, moderate alcohol consumption, good nutrition, and low stress levels contribute significantly to positive physical and mental health ratings later in life and for speedy successful recovery from injury and illness.

Biological Theories of Aging

We are all older today than we were yesterday and younger than we will be tomorrow. How do we age? Intriguing explanations of why we age are provided by five biological theories: evolutionary theory, cellular clock theory, free-radical theory, mitochondrial theory, and hormonal stress theory.

Evolutionary Theory

Recall from Chapter 2 the view that the benefits conferred by evolutionary selection decrease with age (Baltes, 2003). In the **evolutionary theory of aging**, natural selection has not eliminated many harmful conditions and non-adaptive characteristics in older adults (Gems, 2014; Le Couteur & Simpson, 2011; Shokhirev & Johnson, 2014). Why? Because natural selection is linked to reproductive fitness, which is present only in the earlier part of adulthood. For example, consider Alzheimer's disease, an irreversible brain disorder, which does not appear until the late middle adulthood or late adulthood years. In evolutionary theory, if Alzheimer's disease occurred earlier in development, it may have been eliminated many centuries ago. Another concept of the evolutionary theory is culture, that is that we learn from cultural information that is transmitted from generation to generation, enabling one generation to build on what was learned by the previous generation, (Henrich, 2016).

Cellular Clock Theory

Cellular clock theory is Leonard Hayflick's (1977) theory that cells can divide a maximum of about 75 to 80 times, and that as we age our cells become less capable of dividing. Hayflick found that cells extracted from adults in their fifties to seventies divided fewer than 75 to 80 times. Based on the ways cells divide, Hayflick places the upper limit of the human life-span potential at about 120 to 125 years of age.

In the last decade, scientists have tried to fill a gap in cellular clock theory (Ding et al., 2014; Zhao et al., 2014). Hayflick did not know why cells die. The answer may lie at the tips of chromosomes, or *telomeres*, which are DNA sequences that cap chromosomes (Harari et al., 2013; Zhang et al., 2014). Each time a cell divides, the telomeres become shorter and shorter (see Figure 17.1). After about 70 or 80 replications, the telomeres are dramatically reduced and the cell no longer can reproduce. One study revealed that healthy centenarians had longer telomeres than unhealthy centenarians (Terry et al., 2008). Another study found that women with higher intakes of vitamins C and E had longer telomeres than women with lower intakes of these vitamins (Xu et al., 2009). Other studies have found that shorter telomere length is linked to having difficult social relationships, being less optimistic, and showing greater hostility (Uchino et al., 2012; Zalli et al., 2014).

Figure 17.1

Telomeres and Aging

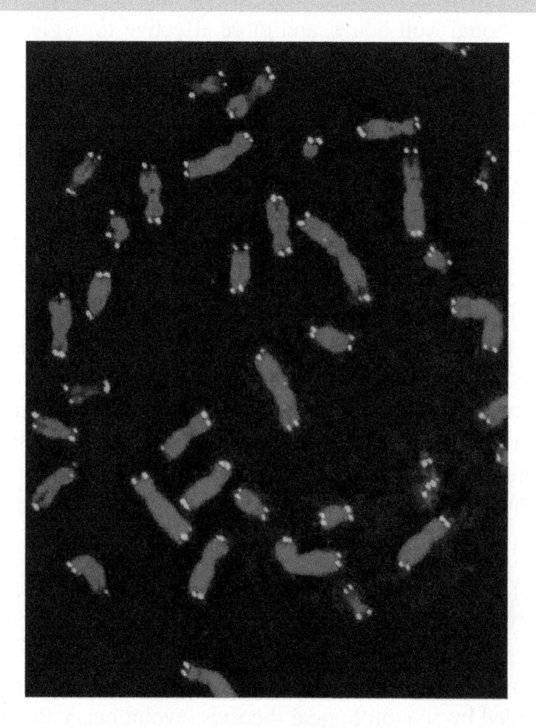

Courtesy of Dr. Jerry Shay, PhD., UT Southwestern Medical Center

The photograph shows actual telomeres lighting up the tips of chromosomes.

Injecting the enzyme telomerase into human cells grown in the laboratory has been found to substantially extend the life of the cells beyond the approximately 70 to 80 normal cell divisions (Harrison, 2012). However, telomerase is present in approximately 85 percent of cancerous cells and thus may not produce healthy life extension of cells (Bertorelle et al., 2014; Fakhoury, Nimmo, & Autexier, 2007). To capitalize on the high presence of telomerase in cancerous cells, researchers currently are investigating gene therapies that inhibit telomerase and lead to the death of cancerous cells while keeping healthy cells alive (Christodoulidou et al., 2013; Londono-Vallejo & Wellinger, 2012). The current focus of these gene therapies is on stem cells and their renewal (Hoffmeyer et al., 2012). Telomeres and telomerase are increasingly thought to be key components of the stem cell regeneration process, providing a possible avenue to restrain cancer and delay aging (Gunes & Rudolph, 2013; Shay, Reddel, & Wright, 2012).

Free-Radical Theory

Another microbiological theory of aging is the **free-radical theory**, which states that people age because, when cells metabolize energy, the by-products include unstable oxygen molecules known as free radicals (Chehab et al., 2008). These molecules ricochet around the cells, damaging DNA and other cellular structures (Bachschmid et al., 2013; da Cruz et al., 2014). The damage can lead to a range of disorders, including cancer and arthritis (Kolovou et al., 2014; Tezil & Basaga, 2014). Overeating is linked with an increase in free radicals, and researchers recently have found that calorie restriction—a diet restricted in calories although adequate in proteins, vitamins, and minerals—reduces the oxidative damage created by free radicals (Cerqueira et al., 2012; Kowaltowski, 2011). In addition to diet, researchers are also exploring the role of exercise in reducing oxidative damage in cells (Sarifakioglu et al., 2014). A study revealed a greater concentration of free radicals in 20- to 80-year-old smokers than in non-smokers (Samjoo et al., 2013).

Mitochondrial Theory

There is increasing interest in the role that mitochondria—tiny bodies within cells that supply essential energy for function, growth, and repair—might play in aging (Arnsburg & Kirstein-Miles, 2014; Shih & Donmez, 2013) (See Figure 17.2). Mitochondrial theory states that aging is due to the decay of mitochondria. It appears that this decay is primarily due to oxidative damage and loss of critical micronutrients supplied by the cell (Christian & Shadel, 2014; Romano et al., 2014; Valcarcel-Ares et al., 2014). **Mitochondrial theory** states that aging is due to the decay of mitochondria. It appears that this decay is primarily due to oxidative damage and loss of critical micronutrients supplied by the cell.

How does this damage and loss of nutrients occur? Among the by-products of mitochondrial energy production are the free radicals we just described. According to the mitochondrial theory, the damage caused by free radicals initiates a self-perpetuating cycle in which oxidative damage impairs mitochondrial function, which results in the generation of even greater amounts of free radicals. The result is that over time, the affected mitochondria become so inefficient that they cannot generate enough energy to meet cellular needs (Schulz et al., 2014; Schiavi & Ventura, 2014). Defects in mitochondria are linked with cardiovascular disease, neurodegenerative diseases such as dementia, and decline in liver functioning (Fabian et al., 2014; Edeas & Weissig, 2013). Mitochondria likely play important roles in neural plasticity (Dorszewska, 2013). However, it is not known whether the defects in mitochondria cause aging or are merely accompaniments of the aging process (Brand, 2011).

Hormonal Stress Theory

The first four biological theories of aging—evolutionary, cellular clock, free-radical, and mitochondrial—focus on changes at the cellular level. A fifth biological theory of aging emphasizes changes at the hormonal level. Hormonal stress theory states that aging in the body's hormonal system can lower resilience to stress and increase the likelihood of disease (Finch & Seeman, 1999).

When faced with external challenges such as stressful situations, the human body adapts by altering internal physiological processes (Almeida et al., 2011). This process of adaptation and adjustment is referred to as allostasis. Allostasis is adaptive in the short term; however, continuous accommodation of physiological systems in response to stressors may result in allostatic load, a wearing down of body systems due to constant activity (Tomiyama et al., 2012).

Normally, when people experience stressors, the body responds by releasing certain hormones. As people age, the hormones stimulated by stress remain at elevated levels longer than when people were younger (Finch, 2011). These prolonged, elevated levels of stress-related hormones are associated with increased risks for cardiovascular disease, cancer, diabetes, and hypertension (Steptoe & Kivimaki, 2012). Researchers are exploring stress buffering strategies, including exercise, in an effort to find ways to weaken some of the negative effects of stress on the ageing process (Bauer et al., 2013).

Figure 17.2
Mitochondria

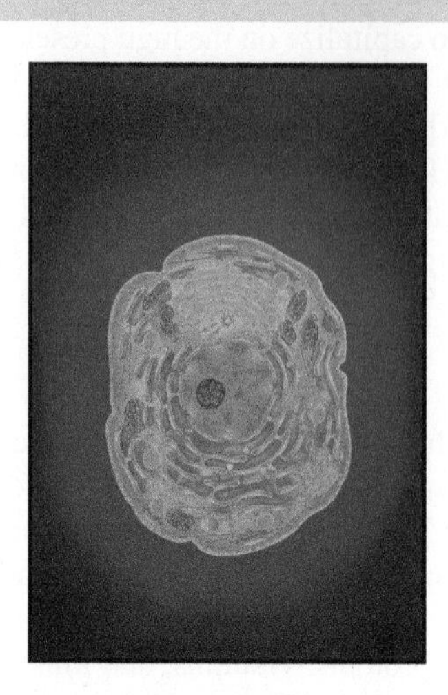

© J. Bavosi/Science Source

This colour-coded illustration of a typical cell shows mitochondria in green. The illustration also includes the nucleus (pink) with its DNA (brown). *In what ways might changes in mitochondria be involved in aging?*

Which of these biological theories best explains aging? That question has not yet been answered. It might turn out that all of these biological processes are involved in aging.

critical thinking

As you have just read, more and more people are living to be centenarians and, although men are closing the life expectancy gap, women still outnumber men in that group. Why do you think women live longer than men? Are there any societal changes that could be made to enable men to live longer? If so, what? Imagine that you live to be a centenarian. What do you think your life would be like? What might be some of the joys? Some of the challenges?

To this point, we have examined a number of ideas about longevity and biological theories of aging. For a review, see the Reach Your Learning Outcomes section at the end of this chapter.

The Course of Physical Development in Late Adulthood

LO2 Describe and give examples of how a person's brain and body change in late adulthood.

- **The Aging Brain**
- **Sleep**
- **The Immune System**
- **Physical Appearance and Movement**
- **Sensory Development**
- **The Circulatory System and Lungs**
- **Sexuality**

The physical decline that accompanies aging usually occurs slowly, and sometimes even lost function can be restored. We will examine the main physical changes behind the losses of late adulthood and describe ways that older adults can age successfully.

The Aging Brain

The brain is a muscle, but unlike other muscles, neurons (the muscle fibres) process and transmit information through synapses that pick up information so that the neurons can compute and store it. In this way, the brain is able to perceive sensations, process information, create and retain memories, and accommodate new information. Dr. Guosong Liu (2012), one of the world's leading experts on cognitive health, compares the synapses of the brain to leaves on a tree, noting that as fall approaches, the tree loses it leaves, much in the same way that the aging brain loses synapses. For most, this change is very gradual and the healthy brain not only plans, analyzes, and organizes information skillfully, but is able to draw on a lifetime of experience to make wise and valid judgments. In this way, the aging brain may even gain a bit or outperform a more youthful brain. To watch an interview with Dr. Liu, go to https://www.youtube.com/watch?v=nDI_nzySNF8.

The Shrinking, Slowing Brain

On average, the brain loses 5 to 10 percent of its weight between the ages of 20 and 90. Brain volume also decreases (Bondare, 2007). One study found that the volume of the brain is 15 percent less in older adults than younger adults (Fjell & Walhovd, 2010). Another study found a decrease in total brain volume and volume in key brain structures such as the frontal lobes and hippocampus from 22 to 88 years of age (Sherwood & others, 2011). Another analysis concluded that in healthy aging the decrease in brain volume is due mainly to shrinkage of neurons, lower numbers of synapses, and reduced length of axons, but only to a minor extent attributable to neuron loss (Fjell & Walhovd, 2010; Slutsky, et al., 2010). Scientists are not sure why these changes occur, but believe they might result from a decrease in dendrites, damage to the myelin sheath that covers axons, or simply the death of brain cells. However, the current consensus is that under normal conditions, adults are unlikely to lose brain cells.

Some areas shrink more than others (Raz et al., 2010). The prefrontal cortex is one area that shrinks with aging, and recent research has linked this shrinkage with a decrease in working memory and other cognitive activities in older adults (Jellinger & Attems, 2013; Rosano et al., 2012). The sensory regions of the brain—such as the primary visual cortex, primary motor cortex, and somatosensory cortex—are less vulnerable to the aging process (Rodrique & Kennedy, 2011). A general slowing of function in the brain and spinal cord begins in middle adulthood and accelerates in late adulthood (Rosano et al., 2012). This slowdown can affect physical coordination and intellectual performance. After age 70, many adults no longer show a knee-jerk reflex, and by age 90, most reflexes are virtually gone (Spence, 1989). The slowing of central nervous system functioning can impair the performance of older adults on intelligence tests, especially timed tests (Lu et al., 2011). For example, one neuroimaging study revealed that older adults are more likely to be characterized by slower processing in the prefrontal cortex during retrieval of information on a cognitive task than are younger adults (Rypma, Eldreth, & Rebbechi, 2007).

Historically, much of the focus on links between brain functioning and ageing has been on volume of brain structures and regions. Today, increased emphasis is being given to changes in myelination and neural networks. More current research indicates that demyelination (a deterioration in the myelin sheath that encases axons, which is associated with information processing) of the brain occurs with aging in older adults (Callaghan et al., 2014; Rodrique & Kennedy, 2011).

Aging has also been linked to a reduction in the production of some neurotransmitters, including acetylcholine, dopamine, and gamma-aminobutyric acid (GABA) (Juraska & Lowry, 2012; Marcello et al., 2012). Reductions in acetylcholine has been linked to small declines in memory functioning, and even with the severe memory loss associated with Alzheimer's disease (Merad et al., 2014). Normal age-related reductions in dopamine may cause problems in planning and carrying out motor activities (Balarajah & Cavanna, 2013). Severe reductions in the production of dopamine have been linked with age-related diseases characterized by a loss of motor control, such as Parkinson's disease (Park et al., 2014). GABA helps to control the preciseness of the signal sent from one neuron to another, decreasing "noise," and its production decreases with aging (Hoshino, 2013).

Research has shown that sensory decline in older adults is linked to a decline in cognitive functioning. One study of individuals in their seventies revealed that visual decline is related to slower speed of processing information, which in turn is associated with greater cognitive decline (Clay et al., 2009). And another study found that hearing loss is associated with a reduction in cognitive functioning in older adults (Lin, 2011).

The Adapting Brain

The story of the aging brain is far from limited to loss and decline in functioning. Unlike a computer, the brain has remarkable repair capability (Karatsoreos & McEwen, 2013). Even in late adulthood, the brain loses only a portion of its ability to function, and the activities older adults engage in can influence the brain's development (Ansado et al., 2013; Kraft, 2012). For example, in a recent fMRI study, higher levels of aerobic fitness were linked with greater volume in the hippocampus, which translates into better memory (Erickson et al., 2009). Researchers have found that **neurogenesis**, the generation of new neurons, occurs in lower mammalian species, such as mice. Also, research indicates that exercise and an enriched, complex environment can generate new brain cells in mice, and that stress reduces their survival rate (Kuipers et al., 2013; Ramirez-Rodriquez et al., 2014) (see Figure 17.3). Interestingly, researchers discovered that if rats are cognitively challenged to learn something, new brain cells survive longer (Shors, 2009). Another study revealed that coping with stress stimulates hippocampal neurogenesis in adult monkeys (Lyons et al., 2010).

Figure 17.3
Generating New Nerve Cells in Adult Mice

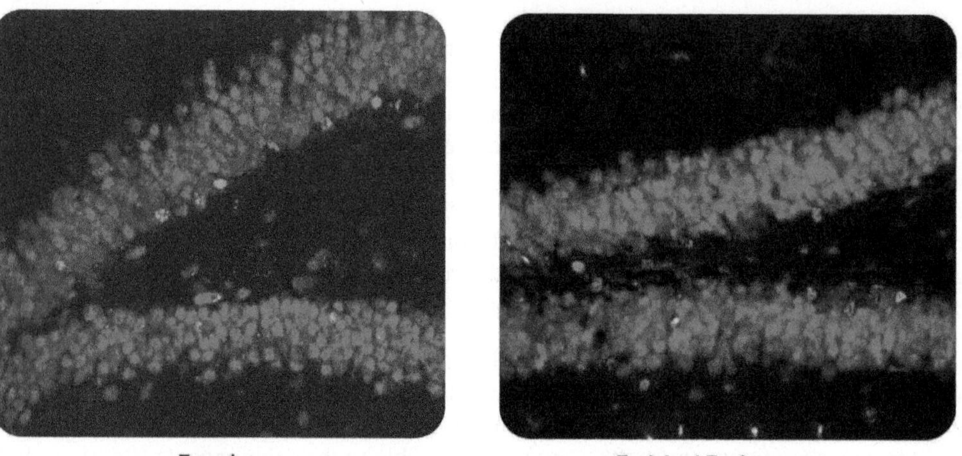

Courtesy of Dr. Fred Gage, The Salk Institute for Biological Studies

Researchers have found that exercise (running) and an enriched environment (a larger cage and many toys) can cause brain cells in adult mice to divide and form new brain cells (Kempermann, van Praag, & Gage, 2000). Cells were labelled with a chemical marker that becomes integrated into the DNA of dividing cells (red). Four weeks later, they were also labelled to mark neurons (nerve cells). As shown here, both the running mice and the mice in an enriched environment had many cells that were still dividing (red) and others that had differentiated into new nerve cells (orange).

Neurogenesis can also occur in humans (Goritz & Frisen, 2012; Ruan et al., 2014). However, researchers have documented neurogenesis in only two brain regions: the hippocampus, which is involved in memory, and the olfactory bulb, which is involved in smell (Brus, Keller, & Levy, 2013; Huart, Rombaux, & Hummel, 2013; Mobley et al., 2014; Rolando & Taylor, 2014). What functions these new brain cells perform remains unknown. Researchers currently are studying factors that might inhibit and promote neurogenesis, including various drugs, stress, and exercise (Gregoire et al., 2014; Schoenfeld & Gould, 2013). Researchers are examining how the grafting of neural stem cells to various regions of the brain, such as the hippocampus, might increase neurogenesis (Farioli-Vecchioli et al., 2014; He et al., 2013). Interest also is being directed to the possible role neurogenesis and loss of synapses might play in neurodegenerative diseases, such as Alzheimer's disease, Parkinson's disease, and Huntington's disease (Benarroch, 2013; Wang & Jin, 2014; Liu, 2012).

Dendritic growth can occur in human adults, possibly even older adults (Eliasieh, Liets, & Chalupa, 2007). Recall from Chapter 5 that dendrites are the receiving portion of the neuron. One study compared the brains of adults at various ages (Coleman, 1986). From the forties through the seventies, the growth of dendrites increased. However, in people in their nineties, dendritic growth no longer occurred. This dendritic growth might compensate for the possible loss of neurons through the seventies, but not in the nineties. Further research is needed to clarify what changes characterize dendrites during aging.

Stanley Rapaport (1994), chief of the neurosciences laboratory at the National Institute on Aging, demonstrated another way in which the aging brain can adapt. He compared the brains of younger and older people engaged in the same tasks. The older brains had rewired themselves to compensate for losses. If one neuron was not up to the job, neighbouring neurons helped to pick up the slack. Rapaport concluded that as brains age, they can shift responsibilities for a given task from one region to another.

Changes in lateralization may provide one type of adaptation in aging adults (Zhu, Zacks, & Slade, 2010). Recall that lateralization is the specialization of function in one hemisphere of the brain or the other. Using neuroimaging techniques, researchers found that brain activity in the prefrontal cortex is lateralized less in older adults than in younger adults when they are engaging in cognitive tasks (Angel et al., 2011; Cabeza, 2002; Manenti, Cotelli, & Miniussi, 2011; Rossi et al., 2005). For example, Figure 17.4 shows that when younger adults are given the task of recognizing words they have previously seen, they process the information primarily in the right hemisphere; older adults are more likely to use both hemispheres (Madden et al., 1999). The decrease in lateralization in older adults might play a compensatory role in the aging brain. That is, using both hemispheres may improve the cognitive functioning of older adults.

Figure 17.4

The Decrease in Brain Lateralization in Older Adults

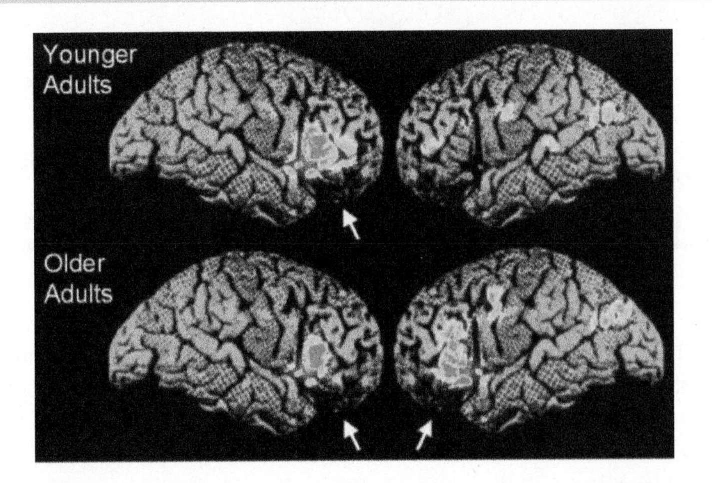

From R. Cabeza, et al., "Age-related differences in neural activity during memory encoding and retrieval: A positron emission tomography study" in *Journal of Neuroscience*, 17, 391-400, 1997.

Younger adults primarily use the right prefrontal region of the brain (top left photo) during a recall memory task, while older adults use both the left and right prefrontal regions (bottom two photos) (Madden et al., 1999).

Of course, individual differences exist in how the brain changes in older adults (Nyberg & Backman, 2011). Consider the successful businessman 85-year-old T. Boone Pickens, who continues to lead a highly active lifestyle, regularly exercising and engaging in cognitively complex work. Pickens recently underwent an fMRI in cognitive neuroscientist Denise Park's laboratory, during which he was presented with various cognitive tasks. Instead of both hemispheres being active, his left hemisphere was still dominant, just as is the case for most younger adults (Helman, 2008). Indeed, as the cognitive tasks became more complex, the more Pickens used the left hemisphere of his brain (see Figure 17.4). Further indication of variation in the link between brain lateralization and cognitive processing was found in a recent study (Manenti, Cotelli, & Miniussi, 2010). Older adults who performed better on memory tasks showed less asymmetry in the prefrontal cortex than their counterparts who performed more poorly on the tasks.

Does staying intellectually challenged affect one's quality of life and longevity? To read further about aging and the brain, see Connections through Research.

CONNECTING through Research

Does Staying Intellectually Challenged Affect One's Quality of Life and Longevity?

The Nun Study, directed by David Snowdon, is an intriguing ongoing investigation of 678 aging nuns who reside in a convent in Mankato, Minnesota (Snowdon, 2003; Pakhomov & Hemmy, 2014; Tyas et al., 2007). In addition to agreeing to donate their brains for scientific research, becoming the largest group of brain donors in the world, each nun agreed to participate in annual assessments of her cognitive and physical functioning. Examination of the nuns' donated brains, as well as others', has led neuroscientists to believe that the brain has a remarkable capacity to change and grow, even in old age. The Sisters of Notre Dame in Mankato lead intellectually challenging lives, and brain researchers believe this contributes to their quality of life as older adults and possibly increases their longevity. Findings from the Nun Study so far include:

- Idea density, a measure of linguistic ability assessed early in the adult years (age 22), is linked with higher brain weight, fewer incidences of mild cognitive impairment, and fewer characteristics of Alzheimer's disease in 75- to 95-year-old nuns (Riley et al., 2005).
- Positive emotions early in adulthood are linked to longevity (Danner, Snowdon, & Friesen, 2001). Handwritten autobiographies from 180 nuns, composed when they were 22 years of age, were scored for emotional content. The nuns whose early writings had higher scores for positive emotional content were more likely to still be alive at 75 to 95 years of age than their counterparts whose early writings were characterized by negative emotional content.
- Sisters who had taught for most of their lives showed more moderate declines in intellectual skills than those who had spent most of their lives in service-based tasks, which supports the notion that stimulating the brain with intellectual activity keeps neurons alive and healthy (Snowdon, 2002).

This and other research provides hope that scientists will discover ways to tap into the brain's capacity to adapt in order to prevent and treat brain diseases (Wirth et al., 2014). For example, scientists might learn more effective ways to improve older adults' cognitive functioning, reduce Alzheimer's disease, and help older adults recover from strokes (Kalladka & Muir, 2014; Wen et al., 2014). Even when areas of the brain are permanently damaged by stroke, new message routes can be created to get around the blockage or to resume the function of that area, indicating that the brain does adapt.

Sister Marcella Zachman (left) stopped teaching at age 97. At 99, she helps ailing nuns exercise their brains by quizzing them on vocabulary or playing a card game called Skip-Bo, at which she deliberately loses. Sister Mary Esther Boor (right), also 99 years of age, is a former teacher who stays alert by doing puzzles and volunteering to work the front desk. The nuns donate their brains for research that explores the effects of stimulation on brain growth.

Sleep

Fifty percent or more of older adults complain of having difficulty sleeping, which can have detrimental effects on their lives (Farajinia et al., 2014; Neikrug & Ancoli-Israel, 2010). One study revealed that sleep time and sleep efficiency decline in older adults (Moraes et al., 2014). Poor sleep is a risk factor for falls, obesity, a lower level of cognitive functioning, and earlier death (Boelens, Hekman, & Verkerke, 2013; Xiao et al., 2013). For example, researchers found that spending more time in sleep benefits older adults' memory (Aly & Moscovitch, 2010). Also, a research review indicated that improving older adults' sleep through behavioural and pharmaceutical treatments may enhance their cognitive skills (Pace-Schott & Spencer, 2011). A further study linked poor quality of sleep with mild cognitive impairment, which in some cases is a precursor for Alzheimer's disease (Hita-Yanez, Atienza, & Cantero, 2013). And another study found that sleep duration of more than 7 hours per night in older adults is linked to longer telomere length, which is similar to the telomere length of middle-aged adults (Cribbet et al., 2014).

Many of the sleep problems of older adults are associated with health problems (Reyes et al., 2013; Rothman & Mattson, 2012). Strategies to help older adults sleep better at night include avoiding caffeine, avoiding over-the-counter sleep remedies, staying physically active during the day, staying mentally active, and limiting naps (Morin, Savard, & Ouellet, 2013). Regular exercise is also linked to improved sleep profiles of older adults (Lira et al., 2011).

The Immune System

Decline in the functioning of the body's immune system with aging is well documented (Cavanaugh, Weyand, & Goronzy, 2012; Stowell, Robles, & Kane, 2013). The extended duration of stress and diminished restorative processes in older adults may accelerate the effects of aging on immunity (Solana et al., 2012). Also, malnutrition involving low levels of protein is linked to a decrease in T-cells that destroy infected cells and hence to deterioration in the immune system (Hughes, 2010). Because of the decline in the functioning of their immune systems, vaccination against influenza is especially important in older adults (Parodi et al., 2011). Exercise can improve immune system functioning (Spielmann et al., 2011).

Physical Appearance and Movement

In Chapter 15, "Physical and Cognitive Development in Middle Adulthood," you read about some changes in physical appearance that occur as we age. The changes are most noticeable in the form of facial wrinkles and age spots. We also get shorter when we get older. Our weight usually drops after we reach 60 years of age. This likely occurs because we lose muscle, which also gives our bodies a more "sagging" look (Evans, 2010). Figure 17.5 shows the declining percentage of muscle and bone from age 25 to age 75, and the corresponding increase in the percentage of fat. A study found that long-term aerobic exercise is linked with greater muscle strength in 65- to 86-year-olds (Crane, Macneil, & Tarnopsolsky, 2013).

Figure 17.5

Changes in Body Composition of Bone, Muscle, and Fat from 25 to 75 Years of Age

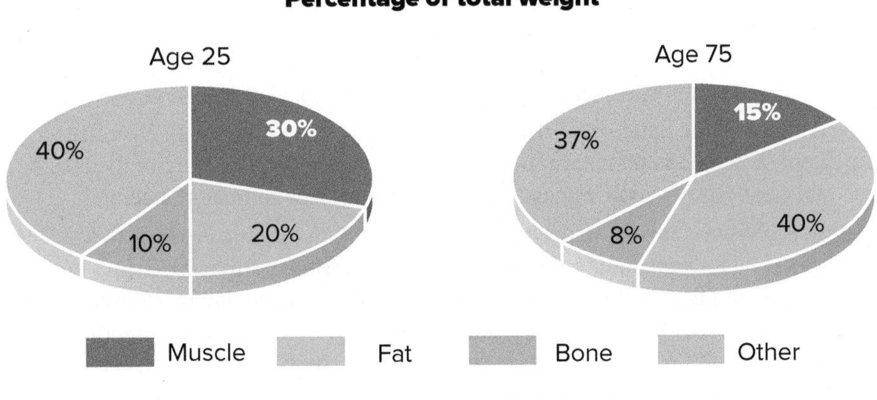

Notice the decrease in bone and muscle and the increase in fat from 25 to 75 years of age.

Older adults move more slowly than young adults, and this slowing occurs for movements with a wide range of difficulty (Davis et al., 2013). Adequate mobility is an important aspect of maintaining an independent and active lifestyle in late adulthood (Clark et al., 2011). Research indicates that obesity contributes to mobility limitation in older adults (Murphy et al., 2014; Vincent, Raiser, & Vincent, 2012). The good news is that regular walking decreases the onset of physical disability and reduces functional limitations in older adults (Mullen et al., 2012; Newman et al., 2006). Also, one study found that a combined program of physical activity and weight loss is linked to preserving mobility in older, obese adults in poor cardiovascular health (Rejeski et al., 2011).

critical thinking

Think of the people you know who are in late adulthood that you believe to be aging gracefully. With that person in mind, describe what the term "aging gracefully" means. How does a person age gracefully? Would you classify his or her functioning levels as "young old," "old old," or "oldest old"? Why? Apart from physical exercise, what can you do to prepare for a positive experience of physical aging?

Sensory Development

Sensory changes in late adulthood involve vision, hearing, taste, smell, touch, and pain. These senses are linked to our ability to perform everyday activities (Hochberg et al., 2012; Schneider et al., 2011). How do vision, hearing, taste, smell, touch, and pain change in late adulthood?

Vision

With aging, visual acuity, colour vision, and depth perception decline. Several diseases of the eye may emerge in aging adults. In late adulthood, the decline in vision that began for most of us in early or middle adulthood becomes more pronounced (Polat et al., 2012). Night driving becomes especially difficult, to some extent, because tolerance for glare diminishes (Gruber et al., 2013). Dark adaptation is slower, meaning that older individuals take longer to recover their vision when going from well-lighted rooms to semi-darkness. The area of the visual field becomes smaller, suggesting that a stimulus's intensity in the peripheral area of the visual field needs to be increased if the stimulus is to be seen. Events taking place away from the centre of the visual field may not be detected (West et al., 2010). This visual decline often can be traced to reduction in the quality or intensity of light reaching the retina (Nag & Wadhwa, 2012). At 60 years of age, the retina receives only about one-third as much light as it did at 20 years of age (Scialfa & Kline, 2007). In extreme old age, these changes may be accompanied by degenerative changes in the retina, causing severe difficulty in seeing. Large-print books and magnifiers may be needed in such cases. The greatest decline in visual perception beyond age 75, and especially beyond age 85, involves glare.

DISEASES OF THE EYE

Cataracts, glaucoma, and macular degeneration are three diseases that can impair the vision of older adults.

- Cataracts involve a thickening of the lens of the eye, which causes vision to become cloudy, opaque, and distorted (Leuschen et al., 2013). By age 70, approximately 30 percent of individuals experience a partial loss of vision due to cataracts. Initially, cataracts can be treated by glasses; if they worsen, the cloudy lens should be surgically removed and replaced with an artificial one (Chung et al., 2009; Michalska-Malecka et al., 2013). Diabetes is a risk factor for the development of cataracts (Olafsdottir, Andersson, & Stefansson, 2012). Cataract surgery is usually very successful.
- Glaucoma involves damage to the optic nerve because of pressure created by a buildup of fluid in the eye, and affects approximately 1 percent of people in their seventies, and 10 percent of people in their nineties (Akpek & Smith, 2013). If untreated, glaucoma can destroy vision. Special eye drops can be used to treat glaucoma.
- Macular degeneration is a disease involving deterioration of the retina that corresponds to the focal centre of the visual field. Individuals with macular degeneration may have relatively normal peripheral vision, but be unable to see clearly what is right in front of them (Taylor, 2012) (see Figure 17.6). This affects one in 25 individuals from 66 to 74 years of age, and one in six who are older. One study revealed that cigarette smoking is a contributing factor in macular degeneration (Schmidt et al., 2006). If the disease is detected early, it can be treated with laser surgery (Sorensen & Kemp, 2010). However, macular degeneration is difficult to treat and is a leading cause of blindness in older adults (Cacho et al., 2010.) Also, there is increased interest in using stem-cell-based therapy for macular degeneration (Eveleth, 2013).

Figure 17.6
Macular Degeneration

© Cordelia Molloy/Science Source

This simulation of the effect of macular degeneration shows how individuals with this eye disease can see their peripheral field of vision, but can't clearly see what is in their central visual field.

Hearing

Although hearing impairment can begin in middle adulthood, it usually does not become much of an impediment until late adulthood (Li-Korotky, 2012). In Canada, 55 percent of people over the age of 12 who have a hearing problem are over the age of 65 (Millar, 2005). Almost a quarter of those individuals over the age of 80 are hearing impaired. Hearing impairments are more common among senior men than women, at 12 percent versus 9 percent, respectively. Many older adults don't recognize that they have a hearing problem, while others deny that they have one or accept it as a part of growing old (Pacala & Yeuh, 2012).

One study found that poor nutrition and a lifetime of smoking are linked to more rapid onset of hearing difficulties in older adults (Heine et al., 2013). Another study found that severity of age-related hearing loss is linked to impaired activities of daily living (Gopinath et al., 2012). And, as mentioned earlier, another study revealed that hearing loss is associated with a reduction in cognitive functioning in older adults (Lin, 2011). Two devices can be used to minimize the problems linked to hearing loss in older adults: (1) hearing aids that amplify sound to reduce middle ear–based conductive hearing loss, and (2) cochlear implants that restore some hearing following neurosensory hearing loss (Pauley et al., 2008).

Earlier, we indicated that life-span developmentalists are increasingly making distinctions between the young old or old age (ages 65 to 74), and the old old or late old age (75 years and older). This distinction is important when considering the degree of decline in various perceptual systems. As indicated in Figure 17.7 the decline in the perceptual systems of vision and hearing is much greater in late old age than in young old age.

Figure 17.7
Vision and Hearing Decline in Old Age and Late Old Age

Perceptual System	Old Age (65–74 Years)	Late Old Age (75 Years and Older)
Vision	There is a loss of acuity even with corrective lenses. Less transmission of light occurs through the retina (half as much as in young adults). Greater susceptibility to glare occurs. Colour discrimination ability decreases.	There is a significant loss of visual acuity and colour discrimination, and a decrease in the size of the perceived visual field. In late old age, people are at significant risk for visual dysfunction from cataracts and glaucoma.

Hearing	There is a significant loss of hearing at high frequencies and some loss at middle frequencies. These losses can be helped by a hearing aid. There is greater susceptibility for background noises to mask what is heard.	There is a significant loss at high and middle frequencies. A hearing aid is more likely to be needed than in old age.

Smell and Taste

Most older adults lose some of their sense of smell or taste, or both (Murphy, 2009). These losses often begin around 60 years of age (Hawkes, 2006). Researchers have found that older adults show a greater decline in their sense of smell than in their taste; in fact the majority of individuals age 80 and older experience a significant reduction in their sense of smell (Lafreniere & Mann, 2009; Schiffman, 2007). Smell and taste decline less in healthy older adults than in their less-healthy counterparts.

critical thinking

Imagine yourself at the age of 65. You have been asked to give a talk about aging to a group of middle-aged adults. Using the information you have just read, construct a list of the five key physical changes or occurrences you would tell them they were most likely to experience in late adulthood. What would you suggest they do to counteract any problems in these areas?

Touch and Pain

Changes in touch and pain are also associated with aging (Arneric et al., 2014; Kemp et al., 2014; Mantyh, 2014). One study found that with aging, individuals are less able to detect touch in the lower extremities (ankles, knees, and so on) than in the upper extremities (wrists, shoulders, and so on) (Corso, 1977). For most older adults, a decline in touch sensitivity is not problematic (Hoyer & Roodin, 2009). One study revealed that older adults who are blind retain a high level of touch sensitivity, which likely is linked to their use of active touch in their daily lives (Legge et al., 2008).

An estimated 60 to 75 percent of older adults report at least some persistent pain (Molton & Terrill, 2014). The most frequent pain complaints of older adults are back pain (40 percent), peripheral neuropathic pain (weakness or numbness, usually in the hands) (35 percent), and chronic joint pain (15 to 25 percent) (Denard et al., 2010). The presence of pain increases with age in older adults, and women are more likely to report having pain than are men (Tsang et al., 2008).

Researchers have found that older adults experience a decrease in brain volume related to pain processing. This decline is most pronounced in the prefrontal cortex and hippocampus and less pronounced in the brain stem (Farrell, 2012). Other physical changes in pain processing occur in the somatosensory pathways (Yezierski, 2012). Although decreased sensitivity to pain can help older adults cope with disease and injury, it can also mask injuries and illnesses that need to be treated.

Perceptual Motor Coupling

Perception and action are coupled throughout the human life span. Driving a car illustrates the coupling of perceptual and motor skills. The decline in perceptual-motor skills in late adulthood makes driving a car difficult for many older adults (Dawson et al., 2010; Stavrinos et al., 2013). Drivers over the age of 65 are involved in more traffic accidents than middle-aged adults because of mistakes such as improper turns, not yielding the right of way, and not obeying traffic signs; their younger counterparts are more likely to have accidents because they are speeding (Lavalliere et al., 2011). Older adults can compensate for declines in perceptual-motor skills by driving shorter distances, choosing less congested routes, and driving only in daylight.

An extensive research review evaluated the effectiveness of two types of interventions in improving older adults' driving: cognitive training and education (Ross, Schmidt, & Ball, 2013).

- *Cognitive training:* Cognitive training programs have shown some success in older adults, including improving their driving safety and making driving less difficult. In one study conducted by Karlene Ball and colleagues (2010), training designed to enhance speed of processing produced more than a 40 percent reduction in at-fault crashes over a six-year period.
- *Education:* Results are mixed with regard to educational interventions that seek to improve older adults' driving ability and to reduce their involvement in traffic accidents (Gaines et al., 2011).

The Circulatory System and Lungs

Cardiovascular diseases (CVD) are chronic, lifelong diseases or injuries of the heart, the blood vessels in the heart, and the veins and arteries throughout the body and within the brain. Stroke, a form of CVD, is the result of a blood flow problem in the brain (Heart and Stroke Foundation, 2013). CVDs are a leading cause of death and hospitalization, as well as the leading driver of prescription medications. The good news is that due to advances in research, improved surgical procedures, drug therapies, and prevention programs, deaths rates from CVDs have declined more than 75 percent in the past 60 years (Heart & Stroke Foundation, 2016).

CVDs are caused by the interaction of genetic predisposition, behaviours, and environment. These diseases increase in late adulthood. According to Public Health Agency of Canada (PHAC), approximately 14.8 percent of seniors between 65 and 74 years of age report having heart disease. For those over 75 years, the percentage climbs to 22.9 percent (PHAC, 2009d).

Today, most experts on aging recommend that consistent blood pressures above 120/80 should be treated to reduce the risk of heart attack, stroke, or kidney disease (Krakoff, 2008). Blood pressure can rise with age because of illness, obesity, anxiety, stiffening of blood vessels, or lack of exercise (Fiocco et al., 2013). The longer any of these factors persists, the higher the individual's blood pressure gets. Lifestyle factors, such as a healthy diet, stress management, exercise, weight management, and various medications can reduce the risk of cardiovascular disease in many older adults (Tselepis, 2014). The Heart and Stroke Foundation notes that 9 out of 10 Canadians have at least one risk factor for heart disease. These factors include:

1. Eating fewer than 5 servings of vegetables and fruit daily
2. Smoking
3. Physical inactivity
4. Overweight or obesity
5. High blood pressure
6. Diabetes
7. Stress

Up to 80 percent of premature heart disease is preventable by adopting healthy behaviours (Heart & Stroke Foundation, 2016).

In the respiratory system, lung capacity drops 40 percent between the ages of 20 and 80, even without disease (Fozard, 1992). Lungs lose elasticity, the chest shrinks, and the diaphragm weakens (Lalley, 2013). Severe impairments in lung functioning and death can result from smoking (Wilhelmsen et al., 2011). The good news, though, is that older adults can improve lung functioning with diaphragm strengthening exercises.

Seniors are more vulnerable to respiratory infections caused by the influenza virus. Consequently, Health Canada advises that people, especially older adults, obtain flu vaccinations each fall and wash their hands carefully as safeguards to becoming infected. Vaccinations are recommended in the fall because the flu season is from November to April (PHAC, 2012).

Sexuality

In the absence of disease, sexuality can be lifelong (Corona et al., 2013; Marshall, 2012). Aging does induce some changes in human sexual performance, moreso in men than women (Gray & Garcia, 2012). Orgasm becomes less frequent in males, occurring in every second to third act of intercourse, rather than every time. More direct stimulation usually is needed to produce an erection.

A large-scale study of individuals from 57 to 85 years of age revealed that sexual activity, a good-quality sexual life, and interest in sex are positively related to health in middle and late adulthood (Lindau & Gavrilova, 2010). Also in this study, these aspects of sexuality are higher for aging males than aging women, and this gap widens with age. Further, sexually active life expectancy is longer for men than women, but men lose more years of sexually active life due to poor health than women. Even when intercourse is impaired by infirmity, other relationship needs persist, among them closeness, sensuality, and being valued (Brock & Jennings, 2007; Hurd Clarke, 2006).

Getty Images/DAL

What are some characteristics of sexuality in older adults? How does sexuality change during late adulthood?

To this point we have discussed a number of ideas about the course of physical development in late adulthood. For a review, see the Reach Your Learning Outcomes section at the end of this chapter.

Physical and Mental Health and Wellness

LO3 Identify factors of health and wellness in late adulthood.

- **Health Problems**
- **Exercise, Nutrition, and Weight**
- **The Nature of Mental Health in Late Adulthood**
- **Dementia, Alzheimer's Disease, and Related Disorders**
- **Health Promotion**

As noted earlier in the chapter, seniors are comprising a larger percentage of the population: 14 percent of those over 65 years, up from 9 percent in the previous census. Immigrants account for 28 percent of the senior population, and Aboriginals 1 percent (Public Health Agency of Canada, 2010b). Although seniors experience the impact of chronic conditions, reduced mobility, and sensory functioning, 44 percent perceive their health to be excellent or very good, and 37 percent report taking action such as changing eating habits or increasing physical activity in order to improve their health (PHAC, 2010b).

Health Problems

In Chapter 15, "Physical and Cognitive Development in Middle Adulthood," chronic disorders were defined as disorders with a slow onset and a long duration. Such conditions are rare in early adulthood, increase in middle adulthood, and become more common in late adulthood.

Women in late adulthood have a higher incidence of arthritis and hypertension, and are more likely to have visual problems but less likely to have hearing problems than are older men. Conflict in relationships has been linked with greater decline in older adults with diabetes or hypertension (Seeman & Chen, 2002). Studies document links between low socio-economic status and health problems (Friedman & Herd, 2010; Yang & Lee, 2010). One study revealed that frailty increased for low-income older adults, regardless of their ethnicity (Szanton et al., 2010).

Causes of Death in Older Adults

More than two-thirds of all older adults die of heart disease, cancer, or cerebrovascular disease (stroke). Chronic lung diseases, pneumonia and influenza, and diabetes round out the six leading causes of death among older adults. For men, the two most significant predictors of death within eight years were chronic disease or widowhood. Men who live with their wives live longer than those whose wives have died.

Arthritis

Arthritis is an inflammation of the joints accompanied by pain, stiffness, and movement problems. It is a highly prevalent, chronic, and painful condition that increases with age, limits mobility, inhibits daily activities, and is linked with falls and fractures. Obesity and the use of multiple medications have been linked with arthritic conditions (Statistics Canada, 2015). There are many different kinds of arthritis, however, two of the most common are osteoarthritis and rheumatoid arthritis.

Osteoarthritis is one of the most prevalent chronic diseases. This chronic, painful condition develops due to the breakdown of the bone-protecting material, cartilage. Hips, knees, hands, and spine joints are the most commonly affected areas. Symptoms include swelling, stiffness, bone-on-bone pain, and reduced range of motion (The Arthritis Society, 2016).

Rheumatoid arthritis (RA) is an autoimmune disorder that targets the lining of joints. Instead of protecting the body, the immune system responds against healthy cells and tissues. In the case of rheumatoid arthritis, the joints become inflamed, swollen, stiff, and so painful that the sufferer may become wheelchair bound (Schlesinger, 2013). Professor El-Gabalawy, in the Department of Medicine and immunology at the University of Manitoba and one of Canada's leading researchers in the field, says, "Our estimate is that rheumatoid arthritis affects about 1 percent of the general population. In the Aboriginal population, it's more like 2 or 3 percent, so it's two to three times higher in this population." Every year about 50 people per 100 000 in Canada are diagnosed with RA, generally more women than men. But among First Nations, the incidence increases to 100 to 150 new cases annually per 100 000 people (Schlesinger, 2013).

Fortunately, medical and surgical advances, including joint replacements, combined with lifestyle changes such as nutritious food and exercise, can reduce the impact of arthritis.

Osteoporisis

Osteoporosis, the silent thief of bone marrow, is a condition that causes the bones to become thin and porous, without apparent symptoms unless a bone is fractured. According to Osteoporosis Canada (2016), fractures from osteoporosis are more common than heart attack, stroke, and breast cancer combined; in fact, 80 percent of all fractures in people over 50 years of age are caused by osteoporosis. The condition can result in disfigurement, reduced mobility, decreased independence, and loss of self esteem (Osteoporosis Canada, 2016).

Accidents

Falls are the leading cause of injury among older Canadians, with 20–30 percent of seniors experiencing one or more falls per year, frequently resulting in injury requiring hospitalization, chronic pain, reduced mobility, loss of independence, and possibly death (PHAC 2015). Falls are related to risk factors such as disease, arthritis, Parkinson's disease, stroke, and blood pressure disorders, as well as physical limitations. Cognitive impairment and alcohol consumption may also contribute to falls (PHAC, 2010b). Falls that occur at home and traffic accidents in which an older adult is the driver or an older pedestrian

Figure 17.8
The Jogging Hog Experiment

Courtesy of Colin M. Bloor

Jogging hogs reveal the dramatic effects of exercise on health. In one investigation, a group of hogs was trained to run approximately 165 km per week (Bloor & White, 1983). Then, the researchers narrowed the arteries that supplied blood to the hogs' hearts. The hearts of the jogging hogs developed extensive alternate pathways for blood supply, and 42 percent of the threatened heart tissue was salvaged, compared with only 17 percent in a control group of non-jogging hogs.

Nutrition and Weight

Seventeenth-century English philosopher and essayist Francis Bacon was the first author to advocate a frugal diet and recommend scientific evaluation of diet and longevity. Such scientific evaluation exists today. For example, studies indicate that calorie restriction works in animals (in most cases rats) by increasing longevity and putting chronic problems such as cardiovascular, kidney, and liver disease in remission (Fontana & Hu 2014; Vera et al., 2005; Robertson & Mitchell, 2013; Yan et al., 2013). Additional research indicates that calorie restriction may provide neuroprotection for an aging central nervous system (Willette et al., 2012). For example, one study revealed that after older adults engaged in calorie restriction for three months, their verbal memory improved (Witte et al., 2009).

Whether similar very-low-calorie diets can stretch the human life span is not known (Stein et al., 2012). For example, the National Institute of Aging (2012) conducted a 25-year longitudinal studies using monkeys and concluded that genes and diet compositions are better predictors of longevity than calorie restriction per se. One study revealed that women who were 20 pounds or more underweight lived longer even after controlling for smoking, hypertension, alcohol intake, and other factors (Wandell, Carlsson, & Theobald, 2009). In this study, underweight men did not live longer when various factors were controlled.

Although several studies have found a link between being overweight and living longer, the majority of studies have revealed that being overweight is a risk factor for the acceleration of diseases and an earlier death (de Hollander et al., 2012; Katzmarzyk et al., 2012; Masters et al., 2013; Preston & Stokes, 2011; Rizzuto & Fratiglioni, 2014; Anton et al., 2013; Perez et al., 2013; Winett et al., 2014). For example, a study of 70- to 75-year-olds reported that a higher body mass index (BMI) is associated with all-cause mortality risk, with the greatest risk occurring for death due to cardiovascular disease (de Hollander et al., 2012).

Researchers consistently find that when individuals are overweight and fit, they have a much better health profile and greater longevity than those who are overweight and not fit (Masters et al., 2013; Matheson, King, & Everett, 2012). Some leading researchers now conclude that inactivity and low cardiorespiratory fitness are greater threats to health and longevity than being overweight (McAuley & Blair, 2011).

Malnutrition is estimated to be as high as 60 percent among seniors living in nursing homes or hospitals; however, seniors living alone are also more prone to malnutrition because they may not feel like cooking or make poor food choices (PHAC, 2010b). Most nutritional experts do not recommend very-low-calorie diets for older adults; rather, they recommend a well-balanced, low-fat diet that includes the nutritional factors needed to maintain good health. Poor nutritional habits among seniors can exacerbate health issues and aggravate symptoms of chronic diseases. In 2008, Statistics Canada reported that 29 percent of seniors were obese, as measured by body mass index (BMI). On the other hand, approximately 18.5 percent of seniors were underweight (PHAC 2010b). Three aspects of nutrition are especially important in older adults: (1) getting adequate nutrition, (2) avoiding overweight and obesity, and (3) the role of calorie restriction in improving health and extending life.

The Growing Controversy over Vitamins and Aging

Traditionally, experts on aging and health have argued that a balanced diet is all that is needed for successful aging; vitamin supplements were not recommended. However, today's research suggests the possibility that some vitamin supplements—mainly a group called *antioxidants*, which includes vitamin C, vitamin E, and beta-carotene—help slow the aging process and improve the health of older adults.

The theory is that antioxidants counteract the cell damage caused by free radicals, which are produced both by the body's own metabolism and by environmental factors, such as smoking, pollution, and bad chemicals in the diet (Gandhi & Abramov, 2012). When free radicals cause damage (oxidation) in one cell, a chain reaction of damage follows. Antioxidants act much like a fire extinguisher, helping to neutralize free-radical activity and reduce oxidative stress (Da Costa, Badawi, & El-Sohemy, 2012).

Some research studies have found links between the antioxidant vitamins and health. For example, a meta-analysis of seven studies concluded that dietary intakes (not vitamin supplements) of vitamin E, C, and beta-carotene were linked to a reduced risk of Alzheimer's disease (Li, Shen, & Ji, 2012).

Long Canadian winters and lack of exposure to the sun have contributed to a deficiency in vitamin D, the sunshine vitamin that enables the body to absorb calcium and is associated with offsetting several diseases including cancer, osteoporosis, autoimmune disease, cardiovascular disease, and infectious disease (Schwalfenberg, 2013). Studies have also shown that people with adequate levels of vitamin D have lower risk of sun damage and, for women, of developing rheumatoid arthritis (Nordqvist, 2009; Sorenson, 2011).

Uncertainty about the role of antioxidant vitamins in health continues to raise questions (Otaegui-Arrazola et al., 2014). For example, which vitamins should be taken, how large a dose should be taken, what are the restraints, if any, and so on. Critics also argue that key experimental studies documenting the effectiveness of the vitamins in slowing the aging process have not been conducted. Other factors—such as exercise, better health practices, and good nutritional habits—might be responsible for the positive findings about vitamins and aging rather than vitamins per se. Also, the free-radical theory is a theory and not a fact, and is only one of a number of theories about why we age.

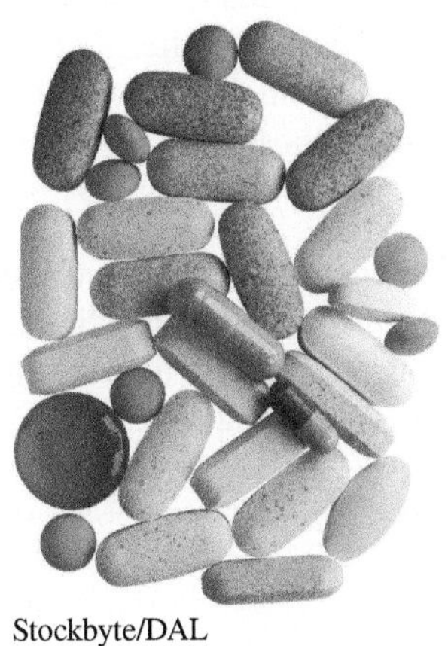

Stockbyte/DAL

Much controversy surrounds the use of vitamin supplements.

The Nature of Mental Health in Late Adulthood

According to Statistics Canada (2015), three-quarters of seniors reported their health to be good, very good, or excellent. Less than one in five reported they were lonely or dissatisfied with life. Seniors between 65 and 74 and women report greater satisfaction with their health and lives than those over 75 years of age and men (Gilmour, 2015). Seniors with higher levels of income and education are more likely to report being satisfied with their health (Statistics Canada, 2015). However, 20 percent of those living in the community have some form of mental health issues which, combined with declining physical strength and loss of autonomy, contribute to feelings of depression, and often go hand-in-hand with substance abuse (PHAC, 2010). Contributing factors to mental health issues include early life experiences, such as those experienced by Aboriginal seniors who attended residential schools, suffering abuse, and low income (PHAC, 2010).

Social Isolation

Social isolation involves a low quantity and quality of social contact and the absence of mutually-rewarding relationships (Seniors' Council of Canada, 2014). Although, on average, seniors are healthier and financially more secure than in past generations, physical, psychological, and cognitive health and well-being are negatively impacted by social isolation. Various studies indicate that older Canadians report feeling socially isolated or at risk of becoming isolated. The Canadian Community Health Survey (2008/09) found that 19 percent of seniors feel left out. Another survey reported that over 30 percent of seniors are at risk of isolation. Isolated seniors are more vulnerable to elder abuse, including financial abuse, depression, social anxiety, loneliness, alcoholism, mental illness, as well as diminished general health. Disabilities can further marginalize people (Seniors' Council of Canada, 2014).

Multiple factors contribute to social isolation, including death of a spouse, retirement, loss of a drivers' license, children relocating for employment opportunities, low income, lack of transportation, unsuitable housing, challenges with technology, and more. According to the Seniors' Council of Canada, specific groups of seniors are the most vulnerable: those with low incomes, with mental and/or physical health issues, as well as seniors who are caregivers, Aboriginal, newcomers or immigrant seniors, seniors separated from family, and those who are lesbian, gay, bisexual, or transgendered.

Depression

Major depression is a mood disorder in which the individual is deeply unhappy, demoralized, self-derogatory, and bored. The individual with major depression does not feel well, loses stamina easily, has a poor appetite, and is listless and unmotivated. Seniors living in residences are twice as likely to suffer major depression or exhibit symptoms of depression than those living in the community (Canadian Psychological Association (CPA) 2015; Seniors' Council of Canada, 2014). Seniors most vulnerable are those with chronic disease, those living in long-term care and nursing homes, those providing care for a family member, such as caring for a spouse suffering from dementia, and those, especially men, who have lost a spouse.

Dr. Leon Kagan, Director of Geriatric Psychiatry at the University of Alberta, says that many seniors cope well with aging; it is when they begin to lose their independence they become at risk for depression (Centre for Suicide Prevention, 2012; Monette, 2012). Loss of autonomy as the result of illness and/or disability, loneliness, and lack of social support increase the likelihood of depression in older age (CPA, 2015). Seniors suffering from depression are two to three times more at risk of death, as depression is a major factor associated with suicide. According to the Centre for Suicide Prevention Resource Toolkit (2012), senior men in general, but particularly those over 80 years of age, have the highest rate of suicide (CPA, 2015; Seniors' Council of Canada, 2014).

Activities and social participation provide benefits including a reduced risk of mortality and depression, better cognitive health, and better self-rated health and health-related behaviours. Statistics Canada reports that four-fifths of seniors who are frequent participants in social activities indicate satisfaction with their health, and this is also true for seniors in institutions who participate in social and recreational activities (Gilmour, 2015).

Socially isolated seniors are vulnerable to depression.

Substance Abuse

In many cases, older adults are taking multiple medications, which can increase the risks associated with consuming alcohol or other drugs. For example, when combined with tranquillizers or sedatives, alcohol use can impair breathing, produce excessive sedation, and be fatal.

Seniors are less likely to use alcohol on a regular basis than younger adults, with 48 percent of seniors drinking alcohol once a month or more versus 67 percent of those aged 25 to 54 (Turcotte & Schellenberg, 2007). Regular low to moderate use of alcohol has been associated with higher self-ratings of excellent or very good health, and may reduce the likelihood of developing certain diseases. However, seniors are more susceptible to the effects of alcohol because their bodies process it more slowly. Further, alcohol exacerbates chronic conditions; causes memory loss, stomach conditions, confusion, liver damage, and diabetes; and increases the probability of injury due to falls. Additionally, high rates of suicide and depression are associated with substance abuse among seniors. The conclusion of a cross-sectional study of older people living in Canadian community dwellings indicated that men suffering from loneliness and depression and lacking engagement in activities are the most vulnerable to alcohol abuse (St. John, Montgomery, & Tyas, 2008).

Substance abuse is a potential major problem at any age, with cognitive, physical, and psychological consequences. However, it often goes undetected in older adults who may abuse not only alcohol and illicit drugs, but prescription drugs as well (PHAC, 2010). Health care professionals may have difficulty identifying substance abuse with seniors as conditions such as memory problems, confusion, lack of self-care, sleep problems, depression, and falls may erroneously be attributed to other medical or psychological conditions (PHAC, 2010; Hoyer & Roodin, 2009).

Researchers have found a protective effect of moderate alcohol use in older adults, especially red wine (Holahan et al., 2012; Smigielski, Bielecki, & Drygas, 2013; O'Keefe et al., 2014). Red wine lowers stress, reduces the risk of heart disease, and is linked to better health and increased longevity (Carrizzo et al., 2013; Rozzini, Ranhoff, & Trabucchi, 2007). A chemical in the skin of red wine grapes—resveratrol—plays a key role in red wine's health benefits. One study found that red wine, but not white, killed several lines of cancer cells (Wallenborg et al., 2009). Scientists are exploring how resveratrol, as well as calorie restriction, increase SIRT1, an enzyme that is involved in DNA repair and aging (Barger, 2013).

critical thinking

Imagine that you suspect a parent or grandparent is suffering from depression or substance abuse. What are some of the behavioural signs that might raise this concern? How do you think you would respond? What would you do? What help might be available? How would this concern impact your well-being?

Dementia, Alzheimer's Disease, and Related Disorders

Among the most debilitating of mental disorders in older adults are the dementias (Clare et al., 2012). In recent years, extensive attention has been focused on the most common dementia, Alzheimer's disease. The Alzheimer's Society of Canada (2015) estimated that in 2011, 747 000 Canadians, or 14.9 percent of Canadians over 65, were living with Alzheimer's disease or other related forms of dementia such as multi-infarct dementia and Parkinson's disease (Alzheimer Society of Canada, 2015; Canadian Health Care Association, 2012).

Dementia

Dementia is a global term for any neurological disorder in which the primary symptoms involve a deterioration of mental functioning. Individuals with dementia often lose the ability to care for themselves and can lose the ability to recognize familiar surroundings and people (including family members) (McMillan et al., 2014; Valkanova & Ebmeier, 2014; Ziso & Larner, 2013).

Multi-Infarct Dementia

Multi-infarct dementia involves a sporadic and progressive loss of intellectual functioning caused by repeated temporary obstruction of blood flow in cerebral arteries. The result is a series of mini-strokes due to "infarct," which is the temporary obstruction of blood vessels. An estimated 15 to 25 percent of dementias involve the vascular impairment of multi-infarct dementia.

Multi-infarct dementia is more common among men with a history of high blood pressure. The clinical picture of multi-infarct dementia is different from that of Alzheimer's disease. Many patients recover from multi-infarct dementia, whereas Alzheimer's disease shows progressive deterioration. The symptoms of multi-infarct dementia include confusion, slurring of speech, writing impairment, and numbness on one side of the face, or in one arm or leg (Hoyer & Roodin, 2009). However, after each occurrence, there is usually a rather quick recovery, although typically each succeeding occurrence is more damaging. Approximately 35 to 50 percent of individuals who have these transient attacks will have a major stroke within five years unless the underlying problems are treated. Exercise, improved diet, and appropriate drugs, which can slow or stop the progression of the underlying vascular disease, are highly recommended (Craft, 2009).

Alzheimer's Disease

One form of dementia is **Alzheimer's disease**, a fatal, progressive, and irreversible disorder characterized by a gradual deterioration of memory, reasoning, language, and eventually, physical functioning. Although aging is a risk factor, Alzheimer's disease is not a normal part of aging (Alzheimer Society, 2013; MediResource, 2010–2011). Women are more likely than men to be diagnosed with Alzheimer's disease, primarily because they live longer.

Alzheimer's disease is described as early-onset (initially occurring in individuals younger than 65 years of age) or late-onset (which has its initial onset in individuals 65 years of age and older). Early-onset Alzheimer's disease is rare (about 7 percent of all cases) and generally affects people 30 to 60 years of age (Dudgeon, 2010). The number of individuals with Alzheimer's disease doubles every five years after the age of 65. Because of changing demographics and the increasing prevalence of Alzheimer's disease, researchers have stepped up their efforts to discover the causes of the disease and to find more effective ways to treat it (Grill & Monsell, 2014; Wilhelmus et al., 2014; Wisse et al., 2014; Zlater et al., 2014).

CAUSES AND TREATMENTS

Alzheimer's disease involves a deficiency in the brain messenger chemical acetylcholine, which plays an important role in memory (Jiang et al., 2014; Mesulam, 2013; Nardone et al., 2014). As Alzheimer's disease progresses, the brain shrinks and deteriorates (see Figure 17.9). The deterioration of the brain in Alzheimer's disease is characterized by the formation of amyloid plaques (dense deposits of protein that accumulate in the blood vessels) and neurofibrillary tangles (twisted fibres that build up in neurons) (Mungas et al., 2014; Taher et al., 2014; Wisnewski & Goni, 2014). Neurofibrillary tangles consist mainly of a protein called tau (Avila et al., 2014; Pooler, Noble, & Hanger, 2014). Currently, there is considerable research interest in the roles that amyloid and tau play in Alzheimer's disease (Tian et al., 2014; Vromman et al., 2013).

Figure 17.9

Two Brains: Alzheimer's Disease and Normal Aging

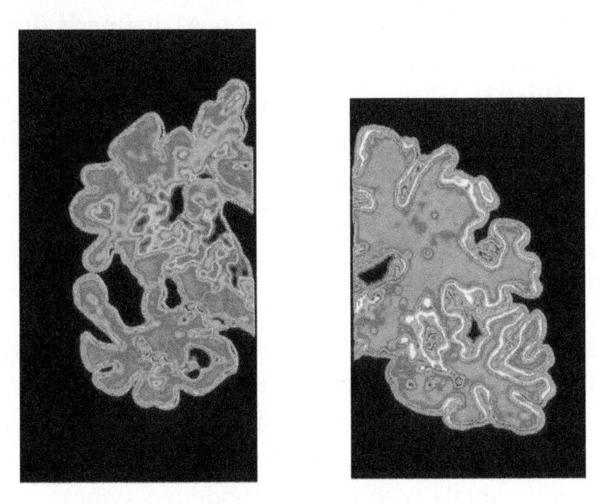

The brain image on the left is from a brain ravaged by Alzheimer's disease. The brain image on the right is from a brain of a normal aging individual. Note the deterioration and shrinking in the Alzheimer brain.

The role that oxidative stress might play in Alzheimer's disease is also of increasing interest. Oxidative stress occurs when the body's antioxidant defences don't cope with the free-radical attacks and oxidation in the body. Recall that earlier you read that free-radical theory is a major theory of biological aging.

Although scientists are not certain what causes Alzheimer's disease, age is an important risk factor, and genes also likely play an important role (Feng et al., 2014; Tang et al., 2014). Peter St. George-Hyslop (2012) of the University of Toronto has identified four genes that influence the inherited susceptibility to Alzheimer's disease. His pioneering work has led to the exploration of proteins that cause the death of nerve cells in the brain. Early detection, before any symptoms appear, and early treatment can be effective in reducing the disease, which once started is irreversible and leads to death (St. George-Hyslop, 2012).

A gene called *apolipoprotein E (ApoE),* which is linked to increasing presence of plaques and tangles in the brain, could play a role in as many as one-third of the cases of Alzheimer's disease (Argyri et al., 2014; Dorey et al., 2014; Osorio et al., 2014). In K. Warner Schaie's (2013) research, individuals who had the ApoE4 allele showed more cognitive decline beginning in middle age. Another study found that the ApoE4 gene creates a cascade of molecular signalling that causes blood vessels to become more porous, allowing toxic substances to leak into the brain and damage neurons (Bell et al., 2012).

Despite links between the presence of the ApoE4 gene and Alzheimer's disease, less than 50 percent of the individuals who are carriers of the ApoE4 gene develop dementia in old age. Advances as a result of the Human Genome Project have resulted in identification of other genes that are risk factors for Alzheimer's disease, although they are not as strongly linked to the disease as the ApoE4 gene (Lillenes et al., 2013).

Although individuals with a family history of Alzheimer's disease are at greater risk, the disease is complex and likely caused by a number of factors, including lifestyle (Jiang et al., 2013). For many years, scientists have known that a healthy diet, exercise, and weight control can lower the risk of cardiovascular disease. Now they are finding that these healthy lifestyle factors may also lower the risk or delay the onset of Alzheimer's disease (Suehs et al., 2014). Researchers have revealed older adults with Alzheimer's disease are more likely to also have cardiovascular disease than are individuals who do not have Alzheimer's disease (Murr et al., 2014; Wang et al., 2013). Recently, more cardiac risk factors have been implicated in Alzheimer's disease—obesity, smoking, atherosclerosis, high cholesterol and lipids (Dublin et al., 2014; Grammas et al., 2014). One of the best strategies for intervening in the lives of people who are at risk for Alzheimer's disease is to improve their cardiac functioning through diet, drugs, and exercise (Tavassoli et al., 2013). For example, one study of older adults found that those who exercised three or more times a week were less likely to develop Alzheimer's disease over a six-year period than those who exercised less (Larson et al., 2006).

EARLY DETECTION OF ALZHEIMER'S DISEASE

Mild cognitive impairment (MCI) represents a transitional state between the cognitive changes of normal aging and very early Alzheimer's disease and other dementias. MCI is increasingly recognized as a risk factor for Alzheimer's disease.

Distinguishing between individuals who merely have age-associated declines in memory and those with MCI is difficult, as is predicting which individuals with MCI will subsequently develop Alzheimer's disease (Poil et al., 2013; Richens et al., 2014). A research review concluded that fMRI measurement of neuron loss in the medial temporal lobe is a predictor of memory loss and eventually dementia (Vellas & Aisen, 2010). Another study revealed that amyloid beta—a protein fragment that forms plaques in the brain—is present in the spinal fluid of approximately 75 percent of individuals with mild cognitive impairment (De Meyer et al., 2010). Every one of the older adults with mild cognitive impairment who had the amyloid beta in their spinal fluid developed Alzheimer's disease within five years.

DRUG TREATMENT OF ALZHEIMER'S DISEASE

Although there is no cure for Alzheimer's disease, several medications can help with symptoms such as memory decline and changes in language, thinking abilities, and motor skills. As Alzheimer's disease progresses, brain cells die, and connections among them are lost. Several drugs called cholinesterase inhibitors are among those most commonly used to lessen or stabilize the symptoms for a limited time, generally two to three years, possibly more. These three cholinesterase—aricept, exelon, and reminyl—are used to help individuals with mild to moderate symptoms. As the disease progresses, ebixa ad aricept may be used. These cholinesterase inhibiters, now approved by Health Canada, may be prescribed by health care professionals to people who meet specific clinical criteria. Unfortunately, the nerve endings eventually degenerate to the point where the drugs are no longer effective (Alzheimer Society Canada, 2016).

MAGNESIUM

Magnesium is an abundant element essential to human health; however, most men and women have an insufficient amount of magnesium in their bodies. People with dementia/Alzheimer's have 40 percent less magnesium in their brain than people without this condition (Wetzel, 2012). New technology has furnished evidence that magnesium plays a vital role in health in numerous ways such as regulating blood pressure, lowering risk of heart attacks, enabling the immune system, and lowering risk of depression. Accumulating evidence indicates that magnesium reduces cognitive deficits by reversing the loss of cell connections between brain cells, enabling memory and learning. This breakthrough has profound implications for Alzheimer's disease as it may offset the progression of the disease, or possibly even contribute to prevention (Maran, 2016). The recommended dietary allowance for women is 310–320 mg/day, and 400–420 mg/day for men; however, over-the-counter magnesium does not get to the brain, where it is most needed. Magnesium Threonate, or Magtein, is the breakthrough magnesium compound that will enhance cognitive functioning and decrease, or possibly reverse, memory decline associated with dementia and Alzheimer's disease (Reynolds, 2014).

CARING FOR INDIVIDUALS WITH ALZHEIMER'S DISEASE

Caring for Alzheimer patients is a special concern (Kamiya et al., 2014). Currently, 55 percent of Canadians aged 65 and over with dementia live in their own homes, with support from their spouse, family members, and/or community-based professionals (Dudgeon, 2010). Psychologists and other health care professionals believe that the family can be an important support system for the Alzheimer patient, but this support has emotional, physical, and financial costs (Carling-Jenkins et al., 2012; Ornstein et al., 2014). One study compared family members' perception of caring for someone with Alzheimer's disease, cancer, or schizophrenia (Papastavrou et al., 2012). In this study, the highest perceived burden was reported for Alzheimer's disease.

Respite care (services that provide temporary relief for those who are caring for individuals with disabilities, illnesses, or the elderly) has been developed to help people who have to meet the day-to-day needs of Alzheimer patients (de la Cuesta-Benjumea, 2011). Caregivers can suffer from excessive workload, depression, guilt, and exhaustion. Various types of respite care are designed to provide caregivers with temporary rest. Respite care include out-of-home respite services and in-home care, including the use of technology, particularly for video chat services. More research is underway to understand the costs, caregiver training, and readiness to use respite care (Canadian Healthcare Association, 2012).

Parkinson's Disease

Another type of dementia is **Parkinson's disease**, a chronic, progressive disease characterized by muscle tremors, slowing of movement, and partial facial paralysis. Parkinson's disease is triggered by degeneration of dopamine-producing neurons in the brain (Catalan et al., 2013). Dopamine is a neurotransmitter that is necessary for normal brain functioning. Why these neurons degenerate is not known.

The main treatment for Parkinson's disease involves administering drugs that enhance the effect of dopamine (dopamine agonists) in the disease's earlier stages and later administering the drug L-dopa, which is converted by the brain into dopamine (Mestre et al., 2014). However, it is difficult to determine the correct level of dosage of L-dopa and it loses efficacy over time (Nomoto et al., 2009).

Another treatment for advanced Parkinson's disease is deep brain stimulation (DBS), which involves implantation of electrodes within the brain (Kim et al., 2014; Pollack, 2013). The electrodes are then stimulated by a pacemaker-like device. Recent studies indicated that deep brain stimulation may provide benefits for individuals with Parkinson's disease (Vedam-Mai et al., 2014). Other studies indicate that certain types of dance, such as the tango, can improve the movement skills of individuals with Parkinson's disease (Kaski et al., 2014; Ransmayr, 2011). Stem cell transplantation and gene therapy also offer hope for treating the disease (Badger et al., 2014; Wyse, Dunbar, & Rossignol, 2014).

Will T Wade Jr. , PacificCoastNe/Newscom

Canadian actor Michael J. Fox has become a leading spokesperson for Parkinson's disease since he was diagnosed with the condition.

Health Promotion

What is the quality of nursing homes and other extended-care facilities for older adults? What is the nature of the relationship between older adults and health-care providers?

Care Options

Statistics Canada (2015) reported that according to the 2011 census report, 92.1 percent of seniors live in private homes: 56.4 percent as couples, 24.6 percent alone, and the remaining with others. As people age, the proportion living in health care facilities or nursing homes increases from 7.1 percent for those 65 years and over, to 29. 6 percent for those 85 years and over. A national study from the University of Alberta reported that two-thirds of residents are female, over 80 years of age, of low-income levels, and have dementia in combination with two other chronic diseases (Estabrooks et al., 2015). Intergenerational programs, discussed in Chapter 15, make a very constructive contribution to seniors living in nursing homes.

In his book *Being Mortal*, Dr. Atul Gawande, a surgeon who spent considerable time assessing life in nursing homes as well as medical treatment of people facing death, concluded that nursing homes are preoccupied with patient safety and doctors are committed to extending life. In both cases, the individual's wishes are often ignored and they may be overly medicated and/or depersonalized (Gawande, 2014). One scenario Gawande describes is the experience of an Emergency Room doctor who became the director of Chase Nursing Home in New York State. As the physician observed and talked to residents, he noted an overriding feeling of sadness and depression. Believing that the residents needed a purpose and a sense of control and autonomy, he persuaded everyone who needed persuasion to allow him to bring in plants for each patient as well as two dogs, four cats, and 100 parakeets. What happened totally transformed the nursing home from an atmosphere of gloom and doom to one where the residents had much more control over activities such as walking the dogs, taking care of the plants, cleaning the kitty-litter, and deciding when and where to eat, who can visit and when, and so forth. Dr. Gawande wrote, "Researchers studied the effects of this program over two years, comparing a variety of measures for Chase residents with these of residents at another nursing home nearby. Their study found that the number of prescriptions required per resident fell to half that of the control nursing home. Psychotrophic drugs for agitation, like Haldol, decreased in particular. The total drug costs fell to just 38 percent of the comparison facility. Deaths fell 15 percent" (Gawande, 2014, p.123).

Prescription Drug Use

Seniors' use of prescribed drugs accounts for 40 percent of all purchases of prescribed medication, a larger share than any other single age group in Canada (Canadian Institute for Health Information, 2010). Inappropriate use of these medications may account for 30 percent of the hospitalizations of people over the age of 65. Multiple prescription drug use is common, with 53 percent of seniors living in institutions being given five or more drugs per day, while 13 percent of those residing in private dwellings take that many drugs per day (Ramage-Morin, 2009). The more drugs used, the greater the risk is for adverse effects. The Canadian Mental Health Association, Ontario (2010) reports that as many as 50 percent of seniors do not take their medications as prescribed, share their medication with spouses, and are unaware of the interaction between their prescription and alcohol.

Therefore, it is critical that seniors and care providers carefully manage their use of prescribed medications. Taking regular inventories of drugs and checking for contraindications, side effects, and interactions is highly recommended. One approach is referred to as the "brown bag" technique, in which the person places all the medication bottles in a brown bag (or other suitable container) and takes them to her/his physician during a regular visit.

CONNECTING through Research

Ursula Franklin (1921–2016)

Celebrated physicist, educator, author, peace advocate, Quaker, and humanitarian Ursula Franklin was born in Germany. As a young adult, she witnessed and experienced first-hand the Nazi work camps—where, because her mother was Jewish, she was imprisoned and forced to work repairing buildings.

She completed her Ph.D. in experimental physics at the Technical University in Berlin, then, in 1948, she immigrated to Canada where she completed her post-doctoral work at the University of Toronto. She worked as a senior scientist at the Ontario Research Foundation. In 1967, Franklin began teaching metallurgy and physics at the University of Toronto, the first woman to do so. In 1984, U of T honoured her with the title of full University Professor and in so doing, she became the university's first female professor (Ursula Franklin Academy [UFA], 2008–2013).

Her research, publications, and teaching career, combined with her tireless advocacy, earned her several awards and honorary degrees, including the Order of Ontario in 1990 and the Companion of the Order of Canada in 1992. She also became a Fellow of the Royal Society of Canada and was inducted into the Canadian Sciences Hall of Fame (UFA, 2008–2013). Toronto honoured her dedication to education by naming one of the city's high schools after her, the Ursula Franklin Academy, where she assumed a role of active participation and leadership, particularly in encouraging young women to enter the sciences and to broaden our understanding of the role of technology in our lives.

Franklin turned her attention to how feminism, language, and social justice contribute to drafting the map that could lead us to peace (Franklin, 2006; Hirsh, 2008). She pointed out that when an earthquake hits any part of the world, we find ways to help each other; however, when we create an enemy, we alienate each other and create war. In our responses to victims of floods or earthquakes, we integrate social justice and peace, and find peaceful maps (Hirsh, 2008). In her acceptance speech for the Pearson Peace Medal from the United Nations Association in Canada (2001), Franklin said, "Peace is not the absence of war. Peace is the presence of justice and the absence of fear" (Geary-Martin, 2013).

Meeting the Mental Health Needs of Older Adults

Mental illnesses have the potential to impact every aspect of an individual's life; however, they often go undetected in seniors. Physical ailments, mobility issues, chronic diseases, widowhood, and changes of income, are among the many variables that are challenging to seniors, often affecting their mental health. Depression, anxiety, dementias, and other mental health issues often go undetected as many seniors have multiple conditions, making diagnosis difficult (Canadian Mental Health Association, 2016). According to Statistics Canada, adults over 65 are more likely than other age groups to use health services for mental illness, and the numbers increase with age, so that by the age of 80, one in four use health services for mental illness (Statistics Canada, 2015).

Treatment and supports are provided by physicians, psychiatrists, hospitals, outpatient programs, clinics and community agencies. More work is needed to understand mental illness, provide more accurate diagnosis and supports, as well as to reduce the stigma attached.

critical thinking

Good physical and mental health appear to share a number of common points. Using the information in this section, construct a six-point list of different ways to help an older adult maintain good mental health. How might you incorporate these points into your life now in an effort to ensure good health in your senior years?

CONNECTING development to life

Health Care Providers and Older Adults

© jonya/E+/Getty Images RF

Almost all seniors in Canada have a doctor (96 percent), and 88 percent have seen their doctor in the previous year (Rotermann, 2005). People over the age of 65 use physicians more than any other group, have more hospital admissions, and have generally longer stays than other age groups (Turcotte & Schellenberg, 2007).

The attitudes of both the health care provider and the older adult are important aspects of the older adult's health care (Agrali & Akyar, 2014). Unfortunately, health care providers too often share society's stereotypes and negative attitudes toward older adults (Eymard & Douglas, 2012). In a health care setting, these attitudes can take the form of avoidance, dislike, and begrudged tolerance rather than positive, hopeful treatment. Health care personnel are more likely to be interested in treating younger persons, who more often have acute problems with a higher prognosis for successful recovery. They often are less motivated to treat older persons, who are more likely to have chronic problems with a lower prognosis for successful recovery.

Not only are physicians less responsive to older patients, but older patients often take a less active role in medical encounters with health care personnel than do younger patients. Older adults should be encouraged to take a more active role in their own health care.

The demand for home-care aides is predicted to increase dramatically in the next several decades because of the likely doubling of the 65-year-and-older population and older adults' preference for remaining out of nursing homes (Moos, 2007). Not only is it important to significantly increase the number of health care professionals available to treat older adults, but it is also very important that they not harbor negative stereotypes of older adults and that they show very positive attitudes toward them.

To this point, we have discussed a number of ideas about physical and mental health and wellness in late adulthood. For a review, see the Reach Your Learning Outcomes section at the end of this chapter.

Cognitive Functioning in Older Adults

LO4 Describe the cognitive functioning of older adults.

- **The Multi-Dimensional, Multi-Directional Nature of Cognition**
- **Education, Work, and Health: Links to Cognitive Functioning**
- **Promoting Cognitive Skills in Later Life: Use It or Lose It**
- **Cognitive Neuroscience and Aging**

The three seniors you read about in the opening vignette—Dr. Arthur B. McDonald, Dr. Roberta Lynn Bondar, and Dr. Buffy Sainte-Marie—are all in their seventies. When Pablo Casals was 95, a reporter asked him why, as the greatest cellist who ever lived, he still practised six hours per day. Mr. Casals replied, "Because I feel like I am making progress" (Canfield & Hansen, 1995). How does cognitive development change in late adulthood?

The Multi-Dimensional, Multi-Directional Nature of Cognition

In thinking about the nature of cognitive change in adulthood, it is important to consider that cognition is a multi-dimensional concept (Dixon et al., 2013). It is also important to consider that while some dimensions of cognition might decline as we age, others might remain stable or even improve.

Cognitive Mechanics and Cognitive Pragmatics.

Paul Baltes (2003; Baltes, Lindenberger, & Staudinger, 2006) clarified the distinction between those aspects of the aging mind that show decline and those that remain stable or even improve. **Cognitive mechanics** are the hardware of the mind and reflect the neurophysiological architecture of the brain developed through evolution. Cognitive mechanics involve the speed and accuracy of the processes involving sensory input, visual and motor memory, discrimination, comparison, and categorization. Because of the strong influence of biology, heredity, and health on cognitive mechanics, their decline with aging is likely. Some researchers conclude that the decline in cognitive mechanics may begin as soon as early mid-life (Salthouse, 2013a, b).

Conversely, **cognitive pragmatics** are the culture-based software programs of the mind. Cognitive pragmatics include reading and writing skills, language comprehension, educational qualifications, professional skills, and also the type of knowledge about the self and life skills that help us master or cope with life. Because of the strong influence of culture on cognitive pragmatics, their improvement into old age is possible. Thus, while cognitive mechanics may decline in old age, cognitive pragmatics may actually improve (see Figure 17.10).

The distinction between cognitive mechanics and cognitive pragmatics is similar to the one between fluid (mechanics) and crystallized (pragmatics) intelligence that was described in Chapter 15. Indeed, the similarity is so strong that some experts now use these terms to describe cognitive aging patterns: fluid mechanics and crystallized pragmatics (Lovden & Lindenberger, 2007).

What factors are most likely to contribute to the decline in fluid mechanics in late adulthood? Among the most likely candidates are processing speed, working memory capacity, and suppressing irrelevant information (inhibition) (Lovden & Lindenberger, 2007).

Now that we have examined the distinction between fluid mechanics and crystallized pragmatics, let us explore some of the more specific cognitive processes that reflect these two general domains.

Figure 17.10

Theorized Age Changes in Cognitive Mechanics and Cognitive Pragmatics

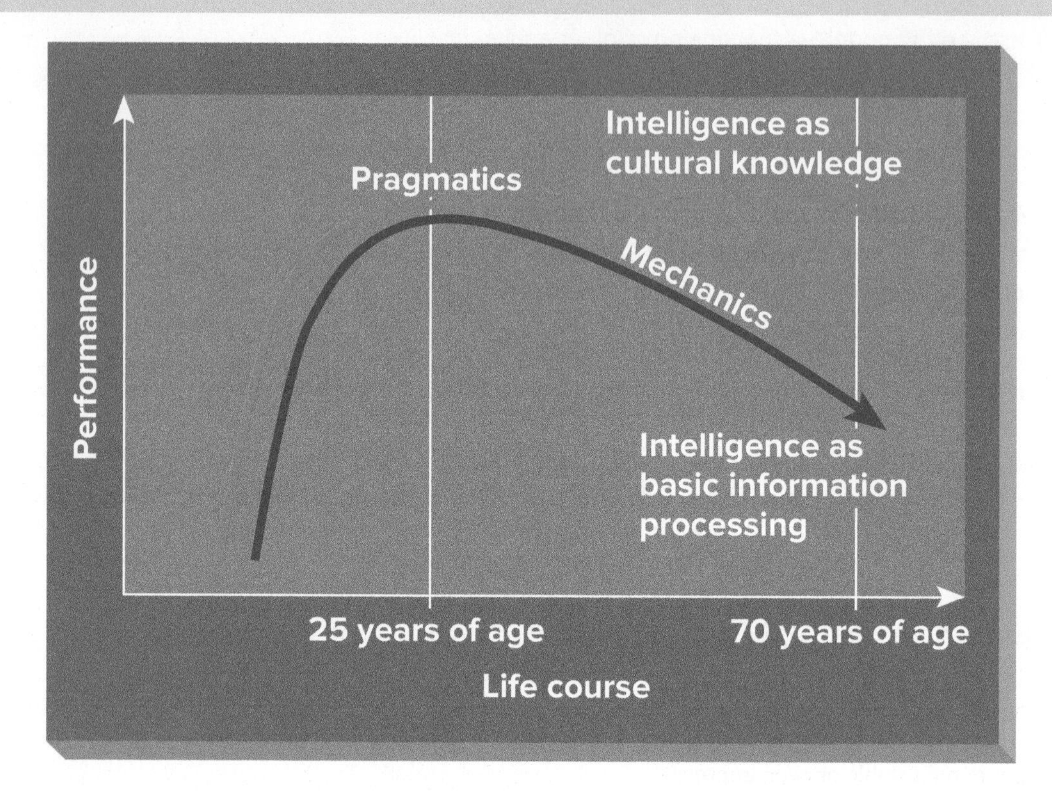

Baltes argues that cognitive mechanics decline during aging, whereas cognitive pragmatics do not. Cognitive mechanics have a biological/genetic foundation; cognitive pragmatics have an experiential/cultural foundation.

Speed-of-Processing Dimensions

That the speed of processing information declines in late adulthood is well accepted, although there is considerable individual variation in this ability (Hartley, 2006). Accumulated knowledge may compensate to some degree for slower processing speed in older adults. For example, one study found that knowledge is more important on a memory task for older adults than younger adults, and that older adults may rely on age-related increases in knowledge to partially compensate for a decline in processing speed (Hoogendam et al., 2014; Robitaille et al., 2013; Salthouse, 2012, 2013a, b). The decline in processing speed in older adults is likely due to a decline in functioning of the brain and central nervous system (Finch, 2009, 2011; Nilsson et al., 2014; Papp et al., 2014, Finch, 2009). Health and exercise may influence how much decline in processing speed occurs (Ellis et al., 2014). Studies have found that aerobic exercise modestly increases attention and processing speed, executive function, and memory, although the effects on working memory are less consistent (Smith et al., 2010).

Attention

Changes in attention are important aspects of cognitive aging (Pierce & Andersen, 2014; Sylvain-Roy, Lungu, & Belleville, 2014). Researchers have found that older adults are less able to ignore distracting information than younger adults, and this distractibility becomes more pronounced as attentional demands increase (Mund, Bell, & Buchner, 2010). Research also indicates that the greater distractibility of older adults is associated with less effective functioning in neural networks running through the frontal and parietal lobes of the brain, which are involved in cognitive control (Campbell et al., 2012). Also, a research review concluded that more active and physically fit older adults are better able to allocate attention when interacting with the environment (Gomez-Pinilla & Hillman, 2013).

In Chapter 7, "Physical and Cognitive Development in Early Childhood," you read about two types of attention—sustained and executive. Here we will discuss those two types of attention in older adults, as well as two additional types of attention: selective and divided attention.

- **Selective attention** is focusing on a specific aspect of experience that is relevant while ignoring others that are irrelevant. An example of selective attention is the ability to focus on one voice among many in a crowded room or a noisy restaurant. Another is making a decision about which stimuli to attend to when making a left turn at an intersection. Generally, older adults are less adept at selective attention than younger adults (Ben-David et al., 2014; Caban-Holt et al., 2012; Quigley & Muller, 2014). In a study, 10 weeks of speed of processing training improved the selective attention of older adults (O'Brien et al., 2013).
- **Divided attention** involves concentrating on more than one activity at the same time. When the two competing tasks are reasonably easy, age differences among adults are minimal or non-existent. However, the more difficult the competing tasks are, the less effectively older adults divide attention when compared to younger adults (Bucur & Madden, 2007). A study conducted by Erin I. Skinner and Myra A. Fernandes of the University of Waterloo investigated the effect of divided attention using study-list repetition. They found that younger adults make fewer errors, whereas older adults are more susceptible to erroneous recall (Skinner & Fernandes, 2009).
- **Sustained attention** is the state of readiness to detect and respond to small changes occurring at random times in the environment. Sometimes sustained attention is referred to as vigilance. On tests of simple vigilance, older adults usually perform as well as younger adults; however, older adults' performance usually drops on complex vigilance tasks (Bucur & Madden, 2007). One study of older adults found that the greater the variability in their sustained attention (vigilance), the more likely they were to experience falls (O'Halloran et al., 2011).
- **Executive attention** involves planning of actions, allocating attention to goals, detecting and compensating for errors, monitoring progress on tasks, and dealing with novel or difficult circumstances. One study found that older adults had deficiencies in executive attention (Mahoney et al., 2010). In this study, a lower level of executive attention in older adults was linked to low blood pressure, which likely is related to reduced blood flow to the brain's frontal lobes.

Memory

The main dimensions of memory and aging that have been studied include episodic memory, semantic memory, cognitive resources (such as working memory and perceptual speed), source memory, and non-cognitive influences such as health education and socio-economic factors.

EPISODIC MEMORY

Episodic memory is the retention of information about the where and when of life's happenings (Tulving, 2000)—for example, what it was like when your younger sister or brother was born, or what happened to you on your first date, or what you were doing when you heard about the devastating fires in Fort McMurray in 2016, or where you were when Justin Trudeau was elected Prime Minister.

Younger adults have better episodic memory than older adults (Friedman, 2013; McDonough & Gallo, 2013; Cansino, 2009). One study of 18- to 94-year-olds revealed that increased age is linked to increased difficulty in retrieving episodic information, facts, and events (Siedlecki, 2007). Older adults report that they can remember older events better than more recent ones; however, the evidence of research contradicts this and reports that in older adults, the older the memory, the less accurate it is.

SEMANTIC MEMORY

Semantic memory is a person's knowledge about the world, including a person's fields of expertise (such as knowledge of chess, for a skilled chess player); general academic knowledge of the sort learned in school (such as knowledge of geometry); and "everyday knowledge" about meanings of words, famous individuals, important places, and common things (such as information about Nelson Mandela, Mahatma Gandhi, and Mohamed Ali). Semantic memory appears to be independent of an individual's personal identity with the past. For example, you can access a fact—such as "Kabul is the capital of Afghanistan"—and not have the foggiest idea of when and where you learned it.

Does semantic memory decline during aging? Among the tasks that researchers often use to assess semantic memory are vocabulary, general knowledge, and word identification (Miotto et al., 2013). Older adults often take longer to retrieve semantic information, but usually they can ultimately retrieve it. However, the ability to retrieve very specific information (such as names) usually declines in older adults (Luo & Craik, 2008). For the most part, episodic memory declines more in older adults than semantic memory (Kuo et al., 2014; Ofen & Shing, 2013; Small et al., 2012b). Although many aspects of semantic memory are reasonably well-preserved in late adulthood, a common memory problem for older adults is the tip-of-the-tongue (TOT) phenomenon, in which individuals can't quite retrieve familiar information but have the feeling that they should be able to (Bucur & Madden, 2007). Researchers have found that older adults are more likely to experience TOT states than younger adults (Bucur & Madden, 2007; Salthouse & Mandell, 2013). A study of older adults found that the most commonly reported errors in memory over the last 24 hours were those involving tip-of-the-tongue (Ossher, Flegal, & Lustig, 2013).

EXPLICIT AND IMPLICIT MEMORY

Researchers have found that aging is linked to changes in explicit memory (Giovanello, 2011; Ward, Berry, & Shanks, 2014). **Explicit memory** is memory of facts and experiences that individuals consciously know and can state. Explicit memory also is sometimes called declarative memory. Examples of explicit memory include being at a grocery store and remembering what you wanted to buy, remembering the capital of Nunavut, or recounting the events of a movie you have seen. **Implicit memory** is memory without conscious recollection; it involves skills and routine procedures that are automatically performed. Implicit memory is sometimes called procedural memory. Examples of implicit memory include unconsciously remembering how to drive a car, swing a golf club, or type on a keyboard.

Implicit memory is less likely to be adversely affected by aging than explicit memory (Norman, Holmin, & Bartholomew, 2011; Nyberg et al., 2012). Thus, older adults are more likely to forget what items they wanted to buy at a grocery store (unless they wrote them down on a list and brought it with them) than they are to forget how to drive a car. Their perceptual speed might be slower in driving the car, but they remember how to do it.

SOURCE MEMORY

Source memory is the ability to remember where one learned something. Failures of source memory increase with age in the adult years and can create awkward situations, such as when an older adult forgets who told a joke and retells it to the source (Davidson et al., 2013; El Haj & Allain, 2012). Lynn Hasher (2003, p. 1301) argues that age differences are substantial in many studies of memory, such as resource memory, when individuals are asked "for a piece of information that just doesn't matter much. But if you ask for information that is important, old people do every bit as well as young adults . . . young people have mental resources to burn. As people get older, they get more selective in how they use their resources."

PROSPECTIVE MEMORY

Prospective memory involves remembering to do something in the future, such as remembering to take your medicine or remembering to do an errand. Although some researchers have found a decline in prospective memory with age (Kelly et al., 2013; Smith & Hunt, 2014), a number of studies show that whether there is a decline is complex and depends on such factors as the nature of the task and what is being assessed (Mullet et al., 2013; Scullin, Bugg, & McDaniel, 2012). For example, age-related deficits occur more often in prospective memory tasks that are time-based (such as remembering to call someone next Friday) than those that are event-based (remembering to tell your friend to read a particular book the next time you see her). Further, declines in prospective memory occur more in laboratory than real-life settings (Bisiacchi, Tarantino, & Ciccola, 2008). Indeed, in some real-life settings, such as keeping appointments, older adults' prospective memory is better than younger adults' (Luo & Craik, 2008).

COGNITIVE RESOURCES: WORKING MEMORY AND PERCEPTUAL SPEED

One view of memory suggests that a limited number of cognitive resources can be devoted to any cognitive task. Two important cognitive resource mechanisms are working memory and perceptual speed (Baddeley, 2012; Nilsson et al., 2014; Salthouse, 2013a, b). Recall from Chapters 9 and 15 that working memory is closely linked to short-term memory but places more emphasis on memory as a place for mental work. Working memory is like a mental "workbench" that allows individuals to manipulate and assemble information when making decisions, solving problems, and comprehending written and spoken language (Baddeley, 2007, 2010, 2012).

Researchers have found a decline in working memory during the late adulthood years (Cansino et al., 2013; Ko et al., 2014; Peich, Husain, & Bays, 2013). A study revealed that working memory continues to decline from 65 to 89 years of age (Elliott et al., 2011). Another study found that multitasking especially produces a disruption in older adults' working memory, likely because of an interruption in retrieving information (Clapp et al., 2011). And in yet another study, verbal and visual working memory declined at similar rates during aging (Kumar & Priyadarshi, 2013). A further, study found that visually encoded working memory is linked to older adults' mobility (Kawagoe & Sekiyama, 2014). Explanations of the decline in working memory in older adults often focus on their less efficient inhibition in preventing irrelevant information from entering working memory and their increased distractibility (Lustig & Hasher, 2009; Yi & Friedman, 2014).

Is there plasticity in the working memory of older adults? An experimental study indicated that moderate exercise results in faster reaction time on a working memory task in older adults (Hogan, Mata, & Carstensen, 2013). Two other studies found that cognitive training and strategy improves older adults' working memory (Borella et al., 2013; Bailey, Dunlosky, & Hertzog, 2014). Thus, there appears to be plasticity in the working memory of older adults.

Perceptual speed is a cognitive resource that involves the ability to perform simple perceptual-motor tasks, such as deciding whether pairs of two-digit or two-letter strings are the same or different. Perceptual speed shows considerable decline in late adulthood, and is strongly linked with decline in working memory (Dirk, 2012; Hoogendam et al., 2014; Salthouse, 2013a). A study revealed that age-related slowing in processing speed is linked to a breakdown in myelin in the brain (Lu et al., 2013). Another study found that 10 hours of visual speed of processing training was effective in improving older adults' speed of processing, attention, and executive function (Wolinksy et al., 2013).

CONCLUSIONS ABOUT MEMORY AND AGING

Some, but not all, aspects of memory decline during late adulthood (Kuo et al., 2014; Nyberg et al., 2012; Schaie, 2013). The decline occurs primarily in explicit, episodic, and working memory, not in semantic memory or implicit memory. A decline in perceptual speed is associated with memory decline (Salthouse, 2013a, b). Successful aging does not mean eliminating memory decline altogether, but it does mean reducing the decline and adapting to it by using certain strategies.

Non-cognitive factors such as health, education, and socio-economic status can influence an older adult's performance on memory tasks (Fritsch et al., 2007; Lachman et al., 2010; Noble et al., 2010). Although such non-cognitive factors as good health are associated with less memory decline in older adults, they do not eliminate it.

Decision Making

Despite declines in many aspects of memory, such as working memory and long-term memory, many older adults preserve decision-making skills reasonably well (Healey & Hasher, 2009). In some cases, though, age-related decreases in memory will impair decision making (Eppinger et al., 2014). However, older adults especially perform well when decision making is not constrained by time pressures and when the decision is meaningful for them (Boyle et al., 2012; Yoon, Cole, & Lee, 2009).

Wisdom

Does wisdom improve with age? If so, what is "wisdom"? One research review found 24 definitions of wisdom, although there was significant overlap in the definitions (Bangen, Meeks, & Jest, 2013). In this review, the following subcomponents of wisdom were commonly cited: knowledge of life, prosocial values, self-understanding, acknowledgment of uncertainty, emotional balance, tolerance, openness, spirituality, and sense of humour. Thus, while there is still some disagreement regarding how wisdom should be defined, the following is the definition that has been used by leading expert Paul Baltes and colleagues (Baltes & Kunzmann, 2007; Baltes & Smith, 2008): **Wisdom** is expert knowledge about the practical aspects of life that permits excellent judgment about important matters.

This practical knowledge involves exceptional insight into human development and life matters, good judgment, and an understanding of how to cope with difficult life problems. Thus, wisdom, more than standard conceptions of intelligence, focuses on life's pragmatic concerns and human conditions (Ferrari & Weststrate, 2013; Jeste & Oswald, 2014; Staudinger & Gluck, 2011; Thomas & Kunzmann, 2014; Webster, Westerhof, & Bohlmeijer, 2014).

In regard to wisdom, research by Baltes and his colleagues (Baltes & Kunzmann, 2007; Baltes & Smith, 2008) has found that:

- *High levels of wisdom are rare.* Few people, including older adults, attain a high level of wisdom. That only a small percentage of adults show wisdom supports the contention that it requires experience, practice, or complex skills.
- *The time frame of late adolescence and early adulthood is the main age window for wisdom to emerge* (Staudinger & Dorner, 2007; Staudinger & Gluck, 2011). No further advances in wisdom have been found for middle-aged and older adults beyond the level they attained as young adults.
- *Factors other than age are critical for wisdom to develop to a high level.* For example, certain life experiences, such as being trained and working in a field concerned with difficult life problems and having wisdom-enhancing mentors,

contribute to higher levels of wisdom. Also, people higher in wisdom have values that are more likely to consider the welfare of others rather than their own happiness.

- *Personality-related factors are better predictors of wisdom than cognitive factors (e.g, intelligence).* Personality-related factors include openness to experience, generativity, and creativity.

Traditional Native elders are carefully selected because one of the essential requirements of being an elder is the ability to use wisdom to guide others. The individual is selected for his or her keen compassion and perceptive abilities. Once selected, the individual goes through years of rigorous mentoring and training, which involves traditional teachings and ceremonies, to be given the combined experiences and accumulated wisdom of other elders (Criger, 2007, interview).

Education, Work, and Health: Links to Cognitive Functioning

Education, work, and health are three important influences on the cognitive functioning of older adults. They are also three of the most important factors involved in understanding why cohort effects need to be taken into account in studying the cognitive functioning of older adults. Indeed, cohort effects are very important considerations in the study of cognitive aging (Hofer, Rast, & Piccinin, 2012; Schaie, 2013).

Education

Successive generations in Canada are better educated. More older adults have gone to college or university than their parents or grandparents; as well, more older adults are returning to college or university today to further their education than in past generations. Educational experiences are positively correlated with scores on intelligence tests and information-processing tasks, such as memory (Muniz-Terrera et al., 2013; Steffener et al., 2014). Older adults might seek more education for a number of reasons, such as enhancing their leisure activities to enable them to make the transition from retirement, or to study something they always wanted to learn but never had time.

Work

More of today's seniors have had work experiences that include a stronger emphasis on cognitively-oriented labour. Our great-grandfathers and grandfathers were more likely to be manual labourers than were our fathers, who are more likely to be involved in cognitively-oriented occupations. As the industrial society continues to be replaced by the information society, younger generations will have more experience in jobs that require considerable cognitive investment. The increased emphasis on information processing in jobs likely enhances an individual's intellectual abilities (Kristjuhan & Taidre, 2010).

Health

Since better treatments for a variety of illnesses (such as hypertension) have been developed, today's seniors are healthier than those of previous generations. Many illnesses, such as stroke or heart disease, have a negative impact on intellectual performance (Chuang et al., 2014; Ganguli et al., 2014; Joosten et al., 2013). Hypertension has been linked to lower cognitive performance in a number of studies in both older, middle aged, and younger adults (Virta et al., 2013). Researchers also have found age-related cognitive decline in adults with mood disorders such as depression (Mackin et al., 2014; van den Kommer et al., 2013). Thus, some of the decline in intellectual performance found for older adults is likely due to health-related factors rather than to age per se (Korten et al., 2014; Morra et al., 2013).

K. Warner Schaie (1994) concluded that although some diseases, such as hypertension and diabetes, are linked to cognitive drop off, they do not directly cause mental decline. Rather, the lifestyles of the individuals with the diseases might be the culprits. For example, overeating, inactivity, and stress are related to both physical and mental decline (Annweiler et al., 2012; Kraft, 2012). In his most recent account of links between health and cognitive factors, Schaie (2013) concluded that the association may be reciprocal. That is, a healthy body facilitates cognitive competence, and cognitive competence facilitates the maintenance of physical health.

A number of research studies have found that lifestyle and exercise are linked to improved cognitive functioning (Kirk-Sanchez & McGough, 2014; Leon et al., 2014; Small et al., 2012a). A research review concluded that physical exercise is a promising non-pharmaceutical intervention to prevent or reduce age-related cognitive decline (Bherer, Erickson, & Liu-Ambrose, 2013). Also recall from earlier in the chapter that a research review concluded that exercise's influence on cognition occurs through changes in molecular events associated with the management of energy metabolism and synaptic plasticity (Gomez-Pinilla & Hillman, 2013). We previously discussed a study that revealed a program involving moderate exercise increases the working memory of older adults (Hogan, Mata, & Carstensen, 2013). Studies have also documented that the mental health of older adults can influence their cognitive functioning.

Here are the results of four other studies linking physical exercise and cognitive development in older adults:

- In a study of healthy 60- to 75-year-olds, those who engaged in a physical training program showed improved centration three months later (Linde & Alfermann, 2014).
- Community-dwelling women 65 years of age and older did not have cognitive impairment or physical limitations when they were initially assessed (Yaffe et al., 2001). Six to eight years later, the women with higher physical activity when they were initially assessed were less likely to experience cognitive decline.
- A higher level of cardiorespiratory fitness in older adults is linked to better performance on a cognitive task through recruitment of neural circuits in the prefrontal and parietal regions of the brain (Prakash et al., 2011).
- A study found that six months of dance intervention was linked to improved cognitive functioning in elderly adults (Kattenstroth et al., 2013).

A final aspect of health that is important to consider in cognitive functioning in older adults is terminal decline. This concept emphasizes that changes in cognitive functioning may be linked more to distance from death or cognition-related pathology than distance from birth (Burns et al., 2014; Hulur et al., 2013; Wilson et al., 2012). A study revealed that on average, a faster rate of cognitive decline occurred on average about 7.7 years prior to death and varied across individuals (Muniz-Terrera et al., 2013). Another study found that a cohort that died in the first decade of the twenty-first century had a steeper terminal decline in cognition than the cohort that preceded it in the 1990s (Hulur et al., 2013). The researchers concluded that this result occurred because of recent increases in "manufacturing" survival by keeping very ill and frail older adults alive through medical advances.

Promoting Cognitive Skills in Later Life: Use It or Lose It

Changes in cognitive activity patterns might result in disuse and consequent atrophy of cognitive skills (de Frias & Dixon, 2014; Gordon, 2013). This concept is captured in the adage, "Use it or lose it." The mental activities that likely benefit the maintenance of cognitive skills in older adults are activities such as reading books, doing crossword puzzles, and going to lectures and concerts. "Use it or lose it" is also a significant component of the engagement model of cognitive optimization that emphasizes how intellectual and social engagement can buffer age-related declines in intellectual development (Park & Bischof, 2011; Park et al., 2014; Park & Reuter-Lorenz, 2009; Stine-Morrow & Basak, 2011). The following studies support the use it or lose it concept and the engagement model of cognitive optimization:

- An analysis of middle-aged and older adults who participated in the Victoria Longitudinal Study found that participation in intellectually engaging activities served as a buffer against cognitive decline (Hultsch et al., 1999). Additional analyses of the participants in this study revealed that engagement in cognitively complex activities was linked to faster and more consistent processing speed (Bielak et al., 2007). Another analysis of older adults over a 12-year period showed that those who reduced their cognitive lifestyle activities (such as using a computer, playing bridge) subsequently showed decline in cognitive functioning in verbal speed, episodic memory, and semantic memory (Small et al., 2012a). The decline in cognitive functioning was linked to subsequent lower engagement in social activities.
- A study revealed that reading daily was linked to reduced mortality in men in their seventies (Jacobs et al., 2008).
- In another study, 488 individuals aged 75 to 85 years were assessed for an average of five years (Hall et al., 2009). At the beginning of the research, the older adults indicated how often they participated in six activities—reading, writing, doing crossword puzzles, playing card or board games, having group discussions, and playing music—on a daily basis. Across the five years of the study, the point at which memory loss accelerated was assessed and it was found that for each additional activity the older adult engaged in, the onset of rapid memory loss was delayed by .18 years. For older adults who participated in 11 activities per week compared to their counterparts who engaged in only 4 activities per week, the point at which accelerated memory decline occurred was delayed by 1.29 years.

If cognitive skills are atrophying in late adulthood, can they be retrained? An increasing number of research studies indicate that they can to a degree (Bailey, Dunlosky, & Hertzog, 2014; Boron, Willis, & Schaie, 2007; Mayas et al., 2014; Willis & Caskie, 2013). Two main conclusions that can be derived from research are: (1) training can improve the cognitive skills of many older adults; but (2) there is some loss in plasticity in late adulthood (Baltes, Lindenberger, & Staudinger, 2006).

In an extensive study by Sherry Willis and her colleagues (2006), older adults were randomly assigned to one of four groups: those training in (1) reasoning, (2) memory, and (3) speed of processing; and (4) a control group that received no training. Each type of training showed an immediate effect in its domain—reasoning training improved reasoning, memory training improved memory, and speed of processing training improved speed of processing. However, the training effects did not transfer across cognitive domains, such that speed of processing training did not benefit the older adults' memory or reasoning, for example. The older adults who were given reasoning training did have less difficulty in the activities of daily living than a control group who did not receive this training. The activities of daily living that were assessed included how independently the older adults were able to prepare meals, do housework, do finances, go shopping, and engage in health maintenance. Each intervention maintained its effects on the specific targeted ability across the five years of the study. However, neither memory nor speed of processing training benefited the older adults' activities of daily living.

Another study of 60- to 90-year-olds found that sustained engagement in cognitively demanding, novel activities improved the older adults' episodic memory (Park et al., 2014). To produce this result, the older adults spent an average of 16.5 hours a week for three months learning how to quilt or how to use digital photography.

A meta-examination of four longitudinal observational studies (Long Beach Longitudinal Study; Origins of Variance in the Oldest-old [Octo-Twin] Study in Sweden; Seattle Longitudinal Study; and Victoria Longitudinal Study in Canada) of older adults' naturalistic cognitive activities found that changes in cognitive activity predicted cognitive outcomes as long as two decades later (Brown et al., 2012; Lindwall et al., 2012; Mitchell et al., 2012; Rebok et al., 2014). When older adults continued to increase their engagement in cognitive and physical activities, they were better able to maintain their cognitive functioning in late adulthood.

The Stanford Center for Longevity (2011) reported information based on a consensus of leading scientists in the field of aging. One of their concerns is the misinformation given to the public touting products to improve the functioning of the mind for which there is no scientific evidence. Nutritional supplements, games, and software products have all been advertised as "magic bullets" to slow the decline of mental functioning and improve the mental ability of older adults. Some of the claims are reasonable but not scientifically tested, while others are unrealistic and implausible. A research review of dietary supplements and cognitive aging did indicate that ginkgo biloba was linked with improvements in some aspects of attention in older adults, and that omega-3 polyunsaturated fatty acids (fish oil) was related to reduced risk of age-related cognitive decline (Gorby, Brownawell, & Falk, 2010). No evidence of cognitive improvements in aging adults who took supplements containing ginseng and glucose was evident in this review. On the other hand, an experimental study with 50- to 75-year-old females found that those who took fish oil for 26 weeks had improved executive function and beneficial effects on a number of areas of brain functioning compared with their female counterparts who took a placebo pill (Witte et al., 2014).

Overall, though, research has not provided consistent plausible evidence that dietary supplements can accomplish major cognitive goals in aging adults over a number of years. However, some software-based cognitive training games have been found to improve older adults' cognitive functioning (Hertzog et al., 2009; Lange et al., 2010; Nouchi et al., 2013). For example, a study of 60- to 85-year-olds found that a multitasking video game that simulates day-to-day driving experiences (NeuroRacer) improved cognitive control skills, such as sustained attention and working memory, after training on the video game and six months later (Anguera et al., 2013). Nonetheless, the training games may improve cognitive skills in a laboratory setting but not generalize to gains in the real world.

In sum, the cognitive vitality of older adults can be improved through cognitive and fitness training (Brown et al., 2012; Mitchell et al., 2012; Rebok et al., 2014; Wolinsky et al., 2013). Further research is needed to determine more precisely which cognitive improvements occur through cognitive and physical fitness training in older adults (Salthouse, 2013a, b).

Cognitive Neuroscience and Aging

On several occasions in this chapter, we have indicated that certain regions of the brain are involved in links between aging and cognitive functioning. Recall from Chapter 2 the substantial increase in interest in the brain's capacity to adapt to trauma, injury, and aging. The field of cognitive neuroscience has emerged as the major discipline that studies links between brain and cognitive functioning (Banuelos et al., 2014; Fletcher & Rapp, 2013; Reuter-Lorenz, 2013; Yuan & Raz, 2014). This field especially relies on brain imaging techniques, such as fMRI (functional magnetic resonance imaging), PET (positron emission tomography), and DTI (diffusion tensor imaging) to reveal the areas of the brain that are activated when individuals are engaging in certain cognitive activities (Leshikar & Duarte, 2014; Toepper et al., 2014). For example, as an older adult is asked to encode and then retrieve verbal materials or images of scenes, the individual's brain activity is monitored by an fMRI brain scan. Recall that in Chapter 15 we discussed how this technique was used by neuroscientists from the University of Montreal and the University of Wisconsin to investigate the impact of prayer and meditation on the brain, broadening the field of neuroscience to include neurospirituality or neurotheology.

Changes in the brain can influence cognitive functioning, and changes in cognitive functioning can influence the brain. For example, aging of the brain's prefrontal cortex may produce a decline in working memory (Reuter-Lorenz, 2013; Takeuchi et al., 2012; Toepper et al., 2014; Smith, 2007). And when older adults do not regularly use their working memory, neural connections in the prefrontal lobe may atrophy. (Recall the concept of "Use It or Lose It".) Further, cognitive interventions that activate older adults' working memory may increase these neural connections.

Although in its infancy as a field, the cognitive neuroscience of aging is beginning to uncover some important links between aging, the brain, and cognitive functioning (Antonenko & Floel, 2014; Ash & Rapp, 2014; Callaghan et al., 2014; Reuter-Lorenz, 2013; Steffener et al., 2014). These links include the following:

- *Neural circuits in specific regions of the brain's prefrontal cortex decline in older adults.* In addition, this decline is linked to poorer performance by older adults on complex reasoning tasks, working memory, and episodic memory tasks (Grady et al. 2006) (see Figure 17.11).

Figure 17.11

The Prefrontal Cortex

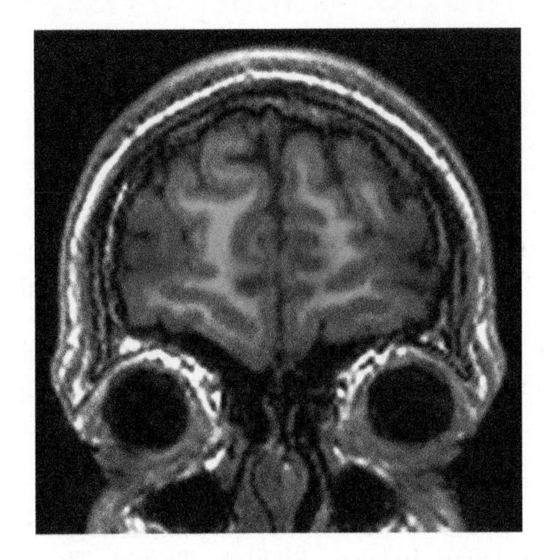

Courtesy of Dr. Sam Gilbert, Institute of Cognitive Neuroscience, UK

Advances in neuroimaging are allowing researchers to make significant progress in connecting changes in the brain with cognitive development. Shown here is an fMRI of the brain's prefrontal cortex. *What links have been found between the prefrontal cortex, aging, and cognitive development?*

- *Older adults are more likely than younger adults to use both hemispheres of the brain to compensate for aging declines in attention, memory, and language* (Dennis & Cabeza, 2008; Davis et al., 2012). Two neuroimaging studies revealed that older adults show better memory performance when both hemispheres of the brain are active in processing information (Angel et al., 2011; Manenti, Cotelli, & Miniussi, 2011).
- *Functioning of the hippocampus declines less than the functioning of the frontal lobes in older adults* (Antonenko & Floel, 2014). In K. Warner Schaie's (2013) research, individuals whose memory and executive function declined in middle age had more hippocampal atrophy in late adulthood, but those whose memory and executive function improved in middle age did not show a decline in hippocampal functioning in late adulthood.
- *Patterns of neural differences with age are larger for retrieval than encoding* (Gutchess et al., 2005). Age differences in neural activation are larger for recall than for recognition.
- *Compared with younger adults, older adults show greater activity in the frontal and parietal regions while they are engaging in tasks that require cognitive control processes such as attention* (Campbell et al., 2012). The findings suggest that distraction may interfere with memory for older adults.
- *Younger adults have better connectivity between brain regions than older adults* (Antonenko & Floel, 2014; Goh, 2011; Waring, Addis, & Kensinger, 2013). For example, a study revealed that younger adults have more connections

between brain activations in frontal, occipital, and hippocampal regions than older adults during a difficult encoding task (Leshikar et al., 2010).

- *An increasing number of cognitive and fitness-training studies include brain-imaging techniques, such as fMRI, to assess the results of this training on brain functioning* (Bherer, Erickson, & Liu-Ambrose, 2013; Kirk-Sanchez & McGough, 2014). In one study, older adults who walked one hour a day three days a week for six months showed increased volume in the frontal and temporal lobes of the brain (Colcombe et al., 2006).

Denise Park and Patricia Reuter-Lorenz (2009) proposed a neurocognitive scaffolding view of connections between the aging brain and cognition. In this view, increased activation in the prefrontal cortex with aging reflects an adaptive brain that is compensating for the challenges of declining neural structures and function, and declines in various aspects of cognition, including working memory and long-term memory. Scaffolding involves the use of complementary neural circuits to protect cognitive functioning in an aging brain. Among the factors that can strengthen brain scaffolding are cognitive engagement and exercise. In the next several decades, we are likely to see increased effort to uncover links among aging, the brain, and cognitive functioning.

To this point, we have discussed several ideas related to cognitive functioning in older adults. For a review, see the Reach Your Learning Outcomes section at the end of this chapter.

Meditation, Religion, and Spirituality in Late Adulthood

LO5 Explain the role of meditation, prayer, and spirituality in the lives of older adults.

In Chapter 15, we described meditation, religion, and spirituality with a special focus on middle age, including links to health and well-being. Here, we continue our exploration by describing its importance in the lives of many older adults.

In many societies around the world, the elderly are the spiritual leaders in their churches and communities. For example, Pope Francis, elected Pope of the Catholic Church in March 2013, was born in 1936; in fact, more popes have been elected in their eighties than any other 10-year period of the life-span. Similarly, the 14th Dalai Lama was born in 1935.

The religious patterns of older adults are being increasingly studied (George et al., 2013; Krause, 2012; Sun et al., 2012). Canada is home to virtually every major world faith or denomination including Aboriginal beliefs, Baha'i faith, Buddhism, Chinese religions, Christianity, Hinduism, Islam, Judaism, Sikhism, Taoism. The most popular religion is Christianity, and most Christians are Catholics. Religious attendance and affiliation have been declining, and Statistics Canada reports that about half of adult Canadians engage in religious activities on their own (Clark & Schellenberg, 2008). In 1971, only 5 percent of Canadians were unaffiliated with any religion; by 2011, the number had risen to 24 percent (The Canadian Encyclopedia, 2016). A longitudinal study found that religious service attendance is stable in middle adulthood, increases in late adulthood, then declines later in the older adult years (Hayward & Krause, 2013b).

Older adults who derive a sense of meaning in life from religion have higher levels of life satisfaction, self-esteem, and optimism. A research review concluded that individuals with a stronger spiritual/religious orientation are more likely to live longer (Lucchetti, Lucchetti, & Koenig. 2011).

Religion and spirituality can meet some important psychological needs in older adults, helping them to face impending death, to find and maintain a sense of meaningfulness in life, and to accept the inevitable losses of old age (George et al., 2013; Koenig, 2004). Socially, the religious community can serve many functions for older adults, such as social activities, social support, and the opportunity to assume teaching and leadership roles (Krause, 2012). A recent study revealed that over a period of seven years, older adults who attended church regularly increased the amount of emotional support they gave and received but decreased the amount of tangible support they gave and received (Hayward & Krause, 2013a).

Throughout the text you have read about many studies demonstrating the interconnection between health and well-being and lifestyle. Dr. Mario Beauregard of the Neuroscience Research Centre at the University of Montreal proposes that the examination of the impact of consciousness on the brain is revolutionizing modern scientific world views, as this research explores the connection between philosophy and science without proposing a religious dogma of any type. In other words, the next frontier of science is an exploration of the mind and consciousness (Beauregard, 2012; Raynauld, 2013).

Through neuroscience, researchers are examining the connection of prayer, meditation, and activities such as Tai Chi or Qigong on the brain, and are observing increases in neurotransmitters, such as serotonin and dopamine, both of which contribute to health and well-being. According to Dr. Herbert Benson, a cardiovascular specialist at Harvard Medical School and a pioneer in the field of mind/body medicine, the "relaxation response" occurs during periods of prayer and meditation. The body's metabolism decreases, the heart rate slows, blood pressure goes down, and we breathe more calmly and regularly (Schiffman, 2012). Andrew Newberg, another pioneer in the study of religious and spiritual experiences on the brain, believes that these studies can help fill the gap between traditional science and spiritual practices in very practical ways. Newberg finds activities such as meditation and prayer to be as fundamental to well-being as fitness training is to an athlete, regardless of their particular sport (Fowler & Rodd, 2013).

Richard Lam/The Canadian Press

During late adulthood, many individuals increasingly engage in prayer. *How might this be linked with longevity?*

To this point, we have discussed a number of ideas about the role of meditation, prayer, and spirituality in late adulthood. For a review, see the Reach Your Learning Outcomes section at the end of this chapter.

Reach Your **Learning Outcomes**

Longevity and Biological Theories of Aging

LO1 Describe longevity and the biological theories of aging.

Life Expectancy and Life Span	▪ Life expectancy refers to the number of years that probably will be lived by an average person born in a particular year. Life span is the maximum number of years any member of a species can live. ▪ Life expectancy has increased dramatically in economically-privileged regions. Life span, however, remains the same. ▪ An increasing number of people are living to be 100 years or older. ▪ Females live on average about six years longer than males do, likely due to biological and social factors; centenarian women outnumber men five to one. ▪ The health adjusted life expectancy indicator (HALE) measures the quality, not the quantity of life.

The Young Old, the Old Old, and the Oldest Old	▪ The young old are 65 to 74 years of age, the old old are 75 years and older, and the oldest old are 85 years and older. ▪ Significant numbers of the oldest old function effectively and are in good health. Negative stereotypes and social reactions, combined with decreased abilities, create challenges for people as they age. ▪ A number of experts believe that when the terms "young old," "old old," and "oldest old" are used, they should refer to functional age, not chronological age. Some 85-year-olds function far better than some 65-year-olds.
The Robust Oldest Old	▪ Early portraits of the oldest old were too negative; there is cause for optimism in the development of new regimens and interventions.
Biological Theories of Aging	▪ *Evolutionary Theory*: Natural selection has eliminated many of the of the harmful conditions to human life. ▪ *Cellular Clock Theory*: Hayflick proposed that cells can divide a maximum of about 75 to 80 times, and that as we age, our cells become less capable of dividing. In the last decade, scientists have found that telomeres likely are involved in explaining why cells lose their capacity to divide. ▪ *Free-Radical Theory*: People age because unstable oxygen molecules called free radicals are produced in cells. ▪ *Mitochondria Theory:* Aging is due to the decay of mitochondria. It appears that this decay is primarily due to oxidative damage and loss of critical micronutrients supplied by the cell. ▪ *Hormone Stress Theory:* Aging in the body's hormonal system can lower resilience to stress and increase the likelihood of disease.

The Course of Physical Development in Late Adulthood

LO2 Describe and give examples of how a person's brain and body change in late adulthood.

The Aging Brain	▪ The brain occupies less of the cranial cavity after 50 years of age. ▪ The aging brain retains considerable plasticity and adaptiveness. ▪ Growth of dendrites can take place in older adults. ▪ The brain has the capacity to virtually rewire itself to compensate for loss in older adults.
The Immune System	▪ A decline in immune system functioning with aging is well documented. ▪ Exercise can improve immune system functioning.
Physical Appearance and Move-ment	▪ The most obvious signs of aging are wrinkled skin and age spots on the skin. ▪ People get shorter as they age, and their weight often decreases after age 60 due to loss of muscle.
Sensory Development	▪ The visual system declines, but the vast majority of older adults can have their vision corrected so that they can continue to work and function in the world. ▪ Hearing decline often begins in middle age, but usually does not become much of an impediment until late adulthood. Hearing aids can diminish hearing problems for many older adults.

	▪ Smell and taste can decline, although the decline is minimal in healthy older adults. ▪ Changes in touch sensitivity are associated with aging, but this does not present a problem for most older adults. ▪ Sensitivity to pain decreases in late adulthood.
The Circulatory System and Lungs	▪ When heart disease is absent, the amount of blood pumped is the same, regardless of an adult's age. ▪ Treatment for cardiovascular diseases (CVD) has improved as a result of research, improved surgical procedures, drug therapies, and prevention programs. ▪ Lung capacity does drop, but older adults can improve lung functioning with diaphragm-strengthening exercises.
Sexuality	▪ Aging in late adulthood does include some changes in sexual performance, more for males than females. Nonetheless, there are no known age limits to sexual activity.

Physical and Mental Health and Wellness

LO3 **Identify factors of health and wellness in late adulthood.**

Health Problems	▪ As we age, our probability of disease or illness increases. ▪ Chronic disorders are rare in early adulthood, increase in middle adulthood, and become common in late adulthood. The most common chronic problem is arthritis. ▪ Nearly three-quarters of older adults die of heart disease, cancer, or stroke. ▪ Arthritis is especially common in older adults. ▪ Osteoporosis is the main reason why many older adults walk with a stoop; women are especially vulnerable. ▪ Accidents are usually more debilitating to older adults than to younger adults.
Exercise, Nutrition, and Weight	▪ The physical benefits of exercise have clearly been demonstrated in older adults. ▪ Aerobic exercise and weightlifting are both recommended if the adults are physically capable. ▪ Food restriction in animals can increase the animals' life span, but whether this works with humans is not known. In humans, being overweight is associated with an increased mortality rate. ▪ Most nutritional experts recommend a well-balanced, low-fat diet for older adults, but do not recommend an extremely low-calorie diet. ▪ Controversy focuses on whether vitamin supplements—especially the antioxidants, vitamin C, vitamin E, and beta-carotene—can slow the aging process and improve older adults' health.
The Nature of Mental Health in Late Adulthood	▪ Twenty percent of seniors in Canada have a mental illness, similar to that of other age groups, while 80 to 90 percent of seniors living in nursing homes are diagnosed with some form of mental illness. ▪ At least 10 percent of older adults have mental health problems sufficient to require professional help. ▪ Depression has been called the "common cold" of mental disorders. However, a majority of older adults with depressive symptoms never receive mental health treatment.

	▪ Older people who are lonely are more vulnerable to late onset alcoholism and substance abuse. ▪ Frequently depression and substance abuse are disregarded or go unnoticed.
Dementia, Alzheimer's Disease, and Related Disorders	▪ Dementia is a global term for any neurological disorder in which the primary symptoms involve a deterioration of mental functioning. ▪ Alzheimer's disease is by far the most common dementia. This progressive, irreversible disorder is characterized by gradual deterioration of memory, reasoning, language, and, eventually, physical functioning. ▪ Special efforts are being made to discover the causes of Alzheimer's and effective treatments for it. Some experts believe Alzheimer's disease is a puzzle with many pieces. ▪ Special brain scans, analysis of spinal fluids, and a sophisticated urine test are being used to detect Alzheimer's before its symptoms appear. ▪ Alzheimer's disease involves a predictable, progressive decline. ▪ An important concern is caring for Alzheimer's patients and the burdens this places on caregivers. ▪ In addition to Alzheimer's disease, other types of dementia are multi-infarct dementia and Parkinson's disease.
Health Promotion	▪ Although only 7 percent of adults over 65 reside in institutions, 32 percent of adults 85 and over do. The quality of nursing homes varies enormously. ▪ Simply giving nursing home residents options for control and teaching coping skills can change their behaviour and improve their health. ▪ The attitudes of both the health-care provider and the older adult patient are important aspects of the older adult's health care. Too often, health-care personnel share society's negative view of older adults.

Cognitive Functioning in Older Adults

LO4 **Describe the cognitive functioning of older adults.**

The Multi-Dimensional, Multi-Directional Nature of Cognition	▪ Baltes emphasizes a distinction between cognitive mechanics (the neurophysiological architecture, including the brain) and cognitive pragmatics (the culture-based software of the mind). ▪ Cognitive mechanics are more likely to decline in older adults than are cognitive pragmatics. ▪ Researchers have found that the speed of processing dimensions declines in older adults. ▪ In selective attention, older adults fare more poorly than younger adults in general, but when tasks are simple and sufficient practice is given, age differences are minimal. Likewise, for divided attention, on simple tasks adult age differences are minimal, but on difficult tasks older adults do worse than younger adults. ▪ Older adults perform as well as middle-aged and younger adults on measures of sustained attention. ▪ Younger adults have better episodic memory than older adults. ▪ Older adults have more difficulty retrieving semantic information, but they usually can retrieve it eventually.

	▪ Researchers have found declines in working memory and perceptual speed in older adults. ▪ Older adults are more likely to show a decline in explicit rather than in implicit memory. ▪ Prospective memory involves remembering what to do in the future; the relation of prospective memory to aging is complex. ▪ An increasing number of studies are finding that people's beliefs about memory play an important role in their memory performance, however some researchers are critical of these findings. ▪ Non-cognitive factors, such as health, education, and socio-economic status, are linked to memory in older adults. ▪ Wisdom is expert knowledge about the practical aspects of life that permits excellent judgments about important matters.
Education, Work, and Health: Links to Cognitive Functioning	▪ Successive generations of Canadians have been better educated. ▪ Education is positively correlated with scores on intelligence tests. Older adults may return to education for a number of reasons. ▪ Successive generations have had work experiences that include a stronger emphasis on cognitively-oriented labour. The increased emphasis on information processing in jobs likely enhances an individual's intellectual abilities. ▪ Poor health is related to decreased performance on intelligence tests in older adults. ▪ Exercise is linked to higher cognitive functioning in older adults.
Promoting Cognitive Skills in Later Life: Use It or Lose It	▪ Researchers are finding that older adults who engage in cognitive activities, especially challenging ones, have higher cognitive functioning than those who do not use their cognitive skills. ▪ Two main conclusions can be derived from research on training cognitive skills in older adults: (1) there is plasticity and training can improve the cognitive skills of many older adults; and (2) there is some loss in plasticity in late adulthood.
Cognitive Neuroscience and Aging	▪ The field of cognitive neuroscience is uncovering important links between aging, the brain, and cognitive functioning.

Meditation, Religion, and Spirituality in Late Adulthood

LO5 **Explain the role of meditation, religion, and spirituality in late adulthood.**

	▪ Many elderly people are spiritual leaders in their religious institutions and community. ▪ Research has found that meditation, religion, and practices in spirituality have a robust impact on the brain. Understanding the interconnection among these practices, the brain, and overall well-being is thought to be the new frontier of neuroscience.

review → connect → reflect

review

1. Identify and define the five biological theories of aging. LO1
2. What are some of physical changes that occur in late adulthood? LO2
3. Identify health problems that face older people and the impact these may have on caregivers. LO3
4. How does education impact aging? LO4
5. What role do meditation, religion, and spirituality play in late adulthood? LO5

connect

In this section, we learned that older adults fare better when they are given more responsibility and control in their lives. At what other age stages is giving individuals more responsibility and control particularly important for their development? In what ways?

reflect

Your Own Personal Journey of Life

What changes in your lifestyle now might help you age more successfully when you become an older adult?

CHAPTER 18

Socio-Emotional Development in Late Adulthood

CHAPTER OUTLINE

Theories of Socio-Emotional Development

LO1 Discuss four theories of socio-emotional development and aging and the social determinants of health.

- **Erikson's Theory**
- **Activity Theory**
- **Socio-Emotional Selectivity Theory**
- **Selective Optimization with Compensation Theory**
- **Social Determinants of Health**

Personality, the Self, and Society

LO2 Describe links between personality and mortality, and identify changes in the self and society in late adulthood.

- **Personality**
- **The Self**
- **Older Adults in Society**

Families and Social Relationships

LO3 Characterize the families and social relationships of aging adults.

- **The Aging Couple**
- **Older Adult Parents and Their Adult Children**
- **Grandparenting and Great-Grandparenting**
- **Friendship**
- **Fear of Victimization, Crime, and Elder Maltreatment**

Social Integration

LO4 Describe social supports and social integration, and understand how altruism, ethnicity, gender, and culture are linked to aging.

- **Social Support and Social Integration**
- **Altruism and Volunteerism**
- **Gender**
- **Ethnicity**
- **Culture**

Successful Aging

LO5 Explain how to age successfully.

"There's nothing pleasant in the realization that my time is running out.
I like it here.
In fact, I like almost everything about the place.
I've been here all my life.
Things fit."

From *Users Guide to a Blank Wall*, 2006, by Editions du Gref. Reprinted with permission.

—THOMAS SCOTT, CANADIAN POET, 2006

© Jonathan Kirn/Riser/Getty Images

The Honourable Michaëlle Jean

Kilpatrick Sean/Abaca/Newscom

The family of Canada's former Governor General, Michaëlle Jean, was one of thousands who fled Haiti during the 1960s to escape the repressive regime of Francois Duvalier or, as he is better known, Papa Doc. Papa Doc's regime was so tyrannical that, as a child, Michaëlle Jean experienced the effects of torture first hand. Her father, a teacher, was abducted and tortured; her uncle, Rene Depestre, a famous Haitian poet, went into exile in Cuba. Seeking asylum in Canada, the Jeans settled in Quebec.

Soon after immigrating to Canada, her parents' marriage fell apart and Michaëlle, her sister, and her mother moved into a basement apartment in Montreal. Although her mother had been a teacher in Haiti, here in Canada, she had to take menial jobs in order to pay the bills. Jean described her father as a "broken man" and bore witness to his abuse of her mother.

Jean studied languages and comparative literature at the University of Montreal, earning both bachelor's and master's degrees. Scholarships enabled her to continue her studies at three universities in Italy, and she is fluent in five languages. Concurrent with her studies, Jean worked in shelters for women and children who were victims of domestic violence and actively contributed to the establishment of a network of emergency shelters throughout Quebec and Canada. As well, she coordinated a study, published in 1987, that examined relationships in which women were the victims of sexual violence at the hands of their spouses.

Michaëlle Jean became a highly regarded journalist and anchor on radio and television. She won many awards, including a Gemini in 2001, as well as awards from The Human Rights League and Amnesty International. She, together with her husband, film director Jean Daniel Lafond, has made numerous documentaries including "Tropique Nord" (1994) about being black in Quebec, and Hot Docs award-winning "Haiti Dans Tous Nos Reves" in 1995. In 1999, they adopted an orphaned Haitian girl, Marie-Eden.

In 2005, Prime Minister Paul Martin named Michaëlle Jean the 27th Governor General of Canada. In her inauguration speech she said, "I know how precious that freedom is ... I, whose ancestors were slaves, who was born into a civilization long reduced to whispers and cries of pain, know something about its price, and I know too, what a treasure it is for us all." Jean brought the inspirational passion of her convictions to the role in an unprecedented and graceful way. For example, during her tenure as Governor General, she and her husband established The Michaëlle Jean Foundation, which is dedicated to supporting initiatives of underserved youth.

Five years later, on September 30, 2010, a few months after the catastrophic earthquake hit Haiti, Michaëlle Jean announced that she would step out of the viceregal role. In her farewell speech she said, "Breaking down solitudes, according to my motto, ending isolation and building on our desire to live together, these were and remain the objectives of the Governor General who stands before you today, a woman born in a country where the social foundations had collapsed, where power was exercised brutally to the detriment of all, a woman who was extraordinarily lucky to be able to pursue her dreams in a country where anything is possible, our country." Shortly after, she became UNESCO's special envoy in Haiti. Since then, Michaëlle Jean continues to give voice to justice and social issues through the arts. For more information about the range and scope of these activities, please visit http://www.fmjf.ca/en/

Michaëlle Jean once described Canada as "a country of enormous possibilities," and her life certainly reflects that belief (CBC News, 2010; Governor General Canada, 2014; University of Ottawa, 2014). Her legacy will continue for generations, and were she to reflect on her life, one might assume that she would do so with satisfaction, thereby, in Erikson's terms, facing her last stage with integrity.

Theories of Socio-Emotional Development

LO1 Discuss four theories of socio-emotional development and aging and the social determinants of health.

- **Erikson's Theory**
- **Activity Theory**
- **Socio-Emotional Selectivity Theory**
- **Selective Optimization with Compensation Theory**
- **Social Determinants of Health**

In this section we will look at the main theories of socio-emotional development that focus on late adulthood: Erikson's theory, activity theory, socio-emotional selectivity theory, and selective optimization with compensation theory. We also examine social determinants of health.

Erikson's Theory

We initially described Erik Erikson's (1968) eight stages of the human life span in Chapter 1, and as we explored different periods of development, we have examined the stages in more detail. Here we will discuss his final stage.

Integrity versus despair is Erikson's eighth and final stage of development, which individuals experience during late adulthood. This involves reflecting on the past and piecing together either a positive or negative review. Through many different routes, the older adult may have developed a positive outlook in each of the preceding periods. If so, retrospective glances and reminiscences will reveal a picture of a life well spent, and the older adult will be satisfied (integrity). However, if the older adult resolved one or more of the earlier stages in a negative way (being socially isolated in early adulthood or stagnated in middle adulthood, for example), retrospective glances about the total worth of his or her life might be negative (despair). Figure 18.1 portrays how positive resolutions of Erikson's eight stages can culminate in wisdom and integrity for older adults.

Life Review

Life review is prominent in Erikson's final stage of *integrity versus despair*. Life review involves looking back at one's life experiences, evaluating them, interpreting them, and often reinterpreting them (George, 2010; Robitaille et al., 2010). A leading expert on aging, Robert Butler, provides this perspective on life review: "... there are chances for pain, anger, guilt, and grief, but there are also opportunities for resolution and celebration, for affirmation and hope, for reconciliation and personal growth" (Butler, 2007, p. 72).

Figure 18.1

Erikson's View of How Positive Resolution of the Eight Stages of the Human Life Span Can Culminate in Wisdom and Integrity in Old Age

From "Erikson's View…Conflict and Resolution: Culmination in Old Age." Copyright © 1988 by *The New York Times*. Reprinted by permission. Photo: © Bettmann/Getty Images

In Erikson's view, each stage of life is associated with a particular psychosocial conflict and a particular resolution. In this chart, Erikson describes how the issues from each of the earlier stages can mature into the many facets of integrity and wisdom in old age. Erikson is shown in this photo with his wife Joan, an artist.

Butler (2007) states that the life review is set in motion as the person looks forward in time and realizes that death is not that far away. Sometimes the life review proceeds quietly; at other times it is intense, requiring considerable work to achieve some sense of personality integration. These thoughts may continue to emerge in brief, intermittent spurts or become essentially continuous. One 76-year-old man commented, "My life is in the back of my mind. It can't be any other way. Thoughts of the past play on me. Sometimes I play with them, encouraging and savouring them; at other times I dismiss them."

Life reviews can include socio-cultural dimensions, such as culture, ethnicity, and gender. Life reviews also can include interpersonal, relationship dimensions, including sharing and intimacy with family members or a friend (Cappeliez & O'Rourke, 2006). And life reviews can include personal dimensions, which might involve the creation and discovery of meaning and coherence. These personal dimensions might unfold in such a way that the pieces do or do not make sense to the older adult. In the final analysis, each person's life review is unique.

As the past marches by in review, the older adult surveys it, observes it, and reflects on it. Reconsideration of previous experiences and their meaning occurs, often with revision or expanded understanding taking place. This reorganization of the past may provide a more valid picture for the individual, providing new and significant meaning to one's life. It may also help prepare the individual for and reduce fear of death (Cappeliez, O'Rourke, & Chaudhury, 2005).

One aspect of life review involves identifying and reflecting on not only the positive aspects of one's life, but also on regrets as part of developing a mature wisdom and self-understanding (Choi & Jun, 2009). The hope is that by examining not only the positive aspects of one's life, but also what an individual has regretted doing, a more accurate vision of the complexity of one's life and possibly increased life satisfaction will be attained (King & Hicks, 2007).

The following is a sampling of recent studies on regrets in older adults:

- For low-income older adults, regrets about education, careers, and marriage are common, but the intensity of regrets is greater for finance/money, family conflict and children's problems, loss and grief, and health (Choi & Jun, 2009). Common indications of pride involve children and parenting, careers, volunteering/informal caregiving, having a long/strong marriage, and personal growth.

- Making downward social comparisons, such as "I'm better off than most people," is linked to a reduction in the intensity of regrets in older adults (Bauer, Wrosch, & Jobin, 2008).
- Following the death of a loved one, resolving regrets is related to lower depression and improved well-being (Torges, Stewart, & Nolen-Hoeksema, 2008). In this study, older adults were more likely to resolve their regrets than were younger adults.

Some clinicians use reminiscence therapy with their older clients. Reminiscence therapy involves discussing past activities and experiences with another individual or group (Peng et al., 2009). The therapy may include the use of photographs, familiar items, and video/audio recordings. Researchers have found that reminiscence therapy improves the mood of older adults (Fiske, Wetherell, & Gatz, 2009). In fact, one study of institutionalized older adults revealed that reminiscence therapy increased their life satisfaction and decreased their depression and loneliness (Chiang et al., 2010).

Robert Peck's Reworking of Erikson's Final Stage

Robert Peck (1968) reworked Erikson's final stage of development, *integrity versus despair,* by describing three developmental tasks, or issues, that men and women face when they age.

Differentiation versus role preoccupation is Peck's developmental task in which older adults must redefine their worth in terms of something other than work roles. Adjustment to retirement involves identifying with new roles and quite often requires an adjustment in relationships as well. Peck believes older adults need to pursue a set of valued activities so that time previously spent in an occupation and with children can be filled.

Body transcendence versus body preoccupation is Peck's developmental task in which older adults must cope with declining physical well-being. As older adults age, they may experience a chronic illness and considerable deterioration in their physical capabilities. For men and women whose identity has revolved around their physical well-being, the decrease in health and deterioration of physical capabilities may present a severe threat to their identity and feelings of life satisfaction. However, while most older adults experience illnesses, many enjoy life through human relationships that allow them to go beyond a preoccupation with their aging body.

Ego transcendence versus ego preoccupation is Peck's developmental task in which older adults must recognize that although death is inevitable and probably not too far away, they feel at ease with themselves. They realize that they have contributed to the future through the competent rearing of their children or through their vocation and ideas.

Activity Theory

Activity theory states that the more active and involved older adults are, the more likely they will be satisfied with their lives. Activity theory suggests that many individuals will achieve greater life satisfaction if they continue their middle-adulthood roles into late adulthood. If these roles are stripped from them (as in early retirement), it is important that they find substitute roles that keep them active and involved.

Researchers since the 1960s have been finding strong support for activity theory (Bielak et al., 2014; Morrow-Howell et al., 2014; Neugarten, Havighurst, & Tobin, 1968; Phillips, Wojcicki, & McAuley, 2013; Solberg et al., 2014). Studies indicate that when older adults are active, energetic, and productive, they age more successfully and happily than if they disengage. A study found that older adults are happiest when they combine effortful social, physical, cognitive, and household activities with restful activities (Oerlemans, Bakker, & Veenhoven, 2011). Another recent study of Canadian older adults revealed that those who are more physically active have higher life satisfaction and greater social interaction than their physically inactive counterparts (Azagba & Sharaf, 2014).

Socio-Emotional Selectivity Theory

Socio-emotional selectivity theory states that older adults become more selective about their social networks. Because they place a high value on emotional satisfaction, older adults often spend more time with familiar individuals with whom they have had rewarding relationships. Developed by Laura Carstensen (1998, 2006, 2008, 2009; Carstebseb et al., 2011), this theory argues that older adults deliberately withdraw from social contact with individuals peripheral to their lives, while they maintain or increase contact with close friends and family members with whom they have had enjoyable relationships. This selective narrowing of social interaction maximizes positive emotional experiences and minimizes emotional risks as individuals become older.

Socio-emotional selectivity theory challenges the stereotype that the majority of older adults are in emotional despair because of their social isolation (Carstensen & Fried, 2012). Rather, older adults consciously choose to decrease the total number of their social contacts in favour of spending increasing time in emotionally rewarding interaction with friends and family. That is, they systematically hone their social networks so that available social partners satisfy their emotional needs.

Research to support socio-emotional selectivity differs in the composition of social networks. Longitudinal studies reveal far smaller social networks for older adults than for younger adults (Charles & Carstensen, 2010; Wrzus et al., 2013). A recent study of individuals from 18 to 94 years of age found that with increasing age, individuals have fewer peripheral social contacts but retain close relationships with people who provide them with emotional support (English & Carstensen, 2014b).

Socio-emotional selectivity theory also focuses on the types of goals that individuals are motivated to achieve (Biggs, Carstensen, & Hogan, 2012; Carstensen et al., 2011). It states that two important classes of goals are (1) knowledge-related and (2) emotional. This theory emphasizes that the trajectory of motivation for knowledge-related goals starts relatively high in the early years of life, peaking in adolescence and early adulthood, and then declining in middle and late adulthood (see Figure 18.2). The emotion trajectory is high during infancy and early childhood, declines from middle childhood through early adulthood, and increases in middle and late adulthood.

Figure 18.2

Idealized Model of Socio-Emotional Selectivity through the Life Span

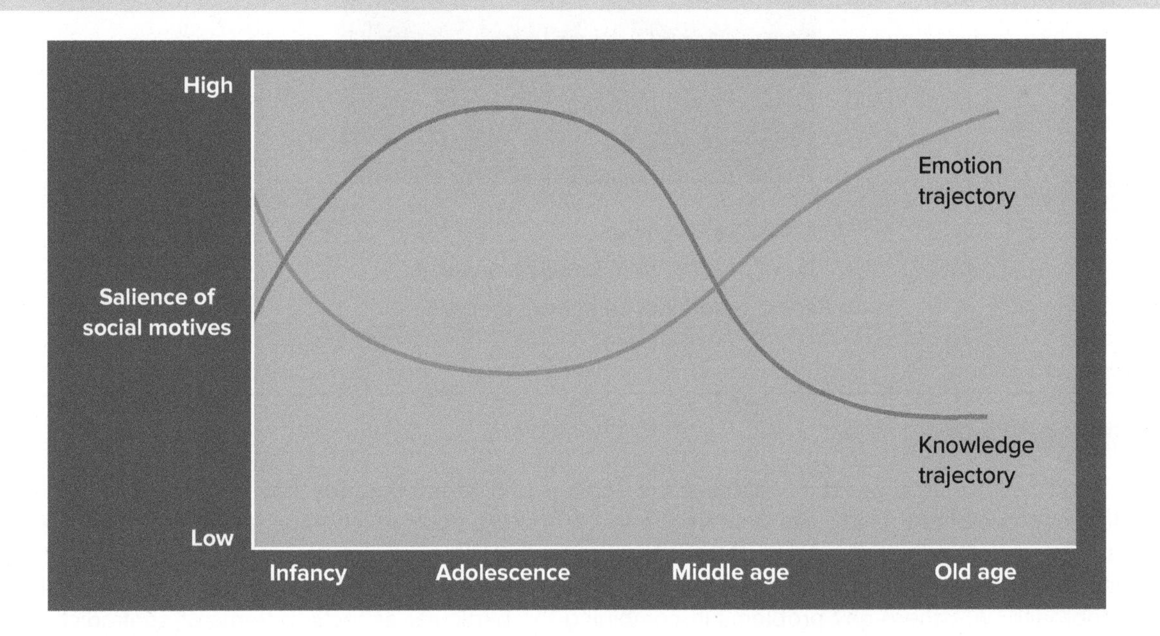

From L. Carstensen, et al., "The Social Context of Emotion" in the *Annual Review of Geriatrics and Gerontology* by Schaie/Lawton, 1997, Vol.17, p.331. Used by permission of Springer Publishing Company, New York, 10012.

According to Carstensen's theory of socio-emotional selectivity, the motivation to reach knowledge-related and emotion-related goals changes across the life span.

One of the main reasons given for these changing trajectories in knowledge-related and emotion-related goals involves the perception of time (Carstensen, 2006; Carstensen et al., 2011). When time is perceived as open-ended, as it is when individuals are younger, people are more strongly motivated to pursue information, even at the cost of emotional satisfaction. But as older adults perceive that they have less time left in their lives, they are motivated to spend more time pursuing emotional satisfaction. Regardless of age and culture, people's perspectives change when faced with mortality. Gaining a sense of how finite your time on this planet may be is key to understanding what matters most in life. When time is open-ended, as with most young people, the knowledge-related goals are prioritized. When time is perceived as limited, then social goals take priority (Kaszniak & Menchola, 2012).

In general, the feelings of older adults mellow. Emotional life is on a more even keel, with fewer highs and lows than young adults. It may be that although older adults have less extreme joy, they have more contentment, especially when they are connected in positive ways with friends and family. Older adults react less to negative circumstances, are better at ignoring irrelevant negative information, and remember more positive than negative information (Mather, 2012).

One study revealed that positive emotion increases and negative emotion (except for sadness) decreases from 50 years of age through the mid-eighties (Stone et al., 2010). In this study, a pronounced decline in anger occurred from the early twenties, and sadness was essentially unchanged from the early twenties through the mid-eighties. Another study found that aging is linked to more positive overall well-being and greater emotional stability (Carstensen et al., 2011). In addition, adults who experienced more positive than negative emotions were more likely to remain alive over a 13-year period. Other research also indicates that happier people live longer (Frey, 2011). A recent study of individuals from 22 to 93 years of age explored emotional experiences in the mornings and evenings (English & Carstensen, 2014a). Older adults reported experiencing more positive emotions than younger adults at both times of the day. Thus, the emotional life of older adults is more positive than stereotypes suggest (Lynchard & Radvansky, 2012; Carstensen & Fried, 2012; Yeung, Wong, & Lok, 2011).

Next, we explore a recently proposed theory that, like socio-emotional selectivity theory, focuses on what is necessary for the realization of developmental goals.

Ryan McVay/Getty Images

What are the main ideas involved in socio-emotional selectivity theory?

critical thinking

An eclectic view would suggest that we take the portions of different theories that are applicable to a given situation and combine them to assist someone to live a more positive life experience. From the theories about aging described in this portion of the chapter, construct an approach to successfully understand the current situation of someone you know who is over 65. Which elements of which theories did you take for your approach? Are there any problems in combining the particular aspects in terms of contradictions in advice to the aging person?

Selective Optimization with Compensation Theory

Selective optimization with compensation theory states that successful aging is linked to three main factors: selection, optimization, and compensation (SOC). The theory describes how people can produce new resources and allocate them effectively to the tasks they want to master (Freund, Nikitin, & Riediger, 2013; Riediger, Li, & Lindenberger, 2006; Staudinger & Jacobs, 2010). *Selection* is based on the concept that older adults have a reduced capacity and loss of functioning, which require a reduction in performance in most life domains. *Optimization* suggests that it is possible to maintain performance in some areas through continued practice and the use of new technologies. *Compensation* becomes relevant when life tasks require a level of capacity beyond the current level of the older adult's performance potential. Older adults especially need to compensate in circumstances with high mental or physical demands, such as when thinking about and memorizing new material very fast, reacting quickly when driving a car, or running fast. When older adults develop an illness, the need for compensation is obvious.

Paul Baltes and his colleagues proposed the selective optimization with compensation theory (Baltes, 2003; Baltes, Lindenberger, & Staudinger, 2006). They describe the life of the late Arthur Rubinstein to illustrate their theory. When he was interviewed at 80 years of age, Rubinstein said that three factors were responsible for his ability to maintain his status as an admired concert pianist into old age. First, he mastered the weakness of old age by reducing the scope of his performances and playing fewer pieces (which reflects *selection*). Second, he spent more time practising than he had earlier in his life (which reflects *optimization*). Third, he used special strategies, such as slowing down before fast segments, thus creating the impression of faster playing (which reflects *compensation*).

The process of selective optimization with compensation is likely to be effective whenever people pursue successful outcomes (Hutchinson & Nimrod, 2012; Freund, Nikitin, & Riediger, 2013; Staudinger & Jacobs, 2010). What makes SOC attractive to aging researchers is that it makes explicit how individuals can manage and adapt to losses. By using SOC, they can continue to live satisfying lives, although in a more restrictive manner. Loss is a common dimension of old age, although there are wide variations in the nature of the losses involved. Because of this individual variation, the specific form of selection, optimization, and compensation likely will vary depending on the person's life history, pattern of interests, values, health, skills, and resources.

In Baltes's view (2003; Baltes, Lindenberger, & Staudinger, 2006), the selection of domains and life priorities is an important aspect of development. Life goals and priorities likely vary across the life course for most people. For many individuals, it is not just the sheer attainment of goals, but rather the attainment of meaningful goals that makes life satisfying.

In one cross-sectional study, the personal life investments of 25- to 105-year-olds were assessed (Staudinger, 1996) (see Figure 18.3). From 25 to 34 years of age, participants said that they personally invested more time in work, friends, family, and independence, in that order. From 35 to 54 and 55 to 65 years of age, family became more important than friends to them in terms of their personal investment. Little changed in the rank ordering of persons 70 to 84 years old, but for participants 85 to 105 years old, health became the most important personal investment. Thinking about life showed up for the first time on the most important list for those who were 85 to 105 years old.

Figure 18.3

Degree of Personal Life Investment at Different Points in Life

Ryan McVay/Getty Images; © Image100/PunchStock; © Image Source/Getty Images; © Corbis; © Image Source/ Getty Images

Shown here are the top four domains of personal life investment at different points in life. The highest degree of investment is listed at the top (for example, work was the highest personal investment from 25 to 34 years of age, family from 35 to 84, and health from 85 to 105).

Social Determinants of Health

Our living conditions play a major role in health. Determinants such as income, education, social inclusion, and housing figure significantly in the health of all, and late adulthood is no exception (Davis, 2011). Poverty factors into each determinant for the young and for those in late adulthood. Among seniors, home ownership is the single most important asset; however, most low-income seniors are renters, and their rent may take up more than 40 percent of their total expenditures. Food accounts for another 20 percent, leaving 40 percent for everything else—transportation, utilities, Internet access, telephone, health care, entertainment, and so on. Those living in urban areas are more hard pressed as rents are higher (National Seniors Council, 2011). As well as contributing to material deprivation, and psychological stress, unemployment often is a pathway to poor health, including depression, anxiety, and increased suicide rates (Mikkonen & Raphael, 2010). Each province has initiated policies in an effort to reduce poverty, yet the problem persists. The economic downturn has further exacerbated the issue.

Fortunately, most seniors are relatively healthy and often are providing care in the form of grandparenting activities for their children. However, as the population ages, and more become seniors—and do so often with less financial security in the form of pensions than today—elder care looms as a major policy issue for both the provinces/territories and the federal government.

To this point, we have studied a number of theories of socio-emotional development that pertain to late adulthood. For a review, see the Reach Your Learning Outcomes section at the end of this chapter.

Personality, the Self, and Society

LO2 Describe links between personality and mortality, and identify changes in the self and society in late adulthood.

- **Personality**
- **The Self**
- **Older Adults in Society**

Is personality linked to mortality in older adults? Do self-perceptions and self-control change in late adulthood? How are older adults perceived and treated by society?

Personality

We described the "big five" factors of personality in Chapter 16, "Socio-Emotional Development in Middle Adulthood." Researchers have found that several of the big five factors of personality continue to change in late adulthood. For example, in one study, conscientiousness continued to develop in late adulthood (Roberts, Donnellan, & Hill, 2013), and in another study older adults were more conscientious and agreeable than middle-aged and younger adults (Allemand, Zimprich, & Hendriks, 2008).

A longitudinal study of more than 1200 individuals across seven decades revealed that the big five personality factor of conscientiousness predicted higher mortality risk from childhood through late adulthood (Martin, Friedman, & Schwartz, 2007). A higher level of conscientiousness has been linked to living a longer life than the other four factors (Hill et al., 2011; Iwasa et al., 2008; Wilson et al., 2004).

Following are the results of two other recent studies of the big five factors in older adults:

- The transition into late adulthood is characterized by increases in these aspects of conscientiousness: impulse control, reliability, and conventionality (Jackson et al., 2009)
- Perceived social support predicts increased conscientiousness in older adults (Hill et al., 2014).
- More severe depression in older adults is associated with higher neuroticism and lower extraversion and conscientiousness (Koorevaar et al., 2013).
- Elevated neuroticism, lower conscientiousness, and lower openness are related to an increased risk of older adults developing Alzheimer's disease across a period of six years (Duberstein et al., 2011).

Affect and outlook on life are also linked to mortality in older adults (Carstensen et al., 2011). Older adults characterized by negative affect don't live as long as those who display more positive affect, and optimistic older adults who have a positive outlook on life live longer than their counterparts who are more pessimistic and have a negative outlook on life (Mosing et al., 2012).

The Self

Our exploration of the self focuses on changes in self-esteem and self-acceptance. In Chapter 12, we described how self-esteem drops in adolescence, especially for girls. How does self-esteem change in the adult years?

Self-Esteem

Self-esteem increases in the twenties, levels off in the thirties and forties, rises considerably in the fifties and sixties, and then drops significantly in the seventies and eighties (see Figure 18.4). Through most of the adult years, the self-esteem of males is higher than the self-esteem of females. However, in the seventies and eighties, the self-esteem of males and females converge.

Figure 18.4

Changes in Self-acceptance across the Adult Years

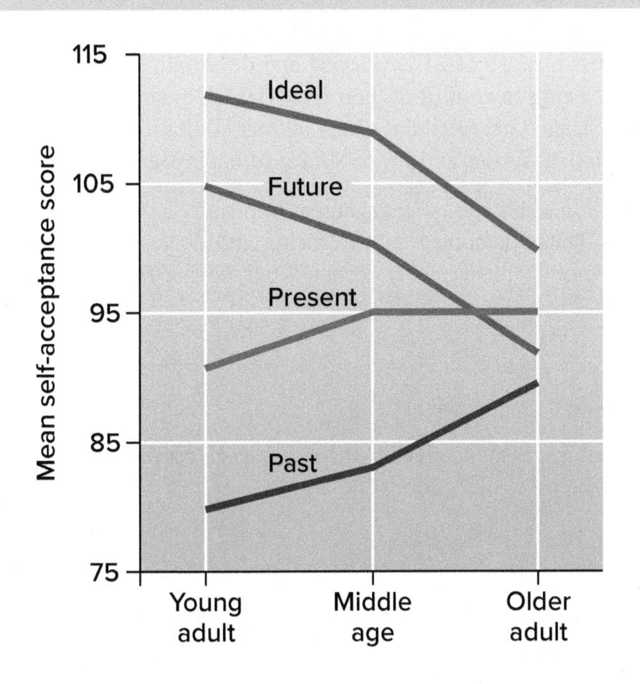

Cite Will come

Acceptance of ideal and future selves decreases with age, acceptance of past selves increases with age, and acceptance of present selves increases slightly in middle age and then levels off.

Why might self-esteem decline in older adults? Explanations include deteriorating physical health and negative societal attitudes toward older adults, although these factors were not examined in the large-scale study just described. Researchers have found that in late adulthood, being widowed, institutionalized, or physically impaired, having a low religious commitment, and experiencing a decline in health are linked to low self-esteem (Giarrusso & Bengtson, 2007).

Although older adults may derive self-esteem from earlier successes in some domains, such as work and family, some aspects of their lives require continued support for self-esteem (Smith, 2009). For example, older adults' self-esteem benefits when they are told they are nice and accepted by others. A recent study revealed that older adults have higher self-esteem when they have a youthful identity and more positive personal experiences (Westerhof, Whitbourne, & Freeman, 2012). And another recent study also found that older adults with higher self-esteem are more likely to be characterized by successful aging factors (Cha, Seo, & Sok, 2012). Boosting self-esteem has also been found to buffer health issues in late adulthood (Liu & Wrosch, 2014).

Self-Acceptance

Another aspect of the self that changes across the adult years is self-acceptance. Self-acceptance is related to possible selves; that is, what individuals might become, what they would like to become, and what they are afraid of becoming (Hoppmann & Smith, 2007). As shown in Figure 18.4, young and middle-aged adults show greater acceptance of their ideal and future selves than their present and past selves. However, in older adults there is little difference in acceptance of various selves because of decreased acceptance of ideal and future selves and increased acceptance of past selves (Ryff, 1991).

One study of older adults (mean age of 81) revealed that hope-related activities have a more positive effect and a higher probability of survival over a 10-year period (Hoppmann et al., 2007). Also in this study, hoped-for selves were linked to more likely participation in these domains. Another study of older adults 70- to 100-plus years found that over time, 72 percent of the older adults added new domains of hope and 53 percent added new fears (Smith & Freund, 2002). In this study, hopes and fears about health were reported more often than ones related to family and social relationships. Also, for some individuals, as middle-aged adults, their possible selves centre on attaining hoped-for selves, such as acquiring material possessions, but as older adults, they become more concerned with maintaining what they have and preventing or avoiding health problems and dependency (Smith, 2009).

Self-Control

Although older adults are aware of age-related losses, most still effectively maintain a sense of self-control (Lewis, Todd, & Xu, 2011). A recent survey across a range of 21 developed and developing countries revealed that a majority of adults in their sixties and seventies report being in control of their lives (HSBC Insurance, 2007). In developed countries such as Denmark, Canada, the United States, and Great Britain, adults in their sixties and seventies said they have more control over their lives than their counterparts in their forties and fifties. Older adults in Denmark reported the highest self-control.

Self-control plays an important role in older adults' engagement in healthy activities. A recent study of 65- to 92-year-olds found that self-control is linked to better outcomes for well-being and depression following a six-week program of yoga (Bonura & Tennenbaum, 2014). Another recent study revealed that self-control is a key factor in older adults' physical activity levels (Franke et al., 2014).

Older Adults in Society

How do the challenges and transitions associated with income, work, retirement, technology, social media, and living conditions affect the lives and well-being of older adults?

Income

Many older adults are understandably concerned about their income (Holden & Hatcher, 2006; Mikkonen & Raphael, 2010). University of British Columbia economist Kevin Milligan (2008) found a significant drop in the number of elderly people living in poverty between the 1970s and the early 2000s (see also Myles & Picot, 2000); however, the Vanier Institute reports that many seniors are outliving their savings, and this, in part is due to the fact that we are living longer. At the same time, Statistics Canada reported that in 2012, 55 percent more seniors were in debt when they retired than in 1999 (Statistics Canada, 2014).

The improvement of pension funds, both government (Canada Pension Plan and Old Age Security) and private (RRSPs) accounts for retirement security. In 2012, the median income for those senior couples with the highest wage-earner being over 65 years, was $52 300. By contrast, the median income for unattached seniors was $25 000 (Statistics Canada, 2014). While the after-tax median incomes are significantly higher than they were a decade ago, Milligan (2008) noted that people aged 55 to 64 who are struggling financially are more likely to experience poverty after age 64. As well, poverty rates among racialized groups are higher than non-racialized groups (Statistics Canada, 2014; Mikkonen & Raphael, 2010).

The income gap between senior men and women closed significantly during the last two decades of the twentieth century, due largely to the increased participation by women in the paid workforce. With increased participation, more women became eligible for the Canadian Pension Plan or the Quebec Pension Plan (CPP/QPP), private pension plans through their employers, and their own retirement savings plans. Having a higher income level allows people to contribute maximum amounts to pensions; thus low income earners in mid-life are less likely to contribute, and therefore will not have access to these pensions later in life.

In 2006, 5.4 percent of people aged 65 and older in Canada lived on what is called a "low income," which indicates they did not have enough money to meet expected monthly expenditures (National Seniors Council, 2011). This number spiked following the economic downturn of 2008 (Friesen, 2010). Living with a partner reduced the chance of living on a low income to an estimated 6.2 percent in 2012, up from 1.4 percent prior to the economic downturn of 2009. During the same period, unattached individuals living at poverty levels rose from 15.5 to 28.5 percent. The median incomes for all Aboriginal peoples continues to fall significantly below of that of the mainstream Canadian population (Mikkonen & Raphael, 2010; Statistics Canada, 2014).

Poverty among seniors poses an additional source of stress for their children who may be trying to ensure their parents have their basic needs met. This trend is particularly hard on new Canadians, many of whom have sponsored their parents to join them in Canada. This concern is especially pronounced in metropolitan areas, such as Montreal, Toronto, and Vancouver (Friesen, 2010). Those most at risk are those who have worked fewer than 10 years, recent immigrants, and Aboriginal peoples (NRC, 2011).

It is important to note that The Conference Board of Canada (2013) reported that poverty among seniors in Canada is one of the lowest in the world. When compared to other countries, Canada ranks number 3. The Netherlands ranks number 1, with an elderly poverty rate of 1.7 percent, whereas in Australia nearly 40 percent of the elderly live in poverty. Both the Netherlands and Canada have universal pension plans. The Conference Board also notes that those most vulnerable are widows over the age of 75, largely due to pension allowances linked to employment history (Conference Board of Canada, 2013). In spite of this, Statistics Canada (2012) reports that 42.5 percent of people over age 65 are in debt, an increase of 55 percent since 1999.

Work and Retirement

What percentage of older adults continue to work? How productive are they? Who adjusts best to retirement? What is the changing pattern of retirement in Canada and around the world? These are some of the questions we will now examine.

The trend toward early retirement evident in the 1990s, when workers appeared to be retiring in their fifties, has reversed. Now, for a variety of reasons such as staying connected to a social network or adding to their financial resources, seniors are increasingly remaining active in the workplace. In fact, work-force participation for seniors has more than doubled from 6.0 percent in 2000 to 13 percent in 2013 (Government of Canada, 2015).

This new trend is creating an important change in older adults' work patterns: working part-time after retiring (Hardy, 2006; Schellenberg & Ostrovsky, 2008b). As noted earlier, mandatory retirement practices and policies are no longer legal as they were found to be discriminatory, and therefore inconsistent with the *Charter of Rights*. In 2012, amendments to the *Canadian Human Rights Act* and the *Canadian Labour Code* prohibited federally-regulated employers from setting a mandatory retirement age unless factors of age such as agility, eyesight, or strength prevent an individual from meeting an occupational requirement (Government of Canada, 2013). Prior to this change, in all sectors of government occupations (with the exclusion of elected officials) and in many organizations and businesses, maintaining employment after age 65 was very difficult. However, Schellenberg and Ostrovsky (2008b) state that most Canadians still set the age of 65 as their retirement mark.

The Special Senate Committee on Aging (2009) heard evidence that most Canadian workers retire before their ability to work is impaired. Cognitive ability is one of the best predictors of job performance in the elderly. Older workers have lower rates of absenteeism, fewer accidents, and increased job satisfaction, compared with their younger counterparts (Warr, 2004). This means that the older worker can be of considerable value to a company, above and beyond the older worker's cognitive competence. Also, recall from our discussion earlier in the chapter that substantively complex work is linked to a higher level of intellectual functioning (Schooler, 2007). This likely is a reciprocal relation; that is, individuals with higher cognitive ability likely continue to work as older adults, and when they work in substantively complex jobs, this likely enhances their intellectual functioning.

An increasing number of middle-aged and older adults are embarking on a second or third career (Moen & Spencer, 2006). In some cases, this is an entirely different type of work or a continuation of previous work but at a reduced level. Employed seniors are more likely to be self-employed: 45 percent of employed seniors report being self-employed compared with 12 percent of people aged 15 to 64 (Duchesne, 2004). In addition, many older adults also participate in unpaid work, as volunteers or active participants in voluntary associations. These options provide older adults with opportunities for productive activity, social interaction, and a positive identity.

RETIREMENT IN CANADA AND OTHER COUNTRIES

The retirement option for older workers is a late-twentieth-century phenomenon in North America (Atchley, 2007). During the economic recession in the 1990s, many older workers were encouraged to take early retirement (before age 65) to reduce the number of layoffs among younger workers or to cut operating costs for struggling organizations. The median retirement age in Canada for 2005 was 62.6 for men and 60 for women (Turcotte & Schellenberg, 2007). The decades following World War II saw the beginning of several pension plans, both private and government-initiated. University of Toronto economist Michael Baker notes that to draw on the maximum benefit of government pensions, people ought to retire at age 60, for later retirement results in a loss.

For those who choose to retire, the number one reason is that it has become financially possible to leave work (Turcotte & Schellenberg, 2007). In cases where people leave involuntarily, poor health accounts for 44 percent of the retirements, compared with 20 percent of the voluntary retirements. Some retirees would continue working if they could reduce the number of days or hours they work, and if it didn't affect the pension they would receive when they fully retire.

ADJUSTMENT TO RETIREMENT

Much of our identity is tied to the work we do. For example, a nurse, teacher, or electrician has internalized his or her profession into their sense of self; therefore, retirement is a process, not an event (Moen, 2007). Not surprisingly, research has found that people with higher incomes and good physical and emotional health adjust to retirement more successfully than those who are ill and have the burden of trying to make ends meet (Donaldson, Earl, & Muratore, 2010). As noted above, retirees who adjust best to retirement are healthy, have adequate income, are active, are better educated, have an extended social network including both friends and family, and usually were satisfied with their lives before they retired (Raymo & Sweeney, 2006; Turcotte & Schellenberg, 2007). Older adults with inadequate income and poor health, and who must adjust to other stress that occurs at the same time as retirement, such as the death of a spouse, have the most difficult time adjusting to retirement (Reichstadt et al., 2007).

Flexibility is also a key factor in whether individuals adjust well to retirement (Baehr & Barnett, 2007). A recent study also found that individuals who had difficulty adjusting to retirement had a strong attachment to work, including full-time jobs and a long work history, lack of control over the transition to retirement, and low self-efficacy (van Solinge & Henkens, 2005). Many seniors are returning to school as many colleges and universities have either lowered or waived tuition costs for seniors; as well, many are returning to the workforce in some capacity.

Planning and then successfully carrying out the plan is an important aspect of adjusting well in retirement. A special concern in retirement planning involves women, who are likely to live longer than men and more likely to live alone (less likely to remarry and more likely to be widowed) (Moen, 2007). About two-thirds of Canadians do make financial plans for retiring during their work life, but this planning takes many forms and has varying degrees of thoroughness, from detailed investment for retirement to a review of what government pensions are available (Schellenberg & Ostrovsky, 2008a, b). Lower income earners and immigrants are more likely not to have an adequate understanding of their post-retirement needs and the government pension system. Financial planning for retirement is important, but equally important is to consider other areas of your life as well (Sener, Terzioglu, & Karabulut, 2007).

Technology and Social Media

The Internet plays an increasingly important role in access to information and communication among adults as well as youth (Cresci, Yarandi, & Morrell, 2010; Cutler, 2009; Rosenberg et al., 2009). A recent study revealed that older adults are clearly capable of being trained to learn new technologies (Hickman, Rogers, & Fisk, 2007).

The growth rates of Internet users have been highest among seniors in Canada. For example, according to one study, Internet use by seniors in 2007 was more than four times as much as in 2000. The three most commonly-used Internet activities include email, games, and downloading music (Veenhof & Timusk, 2014). Information on retirement, health issues, and leisure activities is also sought over the Internet.

Living Arrangements

As noted earlier, housing is one of the primary determinants of health. For over 70 percent of seniors, ownership—that is, ownership of a condominium. townhouse, semi-detached, or fully-detached residence—is mortgage-free. As people age, more reside in special care facilities (Canada Mortgage and Housing Corporation CMHC, 2015). However, for many seniors, housing poses a vulnerability, Seniors suffering from health problems, often related to housing and nutrition, require more formal care than those whose financial position is more secure. Additionally, the needs for seniors requiring more formal care often go unmet. The emotional, physical, and financial strain on the senior who may be isolated, and on his or her family, may impose undue hardship, and the need may go unmet altogether (Lobsinger, 2011).

Multi-generational living has always been a custom for new Canadians and Indigenous peoples, both of which account for a growing share of Canada's population. However, this type of living arrangement is gradually becoming more popular in response to increased housing prices, decreased job security, and increased life-expectancy (Vanier Institute of the Family 2015). The proportion of children under the age of 14 living with a grandparent increased from 3.3 percent in 2001 to 4.8 percent in 2011. In addition, most grandparents who live with their grandchildren also live with at least one middle-generation person (88 percent).

In Aboriginal communities, 9.1 percent of children live in multigenerational homes. Persons aged 45 and over who report an Aboriginal identity and report a Traditional Aboriginal Spirituality have larger proportions of grandparents living with their grandchildren. As well, higher proportions are seen among Sikh (Punjabi-speaking in most cases) and Hindu populations. Of all grandparents living with their grandchildren in 2011, 62 percent were married or in a common-law union. Of those not in couples, 25 percent of co-residing grandparents were widowed, and an additional 14 percent were divorced, separated, or had never been married (Milan, LaFlamme, & Wong, 2015; Battams, 2011). While parents are typically also living in these homes, 12 percent of co-residing grandparents are only living with their grandchildren in "skip-generation" households (Vanier Institute of Family Life, 2015).

Multigenerational living brings many advantages as well as challenges. The advantages include better economic situation, more help with household tasks, provision of daycare, and more company. The major disadvantages are related to the stress of caring for someone who is ill, and the need for personal control and privacy. Adapting the home architecturally is also a factor in addressing the diverse needs of family members. Such living, however, fosters strengthened bonds between family members, and helps address the high cost of housing for families (Vanier Institute of Family Living, 2015; Battams, 2011).

In multigenerational homes, seniors provide and receive care. The majority of the elderly adults in institutions are widows, many of whom cannot physically navigate their environment, are mentally impaired, or are incontinent (cannot control their excretory functions). Of seniors over age 85, 22 percent live on their own (Turcotte & Schellenberg, 2007). Over 50 percent of seniors live with a spouse, and of those between 75 and 85 who live alone, 43 percent are women. Becoming widowed or divorced can have serious financial implications, particularly for women. Widows are more likely to move after the death of a spouse (especially if living in an apartment) than seniors experiencing a divorce (Lin, 2005). But married couples move more often than widowed seniors, and two out of five of the moves involve downsizing to a smaller home.

Most seniors live in urban settings, with 31 percent of Canadian seniors living in Toronto, Montreal, or Vancouver. The oldest (proportionally) communities in Canada are Victoria (British Columbia) and St. Catharines–Niagara (Ontario), both with 17 percent of the population over age 65. Calgary (Alberta) has the lowest population of seniors, at 9 percent (Turcotte & Schellenberg, 2007). Clark (2005) reports that seniors living in large urban areas and immigrants are more likely to have housing affordability problems than those living in smaller communities and people born in Canada, respectively. This is not surprising given that the average price of a home in 2015 was $430 000 across the country, with the highest average at $722 000 in Greater Vancouver (Vanier Institute of Family Living, 2015).

critical thinking

With another student in your class, brainstorm to generate a list of advantages and disadvantages of seniors living in facilities designed by and for them. Consider multi-generational homes. How might they be designed? What may be the advantages and disadvantages to families living in a multi-generational home? What would be the advantages and disadvantages to seniors living in senior residences?

To this point we have discussed a number of issues relating to personality, the self, and society in late adulthood. For a review, see the Reach Your Learning Outcomes section at the end of this chapter.

Families and Social Relationships

LO3 Characterize the families and social relationships of aging adults.

- **The Aging Couple**
- **Older Adult Parents and Their Adult Children**
- **Grandparenting and Great-Grandparenting**
- **Friendship**
- **Fear of Victimization, Crime, and Elder Maltreatment**

The lifestyles of older adults are changing and, like that of younger people, are becoming more and more diverse. Formerly, the later years of life were likely to consist of marriage for men and widowhood for women. With demographic shifts toward marital dissolution characterized by divorce, many adults can now expect to marry, divorce, and remarry during their lifetime. Let's now explore some of the diverse lifestyles of older adults, beginning with those who are married or partnered.

The Aging Couple

The time from retirement until death is sometimes referred to as the "final stage in the marriage process." The number of aging couples has increased significantly, partially due to demographics and partially due to increased acceptance of common-law living arrangements; in fact, the common-law unions for individuals over 65 years rose 66.5 percent between 2006 and 2011, the fastest pace for all age groups (Millan, 2013). The portrait of marriage in the lives of older adults is a positive one for many couples (Piazza & Charles, 2012; Strout & Howard, 2012). A study revealed that marital satisfaction was greater in older adults than middle-aged adults (Henry et al., 2007). In this study, older adults perceived their spouse to be less hostile than did middle-aged adults.

Cohabiting Older Adults

An increasing number of older adults cohabit (Noel-Miller, 2011). In 1960, hardly any older adults cohabited (Chevan, 1996). From 2000 to 2010, cohabitation in adults 50 years and older increased from 1.2 million to 2.5 million (Brown, Bulanda, & Lee, 2012). Still, only a small percentage of older adults cohabit—in 2010, 3 percent of older adults were cohabiting (Mykyta & Macartney, 2012). It is expected that the number of cohabiting older adults will increase further as the large cohort of baby boomers become 65 years of age and older and bring their historically more non-traditional values about love, sex, and relationships to late adulthood. In many cases, the cohabiting is more for companionship than for love. In other cases, such as when one partner faces the potential for expensive care, a couple may decide to maintain their assets separately and thus not marry. One study found that older adults who cohabited had a more positive, stable relationship than younger adults who cohabited, although older adults were less likely to have plans to marry their partner (King & Scott, 2005).

Individuals who are in a marriage or a partnership in late adulthood are usually happier, are less distressed, and live longer than those who are single (Peek, 2009). A recent study of octogenarians revealed that marital satisfaction helps to insulate their happiness from the effects of daily fluctuations in perceived health (Waldinger & Schulz, 2010). Another longitudinal study of adults 75 years of age and older revealed that individuals who are married are likely to live longer than those who are not married (Rasulo, Christensen, & Tomassini, 2005; Manzoli et al., 2007). And a recent study found that marital satisfaction in older adults is linked to whether an individual is depressed or not (Walker et al., 2013).

Retirement alters a couple's lifestyle, requiring adaptation (Price & Nesteruk, 2010). The greatest changes occur in the traditional family in which the husband works and the wife is a homemaker, as each may need to re-learn their roles and help in the upkeep and management of their home. Marital happiness in older adults is also affected by each partner's ability to deal with personal challenges, including aging, illness, and the prospects of widowhood.

Seniors living with a spouse have more immediate access to support and financial security (Turcotte & Schellenberg, 2007). Marital satisfaction is greater for women than for men, possibly because women place more emphasis on attaining satisfaction through marriage than men do. However, as more women develop careers, this gender difference may not continue. In late adulthood, married individuals are more likely to find themselves having to care for a sick partner with a limiting health condition (Blieszner & Roberto, 2012). The stress of caring for a spouse who has a chronic disease can place demands on intimacy.

A recent study explored the quality of marriages in older adults and its link to loneliness (de Jong Gierveld et al., 2009). Two types of loneliness were studied: emotional (the affective state of feeling isolated) and social (a factor of integration in social networks that can provide a sense of connection with others). Approximately 20 to 25 percent of the older adults who were married felt moderate or strong emotional or social loneliness. Stronger emotional and social loneliness appear in older adults whose spouse has health problems, who don't usually get emotional support from their spouse, who rarely converse with their spouse, and who rate their sex life as not very pleasant or not applicable. Emotional loneliness is stronger in older adults in their second marriage, and social loneliness is stronger in husbands with a disabled wife. Also, stronger emotional and social loneliness characterize older adults who have smaller social networks and less contact with their children.

Divorced and Remarried Older Adults

As noted, rising divorce rates, increased longevity, and better health have led to an increase in remarriage by older adults (Ganong & Coleman, 2006). The majority of divorced older adults are women, due to their greater longevity and because men are more likely to remarry, thus removing themselves from the pool of divorced older adults (Peek, 2009). Divorce is far less common in older adults than younger adults, likely reflecting cohort effects rather than age effects since divorce was somewhat rare when current cohorts of older adults were young (Peek, 2009).

What happens when an older adult wants to remarry or does remarry? Reactions to older adults who choose to remarry range from raised eyebrows to outright rejection by adult children (Ganong & Coleman, 2006). As well, an increasing number of older adults cohabit (Mutchler, 2009). However, the majority of adult children support the decision of their older adult parents to remarry. Not all older adults are or ever have been married. At least 8 percent of all individuals who reach the age of 65 have never been married. Contrary to the popular stereotype, older adults who have never been married seem to have the least difficulty coping with loneliness in old age. Many of them discovered long ago how to live autonomously and how to be self-reliant.

A recent study revealed relatively weak ties between older adults and their stepchildren (Noel-Miller, 2013). In this study, older stepparents' social contact with their stepchildren was mainly linked to the stepparent continuing to be married to the stepchildren's biological parent. When divorce occurred in an older adult stepfamily, the divorced stepparent's frequency of contact with stepchildren dropped abruptly.

Romance and Sex in Older Adults' Relationships

Few of us imagine older couples taking an interest in sex or romantic relationships, but as songwriter and singer Leonard Cohen pointed out, "The old are kind but the young are hot. Love may be blind but desire is not (Cohen, 1998)." We might think of seniors as being interested in a game of bridge or a conversation on the porch, but not much else. In fact, a number of older adults date. The increased health and longevity of older adults have resulted in a much larger pool of active older adults. And the increased divorce rate has added more older adults to the senior dating pool.

Older adults may express their sexuality differently from younger adults, especially when engaging in sexual intercourse becomes difficult. Older adults especially enjoy touching and caressing as part of their sexual relationship. When older adults are healthy, they still may engage in sexual activities (Waite, Das, & Laumann, 2009; Waite et al., 2009). For example, a recent U.S. study found that among 75- to 85-year-olds, 40 percent of women and 78 percent of men reported having a stable sexual partner (Waite et al., 2009). The gender differential is likely due to women's higher likelihood of being widowed, age difference in spouses, and the probability of women living longer. With the increased use of drugs to treat erectile dysfunction, older adults can be expected to increase their sexual activity (Aubin et al., 2009; Chevret-Measson et al., 2009). However, companionship often becomes more important than sexual activity in older adults. Older couples often emphasize intimacy over sexual prowess.

Older Adult Parents and Their Adult Children

Parent–child relationships in later life differ from those earlier in the life span (Antonucci, Birditt, & Ajrouch, 2013; Bangerter et al., 2014; Birditt & Wardjiman, 2012; Fingerman & Birditt, 2011; Fingerman et al., 2011a, b; Fingerman, Sechrist, & Birditt, 2013; Kim et al., 2014). They are influenced by a lengthy joint history and extensive shared experiences and memories. Increasingly, diversity characterizes older adult parents and their adult children. Divorce, cohabitation, and non-marital childbearing are more common in the history of older adults today than in the past.

Gender plays an important role in relationships involving older adult parents and their children (Ward-Griffin et al., 2007). Adult daughters, rather than adult sons, are more likely to be the caregivers, and as such are more involved in the lives of aging parents. As discussed in Chapter 16, "Socioemotional Development in Middle Adulthood," middle-aged adults are more likely to provide support if their parents have a disability (Antonucci, Birditt, & Ajrouch, 2013). An extremely valuable task that adult children can perform is to coordinate and monitor services for an aging parent who becomes disabled (Jones et al., 2011). This might involve locating a nursing home and monitoring its quality, procuring medical services, arranging public service assistance, and handling finances. In some cases, adult children provide direct assistance with daily living, including such activities as eating, bathing, and dressing. Even less severely impaired older adults may need help with shopping, housework, transportation, home maintenance, and bill paying.

Researchers have found that ambivalence characterized by both positive and negative perceptions is often present in relationships between adult children and their aging parents (Bangerter et al., 2014; Fingerman & Birditt, 2011; Fingerman, Sechrist, & Birditt, 2013). These perceptions include love, reciprocal help, and shared values on the positive side, and isolation, family conflicts and problems, abuse, neglect, and caregiver stress on the negative side. One study of 1599 adult children's relationships with their older adult parents found that ambivalence is likely to be present when relationships involve in-laws, those in poor health, and adult children with poor parental relationships in early life (Wilson, Shuey, & Elder, 2003). A recent study, however, revealed that affection and support, reflecting solidarity, are more prevalent than ambivalence in intergenerational relationships (Hogerbrugge & Komter, 2012).

Grandparenting and Great-Grandparenting

Let us explore aspects of grandparenting and great-grandparenting: How satisfying are these roles? How do they differ?

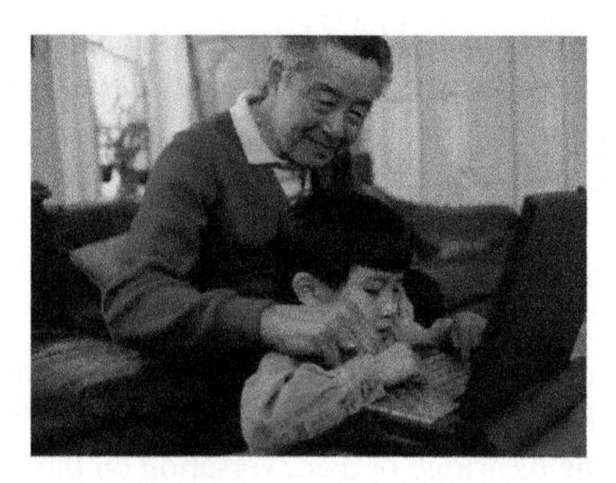

Photodisc/Getty Images

What roles can grandparents play in children's development?

The Changing Profile of Grandparents

Earlier in the text, you read that people are waiting longer to marry and start families. Consequently, the ages of grandparenting and great-grandparenting have increased. Another interesting dynamic is that an increasing number of grandchildren live with their grandparents. This is particularly true in First Nations communities and where the grandmothers are not in the paid labour force (Fuller-Thomson, 2005). Statistics Canada reported that in 2011, more than 75 000 children were being raised by grandparents. Further, most of those caregivers are women (67 percent) caring for two children. Eighty-five percent of children being raised by their grandparent(s) have experienced a crisis situation such as violence, neglect, abandonment, and other forms of parental dysfunction that led to this arrangement. The grandparents face numerous challenges, both physical and financial (Parents Support Services Society of BC, 2011; Fuller-Thomson, 2005).

Grandparent caregivers report a greater degree of closeness to their grandchildren than non-caregivers, and that the health and well-being of the children are similar to those children raised in their parent's home, in spite of poorer economic conditions (Fuller-Thomson, 2005). On the downside, however, studies of grandparents raising their grandchildren in the United States report that the grandparent, usually a grandmother, may also feel isolated, and experience limited physical strength and possible depression. No Canadian study has been conducted to see if this is also the case in Canada (Fuller-Thomson, 2005).

As you read in Chapter 16, grandparents' visitation rights and privileges are also a special concern. Rosenthal and Gladstone (2000) report that a number of self-help and advocacy groups have formed in Canada to address these issues. Such groups as the Grandparents Requesting Access and Dignity (GRAND) society and the Canadian Grandparents Rights Association attempt to raise the public's awareness of child custody and access issues for grandparents, to advocate family law reform to include the rights of grandparents, and to support those involved in access or custody disputes.

Great-Grandparenting

Because of increased longevity, more grandparents today than in the past are also great-grandparents. Today, four-generational families are as common as three-generational families were at the turn of the twentieth century. One contribution of great-grandparents is to transmit family history by telling their children, grandchildren, and great-grandchildren where the family came from, what their members achieved, what they endured, and how their lives changed over the years (Harris, 2002).

There has been little research on great-grandparenting; however, Lillian Troll (2000) has found that older adults who are embedded in family relationships have much less distress than those who are family deprived. Next, we will consider some other aspects of social relationships in late adulthood: friendship and social support.

Friendship

In early adulthood, friendship networks expand as new social connections are made away from home. In late adulthood, new friendships are less likely to be forged, although some adults do seek out new friendships, especially following the death of a spouse (Zettel-Watson & Rook, 2009). As noted earlier in the section on *socio-emotional selectivity theory*, older adults become more selective about their social networks. Noted expert in the field and founding director of the Stanford Center on Longevity, Laura Carstensen, concluded in 1998 that people choose close friends over new friends as they grow older. And, as long as they have several close people in their network, they seem content. Supporting Carstensen's view, recall the more recent study we described earlier in this chapter in which, compared with younger adults, older adults said they experienced less intense positive emotions with new friends and more intense positive emotions with established friends (Charles & Piazza, 2007).

In one study of 128 married older adults, women were more depressed than men if they did not have a best friend, and women who did have a friend reported lower levels of depression (Antonucci, Lansford, & Akiyama, 2001). Similarly, women who did not have a best friend were less satisfied with life than women who did have a best friend.

Three recent studies documented the importance of friendship in older adults:

- In late adulthood friendships are more important than family relationships in predicting mental health (Fiori, Antonucci, & Cortina, 2006). For example, older adults whose social contacts are mainly restricted to their family members are more likely to have depressive symptoms. Friends likely provide emotional intimacy and companionship, as well as integration into the community (Antonucci, Akiyama, & Sherman, 2007).
- Older adults with close ties with friends were less likely to die across a seven-year age span (Rasulo, Christensen, & Tomassini, 2005). The findings were stronger for women than men.
- Activities with friends increase positive affect and life satisfaction in older adults (Huxhold, Miche, & Schuz, 2014).

John Santrock

At the beginning of the twentieth century, the three-generation family was common, but now the four-generation family is common as well. Thus, an increasing number of grandparents are also great-grandparents. The four-generations shown here are members of the Jordan family—author John Santrock's mother-in-law, daughter, granddaughter, and wife.

Fear of Victimization, Crime, and Elder Maltreatment

Stereotyping Older Adults

Ageism is a persistent and destructive prejudice and is fundamentally inconsistent with the values expressed in the Canadian Charter of Rights. **Ageism** is prejudice against others because of their age, especially prejudice against older adults (Jonson, 2013; Lawler et al., 2014). Persons in late adulthood are often perceived as incapable of thinking clearly, learning new things, enjoying sex, contributing to the community, or holding responsible jobs. Many older adults face painful discrimination and might be too polite or timid to attack it. Older adults might not be hired for new jobs or might be eased out of old ones because they are perceived as rigid or feeble-minded, or because employing older adults is not considered cost-effective. A recent study revealed that perceiving themselves as different (self-differentiation) from others in their age group is effective in reducing the impact of negative information on older adults' self-evaluation (Weiss, Sassenberg, & Freund, 2013).

In addition, older adults could be shunned socially, possibly because they are perceived as senile or boring. At other times, they might be perceived as children and described with adjectives such as "cute" and "adorable." The elderly might be edged out of their family life by children who see them as sick and overly demanding. Reg MacDonald (National Advisory Council on Aging, 2001) notes that people over age 65 "are more likely than other groups to be subject to a guardianship or adult protection" legal action, which cast doubts over the elder's mental competence. One study reported that younger Canadians assume that most seniors live in institutions, suffer from dementia, and are responsible for most of the traffic accidents (Kembhavi, 2012). While giving control over someone's life to another person may be warranted to safeguard a person at risk, it may at times be sought as a result of stereotypical misconceptions over the true capacities of the older person.

The personal consequences of negative stereotyping about aging can be serious (Band-Winterstein, 2014; Malinen & Johnston, 2013; Rippon et al., 2014). A physician (60 years old himself) recently told an 80-year-old: "Well, of course, you are tired. You just need to slow down. Don't try to do so much. After all you are very old." Many older adults accept this type of advice, even though it is rooted in age stereotyping rather than medical records. Further, a longitudinal study of adults 70 years of age and older revealed that the older adults who had more negative aging stereotypes at the beginning of the study were more likely to experience hearing decline three years later (Levy, Slade, & Gill, 2006).

Ageism is widespread (Anderson et al., 2013). One study found that men are more likely to negatively stereotype older adults than women (Rupp, Vodanovich, & Crede, 2005). Research indicates that the most frequent form is disrespect for older adults, followed by assumptions about ailments or frailty caused by age (Palmore, 2004). However, the increased number of adults living to an older age has led to active efforts to improve society's image of older adults, obtain better living conditions for older adults, and gain them political clout.

The Canadian Association of Retired Persons (CARP) is dedicated to providing information, social networking, and political advocacy for all retired persons 50 years of age and older. Most provinces and territories have a seniors' organization, such as the Alberta Council on Aging or the New Brunswick Senior Citizens Federation, which aim to address the needs of seniors, improve the quality of life for all older residents in the province/territory, and advise all levels of government on policies and legislation affecting the aged. Most municipalities also have seniors' organizations run through local parks and recreation departments. Local communities organize social networking, fitness activities, or special interest groups such as photography, hiking, bridge, or art for and by seniors.

Nonetheless, there are considerable variations in stereotyping of older adults in different countries. A recent study of European countries found that older adults are perceived as more competent in countries such as Denmark in which they engage in paid or volunteer work, and are perceived as less competent in countries such as Poland in which they are less likely to participate in paid or volunteer work (Bowen & Skirbekk, 2013).

critical thinking

Think of a person you know who is 65 or older. Quickly write down the first five or six words that come to mind when you think of this person. Now think of older people in general and jot down the first five or six words that come to mind. Which list most closely resembles stereotypical images of people in late adulthood?

Policy Issues in an Aging Society

As noted in Chapter 17, Canadians over the age of 65 constitute the fastest growing age group in Canada. To put this growth in perspective, consider that in the 1950s and 1960s, people over 65 accounted for less than 8 percent of the population. Today, according to Statistics Canada, 16.1 percent of the total population is now aged 65 years or older, outnumbering the under-15 age group for the first time in Canada's history. Life expectancy at age 65 is currently at a record high of 22 (87 years old) for women and 19 years (84 years old) for men (Vanier Institute of the Family, 2015).

Policy issues pertaining to older adults are reviewed frequently. For example, in 2007, Canada eliminated mandatory retirement at a specific age, and regulations about individual registered retirement savings plans (RRSP) have been modified (Klassen, 2012; Taylor, 2007). Other policy issues include the status of the economy and the viability of the social insurance system, sources of income, the provision of health care, supports for families who care for older adults, social activities, and generational inequity (Statistics Canada, 2007; Neugarten, 1988).

Health, wellness, and security are crucial elements in the quality of an individual's life and in successful aging (Browne & Braun, 2008; Kane, 2007; Special Senate Committee on Aging, 2009; Turcotte & Schellenberg, 2007). Escalating health-care costs are currently causing considerable concern. Across Canada, provinces/territories have made cuts to the budgets of their ministries of health, and the federal government has made cuts in transfer payments to the provinces. The current view is that the increase in health-care costs is the result of an aging population, and that the future will see costs soar so high that maintaining the health system as it is will harm the nation financially. Older adults are seen as having more illnesses than younger people, even though most older adults view their health as good or very good. Research shows that older adults do visit doctors more often (although we know very little about the nature of these visits), and are hospitalized more frequently and for longer periods of time than other age groups. As noted with other age groups, education and financial security are strong predictors of better health.

Although many raise the concern that health-care costs will rise because of the changing demographics, the Special Senate Committee on Aging (2009) suggested that this increase may not be as overwhelming as some pundits predict. The Committee believes that provinces/territories can handle the costs through a careful integration of the various levels of care available to respond to health needs, including community-based home care, clinics, hospitals, and long-term facilities. This debate between the "common-sense" version of future health-care costs and the evidence from research into health-care costs is of major importance to Canadians. Some politicians lean toward the introduction of a two-tier health system, while the other perspective promotes the continuation of a universal, single-tier health system. The Commission on the Future of Health Care in Canada (Romanow, 2002) recommended a revitalized and sustainable universal health-care system for Canadians. The current federal government has indicated its desire to act on the Romanow Report, although the shape of the future of universal health care in Canada is yet to be fully formed.

A special concern is that although many of the health problems of older adults are chronic rather than acute, the medical system is still based on a "cure" model, rather than a "care" model (Stone, 2006). Chronic illness is long-term, often lifelong, and requires long-term, if not life-term, management (Garasen, Windspoll, & Johnsen, 2008; Nutting et al., 2007). Chronic illness often follows a pattern of an acute period that may require hospitalization, followed by a longer period of remission, and then repetitions of this pattern. The patient's home, rather than the hospital, often becomes the centre of managing the patient's chronic illness. In a home-based system, a new type of cooperative relationship among doctors, nurses, patients, family members, and other service providers needs to be developed (May et al., 2004). Health-care personnel need to be trained and be made available to provide home services, sharing authority with the patient and perhaps yielding to patient authority over the long term.

Eldercare is the physical and emotional caregiving for older members of the family, whether that care is day-to-day physical assistance or responsibility for arranging and overseeing such care. An important issue involving eldercare is how it can best be provided (Trukeschitz et al., 2013; Zacher, Jimmieson, & Winter, 2012). With so many women in the labour market, who will replace them as caregivers? An added problem is that many caregivers are in their sixties, and may not be in perfect health themselves. They may find the responsibility of caring for relatives who are in their eighties or nineties stressful.

Statistics Canada (2008) reported that in 2007, the number of caregivers over the age of 45 providing informal care for seniors rose to 2.7 million people, with 75 percent of these care providers being between the ages of 45 and 64. This means that one in four of those providing eldercare were seniors themselves. Women constitute 57 percent of the informal caregivers, and, in addition to being the primary caregiver, they are more likely to provide care for more than one person. Six of every ten care providers are tending to the needs of a parent or parent-in-law. Fewer than 10 percent said they are taking care of a spouse, but this number may be under-representative as women tend not to report caring for an ill husband as caregiving. About one-third of caregivers are the person's friend, neighbour, or an extended family member.

Not all informal caregivers live in the same community as the person for whom they provide care. Vézina and Turcotte (2010) found 22 percent of those providing informal care live more than an hour's travel time away from the parent they help. Caring from a distance is difficult, as it might interfere with providing assistance for such necessary chores as grocery shopping, taking the parent to doctor's appointments, and the ease of checking in physically with the parent daily, if necessary. People providing care from a distance report having to take time off work (although women were more likely than men to do so), having higher costs in providing care, and not having other siblings with which to share the responsibility of caring for the parent.

The generational equity issue sometimes takes the form of whether the "advantaged" older population is using up resources that should go to disadvantaged younger generation The argument is that older adults are advantaged because they have publicly provided pensions, health care, housing subsidies, tax breaks, and other benefits that younger age groups do not have. This distribution of wealth should not be viewed as one of generational equity, but rather as a major shortcoming of our broader economic and social policies.

Some of the physical decline and limitations that characterize development in late adulthood contribute to a sense of vulnerability and fear among older adults. For some elderly adults, the fear of crime may become a deterrent to travelling, attending social events, and pursuing an active lifestyle. This said, seniors reported feeling more satisfied with their personal safety in 2004 than an earlier sample in 1999—92 percent compared to 89 percent, respectively (Ogrodnik, 2007).

In 2004, 10 percent of Canadian seniors experienced at least one act of victimization during the previous year (Ogrodnik, 2007). This was one-third the rate of victimization for non-seniors; and women are twice as vulnerable to violence than men. In terms of assaults, sexual assaults, and robberies, seniors experience significantly less victimization than non-seniors. Theft of seniors' personal property is less than half that of people aged 55 to 64, and nearly eight times lower than 15- to 24-year-olds. Ogrodnik (2007) found that seniors experience nearly three times fewer break-ins, automobile thefts, and acts of vandalism than non-seniors. Most often, seniors are victimized by a family member (Ogrodnik, 2007).

For more information on elder abuse, see the Connecting through Research feature.

CONNECTING through Research

Elder Abuse

When we become elderly, we hope the principles outlined by the United Nations—independence, participation, care, self-fulfillment, and dignity—will govern our well-being. When these principles are not upheld, when the news reports a story or an exposé about victimization of seniors, for example, we are horrified. Elder abuse is a term that includes all types of mistreatment toward older people, whether an act of commission or omission, and whether intentional or unintentional. According to the Canadian Centre for Elder Law of the University of British Columbia (2011), elder abuse can be broadly categorized as falling into these five categories:

- Physical: causing pain, injury, or harm to health
- Financial: illegal or improper use of funds or assets, such as fraud or theft
- Psychological: infliction of mental anguish or suffering
- Sexual: non-consensual sexual activity or harassing sexual comments
- Neglect: refusal or failure to provide services or necessary care

Such abuse violates the individual's human rights. Not reporting abuse or acknowledging it is a form of abuse in itself, as is neglect (Department of Justice, 2013).

It is not possible to know the extent of elder abuse, as families and institutions may not report incidents. Shame and guilt often prevent victims or families from reporting abuse; however, one in five Canadians are aware of abuse being inflicted on an elder (Government of Canada, 2015). Caregivers in institutions may not be adequately trained, and institutions may not have policies and procedures in place or may turn a blind eye (Department of Justice, 2013). While much abuse goes unreported, police reports on family violence for 2007 represent one-third of the violent crimes against seniors. While family violence against seniors is lower than against those aged 55 to 64 and 25 to 34 (48 versus 104 and 406 per 100 000, respectively), its occurrence is still very troubling (Statistics Canada, 2009).

The types of abuse that are most common result from frustration and financial need. Senior women are more likely than senior men to be victims of family violence. Half of the police-reported cases of family violence against seniors do not result in physical injury, and when it does it tends to be minor injury (91 percent) (Statistics Canada, 2009). The psychological impact of family violence is not assessed in the police reports. Being frail, disabled, and/or suffering from dementia or Alzheimer's disease increases an individual's vulnerability to victimization (Turcotte & Schellenberg, 2007; CNPEA, 2006). Senior women are more likely to be abused by a spouse or adult children, while senior men are abused more often by adult children (Statistics Canada, 2009).

Elder abuse is not confined to Canada; in fact, it is a worldwide occurrence. In 2006, the United Nations, following up on a Plan of Action determined in 2002, declared June 15 World Elder Abuse Day. The Canadian Network for the Prevention of Elder Abuse (CNPEA) is an arm of the International Network (INPEA). Provincial networks are also linked; together, these networks work with governmental and non-governmental groups and individuals around the world to document abuses and provide educational materials in an effort to increase awareness and work toward prevention. For more information, visit the CPNEA's website at http://www.cnpea.ca. The site offers an overview of incidents that have been reported around the world, ranging from malnutrition in nursing homes in one country, to abandonment and neglect in another.

In this section we have discussed families and social relationships in late adulthood. For a review, see the Reach Your Learning Outcomes section at the end of this chapter.

Social Integration

LO4 Describe social supports and social integration, and understand how altruism, ethnicity, gender, and culture are linked to aging.

- **Social Support and Social Integration**
- **Altruism and Volunteerism**
- **Gender**
- **Ethnicity**
- **Culture**

What are the roles of altruism, gender, and ethnicity in aging? What are the social aspects of aging in different cultures?

Social Support and Social Integration

Social support and social integration play important roles in the physical and mental health of older adults (Antonucci, Birditt, & Ajrouch, 2013; Li, Ji, & Chen, 2014; Utz et al., 2014).

In the **convoy model of social relations**, individuals go through life embedded in a personal network of individuals to whom they give and from whom they receive social support (Antonucci, Birditt, & Ajrouch, 2013). Social support can help individuals of all ages cope more effectively and is related to both physical and mental health (Cheng, Lee, & Chow, 2010; Li, Ji, & Chen, 2014; Griffiths et al., 2007). It is linked to a reduction in symptoms of disease, with the ability to meet one's own health care needs, and reduced mortality (Rook et al., 2007). A higher level of social support also is related to a lower probability of an older adult being institutionalized and depressed (Herd et al., 2011; Richardson et al., 2011). Further, a recent study revealed that older adults who experience a higher level of social support show later cognitive decline than their counterparts with a lower level of social support (Dickinson et al., 2011).

In a study of friendships among Canadian seniors, Colin Lindsay (2008) found that 82 percent of people aged 75 and over said they had at least one close friend, compared with 88 percent of those between 65 and 74 and over 90 percent of those in younger age groups. The percentage of seniors aged 75 and over with two close friends was lower (just over 70 percent). Thus, some 18 percent of people over age 75 do not report having a close friend.

Social Integration

Social integration plays an important role in the lives of many older adults (Antonucci, Birditt, & Ajrouch, 2013; Fingerman, Brown, & Blieszner, 2011; Hawkley & Caccioppo, 2012; Stephens, Breheny, & Mansvelt, 2014). Remember from our earlier discussion of socio-emotional selectivity theory that many older adults choose to have fewer peripheral social contacts and more emotionally positive contacts with friends and family (Carstensen et al., 2011). Thus, a decrease in the overall social activity of many older adults may reflect their greater interest in spending more time in the small circle of friends and families where they are less likely to have negative emotional experiences. Researchers have found that older adults tend to report being less lonely than younger adults and less lonely than would be expected based on their circumstances (Schnittker, 2007). Their reports of feeling less lonely than younger adults likely reflect their more selective social networks and greater acceptance of solitude in their lives (Antonucci, Birditt, & Ajrouch, 2013).

Following are the findings of a number of recent research studies on loneliness in older adults:

- The most consistent factor that predicts loneliness in older adults at 70, 78, and 85 years of age is not being married (Stessman et al., 2014).
- For 60- to 80-year-olds, a partner's death is a stronger indicator of loneliness for men than for women (Nicolaisen & Thorsen, 2014).
- Increased use of the Internet by older adults is associated with making it easier to meet new people, feeling less isolated, and feeling more connected with friends and family (Cotten, Anderson, & McCullough, 2013).
- As older adults increase the number of different types of social activities in which they participate, self-perception of their health improves, they feel less lonely, and they are more satisfied with life (Gilmour, 2012).

Recently, researchers also have explored the extent to which loneliness and social isolation are linked to various outcomes in elderly adults (Gerst-Emerson, Shovali, & Markides, 2014; Newall & Menec, 2014; Skingley, 2013). Both loneliness and social isolation are associated with increased health problems and mortality (Cohen-Mansfield & Perach, 2014; Luo et al., 2012). However, a recent study found that social isolation is a better predictor of mortality than loneliness (Steptoe et al., 2013). Another recent study of elderly adults revealed that both loneliness and social isolation were associated with decreases in cognitive functioning four years later (Shankar et al., 2013).

What are some of the benefits of intergenerational programs?

CONNECTING development to life

Intergenerational Programs

In his 1986 essay on autonomy, legal philosopher Ronald Dworkin wrote, "... autonomy makes each of us responsible for shaping our own life according to some coherent and distinctive sense of character, conviction, and interest. It allows us to lead our own lives rather than be led along them, so that each of us can be, to the extent such a scheme of rights can make thus possible, what he has made himself." (Gawande, 2014). Such a philosophy is mirrored in many senior residences and care facilities. Believing that "a good life is one with maximum independence," Dr. William Thomas of New York brought in birds, cats, and dogs to the Chase Memorial Residence New Berlin, NY, in the late 1970s, pioneering a unique and vibrant way of providing care (Gawande, 2014). Such groundbreaking initiatives are gaining momentum around the world and transforming what the British Commission on Housing for the Elderly and Disabled deemed as "care-ghettos" into robust residences (ctvnews, 2014).

University students attending Netherlands University in Deventer, live rent-free in a senior residence in exchange for spending at least 30 hours a month with one of the residents. Students and residents share a variety of activities ranging from conversations, meal preparations, computer lessons, and shopping, to graffiti workshops. This came about because Managing Director Geo Sijikpes saw an opportunity to provide local college students with housing and at the same time enhance the daily lives of the aging adults. The model continues to spread throughout Europe and North America. Such intergenerational initiatives create a powerful feeling of family for both the students and the senior residents (Botek, 2015).

Here in Canada, educator and author Sharon MacKenzie has devoted much of the last thirty years to creating and supporting activities and designing tool kits to facilitate the connection of school-aged children and youth with different generations within the community. MacKenzie founded the Intergenerational Society of Canada, which in 2007 proclaimed June 1 to be Intergenerational Day. Today over 100 cities across the country not only celebrate this day, but have introduced a variety of programs (Intergenerational Society, 2015). One such program, designed by two retirees in Prospect Lake, British Columbia, is the Song Circle. These 90-minute intergenerational choir sessions captured the interest of a group of 7-year-old baseball players, who loved the interaction with their older neighbours so much that they have already signed up for next year's (off-baseball) season (Intergenerational Society, 2015).

MacKenzie also created the Meadows School Project in 2000, where thirty students between 9- and 12-years-of-age connect in a makeshift classroom with seniors living in an assisted living residence. Within two weeks, she realized that such an intergenerational immersion benefitted everyone involved. She observed immediate improvement in the mental, physical, and social health of the seniors. Further, she noted that student engagement and retention of curriculum improved (Szmaus, 2013; Intergenerational Society, 2015). The Meadows School Project has been featured in the documentary, "Whose Grandmother are You?," which can be viewed at http://www.intergenerational.ca/index.php?option=com_content&view=article&id=8:qwhose-grandma-are-youq&catid=36:documentary&Itemid=37.

In programs such as these, not only do connections between seniors and students blossom, but the ripple effect benefits the entire community by building bridges and enhancing understanding. The group Toronto Intergenerational Partnerships (TIGP) has noted many benefits to both seniors and young people of bringing members of different generations together, including enchanced self-esteem, the opportunity to learn new skills, and feelings of usefulness and connectedness with the community (TIGP, 2015). In 2015, the National Seniors' Council made priorities of examining barriers that prevent seniors and communities from reaching out to each other and finding ways to facilitate meaningful contact with socially isolated seniors in their neighbourhoods (National Seniors' Council, 2015). The programs described here are among numerous efforts being made across the country to counteract the isolation so many seniors, especially those living in senior residences, experience.

Altruism and Volunteerism

Two billion hours of volunteer activity occur every year in Canada (Special Senate Committee on Aging, 2009). Just 11 percent of Canadians supply 77 percent of that activity. A common perception is that older adults need to be given help rather than give help themselves. However, the 2003 General Social Survey found that seniors are more likely than younger adults to participate in volunteer activity, contributing a greater number of hours than other age groups (Turcotte & Schellenberg, 2007). The reasons for participating include such things the desire to share skills, to learn new skills, and to give back to their community (Special Senate Committee on Aging, 2009). Researchers recently have found that when older adults engage in altruistic behaviour and volunteering, they benefit from these activities. For example, a recent study revealed that volunteering is linked with less frailty in older adults (Jung et al., 2010). Almost 50 percent of the volunteering efforts of older adults are for services provided by religious organizations (Burr, 2009). Researchers also have found that volunteering as an older adult is associated with a number of positive outcomes (Harootyan, 2007).

A study of 21 000 individuals aged 50 to 79 years in 21 countries revealed that one-third give back to society, saying that they volunteer now or have volunteered in the past (HSBC Insurance, 2007). In this study, about 50 percent who volunteer reported that they do so for at least one-half day each week. And another study found that volunteering steadily increases from 57 to 85 years of age (Cornwell, Laumann, & Schumm, 2008). Among the reasons for the positive outcomes of volunteering are its provision of constructive activities and productive roles, social integration, and enhanced meaningfulness.

Even though seniors represent a significant proportion of volunteers, many report that physical limitations and health prevent them from volunteering. Lack of time is the second most commonly cited reason for not volunteering for both seniors and younger people. Thirdly, seniors cite they have given time to the community over the years, and it is time for younger people to take on that role. Finally, many individuals prefer to donate money instead of making a long-term commitment (Turcotte & Schellenberg, 2007).

The federal government has an initiative to encourage seniors to stay involved within their communities. The New Horizons for Seniors program offers grants up to $25 000 for the creation of community programs that integrate seniors' "skills, experiences and wisdom in support of their community" (Special Senate Committee on Aging, 2009). In its appraisal of the program, the Special Senate Committee on Aging noted the need to bring more young people into the volunteer sector. These grants are to help facilitate the interface of seniors as volunteers with younger people, in part as an effort to instil the value of volunteer activity in the younger group.

Gender

Since women have longer life expectancy, the majority of seniors are women. In 2011, 52 percent of those between 65 and 74 years of age were women; between 75 and 84, the percentage rose to 56 percent; and for those over 85, the percentage jumped to 68 percent. However, the gap is narrowing as men are expected to catch up significantly in terms of life-expectancy in the next decade (Kambhavi, 2012).

Do our gender roles change when we become older adults? Some developmentalists once argued that there is decreasing femininity in women and decreasing masculinity in men when they reach the late adulthood years (Gutmann, 1975). The evidence suggested that older men become more feminine—nurturing, sensitive, and so on—but it appears that older women do not necessarily become more masculine—assertive, dominant, and so on (Turner, 1982). Considering Bronfenbrenner's Bio-ecological Theory, cohort effects are especially important to keep in mind in such areas as gender roles. As socio-historical changes take place and are assessed more frequently in life-span investigations, what were once perceived to be age effects may turn out to be cohort effects, that is, a reflection of changing roles and societal values (Schaie, 2013).

A possible double jeopardy also faces many women—the burden of both ageism and sexism (Meyer & Parker, 2011). Statistics Canada (2014) reports the poverty rate for seniors who live alone to be 28 percent (Statistics Canada, 2014). According to the Canadian Labour Congress (2015), senior women are twice as likely to live in poverty than men and are twice as likely to be reliant solely on Old Age Security and Guaranteed Income Supplement than men.

Not only is it important to be concerned about the double jeopardy of ageism and sexism many older women face, but special attention also needs to be devoted to female ethnic minority older adults (Leifheit-Limson & Levy, 2009). They face what could be described as triple jeopardy—ageism, sexism, and racism. Should the woman also have a disability, her life experience is further jeopardized—a quadruple jeopardy (Ontario Human Rights Commission, 2001). An important research and political agenda for the twenty-first century is increased interest in the aging and the rights of older adult women.

critical thinking

Consider your own cultural or ethnic group's attitudes toward aging. If you are not sure, talk with older family members about their recollections of how older members of the group were treated, what roles they held, restrictions they faced, and any special rights or responsibilities they had. Are there differences in attitudes about aging women and men? With these descriptions in mind, what part of that set of attitudes is positive, and which is potentially negative? How could you change a group's less positive views concerning its older members?

Ethnicity

In 2011, approximately 28 percent of seniors living in Canada were immigrants, the majority from Western Europe and Asia (Kembhavi, 2012). One-quarter of these seniors were members of a visible minority. This is a significant increase over past Canadian demographics, both in terms of the percentage of people identified with a visible minority and the place of origin of immigrants to Canada. Only 3 percent of people aged 65 and over who immigrated to Canada prior to 1991 were members of a visible minority, whereas since 1991 that percentage is 75.6 percent. As we learned earlier, immigrants who arrived in the 1990s have a lower likelihood of retiring before age 65, and when they do retire, their economic situation may be worse than that of Canadian-born seniors (Schellenberg & Ostrovsky, 2008b). The act of immigrating and the economy newcomers join at the time of arrival limits their financial situation. In addition, access to resources to plan for their retirement or to access community services is lower than for non-immigrants.

Sharon Koehn (2006) studied the health-care access of new immigrants in British Columbia. Her study found that immigrants need more care than non-immigrants, and they have a harder time accessing health care. For those whose language is not English, interpreters (both family members and others) often prove unreliable and inaccurate in translation of health information, both about the person's condition and the physician's response. Many immigrants were found to not expect much government provision of health care, and so did not seek it out.

The Aboriginal population in Canada is younger than any other of the country's ethnic groups. Turcotte and Schellenberg (2007) note that even Aboriginal seniors are younger (on average) than non-Aboriginal seniors. The percentage of Aboriginal seniors is expected to grow at a similar rate as the rest of Canada over the next two decades. There are differences between the three groups that constitute the name Aboriginal: the North American Indian, the Métis, and the Inuit. Inuit seniors live predominantly in Northern communities. Just over half of North American Indian seniors live on reservations where the majority of others are North American Indians. Métis seniors are more urbanized, but still less so than non-Aboriginals.

Apart from the problems and prejudices faced by the elderly, individuals from racialized groups may experience the full brunt of ageism, sexism, poverty, and racial or ethnic prejudice.

Culture

What factors are associated with whether older adults are accorded a position of high status in a culture? Seven factors are most likely to predict high status for older adults in a culture (Sangree, 1989):

- Older persons have valuable knowledge.
- Older persons control key family/community resources.
- Older persons are permitted to engage in useful and valued functions as long as possible.
- There is role continuity throughout the life span.
- Age-related role changes involve greater responsibility, authority, and advisory capacity.
- The extended family is a common family arrangement in the culture, and the older person is integrated into the extended family.

In general, respect for older adults is greater in collectivistic cultures (such as China and Japan) than in individualistic cultures (such as Canada). However, some researchers are finding that this collectivistic/individualistic difference in respect for older adults is not as strong as it used to be, and that in some cases older adults in individualistic cultures receive considerable respect (Antonucci, Vandewater, & Lansford, 2000).

To this point, we have discussed several ideas about social integration in late adulthood. For a review, see the Reach Your Learning Outcomes section at the end of this chapter.

Successful Aging

LO5 Explain how to age successfully.

In addition to maintaining both physical and mental fitness, attitude plays a vital role in healthy aging. A study of over 3000 men and women, all over 60 years of age, found that those who reported having fun, doing things that gave them pleasure, and being active developed fewer impairments and showed slower decline than those who were less upbeat. Notably, people with a lower sense of well-being were more than three times as likely as their more positive counterparts to develop problems with routine daily activities (CMAJ, 2014; Gustafson, 2014). With a proper diet, an active lifestyle, mental stimulation and flexibility, positive coping skills, good social relationships and support, and the absence of disease, many of our abilities can be maintained or, in some cases, even improved, as we get older (Antonucci, Birditt, & Ajrouch, 2013). In contrast, people with chronic illnesses such as heart disease, diabetes, arthritis, stroke, and depression experience lower levels of enjoyment with life. Reduced enjoyment of life may be related to future disability or immobility. Even when individuals develop a disease, improvements in medicine mean that increasing numbers of older adults with diseases can still lead active, constructive lives (Steptoee et al., 2014; Siegler et al., 2013a, b).

Being active is especially important in successful aging (Parisi et al., 2014; Solberg et al., 2013). Older adults who optimize their choices and compensate effectively for losses, perhaps by getting out and attending meetings, participating in church and/or community activities, going on trips, and exercising regularly, are more satisfied with their lives than their counterparts who disengage (Berchicci et al., 2014; English & Carstensen, 2014a; Freund, Nikitin, & Riediger, 2013; Kirk-Sanchez & McGough, 2014; Park et al., 2014; Rebok et al., 2014).

Successful aging also involves perceived control over the environment (Bertrand, Graham, & Lachman, 2013; Milte et al., 2014). In Chapter 17, we described how perceived control over the environment has a positive effect on nursing home residents' health and longevity. In recent years, the term self-efficacy has often been used to describe perceived control over the environment and the ability to produce positive outcomes (Bandura, 2010, 2012). Researchers have found that many older adults are quite effective in maintaining a sense of control and have a positive view of themselves (Bertrand, Graham, & Lachman, 2013; Park, Elavsky, & Koo, 2014; Dunbar, Leventhal, & Leventhal, 2007). And one study revealed that maximizing psychological resources (self-efficacy and optimism) is linked to a higher quality of life for older adults (Bowling & Lliffe, 2011).

Cultures vary in the prestige they give to older adults. In the Inuit culture, older adults are especially treated with respect because of their wisdom and extensive life experience. *What are some other factors that are linked to respect for older adults in a culture?*

Examining the positive aspects of aging is an important trend in life-span development and is likely to benefit future generations of older adults (Freund, Nikitin, & Riediger, 2013; Hodge et al., 2014). A very important agenda is to continue to improve our understanding of how people can live longer, healthier, more productive and satisfying lives (Nagamatsu et al., 2014; Park, Han, & Kang, 2014).

critical thinking

On the basis of all that you have read in Chapters 17 and 18, your personal observations and ideas, plus what your professor has discussed, construct a multi-dimensional plan to ensure successful aging. Outline five features of positive aging in each of the following domains: physical, cognitive, and socio-emotional.

To this point, we have studied ideas about successful aging. For a review, see the Reach Your Learning Outcomes section at the end of this chapter.

Reach Your **Learning Outcomes**

Theories of Socio-Emotional Development

LO1 Discuss four theories of socio-emotional development and aging and the social determinants of health.

Erikson's Theory	▪ Erikson's eighth and final stage of development, *integrity versus despair,* involves the process of life-review during which individuals reflect on the past, integrating events positively or negatively, concluding either positively that on the whole one's life has been good, or, negatively, that one's life has not been well spent. ▪ Peck described three developmental tasks that older adults face: (1) differentiation versus role preoccupation, (2) body transcendence versus preoccupation, and (3) ego transcendence versus preoccupation.
Activity Theory	▪ Activity theory states that the more active and involved older adults are, the more likely they will be satisfied with their lives. This theory has been strongly supported by research.
Socio-Emotional Selectivity Theory	▪ The socio-emotional selectivity theory states that older adults become more selective about their social networks. Because they place a high value on emotional satisfaction, they are motivated to spend more time with familiar individuals with whom they have had rewarding relationships. ▪ Knowledge-related and emotion-related goals change across the life span, with emotion-related goals being more important when individuals get older.
Selective Optimization with Compensation Theory	▪ The theory that successful aging is linked to three main factors: (1) selection, (2) optimization, and (3) compensation. These are especially likely to be relevant when loss occurs.
Social Determinants of Health	▪ Social determinants of health include income, education, social inclusion, and housing.

Personality, the Self, and Society

LO2 Describe links between personality and mortality, and identify changes in the self and society in late adulthood.

Personality	▪ The personality traits of conscientiousness and agreeableness increase in late adulthood. ▪ Lower levels of conscientiousness, extroversion, and openness to experience, a higher level of neuroticism, negative affect, pessimism, and a negative outlook on life are related to earlier death in late adulthood.
The Self	▪ In one large-scale study, self-esteem increased through most of adulthood but declined in the seventies and eighties. The stability of self-esteem declines in older adults. ▪ Changes in types of self-acceptance occur through the adult years as acceptance of ideal and future selves decreases with age and acceptance of past selves increases. ▪ Most older adults effectively maintain a sense of self-control, although self-regulation may vary by domain. For example, older adults often show less self-regulation in the physical domain than younger adults.
Older Adults in Society	▪ Ageism is prejudice against others because of their age. Too many negative stereotypes of older adults continue to exist. ▪ Policy issues in an aging society include the status of the economy and the provision of health care, eldercare, and generational inequity. ▪ Of special concern are older adults who are in poverty. Poverty rates are especially high among older women who live alone and seniors from ethnic minority groups and Aboriginals. ▪ Individuals who are healthy, have adequate income, are active, are better educated, have an extended social network of friends and family, and were satisfied with their lives before they retired adjust best to retirement. ▪ Most older adults live in the community, not in institutions. Almost two-thirds of older adults live with family members, usually a spouse.

Families and Social Relationships

LO3 Characterize the families and social relationships of aging adults.

The Aging Couple	▪ Retirement alters a couple's lifestyle and requires adaptation. ▪ Married older adults are often happier than single older adults.
Older Adult Parents and Their Adult Children	▪ Approximately 80 percent of older adults have living children, many of whom are middle-aged. ▪ Adult daughters are more likely than adult sons to be involved in the lives of aging parents. ▪ An important task that adult children can perform is to coordinate and monitor services for an aging parent who becomes disabled. ▪ Ambivalence can characterize the relationships of adult children with their aging parents.

Grandparenting and Great-Grandparenting	▪ Most grandparents are satisfied with their roles. ▪ There are different grandparent roles and styles. The profile of grandparents is changing due to such factors as divorce and remarriage. ▪ Because of increased longevity, more grandparents today are also great-grandparents. One contribution of great-grandparents is family history.
Friendship	▪ There is more continuity than change in friendship for older adults, although there is more change for males than for females.
Fear of Victimization, Crime, and Elder Maltreatment	▪ Seniors experience significantly less assault, sexual assault, robbery, theft, and acts of vandalism than non-seniors. ▪ Maltreatment can take several forms, ranging from neglect to physical abuse, psychological or emotional abuse, or economic or financial abuse, including fraud.

Social Integration

LO4 **Describe social supports and social integration, and understand how altruism, ethnicity, gender, and culture are linked to aging.**

Social Support and Social Integration	▪ Social support and social integration play important roles in both the physical and mental health of people in late adulthood. ▪ Being lonely and socially isolated is a significant health risk factor in late adulthood.
Altruism and Volunteerism	▪ Altruism and volunteerism are beneficial to people in late adulthood.
Gender	▪ There is stronger evidence that men become more feminine (nurturant, sensitive) as older adults than there is that women become more masculine (assertive). ▪ An individual with a physical, emotional, or cognitive disability may experience further prejudice.
Ethnicity	▪ Individuals from racialized groups face special burdens, having to cope with the full brunt of racism, ageism, poverty, and, if they are female, sexism.
Culture	▪ Historically, respect for older adults in China and Japan was high, but today their status is more variable. ▪ Factors that predict high status for the elderly across cultures range from their valuable knowledge to integration into the extended family.

Successful Aging

LO5 **Explain how to age successfully.**

Successful Aging	▪ Increasingly, the positive aspects of older adults are being studied. ▪ Factors that are linked to successful aging include an active lifestyle, positive coping skills, good social relationships and support, and self-efficacy.

review → connect → reflect

review

1. Describe how issues of earlier stages mature into the many facets of integrity and wisdom in late adulthood. LO1
2. Define ageism and cite examples you have observed. LO2
3. How might loneliness be a factor in late adulthood, even for the aging couple? LO3
4. How are altruism, gender, ethnicity, and culture linked to social integration? LO4
5. What are some of the factors linked to successful aging? LO5

connect

In Chapter 16 you read about the big five personality factors, and in this chapter you read about how these factors, particularly low conscientiousness and high neuroticism, may be linked to mortality rates in late adulthood. Why do you think this may be true?

reflect

Your Own Personal Journey of Life

How might your ability to age successfully as an older adult be related to what you are doing in your life now? What behaviours would you like to maintain? What might you change?

SECTION 10

Endings

CHAPTER 19

Death and Grieving

CHAPTER OUTLINE

Defining Death and Life/Death Issues

LO1 Evaluate issues in determining death and decisions regarding death.

- **Issues in Determining Death**
- **Decisions Regarding Life, Death, and Health Care**

Death and Socio-Historical, Cultural Contexts

LO2 Analyze the death system within your personal, cultural, and historical contexts.

- **Changing Historical Circumstances**
- **Death in Different Cultures**

A Developmental Perspective on Death

LO3 Outline death and attitudes from a life-span perspective.

- **Causes of Death and Expectations about Death**
- **Understanding Death from a Life-Span Perspective**

Facing Ones Own Death

LO4 Differentiate the psychological aspects involved in facing ones own death within the contexts in which most people die.

- **Kübler-Rosss Stages of Dying**
- **Perceived Control and Denial**
- **The Contexts in Which People Die**

Coping with the Death of Someone Else

LO5 Identify ways to cope with the death of another person.

- **Communicating with a Dying Person**
- **Grieving**
- **Making Sense of the World**
- **Losing a Life Partner**
- **Forms of Mourning, the Funeral, and Celebration of Life**

"Four parts to life: being born, being young, being a parent, and being dead. Death brings the fourth, the complete, the full, four makes it total, four makes it whole, and the final fourth is with us from birth."

—B.A.CAMERON (CAM HUBERT), CONTEMPORARY CANADIAN WRITER

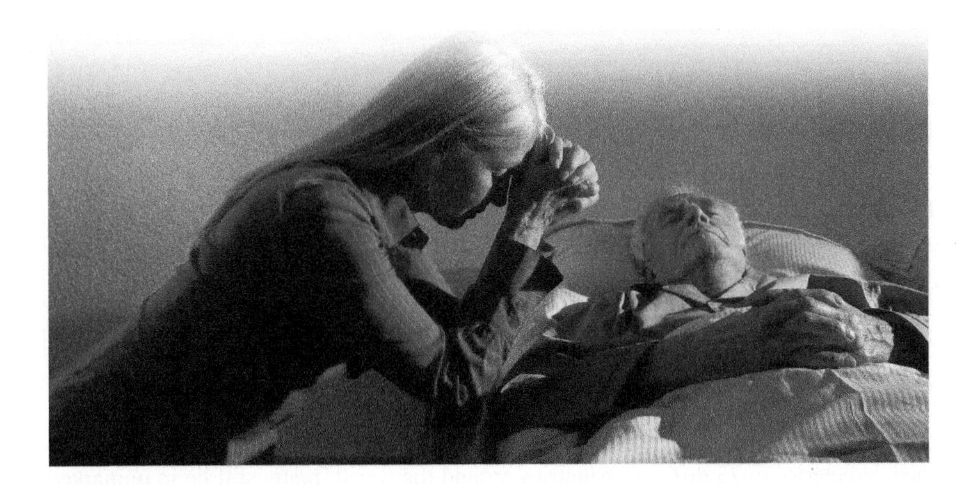

© Hans Neleman/Getty Images

National Mourning

They were young, as we are young,
They served, giving freely of themselves,
To them, we pledge, amid the winds of time,
To carry their torch and never forget.
We will remember them.

—Dakota Brant, youth delegate, 2005 Aboriginal Spiritual Journey

People sat in their cars in the northbound lanes of Toronto's Don Valley Parkway, at the Don Mills exit. Headed home at the end of the day, they were stuck in the usual rush hour traffic. In the southbound lanes, traffic was typically dense, yet moving steadily. Then things changed. Four police motorcycles, lights flashing, appeared in the southbound lanes. They blocked off the nearby on-ramps. The traffic heading south dwindled to nothing, the road left empty. In a moment, five more police motorcycles, lights flashing, in V-formation, were in the left-hand express lane of the barren stretch of highway. They were moving at high speed. No car moved in the northbound lanes. The motorcycles were followed by three police cars, lights flashing. A short distance back was a hearse containing a flag-draped coffin, followed by two black limousines, dark-tinted glass keeping the mourners inside free of the public's gaze. Another three police cars and four more motorcycles, all with lights flashing, brought up the rear. Behind them, southbound traffic moved like a tidal surge in a narrow gorge. The northbound traffic inched forward.

Another Canadian solider, killed in combat in Afghanistan, was being brought home for burial. Two days earlier, his flag-draped coffin had been carried aboard a military transport at the NATO airbase in Kandahar on the shoulders of members of his unit, his comrades in arms. Now, his family was preparing to bury their son and brother; a wife, her husband; children, their father. Along a stretch of Ontario's Highway 401, the signs read "Highway of Heroes," for it is the section that leads from the Canadian Forces Base at Trenton to Toronto. Many of the fallen soldiers and their families have travelled this route on that final trip home. People, strangers to the deceased and their family, line the overpasses as these motorcades pass underneath. Flags wave, banners read "God Bless," hats are removed, veterans salute. Many of these solemn homecoming ceremonies are items on the nightly news. These ceremonies prompt further reflection on our losses, our role in war, and the contrast between the nation's response to soldiers today and its response to those who died in previous wars.

The Canadian War Museum's chart contains the Canadian casualty figures for World Wars I and II, the Korean War, and Afghanistan. In 1917, at Vimy Ridge alone, more than 10 000 Canadian soldiers were killed or wounded. This battle was pivotal because it turned the course of the war (Cook, 2004). According to the *National Post* (Berthiaume, 2012), the total number of Canadian soldiers wounded in action during the mission in Afghanistan from April 2002 to December 2011 was 635. The total number of Canadian soldiers killed was 158 (Berthiaume, 2012).

	Population	**Served**	**Died**	**Wounded**
World War I (1914–1918)	7 800 000	625 825	61 082	154 361
World War II (1939–1945)	11 500 000	1 086 343	42 042	54 414
Korean War (1950–53)	14 000 000	2 751	516	1 072
Afghanistan (2002–2011)	32 000 000	40 000	158	635

Instead of being flown home, soldiers in previous wars were buried on foreign soil. Many of Canada's war dead are buried in carefully maintained cemeteries in 75 different countries around the world; many still lie in unmarked graves. Every five years since 1985, the people of Apeldoorn, Netherlands, have held a parade honouring the Canadian forces that liberated their town from the Nazis in 1945 (Veteran Affairs Canada, 2010). Returning Canadian veterans are paraded through the town on vintage World War II vehicles, feted at dinners, and thanked for freeing the town by Dutch children eagerly waving Canadian flags. A service is held at the monument for the soldiers who died during the war. The number of veterans has declined steadily, and those who go back are now in their eighties and nineties. The parade of 2010 was the last, and from now on the town will remember the sacrifice Canadians made to free their village with an annual "liberation" street festival.

Death closes out the life span. This final chapter will help you explore a topic that many people find difficult.

Defining Death and Life/Death Issues

LO1 Evaluate issues in determining death and decisions regarding death.

- **Issues in Determining Death**
- **Decisions Regarding Life, Death, and Health Care**

Is there one point in the process of dying at which death takes place, or is death a more gradual process? What are some decisions individuals can make about life, death, and health care?

Issues in Determining Death

Thirty years ago, determining if someone was dead was more clear-cut than it is today. The end of certain biological functions, such as breathing and blood pressure, and rigidity of the body (rigor mortis) were considered to be clear signs of death. However, in the past several decades, defining death has become more complex (Kendall et al., 2007; Quesnel et al., 2007).

Brain death is a neurological definition of death, which states that a person is brain dead when all electrical activity of the brain has ceased for a specified period of time. A flat EEG (electroencephalogram) recording for a specified period of time is one criterion of brain death. The higher portions of the brain often die sooner than the lower portions. Because the brain's lower portions monitor heartbeat and respiration, individuals whose higher brain areas have died may continue breathing and have a heartbeat. The definition of brain death currently followed by most physicians includes the death of both the higher cortical functions and the lower brain stem functions (Truog, 2007, 2008).

Some medical experts argue that the criteria for death should include only higher cortical functioning. If the cortical death definition were adopted, physicians could claim a person is dead when he or she has no cortical functioning, even though the lower brain stem is functioning. Supporters of the cortical death policy argue that the functions we associate with being human, such as intelligence and personality, are located in the higher cortical part of the brain. They believe that when these functions are lost, the "human being" is no longer alive. To date, the cortical definition of death is not a legal definition of death anywhere in Canada.

Decisions Regarding Life, Death, and Health Care

With advanced technology, many individuals are living longer with chronic illness. If deterioration occurs in their medical condition, they might not be able to respond adequately to participate in decisions about their medical care. To prepare for this type of situation, some individuals make earlier choices regarding their treatment in the form of an advance directive.

Advance Care Planning and End-of-Life Care

End-of-life decisions may cause significant anxiety for clients and their families. The complexity of multiple life-limiting chronic conditions, which could lead to frequent and prolonged hospitalizations, often create situations in which patients and/or families are asked to make critical decisions about end of life care (Dube, McCarron & Nannini, 2015). Consequently, decisions made during a time of health care-related crisis usually cause added stress and may not accurately reflect the patient's wishes. Furthermore, inexperience in having **advance care planning** discussions may lead to personal anxiety in the patient/family and lead to medical interventions that may not be desired. The prevalence of life-limiting conditions is not age specific. In fact, decisions regarding advance care planning may encompass infants, children of all ages, young and middle-aged people and the elderly. Many studies have indicated that young people in the late stages of their chronic illness and their caregivers frequently claim that they wanted more information, and to be more involved in decision-making that was required (McBride, 2013).

Generally speaking, the process of advance care planning is an interactive and voluntary method of open, person-centred dialogue by which a patient, together with his or her family and the health care team, reflects and contemplates health care decisions and even documents his or her wishes for future care and medical treatment (You, Fowler, & Heyland, 2014). Interactions and discussions with patients and their families to collaborate with them about disease pathways, treatment choices, and the goals and preferences of patients as active participants in their care, are essential to the attainment of the best advance care planning. There is little doubt that advanced care planning is a fundamental component of effective end-of-life care, and that it should be offered to all consenting individuals and their families (Dempsey, 2014). Within such a paradigm, various advance care planning activities will be undertaken, such as the completion of an *advance directive*. An advance directive is a legal document sometimes called the "living will" in which instructions about the treatment an individual would accept, or refuse, are documented (Musa et al., 2015). An advance directive is a written summary of a patient's wishes to be used to guide a substitute decision maker, or proxy, if that person is asked by a physician, or other health care provider, to make a health care treatment decision on behalf of the individual.

A related activity is the *goals of care* discussion, which happens when, for example, the patient is admitted to a hospital or a personal care home (Winnipeg Regional Health Care Authority, n.d.). The health care team will take time to pursue discussions about the individual's current health condition. Providing the health care team with a copy of one's advance care directive or living will guides and informs the advance care planning conversations. The health care team will work with the patient and family to facilitate the decision making process to pursue a goal of care that is most suitable.

The goals of care are three in nature; first is *comfort care,* in which the interventions are directed to maximize comfort, symptom control, and maintenance of quality of life. Attempted cardiopulmonary resuscitation will not be attempted. The second goal of care is *medical care,* which is comprised of appropriate investigations and interventions used to control and treat the medical condition. Again, cardiopulmonary resuscitation will not be attempted. The third goal is *cardiopulmonary resuscitation* (CPR). This goal ensures that appropriate investigation and treatment are used for the medical condition, as well as attempting cardiopulmonary resuscitation (Winnipeg Regional Health Authority, n.d.). Once the patient, family, and health care team have agreed on the goals of care, the health care team will write these goals of care on the Advance Care Planning Goals of Care form. The patient can request changes to his or her goals of care at any time (Winnipeg Regional Health Authority, n.d.).

An Advance Care Planning kit is available for download in every province and territory in Canada (Dying with Dignity Canada Inc., 2015). The kit contains information and questions that help an individual first to think about his or her wishes for care, and secondly to discuss them with the family and/or designated substitute decision-maker. The kit includes province- and territory-specific forms. Currently, Dying with Dignity Canada Inc. (2015) is in the process of developing a new Advance Care Panning toolkit for Quebec.

Dementia in the Canadian population, especially among the elderly, is escalating. This illness significantly influences quality of life, so it is imperative that informed end-of-life care strategies are available that will benefit not only the patient, but family and care providers as well (Stewart-Archer et al., 2015). Although the term *end-of-life care* was originally applied only to terminally ill patients, it now has been broadened to include those with a life-threatening illness who are not imminently at risk of dying, but might have a prognosis of months to years to live. Important medical and social decisions that need to be made for these early stages of dementia include the introduction of an advance directive (Hamann et al., 2011). Quality end-of-life care should be the right of every Canadian (Heyland et al., 2010).

Several benefits of advance care planning have been cited in the literature. One significant benefit is that of increased patient satisfaction with care (Dube, McCarron, & Nannini, 2015). A study conducted by Asagwara (2015) in a mid-Canadian city, found that a sample of 218 registered nurses was well-informed about advance care planning and reported variable levels of involvement in advance care planning with patients and their families. However, despite the known benefits of advance care planning, many barriers exist, such as personal anxiety about the topic and concern about patient acceptance of the discussion (Nelson & Nelson, 2014).

Bravo and colleagues (2011) conducted a postal survey to estimate the frequency with which Canadians communicate the preferences about the health care provided to them, and any research that involves them, should they become incapacitated. These researchers surveyed five populations (older adults, informal caregivers, physicians, researchers in aging and research ethics, and board members) from the provinces of Nova Scotia, Ontario, Alberta, and British Columbia. One of the findings indicated that two out of three respondents had been advised to communicate their health-care preferences in advance. Verbal wishes were more frequent than were written wishes (69 percent versus 49 percent). The researchers concluded that even though advance planning has increased over the last two decades in Canada, further efforts are needed to encourage Canadians to voice their health-care and research preferences in the event of incapacity.

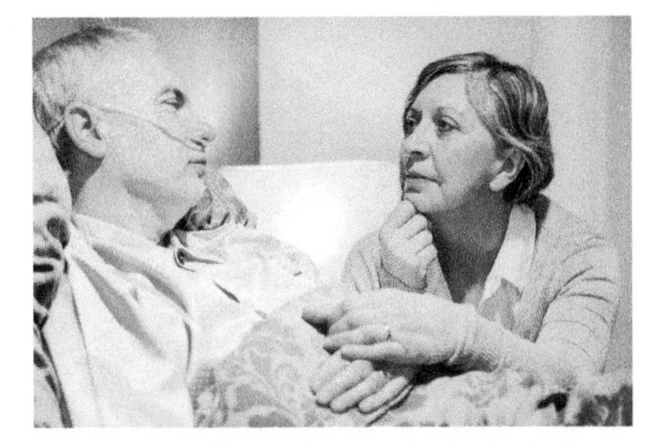

Shutterstock / CandyBox Images

Advances in medical technology have complicated the definition of death. *What is the nature of the controversy about the criteria that should be used for determining when death occurs?*

critical thinking

What are your thoughts about advance care planning? Discuss with a group of peers how health care professionals should approach and engage an individual to develop an advance care directive. What infrastructure is needed in communities to disseminate advance care planning? What can health care providers say to an adolescent about advance care directive for his or her current condition? What is your view of the three goals of advance care planning in regards to an individual who has been admitted to a personal care home?

Euthanasia and Physician-Assisted Dying

Euthanasia *("easy death")* is the act of painlessly ending the lives of individuals who are suffering from an incurable disease or severe disability. Sometimes euthanasia is called "mercy killing" or **physician-assisted dying**. Distinctions are made between two types of euthanasia: passive and active. **Passive euthanasia** occurs when a person is allowed to die by withholding available treatment, such as withdrawing a life-sustaining device. This might involve turning off a respirator or a heart-lung machine, or the removal of a feeding tube. **Active euthanasia** occurs when death is deliberately induced, as when a lethal dose of a drug is injected.

Technological advances in life-support devices raise the issue of quality of life (Fenigsen, 2008; Georges et al., 2008). Should individuals be kept alive in undignified and hopeless states? The trend is toward acceptance of passive euthanasia in the case of terminally ill patients (Truog, 2008). The inflammatory argument that once equated this practice with suicide is rarely heard today. However, experts do not yet entirely agree on the precise boundaries or the exact mechanisms by which treatment decisions should be implemented (Asscher, 2008; Fenigsen, 2008). Can a comatose patient's life-support systems be disconnected when the patient has left no written instructions to that effect? Does the family of a comatose patient have the right to overrule the attending physician's decision to continue life-support systems? These are important questions with no simple or universally agreed-upon answers.

The case of *Sue Rodriguez vs. British Columbia*, in which Sue Rodriguez sought the right to have a physician assist her to commit suicide, dominated the media headlines for weeks in 1993. She had amyotrophic lateral sclerosis and wished to end her life when the quality of that life was severely threatened. The case went all the way to the Supreme Court of Canada, which ruled against her claim. The justices stated, "given the concerns about abuse and the great difficulty in creating appropriate safeguards, the blanket prohibition on assisted suicide is not arbitrary or unfair" (Attorney-General, 1993). Although it was against the law, Sue Rodriguez did have help to commit suicide when she decided to end her life. No charges were laid, since no witness would come forward with information.

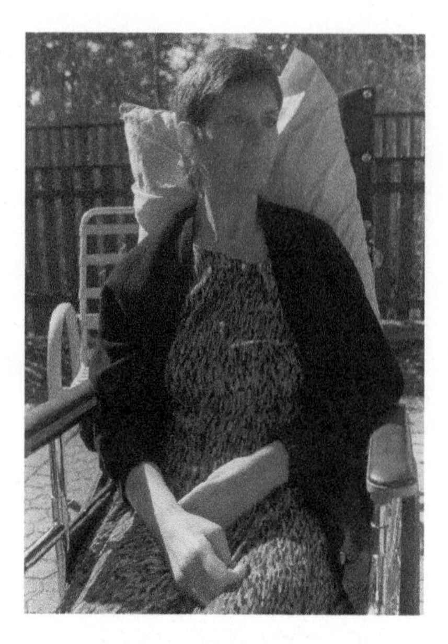

CP Photo Archive/Chuck Studdy

Sue Rodriguez fought for the right to have a physician assist her to commit suicide. Although the Supreme Court of Canada ruled against her, she did commit suicide with assistance.

Although active euthanasia is legal in Belgium (in 2002), the Netherlands (in 2002), Luxembourg (in 2009), and now Canada, it is a criminal offence in most countries, including all states in the United States, except two—Oregon (in 1994) and Washington State (in 2009).

A study on active euthanasia in Flanders, Belgium between June and November 2007 found that 2 percent of all deaths were the result of the administration of life-ending drugs to people who had asked to end their life (Chambaere et al., 2010). They were mainly younger than age 80, had terminal cancer, were in a palliative mode of care, and were largely at home. The study also found that 1.8 percent of the deaths in this area of Belgium during the period were the result of life-ending drugs being given to patients who did not ask to be killed, who tended to be over 80, who did not have cancer, and who were in a hospital at the time of their death. Just over 70 percent were comatose, while 20 percent had dementia. Forty percent of the unrequested euthanized group had, according to the physician, favoured euthanasia in a previous conversation. The authors suggest the unrequested group represents a vulnerable population, people who cannot speak for themselves and need protection. They also suggest that advanced directives could be used to avoid the problem.

Canadian researchers led by Keith Wilson (Wilson et al., 2007) surveyed 379 terminally ill cancer patients on the legalization of euthanasia and/or physician-assisted suicide. They found nearly 63 percent of the patients supported the legalization of one or both, just over 26 percent said no to both, and 11 percent were undecided. Of those 238 who supported one or the other option to end life, 22 patients "indicated a desire to receive a hastened death" (p. 321). Of this small group, 40 percent were assessed as clinically depressed. Wilson and colleagues (2007) noted that these depressed patients ought to be referred for counselling, while the 60 percent who were not depressed counter the often-used argument that only depressed people favour euthanasia or physician-assisted suicide. While loss of dignity was not a significant reason for supporting the hastened termination of life in this study, perceptions of being a burden on others was.

Yun and colleagues (2011), a group of Korean researchers, administered a questionnaire to four groups, one group being oncologists, regarding their attitudes toward end-of-life interventions. The interventions investigated included the following: active euthanasia, physician-assisted suicide, as well as withdrawal of futile life-sustaining treatment, active pain control, and withholding life sustaining measures. The findings revealed that the oncologists had more negative attitudes than those in the other groups toward actively ending life (euthanasia and physician-assisted suicide).

Although Canadian responses to death and dying vary, public support is growing for the decriminalization of physician assisted dying. That is, a substantial majority of Canadians supports the change to the *Criminal Code* that made it legally permissible, subject to cautious regulations, for patients suffering from incurable physical illness to opt for either physician-assisted suicide (PAS) or voluntary active euthanasia (VAE) (Schafer, 2013).

On February 6, 2015, the Supreme Court of Canada rendered its decision (*Carter v Canada*) and unanimously declared that the *Criminal Code* prohibitions on physician-assisted dying (both assisted suicide and voluntary euthanasia) violated the *Canadian Charter of Rights and Freedoms* (Landry, Foreman, & Kekewich, 2015; Supreme Court of Canada, 2015). The Court held that the prohibition on physician-assisted dying deprived the claimants, and others suffering from grievous and irremediable medical condition, of the right to life, liberty, and security of the person. The Court immediately suspending the declaration meant that its decision would not come into effect for 12 months, to allow federal, provincial, and territorial governments to respond, should they so choose, by enacting legislation consistent with the parameters set out in the Supreme Court's decision (Downie, 2015).

Ontario, together with 10 other provinces and territories, established an advisory group of patient, health care professionals, and ethics and legal experts to examine physician-assisted dying (Health Government Ontario, 2015). The end result was that after the advisory group spoke to organizations and experts from around the country, it released its final report and recommendations (Health Government Ontario, 2015). The Advisory Group stated that physician-assisted dying is indeed a critical social policy issue for our generation. A strong belief existed among the participants that physician-assisted dying should be part of a larger discussion about high quality and equitable access to end-of-life care in Canada. They recommended that the federal, provincial, and territorial governments work together to develop a pan-Canadian strategy for palliative and end-of-life care. This strategy would include physician-assisted dying as part of a continuum of services and supports to Canadians at the end of life (Health Government Ontario, 2015).

The Liberal government under Prime Minister Justin Trudeau drafted a new assisted dying law, which received royal assent on June 17, 2016. The new law, Bill C-14, allows physicians or nurse practitioners to provide or administer lethal substances to patients who meet the following five criteria:

1. They are over the age of 18.
2. They have a serious and incurable illness, disease, or disability.
3. They are in an advanced state of irreversible decline in capability.
4. They are enduring physical or psychological suffering that is intolerable to them.
5. Their natural death has become reasonably foreseeable.

These criteria remain controversial to many on all sides of the issue. In summary, physician-assisted dying is new to Canada. A need exists to build and sustain effective capacity, including research and continuing health professional education by all health care providers from different disciplines, as well as public education and engagement.

critical thinking

Differentiate between active and passive euthanasia. What is your position regarding active and passive euthanasia? What are your arguments to defend your position on either active or passive euthanasia? Form a peer group where each member prepares one question and one observation on each type of euthanasia. Then, in group, compare and contrast similarities and differences of opinions. What is your position regarding physician assisted dying? What recommendations would you offer for health authorities to implement a universal palliative care program?

Needed: Better Care for Dying Individuals

The Canadian Hospice Society Palliative Care Association (CHPCA, 2010) states that between 16 and 30 percent of Canadians who die will have access to hospice palliative care depending on where they live in Canada. Interestingly, in two mid-size hospitals in a Canadian city, Cohen and colleagues (2011) used hospital charts of deceased clients to compare the services received by one group who received palliative care to a second group of deceased patients who had not received palliative care. The researchers also compared the care characteristics of both groups. The findings indicated that referral to palliative care services appears to depend upon being admitted to the right hospital. Referral was strongly associated with clients having cancer and being younger. The results suggest that establishing palliative care units or teams of committed health care providers in every hospital could actually increase both referral rates and the equity of access to palliative care services. Collier (2011) states that although some jurisdictions have health centres that give palliative care fairly effectively, no single province or territory stands out as the gold standard for others to copy.

Kaufman (2005) indicates that scientific advances have sometimes made dying harder by delaying the inevitable. Even though analgesics are available, too many individuals experience severe pain during the last days and months of life (Lo & Rubenfeld, 2005). Many health-care providers are increasingly interested in helping individuals experience a "good death" (Brink & Smith, 2008; Lyall, 2007). However, many have not been trained to provide adequate end-of-life care or understand how important it is (Lofmark et al., 2008). End-of-life care should include respect for the goals, preferences, and choices of the patient and his or her family (Harrington & Smith, 2008; Mosenthal et al., 2008).

Chochinov (2007) is a Canadian researcher who is internationally known for his work on death and dying. He claims that health-care providers not only have an important task to conduct, but they also exert a profound effect on how clients experience their illness and on their sense of dignity. He developed a framework for caring to guide health-care professionals toward maintaining client dignity. This framework is called the A (attitude), B (behaviour), C (compassion), and D (dialogue) of dignity conserving care. For example, dialogue should be used routinely to acquaint the health-care providers with poignant moments and experiences of the client's life, with the intent of bolstering the client's sense of meaning and purpose.

Palliative care is a humanized program committed to making the end of life as free from pain, anxiety, and depression as possible. Palliative care can occur in any health-care setting whose aim is to relieve suffering and improve the quality of living and dying (Carstairs, 2010). Past president of the Canadian Medical Association Louis Hugo Francescutti states that palliative care adds quality into the end of life for both patients and families (Lawson, 2014). Whereas a hospital's goals are to cure illness and prolong life, hospice care emphasizes palliative care, which involves reducing pain and suffering and helping individuals die with dignity (Kaasa, 2008; Miyashita et al., 2008). A multidisciplinary team involving health-care and community professionals works together to treat the dying person's symptoms, make the individual as comfortable as possible, show interest in the person and the person's family, and help them cope with death (White et al., 2008). This approach tends to the physical, social, emotional, economic, and spiritual needs of the patient (Moss & Dobson, 2006).

The palliative care movement began toward the end of the 1960s in London, England, when a new kind of medical institution, St. Christopher's Hospice, opened. Little effort is made to prolong life at St. Christopher's—there are no heart-lung machines, and there is no intensive care unit, for example. A primary goal is to bring pain under control and to help dying patients face death in a psychologically healthy way. The hospice also makes every effort to include the dying individual's family. It is believed that this strategy benefits not only the dying individual, but family members as well, probably easing the process of grieving after the loved one's death. The first hospice program in Canada was established in 1974 at St. Boniface Hospital in Winnipeg.

The palliative care movement has grown rapidly in Canada, but advocates continue to underscore the need to develop palliative care options that are available to more Canadians (CHPCA, 2010). Effective palliative care can become possible through building on strengths in palliative care, as well as by addressing existing barriers (Steinstra & Chochinov, 2012). This process involves, first, ensuring physically accessible hospice and palliative care locations, and second, critically thinking about how to include those individuals who have been excluded or stigmatized, such as the vulnerable population. The vulnerable population includes disabled and incarcerated individuals and the homeless who also are in need of palliative care services.

Carstairs (2010), in her report "Raising the Bar—A Roadmap for the Future of Palliative Care in Canada," states that at least 70 percent of Canadians do not have access to palliative care. She points out that Canadians are living longer, but with a multitude of complex health conditions. Further, Canadians who are at end of life and their families need to have access to interdisciplinary health and social services, based on their needs. She claims, however, that for Canadians to have access to quality palliative care, five requirements are needed: a culture of care, sufficient capacity, support for caregivers, integrated services, and leadership. Goals are identified in the report for each requirement. In order to meet these goals, 17 recommendations are stipulated to serve as a road map for the federal, provincial, and territorial governments, as well as for the entire community.

The Canadian Institute for Health Information (2007a) examined the percentage of deaths within hospital-based palliative care in 2003 and 2004 in the four western provinces. They found a range from 13 percent of deaths in Manitoba to 16 percent in Alberta were of people in hospital-based palliative care programs. There are just over 200 palliative care physicians in Canada, some of whom work in the community making house calls in their efforts to support people dying at home (CHPCA, 2010). Whether the hospice program is carried out in the dying person's home, through a combination of home and institutional care, or in an institution, often depends on medical needs and the availability of caregivers, including family and friends (Terry et al., 2006).

Researchers have found that family members provide a large proportion of end-of-life care for their loved ones (CHPCA, 2010). Although this experience can be very rewarding and serve as a source of strength in the time after the patient's death, it is also very demanding. Brazil and colleagues (2009) found gender differences in the nature of the care provided by family members and the impact providing the care had on them. Women were more likely to provide support in toileting-related activity than the males. Men, on the other hand, were more likely to be involved with mobility issues. When the person received care from a woman, they were less likely to receive care from other people.

In terms of stress, not only are physical and mental stress increased for the caregiver, but a recent study found that cognitive functioning can also be impaired (MacKenzie et al., 2007). A study of 209 Canadian palliative care nurses found the group reported lower levels of work stress when compared to other female workers (Fillion et al., 2007). The main sources of stress were worry over self-efficacy, lack of resources, and interpersonal issues with other professionals. It appears that involvement with the person dying and his or her family and friends was generally not a source of stress, but instead was a place where job satisfaction was found.

The Canadian Virtual Hospice, an online resource, was developed to provide support and individualized information about palliative and end-of-life care. It is intended for clients, families, health-care providers, researchers, and educators (Canadian Virtual Hospice, 2013).

Research on cost-effectiveness of palliative care has begun. Johnson and colleagues found that the cost for delivering palliative home care to 434 patients for one year was $2.4 million, or $5586.33 per patient. The average hospital stay time during the period was 64 days. They suggest that home care is cheaper than in-patient hospital care.

Researchers from Alberta and Quebec examined costs a little differently (Dumont et al., 2009). They looked at costs across settings and between those involved in care provision. They found, as expected, that the largest share of the cost was paid by the public health care system (71.3 percent); family costs were next (26.6 percent), followed by not-for-profit organizations (1.6 percent). Hospital costs and home care were the first and second most costly element in care provision, both paid for by the province. Time given by family was the third largest expense.

To this point, we have discussed a number of ideas about defining death and life/death issues. For a review, see the Reach Your Learning Outcomes section at the end of this chapter.

Death and Socio-Historical, Cultural Contexts

LO2 Analyze the death system within your personal, cultural, and historical contexts.

- **Changing Historical Circumstances**
- **Death in Different Cultures**

When, where, and how people die have changed historically in North America, and attitudes toward death vary across cultures.

Changing Historical Circumstances

Until recent decades, the dying process and death were mainly the matter of private decisions made within specific cultures and/or religious frameworks. Currently, questions on how end-of-life decisions are made have become a matter of public policy and ethical debate (Blank, 2011). For example, two things promise to complicate end-of-life decisions in the future: the aging population in most developed countries, and an increasing incidence of AIDS and other chronic diseases in developing countries. Therefore, as a greater proportion of societal resources are exhausted at the life's end, the ethical and policy issues will gain increased momentum. The more we can understand, deliberate upon, and frame the issues right now, the greater will be our opportunities to deal effectively with their rising consequences (Blank, 2011).

Death in Different Cultures

Cultural variations characterize the experience of death and attitudes about death (Baglow, 2007; Walter, 2005). To live a full life and die with glory was the prevailing goal of the ancient Greeks. Individuals are more conscious of death in times of war, famine, and plague. Whereas we in North America are conditioned from early in life to live as though we are immortal, in much of the world this fiction cannot be maintained. Death crowds the streets of Calcutta daily, as it does the scrubby villages of Africa's Sahel. Children live with the ultimate toll of malnutrition and disease; mothers lose as many babies as survive into adulthood; and it is rare that a family remains intact for many years. Even in rural areas where life is better and health and maturity may be reasonable expectations, the presence of dying people in the house, the large attendance at funerals, and the daily contact with aging adults prepare the young for death and provide them with guidelines on how to die.

By contrast, in Canada it is not uncommon to reach adulthood without having seen someone die. Carleton University Professor John Baglow (2007) suggests that the invisibility of real death, which is tucked away in hospitals and handled by professionals, has "generated a proliferation of death discourses" (p. 227). We are more likely to see death in fictional television shows, movies, video games, and, closest to reality, through the lens of the news media.

Most societies throughout history had philosophical or religious beliefs about death, and most societies have a ritual that deals with death (Bruce, 2007) (see Figure 19.1). Death may be seen as a punishment for one's sins, an act of atonement, or a judgment of a just God. For some, death means loneliness; for others, death is a quest for happiness. For still others, death represents redemption, a relief from the trials and tribulations of earthly life. Some embrace death and welcome it; others abhor and fear it. For those who welcome it, death may be seen as the fitting end to a fulfilled life. In many Aboriginal cultures, for example, death is viewed as a natural part of life, as natural as the setting sun. Aboriginal children are not shielded from death; in fact, "It's a good day to die," sums up widespread traditional Aboriginal beliefs. From this perspective, how we depart from Earth is influenced by how we have lived.

Care for the aging and dying is an emerging health issue in Canada, and it affects Aboriginal peoples especially. Hampton and colleagues (2010) conducted a study with Aboriginal elders in Saskatchewan. Their findings add an interesting segment to the growing literature indicating that cultural beliefs, values, and needs are significantly important for dying individuals and for their family members.

Figure 19.1

A Ritual Associated with Death

Family Memorial Day at the national cemetery in Seoul, Korea.

A descriptive cross-sectional study was conducted by Iranmanesh, Hosseini, and Esmaili (2011) to evaluate a good health concept from the bereaved Iranian's family member's perspective. Based on the results, the highest scores belonged to the domains "being respected as an individual," having a "natural death," "religious and spiritual comfort," and "control over the future." The domain perceived by family members as less important was "unawareness of death." The researchers conclude that providing a good death requires that professional caregivers be sensitive and pay attention to the preferences of each person's unique perspectives. Spiritual needs are essential to be considered in the provision of holistic care.

In another study, which explored the Asian American Hindu (AIAH) cultural views related to death and dying, Gupta (2011) conducted interviews with three focus groups. The three groups consisted of senior citizens, middle-aged adults, and young adults. The results of this qualitative study indicate that all three generations were believers in the afterlife and the karmic philosophy. It is interesting to note, however, that the generations exhibited noticeable differences in the degree to which Hindu traditions surrounding death and bereavement have been influenced by the fact that they live in the United States.

Social norms and cultural values shape the meanings attached to values, beliefs, and practices for immigrants who are adapting to a new culture—especially if they are still attached to the beliefs of their country of origin (Gupta, 2011).

In many ways, we in Canada are death avoiders and death deniers. This denial can take many forms, including the following:

- The funeral industry tends to gloss over death and fashion life-like qualities in the dead.
- We often use euphemistic language for death—for example, "exiting," "passing on," "never say die," and "good for life," which implies forever.
- We conduct a persistent search for a "fountain of youth."
- We tend to reject and isolate the aged, who may remind us of death.
- We adopt the concept of a pleasant and rewarding afterlife, suggesting that we are immortal.
- The medical community emphasizes the prolongation of biological life, rather than diminishing human suffering.

critical thinking

What is your personal view of death? Discuss with a group of peers your family rituals associated with death. Design a plan indicating the rituals you would like associated with your own death. Compare and contrast the views of death held by cultures other than your own.

To this point, we have discussed a number of ideas about death in socio-historical, cultural contexts. For a review, see the Reach Your Learning Outcomes section at the end of this chapter.

A Developmental Perspective on Death

LO3 Outline death and attitudes from a life-span perspective.

- **Causes of Death and Expectations about Death**
- **Understanding Death from a Life-Span Perspective**

Do the causes of death vary across the human life span? Do we have different expectations about death as we develop through the life span? What are our attitudes toward death at different points in our development?

Causes of Death and Expectations about Death

In 2012, a total of 246 596 people died in Canada. Of the deaths in 2012, 124 235 were males and 122 361 were females (Statistics Canada, 2012b). The two leading causes of death in Canada in 2012 were cancer and heart disease, which were responsible for half of the deaths. Interestingly, cancer was the leading cause of death in every province and territory. Heart disease was the second leading cause of death in every province and territory except Nunavut, where suicide ranked second (Statistics Canada, 2012b). The other seven leading causes of death, ranked in order, were cerebrovascular diseases (stroke), chronic lower respiratory diseases, accidents (unintentional injuries), diabetes, Alzheimer's disease, influenza and pneumonia, suicide, and kidney disease (Statistics Canada, 2012b).

One of the more interesting historical changes in death is the age group. The infant mortality rate has continued a long-term downward trend, declining from 6.4 infant deaths per 1000 live births in 2001 to 4.8 in 2012. During the same period, the male infant mortality rate decreased from 6.9 to 5.1 deaths per 1000 live births, while for females it decreased from 5.8 to 4.6 (Statistics Canada, 2012m). Life expectancy for seniors has shown an upward trend. A senior in Canada at age 65 could expect to live an additional 20.2 years in 2007–2009, up 2.1 years from 1992–1994 (Statistics Canada, 2012b).

In infants, death is usually the result of complications due to congenital malformations, deformations, as well as chromosomal abnormalities (Statistics Canada, 2012f). Meanwhile, from 2000 to 2009, Alzheimer's disease in older adults had the largest relative increase (24.4 percent) in the number of deaths (Statistics Canada, 2012e).

In both Canada and the United States, three-quarters of all deaths were attributed to the 10 leading causes of death in 2009. However, there were some notable differences. For example, cancer led heart disease as the most common cause of death in Canada in 2009, while in the United States heart disease ranked first as the most common leading cause of death (Statistics Canada, 2012b).

More Aboriginal Canadians die at a younger age than non-Aboriginals. Aboriginal people living in regions where there is a high proportion of other Aboriginal people die at a younger age than those living in areas where there is a low proportion of Aboriginal people (Allard, Wilkins, & Berthelot, 2004). Tjepkema and colleagues (2009) found the life expectancy of Métis men and women age 25 or older was shorter by 3.3 and 5.5 years, respectively, than non-Aboriginals. The rates of cancer among Aboriginal peoples are lower than they are among non-Aboriginal people. Meanwhile, the incidence of heart disease is a leading cause of death for the Aboriginal people (Statistics Canada, 2011d).

Understanding Death from a Life-Span Perspective

The ages of children and adults influence the way they experience and think about death. A mature, adult-like conception of death includes an understanding that death is final and irreversible, that death represents the end of life, and that all living things die. Adults recognize that death comes to all living things, and they know death is the final stage in the human life cycle. Four aspects of death that children and adults do not view in the same way are the following: irreversibility, finality, inevitability, and causality (Willis, 2002). The reality of death is that death is inevitable; it is caused by a breakdown in the functioning of the body (Slaughter, 2005). Most researchers agree that as children grow, they develop a more mature approach to death (Hayslip & Hansson, 2003). Recent research is in general agreement that death is first conceptualized by children as a biological event when they are about 5 or 6 years of age. At that time, children begin to construct a biological model of how the human body functions to maintain "life" (Slaughter, 2005).

Childhood

Unfortunately, children frequently receive negative responses from their parents, other adults, or teachers when they talk about death. Such responses give young children the message that death is a negative concept that they are not to discuss. In fact, when it comes to talking about death, many parents respond in a way that is confusing and potentially harmful to children. It seems that their objective is not to teach, but to protect, their children (Willis, 2002). Most psychologists believe that honesty is the best strategy in discussing death with children.

A study conducted by Cox, Garrett, and Graham (2004–2005) examined the potential influence of Disney films on children's concepts of death. They concluded that certain films may serve as a catalyst to introduce the concept of death into discussions between children and adults or peers. For example, in the film *The Lion King,* death is acknowledged and the young main character grieves and displays a range of typical grieving emotions from self-blame and anger to profound sadness. Lee, Lee, and Moon (2009) state that the concept of death, as a kind of social knowledge, should be included in social cultural contexts.

Death is not well understood during the preschool period. For these children the permanence and finality of death are somewhat problematic to understand. Consequently, death is viewed as an altered temporary state, such as sleep (Hurwitz, Duncan, & Wolfe, 2004). Fortunately, the child is able to interpret meaning from words and images rather than depend solely upon physical interactions (Nielson, 2012). As children enter the school-age period their thoughts become more concrete, organized, and logical (Hurwitz, Duncan, & Wolfe, 2004). Children's perceptions are less egocentric and they are better able to understand the biological basis of death; they begin to comprehend its permanence (Poltorak & Glazer, 2006). This important shift in children's thinking about the biological world allows for a deeper and more detailed account of how the concept of death comes to be understood by childhood (Slaughter, 2005).

A study was conducted by Slaughter and Griffiths (2007) to determine whether or not the developmental acquisition of a mature concept of death—that is, to understand death as a biological event—affects young children's fear of death. The results provided fairly strong empirical support for the widely held belief that discussing death and dying in biological terms is the best way to alleviate fear of dying in young children. Discussing end-of-life issues with the dying child and his or her family can be difficult (Nielson, 2012). However, effective communication, characterized by compassion and openness, has been shown to improve client outcomes and to increase satisfaction (Levetown & American Academy of Pediatrics Committee on Bioethics, 2008). This type of communication must be cognitively informative, and at the same time sensitive to the needs of the client and his or her family. A shift is occurring, with the adoption of the family-centred care model, to include clients, family members, as well siblings in communication efforts regarding end-of-life matters (Harrison, 2010).

An expert on death and dying, Robert Kastenbaum (2007), takes a different view on developmental dimensions of death and dying. He believes, as attachment theorist John Bowlby (1980) does, that even very young children are acutely aware of and concerned about separation and loss. Kastenbaum (2007) also says that many children work hard at trying to understand death. Thus, instead of viewing young children as having illogical perceptions of death, Kastenbaum thinks a more accurate stance is to view them as having concerns about death and striving to understand it.

The following clarification of children's experience with the death of others was provided by Bert Hayslip and Robert Hansson (2003). They concluded that "experiences with the deaths of grandparents, friends, heroes (sports figures, rock stars), and parents are particularly powerful influences on children's awareness of death, as are culturally relevant experiences . . ." (Hayslip & Hansson, 2003, p. 440). School shootings such as the one that occurred at Sandy Hook, terrorist attacks, and the deaths of such public figures as Robin Williams and Prince bring children to a closer understanding of death.

The death of a parent is especially difficult for children (Sood et al., 2006). When a child's parent dies, the child's school performance and peer relationships often worsen. For some children, as well as adults, a parent's death can be devastating and result in a hypersensitivity about death, including a fear of losing others close to the individual. In some cases, loss of a sibling can result in similar negative outcomes (Sood et al., 2006). However, a number of factors, such as the quality of the relationship and type of death (whether due to an accident, long-standing illness, suicide, or murder, for example), can influence the individual's development following the death of a person close to him or her. Stikkelbroek and colleagues (2012) examined the association between parental death during childhood and psychopathology during adulthood. They found that the majority of children overcome the loss of a parent during childhood without experiencing increased mental health problems, reduced functional limitations, or an increased need for mental health services during adulthood.

It is not unusual for terminally ill children to distance themselves from their parents as they approach the final phase of their illness. The distancing may be due to the depression that many dying patients experience, or it may be a child's way of protecting parents from the overwhelming grief they will experience at the death. Most dying children know they have a terminal illness. Their developmental level, social support, and coping skills influence how well they cope with knowing they will die.

Adolescence

During the adolescent years, concepts of death further evolve. However, the understanding of death even among older adolescents may still be more ambiguous and less mature than that of adults (Poltorak & Glazer, 2006). The subject of death may be avoided, glossed over, kidded about, neutralized, and controlled by a cool, spectator-like orientation. This perspective is typical of the adolescent's self-conscious thought; however, some adolescents do show a concern for death, both in trying to fathom its meaning and in confronting the prospect of their own demise (Linebarger, Sahler, & Egan, 2009).

Deaths of friends, siblings, parents, or grandparents bring death to the forefront of adolescents' lives. Deaths of peers who commit suicide "may be especially difficult for adolescents who feel . . . guilty for having failed to prevent the suicide or feel that they should have died, or . . . feel they are being rejected by their friends who hold them responsible for the death" (Hayslip & Hansson, 2003, p. 441). Deaths that result from gang fighting or a random school shooting create fear and trauma, and can lead to depression and anxiety. The adolescent's ability to focus and concentrate on school, jobs, extracurricular activities, and family gatherings may be compromised and counselling may be required.

Adolescents develop more abstract conceptions of death than do children. For example, adolescents describe death in terms of darkness, light, transition, or nothingness (Nielson, 2012). They also develop religious and philosophical views about the nature of death and whether there is life after death.

Recall the concepts of adolescent egocentrism and personal fable from Chapter 11, "Physical and Cognitive Development in Adolescence"—adolescents' preoccupation with themselves and their belief that they are invincible and unique. It is not unusual for adolescents to think that they are somehow immune to death and that death is something that happens to other people but not to them.

Adulthood

Death is the irreversible cessation of all bodily and mental functions. Death is universal for all mankind. Beyond understanding the objective meaning of death, a subjective meaning of death exists at the individual level. These personal meanings of death are constructed by the individual and they are primarily cognitive interpretations of objects and events associated with death that are derived from the personal experiences of the individual. Even though meanings are unique to the individual, certain meanings may be shared with others (King et al., 2006). Meaning in life has been found to be an essential part of the folk concept (Scollon & King, 2004).

Young adults are more realistic about personal mortality than adolescents are. Reactions of young adults to death are influenced by the experience of death of loved ones, as well as whether or not the death was sudden, or had been anticipated. For example, the sudden loss of a loved one appears to shake a young adult's belief in their unique invulnerability. Such an experience can be more traumatic for younger, rather than older adults (Liu & Aaker, 2007). The most frustrating aspect of the grieving process for adults seems to be situations where they have lost a loved one through a violent crime and are unable to find meaning in the event (Currier, Holland, & Neimeyer, 2006). Often, the survivors of loved ones who have been murdered become involved in community or national organizations that support crime victims and survivors of murdered loved ones or those that seek to prevent violence (Stetsone, 2002).

An increase in consciousness about death accompanies individuals' awareness that they are aging, which usually intensifies in middle adulthood. In our discussion of middle adulthood, we indicated that mid-life is a time when adults begin to think more about how much time is left in their lives. Research indicates that middle-aged adults are most fearful of death (Cicirelli, 2006). The inevitability of death has been accepted, and many anxieties are focused on how death will come about. The fact is that to an older person, death is highly important, but it is apparently not as frightening as it was at mid-life. Older adults, though, think about death more and talk about it more in conversation with others than do middle-aged and young adults. They also have more direct experience with death as their friends and relatives become ill and die (Hayslip & Hansson, 2003). Older adults are forced to examine the meaning of life and death more frequently than are younger adults.

In old age, one's own death may take on an appropriateness it lacked in earlier years. Some of the increased thinking and conversing about death, and an increased sense of integrity developed through a positive life review, may help older adults accept death. Older adults are less likely to have unfinished business than are younger adults. They usually do not have children who need to be guided to maturity, their spouses are more likely to be dead, and they are less likely to have work-related projects that require completion. Lacking such anticipations, death may be less emotionally painful to them. Even among older adults, however, attitudes toward death are sometimes as individualized as the people holding them. One 82-year-old woman declared that she had lived her life and was now ready to see it come to an end. Another 82-year-old woman declared that death would be a regrettable interruption to her participation in activities and relationships.

critical thinking

According to the text, our understanding of and attitudes toward death change as we age. How have your ideas about dying and death changed during your lifetime? Has experience played a role in how you now think about death? If you have had no personal experience with death, then where have you gained your information about the topic? Suppose you decide to write your own eulogy to be shared by others at your celebration of life. What would you have the reader of your eulogy say? In what ways might your life experiences change the eulogy you prepared for yourself?

To this point, we have discussed a developmental perspective on death. For a review, see the Reach Your Learning Outcomes section at the end of this chapter.

Facing One's Own Death

LO4 Differentiate the psychological aspects involved in facing one's own death within the contexts in which most people die.

- **Kübler-Ross's Stages of Dying**
- **Perceived Control and Denial**
- **The Contexts in Which People Die**

Most dying individuals want an opportunity to make some decisions regarding their own life and death (Kastenbaum, 2007). Some individuals want to complete unfinished business; they want time to resolve problems and conflicts and to put their affairs in order.

A study examined the concerns of 36 dying individuals from 38 to 92 years of age with a mean age of 68 (Terry et al., 2006). The three areas of concern that consistently appeared were (1) privacy and autonomy, mainly in regard to their families; (2) inadequate information about physical changes and medication as they approached death; and (3) the motivation to shorten their life, which was indicated by all patients.

Kübler-Ross's Stages of Dying

Elisabeth Kübler-Ross (1969) divided the behaviour and thinking of dying persons into five stages: denial and isolation, anger, bargaining, depression, and acceptance. **Denial and isolation** is Kübler-Ross's first stage of dying, in which the person denies that death is really going to take place. The person may say, "No, it can't be me. It's not possible." This is a common reaction to terminal illness. However, denial is usually only a temporary defence, and eventually it is replaced by increased awareness when the person is confronted with such matters as financial considerations, unfinished business, and worry about surviving family members.

Anger is Kübler-Ross's second stage of dying, in which the dying person recognizes that denial can no longer be maintained. Denial often gives way to anger, resentment, rage, and envy. The dying person's question is, "Why me?" At this point, the person becomes increasingly difficult to care for, since anger may become displaced and projected onto physicians, nurses, family members, and even God. The realization of loss is great, and those who symbolize life, energy, and competent functioning are especially salient targets of the dying person's resentment and jealousy.

Bargaining is Kübler-Ross's third stage of dying, in which the person develops the hope that death can somehow be postponed or delayed. Some persons enter into bargaining or negotiation—often with God—as they try to delay their death. Psychologically, the person is saying, "Yes, me, but . . ." In exchange for a few more days, weeks, or months of life, the person promises to lead a reformed life dedicated to God or to the service of others.

Depression is Kübler-Ross's fourth stage of dying, in which the dying person comes to accept the certainty of death. At this point, a period of depression or preparatory grief may appear. The dying person may become silent, refuse visitors, and spend much of the time crying or grieving. This behaviour should be perceived as normal in this circumstance, and is actually an effort to disconnect the self from all love objects. Attempts to cheer up the dying person at this stage should be discouraged, says Kübler-Ross, because the dying person has a need to contemplate impending death.

Acceptance is Kübler-Ross's fifth stage of dying, in which the person develops a sense of peace, an acceptance of one's fate, and, in many cases, a desire to be left alone. In this stage, feelings and physical pain may be virtually absent. Kübler-Ross describes this fifth stage as the end of the dying struggle, the final resting stage before death. A summary of Kübler-Ross's dying stages is presented in Figure 19.2.

What is the current evaluation of Kübler-Ross's approach? According to psychology death expert Robert Kastenbaum (2004), there are some problems with the theory:

- The existence of the five-stage sequence has not been demonstrated by either Kübler-Ross or independent research.
- The stage interpretation neglects the patients' total life situations, including relationship support, specific effects of illness, family obligations, and institutional climate in which they were interviewed.

Because of the criticisms of Kübler-Ross's stages of dying, some psychologists prefer to describe them not as stages, but rather as potential reactions to dying. At any one moment, a number of emotions may wax and wane. Hope, disbelief, bewilderment, anger, and acceptance may come and go as individuals try to make sense of what is happening to them. However, we should not forget Kübler-Ross's pioneering efforts. Her contribution was important in calling attention to people who are attempting to cope with life-threatening illnesses. She did much to encourage giving needed attention to the quality of life for dying persons and their families.

In 1980, Kübler-Ross publicly proclaimed her belief in a life after death. Adding this element to her writing and workshops concerning care for the dying made some of her peers uncomfortable. Some even rejected her work entirely, claiming she was no longer objective. However, many people find her thoughts on life after death comforting and simply an extension of her earlier work, which places death in the context of an entire life.

Figure 19.2

Kübler-Ross's Stages of Dying

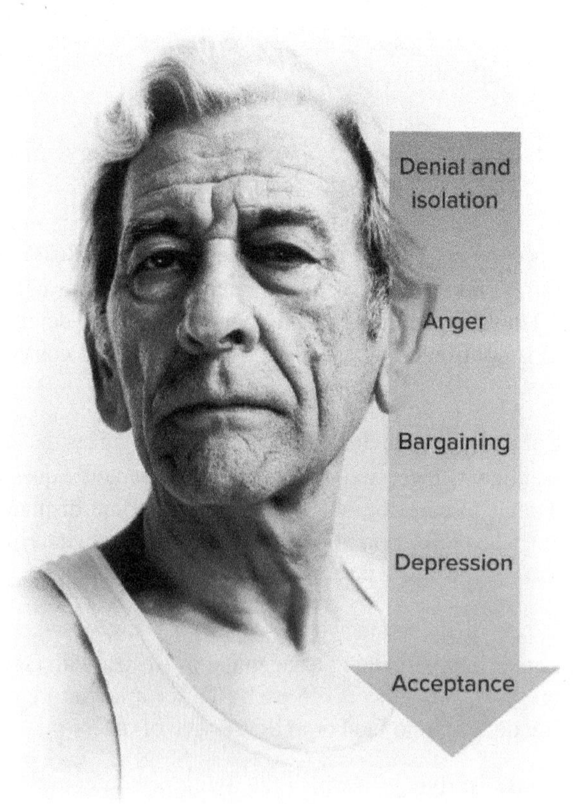

Tim Hall/Getty Images

According to Elisabeth Kübler-Ross, we go through five stages of dying: denial and isolation, anger, bargaining, depression, and acceptance. *Does everyone go through these stages or go through them in the same order? Explain.*

The extent to which people have found meaning and purpose in their lives is linked with the ways in which they approach death. Canadian researchers Sinclair and Chochinov (2012) state that patients and their families facing death identify spiritual and existential needs as vital to their experience at the end of life and they want their health care professionals to address these needs. Spiritual issues have been identified as an important component of quality of life when facing an incurable illness (Grant, Murray, & Sheikh, 2010). Consequently, communicating with patients and their families about their spiritual issues is a core element of comprehensive palliative care (Puchalski et al., 2014).

Based on a study of 50 adult hospice patients, Prince-Paul (2008) reported strong positive correlations among spiritual well-being, communicative acts, and quality of life at the end of life. In another study, 84 percent of the participants indicated a reliance on religious and spiritual beliefs to cope with cancer. These participants considered attention to spiritual concerns by their providers as an important part of their cancer care. These findings highlight the importance of spiritual care in advanced cancer care. (Vallurupalli et al., 2012).

Perceived Control and Denial

Perceived control and denial may work together as an adaptive strategy for some older adults who face death. When individuals are led to believe they can influence and control events—such as prolonging their lives—they may become more alert and cheerful. Even when death is close, a few people never let go of their zest for life. We must respect their denial and follow their lead about what in the moment is vital in their lives (Zerwekh, 2006).

Denial also may be a useful way for some individuals to approach death; it can be adaptive or maladaptive. Denial can be used to avoid the destructive impact of shock by delaying the necessity of dealing with one's death. Denial can also insulate the individual from having to cope with intense feelings of anger and hurt. However, if denial keeps a person from having a life-saving operation, it clearly is maladaptive. Denial is neither good nor bad; its adaptive qualities need to be evaluated on an individual basis.

critical thinking

To explore your own death and dying, respond to the following questions and discuss your answers with several friends or family members. How would you prefer to die, if you have a choice? What are your thoughts about being cremated or buried following your own death? If you were to choose now between cremation or burial following your own death, which would you choose? Why?

The Contexts in Which People Die

Hospitals offer several important advantages to the dying individual—professional staff members are readily available, and the medical technology present may prolong life. Yet, a hospital may not be the best place for many people to die. Population surveys have indicated that most individuals say they would rather die at home (Stajduhar et al., 2008). In examining patient and family preferences for place of dying, Stajduhar and colleagues (2008) found only half preferred home death, while the others preferred to be in a hospital. Further, they found over half of the patients and their families disagreed on where the best place for them to die would be. Stenekes and Streeter (2010) suggest that conversations on the advantages and hurdles each location presents must occur within families, with their loved ones. If available, community-based palliative care can provide necessary supports, in most cases to allow the pending death to take place in the person's home.

To this point, we have discussed a number of ideas about facing one's own death. For a review, see the Reach Your Learning Outcomes section at the end of this chapter.

Coping with the Death of Someone Else

LO5 Identify ways to cope with the death of another person.

- **Communicating with a Dying Person**
- **Grieving**
- **Making Sense of the World**
- **Losing a Life Partner**
- The Funeral

Loss can come in many forms in our lives—divorce, a pet's death, loss of a job. However, no loss is greater than that which comes with the death of a person we love and care for—a parent, sibling, spouse, relative, or friend. In ratings of life's stresses that require the most adjustment, death of a spouse is given the highest number. How should we communicate with a dying individual? How do we cope with the death of someone we love?

Communicating with a Dying Person

Most psychologists believe that it is best for dying individuals and their significant others to know that they are dying so that they can interact and communicate with each other on the basis of this mutual knowledge (Banja, 2005). What are some of the advantages of this open awareness context for the dying individual? The client's hopes can be discussed while anticipation of and preparation for future health states and treatment plans are examined.

Developing an understanding of the client's values and beliefs is essential to help health professionals deliver appropriate client-centred care. The challenges associated with engaging clients and families in meaningful discussions can be made more meaningful by promoting honesty, rapport, trust, and respect (Moore, 2007). In fact, Tulsky (2005) suggests the following for providers: (1) acknowledge the effect, for example "this must be overwhelming for you"; (2) identify loss, for example "it must be difficult to discuss your dependence"; (3) legitimize feelings, for example "being sad is normal under the circumstances"; (4) explore, for example "what scares you most about the future?" Direct discussion and validation of emotion in a supportive way can be highly effective. It is most helpful if health professionals are particularly aware of their own non-verbal behaviour.

In addition to an open communication system, what are some other suggestions for conversing with a dying individual? Some experts believe that conversation should not focus on mental pathology or preparation for death, but should focus on strengths of the individual and preparation for the remainder of life. Since external accomplishments are not possible, communication should be directed more at internal growth. Caring and support for a dying person does not have to come from a mental health professional only; a concerned nurse, an attentive physician, a sensitive spouse, or an intimate friend can provide an important support system (DeSpelder & Strickland, 2005). Figure 19.3 presents some effective strategies for communicating with a dying person.

Figure 19.3

Effective Strategies for Communicating with a Dying Person

1. Establish your presence and be at the same eye level. Do not be afraid to touch the dying person—dying individuals are often starved for human touch.
2. Eliminate distraction. For example, ask if it is okay to turn off the TV. Realize that excessive small talk can be a distraction.

3. Dying individuals who are very frail often have little energy. If the dying person you are visiting is very frail, you may not want to visit for very long.
4. Do not insist that the dying person feel acceptance about death if the dying person wants to deny the reality of the situation. On the other hand, do not insist on denial if the dying individual indicates acceptance.
5. Allow the dying person to express guilt or anger. Encourage the expression of feelings.
6. Do not be afraid to ask the person what the prognosis (expected outcome) for their illness is. Discuss alternatives and unfinished business.
7. Sometimes dying individuals do not have access to others. Ask the dying person if there is anyone he or she would like to see that you can contact.
8. Encourage the dying individual to reminisce, especially if you have memories in common.
9. Talk with the individual when she or he wishes to talk. If this is impossible, make an appointment and keep it.
10. Express your regard for the dying individual. Do not be afraid to express love, and do not be afraid to say good-bye.

Grieving

Our exploration of grief focuses on dimensions of grieving, as well as cultural diversity in healthy grieving.

Dimensions of Grieving

Grief is the emotional numbness, disbelief, separation anxiety, despair, sadness, and loneliness that accompany the loss of someone we love. Grief is not a simple emotional state, but rather it is a complex, evolving process with multiple dimensions (Lund, 2007). In this view, pining for the lost person is one important dimension. Pining or yearning reflects an intermittent, recurrent wish or need to recover the lost person. A recent study revealed that the death of a loved one is most frequently followed by yearning and acceptance, with most of the negative feelings associated with the death diminishing by six months after the death (Maciejewski et al., 2007). In this study, yearning was more common than depression following a loved one's death. Another important dimension of grief is separation anxiety, which not only includes pining and preoccupation with thoughts of the deceased person, but also focuses on places and things associated with the deceased; there is crying or sighing as a type of suppressed cry. Grief may also involve despair and sadness, which include a sense of hopelessness and defeat, depressive symptoms, apathy, loss of meaning for activities that used to involve the person who is gone, and growing desolation. In fact, depression and despair are predictable dimensions of grief (Zerwekh, 2006).

These feelings occur repeatedly shortly after a loss (Moules et al., 2004). As time passes, pining and protest over the loss tend to diminish, although episodes of depression and apathy may remain or increase. The sense of separation anxiety and loss may continue to the end of one's life, but most of us emerge from grief's tears, turning our attention once again to productive tasks and regaining a more positive view of life (Carrington & Bogetz, 2004).

The grieving process is more like a roller-coaster ride than an orderly progression of stages with clear-cut time frames (Lund, 2007). The ups and downs of grief often involve rapidly changing emotions, meeting the challenges of learning new skills, detecting personal weaknesses and limitations, creating new patterns of behaviour, and forming new friendships and relationships (Feldon, 2003). For most individuals, grief becomes more manageable over time, with fewer abrupt highs and lows. But many grieving spouses still report that even though time has brought them some healing, they have never gotten over the loss; they have just learned to live with it.

Cognitive factors are involved in the severity of grief after a loved one has died. One study focused on 329 adults who had suffered the loss of a close relative (Boelen, van den Bout, & van den Hout, 2003). The more negative beliefs and self-blame the adults had, the more severe were their symptoms of traumatic grief, depression, and anxiety.

Long-term grief is sometimes masked and can predispose individuals to become depressed and even suicidal (Kastenbaum, 2007). Good family communication can help reduce the incidence of depression and suicidal thoughts. It is important to remember that each individual processes and recovers from grief in different ways (Zerwekh, 2006). An estimated 80 to 90 percent of survivors experience normal or uncomplicated grief reactions that include sadness and even disbelief or considerable anguish. By six months after their loss, they accept it as a reality, are more optimistic about the future, and function competently in their everyday lives.

However, six months after their loss, approximately 10 to 20 percent of survivors have difficulty moving on with their life, feel numb or detached, believe their life is empty without the deceased, and feel that the future has no meaning. Initially referred to as complicated grief, leading expert Holly Prigerson and her colleagues (Boelen & Prigerson, 2007; Maciejewski et al., 2007) have advocated the use of the term **prolonged grief** to describe this type of grief that involves enduring despair and is still unresolved over an extended period of time. Prolonged grief usually has negative consequences on physical and mental health (Bonanno et al., 2007; Piper et al., 2007; Wortman & Boerner, 2007). A person who loses someone he or she was emotionally dependent on is often at greatest risk for developing prolonged grief (Johnson et al., 2007). A study found that therapy focused on motivational interviewing, emotion coping, and communication skills was effective in reducing prolonged grief (Zuckoff et al., 2006).

Another type of grief is *disenfranchised grief,* which describes an individual's grief over a deceased person that is a socially ambiguous loss that can't be openly mourned or supported (Read & Elliott, 2007; Reilly et al., 2008). Examples of disenfranchised grief include a relationship that isn't socially recognized such as an ex-spouse, a hidden loss such as an abortion, and circumstances of the death that are stigmatized such as death because of AIDS. Disenfranchised grief may intensify an individual's grief because it cannot be publicly acknowledged. This type of grief may be hidden or repressed for many years, only to be reawakened by later deaths.

Dual-Process Model of Coping with Bereavement

The **dual-process model of coping with bereavement** consists of two main dimensions: (1) loss-oriented stressors and (2) restoration-oriented stressors (Stroebe, Schut, & Stroebe, 2005, p. 50). Loss-oriented stressors focus on the deceased individual and can include grief work, as well as positive (such as "relief at the end of suffering") and negative reappraisal ("yearning and rumination") of the meaning of the loss. Restoration-oriented stressors involve the secondary stressors that emerge as indirect outcomes of bereavement. They can include a changing identity (such as from "wife" to "widow") and mastering skills (such as dealing with finances). Restoration rebuilds "shattered assumptions about the world and one's own place in it."

In the dual-process model, effective coping with bereavement often involves an oscillation between coping with loss and coping with restoration (Wijngaards-de Meij et al., 2008). Earlier models often emphasized a sequence of coping with loss through such strategies as grief work as an initial phase, followed by restoration efforts. However, in the dual-process model, coping with loss and engaging in restoration can be carried out concurrently (Richardson, 2007). According to this model, the person coping with death might be involved in grief group therapy while settling the affairs of the loved one. Oscillation might occur in the short term during a particular day as well as across weeks, months, and even years. Although loss and restoration coping can occur concurrently, over time there often is an initial emphasis on coping with loss, followed by greater emphasis on restoration over time (Milberg et al., 2008).

Coping and Type of Death

The impact of death on surviving individuals is strongly influenced by the circumstances under which the death occurs (Hansson & Stroebe, 2007; Wortman & Boerner, 2007). Deaths that are sudden, untimely, violent, or traumatic are likely to have more intense and prolonged effects on surviving individuals and make the coping process more difficult for them (Murphy et al., 2003; Sveen & Walby, 2008). Such deaths often are accompanied by post-traumatic stress disorder (PTSD) symptoms, such as intrusive thoughts, flashbacks, nightmares, sleep disturbance, problems in concentrating, and others (Raphael, Taylor, & McAndrew, 2008). Beliefs about life after death can also impact how individuals cope with death. The Connecting through Research feature explores different views of life after death.

CONNECTING through Research

Life after Death

In this final chapter, we talk about the ending of life, dying and death. Of the over seven billion people on Earth, the vast majority do not believe that the death of the human body is the end of the human being. The world's five major religions, Christianity, Islam, Judaism, Buddhism, and Hinduism, all postulate the continuation of existence after death. Of course, within each major religion, there are differences of practice and belief among subgroups, called sects. Overall, Christians, Muslims, and Jews speak of a resurrection of the person's soul at some point after death. Although each of these three religions offers a different understanding of when and how this resurrection happens, the overall common thread is a day of judgment when the person's life will be reviewed by God. Those who have lived appropriately will enter heaven (a place of comfort and peace) and those who have sinned will be punished (in a place of great pain and sorrow). In the beliefs of some sects of Christianity, the punishment may be temporary, while in others it is permanent. In the Jewish faith, concerns about a life after death are not frequently discussed, as the faith calls its members to focus on living appropriately in the present and to leave to God what will come after life. The Islamic faith is similar to Christianity in tying daily actions with the reward or punishment awaiting their followers after death.

Hinduism and Buddhism approach the idea of life after death in an entirely different way. Both religions see this life as simply one of many that the spirit passes through on its journey of enlightenment. Rather than a day of judgment, these faiths believe that each life you live is connected to what you did or failed to do in the last life or what you need to learn in the present. While Buddhism and Hinduism are different in many respects, the ultimate goal for each is for the spirit to escape the physical ties of the world we know. For Buddhists, this is to escape the ties of pain and desire that the human body has and to reach the state of "Nirvana," or extinction. For Hindus, the goal is to leave the material cycle and become one with Brahman, who is everything physical, spiritual, and conceptual.

Apart from the world's major religions, there are other spiritual or religious practices. Aboriginal cultures around the globe hold beliefs about the existence of spirits after death, whose connection with the living world may be strongly tied to their own behaviours during life or those of the people they left behind. In the past 20 years a "new age" spirituality has arisen in the Western world, which rejects the formal religions and promotes an individualistic approach to spiritual growth. These new age sects often borrow beliefs and practices from a variety of sources, and many believe in a continuation of the spirit after death.

In a text that has offered scientific research to support what is stated about human life-span development, there is little scientific evidence to support what religions or spiritual beliefs say about life after death. Instead, the person is asked to have faith in what their religious or spiritual leader tells them.

Whatever religion or spiritualism people follow can deeply affect the way in which they respond to dying and death. The religions of the world all have specific rituals to perform for the dying person and the dead, to help them transform into whatever comes next. These ceremonies also offer solace and social support for the bereaved.

Cultural Diversity in Healthy Grieving

Contemporary orientations toward grieving emphasize the importance of breaking bonds with the deceased and the return of survivors to autonomous lifestyles.

In the Jewish community, mourning is divided into graduated time periods, each with its appropriate practices (Olyan, 2004). The observance of these practices is required of the spouse and the immediate kin of the deceased. The first period is *aninut*, the period between death and burial. The next two periods make up *avelut*, or mourning proper. The first of these is *shivah*, a period of seven days, which commences with the burial. This is followed by *sheloshim*, the 30-day period following the burial, including shivah. At the end of sheloshim, the mourning process is considered over for all but one's parents. In this case, mourning continues for 11 months, although observances are minimal. The seven-day period of the shivah is especially important in mourning in traditional Judaism.

Grief and mourning rituals are influenced by many factors. Tony Walter (2005) found that in Western Europe and North America, the dominant religious beliefs, type of government and its rules around death and internment of the dead, and the commercial nature of the handling of the dead all influence the nature of the mourning rituals practised. Local variations crop up with the additional influence of sub-cultures and variation in geography and immigration patterns. Thus, while an overall general pattern of grief and bereavement might be suggested for any cultural group, local individual variations will at times create significant differences. This was further examined by Ronald Marshall and University of Toronto Professor Patsy Sutherland (2008), who found that the influence of religion, immigrant culture, and the history of oppression via slavery produced unique local variations in grief and mourning in Jamaica, Trinidad, Grenada, and Barbados. Not only were there differences between the islands, but also within each one.

In summary, people grieve in a variety of ways. The diverse grieving patterns are culturally embedded practices. Thus, there is no one right, ideal way to grieve. There are many different ways to feel about a deceased person, and no set series of stages that the bereaved must pass through to become well adjusted. The stoic widower may need to cry out over his loss at times. The weeping widow may need to put her husband's wishes aside as she becomes the financial manager of her estate. What is needed is an understanding that healthy coping with the death of a loved one involves growth, flexibility, and appropriateness within a cultural context.

Making Sense of the World

Grieving is a healthy and necessary process that individuals must go through to be able to move on with their lives (Heidrich, 2007). Fortunately, most people adapt to bereavement successfully, and such adaptation can even be associated with improving coping, personal growth, and acquiring a new appreciation of life (Dutton & Zisook, 2005). One study found that mourners who express positive themes of hope for a positive future show better adjustment than those who focus on negative themes of pain and suffering (Gamino & Sewell, 2004).

An interesting phenomenon is the near-death experience which is marked by an altered state of consciousness. It generally results from oxygen deprivation, severe trauma, or any number of life-threatening conditions. Individuals who have had near-death experiences often do not fear death (Zerwekh, 2006).

Each individual may offer a piece of death's puzzle. "When I saw him last Saturday, he looked as though he was rallying," says one family member. "Do you think it might have had something to do with his sister's illness?" remarks another. "I doubt it, but I heard from an aide that he fell going to the bathroom that morning," comments yet another. "That explains the bruise on his elbow," says the first individual. "No wonder he told me that he was angry because he could not seem to do anything right," chimes in a fourth family member. So it goes in the attempt to understand why someone who was rallying on Saturday was dead on Wednesday.

When a death is caused by an accident or a disaster, the effort to make sense of it is pursued more vigorously. As pieces of news come trickling in, they are integrated into the puzzle. The bereaved want to put the death into a perspective that they can understand—divine intervention, a curse from a neighbouring tribe, a logical sequence of cause and effect, or whatever it may be. A recent study of more than 1000 post-secondary students found that making sense was an important factor in their grieving of a violent loss by accident, homicide, or suicide (Currier, Holland, & Neimeyer, 2006).

critical thinking

Suppose a friend or relative told you that they were having trouble dealing with the death of a loved one. Using the material in this chapter, what would you do to help them? How will you know whether or not you are helping a grieving family? Compare and contrast strategies you would use if the family's loved one was a child, a young adult, or an older adult. What measures would you take to help the family grieve after you leave the relationship?

Losing a Life Partner

Those left behind after the death of an intimate partner suffer profound grief and often endure financial loss, loneliness, increased physical illness, and psychological disorders, including depression (Kowalski & Bondmass, 2008; Zisook & Kendler, 2007). How they cope with the crisis varies considerably (Ott et al., 2007). A study that included data from 3 years pre-death to 18 months post-death revealed that nearly half of surviving spouses experienced low levels of distress consistently over the four years (Bonanno, Wortman, & Nesse, 2004). Another study found that widowed individuals were more likely to increase their religious and spiritual beliefs following the death of a spouse, and this increase was linked with a lower level of grief (Brown et al., 2004). And a recent study concluded that chronic grief was more likely to characterize bereaved spouses who were highly dependent on their spouse (Ott et al., 2007).

One in two Canadian women over the age of 65 will experience widowhood. Only one in eight Canadian men in the same age group will become widowers. Widowed women are probably the poorest group in North America, despite the myth of huge insurance settlements. Many widows are lonely (Lund, 2007). The poorer and less educated they are, the lonelier they tend to be. The bereaved are also at increased risk for many health problems, including death (Ajdacic-Gross et al., 2008; Elwert & Christakis, 2008).

Optimal adjustment after a death depends on several factors. Women do better than men largely because, in our society, women are responsible for the emotional life of the couple, whereas men usually manage the finances and material goods (Fry, 2001). Thus, women have better networks of friends, closer relationships with relatives, and more experience in taking care of themselves psychologically (Antonucci, Akiyama, & Sherman, 2007). Older widows do better than younger widows, perhaps because they are more prepared for the death of a partner. Men who are widowed usually have more money than their female counterparts, and are much more likely to remarry.

Older adults, however, have unique needs during bereavement. These needs may predispose them to a variety of problems including increased morbidity and mortality (Kowalski & Bondmass, 2008; Stroebe, Schut, & Stroebe, 2007). Finding balance in their completely changed lives is of utmost importance for bereaved caregivers. Re-establishing a balance is a primary objective as they navigate their way through coping with grief and new life circumstances within a complex psychosocial context (Holtslander & Duggleby, 2010). Holtslander, Bally, and Steeves (2011) studied ways in which caregivers who survive the loss of their spouse to cancer find balance in their lives. It was found that bereaved caregivers should be assessed for their risk of losing control of balance, their level of support, and the impact of a difficult caregiving experience. Additional research is required to identify the needs of a wide range of cultural groups, ages, disease states, caregiving experiences, and in varying geographical locations such as rural areas.

How might grieving vary across individuals and cultures?

Social supports help both widows and widowers adjust to the death of a spouse (Schulz, Hebert, & Boerner, 2008; Walsh, 2008; Wortman & Boerner, 2007). Local resources, professional, voluntary, or self-help-oriented programs are available to assist people as they work through their grief. The Bereaved Families of Ontario has chapters across the province providing information, newsletters, social activities, as well as group discussion and support sessions. This organization has a grassroots foundation of people who share their experiences dealing with grief and loss.

Researchers have found that religiosity and coping skills are related to well-being following the loss of a spouse in late adulthood (Leighton, 2008). Further, a study revealed that compared with continually married counterparts, 50-year-old and older adults who experienced the death of a spouse reported a higher participation in volunteer work several years after the death (Li, 2007). The volunteer work helped to protect the spouses from depressive symptoms, and an increase in volunteer hours enhanced their self-efficacy. Another study also found that when older adults helped others following the death of a spouse, they experienced an accelerated decline in depressive symptoms (Brown et al., 2008).

The Funeral

In some cultures, a ceremonial meal is arranged; in others, a black armband is worn for one year following a death. Cultures vary in how they practise mourning.

The funeral is an important aspect of mourning in many cultures. One consideration involves what to do with the body. In Canada, approximately 56 percent of corpses are cremated, while the remaining 44 percent are buried in either the ground or in a vault in a mausoleum (Memorial Society of British Columbia, 2004). Cremation is more popular in British Columbia (at 78 percent) and less popular in Prince Edward Island (at 13 percent). Cremation also is more popular in Canada than in the United States, and most popular of all in Japan and many other Asian countries. The Connecting Development to Life feature discusses the impact of personalizing funerals.

The funeral industry has been the source of controversy in recent years. Funeral directors and their supporters argue that the funeral provides a form of closure to the relationship with the deceased, especially when there is an open casket. Their dissenters, however, stress that funeral directors are just trying to make money; they further argue that the art of embalming is grotesque. One way to avoid being exploited, since bereavement makes us vulnerable to being talked into purchasing more expensive funeral arrangements, is to plan and pay for the funeral in advance. However, most of us do not follow this procedure.

CONNECTING development to life

Personalizing Funerals

War has a way of creating new technologies, often ones to more efficiently kill people. World War I saw its share of new killing technologies, such as tanks, poisonous gases, and improved machine guns. While not invented for or during the war, the airplane made its first combat flight during the conflict. Used in the early months as a means of reconnaissance, it quickly took on machine guns to fight other aircraft and dropped bombs on enemy positions. Flying these machines was not the safest profession, and many of the pilots and crew died after being shot down by enemy aircraft or in crashes due to mechanical problems. According to Florian Schnurer (2008), the public funerals of the pilots took on an overriding political nature as they were used to transmit nationalistic sentiments to the public to sustain the war effort. The political leaders who appeared at these media events became the focus of news reporters' stories, rather than the family of the fallen "hero." Schnurer (2008) claims this was true across Europe; as the war raged on into 1916, every nation used the pilots' funerals as opportunities to communicate with the masses.

At first what took place at the pilots' funerals might seem unnatural, or even offensive. A funeral being used to reinforce a message that a powerful person or persons want the people to believe in does not seem proper. Yet, how we dispose of our dead has always conveyed messages about order and disorder and how to maintain or re-establish the former, and survive or minimize the latter. In the past, religious or spiritual rituals have dominated and shaped the nature of funerals and the mourning process in most cultures in the world (Kastenbaum, 2004; Lynch, 2004). But this is changing.

In the past several decades, funeral directors, clergy, and others have noticed a secularization of the funeral (Emke, 2002; Kastenbaum, 2004, 2007; Lynch, 2004). *Secularization* refers to the removal or downplaying of religious practices within the funeral service. In the place of religion is a *personalization* of the funeral service, focusing on the deceased person's life. Sometimes family members select services are referred to as "celebrations of life," rather than funerals. Many reasons have contributed to this change. As we learned in Chapter 15, fewer people attend religious services and therefore may not know a clergy member to officiate at a funeral. The funeral home can offer to arrange for clergy to lead the service, but the family might ask them to tone down the religious element (Wishart, 2006). Secularization crept into funerals as death was professionalized, with doctors pronouncing it, and funeral directors preparing the body, supplying the location for visitation, the funeral service, and the wake after internment. The customer (the person planning the funeral) is confronted with a line of products to provide "after-death care" to their loved one and to memorialize their life. The marking of a death can be a sizable commercial event.

Robert Kastenbaum (2004) laments this change, suggesting that past death rituals had significant power in marking the endpoint of a life and the starting of a new life for the survivors. Religious services connected the grievers to each other and transferred the deceased from the realm of the living to that of the dead. Today, funeral directors are planning funerals with families that celebrate the individual's life and focus on moving through the event with a minimum of discomfort and pain. Many funeral directors are no longer lowering the casket into the grave in front of the family, seeing it as causes much anguish. Others suggest that lowering the casket is important in accepting the reality of death. The personalization of funerals has been hailed as a mostly positive innovation, allowing families to make a meaningful memorial service for the deceased. In this service, who they were is talked about, their accomplishments hailed, and the personal sense of loss is acknowledged for each of those in attendance.

Today you can pre-arrange your funeral, pay a flat fee for the service, and when you die your family will only need to call the funeral home. Lynch (2004) notes that this is an interesting idea (one in four people over age 60 have made such pre-arrangements), but wonders how it will be received by the children who attend the funeral Mom or Dad planned for themselves and not the one they would have designed for them.

What types of funerals have you attended? How did they seem to you? Were they meaningful? joyous? sad? If you were to plan your own funeral, what would it be like? Would religion or spirituality have a prominent role, or would eulogies by your friends and family dominate? Take a moment and think through these questions. As you do, consider this: some people (for example Kastenbaum, 2007; Wishart, 2006) say that death makes us review all of the deceased person's life and often all of our life up to that point in time. As you think about funerals, yours or another's, what does your life review tell you? It might be interesting to compare notes on funeral plans with your family, friends, or fellow classmates.

critical thinking

Think about the personalization of the funeral service, either your own or that of someone else. In what ways would a celebration of life be appealing to you? On the other hand, what would not be appealing about a celebration of life?

To this point, we have discussed a number of ideas about coping with the death of someone else. For a review, see the Reach Your Learning Outcomes section at the end of this chapter.

Reach Your **Learning Outcomes**

Defining Death and Life/Death Issues

LO1 Evaluate issues in determining death and decisions regarding death.

Issues in Determining Death	▪ Twenty-five years ago, death was assessed and defined in simpler ways. ▪ Brain death is a neurological definition of death, which states that a person is brain dead when all electrical activity of the brain has ceased for a specified period of time. Medical experts debate whether this should mean both the higher and lower brain functions, or just the higher corti-cal functions.
Decisions Regarding Life, Death, and Health Care	▪ Advance care directives are being used by individuals. Advance care planning is an important issue in end of life care. ▪ Euthanasia is the act of painlessly ending the life of a person who is suf-fering from an incurable disease or disability. Distinctions are made be-tween active and passive euthanasia. Physician assisted dying is being examined in Canada. ▪ The need for more humanized care for the dying person includes the de-velopment of palliative care.

Death and Socio-Historical, Cultural Contexts

LO2 Analyze the death system within your personal, cultural, and historical contexts.

Changing Historical Circum-stances	▪ When, where, and why people die have changed historically. Today, death occurs most often among the elderly. ▪ Our exposure to death in the family has been minimized. ▪ Most societies throughout history have had philosophical or religious beliefs about death, and most societies have rituals that deal with death.
Death in Different Cultures	▪ Most cultures do not view death as the end of existence—spiritual life is thought to continue. ▪ Canadian culture has been described as a death-denying and death-avoiding culture.

A Developmental Perspective on Death

LO3 Outline death and attitudes from a life-span perspective.

Causes of Death and Expectations about Death	▪ Although death is more likely to occur in late adulthood, death can come at any point in development. ▪ The deaths of some people, especially children and younger adults, often are perceived to be more tragic than those of others, such as very old adults who have had an opportunity to live a long life. ▪ In children and younger adults, death is more likely to occur because of accidents; in older adults it is more likely to occur because of chronic diseases.
Understanding Death from a Life-Span Perspective	▪ Infants do not have a concept of death. ▪ Preschool children also have little concept of death, often showing little or no upset feelings at the sight of a dead animal or person. Preschool children sometimes blame themselves for a person's death. ▪ In the elementary school years, children develop a more realistic orientation toward death. ▪ Most psychologists believe honesty is the best strategy for helping children cope with death. ▪ Death may be glossed over in adolescence. Adolescents have more abstract, philosophical views of death than children do. ▪ There is no evidence that a special orientation toward death emerges in early adulthood. ▪ Middle adulthood is a time when adults show a heightened consciousness about death and death anxiety. ▪ Older adults often show less death anxiety than middle-aged adults, but older adults experience and converse about death more frequently. ▪ Attitudes about death may vary considerably among adults of any age.

Facing One's Own Death

LO4 **Differentiate the psychological aspects involved in facing one's own death within the contexts in which most people die.**

Kübler-Ross's Stages of Dying	▪ Kübler-Ross proposed five stages: denial and isolation, anger, bargaining, depression, and acceptance. ▪ Not all individuals go through the same sequence, and some individuals may struggle to the end. ▪ Spirituality is an important aspect of holistic care for individuals at end of life care.
Perceived Control and Denial	▪ Perceived control and denial may work together as an adaptive orientation for the dying individual. ▪ Denial can be adaptive or maladaptive, depending on the circumstances.
The Contexts in Which People Die	▪ Most deaths in Canada occur in hospitals; this has advantages and disadvantages. ▪ Many individuals say they would rather die at home, but they worry that they will be a burden and about the lack of medical care.

Coping with the Death of Someone Else

LO5 **Identify ways to cope with the death of another person.**

Communicating with a Dying Person	▪ Most psychologists recommend an open communication system; this system should not dwell on pathology or preparation for death, but should emphasize the dying person's strengths.
Grieving	▪ Grief is the emotional numbness, disbelief, separation anxiety, despair, sadness, and loneliness that accompany the loss of someone we love. ▪ Grief is multi-dimensional and in some cases may last for years. ▪ Complicated grief involves enduring despair that is still unresolved after an extended period of time. ▪ In the dual-process model of coping with bereavement, oscillation occurs between two dimensions: (1) loss-oriented stressors and (2) restoration-oriented stressors. ▪ Grief and coping vary with the type of death. ▪ There are cultural variations in grieving.
Making Sense of the World	▪ The grieving process may stimulate individuals to strive to make sense of their world; each individual may contribute a piece to death's puzzle.
Losing a Life Partner	▪ Usually the most difficult loss is the death of a spouse. ▪ The bereaved are at risk for many health problems. ▪ Social support benefits widows and widowers.
The Funeral	▪ Mourning and funerals vary from culture to culture. ▪ The most important aspect of mourning in most cultures is the funeral. ▪ In recent years, the funeral industry has been the focus of controversy, possibly being replaced with a celebration of life.

review → connect → reflect

review

1. What are some issues regarding the determination of death? LO1
2. What is your personal understanding of death within your own cultural context? LO2
3. What are some variations of death in different cultures? LO2
4. What are some attitudes about death at different points throughout the life span? LO3
5. What is the sequence of stages that an individual goes through when facing death, according to Kübler-Ross? LO3
6. What may be some of your own personal reactions when you face your own death? LO4
7. How would you cope with the pending death of a loved one? LO5

connect

What are the important aspects that you found in the Canadian report on palliative care called "Raising the Bar"?

reflect

Your Own Personal Journey of Life

Have you and your family had a discussion regarding life directives? Have you signed one yet? Explain.

Glossary

A

acceptance Kübler-Ross's fifth stage of dying, in which the person develops a sense of peace, an acceptance of one's fate, and, in many cases, a desire to be left alone.

accommodation In Piaget's theory, individuals adjust to new information.

active (niche-picking) genotype–environment correlations Exist when children seek out environments they find compatible and stimulating.

active euthanasia Occurs when death is deliberately induced, as when a lethal dose of a drug is injected.

activity theory States that the more active and involved older adults are, the more likely they will be satisfied with their lives.

addiction A physical and/or psychological dependence on a drug.

adolescent egocentrism The heightened self-consciousness of adolescents.

advance care planning A process to establish an individual's needs and goals of care for future medical care and treatment

aerobic exercise Sustained exercise (such as jogging, swimming, or cycling) that stimulates heart and lung activity.

affectionate love Also called companionate love, this is the type of love that occurs when individuals desire to have the other person near and have a deep, caring affection for the other person.

afterbirth The third stage of birth when the placenta, umbilical cord, and other membranes are detached and expelled.

ageism Prejudice against others because of their age, especially prejudice against older adults.

agnostic A person who isn't sure whether or not God exists.

AIDS Acquired immune deficiency syndrome; a primarily sexually transmitted disease caused by HIV, which destroys the body's immune system.

alcoholism A disorder that involves long-term, repeated, uncontrolled, compulsive, and excessive use of alcoholic beverages.

altruism Unselfish interest in helping another person.

Alzheimer's disease A fatal, progressive, and irreversible disorder characterized by a gradual deterioration of memory, reasoning, language, and eventually, physical functioning.

amnion A life-support system that is like a bag or envelope containing a clear fluid in which the developing embryo floats.

androgyny The presence of masculine and feminine characteristics in the same individual.

anger Kübler-Ross's second stage of dying, in which the dying person recognizes that denial can no longer be maintained. Denial often gives way to anger, resentment, rage, and envy.

anger cry Similar to the basic cry, with more excess air forced through the vocal chords.

animism The belief that inanimate objects have "lifelike" qualities and are capable of action.

anorexia nervosa (AN) An eating disorder that involves the relentless pursuit of thinness through starvation.

Apgar scale A widely used method to assess the health of newborns at one and five minutes after birth; evaluates infants' heart rate, respiratory effort, muscle tone, body colour, and reflex irritability.

arthritis An inflammation of the joints accompanied by pain, stiffness, and movement problems.

assimilation In Piaget's theory, individuals incorporate new information into their existing knowledge.

atheist A person who does not believe in the existence of God.

attachment A close emotional bond between two people.

attention The focusing of mental resources on select information.

attention deficit hyperactivity disorder (ADHD) A disability in which children consistently show one or more of the following characteristics over a period of time: (1) inattention, (2) hyperactivity, and (3) impulsivity.

authoritarian parenting A restrictive, punitive style in which parents exhort the child to follow their directions and to respect work and effort. The authoritarian parent places firm limits and controls on the child and allows little verbal exchange.

authoritative parenting A style in which parents encourage their children to be independent but still place limits and controls on their actions. Extensive verbal give-and-take is allowed, and parents are warm and nurturing toward the child.

autism spectrum disorder (ASD) A general term for a group of complex disorders of brain development. These disorders are characterized by varying degrees of deficits in communication for social interaction, and repetitive behaviours.

autonomous morality The second stage of moral development, displayed by older children (about 10 years of age and older). By about age 10, children become aware that rules and laws are created by people and that in judging an action one should consider the actor's intentions as well as the consequences.

B

bargaining Kübler-Ross's third stage of dying, in which the person develops the hope that death can somehow be postponed or delayed.

basal metabolism rate (BMR) The minimum amount of energy a person uses in a resting state.

basic cry A rhythmic pattern usually consisting of a cry, a briefer silence, a shorter inspiratory whistle that is higher pitched than the main cry, and then a brief rest before the next cry.

basic-skills-and-phonetics approach An approach to reading instruction that stresses phonetics and basic rules for translating written symbols into sounds. Early reading instruction should involve simplified materials.

Bayley Scales of Infant Development Scales used to assess infant behaviour and predict later development.

becoming parents and a family with children The third stage in the family life cycle that requires adults to move up a generation and become caregivers to the younger generation.

behavioural and social cognitive approach The theory that behaviour, environment, and person/cognitive factors are important in understanding development.

bicultural identity The way adolescents identify in some ways with their cultural group and in other ways with the mainstream culture.

big five factors of personality Consist of openness to experience, conscientiousness, extraversion, agreeableness, and neuroticism (emotional stability) (acronym: OCEAN).

bio-ecological approach Focuses on five environmental systems: microsystem, mesosystem, exosystem, macrosystem, and chronosystem.

biological age A person's age in terms of biological health.

biological processes Changes in an individual's physical nature.

blastocyst The inner mass of cells that develops during the germinal period. These cells later develop into the embryo.

body mass index (BMI) A measure of weight in relation to height.

body transcendence versus body preoccupation Peck's developmental task in which older adults must cope with declining physical well-being.

bonding Close contact, especially physical, between parents and their newborn in the period shortly after birth.

brain death A neurological definition of death, which states that a person is brain dead when all electrical activity of the brain has ceased for a specified period of time; a flat EEG recording for a specified period of time is one criterion of brain death.

brainstorming A technique in which individuals try to come up with ideas and play off each idea. This can be done alone or in a group.

Brazelton Neonatal Behavioral Assessment Scale (NBAS) A test given 24 to 36 hours after birth to assess newborns' neurological development, reflexes, and reactions to people and objects.

breech position The baby's position in the uterus that causes the buttocks to be the first part to emerge from the vagina.

Broca's area An area in the brain's left frontal lobe involved in producing words.

bulimia nervosa (BN) An eating disorder in which the individual consistently follows a binge-and-purge eating pattern.

bullying The use of strength to intimidate or coerce another. Bullying is often repeated or even habitual.

C

Caesarean delivery The baby is removed from the mother's uterus through an incision made in her abdomen.

care perspective Views people in terms of their connectedness with others and emphasizes interpersonal communication, relationships, and concern for others.

case study An in-depth look at a single individual.

cellular clock theory Leonard Hayflick's theory that cells can divide a maximum of about 75 to 80 times, and that as we age, our cells become increasingly less capable of dividing.

centration The focusing, or centring, of attention on one characteristic to the exclusion of all others.

cephalocaudal pattern The sequence in which the greatest growth in size, weight, and feature differentiation gradually works down from top to bottom.

child-centred kindergarten Education that involves the whole child and includes concern for the child's physical, cognitive, and social development.

chlamydia One of the most common STDs. Named for *Chlamydia trachomatis*, an organism that spreads by sexual contact and infects the genitals of both sexes.

chromosomes Threadlike structures that are made up of deoxyribonucleic acid, or DNA.

chronic disorders Conditions characterized by slow onset and long duration; they are rare in early adulthood, increase in middle adulthood, and become common in late adulthood.

chronic stress Stress that is negative, persistent, and as such can be crippling.

chronological age The number of years that have elapsed since a person's birth; what is usually meant by "age."

circadian rhythm Behavioural, physical, and mental changes that occur over roughly 24 hours.

climacteric A term used to describe the midlife transition in which fertility declines.

cognitive mechanics The "hardware" of the mind, reflecting the neurophysiological architecture of the brain developed through evolution; involve the speed and accuracy of the processes involving sensory input, visual and motor memory, discrimination, comparison, and categorization.

cognitive pragmatics The culture-based "software programs" of the mind; include reading and writing skills, language comprehension, educational qualifications, professional skills, and also the type of knowledge about the self and life skills that help us master or cope with life.

cognitive processes Changes in an individual's thought, intelligence, and language.

cognitive theories Emphasize conscious thoughts.

cohort effects Effects that occur due to a person's time of birth or generation but not to actual age.

commitment Personal investment in identity.

concepts A cognitive grouping of similar objects, events, people, or ideas.

congruence The relationship between a person's ideal self and real self as determined by self-selected descriptors.

connectedness Comprises two dimensions: mutuality, sensitivity to and respect for others' views, and permeability, openness to others' views.

consensual validation An explanation of people's attraction to others who are similar to them; our own attitudes and behaviour are supported when someone else's attitudes and behaviour are similar to ours.

conservation Awareness that altering an object's or a substance's appearance does not change its basic properties.

constructive play Play that combines sensorimotor and repetitive activity with symbolic representation of ideas. It occurs when children engage in self-regulated creation or construction of a product or solution.

constructivist approach A learner-centred approach that emphasizes the importance of individuals actively constructing their knowledge and understanding with guidance from the teacher.

contemporary life-events approach Emphasizes that how life events influence the individual's development depends not only on the life event, but also on mediating factors, the individual's adaptation to the life event, the life-stage context, and the socio-historical context.

context The settings, influenced by historical, political, economic, social, and cultural factors, in which development occurs.

continuity–discontinuity issue The debate about whether development involves gradual, cumulative change (continuity) or distinct stages (discontinuity).

conventional reasoning The intermediate level in Kohlberg's theory of moral development. Individuals abide by certain standards (internal), but they are the standards of others (external), such as parents or society.

convergent thinking Produces one correct answer and is characteristic of the kind of thinking required on conventional tests of intelligence.

convoy model of social relations A model in which individuals go through life embedded in a personal network of individuals to whom they give and from whom they receive social support.

coordination of secondary circular reactions Piaget's fourth sensorimotor substage, which develops between 8 and 12 months of age. Actions become more outwardly directed, and infants coordinate schemes and act with intentionality.

correlational research A research design with the goal of describing the strength of the relationship between two or more events or characteristics.

creative thinking The ability to think in novel and unusual ways and to come up with unique solutions to problems.

creativity The process of divergent thinking that requires encounters with the world and a degree of intensity and absorption.

crisis Marcia's term for a period of identity development during which the individual is exploring alternatives.

critical period A period of time in each of Freud's psychosexual stages during which an individual resolves conflicts between sources of pleasure and the demands of reality.

critical thinking Thinking reflectively and productively, and evaluating the evidence.

cross-cultural studies Comparisons of one culture with one or more other cultures; provide information about the degree to which children's development is similar, or universal, across cultures, and the degree to which it is culture-specific.

cross-sectional approach A research strategy in which individuals of different ages are compared at one time.

crystallized intelligence An individual's accumulated information and verbal skills, which continue to increase in the middle adulthood years.

cultural-familial intellectual disability A mental deficit in which no evidence of organic brain damage can be found; IQs range from 50 to 70.

culture The behaviour patterns, beliefs, and all other products of a group that are passed on from generation to generation.

culture-fair tests Tests of intelligence that are intended to be free of cultural bias.

cyberbullying Verbal and written assault through cellphones, Web sites, webcams, chat rooms, email, online profiles, and MUD rooms, as well as altered sexual photographs.

D

deferred imitation Imitation that occurs after a time delay of hours or days.

dementia A global term for any neurological disorder in which the primary symptoms involve a deterioration of mental functioning.

denial and isolation Kübler-Ross's first stage of dying, in which the person denies that death is really going to take place.

depression Experiencing, over a prolonged period of time, a range of symptoms, including fatigue, irritability, inability to make decisions, sleeping problems, lack of interest in daily activities, and suicidal thoughts.

descriptive research A research design used to observe and record behaviour.

developmentally appropriate practice Education based on knowledge of the typical development of children within an age span (age appropriateness) and the uniqueness of the child (individual appropriateness).

differentiation versus role preoccupation Peck's developmental task in which older adults must redefine their worth in terms of something other than work roles.

difficult child Tends to react negatively and cry frequently, engages in irregular daily routines, and is slow to accept new experiences.

direct instruction approach A structured, teacher-centred approach that is characterized by teacher direction and control, maximum time spent on learning tasks, and efforts to keep negative affect to a minimum.

dishabituation The increase in responsiveness after a change in stimulation.

divergent thinking Produces many answers to the same question and is characteristic of creativity.

divided attention Concentrating on more than one activity at the same time.

DNA (deoxyribonucleic acid) A molecule in the shape of a double helix; contains genetic information.

dopamine One of the key brain chemicals that carry and influence messages between nerve cells.

doula A caregiver who provides continuous physical, emotional, and educational support to the mother before, during, and after childbirth.

dual-process model of coping with bereavement Consists of two main dimensions: (1) loss-oriented stressors and (2) restoration-oriented stressors.

dynamic systems theory The perspective that infants assemble motor skills for perceiving and acting.

dyslexia A category of learning disabilities involving a severe impairment in the ability to read and spell.

E

easy child Generally is in a positive mood, quickly establishes regular routines in infancy, and adapts easily to new experiences.

eclectic theoretical orientation An orientation that does not follow any one theoretical approach, but rather selects the best features from each theory.

ego According to Freud, the "executive branch" of the psyche, used for reasoning and decision making.

ego transcendence versus ego preoccupation Peck's developmental task in which older adults must recognize that although death is inevitable and probably not too far away, they feel at ease with themselves by realizing that they have contributed to the future through the competent raising of their children or through their vocation and ideas.

egocentrism The inability to distinguish between one's own perspective and someone else's perspective.

elaboration An important strategy for remembering that involve engaging in more extensive processing of information.

eldercare The physical and emotional caregiving for older members of the family, whether that care is day-to-day physical assistance or responsibility for arranging and overseeing such care.

embryonic period Prenatal development that occurs two to eight weeks after conception, during which the rate of cell differentiation intensifies, support systems for the cells form, and organs appear.

emerging adulthood Arnett's description of young people between the ages of 18 and 25 who have left the dependency of childhood, but have not yet fully assumed the enduring responsibilities of adulthood.

emotion Feeling, or affect, that occurs when a person is in a state or an interaction that is important to him or her, especially to his or her well-being.

emotion regulation Effectively managing arousal to adapt to and reach a goal.

emotional intelligence A form of social intelligence that involves the ability to monitor one's own and others' feelings and emotions, to discriminate among them, and to use this information to guide one's thinking and action.

empty nest syndrome Occurs when marital satisfaction decreases because parents derive considerable satisfaction from their children, and the children's departure leaves parents with empty feelings.

epigenetics The study of ongoing, bidirectional interchange of biological and environmental factors that result in heritable modifications, but which do not alter DNA, our genetic code.

episodic memory The retention of information about the where and when of life's happenings.

episodic stress Stress that is related to an event which, once coped with, is over.

equilibration A mechanism that Piaget proposed to explain how children shift from one stage of thought to the next.

erectile dysfunction The inability to adequately achieve and maintain an erection that results in satisfactory sexual performance.

Erikson's theory Eight stages of psychosocial development unfold throughout the human life span. Each stage consists of a unique developmental task that confronts individuals with a crisis that must be faced.

ethnicity A characteristic based on cultural heritage, nationality characteristics, race, religion, and language.

ethologists Scientists who research the connections between animal and human behaviours.

ethology The study of animals to discover their responses to the environment, their physiological makeup, their communication abilities, and their evolutionary aspects.

euthanasia The act of painlessly ending the lives of individuals who are suffering from an incurable disease or severe disability.

evocative genotype–environment correlations Exist when the child's genotype elicits certain types of physical and social environments.

evolutionary psychology A contemporary approach that emphasizes that behaviour is a function of mechanisms, requires input for activation, and is ultimately related to survival and reproduction.

evolutionary theory of aging This theory states that natural selection has not eliminated many harmful conditions and non-adaptive characteristics in older adults; thus, the benefits conferred by evolution decline with age because natural selection is linked to reproductive fitness.

executive attention Aspects of thinking that include planning actions, allocating attention to goals, detecting and compensating for errors, monitoring progress on tasks, and dealing with novel or difficult circumstances.

executive function An umbrella-like concept that consists of a number of higher-level cognitive processes linked to the development of the brain's frontal cortex. Executive function involves managing one's thought to engage in goal-directed behaviour and self-control.

experiment A carefully regulated procedure in which one or more of the factors believed to influence the behaviour being studied are manipulated, while all other factors are held constant.

expertise Having extensive, highly organized knowledge and understanding of a particular domain.

explicit memory Memory of facts and experiences that individuals consciously know and can state.

external locus of control Events that affect individuals are considered to be the result of fate or higher powers.

F

family in later life The sixth and final stage in the family life cycle, when retirement alters a couple's lifestyle, requiring adaptation. Grandparenting also characterizing many families in this stage.

family nearing the end of life The seventh and final stage in the family life cycle, is characterized by the fact that death is near and the spouse must deal with the loss of a partner, siblings, or other peers.

family with adolescents The fourth stage of the family life cycle in which adolescents push for autonomy and seek to develop their own identities.

fast mapping The ability to make an initial connection between a word and its referent after only limited exposure to the word.

fertilization The process that, in humans, begins when a female gamete (ovum) fuses with a male gamete (sperm) to create a zygote.

fetal period Prenatal development that begins two months after conception and lasts for seven months, on average.

fine motor skills Motor skills that involve more finely tuned movements, such as finger dexterity.

first habits and primary circular reactions Piaget's second sensorimotor substage, which develops between 1 and 4 months of age. In this substage, the infant coordinates sensation and two types of schemes: habits and primary circular reactions.

fluid intelligence An individual's ability to reason abstractly, which begins to decline in the middle adulthood years.

free-radical theory A microbiological theory of aging that states that people age because inside their cells' normal metabolism produces unstable oxygen molecules known as free radicals. These molecules ricochet around inside cells, damaging DNA and other cellular structures.

Freud's five psychosexual stages Freud postulated that as children grow up, their focus of pleasure and sexual impulses shifts from the oral stage to the anal stage, followed by the phallic stage, the latency period, and finally the genital stage.

fuzzy trace theory States that memory is best understood by considering two types of memory representations: (1) verbatim memory trace, and (2) gist. In this theory, older children's better memory is attributed to fuzzy traces created by extracting the gist of information.

G

games Activities engaged in for pleasure that include rules and often involve competition with one or more individuals.

gender The social and psychological dimensions of being male or female.

gender identity The sense of being male or female, which most children acquire by the time they are 3 years old.

gender role A set of expectations that prescribe how females or males should think, act, and feel.

gender schema theory The idea that gender-typing emerges as children gradually develop gender schemas of what is gender-appropriate and gender-inappropriate in their culture.

gender stereotypes Broad categories that reflect general impressions and beliefs about females and males.

gender typing The acquisition of a traditional masculine or feminine role.

generational inequity An aging society's unfairness to its younger members due to older adults piling up advantages by receiving inequitably large allocations of resources.

genes Units of hereditary information composed of DNA; act as a blueprint for cells to reproduce themselves and manufacture the proteins that maintain life.

genital herpes A highly contagious sexually transmitted disease caused by a large family of viruses of different strains. These strains also produce other, non–sexually transmitted diseases, such as chicken pox and mononucleosis.

genotype A person's genetic heritage; the actual genetic material.

germinal period Prenatal development in the first two weeks after conception; includes the creation of the zygote, continued cell division, and the attachment of the zygote to the uterine wall.

gifted Refers to children whose scores on IQ tests indicate that their mental age is considerably higher than their chronological age.

gonads The sex glands—the testes in males and the ovaries in females.

gonorrhea Reported to be one of the most common STIs in Canada, this sexually transmitted disease is caused by a bacterium called *Gonococcus*, which thrives in the moist mucous membranes lining the mouth, throat, vagina, cervix, urethra, and anal tract.

grasping reflex A neonatal reflex that occurs when something touches the infant's palm; the infant responds by grasping tightly.

grief The emotional numbness, disbelief, separation anxiety, despair, sadness, and loneliness that accompany the loss of someone we love.

gross motor skills Involve large muscle activities, such as moving one's arms and walking.

H

habituation Decreased responsiveness to a stimulus after repeated presentations of the stimulus.

heritability The fraction of variance in a population that is attributed to genetics and is computed using correlational techniques.

heteronomous morality The first stage of moral development in Piaget's theory, occurring from approximately 4 to 7 years of age. Justice and rules are conceived of as unchangeable properties of the world, removed from the control of people.

hidden curriculum The moral atmosphere communicated through the school's rules, regulations, deportment, and moral orientation.

hormonal stress theory States that aging in the body's hormonal system can lower resilience to stress and increase the likelihood of disease.

hormones Powerful chemical substances secreted by the endocrine glands and carried through the body by the bloodstream.

HPV A virus (human papillomavirus) that causes warts on people; a few types of the virus cause warts on the genitals.

humanists Psychologists who believe people work hard to become the best they can possibly become.

hypothalamus A structure in the higher portion of the brain that monitors eating, drinking, and sex.

hypotheses Specific assumptions and predictions that can be tested to determine their accuracy.

hypothetical-deductive reasoning A type of problem solving in which an individual creates a hypothesis, deduces implications, and tests implications.

I

id According to Freud, the element of personality consisting of instincts, which are an individual's reservoir of psychic energy.

identity Our self-portraits that develop over our lifetime and are made up of many components, including negations and affirmations of various roles and characteristics.

identity achievement Marcia's term for individuals who have undergone a crisis and have made a commitment.

identity diffusion Marcia's term for individuals who have not yet experienced a crisis (they have not explored meaningful alternatives) or made any commitments.

identity foreclosure Marcia's term for individuals who have made a commitment but have not experienced a crisis.

identity moratorium Marcia's term for individuals who are in the midst of a crisis, but their commitments are either absent or vaguely defined.

imaginary audience Adolescents' belief that others are as interested in them as they themselves are.

imminent justice The concept that if a rule is broken, punishment will be meted out immediately.

implicit memory Memory without conscious recollection; it involves skills and routine procedures that are automatically performed.

incongruity The gap between the real self (the "I am") and the ideal self (the "I should be").

individual differences The stable, consistent ways in which people differ from each other.

individuality Self-assertion, the ability to have and communicate a point of view, and separateness, the use of communication patterns to express how one is different from others.

indulgent parenting A style in which parents are highly involved with their children but place few demands or controls on them.

infant-directed speech A type of speech with a higher-than-normal pitch that involves the use of simple words and sentences.

infinite generativity The ability to produce a seemingly endless number of meaningful sentences using a finite set of words and rules.

information-processing approach Emphasizes that individuals manipulate information, monitor it, and strategize about it. The processes of memory and thinking are central to the approach.

insecure avoidant babies Show insecurity by avoiding the caregiver.

insecure disorganized babies Show insecurity by being disorganized and disoriented.

insecure resistant babies Often cling to the caregiver, then resist by fighting against the closeness, perhaps by kicking or pushing away.

integrity versus despair Erikson's eighth and final stage of development, which individuals experience in late adulthood; involves reflecting on the past and either piecing together a positive review or concluding that one's life has not been well spent.

intellectual disability A condition of limited mental ability in which the individual (1) has low IQ, usually below 70 on a traditional intelligence test, (2) has difficulty adapting to the demands of everyday life, and (3) first exhibits these characteristics by the age of 18.

intelligence Problem-solving skills and the ability to learn from and adapt to life's everyday experiences.

intelligence quotient (IQ) A person's mental age divided by chronological age, multiplied by 100. Depending on the mental age and the chronological age, a person's IQ can be above, equal to, or below 100.

intelligent design The belief that the origin and existence of life and the wondrous miracles of nature are the plan of a supreme intelligence or creator.

intermodal perception The ability to relate and integrate information from two or more sensory modalities, such as vision and hearing.

internal locus of control The belief that the individual can control life events.

internalization The developmental change from behaviour that is externally controlled to behaviour that is controlled by internal standards and principles.

internalization of schemes Piaget's sixth and final sensorimotor substage, which develops between 18 and 24 months of age. In this substage, the infant develops the ability to use primitive symbols.

intimacy in friendships Self-disclosure and the sharing of private thoughts.

intuitive thought substage Occurs between approximately 4 and 7 years of age, when children begin to use primitive reasoning and want to know the answers to all sorts of questions.

J

justice perspective Focuses on the rights of the individual; individuals independently make moral decisions.

K

kwashiorkor A condition caused by a deficiency in protein, in which the child's abdomen and feet swell with water.

L

laboratory A controlled setting where many of the complex factors of the "real world" are absent.

language A form of communication, whether spoken, written, or signed, that is based on a system of symbols.

language acquisition device (LAD) A biological endowment that enables the child to detect certain language categories, such as phonology, syntax, and semantics.

lateralization Specialization of function in one hemisphere of the cerebral cortex or the other.

launching The process by which youths move into adulthood and exit their family of origin.

launching children and moving on The fifth stage in the family life cycle, a time of launching children, playing an important role in linking generations, and adapting to mid-life changes in development.

learning disability A disability that involves (1) normal intelligence or above, (2) difficulties in at least one academic area and usually several, and (3) no other problem or disorder, such as mental retardation, that can be determined as causing the difficulty.

leaving home and becoming a single adult The first stage in the family life cycle, which involves launching.

leisure The pleasant times after work when individuals are free to pursue activities and interests of their own choosing.

life expectancy The number of years that probably will be lived by the average person born in a particular year.

life span The upper boundary of life, the maximum number of years an individual can live. The maximum life span of human beings is about 120 years.

life-span development The pattern of change that begins at conception and continues through the life cycle.

life-span perspective The view that development is lifelong, multidimensional, multidirectional, plastic, contextual, and multidisciplinary and involves growth, maintenance, and regulation.

locus of control The perceived extent to which individuals believe they have control over the events that affect them.

long-term memory The memory component in which individuals retain information for a long period of time, even indefinitely.

long-term memory A relatively permanent and unlimited type of memory that increases with age during middle and late childhood.

longitudinal approach A research strategy in which the same individuals are studied over a period of time, usually several years or more.

low-birth-weight infant Born after a regular period of gestation (the length of time between conception and birth) of 38 to 42 weeks but who weighs less than 2.5 kg.

M

mainstreaming Educating a child with special education needs in a regular classroom.

major depression A mood disorder in which the individual is deeply unhappy, demoralized, self-derogatory, and bored. The individual with major depression does not feel well, loses stamina easily, has a poor appetite, and is listless and unmotivated.

MAMA cycles The identity status changes from moratorium, to achievement, to moratorium, to achievement that are repeated throughout life.

marasmus A wasting away of body tissues in the infant's first year, caused by severe protein-calorie deficiency.

meditation A variety of practices intended to foster clarity of thought, well-being, and relief from stress by focusing attention with calmness and concentration.

meiosis The process of cellular division that divides sex cells and produces four daughter cells, each with 23 single chromosomes.

menarche A girl's first menstruation.

menopause The time in middle age, usually in the late forties or early fifties, when a woman's menstrual periods completely cease.

mental age (MA) An individual's ability to solve problems on a diagnostic instrument relative to others of the same chronological age.

metacognition Cognition about cognition, or knowing about knowing metalinguistic awareness Knowledge about language, such as knowing what a preposition is or the ability to discuss the sounds of language.

middle adulthood Generally considered to be the developmental period beginning at approximately 40 years of age and extending to about 60 or 65 years of age.

midwife A responsible and accountable professional who works in partnership with women to give the necessary support, care, and advice during pregnancy, labour, and the postpartum period.

mitochondrial theory States that aging is due to the decay of mitochondria. It appears that this decay is primarily due to oxidative damage and loss of critical micronutrients supplied by the cell.

mitosis The process of cellular division during which cellular material is duplicated and two daughter cells are formed.

Montessori approach An educational philosophy in which children are given considerable freedom and spontaneity in choosing activities.

moral development Thoughts and feelings regarding standards of right and wrong and behaviours regarding rules and conventions about what people should do in their interactions with others.

moral reasoning Rules that focus on ethical issues and morality. They are obligatory, widely accepted, and somewhat impersonal.

Moro reflex A neonatal startle response that occurs in reaction to a sudden, intense noise or movement. When startled, the newborn arches its back, throws its head back, and flings out its arms and legs. Then the newborn rapidly draws its arms and legs close to the centre of the body.

multi-infarct dementia Involves a sporadic and progressive loss of intellectual functioning caused by repeated temporary obstruction of blood flow in cerebral arteries.

multiculturalism The coexistence of distinct ethnic and cultural groups in the same society.

myelination The process in which nerve cells are covered and insulated with a layer of fat cells, increasing the speed at which information travels through the nervous system.

N

natural childbirth Developed in 1914 by Dick-Read, this method attempts to reduce the mother's pain by decreasing her fear through education about childbirth and relaxation techniques during delivery.

naturalistic observation Observing behaviour in real-world settings, making no effort to manipulate or control the situation.

nature An organism's biological inheritance.

nature-nurture controversy Debate about whether development is primarily influenced by nature or nurture.

neglectful parenting A style in which the parent is very uninvolved in the child's life.

Neonatal Intensive Care Unit Network Neurobehavioral Scale (NNNS) Provides a more comprehensive analysis of the newborn's behaviour, neurological and stress responses, and regulatory capacities; an offspring of the NBAS.

neurogenesis The generation of new neurons.

neuron Nerve cell that handles information processing at the cellular level.

neuroscience Scientific study of the brain, the nervous system, and the spinal cord in an effort to understand how these organs and systems work as well as how to respond when they malfunction.

new couple The second stage in the family life cycle, in which two individuals from separate families of origin unite to form a new family system.

non-shared environmental experiences The child's own unique experiences, both within the family and outside the family, that are not shared by another sibling. Thus, experiences occurring within the family can be part of the "non-shared environment."

normal distribution A symmetrical distribution with most scores falling in the middle of the possible range of scores and a few scores appearing toward the extremes of the range.

nurture An organism's environmental experiences.

O

obesity According to the World Health Organization (WHO), obesity is defined as having a body mass index (BMI) equal to or more than 30.

object permanence The Piagetian term for one of an infant's most important accomplishments: understanding that objects and events continue to exist even when they cannot directly be seen, heard, or touched.

observation A systematic and scientific inquiry into behaviour that may be conducted in a natural environment or a laboratory setting.

operations In Piaget's theory, an internalized set of actions that allow a child to do mentally what before he or she did physically.

organic intellectual disability A genetic disorder or condition involving brain damage that is linked to a low level of intellectual functioning.

organization Piaget's concept of grouping isolated behaviours and thoughts into a higher-order system.

organogenesis Organ formation that takes place during the first two months of prenatal development.

osteoporosis An aging disorder involving an extensive loss of bone tissue. It is the main reason many older adults walk with a marked stoop.

P

pain cry A sudden appearance of loud crying without preliminary moaning and a long initial cry followed by an extended period of breath holding.

palliative care A humanized program committed to making the end of life as free from pain, anxiety, and depression as possible.

Parkinson's disease A chronic, progressive disease characterized by muscle tremors, slowing of movement, and partial facial paralysis.

passive euthanasia Occurs when a person is allowed to die by withholding available treatment, such as withdrawing a life-sustaining device.

passive genotype–environment correlations Exist when the natural parents, who are genetically related to the child, provide a rearing environment for the child.

perception The interpretation of what is sensed.

personal fable The part of adolescent egocentrism that involves an adolescent's sense of uniqueness and invincibility.

perspective taking The ability to assume other people's perspectives and understand their thoughts and feelings.

phenotype The way an individual's genotype is expressed in observed and measurable characteristics.

phonology The study of how sounds are organized and used.

physician assisted dying Medical professionals helping patients to achieve the death they want.

Piaget's theory Children actively construct their understanding of the world and go through four stages of cognitive development.

pituitary gland An important endocrine gland that controls growth and regulates other glands.

placenta A life-support system that consists of a disc-shaped group of tissues in which small blood vessels from the mother and offspring intertwine but do not join.

plasticity The capacity for change.

positive psychology This approach contends that understanding happiness can facilitate human grown and development.

post-formal thought Involves understanding that the correct answer to a problem requires reflective thinking and can vary from one situation to another, and that the search for truth is often an ongoing, never-ending process.

postconventional reasoning The highest level in Kohlberg's theory of moral development. Morality is completely internalized and is not based on others' standards.

postpartum depression A major depressive episode that typically occurs about four weeks after delivery. Women with postpartum depression have such strong feelings of sadness, anxiety, or despair, that for at least a two-week period they have trouble coping with daily tasks.

postpartum period Occurs after childbirth when the mother adjusts, both physically and psychologically, to the process of childbirth; lasts for about six weeks or until her body has completed its adjustment and returned to a near pre-pregnant state.

practice play The repetition of behaviour when new skills are being learned or when physical or mental mastery and coordination of skills are required for games or sports.

preconventional reasoning The lowest level in Kohlberg's theory of moral development. The individual shows no internalization of moral values—moral reasoning is controlled by external rewards and punishment.

preoperational stage Piaget's second stage, lasting from 2 to 7 years of age, during which children begin to represent the world with words, images, and drawings. They form stable concepts and begin to reason.

prepared childbirth A childbirth strategy similar to natural childbirth but that includes a special breathing technique to control pushing in the final stages of labour and a more detailed anatomy and physiology course; developed by Fernand Lamaze.

pretense/symbolic play Play in which the child transforms the physical environment into a symbol.

preterm infant Born prior to 38 weeks after conception.

primary emotions Present in humans and other animals and emerge early in life; examples are joy, anger, sadness, fear, and disgust.

prolonged grief Grief that involves enduring despair and is still unresolved over an extended period of time.

prospective memory Involves remembering to do something in the future.

proximodistal pattern The sequence in which growth starts at the centre of the body and moves toward the extremities.

psychoanalytic approach Development is primarily unconscious and heavily coloured by emotion. Behaviour is merely a surface characteristic. It is important to analyze the symbolic meanings of behaviour. Early experience is important to development.

psychoanalytic theory of gender Derived from Freud's view that the preschool child develops a sexual attraction to the opposite-sex parent, renounces this attraction by approximately 5 or 6 years of age because of anxious feelings, and subsequently identifies with the same-sex parent, unconsciously adopting the same-sex parent's characteristics.

psychological age An individual's adaptive capacities compared with those of other individuals of the same chronological age.

psychosocial moratorium Erikson's term for the gap between childhood security and adult autonomy that adolescents experience as part of their identity exploration.

puberty A period of rapid skeletal and sexual maturation involving hormonal and bodily changes that occur primarily in early adolescence.

R

race A classification of people according to real or imagined biological characteristics, such as skin colour and blood group.

reciprocal socialization The idea that children socialize parents, just as parents socialize children.

reflexes Built-in reactions to stimuli; they govern the newborn's movements, which are automatic and beyond the newborn's control.

reflexive smile Does not occur in response to external stimuli. It happens during the month after birth, usually during irregular patterns of sleep.

relational aggression Such behaviours as trying to make others dislike a certain child by spreading malicious rumours about the child or ignoring another child when angry with him or her relative age The differences in development among children of the same age group.

relative age effect The consequences of developmental differences among children of the same age group.

religion An organized set of beliefs about how the universe originated, as well as the nature and the purpose of the universe.

REM (rapid eye movement) sleep A recurring sleep stage during which vivid dreams commonly occur.

restrained eaters Individuals who chronically restrict their food intake to control their weight. Restrained eaters are often on diets, are very conscious of what they eat, and tend to feel guilty after splurging on sweets.

rite of passage A ceremony or ritual that marks an individual's transition of from one status to another.

romantic love Also called "passionate love" or "eros," romantic love has strong components of sexuality and infatuation and often predominates in the early part of a love relationship.

rooting reflex When the infant's cheek is stroked or the side of the mouth is touched, the infant turns its head toward the side that was touched in an apparent effort to find something to suck.

rules of morphology The study of the structure and form of words, including inflection, derivation, and compound words.

S

scaffolding In cognitive development, Vygotsky used this term to describe the changing support over the course of a teaching session, with the more-skilled person adjusting the amount of guidance to fit the child's current performance level.

scheme In Piaget's theory, a cognitive structure that helps individuals organize and understand their experiences.

secondary circular reactions Piaget's third sensorimotor substage, which develops between 4 and 8 months of age. In this substage, the infant becomes more object-oriented, moving beyond preoccupation with the self.

securely attached babies Use the caregiver as a secure base from which to explore the environment.

selective attention Focusing on a specific aspect of experience that is relevant while ignoring others that are irrelevant.

selective optimization with compensation theory States that successful aging is linked to three main factors: selection, optimization, and compensation (SOC).

self-actualization The individualized expression of self in terms of reaching one's fullest potential without concern for praise or rewards.

self-concept Domain-specific evaluations of the self.

self-conscious emotions Require self-awareness, especially consciousness and a sense of "me"; examples include jealousy, empathy, and embarrassment.

self-efficacy The belief that one can master a situation and produce favourable outcomes.

self-esteem The global evaluative dimension of the self; also referred to as self-worth or self-image.

self-understanding The child's cognitive representation of self, the substance and content of self-conceptions.

semantic memory A person's knowledge about the world—including fields of expertise, general academic knowledge of the sort learned in school, and "everyday knowledge."

semantics The meaning of words.

sensation Occurs when a stimulus reaches sensory receptors—the eyes, ears, tongue, nostrils, and skin.

sensorimotor play Behaviour engaged in by infants that lets them derive pleasure from exercising their existing sensorimotor schemas.

separation protest An infant's crying when the caregiver leaves.

sequential approach A combined cross-sectional, longitudinal design.

seriation The concrete operation that involves ordering stimuli along a quantitative dimension (such as length).

service-learning A form of education intended to promote social responsibility and service to the community.

sexual identity An individual's inner conviction about his or her male or femaleness.

sexual orientation An individual's sexual interests; that is, whether or not a person is sexually and romantically attracted to others of the same sex, the opposite sex, or both sexes.

sexually transmitted infections (STIs) Infections and diseases that are contracted primarily through sexual contact, which is not limited to sexual intercourse. Oral–genital and anal–genital contact also can transmit STIs and STDs.

shared environmental experiences Children's common environmental experiences that are shared with their siblings, such as their parents' personalities and intellectual orientation, the family's social class, and the neighbourhood in which they live.

short-term memory The memory component in which individuals retain information for 15 to 30 seconds, assuming there is no rehearsal.

simple reflexes Piaget's first sensorimotor substage, which corresponds to the first month after birth. In this substage, sensation and action are coordinated primarily through reflexive behaviours.

sleep apnea A serious condition that prevents a person from sleeping; a temporary cessation of breathing caused when the airways become blocked.

slow-to-warm-up child Has a low activity level, is somewhat negative, shows low adaptability, and displays a low intensity of mood.

small-for-date infants Born with birth weight below normal when length of the pregnancy is considered; may be preterm or full-term; also called *small-for-gestational-age infants*.

social age Social roles and expectations related to a person's age.

social clock The timetable according to which individuals are expected to accomplish life's tasks, such as getting married, having children, or establishing themselves in a career and retiring.

social cognitive theory of gender Explains that children's gender development occurs through observing and imitating what other people say and do, and through being rewarded and punished for gender-appropriate and gender-inappropriate behaviour.

social constructivist approach An approach that emphasizes that both learning and the construction of knowledge occur in social contexts.

social conventional reasoning Conventional rules that have been established by social consensus to control behaviour and maintain the social system.

social play Play that involves social interaction with peers.

social policy A national government's course of action designed to influence the welfare of its citizens.

social referencing Involves "reading" emotional cues in others to help determine how to act in a particular situation.

social role theory A theory that gender differences result from the contrasting roles of men and women.

social smile Occurs in response to an external stimulus, which, early in development, typically is a face.

socio-emotional processes Changes in an individual's relationships with other people, emotions, and personality.

socio-emotional selectivity theory States that older adults become more selective about their social networks. Because they place a high value on emotional satisfaction, older adults often spend more time with familiar individuals with whom they have had rewarding relationships.

source memory The ability to remember where one learned something.

spirituality Efforts to find meaning in life.

stability–change issue The debate about whether development is best described as involving stability or as involving change; involves the degree to which we become older renditions of our early experience or, instead, develop into someone different from who we were at an earlier point in development.

standardized test A data collection method with uniform procedures for administration and scoring.

Strange Situation An observational measure of infant attachment that requires the infant to move through a series of introductions, separations, and reunions with the caregiver and an adult stranger in a prescribed order.

stranger anxiety An infant's fear and wariness of strangers; it tends to appear in the second half of the first year of life.

strategies Deliberate mental activities that improve the processing of information.

stress The non-specific response of the body to any demand made upon it.

sucking reflex A newborn automatically sucks an object placed in its mouth.

sudden infant death syndrome (SIDS) A condition that occurs when an infant stops breathing, usually during the night, and suddenly dies without apparent cause.

superego According to Freud, the moral branch of the personality, which takes into account whether something is right or wrong.

sustained attention Focused and extended engagement with an object, task, event, or other aspect of the environment.

symbolic function substage Piaget's first substage of preoperational thought, in which the child gains the ability to mentally represent an object that is not present (occurs between 2 and 4 years of age).

syntax The formation of grammatically correct sentences.

syphilis A sexually transmitted disease caused by the bacterium *Treponema pallidum*, a member of the spirochete family.

T

telegraphic speech The use of short and precise words to communicate.

temperament An individual's behavioural style and characteristic way of emotionally responding.

teratogen Any agent that causes a birth defect or negatively alters cognitive and behavioural outcomes. The field of study that investigates the causes of birth variations is called *teratology.* From the Greek word *tera,* meaning "monster."

tertiary circular reactions, novelty, and curiosity Piaget's fifth sensorimotor substage, which develops between 12 and 18 months of age. In this substage, infants become intrigued by the many properties of objects and by the many things that they can make happen to objects.

theory An interrelated, coherent set of ideas that help explain and make predictions.

theory of mind The awareness of one's own mental processes and the mental processes of others.

transitivity In concrete operational thought, a mental concept that underlies the ability to combine relations logically in order to understand certain conclusions.

triangular theory of love Sternberg's theory that love can be thought of as having three main dimensions: passion, intimacy, and commitment.

triarchic theory of intelligence Sternberg's theory that intelligence comes in three forms: analytical, creative, and practical.

trophoblast The outer layer of cells that develops in the germinal period to provide nutrition and support for the embryo.

U

umbilical cord A life-support system containing two arteries and one vein that connects the baby to the placenta.

V

visible minority The term used by the Canadian census for people who are neither Aboriginal nor Caucasian.

Vygotsky's theory A socio-cultural cognitive theory that emphasizes developmental analysis, the role of language, and social relations.

W

Wernicke's area A region of the brain's left hemisphere involved in language comprehension.

whole-language approach An approach to reading instruction based on the idea that instruction should parallel children's natural language learning. Reading materials should be whole and meaningful.

wisdom Expert knowledge about the practical aspects of life that permits excellent judgment about important matters.

working memory The concept currently used to describe short-term memory as a place for mental work. Working memory is like a "workbench" where individuals can manipulate and assemble information when making decisions, solving problems, and comprehending written and spoken language.

Y

young offenders Young people between the ages of 12 and 18 who commit criminal acts.

Z

zone of proximal development Vygotsky's term for the range of tasks too difficult for a child to master alone but that can be learned with the guidance and assistance of adults or more-skilled children.

zygote A single cell formed when an ovum is fertilized by a sperm.

References

A

Aalsma, M., Lapsley, D. K., & Flannery, D. (2006). Narcissism, personal fables, and adolescent adjustment. *Psychology in the Schools, 43*, 481–491.

Abar, B., Laglasse, L., Newman, E., Smith, L., Huestis, M., Neal, C., Derauf, C., Shah, R., Arria, A., Grotta, S. & Dansereau, L., & Lester, B. (2012). Examining the relationships between prenatal methamphetamine exposure, early adversity, and child neurobehavioral disinhibition. *Psychology of Addictive Behaviors, 27*(1), 662–673.

Abbott, R. D., White, I. R., Ross, G. W., Masaki, K. H., Curb, J. D., & Petrovitch, H. (2004). Walking and dementia in physically capable elderly men. *Journal of the American Medical Association, 292*, 1447–1453.

Abdo, C. H., Afif-Abdo, J., Otani, F., & Machado, A. C. (2008). Sexual satisfaction among patients with erectile dysfunction treated with counseling, sildenafil, or both. *Journal of Sexual Medicine, 5*(7), 1720–1726.

Abdou, C., Dunkel Schetter, C., Campos, B., Hilmert, C., Dominguez, T. .... Sandman, C. (2010). Communalism predicts prenatal affect, stress, and physiology better than ethnicity and SES. *Cultural Diversity and Ethnic Minority Psychology*, 16, 395–403.

Abel, T., Havekes, R., Saletin, J. M., & Walker, M. P. (2013). Sleep, plasticity, and memory from molecules to whole-brain networks. *Current Biology, 23*, R774–R788.

Abellan van Kan, G., Rolland, Y., Nourhashemi, F., Coley, N., Andrieu, S., & Vellas, B. (2009). Cardiovascular disease risk factors and progression of Alzheimer's disease. *Dementia and Geriatric Cognitive Disorders, 27*, 240–246.

Abeykoon, H., & Lucyk, K. (Winter 2015/ 2015). Sex and Seniors: A Perspective. Canada's Public Health Association (CPHA). Volume XXXIX, Number 4 Retrieved from http://www.cpha.ca/en/about/digest/39-4/15.aspx.

Aboriginal Affairs and Northern Development Canada (AANDC). (2010). Statement of apology: Prime Minister Harper offers full apology on behalf of Canadians for the Indian Residential Schools system. Retrieved from http://www.aadnc-aandc.gc.ca/eng/1100100015644/1100100015649.

Aboud, F. E., Mendelson, M. J., & Purdy, K. T. (2003). Cross-race peer relations and friendship quality. *International Journal of Behavioral Development, 27*(2), 165–173.

Abouguendia, M., & K. A. Noels. (2001). General and acculturation-related daily hassles and psychological adjustment in first- and second-generation South Asian immigrants to Canada. *International Journal of Psychology, 36*(3), 163–173.

Abrams, L. (2009). Exploring the generality of retest effects: Commentary on "When does age-related cognitive decline begin?" *Neurobiology of Aging, 30*, 525–527.

Abruscato, J. A., & DeRosa, D. A. (2010). *Teaching children science: A discovery approach* (7th ed.). Boston: Allyn & Bacon.

Abyzov, A., et al. (2013). Analysis of variable retroduplications in human populations suggests coupling of retrotransposition to cell division. Genome Research, 23, 2042–2052.

Accornero, V. H., Amado, A. J., Morrow, C. E., Xue, L., Anthony, J. C., & Bandstra, E. S. (2007). Impact of prenatal cocaine exposure on attention and response inhibition as assessed by continuous performance tests. *Journal of Developmental and Behavioral Pediatrics, 28*, 195–205.

Acevedo, B., & Aron, A. (2009). Does a long term relationship kill romantic love? *Review of General Psychology, 13*, 59–65.

Active Healthy KidsCanada. (2012). *Is active play extinct? The Active Healthy Kids Canada 2012 Report Card on Physical Activity for Children and Youth.* Toronto: Active Healthy Kids Canada.

Adamson, P. (2013) Child Wellbeing in Rich Countries - A Comparative Overview. Innocenti Report Card 11 UNICEF. Retrieved from http://www.unicef.ca/sites/default/files/imce_uploads/DISCOVER/OUR%20WORK/ADVOCACY/DOMESTIC/POLICY%20ADVOCACY/DOCS/unicef_report_card_11.pdf.

Adler, A. (1927). *The Practice and Theory of Individual Psychology.*

Adolph, K. E. (2008). Motor and physical development: Locomotion. In M. M. Haith & J. B. Benson (Eds.), *Encyclopedia of infant and early childhood development.* Oxford, UK: Elsevier.

Adolph, K. E., & Joh, A. S. (2007). Motor development: How infants get into the act. In A. Slater & M. Lewis (Eds.), *Infant Development.* New York: Oxford University Press.

Adolph, K. E., & Joh, A. S. (2008). Multiple learning mechanisms in the development of action. In A. Needham & A. Woodward (Eds.), *Learning and the infant mind.* New York: Oxford University Press.

Adolph, K., Karasik, L. & Tamis-LeMonda. (2010). Using social information to guide action: Infants' locomotion. *Neural Networks, 23*, 1033–1042.

Adolph, K., Kretch, K. & LoBue, V. (2014). Fear of heights in infants? *Current Directions in Psychological Science, 23*, 60–66.

Adoption Council of Canada. (2003). Canadians adopt almost 20,000 children from abroad.

Afifi, T. O. (2011). Child maltreatment in Canada: An understudied public health problem. Canadian *Journal of Public Health*, 456–461.

Afifi, T. O., et al. (2016). Health Reports - Child abuse and physical health in adulthood. Public Health Agency of Canada. Retrieved from http://www.statcan.gc.ca/pub/82-003-x/2016003/article/14339-eng.htm.

Afifi, T. O., et al. (2014) Child abuse and mental disorders in Canada. *Canadian Medical Association Journal*. Retrieved from http://www.cmaj.ca/content/early/2014/04/22/cmaj.131792.

Agras, W. S., et al. (2004). Report of the National Institutes of Health workshop on overcoming barriers to treatment research in anorexia nervosa. *International Journal of Eating Disorders, 35*, 509–521.

Agrillo, C., & Netini, C. (2008). Childfree by choice: A review. *Journal of Cultural Geography, 25*(3), 347–363.

Aguiar, A., & Baillargeon, R. (2002). Development in young infants' reasoning about occluded objects. *Cognitive Psychology, 45*, 267–336.

Aguiar, C., & Jennings. L. (2015). Impact of male partner antenatal accompaniment on perinatal health outcomes in developing countries: A systematic literature review. *Maternal and Child Health Journal*, *19*, 2012–2019.

Aguiar, E., Morgan, P., Collins, C., Plotikoff, R., & Callister, R. (2014). Efficacy of interventions that include diet, aerobic and resistance training components for type 2 diabetes prevention: A systematic review with meta-analysis. *Journal of Behavioural Nutrition and Physical Activity, 11*(2), 2–10.

Ahern, E. C., & Lamb, M. E. (2014, in press). Research-based child investigative interviewing. *Community Care Information*.

Ahlin, E., & Lobo Antunes, M. (2015). Locus of control orientation: Parents, peers, and places. *Journal of Youth and Adolescence, 44*, 1803–1818.

Ahrons, C. (2004). *We're still family.* New York: HarperCollins.

Aiken Morgan, A. T., Sims, R. C., & Whitfield, K. E. (2010). Cardiovascular health and education as sources of individual variability in cognitive aging among African Americans. *Journal of Aging and Health, 22*, 477–503.

Ailshire, J. A., & Burgard, S. A. (2012). Family relationships and troubled sleep among U.S. adults: Examining the influences of contact frequency and relationship quality. *Journal of Health and Social Behavior, 53*, 248–262.

Aina, O. E., & Cameron, P. A. (2011). Why Does Gender Matter? Counteracting Stereotypes With Young Children. *Dimensions of Early Childhood*, 39(3). Retrieved from http://www.southernearlychildhood.org/upload/pdf/Why_Does_Gender_Matter_Counteracting_Stereotypes_With_Young_Children_Olaiya_E_Aina_and_Petronella_A_Cameron.pdf.

Ainsworth, M. D. S. (1979). Infant-mother attachment. *American Psychologist, 34*, 932–937.

Aizawa, K., Shoemaker, J. K., Overend, T. J., & Petrella, R. J. (2010). Longitudinal changes in central artery stiffness with lifestyle modification, washout, and drug treatment in individuals at risk for cardiovascular disease. *Metabolic Syndrome and Related Disorders, 8*(4), 323.

Ajdacic-Gross, V., Ring, M., Gadola, E., Lauber, C., Bopp, M., Gutzwiller, F., & Rossler, W. (2008). Suicide after bereavement: An overlooked problem. *Psychology and Medicine, 38*, 673–676.

Akhtar, N., & Herold, K. (2008). Pragmatic development. In M. M. Haith & J. B. Benson (Eds.), *Encyclopedia of infant and early childhood development.* Oxford, UK: Elsevier.

Akhter, M., Nishino, Y., Nakaya, N., Kurashima, K., Sato, Y., Kuriyama, S., et al. (2007). Cigarette smoking and the risk of colorectal cancer among men: A prospective study in Japan. *European Journal of Cancer Prevention, 16*, 102–107.

Akinsanya, S. (Interview, March 9, 2016)

Akpek, E. K., & Smith, R. A. (2013). Current treatment strategies for age-related ocular conditions. *American Journal of Managed Care, 19*(5, Suppl.), S76–S84.

Alasia, A. (2010). Population change across Canadian communities 1981–2006. *Rural and Small Town Canada Analysis Bulletin, 8*(4), 1–32.

Albury, K., & Crawford, K. (2012). Sexting, consent and young people's ethics: Beyond Megan's story. *Continuum: Journal of Media and Cultural Studies, 26*(3), 463–473.

Alcoholics Anonymous. (2013). *Information on A.A.* Retrieved from http://www.aa.org/

Allaire, J. C. (2012). Everyday cognition. In S. K. Whitbourne & M. Sliwinski (Eds.), Wiley-Blackwell handbook of adult development and aging. New York: Wiley.

Allard, Y., Wilkins, R., & Berthelot, J. (2004). Premature mortality in health regions with high Aboriginal populations. *Health Reports, 15*(1), 51–60.

Allen, J. (2008). The attachment system in adolescence. In J. Cassidy & P. Shaver (Eds.), *Handbook of attachment: Theory, research, and clinical applications* (2nd ed.) (pp. 419–435). New York, NY: Guilford.

Allen, J. P., & Antonishak, J. (2008). Adolescent peer influences: Beyond the dark side. In M. J. Prinstein & K. A. Dodge (Eds.), *Understanding peer influence in children and adolescents.* New York: Guilford.

Allen, J. P., Kuperminc, G. P., & Moore, C. (2005, April). *Stability and predictors of change in attachment security across adolescence.* Paper presented at the meeting of the Society for Research on Child Development, Atlanta.

Allen, K. L., Byrne, S. M., McLean, N. J., & Davis, E. A. (2008). Overconcern with weight and shape is not the same as body dissatisfaction: Evidence from a prospective study of pre-adolescent boys and girls. *Body Image, 5*(3), 261–270.

Allen, K. R., Blieszner, R., & Roberto, K. A. (2000). Families in middle and later years: A review and critique of research in the 1990s. *Journal of Marriage and the Family, 62*, 911–926.

Allen, M. (2013). *Youth Bilingualism in Canada.* Statistics Canada. Retrieved from http://www.statcan.gc.ca/pub/81-004-x/2008004/article/10767-eng.htm.

Allen, M. C. (2008). Neurodevelopmental outcomes of preterm infants. *Current Opinion in Neurology, 21*, 123–128.

Alleyne, R. (2010, May 16). Lying children will grow up to be successful citizens. *The Telegraph.* Retrieved from http://www.telegraph.co.uk/science/7730522/Lying-children-will-grow-upto-be-successful-citizens.html

Alm, B., Lagercrantz, H., & Wennergren, G. (2006). Stop SIDS—sleeping solitary supine, sucking smoother, stopping smoking substitutes. *Acta Paediatrica, 95*, 260–262.

Almas, A., Degaan, K., Radulesscu, A., Nelson, C., Zeanah, C. & Fox, N. (2012). Effects of early intervention and moderating effects of brain activity on institutionalized children's social skills at age 8. *Proceedings of the National Academy of Science, 109*, 17228–17231.

Almeida, D. M., Piazza, J. R., Stawski, R. S., & Klein, L. C. (2011). The speedometer of life: Stress, health, and aging. In K. W. Schaie & S. L. Willis (Eds.), *Handbook of the Psychology of Aging* (7th ed.). New York: Elsevier.

Al-Safi, Z. A., & Santoro, N. (2014, in press). Menopausal hormone therapy and menopausal symptoms. Fertility and Sterility.

Al-Sahab, B., Saqib, M., Hauser, G., & Tamim, H. (2010). Prevalence of smoking during pregnancy and associated risk factors among Canadian women: A national survey. *BMC Pregnancy and Childbirth, 10*(24), 1–9.

Althof, S. E., Rubio-Aurioles, E., Kingsberg, S., Zeigler, H., Wong, D. G., & Burns, P. (2010). Impact of tadalafil once daily in men with erectile dysfunction—including a report of the partner's evaluation. *Urology, 75*(6), 1358–1363.

Altimer, L. (2008). Shaken baby syndrome. *Journal of Perinatal and Neonatal Nursing, 22*, 68–76.

Aly, M., & Moscovitch, M. (2010). The effects of sleep on episodic memory in older and younger adults. Memory, 18, 327–334.

Al-Yagon, M., Kopelman-Rubin, D., Brunstein, K., & Mikulincer, M. (2016). Four-model approach to adolescent-parent attachment relationships and adolescents' loneliness, school belonging, and teacher appraisal. *Personal Relationships, 23*, 141–158.

Alzheimer Society of Canada (2015). Dementia numbers in Canada. Retrieved from http://www.alzheimer.ca/en/About-dementia/What-is-dementia/Dementia-numbers.

Alzheimer Society of Canada (2016). Drugs approved for Alzheimer's disease. Retrieved from http://www.alzheimer.ca/en/About-dementia/Treatment-options/Drugs-approved-for-Alzheimers-disease#navigation.

Alzheimer Society of Canada. (2013). Alzheimer's disease. Retrieved from http://www.alzheimer.ca/en/About-dementia/Alzheimer-s-disease/What-is-Alzheimer-s-disease

Amabile, T. M. (1993). Commentary. In D. Goleman, P. Kaufman, & M. Ray, *The creative spirit.* New York: Plume.

Amato, P. R. (2007). Transformative processes in marriage: Some thoughts from a sociologist. *Journal of Marriage and the Family, 69*, 305–309.

Amato, P. R., & Cheadle, J. (2005). The long reach of divorce: Divorce and child well-being across three generations. *Journal of Marriage and the Family, 67*, 191–206.

Amato, P. R., & Dorius, C. (2010). Fathers, children, and divorce. In M.E. Lamb (Ed.), *The role of the father in child development* (5th ed.). New York: Wiley.

Ambert, A. (1998). *Divorce: Facts, figures, and consequences.* Vanier Institute of the Family: Child and Family Canada.

Ambert, A. (2003). *The negative social construction of adoption: Its effects on children and parents.*

Ambert, A. (2005). *Divorce, facts, causes & consequences.* The Vanier Institute of the Family. Retrieved from http://www.vifamily.ca/library/cft/divorce_05.html#What_causes.

Ambert, A. M. (2007). *The rise in the number of children and adolescents who exhibit problematic behaviours: Multiple causes.* Vanier Institute of the Family.

Ambrose, D., Sternberg, R. J., & Sriraman, B. (2012). Considering the effects of dogmatism on giftedness and talent development. In D. Ambrose, R. J. Sternberg, & B. Sriraman (Eds.), *Confronting dogmatism in gifted education.* New York: Taylor & Francis.

American Academy of Paediatrics. (2016). Gender Identity Development in Children. What's the Difference Between Gender and Sex? Retrieved from https://www.healthychildren.org/English/ages-stages/gradeschool/Pages/Gender-Identity-and-Gender-Confusion-In-Children.aspx.

American Psychological Association (APA). (2006). Answers to Your Questions About Individuals With Intersex Conditions. APA. Retrieved from https://www.apa.org/topics/lgbt/intersex.pdf.

American Psychological Association. (2007). *Stress in America.* Washington, DC: Author.

American Public Health Association. (2006). *Understanding the health culture of recent immigrants to the United States.* Retrieved from http://www.apha.org/

Ames, E. A. (1997, January 1). *The development of Romanian orphanage children adopted to Canada: Final report.* Simon Fraser University.

Amnesty International. (2014). *Violence against indigenous women and girls in Canada.* Retrieved from http://www.anmesty.ca

Amoroso, J. (2010). From women to children: Reframing child care in Canada. *Queen's Policy Review, 1*(1), 30–46.

Amos, H. (June 2, 2011). Turning your genes on and off - Researchers of the GECKO Project lead the first study of how life experiences shape who we are. UBS News: The University of British Columbia Retrieved from http://news.ubc.ca/2011/06/02/turning-your-%E2%80%A8genes-on-and-off/.

Amsterdam, B. K. (1968). *Mirror behavior in children under two years of age.* Unpublished doctoral dissertation, University of North Carolina, Chapel Hill.

Andersen, S. L., Sebastiani, P., Dworkis, D. A., Feldman, L., & Perls, T. T. (2012). Health span approximates life span among many supercentenarians: Compression of morbidity at the approximate limit of life span. *Journals of Gerontology A: Biological Sciences and Medical Sciences, 67A*, 395–405.

Anderson, K., Nisenblat, V. & Norman, R. (2010). Lifestyle factors in people seeking infertility treatment–a review. *Australian New Zealand Journal of Obstetrics and Gynaecology, 5*, 8–20.

Anderson, S. A., & Sabatelli, R. M. (2007). *Family interaction* (4th ed.). Boston: Allyn & Bacon.

Andersson, U. (2010). The contribution of working memory capacity to foreign language comprehension in children. *Memory, 18*, 458–472.

Anetzberger, G. J., & Teaster, P. B. (2010). Future directions for social policy and elder abuse: Through the looking glass of generational characteristics. *Journal of Elder Abuse and Neglect, 22*, 207–215.

Angel, L., Fay, S., Bouazzaoui, B., & Isingrini, M. (2011). Two hemispheres for better memory in old age: Role of executive functioning. *Journal of Cognitive Neuroscience, 23*(12), 3767–3777.

Anguera, J. A., et al. (2013). Video game training enhances cognitive control in older adults. *Nature, 501*, 97–101.

Angus Reid. (2009). *Mortality.* Retrieved from http://www.visioncritical.com.

Anita, J., O'Leary, K., & Moyer, A. (2010). Does premarital cohabitation predict subsequent marital stability and marital quality? A meta-analysis. *Journal of Marriage and Family, 72*(1), 105–116.

Annett, E. (2015, Dec. 8). Justin and Sophie The family album. *The Globe and Mail.* Retrieved from http://www.theglobeandmail.com.

Ansado, J., et al. (2013). Coping with task demand in aging using neural compensation and neural reserve triggers primarily intra-hemispheric-based neurofunctional reorganization. *Neuroscience Research, 75*, 295–304.

Anspaugh, D. J., Hamrick, M. H., & Rosato, F. D. (2009). *Wellness* (7th ed.). New York: McGraw-Hill.

Antonenko, D., & Floel, A. (2014). Healthy aging by staying selectively connected: A mini-review. *Gerontology, 60*(1), 3–9.

Antonucci, T. C., Akiyama, H., & Sherman, A. M. (2007). Social networks, support, and integration. In J. E. Birren (Ed.), *Encyclopedia of gerontology* (2nd ed.). San Diego: Academic Press.

Antonucci, T. C., Birditt, K. S., & Akiyama, H. (2009). Convoys of social relations: An interdisciplinary approach. In V. L. Bengtson, D. Gans, N. M. Putney, & M. Silverstein (Eds.), *Handbook of theories of aging* (2nd ed.). New York: Springer.

Antonucci, T. C., Fiori, K. L., Birditt, K., & Jackey, L. M. H. (2011). Convoys of social relations: Integrating life-span and life-course perspectives. In R.M. Lerner, W. F. Overton, A. M. Freund, & M. E. Lamb (Eds.), *Handbook of life-span development.* New York: Wiley.

Antonucci, T. C., Lansford, J. E., & Akiyama, H. (2001). The impact of positive and negative aspects of marital relationships and friendships on the well-being of older adults. In J. P. Reinhardt (Ed.), *Negative and positive support.* Mahwah, NJ: Erlbaum.

Antonucci, T. C., Vandewater, E. A., & Lansford, J. E. (2000). Adulthood and aging: Social processes and development. In A. Kazdin (Ed.), *Encyclopedia of psychology.* Washington, DC: American Psychological Association and Oxford University Press.

Applebaum, M. (2008). Why diets fail—expert diet advice as a cause of diet failure. *American Psychologist, 63*, 200–202.

Appleton, J. V., & Stanley, N. (2009). Editorial: Childhood outcomes. *Child Abuse Review, 18*, 1–5.

Arai, A. B. (2000). Reasons for home schooling in Canada. *Canadian Journal of Education, 25*(3), 204–217.

Archibald, M. & Fraser, K. (2013). The potential for nurse practitioners in health care reform. *Journal of Professional Nursing, 29*(5), 270–275.

Arens, A., & Hasselhorn, M. (2014). Age and gender differences in the relation between self-concept facets and self-esteem. *Journal of Early Adolescence, 34*(6), 760–791.

Armour, S., & Haynie, D. L. (2007). Adolescent sexual debut and later delinquency. *Journal of Youth and Adolescence, 36*, 141–152.

Armstrong, M. L. (1995). Adolescent tattoos: Educating and pontificating. *Pediatric Nursing, 21*(6), 561–564.

Armstrong, M. L., Roberts, A. E., Owen, D. C., & Koch, J. R. (2004). Contemporary college students and body piercing. *Journal of Adolescent Health, 35*, 58–61.

Arnett, J. J. (2004). *Emerging adulthood.* New York: Oxford University Press.

Arnett, J. J. (2006). Emerging adulthood: Understanding the new way of coming of age. In J. J. Arnett & J. L. Tanner (Eds.), *Emerging adults in America.* Washington, DC: American Psychological Association.

Arnett, J. J. (2007). Socialization in emerging adulthood. In J. E. Grusec & P. D. Hastings (Eds.), *Handbook of socialization.* New York: Guilford.

Arnett, J., & Galambos, N. (2003). Culture and conceptions of adulthood. In J. Arnett & N. Galambos (Eds.), *New directions for child and adolescent development: Exploring cultural conceptions of the transition to adulthood* (No. 100, pp. 63–76). San Franscisco: Jossey-Bass.

Arnold, A. (2012, April). *Reframing sexual differentiation in the brain.* Paper presented at the Gender Development Research conference, San Francisco.

Arnsburg, K., & Kirstein-Miles, J. (2014). Interrelation between protein synthesis, proteostasis, and life span. *Current Genomics, 15*, 66–75.

Aron, A., Aron, E., & Coupos, E. (2008). *Statistics for the behavioral and social sciences.* Upper Saddle River, NJ: Prentice Hall.

Aronson, S., & Huston, A. (2004). The mother-infant rerlationship in single, cohabiting, and married families: A case for marriage? *Journal of Family Psychology, 18*(1), 5–18.

Arpanantikul, M. (2004). Midlife experiences of Thai women. *Journal of Advanced Nursing, 47*, 49–56.

Arseth, A., Kroger, J., Martinussen, M., & Marcia, J. (2009). Meta-analytic studies of identity status and the relational issues of attachment and intimacy. *Identity, 9*, 1–32.

Arthritis Society of Canada. (2016). *Rheumatoid Arthritis*. Retrieved from http://arthritis.ca/understand-arthritis/types-of-arthritis/rheumatoid-arthritis.

Arthritis Society of Canada. (2016). *Osteoarthritis*. Retrieved from http://arthritis.ca/understand-arthritis/types-of-arthritis/osteoarthritis.

Asagwara, O. (2015). The knowledge, attitudes and experiences of medical surgical nurses in Winnipeg, Manitoba, Canada. (Doctoral dissertation). Retrieved from http://www.handle.net/1993/30723?show=full

Asbury, K., & Plomin, R. (2014). *G is for genes: The impact of genetics on education and achievement.* New York: Wiley.

Asendorph, J. B. (2008). Shyness. In M. M. Haith & J. B. Benson (Eds.), *Encyclopedia of infant and early childhood development.* Oxford, UK: Elsevier.

Asendorph, J., Denissen, J., & van Aken, M. (2008). Inhibited and aggressive preschool children at 23 years of age: Personality and social transition into adulthood. *Developmental Psychology, 44*, 997–1011.

Ash, J. A., & Rapp, P. R. (2014 in press). *A quantitative neural network approach to understanding aging phenotypes.* Aging Research Reviews.

Asian, Y., et al. (2014, in press). *The impact of metabolic syndrome on serum total testosterone level in patients with erectile dysfunction.* Aging Male.

Aslan, A., Zellner, M., & Bauml, K. H. (2010). Working memory capacity predicts listwise directed forgetting in adults and children. *Memory, 18*(4), 442–450.

Aslin, R. N., & Lathrop, A. L. (2008). Visual perception. In M. M. Haith & J. B. Benson (Eds.), *Encyclopedia of infant and early childhood development.* Oxford, UK: Elsevier.

Asscher, J. (2008). The moral distinction between killing and letting die in medical cases. *Bioethics, 22*(5), 278–285.

Association of Chief Psychologists with Ontario School Boards (ACPOSB). (2004). *Attention deficit hyperactivity disorder.* Retrieved from http://www.acposb.on.ca/ADHD.html.

Association of Professional Piercers. (nd). *Body piercing aftercare*. Retrieved from http://www.safepiercing.org.

Astington, J. W., & Hughes, C. (2013). Theory of mind: Self-reflection and social understanding. In P. D. Zelazo (Ed.), *Handbook of developmental psychology.* New York: Oxford University Press.

Ata, R. N., Ludden, A. B., & Lally, M. M. (2007). The effect of gender and family, friend, and media influences on eating behaviors and body image during adolescence. *Journal of Youth and Adolescence, 36*, 1024–1037.

Atchley, R. C. (2007). Retirement. In J. E. Birren (Ed.), *Encyclopedia of gerontology* (2nd ed.). San Diego: Academic Press.

Atkinson, L., Raval, V., Benoit, D., Poulton, L., Gleason, K., Goldberg, S., et al. (2005). On the relation between maternal state of mind and sensitivity in the prediction of infant attachment security. *Developmental Psychology, 41*(1), 42–53.

Attorney-General. (1993). Decisions: Supreme Court judgments. *Rodriguez v. British Columbia (Attorney General),* [1993] 3 S.C.R. 519.

Aubin, S., Heiman, J. R., Berger, R. E., Murallo, A. V., & Yung-Wen, L. (2009). Comparing Sildenafil alone vs. Sildenafil plus brief couple therapy on erectile dysfunction and couples' sexual and marital quality of life: A pilot study. *Journal of Sexual and Marital Therapy, 35*, 122–143.

Aubrey, T., Klodawsky, F., & Coulombe, D. (2012). Comparing the housing trajectories of different classes within a diverse homeless population. *American Journal of Community Psychology, 49*, 142–155.

Autism Speaks (2016). DSM-5 Diagnostic Criteria. Retrieved from https://www.autismspeaks.org/what-autism/diagnosis/dsm-5-diagnostic-criteria.

Autism Speaks Canada (2016). Facts and Statistics. Retrieved from http://www.autismspeaks.ca/about-autism/facts-and-faqs/.

Averett, S., Argys, L., & Sorkin, J. (2013). In sickness and in health: An examination of relationship status and health using data from the Canadian national public health survey. *Review of Economics of the Household, 11*, 599–633.

AVERT. (2015). HIV and AIDS in sub-Saharan Africa regional overview. Retrieved from http://www.avert.org.

Avila, J., et al. (2014, in press). Sources of extracellular tau and its signaling. *Journal of Alzheimer's Disease*.

B

B.C. Council for Families. (2007). Quick facts on grandparenting.

Bachman, J. G., O'Malley, P. M., Schulenberg, J. E., Johnston, L. D., Bryant, A. L., & Merline, A. C. (2002). *The decline of substance abuse in young adulthood.* Mahwah, NJ: Erlbaum.

Bachman, J. G., O'Malley, P. M., Schulenberg, J. E., Johnston, L. D., Freedman-Doan, P., & Messersmith, E. E. (2008). *The education-drug use connection.* Clifton, NJ: Psychology Press.

Bachschmid, M. M., et al. (2013). Vascular aging: Chronic oxidative stress and impairment of redox signaling—consequences for vascular homeostatis and disease. *Annals of Medicine, 45*(1), 17–36.

Backhans, M., & Hemmingsson, T. (2012). Unemployment and mental health—Who is (not) affected. *European Journal of Public Health, 22*, 429–433.

Backman, L., Small, B. J., & Wahlin, A. (2001). Aging and memory: Cognitive and behavioral processes. In J. E. Birren & K. W. Schaie (Eds.), *Handbook of the*

psychology of aging (5th ed.). San Diego: Academic Press.

Baddeley, A. D. (1990). *Human memory: Theory and practice.* Boston: Allyn & Bacon.

Baddeley, A. D. (2001). *Is working memory still working?* Paper presented at the meeting of the American Psychological Association, San Francisco.

Baddeley, A. D. (2007a). *Working memory, thought, and action.* New York: Oxford University Press.

Baddeley, A. D. (2007b). Working memory: Multiple models, multiple mechanisms. In H. L. Roediger, Y. Dudai, & S. M. Fitzpatrick (Eds.). *Science of memory: concepts.* New York: Oxford University Press.

Baddeley, A. D. (2010). Working memory. *Current Biology, 20,* 136–140.

Baddeley, A. D. (2012). Working memory: Theories, models, and controversies. *Annual Review of Psychology* (Vol. 63). Palo Alto, CA: Annual Reviews.

Badger, J. L., et al. (2014). Parkinson's disease in a dish—using stem cells as a molecular tool. *Neuropharmacology, 76* Pt. A, 88–96.

Badowski, M., et al. (2014, in press). The influence of intrinsic and extrinsic factors on immune system aging. *Immunobiology.*

Baehr, T. A., & Barnett, M. M. (2007). Examining retirement from a multi-level perspective. In K. S. Shultz & G. A. Adams (Eds.), *Aging and work in the 21st century.* Mahwah, NJ: Erlbaum.

Baer, J., & Kaufman, J. C. (2013). *Being creative inside and outside the classroom.* The Netherlands: Sense Publishers.

Baghurst, T., & Kelley, B. (2014). An examination of stress in college students over the course of a semester. *Health Promotion Practice, 15*(3), 438–447.

Baglow, J. S. (2007). The rights of the corpse. *Mortality, 12*(3), 223–239.

Bahrick, L. (2006). Development of intermodal perception. *Encyclopedia of Cognitive Science.* Retrieved from http://www.onlinelibrary.wiley.com/

Bahrick, L. E., & Hollich, G. (2008). Intermodal perception. In M. M. Haith & J. B. Benson (Eds.), *Encyclopedia of infant and early childhood development.* Oxford, UK: Elsevier.

Bailes, C. N., Erting, C. J., Erting, L. C., & Thumann-Prezioao, C. (2009). Language and literacy acquisition through parental mediation in American Sign Language. *Sign Language Studies, 9*(4), 417–456.

Bailey, D. M., et al. (2013). Elevated aerobic fitness sustained throughout the adult lifespan is associated with improved cerebral hemodynamics. *Stroke, 44*(11), 3235–3238.

Bailey, H. N., Moran, G., Pederson, D. R., & Bento, S. (2007). Understanding the transmission of attachment using variable-and relationship-centered approaches. *Development and Psychopathology, 19,* 313–343.

Bailey, H. R., Dunlosky, J., & Hertzog, C. (2014, in press). *Does strategy training reduce age-related deficits in working memory?* Gerontology.

Bailey, S. (2016). *What's the Best Way to Discipline a Toddler? Baby Center, Expert Advice.* Retrieved from http://www.babycenter.com/404_whats-the-best-way-to-discipline-a-toddler_6895.bc.

Baillargeon, R. (2004). Infants' reasoning about hidden objects: Evidence for event-general and event-specific expectations. *Developmental Science, 7*(4), 391–424.

Bain, J. (2010). Testosterone and the aging male: To treat or not to treat? *Maturitas, 66*(1), 16–22.

Bajoghli, H., Keshavarzi, Z., Mohammadi, M., Schmidt, N., Norton, P., Holsboer-Trachsler, E., & Brand, S. (2014). "I love you more than I can stand!" – Romantic love, symptoms of depression and anxiety, and sleep complaints are related among young adults. *International Journal of Psychiatry in Clinical Practice, 18*(3), 169–174.

Baker, D. A. (2007). Consequences of herpes simplex virus in pregnancy and their prevention. *Current Opinions in Infectious Diseases, 20,* 73–76.

Baker, J. K., Fenning, R. M., & Crnic, K. A. (2011). Emotion socialization by mothers and fathers: Coherence among behaviors and associations with parent attitudes and children's competence. *Social Development, 20,* 412–430.

Baker, J., Thorton, L., Lichtenstein, P. Bulik, C. (2012). Pubertal development predicts eating behaviours in adolescents. *International Journal of Eating Disorders, 45*(7), 819–826.

Bakermans-Kranenburg, M. J., Breddels-Van Bardewijk, F., Juffer, M. K., Velderman, M. H., & van IJzenddorn, M. H. (2007). Insecure mothers with temperamentally reactive infants. In F. Juffer, M. J. Bakermans-Kranenburg, & M. H. van IJzendoorn (Eds.), *Promoting positive parenting.* Mahwah, NJ: Erlbaum.

Bakermans-Kranenburg, M., & van IJzendoorn, M. (2009). The first 10,000 attachment interviews: Distribution of adult attachment representations in clinical and non-clinical groups. *Attachment & Human Development, 11*(3), 223–263.

Balarajah, S., & Cavanna, A. E. (2013). The pathophysiology of impulse control disorders in Parkinson disease. *Behavioral Neurology, 26*(4), 237–244.

Baldwin, S., & Hoffman, J. P. (2002). The dynamics of self-esteem: A growth curve analysis. *Journal of Youth and Adolescence, 31,* 101–113.

Ball, J. (2009). Supporting young indigenous children's language development in Canada: A review of research on needs and promising practices. *The Canadian Modern Language Review, 66*(1), 19–47.

Ball, J. W., Bindler, R. C., & Cowen, K. J. (2014, in press). *Child health nursing* (3rd ed.). Upper Saddle River, NJ: Pearson.

Ball, K., Edwards, J. D., Ross, L. A., & McGwin, G. (2010). Effects of cognitive training interventions with older adults: a randomized controlled trial. *Journal of the American Geriatrics Society, 55,* 1–10.

Balsano, A., Phelps, E., Theokas, C., Lerner, J. V., & Lerner, R. M. (2008). Patterns of early adolescents' participation in youth developing programs having positive youth development. *Journal of Research on Adolescence, 19*(2), 249–259.

Baltes, P. B. (2003). On the incomplete architecture of human ontogeny: Selection, optimization, and compensation as foundation for development theory. In U. M. Staudinger & U. Lindenberger (Eds.), *Understanding human development.* Boston: Kluwer.

Baltes, P. B. (2006). *Facing our limits: The very old and the future of aging.* Unpublished manuscript, Max Planck Institute, Berlin.

Baltes, P. B. (2009). Aging and wisdom. In D. C. Park & N. Schwarz (Eds.), *Cognitive aging* (2nd ed.). Clifton, NJ: Psychology Press.

Baltes, P. B., & Kunzmann, U. (2007). Wisdom and aging: The road toward excellence in mind and character. In D. C. Park & N. Schwarz (Eds.), *Cognitive aging: A primer* (2nd ed.). Philadelphia: Psychology Press.

Baltes, P. B., & Smith, J. (2003). New frontiers in the future of aging: From successful aging of the young old to the dilemmas of the fourth age. *Gerontology, 49,* 123–135.

Baltes, P. B., & Smith, J. (2008). The fascination of wisdom: Its nature, ontogeny, and function. *Perspectives in Psychological Sciences, 3,* 56–64.

Baltes, P. B., Lindenberger, U., & Staudinger, U. (2006). Lifespan theory in developmental psychology. In W. Damon & R. Lerner (Eds.), *Handbook of child psychology* (6th ed.). New York: Wiley.

Baltes, P. B., Reuter-Lorenz, P., & Rösler, F. (Eds.). (2006). *Lifespan development and* *the brain.* New York: Cambridge University Press.

Banasik, J. (2013a). Endocrine physiology and mechanisms of hypothalamic-pituitary regulation. In L. Copstead, & J. Banasik (Eds.) *Pathophysiology* (5th ed.) (pp. 790–792). St. Louis: Elsevier.

Banasik, J. (2013b). Structure and function of the nervous system. In L. Copstead, & J. Banasik (Eds.) *Pathophysiology* (5th ed.) (pp. 857–897). St. Louis: Elsevier.

Bandura, A. (1977). *Social learning theory.* Englewood Cliffs, NJ: Prentice Hall.

Bandura, A. (1986). *Social foundations of thought and action: A social cognitive theory.* Englewood Cliffs, NJ: Prentice Hall.

Bandura, A. (1998, August). *Swimming against the mainstream: Accentuating the positive aspects of humanity.* Paper presented at the meeting of the American Psychological Association, San Francisco.

Bandura, A. (2001). Social cognitive theory. *Annual Review of Psychology.* Palo Alto, CA: Annual Reviews.

Bandura, A. (2002). Selective moral disengagement in the exercise of moral agency. *Journal of Moral Education, 31,* 101–119.

Bandura, A. (2004, May). *Toward a psychology of human agency.* Paper presented at the meeting of the American Psychological Society, Chicago.

Bandura, A. (2006). Going global with social cognitive theory: From prospect to paydirt. In S. I. Donaldson, D. E. Berger, & K. Pezdek (Eds.), *The rise of applied psychology: New frontiers and rewarding careers.* Mahwah, NJ: Erlbaum.

Bandura, A. (2008). Reconstrual of "free will" from the agentic perspective of social cognitive theory. In J. Baer, J. C. Kaufman, & R. F. Baumeister (Eds.), *Are we free? Psychology and free will.* Oxford, UK: Oxford University Press.

Bandura, A. (2009a). Social and policy impact of social cognitive theory. In M. Mark, S. Donaldson, & B. Campell (Eds.), *Social psychology and program/policy evaluation.* New York: Guilford.

Bandura, A. (2009b). Self-efficacy. In D. Carr (Ed.), *Encyclopedia of the life course and human development.* Boston: Gale Cengage.

Bandura, A. (2010a). Self-efficacy. In D. Matsumoto (Ed.), *Cambridge dictionary of psychology.* New York: Cambridge University Press.

Bandura, A. (2010b). Vicarious learning. In D. Matsumoto (Ed.), *Cambridge dictionary of psychology.* New York: Cambridge University Press.

Bandura, A. (2012). Social cognitive theory. *Annual Review of Clinical Psychology* (Vol. 8). Palo Alto, CA: Annual Reviews.

Banerjee, S. (2011). Hearing aids in the real world: Use of multimemory and multivolume controls. *Journal of the American Academy of Audiology, 22,* 359–374.

Bangen, K. J., Meeks, T. W., & Jeste, D. V. (2013). Defining and assessing wisdom: A review of the literature. *American Journal of Geriatric Psychiatry, 21,* 1254–1266.

Banja, J. (2005). Talking to the dying. *Case Manager, 16,* 37–39.

Bank, L., Burraston, B., & Snyder, J. (2004). Sibling conflict and ineffective parenting as predictors of adolescent boys' antisocial behavior and peer difficulties: additive and interactive effects. *Journal of Research on Adolescence, 14,* 99–125.

Banks, J. A. (2008). *Introduction to multicultural education* (4th ed.). Boston: Allyn & Bacon.

Banuelos, C., et al. (2014). Prefrontal cortical GABAergic dysfunction contributes to age-related working memory impairment. *Journal of Neuroscience, 34,* 3457–3466.

Barbarin, O. A., & Miller, K. (2009). Developmental science and early education: An introduction. In O. A. Barbarian & B. H. Wasik (Eds.), *Handbook of child development and early education.* New York: Guilford.

Barger, J. L. (2013). An adipocentric perspective of resveratrol as a calorie restriction mimetic. *Annals of the New York Academy of Sciences, 1290,* 122–129.

Bargh, J., & McKenna, K. (2004). The Internet and social life. *Annual Review of Psychology* (Vol. 55). Palo Alto, CA: Annual Reviews.

Baringa, M. (2003, January 3). Newborn neurons search for meaning. *Science, 299,* 32–34.

Barker, E. D., Boivin, M., Brendgen, M., Fontaine, N., Arseneault, L., Vitaro, F., et al. (2008). Predictive validity and early predictions of peer-victimization trajectories in preschool. *Archives of General Psychiatry, 65*(10), 1185–1192.

Barker, E., & Galambos, N. (2005). Adolescents' implicit theories of maturity. *Journal of Adolescent Research, 20*(5), 557–576.

Barnes, K. (2003). *Pregnancy (Gestational) Diabetes: Health Canada.* Retrieved from http://www.hc-sc.gc.ca/pphb-dgspsp/ccdpccpcmc/diabetes-diabete/english/whatis/pregnancy.html.

Barnes, L. L., de Leon, C. F., Lewis, T. T., Bienias, J. L., Wilson, R. S., & Evans, D. A. (2008). Perceived discrimination and mortality in a population-based study of older adults. *American Journal of Public Health, 98,* 1241–1247.

Barnett, J. E., & Francis, A. L. (2012). Using higher order thinking questions to foster critical thinking: A classroom study. *Educational Psychology, 32,* 201–211.

Baron, C. (2012). Using the gradient of human cortical bone properties to determine age-related bone changes via ultrasonic guided waves. *Ultrasound in Medicine and Biology, 38,* 972–981.

Barone, D., Hardman, D., & Taylor, J. (2006). *Reading first in the classroom.* Boston: Allyn & Bacon.

Barrett, A. (2012). Feeling young–A Prescription for growing older? *Aging Today, 33,* 3–4.

Barrett, A. E., & Turner, R. J. (2005). Family structure and mental health: The mediating effects of socioeconomic status, family process, and social stress. *Journal of Health and Social Behavior, 46,* 156–169.

Barrett, L. F., Mesquita, B., Ochsner, K. N., & Gross, J. J. (2007). The experience of emotion. *Annual Review of Psychology* (Vol. 58). Palo Alto, CA: Annual Reviews.

Barrett, T. M., Davis, E. F., & Needham, A. (2007). Learning about tools in infancy. *Developmental Psychology, 43,* 352–368.

Barron, J., Petrilli, F., Strath, L., & McCaffrey, R. (2007). Successful interventions for smoking cessation in pregnancy. *MCN American Journal of Maternal and Child Nursing, 32,* 42–47.

Bart, W. M., & Peterson, D. P. (2008). Stanford-Binet test. In N. J. Salkind (Ed.), *Encyclopedia of educational psychology.* Thousand Oaks, CA: Sage.

Bartel, M. A., Weinstein, J. R., & Schaffer, D. V. (2012). Directed evolution of novel adeno-associated viruses for therapeutic gene delivery. *Gene Therapy, 19*(6), 694–700.

Bartel, M., Weinstein, J., & Schaffer, D. (2012). Directed evolution of novel adeno-associated viruses for therapeutic gene delivery. *Gene Therapy, 19*(6), 694–700.

Bartlett, E. (2004). The effects of fatherhood on the health of men: A review of the literature. *Journal of Men's Health and Gender, 1*(2–3), 159–169.

Basaran, A. (2007). Progesterone to prevent preterm delivery: Enigma or ready? *American Journal of Obstetrics and Gynecology, 197,* 686.

Bateman, B. T., & Simpson, L. L. (2006). Higher rate of stillbirth at the extremes of reproductive age: A large nationwide sample of deliveries in the United States. *American Journal of Obstetrics and Gynecology, 194,* 840–845.

Bates, J. E. & Pettit, G. S. (2007). Temperament, parenting, and socialization. In J. E. Grusec & P. D. Hastings (Eds.), *Handbook of socialization.* New York: Guilford.

Battams, N. (2011). *In it together. Multigenerational living in Canada.* Transition. Vanier Institute of the Family. Volume 43, Number 3 http://www.vanierinstitute.ca/include/get.php?nodeid=3538.

Bauer, I., Wrosch, C., & Jobin, J. (2008). I'm better off than most people: The role of social comparisons for coping with regret in young adulthood and old age. *Psychology and Aging, 23*, 800–811.

Bauer, P. J. (2007). *Remembering the times of our lives.* Mahwah, NJ: Erlbaum.

Bauer, P. J. (2008). Learning and memory: Like a horse and carriage. In A. Netdham & A. Woodward (Eds.), *Learning and the infant mind.* New York: Oxford University Press.

Bauer, P. J. (2009). Neurodevelopmental changes in infancy and beyond: Implications for learning and memory. In O. A. Barbarin & B. H. Wasik (Eds.), *Handbook of child development and early education.* New York: Guilford.

Bauer, P. J. (2013). Memory. In P. D. Zelazo (Ed.), *Oxford handbook of developmental psychology.* New York: Oxford University Press.

Bauer, P. J., & Fivush, R. (Eds.) (2014). *Wiley-Blackwell handbook of children's memory.* New York: Wiley.

Bauer, P. J., Wenner, J. A., Dropik, P. L., & Wewerka, S. S. (2000). Parameters of remembering and forgetting in the transition from infancy to early childhood. *Monographs of the Society of Research in Child Development, 65* (4, Serial No. 263).

Bauer, P., & Zelazo, P. D. (2013). X. NIH Toolbox Cognition Battery (CB): Summary, conclusions, and implications for cognitive development. *Monographs of the Society for Research in Child Development, 78*, 133–146.

Bauman, R. W. (2015, in press). *Microbiology with diseases by body system* (4th ed.). Upper Saddle River, NJ: Pearson.

Baumeister, R. F., & Vohs, K. D. (2002). The pursuit of meaningfulness in life. In C. R. Snyder & S. J. Lopez (Eds.), *Handbook of positive psychology.* New York: Oxford University Press.

Baumeister, R. F., Campbell, J. D., Krueger, J. I., & Vohs, K. D. (2003). Does high self-esteem cause better performance, interpersonal success, happiness, or healthier lifestyles? *Psychological Science in the Public Interest, 4*(1), 1–44.

Baumrind, D. (1971). Current patterns of parental authority. *Developmental Psychology Monographs, 4*(1, Pt. 2).

Baumrind, D. (1991). Effective parenting during the early adolescent transition. In P. A. Cowan & E. M. Hetherington (Eds.), *Advances in family research* (Vol. 2). Hillsdale, NJ: Erlbaum.

Bayley, N. (1969). *Manual for the Bayley Scales of infant development.* New York: Psychological Corporation.

Bayley, N. (1993). *Bayley Scales of infant development* (2nd ed.). San Antonio: The Psychological Corporation.

Bayley, N. (2005). *Bayley Scales of infant and toddler development* (3rd ed.) (Bayley—III). Upper Saddle River, NJ: Pearson.

Baysinger, C. L. (2010). Imaging during pregnancy. *Anesthesia and Analgesia, 110*, 863–867.

Beach, J., & Bertrand, J. (2009, December). Early childhood programs and the education system. *Paediatric Child Health, 14*(10), 666–668.

Beach, J., et al. (2009). *Early childhood education and care in Canada, 2008* (8th ed.). Child Care Canada: Childcare Resource and Research Unit.

Bearman, S. K., Presnall, K., Martinez, E., & Stice, E. (2006). The skinny on body dissatisfaction: A longitudinal study of adolescent girls and boys. *Journal of Youth and Adolescence, 35*, 217–229.

Beaupré, P., & Cloutier, E. (2006). *Navigating family transitions: Evidence from the general social survey.* Ottawa: Social and Aboriginal Statistics Division, Statistics Canada.

Beauregard, M. (2012, May 4). *The neuroscience of spiritual experiences.* Psychiatry Department, McGill University.

Beck, C. T. (2006). Postpartum depression: It isn't just the blues. *American Journal of Nursing, 106*, 40–50.

Bedford, V. H. (2009). Sibling relationships: Adulthood. In D. Carr (Ed.), *Encyclopedia of the life course and human development.* Boston: Gale Cengage.

Beeghly, M., Martin, B., Rose-Jacobs, R., Cahral, H., Heeren, T., Augustyn, M., et al. (2006). Prenatal cocaine exposure and children's language functioning at 6 and 9.5 years: Moderating effects of child age, birth weight, and gender. *Journal of Pediatric Psychology, 31*, 98–115.

Beets, M. W., & Foley, J. T. (2008). Association of father involvement and neighborhood quality with kindergartners' physical activity: A multilevel structural equation model. *American Journal of Health Promotion, 22*, 195–203.

Behrens, H. (2012). Grammatical categories. In E. L. Bavin (Ed.), *Cambridge handbook of child language*. New York: Cambridge University Press.

Behrman, S., & Ebemeier, K. (2014). Can exercise prevent cognitive decline? *Practitioner, 258*, 17–21.

Belic, R. (2011). *Happy*. Retrieved from http://www.thehappymovie.com/film/.

Bell, L., et al. (2013). Body mass index and waist circumference: Relationship to cardiovascular risk factors in children—Busselton Health Study 2005–2007. *Journal of Pediatrics and Child Health*, *49*(11), 955–962.

Bell, M. A., & Cuevas, K. (2014). Psychobiology of executive function in early development. In J. A. Griffin, L. S. Freund, & P. McCardle (Eds.), *Executive function in preschool children*. Washington, DC: American Psychological Association.

Bell, M. A., & Wolfe, C. D. (2007). The cognitive neuroscience of early socioemotional development. In C. A. Brownell & C. B. Kopp (Eds.), *Socioemotional development in the toddler years.* New York: Guilford.

Bell, N., & Baron, E. (2015). Resistance to peer influence during adolescence: Proposing a sociocultural-developmental framework. *New Ideas in Psychology, 39*, 53–62.

Bell, R. D., et al. (2012). Apolipoprotein E controls cerebrovascular integrity via cyclophilin A. *Nature*, *485*(7399), 512–516.

Belsky, J. (1981). Early human experience: A family perspective. *Developmental Psychology, 17*, 3–23.

Belsky, J. (2009). Social-contextual determinants of parenting. In R. E. Tremblay, R. deV Peters, M. Boivin, & R. G. Barr (Eds.), *Encyclopedia on early childhood development.* Montreal: Centre of Excellence for Early Childhood Development.

Belsky, J. (2010). *Experiencing the lifespan* (2nd ed.). New York: Worth.

Belsky, J. (2013). *Experiencing the lifespan* (3rd ed). New York: Worth.

Belsky, J., & Pasco Fearon, R. (2002a). Early attachment security, subsequent maternal sensitivity, and later child development: Does continuity in development depend on continuity of care-giving? *Attachment & Human Development, 4*, 361–387.

Belsky, J., Burchinal, M., McCartney, K., Vandell, D., Clarke-Stewart, K. & Owen, M. (2007). Are there long-term effects of early child care? *Child Development, 78*(2), 681–701.

Bem, S. L. (1977). On the utility of alternative procedures for assessing psychological androgyny. *Journal of Consulting and Clinical Psychology, 45*, 196–205.

Benarroch, E. E. (2013). Adult neurogenesis in the dentate gyrus: General concepts and potential implications. *Neurology, 81*(16), 1443–1452.

Ben-David, B. M., Tewari, A., Shakuf, V., & van Lieshout, P. H. (2014). Stroop effects in Alzheimer's disease: Selective attention speed of processing, or color-naming? A meta-analysis. *Journal of Alzheimer's Disease, 38*(4), 923–938.

Bender, H. L., et al. (2007). Use of harsh discipline and developmental outcomes in adolescence. *Development and Psychopathology, 19*, 227–242.

Benegbi, M. (2007, Winter). 45 years later . . . Where do we stand? *Canadian Journal of Clinical Pharmacology, 14*(1), e37–e39.

Benenson, J. F., & Heath, A. (2006). Boys withdraw more in one-on-one situations, whereas girls withdraw more in groups. *Developmental Psychology, 42*, 272–282.

Benenson, J. F., Apostoleris, N. H., & Parnass, J. (1997). Age and sex differences in dyadic and group interaction. *Developmental Psychology, 33*, 538–543.

Bener, A., et al. (2013). Obesity index that better predicts metabolic syndrome: Body mass index, waist circumference, waist hip ratio, or waist height ratio. *Journal of Obesity*, 269038.

Bengtsson, H., & Arvidsson, A. (2011). The impact of developing social perspective-taking skills on emotionality in middle and late childhood. *Social Development, 20*, 353–375.

Bennet, T., Szatmari, P., Georgiades, K., Hanna, S., Janus, M.......The Pathways in ASD Study Team. (2015). Do reciprocal associations exist between social and language pathways in preschoolers with autism spectrum disorders. *Journal of Child Psychology and Psychiatry, 56*(8), 874–883.

Bennett, P. W. (April 7, 2012) *Full Inclusion in Public Schools: Is It Best for all Special Needs Kids?* Retrieved from https://educhatter.wordpress.com/2012/04/07/full-inclusion-in-public-schools-is-it-best-for-all-special-needs-kids/

Bennett, S. (2015). Prescribing in pregnancy: Effects on the fetus. *Nurse Prescribing, 13*(1). 24–29.

Bennetts, B. (2014). Update on molecular genetic testing methodologies. Pathology, 46(1, Suppl.), S38.

Benninghoven, D., Tetsch, N., Kunzendorf, S., & Jantschek, G. (2007). Body image in patients with eating disorders and their mothers, and the role of family functioning. *Comprehensive Psychiatry, 48*, 118–123.

Benoit, D. (2009). Efficacy of attachment-based interventions. In R. E. Tremblay, R. deV Peters, M. Boivin, & R. G. Barr (Eds.), *Encyclopedia on early childhood development.* Montreal: Centre of Excellence for Early Childhood Development.

Benoit, D., Coolbear, J., & Crawford, A. (2008). Abuse, neglect, and maltreatment of infants. In M. M. Haith & J. B. Benson (Eds.), *Encyclopedia of infant and early childhood development.* Oxford, UK: Elsevier.

Benokraitis, N. (2008). *Marriages and families* (6th ed.). Upper Saddle River, NJ: Prentice Hall.

Benowitz-Fredericks, C., Garcia, K., Massey, M., Vassagae, B. & Borzekowski, D. (2012). Body image, eating disorders, and the relationship to adolescent media use. *Pediatric Clinics of North America, 59*, 693–704.

Benson, J. E., Sabbagh, M. A., Carlson, S. M., & Zelazo, P. D. (2014, in press). Individual differences in executive functioning predict preschoolers' improvement from theory-of-mind training. *Developmental Psychology.*

Benson, M., & Buehler, C. (2012). Family process and peer deviance influences on adolescent aggression: longitudinal effects across early and middle adolescence. *Child Development, 83*, 1213–1228.

Benson, P. L., Roehlkepartain, E. C., & Hong, K. L. (2008). Spiritual development. *New Directions for Youth Development, 118.*

Benson, P., & Scales, P. (2009). The definition of preliminary measurement of thriving in adolescence. *Journal of Positive Psychology, 41*(1), 85–104.

Benzies, K., Tough, S. W., Tofflemire, K., Frick, C., Faber, A., & Newburn-Cook, C. (2006). Factors influencing women's decisions about timing of motherhood. *Journal of Obstetric Gynecologic & Neonatal Nursing, 35*(5), 625–633.

Berardi, N., Sale, A., & Maffei, L. (2015). Brain structural and functional development: Genetics and experience. *Developmental Medicine and Child Neurology, 57(2)*, 4–9.

Berger, J. T. (2010). What about process? Limitations in advanced directives, care planning, and noncapacitated decision making. *American Journal of Bioethics, 10*, 33–34.

Berger, J., Motte, A., & Parkin, A. (2007). *The price of knowledge 2006–7: Chapter 1—Why access matters.* Montreal: The Canadian Millennium Scholarship Foundation.

Berger, K. & Chuang, S. (2014). *Invitation to the lifespan*. (Canadian ed.). New York, NY: Worth.

Berger, K. (2011). *The developing person through the life span* (8th ed). New York: Worth.

Berger, K. (2014). *Invitation to the life span* (2nd ed). New York: Worth.

Bergeson, T. R., & Trehub, S. E. (2007). Signature tunes in mothers' speech to infants. *Infant Behavior & Development, 30*, 648–654.

Berk, L. E., & Spuhl, S. T. (1995). Maternal interaction, private speech, and task performance in preschool children. *Early Childhood Research Quarterly, 10*, 145–169.

Berko-Gleason, J. (1958). The child's learning of English morphology. *Word, 14*, 150–177.

Berkowitz, R. L., Roberts, J., & Minkoff, H. (2006). Challenging the strategy of maternal age-based prenatal genetic counseling. *Journal of the American Medical Association*, 1446–1448.

Berman, S., O'Neill, J., Fears, S., Bartzokis, G. & London, E. (2008). Abuse of amphetamines and structural abnormalities in the brain. *Annals of the New York Academy of Sciences, 1141*, 195–150.

Bernard, K., & Dozier, M. (2008). Adoption and foster placement. In M. M. Haith & J. B. Benson (Eds.), *Encyclopedia of infant and early childhood development.* Oxford, UK: Elsevier.

Bernard, K., Dozier, M., Bick, J., Lewis-Morrarty, E., Lindheim, O. & Carson, E. (2012). Enhancing attachment organization among maltreated children: Results of a randomized clinical trial. *Child Development, 83*(2), 623–636.

Berndt, T. J. (2002). Friendship quality and social development. *Current Directions in Psychological Science, 11*, 7–10.

Berndt, T. J., & Perry, T. B. (1990). Distinctive features and effects of early adolescent friendships. In R. Montemayor (Ed.), *Advances in adolescent research.* Greenwich, CT: JAI Press.

Berninger, V., & Dunn, M. (2012). Brain and behavioral response to intervention for specific reading, writing, and math disabilities: What works for whom? In B. Wong, & D. Butler (Eds.), *Learning about LD* (4th ed.). New York: Elsevier.

Bernstein, A. (2012, March 7). If Canada's game is hockey, its science is stem cells. *The Globe and Mail.* Retrieved from http://www.theglobeandmail.com/commentary/if-canadas-game-is-hockey-its-science-is-stem-cells/article551653/

Berscheid, E. (2010). Love in the fourth dimension. *Annual Review of Psychology* (Vol. 61). Palo Alto, CA: Annual Reviews.

Berthiaume, L. (2012, Feb. 2). Over 2000 Canadians were wounded in Afghan mission: report. *The National Post.* Retrieved from http://www.news.*nationalpost*.com

Bertorelle, R., et al. (2014). Telomeres, telomerase, and colorectal cancer. *World Journal of Gastroenterology, 20*, 1940–1950.

Bertrand, R. M., & Lachman, M. E. (2003). Personality development in adulthood and old age. In I. B. Weiner (Ed.). *Handbook of psychology,* Vol. VI. New York: John Wiley.

Bertrand, R., Graham, E. K., & Lachman, M. E. (2013). Personality development in adulthood and old age. In I. B. Weiner et al. (Eds.), *Handbook of aging* (2nd ed., Vol. 6). New York: Wiley.

Beverly, C., Burger, S. G., Maas, M. L., & Specht, J. K. (2010). Aging issues: Nursing imperatives for healthcare reform. *Nursing Administration Quarterly, 34*, 95–109.

Beyene, Y. (1986). Cultural significance and physiological manifestations of menopause: A biocultural analysis. *Culture, Medicine and Psychiatry, 10*, 47–71.

Beyers, E., & Seiffge-Krenke, I. (2010). Does identity precede intimacy? Testing Erikson's theory on romantic development in emerging adults of the 21st century. *Journal of Adolescent Research, 25*, 387–415.

Beyers, W., & Goossens, L. (2008). Dynamics of perceived parenting and identity formation in late adolescence. *Journal of Adolescence, 31*, 165–184.

Bezanson, K. (2010). The "great recession," families and social reproduction. *Transition: The Vanier Institute of the Family, 40*(1).

Bialystok, E. (2007). Cognitive effects of bilingualism: How linguistic experience leads to cognitive change. *International Journal of Bilingual Education and Bilingualism, 10*(3), 210–223.

Bianchi, S., Robinson, J., & Milkie, M. (2006). *Changing rhythms life* (Rose series in sociology). New York: Russell Sage Foundation Publications.

Bianco, I. H., Carl, M., Russell, C., Clarke, J. D., & Wilson, S. W. (2008). Brain asymmetry is encoded at the level of axon terminal morphology. *Neural Development, 3*, 9.

Bibby, R. (2009, May). *Restless gods and restless youth: An update on the religious situation in Canada.* Paper presented at the Annual Meeting of the Canadian Sociological Association, Ottawa.

Bibby, R. (2010). Beyond the stereotypes–an inside look at Canada's emerging millennials. *Canadian Education Association.* Education Canada, Vol. 50(1).

Bibby, R. (2011). Reginald Bibby: Study predicting religion's demise is way off the mark. *National Post.* Retrieved from http://www.nationalpost.com

Bielak, A. A. M., Hughes, T. F., Small, B. J., & Dixon, R. A. (2007). It's never too late to engage in lifestyle activities: Significant concurrent but not change relationships between lifestyle activities and cognitive speed. *Journals of Gerontology B: Psychological Sciences and Social Sciences, 62*, P331–P339.

Bigelow, A. E. (2003). The development of joint attention in blind infants. *Development and Psychopathology, 15*, 59–275.

Billari, F., et al. (2011). Social age deadlines for the childbearing of women and men. *Human Reproduction, 26*(3), 616–622.

Binder, T., & Vavrinkova, B. (2008). Prospective randomized comparative study of the effect of buprenorphine, methadone, and heroin on the course of pregnancy, birthweight of newborns, early postpartum adaptation, and the course of neonatal abstinence syndrome (NAS). *Neuroendocrinology Letters, 29*, 80–86.

Biography.com. (2013). *Leonard Cohen biography*. Arts & Entertainment Network. Retrieved from http://www.biography.com/people/leonard-cohen-9252529

Birch, S. A. J. (2005). When knowledge is a curse: Childrens' and adults' reasoning about mental states. *Current Directions in Psychological Science, 14*, 25–29.

Birditt, K. S. (2009). Spousal caregiving. In D. Carr (Ed.), *Encyclopedia of the life course and human development.* Boston: Gale Cengage.

Birditt, K. S., & Wardjiman, E. (2012a). Intergenerational relationships and aging. In S. K. Whitbourne & M. J. Sliwinski (Eds.), *Wiley-Blackwell handbook of adult development and aging*. New York: Wiley.

Birditt, K. S., & Wardjiman, E. (2012b). Partners and friends in adulthood. In S. K. Whitbourne & M. Sliwinski (Eds.), *Wiley-Blackwell handbook of adult development and aging*. New York: Wiley.

Birkeland, M. S., Melkevick, O., Holsen, I., & Wold, B. (2012). Trajectories of global self-esteem development during adolescence. *Journal of Adolescence, 35*, 43–54.

Birken, C., Parkin, P., To, T., & Macarthur C. (2006). Trends in the rates of death from unintentional injury among Canadian children in urban areas: Influence of socioeconomic status. *Canadian Medical Association Journal, 175*(8), 867–868.

Birren, J. E. (Ed.). (1996). *Encyclopedia of gerontology.* San Diego: Academic Press.

Birren, J. E. (Ed.). (2007). *Encyclopedia of gerontology* (2nd ed.). San Diego: Academic Press.

Bisiacchi, P. S., Tarantino, V., & Ciccola, A. (2008). Aging and prospective memory: The role of working memory and monitoring processes. *Aging: Clinical and Experimental Research, 20*, 569–577.

Bisson, M., & Levine, T. (2009). Negotiating a friends with benefits relationship. *Archives of Sexual Behavior, 25*, 125–140.

Bjorklund, D. F. (2008). Advances in memory in childhood: Strategies, knowledge, and meta cognition. In M. Courage & N. Cowan (Eds.), *The development of memory in infancy and childhood.* Philadelphia: Psychology Press.

Bjorklund, D. F. (2013). Cognitive development: An overview. In P. D. Zelazo (Ed.), *Oxford handbook of developmental psychology*. New York: Oxford University Press.

Blackstone, A., & Stewart, M. (2012). Choosing to be childfree: Research on the decision not to parent. *Sociology Compass, 6*(9), 718–727.

Blair, C., & Razza, R. P. (2007). Relating effortful control, executive functioning, and false belief understanding to emerging math and literacy ability in kindergarten. *Child Development, 78*, 647–663.

Blair, C., Raver, C. C., & Berry, D. J. (2014). Two approaches estimating the effect of parenting on the development of executive function in early childhood. *Developmental Psychology, 50*, 554–565.

Blair, M., & Somerville, S. C. (2009). The importance of differentiation in young children's acquisition of expertise. *Cognition, 112*, 259–280.

Blair, P., Platt, M., Smith, I. & Fleming, P. (2006). Sudden infant death syndrome and sleeping position in pre-term and low birth weight infants: an opportunity for targets intervention. *Archives of Disease in Childhood, 91*(2), 101–106.

Blake, J., Munoz, K., & Volpe, S. (2014). *Nutrition: From science to you plus mastering nutrition with e-text* (2nd ed.). Upper Saddle River, NJ: Pearson.

Blanchard-Fields, F., & Coats, A. (2007). *Emotions in everyday problems: Age differences in elicitation and regulation.* Paper submitted for publication. Atlanta: Department of Psychlogy, Georgia Tech University.

Blanco, C., et al. (2014, in press). Risk factors for anxiety disorders: Common and specific effects in a national sample. *Depression and Anxiety.*

Blandon, A., Calkins, S., Keane, S. & O'Brien, M. (2010). Contributions of child's pjysiology and maternal behaviour to children's trajectories of temperament reactivity. *Developmental Psychology, 46*(5), 1089–1102.

Blank, R. (2011). End-of-life decision making across cultures. *Journal of Law, Medicine & Ethics, 39*(2), 201–214.

Blieszner, R. (2009). Friendship, adulthood. In D. Carr (Ed.). *Encyclopedia of the life course and human development.* Boston: Gale Cengage.

Blieszner, R., & Roberto, K. A. (2012a). Intergenerational relationships and aging. In S. K. Whitbourne & M. Sliwinski (Eds.), *Wiley-Blackwell handbook of adult development and aging*. New York: Wiley.

Blieszner, R., & Roberto, K. A. (2012b). Partner and friend relationships in adulthood. In S. K. Whitbourne & M. Sliwinski (Eds.), *Wiley-Blackwell handbook of adult development and aging*. New York: Wiley.

Block, J. (1993). Studying personality the long way. In D. Funder, R. D. Parke, C. Tomlinson-Keasey, & K. Widaman (Eds.), *Studying lives through time.* Washington, DC: American Psychological Association.

Bloom, L. (1998). Language acquisition in developmental context. In W. Damon (Ed.), *Handbook of child psychology* (5th ed., Vol. 5). New York: Wiley.

Bloom, L., Lifter, K., & Broughton, J. (1985). The convergence of early cognition and language in the second year of life: Problems in conceptualization and measurement. In M. Barrett (Ed.), *Single word speech.* London: Wiley.

Bloor, C., & White, F. (1983). Unpublished manuscript. University of California at San Diego, LaJolla, CA.

Blum, J. W., Beaudoin, C. M., & Caton-Lemos, L. (2005). Physical activity patterns and maternal well-being in postpartum women. *Maternal and Child Health Journal, 8*, 163–169.

Blum, R., & Nelson-Mmari, K. (2004). Adolescent health from an international perspective. In R. Lerner & L. Steinberg (Eds.), *Handbook of adolescent psychology.* New York: Wiley.

Blumel, J. E., Lavin, P., Vellejo, M. S., & Sarra, S. (2014, in press). Menopause or climacteric, just a semantic discussion or has it clinical implications? *Climacteric.*

Blustein, D. L. (2008). The role of work in psychological health and well-being. *American Psychologist, 63*, 228–240.

Boden, J., Fergusson, D. & Horwood, L. (2008). Does adolescent self-esteem predict later life outcomes? A test of the causal role of self-esteem. *Development and Psychopathology, 20*, 319–339.

Boelen, P. A., & Prigerson, H. G. (2007). The influence of symptoms of prolonged grief disorder, depression, and anxiety on quality of life among bereaved adults: A prospective study. *European Archives of Psychiatry and Clinical Neuroscience, 257*, 444–452.

Boelen, P. A., van den Bout, J., & van den Hout, M. A. (2003). The role of cognitive variables in psychological functioning after the death of a first degree relative. *Behavior Research and Therapy, 41*, 1123–1136.

Boelens, C., Hekman, E. E., & Verkerke, G. J. (2013). Risk factors for falls of older citizens. *Technology and Health Care, 21*, 521–533.

Boerce, G. C. (2006). *Carl Jung, 1987–1961.* Retrieved from http://webspace.ship.edu/cgboer/jung.html.

Boerleider, A., Wiegers, T., Manniën, J. Francke, A., & Devillé, W. (2013). Factors affecting the use of prenatal care by non-western women in industrialized western countries. A systematic review. *BMC Pregnancy and Childbirth, 13*, 81. Retrieved from http://www.biomedcentral.com/

Bogle, K. (2008). *Hooking up: Sex, dating, and relationships on campus.* New York: University Press.

Bohlin, G. & Hagekull, B. (2009). Socio-emotional development from infancy to young adulthood. *Scandinavian Journal of Psychology, 50*, 592–601.

Boisvert, J., & Harrell, W. (2009). Homosexuality as a risk factor for eating disorder symptomology in men. *The Journal of Men's Studies, 17*, 210–225.

Bombak, A. (2014). Obesity, health at every size, and public policy. *American Journal of Public Health, 104*, e60–e67.

Bonanno, G. A., Neria, Y., Mancini, A., Coiofman, K. G., Litz, B., & Insel, B. (2007). Is there more to complicated grief than depression and posttraumatic stress disorder? *Journal of Abnormal Psychology, 116*, 342–351.

Bonanno, G. A., Wortman, C. B., & Nesse, R. M. (2004). Prospective patterns of resilience and maladjustment during widowhood. *Psychology and Aging, 19*, 260–271.

Bondare, W. (2007). Brain and central nervous system. In J. E. Birren (Ed.), *Encyclopedia of gerontology* (2nd ed.). San Diego: Academic Press.

Bone and Joint Canada. (2014). *Osteoarthritis*. Retrieved from http://boneandjointcanada.com/osteoarthritis/.

Bonell, C., et al. (2013). The effects of school environment on student health: A systematic review of multi-level studies. *Health & Place, 21*, 180–191.

Bonvillian, J. (2005). Unpublished review of J. W. Santrock's *Topical life-span development* (3rd ed.). New York: McGraw-Hill.

Booth, A. (2006). Object function and categorization in infancy: Two mechanisms of facilitation. *Infancy, 10*, 145–169.

Booth, D., Elliott, S., & Bruce, F. (2009). Boys' literacy attainment: Research and related practice. Retrieved from http://www.edu.gov.on.ca/eng/research/boys_literacy.pdf.

Booth, M. (2002). Arab adolescents facing the future: Enduring ideas and pressures to change. In B. B. Brown, R. W. Larson, & T. S. Saraswathi (Eds.), *The world's youth.* New York: Cambridge University Press.

Bor, W., McGee, T. R., & Fagan, A. A. (2004). Early risk factors for adolescent antisocial behavior: An Australian longitudinal study. *Australian and New Zealand Journal of Psychiatry, 38*, 365–372.

Borella, E., Caretti, B., Zanoni, G., Zavagnin, M., & De Beni, R. (2013). Working memory training in old age: An examination of transfer and maintenance effects. *Archives of Clinical Neuropsychology, 28*, 331–347.

Bornstein, M. H., & Bohr, Y. (2011). Immigration, Acculturation, and Parenting. *Encyclopedia on Early Childhood Development.* Retrieved from http://www.child-encyclopedia.com/Pages/PDF/Bornstein-BohrANGxp1.pdf.

Bornstein, M. (2014). Human infancy....and the rest of the lifespan. *Annual Review of Psychology, 65*, 121–158.

Bornstein, M. H. (1975). Qualities of color vision in infancy. *Journal of Experimental Child Psychology, 19*, 401–409.

Bornstein, M. H. (2006). Parenting science and practice. In W. Damon & R. Lerner (Eds.), *Handbook of child psychology* (6th ed.). New York: Wiley.

Bos, A., Huijding, J., Muris, P., Vogel, L., & Biesheuvel, J. (2010). Global, contingent and implicit self-esteem and psychopathological symptoms in adolescents. *Personality and Individual Differences, 48*, 311–316.

Bos, H. M. W., Sandfort, T. G. M., de Bruyn, E. H., & Hakvoort, E. M. (2008). Same-sex attraction, social relationships, psychosocial functioning, and school performance. *Developmental Psychology, 44*, 102–116.

Bos, H., van Balen, F., & van den Boom, D. (2005). Lesbian families and family functioning: an overview. *Patient Education and Counselling, 59*, 263–275.

Botek, A. (2015). Why these college students love living in a retirement home. *Aging Care*. Retrieved from https://www.agingcare.com/Articles/college-students-living-in-nursing-home-179924.htm.

Bouchard, T. J., Lykken, D. T., McGue, M., Segal, N. L., & Tellegen, A. (1990). Source of human psychological differences. The Minnesota Study of Twins Reared Apart. *Science, 250*, 223–228.

Boukydis, C. F., & Lester, B. M. (2008). Mother-infant consultation during drug treatment: Research and innovative clinical practice. *Harm Reduction Journal, 5*(6).

Bowen, A., & Muhajarine, N. (2006). Prevalence of antenatal depression in women enrolled in an outreach program in Canada. *Journal of Obstetrics, Gynecologic and Neonatal Nursing, 35*(4), 491–498.

Bowen, A., Bowen, R., Maslany, G., & Muhajarine, N. (2008, July). Anxiety in a socially high-risk sample of pregnant women in Canada. *The Canadian Journal of Psychiatry, 53*(7), 435–440.

Bowers, G., & Lopez, W. (2013). Which way to the restroom? – Respecting the rights of transgender youth in the school system: A North American perspective. *Education and Law Journal, 22*(3), 243–266.

Bowker, A. (2006). Relationship between sports participation and self-esteem during early adolescence. *Canadian Journal of Behavioural Science, 38*, 214–229.

Bowlby, J. (1969). *Attachment and loss (Vol. 1)*. London: Hogarth Press.

Bowlby, J. (1980). *Attachment and loss (Vol. 3): Loss, sadness, and depression*. New York: Basic Books.

Bowlby, J. (1989). *Secure and insecure attachment*. New York: Basic Books.

Bowman, M. A., Prelow, H. M., & Weaver, S. R. (2007). Parenting behaviors, association with deviant peers, and delinquency in African American adolescents: A mediated-moderation model. *Journal of Youth and Adolescence, 36*, 517–527.

Bowman, N. (2010). The development of psychological well-being in first year college students. *Journal of College Student Development, 51*, 180–200.

Boyce, W., Doherty-Poirier, M., MacKinnon, D., Fortin, H., King, M. & Gallupe, O. (2006). Sexual health of Canadian youth: Findings from the Canadian youth, sexual health and HIV/AIDS study. *The Canadian Journal of Human Sexuality, 15(2)*, 59–68.

Boyer, K., & Diamond, A. (1992). Development of memory for temporal order in infants and young children. In A. Diamond (Ed.), *Development and neural bases of higher cognitive function*. New York: New York Academy of Sciences.

Boykin McElhaney, K., Allen, J., Stephenson, C., & Hare, A. (2006). Attachment and autonomy during adolescence. In R. Lerner & L. Steinberg (Eds.), *Handbook of adolescent psychology* (3rd ed.) Vol. 1 (pp. 358–403). Hoboken, NJ: Wiley.

Boyle, P. A., Yu, L., Buchman, A. S., & Bennett, D. A. (2012). Risk aversion is associated with decision making among community-based older persons. *Frontiers in Psychology, 3*, 205.

Bozhovich, L. (2009). The social situation of child development. *Journal of Russian & East European Psychology, 47*, 59–86.

Bradley, L. (2012). *Sharing my vision—Changing directions, changing lives: The mental health strategy for Canada unveiled*. Mental Health Commission of Canada. Retrieved from http://www.mentalhealthcommission.ca/

Bradley, R. E., & Webb, R. (1976). Age-related differences in locus of control orientation in three behavior domains. *Human Development, 19*, 49–55.

Brain Canada Foundation. *The news*. (August, 2012). Retrieved from http://braincanada.ca.

Brainerd, C. J., & Reyna, V. E. (1993). Domains of fuzzy-trace theory. In M. L. Howe & R. Pasnak (Eds.), *Emerging themes in cognitive development*. New York: Springer.

Braithwaite, D., Emery, J., Walter, F., Prevost, A. T., & Sutton, S. (2004, January 21). Psychological impact of genetic counseling for familial cancer: A systematic review and meta-analysis. *Journal of the National Cancer Institute, 96*(2), 122–133.

Brand, J. (2014). Social consequences of job loss and unemployment. *Annual Review of Sociology* (Vol. 40). Palo Alto, CA: Annual Reviews.

Brand, M. (2011). Mitochondrial functioning and aging. In E. Masoro & S. Austad (Eds.), *Handbook of the biology of aging* (7th ed.). New York: Elsevier.

Brandstädter, J., & Renner, G. (1990). Tenacious goal pursuit and flexible goal adjustment: Explication and age-related analysis of assimilative and accommodative strategies of coping. *Psychology and Aging, 5*, 58–67.

Brannen, C., Dyck, K., Hardy, C., & Mushquash, C. (2012). Rural mental health services in Canada: A model for research and practice. In J. Kulig & A. Williams (Eds.), *Health in rural Canada* (pp. 239–257). Vancouver: UBC Press.

Brannen, C., McGrath, P., Johnston, C., Dozois, D., Elgar, F., & Whitehead, M. (2006). *Managing our mood (MOM): Distance treatment for post-partum depression in rural Nova Scotia*. Paper presented at the Annual Conference of the Canadian Rural Health Research Society, Prince George, BC.

Bransford, J., et al. (2006). Learning theories in education. In P. A. Alexander & P. H. Winne (Eds.), *Handbook of educational psychology* (2nd ed.). Mahwah, NJ: Erlbaum.

Branswell, H. (2013, Apr 17). *Herpes virus has infected nearly one in 5 Canadians over age 35, most unaware they have it: Study*. The Canadian Press. Retrieved from http://www.news.nationalpost.com.

Brassard, A., Pèloquin, K., Dupuy, E., Wright, J., & Shaver, P. (2012). Romantic attachment insecurity predicts sexual dissatisfaction in couples seeking marriage therapy. *Journal of Sex and Marital Therapy, 38*(3), 245–262.

Brault, M. C., & Lacourse, É. (February, 2012). Prevalence of prescribed attention-deficit hyperactivity disorder medications and diagnosis among Canadian preschoolers and school-age children: 1994–2007. *Canadian Journal of Psychiatry, 57*(2), 93–101. Retrieved from http://www.ncbi.nlm.nih.gov/pubmed/22340149.

Braver, S., & Lamb, M. (2013). Marital dissolution. In G. Peterson & K. Bush (Eds.) *Handbook of marriage and the family* (3rd ed) (pp. 487–516). New York, NY: Springer.

Bravo, G., et al. (2011). Are Canadians providing advance directives about health care and research participation in the event of decisional incapacity? *The Canadian Journal of Psychiatry, 56*(4), 209–218.

Bravo, I., & Noya, M. (2014). Cultures in prenatal development: Parental attitudes, availability of care, expectations, values and nutrition. *Child Youth Care Forum*, 43, 521–538.

Brazelton, T. B. (2004). Preface: The neonatal intensive care unit network neurobehavioral scale. *Pediatrics, 113* (Suppl.) S632–S633.

Brazil, K., Thabane, L., Foster, G., & Bédard, M. (2009). Gender differences among Canadian spousal caregivers at the end of life. *Health and Social Care in the Community, 17*(2), 159–166.

Breaslau, N., Paneth N. S., & Lucia, V. C. (2004). The lingering academic deficits of low birth weight children. *Pediatrics, 114*, 1035–1040.

Brechwald, W. A., & Prinstein, M. J. (2011). Beyond homophily: A decade of advances in understanding peer influence processes. *Journal of Research on Adolescence, 21*, 166–179.

Bredekamp, S. (2011). *Effective practices in early childhood education.* Upper Saddle River, NJ: Merrill.

Bregman, H., Malik, N., Page, M., Makynen, E., & Lindahl, K. (2013). Identity profiles in lesbian, gay, and bisexual youth: The role of family influences. *Journal of Youth and Adolescence, 42*, 417–430.

Bremner, G. (2007). Perception and knowledge of the world. In A. Slater & M. Lewis (Eds.), *Introduction to infant development* (2nd ed.). Malden, MA: Blackwell.

Brenna, V., Proietti, V., Montirosso, R. & Turati, C. (2012). Positive, but not negative, facial expressions facilitate 3-month-olds' recognition of an individual face. *International Issue of Behavioural Development, 37*(2), 137–142.

Brennan, S. (2011). *Violent victimization of Aboriginal women in the Canadian provinces, 2009.* Retrieved from http://www.statca.gc.ca.

Brenner-Shuman, A. & Waren, W. (2013). Age at menarche and choice of college major: Implications for STEM majors. *Bulletin of Science, Technology & Society, 33*(11-2), 28–34.

Breslau, J., Miller, E., Jin, R., Sampson, N., Alonso, J., Andrade, L.,... Kessler, R. (2011). A multinational study of mental disorders, marriage, and divorce. *Acta Psychiatria Scandinavica, 124*, 474–486.

Bretherton, I. (2012). Afterword. In K. H. Brisch, *Treating attachment disorders* (2nd ed.). New York: Guilford.

Bretscher, P. (Interview on February 10, 2106).

Brez, C., Colombo, J. & Cohen, L. (2012). *Infant Behaviour and Development, 35*, 705–710.

Brice, A., Miller, K., & Brice, R. (2006). Language in the English as a second language and general education classrooms: A tutorial. *Communication Disorders Quarterly, 27*, 240–247.

Briem, V., Radeborg, K., Salo, I., & Bengtsson, H. (2004). Developmental aspects of children's behavior and safety while cycling. *Journal of Pediatric Psychology, 29*, 369–377.

Brim, G. (1992, December 7). Commentary, *Newsweek*, p. 52.

Brim, G., Ryff, C. D., & Kessler, R. (Eds.). (2004). *How healthy are we? A national study of well-being at midlife.* Chicago: University of Chicago Press.

Brink, P., & Smith, T. F. (2008). Determinants of home death in palliative home care: Using the interRAI palliative care to assess end-of-life care. *American Journal of Hospice and Palliative Medicine, 25*(4), 263–270.

Brislin, R. W. (2000). Cross-cultural training. In A. Kazdin (Ed.), *Encyclopedia of psychology.* Washington, DC: American Psychological Association and Oxford University Press.

Brock, L. J., & Jennings, G. (2007). Sexuality and intimacy. In J. A. Blackburn & C. N. Dulmas (Eds.), *Handbook of gerontology.* New York: Wiley.

Brockie, J., et al. (2014, in press). EMAS position statement: Menopause for medical students. *Maturitas.*

Broderick, R. (2003, July/August). A surgeon's saga. *Minnesota: The Magazine of the University of Minnesota Alumni Association*, 26–31.

Broekhuizen, L. N., et al. (2011). Physical activity, metabolic syndrome, and coronary risk: The EPIC-Norfolk prospective population study. *European Journal of Cardiovascular Prevention and Rehabilitation, 18*, 209–217.

Bronfenbrenner, U. (1979). *The ecology of human development. Experiments by nature and design.* Cambridge, MA: Harvard University Press.

Bronfenbrenner, U. (1986). Ecology of the family as a context for human development: Research perspectives. *Developmental Psychology, 22*, 723–742.

Bronfenbrenner, U. (2000). Ecological theory. In A. Kazdin (Ed.), *Encyclopedia of psychology.* Washington, DC: American Psychological Association and Oxford University Press.

Bronfenbrenner, U. (2004). *Making human beings human.* Thousand Oaks. CA: Sage.

Bronfenbrenner, U., & Morris, P. (1998). The ecology of developmental processes. In W. Damon (Ed.), *Handbook of child psychology* (5th ed., Vol. 1). New York: Wiley.

Bronfenbrenner, U., & Morris, P. A. (2006). The ecology of human development. In W. Damon & R. Lerner (Eds.), *Handbook of child psychology* (6th ed.). New York: Wiley.

Bronstein, P. (2006). The family environment: Where gender role socialization begins. In J. Worell & C. D. Goodheart (Eds.), *Handbook of girl's and women's psychological health.* New York: Oxford University Press.

Brooker, R. J. (2015). *Genetics* (5th ed.). New York: McGraw-Hill.

Brooker, R. J., Widmaier, E. P., Grham, L., & Stiling, P. (2015). *Principles of biology.* New York: McGraw-Hill.

Brooker, R., Buss, K., Lemery-Chalfant, K., Aksan, N., Davidson, R. & Hill Goldsmith, H. (2013). The development of stranger fear in infancy and toddlerhood: Normative development, individual differences, antecedents, and outcomes. *Developmental Science, 16*(6), 864–878.

Brookfield, S. (2011). *Teaching for critical thinking: Tools and techniques to help students question their assumptions.* San Francisco: Jossey-Bass.

Brooks, J. G., & Brooks, M. (2001). *The case for constructivist classroom* (2nd ed.). Upper Saddle River, NJ: Erlbaum.

Brooks-Gunn, J. (2003). Do you believe in magic? What we can expect from early childhood programs. *Social Policy Report, Society for Research in Child Development, XVII* (No. 1), 1–13.

Brooks-Gunn, J., & Warren, M. P. (1989). The psychological significance of secondary sexual characteristics in 9- to 11-year-old girls. *Child Development, 59*, 161–169.

Brown, B. B. (1999). Measuring the peer environment of American adolescents. In S. L. Friedman & T. D. Wachs (Eds.), *Measuring environment across the life span.* Washington, DC: American Psychological Association.

Brown, B. B. (2011). Popularity in peer group perspective: The role of status in adolescent peer systems. In A. H. N Cillessen, D. Schwartz, & L. Mayeux (Eds.), *Popularity in the peer system* (pp. 165–192). New York, NY: Guilford.

Brown, B. B., & Larson, R. W. (2002). The kaleidoscope of adolescence: Experiences of the world's youth at the beginning of the 21st century. In B. B. Brown, R. W. Larson, & T. S. Saraswathi (Eds.), *The world's youth.* New York: Cambridge University Press.

Brown, B. B., & Bakken, J. (2011). Parenting and peer relationships: Reinvigorating research on family—peer linkages in adolescence. *Journal of Research and Adolescence, 21*, 153–165.

Brown, B. B., Bakken, J. P., Amerigner, S. W., & Mahon, S. D. (2008). A comprehensive conceptualization of the peer influence process in adolescence. In M. J. Prinstein & K. A. Dodge (Eds.), *Understanding peer influence in children and adolescents.* New York: Guilford.

Brown, D., Hawkins Rodgers, Y. & Kapadia, K. (2008). Multicultural considerations for the application of attachment theory. *American Journal of Psychotherapy, 62*(4), 353–363.

Brown, J. D., Keller, S., & Stern, S. (2009). Sex, sexuality, sexting and sexed: Adolescents and the media. *The Prevention Researcher, 16*(4), 12–16.

Brown, K., Cassidy, W., & Jackson, M. (2006). Cyber-bullying: Developing policy to direct responses that are equitable and effective in addressing this special form of bullying. *Canadian Journal of Educational Administration and Policy, 57.* Retrieved from http://www.umanaitoba.ca/publications/cjeap/articles/brown_jackson_cassidy.html

Brown, L., Hansen, C., Huberty, A., & Castonquay, T. (2011). Traits of the metabolic syndrome after corpulent obesity in LAN, SHR and DSS rats: Behavioral and metabolic interactions with adrenalectomy. *Physiology and Behavior, 103*, 98–103.

Brown, M. (2003, July 10). Parents bring class home. *The Markham Economist & Sun*, 14–15.

Brown, S. L., Brown, R. M., House, J. S., & Smith, D. M. (2008). Coping with spousal loss: Potential buffering effects of self-reported helping behavior. *Personality and Social Psychology Bulletin, 34*, 849–861.

Brown, S. L., Bulanda, J. R., & Lee, G. R. (2005). The significance of nonmarital cohabitation: Marital status and mental health benefits among middle-aged and older adults. *Journals of Gerontology B: Psychological Sciences and Social Sciences, 60*, S21–S29.

Brown, S. L., Nesse, R. M., House, J. S., & Utz, R. L. (2004). Religion and emotional compensation: Results from a prospective study of widowhood. *Personality and Social Psychology Bulletin, 30*, 1165–1174.

Browne, C. V., & Braun, K. L. (2008). Globalization, women's migration, and the long-care workforce. *Gerontologist, 48*, 16–24.

Brownell, C. A., & Kopp, C. B. (Eds.). (2007). *Socioemotional development in the toddler years.* New York: Guilford.

Brownell, C. A., Ramani, G. B., & Zerwas, S. (2006). Becoming a social partner with peers: Cooperation and social understanding in one- and two-year-olds. *Child Development, 77*, 803–821.

Bruce, A. (2007). Time(lessness): Buddhist perspectives and end-of-life. *Nursing Philosophy, 8*, 151–157.

Bruck, M., & Ceci, S. J. (2012). Forensic developmental psychology in the courtroom. In D. Faust & M. Ziskin (Eds.), *Coping with psychiatric and psychological testimony*. New York: Cambridge University Press.

Bruck, M., & Ceci, S. J. (2014, in press). *Expert testimony in a child sex abuse case: Translating memory development research*. Memory.

Bruin, J., Gerstein, H., & Holloway, A. (2010). Long-term consequence of fetal and neonatal nicotine exposure: A critical review. *Toxicological Sciences, 116*(2), 364–374.

Brumariu, L. E., & Kerns, K. A. (2010). Parent-child attachment and internalizing symptomatology in childhood and adolescence: A review of empirical findings and future direction. *Development and Psychopathology, 22*, 177–203.

Brumariu, L. E., & Kerns, K. A. (2014, in press). Pathways to anxiety: Contributions to attachment history, temperament, peer competence, and ability to manage intense emotions. *Child Psychiatry and Human Development*.

Brumariu, L. E., Kerns, K. A., & Seibert, A. C. (2012). Mother-child attachment, emotion regulation, and anxiety symptoms in middle childhood. *Personal Relationships, 19*(3), 569–585.

Brummelman, E., et al. (2014). "That's not beautiful—That's incredibly beautiful!" The adverse impact of inflated praise on children with low self-esteem. *Psychological Science, 25*, 728–735.

Brune, C. W., & Woodward, A. L. (2007). Social cognition and social responsiveness in 10-month-old infants. *Journal of Cognition and Development, 2*, 3–27.

Brunstein Klomek, A., Marrocco, F., Kleinman, M., Schofeld, I. S., & Gould, M. S. (2007). Bullying, depression, and suicidality in adolescents. *Journal of the American Academy of Child and Adolescent Psychiatry, 46*, 40–49.

Brus, M., Keller, M., & Levy, F. (2013). Temporal features of adult neurogenesis: Differences and similarities across mammalian species. *Frontiers in Neuroscience, 7*, 135.

Bryant, J. A. (Ed.). (2007). *The children's television community.* Mahwah, NJ: Erlbaum.

Bryant, J. B. (2012). Pragmatic development. In E. L. Bavin (Ed.), *Cambridge handbook of child language*. New York: Cambridge University Press.

Brym, R., Roberts, L., Lie, J., & Rytina, S. (2013). *Sociology: Your compass for a new world.* Toronto: Nelson.

Brym, R., Roberts, L., Strohschein, L. & Lie, J. (2016). *Sociology My Compass for a New World* (5th Canadian Ed.). Toronto: Nelson.

Buchanan, S. L., et al. (2012). Trends in morbidity associated with oxytocin use in labor in nulliparas at term. *Australian and New Zealand Journal of Obstetrics and Gynecology, 52*, 173–178.

Buchman, S. (2008). *Do not resuscitate confirmation form.* Newsbriefs: The Ontario College of Family Physicians. Retrieved from http://www.ocfp.on.ca

Buckner, J. C., Mezzacappa, E., & Beardslee, M. R. (2009). Self-regulation and its relations to adaptive functioning in low income youths. *American Journal of Orthopsychiatry, 79*, 19–30.

Budworth, M., Enns, J. & Rowbotham, K. (2007). Shared identity and strategic choice in dual-career couples. *Gender in Management: An International Journal, 23*(2), 103–119.

Buhling, K. J., et al. (2014). The use of complementary and alternative medicine by women transitioning through menopause in Germany: Results of a survey of women aged 45–60 years. *Complementary Therapies in Medicine*, 22, 94–98.

Buhrmester, D. (1998). Need fulfillment, interpersonal competence, and the developmental contexts of early adolescent friendship. In W. M. Bukowski & A. F. Newcomb (Eds.), *The company they keep: Friendship in childhood and adolescence:* New York: Cambridge University Press.

Buhrmester, D. (2005, April). *The antecedents of adolescents' competence in close relationships: A six-year-study.* Paper presented at the meeting of the Society for Research in Child Development, Atlanta.

Bukowski, W. M., Velasquez, A. M., & Brendgen, M. (2008). Variation in patterns of peer influence: Considerations of self and other. In M. J. Prinstein & K. A. Dodge (Eds.), *Understanding peer influence in children and adolescents.* New York: Guilford.

Bulik, C. M., Berkman, N. D., Brownley, K. A., Sedway, J. A., & Lohr, K. N. (2007). Anorexia nervosa treatment: A systematic review of randomized controlled trials. *International Journal of Eating Disorders, 40*, 310–320.

BullyingCanada. (2016). *What is bullying*. Bullying Canada Inc. Retrieved from https://www.bullyingcanada.ca

Buratti, S., Allwood, C. M., & Johansson, M. (2014). Stability in the metamemory realism of eyewitness confidence judgments. *Cognitive Processing, 15*, 39–53.

Burck, J. R., Vena, M., Jolicoeur, M., & Jolicoeur, L. E. (2007). At a threshold: Making decisions when you don't have all the answers. *Physical Medicine and Rehabilitation Clinics of North America, 18*, 1–25.

Burney, R., & Leerkes, E. (2010). Links between mothers' and fathers' perception of infant temperament and coparenting. *Infant Behavior & Development, 33*, 125–135.

Burns, C. (2008). In C. Burns, M. Brady, A. Dunn C. Blosser, & B. Starr (Eds). *Pediatric primary care: A handbook for*

nurse practitioners (4th ed.). (pp. 304–319). St. Louis: Sanders.

Burns, C., Dunn, A., Brady, M., Starr, N., & Blosser, C. (2013). *Pediatric primary care.* St. Louis: Elsevier.

Burns, L., Mattick, R. P., Lim, K., & Wallace, C. (2007). Methadone in pregnancy: Treatment retention and neonatal outcomes. *Addiction, 102*, 264–270.

Burns, R. A., Mitchell, P., Shaw, J., & Anstey, K. J. (2014). Trajectories of cognitive decline in the well-being of older women: The DYNOPTA project. *Psychology and Aging*, 29, 44–56.

Burr, J. (2009). Volunteering, later life. In D. Carr (Ed.), *Encyclopedia of the life course and human development.* Boston: Gale Cengage.

Burt, K., & Paysnick, A. (2012). Resilience in the transition to adulthood. *Development of Psychopathology, 24*, 493–505.

Burt, S. A. (2014, in press). *Research review: The shared environment as a key source of variability in child and adolescent psychopathology.* Journal of Child Psychology and Psychiatry.

Burton, P., Lethbridge, L., & Phipps, S. (2006). *Children with disabilities and chronic conditions and longer-term parental health.* Retrieved from http://atlanticresearchdatacentre.dal.ca/

Burton, P., Phipps, S., & Curtis, L. (2005). *All in the family: A simultaneous model of parenting style and child conduct.* Ottawa: Family and Labour Studies Division, Statistics Canada.

Busch, H., & Hofer, J. (2012). Self-regulation and milestones of adult development: Intimacy and generativity. *Developmental Psychology, 48*, 282–293.

Bush, K. R., & Peterson, G. W. (2013). Parent-child relationships in diverse contexts. In G. W. Peterson & K. R. Bush (Eds.), *Handbook of marriage and the family* (3rd ed.). New York: Springer.

Buss, D. M. (1999). *Evolutionary psychology: The new science of the mind.* Boston: Allyn & Bacon.

Buss, D. M. (2000). Evolutionary psychology. In A. Kazdin (Ed.), *Encyclopedia of psychology.* Washington, DC: American Psychological Association and Oxford University Press.

Buss, D. M. (2012). *Evolutionary psychology* (4th ed.). Boston: Allyn & Bacon.

Buss, K. (2011). Which fearful toddlers should we worry about? Context, fear regulation, and anxiety risk. *Developmental Psychology, 47,* 804–819.

Buss, K. A., & Goldsmith, H. H. (2007). Biobehavioral approaches to early socioemotional development. In C. A. Brownell & C. B. Kopp (Eds.), *Socioemotional development in the toddler years.* New York: Guilford.

Bussey, K., & Bandura, A. (1999). Social cognitive theory of gender development and differentiation. *Psychological Review, 106*, 676–713.

Butler, R. N. (2007). Life review. In J. E. Birren (Ed.), *Encyclopedia of gerontology* (2nd ed.). San Diego: Academic Press.

Buttelmann, D., Over, H., Carpenter, M., & Tomasello, M. (2014). Eighteen-month-olds understand false beliefs in an unexpected-contents task. *Journal of Experimental Child Psychology, 119*, 120–126.

Byrnes, H. F., Chen, M. J., Miller, B. A., & Maguin, E. (2007). The relative importance of mothers' and youths' neighborhood perceptions for youth alcohol use and delinquency. *Journal of Youth and Adolescence, 36*, 649–659.

Byrnes, J. P. (2008). Piaget's cognitive developmental theory. In M. M. Haith & J. B. Benson (Eds.), *Encyclopedia of infant and early childhood development.* Oxford, UK: Elsevier.

C

Caban-Holt, A., et al. (2012). Age-expanded normative data for the Ruff 2&7 Selective Attention Test: Evaluating cognition in older males. *Clinical Neuropsychology, 26*(5), 751–768.

Cabrera, N., Fagan, J. & Farrie, A. (2008). Explaining the long reach of fathers' prenatal involvement on later paternal engagement with children. *Journal of Marriage and Family, 55*, 987–1000.

Cabrera, N., Hofferth, S., & Chae, S. (2011). Patterns and predictors of father-infant engagement across race/ethnic groups. *Early Childhood Research Quarterly, 26*, 365–375.

Cabrera, N., Hutchens, R., & Peters, H. E. (Eds.). (2006). *From welfare to childcare.* Mahwah, NJ: Erlbaum.

Cacho, I., Dickinson, C. M., Smith, H. J., & Harper, P. A. (2010). Clinical impairment measures and reading performance in a large age-related macular degeneration group. *Optometry and Vision Science, 87*(5), 344–349.

Cahill, K.E., Giandrea, M.D., & Quinn, J.F. (2014, in press). Retirement patterns and the macroeconomy, 1992–2010: The prevalence and determinants of bridge jobs, retirement, and reentry among three recent cohorts of older Americans. *Gerontologist.*

Cai, L., Chan, J. S., Yan, J. H., & Peng, K. (2014). Brain plasticity and motor practice in cognitive aging. *Frontiers in Aging Neuroscience*, 6, 31.

Cain, S. (2012). *Quiet—The power of introverts in a world that can't stop talking.* New York: Crown Publishers.

Caley, L., Syms, C., Robinson, L., Cederbaum, J., Henry, M., & Shipkey, N. (2008). What human service professionals know and want to know about fetal alcohol syndrome. *Canadian Journal of Clinical Pharmacology, 15*, e117–e123.

Calkins, S. & Leerkes, E. (2010). Early attachment processes and the development of emotional self-regulation. In K. Vohs & R. Baumeister (Eds.), *Handbook of self regulation; Research, theory and applications* (2nd ed.) (pp. 355–373). New York, NY; Guilford Press.

Calkins, S. D. (2007). The emergence of self-regulation: Biological and behavioral control mechanisms supporting toddler competencies. In C. A. Brownell & C. B. Kopp (Eds.), *Socioemotional development in the toddler years.* New York: Guilford.

Callaghan, M. E., et al. (2014, in press). *Widespread age-related differences in the human brain microstructure revealed by quantitative magnetic resonance imaging.* Neurobiology of Aging.

Cameron, J. R., Hansen, R., & Rosen, D. (1989). Preventing behavioral problems in infancy through temperament assessment and parental support programs. In W. B. Carey & S. C. McDevitt (Eds.), *Clinical and education applications of temperament research.* Amsterdam: Swets & Zeitlinger.

Camp, J. (2013). Postpartum depression 101: Teaching and supporting the family. *International Journal of Childbirth, 28*(4) 45–49.

Campaign 2000. (2009). Report card on child and family poverty in Canada: 1989–2009. Keep the Promise: Make Canada poverty-free. Retrieved from http://www.campaign2000.ca/reportcards.html

Campaign 2000. (2012). Needed: A federal action plan to end child and family poverty in Canada. Retrieved from http://www.campaign2000.ca/reportcards.html

Campaign 2000. (2015). Campaign 2000 Report Card on Child & Family Poverty in Canada. Retrieved from http://www.campaign2000.ca/reportCards/2015RepCards/NationalReportCardEn2015.pdf.

Campanella, J., & Rovee-Collier, C. (2005). Latent learning and deferred imitation at 3 months. *Infancy, 7*(3), 243–262.

Campbell, D. A., Lake, M. F., Falk, M., & Backstrand, J. R. (2006). A randomized-controlled trial of continuous support by a lay doula. *Journal of*

Obstetrics and Gynecology: Neonatal Nursing, 35, 456–464.

Campbell, D., Scott, K. D., Klaus, M. H., & Falk, M. (2007). Female relatives or friends trained as labor doulas: Outcomes at 6 to 8 weeks postpartum. *Birth, 34*, 220–227.

Campbell, K. L., Grady, C. L., Ng, C., & Hasher, L. (2012). Age differences in the frontoparietal cognitive control network: Implications for distractibility. *Neuropsychologia, 50*(9), 2212–2223.

Campos, J. J. (2005). Unpublished review of J. W. Santrock's *Life-span development* (10th ed.). New York: McGraw-Hill.

Campos, J. J., Langer, A., & Krowitz, A. (1970). Cardiac responses on the visual cliff in prelocomotor human infants. *Science, 170*, 196–197.

Canada Centre on Substance Abuse. (2011). Cross-Canada report on student alcohol and drug use. Retrieved from http://www.ccsa.ca

Canada Labour Code. (2013). Information on Labour Standard - Maternity and Parental Leave. Retrieved from http:///www.12.hrsdc.gc.ca

Canada Statistics. (2009). *Trends in police-reported drug offence in Canada* (No. 85-002-X). Retrieved from http://www.statcan.gc.ca.

Canada Without Poverty. (2016a). *Poverty*. Retrieved from http://www.cwp-csp.ca/poverty/.

Canada Without Poverty. (2016b). *Just the Facts*. Retrieved from http://www.cwp-csp.ca/poverty/just-the-facts/

Canada Year Book. (2008). *Income, pensions, spending and wealth*. Ottawa: Statistics Canada.

Canadian Association for Neuroscience. (2012). *Canadian neuroscience news*. Retrieved from http://www.can-acn.org/page/4.

Canadian Association of Genetic Counsellors. (2016). *What is a genetic counsellor*. Retrieved from http://www.cagc-accg.ca/.

Canadian Blood Services. (2012). *Types and Rh system*. Retrieved from http://www.blood.ca/.

Canadian Broadcasting Company (CBC). (2012a, September 24). Barbara Coloroso on bullying. *Information Morning on CBC Fredrickton*. Retrieved from http://www.cbc.cainformationmorningfredericton/2012/09/24/barbara-coloroso-on-bullying/.

Canadian Broadcasting Company (CBC). (2012b, September 17). Robert Latimer gets OK to travel to U.K. for panel talk. Retrieved from http://www.cbc.ca/news/.

Canadian Broadcasting Company (CBC). (2012c, October 17). Robert Latimer visa problems scuttle U.K. trip, debate groups says. Retrieved from http://www.cbc.ca/news/.

Canadian Cancer Society. (2016a). *Eating Habits*. Retrieved from http://www.cancer.ca/en/prevention-and-screening/live-well/healthy-habits-for-families/eating-habits/?region=pe.

Canadian Cancer Society. (2016b). *Hormone Replacement Therapy*. Retrieved from http://www.cancer.ca/en/prevention-and-screening/be-aware/artificial-hormones/hormone-replacement-therapy/?region=on.

Canadian Cancer Society. (2016c). *Tobacco*. Retrieved from http://www.cancer.ca.

Canadian Centre on Substance Abuse. (2015). *Prescriptions opioids*. Retrieved from http://www.ccsa.ca.

Canadian Child Care Federation. (2009). Ages and stages of numeracy development. Retrieved from http://www.ccf-fcsge.ca

Canadian Child Care Federation. (2013). About Canadian Child Care Federation (CCCF). Retrieved from http://www.cccf.fcsge.ca/

Canadian Conference Board of Canada. (2016). Centre for the future of health. Retrieved from http://www.conferenceboaard.ca/

Canadian Council for Refugees. (2012). Family reunification. Retrieved from http://ccrweb.ca/en/family-reunification

Canadian Council for Refugees. (2015). Refugee and immigration issues: Key priorities for the next government. Retrieved from http://www.ccrweb.ca/sites/ccrweb.ca/

Canadian Council on Learning (CCL). (2006). Working to learn: Meeting university and college costs. *Lessons in Learning*. Retrieved from http://www.ccl-cca.ca/

Canadian Council on Learning (CCL). (2007). State of learning in Canada: No time for complacency. Retrieved from http://www.ccl-cca.ca

Canadian Council on Learning (CCL). (2008). *Bullying in Canada: How intimidation affects learning*. Retrieved from http://www.cci-cca.ca/

Canadian Council on Learning (CCL). (2009). Learning about sex and sexual health. Retrieved from http://www.cci-cca.ca/

Canadian Council on Social Development (CCHD). (2006). *Families: A Canadian profile*. Retrieved from http://www.ccsd.ca/

Canadian Council on Social Development (CCSD). (2003). Persons with disabilities and medication uses. CCSD's disability information sheet (no. 11) [electronic version]. Retrieved from http://www.ccsd.ca/drip/research/dis11/dis11.pdf

Canadian Education Association. (March 2013). *Inclusive Education - Are we Getting it Right?* Canadian Education. Retrieved from http://www.cea-ace.ca/education-canada/article/school-inclusion on March 7, 2016

Canadian Federation of Students. (2015). *Sexual violence on campus*. Retrieved from http://www.cfs-fcee.ca/

Canadian Fertility and Andrology Society. (2012). Fertility FAQ. Retrieved from http://www.cfas.ca/index.php?option=com_content&view=article&id=1126&Itemid=692

Canadian Fitness and Lifestyle Research Institute. (2005). CFLRI 2005 physical activity monitor. Retrieved from http://www.cflri.ca/pub_page/106

Canadian Healthcare Association. (2012) Respite care in Canada. Retrieved on September 15, 2013 from http://www.cha.ca/wp-content/uploads/2012/11Respite_Care_in_Canada_EN_web.pdf

Canadian Hospice Palliative Care Association (CHPCA). (2010). Fact sheet: Hospice palliative care in Canada. Retrieved from http://www.chpca.net/resource_doc_library/Fact_sheet_HPC_in-Canada.pdf

Canadian Housing & Mortgage Company (CHMC). (2015) Housing for Older Canadians- The Definitive guide to the Over 55 Market. Retrieved from http://www.cmhc-schl.gc.ca/odpub/pdf/67514.pdf.

Canadian Institute for Health Information (CIHI). (2004). Chapter 4—Aboriginal peoples' health. *Improving the Health of Canadians*. Retrieved from http://www.cihi.ca

Canadian Institute for Health Information (CIHI). (2006). How healthy are rural Canadians? Ottawa: Author.

Canadian Institute for Health Information (CIHI). (2007). *Health care use at the end of life in Western Canada*. Ottawa: CIHI.

Canadian Institute for Health Information (CIHI). (2010). *Drug use among seniors on public drug programs in Canada, 2002 to 2008*. Ottawa: CIHI.

Canadian Institute for Health Information (CIHI). (2011). Obesity in Canada.

Canadian Institute of Health Information. (2012). Highlights of 2010-2011 selected indicators describing the birthing process in Canada. Retrieved from http://www.cihi.ca/

Canadian Institute of Health Information. (2014a). Inpatient hospitalizations, surgeries and chilodbirth indicators in 2013-2014. Retrieved from http://www.cihi.ca/

Canadian Institute of Health Information. (2014b). Premature birth in Canada: An environmental scan-Final Report. Retrieved from http://www.cihi.ca/

Canadian Institute of Health Information. (2016). CIHI Data Sheds light on the system's smallest patient. Retrieved from http://www.cihi.ca/

Canadian Institutes of Health Research (CIHR). (2006). Improving the health of Canadians. Retrieved from http://www.cihi.ca

Canadian Institutes of Health Research (CIHR). (2012a). Fact sheet—Suicide prevention. Retrieved from http://www.cihrirsc.gc.ca

Canadian Institutes of Health Research (CIHR). (2012b, June 30). Guidelines for human pluipotent stem cell research, June 29, 2007. Retrieved from http://www.cihr-irsc.gc.ca/

Canadian Institutes of Health Research, Natural Sciences and Engineering Research Council of Canada, and Social Sciences and Humanities Research Council of Canada. (2010). *Tri-Council policy statement: Ethical conduct for research involving humans.*

Canadian Labour Congress. (2015). Did you know senior women are twice as likely to live in poverty as men? Retrieved from http://canadianlabour.ca/issues-research/did-you-know-senior-women-are-twice-likely-live-poverty-men

Canadian Medical Association (CMA). (2007). Euthanasia and assisted suicide (update 2007). Retrieved from http://policybase.cma.ca/dbtw-wpd/Policypdf/PD07-01.pdf

Canadian Mental Health Association (CAMH). (2012). Fast facts about mental illness. Retrieved from http://www.cmha.ca/media/fast-factsabout-mental-illness/#.Ui83axYTu8o

Canadian Mental Health Association. (2016). Seniors' Mental Health. Retrieved from http://mentalhealthweek.cmha.ca/your-mental-health/seniors-mental-health/.

Canadian Mental Health Association, Ontario. (2010). *Mental health and addictions issues for older adults: Opening the doors to a strategic framework.* Toronto: CMHA Ontario.

Canadian Midwifery Regulators Consortium. (2012). What is a Canadian registered midwife? Retrieved from http://cmrc-ccosf.ca/node/18

Canadian Nurses Association. (2009, June 10). *Federal contribution to reducing poverty in Canada.* Brief to the House of Commons Standing Committee on Human Resources, Skills and Scoial Development and the Status of Persons with Disabilities (HUMA). Ottawa.

Canadian Obesity Network (2014) Obesity in Canada. Retrieved from http://www.obesitynetwork.ca/obesity-in-canada

Canadian Paediatric Society. (2003). Position statement: Adolescent pregnancy. Retrieved from http://www.cps.ca/documents/position/adolescent-pregnancy

Canadian Paediatric Society. (2012). Position statement: Gambling in children and adolescents. Retrieved from http://www.cps.ca/

Canadian Paediatric Society. (2016). *Language Acquisition in Immigrant and Refugee Children: First Language and Bilingualism.* Caring for Kids New to Canada. Retrieved from http://www.kidsnewtocanada.ca/screening/language-acquisition.

Canadian Psychological Association. (2000). *Canadian Code of Ethics for Psychologists,* 3rd edition.

Canadian Psychological Association (CPA). (2015). "Psychology Works" Fact Sheet: Depression Among Seniors. Retrieved from http://www.cpa.ca/docs/File/Publications/FactSheets/PsychologyWorksFactSheet_DepressionAmongSeniors.pdf.

Canadian Psychological Association. (2016). Code of ethics for psychologists. Retrieved from http://www.cpa.ca/

Canadian Public Health Association (CPHA). (2004). *Assessment toolkit for bullying: Harassment and peer relations at school: Definitions, Bullying, 2004.* Retrieved from http://www.cpha.ca

Canadian Research Institute for Social Policy. (2016a). Lucia Tremonte Biography. Retrieved from http://unb.ca/research/insitute/crisp/

Canadian Research Institute for Social Policy. (2016b). J. Douglas Willms, PhD. Biography. Retrieved from http://unb.ca/reserach/insitute/crisp/

Canadian Space Agency. (2003). Biography of Roberta Lynn Bondar Retrieved from http://www.asc-csa.gc.ca/eng/astronauts/biobondar.asp

Canadian Teachers' Federation (CTF). (2009). Supporting education building Canada—Child poverty and schools. Retrieved from http://www.ctf-fce.ca/publications/Briefs/FINAL_Hilldayleavebehind_eng.pdf

Canadian Virtual Hospice. (2013). Canadian Virtual Hospice: Features and content. Retrieved from http://www.virtualhospice.ca/

Canfield, J., & Hansen, M. V. (1995). *A second helping of chicken soup for the soul.* Deerfield Beach, FL: Health Communications.

Canfield, R. L., & Haith, M. M. (1991). Young infants' visual expectations for symmetric and asymmetric stimulus sequences. *Developmental Psychology, 27,* 198–208.

Cansino, S. (2009). Episodic memory decay along the adult lifespan: A review of behavioral and neurophysiological evidence. *International Journal of Psychophysiology, 71,* 64–69.

Cansino, S., et al. (2013). The decline of verbal and visuospatial working memory across the life span. *Age, 35,* 2283–2302.

Canterino, J. C., Ananth, C. V., Smulian, J., Harrigan, J. T., & Vintzileos, A. M. (2004). Maternal age and risk of fetal death in singleton gestation: United States, 1995–2000. *Obstetrics and Gynecology Survey, 59,* 649–650.

Cappeliez, P., & O'Rourke, N. (2006). Empirical validation of model of reminiscence and health in later life. *Journals of Gerontology B: Psychological and Social Sciences, 61,* P237–P244.

Cappeliez, P., O'Rourke, N., & Chaudhury, H. (2005). Functions of reminiscence and mental health in later life. *Aging and Mental Health, 9,* 295–301.

Capponi, P. (1997). *Dispatches from the poverty line.* Toronto: Penguin.

Cardinal, B., Sorensen, S., & Cardinal, M. (2013). Historical perspective and current status of the physical education graduation requirement at American 4-year colleges and universities. *Research Quarterly for Exercise and Sport, 83,* 503–512.

Carling-Jenkins, R., Torr, J., Iacono, T., & Bigby, C. (2012). Experiences of supporting people with Down syndrome and Alzheimer's disease in aged care and family environments. *Journal of Intellectual and Developmental Disability, 37,* 54–60.

Carlisle, J., Kenney, C., & Vereb, A. (2013). Vocabulary instruction for students with or at risk for learning disabilities: Promising approaches for learning words from text. In B. G. Cook & M. G. Tankersley (Eds.), *Research-based practices in special education.* Upper Saddle River, NJ: Pearson.

Carlson, S. M., Claxton, L. J., & Moses, L. J. (2014, in press). The relation between executive function and theory of mind is more than skin deep. Journal of *Cognition and Development.*

Carlson, S. M., White, R., & Davis-Unger, A. C. (2014, in press). Evidence for a relation between executive function and pretense representation in preschool children. *Cognitive Development.*

Carlson, S. M., Zelazo, P. D., & Faja, S. (2013). Executive function. In P. D. Zelazo (Ed.), *Oxford handbook of developmental psychology*. New York: Oxford University Press.

Carlsson, N., Johansson, A., Abrahamsson, A., & Andersson Gare, B. (2013). How to minimize children's environmental tobacco smoke exposure: An intervention in a clinical setting in high risk areas. *BMC Pediatrics, 13*(1), 76.

Carolan, M., & Nelson, S. (2007). First mothering over 35 years: Questioning the association of maternal age and pregnancy risk. *Health Care for Women International, 28*, 534–555.

Carpendale, J., & Lewis, C. (2004). Constructing an understanding of mind: The development of children's social understanding within social interaction. *Behavioral and Brain Science, 27*, 79–96.

Carpendale, J., Muller, U., & Bibok, M. B. (2008). Piaget's theory of cognitive development. In N. J. Salkind (Ed.), *Encyclopedia of educational psychology.* Thousand Oaks, CA: Sage.

Carrington, N. A., & Bogetz, J. E. (2004). Normal grief and bereavement. *Journal of Palliative Medicine, 7*, 309–323.

Carrizzo, A., et al. (2013). Antioxidant effects of resveratrol in cardiovascular, cerebral, and metabolic diseases. *Food and Chemical Toxicology, 61*, 215–226.

Carroll, D., et al. (2011). Low cognitive ability in early adulthood is associated with reduced lung function in middle age: The Vietnam Experience Study. *Thorax, 66*, 884–888.

Carroll, J. L. (2007). *Sexuality now* (2nd ed.). Belmont, CA: Wadsworth.

Carskadon, M. A. (2004). Sleep difficulties in young people. *Archives of Pediatrics and Adolescent Medicine, 158*, 597–598.

Carskadon, M. A. (2005). Sleep and circadian rhythms in children and adolescents: Relevance for athletic performance of young people. *Clinical Sports Medicine, 24*, 319–328.

Carskadon, M. A. (2006, March). *Too little, too late: Sleep bioregulatory processes across adolescence.* Paper presented at the meeting of the Society for Research on Adolescence, San Francisco.

Carstairs, S. (2010). *Raising the bar: A roadmap for the future of palliative care in Canada.*

Carstensen, L. L. (1998). A life-span approach to social motivation. In J. Heckhausen & C. Dweck (Eds.), *Motivation and self-regulation across the life span.* New York: Cambridge University Press.

Carstensen, L. L. (2006). The influence of a sense of time on human development. *Science, 312*, 1913–1915.

Carstensen, L. L. (2008, May). *Long life in the 21st century.* Paper presented at the meeting of the Association of Psychological Science, Chicago.

Carter, B., & McGoldrick, M. (2005). Overview: The expanded family life cycle, individual, family and social perspectives. In B. Carter & M. McGoldrick (Eds.). *The expanded family life cycle: Individual, family and social perspectives* (3rd ed.). Toronto: Pearson.

Carter, S., & Buckwalter, J. (2009). Enhancing mate selection through the internet: A comparison of relationship quality between marriages arising from an online matchmaking system and marriages arising from unfettered selection. *Interpersona: An International Journal on Personal Relationships, 3*, 105–125.

Carver, C. S., & Connor-Smith, J. (2010). Personality and coping. *Annual Review of Psychology* (Vol. 61). Palo Alto, CA: Annual Reviews.

Carver, K., Joyner, K., & Udry, J. R. (2003). National estimates of romantic relationships. In P. Florsheim (Ed.), *Adolescent romantic relations and sexual behavior.* Mahwah, NJ: Erlbaum.

Carver, L. J., & Bauer, P. J. (2001). The dawning of a past: The emergence of long-term explicit memory in infancy. *Journal of Experimental Psychology: General, 130*, 726–745.

CASA. (2007, September). The importance of family dinners IV. Retrieved from http://www.casacolumbia.org/articlefiles/380-Importance%20of%20Family%20Dinners%20IV.pdf

Casalin, S., Luyten, P., Vliegen, N. & Meurs, P. (2012). The structure and stability of temperament from infancy to toddlerhood: A one-year prospective study. *Infant Behaviour & Development, 35*, 94–108.

Case, R., & Mueller, M. P. (2001). Differentiation, integration, and covariance mapping as fundamental processes in cognitive and neurological growth. In J. L. McClelland & R. S. Siegler (Eds.), *Mechanisms of cognitive development.* Mahwah, NJ: Erlbaum.

Casey, B. J., Getz, S., & Galvan, A. (2008). The adolescent brain. *Developmental Review, 28*, 42–77.

Casey, P. H. (2008). Growth of low birth weight preterm children. *Seminars in Perinatology, 32*, 20–27.

Casper, L. M., & Bianchi, S. M. (2007). Cohabitation. In A. S. Skolnick & J. H. Skolnick (Eds.), *Family in transition* (14th ed.). Boston: Allyn & Bacon.

Caspers, K., et al. (2009). Association between the serotonin transporter polymorphism (5-HTTLPR) and adult unresolved attachment. *Developmental Psychology, 45*, 64–76.

Caspi, A. (1998). Personality development across the life course. In W. Damon (Ed.), *Handbook of child psychology* (Vol. 3). New York: Wiley.

Caspi, A., & Roberts, B. W. (2001). Personality development across the life course: The argument for change and continuity. *Psychological Inquiry, 12*, 49–66.

Caspi, A., & Shiner, R. L. (2006). Personality development. In W. Damon & R. Lerner (Eds.), *Handbook of child psychology* (6th ed.). New York: Wiley.

Cass, A. (2007). Routine activities and sexual assault: An analysis of individual- and school-level factors. *Journal of Violence and Victims, 22*(3), 350–364.

Cassidy, J. (2009). The nature of the child's ties. In J. Cassidy & P. R. Shaver (Eds.), *Handbook of attachment* (2nd ed.). New York: Guilford.

Cassidy, J., & Berlin, L. J. (1994). The insecure/ambivalent pattern of attachment: Theory and research. *Child Development, 65*, 971–991.

Catalan, M. J., et al. (2013). Levodopa infusion improves impulsivity and dopamine dysregulation syndrome in Parkinson's disease. *Movement Disorders, 28*, 2007–2010.

Catarino, A., et al. (2013, in press). Task-related functional connectivity in autism spectrum conditions: An EEG study using wavelet transform coherence. *Molecular Autism.*

CATIE. (2016). *The epidemiology of HIV in Canada.* Retrieved from http://www.catie.ca.

Caulfield, R. A. (2001). *Infants and toddlers.* Upper Saddle River, NJ: Prentice Hall.

Cavanagh, S. E. (2004). The sexual debut of girls in early adolescence: The intersection of race, pubertal timing, and friendship group characteristics. *Journal of Research on Adolescence, 14*, 285–312.

Cavanaugh, M. M., Weyand, C. M., & Goronzy, J. J. (2012). Chronic inflammation and aging: DNA damage tips the balance. *Current Opinion in Immunology, 24*(4), 488–493.

Caylak, E. (2012). Biochemical and genetic analyses of childhood attention deficit/hyperactivity disorder. *American Journal of Medical Genetics B: Neuropsychiatric Genetics, 159B*(6), 613–627.

CBC News. (2010, April 29). Omar Kadhr: Coming of age in a Guantanamo Bay jail cell. Retrieved from http://www.cbc.ca/world/story/2009/01/13/f-omar-khadr.html

CBC News. (2015, Sept 30). Justin Trudeau promises new health accord, improved home care. *Canadian Broadcasting Corporation,* Retrieved from http://www.cbcnews.ca/

CBC News. (2016, Feb 18). Omar Khadr to stay out on bail after federal government drops appeal. *CBC News.* Retrieved from http://www.cbcnews.ca

CBC Newsworld. (2003). The life and times of Jean Chrétien. Canadian Broadcasting Corporation.

CBC Sports. (2010, February 26). IOC rep downplays women's hockey party; Hockey Canada apologizes for party on ice. Retrieved from http://www.cbc.ca/

CCSA. (2014). *Alcohol.* Retrieved from www.ccsa.ca

CDC. (2014). *What can I do to reduce my risk of cervical cancer?* Retrieved from http://www.cdc.gov.

Ceci, S. J. (2000). Bronfenbrenner, Urie. In A. Kazdin (Ed.), *Encyclopedia of psychology.* Washington, DC: American Psychological Association and Oxford University Press.

Ceci, S. J., & Gilstrap, L. L. (2000). Determinants of intelligence: Schooling and intelligence. In A. Kazdin (Ed.), *Encyclopedia of psychology.* Washington, DC: American Psychological Association and Oxford University Press.

Ceci, S. J., & Klemfuss, J. Z. (2010). Children's suggestibility: Knowns and unknowns. *The Advocate: Division 37 of APA, 33,* 3–7.

Cederborg, A-C., Alm, C., Da Silva Nises, D. L., & Lamb, M. E. (2014, in press). Investigative interviewing of alleged child abuse victims: Evaluation of a new training program for investigative interviewers. *Police Practice and Research.*

Census Shows New Face of the Canadian Family. (2012, September 19). *The Canadian Press.* Retrieved from http://www.cbc.ca/

Centers for Disease Control and Prevention (CDC). (2011). Vital signs: Teen pregnancy—United States 1991–2009, *Morbidity and Mortality Report Weekly Report, 60*(13), 414–420.

Central Intelligence Agency (CIA). (2016). The World Factbook. Retrieved from https://www.cia.gov/library/publications/resources/the-world-factbook/fields/2102.html#138.

Centre for Addiction and Mental Health (CAMH). (2003). Press release: Ecstasy use down, cigarettes and LSD continue to decline, but heavy drinking remains a problem. Retrieved from http://www.camh.ca

Centre for Addiction and Mental Health (CAMH). (2011). Drug use among Ontario students, 1977–2011 (no. 33). Retrieved from http://www.camh.net

Centre for Addiction and Mental Health (CAMH). (2013). VISION 2020: Tomorrow. today. Retrieved from http://www.camh.ca/

Centre for Disease Control and Prevention. (2015). *Physical activity and health.* Retrieved from https://www.cdc.gov

Centre for Suicide Prevention. (2012). Teen suicide resource toolkit. Retrieved from http://www.suicideinfo.ca

Cerqueira, F. M., Cunha, F. M., Laurindo, F. R., & Kowaltowski, A. J. (2012). Calorie restriction increases cerebral mitochondrial respiratory capacity in a NO mediated mechanism: Impact on neuronal survival. *Free Radical and Biological Medicine, 52,* 1236–1241.

CESP. (2011). *Canada physical activity guidelines.* Retrieved from http://www.csep.ca

Chalmers, B., & Wen, S. W. (2003). Perinatal care in Canada. In M. DesMeules & D. Stewart (Eds.), *Women's Health Surveillance Report.* Ottawa: Canadian Institute for Health Information. Retrieved from http://www.hc-sc.gc.ca/pphb-dgspsp/publicat/whsr-rssf/index.html

Chalmers, B., Kaczorowski, J., O'Brien, B., & Royle, C. (2012). Cesarean and vaginal birth in Canadian women: a comparison of experiences. *Birth, 39*(3), 203–210.

Chalmers, B., Levitt, C., Heaman, M., O'Brien, B., Sauve, R., & Kaczorowski, J. (2009). Breastfeeding rates and hospital feeding practices in Canada: A national survey of women. *Birth, 36*(2), 122–132.

Chambaere, K., Bilsen, J., Cohen, J., Onwuteake-Philipsen, B. D., Mortier, F., & Deliens, L. (2010). Physician-assisted deaths under the euthanasia law in Belgium: A population-based survey. *Canadian Medical Association Journal* [online].

Chan, C., Ting, T., Chen, C., Chen, Chen, & Chen, W. (2015). *Sexual initiation and emotional/behavioural problems in Tiawanese adolescents: A multivariate response profile analysis.* Retrieved from http://www.newsrx.com/newsletters/Life-Science-Weekly.html

Chan, H. C., et al. (2013). Highly electronegative LDL from patients with ST-elevation myocardial infarction triggers platelet activation and aggregation. *Blood, 211,* 3632–3641.

Chandler, M., & LaLonde, C. (2008). Cultural continuity as a moderator of suicide risk among Canada's First Nations. In L. Kirmayer & G. Valaskakis (Eds.), *Healing traditions: The mental health of Aboriginal peoples in Canada* (pp. 221–248). Vancouver: UBC Press.

Chao, R., & Tseng, V. (2002). Parenting of Asians. In M. H. Bornstein (Series Ed.), *Handbook of parenting (vol. 4.): Social conditions and applied parenting* (2nd ed.). Mahwah, NJ: Erlbaum.

Charles, S. C., & Piazza, J. R. (2007). Memories of social interactions: Age differences in emotional intensity. *Psychology and Aging, 22,* 300–309.

Charles, S. T., & Carstensen, L. L. (2009). Socioemotional selectivity theory. In H. Reis & S. Specher (Eds.), *Encyclopedia of Human Relationships.* Thousand Oaks, CA: Sage.

Charles, S. T., & Carstensen, L. L. (2010). Social and emotional aging. *Annual Review of Psychology* (Vol. 61). Palo Alto, CA: Annual Reviews.

Charles, S. T., Piazza, J. R., Mogle, J., Sliwinski, M. J., & Almeida, D. M. (2013). The wear and tear of daily stressors on mental health. *Psychological Science, 24,* 733–741.

Charles, S., & Luong, G. (2011). Emotional experience across the lifespan. In K. Fingerman, C. Berg, J. Smith & T. Antonucci (Eds.). *Handbook of Life-Span Development* (pp. 531–560). New York, NY: Springer.

Charness, N., & Krampe, R. T. (2008). Expertise and knowledge. In D. F. Alwin & S. M. Hofer (Eds.), *Handbook on cognitive aging.* Thousand Oaks, CA: Sage.

Charpak, N., et al. (2005). Kangaroo mother care: 25 years after. *Acta Paediatrica, 94,* 514–522.

Chassin, L., Presson, C., Seo, D. C., Sherman, S. J., Macy, J., Wirth, R. J., et al. (2008). Multiple trajectories of cigarette smoking and the intergenerational transmission of smoking: A multigenerational, longitudinal study of a Midwestern community sample. *Health Psychology, 27,* 819–828.

Chatzimichael, A., Tsalkidis, A., Cassimos, D., Gardikis, S., Tripsianis, G., Deftereos, S., et al. (2007). The role of breastfeeding and passive smoking on the development of severe bronchiolitis in infants. *Minerva Pediatrica, 59,* 199–206.

Chehab, O., Ouertani, M., Souiden, Y., Chaieb, K., & Mahdouani, K. (2008). Plasma antioxidants and human aging: A study on healthy elderly Tunisian population. *Molecular Biotechnology, 40*(1), 27–37.

Chen, J. J., & Dashtipour, K. (2013). Abo-, ino-, ona-, and rima-botulinum toxins in clinical therapy: A primer. *Pharmacotherapy, 33*, 304–318.

Chen, X. (2011). Culture and children's socioeconomic functioning. A contextual-developmental perspective. In X. Chen & H. Rubin (Eds.). *Socioemotional development in cultural context* (pp. 29–52). New York, NY: Guilford Press.

Chen, X. K., Wen, S. W., Yang, Q., & Walker, M. C. (2007). Adequacy of prenatal care and neonatal mortality in infants born to mothers with and without antenatal high-risk conditions. *Australian and New Zealand Journal of Obstetrics and Gynecology, 47*, 122–127.

Chen, X., Chung, J., Lechccier-Kimel, R., & French, D. (2011). Culture and social development. In P. K. Smith & C. H. Hart (Eds.), *Wiley-Blackwell perspectives on childhood social development* (2nd ed.). New York: Wiley.

Chen, X., DeSouza, A. T., Chen, H., & Wang, L. (2006). Reticent behaviour and experiences in peer inteactions in Chinese and Canadian children. *Developmental Psychology, 42*, 656–665.

Chen, X., Hastings, P. D., Rubin, K. H., Chen, H., Cen, G., & Stewart, S. L. (1998). Child-rearing attitudes and behavioral inhibition in Chinese and Canadian toddlers: A cross-cultural study. *Developmental Psychology, 34*, 677–686.

Chen, Z., & Siegler, R. E. (2000). Across the great divide: Bridging the gap between understanding of toddlers' and older children's thinking. *Monograph of the Society for Research in Child Development, 65*(2).

Cherlin, A. J. (2007). The deinstitutionalization of marriage. In S. J. Ferguson (Ed.), *Shifting the center: Understanding contemporary families* (3rd ed.). New York: McGraw-Hill.

Chess, S., & Thomas, A. (1977). Temperamental individuality from childhood to adolescence. *Journal of Child Psychiatry, 16*, 218–226.

Chess, S., & Thomas, A. (1987). *Origins and evolution of behavior disorders.* Cambridge, MA: Harvard University Press.

Cheung, Y. T., Chau, P. H., & Yip, P. S. (2008). A revisit of older adults' suicides and severe acute respiratory syndrome (SARS) epidemic in Hong Kong. *International Journal of Geriatric Psychiatry, 23*(12), 1231–1238..

Chevret-Measson, M., Lavallee, E., Troy, S., Arnould, B., Oudin, S., & Cuzin, B. (2009). Improvement in quality of sexual life in female partners of men with erectile dysfunction treated with sildenafil citrate: Findings of the Index of Sexual Life (ISL) in a couple study. *Journal of Sexual Medicine, 6*, 761–769.

Chi, M. T. (1978). Knowledge structures and memory development. In R. S. Siegler (Ed.), *Children's thinking: What develops?* Hillsdale, NJ: Erlbaum.

Chia, P., Sellick, K., & Gan, S. (2006). The attitudes and practices of neonatal nurses in the use of kangaroo care. *Australian Journal of Advanced Nursing, 23*, 20–27.

Chiang, K. J., et al. (2010). The effects of reminiscence therapy on psychological well-being, depression, and loneliness among the institutionalized aged. *International Journal of Geriatric Psychiatry, 25*, 380–388.

Chida, Y., & Steptoe, A. (2008). Positive psychological well-being and mortality: A quantitative review of prospective observational studies. *Psychosomatic Medicine, 70*, 741–756.

Chiefs Assembly on Education. (2012). A Portrait of First Nations and Education. Palais des Congres de Gatineau. Retrieved from http://www.afn.ca/uploads/files/events/fact_sheet-ccoe-3.pdf

Child Care Canada. (2010). 2016 Federal Budget. Retrieved from http://www.childcarecanada.org/

Child Welfare Information Gateway. (2009). Understanding the effects of maltreatment on brain development. Retrieved from http://www.childtrauma.org.

Childers, J. B., & Tomasello, M. (2002). Two-year-olds learn novel nouns, verbs, and conventional actions from massed or distributed exposures. *Developmental Psychology, 38*, 967–978.

Children's Hospital of Eastern Ontario (CHEO). (2016). Gender Identity and Diversity. Retrieved from http://www.cheo.on.ca/en/genderidentity.

Chochinov, H. (2007). Dignity and the essence of medicine: The A, B, C, and D of dignity conserving care. *British Medical Journal, 335*, 184–187.

Choi, N. G., & Jun, J. (2009). Life regrets and pride among low-income older adults: Relationships with depressive symptoms, current life stressors, and coping resources. *Aging and Mental Health, 13*, 213–225.

Chomsky, N. (1957). *Syntactic structures.* The Hague: Mouton.

Chow, J., Ateah, C., Scott, S., Ricci, S., & Kyle, T. (2013). *Canadian maternity and pediatric nursing.* Philadelphia: Lippincott Williams & Wilkins.

Christian, B. E., & Shadel, G. S. (2014). Aging: It's SIRTainly possible to restore mitochondrial dysfunction. *Current Biology, 24*, R206–R208.

Christianson, M. S., & Shen, W. (2013). Osteoporosis prevention and management: Nonpharmacologic and lifestyle options. *Clinical Obstetrics and Gynecology, 56*, 703–710.

Christie, J., Enz, B. J., Vukelilch, C., & Roskos, K. A. (2014). *Teaching language and literacy* (5th ed.). Upper Saddle River, NJ: Pearson.

Christodoulidou, A., et al. (2013). The roles of telomerase in the generation of polyploidy during neoplastic cell growth. *Neoplasia, 15*, 156–168.

Christofides, A., Schauer, C., & Zlotkin, S. H. (2005). Iron deficiency and anemia prevalence and associated etiologic factors in First nations and Inuit communities in northern Ontario and Nunavut. *Canadian Journal of Public Health, 96*, 304–307.

Chuang, S. & Su, Y. (2008). Says who? Decision-making and conflicts among Chinese-Canadian Mainland Chinese parents of young children. *Sex Roles, 60*, 527–536.

Chuang, S. (2013). Fathering roles and responsibilities of cocntemporary Chinese fathers in Canada and China. In S. S. Chuang & C. Tamis-LeMonda (Eds.). *Gender roles in immigrant families* (pp. 27–42). New York, NY: Springer.

Chuang, S. S., Rasmi, S., & Friesen, C. (2011). Service providers' perspectives on the pathways of adjustment for newcomer children and youth in Canada. In S. S. Chuang & R. P. Moreno (Eds.), *Immigrant children: Change, adaptation, and cultural transformation* (pp. 149–170). Lanham, MD: Lexington Books.

Chuang, S., & Canadian Immigrant Settlement Sector Alliance (CISSAACSEI). (2010). *New start for youth study: An examination of the settlement pathways of newcomer youth.* CISSA-ACSEI. Toronto: Lexington Books.

Chuang, Y. F., et al. (2014). Cardiovascular risks and brain function: A functional magnetic resonance imaging study of executive function in older adults. *Neurobiology of Aging, 35*, 1396–1403.

Chung, J. K., Park, S. H., Lee, W. J., & Lee, S. J. (2009). Bilateral cataract surgery: A controlled clinical trial. *Japan Journal of Ophthalmology, 53*, 107–113.

CIA World Factbook. (2012). Retrieved from https://www.cia.gov/library/publications/the-world-factbook/geos/ca.html

Cicchetti, D., & Toth, S. L. (2006). Developmental psychopathology and preventive intervention. In W. Damon & R. Lerner (Eds.), *Handbook of child psychology* (6th ed.). New York: Wiley.

Cicchetti, D., & Toth, S. L. (2011). Child maltreatment: The research imperative and the exploration of results to clinical contexts. In B. Lester & J. D. Sparrow

(Eds.), *Nurturing children and families.* New York: Wiley.

Cicchetti, D., & Toth, S. (2015). A multilevel perspective on child maltreatment. In R. Learner (Ed.) *Handbook of Child Psychology and Developmental Science* (7th ed., vol 3) (pp. 513–563). New York, NY: Wiley.

Cicchetti, D., Rogosch, F. A., Gunnar, M. R., & Toth, S. L. (2010). The differential impacts of physical and sexual abuse and internalizing problems on daytime cortisol rhythm in school-aged children. *Child Development, 81,* 252–269.

Cicchetti, D., Toth, S. L. & Rogosch, F. A. (2005). *A prevention program for child maltreatment.* Unpublished manuscript. University of Rochester, Rochester, N.Y.

Cicirelli, V. (2001). Personal meanings of death in older adults and young adults in relations to their fears of death. *Death Studies, 25,* 663–683.

Cicirelli, V. (2006). Fear of death in mid-old age. *Journals of Gerontology: Series B: Psychological and Social Sciences, 61*(B), 75–81.

Cicirelli, V. G. (1991). Sibling relationships in adulthood. *Marriage and Family Review, 16,* 291–310.

CIHR (Canadian Institutes of Health Research). (2012). *Canadian bullying statistics.* Retrieved from http://www.cihr-irsc.gc.ca/

Cillessen, A. H. N., & van den Berg, Y. H. M. (2012). Popularity and school adjustment. In A. M. Ryan & G. W. Ladd (Eds.), *Peer relationships and adjustment at school.* Charlotte, NC: Information Age Publishing.

Clapp, W. C., Rubens, M. T., Sabharwal, J., & Gazzaley, A. (2011). Deficit switching between functional brain networks underlies the impact of multitasking on working memory in older adults. *Proceedings of the National Academy of Sciences U.S.A., 108,* 7212–7217.

Clare, L., et al. (2012). Longitudinal trajectories of awareness and early-stage dementia. *Alzheimer Disease and Associated Disorders, 26,* 140–147.

Clark, D. J., et al. (2011). Muscle performance and physical function are associated with voluntary rate of neuromuscular activation in older adults. *Journals of Gerontology A: Biological Sciences and Medical Sciences, 66A,* 115–121.

Clark, E. (1993). *The lexicon in acquisition.* New York: Cambridge University Press.

Clark, E. V. (2012). Lexical meaning. In E. L. Bavin (Ed.), *Cambridge handbook of child language.* New York: Cambridge University Press.

Clark, F. (2014). Discrimination against LGBT people triggers health concerns. *Lancet, 383,* 500–502.

Clark, M. D., & Carroll, M. H. (2008). Acquaintance rape scripts of women and men: Similarities and differences. *Sex Roles, 58,* 616–625.

Clark, W. (2005). What do seniors spend on housing? *Canadian Social Trends, 85*(Autumn), 2–7.

Clark, W. (2009). *Delayed transitions of young adults.* Ottawa: Statistics Canada.

Clark, W., & Schellenberg, G. (2006). Who's religious? *Canadian Social Trends, 81,* 2–9.

Clarke, B. (2009). Friends forever: How young adolescents use social-networking sites. *Society Online, 24*(6), 22–26.

Clarke-Stewart, A. K., & Miner, J. L. (2008). Child and day care, effects of. In M. M. Haith & J. B. Benson (Eds.), *Encyclopedia of infant and early childhood development.* Oxford, UK: Elsevier.

Clarke-Stewart, A. K., & Parke, R. D. (2014a). *Future families.* New York: Wiley.

Clarke-Stewart, A. K., & Parke, R. D. (2014b). *Social development* (2nd ed.). New York: Wiley.

Clausen, J. A. (1993). *American lives.* New York: Free Press.

Claxton, L. J., Keen, R., & McCarty, M. E. (2003). Evidence of motor planning in infant reaching behavior. *Psychological Science, 14,* 354–356.

Clay, O. J., et al. (2009). Visual function and cognitive speed of processing mediate age-related decline in memory span and fluid intelligence. *Journal of Aging and Health, 21,* 547–566.

Clearfield, M., Osborne, C. & Mullen, M. (2008). Learning by looking: Infant's social looking behavior across the transition from crawling to walking. *Journal of Experimental Child Psychology, 100,* 297–307.

Clements, M., Stanley, S., & Markman, H. (2004). Before they said "I do": Discriminating among marital outcomes over 13 years. *Journal of Personality and Social Psychology, 66,* 613–626.

Cleveland, L., Minter, M., Cobb, K., Scott, A., & German, V. (2008). Lead hazards for pregnant women and children: Part 2. *American Journal of Nursing, 108*(11), 40–47.

Coats, A., & Blanchard-Fields, F. (2008). Emotion regulation in interpersonal problems: The role of cognitive-emotional complexity, emotion regulation goals, and expressivity. *Psychology and Aging, 23,* 39–51.

Cobb, M. (2011). *Single: Arguments for the uncoupled.* New York, NY: University Press.

Cochran, S. D., & Mays, V. M. (1990). Sex, lies, and HIV. *New England Journal of Medicine, 322*(11), 774–775.

Coghlan, K. (December 21, 2015). Children's rights groups will be thankful to see 'spanking law' repealed. *Global News.* Retrieved from http://globalnews.ca/news/2413962/childrens-rights-groups-will-be-thankful-to-see-spanking-law-repealed/.

Cohen, D. (2012). *How the child's mind develops* (2nd ed.). New York: Psychology Press.

Cohen, D., & Belsky, J. (2008). Avoidant romantic attachment and female orgasm: Testing an emotion-regulation hypothesis. *Attachment and Human Development, 10,* 1–10.

Cohen, J., Wilson, D., Thurston, A., Macleod, R. & Deliens, L. (2011). Access to palliative care services in hospital a matter of being in the right hospital: Hospital charts study in a Canadian city. *Palliative Medicine, 26*(1), 89–94.

Cohen, L. B., & Cashon, C. H. (2003). Infant perception and cognition. In I. B. Weiner (Ed.), *Handbook of psychology* (Vol. VI). New York: Wiley.

Cohen, S., & Janicki-Deverts, D. (2012). Who's stressed? Distributions of psychological stress in the United States: Probability samples from 1983, 2006, and 2009. *Journal of Applied Social Psychology, 42,* 1320–1332.

Cohen, S., & Shachar, I. (2012). Cytokines as regulators of proliferation and survival of healthy and malignant peripheral B cells. *Cytokine, 60,* 13–22.

Cohen, S., et al. (2013). Association between telomere length and experimentally induced upper viral infection in healthy adults. *Journal of the American Medical Association, 309,* 699–705.

Cohen, S., Janicki-Deverts, D., Crittenden, C. N., & Sneed, R. S. (2012). Personality and human immunity. In S. C. Segerstrom (Ed.), *Oxford handbook of psychoneuroimmunology.* New York: Oxford University Press.

Cohen-Woods, S., Craig, I. W., & McGuffin, P. (2012). The current state of play on molecular genetics of depression. *Psychological Medicine, 43*(4), 673–687.

Coie, J. (2004). The impact of negative social experiences on the development of antisocial behavior. In J. B. Kupersmidt & K. A. Dodge (Eds.), *Children's peer relations: From development to intervention.* Washington, DC: American Psychological Association.

Colby, A., Kohlberg, L., Gibbs, J., & Lieberman, M. (1983). A longitudinal study of moral judgment. *Monographs of the Society for Research in Child Development* (Serial No. 201).

Colcombe, S. J., Erickson, K. I., Scalf, P. E., Kim, J. S., Prakash, R., McAuely, E., et al. (2006). Aerobic exercise training increase brain volume in aging humans.

Journals of Gerontology A: Medical Sciences, 61, 1166–1170.

Cole, M. (2006). Culture and cognitive development in phylogenetic, histroical, and ontogenetic perspective. In W. Damon & R. Lerner (Eds.), *Handbook of child psychology* (6th ed.). New York: Wiley.

Cole, P. M., & Hall, S. E. (2012). Emotion dysregulation as a risk factor for psychopathology. In T. Beauchaine & S. Hinshaw (Eds.), *Developmental psychopathology*. New York: Wiley.

Cole, P. M., Dennis, T. A., Smith-Simon, K. E., & Cohen, L. H. (2009). Preschoolers' emotion regulation strategy understanding: Relations with maternal socialization and child behavior. *Social Development*, *18*(2), 324–352.

Coleman, M., Ganong, L., & Fine, M. (2004). Communication in stepfamilies. In A. L. Vangelisti (Ed.), *Handbook of family communication.* Mahwah, NJ: Erlbaum.

Coley, R., MaPherran Lombardi, C., Doyle Lynch, A., Makalik, J. & Sims, J. (2013). Sexual partner accumulation from adolescence through early adulthood: The role of family, peer, and school social norms. *Journal of Adolescent Health, 53*, 91–97.

Collaku, A., Rankinen, T., Rice, T., Leon, A. S., Rao, D. C., Skinner, J. S., et al. (2004). A genome-wide linkage scan for dietary energy and nutrient intakes. *American Journal of Clinical Nutrition, 79*, 881–886.

Collaku, A., Rankinen, T., Rice, T., Leon, A., Rao, D., Skinner, J.,...Bouchard, C. (2004). A genome-wide linkage scan for dietary energy and nutrient intakes: The health, risk factors, exercise training, and genetics (HERITAGE) family study. *American Journal of Clinical Nutrition, 79*(5), 881–886.

Colley, R., Garriguet, D., Janssen, I., Craig, C.L., Clarke, J., & Tremblay, M.S. (2015). *Physical Activity of Canadian Children and Youth: Accelerometer Results from the 2007 to 2009 Canadian Health Measures Survey*. Statistics Canada. Retrieved from http://www.statcan.gc.ca/pub/82-003-x/2011001/article/11397-eng.htm.

Collier, R. (2011). Access to palliative care varies widely across Canada. *Canadian Medical Association Journal, 183*(2), E87–E88.

Collier, R. (2014). 10 health stories that mattered: Nov. 11-15. *Canadian Medical Association Journal, 186*(1), E6.

Collins, R. L., Elliott, M. N., Berry, S. H., Kanocouse, D. E., Kunkel, D., Hunter, S. B., et al. (2004). Watching sex on television predicts adolescent initiation of sexual behavior. *Pediatrics, 114*, e280–e289.

Collins, W. A., & Steinberg, L. (2006). Adolescent development in interpersonal context. In W. Damon & R. Lerner (Eds.), *Handbook of child psychology* (6th ed.). New York: Wiley.

Collins, W., Welsh, D., & Furman, W. (2009). Adolescent romantic relationships. *Annual Review of Psychology, 60*, 631–652.

Colombo, J. & Mitchell, D. (2009). Infant visual habituation. *Neurobiology of Learning and Memory: Special Issue: Habituation, 92*, 225–234.

Colonnesi, C., Stams, G., Koster, L. & Noom, M. (2010). The relation between pointing and language development.: A meta-analysis. *Developmental Review, 30*, 352–366.

Coloroso, B. (2003). *The bully, the bullied, and the bystander.* Toronto: HarperCollins.

Committee on Hospital care and Institute for Patient and Family-Centred Care. (2012). Patient and family - centred care and the pediatrician's role. *Pediatrics, 129*, 394–404.

Commoner, B. (2002). Unraveling the DNA myth: The spurious foundation of genetic engineering. *Harper's Magazine, 304*, 39–47.

Commons, M. L., & Bresette, L. M. (2006). Illuminating major creative scientific innovators with postformal stages. In C. Hoare (Ed.), *Handbook of adult development and learning.* New York: Oxford University Press.

Conference Board of Canada. (2013). Elderly poverty. Retrieved from http://www.conferenceboard.ca/hcp/details/society/elderly-poverty.aspx

Conference Board of Canada. (2016a). Life Expectancy, Provincial and Territorial Ranking Retrieved from http://www.conferenceboard.ca/hcp/provincial/health/life.aspx.

Conference Board of Canada. (2016b). Education and Skills- Canada Benchmarked Against 15 Other Countries. Conference Board of Canada. Retrieved from http://www.conferenceboard.ca/hcp/details/education.aspx.

Connolly, J. A., & McIsaac, C. (2009). Romantic relationships in adolescence. In R. Lerner & L. Steinberg (Eds.), *Handbook of adolescent psychology* (3rd ed.). New Jersey: Wiley.

Connor, S. (2009, April). Fertility expert: "I can clone a human being." Controversial doctor filmed creating embryos before injecting them into wombs of women wanting cloned babies. Retrieved from http://www.independent. co.uk/news/science/fertility-expert-i-canclone-a-human-being-1672095.html

Conry-Murray, C., Kim, J. M., & Turiel, E. (2012, April). *U.S. and Korean children's judgments of gender norm violations.* Paper presented at the Gender Development Research conference, San Francisco.

Contant, T. L., Bass, J. E., & Carin, A. A. (2015, in press). *Teaching science through inquiry and investigation* (12th ed.). Upper Saddle River, NJ: Pearson.

Conway, K. P., Swendsen, J. D., & Merikangas, K. R. (2003). Alcohol expectancies, alcohol consumption, and problem drinking: The moderating role of family history. *Addictive Behaviors, 28*, 823–836.

Conway, K. S., & Kutinova, A. (2006). Maternal health: Does prenatal care make a difference? *Health Economics, 15*, 461–488.

Cook, E., Buehler, C., & Blair, B. (2013). Adolescents' emotional reactivity across relationship contexts. *Developmental Psychology, 49*(2), 341–352.

Cook, T. D., Deng, Y., & Morgano, E. (2007). Friendship influences during early adolescence: The special role of friends' grade point average. *Journal of Research on Adolescence, 17*, 325–356.

Cooper, A. R., & Moley, K. H. (2008). Maternal tobacco use and its preimplantation effects on fertility: More reasons to stop smoking. *Seminars in Reproductive Medicine, 26*, 204–212.

Cooper, C. R., & Grotevant, H. D. (1989, April). *Individuality and connectedness in the family and adolescent's self and relational competence.* Paper presented at the meeting of the Society for Research in Child Development, Kansas City.

Cooper, C. R., Behrens, R., & Trinh, N. (2008). Identity development. In R. A. Shweder, T. R. Bidell, A. C. Daily, S. D. Dixon, P. J. Miller, & J. Model (Eds.), *The Chicago companion to the child.* Chicago: University of Chicago Press.

Cope, M., & Allison, D. (2008). Critical review of the World Health Organization's 2007 report on "evidence of the long-term effects of breastfeeding: Systematic reviews and meta-analysis" with respect to obesity. *Obesity Reviews, 9*, 594–605.

Coplan, R J. & Graham, A. (2012). Shyness, sibling relationships, and young children's socioemotional adjustment to preschool. *Journal of Research in Childhood Education*. Retrieved from http://www.freepatentsonline.com/article/Journal-Research-in-Childhood-Education/306971659.html

Coplan, R. J., & Arbeau, K. A. (2009). Peer interactions and play in early childhood.

In K. H. Rubin, W. M. Bukowski, & B. Laursen (Eds.), *Handbook of peer interactions, relationships, and groups*. New York: Guilford.

Coplan, R. J., & Armer, M. (2005). Talking yourself out of being shy: Shyness, expressive vocabulary, and socioemotional adjustment in preschool. *Merrill-Palmer Quarterly, 51*, 20–41.

Coplan, R. J., Prakash, K., O'Neil, K., & Armer, M. (2004). Do you "want" to play? Distinguishing between conflicted shyness and social disinterest in early childhood. *Developmental Psychology, 40*(2), 244–258.

Corbetta, D. & Snapp-Childs, W. (2009). Seeing and touching: The role of sensory-motor experience on the development of infant reaching. *Infant Behaviour and Development, 32*, 44–58.

Corbin, C. B., Welk, G. J., Corbin, W. R., & Welk, K. A. (2008). *Concepts of physical fitness* (14th ed.). New York: McGraw-Hill.

Cordier, S. (2008). Evidence for a role of paternal exposure in developmental toxicity. *Basic and Clinical Pharmacology and Toxicology, 102*, 176–181.

Cornelius, J. R., Clark, D. B., Reynolds, M., Kirisci, L., & Tarter, R. (2007). Early age of first sexual intercourse and affiliation with deviant peers predict development of SUD: A prospective longitudinal study. *Addictive Behavior, 32*, 850–854.

Cornew, L., Dobkins, K., Akshoomoff, N., McCleaerly, J & Carver, L. (2012). Atypical social referencing in infants siblings of children with autism spectrum disorders. *Journal of Autism Developmental Disorders. 42*, 2611–2621.

Cornwell, B., Laumann, E. O., & Schumm, L. P. (2008). The social connectedness of older adults: A national profile. *American Sociological Review, 73*, 185–203.

Corona, G., Rastrelli, G., Maseroli, E., Forti, G., & Maggi, M. (2013). Sexual functioning of the aging male. *Best Practices & Research: Clinical Endocrinology and Metabolism, 27*, 581–601.

Corsi, D., Boyle, M., Lear, S., Chow, C., Teo, K., & Subramaian, S. (2014). Trends in smoking in Canada from 1950 to 2011: Progression of the tobacco epidemic according to socioeconomic status and geography. *Cancer Causes Control, 25*, 45–57.

Corsini, R. (1999). *The dictionary of psychology.* Philadelphia: Brunner/Mazel.

Corso, J. F. (1977). Auditory perception and communication. In J. E. Birren & K. W. Schaie (Eds.), *Handbook of the psychology of aging* (2nd ed.). New York: Van Nostrand Reinhold.

Costa, P. T., & McCrae, R. R. (1995). Solid ground on the wetlands of personality: A reply to Black. *Psychological Bulletin, 117*, 216–220.

Costa, P. T., Jr., & McCrae, R. R. (2000). Contemporary personality psychology. In C. E. Coffey & J. L. Cummings (Eds.). *Textbook of geriatric neuropsychiatry.* Washington, DC: American Psychiatric Press.

Costa, R., & Figueiredo, B. (2011). Infant's psychophysiological profile and temperament at 3 and 12 months. *Infant Behavior & Development, 34*, 270–279.

Costa-Glomi, Eugena (2015) The Long-Term Effects of Childhood Music Instruction on Intelligence and General Cognitive Abilities. *Sage Journals*. Retrieved from http://upd.sagepub.com/content/33/2/20.abstract.

Costley, K. C. (2012). *An overview of the life, central concepts, including classroom applications for Lev Vygotsky*. ERIC, ED529565.

Cote, J. E. (2006). Emerging adulthood as an institutionalized moratorium: Risks and benefits to identity formation. In J. J. Arnett & J. L. Tanner (Eds.), *Emerging adults in America.* Washington, DC: American Psychological Association.

Côté, S. M., Boivin, M., Nagin, D. S., Japel, C., Xu, Q., Zoccolillo, M., et al. (2007). The role of maternal education and nonmaternal care services in the provision of children's physical aggression problems. *Archives of General Psychiatry, 64*(11), 1305–1312.

Cotton, S., Zebracki, M. A., Rosenthal, S. L., Tsevat, J., & Drotar, D. (2006). Religion/spirituality and adolescent health outcomes: A review. *Journal of Adolescent Health, 38*, 472–480.

Council of Ministers of Education Canada (CMEC). (2003). Canadian youth sexual health & HIV/AIDS study: Factors influencing knowledge, attitudes and behaviours. Retrieved from http://www.cmec.ca/

Council of Ministers of Education, Canada (2008). Report One: The Education Systems in Canada - Facing Challenges of the Twenty-First Century; Report Two: Inclusive Education in Canada: The Way of the Future. Retrieved from http://www.cmec.ca/Publications/Lists/Publications/Attachments/122/ICE2008-reports-canada.en.pdf.

Courage, M. & Howe, M. (2010). To watch or not to watch: Infants and toddlers in a brave new electronic world. *Developmental Review, 30.* 101–115.

Courage, M. & Setliff, A. (2010). When babies watch television: Attention-getting, attention-holding, and the implications from video material. *Developmental Review, 30*, 220–238.

Courage, M. L., & Richards, J. E. (2008). Attention. In M. M. Haith & J. B. Benson (Eds.), *Encyclopedia of infant and early childhood development.* Oxford, UK: Elsevier.

Courage, M. L., Reynolds, G. D., & Richards, J. E. (2006). Infants' attention to patterned stimuli: Developmental changes from 3 to 12 months of age. *Child Development, 77*(3), 680–695.

Court, F., et al. (2014, in press). Genome-wide parent-of-origin DNA methylation analysis reveals the intricacies of the human imprintome and suggests a germline methylation independent establishment of imprinting. *Genome Research.*

Cousineau, T., Goldstein, M., & Franco, D. (2005). A collaborative approach to nutrition education for college students. *Journal of American College Health, 53*, 79–84.

Cowan, C. P., & Cowan, P. A. (2000). *When partners become parents.* Mahwah, NJ: Erlbaum.

Cowan, M. K. (2015, in press). *Microbiology* (4th ed.). New York: McGraw-Hill.

Cowan, N. (2014). Short-term and working memory in childhood. In P. Bauer & R. Fivush (Eds.), *Wiley-Blackwell handbook of children's memory.* New York: Wiley.

Cowan, P., Cowan, C., Ablow, J., Johnson, V. K., & Measelle, J. (2005). *The family context of parenting in children's adaptation to elementaly school.* Mahwah, NJ: Lawrence Erlbaum Associates.

Cox, J. (2006). Postnatal depression in fathers. *Lancet, 366*, 982.

Cox, M., Garrett, E., & Graham, J. (2004–2005). Death in Disney films: Implications for children's understanding of death. *Omega—Journal of Death and Dying, 50*(4), 267–280.

Coyne, S. M., Nelson, D. A., & Underwood, M. K. (2011). Aggression in children. In P. K. Smith & C. H. Hart (Eds.), *Wiley-Blackwell handbook of childhood social development* (2nd ed.). New York: Wiley.

Craft, C. S., et al. (2014, in press). The extracellular matrix protein MAGP1 suppports thermogenesis and protects against obesity and diabetes through regulation of TGFB. *Diabetes.*

Craft, S. (2009). The role of metabolic disorders in Alzheimer disease and vascular dementia: Two roads converged. *Archives of Neurology, 66*, 300–305.

Craik, F.I.M., Bialystok, E., & Freedman, M. (2010, November 9). Delaying the onset of Alzheimer disease—Bilingualism as a form of cognitive reserve. *Neurology, 75*(19), 1726–1729.

Crain, S. (2012). Sentence scope. In E. L. Bavin (Ed.), *Cambridge handbook of child* *language*. New York: Cambridge University Press.

Crane, J. D., Macneil, L. G., & Tarnopolsky, M. A. (2013). Long-term aerobic exercise is associated with greater muscle strength throughout the life span. *Journals of Gerontology A: Biological Sciences and Medical Sciences, 68,* 631–638.

Cranswick, K., & Dosman, D. (2008). Eldercare: What we know today. *Canadian Social Trends, 90*(Autumn), 48–56.

Craparo, G., Gori, A., Petruccelli, I., Cannella, V., & Simonelli, C. (2014). Intimate partner violence: Relationships between alexithymia, depression, attachment styles, and coping strategies of battered women. *Journal of Sexual Medicine, 11,* 1484–1494.

Crawford, A. (2013, March 9). How 20 years has changed the debate over assisted suicide. CBC News Politics. Retrieved from http://www.cbc.ca/

Cresci, M. K., Yarandi, H. N., & Morrell, R. W. (2010). The digital divide and urban older adults. *Computers, Informatics, Nursing, 28,* 88–94.

Creswell, J. W. (2008). *Educational research* (3rd ed.). Upper Saddle River, NJ: Prentice Hall.

Crick, N. R., Murray-Close, D., Marks, P. E. L., & Mohajeri-Nelson, N. (2009). Aggression and peer relationships in school-age children: Relational and physical aggression in group and dyadic contexts. In K. H. Rubin, W. M. Bukowski, & B. Laursen (Eds.), *Handbook of peer interactions, relationships, and groups.* New York: Guilford.

Cristi, C., et al. (2014, in press). Whole-body vibration training increases physical fitness measures without alteration of inflammatory markers in older adults. *European Journal of Sport Science.*

Crocetti, E., Rubini, M., Luyckx, K., & Meeus, W. (2008). Identity formation in early and middle adolescents from various ethnic groups: From three dimensions to five statuses. *Journal of Youth and Adolescence, 37,* 983–996.

Crocker, B., et al. (2011). Very high vitamin D supplementation rates among infants aged 2 months in Vancouver and Richmond, British Columbia, Canada. *BMC Public Health, 11,* 1–8.

Crompton, S., & Keown, L. (2009, Winter). Do parental benefits influence fertility decisions? *Canadian Social Trends, 88,* 46–53.

Crone, E. A., & Dahl, R. E. (2012). Understanding adolescence as a period of social-affective engagement and goal flexibility. *Nature Reviews: Neuroscience, 13,* 636–650.

Crosnoe, R. & Johnson, M. (2011). Research on adolescence in the twenty-first century. *Annual Review of Sociology, 37,* 439–460.

Crosnoe, R., Riegle-Crumb, C., Field, S., Frank, K., & Muller, C. (2008). Peer group contexts of girls' and boys' academic experiences. *Child Development, 79,* 139–155.

Crosnoe, R., Wirth, R., Pianta, R. Leventhal, T. & Pierce, K. (2010). Family socioeconomic status and consistent environmental stimulation in early childhood. *Child Development, 81*(3), 972–987.

Crowell, J. A., Treboux, D., & Brockmeyer, S. (2009). Parental divorce and adult children's attachment representations and marital status. *Attachment and Human Development, 11,* 87–101.

Crowell, J. A., Treboux, D., Gao, Y., Fyffe, C., Pan, H., & Water, E. (2002). Assessing secure base behavior in adulthood: Development of a measure, links to adult attachment representations, and relations to couples' communication and reports of relationships. *Developmental Psychology, 38,* 679–693.

Crowley, K., Callahan, M. A., Tenenbaum, H. R., & Allen, E. (2001). Parents explain more to boys than to girls during shared scientific thinking. *Psychological Science, 12,* 258–261.

Croyle, R. T. (2000). Genetic counseling. In A. Kazdin (Ed.), *Encyclopedia of psychology.* Washington, DC: American Psychological Association and Oxford University Press.

Cruchaga, C., et al. (2014). Rare encoding variants in the phospholipase D3 gene confer risk for Alzheimer's disease. *Nature, 505,* 550–554.

CSEP. (2012). Canadian physical activity guidelines. Retrieved from http://www.csep.ca/

Csikszentmihalyi, M. (1995). *Creativity.* New York: HarperCollins.

Csikszentmihalyi, M. (2000). Creativity: An overview. In A. Kazdin (Ed.), *Encyclopedia of psychology.* Washington, DC: American Psychological Association and Oxford University Press.

Cuenca-Garcia, M., et al. (2014). Dietary indices, cardiovascular risk factors, and mortality in middle-aged adults: Findings from the Aerobics Center Longitudinal Study. *Annals of Epidemiology, 24,* 297–303.

Cuevas, K. (2015). Obituary: Carolyn Rovee-Collier. *Infancy, 20*(3), 237–241.

Cuevas, K., Rovee-Collier, C., & Learmonth, A. (2006). Infants form associations between memory representatives of stimuli that are absent. *Psychological Science, 17,* 543–549.

Cummings, M. (2014). *Human heredity* (10th ed.). Boston: Cengage.

Cunningham, P. M. (2013). *Phonics they use: Words for reading and writing* (6th ed.). Boston: Allyn & Bacon.

Cunningham, S. A., Kramer, M. R., & Narayan, K. M. (2014). Incidence of child obesity in the United States. *New England Journal of Medicine, 370,* 403–411.

Cunningham, W., & Hyson, D. (2006). The skinny on high-protein, low-carbohydrate diets. *Preventive Cardiology, 9,* 166–171.

Currie, C., Ahluwalia, N., Godeau, E., Gabhainn, S., Due, P. & Currie, D. (2012). Is obesity at individual and national levels associated with lower age at menarche? Evidence from 34 countries in the health behaviour in school-aged children study. *Journal of Adolescent Health, 50,* 621–626.

Currier, J. M., Holland, J. M., & Neimeyer, R. A. (2006). Sense-making, grief, and the experience of violent loss: Toward a mediational model. *Death Studies, 30,* 403–428.

Curry, B., & Friesen, J. (2012, August 23). Low-income seniors threatened by changes to federal income support. *The Globe and Mail.* Retrieved from http://www.theglobeandmail.com/news/politics/low-income-seniors-threatenedby-changes-to-federal-income-support/article1315681/

Curtin, S. (2010). Young infants encode lexical stress in newly encountered words. *Journal of Experimental Child Psychology, 105,* 376–385.

Cutler, S. J. (2006). Technological change and aging. In R. H. Binstock & L. K. George (Eds.), *Handbook of aging and the social sciences* (6th ed.). San Diego: Academic Press.

Cutler, S. J. (2009). Media and technology use, later life. In D. Carr (Ed.), *Encyclopedia of the life course and human development.* Boston: Gale Cengage.

Cuzon, V. C., Yeh, P. W., Yanagawa, Y., Obata, K., & Yeh, H. H. (2008). Ethanol consumption during early pregnancy alters the disposition of tangentially migrating GAB Aergic interneurons in the fetal cortex. *Journal of Neuroscience, 28,* 1854–1864.

Czoli, C., Hammond, D., & White C. (2014). Electronic cigarettes in Canada: prevalence of use and perceptions among youth and young adults. *Canadian Journal of Public Health, 105*(2), e97–e102.

Czyzewski, K. (2011). The Truth and Reconciliation Commission of Canada: Insights into the goal of transformative education. *The International Indigenous Policy Journal, 2*(3), 4.

D

D'Entremont, B., & Hartung, C. (2003). *A longitudinal investigation of joint attention, emotion regulation and attachment.* Poster presentation at the Society for Research in Child Development, Tampa, FL.

D'souza, B. (May 30, 2011). Children of immigrants and their challenges. Canadian Immigrant. Retrieved from http://canadianimmigrant.ca/featured/children-of-immigrants-and-their-challenges.

Da Costa, L. A., Badawi, A., & El-Sohemy, A. (2012). Nutrigenetics and modulation of oxidative stress. *Annals of Nutrition and Metabolism* (3, Suppl.), S27–S36.

da Cruz, A. C., et al. (2014). Oxidative stress and aging: Correlation with clinical parameters. *Aging: Clinical and Experimental Research*, *26*, 7–12.

Daddis, C. (2010). Adolescent peer crowds and patterns of belief in the boundaries of personal authority. *Journal of Adolescence, 33*, 699–708.

Dahl, R. (2004). Adolescent brain development: A period of vulnerabilities and opportunities. Keynote address. In R.E. Dahl & L.P. Spear (Eds.), *Adolescent brain development: Vulnerabilities and opportunities* (Vol. 1021, pp. 1–22). New York, NY: Teachers College Press.

Dahl, R. E. (2004). Adolescent brain development: A period of vulnerabilities and opportunities. *Annals of the New York Academy of Sciences, 1021*, 1–22.

Dainkeh, S. (2010, May). Interview.

Dakin, E., & Pearlmutter, S. (2009). Older women's perceptions of elder maltreatment and ethical dilemmas in adult protective services: A cross-cultural, exploratory study. *Journal of Elder Abuse and Neglect, 21*, 15–57.

Daley, A. J., Macarthur, C., & Winter, H. (2007). The role of exercise in treating postpartum depression: A review of the literature. *Journal of Midwifery & Women's Health, 52*, 56–62.

Dalton, T. C., & Bergenn, V. W. (2007). *Early experience, the brain, and consciousness.* Mahwah, NJ: Erlbaum.

Daltro, P., et al. (2010). Congenital chest malformations: A multimodality approach with emphasis on fetal MRI imaging. *Radiographics, 30*, 385–395.

Danne, T., & Becker, D. (2007). Pediatric diabetes: Achieving practical, effective insulin therapy in type 1 and 2 diabetes. *Acta Pediatrica, 96*, 1560–1570.

Danner D., Snowdon D., & Friesen W. (2001). Positive emotions in early life and longevity: Findings from the Nun Study. *Journal of Personality and Social Psychology, 80*(5), 814–813.

Darling-Hammond, L., & Bransford, J. (with LePage, P., Hammerness, K., & Duffy, H.). (2005). *Preparing teachers for a changing world: What teachers should learn and be able to do.* San Francisco: Jossey-Bass.

Das, A. (2008). Sexual harassment at work in the United States. *Archives of Sexual Behavior, 38*, 909–921.

Dastani, Z., et al. (2012). Novel loci for adiponectin levels and their influence on type 2 diabetes and metabolic traits: A multi-ethnic meta-analysis of 45,891 individuals. *PLoS One, 8*(3), e1002607.

Daubenmier, J. J., Weidner, G., Sumner, M. D., Mendell, N., Merritt-Worden, T., Studley, J., et al. (2007). The contribution of changes in diet, exercise, and stress management to changes in coronary risk in women and men in the multisite cardiac lifestyle intervention program. *Annals of Behavior Medicine, 33*, 57–68.

David, P., & Stafford, L. (2015). A relational approach to religion and marriage: The role of couples' religious communication in marital satisfaction. *Journal of Family Issues, 36*(2), 232–249.

Davidson, J. (2000). Giftedness. In A. Kazdin (Ed.), *Encyclopedia of psychology.* Washington, DC, & New York: American Psychological Association and Oxford University Press.

Davidson, J. (2015). *Binge drinking by young women raises future health risks. CBC News.* Retrieved from http://www.cbc.ca

Davidson, M. R., London, M. L., & Ladewig, P. A. (2008). *Olds' maternal-newborn nursing and women's health across the lifespan* (8th ed.). Upper Saddle River, NJ: Prentice Hall.

Davidson, P. S., et al. (2013). Source memory in normal aging and Parkinson's disease. *Journal of Neuropsychology*, *7*, 179–192.

Davies, G. A. L., Wolfe, L. A., Mottola, M. F., & MacKinnon, C. (2003). Joint SOGC/CSEP clinical practice guideline: Exercise in pregnancy and the post partum period. *Canadian Journal of Applied Physiology, 28*(3), 329–341.

Davies, G., et al. (2011). Genome-wide association studies establish that human intelligence is highly heritable and polygenic. *Molecular Psychiatry*, *16*, 996–1005.

Davis, K. (2011, May 13). Social determinants of health in Canada: A treadmill of progress. *Ontario Health Promotion E-Bulletin No. 708.* Retrieved from http://www.ohpe.ca/node/12295

Davis, M. C., Burke, H. M., Zautra, A. J., & Stark, S. (2013). Arthritis and musculoskeletal conditions. In I. B. Weiner et al. (Eds.), *Handbook of psychology* (2nd ed., Vol. 9). New York: Wiley.

Davis, S. W., Kragel, J. E., Madden, D. J., & Cabesa, R. (2012). The architecture of cross-hemispheric communication in the aging brain: Linking behavior to functional and structural connectivity. *Cerebral Cortex*, *22*, 232–242.

Davis-Kean, P. E., Jager, J., & Collins, W. A. (2009). The self in action: An emerging link between self-beliefs and behaviors in middle childhood. *Child Development Perspectives, 3*, 184–188.

Davison, G. (2005). Issues and nonissues in the gay affirmative treatment of patients who are gay, lesbian, or bisexual. *Clinical Psychology: Science and Practice, 12*, 25–28.

Daws, D. (2000). *Through the night.* San Francisco: Free Association Books.

Dawson, G., Munson, J., Estes, A., Osterling, J., McPartland, J., Toth, K.....Varley, J. (2010). Randomized controlled trial of an intervention for toddlers with autism: The Early Start Denver Model. *Pediatrics, 125*, e17–e23.

Dawson, J. D., Uc, E. Y., Anderson, S. W., Johnson, A. M., & Rizzo, M. (2010). Neuropsychological predictors of driving errors in older adults. Journal of the American *Geriatric Society*, *58*(6), 1090–1096.

Day, N. L., Goldschmidt, L., & Thomas, C. A. (2006). Prenatal marijuana exposure contributes to the prediction of marijuana use at age 14. *Addiction, 101*, 1313–1322.

Day, N., Goldschmidt, L. Day, R. Larkby, C. & Richardson, G. (2015). Prenatal marijuana exposure, age of marijuana initiation, and the development of psychotic symptoms in young adults. *Psychological Medicine, 48*, 1779–1787.

De Brouwer, W. (2012). Life meets trek: Walter De Brouwer at TEDxSanJoseCA 2012. Retrieved from http://www.youtube.com/watch?v=BSZJjN7o8Ck

de Frias, C. M., & Dixon, R. A. (2014). Lifestyle engagement affects cognitive status differences and trajectories on executive functions in older adults. *Archives of Clinical Neuropsychology*, *29*, 16–25.

De Guzman, N. & Nishina, A. (2014). A longitudinal study of body dissatisfaction and pubertal timing in an ethnically diverse adolescent sample. *Body Image, 11*, 68–71.

de Haan, M., & Martinos, M. (2008). Brain function. In M. M. Haith & J. B. Benson (Eds.), *Encyclopedia of infant and early childhood development.* Oxford, UK: Elsevier.

de Hollander, E. L., et al. (2012). The association between waist circumference and risk of mortality considering body mass index in 65- to 74-year-olds: A meta-analysis of 29 cohorts involving more than 58,000 elderly persons. *International Journal of Epidemiology*, *41*(3), 805–817.

de Jong Gierveld, J., & Merz, E-M. (2013). Parents' partnership decision making after divorce or widowhood: The role of (step) children. *Journal of Marriage and Family*, *75*, 1098–1113.

de Jong Gierveld, J., Broese van Groenou, M., Hoogendoorn, A. W., & Smit, J. H. (2009). Quality of marriages in later life and emotional and social loneliness. *Journals of Gerontology B: Psychological Sciences and Social Sciences, 64*(B), 497–506.

de la Cuesta-Benjumea, C. (2011). Strategies for the relief of burden in advanced dementia care-giving. *Journal of Advanced Nursing*, *67*, 1790–1799.

de Lauzon-Guillain et al. (2006). Is restrained eating a risk factor for weight gain in a general population? *American Journal of Clinical Nutrition, 83*(1), 132–138.

de Luis, D. A., Aller, R., Izaola, O., Gonzales Sagrado, M., Bellioo, D., & Conde, R. (2007). Effects of a low-fat versus a low-carbohydrate diet on adipocytokines in obese adults. *Hormone Research, 67*, 296–300.

de Rosnay, M., Cooper, P. J., Tsigaras, N., & Murray, L. (2006). Transmission of social anxiety from mother to infant: An experimental study using a social referencing paradigm. *Behavior Research and Therapy, 44*, 1165–1175.

de Villiers, J., & de Villiers, P. (2013). Syntax acquisition. In P. D. Zelazo (Ed.), *Oxford handbook of developmental psychology*. New York: Oxford University Press.

de Vres, S., Hoeve, M., Stams, G., & Asscher, J. (2016). Adolescent-parent attachment and externalizing behaviour: The mediating role of individual and social factors. *Journal of Abnormal Child Psychology, 44*, 283–294.

de Wind, A. W., et al. (2014). Health, job characteristics, skills, and social and financial factors in relation to early retirement—results from a longitudinal study in the Netherlands. Scandinavian *Journal of Work, Environment, and Health*, *40*, 186–194.

Deák, G., Krasno, A., Triesch, J., Lewis, J. & Sepeta, L. (2014). Watch the hands: Infants can learn to follow gaze by seeing adults manipulate objects. *Developmental Science*, *17*(2), 270–281.

Deary, I. J. (2012). Intelligence. *Annual Review of Intelligence* (Vol. 63). Palo Alto, CA: Annual Reviews.

DeCasper, A. J., & Spence, M. J. (1986). Prenatal maternal speech influences newborn's perception of speech sounds. *Infant Behavior and Development, 9*, 133–150.

Decety, J., et al. (November 16, 2015). The negative associaltion between religiousness and children's altruism across the world. *Current Biology, 25*(22), 2951–2955. Retrieved from http://www.cell.com/current-biology/fulltext/S0960-9822(15)01167-7.

Declercq, E., Cunningham, D. K., Johnson, C., & Sakala, C. (2008). Mothers' reports of postpartum pain associated with vaginal and cesarean deliveries: Results of a national survey. *Birth, 35*, 16–24.

Dedon, P. C., & Begley, T. H. (2014, in press). A system of RNA modifications and biased codon use control cellular stress response at the level of transition. *Chemical Research in Toxicology*.

Deeg, D. J. H. (2005). The development of physical and mental health from late midlife to early old age. In S. L. Willis & M. Martin (Eds.), *Middle adulthood*. Thousand Oaks, CA: Sage.

DeGenova, M. K., & Rice, F. P. (2008). *Intimate relationships, marriages, and families* (7th ed.). New York: McGraw-Hill.

Del Guidice, M. (2011). Sex differences in romantic attachment: A meta-analysis. *Personality and Social Psychology Bulletin, 37*, 193–214.

Del Tredici, K., & Braak, H. (2008). Neurofibrillary changes of the Alzheimer type in very elderly individuals: Neither inevitable nor benign. Commentary on no disease in the brain of a 115-yearold woman. *Neurobiology of Aging, 29*, 1133–1136.

DeMarie, D., & Lopez, L. (2014). Memory in school. In R. Fivush & P. Bauer (Eds.), *Wiley-Blackwell handbook of the development of children's memory*. New York: Wiley.

Dempsey, D. (2014). Advance care planning: taking time now will save time later. *Nursing and Residential Care, 16*(5), 269–272.

Dempster, F. N. (1981). Memory span: Sources of individual and developmental differences. *Psychological Bulletin, 80*, 63–100.

den Hollander, B., et al. (2012). Preliminary evidence of hippocampal damage in chronic users of ecstasy. *Journal of Neurology Neurosurgery and Psychiatry, 83*, 83–85.

Denburg, N. L., et al. (2009). Poor decision making among older adults is related to elevated levels of neuroticism. *Annals of Behavioral Medicine, 37*, 164–172.

Denham, J., et al. (2013). Longer leukocyte telomeres are associated with ultra-endurance exercise independent of cardiovascular factors. *PLoS One, 8*(7), e69377.

Denham, S., et al. (2012). Preschoolers' emotion knowledge: Self-regulatory foundations and predictors of school success. *Cognition and Emotion*, *26*(4), 667–679.

Denney, N. W. (1986, August). *Practical problem solving.* Paper presented at the meeting of the American Psychological Association, Washington, DC.

Denney, N. W. (1990). Adult age differences in traditional and practical problem solving. *Advances in Psychology, 72*, 329–349.

Dennis, N. A., & Cabeza, R. (2008). Neuroimaging of healthy cognitive aging. In F. I. M. Craik & T. A. Salthouse (Eds.), *Handbook of aging and cognition* (3rd ed.). Mahwah, NJ: Erlbaum.

Dennison, S., Reede, C., & Xu, F. (2013). The emergence of probabilistic reasoning in very young infants. Evidenced from 4-, 5- and 6-month-olds. *Developmental Psychology, 49*, 243–249.

Department of Indian and Northern Affairs Canada. (1996). *A Word from Commissioners.* Royal Commission on Aboriginal Peoples. Retrieved from http://www.iainc-inac.gc.ca/

Department of Justice Canada. (2013). *Government of Canada announces continued support to youth justice services.* Retrieved from http://www.justice.gc.ca/

DePaulo, B. (2006). *Singled out.* New York, NY: St. Martin's Press.

DePaulo, B. (2011). Living single: Lightening up those dark, dopey myths. In W. Cupach & B. Spitzberg (Eds.) *The dark side of relationships II* (pp. 409–439). New York, NY: Routledge.

Depp, C., & Jeste, D. V. (2010). Successful aging. *Annual Review of Clinical Psychology* (Vol. 6). Palo Alto, CA: Annual Reviews.

Derbyshire, E. (2007a). Nutrition in pregnant teenagers: How nurses can help. *British Journal of Nursing, 16*, 144–145.

Derbyshire, E. (2007b). The importance of adequate fluid and fiber intake during pregnancy. *Nursing Standard, 21*, 40–43.

DeRosa, D. A., & Abruscato, J. (2015, in press). *Teaching children science* (8th ed.). Upper Saddle River, NJ: Pearson.

DeRose, L., & Brooks-Gunn, J. (2008). Pubertal development in early adolescence: Implications for affective processes. In N. B. Allen & L. Sheeber (Eds.), *Adolescent emotional development and the emergence of depressive disorders.* New York: Cambridge University Press.

Deschesnes, M., Fines, P., & Demers, S. (2006). Are tattooing and body piercing indicators of risk-taking behaviours among high school students? *Journal of Adolescence, 29*, 379–393.

DesMeules, M., Pong, R. W., Read Guernsey, J., Wang, F., Luo, W., & Dressler, M. P. (2012). Rural health status and determinants in Canada. In J. C. Kulig & A. M. Williams (Eds.), *Health in Rural Canada* (pp. 23–43). Vancouver: UBC Press.

DeSpelder, L. A., & Strickland, A. L. (2005). *The last dance: Encountering death and dying* (6th ed., rev. update). Mountain View, CA: Mayfield.

Desrosiers, H., Cardin, J. F., & Belleau, L. (2013). The Impact of Parental Separation on Young Children's Mental Health. In *Québec Longitudinal Study of Child Development (QLSCD 1998–2010) – From Birth to 10 Years of Age*, Institut de la statistique du Québec, Vol. 6, Fascicle 3.

Diamond, A. (2001). A model system for studying the role of dopamine in the prefrontal context during early development in humans: Early and continuously treated phenylketonuria. In C. Nelson & M. Luciana (Eds.), *Handbook of developmental cognitive neuroscience.* Cambridge, MA: MIT Press.

Diamond, A. (2009). The interplay of biology and the environment broadly defined. *Developmental Psychology, 45*, 1–8.

Diamond, A. (2013). Executive functions. *Annual Review of Psychology* (Vol. 64). Palo Alto, CA: Annual Reviews.

Diamond, A. D. (2007). Interrelated and interdependent. *Developmental Science, 10*, 152–158.

Diamond, A., & Lee, K. (2011). Interventions shown to aid executive function development in children 4 to 12 years old. *Science, 333*, 959–964.

Diamond, A., Barnett, W. S., Thomas, J., & Munro, S. (2007). Preschool program improves cognitive control. *Science, 318*, 1387–1388.

Diamond, L. & Savan-Williams, R. (2015). Same sex activity in adolescence: Multiple meanings and implications. In R.F. Fassinger & S. L. Morrow (Eds.), *Sex in the margins*. Washington, DC: American Psychological Association.

Diamond, L. M. (2008). Female bisexuality from adolescence to adulthood: Results from a 10-year longitudinal study. *Developmental Psychology, 44*, 5–14.

DiBlasio, S. (April 30, 2014) Working poor? Immigrant survival jobs and poverty. Canadian Immigrant Retrieved from http://canadianimmigrant.ca/category/immigrant-stories.

Dickens, B. M. (2014). Ethical and legal aspects of noninvasive prenatal genetic diagnosis. *International Journal of Gynecology and Obstetrics, 124*, 181–184.

Dietz, P., et al. (2010). Estimates of nondisclosure of cigarette smoking among pregnant and nonpregnant women of reproductive age in the United States. *American Journal of Epidemiology, 173*(3), 355–359.

Dillon, J. (2003). Reincarnation: The technology of death. In C. D. Bryant (Ed.), *Handbook of death and dying.* Thousand Oaks, CA: Sage.

Dimmitt, C., & McCormick, C. B. (2012). Metacognition in education. In K. R. Harris, S. Graham, & T. Urdan (Eds.), *Handbook of educational psychology*. Washington, DC: American Psychological Association.

Dindia, K. (2006). Men are from North Dakota, women are from South Dakota. In K. Dindia & D. J. Canary (Eds.), *Sex differences and similarities in communication.* Mahwah, NJ: Erlbaum.

Dine, A., Kizilkaya Beji, N., & Yalcin, O. (2009). Effect of pelvic floor muscle exercises in the treatment of urinary incontinence during pregnancy and the postpartum period. *International Urogynecology Journal, 20*(120), 1223–1231.

Ding, Z., et al. (2014, in press). Estimating telomere length from whole genome sequence data. *Nucleic Acids Research.*

Dinger, M., Brittain, D., & Hutchinson, S. (2014). Associations between physical activity and health-related factors in a national sample of college students. *Journal of American College Health, 62*, 67–74.

Dirk, J. (2012). Processing speed. In S. K. Whitbourne & M. Sliwinski (Eds.), *Wiley-Blackwell handbook of adulthood and aging.* New York: Wiley.

Dishion, T. J., & Piehler, T. F. (2009). Deviant by design: Peer contagion in development, interventions, and schools. In K. H. Rubin, W. M. Bukowski, & B. Laursen (Eds.), *Handbook of peer interactions, relationships, and groups.* New York: Guilford.

DiTommaso, E., Brannen-McNulty, C., Ross, L. & Burgess, M. (2003), Attachment styles, social skills and loneliness in young adults. *Personality and Individual Differences, 35*, 303–312.

Divall, S. A., & Radovick, S. (2008). Pubertal development and menarche. *Annals of the New York Academy of Sciences, 1135*, 19–28.

Divecha, D. (2015) The Only Parenting Model You Need. Developmental Science. Retrieved from http://www.developmentalscience.com/blog/2015/6/28/the-only-parenting-model-you-need.

Division of British Columbia Law Institute. (2011) A practical guide to elder abuse and neglect law in Canada. Canadian Centre for Elder Law. Retrieved from http://www.bcli.org/sites/default/files/Practical_Guide_English_Rev_JULY_2011.pdf.

Dixon, D. (2008). Informed consent or institutionalized eugenics? How the medical profession encourages abortion of fetuses with Down Syndrome. *Issues in Law & Medicine, 24*(1), 3–59.

Dixon, R. A., McFall, G. P., Whitehead, B. P., & Dolcos, S. (2013). Cognitive development in adulthood and aging. In I. B. Weiner et al. (Eds.), *Handbook of psychology* (2nd ed., Vol. 6). New York: Wiley.

Dobkins, K. & Harms, R. (2014). The face inversion effect in infants is driven by high, and not low, spatial frequencies. *Journal of Vision, 14*(1), 1–17.

Doblado, M., & Moley, K. H. (2007). Glucose metabolism in pregnancy and embryogenesis. *Current Opinion in Endocrinology, Diabetes, and Obesity, 14*, 488–493.

Dobson, J., Maheux, H., Chui, T. (2015). Generation status: Canadian born Children of Immigrants. Statistics Canada. Retrieved from https://www12.statcan.gc.ca/nhs-enm/2011/as-sa/99-010-x/99-010-x2011003_2-eng.cfm.

Dodge, K. A. (1983). Behavioral antecedents of peer social status. *Child Development, 54*, 1386–1399.

Dodge, K. A. (2011a). Context matters in child and family policy. *Child Development, 82*, 433–442.

Dodge, K. A. (2011b). Social information processing models of aggressive behavior. In M. Mikulincer & P. R. Shaver (Eds.), *Understanding and reducing aggression, violence, and their consequences*. Washington, DC: American Psychological Association.

Dodson, L. J., & Davies, A. P. C. (2014). Different challenges, different well-being: A comparison of psychological well-being across stepmothers and biological mothers and across four categories of stepmothers. *Journal of Divorce & Remarriage*, 55, 49–63.

Doey, L., Coplan, R. J., & Kingsbury, M. (2014). *Bashful Boys and Girls: A Review of Gender Differences in Childhood Shyness*. Springer US. Retrieved from http://link.springer.com/article/10.1007/s11199-013-0317-9.

Doherty, T., Chopra, M., Nkonki, L., Jackson, D., & Greiner, T. (2006). Effects of the HIV epidemic on infant feeding in South Africa: "When they see me coming with the tins they laugh at me." *Bulletin of the World Health Organization, 84*, 90–96.

Dohnt, H. & Tiggemann, M. (2006). The contribution of peer and media influences to the development of body satisfaction and self-esteem in young girls: A prospective study. *Developmental Psychology, 42*, 929–936.

Doidge, N. (2006, May 8). The doctor is totally in. *Maclean's*, 40–42.

Doidge, N. (2007). *The brain that changes itself.* Toronto: James H. Silberman Books.

Doll, C. A., & Broadie, K. (2014). Impaired activity-dependent neural circuit assembly and refinement in autism spectrum disorder genetic models. *Frontiers in Cellular Neuoroscience, 8*, 30.

Donaldson, T., Earl, J. K., & Muratore, A. M. (2010). Extending the integrated model of retirement adjustment: Incorporating mastery and retirement planning. *Journal of Vocational Behavior, 77*(2), 279–289. Retrieved from http://www.sciencedirect.com/science/article/pii/S0001879110000679

Dondi, M., Simion, F., & Caltran, G. (1999). Can newborns discriminate between their own cry and the cry of another newborn infant? *Developmental Psychology, 35*(2), 418–426.

Donnellan, M. B., Hill, P. L., & Roberts, B. W. (2014, in press). Personality development across the life span: Current findings and future directions. In L. Cooper & M. Mikulincer (Eds.), *Handbook of personality and social psychology.* Washington, DC: American Psychological Association.

Dontigny, L., Arsenault, M. Y., Martel, M. J., Biringer, A., Cormier, J., Delaney, M., et al. (2008). Rubella in pregnancy. *Journal of Obstetrics and Gynecology Canada, 30*, 152–168.

Dorey, E., Chang, N., Liu, Q. Y., Yang, Z., & Zhang, W. (2014, in press). Apolipoprotein E., amyloid-beta, and neuroinflammation in Alzheimer's disease. *Neuoroscience Bulletin.*

Dorn, L. D., Dahl, R. E., Woodward, H. R., & Biro, F. (2006). Defining the boundaries of early adolescence: A user's guide to assessing pubertal status and pubertal timing in research with adolescents. *Applied Developmental Science, 10*, 30–56.

Dorszewska, J. (2013). Cell biology of normal brain aging: Synaptic plasticity-cell death. *Aging: Clinical and Experimental Research, 25*, 25–34.

Dorval, V., Ritchie, K., & Gruslin, A. (2007). Screening HIV in pregnancy. *Canadian Journal of Public Health, 98*(5), 379–382.

Doty, R. L., & Shah, M. (2008). Taste and smell. In M. M. Haith & J. B. Benson (Eds.), *Encyclopedia of infant and early childhood development.* Oxford, UK: Elsevier.

Dougall, A. L., Biglan, C. W., Swanson, J. N., & Baum, A. (2013). Stress, coping, and immune function. In I. B. Weiner et al. (Eds.), *Handbook of psychology* (2nd ed., Vol. 3). New York: Wiley.

Doumen, S., Smits, I., Luyckx, K., Duriez, B., Vanhalst, J., Verschueren, K., & Goossens, L. (2012). Identity and perceived peer relationship quality in emerging adulthood: The mediating role of attachment – related emotions. *Journal of Adolescence, 35*(6), 1417–1425.

Dow, B. J., & Wood, J. (Eds.). (2006). *The Sage handbook of gender and communication.* Thousand Oaks, CA: Sage.

Dowling, J. (2004). *The great debate: Nature or nurture?* Washington, DC: Joseph Henry Press.

Downie, J. (2015). Carter v. Canada: What's next for physicians? *Canadian Medical Association Journal, 187*(7), 481–482.

Dozier, M., Stovall-McClough, K. C., & Albus, K. E. (2009). Attachment and psychopathogy in adulthood. In J. Cassidy & P. R. Shaver (Eds.), *Handbook of attachment* (2nd ed.). New York: Guilford.

Draghi-Lorenz, R. (2007, July). *Self-conscious emotions in young infants and the direct perception of self and others in interaction.* Paper presented at the meeting of the International Society for Research on Emotions, Sunshine Coast, Australia.

Draghi-Lorenz, R., Reddy, V., & Costall, A. (2001). Rethinking the development of "nonbasic" emotions: A critical review of existing theories. *Developmental Review, 21*, 263–304.

Dryfoos, J. G., & Barkin, C. (2006). *Growing up in America today.* New York: Oxford University Press.

Dube, M., McCarron, A. & Nannini, A. (2015). Advance care planning complexities for nurse practitioners. *Journal for Nurse Practitioners, 11*(8), 766–772.

Dube, S., Boily, M. C., Mugurungi, O., Mahomva, A., Chikhata, F., & Gregson, F. (2008). Estimating vertically acquired HIV infections and the impact of the prevention of mother-to-child transmission program in Zimbabwe: Insights from decision analysis models. *Journal of Acquired Immune Deficiency Syndrome, 48*(1), 72–81.

Dublin, S., et al. (2014, in press). Neuropathologic changes associated with atrial fibrillation in a population-based autopsy cohort. *Journals of Gerontology A: Biological Sciences and Medical Sciences.*

Dubois, J., Dehaene-Lambertz, G., Perrin, M., Mangin, J. F., Cointepas, Y., Duchesnay, E., et al. (2007). Asynchrony of the early maturation of white matter bundles in healthy infants: Quantitative landmarks revealed noninvasively by diffusion tensor imaging. *Human Brain Mapping, 29*, 14–27.

Duchesne, D. (2004). More seniors at work. *Perspectives on Labour and Income, 5*(2), 5–17.

Duczkowska, A., et al. (2010). Magnetic resonance imaging in the evaluation of fetal spinal canal contents. *Brain Development, 33*, 10–20.

Duffy, T. M., & Kirkley, J. R. (Eds.) (2004). *Learner-centered theory and practice in distance education.* Mahwah, NJ: Erlbaum.

Dufour-Rainfray, D., Vourc'h, P., Tourlet, S., Guilloteau, D., Chalon, S. & Andres, C. (2011). Featal exposure to teratogens: Evidence of genes involved in autism. *Neuroscience and Biobehavioural Reviews, 36*, 1254–1265.

Dumas, T. M., Ellis, W. E., & Wolfe, D. A. (2012). Identity development as a buffer of adolescent risk behaviors in the context of peer group pressure and control. *Journal of Adolescence, 35*, 917–927.

Dumont, S., Jacobs, P., Fassbender, K., Anderson, D., Turcotte, V., & Harel, F. (2009). Costs associated with resource utilization during the palliative phase of care: A Canadian perspective. *Palliative Medicine, 23*(8), 708–717.

Dunbar, L., Leventhal, H., & Leventhal, E. A. (2007). Self-regulation, health, and behavior. In J. E. Birren (Ed.), *Encyclopedia of gerontology* (2nd ed.). San Diego: Academic Press.

Duncan, E. & Forbes-McKay, K. (2012). Alcohol use during pregnancy: An application of the theory of planned behaviours. *Journal of Applied Social Psychology.* 42, 1887–1903.

Dunn, J. (2005). Commentary: Siblings in their families. *Journal of Family Psychology, 19*, 654–657.

Dunn, J. (2007). Siblings and socialization. In J. E. Grusec & P. D. Hastings (Eds.), *Handbook of socialization.* New York: Guilford.

Dunn, M., & O'Brien, K. (2013). Work-family enrichment among dual-earner couples: Can work improve our family life? *Journal of Counseling Psychology, 60*(4), 634–640.

Dunn, S. (2009). Upstanders could bring peace to playgrounds everywhere. University of Alberta news archives. Retrieved from http://www.archives.expressnews.ualberta.ca/article/2009/04/10146.html

Dunsmore, J. C., Booker, J. A., & Ollendick, T. H. (2013). Parental emotion coaching and child emotion regulation as protective factors for children with oppositional defiant disorder. *Social Development, 22*(3), 444–466.

Dupre, M. E., & Meadows, S. O. (2007). Disaggregating the effects of marital trajectories on health. *Journal of Family Issues, 28*, 623–652.

Durrant, J. E. (2008). Physical punishment, culture, and rights: Current issues for professionals. *Journal of Developmental and Behavioral Pediatrics, 29*, 55–66.

Durrant, R., & Ellis, B. J. (2013). Evolutionary psychology. In I. B. Weiner et al. (Eds.), *Handbook of psychology* (2nd ed., Vol. 3). New York: Wiley.

Durston, S., & Casey, B. J. (2006). What have we learned about cognitive development from neuroimaging. *Neuropsychologia, 44*, 2149–2157.

Dutton, Y., & Zisook, S. (2005). Adaptation to bereavement. *Death Studies, 29*(10), 877–903.

Dvornyk, V. & Waqar-ul-Haq, H. (2012). Genetics of age at menarche: A systematic review. *Human Reproduction Update. 18*, 198–210.

Dying with Dignity Canada, Inc. (2015). Advance care planning. Retrieved from http://www.dyingwithdignity.ca

Dyl, J., Kittler, J., Phillips, K. A., & Hunt, J. I. (2006). Body dysmorphic disorder and other clinically significant body image concerns in adolescent psychiatric inpatients: Prevalence and clinical characteristics. *Child Psychiatry and Human Development, 36*, 369–382.

Dysart-Gale, D. (2010). Social justice and social determinants of health: Lesbian, gay, bisexual, transgendered, intersexed, and queer youth in Canada. *Journal of Child and Adolescent Psychiatric Nursing, 23*(1), 23–28.

E

Early Childhood Education and Care. (2016). Early Childhood Education and Care. Retrieved from http://www.oecd.org/edu/school/earlychildhoodeducationandcare.htm

Easterbrooks, M. A., Bartlett, J. D., Beeghly, M., & Thompson, R. A. (2013). Social and emotional development in infancy. In I. B. Weiner et al. (Eds.), *Handbook of psychology* (2nd ed., Vol.6). New York: Wiley.

Eastwick, P. W., & Finkel, E. J. (2008). Sex differences in mate preferences revisited: Do people know what they initially desire in a romantic partner? *Journal of Personality and Social Psychology, 94*, 245–264.

Eby, J. W., Herrell, A. L., & Jordan, M. L. (2011). *Teaching in elementary school: A reflective approach* (6th ed.). Boston: Allyn & Bacon.

Eccles, J. S. (2014). Gender and achievement choices. In E. T. Gershoff, R. S. Mistry, & D. A. Crosby (Eds.), *Societal contexts of child development.* New York: Oxford University Press.

Eccles, J. S., & Goodman, J. (Eds.). (2002). *Community programs to promote youth development.* Washington, DC: National Academy Press.

Eccles, J. S., Brown, B. V., & Templeton, J. (2008). A developmental framework for selecting indicators of well-being during the adolescent and young adult years. In B. V. Brown (Ed.), *Key indicators of child and youth well-being.* Clifton, NJ: Psychology Press.

Eccles, J., & Roesner, R. (2009). Schools, academic motivation, and stage–environment fit. In R. Lerner & L. Steinberg (Eds.), *Handbook of adolescent psychology* (3rd ed.) (Vol. 1) (pp. 404–434). New York: Wiley.

Eckstein, C. (2007). History of euthanasia in Canada, part II. Compassionate Healthcare Network International. Retrieved from http://www.chninternational.com/history_of_euthanasia_in_canada%20part2.htm

Edeas, M., & Weissig, V. (2013). Targeting mitochondria: Strategies, innovations, and challenges: The future of medicine will come through mitochondria. *Mitochondrion, 13*, 1389–1390.

Edwards, C., Sheridan, S., & Knoche, L. (2010). Parent-child relationships in early learning. In E. Baker, P. Peterson & B. McGraw (Eds). *International encyclopedia of education* (pp. 438–443). Oxford, England: Elsevier.

Egan, S. K., & Perry, D. G. (2001). Gender identity: A multidimensional analysis with implications for psychosocial adjustment. *Developmental Psychology, 37*, 451–463.

Egeland, B. (2009). Attachment-based interventions on the quality of attachment among infants and young children. In R. E. Tremblay, R. deV Peters, M. Boivin, & R. G. Barr (Eds.), *Encyclopedia on early childhood development.* Montreal: Centre of Excellence for Early Childhood Development.

Eichorn, D. H., Clausen, J. A., Haan, N., Honzik, M. P., & Mussen, P. H. (Eds.). (1981). *Present and past in middle life.* New York: Academic Press.

Eiferman, R. R. (1971). Social play in childhood. In R. Herron & B. Sutton-Smith (Eds.), *Child's play.* New York: Wiley.

Einarson, A., & Ito, S. (2007). Re: Use of contemporary antidepressants during breastfeeding: A proposal for a specific safety index. *Drug Safety, 30*, 643.

Eisenberg, N., & Morris, A. S. (2004). Moral cognitions and social responding in adolescence. In R. Lerner & L. Steinberg (Eds.), *Handbook of adolescent psychology.* New York: Wiley.

Eisenberg, N., & Spinrad, T. L. (2014). Multidimensionality of prosocial behavior: Rethinking the conceptualization and development of prosocial behavior. In L. Padilla-Walker & G. Carlo (Eds.), *Prosocial behavior.* New York: Oxford University Press.

Eisenberg, N., Fabes, R. A., Guthrie, I. K., & Reiser, M. (2002). The role of emotionality and regulation in children's social competence and adjustment. In L. Pulkkinen & A. Caspi (Eds.), *Paths to successful development.* New York: Cambridge University Press.

Eisenberg, N., Morris, A. S., McDaniel, B., & Spinrad, T. L. (2009). Moral cognitions and prosocial responding in adolescence. In R. M. Lerner & L. Steinberg (Eds.), *Handbook of adolescent psychology* (3rd ed.). New York: Wiley.

Eisenberg, N., Spinrad, T. L., & Morris, A. S. (2013). Prosocial development. In P. D. Zelazo (Ed.), *Oxford handbook of developmental psychology.* New York: Oxford University Press.

El Haj, M., & Allain, P. (2012). Relationship between source monitoring in episodic memory and executive function in normal aging. *Geriatrie et Psychologie Neuropsychiatrie du Viellissement, 10*, 197–205.

Elder, G. H., & Shanahan, M. J. (2006). *The life course and human development.* New York: John Wiley & Sons.

Eliasieh, K., Liets, L. C., & Chalupa, L. M. (2007). Cellular reorganization in the human retina during normal aging. *Investigative Ophthalmology and Visual Science, 48*, 2824–2830.

Elkind, D. (1970, April 5). Erik Erikson's eight ages of man. *New York Times Magazine.*

Elkind, D. (1976). *Child development and education: A Piagetian perspective.* New York: Oxford University Press.

Elliott, E. M., et al. (2011). Working memory in the oldest-old: Evidence from output serial position curves. *Memory and Cognition, 39*(8), 1423–1434.

Elliott, S. L. (November 2011). Hot topics in erectile dysfunction. *British Columbia Medical Journal, 53*(9). Retrieved from http://www.bcmj.org/articles/hot-topics-erectile-dysfunction.

Elliott, V. S. (2004). Methamphetamine use increasing. Retrieved from http://www.amaasson.org/

Ellis, B., Shirtcliff, E., Boyce, W., Deardoeff, J. & Essex, M. (2011). Quality of early family relationships and the timing and tempo of puberty: Effects depend on biological sensitivity to context. *Development and Psychopathology, 23*, 85–99.

Ellis, M. L., et al. (2014, in press). Effects of cognitive speed of processing training among older adults with heart failure. *Journal of Aging and Health*.

Else-Quest, N. Hyde, J., Goldsmith, H., & Van Hulle, C. (2006). Gender differences in temperament: A meta - analysis. *Psychological Bulletin, 132*(1), 33–72.

Eltis, K. (2007, Summer). Genetic determinism and discrimination: A call to re-orient prevailing human rights discourse to better comport with the public implications of individual genetic testing. *The Journal of Law, Medicine & Ethics, 35*(2), 282–294.

Elwert, F., & Christakis, N. A. (2008). The effect of widowhood on mortality by the causes of death of both spouses. *American Journal of Public Health, 98*(11), 2092–2098.

Emery, C. F., Anderson, D. R., & Goodwin, C. L. (2013). Coronary heart disease and hypertension. In I. B. Weiner et al. (Eds.), *Handbook of psychology* (2nd ed., Vol. 9). New York: Wiley.

Emke, I. (2002). Why the sad face? Secularization and the changing function of funerals in Newfoundland. *Mortality, 7*(3), 269–284.

Endicott, O. (2003). Legalizing physician-assisted death: Can safeguards protect the interests of vulnerable persons? Council of Canadian with Disabilities. Retrieved from http://www.ccdonline.ca/en/humanrights/endoflife/euthanasia/lpad

Engler, A. J., Ludington-Hoe, S. M., Cusson, R. M., Adams, R., Bahnsen, M., Brumbaugh, E., et al. (2002). Kangaroo care: National survey of practice, knowledge, barriers, and perceptions. *American Journal of Maternal/Child Nursing, 27*, 146–153.

Eni, R., & Phillips-Beck, W. (2013). Teenage pregnancy and parenthood perspectives of First Nation Women. *The International Indigenous Policy Journal, 4*(1). Retrieved from http://www.ir.lib.uwo.ca/

Ennett, S. T., Bauman, K. E., Hussong, A., Faris, R., Foshee V. A., & Cai, L. (2006). The peer context of adolescent substance use: Findings from social network analysis. *Journal of Research on Adolescence, 16*, 159–186.

Enough-Is-Enough. (2009–2013). Online bullying. Retrieved from http://www.internetsafety101.org/

Ensor, R., Spencer, D., & Hughes, C. (2011). You feel sad? Emotional understanding mediates effects of verbal ability and mother-child mutuality on prosocial behaviors: Findings from 2 to 4 years. *Social Development, 20*, 93–100.

Eppinger, B., Walter, M., Heekeren, H. R., & Li, S. C. (2013). Of goals and habits: Age-related and individual differences in goal-directed decision-making. *Frontiers in Neuroscience, 7*, 253.

Erickson, K. I., & Kramer, A. F. (2009). Aerobic exercise effects on cognitive and neural plasticity in older adults. *British Journal of Sports Medicine, 43*, 22–24.

Erickson, K. I., et al. (2011). Exercise training increases the size of the hippocampus and improves memory. *Proceedings of the National Academy of Sciences U.S.A., 108*, 3017–3022.

Ericsson, K. A. (2014). Creative genius: A view from the expert-performance approach. In D. K. Simonton (Ed.), *Wiley-Blackwell handbook of genius*. New York: Wiley.

Erikson, E. H. (1968). *Identity: Youth and crisis*. New York: W. W. Norton.

Eriksson Sorman, D., Sunderstrom, A., Ronnlund, M., Adolfsson, R., & Nilsson, L. G. (2014, in press). Leisure activity in old age and risk of dementia: A 15-year prospective study. *Journals of Gerontology B: Psychological Sciences and Social Sciences*.

Erixon-Lindroth, N., Farde, L., Robins Whalin, T. B., Sovago, J., Halldin, C., & Backman, L. (2005). The role of the striatal dopamine transporter in cognitive aging. *Psychiatry Research: Neuroimaging, 138*, 1–12.

Erol, R., & Orth, U. (2011). Self-esteem development from age 14 to 30 years: A longitudinal study. *Journal of Personality and Social Psychology, 101*, 607–609.

ESHRE Capri Workshop Group (2011). Perimenopausal risk factors and future health. *Human Reproduction Update, 17*, 706–717.

Esposito, K., et al. (2009). Effects of intensive lifestyle changes on erectile dysfunction in men. *Journal of Sexual Medicine, 6*, 243–250.

Essau, C., Lewinsohn, P., Seeley, J., & Sasagawa, S. (2010). Gender differences in the development course of depression. *Journal of Affective Disorders, 127*, 185–190.

Estabrooks, C.A., Hoben, M., Poss, J.W., Chamberlain, S.A., Thompson, G.N., Silvius, J.L., Norton, P.G. (2015). Dying in a nursing home: Treatable symptom burden and its link to modifiable features of work context. *Journal of the American Medical Directors Association, 16*(6), 515–520. Retrieved from http://cahs-acss.ca/wp-content/uploads/2015/09/Estabrooks_CAHS-Dementia-Forum-presentation-Caregivers-Sep-13-2015.pdf

Etaugh, C., & Bridges, J. S. (2010). *Women's lives* (2nd ed.). Boston: Allyn & Bacon.

Evanoo, G. (2007). Infant crying: A clinical conundrum. *Journal of Pediatric Care, 21*, 333–338.

Evans, S. E. (2004). *Forgotten crimes: The Holocaust and people with disabilities.* Chicago: Ivan R. Dee.

Evans, W. J. (2010). Skeletal muscle loss: Cachexia, sarcopenia, and inactivity. *American Journal of Clinical Nutrition, 91*, S1123–S1127.

Eveleth, D. D. (2013). Cell-based therapies for ocular disease. *Journal of Occupational and Pharmacological Therapeutics, 29*, 844–854.

Everingham, C., Stevenson, D. & Warner-Smith, P. (2007). "Things are getting better all the time?" Challenging the narrative of women's progress from a generational perspective. *Sociology, 41*(3), 419–437.

Evers, A. W., et al. (2014, in press). Does stress affect the joints? Daily stressors, stress vulnerability, immune and HPA axis activity, and short-term disease and symptom fluctuations in rheumatoid arthritis. *Annals of the Rheumatic Diseases*.

Ewanchuk, M., & Brindley, P. G. (2006). Ethics review: Perioperative do-not-resuscitate orders—doing "nothing" when "something" can be done. *Critical Care, 10*(219) [online] doi:10.1186/cc4929.

Ezkurdia, L., et al. (2014). The shrinking human protein coding complement: Are there fewer than 20,000 genes? *bioRxiv*, doi:10.1101/001909.

F

Fabian, S. G., et al. (2014, in press). Mitochondrial biogenesis in health and disease. Molecular and therapeutic approaches. *Current Pharmaceutical Design*.

Fagan, J. F. (1992). Intelligence: A theoretical viewpoint. *Current Directions in Psychological Science, 1*, 82–86.

Fagan, J., Holland, C., & Wheeler, K. (2007). The prediction from infancy, of adult IQ and achievement. *Intelligence, 35*(3), 225–231.

Fagot, B. I., Rogers, C. S., & Leinbach, M. D. (2000). Theories of gender socialization. In T. Eckes & H. M. Trautner (Eds.), *The developmental social psychology of gender.* Mahwah, NJ: Erlbaum.

Fagundes, C. P., et al. (2013). Depressive symptoms enhance stress-induced inflammatory responses. *Brain, Behavior, and Immunity, 31*, 172–176.

Fahey, T. D., Insel, P. M., & Roth, W. T. (2009). *Fit and well* (8th ed.). New York: McGraw-Hill.

Fakhoury, J., Nimmo, G. A., & Autexier, C. (2007). Harnessing telomerase in cancer therapeutics. *Anti-cancer Agents in Medicinal Chemistry, 7*, 475–483.

Falci, D. (2011). Self-esteem and mastery trajectories in high school by social class and gender. *Journal of Social Science Research, 40*, 586–601.

Fallows, M. (2011, April). Insomnia: How do I beat it? *The Teacher, 49*(6), 6. Retrieved from http://www.nstu.ca/images/pklot/wellteacherAPR11.pdf

Fang, L., Wang, Y., & He, X. (2013). Theoretical analysis of wavefront aberration caused by treatment decentration and transition zone after custom myopic laser refractive surgery. *Journal of Cataract and Refractive Surgery, 39*, 1336–1347.

Fantz, R. L. (1963). Pattern vision in newborn infants. *Science, 140*, 296–297.

Farioli-Vecchioli, S., et al. (2014, in press). Running rescues defective adult neurogenesis by shortening the length of the cell cycle of neural stem and progenitor cells. *Stem Cells.*

Farley, M., Lynne, J., & Cotton, A. J. (2005). Prostitution in Vancouver: Violence and the colonization of First Nations Women. *Transcultural Psychiatry, 42*(2), 242–271.

Farr, R. & Patterson, C. (2013). Coparenting among lesbian gay, and heterosexual couples: Association with adopted children outcomes. *Child Development, 84*, 1226–1240.

Farrell, M. J. (2012). Age-related changes in the structure and function of brain regions involved in pain processing. *Pain Medicine, 13*(2, Suppl.), S37–S43.

Farrington, D. P. (2004) Criminological psychology in the 21st century. *Criminal Behaviour and Mental Health, 14*, 152–166.

Fatusi, N., & Hindin, M. (2010). Adolescents and youths in developing countries: Health and development issues in context. Health and Development in Issues in Context. *Journal of Adolescence, 35*(5), 1191–1201.

Fausto-Sterling, A. (2011). In praise of Esther Thelen. *Psychology Today.* Retrieved from http://www.psychologytoday.com/blog/sexing-the-body/201106/in-praise-esther-thelen

Feeney, B. C., & Collins, N. L. (2007). Interpersonal safe haven and secure base caregiving processes in adulthood. In W. S. Rholes & J. A. Simpson (Eds.), *Adult attachment.* New York: Guilford.

Feeney, J. A. (2009). Adult romantic attachment: Developments in the study of couple relationships. In J. Cassidy & P. R. Shaver (Eds.), *Handbook of attachment* (2nd ed.). New York: Guilford.

Feeney, J. A., & Monin, J. K. (2009). An attachment theoretical perspective on divorce. In J. Cassidy & P. R. Shaver (Eds.), *Handbook of attachment* (2nd ed.). New York: Guilford.

Feeney, S., Moravcik, E., & Nolte, S. (2013). *Who am I in the lives of children?* (9th ed.). Upper Saddle River, NJ: Pearson.

Feig, D., Hwee, J., Shah, B., Booth, G., Bierman, A. & Lipscombe, L. (2014). Trends in incidence of diabetes in pregnancy and serious perintal outcomes: A large population-based study in Ontario, Canada, 1996–2010. *Diabetic Care,* 37, 1590–1596.

Feinberg, M. E., Button, T. M., Neiderhiser, J. M., Reiss, D., & Hetherington, E. M. (2007). Parenting and antisocial behavior and depression: Evidence of genotype x parenting environment interaction. *Archives of General Psychiatry, 64*, 457–465.

Feldman, D. H. (2013). Cognitive development in childhood: A contemporary perspective. In I. B. Weiner et al. (Eds.), *Handbook of psychology* (2nd ed., Vol. 6). New York: Wiley.

Feldman, R. (2007). Parent-infant synchrony. *Current Directions in Psychological Science, 16*, 340–345.

Feldman, R., & Eidelman, A. (2003). Skin-to-skin contact (kangaroo care) accelerates autonomic and neuro-behavioral maturation in preterm infants. *Developmental Medicine and Child Neurology, 45*, 274–281.

Feldman, R., & Eidelman, A. I. (2007). Maternal postpartum behavior and the emergence of infant-mother and infant-father synchrony in preterm and full-term infants: The role of neonatal vagal tone. *Developmental Psychobiology, 49*, 290–302.

Feldman, R., & Landry, O. (2014). *Discovering the lifespan* (Canadian ed.). Don Mills, ON: Pearson.

Feldman, R., Weller, A., Sirota, L., & Eidelman, A. I. (2003). Testing a family intervention hypothesis: The contribution of mother-infant skin-to-skin (kangaroo care) to family interaction, proximity, and touch. *Journal of Family Psychology, 17*, 94–107.

Feldon, J. M. (2003). Grief as a transformative experience: Weaving through different lifeworlds after a loved one has committed suicide. *International Journal of Mental Health Nursing, 12*, 74–85.

Felmlee, D., Sweet, E., & Sinclair, H. (2012). Gender rules: Same- and cross-gender friendships norms. *Sex Roles, 66*, 518–529.

Fenesi, B., & Sana, F. (2015). What is your degree worth? The relationship between post-secondary programs and employment outcomes. *Canadian Journal of Higher Education, 45*(4), 383–399.

Feng, X., et al. (2014, in press). Robust gene dysregulation in Alzheimer's disease brains. *Journal of Alzheimer's Disease.*

Fenigsen, R. (2008). Other people's lives: Reflections on medicine, ethics, and euthanasia. *Issues in Law and Medicine, 23*, 281–297.

Ferber, S. G., & Makhoul, I. R. (2008). Neurobehavioral assessment of skin-to-skin effects on reaction to pain in preterm infants: A randomized, controlled within-subject trial. *Acta Pediatrica, 97*, 171–176.

Ferguson, D. M., Harwood, L. J., & Shannon, F. T. (1987). Breastfeeding and subsequent social adjustment in 6- to 8-year-old children. *Journal of Child Psychology and Psychiatry, 28*, 378–386.

Ferguson, K., Bender, K., Thompson, S., Maccio, E., Xie, B. & Pollio, D. (2011). Correlates of street survival behaviours in homeless young adults in four U.S. cities. *American Journal of Orthopsychiatry, 81*(3), 401–409.

Ferrari, M., & Weststrate, N. (Eds.) (2013). *Personal wisdom.* New York: Springer.

Ferris, M. (2010). Voices from the field—Aboriginal children and obesity. In R.E. Tremblay, R. G. Barr, R. DeV. Peters, & M. Boivin (Eds.), *Encyclopedia on Early Childhood Development* [online]. Montreal, Quebec: Centre of Excellence for Early Childhood Development, (1–6). Retrieved from http://www.child-encyclopedia.com/documents/FerrisANGps.pdf

Fertility Matters Canada. (2016). IVF funding by province. Retrieved from http://fertilitymatters.ca.

Fiedorowicz, C., Craig, J., Phillips, M., Price A., & Bullivant, G. (2015). Position Paper - to Revise or Not to Revise: The Official LDAC Definition of Learning Disabilities Versus DSM-5 Criteria. Learning Disabilities Association of Canada (LDAC) Retrieved from http://www.ldac-acta.ca/downloads/pdf/media_release/LDAC-DSM-5-Statement-March-2015-FINAL-CL.pdf

Field, D. (1996). Review of relationships in old age by Hansson & Carpenter. *Contemporary Psychology, 41*, 44–45.

Field, R. D., England, D. E., Andrews, C. Z., Martin, C. L., & Zosuls, K. M. (2012, April). *"I understand girls but not boys": Assessing gender-based relationship efficacy.* Paper presented at the Gender

Development Research conference, San Francisco.

Field, T. M. (2007). *The amazing infant.* Malden, MA: Blackwell.

Field, T. M. (2008). Breastfeeding and antidepressants. *Infant Behavior and Development, 31*(3), 481–487.

Field, T. M., & Hernandez-Reif, M. (2008). Touch and pain. In M. M. Haith & J. B. Benson (Eds.), *Encyclopedia of infant and early childhood development.* Oxford, UK: Elsevier.

Field, T. M., Hernandez-Reif, M., Feije, L., & Freedman, J. (2006). Prenatal, perinatal, and neonatal stimulation, *Infant Behavior and Development, 29*, 24–31.

Fielding, K. & Forchuk, C. (2013). Exploring the factors associated with youth homelessness and arrests. *Journal of Child and Adolescent Psychiatric Nursing, 26*, 225–233.

FIERA (Father Involvement Research Alliance). (2016). Research clusters: New Fathers. Retrieved from http://www.fira.ca/

Fiese, B. H., & Winter, M. A. (2008). Family influences. In M. M. Haith & J. B. Benson (Eds.), *Encyclopedia of infant and early childhood development.* Oxford, UK: Elsevier.

Figueiredo, R., Hwang, S. & Quiñonez, C. (2013). Dental health of homeless adults in Toronto, Canada. *Journal of Public Health Dentistry, 73*, 74–78.

Fillion, L., Tremblay, I., Truchon, M., Côté, D., Sutruthers, C. W., & Dupuis, R. (2007). Job satisfaction and emotional distress among nurses providing palliative care: Empirical evidence for an integrative occupational stress-model. *International Journal of Stress Management, 13*(1), 1–25.

Finch, C. E. (2011). Inflammation and aging. In E. Masoro & S. Austad (Eds.), Handbook of the biology of aging (7th ed.). New York: Elsevier.

Finch, C. E., & Seeman, T. E. (1999). Stress theories of aging. In V. L. Bengtson, & K. W. Schaie (Eds.). *Handbook of theories of aging.* New York: Springer.

Fincham, F. D., Stanley, S. M., & Beach, S. R. H. (2007). Transformative processes in marriage: An analysis of emerging trends. *Journal of Marriage and the Family, 69*, 275–292.

Finding Quality Child care (n.d.) What to look for- A checklist. Retrieved from http://www.findingqualitychildcare.ca/

Finger, B., Hans, S., Bernstein, V. & Cox, S. (2009). Parent relationship quality and infant-mother attachment. *Attachment and Human Development, 11*, 285–306.

Fingerhut, A., & Peplau, L. (2013). Same-sex romantic relationships. In C.J. Patterson & A. R. D'Augelli (Eds.), *Handbook of psychology and sexual orientation* (pp. 165-178). New York, NY: Oxford University Press.

Fingerman, K. L., & Baker, B. (2006). Socioemotional aspects of aging. In J. Wilmouth & K. Ferraro (Eds.), *Perspectives in gerontology* (3rd ed.). New York: Springer.

Fingerman, K. L., Birditt, K. S., Nussbaum, J., & Schroeder, D. (2014, in press). Generational juggling: Midlife. In A. L. Vangelisti (Ed.), *Handbook of family communication* (2nd ed.). New York: Elsevier.

Fingerman, K. L., Brown, B. B., & Blieszner, R. (2011). Informal ties across the lifespan: Peers, consequential strangers, and people we encounter in daily life. In K. L. Fingerman, C. A. Berg, J. Smith, & T. C. Antonucci (Eds.), *Handbook of life-span development.* New York: Springer.

Fingerman, K. L., Whiteman, S. D., & Dotterer, A. M. (2009). Mother-child relationships in adolescence and old age. In H. T. Reis & S. K. Sprecher (Eds.), *Encyclopedia of human relationships.* Thousand Oaks, CA: Sage.

Finnegan, L. (2013). Licit and illicit drug use during pregnancy: Maternal, neonatal and Early childhood consequences. *Canadian Center on Substance Abuse.* Retrieved from http://www.CCJA.Ca/

Finnie, R. (2012). Access to post-secondary education: The importance of culture. *Children and Youth Services Review, 34*(6), 1161–1170.

Fiocco, A. J., et al. (2013). The effects of an exercise and lifestyle intervention program on cardiovascular, metabolic factors, and cognitive performance in middle-aged adults with Type II diabetes: A pilot study. *Canadian Journal of Diabetes, 37*, 214–219.

Fiori, K. L., Antonucci, T. C., & Cortina, K. S. (2006). Social network typologies and mental health among older adults. *Journals of Gerontology B: Psychological Sciences and Social Sciences, 61*, P25–P32.

Fiori, K. L., Smith, J., & Antonucci, T. C. (2007). Social network types among older adults: A multidimensional approach. *Journals of Gerontology B: Psychological Sciences and Social Sciences, 62*, P322–P330.

FIRA. (2012). Brand new Canadian website for new dads. Retrieved from http://www.fira.ca/

Firbank, O. (2011). Framing home-care policy: A case study of reforms in a Canadian jurisdiction. *Journal of Aging Studies, 25*, 36–44.

Fischer, K. W., & Bidell, T. R. (2006). Dynamic development of action, thought, and emotion. In W. Damon & R. M. Lerner (Eds.), *Handbook of child psychology: Theoretical models of human development* (6th ed.). New York: Wiley.

Fischer, K. W., & Immordino-Yang, M. H. (2008). The fundamental importance of the brain and learning for education. *The Jossey-Bass reader on the brain and learning.* San Francisco: Jossey-Bass.

Fisher, C. B., Busch-Rossnagel, N. A., Jopp, D. S., & Brown, J. L. (2013). Applied developmental science: Contributions and challenges for the 21st century. In I. B. Weiner et al. (Eds.), *Handbook of psychology* (2nd ed., Vol. 6). New York: Wiley.

Fisher, M. (2001). Alfred Adler. Retrieved from http://www.muskingum.edu/~psych/psycweb/history/adler.htm

Fisher, P. A. (2005, April). *Translational research on underlying mechanisms of risk among foster children: Implications for prevention science.* Paper presented at the meeting of the Society for Research in Child Development, Washington, DC.

Fitzgerald, D. (November 11, 2015). Ireland Becomes 47th Country to BanCorporal Punishment. UN Tribune Independent. Retrieved from http://untribune.com/ireland-becomes-47th-country-to-ban-corporal-punishment/

Fitzgerald, E. F., et al. (2004). Fish consumption and other environmental exposures and their associations with serum PCB concentrations among Mohawk women at Akwesasne. *Environmental Research, 94*(2), 160–170.

Flannagan, D., Marsh, D., & Fuhrman, R. (2005). Judgments about the hypothetical behaviors of friends and romantic partners. *Journal of Social and Personal Relationships, 22*, 797–815.

Flannery, D. J., Hussey, D., Biebelhausen, L., & Wester, K. (2003). Crime, delinquency, and youth gangs. In G. Adams & M. Berzonsky (Eds.), *Blackwell handbook of adolescence.* Malden, MA: Blackwell.

Flavell, J. H. (2004). Theory-of-mind development: Retrospect and prospect. *Merrill-Palmer Quarterly, 50*, 274–290.

Flavell, J. H., Friedrichs, A., & Hoyt, J. (1970). Developmental changes in memorization processes. *Cognitive Psychology, 1*, 324–340.

Flavell, J., Mumme, D., Green, F., & Flavell E. (1992). Young children's understanding of different types of beliefs. Child Development, 63, 960–977.

Flegal, W. A. (2007). Blood group genotyping in Germany. *Transfusion, 47* (Suppl. 1), S47–S53.

Flegel, K., MacDonald, N., & Hèbert, P. (2011). Binge drinking: All too prevalent and hazardous. *Canadian Medical Association Journal, 183*(4), 411.

Fleming, L. M., & Tobin, D. J. (2005). Popular child-rearing books: Where is daddy? *Psychology of Men and Masculinity, 6*, 18–24.

Fletcher, A. C., Steinberg, L., & Williams-Wheeler, M. (2004). Parental influences on adolescent problem behavior: Revisiting Stattin and Kerr. *Child Development, 75*, 781–796.

Fletcher, B. R., & Rapp, P. R. (2013). Normal neurocognitive aging. In I. B. Weiner et al. (Eds.), *Handbook of psychology* (2nd ed., Vol. 3). New York: Wiley.

Fletcher, G., Simpson, J., Campbell, L., & Overall, N. (2015). Pair-bonding, romantic love, and evolution: The curious case of homo sapiens. *Perspectives on Psychological Science, 10*(1), 20–36.

Flint, M. S., Baum, A., Chambers, W. H., & Jenkins, F. J. (2007). Induction of DNA damage, alteration of DNA repair, and transcriptional activation by stress hormones. *Psychoneuroen-docrinology, 32*, 470–479.

Flom, R., & Pick, A. (2012). Dynamics of infant habituation: Infant's discrimination of musical excerpts. *Infant Behaviour and Development. 35*, 697–704.

Florsheim, P. (2003). Adolescent romantic and sexual behavior: What we know and where we go from here. In P. Florsheim (Ed.), *Adolescent romantic relations and sexual behavior: Theory, research and practical implications.* Mahwah, NJ: Erlbaum.

Florsheim, P., Moore, D., & Edgington, C. (2003). Romantic relationships among pregnant and parenting adolescents. In P. Florsheim (Ed.), *Adolescent romantic relations and sexual behavior.* Mahwah, NJ: Erlbaum.

Flouri, E., Midouhas, E., & Joshi, H. (2014, in press). Family poverty and trajectories of children's emotional and behavioral problems: The moderating role of self-regulation and verbal cognitive ability. *Journal of Abnormal Child Psychology.*

Flynn, J. R. (1999). Searching for justice: The discovery of IQ gains over time. *American Psychologist, 54*, 5–20.

Flynn, J. R. (2007). The history of the American mind in the 20th century: A scenario to explain IQ gains over time and a case for the relevance of *g.* In P. C. Kyllonen, R. D. Roberts, & L. Stankov (Eds.), *Extending intelligence.* Mahwah, NJ: Erlbaum.

Flynn, J. R. (2011). Secular changes in intelligence. In R. J. Sternberg & S. B. Kaufman (Eds.), Cambridge handbook of intelligence. New York: Cambridge University Press.

Flynn, J. R. (2013). Are we getting smarter? New York: Cambridge University Press. Fox, B. J. (2014). *Phonics and word study for the teacher of reading* (11th ed.). Upper Saddle River, NJ: Pearson.

Fong, P. (2013, March 18). Protecting the vulnerable still the goal, says government lawyer in B.C. right-to-die case. *The Star.* Retrieved from http://www.thestar.com/

Fonseca, E. B., Celik, E., Parra, M., Singh, M., Nicolaides, K. H., & the Fetal Medicine Foundation Second Trimester Screening Group. (2007). Progesterone and the risk of preterm birth among women with a short cervix. *New England Journal of Medicine, 357*, 462–469.

Fontana, L. (2009). The scientific basis of caloric restriction leading to longer life. *Current Opinion in Gastroenterology, 25*, 144–150.

Fontana, L., & Hu, F. B. (2014, in press). Optimal body weight for health and longevity: Bridging basic, clinical, and population research. *Aging Cell.*

Food Banks Canada. (2016). Hunger count 2015. Retrieved from https://www.foodbankscanada.ca/hungercount2015.

Food Banks Canada. (2012). Hunger count 2012. Retrieved from http://foodbankscanada.ca/getmedia/3b946e67-fbe2-490e-90dc-4a313dfb97e5/HungerCount2012.pdf.aspx

Forbes, J., et al. (2011). A national review of vertical HIV transmission. *AIDS, 26*, 757–763.

Forester, M. B., & Merz, R. D. (2007). Risk of selected birth defects with prenatal illicit drug use, Hawaii, 1986–2002. *Journal of Toxicology and Environmental Health, 70*, 7–18.

Forget-Dubois, N., Dionne, G., Lemelin, J-P., Perusse, D., Tremblay, R. E., & Boivan, M. (2009). Early child language mediates the relation between home environment and school readiness. *Child Development, 80*, 736–749.

Fosco, G., Frank, J., & Dishion, T. (2012). Coercion and contagion in family and school environments: Implications for educating and socializing youth. In S. R. Jimerson, A. B. Nickerson, M. J. Mayer, & M. J. Furlong (Eds.), *Handbook of school violence and school safety* (2nd ed.) (pp. 69–80). New York, NY: Routledge.

Foster, H., & Brooks-Gunn, J. (2008). Role strain in the transition to adolescence: Pubertal timing associations with behavior problems by gender and race/ethnicity. *Developmental Psychology.*

Foster-Cohen, S., Edgin, J. O., Champion, P. R., & Woodward, L. J. (2007). Early delayed language development in very preterm infants: Evidence from the MacArthur-Bates CDI. *Journal of Child Language, 34*, 655–675.

Fouad, N. A., & Bynner, J. (2008). Work transitions. *American Psychologist, 63*, 241–251.

Fowler, G. (1999). *As we grow old: How adult children and their parents can face aging with candor and grace.* Valley Forge, PA: Judson Press.

Fowler, J., & Rodd, E. (Eds.). (2013). The neuroscience of religious experience: Andrew Newberg LIVE on Big Think. Retrieved from http://bigthink.com/

Fox, N., Snidman, N., Haas, S., Degnan, K., & Kagan, J. (2015). The relations between reactivity at 4 months and behavioural inhibition in the second year: Replication across three independent samples. *Infancy, 20*(1), 98–114.

Fozard, J. (1992, December 6). Commentary in "We can age successfully." *Parade Magazine*, 14–15.

Francis, J., Fraser, G., & Marcia, J. E. (1989). *Cognitive and experimental factors in moratorium-achievement (MAMA) cycles.* Unpublished manuscript, Department of Psychology, Simon Fraser University, Burnaby, British Columbia.

Franke, S. (2003). Studying and working: The busy lives of students with paid employment (Cat. No. 11-008). *Canadian Social Trends, 68*(Spring), 22–25.

Frankel, L. (2005). An appeal for additional research about the development of heterosexual male sexual identity. *Journal of Psychology and Human Sexuality, 16*, 1–16.

Frankl, V. (1984). *Man's search for meaning.* New York: Basic Books.

Franklin, C. & Kercher, G. (2012). The intergenerational transmission of intimate partner violence: Differentiating correlates in a random community sample, *Journal of Family Violence, 27*, 187–199.

Franklin, U. (2006). *The Ursula Franklin reader: Pacifism as a map.* Toronto: Between the Lines Publishing.

Frederick, I. O., Williams, M. A., Sales, A. E., Martin, D. P., & Killien, M. (2008). Pre-pregnancy body mass index, gestational weight gain, and other maternal characteristics in relation to infant birth weight. *Maternal Child Health Journal, 12*(5), 557–567.

Frederikse, M., et al. (2000). Sex differences in inferior lobule volume in schizophrenia. *American Journal of Psychiatry, 157*, 422–427.

Free Omar. (2016). Omar Khadr in Edmonton court, has bail conditions relaxed. Retrieved from http://www.freeomar.ca

Freeman, J. (2009) *"Very young and gifted": Young gifted and talented web-site.* CfBT Education Trust.

French, D. C., Eisenberg, N., Vaughan, J., Purwono, U., & Suryanti, T. A. (2008). Religious involvement and the social competence and adjustment of Indonesian Muslim adolescents. *Developmental Psychology, 44*, 597–611.

Fretts, R. C., Zera, C., & Heffner, C. Z. (2008). Maternal age and pregnancy. In M. M. Haith & J. B. Benson (Eds.), *Encylopedia of infancy and early childhood*. London, UK: Elsevier.

Freund, A. M., & Lamb, M. E. (2011). Introduction: Social and emotional development across the life span. In R. M. Lerner, W. F. Overton, A. M. Freund, & M.E. Lamb (Eds.), *Handbook of life-span development*. New York: Wiley.

Frey, K. S., Hirschstein, M. K., Snell, J. L., Van Schoiack Edstrom, L., MacKenzie, E. P., & Broderick, C. J. (2005). Reducing playground bullying and supporting beliefs: An experimental trial of the Steps to Respect Program. *Developmental Psychology, 41*, 479–490.

Freyer-Adam, J., Gaertner, B., Tobschall, S. & John, U. (2011). Health risk factors and self-rated health among job-seekers. *BMC Public Health, 11*, 659.

Freytag. S., et al. (2014). A network-based kernel machine test for the identification of risk pathways in genome-wide association studies. *Human Heredity*, *76*, 64–75.

Friedlander, L., Connolly, J., Pepler, D., & Craig, W. (2007). Biological, familial, and peer influences on dating in early adolescence, *Archives of Sexual Behavior, 36*, 821–830.

Friedman, D. (2013). The cognitive aging of episodic memory: A view based on the event-related brain potential. *Frontiers in Behavioral Neuroscience, 7*, 111.

Friedman, E. M., & Herd, P. (2010). Income, education, and inflammation: Differential associations in a national probability sample (the MIDUS study). *Psychosomatic Medicine, 72*(3), 290–300.

Friedman, R. (2006). Uncovering an epidemic–screening for mental illness in teens. *The New England Journal of Medicine, 355*(26), 2717–2719.

Friedman, W. J. (2014). Development of memory for the times of past events. In P. Bauer & R. Fivush (Eds.), *Wiley handbook of children's memory*. New York: Wiley.

Friendly, M., Doherty, G., & Beach, J. (2006). *Quality by design: What do we know about quality in early learning and child care, and what do we think? A literature review.* Childcare Resource and Research Unit, University of Toronto. Retrieved from http://www.childcarequality.ca/wdocs/QbD_LiteratureReview.pdf

Friesen, J. (2010, November 25). Number of seniors living in poverty soars nearly 25%. *The Globe and Mail.* Retrieved from http://www.theglobeandmail.com/news/national/number-of-seniorsliving-in-poverty-soars-nearly-25/article1315450/

Fritsch, T., McClendon, M. J., Smyth, K. A., Lerner, A. J., Friedland, R. P., & Larson, J. D. (2007). Cognitive functioning in healthy aging: The role of reserve and lifestyle factors early in life. *Gerontologist, 47*, 307–322.

Fritschmann, N. S., & Solari, E. J. (2008). Learning disabilities. In N. J. Salkind (Ed.), *Encyclopedia of educational psychology.* Thousand Oaks, CA: Sage.

Fromm, E. (1956). *The art of loving.* New York: Harper & Row Publishers.

Fry, P. S. (2001). The unique contribution of key existential factors to the prediction of psychological well-being of older adults following spousal loss. *The Gerontologist, 41*, 69–81.

Frye, D. (1999). Development of intention: The relation of executive function of theory of mind. In P. D. Zelazo, J. W. Astington, & D. R. Oison (Eds.), *Developing theories of intention: Social understanding and self-control.* Mahwah, NJ: Erlbaum.

Fu, G., Xu, F., Cameron, C. A., Heyman, G., & Lee, K. (2007). Cross-cultural differences in children's choices, categorizations, and evaluations of truths and lies. *Developmental Psychology, 43*, 278–293.

Fujita, A., et al. (2014, in press). A novel WTX mutation in a female patient with osteopathia striata with cranial sclerosis and hepatoblastoma. *American Journal of Medical Genetics A*.

Fuligni, A. (2012). Gaps, conflicts, and arguments between adolescents and their parents. New *Directions for Child and Adolescent Developments, 135*, 105–110.

Fuligni, A. J., & Witkow, M. (2004). The postsecondary educational progress of youth from immigrant families. *Journal of Research on Adolescence, 14*, 159–183.

Fuligni, A.J., Witkow, M., & Garcia, C. (2005). Ethnic identity and the academic adjustment of adolescents from Mexican, Chinese, and European backgrounds. *Developmental Psychology, 41*, 799–811.

Fuller-Thomson, E. (2005). Grandparents raising grandchildren in Canada: Profile of a skipped generation. Social and economic dimensions of an aging population (SEDAP). Retrieved from http://socserv2.mcmaster.ca/sedap/p/sedap132.pdf

Fuller-Thomson, E., & Minkler, M. (2001). American grandparents providing extensive care to their grandchildren: Prevalence and profile. *The Gerontologist, 41*(2), 201–209.

Funai, E. F., Evans, M., & Lockwood, C. J. (2008). *High risk obstetrics.* Oxford, UK: Elsevier.

Furlong, A., & Cartmel, F. (2007). *Young people and social change: Individualism and risk in late modernity* (2nd ed). Buckingham: Open University.

Furlong, M., et al. (2003). Multiple contexts of school engagement: Moving toward a unifying framework for educational research and practice. *The California School Psychologist, 8*, 99–113.

Furman, E. (2005). *Boomerang nation.* New York: Fireside.

Furman, W. C., & Simon, V. A. (2008). Homophily in adolescent romantic relationships. In M. J. Prinstein & K. A. Dodge (Eds.), *Understanding peer influences in children and adolescents.* New York: Guilford.

Furman, W. C., Ho, M., & Low, S. (2005, April). *Adolescent dating experiences and adjustment.* Paper presented at the meeting of the Society for Research in Child Development, Atlanta.

Furman, W., Low, S., & Ho, M. (2009). Romantic experience and psychosocial adjustment in middle adolescence. *Journal of Clinical Child and Adolescent Psychology, 38*, 75–90.

Furth, H. G., & Wachs, H. (1975). *Thinking goes to school.* New York: Oxford University Press.

G

Gaff, C. & Hodgson, J. (2014). A genetic counselling intervention to facilitate family communication about inherited conditions. *Journal of Genetic Counselling, 23*(8), 814–823.

Gaffin, E., Martins, C., Healy, S. & Murray, L. (2010). Early social experience and individual differences in infants' joint attention. *Social Development, 19*(2), 369–393.

Gainer, J. (2012). Critical thinking: Foundational for digital literacies and democracy. *Journal of Adolescent & Adult Literacy, 58*(1), 14–17.

Gaines, J. M., Burke, K. L., Marx, K. A., Wagner, M., & Parrish, J. M. (2011). Enhancing older driver safety: A driving survey and evaluation of the CarFit program. *Journal of Safety Research*, *42*, 351–358.

Gajdos, Z., Hirschhorn, J., & Palmert, M. (2009). What controls the timing of puberty? An update on progress from genetic investigation. *Current Opinion in Endocrinology, Diabetes & Obesity, 16*, 16–24.

Galambos, N. L., Barker, E. T., & Tilton-Weaver, L. C. (2003). Who gets caught at maturity gap? A study of pseudomature, immature, and mature adolescents. *International Journal of Behavioural Development 2003, 27*(3), 253–263.

Galambos, N. L., Leadbeater, B. J., & Barker, E. T. (2004). Gender differences in and risk factors for depression in adolescence: A 4-year longitudinal study. *International Journal of Behavioural Development 2004, 28*(1), 16–25. Retrieved from http://www.tandf.co.uk/journals

Galambos, N., MacDonald, S., Naphtali, C., Cohen, S. A., & deFrias, C. (2005). Cognitive performance differentiates selected aspects of psychosocial maturity of adolescence. *Developmental Neuropsychology, 28*(1), 473–492.

Gallagher, J. (2016). Scientists get 'gene editing' go-ahead. *BBC News.* Retrieved from http://www.bbc.com/news/health-35459054.

Gallicano, G. (2010). Alcohol and its effect on fetal development: What do we know? *Pediatric Health, 4*(5), 459.

Gallo, L. C., Troxel, W. M., Matthews, K. A., & Kuller, L. W. (2003). Marital status and quality in middle-aged women: Associations with levels and trajectories of cardiovascular risk factors. *Health Psychology, 22*, 453–463.

Gallo, W. T., Bradley, E. H., Dubin, J. A., Jones, R. N., Falba, T. A., Teng, H. M., et al. (2006). The persistence of depressive symptoms in older workers who experience involuntary job loss: Results from the health and retirement survey. *Journal of Gerontology B: Psychological Sciences and Social Sciences, 61*, S221–S228.

Gamino, L. A., & Sewell, K. W. (2004). Meaning constructs as predictors of bereavement adjustment: A report from the Scott & White Grief Study. *Death Studies, 28*, 397–421.

Gandhi, S., & Abramov, A. Y. (2012). Mechanism of oxidative stress in neurodegeneration. *Oxidative Medicine and Cellular Longevity*, 428010.

Ganguli, M., et al. (2014). Vascular risk factors and cognitive decline in a population sample. *Alzheimer Disease and Associated Disorders*, *28*, 9–15.

Ganiban, J., Saudino, K., Ulbricht, J., Neiderhiser, J., & Reiss, D. (2008). Stability and change in temperament across adolescence. *Journal of Personality and Social Psychology, 95*, 222–236.

Ganong, L., & Coleman, M. (2006). Obligations to step-parents acquired in later life: Relationship quality and acuity of needs. *Journals of Gerontology B: Psychological Sciences and Social Sciences, 61*, S80–S88.

Ganong, L., Coleman, M., & Hans, J. (2006). Divorce as prelude to stepfamily living and the consequences of re-divorce. In M. A. Fine & J. H. Harvey (Eds.), *Handbook of divorce and relationship dissolution.* Mahwah, NJ: Erlbaum.

Garasen, H., Windspoll, R., & Johnsen, R. (2008). Long-term patients' outcomes after intermediate care at a community hospital for elderly patients: 12-month follow-up of a randomized controlled trial. *Scandinavian Journal of Public Health, 36*, 197–204.

Garcia-Bournissen, F., Tsur, L., Goldstein, L., Staroselsky, A., Avner, M., Asrar, F., et al. (2008). Fetal exposure to isotretinoin—an international problem. *Reproductive Toxicology, 25*, 124–128.

Garcia-Sierra, A., Rivera-Gaxiola, Conboy, B., Romo, H. Klarman, L. & Kuhl, P. (2009). Brain, behavioural, and sociocultural factors in bilingual language. *The Journal of Acoustical Society of America, 125*, 2779.

Gardner, D. S., Hosking, J., Metcalf, B. S., An, J., Voss, L. D., & Wilkin, T. J. (2009). Contribution of early weight gain to childhood overweight and metabolic health: A longitudinal study (Early Bird 36). *Pediatrics, 123*, e67–e73.

Gardner, H. (1983). *Frames of mind.* New York: Basic Books.

Gardner, H. (1993). *Multiple intelligences.* New York: Basic Books.

Gardner, H. (2002). The pursuit of excellence through education. In M. Ferrari (Ed.), *Learning from extraordinary minds.* Mahwah, NJ: Erlbaum.

Gardner, M., & Steinberg, L. (2005). Peer influence on risk taking, risk preference, and risky decision making in adolescence and adulthood. *Developmental Psychology, 41*, 625–635.

Garolla, A., Pizzol, D., & Foresta, C. (2011). The role of human papillomavirus on sperm function. *Current Opinions in Obstetrics and Gynecology, 23*, 232–237.

Garrett, D. D., Tuokko, H., Stajduhar, K. I., Lindsay, J., & Buehler, S. (2008). Planning for end-of-life care: Findings from the Canadian Study of Health and Aging. *Canadian Journal of Aging, 27*, 11–21.

Gartner, L. M., Morton, J., Lawrence, R. A., Naylor, A. J., O'Hare, D., & the American Academy of Pediatrics Section on Breastfeeding. (2005). Breastfeeding and the use of human milk. *Pediatrics, 115*, 496–506.

Gartstein, M., Bridgett, D., Rothbart, M., Robertson, C., Iddins, E., Ramsey, K. & Schlect, S. (2016). A latent growth examination of fear development in infancy: Contributions of maternal depression and the risk for toddler ansiety. *Developmental Psychology, 46*(1), 651–668.

Garvey, C. (2000). *Play* (enlarged ed.). Cambridge, MA: Harvard University Press.

Gathercole, S., Pickering, S., Ambridge, B., & Wearing, H. (2004). The structure of working memory from 4 to 15 years of age. *Developmental Psychology, 40*, 177–190.

Gathercole, V. C. M., & Hoff, E. (2007). Input and the acquisition of language: Three questions. In E. Hoff & M. Shatz (Eds.), *Blackwell handbook of language development.* Malden, MA: Blackwell.

Gauri, C. (July 2007). Cree Bilingual Program Named After Local Elder. *Alberta Sweetgrass*, *14*(8), 14. Retrieved from http://connection.ebscohost.com/c/articles/25576618/cree-bilingual-program-named-after-local-elder.

Gauvain, M. (2008). Vygotsky's sociocultural theory. In M. M. Haith & J. B. Benson (Eds.), *Encyclopedia of infant and early childhood development.* Oxford, UK: Elsevier.

Gauvain, M. (2013). Sociocultural contexts of development. In P. D. Zelazo (Ed.), *Oxford handbook of developmental psychology.* New York: Oxford University Press.

Gawande, A. (2015). *Being Mortal - Medicine and What Matters in the End*. Doubleday Canada.

Geary-Martin, C. (2013). Dr. Ursula M. Franklin, c.c. frsc. bronze. Retrieved from http://camie.ca/wordpress/galleries/commissions/ursula-franklin/

Gee, C. L., & Heyman, G. D. (2007). Children's evaluations of other people's self-descriptions. *Social Development*, *16*, 800–818.

Gee, E. M., & Prus. S. G. (2000). Income inequality in Canada: A "racial divide". In M. A. Kalbach, & W. E. Kalhach (Eds.). *Perspectives on ethnicity in Canada.* Toronto: Harcourt Canada.

Geers, A., Kosbab, K., Helfer, S., Weiland, P. & Wellman, J. (2007). Further evidence for individual differences in placebo responding: An interactionist perspective. *Journal of Psychosomatic Research, 62*, 563–570.

Gelman, R. (1969). Conservation acquisition: A problem of learning to attend to relevant attributes. *Journal of Experimental Child Psychology, 7*, 67–87.

Gelman, S. A. (2009). Learning from others: Children's construction of concepts. *Annual Review of Psychology, 60*, 115–140.

Gelman, S. A. (2013). Concepts in development. In P. Zelazo (Ed.), *Oxford handbook of developmental psychology.* New York: Oxford University Press.

Gelman, S. A., & Kalish, C. W. (2006). Conceptual development. In W. Damon &

R. Lerner (Eds.), *Handbook of child psychology* (6th ed.). New York: Wiley.

Gems, D. (2014). Evolution of sexually dimorphic longevity in humans. *Aging, 6*, 84–91.

Genesee, F. (2001). Bilingual first language acquisition: Exploring the limits of the language faculty. In M. McGroarty (Ed.) *Annual Review of Applied Linguistics: Language and Psychology,* Vol. 21 (pp. 153–168). New York: Cambridge University Press.

Genesee, F., & Jared, D., (2008). Literacy Development in Early French Immersion Programs. *Canadian Psychology*, *49*(2), 140–147. Retrieved from http://www.psych.mcgill.ca/perpg/fac/genesee/19.pdf

Genome Canada. (2012). Did you know? Retrieved from http://www.genomecanada.ca/en/info/dna/know.aspx

Genovese, J. E. C. (2003, June). Piaget, pedagogy, and evolutionary psychology. *Evolutionary Psychology, 1*, 127–137. Retrieved from http://www.human-nature.com/ep

Gentzler, A. L., & Kerns, K. A. (2004). Associations between insecure attachment and sexual experiences. *Personal Relationships, 11*, 249–266.

Geoffroy, M., Côté, S. M., Parent, S., & Séguin, J. R. (2006, August). Daycare attendance, stress, and mental health. *Canadian Journal of Psychiatry, 51*(9), 607–615.

George, L. G., Helson, R., & John, O. P. (2011). The "CEO" of women's work lives: How big five conscientiousness, extraversion, and openness predict 50 years of work experiences in a changing sociocultural context. *Journal of Personality and Social Psychology*, *101*, 812–830.

George, L. K. (2010). Still happy after all these years: Research frontiers on subjective wellbeing in later life. *Journals of Gerontology B: Psychological Sciences and Social Sciences, 65*(B), 331–339.

George, L. K., et al. (2013). Why gerontologists should care about empirical research on religion and health: Transdisciplinary perspectives. *Gerontologist*, *53*, 898–906.

George, M., Cummings, E. & Davies, P. (2010). Positive aspects of fathering and mothering, and children's attachment in kindergarten. *Early Childhood Development and Care, 180,* 107–119.

Georges, J. J., The, A. M., Onwuteaka-Philipsen, B. D., & van der Wal, G. (2008). Dealing with requests for euthanasia: A qualitative study investigating the experience of general practitioners. *Journal of Medical Ethics, 34*, 150–155.

Gerards, F. A., Twisk, J. W., Fetter, W. P., Wijnaendts, L. C., & van Vugt, J. M. (2008). Predicting pulmonary hypoplasia with 2-or-3 dimensional ultrasonography in complicated pregnancies. *American Journal of Gynecology and Obstetrics, 198*, e1–e6.

Gerber, L. (2014). Education, employment, and income polarization among Aboriginal men and women in Canada. *Canadian Ethnic Studies, 46*(1), 121–144.

Gerrard, M., Gibbons, F. X., Houihan, A. E., Stock, M. L., & Pomery, E. A. (2008). A dual-process approach to health risk decision-making. *Developmental Review, 28*, 29–61.

Gershoff, E. T., Mistry, R. S., & Crosby, D. A. (Eds.) (2014). *Societal contexts of child development*. New York: Oxford University Press.

Gerstenberg, F. X., Imhoff, R., Banse, R., & Schmitt, M. (2014). Discrepancies between implicit and explicit self-concepts of intelligence: Relations to modesty, narcissism, and achievement motivation. *Frontiers in Psychology*, *5*, 85.

Gervain, J. & Mehler, J. (2010). Speech perception and language acquisition in the first year of life. *Annual Review of Psychology, 61*, 191–218.

Gettler, L., McDade, T., Feranil, A., & Kuzawa, C. (2011). Longitudinal evidence that fatherhood decreases testosterone in human males. *Proceedings of the National Academy of Science, 108*(39), 16194–16199.

Ghetti, S., & Alexander, K. W. (2004). "If it happened, I would remember it": Strategic use of event memorability in the rejection of false autobiographical events. *Child Development, 75*, 542–561.

Giangregorio, L. M., et al. (2014, in press). Too fit to fracture: A consensus on future research priorities in osteoporosis and exercise. *Osteoporosis International.*

Giannarelli, F., Sonenstein, E., & Stagner, M. (2006). Child care arrangements and help for low-income families with young children: Evidence from the National Survey of America's Families. In N. Cabrera, R. Hutchens, & H. E. Peters (Eds.), *From welfare to childcare.* Mahwah, NJ: Erlbaum.

Giarrusso, R., & Bengtson, V. L. (2007). Self-esteem. In J. E. Birren (Ed.), *Encyclopedia of gerontology* (2nd ed.). San Diego: Academic Press.

Gibbs, J. C. (2014). *Moral development and reality: Beyond the theories of Kohlberg and Hoffman* (3rd ed.). New York: Oxford University Press.

Gibbs, J. C., Basinger, K. S., Grime, R. L., & Snarey, J. R. (2007). Moral judgment development across cultures: Revisiting Kohlberg's universality claims. *Developmental Review, 27*, 443–500.

Gibson, E. J. (2001). *Perceiving the affordances.* Mahwah, NJ: Erlbaum.

Gibson, E. J., & Walk, R. D. (1960). The "visual cliff." *Scientific American, 202*, 64–71.

Gibson, E. S., Powles, A. C. P., Thabane, L., O'Brien, S., Molnar, D.S., Trajanovic, N., et al. (2006). Sleepiness is serious in adolescence: Two surveys of 3235 Canadian students. *BMC Public Health, 6*, 116.

Giedd, J. N. (2007, September). Commentary in S. Jayson "Teens driven to distraction." *USA Today,* pp. D1–2.

Giedd, J. N. (2008). The teen brain: Insights from neuroimaging. *Journal of Adolescent Medicine, 42*, 335–343.

Giedd, J. N. (2012). The digital revolution and the adolescent brain. *Journal of Adolescent Health*, *51*, 101–105.

Giedd, J. N., Blumenthal, J., Jeffries, N. O., Castellanos, F. X., Liu, H., Zijdenbos, T. P., et al. (1999, October). Brain development during childhood and adolescence: A longitudinal MRI study. *Nature Neuroscience, 2*(10), 861–863.

Giedd, J. N., et al. (2006). Puberty-related influences on brain development. *Molecular and Cellular Endocrinology, 25*, 154–162.

Giedd, J. N., et al. (2012). Anatomic magnetic resonance imaging of the developing child and adolescent brain. In V. F. Reyna et al. (Eds.), *The adolescent brain*. Washington, DC: American Psychological Association.

Gielen, S., Sandri, M., Erbs, S., & Adams, V. (2011). Exercise-induced modulation of endothelial nitric oxide production. *Current Pharmaceutical Biotechnology, 12*(9), 1375–1384.

Giger, J., & Davidhizar, R. (2004). Introduction to transcultural nursing. In M. S. Ledbetter (Ed.), *Transcultural nursing: Assessment and intervention* (4th ed.) (pp. 3–19). St. Louis: CV Mosby.

Gilber, N., Auger, N., Wilkins, R. & Kramer, M. (2013). Neighbourhood income and neonatal, postnatal and Sudden Infant Death Syndrome (SIDS) Mortatlity in Canada, 1991-2005. *Canadian Journal of Public Health, 104*(3), e187–e192.

Giles, A., & Rovee-Collier, C. (2011). Infant long-term memory for associations formed during mere exposure. *Infant Behavior and Development, 34*, 327–338.

Gillam, M., Stockman, M., Malek, M., Sharp, W., Greenstein, D., Lalonde, F., ... Shaw, P. (2011). Developmental trajectories of the corpus callosum in attention-deficit/hyperactivity disorder. *Biological Society, (69)*, 839–846.

Gillen, M., Lefkowitz, E., & Shearer, C. (2006). Does body image play a role in risky sexual behavior and attitudes? *Journal of Youth and Adolescence, 35*, 230–242.

Gilligan, C. (1982, 1993). *In a different voice: Psychological theory and women's development.* Cambridge, MA: Harvard University Press.

Gilligan, C. (1992, May). *Joining the resistance: Girls' development in adolescence.* Paper presented at the symposium on development and vulnerability in close relationships, Montreal.

Gilligan, C. (1996). The centrality of relationships in psychological development: A puzzle, some evidence, and a theory. In G. G. Noam & K. W. Fischer (Eds.), *Development and vulnerability in close relationships.* Hillsdale, NJ: Erlbaum.

Gilligan, C., Spencer, R., Weinberg, M. K., & Bertsch, T. (2003). On the listening guide: A voice-centered relational model. In P. M. Carnic & J. E. Rhodes (Eds.), *Qualitative research in psychology* Washington, DC: American Psychological Association.

Gilliland, A. (2010). After praise and encouragement: Emotional support strategies used by birth doulas in the USA and Canada. *Midwifery, 27*, 525–531.

Gillum, R. F., & Ingram, D. D. (2007). Frequency of attendance at religious services, hypertension, and blood pressure: The third national health and nutrition examination survey. *Psychosomatic Medicine, 68*, 382–385.

Gillum, R. F., & Ingram, D. D. (2007). Frequency of attendance at religious services, hypertension, and blood pressure: The Third National Health and Nutrition Examination Survey. *Psychosomatic Medicine, 68*, 382–385.

Gilmore, J. (2009). *The immigrant labour force analysis: The 2008 Canadian immigrant labour market—Analaysis of quality of employment.* Ottawa: Statistics Canada, catalogue no. 71-606-X. Retrieved from http://www.statcan.gc.ca/pub/71-606-x/71-606-x2009001-eng.pdf

Gilmour, H. (2015). Social participation and the health of seniors. Statistics Canada. Retrieved from http://www.statcan.gc.ca/pub/82-003-x/2012004/article/11720-eng.htm.

Gimovsky, A., Khodak-Gelman, S., & Larsen, J. (2014). Making chorionic villus sampling painless for both the patient and the physician. *Journal of Ultrasound Medicine*, *33*, 355–357.

Gionet, L. (2015), Breastfeeding trends in Canada. Statistics Canada Catalogue 82-624-X. Retrieved from http://www.statcan.gc.ca/

Girling, A. (2006). The benefits of using the Neonatal Behavioral Assessment Scale in health visiting practice. *Community Practice, 79*, 118–120.

Gjerdingen, D., Katon, W., & Rich, D. E. (2008). Stepped care treatment of postpartum depression: A primary care-based management model. *Women's Health Issues, 18*, 44–52.

Gladwell, M. (2008). *The Outliers.* New York: Little, Brown and Company.

Glantz, J. C. (2005). Elective induction vs. spontaneous labor associations and outcomes. *Journal of Reproductive Medicine, 50*, 235–240.

Glick, G. C. (2004). On the demographic stratification in U.S. teenage pregnancy rates. Retrieved from http://artsci.drake.edu/dussj/2004/Glick.pdf

Gliori, G., Imm, P., Anderson, H. A., & Knobeloch, L. (2006). Fish consumption and advisory awareness among expectant women. *Wisconsin Medicine Journal, 105*, 41–44.

Glozah, F., & Lawani, S. (2014). Social change and adolescent rites of passage: A cross cultural perspective. *Journal of Human Sciences, 11*(1), 1188–1197.

Glynn, L. M., Schetter, C. D., Hobel, C. J., & Sandman, C. A. (2008). Pattern of perceived stress and anxiety in pregnancy predicts preterm birth. *Health Psychology, 27*, 43–51.

Godding, V., Bonnier, C., Fiasse, L., Michel, M., Longueville, E., Lebecque, P., et al. (2004). Does in utero exposure to heavy maternal smoking induce nicotine withdrawal symptoms in neonates? *Pediatric Research, 55*, 645–651.

Goel, A., Sinha, R. J., Dalela, D., Sankhwar, S., & Singh, V. (2009). Andropause in Indian men: A preliminary cross-sectional study. *Urology Journal, 6*, 40–46.

Gogtay, N., & Thompson, P. M. (2010). Mapping gray matter development: Implications for typical development and vulnerability to psychopathology. *Brain and Cognition, 72*, 6–15.

Goh, J. O. (2011). Functional dedifferentiation and altered connectivity in older adults: Neural accounts of cognitive aging. *Aging and Disease, 2*, 30–48.

Goh, V. I., & Koren, G. (2008). Folic acid in pregnancy and fetal outcomes. *Journal of Obstetrics and Gynecology, 28*, 3–13.

Goldberg, A., Smith, J., & Perry-Jenkins, M. (2012). The division of labor in lesbian, gay, and heterosexual adoptive parents. *Journal of Marriage and Family, 74*(4), 812–828.

Goldenberg, R. L., & Culhane, J. F. (2007). Low birth weight in the United States. *American Journal of Clinical Nutrition, 85* (Suppl.), S584–S590.

Goldschmidt, L., Richardson, G. A., Willford, J., & Day, N. L. (2008). Prenatal marijuana exposure and intelligence test performance at age 6. *Journal of the American Academy of Child and Adolescent Psychiatry.*

Goldstein, A. L., Amiri, T., Vilhena, N., Wekerle C., Thornton, T., & Tonmyr, L. (2012, December 13). Youth on the street and youth involvement in welfare: Maltreatment, mental health and substance use. Public Health Agency. Retrieved from http://www.phac-aspc.gc.ca/

Goldstein, M. H., King A. P., & West, M. J. (2003). Social interaction shapes babbling: Testing parallels between birdsong and speech. *Proceedings of the National Academy of Sciences, 100*(13), 8030–8035.

Gollnick, D. M., & Chinn, P. C. (2009). *Multicultural education in a pluralistic society* (8th ed.). Boston: Allyn & Bacon.

Golombok, S. (2011a). Children in new family forms. In R. Gross (Ed.), *Psychology* (6th ed.). London: Hodder Education.

Golombok, S. (2011b). Why I study lesbian families. In S. Ellis, V. Clarke, E. Peel, & D. Riggs (Eds.), *LGBTQ psychologies.* New York: Cambridge University Press.

Golombok, S., Rust, J., Zervoulis, K., & Croudace, T., Golding, J., & Hines, M. (2008). Developmental trajectories of sex-typed behavior in boys and girls: A longitudinal general population study of children aged 2.5–8 years. *Child Development, 79*, 1583–1593.

Gomez-Pinilla, F., & Hillman, C. (2013). The influence of exercise on cognitive abilities. *Comprehensive Physiology*, *3*, 403–428.

Gonzales-Backen, M. (2013). An application of ecological theory to ethnic identity formation among biethnic adolescents. *Interdisciplinary Journal of Applied Family Studies, 62*, 92–108.

Good, M., & Willoughby, T. (2008). Adolescence as a sensitive period for spiritual development. *Child Development Perspectives, 2*, 32–37.

Goodman, G. S., Ghetti, S., Quas, J. A., Edelstein, R. S., Alexander, K. W., Redlich, A. D., Cordon, I. M., & Jones, D. P. H. (2003). A prospective study of memory for child sexual abuse: New findings relevant to the repressed-memory controversy. *Psychological Science, 14*(2), 113–118.

Goodridge, D. (2010). End of life policies: Do they make a difference in practice? *Social Science & Medicine, 70*, 1166–1170.

Goodvin, R., Meyer, S., Thompson, R. A., & Hayes, R. (2008). Self-understanding in early childhood: Associations with child attachment security and maternal negative affect. *Attachment and Human Development, 10*, 433–450.

Goodvin, R., Winer, A. C., & Thompson, R. A. (2014, in press). The individual child: Temperament, emotion, self, and personality. In M. Bornstein & M. E. Lamb (Eds.), *Developmental science* (7th ed.). New York: Psychology Press.

Gorby, H. E., Brownawell, A. M., & Falk, M. C. (2010). Do specific dietary constituents and supplements affect mental energy? Review of the evidence. *Nutrition Reviews, 68*, 697–718.

Gorchoff, S. M., John, O. P., & Helson, R. (2008). Contextualizing change in marital satisfaction during middle age: An 18-year longitudinal study. *Psychological Science, 19*, 1194–1200.

Gordith, A., Brkic, S., & Soderpalm, B. (2011). Stress and consumption of alcohol in humans with a type I family history of alcoholism in an experimental laboratory setting. *Pharmacology, Biochemistry and Behaviour, 68*, 377–382.

Gordon, A. (2007, January 6). Time to let dads in. *Toronto Star*, pp. L1–L2.

Goritz, C., & Frisen, J. (2012). Neural stem cells and neurogenesis in the adult. *Cell: Stem Cell, 10*, 657–659.

Gosselin, J. (2010). Individual and family factors related to psychosocial adjustment in stepmother families with adolescents. *Journal of Divorce and Remarriage, 51*, 108–123.

Gostic, C. L. (2005). The crucial role of exercise and physical activity in weight management and functional improvement for seniors. *Clinical Geriatric Medicine, 21*, 747–756.

Gottleib, G., Wahlsten, D., & Lickliter, R. (2006). The significance of biology for human development: A developmental psychobiological systems view. In W. Damon & R. Lerner (Eds.), *Handbook of child psychology* (6th ed.). New York: Wiley.

Gottman, J. (2011). *The science of trust*. New York, NY: Norton.

Gottman, J. M. (1994). *Why marriages succeed or fail*. New York: Simon & Schuster.

Gottman, J. M. (2006, April 29). Secrets of long term love. *New Scientist, 2549*, 40.

Gottman, J. M. (2007). The magic relationship ratio. Retrieved from http://www.youtube.com/watch?v=Xw9SE315GtA

Gottman, J. M., & Gottman, J. S. (2009). Gottman method of couple therapy. In A. S. Gurman (Ed.), *Clinical handbook of couple therapy* (4th ed.). New York: Guilford.

Gottman, J. M., & Levenson, R. W. (2000). The timing of divorce: Predicting when a couple will divorce over a 14-year period. *Journal of Marriage and the Family, 62*, 737–745.

Gottman, J. M., & Parker, J. G. (Eds.). (1987). *Conversations of friends*. New York: Cambridge University Press.

Gottman, J. M., Gottman, J. S., & Declaire, J. (2006). *10 lessons to transform your marriage: America's love lab experts share their strategies for strengthening your relationship*. New York: Random House.

Gouin, K., Murphy, K., Prakesh and the Knowledge Synthesis Group on Determinanats of Low Birth Weight and Preterm Births. (2011). Effects of cocaine use during pregnancy on low birthweight and preterm birth: systematic review and metaanalysis. *American Journal of Obstetrics and Gynecology*, 204, 340e1–12.

Gould, M., Greenberg, T., Velting, D., & Shaffer, D. (2003). Youth suicide risk and preventative interventions: A review of the past 10 years. *Journal of the American Academy of Child and Adolescent Psychiatry, 42*, 386–405.

Goulet, C., Frappier, J., Fortin, S., Lampton, A., & Boulanger, M. (2009). Development and evaluation of a shaken baby syndrome prevention program. *Journal of Obstetric, Gynecologic and Neonatal Nursing, 38*, 7–21.

Gouvernment du Canada. (2013). Fertility. Retrieved from http://healthycanadians.gc.ca/healthy-living-vie-saine/pregnancy-grossesse/fertility-fertilite/fert-eng.php.

Government of Alberta. (2011). Employment standards: Adolescent and young persons. Retrieved from http://www.employment. alberta.ca/

Government of Alberta. (2014). Employment standards: Adolescents and young persons. Retrieved from http://www.work.alberta.ca

Government of Canada News Release. (2015). *Government of Canada launches inquiry into missing and murdered indigenous women and girls*. Retrieved from http://www.news.gc.ca.

Government of Canada. (2011). Early Childhood Development. Retrieved from http://www.dpe-agje-ecd-elcc.ca/eng/ecd/well-being/page11.shtml

Government of Canada. (2012). Chapter 9 - What Do We Know About Children with Disabilities in Canada? The Well-being of Canada's Young Children:

Government of Canada. (2013a). Eliminating mandatory retirement age. Canada's economic action plan. Retrieved from http://actionplan.gc.ca/en

Government of Canada. (2013b). Genetic testing and screening. Retrieved from http://www.healthycanadians.gc.ca/

Government of Canada. (2014). National dementia research and prevention Retrieved from http://healthycanadians.gc.ca/diseases-conditions-maladies-affections/disease-maladie/dementia-demence/plan-eng.php.

Government of Canada. (2015a). Autism Spectrum Disorder. Retrieved from http://healthycanadians.gc.ca/diseases-conditions-maladies-affections/disease-maladie/autism-eng.php

Government of Canada. (2015b). Childhood Obesity. http://healthycanadians.gc.ca/healthy-living-vie-saine/obesity-obesite/risks-risques-eng.php

Government of Canada. (2015c). Action for seniors report Retrieved from http://www.aines.gc.ca/eng/report/index.shtml#tc2a.

Government of Canada. (2015d). Report from the Canadian Chronic Disease Survey of Mental Illness in Canada, 2015. Retrieved from http://healthycanadians.gc.ca/publications/diseases-conditions-maladies-affections/mental-illness-2015-maladies-mentales/index-eng.php.

Government of Canada. (2015e). Elder abuse: It's time to face the reality. Retrieved from http://www.seniors.gc.ca/eng/pie/eaa/elderabuse.shtml

Government of Canada. (2016a). Family Life - Divorce Employment and Social Development Canada Retrieved from http://well-being.esdc.gc.ca/misme-iowb/.3ndic.1t.4r@-eng.jsp?iid=76

Government of Canada. (2016b). Canadians in Context- Households and Families. Retrieved from http://well-being.esdc.gc.ca/misme-iowb/.3ndic.1t.4r@-eng.jsp?iid=37

Government of Manitoba. (2016c). For the Sake of the Children Progam for Parents. Retrieved from https://www.gov.mb.ca/fs/childfam/for_sake_of_children.html

Goyal, M., Hersh, A., Badolato, G., Luan, X., Trent, M. Zaoutis, T. & Chamberlain, J. (2015). Underuse of pregnancy testing for women prescribed teratogenic medications in the emergency department. *Academic Emergency Medicine, 22*, 192–196.

Graber, J. (2013), Pubertal timing and the development of psychopathology in adolescence and beyond. *Hormones and Behaviour, 64*, 262–269.

Graber, J. A. (2008). Pubertal and neuroendocrine development and risk for depressive disorders. In N. B. Allen & L. Sheeber (Eds.), *Adolescent emotional development and the emergence of depressive disorders.* New York: Cambridge University Press.

Graber, J. A., & Brooks-Gunn, J. (2002). Adolescent girls' sexual development. In G. M. Wingood & R. J. DiClemente (Eds.), *Handbook of women's sexual and reproductive health.* New York: Kluwer Academic/Plenum Publishers.

Grady, C. L., Springer, M. V., Hongwanishkul, D., McIntosh, A. R., & Winocur, G. (2006). Age-related changes in brain activity across the adult lifespan. *Journal of Cognitive Neuroscience, 18,* 227–241.

Grafenhain, M., Behne, T., Carpenter, M., & Tomasello, M. (2009). Young children's understanding of joint commitments. *Developmental Psychology, 45,* 1430–1443.

Graham, G. M., Holt-Hale, S., & Parker, M. A. (2013). *Children moving* (9th ed.). New York: McGraw-Hill.

Graham, J. (2011). Measuring love in romantic relationships: A meta-analysis. *Journal of Social and Personal Relationships, 28*(6), 748–771.

Graham, S. (2005, February 16). Commentary in USA TODAY, p. 20.

Graham, S. (Ed.). (2006). Our children too: A history of the first 25 years of the Black caucus of the Society for Research in Child Development. *Monographs of the Society for Child Development, 71* (1, Serial No. 283).

Grambs, J. D. (1989). *Women over forty* (rev. ed.). New York: Springer.

Grammas, P., et al. (2014, in press). A new paradigm for the treatment of Alzheimer's disease: Targeting vascular activation. *Journal of Alzheimer's Disease.*

Grandner, M. A., Sands-Lincoln, M. R., Pak, V. M., & Garland, S. N. (2013). Sleep duration, cardiovascular disease, and proinflammatory biomarkers. *Nature Science: Sleep, 5,* 93–107.

Grant, L., Murray, S.A., & Sheikh, A. (2010). Spiritual dimensions of dying in pluralist societies. *British Medical Journal, 341,* 659–662.

Grant, N., Wardel, J., & Steptoe, A. (2009). The relationship between life satisfaction and health behaviour: A cross-cultural analysis of young adults. *International Journal of Behavioural Medicine, 7,* 259–268.

Graven, S. (2006). Sleep and brain development. *Clinical Perinatology, 33,* 693–706.

Gray, K. A., Day, N. L., Leech, S., & Richardson, G. A. (2005). Prenatal marijuana exposure: Effect on child depressive symptoms at ten years of age. *Neurotoxicology and Teratology, 27,* 439–448.

Gray, P. B., & Garcia, J. R. (2012). Aging and human sexual behavior: Biocultural perspectives—a mini-review, *Gerontology, 58*(5), 446–452.

Gredler, M. E. (2008). Vygotsky's cultural historical theory of development. In N. J. Salkind (Ed.), *Encyclopedia of educational psychology.* Thousand Oaks, CA: Sage.

Gredler, M. E. (2012). Understanding Vygotsky for the classroom: Is it too late? *Educational Psychology Review, 24,* 113–131.

Green, M. J., Espie, C. A., Hunt, K., & Benzeval, M. (2012). The longitudinal course of insomnia symptoms: Inequalities by sex and occupational class among two different age cohorts followed for 20 years in the west of Scotland. *Sleep, 35,* 815–823.

Green, R. J., & Mitchell, V. (2009). Gay and lesbian couples in therapy. In A. S. Gurman (Ed.), *Clinical handbook of couple therapy* (4th ed.). New York: Guilford.

Greener, M. (2011a). Thalidomide's shadow: Drug-induced teratogenicity. *Nurse Prescribing, 9*(5), 228–232.

Greener, M. (2011b). The tragedy of congenital abnormalities. *Nursing Prescribing, 9*(3), 117–121.

Greenfield, P., Keller, H., Fuligni, A., & Maynard, A. (2003). Cultural pathways through universal development. *Annual Review of Psychology (54)* 461–490. Palo Alto, CA: Annual Reviews.

Greenman, P., & Johnson, S. (2012). United we stand: Emotionally focused therapy for couples in the treatment of posttraumatic stress disorder. *Journal of Clinical Psychology, 68,* 561–569.

Greenough, A. (2007). Late respiratory outcomes after preterm birth. *Early Human Development, 83,* 785–788.

Greenstein, T. N. (2000). Economic dependence, gender, and the division of labor in the home: A replication and extension. *Journal of Marriage and the Family, 62,* 322–335.

Greer, F. R., Sicherer, S. H., Burks, A. W., & the Committee on Nutrition and Section on Allergy and Immunology. (2008). Effects of early nutritional interventions on the development of atopic disease in infants and children: The role of maternal dietary restriction, breast feeding, timing of introduction of complementary foods, and hydrolyzed formulas. *Pediatrics, 121,* 183–191.

Gregoire, C. A., et al. (2014). Untangling the influence of voluntary running, environmental complexity, social housing, and stress on adult hippocampal neurogenesis. *PLoS One, 9*(1), e86237.

Griffin, K. (2001, June 7). Educators spread antibullying message to elementary level. *Economist & Sun/Tribune.*

Griffiths, R., Horsfall, J., Moore, M., Lane, D., Kroon, V., & Langdon, R. (2007). Assessment of health, well-being, and social connections: A survey of woman living in western Sydney. *International Journal of Nursing Practice, 13,* 3–13.

Grigorenko, E. L., & Takanishi, R. (Eds.) (2012). *Immigration, diversity, and education.* New York: Routledge.

Grigoriadis, S., & Kennedy, S. H. (2002). Role of estrogen in the treatment of depression. *American Journal of Therapy, 9,* 503–509.

Grigsby, T., Forster, M., Baezconde-Garbanati, L., Soto, D., & Unger, J. (2014). Do adolescent drug use consequences predict externalizing and internalizing problems in emerging adulthood as well as traditional drug use measures in a Hispanic sample? *Addictive Behaviours, 39,* 644–651.

Grill, J. D., & Monsell, S. E. (2014). Choosing Alzheimer's disease prevention clinical trial populations. *Neurobiology of Aging, 35,* 466–471.

Groen, R., Bae, J., & Lim, K. (2012). Fear of the unknown: Ionizing radiation exposure during pregnancy. *American Journal of Obstetrics & Gynecology, 206*(6), 456–462.

Groer, M. W., & Morgan, K. (2007). Immune, health, and endocrine characteristics of depressed postpartum mothers. *Psycohoneuroimmunology, 32,* 133–138.

Grossman, K., & Grossman, K. E. (2009). The impact of attachment to mother and father at an early age on children's psychosocial development through early adulthood. In R. E. Tremblay, R. deV Peters, M. Boivin, & R. G. Barr (Eds.), *Encyclopedia on early childhood development.* Montreal: Centre of Excellence for Early Childhood Development.

Grotevant, H. D., & McDermott, J. M. (2014). Adoption: Biological and social processes linked to adaptation. *Annual Review of Psychology* (Vol. 65). Palo Alto, CA: Annual Reviews.

Grotevant, H. D., McRoy, R. G., Wrobel, G. M., & Ayers-Lopez, S. (2013). Contact between adoptive and birth families: Perspectives from the Minnesota/Texas Adoption Research Project. *Child Development Perspectives, 7*(3), 193–198.

Gruber, N., Mosimann, U. P., Muri, R., & Nef. T. (2013). Vision and night driving abilities of elderly drivers. *Traffic Injury Prevention, 15*, 477–485.

Grusec, J. E., Chaparro, M. P., Johnston, M., & Sherman, A. (2013). Social development and social relationships in middle childhood. In I. B. Weiner et al. (Eds.), *Handbook of psychology* (2nd ed., Vol. 6). New York: Wiley.

Gu, D., Dupre, M. E., Sautter, J., Zhu, H., Liu, Y., & Yi, Z. (2009). Frailty and mortality among Chinese at advanced ages. *Journals of Gerontology A: Biological Sciences and Medical Sciences, 64*, 279–289.

Gueguen, J., et al. (2012). Severe anorexia nervosa in men. Comparison with severe AN in women and analysis of mortality. *International Journal of Eating Disorders, 45*(4), 537–545.

Guelinckx, I., Devlieger, R., Beckers, K., & Vansant, G. (2008). Maternal obesity: Pregnancy complications, gestational weight gain, and nutrition. *Obesity Review, 9*, 140–150.

Guerrero, L., Anderson, P., & Afifi, W. (2011). *Close encounters: Communication in relationships* (3rd ed.). Thousand Oaks: Sage.

Guffanti, G., et al. (2013). Genome-wide association study implicates a novel RNA gene, the lincRNA AC068718.1, as a risk factor for post-traumatic stress disorder in women. *Psychoneuroendocrinology, 38*, 3029–3038.

Guilford, J. P. (1967). *The structure of intellect.* New York: McGraw-Hill.

Guirado, G. N., et al. (2012). Combined exercise training in asymptomatic elderly with controlled hypertension: Effects on functional capacity and cardiac diastolic function. *Medical Science Monitor, 28*, CR461–CR465.

Gump, B., & Matthews, K. (2000, March). *Annual vacations, health, and death.* Paper presented at the meeting of American Psychosomatic Society, Savannah, GA.

Gunderson, E. P., Rifas-Shiman, S. L., Oken, E., Rich-Edwards, J. W., Kleinman, K. P., Taveras, E. M., et al. (2008). Association of fewer hours of sleep at 6 months postpartum with substantial weight retention at 1 year postpartum. *American Journal of Epidemiology, 167*, 178–187.

Gunes, C., & Rudolph, K. L. (2013). The role of telomeres in stem cells and cancer. *Cell, 152*, 390–393.

Gunnar, M. R., & Quevado, K. (2007). The neurobiology of stress and development. *Annual Review of Psychology* (Vol. 58). Palo Alto, CA: Annual Reviews.

Gunnar, M. R., Fisher, P. A., & the Early Experience, Stress, and Prevention Network. (2006). Bringing basis research on early experience and stress neurobiology to bear on preventive interventions for neglected and maltreated children. *Development and Psychopathology, 18*, 651–677.

Gunning, T. G. (2013). *Creating literacy instruction for all children in grades pre-K to 4* (2nd ed.). Boston: Allyn & Bacon.

Gupta, R. (2011). Death beliefs and practices from an Asian Indian American Hindu perspective. *Death Studies, 35*, 244–266.

Gupta, R. P., de Wit, M. L., & McKeown, D. (2007, October). The impact of poverty on the current and future health status of children. *Paediatric Child Health, 12*(8), 667–672.

Gurrero, L., Anderson, P., & Afifi, W. (2011). *Close encounters: Communication in relationships* (3rd ed.). Thousand Oaks, CA: Sage.

Gurwitch, R. H., Silovsky, J. F., Schultz, S., Kees, M., & Burlingame, S. (2001). *Reactions and guidelines for children following trauma/disaster.* Norman, OK: Department of Pediatrics, University of Oklahoma Health Sciences Center.

Gustafson, T. (2014). Outlook on life may influence longevity, study finds. *Food and Health.* Solstice Publications.

Gustafsson, J. E. (2007). Schooling and intelligence: Effects of track of study on level and profile of cognitive abilities. In P. C. Kyllonen, R. D. Roberts, & L. Stankov (Eds.), *Extending intelligence.* Mahwah, NJ: Erlbaum.

Gutchess, A. H., Welsch, R. C., Hedden, T., Bangert, A., Minear, M., Liu, L. L., et al. (2005). Aging and the neural correlates of successful picture encoding: Frontal activations compensate for decreased medial-temporal activity. *Journal of Cognitive Neuroscience, 17*, 84–96.

Gutmann, D. L. (1975). Parenthood: A key to the comparative study of the life cycle. In N. Datan & L. Ginsberg (Eds.), *Life-span developmental psychology: Normative life crises.* New York: Academic Press.

Guttmacher Institute. (2006). Adolescents in Malawi, Uganda, and Ghana. Retrieved from http://www.guttmacher.org/

Guzzo, K. (2014). Trends in cohabitation outcomes: Compositional changes and engagement among never-married young adults. *Journal of Marriage and Family, 76*, 826–842.

H

Haaf, W. (2015). IVF & Infertility Clinics Across Canada - How much are we paying to get pregnant? Retrieved from http://www.wdish.com/health/ivf-infertility-clinic-costs-across-canada-how-much-are-we-paying-get-pregnant.

Habel, C., Feeley, N., Hayton, B. & Zelkowitz, P. (2015). *Midwifery, 31*, 728–734.

Hadders-Algra, M. (2011). Challenges and limitations in early intervention. *Developmental Medicine and Child Neurology, 53(Supp)*, 52–55.

Hadfield, J. C. (2014, in press). The health of grandparents raising grandchildren: A literature review. *Journal of Gerontological Nursing.*

Hahn, D. B., Payne, W. A., & Lucas, E. B. (2009). *Focus on health* (9th ed.). New York: McGraw-Hill.

Hahn, W. K. (1987). Cerebral lateralization of function: From infancy through childhood. *Psychological Bulletin, 101*, 376–392.

Hair, E. C., Moore, K. A., Garrett, S. B., Ling, T., & Cleveland, K. (2008). The continued importance of quality parent-adolescent relationships during late adolescence. *Journal of Research on Adolescence, 18*, 187–200.

Haith, M. M., Hazen, C., & Goodman, G. S. (1988). Expectation and anticipation of dynamic visual events by 3.5 month old babies. *Child Development, 59*, 467–479.

Hajek, P., Etter, J-F., Benowitz, N., Eissenberg, T., & McRobbie, H. (2014). Electronic cigarettes: review of use, content, safety, effects on smokers and potential harm and benefits. *Addiction, 109*, 1801–1810.

Halchuk, R., Makinen, J., & Johnson, S. (2010). Resolving attachment injuries in couples using emotionally focused therapy: A three-year follow-up. *Journal of Couple and Relationship Therapy, 9*, 31–47.

Halford, G. S. (2008). Cognitive developmental theories. In M. M. Haith & J. B. Benson (Eds.), *Encyclopedia of infancy and early childhood.*

Hall, C. B., Lipton, R. B., Sliwinski, M., Katz, M. J., Derby, C. A., & Verghese, J. (2009). Cognitive activities delay onset of memory decline in persons who develop dementia. *Neurology, 73*, 356–361.

Halonen, J., & Santrock, J. (2013). *Your guide to college success* (7th ed.). Boston, MA. Cengage Learning.

Halpern, D. F., Benbow, C. P., Geary, D. C., Gur, R. C., Hyde, J. S., & Gernsbacher, M. A. (2007). The science of sex differences in science and mathematics. *Psychological Science in the Public Interest, 8*, 1–51.

Halpern, I. F., & Brand, K. L. (1999, April). *The role of temperament in children's emotion reactions and coping responses to stress.* Paper presented at the meeting of the Society for Research in Child Development, Albuquerque.

Halseth, R. (2013). Aboriginal women in Canada: Gender, socio-economic determinants of health, and initiatives close the wellness gap. *National Collaborating Centre for Aboriginal Health*. Prince George, BC. Retrieved from http://www.nccah-ccnsa.ca.

Haltiwanger, E. P. (2013). Preventing falls. *Diabetes self-management, 30*, 10–12.

Hamamura, T., Heine, S. J., & Paulhus, D. L. (2008). Cultural differences in response styles: The role of the dialectical thinking. *Personality and Individual Differences, 44*, 932–942. Retrieved from http://www2.psych.ubc.ca/~heine/docs/2008DialecticalResponses.pdf http://www2.psych.ubc.ca/~heine/docs/2008DialecticalResponses.pdf

Hamann, J., Bronner, K., Margull, J., Mendel, R., Diel-Schmid, J., Buhner, M., Klein, R., Schneider, A. Kurz, A. & Perneczkey, R. (2011). Patient participation in medical and social decisions in Alzheimer's disease. *Journal of American Geriatric Society, 59*(11), 2045–2052.

Hamilton, J., Hamlat, E., Stange, J., Abramson, L. & Alloy, L. (2014). Pubertal timing and vulnerabilities to depression in early adolescence: Differential pathways to depressive symptoms by sex. *Journal of Adolescence, 37*, 165–174.

Hamilton, L. D., & Julian, A. M. (2014, in press). The relationship between daily hassles and sexual function in men and women. *Journal of Sex and Marital Therapy*.

Hamilton, M. A., & Hamilton, S. F. (2004). Designing work and service for learning. In S.F. Hamilton & M. A. Hamilton (Eds.), *The youth development handbook: Coming of age in American communities* (pp. 147–169). Thousand Oaks, CA: Sage.

Hamlin, J. K., Hallinan, E. V., & Woodward, A. L. (2008). Do as I do: 7-month-old infants selectively reproduce others' goals. *Developmental Science 11*(4), 487–494.

Hampton, et al. (2010). Completing the circle: Elders speak about end of life care with Aboriginal families in Canada. *Journal of Palliative Care, 6*(1), 6–14.

Hanish, L. D., & Guerra, N. G. (2004). Aggressive victims, passive victims, and bullies: Developmental continuity or developmental change? *Merrill-Palmer Quarterly, 50*, 17–38.

Hankin, B. L., Kassel, J. D., & Abela, J. R. (2005). Adult attachment dimensions and specificity of emotional distress symptoms: Prospective investigations of cognitive risk and interpersonal stress generation as mediating mechanisms. *Personality and Social Psychology Bulletin, 31*, 136–151.

Hannon, E., & Trehub, S. (2005). Tuning in to musical rhythms: Infants learn more readily than adults. *Proceedings of the National Academy of Science, 102*, 12639–12643.

Hansson, R. O., & Stroebe, M. S. (2007). *Bereavement in late life: Development, coping and adaptation*. Washington, DC: American Psychological Association.

Hanusaik, N., Maximova, K., Kishchuk, N., Tremblay, M., Parades, G., & O'Loughlin, J. (2012). Does level of tobacco control relate to smoking prevalence in Canada: A national survey of public health organizations. *Canadian Journal of Public Health, 103*(3), 195–201.

Hanvey, L. (2015). *Child and Youth with Special Needs*. Canadian Council on Social Development Retrieved from http://www.ccsd.ca/images/research/DisabilityResearch/PDF/ChildrenYouthSpecialNeeds_2001.pdf.

Harari, Y., Romano, G. H., Ungar, L., & Kupiec, M. (2013). Nature vs. nurture: Interplay between the genetic control of telomere length and environmental factors. *Cell Cycle, 12*, 3465–3470.

Harder, G., Rash, J., Holyk, T., Jovel, E., & Harder, K. (2012). Indigenous youth suicide: A systematic review of the literature. *Pimatisiwin: A Journal of Aboriginal and Indigenous Community Health, 10*(1), 125–142.

Hardy, M. (2006). Older workers. In R. H. Binstock & L. K. George (Eds.), *Handbook of aging and the social sciences* (6th ed.). San Diego: Academic Press.

Hargreaves, D. A., & Tiggemann, M. (2004). Idealized body images and adolescent body image: "Comparing" boys and girls. *Body Image, 1*, 351–361.

Harkins, S. W., Price, D. D., & Martinelli, M. (1986). Effects of age on pain perception. *Journal of Gerontology, 41*, 58–63.

Harley, T. A. (2009). *The psychology of language*. Philadelphia: Psychology Press.

Harlow, H. F. (1958). The nature of love. *American Psychologist, 13*, 673–685.

Harootyan, R. A. (2007). Volunteer activity in older adults. In J. E. Birren (Ed.), *Encyclopedia of gerontology* (2nd ed.). San Diego: Academic Press.

Harrington, S. E., & Smith, T. J. (2008). The role of chemotherapy at the end of life: "When is enough, enough?" *Journal of the American Medical Association, 299*, 2667–2678.

Harris, J., Golinkoff, R. M., & Hirsh-Pasek, K. (2011). Lessons from the crib for the classroom: How children really learn vocabulary. In S. B. Neuman & D. K. Dickinson (Eds.), *Handbook of early literacy research* (Vol. 3). New York: Guilford.

Harris, K. M., Gorden-Larsen, P., Chantala, K., & Udry, J. R. (2006). Longitudinal trends in race/ethnic disparities in leading health indicators from adolescence to young adulthood. *Archives of Pediatrics and Adolescent Medicine, 160*, 74–81.

Harris, K. R., Graham, S., Brindle, M., & Sandmel, K. (2009). Metacognition and children's writing. In D. J. Hacker, J. Dunlosky, & A. Graesser (Eds.), *Handbook of Metacognition in Education*. New York: Elsevier.

Harris, P. L. (2000). *The work of the imagination*. Oxford: Oxford University Press.

Harris, Y. R., & Graham, J. A. (2007). *The African American child*. New York: Springer.

Harrison, C. (2012). Aging: Telomerase gene therapy increases longevity. Nature Reviews. *Drug Discovery, 11*, 518.

Harrison, T. (2010). Family-centred pediatric nursing care. State of the science. *Journal of Pediatric Nursing, 25*, 335–343.

Hart, D., Atkins, R., & Donnelly, T. M. (2006). Community service and moral development. In M. Killen & J. Smetana (Eds.), *Handbook of moral development*. Mahwah, NJ: Erlbaum.

Hart, S. (2010). The ontogenesis of jealousy in the first year of life: A theory of jealolusy as a biologically based dimension of temperament. In S, Hart & M. Legerstee (Eds.), *Handbook of jealousy: Theory research and multidisciplinary approaches* (pp. 57–82). Malden, MA: Wiley-Blackwell.

Hart, S. & Behrens, K. (2013). Regulation of jealousy protest in the context of reunion following differential treatment. *Infancy, 18*(6), 1076–1110.

Hart, S., & Carrington, H. (2002). Jealousy in 6-month-old infants. *Infancy, 3*, 395–402.

Harter, S. (2012). *The construction of the self* (2nd ed.). New York: Wiley.

Harter, S. (2013). The development of self-esteem. In M. H. Kernis (Ed.), *Self-esteem issues and answers*. New York: Psychology Press.

Hartley, A. (2006). Changing role of the speed of processing construct in the cognitive psychology of human aging. In J. E. Birren & K. W. Schaie (Eds.), *Handbook of the psychology of aging* (6th ed.). San Diego: Academic Press.

Hartup, W. W. (1983). The peer system. In P. H. Mussen (Ed.), *Handbook of child psychology* (4th ed., Vol. 4). New York: Wiley.

Hartup, W. W. (1996). The company they keep: Friendships and their development significance. *Child Development, 67*, 1–13.

Hartup, W. W. (2009). Critical issues and theoretical viewpoints. In K. H. Rubin, W. M. Bukowski, & B. Laursen (Eds.), *Handbook of peer interactions, relationships, and groups.* New York: Guilford.

Hasher, L. (2003, February 28). Commentary in "The wisdom of the wizened." *Science, 299*, 1300–1302.

Hass, J. (2001). Rocking in the real world. *Canadian Medical Association Journal, 165*(9), 1288.

Hatfield, E., Rapson, R., & Martel, L. (2007). Passionate love and sexual desire. In S. Kitayama & D. Cohen (Eds.), *Handbook of cultural psychology* (pp. 760–779). New York: Guilford Press.

Hatzenbuehler, M., McLaughlin, K., & Nolen-Hoeksema, S. (2008). Emotional regulation and internalizing symptoms in a longitudinal study of sexual minority and heterosexual adolescents. *Journal of Child Psychology and Psychiatry, 49*, 1270–1278.

Hauser Kunz, J., & Grych, J. (2013). Parental psychological control and autonomy granting: Distinctions and associations with child and family. *Science and Practice, 13*(2), 77–94.

Hawkes, C. (2006). Olfaction in neurogenerative disorder. *Advances in Otorhinollaryngology, 63*, 133–151.

Hawkley, L. C., Thisted, R. A., Masi, C. M., & Cacioppo, J. T. (2010). Loneliness predicts increased blood pressure: 5-year cross-lagged analyses in middle-aged and older adults. *Psychology and Aging, 25*, 132–141.

Hayatbakhsh, R., et al. (2013). Early childhood predictors of early onset of smoking: A birth prospective study. *Addictive Behaviors*, *38*, 2513–2519.

Hayflick, L. (1977). The cellular basis for biological aging. In C. E. Finch & L. Hayflick (Eds.), *Handbook of the biology of aging.* New York: Van Nostrand.

Hayslip, B., & Hansson, R. (2003). Death awareness and adjustment across the life span. In C. D. Bryant (Ed.), *Handbook of death and dying.* Thousand Oaks, CA: Sage.

Hayward, I., Halinka Malcoe, L., Cleathero, L., Janssen, P., Lanphear, B., Hayes, M., Mattman, A., Pampalon, R. & Venners, S. (2012). Investigating maternal risk factors as potential targets of intervention to reduce socioeconomic inequality in small for gestational age: a population-based study. *Biomed Central Public Health, 12*, 1–13.

Hayward, R. D., & Krause, N. (2013b). Patterns of change in religious service attendance across the life course: Evidence from a 34-year longitudinal study. *Social Science Research, 42*, 1480–1489.

Hazan, C., & Shaver, P. R. (1987). Romantic love conceptualized as an attachment process. *Journal of Personality and Social Psychology, 52*, 522–524.

He, C., Hotson, L., & Trainor, L. J. (2009). Development of infant mismatch responses to auditory pattern changes between 2 and 4 months of age. *European Journal of Neuroscience, 29*, 861–867.

He, N., Wang, Z., Wang, Y., Shen, H., & Yin, M. (2013). ZY-1, a novel nicotinic analog, promotes proliferation and migration of adult hippocampal neural stem/ progenitor cells. *Cellular and Molecular Neurobiology*, *33*, 1149–1157.

Healey, J. F. (2009). *Race, ethnicity and class* (5th ed.). Thousand Oaks, CA: Sage.

Health Canada. (2005). Sudden infant death syndrome (SIDS). Retrieved from http://www.hc-sc.gc.ca/

Health Canada. (2007a). Eating well with Canada's Food Guide. Retrieved from http://www.hc-sc.gc.ca/

Health Canada. (2007b). Human papillomavirus (HPV). Retrieved from www.hc-sc.gc.ca/

Health Canada. (2007c). Canada's Food Guide. Retrieved from http://hc-sc.gc.ca/fn-an/food-guide-aliment/basics-base/quantit-eng.php.

Health Canada. (2010). Healthy Canadians: A federal report on comparable health indicators 2010. Retrieved from http://www.hc-sc.gc.ca/hcs-sss/pubs/system-regime/2010-fed-comp-indicat/index-eng.php

Health Canada. (2011a). Welcome to eat well and be active toolkit. Retrieved from http://www.hc-sc.gc.ca

Health Canada. (2011b). Lead and health. Retrieved from http://www.hc-sc.gc.ca/

Health Canada. (2011c). Lead-based paint. Retrieved from http://www.hc-sc.gc.ca/

Health Canada (2012a). Brain: Canada's brain research fund. Factsheet. Retrieved from http://www.hc-sc.gc.ca/ahc-asc/media/nr-cp/_2012/2012-60fs-eng.php

Health Canada. (2012b). Nutrition for healthy term infants: Recommendations from birth to six months. Statement of the Infant Feeding Joint Working Group: Canadian Paediatric Society, Dietitians of Canada and Health Canada. Retrieved from http://www.hc-sc.gc.ca/fn-an/nutrition/infant-nourisson/recom/index-eng.php

Health Canada. (2012c). First Nations and Inuit health: Fetal alcohol syndrome/Fetal alcohol effects. Retrieved from http://www.hc-sc.gc.ca/

Health Canada. (2012d). Food and nutrition: Principles and recommendations for infant feeding from birth to six months. Retrieved from http://www.hc-sc.gc.ca/

Health Canada. (2012e). Summary of results of the 2010–2011 Youth Smoking Survey. Retrieved from http://www.hc-ps/

Health Canada. (2013a). National native alcohol and drug abuse program. Retrieved from http://www.hc-sc.gc.ca/

Health Canada. (2013b). Retrieved from http://www.phac-aspc.gc.ca/cphorsphc-respcacsp/2009/fr-rc/pdf/cphorsphc-respcacsp-eng.pdf,

Health Canada. (2014). Summary Safety Review - Testosterone Replacement Products - Cardiovascular Risk. Retrieved from http://www.hc-sc.gc.ca/dhp-mps/medeff/reviews-examens/testosterone-eng.php.

Health Canada. (2015). Nutrition for healthy term infants: Recommendations from birth to six months. Retrieved from http://www.hc-sc.gc.ca/

Health Canada. (2016). First Nations and Inuit Health. Retrieved from www.hc-sc.gc.ca

Health Government Ontario. (2015*). Doctor-assisted dying end-of-life decisions*. Retrieved from http://www.ontario.ca/page/doctor-assisted-dying-and-end-life-decisions-consultation

Health, V. (2014). Genes and a hearty appetite conspire to increase childhood obesity risk. *Nature Reviews Endocrinology, 10*, 187.

Healthy Canada. (2011). Tetracycline. Retrieved from http://www.healthycanada.com

Healthy Child Manitoba. (2012). *Position paper: Developing a national prevalence plan for FASD in Canada.* Retrieved from http://www.canfasd.ca/.

Heaney, J. L. J., Carroll, D., & Phillips, A. C. (2014). Physical activity, life events stress, cortisol, and DHEA in older adults: Preliminary findings that physical activity may buffer against the negative effects of stress. *Journal of Aging and Physical Activity.*

Heart & Stroke Foundation. (2016). Statistics. Retrieved from http://www.heartandstroke.com/site/c.ikIQLcMWJtE/b.3483991/k.34A8/Statistics.htm

Heidrich, D. (2007). *The dying process.* In K. Kuebler, D. Heinrich, & P. Esper (Eds.), *Palliative and end-of-life-care* (2nd ed.) (pp. 33–45). St. Louis: Elsevier.

Heimann, M., Strid, K., Smith, L., Tjus, T., Ulvund, S. E., & Meltzoff, A. N. (2006). Exploring the relation between memory, gestural communication, and the emergence of language in infancy: A longitudinal study. *Infant and Child Development, 15*, 233–249.

Heine, C., Browning, C., Cowlishaw, S., & Kendig, H. (2013). Trajectories of older adults' hearing difficulties: Examining the influence of health behaviors and social activity over ten years. *Geriatrics and Gerontology International, 13*, 911–918.

Helgeson, V. (2012). *Psychology of gender* (4th ed.). Upper Saddle River, NJ: Pearson.

Helman, C. (2008). Inside T. Boone Pickens' brain. *Forbes.* Retrieved from http://www.forbes.com/

Helson, R. (1997, August). *Personality change: When is it adult development?* Paper presented at the meeting of the American Psychological Association, Chicago.

Helson, R., & Wink, P. (1992). Personality change in women from the early 40s to early 50s. *Psychology and Aging, 7*, 46–55.

Helwig, C. C., & Turiel, E. (2011). Children's social and moral reasoning. In P. K. Smith & C. H. Hart (Eds.), *Wiley-Blackwell handbook of childhood social development* (2nd ed.). New York: Wiley.

Henchoz, Y., Baggio, S., N'Goran, A., Studer, J., Deline, S., Mohler-Kuo, M., … Gmel, G. (2014). Health impact of sport and exercise in emerging adult men: A prospective study. *Quality of Life Research, 23*(8), 2225–2234.

Hendershot, C., Witkiewitz, K., George, W., & Marlatt, G. (2011). Relapse prevention for addictive behaviours. *Substance Abuse Treatment, Prevention, and Policy, 6*, 1–17.

Henderson, A. J. (2008). The effects of tobacco smoke exposure on respiratory health in school-aged children. *Pediatric Respiratory Review, 9*, 21–28.

Henderson, V. W. (2011). Gonadal hormones and cognitive aging: A midlife perspective. *Women's Health, 7*, 81–93.

Hennessey, B. A. (2011). Intrinsic motivation and creativity: Have we come full circle? In R. A. Beghetto & J. C. Kaufman (Eds.), *Nurturing creativity in the classroom.* New York: Cambridge University Press.

Henninger, M. L. (2013). *Teaching young children* (5th ed.). Upper Saddle River, NJ: Pearson.

Henretta, J. (2010). Lifetime marital history and mortality after age 50. *Journal of Aging and Health, 22*(8), 1198–1212.

Henrich, J. (2016). *The Secret of Our Success: How Culture is Driving Human Evolution, Domesticating our Species, and Making us Smarter.* Princeton University Press.

Henriksen, T. B., Hjollund, N. H., Jensen, T. K., Bonde, J. P., Andersson, A. M., Kolstad, H., et al. (2004). Alcohol consumption at the time of conception and spontaneous abortion. *American Journal of Epidemiology, 160*, 661–667.

Henry, N. J. M., Berg, C. A., Smith, T. W., & Florsheim, P. (2007). Positive and negative characteristics of marital interaction and their association with marital satisfaction in middle aged and older couples. *Psychology and Aging, 22*, 428–441.

Hepper, P. (2007). The foundations of development. In A. Slater & M. Lewis, *Introduction to infant development* (2nd ed.). New York: Oxford University Press.

Herbison, A. E., Porteus, R., Paper, J. R., Mora, J. M., & Hurst, P. R. (2008). Gonadotropin-releasing hormone neuron requirements for puberty, ovulation, and fertility. *Endocrinology, 149*, 597–604.

Herdt, G., & Polen-Petit, N. (2014). *Human sexuality.* New York: McGraw-Hill.

Herek, G. M. (2008). Hate crimes and stigma-related experiences among sexual minority adults in the United States: Prevalence estimates from a national probability sample. *Journal of Interpersonal Violence, 24*(1), 54–74.

Herman, C. P., van Strien, T., & Polivy, J. (2008). Undereating or eliminating overeating. *American Psychologist, 63*, 202–203.

Hermann-Giddens, M. E. (2006). Recent data on pubertal milestones in United States children: The secular trend toward earlier development. *International Journal of Andrology, 29*, 241–246.

Hermann-Giddens, M. E. (2007). The decline in the age of menarche in the United States: Should we be concerned? *Journal of Adolescent Health, 40*, 201–203.

Hernandez-Reif, M. (2007). Unpublished review of J. W. Santrock, *Life-span development* (12th ed.). New York: McGraw-Hill.

Hernandez-Reif, M., Diego, M., & Field, T. (2007). Preterm infants show reduced stress behaviors and activity after 5 days of massage therapy. *Infant Behavior and Development, 30*, 557–561.

Heroines.ca (2004). Biographies, Buffy Sainte-Marie (1941-). Musician, artist, and activist. A Guide to Women in Canadian History. Retrieved from http://www.heroines.ca/people/saintemarie.html.

Hertzman, C. (2009, December). The state of child development in Canada: Are we moving toward, or away from, equity from the start? *Paediatric Child Health, 14*(10), 673–676.

Hertzog, C., Kramer, A. F., Wilson, R. S., & Lindenberger, U. (2009). Enrichment effects on adult cognitive development. *Psychological Perspectives in the Public Interest, 9*, 1–65.

Hertz-Picciotto, I., Park, H. Y., Dostal, M., Kocan, A., Trnovec, T., & Sram, R. (2008). Prenatal exposure to persistent and non-persistent organic compounds, and effects on immune system development. *Basic and Clinical Pharmacology and Toxicology, 102*, 146–154.

Hetherington, E. M., & Kelly, J. (2002). *For better or for worse: Divorce reconsidered.* New York: Norton.

Hetherington, E. M., & Stanley-Hagan, M. (2002). Parenting in divorced and remarried families. In M. H. Bornstein (Ed.), *Handbook of parenting* (2nd ed., Vol. 3). Mahwah, NJ: Erlbaum.

Heyland, D., Cook, D., Rocker, G., Dodek, P., Kutsogiannis, D., Skrobik, Y., Jiang, X., Day, A. & Cohen, R. (2010). Defining priorities for improving end-of-life care in Canada. *Canadian Medical Association Journal, 182*(16), E747–E752.

Heyman, G. D., & Legare, C. H. (2005). Children's evaluation of sources of information about traits. *Developmental Psychology, 41*, 636–647.

Heyman, G. D., Fu, G., & Lee, K. (2013). Selective skepticism: American and Chinese children's reasoning about evaluative feedback. *Developmental Psychology, 49*, 543–553.

Hibbert, L., & Best, D. (2011). Assessing recovery and functioning in former problem drinkers at different stages of their recovery journeys. *Drug and Alcohol Review, 30*, 12–20.

Hickman, J. M., Rogers, W. A., & Fisk, A. D. (2007). Training older adults to use a new technology. *Journals of Gerontology B: Psychological Sciences and Social Sciences, 62* (Special Issue), P77–P84.

Higginbotham, B., et al. (2012). Stepfathers and stepfamily education. *Journal of Divorce & Remarriage, 53*, 76–90.

Higo, M., & Williamson, J. B. (2009). Retirement. In D. Carr (Ed.), *Encyclopedia of the life course and human development.* Boston: Gale Cengage.

Hilbrecht, M., Zuzanek, J., & Mannell, C. (2008). Time use, time pressure and gendered behaviour in early and late adolescence. *Sex Roles, 58*, 342–357.

Hill, M. A. (2007). Early human development. *Clinical Obstetrics and Gynecology, 50*, 2–9.

Hines, M. (2013). Sex and sex differences. In P.D. Zelazo (Ed.) *The Oxford Handbook of Developmental Psychology* (pp. 164–201). New York, NY: Oxford University Press.

Hingson, R. W., Heeren, T., & Winter, M. R. (2006). Age at drinking onset and alcohol dependence: Age at onset, duration, and severity. *Archives of Pediatric and Adolescent Medicine, 160*, 739–746.

Hirsh, J. (2008, January 2). 3-D dialogue: Ursula Franklin and pacifism. Retrieved from http://www.youtube.com/

Hirsh-Pasek, K., & Golinkoff, R. M. (2014, in press). Early language and literacy: Six principles. In S. Gilford (Ed.), *Head Start teacher's guide*. New York: Teacher's College Press.

Hirsh-Pasek, K., Golinkoff, R. M., Singer, D., & Berk, L. (2009). *A mandate for playful learning in preschool: Presenting the evidence*. New York: Oxford University Press.

Hita-Yanez, E., Atienza, M., & Cantero, J. L. (2013). Polysomnographic and subjective sleep markers of mild cognitive impairment. *Sleep, 36*, 1327–1334.

HLWIKI International. (2014). Constructivism. Retrieved from http://hlwiki.slais.ubc.ca/index.php/Constructivism

Hochberg, C., et al. (2012). Association of vision loss in glaucoma and age-related macular degeneration with IADL disability. *Investigative Ophthalmology and Visual Science, 53*, 3201–3206.

Hock, R. (2012). *Human sexuality* (3rd ed.). Upper Saddle River, NJ: Pearson.

Hockenberry, M., & Wilson, D. (2013). *Wong's essentials of pediatric nursing* (9th ed). St. Louis: Elsevier.

Hodapp, R. M., Griffin, M. M., Burke, M., & Fisher, M. H. (2011). Intellectual disabilities. In R. J. Sternberg & S. B. Kaufman (Eds.), *Cambridge handbook of intelligence*. New York: Cambridge University Press.

Hoefnagels, M. (2015, in press). *Biology* (3rd ed.). New York: McGraw-Hill.

Hoeger, W. W. K., & Hoeger, S. A. (2008). *Principles and labs for physical fitness* (6th ed.). New York: McGraw-Hill.

Hoek, H. W. (2006). Incidence, prevalence and mortality of anorexia nervosa and other eating disorders. *Current Opinion in Psychiatry, 19*, 389–394.

Hoelter, L. (2009). Divorce and separation. In D. Carr (Ed) *Encyclopedia of the life course and human development*. Boston, MA: Gale Cengage.

Hofer, S. M., Rast, P., & Piccinin, A. M. (2012). Methodological issues in research on adult development and aging. In S. K. Whitbourne & M. J. Sliwinski (Eds.), *Wiley-Blackwell handbook of adult development and aging*. New York: Wiley.

Hofer, T., Hohenberger, A., Hauf, P., & Aschersleben, A. (2008). The link between maternal interaction style and infant action understanding. *Infant Behaviour and Development, 31*, 115–126.

Hoff, E. (2014). *Language development* (5th ed.). Boston: Cengage.

Hoffmeyer, K., et al. (2012). Wnt/B-catenin signaling regulates telomerase in stem cells and cancer cells. *Science, 336*, 1549–1554.

Hofheimer, J. A., & Lester, B. M. (2008). Neuropsychological assessment. In M. M. Haith & J. B. Benson (Eds.), *Encyclopedia of infancy and early childhood.* Oxford, UK: Elsevier.

Hogan, C. L., Mata, J., & Carstensen, L. L. (2013). Exercise holds immediate benefits for affect and cognition in younger and older adults. *Psychology and Aging, 28*, 587–594.

Hogerbrugge, M. J., & Komter, A. E. (2012). Solidarity and ambivalence: Comparing two perspectives on intergenerational relations using longitudinal panel data. *Journals of Gerontology B: Psychological Sciences and Social Sciences, 67*, 372–383.

Hohenberger, A., Elsabbagh, M., Serres, J., de Schoenen, S., Karmiloff-Smith & Aschersleben, G. (2012). Understanding goal-directed human actions and physical casusality: The role of mother-infant interaction. *Infant Behaviour and Development, 35*, 898–911.

Holahan, C. J., et al. (2012). Wine consumption and 20-year mortality among late-life moderate drinkers. *Journal of Studies in Alcohol and Drugs, 73*, 80–88.

Holden, K., & Hatcher, C. (2006). Economic status of the aged. In R. H. Binstock & L. K. George (Eds.), *Handbook of aging and the social science* (6th ed.). San Diego: Academic Press.

Holden, S. (2013, January 17). When they hammered out justice in the 60's—Greenwich Village: Music that defined a generation. *New York Times.* Retrieved from http://movies.nytimes.com/

Holden, T. (2012). Addiction is not a disease. *Canadian Medical Association Journal, 184*(6), 679.

Holder, M. & Blaustein, J. (2014). Puberty and adolescence as a time of vulnerability to stressors that alter neurobehavioral processes. *Frontiers in Neuroscience, 35*, 89–110.

Hollich, G., Newman, R. S., & Jusczyk, P. W. (2005). Infants' use of synchronized visual information to separate streams of speech. *Child Development, 76*, 598–613.

Hollier, L., & Wendel, G. (2008). Third trimester antiviral prophylaxis for preventing maternal genital herpes simplex virus (HSV) recurrences and neonatal infection. *Cochrane Database of Systematic Reviews, 1*, CD004946.

Holmes, L. (2011). Human teratogens: Update 2010. *Birth Defects Research (Part A), 91*, 1–7.

Holmes, T. H., & Rahe, R. H. (1967). The social readjustment rating scale. *Journal of Psychosomatic Research, 11*, 213–218.

Holsen, I., Carlson Jones, D. & Skogbrott Birkeland, M. (2012). Body image satisfaction among Norwegian adolescents and young adults: A longitudinal study of the influence of interpersonal relationships and BMI. *Body Image, 9*, 201–208.

Holtslander, L., & Duggleby, W. (2010). The hope experienced of older bereaved women who cared for a spouse with terminal cancer. *Qualitative Health Research, 19*, 388–400.

Holtslander, L., Bally, J., & Steeves, M. (2011). Walking a fine line: An exploration of the experience of findings balance for older persons bereaved after caregiving for a spouse with advanced cancer. *European Journal of Oncology Nursing, 15*, 254–259.

Holtz, M. (2015, October, 22). Buoyed by election, Canadians roll out welcome mat to Syrian refugees. *The Christian Science Monitor.* Retrieved from http://www.csmonitor.com

Hoogendam, Y. Y., et al. (2014). Patterns of cognitive functioning in aging. *The Rotterdam Study, 29*, 133–140.

Hooley, J., Ho, D. E., Slater, J., & Lockshin, A. (2010). Pain perception and non-suicidal self-injury. *Personality Disorder: Theory, Research, and Treatment, 1*, 170–179.

Hopkins, J. R. (2000). Erikson, E. H. (2000). In A. Kazdin (Ed.), *Encyclopedia of psychology.* Washington, DC: American Psychological Association and Oxford University Press.

Hoppmann, C. A., Gerstorf, D., Smith, J., & Klumb, P. L. (2007). Linking possible selves and behavior: Do domain-specific hopes and fears translate into daily activities in very old age? *Journals of Gerontology B: Psychological Sciences and Social Sciences, 62*, P104–P111.

Hoppmann, C., & Smith, J. (2007). Life-history related differences in possible selves in very old age. *International Journal of Aging and Human Development, 64*, 109–127.

Horn, J. L., & Donaldson, G. (1980). Cognitive development II: Adulthood development of human abilities. In O. G. Brim & J. Kagan (Eds.), *Constancy and change in human development.* Cambridge, MA: Harvard University Press.

Horne, R. S., Franco, P., Adamson, T. M., Groswasser, J., & Kahn, A. (2002). Effects of body position on sleep and arousal characteristics in infants. *Early Human Development, 69*, 25–33.

Horney, K. (1967). *Feminine psychology.* New York: W.W. Norton & Company, Inc.

Horowitz, F. D. (2009). Introduction: A developmental understanding of giftedness and talent. In F. D. Horowitz, R. F. Subotnik, & D. J. Matthews (Eds.), *The development of giftedness and talent across the life span.* Washington, DC: American Psychological Association.

Horowitz, J. A., & Cousins, A. (2006). Postpartum depression treatment rates for at-risk women. *Nursing Research, 55* (Suppl. 2), S23–S27.

Hoshino, O. (2013). Ambient GABA responsible for age-related changes in multistable perception. *Neural Computation, 25*, 1164–1190.

House, J. S., Landis, K. R., & Umberson, D. (1988). Social relationships and health. *Science, 241*, 540–545.

Houston, D., & Bergeson, T. (2014). Hearing versus listening: Attention to speech and its role in language acquisition in deaf infants with cochlear implants. *Science, 139*, 10–25.

How, N., Jacobs, E., Vukelich, G., & Recchia, H. (2013). Canadian parents' knowledge and satisfaction regarding their child's day-care experience. *Journal of Early Childhood Research, 1*(2), 133–148.

Howard, A., & Rogers, A. N. (2014, in press). Role of translation factor 4G in lifespan regulation and age-related health. *Aging Research Reviews.*

Howard, A., Galambos, N., & Krahn, H. (2010). Paths to success in young adulthood from mental health and life transitions in emerging adulthood. *International Journal of Behavioural Development, 34*(6), 538–546.

Howard, A., Patrick, M., & Maggs, J. (2015). College student affect and heavy drinking: Variable associations across days, semesters, and people. *Psychology of Addictive Behaviours, 29*(2), 430–443.

Howe, M. L., & Courage, M. L. (2004). Demystifying the beginnings of memory. *Developmental Review, 24*, 1–5.

Howell, D. (2014). *Fundamental statistics for the behavioural science.* (8ed.). Boston: Cengage.

Howes, C. (2008). Friends and peers. In M. M. Haith & J. B. Benson (Eds.), *Encyclopedia of infant and early childhood development.* Oxford, UK: Elsevier.

Hoyer, W. J., & Roodin, P. A. (2003). *Adult development and aging* (5th ed.). New York: McGraw-Hill.

Hoyer, W. J., Rybash, J. M., & Roodin, P. A. (1999). *Adult development and aging* (4th ed.). New York: McGraw-Hill.

Hoyert, D. L., Mathews, T. J., Menacker, F., Strobino, D. M., & Guyer, B. (2006). Annual summary of vital statistics: 2004, *Pediatrics, 117*, 168–183.

Hoyt, M. A., & Stanton, A. (2012). Adjustment to chronic illness. In A. Baum, T. A. Revenson, & J. Singer (Eds.), *Handbook of health psychology* (2nd ed.). New York: Psychology Press.

HSBC Insurance. (2007). *The future of retirement: The new old age-global report.* London: Author.

HSLDA. (2016). Canadian Homeschool Research. Home School Legal Defense Association. Retrieved from http://www.hslda.ca/research.

Hsu, H. C. (2004). Antecedents and consequences of separation anxiety in first-time mothers: Infant, mother, and social-contextual characteristics. *Infant Behavior and Development, 27*, 113–133.

Hsu, J. L., et al. (2008). Gender differences and age-related white matter changes of the human brain: A diffusion tensor imaging study. *NeuroImage, 39*, 566–577.

Hsu, W. L., Chen, C. Y., Tsauo, J. Y., & Yang, R. S. (2014, in press). Balance control in elderly people with osteoporosis. *Journal of the Formosa Medical Association.*

Hu, H., et al. (2006). Fetal lead exposure at each stage of pregnancy as a predictor of infant mental development. *Environmental Health Perspectives, 114*, 1730–1735.

Hu, J. K., Wang, X., & Wang, P. (2014). Testing gene-gene interactions in genome-wide association studies. *Genetic Epidemiology, 38*, 123–134.

Huang, G., Unger, J., Soto, D., Fujimoto, K., Pentz, M., Jordan-Marsh, M., & Valente, T. (2014). Peer influences: The impact of online and offline friendship networks on adolescent smoking and alcohol use. *Journal of Adolescent Health, 54*, 508–514.

Huang, J., Dejong, W., Towvim, L., & Schnieder, S. (2009). Sociodemographic and psychobehavioural characteristics of US college students who abstain from alcohol. *Journal of American College Health, 57*(4), 395–410.

Huang, K., et al. (2014). MetaRef: A pan-genomic database for comparative and community microbial genomics. *Nucleic Acids Research, 42*, D618–D624.

Huart, C., Rombaux, O. P., & Hummel, T. (2013). Plasticity of the human olfactory system: The olfactory bulb. *Molecules, 18*, 11586–11600.

Hudson, A., Nyamathi, A., Greengold,B., Slagle, A., Koniak-Griffin, D., Khalilifard, E., & Getzoff, D. (2010). Health-seeking challenges among homeless youth. *Nursing Research, 59*(3), 212–218.

Hughes, C., & Ensor, R. (2007). Executive function and theory of mind.: Predictive relations from ages 2 to 4. *Developmental Psychology, 43*, 1447–1459.

Hughes, M. E., Waite, L. J., LaPierre, T. A., & Luo, Y. (2007). All in the family: The impact of caring for grandchildren on grandparents' health. *Journals of Gerontology B: Psychological Sciences and Social Sciences, 62*, S108–S119.

Hughes, M., Morrison, K., & Asada, K. (2005). What's love got to do with it? Exploring the impact of maintenance rules, love attitudes, and network support of friends with benefits relationships. *Western Journal of Communication, 69*, 49–66.

Hughes, T. F. (2010). Promotion of cognitive health through cognitive activity in the aging population. *Aging and Health, 6*, 111–121.

Hui, W. S., Liu, Z., & Ho, S. C. (2010). Metabolic syndrome and all-cause mortality: A meta-analysis of prospective cohort studies. *European Journal of Epidemiology, 25*(6), 375–384.

Huizink, A. C., & Mulder, E. J. (2006). Maternal smoking, drinking, or cannibis use during pregnancy and neurobehavioral and cognitive functioning in human offspring. *Neuroscience and Biobehavioral Research, 30*, 24–41.

Hultsch, D. F., Hertzog, C., Small, B. J., & Dixon, R. A. (1999). Use it or lose it: Engaged lifestyle as a buffer of cognitive decline in aging? *Psychology and Aging, 14*, 245–263.

Hulur, G., Infuma, F. J., Ram, N., & Gerstorf, D. (2013). Cohorts based on decade of death: No evidence for secular trends favoring later cohorts in cognitive aging and terminal decline in the AHEAD study. *Psychology and Aging, 28*, 115–127.

Human Cloning Foundation. (2012). Welcome to the official website of the Human Cloning Foundation. Retrieved from http://www.humancloning.org

Human Genome Project Information. (2009). Cloning fact sheet. U.S. Department of Energy Office of Science, Office of Biological and Environmental Research, Human Genome Program. Retrieved from http://www.ornl.gov/

Human Resources and Skills Development Canada. (2008). *Special reports—What difference does learning make to financial security?* Retrieved from http://www4.hrsdc.gc.ca/.3ndic.1t.4r@-eng.jsp?iid=54

Human Resources and Skills Development Canada. (2012a). *Chapter 2—The new economy, a changing society and a renewed agenda for labour standards.* Ottawa: Author. Retrieved from http://www.hrsdc.gc.ca/eng/labour/employment_standards/fls/final/page07.shtml

Human Resources and Skills Development Canada. (2012b). *Family life—Age of mother at childbirth.* Retrieved from http://www4.hrsdc.gc.ca/

Human Resources and Skills Development Canada. (2012c). *Indicators of well-being in Canada: Work–employment rate.* Retrieved from http://www4.hrsdc.gc.ca/.3ndic.1t.4r@-eng.jsp?iid=13#M_7

Hunt, C. E., & Hauck, F. (2006, June 20). Sudden infant death syndrome. *Canadian Medical Association Journal, 174*(13), 1861–1869.

Hur, K., Liang, J., & Lin, S. Y. (2014). The role of secondhand smoke in allergic rhinitis: A systematic review. *International Forum of Allergy and Rhinology, 4*, 110–116.

Hurd Clarke, L. (2006). Older women and sexuality: Experiences in marital relationships across the life course. *Canadian Journal of Aging, 25*, 129–140.

Hurt, H., Brodsky, N. L., Roth, H., Malmud, F., & Giannetta, J. M. (2005). School performance of children with gestational cocaine exposure. *Neurotoxicology and Teratology, 27*, 203–211.

Hurwitz, C., Duncan, J., & Wolfe, J. (2004). Caring for the child with cancer at the close of life. *Journal of the American Medical Association, 292*, 2141–2149.

Hutchins, A. (2015). What Canadians really believe: A surprising poll. *Maclean's*. Retrieved from http://www.macleans.ca

Hutchinson, D. M., & Rapee, R. M. (2007). Do friends share similar body image and eating problems? The role of social networks and peer influences in early adolescence. *Behavior Research and Therapy, 45*, 1557–1577.

Hwang, S.W., et al. (October 27, 2009). Mortality among residents of shelters, rooming houses, and hotels in Canada: 11 year follow-up study. *British Medical Journal, 339*, b4036. Retrieved from http://www.bmj.com/content/339/bmj.b4036.full.

Hyde, J. & DeLamater, J. (2014). *Understanding human sexuality* (12th ed.). New York: McGraw-Hill.

Hyde, J. S. (2005). The gender similarities hypothesis. *American Psychologist, 60*, 581–592.

Hyde, J. S. (2007a). *Half the human experience* (7th ed.). Boston: Houghton Mifflin.

Hyde, J. S. (2007b). New directions in the study of gender similarities and differences. *Current Directions in Psychological Science, 16*, 259–263.

Hyde, J. S. (2014). Gender similarities and differences. *Annual Review of Psychology* (Vol. 66). Palo Alto, CA: Annual Reviews.

Hyde, J. S., & Else-Quest, N. (2013). *Half the human experience* (8th ed.). Boston: Cengage.

Hyde, J. S., & Price, M. (2007, November). *When two isn't better than one: Predictors of early sexual activity in adolescence using a cumulative risk model.* Paper presented at the meeting of the Society for the Scientific Study of Sexuality, Indianapolis.

Hyman, I. E., & Loftus, E. F. (2001). False childhood memories and eye-witness errors. In M. L. Eisen, J. A. Quas, & G. S. Goodman (Eds.), *Memory and suggestibility in the forensic interview.* Mahwah, NJ: Erlbaum.

Hyson, M. C., Copple, C., & Jones, J. (2006). Early childhood development and education. In W. Damon & R. Lerner (Eds.), *Handbook of child psychology* (6th ed.). New York: Wiley.

I

Iacono, M. V. (2007). Osteoporosis: A national public health priority. *Journal of Perianesthesia Nursing, 223*, 175–180.

ICM. (2011). *ICM international definition of the midwife*. The Hague: International Confederation of Midwives.

Igarashi, H., Hooker, K., Coehlo, D. P., & Manoogian, M. M. (2013). "My nest is full": Intergenerational relationships at midlife. *Journal of Aging Studies, 27*, 102–112.

Ikeda, A., et al. (2007). Marital status and mortality among Japanese men and women: The Japanese Collaborative Cohort Study. *BMC Public Health, 7*, 73.

Imada, T., Zhang, Y., Cheour, M., Taulu, S., Ahonen, A., & Kuhl, P. K. (2007). Infant speech perception activates Broca's area: A developmental magnetoencephalography study. *Neuroreport, 17*, 957–962.

Impett, E. A., Schooler, D., Tolman, L., Sorsoli, L., & Henson, J. M. (2008). Girls' relationship authenticity and self-esteem across adolescence. *Developmental Psychology, 44*, 722–733.

Indian Residential Schools Agreement. (2011). Schedule "N." Mandate for the truth and Reconciliation Commission. Retrieved from http://www.trc.ca/websites/trcintitution/File/pdfs/SCHEDULE_N_.pdf.

Insel, P. M., & Roth, W. T. (2008). *Core concepts in health* (10th ed.). New York: McGraw-Hill.

Institute of Marriage and Family Canada. (2013). *Cohabitation in Canada.* Retrieved from http://www.statcan.gc.ca.

International Clearinghouse for Birth Defects Monitoring Systems. (2001). *Annual Report.* Rome, Italy.

Intersex Society of North America. (2008). How Common is Intersex? Retrieved from http://www.isna.org/faq/frequency.

Iolascon, G., et al. (2013). Osteoporosis drugs in real-world clinical practice: An analysis of persistence. *Aging: Clinical and Experimental Research, 25*(1, Suppl.), S137–S141.

Iovannone, R. (2013). Teaching students with autism spectrum disorders. In B. G. Cook & M. G. Tankerslee (Ed.), *Research-based practices in special education.* Upper Saddle River, NJ: Pearson.

Ip, S., Chung, M., Raman, G., Chew, P., Magula, N., Devine, D., et al. (2007). Breastfeeding and maternal and infant health outcomes in developed countries. *Evidence Report/Technology Assessment, 153*, 1–86.

Iranmanesh, S., Hosseini, H., & Esmaili, M. (2011). Evaluating the "good death" concept from Iranian bereaved family members' perspective. *The Journal of Supportive Oncology, 9*(2), 59–63.

Isayama, T., Shoo, K., Mori, R., Kusuda, S., Fujimura, M., Xiang Y., ... Neonatal Research Network of Japan. (2012). Comparison of mortality and morbidity of very low birth weight infants between Canada and Japan. *Pediatrics, 130*, E957–E965.

Isidori, A. M., et al. (2014). A critical analysis of the role of testosterone in erectile function: From pathophysiology to treatment—a systematic analysis. *European Urology, 65*(1), 99–112.

Izard, C. (2009). Emotion theory and research: Highlights, unanswered question, and emerging issues. *Annual Review of Psychology, 60*, 1–25.

J

Jack, S. (2011). Child maltreatment in Canada. National Clearinghouse on Family Violence. Public Health Agency of Canada. Retrieved from http://www.phac-aspc.gc.ca/ncfv-cnivf/pdfs/nfnts-2006-maltr-eng.pdf

Jackson, J. J., et al. (2009). Not all conscientiousness scales change alike: A multimethod, multisample study of age differences in the facets of conscientiousness. *Journal of Personality and Social Psychology, 96*, 446–459.

Jackson, S. L. (2008). *Research methods.* Belmont, CA: Wadsworth.

Jacobs, J. M., Hammerman-Rozenberg, R., Cohen, A., & Stressman, J. (2008). Reading daily predicts reduced mortality among men from a cohort of community-dwelling 70-year-olds. *Journals of*

Gerontology B: Psychological Sciences and Social Sciences, 63, S73–S80.

Jacobs-Lawson, J. M., Hershey, D. A., & Neukam, K. A. (2005). Gender differences in factors that influence time spent planning for retirement. *Journal of Women and Aging, 16*, 55–69.

Jaeggi, S. M., Berman, M. G., & Jonides, J. (2009). Training attentional processes. *Trends in Cognitive Science, 37*, 644–654.

Jaffee, S. R., et al. (2013). Safe, stable, nurturing relationships break the intergenerational cycle of abuse: A nationally representative cohort of children in the United Kingdom. *Journal of Adolescent Health, 53*(4, Suppl.), S4–S10.

Jaffee, S., & Hyde, J. S. (2000). Gender differences in moral orientation: A metaanalysis. *Psychological Bulletin, 126*, 703–726.

Jain, M. M., Joshi, A., Tayade, N. G., Jaiswar, S. R., & Thakkar, K. B. (2013, January 16). Knowledge, attitude, and practices regarding "The role of spirituality in current medical practice amongst medical professionals" in a tertiary care hospital. *Journal of Medical and Dental Sciences.* Retrieved from http://www.jemds.com/

Jalongo, M. R. (2014). *Early childhood language arts* (6th ed.). Upper Saddle River, NJ: Pearson.

James, A. H., Brancazio, L. R., & Price, T. (2008). Aspirin and reproductive outcomes. *Obstetrical and Gynecological Survey, 63*, 49–57.

James, W. H. (2005). Biological and psychosocial determinants of male and female human sexual orientation. *Journal of Biosocial Science, 37*, 555–567.

Jamshidi, Y., Snieder, H., Ge, D., Spector, T. D., & O'Dell, S. D. (2007). The SH2B gene is associated with serum leptin and body fat in normal female twins. *Obesity, 15*, 5–9.

Janacek, R. J., Anderson, N., Liu, M., Zheng, S., Yang, Q., & Tso, P. (2005). Effects of yo-yo diet, caloric restriction, and olestra on tissue distribution of hexachlorobenzene. *American Journal of Physiology and Gastrointestinal Liver Physiology, 288*, G292–G299.

Janssen, P., Saxell, M., Page, L., Klein, M., Liston, R., & Lee, S. (2009). Outcomes of planned home births with registered midwife versus planned hospital birth with midwife or physician. *Canadian Medical Association Journal, 181*(6–7), 377–383.

Janus, M, Duku, E. Schell, A. (2012) The Full Day Kindergarten Early Learning Program Final Report. Offord Centre for Child Studies, McMaster University. Retrieved from http://www.edu.gov.on.ca/kindergarten/ELP_FDKFall2012.pdf

Jaremka, L. M., et al. (2013b). Loneliness promotes inflammation during acute stress. *Psychological Science, 24*, 1089–1097.

Jaremka, L. M., et al. (2014, in press). Pain, depression, and fatigue: Loneliness as a longitudinal risk factor. *Health Psychology*.

Jaremka, L. M., Glaser, R., Malarkey, W. B., & Kiecolt-Glaser, J. K. (2013a). Marital distress prospectively predicts poorer cellular immune function. *Psychoneuroendocrinology, 38*(11), 2713–2719.

Jarosinka, D., Polanska, K., Woityniak, B., & Hanke, W. (2014, in press). Toward estimating the burden of disease attributable to second-hand smoke exposure in Polish children. *International Journal of Occupational Medicine and Environmental Health*.

Jarry, V., Gagnon, A., Bourbeau, R. (2012) The advantage of siblings and spouses of centenarians in the 20th century. *Canadian Studies in Population, 39*(3-4). Retrieved from https://ejournals.library.ualberta.ca/index.php/csp/article/view/18970.

Jasik, C. B., & Lustig, R. H. (2008). Adolescent obesity and puberty: The "perfect storm." *Annals of the New York Academy of Sciences, 1135*, 265–279.

Javo, C., Rønning, J. A., & Heyerdahl, S. (2004). Child-rearing in an indigenous Sami population in Norway: A cross-cultural comparison of parental attitudes and expectations. *Scandinavian Journal of Psychology, 45*, 67–78.

Jellinger, K. A., & Attems, J. (2013). Neuropathological approaches to cerebral aging and neuroplasticity. *Dialogues in Clinical Neuroscience, 15*, 29–43.

Jensen, P. S., et al. (2007). Three-year follow-up of the NIMH MTA study. *Journal of the American Academy of Child and Adolescent Psychiatry, 46*, 989–1002.

Jeschonek, S., Pauen, S. & Baboscai, L. (2013). Cross-modal mapping of visual and acoustic displays in infants: The effect of dynamic static components. *European Journal of Developmental Psychology. 10*(3), 337–358.

Jessberger, S., & Gage, F. H. (2008). Stem-cell-associated structural and functional plasticity in the aging hippocampus. *Psychology and Aging, 23*, 684–691.

Jeste, D. V., & Oswald, A. J. (2014, in press). Individual and societal wisdom: Explaining the paradox of human aging and high well-being. *Psychiatry.*

Jeste, D. V., et al. (2013). Association between older and more successful aging: Critical role of resilience and depression. *American Journal of Psychiatry, 170*, 188–196.

Jha, A. (2012, October 14). Childhood stimulation key to brain development, study finds. *Special Needs Digest, 20*(5), 530–537.

Ji, C. Y., & Chen, T. J. (2008). Secular changes in stature and body mass index for Chinese youth in sixteen major cities, 1950s–2005. *American Journal of Human Biology, 67*(2), 387–395.

Jiang, T., Yu, J. T., Tian, Y., & Tan, L. (2013). Epidemiology and etiology of Alzheimer's disease: From genetic to non-genetic factors. *Current Alzheimer Research, 10*, 852–867.

Jimeno, C. et al. (2010). *Immigrant children, youth & families: A qualitative analysis of the challenges of integration*. Families in Community - A project of the Social Planning Council of Ottawa. Retrieved from http://www.spcottawa.on.ca/sites/all/files/pdf/2010/Publications/Immigrant-Family-Report-English.pdf.

Jinyao, Y., Xiongzhao, Z., Auerbach, R., Gardiner, C., Lin, C., Yuping, W., Shuqiao, Y. (2012). Insecure attachment as a predictor of depressive and anxious symptomology. *Depression and Anxiety, 29*, 789–796.

Johnson, C. L., & Troll, L. E. (1992). Family functioning in late life. *Journals of Gerontology, 47*, S66–S72.

Johnson, F., & Wardle, J. (2005). Dietary restraint, body dissatisfaction, and psychological distress: a prospective analysis. *Journal of Abnormal Psychology, 114*(1), 119.

Johnson, G. B. (2015, in press). *The living world* (8th ed.). New York: McGraw-Hill.

Johnson, H. L., Erbelding, E. J., & Ghanem, K. G. (2007). Sexually transmitted infections during pregnancy. *Current Infectious Disease Reports, 9*, 125–133.

Johnson, H., & Colpitts, E. (2013). Fact sheet: Violence against women in Canada. *CIRAW*. Retrieved from http://www.ciraw-icref.ca.

Johnson, J. A., Musial, D. L., Hall, G. E., & Gollnick, D. M. (2011). *Foundations of American education* (15th ed.). Upper Saddle River, NJ: Prentice Hall.

Johnson, J. G., Zhang, B., Greer, J. A., & Prigerson, H. G. (2007). Parental control, partner dependency, and complicated grief among widowed adults in the community. *Journal of Nervous and Mental Disease, 195*, 26–30.

Johnson, K., & Daviss, B. (2005). Outcomes of planed home births with certified professional midwives: Large prospective study in North America. *British Medical Journal, 330*(7505), 1416.

Johnson, M., Anderson, J., & Aducci, C. (2011). Understanding the decision to marry versus cohabit: The role of interpersonal dedication and constraints and the impact on life satisfaction. *Marriage and Family Review, 47*, 73–89.

Johnson, M., Crosnoe, R. & Elder, Jr. G. (2011). Insights on adolescence from a life course perspective. *Journal of Research on Adolescence, 21*(1), 273–280.

Johnson, S. (2004), *The practice of emotionally focused marital therapy: Creating connections* (2nd ed.). New York: Brunner/Mazel.

Johnson, S. (2007). Cognitive and behavioral outcomes following very preterm birth. *Seminars in Fetal and Neonatal Medicine, 12*, 363–373.

Johnson, S. (2016). *About Dr. Sue Johnson*. Retrieved from http://www.drsuejohnson.com.

Johnson, S., Dariotis, J. & Wang, C. (2012). Adolescent risk taking under stressed and nonstressed conditions: Conservative, calculating, and impulsive types. *Journal of Adolescent Health, 51*, S34–S40.

Johnson-Agbakwu, C., Flynn, P., Asiedu, G., Hedberg, E., & Radecki Breitkopf, C. (2016). Adaptation of an acculturation scale for African refugee women. *Journal of Immigrant Minority Health, 18*, 252–262.

John-Steiner, V. (2007). Vygotsky on thinking and speaking. In H. Daniels, J. Wertsch, & M. Cole (Eds.), *The Cambridge companion to Vygotsky*. New York: Cambridge University Press.

Johnston, A. M., Barnes, M. A., & Desrochers, A. (2008). Reading comprehension: Developmental processes, individual differences, and interventions. *Canadian Psychology, 49*(2), 125–132.

Johnston, B. B. (2008). Will increasing folic acid in fortified grain products further reduce neural tube defects without causing harm? Consideration of the evidence. *Pediatric Research, 63*, 2–8.

Johnston, L. D., O'Malley, P. M., Bachman, J. G., & Schulenberg, J. E. (2007). *Monitoring the future national survey results on drug use, 1975–2006. Vol. II: College students and adults ages 19–45* (NIH Publication No. 07-6206). Bethesda, MD: National Institute on Drug Abuse.

Johnston, L., O'Malley, P., Bachman, J., Schulenberg, J., & Miech, R. (2015). *Monitoring the Future national survey results on drug use, 1975-2014: Volume II, college students and adults ages 19-55.* Ann Arbor: Institute for Social Research, The University of Michigan. Retrieved from http://www.monitoringthefuture.org.

Joint Economic Committee. (2007, February). *Investing in raising children.* Washington, DC: U.S. Senate.

Jolley, S. N., Ellmore, S., Barnard, K. E., & Carr, D. B. (2007). Dysregulation of the hypothalamic-pituitary-adrenal axis in postpartum depression. *Biological Research for Nursing, 8*, 210–222.

Jolly, C. A. (2005). Diet manipulation and prevention of aging, cancer, and autoimmune disease. *Current Opinions in Clinical Nutrition and Metabolic Care, 8*, 382–387.

Jones, B. F., Reedy, E. J., & Weinberg, B. A. (2014). Age and scientific genius. In D. K. Simonton (Ed.), *Wiley-Blackwell handbook of genius*. New York: Wiley.

Jones, D. C., Bain, N., & King, S. (2008). Weight and muscularity concerns as longitudinal predictors of body image among early adolescent boys: A test of the dual path model. *Body Image, 5*, 195–204.

Jones, J., & Augustine, S. (2015). Creating an anti-bullying culture in secondary schools: Characterists to consider when constructing appropriate anti-bullying programs. *American Secondary Education, 43*(3), 73–84.

Jones, M. D., & Galliher, R. V. (2007). Ethnic identity and psychosocial functioning in Navajo adolescents. *Journal of Research on Adolescence, 17*, 683–696.

Jones, M. H., West, S. D., & Estell, D. B. (2006). The Mozart effect: Arousal, preference, and spatial performance. *Psychology of Aesthetics, Creativity, and the Arts, 5*, 26–32.

Jones, N. (2012), Delayed reactive cries demonstrates emotional and physiological dysregulation in newborns of depressed mothers. *Biological Psychology, 80*, 374–381.

Joosten, H., et al. (2013). Cardiovascular risk profile and cognitive function in young, middle-aged, and elderly subjects. *Stroke, 44*, 1543–1549.

Jopp, D., & Rott, C. (2006). Adaptation in very old age: Exploring the role of resources and attitudes for centenarians' happiness. *Psychology and Aging, 21*, 266–280.

Jordan, C. H., & Zeigler-Hill, V. (2013). Secure and fragile forms of self-esteem. In V. Zeigler-Hill (Ed.), *Self-esteem*. New York: Psychology Press.

Jordan, S. J., et al. (2008). Serious ovarian, fallopian tube, and primary peritoneal cancers: A comprehensive epidemiological analysis. *International Journal of Cancer.*

Joseph, J. (2006). *The missing gene*. New York: Algora.

Joseph, K., Allen, A., Dodds, L., Turner, L., Scott, H., & Liston, R. (2005). The perinatal effects of delayed childbearing. *Obstetrics & Gynecology, 105*, 1410–1418.

Joshi, S., & Kotecha, S. (2007). Lung growth and development. *Early Human Development, 83*, 789–794.

Juang, L., & Umaña-Taylor, A. (2012). Family conflict among Chinese- and Mexican-origin adolescents and their parents in the U.S: An introduction. *New Directions in Child and Adolescent Developments, 135*, 1–12.

Judd, F. K., Hickey, M., & Bryant, C. (2012). Depression and midlife: Are we overpathologising the menopause? *Journal of Affective Disorders, 136*, 199–211.

Juffer, F., Bakermans-Kranenburg, M. J., & van IJzendoorn, M. H. (2007). *Promoting positive parenting.* Mahwah, NJ: Erlbaum.

Julian, M. M. (2013). Age at adoption from institutional care as a window into the lasting effects of early experience. *Clinical Child and Family Psychology Review, 16*(2), 101–145.

Jumah, N., Graves, L. & Kahan, M. (2015). The management of opioid dependence during pregnancy in rural and remote settings. *Canadian Medical Association Journal, 187*(1), E41–E46.

Jung, C. (1933). *Modern man in search of a soul.* New York: Harcourt Brace.

Jung, Y., Gruenewald, T. L., Seeman, T. E., & Sarkisian, C. A. (2010). Productive activities and development of frailty in older adults. *Journals of Gerontology B: Psychological Sciences and Social Sciences, 65*(B), 256–261.

Juraska, J. M., & Lowry, N. C. (2012), Neuroanatomical changes associated with cognitive aging. *Current Topics in Behavioral Neuroscience, 10*, 137–162.

Just, M. A., Keller, T. A., Malave, V. L., Kana, R. K., & Varma, S. (2012). Autism as a neural system disorder: A theory of frontal-posterior underconnectivity. *Neuroscience and Biobehavioral Reviews, 36*, 1292–1313.

Justice for Children and Youth (JFCY) (2012). Is spanking legal? Justice for Children and Youth. Retrieved from http://yourlegalrights.on.ca/sites/all/files/Section43June2012.pdf

Jutras-Aswald, D., NiNieri, J., Harkany, T. & Hurd, Y. (2009). Neurobiological consequences of maternal cannabis on human fetal development and its neuropsychiatric outcome. *European Archives of Psychiatry and Clinical Neuroscience, 259*(7), 395–412.

K

Kaasa, S. (2008). Editorial: Palliative care research—Time to intensify international collaboration. *Palliative Medicine, 22*, 301–302.

Kagan, J. (1987). Perspectives on infancy. In J. D. Osofsky (Ed.), *Handbook on infant development* (2nd ed.). New York: Wiley.

Kagan, J. (2000). Temperament. In A. Kazdin (Ed.), *Encyclopedia of psychology.* Washington, DC: American Psychological Association and Oxford University Press.

Kagan, J. (2002). Behavioral inhibition as a temperamental category. In R. J. Davidson, K. R. Scherer, & H. H. Goldsmith (Eds.), *Handbook of affective sciences.* New York: Oxford University Press.

Kagan, J. (2008). Fear and wariness. In M. M. Haith & J. B. Benson (Eds.), *Encyclopedia of infant and early childhood development.* Oxford, UK: Elsevier.

Kagan, J. (2010). *The temperamental thread: How genes culture, time, and luck make us who we are.* New York, NY: Dana Press.

Kagan, J. (2011). Emotions and temperament. In M. Burnstein (Ed.) *Handbook of Cultural Developmental Science* (pp. 175–194). New York, NY: Psychology Press.

Kagan, J. (2012). The biography of behavioural inhibition. In M. Zentner & R. Sniner (Eds.). *Handbook of temperament* (pp. 69–82). New York, NY: Guilford.

Kagan, J. (2013). Temperamental contributions to inhibited and uninhibited profiles. In P. Zelazo (Ed.) *Oxford Handbook of Developmental Psychology* (vol. 2) (pp. 142–166). New York, NY: Oxford University Press.

Kagan, J., Snidman, N., Kahn, V., & Towsley, S. (2007). The preservation of two infant temperaments into adolescence. *Monographs of the Society for Research in Child Development, 72*(2), 1–75.

Kagitani, H., Asou, Y., Ishihara, N., Hoshide, S., & Kario, K. (2014). Hot flashes and blood pressure in middle-aged Japanese women. *American Journal of Hypertension, 27*, 503–507.

Kahan, M., Wilson, L., Mailis-Gagnon, A. & Srivastava, A. (2011). Canadian guidelines for safe and effective use of opioids for chronic cancer pain. *Canadian Family Physician,* 57, 1269–1276.

Kalladka, D., & Muir, K. W. (2014). Brain repair: Cell therapy in stroke. *Stem Cells and Cloning, 7*, 31–44.

Kalousova, L., & Burgard, S. (2014). Unemployment measured and perceived decline of economic resources: Contrasting three measures of recessionary hardships and their implications for adopting negative health behaviors. *Social Science and Medicine, 106*, 28–34.

Kambhavi, R. (Nov. 2012). Research Note - Canadian Seniors: A Demographic Profile. Elections Canada, http://www.elections.ca/content.aspx?section=res&dir=rec/part/sen&document=index&lang=e

Kamerman, S. B. (1989). Child care, women, work, and the family: An international overview of child-care services and related policies. In J. S. Lande, S. Scarr, & N. Gunzenhauser (Eds.), *Caring for children: Challenge to America.* Hillsdale, NJ: Erlbaum.

Kamerman, S. B. (2000a). Parental leave policies. *Social Policy Report of the Society for Research in Child Development, XIV* (No. 2), 1–15.

Kamerman, S. B. (2000b). From maternity to paternity child leave policies. *Journal of the Medical Women's Association, 55*, 98–99.

Kamiya, M., Sakurai, T., Ogama, N., Maki, Y., & Toba, K. (2014). Factors associated with increased caregivers' burden in several cognitive stages of Alzheimer's disease. *Geriatrics and Gerontology International, 14*(2, Suppl.), S45–S55.

Kan, P. F. (2014). Novel word retention in sequential bilingual children. *Journal of Child Language, 41*, 416–438.

Kane, R. L. (2007). Health care and services. In J. E. Birren (Ed.), *Encyclopedia of gerontology* (2nd ed.). San Diego: Academic Press.

Kantak, C., et al. (2014, in press). Lab-on-a-chip technology: Impacting non-invasive prenatal diagnostics (NIPD) through miniaturization. *Lab on a Chip.*

Kaplan, D. L., Jones, E. J., Olson, E. C., & Yunzal-Butler, C. B. (2013). Early age of first sex and health risk in an urban adolescent population. *Journal of School Health, 83*, 350–356.

Karasik, L., Adolph, K., Tamis-LeMonda & Zukerment, A. (2012). Carry on: Spontaneous object carrying in 13-month-old-crawling and walking infants. *Developmental Psychology, 48*(2), 389–397.

Karasik, L., Tamis-LeMonda, C. & Adolph, K. (2011). Transition from crawling to walking and infants' actions with objects and people. *Child Development, 82*(4), 1199–1209.

Karasik, L., Tamis-LeMonda, C. & Adolph, K. (2014). Crawling and walking infants elicit different verbal responses from mothers. *Developmental Science, 17*(3), 388–395.

Karasik, L., Tamis-LeMonda, C., Adolphe, K. & Bornstein, M. (2015). Places and posture: A cross-cultural comparison of sitting in 5-month-olds. *Journal of Cross-Cultural Psychology, 46*(8). 1023–1038.

Karasu, S. R. (2007). The institution of marriage: Terminable or interminable? *American Journal of Psychotherapy, 61*, 1–16.

Karatsoreos, I. N., & McEwen, B. S. (2013). Annual research review: The neurobiology and physiology of resilience and adaptation across the life course. *Journal of Child Psychology and Psychiatry, 54*, 337–347.

Karavia, E. A., et al. (2014). HDL quality and functionality: What can proteins and genes predict? *Expert Review of Cardiovascular Therapy, 12*, 521–532.

Karlamangia, A. S., et al. (2014). Biological correlates of adult cognition: Midlife in the United States (MIDUS). *Neurobiology of Aging, 35*(2), 387–394.

Karney, B. R., & Bradbury, T. N. (2005). Contextual influences on marriage. *Current Directions in Psychological Science, 14*, 171–175.

Karniol, R., Grosz, E., & Schorr, I. (2003). Caring, gender-role orientation, and volunteering. *Sex Roles, 49*, 11–19.

Kaski, D., Allum, J. H., Bronstein, A. M., & Dominguez, R. O. (2014, in press). Applying anodal tDCS tango dancing in a patient with Parkinson's disease. *Neuroscience Letters.*

Kassahn, K. S., Scott, H. S., & Fletcher, J. M. (2014). Ensuring clinical validity—modernizing genetic testing services. *Pathology, 46*(1, Suppl.), S27–S28.

Kastenbaum, R. J. (2004). *Death, society, and human experience* (8th ed.). Boston: Allyn & Bacon.

Kastenbaum, R. J. (2007). *Death, society, and human experience* (9th ed.). Boston: Allyn & Bacon.

Katimavik. (2010). http://www.katimavik.org/

Kato, T. (2005). The relationship between coping with stress due to romantic break-ups and mental health. *Japanese Journal of Social Psychology, 20*, 171–180.

Kattenstroth, J. C., Kalisch, T., Holt, S., Tegenthoff, M., & Dinse, H. R. (2013). Six months of dance intervention enhances postural, sensorimotor, and cognitive performance in elderly without affecting cardio-respiratory functions. *Frontiers in Aging Neuroscience, 5*, 5.

Katz, P. R., Karuza, J., Intrator, O., & Mor, V. (2009). Nursing home physician specialists: A response to the workforce crisis in long-term care. *Annals of Internal Medicine, 150*, 411–413.

Kaufman, J. C., & Sternberg, R. J. (2013). The creative mind. In C. Jones, M. Lorenzen, & R. F. Proctor (Eds.), *Handbook of psychology: Experimental psychology* (Vol. 4). New York: Wiley.

Kaufman, S. R. (2005). *And a time to die.* New York: Scribner.

Kavsek, M. (2004). Predicting IQ from infant visual habituation and dishabituation: A metaanalysis. *Journal of Applied Developmental Psychology, 25,* 369–393.

Kawagoe, T., & Sekiyama, K. (2014, in press). Visually encoded working memory is closely associated with mobility in older adults. *Experimental Brain Research.*

Keating, D. P. (2004). Cognitive and brain development. In R. Lerner & L. Steinberg (Eds.), *Handbook of Adolescent Psychology.* New York: Wiley.

Keating, D. P. (2007). Understanding adolescent development: Implications for driving safety. *Journal of Safety Research, 38,* 147–157.

Keating, D. P. (2009). Developmental science and giftedness: An integrated life-span framework. In F. D. Horowitz, R. F. Subotnik, & D. J. Matthews (Eds.), *The development of giftedness and talent across the life span.* Washington, DC: American Psychological Association.

Keatings, M., & Smith, O. (2010). *Ethical & legal issues in Canadian nursing* (3rd ed.). Toronto: Mosby.

Keen, R. (2005). Unpublished review of J. W. Santrock's *Topical life-span development* (3rd ed.). New York: McGraw-Hill.

Kehle, T. J., & Bray, M. A. (2014). Individual differences. In M. A. Bray & T. J. Kehle (Eds.), *Oxford handbook of school psychology.* New York: Oxford University Press.

Kell, H. J., & Lubinski, D. (2014). The study of mathematically precocious youth at maturity: Insights into elements of genius. In D. K. Simonton (Ed.), *Wiley-Blackwell handbook of genius.* New York: Wiley.

Keller, H. (2002). Culture and development: Developmental pathways to individualism and interrelatedness. In W. J. Lonner, D. L. Dinnel, S. A. Hayes, & D. N. Sattler (Eds.), *Online readings in psychology and culture* (Unit 11, Chapter 1). Bellingham, Washington: Center for Cross-Cultural Research, Western Washington University. Retrieved from http://www.wwu.edu/

Keller, H., et al. (2004b). The bio-culture of parenting: Evidence from five cultural communities. *Parenting: Science and Practice, 4,* 25–50.

Keller, H., Yovsi, R., Borke, J., Kartner, J., Jensen, H. & Papligoura, Z. (2004a). Developmental Consequences of early parenting experiences: Self-recognition and self-regulation in three cultural communities. *Child Development, 75*(6), 1745–1760.

Kellman, P. J., & Arterberry, M. E. (2006). Infant visual perception. In W. Damon & R. Lerner (Eds.), *Handbook of child psychology* (6th ed.). New York: Wiley.

Kelly, D., Quinn, P., Slater, A., Lee, K., Ge, L. & Pascalis, O. (2008). The other-race effect develops during infancy: Evidence of perceptual narrowing. *Psychological Science, 18*(12), 1084–1089.

Kelly, G. F. (2008). *Sexuality today* (9th ed.). New York: McGraw-Hill.

Kelly, L., et al. (2009). Palliative care of First Nations people: A qualitative study of bereaved family members. *Canadian Family Physician, 55,* 394–395.

Kelly, M. (2012). Comparison of functional status of 8-to 12-year-old children born ;prematurely: An integrative review of literature. *Journal of Pediatric Nursing, 27,* 299–309.

Kelly, M. B. (2013). Divorce cases in civil court 2010/2011. Statistics Canada (2013). Retrieved from http://statcan.gc.ca/pub/85-002-x/2012001/article/11634-eng.htm

Kelly, M. E., et al. (2014). The impact of cognitive training and mental stimulation on cognitive and everyday functioning of healthy older adults: A systematic review and meta-analysis. *Aging Research Reviews, 15C,* 28–43.

Kelly, P. & Quesnelle, H. (2016). *Nursing leadership and management* (3rd Canadian edition). Toronto, ON: Nelson.

Kelly, S., Sprague, A., Deshayne, B., Murphy, P., Aelicks, N., Yanfang, G.,...Walker, M. (2013). *Journal of Obstetricians and Gynaecologists, 35*(3), 206–214.

Kelly, Y., et al. (2013). Light drinking versus abstinence in pregnancy—behavioral and cognitive outcomes in 7-year-old children: A longitudinal cohort study. *International Journal of Obstetrics and Gynaecology, 120,* 1340–1347.

Kemp, J., Despres, O., Pebayle, T., & Dufour, A. (2014). Age-related decrease in sensitivity to electrical stimulation is unrelated to skin conductance: An evoked potentials study. *Clinical Neurophysiology, 125,* 602–607.

Kendall, M., Harris, F., Boyd, K., Sheikh, A., Murray, S. A., Brown, D., et al. (2007). Key challenges and ways forward in researching the "good death": Qualitative in-depth interview and focus group study. *British Medical Journal, 334,* 485–486.

Kendrick, K., Jutengren, G., & Stattin, H. (2012). The protective role of supportive friends against bullying perpetration and victimization. *Journal of Adolescence, 35*(4), 1069–1080.

Kennedy, S., & Bumpass, L. (2008). Cohabitation and children's living arrangements: New estimates from the United States. *Demographic Research, 19,* 1663–1692.

Kennell, J. H. (2006). Randomized controlled trial of skin-to-skin contact from birth versus conventional incubator for physiological stabilization in 1200 g to 2199 g newborns. *Acta Paediatica (Sweden), 95,* 15–16.

Kennis, E., et al. (2013). Long-term impact of strength training on muscle strength characteristics in older adults. *Archives of Physical Medicine and Rehabilitation, 94,* 2054–2060.

Keon, W. J. (2009, December). Early childhood education and care: Canada's challenges and next steps. *Paediatric Child Health, 14*(10), 660–661.

Kerns, K. A., & Seibert, A. C. (2012). Finding your way through the thicket: Promising approaches to assessing attachment in middle childhood. In E. Waters & B. Vaughn (Eds.), *Measuring attachment.* New York: Guilford.

Kerns, K. A., Siener, S., & Brumariu, L. E. (2011). Mother-child relationships, family context, and child characteristics as predictors of anxiety symptoms in middle childhood. *Development and Psychopathology, 23,* 593–604.

Keyes, C. L. M., & Ryff, C. D. (1998). Generativity in adult lives: Social structure contours and quality of life consequences. In D. P. McAdams & E. de St. Aubin (Eds.), *Generativity and adult development: How and why we care for the next generation.* Washington, DC: American Psychological Association.

Khalil, A., & O'Brien, P. (2010). Alcohol and pregnancy. *Obstetrics, Gynaecology and Reproductive Medicine, 20*(10), 311–313.

Khera, M., Crawford, D., Morales, A., Salonia, A., & Morgentaler, A. (2014). A new era of testosterone and prostate cancer: From physiology to clinical implications. *European Urology, 65*(1), 115–123.

Kiang, L., Witkow, M., & Champagne, M. (2013). Normative changes in ethnic and American identities and links with adjustment among Asian American adolescents. *Developmental Psychology, 17,* 1713–1722.

Kilkenny C. (April 27, 2016). UNICEF Canada: education fro Syrian refugee children. Retrieved from http://www.rcinet.ca/en/2016/04/27/unicef-canada-education-for-syrian-refugee-children/.

Killen, M., & Smetana, J. G. (Eds.) (2014). *Handbook of moral development* (2nd ed.). New York: Psychology Press.

Kim, H., Schimmack, U., & Oishi, S. (2012). Cultural differences in self- and other-evaluations and well-being: A study of European and Asian Canadians. *Journal of Personality and Social Psychology, 102*(4), 856–873.

Kim, S. Y., Su, J., Yancurra, L., & Yee, B. (2009). Asian American and Pacific Islander families. In N. Tewari & A. Alvarez (Eds.), *Asian American psychology.* Clifton, NJ: Psychology Press.

Kim-Fuchs, C., et al. (2014, in press). Chronic stress accelerates pancreatic cancer growth and invasion: A critical role for beta-adrenergic signaling in the pancreatic microenvironment. *Brain, Behavior, and Immunity*.

King, B. & Regan, P. (2014). *Human sexuality today* (8th ed.) Upper Saddle River, NJ: Pearson.

King, K. M., & Chassin, L. (2007). A prospective study of the effects of age of initiation of alcohol and drug use on young adult substance dependence. *Journal of Studies on Alcohol and Drugs, 68*, 256–265.

King, L. A., & Hicks, J. A. (2007). Whatever happened to "What might have been?" Regrets, happiness, and maturity. *American Psychologist, 62*, 625–636.

King, L., Hicks, J., Krull, J., & Del Gaiso, A. (2006). Positive affect and the experience of meaning in life. *Journal of Personality and Social Psychology, 90*(1), 174–196.

King, W. J., MacKay, M., Sirnick, A., & Canadian Shaken Baby Study Group. (2003). Shaken baby syndrome in Canada: Clinical characteristics and outcomes of hospital cases. *Canadian Medical Association Journal, 168*(2), 155–159.

Kingston, N. (2008). Standardized tests. In N. J. Salkind (Ed.), *Encyclopedia of educational psychology.* Thousand Oaks, CA: Sage.

Kinney, J. (2009). *Loosening the grip* (9th ed.). New York: McGraw-Hill.

Kinney, J. (2012). *Loosing the grip: A handbook of alcohol information (10th ed.).* New York, NY: McGraw-Hill.

Kirk, R. E. (2003). Experimental design. In I.B. Weiner (Ed.), *Handbook of psychology* (Vol. II). New York: John Wiley.

Kirsch, G., McVey, G., Tweed, S., & Katzman, D. K. (2007). Psychosocial profiles of young, adolescent females seeking treatment for an eating disorder. *Journal of Adolescent Health, 40*, 351–356.

Kisilevsky, B. S., Hains, S. M., Jacquet, A. Y., Granier-Deferre, C., & Lecanuet, J. P. (2004). Maturation of fetal responses to music. *Developmental Science, 7*, 550–559.

Kisilevsky, B. S., Hains, S. M., Lee, K., Xie, X., Huang, H., Ye, H. H., et al. (2003). Effects of experience on fetal voice recognition. *Psychological Science, 14*, 220–224.

Kisilevsky, B., Hains, S., Brown, C., Lee, C., Cowpwerthwaite, B., Stutzman, S., Swansburg, M., Lee, K., Xie, X., Huang, H. Ye, H., Zhang, K. & Wang, Z. (2009). Fetal sensitivity to properties of maternal speech and language. *Infant Behaviour & Development, 32,* 59–71.

Kit, B. K., Simon, A. E., Brody, D. J., & Akinbami, L. J. (2013). U.S. prevalence and trends in tobacco smoke exposure among children and adolescents with asthma. *Pediatrics, 131*, 407–414.

Kitchener, K. S., King, P. M., & DeLuca, S. (2006). The development of reflective judgment in adulthood. In C. Hoare (Ed.), *Handbook of adult development and learning.* New York: Oxford University Press.

Kitchin, B. (2013). Nutrition counseling for patients with osteoporosis: A personal approach. *Journal of Clinical Densitometry, 16*, 426–231.

Klahr, A. M., & Burt, S. A. (2014, in press). Elucidating the etiology of individual differences in parenting: A meta-analysis of behavioral genetic research. *Psychological Bulletin.*

Klassen, T. R. (2012, February). The future of mandatory contractual retirement in South Korea. Canadian Labour Market and Skills Research Network. Retrieved from http://www.clsrn.econ.ubc.ca/workingpapers/CLSRN%20Working%20Paper%20no.%2093%20-%20Klassen.pdf

Kleinberg, E. (2012). *Going solo: The extraordinary rise and surprising appeal of living alone*. New York, NY: The Penguin Press.

Klieger, C., Pollex, E., & Koren, G. (2008). Treating the mother—protecting the newborn: The safety of hypoglycemic drugs in pregnancy. *Journal of Maternal-Fetal and Neonatal Medicine, 21*, 191–196.

Kline, G. H., Stanley, S. M., Markman, H. J., Olmos-Gallo, P. A., S. Peters, M., Whitton, S. W., et al. (2004). Timing is everything: Pre-engagement cohabitation and increased risk for poor marital outcomes. *Journal of Family Psychology, 18*, 311–318.

Klinenberg, E. (2016). Social isolation, loneliness, and living alone: Identifying risks for public health. *American Journal of Public Health, 106*(5), 786–787.

Klodawsky, F. (2006). Landscapes on the margin: Gender and homelessness in Canada. *Gender Place and Culture, 13*, 365–381.

Klomek, A. B., Sourander, A., & Gould, M. (2010). The association of suicide and bullying in childhood to young adulthood: A review of cross-sectional and longitudinal research findings. *Canadian Journal of Psychiatry, 55*(5), 282–288.

Knight, B. G., & Sayegh, P. (2010). Cultural values and caregiving: The updated sociocultural stress and coping model. *Journal of Gerontology: Psychological Sciences, 65*(B), 5–13.

Knight, G., Basilio, C., Cham, H., Gonzales, N., Liu, Y., & Umaña-Taylor, A. (2014). Trajectories of Mexican American and mainstream cultural values among Mexican American adolescents. *Journal of Youth Adolescence, 43*, 2012–2027.

Ko, P. C., et al. (2014, in press). Understanding age-related reductions in visual working memory capacity: Examining the stages of change detection. *Attention, Perception, and Psychophysics*.

Kochanska, G., & Kim, S. (2012). Toward a new understanding of the legacy of early attachments for future antisocial trajectories: Evidence from two longitudinal studies. *Development and Psychopathology, 24*(3), 783–806.

Kochanska, G., & Kim, S. (2013). Early attachment organization with both parents and future behavior problems: From infancy to middle childhood. *Child Development, 84*(1), 283–296.

Kochanska, G., Barry, R. A., Jimenez, N. B., Hollatz, A. L., & Woodard, J. (2009). Guilt and effortful control: Two mechanisms that prevent disruptive developmental trajectories. *Journal of Personality and Social Psychology, 97*, 322–333.

Koehler-Platten, K., Grow, L. L., Schulze, K. A., & Bertone, T. (2013). Using a lag reinforcement to increase phonemic variability in children with autistic spectrum disorders. *Analysis of Verbal Behavior, 29*, 71–83.

Koehn, S. (2006). Ethnic minority seniors face a "double whammy" in health care access. *GRC News, 25*(2), 1–2.

Koenig, H. G. (2004). Religion, spirituality, and medicine: Research findings and implications for clinical practice. Southern Medical Journal, 97, 1194–2000.

Koenig, H. G. (2007). Religion and remission of depression in medical inpatients with heart failure/pulmonary disease. *Journal of Nervous and Mental Disease, 195*, 389–395.

Koenig, L. B., McGue, M., & Iacono, W. G. (2008). Stability and change in religiousness during emerging adulthood. *Developmental Psychology, 44*, 523–543.

Koh, A., & Ross, L. (2006). Mental health issues. A comparison of lesbian, bisexual,and heterosexual women. *Journal of Homosexuality, 51*, 33–57.

Kohen, D., Uppal, S., Guevremont, A., & Cartwright, F. (2008) Children with disabilites and the educational system - a provincial perspective. Statistics Canada.

Retrieved from http://www.statcan.gc.ca/pub/81-004-x/2007001/9631-eng.htm

Kohlberg, L. (1958). *The development on modes of moral thinking and choice in the years 10 to 16*. Unpublished doctoral dissertation, University of Chicago.

Kohlberg, L. (1969). Stage and sequence: The cognitive-developmental approach to socialization. In D. A. Goslin (Ed.), *Handbook of socialization theory and research*. Chicago: Rand McNally.

Kohlberg, L. (1986). A current statement of some theoretical issues. In S. Modgil & C. Modgil (Eds.), *Lawrence Kohlberg*. Philadelphia: Falmer.

Kohut, R., & Rouleau, J. (2013). Chapter 2 - Down syndrome. Congenital Abnormalities in Canada - A perinatal Health Surveillance Report. Public Health Agency of Canada. Retrieved from http://www.aphp.ca/pdf/CAC%20report%202013%20EN.pdf

Kollar, L., Jordan, K., & Wilson, D. (2013). Health problems of school-age children and adolescents. In M. Hockenberry & D. Wilson (Eds.), *Wong's Essential of pediatric nursing* (9th ed.) (pp.498–535). Philadelphia: Elsevier.

Kolovou, G., et al. (2014, in press). Aging mechanisms and associated lipid changes. *Current Vascular Pharmacology*.

Konik, J., & Stewart, A. (2004). Sexual identity development in the context of compulsory heterosexuality. *Journal of Personality, 72*, 815–844.

Konopka, A. R., Suer, M. K., Wolff, C. A., & Harber, M. P. (2014). Markers of human skeletal muscle mitochondrial biogenesis and quality control: Effects of age and aerobic training. *Journals of Gerontology A: Biological Sciences and Medical Sciences, 69*, 371–388.

Koolhof, R., Loeber, R., Wei, E. H., Pardini, D., & D'escury, A. C. (2007). Inhibition deficits of serious delinquent boys of low intelligence. *Criminal Behavior and Mental Health, 17*, 274–292.

Kopp, C. B. (2008). Self-regulatory processes. In M. M. Haith & J. B. Benson (Eds.), *Encyclopedia of infant and early childhood development*. Oxford, UK: Elsevier.

Koran, M. E., Hohman, T. J., Meda, S. A., & Thornton-Wells, T. A. (2014). Genetic interactions with inositol-related pathways are associated with longitudinal changes in ventricle size. *Journal of Alzheimer's Disease, 38*, 145–154.

Korat, O. (2009). The effect of maternal teaching talk on children's emergent literacy as a function of type of activity and maternal education level. *Journal of Applied Developmental Psychology, 30*, 34–42.

Koropeckyj-Cox, T. (2009). Singlehood. In D. Carr (Ed.), *Encyclopedia of the life course and human development*. Boston: Gale Cengage.

Korrick, S. A., & Sagiv, S. K. (2008). Polychlorinated biphenyls, organopesticides, and neurodevelopment. *Current Opinion in Pediatrics, 20*, 198–204.

Korten, N. C., et al. (2014, in press). Heterogeneity of late-life depression: Relationship with cognitive functioning. *International Psychogeriatrics*.

Kostelnik, M. J., Soderman, A. K., & Whiren, A. P. (2011). *Developmentally appropriate curricula* (5th ed.). Upper Saddle River, NJ: Merrill.

Kostelnik, M. J., Soderman, A. K., Whiren, A. P., & Rupiper, M. (2015, in press). *Developmentally appropriate curriculum* (6th ed.). Upper Saddle River, NJ: Pearson.

Kostenuik, M., & Ratnapalan, M. (2010). Approach to adolescent suicide prevention. *Canadian Family Physician, 56*, 755–760.

Kotovsky, L., & Baillargeon, R. (1994). Calibration-based reasoning about collision events in 11-month-old infants. *Cognition, 51*, 107–129.

Kottak, C. P. (2004). *Cultural anthropology* (10th ed.). New York: McGraw-Hill.

Koukoura, O., Sifakis, S., Stratoudakis, G., Manta, N., Kaminopetros, P., & Koumantakis, E. (2006). A case report of recurrent anencephaly and literature review. *Clinical and Experimental Obstetrics and Gynecology, 33*, 185–189.

Kowalski, S. D., & Bondmass, M. D. (2008). Physiological and psychological symptoms of grief in widows. *Research in Nursing and Health, 31*, 23–30.

Kowaltowski, A. J. (2011). Caloric restriction and redox state: Does this diet increase or decrease oxidant production? *Redox Report, 16*, 237–241.

Kozbelt, A. (2014). Musical creativity over the lifespan. In D. K. Simonton (Ed.), *Wiley-Blackwell handbook of genius*. New York: Wiley.

Kozier, et al. (2010). *Fundamentals of Canadian nursing* (2nd Canadian ed.). Toronto: Pearson.

Kraft, E. (2012). Cognitive function, physical activity, and aging: Possible biological links and implications for multimodal interventions. *Neuropsychology, Development, and Cognition: Section B, Aging, Neuropsychology, Cognition, 19*, 248–263.

Krakoff, L. R. (2008). Older patients need better guidelines for optimal treatment of high blood pressure: 1 size fits few. *Hypertension, 51*, 817–818.

Kramer, K., Kelly, E. & McCulloch, J. (2015). Stay-At-Home fathers: Definition and characteristics based on 34 years of CPS data. *Journal of Family Issues, 36*(12), 1651–1673.

Kramer, L., & Bank, L. (2005). Sibling relationship contributions to individual and family wellbeing: Introduction to the special issue. *Journal of Family Psychology, 19*, 483–485.

Kramer, M., et al. (2008). Effects of prolonged and exclusive breastfeeding on child behaviour and maternal adjustment: Evidence from a large, randomized trial. *Pediatrics, 121*, e435–e440.

Kranz Graham, E., & Lachman, M. E. (2014, in preparation). *The associations between facet level personality and cognitive performance: What underlying characteristics drive trait level predictors across the adult lifespan?* Unpublished manuscript, Department of Psychology, Brandeis University, Waltham, MA.

Kraska, M. (2008). Quantitative research methods. In N. J. Salkind (Ed.), *Encyclopedia of educational psychology*. Thousand Oaks, CA: Sage.

Krause, N. (2012). Valuing the life experience of old adults and change in depressive symptoms: Exploring an overlooked benefit of involvement in religion. *Journal of Aging Health, 24*, 227–247.

Krauss, S., Hamzah, A., Ishmail, A., Suandi, T., Raba'ah Hamzah, S., Dahalan, D., & Idris, F. (2016). Parenting, community, and positive religious predictors of positive and negative developmental outcomes among Muslim adolescents. *Journal of Youth and Society, 46*(2), 201–227.

Kreutzer, M., Leonard, C., & Flavell, J. H. (1975). An interview study of children's knowledge about memory. *Monographs of the Society for Research in Child Development, 40*(1, Serial No. 159).

Kriebs, J. M. (2009). Obesity as a complication of pregnancy and labor. *Journal of Perinatal and Neonatal Nursing, 23*(1), 15–22.

Krimer, L. S., & Goldman - Rakic, P. S. (2001). Prefrontal microcircuits. *Journal of Neuroscience, 21*, 3788–3796.

Krist, H. & Krüger M. (2012). Towards a new method for bridign the gap between "smart" infants and "dumb" Preschoolers. *European Journal of Developmental Psychology, 9*(5), 631–637.

Kristjuhan, U., & Taidre, E. (2010). Postponed aging in university teachers. *Rejuvenation Research, 13*(2–3), 353–355.

Kroger, J. (2007). *Identity development: Adolescence through adulthood*. Thousand Oaks, CA: Sage.

Kroger, J., Martinussen, M., & Marcia, J. (2010). Identity status change during adolescence and young adulthood: A metanalysis. *Journal of Adolescence, 33,* 683–698.

Kruger, J., Blanck, H. M., & Gillespie, C. (2006). Dietary and physical activity behaviors among adults successful at weight loss management. *International Journal of Behavioral Nutrition and Physical Activity, 3,* 17.

Krushkal, J., et al. (2014, in press). Epigenetic analysis of neurocognitive development at 1 year of age in a community-based pregnancy cohort. *Behavior Genetics.*

Ksir, C. J., Hart, C. L., & Ray, O. S. (2008). *Drugs, society, and human behavior* (12th ed.). New York: McGraw-Hill.

Kübler-Ross, E. (1969). *On death and dying.* New York: Macmillan.

Kuebli, J. (1994, March). Young children's understanding of everyday emotions. *Young Children,* 36–48.

Kuhl, P. (2009). Linking infant speech perception to language acquisition: Phonetic learning predicts language growth. In J. Colombo, P. McCardle & L. Fruend. *Infant pathways to language: Methods, models and research directions.* (pp. 99–118). New York: Psychology Press.

Kuhl, P. (2010). Brain mechanisms in early language acquisition. *Neuron, 67*(5), 713-727.

Kuhl, P. (2011a) Early language learning and literacy: Neuroscience implications for education. *Mind, Brain and Education,* 5(3), 128–142.

Kuhl, P. (2011b), Social mechanisms in early language acquisition: Understanding integrated brain systems supporting language. In J. Decety & J. Cacioppo (Eds). *The handbook of neuroscience* (pp. 649–667) Oxford: Oxford University Press.

Kuhl, P. K. (2007). Is speech learning "gated" by the social brain? *Developmental Science, 10,* 110–120.

Kuhn, D., & Franklin, S. (2006). The second decade: What develops (and how)? In W. Damon & R. Lerner (Eds.), *Handbook of child psychology* (6th ed.). New York: Wiley.

Kuipers, S., Trentani, A., van der Zee, E. A., & den Boer, J. A. (2013). Chronic stress-induced changes in the rat brain: Role of sex differences and effect of long-term tianeptine treatment. *Neuropharmacology, 75C,* 426–436.

Kulkofsky, S., & Klemfuss, J. Z. (2008). What the stories children tell can tell about their memory: Narrative skill and young children's suggestibility. *Developmental Psychology, 44,* 1442–1456.

Kulmala, J., et al. (2013). Perceived stress symptoms in midlife predict disability in old age: A 28-year prospective study. *Journals of Gerontology A: Biological Sciences and Medical Sciences, 68,* 984–991.

Kumar, N., & Priyadarshi, B. (2013). Differential effect of aging on verbal and visuo-spatial working memory. *Aging and Disease, 12,* 170–177.

Kunz Stansbury, J. & Wilson, D. (2015). The child with neuromuscular or muscular dysfunction. In M. Hockenberry & D. Wilson (Eds.) *Wong's nursing care of infants and children* (10th ed.). (pp. 1615–1672). St. Louis: Elsevier.

Kunzweiler, C. (2007). Twin individuality. *Fresh ink: Essays from Boston College's first-year writing seminar, 9*(1), 2–3.

Kuo, M. C., Kiu, I. P., Ting, K. H., & Chan, C. C. (2014). Age-related effects on perceptual and semantic encoding in memory. *Neuroscience, 261,* 95–106.

Kuppens, S., Grietens, H. Onghena, P., & Michiels, D. (2009). Relations between parental psychological control and childhood relational aggression: Reciprocal in nature? *Journal of Clinical Child and Adolescent Psychology, 38,* 117–131.

Kurdek, L. A. (1997). Adjustment to relationship dissolution in gay, lesbian, and heterosexual partners. *Personal Relationships, 4,* 145–161.

Kurdek, L. A. (2006). Differences between partners from heterosexual, gay, and lesbian cohabiting couples. *Journal of Marriage and the Family, 68,* 509–528.

Kurdek, L. A. (2007). The allocation of household labor between partners in gay and lesbian couples. *Journal of Family Issues, 28,* 132–148.

Kutcher, S., & Szumilas, M. (2008). Youth suicide prevention. *CMAJ, 178*(3), 282–285.

Kwok, S., & Shek, D. (2010). Hopelessness, parent - adolescent communication, and suicidal ideation among Chineses adolescents in Hong Kong. *Suicide and Life Threatening Behaviour, 40,* 224–233.

L

La Greca, A. M., & Harrison, H. M. (2005). Adolescent peer relations, friendships, and romantic relationships: Do they predict social anxiety and depression? *Journal of Clinical Child and Adolescent Psychology, 34,* 49–61.

Labouvie-Vief, G. (1986, August). *Modes of knowing and life-span cognition.* Paper presented at the meeting of the American Psychological Association, Washington, DC.

Labouvie-Vief, G. (2006). Emerging structures of adult thought. In J. J. Arnett & J. L. Tanner (Eds.), *Emerging adults in America.* Washington, DC: American Psychological Association.

Labouvie-Vief, G., & Diehl, M. (1999). Self and personality development. In J. C. Kavanaugh & S. K. Whitbourne (Eds.), *Gerontology: An interdisciplinary perspective.* New York: Oxford University Press.

Lachlan, R. F., & Feldman, M. W. (2003). Evolution of cultural communication systems. *Journal of Evolutionary Biology, 16,* 1084–1095.

Lachman, M. E. (2006). Perceived control over aging-related declines. *Current Directions in Psychological Science, 15,* 282–286.

Lachman, M. E., & Firth, K. (2004). The adaptive value of feeling in control during midlife. In G. O. Brim., C. D. Ryff, & R. C. Kessler (Eds.), *How healthy are we? A national study of well-being at midlife.* Chicago: University of Chicago Press.

Lachman, M. E., Agrigoroaei, S., Murphy, C., & Tun, P. A. (2010). Frequent cognitive activity compensates for education differences in episodic memory. *American Journal of Geriatric Psychiatry, 18,* 4–10.

Lachman, M. E., Rosnick, C., & Rocke, C. (2009). The rise and fall of control beliefs predict exercise behavior during and after an exercise intervention. *Journal of Aging and Physical Activity, 16,* 1–16.

LaCour, D., & Trimble, C. (2012). Humanpapillomavirus in infants: Transmission, prevalence, and persistence. *Journal of Pediatric Adolescent Gynecology, 25,* 93–97.

Lacroix, V., Pomerleau, A., Malcuit, G., Séguin, R., & Lamarre, G. (2001). Cognitive and language development of children during the first three years of life with respect to maternal vocalizations and toys at home: Longitudinal study of a high risk population. *Canadian Journal of Behavioural Science, 33*(2), 65–76.

Lafreniere, D., & Mann, N. (2009). Anosmia: Loss of smell in the elderly. *Otolaryngologic Clinics of North America, 42,* 123–131.

Laible, D., & Karahuta, E. (2014). Prosocial behaviors in early childhood: Helping others, responding to the distress of others, and working with others. In L. Padilla-Walker & G. Carlo (Eds.), *Prosocial behavior.* New York: Oxford University Press.

Laird, R. D., Criss, M. M., Pettit, G. S., Dodge, K. A., & Bates, J. E. (2008). Parents' monitoring knowledge attenuates the link between antisocial friends and adolescent delinquent behavior. *Journal of Abnormal Child Psychology, 36*, 299–310.

Lalley, P. M. (2013). The aging respiratory system—pulmonary structure, function, and neural control. *Respiratory Physiology and Neurology, 187*, 199–210.

Lalonde, C., Chandler, M. J., Hallett, D., & Paul, D. (2001). Personal persistence, identity development, and suicide: A study of native and non-native North American adolescents. April 2003. *Monographs of the Society for Research in Child Development.*

Lamb, M. (2012). Mothers, fathers, families, and circumstances: Factors affecting children's adjustment. *Applied Developmental Science, 16*(2), 98–111.

Lamb, M. (Ed.). (2010). *The role of the father in child development* (5th ed.). Hoboken, NJ: Wiley.

Lamb, M. E. (1994). Infant care practices and the application of knowledge. In C. B. Fisher & R. M. Lerner (Eds.), *Applied developmental psychology.* New York: McGraw-Hill.

Lamb, M. E. (2005). Attachments, social networks, and developmental contexts. *Human Development, 48*, 108–112.

Lamb, M. E., Malloy, L. C., Hershkowitz, I., & La Rooy, D. (2015, in press). Children and the law. In R. E. Lerner (Ed.), *Handbook of child psychology and developmental science* (7th ed.). New York: Wiley.

Lamb, M., & Lewis, C. (2010). The development and significance of father-child relationships in two-parent families. In M. Lamb (Ed.), *The role of the father in child development* (4th ed.), (pp. 94–153). Hoboken, NJ: Wiley.

Lamb, M., & Lewis, C. (2011). The role of parent-child relationships in two-parent families. In M. Bornstein & M. Lamb (Eds.), *Developmental science: An advanced textbook* (6th ed.), (pp. 469–517). New York: Taylor & Francis.

Lambert, C. (January-February, 2007) The Science of Happiness - Psychology explores humans at their best. Harvard Magazine Retrieved from http://harvardmagazine.com/2007/01/the-science-of-happiness.html.

Lamont, R. F., & Jaggat, A. N. (2007). Emerging drug therapies for preventing spontaneous labor and preterm birth. *Expert Opinion on Investigational Drugs, 16*, 337–345.

Lamy, S., et al. (2014, in press). Psychosocial and organizational work factors and incidence of arterial hypertension among female healthcare workers: Results of the Organisation des soins et santé des soignants cohort. *Journal of Hypertension.*

Landa, R. & Kalb, L. (2012). Long-term outcomes of toddlers with autism spectrum disorders: A prospective study. *Journal of Child Psychology and Psychiatry, 47*, 629–638.

Landau, L. I. (2008). Tobacco smoke exposure and tracking of lung function into adult life. *Pediatric Respiratory Reviews, 9*, 39–44.

Landoll, R., Schwartz-Mette, R., Rose, A., & Prinstein, M. (2012). Girls' and boys' disclosure about problems as a predictor of changes in depressive symptoms over time. *Sex Roles, 65*, 410–420.

Landrum, A. R., Mills, C. M., & Johnston, A. M. (2013). When do children trust the expert? Benevolence information influences children's trust more than expertise. *Developmental Science, 16*, 622–638.

Landry, J. T., Foreman, T., & Kekewich, M. (2015). Ethical considerations in the regulation of euthanasia and physician-assisted death in Canada. *Health Policy, 119*(11), 1490–1498.

Landsberg, L., et al. (2013). Obesity-related hypertension: Pathogenesis, cardiovascular risk, and treatment—A position paper of the Obesity Society and the American Society of Hypertension. *Obesity, 21*(1), 8–24.

Landy, F. & Conte, J. (2007). *Work in the 21st century: An instruction to industrial and organizational psychology* (2nd ed.). Malden, MA: Blackwell.

Lang, F. R., & Carstensen, L. L. (1994). Close emotional relationships in late life: Further support for proactive aging in the social domain. *Psychology and Aging, 9*, 315–324.

Lange, B. S., et al. (2010). The potential of virtual reality and gaming to assist successful aging with disability. *Physical Medicine and Rehabilitation Clinics of North America, 21*, 339–356.

Langer, E. (2005). *On becoming an artist.* New York: Ballantine.

Langille, D. (2007). Teenage pregnancies: Trends, contributing factors and the physician's role. *Canadian Medical Association Journal, 176*(11), 1601–1602.

Lango Allen, H., et al. (2014, in press). Next generation sequencing of chromosomal rearrangements in patients with split-hand/split-foot malformation provides evidence for DYNC1L1 exonic enhancers of DLX5/6 expression in humans. *Journal of Medical Genetics.*

Lanius, R. A., et al. (2004). The nature of traumatic memories: A 4 - TfMRI functional connectivity analysis. *American Journal of Psychiatry, 161*(1), 36–44.

Lansford, J. E., Miller-Johnson, S., Berlin, L. J., Dodge, K. A., Bates, J. E., & Pettit, G. S. (2007). Early physical abuse and later violent delinquency: A prospective longitudinal study. *Child Maltreatment, 12*, 233–245.

Lapsley, D. K, & Yeager, D. (2013). Moral-character education. In I. B. Weiner et al. (Eds.), *Handbook of psychology* (2nd ed., Vol. 7). New York: Wiley.

Larimer, M., Palmer, R., & Marlatt, G. (1999). *An overview of Marlatt's cognitive-behavioural model. Relapse Prevention, 23*(2), 151–160.

Larke, I. (2006). The relationship between bullying and social skills in primary school students. *Issues in Educational Research, 16*, 38–51.

LaRochelle-Côté, S., & Dionne, C. (2009, Autumn). Family working patterns. *Perspectives on Labour and Income, 9*, 15–26.

Larson, F. B., Wang, L., Bowen, J. D., McCormick, W. C., Teri, L., Crane, P., et al. (2006). Exercise is associated with reduced risk for incident dementia among persons 65 years of age and older. *Annals of Internal Medicine, 144*, 73–81.

Larson, R. W., & Verma, S. (1999). How children and adolescents spend time across the world: Work, play, and developmental opportunities. *Psychological Bulletin, 125*, 701–736.

Larson, R. W., & Wilson, S. (2004). Adolescence across place and time: Globalization and the changing, pathways to adulthood. In R. Lerner & L. Steinberg (Eds.), *Handbook of adolescent psychology.* New York: Wiley.

Larson, R., & Angus, R. (2011). Adolescents' development of skills for agency in youth programs: Learning to think strategically. *Child Development, 82*, 277–294.

Larson, R., & Dawes, N. (2014). Cultivating adolescents' motivation. In Joseph, S. (Ed) Positive *Psychology in Practice: Promoting Human Flourishing in Work, Health, Education, and Everyday Life* (pp. 313–326). Hoboken, NJ: Wiley.

Larson, R., Pearce, N., Sullivan, P., & Jarrett, R. L. (2007). Participation in youth programs as a catalyst for negotiation of family autonomy with connection. *Journal of Youth and Adolescence, 36*(1), 31–45.

Larson, R., Wilson, S., & Rickman, A. (2009). Globalization, societal change, and adolescence across the world. In R. M. Learner & L. S. Steinberg (Eds.) *Handbook of Adolescent Psychology* (3rd ed) (pp. 590–622). New York, NY: Wiley.

Lasker, J. N., Coyle, B., Li, K., & Ortynsky, M. (2005). Assessment of risk factors for low birth weight deliveries. *Health Care for Women International, 26*, 262–280.

Latt, E., Mäestu, J., Rääsk, T., Purge, P., Jürimă,T. & Jürimă, J. (2015). Maturity-related differences in moderate, vigourous, and moderate-to-vigorous physical activity in 10-14-year-old boys. *Perceptual & Motor Skills Physical Development & Measurement, 120*(2), 659–670.

Lauer, R., & Lauer, J. C. (2007). *Marriage and family: The quest for intimacy* (6th ed.). New York: McGraw-Hill.

Laursen, B., & Collins, W. (2009). Parent-child relationships during adolescence. In R. M. Lerner & L. D. Steinberg (Eds.), *Handbook of Adolescent Psychology: Vol 2. Contextual Influences on Adolescent Development* (3rd ed.) (pp. 3–42). Hoboken, NJ: Wiley.

Laursen, B., & Pursell, G. (2009). Conflict in peer relationships. In K. H. Rubin, W. M. Bukowski, & B. Laursen (Eds.), *Handbook of peer interactions, relationships, and groups*. New York: Guilford.

Lavalliere, M., et al. (2011). Changing lanes in a simulator: Effects of aging on the control of the vehicle and visual inspection of mirrors and the blind spot. *Traffic Injury Prevention, 12*, 191–200.

Lawson, C. & Rakison, D. (2013). Expectations about single event probabilities in the first year of life: The influence of perceptual and statistical information. *Infancy, 18*(6), 961–982.

Lawson, J. (2014). Canada needs a 'dialogue about death" says CMA President. *Canadian Medical Association Journal, 186*(6), E183.

Lazaruk, W. (2013). Linquistic, Academic, and Cognitive Benefits of French Immersion. *The Canadian Modern Language Review, 63*(5), 605–627. University of Toronto Press. Project Muse. Retrieved from http://languages.sd62.bc.ca/files/2013/09/September-2013-Benefits-of-FI.pdf.

Le Couteur, D. G., & Simpson, S. J. (2011). Adaptive senectitude: The prolongevity effects on aging. *Journals of Gerontology A: Biological Sciences and Medical Sciences, 66A*, 179–182.

Leahy-Warren, P., & McCarthy, G. (2011). Maternal parental self - efficacy in the postpartum period . *Midwifery, 27*, 802–811.

Leaper, C. (2013). Gender development during childhood. In P. D. Zelazo (Ed.), *Oxford handbook of developmental psychology*. New York: Oxford University Press.

Leaper, C., & Bigler, R. S. (2011). Gender. In M. H. Underwood & L. H. Rosen (Eds.), *Social development.* New York: Guilford.

Leaper, C., & Brown, C. S. (2008). Perceived experience of sexism among adolescent girls. *Child Development, 79*, 685–704.

Lee, J. H., Jang, A. S., Park, S. W., Kim, D. J., & Park, C. S. (2014). Gene-gene interaction between CCR3 and Eotaxin genes: The relationship with blood eosinophilia in asthma. *Allergy, Asthma, and Immunology Research, 6*, 55–60.

Lee, J., Lee, J., & Moon, S. (2009). Exploring children's understanding of death concepts. *Asia Pacific Journal of Education, 29*(2), 251–264.

Lee, K. (2010). Does your child tell lies? Here are some answers about children's lies. *Child Development Research Group Institute of Child Study.*

Lee, K. Y., et al. (2011). Effects of combined radiofrequency radiation exposure on the cell cycle and its regulatory proteins. *Bioelectromagnetics, 32*, 169–178.

Lee, K., Cameron, C. A., Doucette, J., & Talwar, V. (2002). Phantoms and fabrications: Young children's detection of implausible lies. *Child Development, 73*, 1688–1702.

Lee, K., Cameron, C. A., Xu, F., Fu, G., & Board, J. (1997). Chinese and Canadian children's evaluations of lying and truth telling: Similarities and differences in the context of pro- and antisocial behaviors. *Child Development, 68*, 924–934.

Lee, R. M., Grotevant, H. D., Hellerstedt, W. L., Gunnar, M. R., & the Minnesota International Adoption Project Team. (2006). Cultural socialization in families with internationally adopted children. *Journal of Family Psychology, 20*, 571–580.

Lee, S., Lee, B., Kim, J., Vi, J., & Choi, I. (2013). Association between alcoholism and family history and alcohol screening scores among alcohol-dependent patients. *Clinical Psychopharmacology and Neuroscience, 11*, 89–95.

Leerkes, E., Parade, S. & Gudmundson, J. (2011). Mothers' emotional reaction to crying pose risk for subsequent attachment insecurity. *Journal of Family Psychology, 25*, 635–643.

Lefkowitz, E. S., & Gillen, M. M. (2006). "Sex is just a normal part of life": Sexuality in emerging adulthood. In J. J. Arnett & J. L. Tanner (Eds.), *Emerging adults in America.* Washington, DC: American Psychological Association.

Legge, G. E., Madison, C., Vaughn, B. N., Cheong, A. M., & Miller, J. C. (2008). Retention of high tactile acuity throughout the lifespan in blindness. *Perception and Psychophysics, 70*, 1471–1488.

Leifheit-Limson, E., & Levy, B. (2009). Ageism/age discrimination. In D. Carr (Ed.), *Encyclopedia of the life course and human development.* Boston: Gale Cengage.

Leighton, S. (2008). Bereavement therapy with adolescents: Facilitating a process of spiritual growth. *Journal of Child and Adolescent Psychiatric Nursing, 21*, 24–34.

Lemstra, M. E., Nielsen, G., Rogers, M. R., Thompson, A. T., & Moraros, J. S. (2012). Risk indicators and outcomes associated with bullying in youth aged 9–15 years. *Canadian Journal of Public Health, 103*(1), 9–13.

Lennon, E. M., Gardner, J. M., Karmel, B. Z., & Flory, M. J. (2008). Bayley Scales of Infant Development. In M. M. Haith & J. B. Benson (Eds.), *Encyclopedia of infant and early childhood development.* Oxford, UK: Elsevier.

Lenroot, R. K., & Giedd, J. N. (2006). Brain development in children and adolescents: Insights from anatomical magnetic resonance imaging. *Neuroscience and Biobehavioral Reviews, 30*, 718–729.

Leon, J., et al. (2014, in press). A combination of physical and cognitive exercise improves reaction time in 61-84-years-old persons. *Journal of Aging and Physical Activity.*

Leonardi-Bee, J. A., Smyth, A. R., Britton, J., & Coleman, T. (2008). Environmental tobacco smoke and fetal health: Systematic review and analysis. *Archives of Disease in Childhood: Fetal and Neonatal Edition.*

Leone, J., Mullin, E., Maurer-Starks, S. & Rovito, M. (2014). The adolescent body image satisfaction scale for males: Exploratory factor analysis and implications for strength and conditioning professional. *Journal of Strength and Conditioning Research, 28*(9), 2657–2668.

Leon-Guerrero, A. (2009). *Social problems* (2nd ed.). Thousand Oaks, CA: Sage.

Leppanen, J. M., Moulson, M., Vogel-Farley, V. K., & Nelson, C. A. (2007). An ERP study of emotional face processing in the adult and infant brain. *Child Development, 78*, 232–245.

Lerner, H. (1989). *The dance of intimacy.* New York: Harper & Row.

Lerner, H. (1998). *The mother dance: How children change your life.* New York: Harper Perennial.

Lerner, R. M., Boyd, M., & Du, D. (2008). Adolescent development. In I. B. Weiner & C. B. Craighead (Eds.), *Encyclopedia of psychology* (4th ed). Hoboken, NJ: Wiley.

Lerner, R. M., Roeser, R. W., & Phelps, E. (Eds.). (2009). *Positive youth development and spirituality: From theory to research.* West Conshohocken, PA: Templeton Foundation Press.

Lerner-Geva, L., Boyko, V., Blumstein, T., & Benyamini, Y. (2010). The impact of education, cultural background, and lifestyle on symptoms of the menopausal transition: The Women's Health at Midlife Study. *Journal of Women's Health, 19*, 975–985.

Leshikar, E. D., & Duarte, A. (2014). Medial prefrontal cortex supports source memory for self-referenced materials in young and older adults. *Cognitive, Affective, and Behavioral Neuroscience, 14*, 236–252.

Leshikar, E. D., Gutchess, A. H., Hebrank, A. C., Sutton, B. P., & Park, D. C. (2010). The impact of increased relational encoding demands in frontal and hippocampal function in older adults. *Cortex, 46*, 507–521.

Lester, B. (2000). Unpublished review of J. W. Santrock's *Life-span development* (8th ed.). New York: McGraw-Hill.

Lester, B., & Lafasse, L. (2010). Children of addicted women, *Journal of Addictive Diseases,* 29. 259–276.

Lester, B. M., Tronick, E. Z., & Brazelton, T. B. (2004). The Neonatal Intensive Care Unit Network neurobehavioral scale procedures. *Pediatrics, 113* (Suppl.), S641–S667.

Lester, D. (2006). Sexual orientation and suicidal behaviour. *Psychological Reports, 99*, 923–924.

Letourneau, N. L., Hungler, K. M., & Fisher, K. (2005). Low-income Canadian Aboriginal and non-Aboriginal parent-child interactions. *Child: Care, Health & Development, 31*, 545–554.

Leuschen, J., et al. (2013). Association of statin use with cataracts: A propensity score-matched analysis. *Journal of the American Medical Association Ophthalmology, 131*, 1427–1431.

Levant, R. F. (2002). Men and masculinity. In J. Worell (Ed.), *Encyclopedia of women and gender.* San Diego: Academic Press.

LeVay, S., & Valente, S. (2003). *Human sexuality.* Sunderland, MA: Sinauer Associates.

Levetown, M., & American Academy of Pediatrics Committee on Bioethics. (2008). Communicating with children and families: From everyday interactions to skill in conveying distressing information. *Pediatrics, 121*, e1441–e1460.

Levin, M. F. (2011) Can virtual reality offer enriched environments for rehabilitation? Expert Review. Ltd. Retrieved from https://www.researchgate.net/profile/Mindy_Levin/publication/49822047_Can_virtual_reality_offer_enriched_environments_for_rehabilitation/links/0046353c979b57b9d6000000.pdf

Levine, D. (2013). Office-based care for lesbian, gay, bisexual, transgender, and questioning youth. *American Academy of Pediatrics, 132*(1), e297–e313.

LeVine, S. (1979). *Mothers and wives: Gusii women of East Africa.* Chicago: University of Chicago Press.

Levinson, D. J. (1978). *The seasons of a man's life*. New York: Knopf.

Levinson, D. J. (1996). *Seasons of a woman's life.* New York: Alfred Knopf.

Levitt, C., Hanvey, L., Kaczorowski, J., Chalmers, B., Heaman, M., & Bartholomew, S. (2011). Breastfeeding policies and practices in Canadian hospitals: Comparing 1993 with 2007. *Birth, 38*(3), 228–237.

Levy, B. R., Slade, M. D., & Gill, T. (2006). Hearing decline predicted by elders' age stereotypes. *Journal of Gerontology B: Psychological Sciences and Social Sciences, 61*, P82–P87.

Levy, B. R., Slade, M. D., Kunkel, S. R., & Kasl, S. V. (2002). Longevity increased by positive self-perceptions of aging. *Journal of Personality and Social Psychology, 83*, 261–270.

Lewis, A., Huebner, E., Malone, P., & Valois, R. (2011). Life satisfaction and student engagement in adolescence. *Journal of Youth and Adolescence, 40*, 249–262.

Lewis, M. (2005). The child and its family: The social network model. *Human Development, 33*, 48–61.

Lewis, M. (2007). Early emotional development. In A. Slater & M. Lewis (Eds.), *Introduction to infant development* (2nd ed.). New York: Oxford University Press.

Lewis, M. (2011). Inside and outside: The relation between emotional states and expressions. *Emotion Review, 3*, 189–196.

Lewis, M. D. (2000, January/February). The dynamic systems approaches for an integrated account of human development. *Child Development 71*(1), 36–43. Retrieved from http://www.psych.yorku.ca/adler/courses/4010/documents/LewisChDev2000.pdf.

Lewis, M. D. (2012) Memoirs of an addicted brain. Retrieved from http://www.youtube.com/watch?v=MBPBcJIZIsA

Lewis, M., & Brooks-Gunn, J. (1979). *Social cognition and the acquisition of the self.* New York: Plenum.

Lewis, M., Feiring, C., & Rosenthal, S. (2000). Attachment over time. *Child Development, 71*, 707–720.

Lewis, R. (2010). *Human genetics* (9th ed.). New York: McGraw-Hill.

Lewis, R. (2012). *Human genetics* (10th ed.). New York: McGraw-Hill.

Lewis, T., & Maurer, D. (2009). Effects of early pattern deprivation on visiual development. *Optometry and Vision Science, 86*(6), 640–646.

Li, B., Jiang, Y. Yuan, F. & Ye, H. (2010). Exchange transfusion of least incompatable blood for sever hymolytic disease of the newborn due to anti-Rh17. *Transfusion Medicine, 20*, 66–69.

Li, C., Goran, M. I., Kaur, H., Nollen, N., & Ahluwalia, J. S. (2007). Developmental trajectories of overweight during childhood: Role of early life factors. *Obesity, 15*, 760–761.

Li, D. K., Willinger, M., Petitti, D. B., Odulil, R. K., Liu, L., & Hoffman, H.J. (2006). Use of a dummy (pacifier) during sleep and risk of sudden infant death syndrome (SIDS): Population based case-control study. *British Medical Journal, 332*, 18–22.

Li, F. J., Shen, L., & Ji, H. F. (2012). Dietary intakes of vitamin E, vitamin C, and b-carotene, and risk of Alzheimer's disease: A meta-analysis. *Journal of Alzheimer's Disease, 31*, 753–758.

Li, J. (2013). It's complicated: Teens' relationship with religion. *The Source, 13*(22), 1–2.

Li, P. Q., et al. (2014, in press). Development of noninvasive prenatal diagnosis of trisomy 21 by RT-MLPA with a new set of SNP markers. *Archives of Gynecology and Obstetrics.*

Li, Q. (2005, April). *Cyberbullying in schools: Nature and extent of Canadian adolescents experience.* Paper presented at the conference of the American Education Research Association, Montreal.

Li, Q. (2006). Cyberbullying in schools: A research of gender differences. *School Psychology International, 27*, 157–170.

Li, X. P., et al. (2013). The influence of statin-fibrate combination therapy on lipids profile and apolipoprotein A5 in patients with acute coronary syndrome. *Lipids in Health and Disease, 12*, 133.

Li, X., Kim, P., & Gilbert, M. (2008, June 19). Trends in herpes simplex virus cases in British Columbia 1992–2006: STI and HIV prevention and control. BC Centre of Disease Control. Retrieved from http://www.bccdc.ca/

Li, Y. (2007). Recovering from spousal bereavement in later life: Does volunteer participation play a role? *Journals of Gerontology B: Psychological Sciences and Social Sciences, 62*, S257–S266.

Li, Y. (2016) Canada Research Chair in Directed Evolution of Nucleic Acids. *McMaster University News* (2016). http://fhs.mcmaster.ca/main/canada_chairs/directed_evolution_chair.html

Liben, L. S. (2009). Giftedness during childhood: The spatial-graphic domain. In F. D. Horowitz, R. F. Subotnik, & D. J. Matthews (Eds.), *The development of giftedness and talent across the life span.* Washington, DC: American Psychological Association.

Liben, L. S., Bigler, R. S., & Hilliard, L. J. (2014). Gender development: From universality to individuality. In E. T. Gershoff, R. S. Mistry, & D. A. Crosby (Eds.), *Societal contexts of child development.* New York: Oxford University Press.

Liberal Party of Canada. (2016). Marijuana. Retrieved from http://www.liberal.ca/realchange/marijuana/

Licata, M., Paulus, M., Thoermer, C., Kristen, S., Woodward, A. & Sodian, B. (2014). Mother-infant interaction quality and infant's ability to encode actions as goal-directed. *Social Development, 23*(2), 340–356.

Lie, E., & Newcombe, N. (1999). Elementary school children's explicit and implicit memory of faces of preschool classmates. *Developmental Psychology, 35*, 102–112.

Liegeois, F., Connelly, A., Baldeweg, T., & Vargha-Khadem, F. (2008). Speaking with a single cerebral hemisphere: fMRI language organization after hemispherectomy in childhood. *Brain and Language, 106*(3), 195–203.

Li-Korotky, H. S. (2012). Age-related hearing loss: Quality of care for quality of life. *Gerontologist, 52*, 265–271.

Lillard, A. (2006). Pretend play in toddlers. In C. A. Brownell & C. B. Kopp (Eds.), *Socioemotional development in the toddler year.* New York: Oxford University Press

Lillard, A. S., & Kavanaugh, R. D. (2014, in press). The contribution of symbolic skills to the development of explicit theory of mind. *Child Development.*

Lillenes, M. S., et al. (2013). Transient OGG1, APE1, PARP1, and PolB expression in an Alzheimer's disease mouse model. *Mechanisms of Aging and Development, 34*, 467–477.

Lim, J. H., Park, S. Y., & Ryu, H. M. (2013). Non-invasive prenatal diagnosis of fetal trisomy 21 using cell-free fetal DNA in maternal blood. *Obstetrics and Gynecology Science, 56*, 58–66.

Lin, C. C., et al. (2013). In utero exposure to environmental lead and manganese and neurodevelopment at 2 years of age. *Environmental Research, 123*, 52–57.

Lin, F. R. (2011). Hearing loss and cognition among older adults in the United States. *Journals of Gerontology A: Biological Sciences and Medical Sciences, 66*, 1131–1136.

Lin, J. (2005). The housing transitions of seniors. *Canadian Social Trends,* 85 (Winter), 22–26.

Lindau, S. T., & Gavrilova, N. (2010). Sex, health, and years of sexually active life gained due to good health: Evidence from two U.S. population based cross sectional surveys of aging. *British Medical Journal, 340,* c810.

Lindblad, F., Hjern, A., & Vinnerljung, B. (2003). Intercountry adopted children as young adults—A Swedish cohort study. *American Journal of Orthopsychiatry, 73,* 190–202.

Linde, K., & Alfermann, D. (2014, in press). Single versus combined cognitive and physical activity effects on fluid cognitive abilities of healthy older adults: A 4-month randomized controlled trial with follow-up. *Journal of Aging and Physical Activity.*

Lindwall, M., et al. (2012). Dynamic associations of change in physical activity and change in cognitive function: Coordinated analyses across four studies with up to 21 years of longitudinal data. *Journal of Aging Research.*

Linebarger, J., Sahler, O., & Egan, K. (2009). Coping with death. *Pediatrics in Review, 30*, 350–356.

Lio, G. (2012) You need more magnesium. Retrieved from https://www.youtube.com/watch?v=nDI_nzySNF8

Lippman, L. A., & Keith, J. D. (2006). The demographics of spirituality among youth: International perspectives. In E. Roehlkepartain, P. E. King, L. Wagener, & P. L. Benson (Eds.), *The handbook of spirituality in childhood and adolescence.* Thousand Oaks, CA: Sage.

Lira, F. S., et al. (2011). Exercise training improves sleep pattern and metabolic profile in elderly people in a time-dependent manner. *Lipids in Health and Disease, 10*, 1–6.

Lisonkova, S., Sabr, Y., Butler, B. & Joseph, K. (2012). International comparisons of preterm birth: higher rates of late preterm birth are associated with lower rates of stillbirth and neonatal death. International *Journal of Obstetrics and Gynaecology, 119*(13), 1630–1639.

Liston, F., Allen, V., O'Connell, C., & Jangaard, K. (2008). Neonatal outcomes with caesarean delivery at term. *Archives of Disease in Childhood - Fetal and Neonatal Edition, 93*, F176–F182.

Little, T., Card, N., Preacher, K. & McConnell, E. (2009). Modeling longitudinal data from research on adolescence. In R. Lerner & L. Steinberg, (Ed.). *Handbook of Adolescent Psychology* (3rd ed., pp. 15–54). New York, NY: Wiley.

Liu, A., Hu, X., Ma, G., Cui, Z., Pan, Y., Chang, S., et al. (2008). Evaluations of a classroom-based physical activity promoting program. *Obesity Reviews, 9* (Suppl. 1), S130–S134.

Liu, P., Lu, Y., Recker, R. R., Deng, H. W., & Dvornyk, V. (2010). ALOX12 gene is associated with the onset of natural menopause in white women. *Menopause, 17*, 152–156.

Liu, R., & Mustanski, B. (2012). Suicidal ideation and self-harm in lesbian, gay, bisexual, and transgender youth. *American Journal of Preventative Medicine, 42*(3), 221–228.

Liu, S., Liston, R., Joseph, K., Heaman, M., Sauve, R., & Kramer, M. (2007). Maternal mortality and severe morbidity associated with low-risk planned caesarian delivery versus planned vaginal delivery at term. *Canadian Medical Association, 176*(4) 455–460.

Liu, S., Wrosh,C., Miller, G., & Pruessner, J. (2014) Self-esteem change and diurnal cortisol secretion in older adulthood. *Psychoneuroendocrinology, 41*, 111–120.

Liu, W., & Aaker, J. (2007). Do you look to the future or focus on today? The impact of life experiences on intertemporal decisions. *Organizational Behaviour and Human Decision Processes, 102*, 212–225.

Liu, Y. J., Xiao, P., Xiong, D. H., Recker, R. R., & Deng, H. W. (2005). Searching for obesity genes: Progress and prospects. *Drugs Today, 41*, 345–362.

Lloyd, J. W., et al. (2015, in press). *Evidence-based reading instruction for ALL learners.* Upper Saddle River, NJ: Pearson.

Lo, B., & Rubenfeld, G. (2005). Palliative sedation in dying patients: "We turn to it when everything else hasn't worked." *Journal of the American Medical Association, 294*, 1810–1816.

LoBiondo, G., Haber, J. & Singh, M. (2013). Nonexperimental designs. In G. LoBiondo-Wood, J, Haber, C, Cameron, & M. Singh (Eds.) *Nursing research in Canada.* (3rd Canadian ed.) (pp. 234–252). Toronto: Elsevier.

Lobsinger, T. (2011, Spring). Eldercare: By seniors for seniors. *The Vanier Institute of the Family: Transition, 41*(1), 1.

Lochman, J., Powell, N., Boxmeyer, C., Young, L., & Baden, R. (2010). Historical conceptions or risk subtyping among children and adolescents. In R.T. Salekin, & D. R. Lynam (Eds.), *Handbook of Child and Adolescent Psychopathy* (pp. 49–78). New York, NY: The Guliford Press.

Lockenhoff, C. E., Costa, P. T., & Lane, R. D. (2008). Age differences in descriptions of emotional experiences in oneself and others. *Journals of Gerontology B: Psychological Sciences and Social Sciences, 63*, P62–P99.

Loeber, R., Pardini, D. A., Stouthamer-Loeber, M., & Raine, A. (2007). Do cognitive, physiological, and psychosocial risk and promotive factors predict desistance from delinquency in males? *Development and Psychopathology, 19*, 867–887.

Loehlin, J. C., Horn, J. M., & Ernst, J. L. (2007). Genetic and environmental influences on adult life outcomes: Evidence from the Texas adoption project. *Behavior Genetics, 37*, 463–476.

Loehlin, J., Neiderhiser, J., & Reiss, D. (2003). The behavior genetics of personality and the NEAD study. *Journal of Research in Personality, 37*, 373–387.

Loessi, B., Valerius, G., Kopasz, M., Hornyak, M., Riemann, D., & Voderholzer, U. (2008). Are adolescents chronically sleep-deprived? An investigation of sleep habits of adolescents in the Southwest of Germany. *Child Care Health and Development, 34*(5), 549–556.

Lofmark, R., et al. (2008). Physicians' experiences with end-of-life decision-making: Survey in six European countries and Australia. *BMC Medicine, 12*, 4.

Logan, A. G. (2011). Hypertension in aging patients. Expert Review of Cardiovascular Therapy, 9, 113–120.

Loiselle, C. G., Profetto-McGrath, J., Polit, D. F., & Beck, C.T. (2011). *Canadian essentials of nursing research* (3rd ed). New York: Wolters Kluwer Health/ Lippincott, Williams & Wilkins.

Lombardo, P. A. (2008). *Three generations, no imbeciles: Eugenics, the Supreme Court, and Buck v. Bell.* Baltimore: Johns Hopkins University Press.

London, M. L., Ladewig, P. A., Ball, J. W., & Bindler, R. A. (2007). *Maternal and child nursing care* (2nd ed.). Upper Saddle River, NJ: Prentice Hall.

Londono-Vallejo, J. A., & Wellinger, R. J. (2012). Telomeres and telomerase dance to the rhythm of the cell cycle. Trends in Biochemical Science, 37(9), 391–399.

Longman, P. (1987). *Born to pay: The new politics of aging in America.* Boston: Houghton-Mifflin.

Loponen, M., Hublin, C., Kalimo, R., Manttari, M., & Tenkanen, L. (2010). Joint effect of self-reported sleep problems and three components of the metabolic syndrome on risk of coronary heart disease. *Journal of Psychosomatic Research, 68*, 149–158.

Lorenz, K. Z. (1965). *Evolution and the modification of behavior.* Chicago: University of Chicago Press.

Lou, J., Agley, J., Hendryx, M., Gassman, R., & Lohrmann, D. (2015). Risk patterns among college youth: Identification and implications for prevention and treatment. *Health Promotion Practice, 16*(1), 132–141.

Loutfy, M., et al. (2012). High prevalence of unintended pregnancies in HIV-positive women of reproductive age in Ontario, Canada: A retrospective study. *HIV Medicine, 13*, 107–113.

Love, J. M., Chazan-Cohen, R., Raikes, H., & Brooks-Gunn, J. (2013). What makes a difference: Early Head Start evaluation findings in a developmental context. Monographs of the Society for Research in Child Development, 78, 1–173.

Low, J., & Simpson, S. (2012). Effects of labeling on preschoolers' explicit false belief performance: Outcomes of cognitive flexibility or inhibitory control? *Child Development, 83*(3), 1072–1084.

Lowe, J., MacLean, P., Duncan, A., Aragón, C., Schrader, R., Caprihan, S. & Phillips, J. (2012). Association of maternal interaction with emotional regulation in 4-and 9- month infants during the Still Face Paradigm. *Infant Behaviour and Development, 35*, 295–302.

Lowe, M., & Kral, T. (2005, 2006). Stress-induced eating in restrained eaters may not be caused by stress or restraint. *Appetite, 46*, 16–21.

Lowry, R.B., & León, J.A. (2013).Introduction - Congenital anolmalies surveillance in Canada. *Congenital Anomalies in Canada 2013 - A Perinatal Health Surveillance Report- Protecting Canadians from Illness.* Public Health Agency of Canada. Retrieved from http://www.aphp.ca/pdf/CAC%20report%202013%20EN.pdf.

Lu, C. J., Yu, J. J., & Deng, J. W. (2012). Disease-syndrome combination clinical study of psoriasis: Present status, advantages, and prospects. *China Journal of Integrative Medicine, 18*, 166–171.

Lu, M. C., & Lu, J. S. (2008). Prenatal care. In M. M. Haith & J. B. Benson (Eds.), *Encyclopedia of infancy and early childhood development.* Oxford, UK: Elsevier.

Lu, P. H., et al. (2011). Age-related slowing in cognitive processing speed is associated with myelin integrity in a very healthy elderly sample. *Journal of Clinical and Experimental Neuropsychology, 33*, 1059–1068.

Lu, P. H., et al. (2013). Myelin breakdown mediates age-related slowing in cognitive processing speed in healthy elderly men. *Brain and Cognition, 81*(1), 131–138.

Lucas, R. E., & Donnellan, M. B. (2011). Personality development across the life span: Longitudinal analyses with a national sample in Germany. *Journal of Personality and Social Psychology, 101*, 847–861.

Lucas, R. E., Clark, A. E., Yannis, G., & Diener, E. (2004). Unemployment alters the setpoint for life satisfaction. *Psychological Science, 15*, 8–13.

Lucchetti, G., Lucchetti, A. L., & Koenig, H. G. (2011). Impact of spirituality/religiosity on mortality: Comparison with other health interventions. *Explore, 7*, 234–238.

Ludington-Hoe, S. (2011). Thirty years of kangaroo care science and practice. *Neonatal Network: The Journal of Neonatal Nursing, 30*, 357–362.

Ludington-Hoe, S. M., Lewis, T., Morgan, K., Cong, X., Anderson, L., & Reese, S. (2006). Breast and infant temperatures with twins during kangaroo care. *Journal of Obstetric, Gynecologic, and Neonatal Nursing, 35*, 223–231.

Luhmann, M., Hofmann, W., Eid, M., & Lucas, R. E. (2012). Subjective well-being and adaptation to life events: A meta-analysis. *Journal of Personality and Social Psychology 102*, 592–615.

Lukowski, A. F., & Bauer, P. J. (2014). Long-term memory in infancy and early childhood. In P. J. Bauer & R. Fivush (Eds.), *Wiley-Blackwell handbook of children's memory.* New York: Wiley.

Lumpkin, A. (2011). *Introduction to physical education, exercise science, and sport studies* (8th ed.). New York: McGraw-Hill.

Luna, B., Padmanabhan, A., & Axelsson, B. (2011). Information of imminent death or not: Does it make a difference? *Journal of Clinical Oncology, 29*, 3927–3931.

Lunau, K. (2012). Campus crisis: the broken generation. *Maclean's.* Retrieved from http://www2.macleans.ca/2012/09/05/the-broken-generation/

Lund, D. A. (2007). Bereavement and loss. In J. E. Birren (Ed.), *Encyclopedia of gerontology* (2nd ed.). San Diego: Academic Press.

Lundervold, A. J., Wollschlager, D., & Wehling, E. (2014, in press). Age and sex-related changes in episodic memory function in middle aged and older adults. *Scandinavian Journal of Psychology.*

Lundin, A., Falkstedt, D., Lundberg, L. & Hemmingsson, T. (2014). Unemployment and coronary heart disease among middle-men I Sweden: 39,243 men followed for 8 years. *Occupational and Environmental Medicine, 71*, 183–188.

Lung, F., Shu, B., Chiang, T. & Lin, S. (2010). Maternal mental health and childrearing context in the development of children at 6. 18 and 36 months: a Taiwan birth cohort study. *Child: care, health and development, 37*(2), 211–223.

Luo, L., & Craik, F. I. M. (2008). Aging and memory: A cognitive approach. *Canadian Journal of Psychology, 53*, 346–353.

Luo, L., Kaufman, L. & Baillargeon, R. (2009). Young infants' reasoning about events involving inert and self-propelled objects. *Cognitive Psychology, 58,* 441–486.

Luo, Y. & Baillargeon, R. (2010). Toward a mentalistic account of early psychological reasoning. *Current Directions in Psychological Science, 19,* 301–307.

Luo, Z., Wilkins, R. R., Platt, R. W., & Kramer, M. S. (2004). Risks of adverse pregnancy outcomes among Inuit and North American Indian women in Quebec, 1985–97. *Paediatric and Perinatal Epidemiology, 18,* 40–50.

Luque-Contreras, D., et al. (2014). Oxidative stress and metabolic syndrome: Cause or consequence of Alzheimer's disease. *Oxidative Medicine and Cellular Longevity,* 497802.

Lusardi, A., Mitchell, O. S., & Curto, V. (2012). Financial sophistication in the older population. Retrieved from http://www.pensionresearchcouncil.org/publications/document.php?fi

Lustig, C., & Hasher, L. (2009). Interference. In R. Schulz, L. Noelker, K. Rockwood, & R. Sprott (Eds.), *Encyclopedia of aging* (4th ed.). New York: Springer Publishing.

Luyckx, K., Schwartz, S. J., Goossens, L., Soenens, B., & Beyers, W. (2008a). Developmental typologies of identity formation and adjustment in female emerging adults: A latent class growth analysis approach. *Journal of Research on Adolescence, 18*(4), 595–619.

Luyckx, K., Soenens, B., Goossens, L., & Vansteenkiste, M. (2007). Parenting, identity formation, and college adjustment: A mediation model with longitudinal data. *Identity, 7,* 309–330.

Luyckx, K., Soenens, B., Vansteenkiste, M., Goossens, L., & Berzonsky, M. D. (2008c). Parental psychological control and dimensions of identity formation in emerging adulthood. *Journal of Family Psychology, 21,* 546–550.

Lyall, J. (2007). What is a good death? *Nursing Older People, 19,* 6–8.

Lye, J. (1995). *Fiction and the immigrant experience.* Brock University. Retrieved from http://www.brocku.ca/

Lykken, D. (2001). *Happiness: What studies on twins show us about nature, nurture, and the happiness set point.* New York: Golden Books.

Lynch, T. (2004). Funerals-R-Us: From funeral home to mega-industry. *Generations, 28*(2), 11–14.

Lyndaker, C., & Hulton, L. (2004). The influence of age on symptoms of perimenopause. *Journal of Obstetric, Gynecological, and Neonatal Nursing, 33,* 340–347.

Lyon, T. D., & Flavell, J. H. (1993). Young children's understanding of forgetting over time. *Child Development, 64,* 789–800.

M

Ma, X., & Klinger, D. A. (2000). Hierarchical linear modelling of student and school effects on academic achievement. *Canadian Journal of Education, 25*(1), 41–55.

Maas, J. B. (1998). *Power sleep.* New York: Villard Books.

Maccoby, E. E., & Martin, J. A. (1983). Socialization in the context of the family: Parent-child interaction. In P. H. Mussen (Ed.), *Handbook of child psychology* (4th ed., Vol. 4). New York: Wiley.

MacDonald, H., MacKeigan, K., & Weaver, A. (2011). Experiences and perceptions of young adults in friends with benefits relationships: A qualitative study. *The Canadian Journal of Human Sexuality, 20*(1–2), 41.

Machado-Vidotti, H. G., et al. (2014). Cardiac autonomic responses during upper versus lower limb resistance exercise in healthy men. *Brazilian Journal of Physical Therapy, 18,* 1–18.

Maciejewski, P. K., Zhang, B., Block, S. D., & Prigerson, H. G. (2007). An empirical examination of the stage theory of grief. *Journal of the American Medical Association, 297,* 716–723.

Macionis, J., & Gerber, L. (2011). *Sociology.* Toronto: Pearson.

Macionis, J., & Gerber, L. (2014). *Sociology* (8th Canadian Ed.). Upper Saddle River, NJ: Pearson.

Macionis, J., Jansson, S. W. & Benoit, C. (2013). *Society: The basics* (5th Canadian ed.). Toronto: Pearson.

MacKenzie, C. S., Smith, M. C., Hasher, L., Leach, L., & Behl, P. (2007). Cognitive functioning under stress: Evidence from informal caregivers of palliative patients. *Journal of Palliative Medicine, 10*(3), 749–758.

Mackin, R. S., et al. (2014, in press). Association of age at depression onset with cognitive functioning in individuals with late-life depression and executive dysfunction. *American Journal of Geriatric Psychiatry.*

Mackoff, R., Iverson, E., Kicket, P., Dorey, F., Upperman, J., & Metzenberg, A. (2010). Attitudes of genetic counsellors towards genetic susceptibility testing in children. *Journal of Genetic Counselling, 19,* 402–416.

MacMartin, C. (2004). Judicial constructions of the seriousness of child sexual abuse. *Canadian Journal of Behavioural Science, 36,* 66–80.

Macmillan, H. L., Wathen, C. N., Barlow, J., Fergusson, D. M., Leventhal, J. M.,& Taussig, H. N. (2009). Interventions to prevent child maltreatment and associated impairment. *Lancet, 373,* 250–266.

Macmillan, R., & Meyer, M. J. (2006). Inclusion and guilt: The emotional fallout for teachers. *Exceptionality Education Canada, 16,* 25–43.

MacNeil, M. (2008). An epidemiologic study of Aboriginal adolescent risk in Canada: The meaning of suicide. *Journal of Child and Adolescent Psychiatric Nursing, 21*(1), 3–12.

Maconochie, N., Doyle, P., Prior, S., & Simmons, R. (2007). Risk factors for first trimester miscarriage—Results from a UK-population-based case-control study. *British Journal of Obstetrics and Gynecology, 114,* 170–176.

Mactier, H. (2011). The management of heroin misuse in pregnancy: Time for a rethink? *Arch Dis Child Fetal Neonatal Ed, 96,* F457–F460.

Madden, D. J., Gottlob, L. R., Denny, L. L., Turkington, T. G., Provenzale, J. M., Hawk. T. C., et al. (1999). Aging and recognition memory: Changes in regional cerebral blood flow associated with components of reaction time distributions. *Journal of Cognitive Neuroscience, II,* 511–520.

Madigan, S., Moran, G. & Pederson, D. (2006). Unresolved states of mind, disorganized attachment relationships, and disrupted interactions of adolescent mothers and their infants. *Developmental Psychology, 42,* 293–304.

Maggi, S. (2010). Vaccination and healthy aging. *Expert Review of Vaccines, 9* (Suppl. 3), S3–S6.

Maher, J., Doerksen, S., Elavsky, S., Hyde, A., Pincus, A., Ram, N., & Conroy, D. (2013). A daily analysis of physical activity and satisfaction with life in emerging adults. *Health Psychology, 23*(6), 647–656.

Mahler, M. (1979). *Separation-individuation* (Vol. 2). London: Jason Aronson.

Mahn, H., & John-Steiner, V. (2013). Vygotsky and sociocultural approaches to teaching and learning. In I. B. Weiner et al. (Eds.), *Handbook of psychology* (2nd ed., Vol. 7). New York: Wiley.

Maholmes, V., & King, R. B. (Eds.) (2012). *Oxford handbook of poverty and child development.* New York: Oxford University Press

Mahoney, J. R., Verghese, J., Goldin, Y., Lipton, R., & Holtzer, R. (2010). Altering orienting and executive attention in older adults. *Journal of the International Neuropsychological Society, 16*(5), 877–889.

Maillard, P., et al. (2012). Effects of systolic blood pressure on white-matter integrity in young adults in the Framington Heart Study: A cross-sectional study. *Lancet Neurology, 11*, 1039–1047.

Maimoun, L., & Sultan, C. (2010). Effects of physical activity on bone remodeling. *Metabolism, 60*(3), 373–388.

Maindonald, E. (2005). Sudden infant death syndrome (SIDS). *Nursing, 35*(7), 53.

Maki, A. (2014, Feb 21). Women's hockey final: A monumental rivalry, a spectacular finish for Canada. *The Globe and Mail*. Retrieved from http://www.theglobeandmail.com

Makinen, J., & Johnson, S. (2006). Resolving attachment injuries in couples using emotionally focused therapy: Steps toward forgiveness and reconciliation. *Journal of Consulting and Clinical Psychology, 74*(6), 1055–1064.

Malamitsi-Puchner, A., & Boutsikou, T. (2006). Adolescent pregnancy and perinatal outcome. *Pediatric Endocrinology Reviews, 3* (Suppl. 1), 170–171.

Malatesta, V. J. (2007). Sexual problems, women, and aging: An overview. *Journal of Women and Aging, 19*, 139–154.

Maloy, R. W., Verock-O'Loughlin, R-E., Edwards, S. A., & Woolf, B. P. (2014). *Transforming learning with new technologies* (2nd ed.). Upper Saddle River, NJ: Pearson.

Malti, T., Dys, S.P., & Zuffianò, A. (2015. Prosocial behaviour. *Encyclopedia on Early Childhood Development.* Retrieved from http://www.child-encyclopedia.com/prosocial-behaviour/according-experts/moral-foundations-prosocial-behaviour.

Mamtani, M., Patel, A., & Kulkarni, H. (2008). Association of the pattern of transition between arousal states in neonates with the cord blood lead level. *Early Human Development, 84*, 231–235.

Mandal, S., Abebe, F., & Chaudhary, J. (2014). –174G/C polymorphism in the interleukin-6 promoter is differently associated with prostate cancer incidence depending on race. *Genetics and Molecular Research, 13*, 139–151.

Mandler, J. (2012). On the spatial foundations of the conceptual system and its enrichment. *Cognitive Science, 36*, 421–451.

Mandler, J. M. (2006). *Jean Mandler.* Retrieved from http://cogsci.ucsd.edu/~jean/

Mandler, J. M., & DeLoache, J. (2012). The beginnings of conceptual development. In S. Pauen & M. Bornstein (Eds.), *Early child development and later outcome.* New York: Cambridge University Press.

Manenti, R., Cotelli, M., & Miniussi, C. (2011). Successful physiological aging and episodic memory: A brain stimulation study. *Behavioral Brain Research, 216*, 153–158.

Mang,C. S., Campbell, K. L., Ross, C. J. D., and Boyd, L. (2013). Variation on Brain-Derived Neurotrophic Factor. Physical Therapy. *Journal of the American Physical Therapy Association.* Retrieved from http://ptjournal.apta.org/content/93/12/1707.short.

Mangeni, J., Mwangi, A., Mbugua, S. & Mukthar, V. (2013). Male involvement min maternal health care as a determinant of utilization of skilled birth attendants in Kenya. Retrieved from http://www.ncbi.nim.gov

Manitoba Scool Improvement Program (MSIP). (2011). Manitoba school improvement program: Annual report. Retrieved from http://www.msip.ca/

Mann, J., et al. (2005). Suicide prevention strategies: A systematic review. *Journal of the American Medical Association, 294*(16), 2064–2074.

Mann, T., Tomiyama, J., Westling, E., Lew, A., Samuels, B., & Chatman, J. (2007). Medicare's search for effective obesity: Diets are not the answer. *American Psychologist, 62*(3), 220–233.

Mantyh, P. W. (2014). The neurobiology of skeletal pain. *European Journal of Neuroscience, 39*, 508–519.

Manzoli, L., Villari, P., Pirone, M., & Boccia, A. (2007). Marital status and mortality in the elderly: A systematic review and meta-analysis. *Social Science Medicine, 64*, 77–94.

Marano, H. E. (May/June 2016) An element of protetion - Magnesium is a mineral essential to mental health. *Psychology Today, 49*(3).

Marceau, K., Dorn, L. & Susman, E. (2012). Stress and puberty-related hormone reactivity, negative emotionality, and parent-adolescent relationships. *Psychoneuroimmunology, 37*(8), 1286–1298.

Marcia, J. E. (1980). Ego identity development. In J. Adelson (Ed.), *Handbook of adolescent psychology.* New York: Wiley.

Marcia, J. E. (1994). The empirical study of ego identity. In H. A. Bosma, T. L. G. Graafsma, H. D. Grotevant, & D. J. De Levita (Eds.), *Identity and development.* Newbury Park, CA: Sage.

Marcia, J. E. (2002). Identity and psychosocial development in adulthood. *Identity, 2*, 7–28.

Marcia, J., & Josselson R. (2013). Eriksonian personality research and its implications for psychotherapy. *Journal of Personality, 81*(6), 617–629.

Mares, M-L., & Pan, Z. (2013). Effects of Sesame Street: A meta-analysis of children's learning in 15 countries. *Journal of Applied Developmental Psychology, 34*, 140–151.

Margolis, R., & Iciaszczyk, N. (2015). The Changing Health of Canadian Granparents. *Candian Studies in Population, 42*(3-4), 63–76. Retrieved from https://ejournals.library.ualberta.ca/index.php/csp/article/viewFile/24598/18944.

Marin, L., & Halpern, D. (2011). Pedagogy for developing critical thinking in adolescents: Explicit instruction produces greatest gains. *Thinking Skills and Creativity, 6*, 1–13.

Markant, J. C., & Thomas, K. M. (2013). Postnatal brain development. In P. D. Zelazo (Ed.), *Oxford handbook of developmental psychology.* New York: Oxford University Press.

Markides, K. S., Rudkin, L., & Wallace, S. P. (2007). Ethnicity and minorities. In J. E. Birren (Ed.), *Encyclopedia of gerontology* (2nd ed.). San Diego: Academic Press.

Marks, A. K., Patton, F., & García Coll, C. (2011). Being bicultural: A mixed-methods study of adolescents' implicitly and explicitly measured multiethnic identities. *Developmental Psychology, 47*(1), 270–288.

Marks, B. L., Katz, L. M., & Smith, J. K. (2009). Exercise and the aging mind: Buffing the baby boomer's body and brain. *The Physician and Sportsmedicine, 37*, 119–125.

Markus, H. R., Ryff, C. D., Curhan, K., & Palmersheim, K. (2004). In their own words: Well-being among high school and college-educated adults. In G. Brim, C. D. Ryff, & R. Kessler (Eds.), *How healthy are we? A national study of well-being in midlife.* Chicago: University of Chicago Press.

Marlatt, G. (1996). Taxonomy of high-risk situations for alcohol relapse: Evolution and development of a cognitive-behavioural model. *Addiction, 91*, S37–S49.

Marlow, N., Hennessy, E. M., Bracewell, M. A., Wolke, D., & the EPICure Study Group. (2007). Motor and executive function at 6 years of age after extremely preterm birth. *Pediatrics, 120*, 793–804.

Maroney, T. (2009). The false promise of adolescent brain science in juvenile justice. *Notre Dame Law Review, 85*(1), 88–177.

Marquart, B., Nannini, D., Edwards, R., Stanley, L., & Wayman, J. (2007). Prevalence of dating violence: Regional and gender differences. *Adolescence, 42*, 645–657.

Marsh, H. W., Martin, A. J., & Xu, M. (2012). Self-concept: Synergy of theory, mind, and application. In K. R. Harris, S. Graham, & T. Urdan (Eds.), *APA*

educational psychology handbook. Washington, DC: American Psychological Association.

Marsh, H., Ellis, L., & Craven, R. (2002). How do preschool children feel about them selves? Unraveling measurement and multidimensional self-concept structure. *Developmental Psychology, 38,* 376–393.

Marsh, I., Keating, M., Punch, S., & Harden, J. (2009). *Sociology: Making sense of society.* (4th ed.) London: Pearson Education/Prentice-Hall.

Marshall, K. (2003). Parental leave: More time off for baby. *Canadian Social Trends,* Winter 2003, Statistics Canada Catalogue no. 11-008, 13–18.

Marshall, K. (2008). Fathers' use of paid parental leave. Retrieved from http://www.statcan.gc.ca/pub/75-001-x/2008106/article/10639-eng.htm

Marshall, R., & Sutherland, P. (2008). The social relations of bereavement in the Caribbean. *Omega (Westport), 57*(1), 21–34.

Marshall, W. (2010). The role of attachments, intimacy, and loneliness in the etiology and maintenance of sexual offending. *Sexual and Relationship Therapy, 25*(1), 73–85.

Marsiske, M., Klumb, P. L., & Baltes, M. M. (1997). Everyday activity patterns and sensory functioning in old age. *Psychology and Aging, 12,* 444–457.

Martell, L. (2003). Postpartum women's perceptions of the hospital environment. *Journal of Obstetric Gynecologic & Neonatal Nursing, 32*(4), 478–485.

Martin, C., & Evaldsson, A-C. (2012). Affordances for participation: Children's appropriation of rules in a Reggio Emilia school. *Mind, Culture, and Activity, 19,* 51–74.

Martin, L. R., Friedman, H. S., & Schwartz, J. E. (2007). Personality and mortality risk across the life span: The importance of conscientiousness as a biopsychosocial attribute. *Health Psychology, 26,* 428–436.

Martin, M., Grünendahl, M., & Martin, P. (2001). Age differences in stress, social-resources, and well-being in middle and older age. *Journals of Gerontology: Psychological Sciences and Social Sciences, 56B,* P214–P222.

Martinez, M. E. (2010). *Learning and cognition.* Upper Saddle River, NJ: Merrill.

Martins, W. P., et al. (2014). Hormone therapy for female sexual function during perimenopause and postmenopause: A Cochrane review. *Climacteric, 17*(2), 133–135.

Masche, J. (2010). Explanation of normative declines in parent's knowledge about their adolescent children. *Journal of Adolescence, 33,* 271–284.

Maslow, A. H. (1954, 1968). *Toward a psychology of being.* Toronto: Van Nostrand Reinhold, Ltd.

Maslow, A. H. (1970). *Motivation and personality.* New York: Harper and Row.

Mason, K. A., Johnson, G. B., Losos, J. B., & Singer, S. (2015, in press). *Understanding biology.* New York: McGraw-Hill.

Masoro, E. J. (2006). Are age-associated diseases an integral part of aging? In E. J. Masoro & S. N. Austad (Eds.), *Handbook of the biology of aging* (6th ed.). San Diego: Academic Press.

Massey, Z., Rising, S. S., & Ickovics, J. (2006). Centering Pregnancy group prenatal care: Promoting relationship-centered care. *Journal of Obstetric, Gynecologic, and Neonatal Nursing, 35,* 286–294.

Masten, A. S. (2012). Faculty profile: Ann Masten. The Institute of Child Development further developments. Minneapolis: School of Education.

Masten, A. S. (2013). Risk and resilience in development. In P. D. Zelazo (Ed.), *Oxford handbook of developmental psychology.* New York: Oxford University Press.

Masten, A. S. (2014a). Global perspectives on resilience in children and youth. *Child Development, 85,* 6–20.

Masten, A. S. (2014b, in press). *Ordinary magic: Resilience in development.* New York: Guilford.

Masten, A. S., & Narayan, A. J. (2012). Child development in the context of disaster, war, and psychopathology: The legacy of Norman Garmezy. *Annual Review of Psychology* (Vol. 63). Palo Alto, CA: Annual Reviews.

Masten, A. S., Obradovic, J., & Burt, K. B. (2006). Resilience in emerging adulthood: Developmental perspectives on continuity and transformation. In J. J. Arnett & J. L. Tanner (Eds.), *Emerging adults in America.* Washington, DC: American Psychological Association.

Masten, A., & Tellegen, A. (2012). Resilience in developmental psychopathology: Contributions of the project competence longitudinal study. *Development and Psychopathology, 24,* 345–361.

Mastropieri, M. & Scruggs, T. (2004). *The inclusive classroom: Strategies for effective instruction* (2nd ed). Upper Saddle River, NJ: Pearson.

Masui, Y., Gondo, Y., Inagaki, H., & Hirose, N. (2006). National Library of Medicines National Instituted of Health. 28(4) Retrieved from http://www.ncbi.nlm.nih.gov/pmc/articles/PMC3259156/

Mate, I., Madrid, J. A., & la Fuente, M. D. (2014, in press). Chronobiology of the neuroimmunoendocrine system and aging. *Current Pharmaceutical Design.*

Mathole, T., Lindmark, G., Majoko, F., & Ahlberg, B. M. (2004). A qualitative study of women's perspectives of antenatal care in rural areas of Zimbabwe. *Midwifery, 20,* 122–132.

Matlin, M. W. (2004). *The psychology of women* (5th ed.). Belmont, CA: Wadsworth.

Matthews, C. E., Jurj, A. L., Shu, X. O., Yang, G., Li, Q., Gao, Y. T., et al. (2007). Influence of exercise, walking, cycling, and overall nonexercise physical activity on mortality in Chinese women. *American Journal of Epidemiology, 165,* 1343–1350.

Maxmen, A. (August, 2015). Easy DNA Editing Will Remake the World. Buckle Up. *Wired.* Retrieved from http://www.wired.com/2015/07/crispr-dna-editing-2/.

Maxson, S. C. (2013). Behavioral genetics. In I. B. Weiner et al. (Eds.), *Handbook of psychology* (2nd ed., Vol. 3). New York: Wiley.

May, R. (1975) *The courage to create.* New York: Bantam Books.

May, V., Onarcan, M., Oleschowski, C., & Mayron, Z. (2004). International perspectives on the role of home care and hospice in aging and long-term care. *Caring, 23,* 14–17.

Mayas, J., Parmentier, F. B., Andres, P., & Ballesteros, S. (2014). Plasticity of attentional functions in older adults after non-action video game training: A randomized controlled trial. *PloS One, 9*(3), e92269.

Mayer, A. (2011, September 28). Interview: Who's a bully? Psychologist Tracy Vaillancourt on kids who bully and what parents can do. CBC News Canada. Retrieved from http://www.cbc.ca/news/canada/story/2011/09/28/f-bullying-q-and-a.html

Mayer, D. (2009). The importance of work. *Clinical Journal of Oncology Nursing, 13*(6), 607.

Mayer, J. D. (2004). Who is emotionally intelligent—and how does it matter? Retrieved from http://www.unh.edu/emotional_intelligence/EI%20Assets/Reprints...EI%20Proper/EI2004MayerSaloveyCarusotarget.pdf

Mayer, J. D., Salovey, P., & Caruso, D. R. (2004). Emotional intelligence, theory, findings, and applications. *Psychological Inquiry, 15*(3), 197–215.

Mayer, K., Garofalo, R. & Makadon, H. (2014). Promoting the successful development of sexual and gender minority youth. *American Journal of Public Health, 104*(6), 976–981.

Mayers, L. B., & Chiffriller, S. H. (2008). Body art (body piercing and tattooing) among university undergraduate students: "Then and now." *Journal of Adolescent Health, 42*, 201–203.

Mayo Clinic. (2013). *Male hypogonadism*. Rochester, MN: Mayo Clinic.

Mayo Clinic Staff. (2016). Arthritis. Retrieved from http://www.mayoclinic.org/diseases-conditions/arthritis/home/ovc-20168903

Mayo Clinic. (2012). Teen eating disorders: Tips to protect your teen. Retrieved from http://www.mayoclinic.com/

Mayseless, O., & Scharf, M. (2007). Adolescents' attachment representation and their capacity for intimacy in close relationships. *Journal of Research on Adolescence, 17*, 23–50.

Mbonye, A. K., Neema, S., & Magnussen, P. (2006). Treatment-seeking practices for malaria in pregnancy among rural women in Mukono district, Uganda. *Journal of Biosocial Science, 38*, 221–237.

McAlister, A., & Peterson, C. (2007). A longitudinal study of child siblings and theory of mind development. *Cognitive Development, 22*, 258–270.

McAnarney, E. R. (2008). Editorial: Adolescent brain development: Forging new links? *Journal of Adolescent Health, 42*, 321–323.

McBride, D. (2013). Advance care planning discussions with adolescents and young adults with cancer. *Journal of Pediatric Nursing, 28*(4), 406–407.

McCabe, D. P., & Loaiza, V. M. (2012). Working memory. In S. K. Whitbourne & M. Sliwinski (Eds.), *Wiley-Blackwell handbook of adult development and aging*. New York: Wiley.

McCall, J., & Vicol, L. (2011). HIV infection and contraception. *Journal of the Association of Nurses in AIDS Care, 22*(3), 193–201.

McCartney, K. (2009). Current research on childcare effects. In R. E. Tremblay, R. deV Peters, M. Boivan, & R. G. Barr (Eds.), *Encyclopedia on early childhood development*. Montreal: Center of Excellence for Early Childhood Development.

McCartney, K., Dearing, E., Taylor, B. A., & Bub, K. L. (2007). Quality child care supports the achievement of low-income children: Direct and indirect pathways through caregiving and the home environment. *Journal of Applied Developmental Psychology, 28*, 411–426.

McClain, C. S., Rosenfeld, B., & Breitbart, W. S. (2003, March). *The influence of spirituality on end-of-life despair in cancer patients close to death.* Paper presented at the meeting of American Psychosomatic Society, Phoenix.

McClelland, K., Bowles, J., & Koopman, P. (2012). Male sex determination: Insights into molecular mechanisms. *Asian Journal of Andrology, 14*, 164–171.

McClosky, D. (2003–2004, Winter). Introduction to Canada's stepfamilies. *Transition Magazine, 33*(4). Montreal: The Vanier Institute of the Family.

McCormick, C. B., Dimmitt, C., & Sullivan, F. R. (2013). Metacognition, learning, and instruction. In I. B. Weiner et al. (Eds.), *Handbook of psychology* (2nd ed., Vol. 7). New York: Wiley.

McCoy, M. L., & Keen, S. M. (2014, in press). *Child abuse and neglect* (2nd ed.). New York: Psychology Press.

McCrae, R. R., & Costa, P. T. (2003). *Personality in adulthood* (2nd ed.). New York: Guilford.

McCrae, R. R., & Costa, P. T. (2006). Cross-cultural perspectives on adult personality trait development. In D. K. Mroczek & T. D. Little (Eds.), *Handbook of personality development.* Mahwah, NJ: Erlbaum.

McCrae R. R., Costa, P. T., et al. (1998). Age differences in personality across the adult lifespan: Parallels in five cultures. *Developmental Psychology, 35*, 466–477.

McCrae, R. R., Gaines, J. F., & Wellington, M. A. (2013). The five-factor model in fact and fiction. In I. B. Weiner et al. (Eds.), *Handbook of psychology* (2nd ed., Vol. 5). New York: Wiley.

McCreary Centre Society. (1999, June 14). Press release: B.C. study shows gay youth face high suicide risk. Retrieved from http://www.mcs.bc.ca

McCreary Centre Society. (2001). *Street youth not just an urban issue in B.C.* Retrieved from http://www.msc.bc.ca

McCreary Centre Society. (2015). Our communities, our youth: The health of homeless and street involved youth in B.C. Retrieved from http://www.mcs.bc.ca

McCuaig, K. (2014) Kindergarten in Canada. Atkinson Centre for Society and Child Development. Retrieved from https://www.oise.utoronto.ca/atkinson/UserFiles/File/Policy%20Commentaries/PolicyUpdate-FDKinCanada.pdf.

McCullough, A. R., Steidle, C. P., Klee, B., & Tseng, L. J. (2008). Randomized, double-blind, cross-over trial of sildenafil in men with moderate erectile dysfunction: Efficacy at 8 and 12 hours postdose. *Urology, 71*, 686–692.

McDonald, E., & Brown, S. (2013). Does method of birth make a difference to when women resume sex after childbirth? *An International Journal of Obstetrics and Gynaecology, 120970*, 823–830.

McDonald, S. D., et al. (2009). Preterm birth and low birth weight among in vitro fertilization singeltons: A systematic review and metaanalyses. *European Journal of Obstetrics, Gynecology, and Reproductive Biology, 146*, 138–148.

McDonald, S. D., et al. (2010). Preterm birth and low birth weight among in vitro fertilization twins: A systematic review and meta-analyses. *European Journal of Obstetrics, Gynecology, and Reproductive Biology, 148*, 105–113.

McDonough, I. M., & Gallo, D. A. (2013). Impaired retrieval monitoring for past and future autobiographical events in older adults. *Psychology and Aging, 28*, 457–466.

McDowell, M. A., Brody, D. J., & Hughes, J. P. (2007). Has age of menarche changed? Results from the National Health and Nutrition Examination Survey. *Journal of Adolescent Health, 40*, 227–231.

McElwain, N. L., & Booth-LaForce, C. (2006). Maternal sensitivity to infant distress and nondistress as predictors of infant-mother attachment security. *Journal of Family Psychology, 2*, 247–255.

McFarlane, M., Ross, M., & Elford, J. (2004). The Internet and HIV/STD prevention. *AIDS Care, 16*(8), 929–930.

McGoldrick, M., Carter, B., & Garcia-Preto, N. (2011). *The expanded family life cycle: Individual, family, and social perspectives.* Boston, MA: Pearson.

McIntosh, E., Gillanders, D., & Rodgers, S. (2010). Rumination, goal linking, daily hassles, and life events in major depression. *Clinical Psychology and Psychotherapy, 17*, 33–43.

McIntyre, M. (2009). Universities must help students with depression. Children's Mental Health Ontario. Retrieved from http://www.kidsmentalhealth.ca/news_and_events/view_html_article.php?id=796#top

McKay, A. (2006). Trends in teen pregnancy in Canada with comparison to USA and England/Wales. *The Canadian Journal of Human Sexuality, 15*(3–4), 157–161.

McKay, A. S., & Kaufman, J. C. (2014). Literary geniuses: Their life, work, and death. In D. K. Simonton (Ed.), *Wiley-Blackwell handbook of genius*. New York: Wiley.

McKenna, L., Kodner, I. J., Healy, G. G., & Keune, J. D. (2013). Sleep deprivation: A call for institutional rules. *Surgery, 154*, 118–122.

McKenzie, Marika. (2016) Father Goose. *Canadian Geographic*. Retrieved from http://www.canadiangeographic.ca/magazine/dec13/lishman-teaching-birds-to-migrate.asp.

McKeough, A., Bird, S., Tourigny, E., Romaine, A., Graham, S., Ottmann, J., et al. (2008). Storytelling as a foundation to literacy development for Aboriginal children: Culturally and developmentally appropriate practices. *Canadian Psychology, 49*(2), 148–154.

McKeown, J. (2015). "I will not be wearing heels tonight!": A feminist exploration of singlehood, dating, and leisure. *Journal of Leisure Research, 47*(4), 485–500.

McLaren, C. (2009). Alberta creates electronic registry for personal directives. *Canadian Medical AssociationJournal, 180*(7), 708.

McLeod, S. (2012). Carl Rogers. *Simply Psychology*. Retrieved from http://www.simplypsychology.org/carl-rogers.html.

McMahon, T. (2013, March 11). The smartphone will see you now–Putting medical technology in the hands of patients could revolutionize medicine. *McLean's*.

McMillan, C. T., et al. (2014, in press). The power of neuroimaging biomarkers for screening frontotemporal dementia. *Human Brain Mapping*.

McMillan, J. H. (2008). *Educational research* (5th ed.). Boston: Allyn & Bacon.

McMillen, I. C., MacLaughlin, S. M., Muhlhausler, B. S., Gentili, S., Duffield, J. L., & Morrison, J. L. (2008). Developmental origins of adult health and disease: The role of periconceptional and fetal nutrition. *Basic and Clinical Pharmacology and Toxicology, 102*, 82–89.

McNamara, F., & Sullivan, C. E. (2000). Obstructive sleep apnea in infants. *Journal of Pediatrics, 136*, 318–323.

McNamara, F., Lijowska, A. S., & Thach, B. T. (2002). Spontaneous arousal activity in infants during NREM and REM sleep. *Journal of Physiology, 538*, 263–269.

McPherson, M., Weissman, G., Strickland, B., van Dyck, P., Blumberg, S., & Newacheck, P. (2004). Implementing community-based systems of services for children and youths with special health care needs: How well are we doing? *Pediatrics, 113*(5 supp.), 1538–1544.

McRae, K., et al. (2012). The development of emotion regulation: An fMRI study of cognitive reappraisal in children, adolescents, and adults. *Social Cognitive and Affective Neuroscience, 7*, 11–22.

McShane, K., & Hastings, P. (2004). Culturally sensitive approaches to research on child development and family practices in first peoples communities. *First Peoples Child and Family Review, 1*(1), 38–44.

McShane, K., Smylie, J., & Adomako, P. (2009). Health of First Nations, Inuit, and Métis children in Canada. In J. Smylie & P. Adomako (Eds.), *Indigenous children's health report: Health assessment in action.* Toronto: Centre for Research on Inner City Health, Keenan Research Center.

Media Awareness Network. (2005). Young Canadians in a wired world Phase II: Student survey. Retrieved from http://www.media-awareness.ca/english/research/YCWW/phaseII/upload/YCWWII_Student_Survey.pdf

Medical News Today. (2009, August 24). What is vitamin D? What are the benefits of vitamin D? *Medical News Today*. Retrieved from http://www.medicalnewstoday.com/articles/161618.php

MediResource. (2010–2011). Alzheimer's disease. Canada.com. Retrieved from http://bodyandhealth.canada.com/channel_condition_info_details.asp?disease_id=218&channel_id=11&relation_id=10899

Meerlo, P., Sgoifo, A., & Suchecki, D. (2008). Restricted and disrupted sleep: Effects on autonomic function, neuroendocrine stress systems, and stress responsivity. *Sleep Medicine Review, 12*, 197–210.

Mehrotra, C. M., & Wagner, L. S. (2009). *Aging and diversity.* Clifton, NJ: Psychology Press.

Meikle, J., Al-Sarraf, A., Li, M., Grierson, K., & Frohlich, J. (2013). Exercise in a healthy heart program: A cohort study. *Clinical Medicine Insights: Cardiology, 7*, 145–151.

Meinhard, A. G., Foster, M. K. & Wright, C. (2006, Winter). Rethinking school-based community service: The importance of a structured program. *The Philanthropist.*

Meins, E., et al. (2013). Mind-mindedness and theory of mind: Mediating processes of language and perspectival symbolic play. *Child Development, 84*, 1777–1790.

Meins, E., Fernyhough, Arnott, B., Vittorini, L., Turner, M., Leeham, S., & Parkinson, K. (2011). Individual differences in infants' joint attention behaviours with mother and a new social partner. *Infancy, 16*(6), 587–610.

Mellon, N., Niparko, J., Rathmann, C., Mathur, G., Humpries, T. ... Lantos, J. (2015). Should all deaf children learn sign language. *Pediatrics, 136*(1), 176.

Meltzer, A., McNulty, J., Jackson, G., & Karney, B. (2014). Sex differences in the implications of partner physical attractiveness for the trajectory of marital satisfaction. *Journal of Personality and Social Psychology, 106*, 418–428.

Meltzoff, A. N. (1988). Infant imitation and memory: Nine-month-old infants in immediate and deferred tests. *Child Development, 59*, 217–225.

Meltzoff, A. N. (2004). Imitation as a mechanism of social cognition: Origins of empathy, theory of mind, and the representation of action. In U. Goswami (Ed.), *Blackwell handbook of childhood cognitive development.* Malden, MA: Blackwell.

Meltzoff, A. N. (2005). Imitation. In B. Hopkins (Ed.), *Cambridge encyclopedia of child development.* Cambridge: Cambridge University Press.

Meltzoff, A. N. (2007). Infants' causal learning. In A. Gopnik & L. Schulz (Eds.), *Causal learning.* New York: Oxford University Press.

Meltzoff, A. N., & Moore, M. K. (1999). A new foundation for cognitive development: The birth of the representational infant. In E. K. Skolnick, K. Nelson, S. A. Gelman, & P. H. Miller (Eds.), *Conceptual development.* Mahwah, NJ: Erlbaum.

Meltzoff, A. N., & Williamson, R. A. (2008). Imitation and modeling. In M. M. Haith & J. B. Benson (Eds.), *Encyclopedia of infant and early childhood development.* Oxford, UK: Elsevier.

Meltzoff, A., Kuhl, P., Movellan, J. & Sejnowski, T. (2009). Foundations for a new science of learning. *Science, 35,* 284–288.

Meltzoff, A., Waismeyer, A. & Gopnik, A. (2012). Learning about causes from people: Observational causal learning in 24-month-old infants. *Developmental Psychology, 48*(5), 1215–1228.

Memorial Society of British Columbia. (2004). Public health impact of crematoria. Retrieved from http://www.memorialsocietybc.org/c/g/cremationreport.html

Mendelson, M. (2008). *Improving education on reserves: A First Nations education authority act.* The Caledon Institute of Social Policy. Retrieved from http://www.caledoninst.org/publications/pdf/684eng.pdf

Menec, V. H. (2003). The relation between everyday activities and successful aging: A 6-year longitudinal study. *Journal of Gerontology B: Psychological Sciences and Social Sciences, 58*, 574–582.

Menias, C. O., Elsayes, K. M., Peterson, C. M., Huete, A., Gratz, B. I., & Bhalla, S. (2007). CT of pregnancy-related complications. *Emergency Radiology, 13,* 299–306.

Menn, L., & Stoel-Gammon, C. (2009). Phonological development: Learning sounds and sound patterns. In J. Berko Gleason (Ed.), *The development of language* (7th ed.). Boston: Allyn & Bacon.

Mennecke, A., Gossler, A., Hammen, T., Dörfler, A., Stadlebaure, A., Rösch, J.,.... Thürauf, N. (2014). Physiological effects of cigarette smoking in the limbic system revealed by 3 tesla magnetic resonance spectroscopy. *Journal of Neural Transmission, 121*, 1211–1299.

Menon, M., Tobin, D. D., Corby, B. C., Menon, M., Hodges, E. V. E., & Perry, D. G. (2007). The developmental costs of high self-esteem in aggressive children. *Child Development, 78*, 1627–1639.

Menon, R., et al. (2014, in press). Amniotic fluid metabolomic analysis in spontaneous preterm birth. Reproductive Sciences.

Mensah, G. A., & Brown, D. W. (2007). An overview of cardiovascular disease burden in the United States. *Health Affairs, 26*, 38–48.

Merad, M., et al. (2014, in press). Molecular interaction of acetylcolinesterase with carnosic acid derivaties: A neuroinformatics study. *CNS & Neurological Disorders Drug Targets.*

Meraz-Rios, M. A., et al. (2014). Early onset Alzheimer's disease and oxidative stress. *Oxidative Medicine and Cellular Longevity, 2014*, 375968.

Mercer, M., Drodge, S., Courage, M. & Adams, R. (2014). A pseudoischrromatic test of color vision for human infants. *Vision Research, 100*, 72–77.

Meristo, M., Falkman, K. W., Hjelmquist, E., Tedoldi, M., Surian, L., & Siegal, M. (2007). Language access and theory of mind reasoning: Evidence from deaf children in bilingual and oral environments. *Developmental Psychology, 43*(5), 1156–1169.

Merrill, D. M. (2009). Parent-child relationships: Later-life. In D. Carr (Ed.), *Encyclopedia of the life course and human development.* Boston: Gale Cengage.

Mesch, G., Talmud, I., & Quan-Haase, A. (2012). IM social networks: Individual, relational and cultural characteristics. *Journal of Social and Personal Relationships.*

Messinger, D. (2008). Smiling. In M. M. Haith & J. B. Benson (Eds.), *Encyclopedia of infant and early childhood development.* Oxford, UK: Elsevier.

Mestre, T. A., et al. (2014, in press). Reluctance to start medication for Parkinson's disease: A mutual misunderstanding by patients and physicians. *Parkinsonism and Related Disorders.*

Mesulam, M. M. (2013). Cholinergic circuitry of the human nucleus basalis and its fate in Alzheimer's disease. *Journal of Comparative Neurology and Psychology, 521*, 4124–4144.

Metts, S., & Cupach, W. R. (2007). Responses to relational transgressions. In M. Tafoya & B. H. Spitzberg (Eds.), *The dark side of interpersonal communication.* Mahwah, NJ: Erlbaum.

Meyer, I. H. (2003). Prejudice, social stress, and mental health in gay, lesbian, and bisexual populations: Conceptual issues and research evidence. *Psychological Bulletin, 129*, 674–697.

Michalska-Malecka, K., et al. (2013). Results of cataract surgery in the very elderly population. *Clinical Interventions in Aging, 8*, 1041–1046.

Miech, R., Johnston, L., O'Malley, P., Bachman, J., & Schulenberg, J. (2016). *Monitoring the Future national survey results on drug use, 1975-2015: Volume I, Secondary school students.* Ann Arbor: Institute for Social Research, The University of Michigan. Retrieved from http://www.monitoringthefuture.org

Mikkonen, J., & Raphael, D. (2010). Social determinants of health: The Canadian facts. Toronto: York University School of Health Policy and Management. Retrieved from http://www.thecanadianfacts.org/

Mikkonen, J., & Raphael, D. (2010). *Social determinants of health: The Canadian facts.* Retrieved from http://www.thecanadianfacts.org/

Mikulincer, M., & Shaver, P. (2007). Reflections on security dynamics: Core constructs, psychological mechanisms, relational contexts, and the need for an integrative theory. *Psychological inquiry, 18*, 197–209.

Mikulincer, M., & Shaver, P. R. (2007). *Attachment in adulthood.* New York: Guilford.

Mikulincer, M., & Shaver, P. R. (2009). Adult attachment and affect regulation. In J. Cassidy & P. R. Shaver (Eds.), *Handbook of attachment* (2nd ed.). New York: Guilford.

Mikulincer, M., Shaver, P., Bar-on, N., & ein-Dor, T. (2010) The push and pulls of close relationships: Attachment insecurities and relational ambivalence. *Journal of Personality and Social Psychology, 98*, 450–468.

Milan, A. (2013). *Marital status: Overview, 2011.* Statistics Canada. Retrieved from http://www.statcan.gc.ca.

Milan, A. (2015). *Women in Canada: A gender-based statistical report.* Retrieved from http://www.statcan.gc.ca.

Milan, A., & Hamm, B. (2003). Across the generations: Grandparents and grandchildren. *Canadian Social Trends, 71*, 2–7.

Milan, A., Hou, F., & Wong, I. (2006). Learning disabilities and child altruism, anxiety and aggression. *Canadian Social Trends* (Catalogue no. 11-008), 16–20.

Milan, A., Keown, L.A., & Urquijo, C. R. (2015). *Families, Living Arrangements and Unpaid Work.* Statistics Canada Retrieved from http://www.statcan.gc.ca/pub/89-503-x/2010001/article/11546-eng.htm.

Milan, A., Laflamme, N., & Wong, I. (2015a). Grandparents living with their grandchildren. Statistics Canada. Retrieved from http://www.statcan.gc.ca/daily-quotidien/150414/dq150414a-eng.htm.

Milan, A., Laflamme, N., & Wong, I. (2105b). Diversity of grandparents living with grandchildren. Statistics Canada. Retrieved from http://www.statcan.gc.ca/pub/75-006-x/2015001/article/14154-eng.htm

Milberg, A., Olsson, E. C., Jakobsson, M., Olsson, M., & Friedrichsen, M. (2008). Family members' perceived needs for bereavement follow-up. *Journal of Pain and Symptom Management, 35*, 58–69.

Miles, M. F., & Williams, R. W. (2007). Meta-analysis for microarray studies of the genetics of complex traits. *Trends in Biotechnology, 25*, 45–47.

Milke, M. A., & Peltola, P. (2000). Playing all the roles: Gender and the work-family balancing act. *Journal of Marriage and the Family, 61*, 476–490.

Miller, B. C., Bayley, B. K., Christensen, M., Leavitt, S. C., & Coyl, D. D. (2003). Adolescent pregnancy and childbearing. In G. Adams & M. Berzonsky (Eds.), *Blackwell handbook of adolescence.* Malden, MA: Blackwell.

Miller, C. F., Lurye, L. E., Zusuls, K. M., & Ruble, D. N. (2009). Accessibility of gender stereotype domains: Developmental and gender differences in children. *Sex Roles, 60*, 870–881.

Miller, J. B. (1986). *Toward a new psychology of women* (2nd ed.). Boston: Beacon Press.

Miller, J. G., & Bland, C. G. (2014). A cultural perspective on moral development. In M. Killen & J. G. Smetana (Eds.), *Handbook of moral development* (2nd ed.). New York: Psychology Press.

Miller, K., Couchie, R., Ehman, W., Graves, L., Grzybowski, S., & Medves, J. (2012). Joint position paper on rural maternity care. *Canadian Journal of Rural Medicine, 17*(4), 135–141.

Miller, P. H. (2014). The history of memory development research: Remembering our roots. In P. Bauer & R. Fivush (Eds.), *Wiley handbook on the development of children's memory.* New York: Wiley.

Miller, R. B., Hollist, C. S., Olsen, J., & Law, D. (2013). Marital quality and health over 20 years: A growth curve analysis. *Journal of Marriage and the Family, 75*, 667–680.

Miller, R., Sullivan, M., Hawes, K. & Marks, A. (2009). The effects of perinatal morbidity and environmental factors on health status pf preterm children at age 12. *Journal of Pediatric Nursing, 24*, 101–114.

Miller-Perrin, C. L., Perrin, R. D., & Kocur, J. L. (2009). Parental, physical, and psychological aggression: Psychological symptoms in young adults. *Child Abuse and Neglect, 33*, 1–11.

Milligan, K. (2008). The evolution of elderly poverty in Canada. *IDEAS, 34*(1), 79–94.

Milligan, K., Atkinson, L., Trehub, S. E., Benoit, D., & Poulton, L. (2003). Maternal attachment and the communication of emotion through song. *Infant Behavior & Development, 26*, 1–13.

Mills, A., Schmied, V., Taylor, C., Dahlen, H., Shuiringa, W. & Hudson, M. (2012). Someone to talk to: a young mothers' experience of participating in a young parents support program. *Scandinavian Journal of Caring Sciences, 27*(3), 551–559.

Mills, C. M., & Landrum, A. R. (2012). Judging judges: How do children weigh the importance of capability for being a good decision maker? *British Journal of Developmental Psychology, 30*(3), 383–414.

Mills, C. M., Elashi, F. B., & Archacki, M. A. (2011, March). *Evaluating sources of information and misinformation: Developmental and individual differences in the elementary school years.* Paper presented at the biennial meeting of the Society for Research in Child Development, Montreal.

Mills, D., & Mills, C. (2000). *Hungarian kindergarten curriculum translation.* London: Mills Production.

Minde, K., & Zelkowitz, P. (2008). Premature babies. In M. M. Haith & J. B. Benson (Eds.), *Encylopedia of infancy and early childhood development.* Oxford, UK: Elsevier.

Mindell, J., Sadeh, A., Wiegand, B., How, T., & Goh, D. (2010). Cross-cultural differences in infant and toddler sleep. *Sleep Medicine, 11*, 274–280.

Miner, M. M., Bhattacharya, R. K., Blick, G., Kushner, H., & Khera, M. (2013). 12-month observation of testosterone replacement effectiveness in a general population of men. *Postgraduate Medicine, 125*, 8–18.

Minister of Public Works and Government Services Canada. (2010). *The current state of multiculturalism in Canada and research themes on Canadian multiculturalism 2008–2010.* Ottawa: Citizenship and Immigration Canada. Retrieved from http://www.cic.gc.ca/english/pdf/pub/multi-state.pdf

Minnes, S., Min, M., Singer, L., Edguer, M., Wu, M. & Thi, P. (2012). Cocaine use during pregnancy and health outcomes after 10 years. *Drug and Alcohol Dependence*, 126, 71–79.

Minnesota Centre for Twin Research. (2012). Sir Francis Galton and twin research. Retrieved from https://mctfr.psych.umn.edu/research/Sir%20Galton.html

Minnotte, K., Minnotte, M. & Pedersen, D. (2013). Marital satisfaction among dual-earner couples: Gender ideologies and family-to-work conflict. *Family Relations: Interdisciplinary Journal of Applied Family Studies. 62*, 686–698.

Minzi, M. (2010). Genders and cultural patterns pf mothers' and fathers' attachment and links with children's self-competence, depression and loneliness in middle and late childhood. *Early Childhood Development and Care, 180*, 193–209.

Miotto, E. C., et al. (2013). Semantic strategy training increases memory performance and brain activity in patients with prefrontal cortex lesions. *Clinical Neurology and Neurosurgery, 115*(3), 309–316.

Miranda, M. L. (2004). The implications of developmentally appropriate practices for the kindergarten general music classroom. *Journal of Research in Music Education, 52*, 43–53.

Mischel, W. (2004). Toward an integrative science of the person. *Annual Review of Psychology* (Vol. 55). Palo Alto, CA: Annual Reviews.

Mischel, W., et al. (2011). 'Willpower' over the life span: Decomposing self-regulation. *Social Cognitive and Affective Neuroscience, 6*, 252–256.

Mischel, W., Shoda, Y., & Ayduk, O. (2008). *Introduction to personality: Toward an integrative science of the person* (8th ed.). New York: Wiley.

Mishra, G. D., Cooper, R., Tom, S. E., & Kuh, D. (2009). Early life circumstances and their impact on menarche and menopause. *Women's Health, 5*, 175–190.

Mitchell, E. A., Stewart, A. W., Crampton, P., & Salmond, C. (2000). Deprivation and sudden infant death syndrome. *Social Science and Medicine, 51*, 147–150.

Mitchell, M. B., et al. (2013). Norms for the Georgia Centenarian Study: Measures of verbal abstract reasoning, fluency, memory, and motor function. *Neuropsychology, Development, and Cognition B: Aging, Neuropsychology, and Cognition, 20*, 620–637.

Mitchell, M. S., Koien, C. M., & Crow, S. M. (2008). Harassment: It's not (all) about sex! Part I: The evolving legal framework. *Health Care Management, 27*, 13–22.

Miyashita, M., Sato, K., Morita, T., & Suzuki, M. (2008). Effect of a population-based educational intervention focusing on end-of-life home care, life-prolonging treatment, and knowledge about palliative care. *Palliative Medicine, 22*, 376–382.

Mize, K. & Jones, N. (2012). Infant physiological and behavioural responses to loss of maternal attention to a social-rival. *International Journal of Psychophysiology, 83*, 16–23.

Mobley, A. S., Rodriquez-Gil, D. J., Imamura, F., & Greer, C. A. (2014). Aging in the olfactory system. *Trends in Neuroscience, 37*, 37–44.

Moen, P. (2007). Unpublished review of J. W. Santrock's *Life-span development* (12th ed.). New York: McGraw-Hill.

Mohr, J. J. (2009). Same-sex romantic attachment. In J. Cassidy & P. R. Shaver (Eds.), *Handbook of attachment* (2nd ed.). New York: Guilford.

Moise, K. J. (2005). Fetal RhD typing with free DNA I maternal plasma. *American Journal of Obstetrics and Gynecology, 192*, 663–665.

Moise, K. J., et al. (2013). Circulating cell-free DNA for the detection of RHD status and sex using reflex fetal identifiers. *Prenatal Diagnosis*.

Moksnes, U., Moljord, I., Espnes, G., & Byrne, D. (2010). The association between stress and emotional states in adolescents: The role of gender and self-esteem. *Personality and Individual Differences, 49*, 430–435.

Mollee, P. (2014, in press). New diagnostic strategies for assessment of amyloidosis and myeloma. *Pathology*.

Molnar, B. E., Cerda, M., Roberts, A. L., & Buka, S. L. (2007). Effects of neighborhood resources on aggressive and delinquent behaviors among urban youths. *American Journal of Public Health, 98*, 1086–1093.

Molton, I. R., & Terrill, A. L. (2014). Overview of persistent pain in older adults. *American Psychologist, 69*, 197–207.

Mondloch, C., Geldart, S., Maurer, D., & Le Grand, R. (2003). Developmental changes in face processing skills. *Journal of Experimental Psychology, 86*, 67–84.

Monge, P., Wesseling, C., Guardado, J., Lundberg, II, Ahlbom, A., Cantor, K. P., et al. (2007). Parental occupation exposure to pesticides and the risk of childhood leukemia in Costa Rica. *Scandinavian Journal of Work, Environment, and Health, 33*, 293–303.

Monserud, M. A. (2008). Intergenerational relationships and affectual solidarity between grandparents and young adults. *Journal of Marriage and the Family, 70*, 182–195.

Moon, C., Lagercrantz, H. & Kuhl, P. (2009). Newborn infant perception of vowels is affected by ambient language. *The Journal of Acoustical Society of America, 125*, 2778.

Moore, C. (2007). *Advance care planning and end-of-life decision making.* In K. Kuebler, D. Heidrich, & P. Esper (Eds.), *Palliative and endof-life care* (2nd ed.) (pp. 49–62). St. Louis: Elsevier.

Moore, D. S. (2013). Behavioral genetics, genetics, and epigenetics. In P. D. Zelazo (Ed.), *Handbook of developmental psychology*. New York: Oxford University Press.

Moore, S., D'Aoust, K., Robertson, D., Savage, C., & Jiwani, Y. (2009). Swallowing the hurt: Exploring the links between anorexia, bulimia and violence against women and girls. Public Health Agency of Canada (PHAC). Retrieved from http://www.phac-aspc.gc.ca/ncfv-cnivf/publications/femrav-eng.php

Moore, S., Harden, K & Mendel, J. (2014). Pubertal timing and adolescent sexual behaviour in girls, *Developmental Pychology, 50*(6), 1734–1745.

Moos, M. K. (2006). Prenatal care: Limitations and opportunities. *Journal of Obstetric, Gynecologic, and Neonatal Nursing, 35*, 278–285.

Moraes, W., et al. (2014, in press). Effects of aging on sleep structure throughout adulthood: A population-based study. *Sleep Medicine*.

Moran S., & Gardner, H. (2006). Extraordinary achievements. In W. Damon & R. Lerner (Eds.), *Handbook of child psychology* (6th ed.). New York: Wiley.

Moran, S., & Gardner, H. (2007). Hill, skill, and will: Executive function from a multiple intelligences perspective. In L. Meltzer (Ed.), *Executive function in education.* New York: Guilford.

Morasch, K. & Bell, M. (2012). Self-regulation of negative affect at 5 and 10 months. *Developmental Psychology, 54*, 215–221.

Moreau, C., Beltzer, N., Bozon, M., Bajos, N., & the CSF Group. (2011). Sexual risk taking following relationship break-ups. *European Journal of Contraception and Reproductive Health, 16*, 95–99.

Moreira, S. R., Lima, R. M., Silva, K. E., & Simoes, H. G. (2014). Combined exercise circuit session acutely attenuates stress-induced blood pressure reactivity in healthy adults. *Brazilian Journal of Physical Therapy, 18*, 38–46.

Moreno, A., Posada, G. E., & Goldyn, D. T. (2006). Presence and quality of touch influence coregulation in mother-infant dyads. *Infancy, 9*, 1–20.

Morgan, E. (2012). Not always a straight path: College students' narratives of heterosexual identity development. *Sex Roles, 66*(1–2), 79–93.

Morgan, J. D. (2003). Spirituality. In C. D. Bryant (Ed.), *Handbook of death and dying*. Thousand Oaks, CA: Sage.

Morin, C. M., Savard, J., & Ouellet, M-C. (2013). Nature and treatment of insomnia. In I. B. Weiner et al. (Eds.), *Handbook of psychology* (2nd ed., Vol. 9). New York: Wiley.

Morissette, R., & Ostrovsky, Y. (2007). Pensions and retirement savings of families. *Perspectives on Labour and Income* (Winter), 43–56.

Morokuma, S., Doria, V., Ierullo, A., Kinukawa, N., Fukushima, K., Nakano, H., Arulkumaran, S., & Papageorghiou, A. (2008). Developmental change in fetal response to repeated low-intensity sound. *Developmental Science, 11*(1), 47–52.

Morra, L., Zade, D., McGlinchey, R. E., & Milberg, W. P. (2013). Normal aging and cognition: The unacknowledged contribution of cerebrovascular risk factors. *Neuropsychology, Development, and Cognition B: Aging, Neuropsychology, and Cognition, 20*(3), 271–297.

Morra, S., Gobbo, C., Marini, Z., & Sheese, R. (2008). *Cognitive development: Neo Piagetian perspectives.* Mahwah, NJ: Erlbaum.

Morris, R. J., Thompson, K. C., & Morris, Y. P. (2013). Child psychotherapy. In I. B. Weiner et al. (Eds.), *Handbook of psychology* (2nd ed., Vol. 8). New York: Wiley.

Morrison, G. S. (2014). *Fundamentals of early childhood education* (7th ed.). Upper Saddle River, NJ: Pearson.

Morrison, G. S. (2015, in press). *Early childhood education today* (13th ed.). Upper Saddle River, NJ: Pearson.

Morrissey, M. V. (2007). Suffer no more in silence: Challenging the myths of women's mental health in childbearing. *International Journal of Psychiatric Nursing Research, 12*, 1429–1438.

Morrongiello, B., & Dawber, T. (2004). Identifying factors that relate to children's risk-taking decisions. *Canadian Journal of Behavioural Science, 36*, 255–266.

Mortensen, J., & Mastergeorge, A. (2014). A meta-analytical review of relationship-based interventions for low-income families with infants and toddlers: Facilitating supportive parent-child interactions. *Infant Mental Health Journal, 35*(4), 336–353.

Mortimer, J., Vuolo, M., Staff, J., Wakefield, S., & Xie, W. (2008). Tracing the timing of "career" acquisition in a contemporary youth cohort. *Work and Occupations, 35*, 44–84.

Morton, D., & Weinfeld, M. (1998). *Who speaks for Canada? Words that shape a country.* Toronto: McClelland & Stewart.

Morton, J. (2003). Targeting generation X. *Public Relations Quarterly, 48*(4), 43–45.

Moschonis, G., Grammatikaki, E., & Manios, Y. (2008). Perinatal predictors of overweight at infancy and preschool childhood: The GENESIS study. *International Journal of Obesity, 32*(1), 39–47.

Mosenthal, A. C., Murphy, P. A., Barker, L. K., Lavery, R., Retano, A., & Livingston, D. H. (2008). Changing the culture around end-of-life care in the trauma intensive care unit. *Journal of Trauma, 64*, 1587–1593.

Moshman, D. (2006). Theories of adult development. In J. Demick & C. Andreoletti (Eds.), *Handbook of adult development* (pp. 42–60). New York: Springer.

Moss, E. L., & Dobson, K. S. (2006). Psychology, spirituality, and end-of-life care: An ethical integration? *Canadian Psychology, 47*(4), 284–299.

Moss, E., Cyr, C., Bureau, J. F., Tarabulsy, G. M., & Dubois-Comtois, K. (2005). Stability of attachment during the preschool period. *Developmental Psychology, 41*, 773–783.

Moss, K. (2003). Witnessing violence—Aggression and anxiety in young children. *Supplement to Health Reports, 14* (Catalogue 82-003). Ottawa: Statistics Canada.

Mota, P., Pascoal, A., Carita, A., & Bø, K. (2015). The immediate effects on inter-rectus distance of abdominal crunch and drawing-in exercises during pregnancy and the post-partum period. *Journal of Orthopaedic Sports Therapy, 45*(10), 781–788.

Motherrisk. (2012). *Drugs in pregnancy.* Retrieved from http://www.motherrisk.org/

Mothers Against Drunk Drivers (MADD). (2012). Statistics. Retrieved from http://www.madd.org/

Moules, N. J., Simonson, K., Prins, M., Angus, P., & Bell, J. M. (2004). Making room for grief. *Nursing Inquiry, 11*, 99–107.

Moulson, M. C., & Nelson, C. A. (2008). Neurological development. In M. M. Haith & J. B. Benson (Eds.), *Encyclopedia of Infant and Early Childhood Development.* Oxford, UK: Elsevier.

Moussaly, K. (2010). *Participation in private retirement savings plans, 1997 to 2006.* Ottawa: Statistics Canada. Catalogue no. 13F0026M, no. 1.

Mowafaghian, D. (2014). *Working together to advance health through research and treatment.* Centre for Brain Health.

University of British Columbia. Retrieved from http://www.brain.ubc.ca.

Moyer, R. H., Hackett, J. K., & Everett, S. A. (2007). *Teaching science as investigations.* Upper Saddle River, NJ: Prentice Hall.

Mroczek, D. K., Spiro, A., & Griffin, P. W. (2006). Personality and aging. In J. E. Birren & K. W. Schale (Eds.), *Handbook of the psychology of aging* (6th ed.). San Diego: Academic Press.

Muehlenkamp, J., & Brausch, A. (2012). Body image as a mediator of non-suicidal self-injury in adolescents. *Journal of Adolescence, 35*(1), 1–9.

Muffels, R., & Luijks, R. (2008). Labour market mobility and employment security of male employees in Europe: 'Trade-off' or 'flexicurity'. *Work Employment Society, 22*, 221–242.

Muir, D., & Hains, S. (1999). Young infants' perception of adult intentionality: Adult contingency and eye direction. In P. Rochat (Ed.), *Early social cognition: Understanding others in the first months of life* (pp. 155–188).

Muir, D., & Lee, K. (2003). The still-face effect: methodological issues and new application. *Infancy, 4*, 483–491.

Mullen, S. P., et al. (2012). Physical activity and functional limitations in older adults: The influence of self-efficacy and functional performance. *Journals of Gerontology B: Psychological Sciences and Social Sciences, 67*, 354–361.

Mullet, H. G., et al. (2013). Prospective memory and aging: Evidence for preserved spontaneous retrieval with exact but not related cues. *Psychology and Aging, 28*, 910–922.

Mullinax, M. (2013). *Talk about testing: What sexual partners discuss in relations to STI status and why.* 141st APHA Annual Meeting: American Public Health Association: Retrieved from https://apha.confex.com.

Mullins, L. (2007). Loneliness in old age. In J. E. Birren (Ed.), *Encyclopedia of gerontology* (2nd ed.). Oxford, UK: Elsevier.

Mullis, P. E., & Tonella, P. (2008). Regulation of fetal growth: Consequences and impact of being born small. *Best Practice Research: Clinical Endocrinology and Metabolism, 22*, 173–190.

Mund, I., Bell, R., & Buchner, A. (2010). Age differences in reading with distraction: Sensory or inhibitory deficits. *Psychology and Aging, 25*, 886–897.

Mundt, M., Zaklestskaia, L., & Fleming, M. (2009). Extreme college drinking and alcohol-related injury risk. *Alcoholism: Clinical & Experimental Research, 33*(9), 1532–1538.

Mungas, D., et al. (2014). A 2-process model for neuropathology and Alzheimer's disease. *Neurobiology of Aging, 35*, 301–308.

Muniz-Terrera, G., et al. (2013). Investigating terminal decline: Results from a UK population-based study of aging. *Psychology and Aging, 28*, 377–385.

Munro, S., Kornelson, J., & Hutton, E. (2009). Decision-making in patient-initiated elective caesarean delivery: The influence of birth stories. *Journal of Midwifery & Women's Health, 54*(5), 373–379.

Murphy, B., Zhang, X., & Dionne, C. (2012). Low income in Canada: A multipline and multi-index persepctive. Catalogue no. 75F0002M–No. 001. Statistics Canada. Retrieved from http://www.statcan.gc.ca/pub/75f0002m/75f0002m2012001-eng.pdf

Murphy, D., Brecht, M., Huang, D., & Herbeck, D. (2012). Trajectories of delinquency from age 14-23 in the *National longitudinal survey of youth sample, 17*, 47–62.

Murphy, E., & Carr, D. (2007). *Powerful partners: Adolescent girls' education and delayed childbearing.* Retrieved from http://www.prb.org

Murphy, N., Carbone, P., & Council on Children with Disabilities. (2011). Parent provider-community partnerships: Optimizing outcomes for children with disabilities. *Pediatrics, 128*(4), 795–802.

Murphy, R. A., et al. (2014, in press). Associations of BMI and adipose tissue area and density with incident mobility limitation and poor performance in older adults. *American Journal of Clinical Nutrition.*

Murphy, S. A., Johnson, L. C., Chung, I., & Beaton, R. D. (2003). The prevalence of PTSD following the violent death of a child and predictors of change 5 years later. *Journal of Traumatic Stress, 16*, 17–25.

Murphy-Hoefer, R., Alder, S., & Higbee, C. (2004). Perceptions about cigarette smoking and risks among college students. *Nicotine and Tobacco Research, 6* (Suppl. 3), S371–S374.

Murray, J. P. (2007). TV violence: Research and controversy. In N. Pecora, J. P. Murray, & E. A. Wartella (Eds.), *Children and television.* Mahwah, NJ: Erlbaum.

Murray, S., McKenny, E. & Murray, S. (2010). *Foundations of maternal-newborn and women's health nursing* (5th ed.). Maryland Heights, Saunders Elsevier.

Musa, I., Seymour, J., Narayanasamy, M., Wada, T. &Conroy, S. (2015). A survey of older peoples' attitudes towards advance care planning. *Age and Ageing, 44*(3), 371–376.

Musch, J., & Grodin, S. (2001). Unequal competition as an impediment to personal development: A review of the relative age effect in sport. *Developmental Review, 21*, 147–167.

Mustard, J. F. (2009, December). Canadian progress in early child development-putting science into action. *Paediatric Child Health, 14*(10), 689–690.

Mutchler, J. E. (2009). Family and household structure, later life. In D. Carr (Ed.), *Encyclopedia of the life course and human development.* Boston: Gale Cengage.

Myatchin, I., & Lagae, O. (2013, in press). Developmental changes in visuo-spatial working memory in normally developing children: Event-related potentials study. *Brain Development.*

Myles, J., & Picot, G. (2000). Poverty indices and policy analysis. *The Review of Income and Wealth, 46*(2), 161–179.

N

Nabe-Nielsen, K., et al. (2009). Differences between day and noonday workers in exposure to physical and psychological work factors in the Danish eldercare sector. *Scandinavian Journal of Work, Environment, and Health, 35*, 48–55.

Nabet, C., Lelong, N., Ancel, P. Y., Saurel-Cubizolles, M. J., & Kaminski, M. (2007). Smoking during pregnancy according to obstetric complications and parity: Results of the EUROPOP study. *European Journal of Epidemiology, 22*, 715–721.

Nag, T. C., & Wadhwa, S. (2012). Ultrastructure of the human retina in aging and various pathological states. *Micron, 43*, 759–781.

Nagashima, J., et al. (2010). Three-month exercise and weight loss program improves heart rate recovery in obese persons along with cardiopulmonary function. *Journal of Cardiology, 56*(1), 79–84.

Nagy, R. (2014). The Truth and Reconciliation Commission of Canada: Genesis and design. *Canadian Journal of Law and Society, 29*(2), 199–217.

Nakamura, K., Sheps, S., & Clara Arck, P. (2008). Stress and reproductive failure: Past notions, present insights, and future directions. *Journal of Assisted Reproduction and Genetics, 25*(2–3), 47–62.

Nakata, T. & Trehub, S. (2011). Expressive timing and dynamics in infant-directed and non-infant-directed sining. *Psychomusicology, Music, Mind & Brain, 21*(1 & 2), 45–52.

Nakata, T., & Trehub, S. E. (2004). Infants' responsiveness to maternal speech and singing. *Infant Behavior & Development, 27*, 455–464.

Nakayama, H. (2010). Development of infant crying behavior: A longitudinal case study. *Infant behavior and Development, 33*, 463–471.

Nanovskaya, T. N., Nekhayeva, I. A., Hankins, G. D., & Ahmed, M. S. (2008). Transfer of methadone across the dually perfused preterm human placental lobule. *American Journal of Obstetrics and Gynecology, 198*, e1–e4.

Nansel, T. R., Overpeck, M., Pilla, R., Ruan, W., Simons-Morton, B., & Scheidt, P. (2001). Bullying behaviors among U.S. youth. *Journal of the American Medical Association, 285*, 2094–2100.

Narayan, C., Werker, J., & Beddor, P. (2010). The interaction between acoustic salience and language experience in developmental speech perception. Evidence from nasal place discrimination. *Developmental Science, 13*, 407–420.

Narberhaus, A., Segarra, D., Caldu, X., Gimenez, M., Junque, C., Pueyo, R., et al. (2007). Gestational age at preterm birth in relation to corpus callosum and general cognitive outcome in adolescents. *Journal of Child Neurology, 22*, 761–765.

Nardone, R., et al. (2014, in press). Dopamine differentially modulates central cholinergic circuits in patients with Alzheimer disease and CADASIL. *Journal of Neural Transmission.*

Narducci, A., Einarson, A., & Bozzo, P. (2012). Human papillomavirus vaccine and pregnancy. *Canadian Family Physician, 58*, 268–269.

Narvaez, D. (2014, in press). *The neurobiology and development of human morality.* New York: Norton.

Nascimento Dda, C., et al. (2014). Sustained effect of resistance training on blood pressure and hand grip strength following a detraining period in elderly hypertensive women: A pilot study. *Clinical Interventions in Aging, 9*, 219–225.

Natali, A., Pucci, G., Boldrini, B., & Schillaci, G. (2009). Metabolic syndrome: At the crossroads of cardiorenal risk. *Journal of Nephrology, 22*, 29–38.

Natalizia, A., Casale, M., Guglielmelli, E., Rinaldi, V., Vressi, F., & Savinelli, F. (2010). An overview of hearing impairment in older adults: Perspectives for rehabilitation with-hearing aids. *European Review for Medical and Pharmaceutical Sciences, 14*, 223–229.

National Aboriginal Health Organization. (2012). *Midwifery.* Retrieved from http://www.naho.ca/

National Advisory Council on Aging. (2001, Summer). Seniors and the law. *Bulletin of the National Advisory Council on Aging, 14*(3).

National Clearinghouse on Family Violence. (2006). *Violence in dating relationships.* Government of Canada, (No. HP20-3/2006E). Retrieved from http://www.phac-aspc.gc.ca/

National Collaborating Centre of Aboriginal Health (NCCAH) (July 18, 2013). An Overview of Aboriginal Health in Canada. Retrieved from http://www.nccah-ccnsa.ca/en/publications.aspx?sortcode=2.8.10&publication=101'.

National Council of Welfare Reports (2013). Poverty Profile: Special Edition. Snapshop of racialized poverty in Canada. Retrieved from http://www.esdc.gc.ca/eng/communities/reports/poverty_profile/snapshot.shtml

National Eating Disorder Information Centre (NEDIC). (2008). Understanding statistics on eating disorders. Retrieved from http://www.nedic.ca/knowthefacts/statistics.shtml

National Eating Disorder Information Centre. (2014). Statistics - Understanding Statistics on Eating Disorders. Retrieved from http://nedic.ca/know-facts/statistics.

National Epidemiological Database for the Study of Autism in Canada (NEDSAC). (2012). Findings from the National Epidemiological Database for the Study of Autism in Canada: Changes in the prevalence of autism spectrum disorders in Newfoundland and Labrador, Prince Edward Island, and Southeastern Ontario. Retrieved from http://www.nedsac.ca/

National Sleep Foundation. (2006). *Sleep in America poll.* Washington, DC: Author.

Native Women's Association of Canada. (2010). *What their stories tell us: Research findings from the Sisters in Spirit Initiative.* Retrieved from http://www.nwac.ca/

Navaneelan, T., & Janz., T. (2015) Adjusting the scale: Obesity in the Canadian population after correcting for responder bias. Health at a Glance. Statistics Canada. Retrieved from http://www.statcan.gc.ca/pub/82-624-x/2014001/article/11922-eng.htm.

Nava-Ocampo, A. A., & Koren, G. (2007). Human teratogens and evidence-based teratogen risk counseling: The Motherisk approach. *Clinical Obstetrics and Gynecology, 50*, 123–131.

Naylor, C. (1999, May). How does working part-time influence secondary students' achievement and impact on their overall well-being? *BCTF Research Report.* Retrieved from http://www.bctf.ca/uploadedfiles/publications/research_reports/99ei02.pdf

Neal, J. W., Neal, Z. P., & Cappella, E. (2014, in press). I know who my friends are, but do you? Predictors of self-reported and peer-inferred relationships. *Child Development.*

Needham, A. (2008). Learning in infants' object perception, object-directed action, and tool use. In A. Needham & A. Woodward (Eds.), *Learning and the infant mind.* New York: Oxford University Press.

Needle, D. (2001, March 6). Website honors "Thinker of the Year." *Internetnews.com.*

Neikrug, A. B., & Ancoli-Israel, S. (2010). Sleep disorders in the older adult: A mini-review. *Gerontology, 56*, 181–189.

Nelson, C. A. (2003). Neural development and lifelong plasticity. In R. M. Lerner, F. Jacobs, & D. Wertlieb (Eds.), *Handbook of applied developmental science* (Vol. 1). Thousand Oaks, CA: Sage.

Nelson, C. A. (2009). Brain development and behavior. In A. M. Rudolph, C. Rudolph, L. First, G. Lister, & A. A. Gersohon (Eds.), *Rudolph's pediatrics* (22nd ed.). New York: McGraw-Hill.

Nelson, C. A., Thomas, K. M., & de Haan, M. (2006). Neural bases of cognitive development. In W. Damon, R. Lerner, D. Kuhn, & R. Siegler (Eds.), *Handbook of child psychology* (6th ed., Vol. 2). New York: Wiley.

Nelson, C. A., Zeanah, C., & Fox, N. A. (2007). The effects of early deprivation on brain-behavioral development: The Bucharest Early Intervention Project. In D. Romer & E. Walker (Eds.), *Adolescent psychopathology and the developing brain: Integrating brain and prevention science.* New York: Oxford University Press.

Nelson, H., Kendall, G. & Shields, L. (2014). Neurological and biological foundations of children's social and emotional development: An integrated literature review. *Journal of School Nursing, 30*(4), 240–250.

Nelson, J. A., et al. (2012). Maternal expressive style and children's emotional development. *Infant and Child Development, 3*, 267–286.

Nelson, J. A., et al. (2013). Preschool-aged children's understanding of gratitude: Relations with emotion and mental state knowledge. *British Journal of Developmental Psychology, 31*, 42–56.

Nelson, J., & Nelson, T. (2014). Advance directives: empowering patients at the end of life. *Nurse Practitioner,* (39)11, 34–40.

Nelson, K. (2013). Introduction to the special issue. *Cognitive Development, 28*, 175–177.

Nelson, R., & DeBecker, T. (2008). Achievement motivation in adolescents: The role of peer climate and best friends. *Journal of Experimental Education, 76*, 170–189.

Nelson, T. D., & Nelson, J. M. (2010). Evidence-based practice and the culture of adolescence. *Professional Psychology: Research and Practice, 41*(4), 305–311.

Ness, A., Dias, T., Damus, K., Burd, I., & Berghella, V. (2006). Impact of recent randomized trials on the use of progesterone to prevent preterm birth: A 2005 follow-up survey. *American Journal of Obsterics and Gynecology, 195*, 1174–1179.

Neufeld, G., & Mate, G. (2004). *Hold on to your kids: Why parents matter.* Toronto: Knopf.

Neugarten, B. L. (1986). The aging society. In A. Pifer & L. Bronte (Eds.), *Our aging society: Paradox and promise.* New York: W. W. Norton.

Neugarten, B. L. (1988, August). *Policy issues for an aging society.* Paper presented at the meeting of the American Psychological Association, Atlanta.

Neugarten, B. L., & Weinstein, K. K. (1964). The changing American grandparent. *Journal of Marriage and the Family, 26*, 199–204.

Newburg, D. S., & Walker, W. A. (2007). Protection of the neonate by the innate immune system of developing gut and of human milk. *Pediatric Research, 61*, 2–8.

Newcombe, N. (2008). The development of implicit and explicit memory. In N. Cowan & M. Courage (Eds.), *The development of memory in childhood.* Philadelphia: Psychology Press.

Newcombe, N. S. (2007). Developmental psychology meets the mommy wars. *Journal of Applied Developmental Psychology, 28*, 553–555.

Newell, K., Scully, D. M., McDonald, P. V., & Baillargeon, R. (1989). Task constraints and infant grip configurations, *Developmental Psychobiology, 22*, 817–832.

Newman, A. B., et al. (2006). Association of long-distance corridor walk performance with mortality, cardiovascular disease, mobility limitation, and disability. *Journal of the American Medical Association, 295*, 2018–2026.

Newton, N. J., & Stewart, A. J. (2012). Personality development in adulthood. In S. K. Whitbourne & M. Sliwinski (Eds.), *Wiley-Blackwell handbook of adult development and aging.* New York: Wiley.

Ng, C. (2014, Feb 20). *Best game ever? What the players think about a gold medal game 'for the ages'.* Retrieved from http://www.olympics.ca

NHS. (2011a). *Immigration and ethnocultural diversity in Canada.* Retrieved from http://www.statcan.gc.ca

NHS. (2011b). *Religions in Canada.* Retrieved from http://www.statcan.gc.ca

NICHD Early Child Care Research Network. (2005). Predicting individual differences in attention, memory, and planning in first graders from experiences at home, child care, and school. *Developmental Psychology, 41*, 99–114.

NICHD Early Child Care Research Network. (2009). Family-peer linkages: The mediational role of attentional processes. *Social Development, 18*(4), 875–895.

Nicolaisen, M., Thorsen, K., & Eriksen, S. H. (2012). Jump into the void? Factors related to a preferred retirement age: Gender, social interests, and leisure activities. *International Journal of Aging and Human Development, 75*, 239–271.

Nielson, D. (2012). Discussing death with pediatric patients: Implications for nurses. *Journal of Pediatric Nursing, 27*, e59–e64.

NIH. (2015). *College Drinking.* Retrieved from https://www.niaaa.hih.gov.

Nijmeijer, J. S., et al. (2014, in press). Quantitative linkage for autism spectrum disorders symptoms in attention-deficit/hyperactivity disorder: Significant locus on chromosome 7Q11. *Journal of Autism and Developmental Disorders.*

Nisbett, R. (2003). *The geography of thought.* New York: Free Press.

Noble, J. M., et al. (2010). Association of C-reactive protein with cognitive impairment. *Archives of Neurology, 67*, 87–92.

Noftle, E. E., & Robins, R. W. (2007). Personality predictors of academic outcomes: Big five correlates of GPA and SAT scores. *Journal of Personality and Social Psychology, 93*, 116–130.

Nohr, E. A., Bech, B. H., Davies, M. J., Fryenberg, M., Henriksen, T. B., & Olsen, J. (2005). Prepregnancy obesity and fetal death: A study with the Danish National Birth Cohort. *Obstetrics and Gynecology, 106*, 250–259.

Noland, J. S., Singer, L. T., Short, E. J., Minnes, S., Arendt, R. E., Kirchner, H. L., et al. (2005). Prenatal drug exposure and selective attention in preschoolers. *Neurotoxicology and Teratology, 27*, 429–438.

Nomoto, M., et al. (2009). Inter- and intra-individual variation in L-dopa pharmacokinetics in the treatment of Parkinson's disease. *Parkinsonism and Related Disorders, 15*(1, Suppl.), S21–S24.

Nordqvist, C. (2009, August 24). What is vitamin D? What are the benefits of vitamin D? *Medical News Today.* Retrieved from http://www.medicalnewstoday.com/articles/161618.php

Nores, M. & Barnett, W. (2010). Benefits of early childhood interventions across the world: (Under) investing in the very young. *Economics of Education Review. 29*(2), 271–282.

Norgard, B., Puho, E., Czeilel, A. E., Skriver, M. V., & Sorensen, H. T. (2006). Aspirin use during early pregnancy and the risk of congenital abnormalities. *American Journal of Obstetrics and Gynecology, 192*, 922–923.

Norman, J. F., Holmin, J. S., & Bartholomew, A. N. (2011). Visual memories for perceived length are well preserved in older adults. *Vision Research, 51*, 2057–2062.

Norton, W., Fisher, J., Amico, K., Dovidio, J., & Johnson, B. (2012). Relative efficacy of a pregnancy, sexually transmitted infection, or human immunodeficiency virus, prevention-focused interventions on changing sexual risk behavior among young adults. *Journal of American College Health, 60*, 574–582.

Nottelmann, E. D., Susman, E. J., Blue, J. H., Inoff - Germain, G., Dorn, L. D., Loriaux, D. L., et al. (1987). Gonadal and adrenal hormone correlates of adjustment in early adolescence. In R. M. Lerner & T. T. Foch (Eds.), *Biological-psychological interactions in early adolescence.* Hillsdale, NJ: Erlbaum.

Nouchi, R., et al. (2013). Brain training game boosts executive functions, working memory, and processing speed in young adults: A randomized controlled trial. *PLoS, 8*(2), e55518.

Nova Scotia Advisory Council on the Status of Women. (2013). *Nova Scotia Advisory Council on the Status of Women.* Retrieved from http://women.gov.ns.ca/

Novo-Veleiro, I., González-Sarmiento, R., Cieza-Borrella, C., Pastor, I., Laso, F., & Marcos, M. (2014). A genetic variant in the miroRNA-146a gene is associated with susceptibility to alcohol use disorders. *European Psychiatry, 29*(5), 288–292.

Nowakowski, M. (2009). *Temperament and joint attention: Stability, continuity, and predictive outcomes in children's socioemotional development* (Doctoral Dissertation). Retrieved from Proquest Dissertation and Theses Database (AAT NR65903).

Nussbaum, R., McInnes, R., & Willard, H. (2007). *Thompson & Thompson: Genetics in medicine* (7th ed). Philadelphia: Saunders Elsevier.

Nutt, S. (2007). Speech presented to the University Women's Club in Georgetown, ON, and from personal interview in May 2007.

Nutt, S. (2016). *Samantha Nutt: Damned nations.* Retrieved from http://www.samanthanutt.com.

Nutting, P. A., Dickinson, W. P., Dickinson, L. M., Nelson, C. C., King, D. K.,

Crabtree, B. F., et al. (2007). Use of chronic care model elements is associated with higher-quality care for diabetes. *Annals of Family Medicine, 5*, 14–20.

Nyberg, L., & Backman, L. (2011). Influences of biological and self-initiated factors on brain and cognition in adulthood and aging. In P. B. Baltes, P. A. Reuter-Lorenz, & F. Rosler (Eds.), *Lifespan development and the brain.* New York: Cambridge University Press.

Nyberg, L., Lovden, M., Rilund, K., Lindenberger, U., & Backman, L. (2012). Memory aging and brain maintenance. *Current Trends in Cognitive Science, 16*, 292–305.

Nygard, C.-H. (2013). The ability to work peaks in middle age. Interview. Retrieved from http://researchandstudy.uta.fi/2013/09/12/the-ability-to-work-peaks-in-middle-age/

O

O'Brien, B., Chalmers, B., Fell, D., Heaman, M., Darling, E., & Herbert, P. (2011). The experience of pregnancy and birth with midwives: Results from the Canadian Maternity Experiences Survey. *Birth, 38*(3), 207–215.

O'Brien, E. J., Bartoletti, M., & Leitzel, J. D. (2013). Self-esteem, psychopathology, and psychotherapy. In M. H. Kernis (Ed.), *Self-esteem issues and answers*. New York: Psychology Press.

O'Brien, J. L., et al. (2013). Cognitive training and selective attention in the aging brain: An electrophysiological study. *Clinical Neurophysiology, 124*, 2198–2208.

O'Brien, M. (2009). Fathers, parental leave policies, and infant quality of life, International perspectives and policy impact. *Annals of the American Academy of Political and Social Science, 624*, 190–213.

O'Connor, A. B., & Roy, C. (2008). Electric power plant emissions and public health. *American Journal of Nursing, 108*, 62–70.

O'Connor, D. B., Conner, M., Jones, F., McMillan, B., & Ferguson, E. (2009). Exploring the benefits of conscientiousness: An investigation of the role of daily stressors and health benefits. *Annals of Behavioral Medicine, 37*, 184–196.

O'Connor, E., & McCartney, K. (2007). Attachment and cognitive skills: An investigation of mediating mechanisms. *Journal of Applied Developmental Psychology, 28*, 458–476.

O'Donnell, E., Kirwan, L. D., & Goodman, J. M. (2009). Aerobic exercise training in healthy postmenopausal women: Effects of hormone therapy. *Menopause, 16*, 770–776.

O'Halloran, A. M., et al. (2011). Falls and fall efficacy: The role of sustained attention in older adults. *BMC Geriatrics, 11*, 85.

O'Hara, W., & McGabe, J. (2013). Postpartum depression: current status and future directions. *Annual Reviews Clinical psychology, 9*, 379–407.

O'Kane, J. (2012). Canada's work-life balance more off-kilter than ever. *Globe and Mail.* Retrieved from http://www.theglobeandmail.com.

O'Keefe, J. H., Schnohr, P., & Lavie, C. J. (2013). The dose of running that best confers longevity. *Heart, 99*, 588–590.

O'Malley, P. (2014). A review of studies of drinking patterns in the United States since 1940. *Journal of Studies on Alcohol and Drugs, 75*(17, Suppl.), S18–S25.

O'Neill, D. K., Main, R. M., & Ziemski, R. A. (2009). "I like Barney": Preschoolers' spontaneous conversational initiations with peers. *First Language, 29*(4), 401–425.

O'Sullivan, L. F., Cheng, M. M., Harris, K. M., & Brooks-Gunn, J. (2007). I wanna hold your hand: The progression of social, romantic, and sexual events in adolescent relationships. *Perspectives on Sexual and Reproductive Health, 39*, 100–107.

Oakes, L. M. (2008). Categorization skills and concepts. In M. M. Haith & J. B. Benson (Eds.), *Encyclopedia of infant and early childhood development.* Oxford, UK: Elsevier.

Oakes, L. M., Kannass, K. N., & Shaddy, D. J. (2002). Developmental changes in endogenous control of attention: The role of target familiarity on infants' distraction latency. *Child Development, 73*, 1644–1655.

Obenauer, S., & Maestre, L. A. (2008). Fetal MRI of lung hypoplasia: Imaging findings. *Clinical Imaging, 32*, 48–50.

Odom, S., Boyd, B., Hall, L. J., & Hume, K. A. (2014). Comprehensive treatment models for children and youth with autism. In F. R. Volkmar et al. (Eds.), *Handbook of autism and pervasive developmental disorders.* New York: Wiley.

OECD. (2010). Executive summary. In F. Sassi (Ed.) *Obesity and the Economics of Prevention: Fit not Fat* (pp. 15-22). Paris, France: OECD Publishing.

OECD. (2015). Education Policy Outlook Canada. Retrieved from http://www.oecd.org/

Ofen, N., & Shing, Y. L. (2013). From perception to memory: Changes in memory systems across the lifespan. *Neuroscience and Biobehavioral Reviews, 37*, 2258–2267.

Ogden, C. L., Carroll, M. D., Kit, B. K., & Flegal, K. M. (2014). Prevalence of childhood and adult obesity in the United States, 2011–2012. *Journal of the American Medical Association, 311*, 308–314.

Ogrodnik, L. (2007). *Seniors as victims of crime 2004 and 2005.* Canadian Centre for Justice Profile Series. Ottawa: Statistics Canada.

Oiestad, B. E., et al. (2013). Efficacy of strength and aerobic exercise on patient-reported outcomes and structural changes in patients with knee osteoarthritis: Study protocol for a randomized trial. *BMC Musculoskeletal Disorders, 14*(1), 266.

Okada, H. C., Alleyne, B., Varghai, K., Kinder, K., & Guyuron, B. (2013). Facial changes caused by smoking: A comparison between smoking and non-smoking identical twins. *Plastic and Reconstructive Surgery, 132*(5), 1085–1092.

Okada, K., et al. (2014, in press). Comprehensive evaluation of androgen replacement therapy in aging Japanese men with late-onset hypogonadism. *Aging Male*.

Okpik, A. (2005). *We call it survival: Nunavut Arctic College.*

Okun, N., et al. (2014). Pregnancy outcomes after assisted human reproduction. *Journal of Obstetrics and Gynecology Canada*.

Olafsdottir, E., Andersson, D. K., & Stefansson, E. (2012). The prevalence of cataract in a population of with and without type 2 diabetes mellitus. *Acta Ophthalmologica, 90*, 334–340.

Olesen, J., et al. (2014, in press). Exercise training, but not resveratrol, improve metabolic and inflammatory status in skeletal muscle of aged men. *Journal of Physiology*.

Olmstead, S., Futris, T. & Pasley, K. (2009). An exploration of married and divorced non-resident men's perception and organization of their father's role identity. *Fathering, 7*, 249–268.

Olson, H. C., King, S., & Jirikowic, T. (2008). Fetal alcohol spectrum disorders. In M. M. Haith & J. B. Benson (Eds.), *Encyclopedia of infancy and early childhood.* Thousand Oaks, CA: Sage.

Olszewski-Kubilius, P., & Thomson, D. (2013). Gifted education programs and procedures. In I. B. Weiner et al. (Eds.), Handbook of psychology (2nd ed., Vol. 7). New York: Wiley.

Olyan, S. M. (2004). *Biblical mourning: Ritual and social dimension.* New York: Oxford Press.

Oman, D., & Thoresen, C. E. (2006). Do religion and spirituality influence health? In R. F. Paloutzian & C. L. Park (Eds.), *Handbook of the psychology of religion and spirituality.* New York: Guilford.

Ontario Human Rights Commission. (2006–2007). *Discussion paper: Toward a commission policy on gender identity.* Appendix 2. Retrieved from www.ohrc.on.ca/en/

Operation Migration. (2016). OM's Co-founders. Retrieved from http://www.operationmigration.org/work_bios.html

Opitz, B., & Friederici, A. D. (2007). Neural basis of processing sequential and hierarchical structures. *Human Brain Mapping, 28,* 585–592.

Orbe, M. P. (2008). Theorizing multidimensional identity negotiation: Reflections on the lived experiences of first-generation college students. In M. Azmitia, M. Syed, & K. Radmacher (Eds.), *The intersections of personal and social identities. New Directions for Child and Adolescent Development, 120,* 81–95.

Orecchia, R., Lucignani, G., & Tosi, G. (2008). Prenatal irradiation and pregnancy: The effects of diagnostic imaging and radiation therapy. *Recent Results in Cancer Research, 178,* 3–20.

Orford, J., Velleman, R., Natera, G., Templeton, L., & Copello, A. (2013). Addiction in the family is a major but neglected contributor to the global burden of adult ill-health. *Social Science and Medicine, 78,* 70–77.

Organisation for Economic Co-operation and Development (OECD). (2010). *Programme for International Student Assessment (PISA).* Retrieved from http://www.oecd.org/edu/school/programmeforinternationalstudentassessmentpisa/pathwaystosuccess-howknowledgeandskillsatage15shapefuturelivesinca nada.htm

Organization for Economic Cooperation and Development (OECD). (2014). Obesity and the Economics of Prevention: Fit Not Fit. Key Facts - Canada, Update 2014. Retrieved from http://www.oecd.org/canada/Obesity-Update-2014-CANADA.pdf.

Ornstein, K., et al. (2013). The differential impact of unique behavioral and psychological symptoms for the dementia caregiver: How and why do patients' individual symptom clusters impact caregiver depressive symptoms? *American Journal of Geriatric Psychiatry, 21,* 1277–1286.

Ornstein, P. A., Coffman, J. L., & Grammer, J. K. (2007, April). *Teachers' memory-relevant conversations and children's memory performance.* Paper presented at the biennial meeting of the Society for Research in Child Development, Boston.

Orrange, R. M. (2007). *Work, family, and leisure: Uncertainty in a risk society.* Boulder, CO: Rowman & Littlefield.

Ory, M. G., et al. (2013). National study of chronic disease self-management: Six-month outcome findings. *Journal of Aging and Health, 25,* 1258–1274.

Osorio, R. S., et al. (2014). Imaging and cerebrospinal fluid biomarkers in the search for Alzheimer's disease mechanisms. *Neurogenerative Diseases, 13,* 163–165.

Ossher, L., Flegal, K. E., & Lustig, C. (2013). Everyday memory errors in older adults. *Neuropsychology, Development, and Cognition, B: Aging, Neuroscience, and Cognition, 20,* 220–244.

Osteoporosis Canada. (2016). Osteoporosis facts & statistics. Retrieved from http://www.osteoporosis.ca/osteoporosis-and-you/osteoporosis-facts-and-statistics/.

Osterberg, E. C., Bernie, A. M., & Ramasamy, R. (2014). Risk of replacement testosterone therapy in men. *Indian Journal of Urology, 30,* 2–7.

Ostfeld, B., Esposito, L., Perl, H., & Hegyi, T. (2010). Concurrent risks in sudden infant death syndrome. *Pediatrics, 125*(3), 447–453.

Otaegui-Arrazola, A., et al. (2014). Diet, cognition, and Alzheimer's disease: Food for thought. European *Journal of Nutrition, 53,* 1–23.

Ott, C. H., Lueger, R. J., Kelber, S. T., & Prigerson, H. G. (2007). Spousal bereavement in older adults: Common, resilient, and chronic grief with defining characteristics. *Journal of Nervous and Mental Disease, 195,* 332–341.

Ouellet-Morin, I., Dionne, G., Lupien, S., Muckle, G., Côté, S., Pérusse, D., Tremblay, R., & Noivin, M. (2011). Prenatal alcohol exposure and cortisol activity in 19-month-old toddlers: an investigation of the moderating effects of sex and testosterone. *Psychopharmocoly, 214,* 297–307.

Ouellette-Kuntz, H., Coo, H., Yu, C., Lewis, M., Dewey, D., Hennessey, P. ....Holden, J. Status report. National Epidemiological Database for the Study of Autism in Canada (NEDSAC). (2012). *Chronic Diseases and Injuries in Canada, 32*(2), 84–89.

Owen, J., & Fincham, F. (2011). Effects of gender and psychosocial factors on "Friends with Benefits" relationships among young adults. *Archives of Sexual Behavior, 40*(2), 311–320.

Oyserman, D., & Destin, M. (2010). Identity-based motivation: implications for interventions. *The Counselling Psychologist, 38,* 1001–1043.

P

Pacala, J. T., & Yeuh, B. (2012). Hearing defects in the older patient: "I didn't notice anything." *Journal of the American Medical Association, 307,* 1185–1194.

Pace-Schott, E. F., & Spencer, R. M. (2011). Age-related changes in the cognitive function of sleep. *Progress in Brain Research, 191,* 75–89.

Padilla-Walker, L., & Carlo, G. (Eds.) (2014). *Prosocial behavior.* New York: Oxford University Press.

Pagani, L. S., Jalbert, J., Lapointe, P., & Hébert, M. (2006). Effects of junior kindergarten on emerging literacy in children from low-income and linguistic-minority families. *Early Childhood Education Journal, 33,* 209–215.

Pageon, H., et al. (2014). Skin aging by glycation: Lessons from the reconstructed skin model. *Clinical Chemistry and Laboratory Medicine, 52*(1), 169–174.

Pakhomov, S. V., & Hemmy, L. S. (2014, in press). A computational linguistic measure of clustering behavior on semantic verbal fluency task predicts risk of future dementia in the Nun Study. *Cortex.*

Pakpreo, P., Ryan, S., Auinger, P., & Aten, M. (2005). The association between parental lifestyle behaviors and adolescent knowledge, attitudes, intentions, and nutritional and physical activity behaviors. *Journal of Adolescent Health, 34,* 129–130.

Palda, V. A., Guise, J. M., Wayhen, C. N., with the Canadian Task Force on Preventive Health Care. (2004). Interventions to promote breastfeeding: Applying the evidence in clinical practice. *Canadian Medical Association Journal, 170,* 976–978.

Palmore, E. B. (2004). Research note: Ageism in Canada and the United States. *Journal of Cross Cultural Gerontology, 19,* 41–46.

Pan, Z., & Chang, C. (2012). Gender and the regulation of longevity: Implications for autoimmunity. *Autoimmunity Reviews, 11,* A393–A403.

Panigrahy, A., Borzaga, M., & Blumi, S. (2010). Basic principles and concepts underlying recent advances in magnetic resonance imaging of the developing brain. *Seminars in Perinatology, 34,* 3–19.

Panizzon, M. S., et al. (2014, in press). Interaction of APOE genotype and testosterone on episodic memory in middle-aged men. *Neurobiology of Aging.*

Pannikar, V. (2003). The return of thalidomide: New uses and renewed concerns. *Leprosy Review, 74*(3), 286–288.

Panscofar, N. & Vernon-Feagans, L. (2010). Fathers' early contribution to children's language development in families from low-income rural communities. *Early Childhood Research Quarterly, 25*(4), 450–463.

Paoli, A., et al. (2014, in press). Effects of high-intensity circuit training, low-intensity circuit training, and endurance training on blood pressure and lipoproteins in middle-aged overweight men. *Lipids in Health and Disease.*

Papastavrou, E., Charlalambous, A., Tsangari, H., & Karayiannis, G. (2012). The burdensome and depressive experience of caring: What cancer, schizophrenia, and Alzheimer's disease caregivers have in common. *Cancer Nursing, 35*, 187–194.

Parade, S., Leerkes, E., & Blankson, A. (2010). Attachment to parent, social anxiety and close relationships of female students over the transition to college. *Journal of Youth and Adolescence, 39*, 127–137.

Paredes, I., Hidalgo, L., Chedraui, P., Palma, J., & Eugenio, J. (2005). Factors associated with inadequate prenatal care in Ecuadorian women. *International Journal of Gynecology and Obstetrics, 88*, 168–172.

Parent Support Services of BC. (2011). Retrieved from http://www.interprofessional.ubc.ca/EarlyYears2014/documents/B5%20Ross.pdf.

Parish-Morris, J., Golinkoff, R. M., & Hirsh-Pasek, K. (2013). From coo to code: A brief story of language development. In P. D. Zelazo (Ed.), *Handbook of developmental psychology*. New York: Oxford University Press.

Park, C. J., Yelland, G. W., Taffe, J. R., & Gray, K. M. (2012). Morphological and syntactic skills in language samples of pre-school aged children with autism: Atypical development? *International Journal of Speech and Language Pathology, 14*, 95–108.

Park, D. (2001). Commentary in Restak, R. *The secret life of the brain.* Washington, DC: Joseph Henry Press.

Park, D., & Bischof, G. (March 15, 2013). The aging mind: neuroplasticity in response to cognitive training. *Dialogues in Clinical Neurosience, 15*(1), PMC3622463. Retrieved from http://www.ncbi.nlm.nih.gov/pmc/articles/PMC3622463/.

Park, D. C., & Bischof, G. N. (2011). Neuroplasticity, aging, and cognitive function. In K. W. Schaie & S. L. Willis (Eds.), *Handbook of the psychology of aging* (7th ed.). New York: Elsevier.

Park, D. C., & Gutchess, A. H. (2005). Long-term memory and aging: A cognitive neuroscience perspective. In R. Cabeza, L. Nyberg, & D. Park, (Eds.), *Cognitive neuroscience of aging: Linking cognitive and cerebral aging.* New York: Oxford University Press.

Park, D. C., & Schwarz, N. (Eds.). (2009). *Cognitive aging* (2nd ed.). Clifton, NJ: Psychology Press.

Park, D. W., Baek, K., Kim, J. R., Lee, J. J., Ryu, S. H., Chin, B. R., et al. (2009). Resveratrol inhibits foam cell formation via NADPH oxidase 1-mediated reactive oxygen species and monocyte chemotatic protein-1. *Experimental Molecular Medicine, 41*, 171–179.

Park, M. J., Brindis, C. D., Chang, F., & Irwin, C. E. (2008). A midcourse review of the healthy people 2010: 21 critical health objectives for adolescents and young adults. *Journal of Adolescent Health, 42*, 329–334.

Park, N. S., et al. (2013). Typologies of religiousness/spirituality: Implications for health and well-being. *Journal of Religion and Health, 52*, 828–839.

Parke, R. D. (2004). Development in the family. *Annual Review of Psychology* (Vol. 55). Palo Alto, CA: Annual Reviews.

Parke, R. D., & Clarke-Stewart, A. K. (2011). *Social development*. New York: Wiley.

Parke, R. D., Leidy, M. S., Schofield, T. J., Miller, M. A., & Morris, K. L. (2008). Socialization. In M. M. Haith & J. B. Benson (Eds.), *Encyclopedia of infant and early childhood development.* Oxford, UK: Elsevier.

Parkin, C., & Kuczynski, L. (2012). Adolescent perspectives on rules and resistance within the parent-child relationship. *Journal of Adolescent Research, 27*(5), 632–658.

Parodi, V., de Florentiis, D., Martini, M., & Ansaldi, F. (2011). Inactivated influenza vaccines: Recent progress and implications for the elderly. *Drugs and Aging, 28*, 93–106.

Parr, E. B., Coffey, V. G., & Hawley, J. A. (2013). 'Sarcobesity': A medical conundrum. *Maturitas, 74*, 109–113.

Parten, M. (1932). Social play among preschool children. *Journal of Abnormal and Social Psychology, 27*, 243–269.

Participaction Report Card. (2015). The Biggest Risk is Keeping Kids Indoors. Partipaction Report Card on Physical Activity for Children and Youth. Retrieved from http://www.participaction.com/report-card-2015/.

Pasiak, C. & Menna, R. (2015). Mother-child synchrony: Implications for young children's aggression and social competence. *Journal of Family Studies, 24*, 3079–3092.

Pasley, K., & Moorefield, B. S. (2004). Stepfamilies. In M. Coleman & L. Ganong (Eds.), *Handbook of contemporary families.* Thousand Oaks, CA: Sage.

Pasoli, K. (2015). Comparing child care policies in the Canadian provinces. *Canadian Political Science Review, 9*(2), 63–78.

Passini, S. (2012). The delinquency-drug relationship: The influence of social reputation and moral disengagement. *Addictive Behaviours, 37*, 577–579.

Passuth, P. M., Maines, D. R., & Neugarten, B. L. (1984). *Age norms and age constraints twenty years later.* Paper presented at the annual meeting of the Midwest Sociological Society, Chicago.

Patchin, J.W., & Hinduja, S. (2010). Changes in adolescent online social networking behaviors from 2006 to 2009. *Computers in Human Behavior, 26*, 1818–1821.

Pathman, T., & St. Jacques, P. L. (2014). Locating events in personal time: Time in autobiography. In P. Bauer & R. Fivush (Eds.), *Wiley-Blackwell handbook of children's memory*. New York: Wiley.

Patterson, C. J. (2009b). Children of lesbian and gay parents: Psychology, law, and policy. *American Psychologist, 64*, 727–736.

Patterson, C. J., & Hastings, P. D. (2007). Socialization in the context of family diversity. In J. E. Grusec & P. D. Hastings (Eds.), *Handbook of socialization.* New York:

Patterson, M. L., & Werker, J. F. (2003). Two-month-old infants match phonetic information in lips and voice. *Developmental Science, 6*, 191–196.

Paulhus, D. L. (2008). Birth order. In M. M. Haith & J. B. Benson (Eds.), *Encyclopedia of infant and early childhood development.* Oxford, UK: Elsevier.

Paulson, J. F., Dauber, S., & Leiferman, J. A. (2006). Individual and combined effects of postpartum depression in mothers and fathers on parenting behavior. *Pediatrics, 118*, 659–668.

Paus, T., Toro, R., Leonard, G., Lerner, J. V., Lerner, R. M., Perron, M., et al. (2008). Morphological properties of the action-observation cortical network in adolescents with low and high resistance to peer influence. *Social Neuroscience, 3*(3–4), 303–316.

Pavone, C., Curto, F., Anello, G., Serretta, V., Almasio, P. L., & Pavone-Macaluso, M. (2008). Prospective, randomized crossover comparison of sublingual apopmorphine (3 mg) with oral sildenafil (50 mg) for male erectile dysfunction. *Journal of Urology, 179* (Suppl. 5), S92–S94.

Pavot, W., & Diener, E. (2008). The satisfaction with life scale and the emerging construct of life satisfaction. *The Journal of Positive Psychology, 3*, 137–152.

Pearlman, E. (2013). Twin psychological development. Retrieved from http://christinabaglivitinglof.com/twin-pregnancy/six-twin-experts-te

Peck, R. C. (1968). Psychological developments in the second half of life. In B. L. Neugarten (Ed.), *Middle age and aging.* Chicago: University of Chicago Press.

Peek, M. K. (2009). Marriage in later life. In D. Carr (Ed.), *Encyclopedia of the life course and human development.* Boston: Gale Cengage.

Peich, M. C., Husain, M., & Bays, P. M. (2013). Age-related decline of precision and binding in visual working memory. *Psychology and Aging, 28*, 729–743.

Pelaez, M., Virues-Ortega, J., & Gewirtz, J. (2012). Acquisition of social referencing via discrimination training in infants. *Journal of Applied Behavior Analysis, 45*, 23–36.

Pelayo, R., Owens, J., Mindell, J., & Sheldon, S. (2006). Bed sharing with unimpaired parents is not an important risk for sudden infant death syndrome: Letter to the editor. *Pediatrics, 117*, 993–994.

Pellicano, E. (2010). Individual differences in executive function and central coherence predict developmental changes in theory of mind in autism. *Developmental Psychology, 46*, 530–544.

Pendakur. R. (2000, January–February). Immigrants and the labour force: Policy, regulation and impact. *Canadian Journal of Sociology Online.*

Peng, P., & Fuchs, D. (2014, in press). A meta-analysis of working memory deficits in children with learning difficulties: Is there a difference between the verbal domain and numerical domain? *Journal of Learning Disabilities.*

Peng, X. D., Huang, C. Q., Chen, L. J., & Lu, Z. C. (2009). Cognitive behavioral therapy and reminiscence techniques for the treatment of depression in the elderly: A systematic review. *Journal of International Medical Research, 37*, 975–982.

Peplau, L. A., & Beals, K. P. (2002). Lesbians, gays, and bisexuals in relationships. In J. Worrell (Ed.), *Encyclopedia of women and gender.* San Diego: Academic Press.

Peplau, L. A., & Fingerhut, A. W. (2007). The close relationships of lesbians and gay men. *Annual Review of Psychology* (Vol. 58). Palo Alto, CA: Annual Reviews.

Pepler, D. (2009). Bullying. No Way! Retrieved from www.bullyingnoway.com.au/talkout/profiles/researchers/debraPepler.shtm

Pepler, D., et al. (2011, April). Why worry about bullying. *Health Care Quarterly, 14*, special issue. Retrieved from http://www.longwoods.com/articles/images/HQ_vol14_ChildHealth_Issue2_Pepler.pdf

Perelli-Harris, B., Kreyenfeld, M., Sigle-Rushton, W., Keizer, R., Laapegard, T., Jasilioneone, A.,... di Guilio, P. (2012). Changes in union status during the transition to parenthood in eleven European countries, 1970's to Early 2000's. *Populations Studies: A Journal of Demography, 66*, 167–182.

Perez, S. M., & Gauvain, M. (2007). The sociocultural context of transitions in early socioemotional development. In C. A. Brownell & C. B. Kopp (Eds.), *Socioemotional development in the toddler years.* New York: Guilford.

Perkins, T. (2006, November 23). Give a little love, says Hannah. *Toronto Star,* p. C3.

Perlman, M., & Ross, H. S. (2005). If-then contingencies in children's sibling conflicts. *Merrill-Palmer Quarterly, 51*, 42–66.

Perls, T. T. (2007). Centenarians. In J. E. Birren (Ed.), *Encyclopedia of gerontology* (2nd ed.). San Diego: Academic Press.

Perls, T. T. (2009). Health and disease in 85 year olds: Baseline findings from the Newcastle 851 cohort study. *British Medical Journal, 339*, b4904.

Perner, J., Stummer, S., Sprung, M., & Doherty, M. (2002). Theory of mind finds its Piagetian perspective: Why alternative naming comes with understanding belief. *Cognitive Development, 17*, 1451–1472.

Perosa, L., Perosa, S., & Tam, H. (2002). Intergenerational system theory and identity development in young adult women. *Journal of Adolescent Research, 17*, 235–259.

Perrault, S. (2015). *Criminal victimization in Canada, 2014.* Retrieved from http://www.statcan.gc.ca.

Perrin, J., et al. (2007). A family-centered, community-based system of services for children and youth with special health care needs. *Archives of Pediatric & Adolescent Medicine, 161*(10), 933–936.

Perry, B. (2003). Effects of traumatic events on children. Retrieved from http://www.childtrauma.org

Perry, B. (2004). Maltreatment and the developing child: How early childhood experience shapes child and culture. Retrieved from www.lfcc.on.ca

Perry, B. D. (2002–2003). *Risk and vulnerability.* Kaiser Foundation. Retrieved from www.kaiserfoundation.ca/modules/document.asp?locid=414&docid=986

Perry, N. B., et al. (2012). The relation between maternal emotional support and child physiological regulation across the preschool years. *Developmental Psychobiology, 55*(4), 382–394.

Perry, N. B., et al. (2013). *Early cardiac vagal regulation predicts the trajectory of externalizing behaviors across the preschool periods.* Unpublished manuscript, University of North Carolina—Greensboro.

Perry, W. G. (1999). *Forms of ethical and intellectual development in the college years: A scheme.* San Francisco: Jossey Bass.

Pessia, E., et al. (2012). Mammalian X chromosome inactivation evolved as a dosage-compensation mechanism for dosage-sensitive genes on the X chromosome. *Proceedings of the National Academy of Sciences USA, 109*, 5346–5351.

Peterson, C. (1996). The ticking of the social clock: Adults' beliefs about the timing of transition events. *International Journal of Aging and Human Development, 42*, 189–203.

Peterson, C. C. (2005). Mind and body: Concepts of human cognition, physiology and false belief in children with autism or typical development. *Journal of Autism and Developmental Disorders, 35*, 487–497.

Peterson, C., & McCabe, A. (1994). A social interactionist account of developing decontextualized narrative skill. *Developmental Psychology, 30*(6), 937–948.

Peterson, C., & Roberts, C. (2003). Like mother, like daughter: Similarities in narrative style. *Developmental Psychology, 39*(3), 551–562.

Peterson, C., & Wang, Q., (January 12, 2016). The Fate of Childhood Memories: Children Postdated Their Earliest Memories as They Grew Older. *Frontiers in Psychology.*

Peterson, C., Morris, G., Baker-Ward, L., & Flynn, S. (2013, June 3). Predicting Which Childhood Memories Persist: Contributions of Memory Characteristics. *Developmental Psychology.* Advance online publication.

Peterson, C., Warren, K. & Short, M. (2011). Infantile Amnesia Across the Years: A 2-Year Follow-up of Children's Earliest Memories. *Child Development, 82*(4), 1092–1105.

Peterson., C. (2012). Children's autobiographical memories across the years: Forensic implications of childhood amnesia and eyewitness memory for stressful events. *Developmental Review, 32*(3), 287–306.

Petitclerc, C. (May 12, 2016). Presentation for Pinehurst Breakfast Club. Sleeping Children Around the World.

Petitto, L., & Marentette, P. (1991). Babbling in the manual mode: Evidence for the ontogeny of language. *Science, 251*, 1493–1496.

Petitto, L., Berens, M., Kovelman, I. Dubins, M., Jasinka, K. & Shalinsky, M. (2012). The "Perceptual Wedge Hypothesis" as the basis for bilingual babies phonetic processing advantage: new insights from fNIRS brain imaging. *Brain Language, 121,* 130–143.

Petrick-Steward, E. (2012). *Beginning writers in the zone of proximal development.* New York: Psychology Press.

Pfeffer, J. (2007). Human resources from an organizational behavior perspective. Some paradoxes explained. *Journal of Economic Perspectives, 21,* 115–134.

Pfefferbaum, B., Newman, E., & Nelson, S.D. (2014). Mental health interventions for children exposed to disasters and terrorism. *Journal of Child and Adolescent Psychopharmacology, 24,* 24–31.

Pfeifer, M., Goldsmoth, H. H., Davidson, R. J., & Rickman, M. (2002). Continuity and change in inhibited and uninhibited children. *Child Development, 73,* 1474–1485.

PHAC & CIHI. (2011). Obesity in Canada: Health and economic implications. Retrieved from http://www.phac-aspc.gc.ca

PHAC. (2008). *Canadian Perinatal Health Report, 2008.* Ottawa, Canada.

PHAC. (2011). *Human papillomavirus (HPV) prevention and HPV vaccines: Questions and answers.* Retrieved from http://www.phac-aspc.gc.ca.

PHAC. (2012a). *Canadian communicable disease report: Update on human papillomavirus (HPV) vaccines.* Retrieved from http://www.phac-aspc.gc.ca.

PHAC. (2012b). Joint statement on safe sleep: Preventing sudden infant deaths in Canada. Retrieved from http://www.phac-aspc.gc.ca/

PHAC. (2012c). *Physical activity tips for adults (18-64 years).* Retrieved from http://www.phac-aspc.gc.ca

PHAC. (2013a). *Chief public health officer's report on the state of public health in Canada 2013: Infectious diseases – the never ending threat.* Retrieved from http://www.phac-aspc.gc.ca.

PHAC. (2013b). *Canadian guidelines on sexually transmitted infections.* Retrieved from http://www.phac-aspc.gc.ca.

PHAC. (2014a). Breastfeeding and infant nutrition . Retrieved from http://www.phac-aspc.gc.ca/

PHAC. (2014b). Sudden infant death syndrome (SIDS) in Canada. Retrieved from http://www.phac-aspc.gc.ca/

PHAC. (2014c). *Summary: Estimates of HIV incidence, prevalence and proportion undiagnosed in Canada, 2014.* Retrieved from http://www.phac-aspc.gc.ca.

PHAC. (2015a). *Report on sexually transmitted infections in Canada: 2012.* Retrieved from http://www.phac-aspc.gc.ca.

PHAC. (2015b). *Sexually transmitted infections.* Retrieved from http://www.phac-aspc.gc.ca.

Phillipp, B., & Merewood, A. (2004). The baby-friendly way: The best breastfeeding start. *Pediatric Clinics North America, 51,* 761–783.

Phillips, A. C., Burns, V. E., & Lord, J. M. (2007). Stress and exercise: Getting the balance right for aging immunity. *Exercise and Sport Sciences Reviews, 35,* 35–39.

Phillips, D. & Lowenstein, A. (2011). Early Care, education and child development. *American Review of Psychology, 62,* 483–500.

Phillips, L. M., Norris, S. P., & Anderson, J. (2008). Unlocking the door: Is parents' reading to children the key to early literacy development? *Canadian Psychology, 49*(2), 82–88.

Phinney, J. S. (2006). Ethnic identity exploration in emerging adulthood. In J. J. Arnett & J. L. Tanner (Eds.), *Emerging adults in America.* Washington, DC: American Psychological Association.

Phinney, J. S. (2008). Bridging identities and disciplines: Advances and challenges in understanding multiple identities. In M. Azmitia, M. Syed, & K. Radmacher (Eds.), *The intersections of personal and social identities. New Directions for Child and Adolescent Development, 120,* 81–95.

Phinney, S., & Ong, A. (2007). Ethnic identity in immigrant families. In J. Lansford, K. Deater-Deckard, & M. Bornstein (Eds), *Immigrant families in contemporary society* (pp. 51–68). New York: Guilford.

Piaget, J. (1932). *The moral judgment of the child.* New York: Harcourt Brace Jovanovich.

Piaget, J. (1952). *The origins of intelligence in children.* New York: International Universities Press.

Piaget, J. (1954). *The construction of reality in the child.* New York: Basic Books.

Piaget, J. (1962). *Play, dreams, and imitation.* New York: W. W. Norton.

Piaget, J., & Inhelder, B. (1969). *The child's conception of space* (F. J. Langdon & J. L. Lunger, Trans.). New York: W. W. Norton.

Piazza, J. R., Charles, S. T., Sliwinski, M. J., Mogle, J., & Almeida, D. M. (2013). Affective reactivity to daily stressors and long-term risk of reporting chronic physical health condition. Annals of Behavior Medicine, 45, 110–120.

Picot, G., & Hou, F. (2014) Immigration, Poverty, and Inequality in Canada: What is New in the 2000'? Statistics Canada Retrieved from http://irpp.org/wp-content/uploads/assets/Uploads/picot-hou.pdf.

Pieperhoff, P., Homke, L., Schneider, F., Habel, U., Shah, N. J., Zilles, K., et al. (2008). Deformation field morphometry reveals age-related structural differences between the brains of adults up to 51 years. *Journal of Neuroscience 28,* 828–842.

Pierce, R. S., & Anderson, G. J. (2014). The effects of age and workload on 3D spatial attention in dual-task driving. Accident Analysis and Prevention, 67C, 96–104.

Pinette, M., Wax, J., & Wilson, E. (2004). The risks of underwater birth. *American Journal of Obstetrics and Gynecology, 190,* 1211–1215.

Ping, H., & Hagopian, W. (2006). Environmental factors in the development of type 1 diabetes. *Reviews in Endocrine and Metabolic Disorders, 7,* 149–162.

Pinheiro, R. T., Magalhaes, P. V., Horta, B. L., Pinheiro, K. A., da Silva, R. A., & Pinto, R. H. (2006). Is paternal postpartum depression associated with maternal postpartum depression? Population-based study in Brazil. *Acta Psychiatrica Scandinavia, 113,* 230–232.

Piper, W. E., Ogrodniczuk, J. S., Joyce, A. S., Weideman, R., & Rosie, J. S. (2007). Group composition and group therapy for complicated grief. *Journal of Consulting and Clinical Psychology, 75,* 116–125.

Pitkanen, T., Lyyra, A. L., & Pulkkinen L. (2005). Age of onset of drinking and the use of alcohol in adulthood: A follow-up study from age 8–42 for females and males. *Addiction, 100,* 652–661.

Pitman, E., & Matthey, S. (2004). The SMILES program: A group program for children with mentally ill parents or siblings. *American Journal of Orthopsychiatry, 74,* 383–388.

Pitt-Catsouphes, M., Kossek, E. E., & Sweet, S. (Eds.). (2006). *The work and family handbook.* Mahwah, NJ: Erlbaum.

Pitzer, L. M., Fingerman, K. L., & Lefkowitz, E. S. (2014, in press). Support and negativity in the adult parent tie: Development of the Parent Adult Relationship Questionnaire (PARQ). *International Journal of Aging and Human Development.*

Pleck, J. H. (1995). The gender-role strain paradigm. In R. F. Levant & W. S. Pollack (Eds.), *A new psychology of men.* New York: Basic Books.

Pliszka, S. R. (2007). Pharmacologic treatment of attention deficit hyperactivity disorder: Efficacy, safety, and mechanisms of action. *Neuropsychology Review, 17,* 61–72.

Plomin, R. (2004). Genetics and developmental psychology. *Merrill-Palmer Quarterly, 50*, 341–352.

Plomin, R., DeFries, J. C., & Fulker, D. W. (2007). Nature and nurture during infancy and early childhood. New York: Cambridge University Press.

Plomin, R., DeFries, J. C., Craig, I. W., & McGuffin, P. (Eds.). (2003). *Behavioral genetics in the postgenomic era.* Washington, DC: APA Books.

Plomin, R., DeFries, J., McLearn, G., & McGuffin, P. (2009). *Behavioural genetics* (5th ed.). New York, NY: Freeman.

Pohanka, M. (2013). Alzheimer's disease and oxidative stress: A link to etiology? A review. *Current Medicinal Chemistry, 21*, 356–364.

Pohlhaus, J. R., et al. (2011). Sex differences in application, success, and funding rates for NIH extramural programs. *Academic Medicine, 86*(6), 759–767.

Poil, S. S., et al. (2013). Integrative EEG biomarkers predict progression in Alzheimer's disease at the MCI stage. *Frontiers in Aging Neuroscience, 5*, 58.

Polan, E., & Taylor, D. (2011). *Journey across the lifespan: Human development and health promotion* (4th ed). Philadelphia: Davis.

Polat, U., et al. (2012). Training the brain to overcome the effect of aging on the human eye. *Science Reports, 2*, 278.

Polit, D., & Beck, C. (2010). *Nursing research: Appraising evidence for nursing practice* (7th ed.). Philadelphia: Lippincott Williams & Wilkins.

Pollack, P. (2013). Deep brain stimulation for Parkinson's disease—patient selection. *Handbook of Clinical Neurology, 116C*, 97–105.

Pollack, W. (1999). *Real boys.* New York: Owl Books.

Pollard, I. (2007). Neuropharmacology of drugs and alcohol in mother and fetus. *Seminars in Fetal and Neonatal Medicine, 12*, 106–113.

Polo-Kantola, P. (2011). Sleep problems in midlife and beyond. *Maturitas, 68*, 224–232.

Poltorak, D., & Glazer, J. (2006). The development of children's understanding of death: Cognitive and psychodynamic considerations. *Child and Adolescent Psychiatric Clinics of North America, 15*, 567–573.

Pomerantz, E. M. (2013). Center for Parent-Child Studies. Retrieved from http://labs.psychology.illinois.edu/cpcs/

Pomerleau, A., Scuccumarri C., & Malcuit, G. (2003). Mother-infant behavioural interactions in teenage and adult mothers during the first six months postpartum: Relations with infant development. *Infant Mental Health Journal, 24*, 495–509.

Pomfrey, E. (2012). What is stress? Natural Health and Meditation Resource Page. Retrieved from http://www.tm.org/resource-pages/60-what-is-stress

Ponton, L. E. (1997). *The romance of risk: Why teenagers do the things they do.* New York: Basic Books.

Pooler, A. M., Noble, W., & Hanger, D. P. (2014). A role for tau at the synapse in Alzheimer's disease pathogenesis. *Neuropharmacology, 76*, Pt. A, 1–8.

Popenoe, D. (2007). *The state of our unions: 2007.* Piscataway, NJ: The National Marriage Project, Rutgers University.

Popenoe, D. (2008). *Cohabitation, marriage, and child wellbeing: A cross-national perspective.* Piscataway, NJ: The National Marriage Project, Rutgers University.

Poranganel, L., Titley, K., & Kulkarni, G. (2006). Establishing a dental home: A program for promoting comprehensive oral health starting from pregnancy through childhood. *Oral Health, 96*, 10–14.

Porath-Walker, A. (2015). Clearing the smoke on cannabis-Maternal cannabis use during pregnancy – An update. Retrieved from http://www.ccsa.ca/

Porterfield, S. (2011). Vertical transmission of human papillomavirus from mother to fetus: Literature review. *The Journal of Nurse Practitioners, 7*(8), 665–670.

Posada, G. (2008). Attachment. In M. M. Haith & J. B. Benson (Eds.), *Encyclopedia of infancy and early childhood.* Oxford, UK: Elsevier.

Pot, A. M., et al. (2010). The impact of life review on depression in older adults: A randomized controlled trial. *International Psychogeriatrics, 22*(4), 572.

Poulin, F., & Pedersen, S. (2007). Developmental changes in gender composition of friendship networks in adolescent girls and boys. *Developmental Psychology, 43*, 1484–1496.

Poulin-Dubois, D., & Héroux, G. (1994). Movement and children's attributions of life properties. *International Journal of Behavioral Development, 17*(2), 329–347.

Powell, B., Cooper, G., Hoffman, K., & Marvin, B. (2014), *The circle of security intervention.* New York: Guilford.

Power, T. G. (2011). Social play. In P. K. Smith & C. H. Hart (Eds.), *Wiley-Blackwell handbook of childhood social development* (2nd ed.). New York: Wiley

Powers, C. J., & Bierman, K. L. (2013). The multifaceted impact of peer relations on aggressive-disruptive behavior in early elementary school. *Developmental Psychology, 49*(6), 1174–1186.

Prakash, R. S., et al. (2011). Cardiovascular fitness and attentional control in the aging brain. *Frontiers in Human Neuroscience, 4*(229), 1–12.

Pressley, M., Raphael, L., Gallagher, D., & DiBella, J. (2004). Providence–St. Mel School: How a school that works for African-American students works. *Journal of Educational Psychology, 96*, 216–235.

Pressley, M., Wharton-MacDonald, R., Allington, R., Block, C. C., Morrow, L., Tracey, D., et al. (2001). A study of effective first grade literacy instruction. *Scientific Studies of Reading, 15*, 35–58.

Preston, S. H., & Stokes, A. (2011). Contribution of obesity to international differences in life expectancy. *American Journal of Public Health, 101*, 2137–2143.

Price, C. A., & Joo, E. (2005). Exploring the relationship between marital status and women's retirement satisfaction. *International Journal of Aging and Human Development, 61*, 37–55.

Price, C. A., & Nesteruk, O. (2010). Creating retirement paths: Examples from the lives of women. *Journal of Women and Aging, 22*, 136–149.

Pride Toronto. (2016). *Pride parade*. Retrieved from http://www.pridetoronto.com.

Prince-Paul, M. (2008). Relationships among communicative acts, social well-being, and spiritual well-being on the quality of life at the end of life in patients with cancer enrolled in hospice. *Journal of Palliative Medicine, 11*(1), 20–25.

Princess Margaret Hospital. (2005). Do not resuscitate orders. Caring to the End of Life Series. Toronto: University Health Network. Retrieved from http://www.caringtotheend.ca/body.php?id=515&cc=1

Prinstein, M. (2007). Moderators of peer contagion: A longitudinal examination of depression socialization between adolescents and their best friends. *Journal of Clinical Child & Adolescent Psychology, 36*(2), 159–170.

Prinstein, M. J., & Dodge, K. A. (Eds.). (2008). *Understanding peer influence in children and adolescents.* New York: Guilford.

Prinz, R. J., Sanders, M. R., Shapiro, C. J., Witaker, D. J., Lutzker, J. R. (2009). Population-based prevention of child maltreatment: The U.S. Triple P System Population Trial. *Prevention Science, 10*, 1–13.

Problem Gambling Institute of Ontario. (2010). Ontario youth gambling report: Data from the 2009 Ontario student drug use and health survey. Retrieved from http://www.problemgambling.ca

Promislow, D. E. L., Fedorka, K. M., & Burger, J. E. P. (2005). Evolutionary biology of aging: Future directions. In S. Austad & E. Masoro (Eds.), *The Handbook of the Biology of Aging* (6th ed.).

Proulx, C., & Snyder-Rivas, L. (2013). The longitudinal association between marital happiness, problems, and self-rated health. *Journal of Family Psychology, 27*, 194–202.

Province of British Columbia. (2015.) Intergenerational connections Retrieved from http://www2.gov.bc.ca/gov/content/family-social-supports/seniors/health-safety/active-aging/intergenerational-connections

Pryor, J. H. Y., Hurtado, S., Harkness, J., & Korn, W. S. (2007). *The American freshman: National norms for fall, 2007.* Los Angeles: Higher Education Research Institute, UCLA.

Public Health Agency of Canada (PHAC). (2007, November). HIV/AIDS epi updates. Canada. Retrieved from http://www.phac-aspc.gc.ca/

Public Health Agency of Canada (PHAC). (2008a). *Canadian guidelines for sexual health education.* Ottawa. Retrieved from http://www.phac-aspc.gc.ca/publicat/cgshe-ldnemss/

Public Health Agency of Canada (PHAC). (2008b). *Canadian perinatal health report 2008 edition.* Ottawa.

Public Health Agency of Canada (PHAC). (2009a). Breastfeeding & infant nutrition. Retrieved from http://www.phac-aspc.gc.ca/dca-dea/prenatal/nutrition-eng.php

Public Health Agency of Canada (PHAC). (2009b). Childhood cancers: Ages 1–14. Retrieved from http://www.phac-aspc.gc.ca/

Public Health Agency of Canada (PHAC). (2009c). *What mothers say: The Canadian maternity experiences survey.* Retrieved from http://www.publichealth.gc.ca/mes

Public Health Agency of Canada (PHAC). (2010a). Life with arthritis in Canada: A personal and public health challenge. Retrieved from http://www.phac-aspc.gc.ca/cd-mc/arthritis-arthrite/lwaic-vaaac-10/4-eng.php#Sel

Public Health Agency Canada (PHAC). (2010b). The Chief Public Health Officer's Report on the State of Public Health in Canada 2010 PHAC. Retrieved from http://www.phac-aspc.gc.ca/cphorsphc-respcacsp/2010/fr-rc/cphorsphc-respcacsp-06-eng.php

Public Health Agency of Canada (PHAC). (2010c). *Report on sexually transmitted infections in Canada: 2008.* Retrieved from http://www.phac-aspc.gc.ca/

Public Health Agency of Canada (PHAC). (2010d). What is the impact of sleep apnea on Canadians? Retrieved from http://www.phac-aspc.gc.ca/cd-mc/sleepapnea-apneesommeil/ff-rr-2009-eng.php

Public Health Agency of Canada (PHAC). (2011a). Joint statement on safe sleep: Preventing sudden infant deaths in Canada. Retrieved from http://www.phacaspc.gc.ca

Public Health Agency of Canada (PHAC). (2011b). Shaken baby syndrome (SBS). Retrieved from http://www.phacaspc.gc.ca

Public Health Agency of Canada (PHAC). (2011c). *The Chief Public Health Officer's report on the state of public health in Canada, 2011.* Retrieved from http://www.phac-aspc.gc.ca/

Public Health Agency of Canada (PHAC). (2011d). *HIV/AIDS epi updates—*July 2010. Retrieved from http://www.sogc.org/

Public Health Agency of Canada (PHAC). (2011e). Reported cases and rates of chlamydia by age group and sex, 1991 to 2009. Retrieved from http://www.phac-aspc.gc.ca/

Public Health Agency of Canada (PHAC). (2011f). Human papillomavirus (HPV) prevention and HPV vaccines: Questions and answers. Retrieved from http://www.phac-aspc.gc.ca/

Public Health Agency of Canada (PHAC). (2011g). *The sensible guide to a healthy pregnancy.* Retrieved from http://www.healthycanadians.ca/

Public Health Agency Canada (PHAC). (2011h). Chapter 7 Eating Disorders. Public Health Agency Canada. Retrieved from http://www.phac-aspc.gc.ca/publicat/human-humain06/10-eng.php.

Public Health Agency Canada (PHAC). (2012a). Cancer in Children in Canada (0-14 years). Public Health Agency Canada. Retrieved from http://www.phac-aspc.gc.ca/cd-mc/cancer/fs-fi/cancer-child-enfant/index-eng.php.

Public Health Agency of Canada (PHAC). (2012b). Evaluation of the Aboriginal Head Start in Urban and Northern Communities Program at the Public Health Agency of Canada. Retrieved from http://www.phac-aspc.gc.ca/about_apropos/evaluation/reports-rapports/2011-2012/ahsunc-papacun/summary-resume-eng.php#executive_summary

Public Health Agency of Canada (PHAC). (2012c). The Human Face of Mental Health and Mental Illness in Canada 2006. Retrieved from http://www.phac-aspc.gc.ca/publicat/human-humain06/index-eng.php.

Public Health Agency of Canada (PHAC). (2012d). Executive summary. *Report on sexually transmitted infections in Canada: 2009.* Retrieved from http://www.phacaspc.gc.ca/

Public Health Agency of Canada (PHAC). (2012e). Canadian perinatal surveillance system. Retrieved from http://www.phac-aspc.gc.ca/

Public Health Agency of Canada (PHAC). (2012f). *Perinatal health indicators for Canada, 2011.* Retrieved from http://www.phac-asap.gc.ca/

Public Health Agency of Canada (PHAC). (2012g). *The health of Canada's young people: A mental health focus.* Retrieved from http://www.phac-aspc.gc/

Public Health Agency Canada (PHAC). (2014). Seniors' Falls in Canada - Infographic. Retrieved from http://www.phac-aspc.gc.ca/seniors-aines/publications/public/injury-blessure/seniors_falls-chutes_aines/infographic-infographie_2015-eng.php.

Public Health Agency Canada (PHAC). (2016a). Leading Causes of Death and Hospitialization in Canada. Retrieved from http://www.phac-aspc.gc.ca/publicat/lcd-pcd97/index-eng.php.

Public Health Agency Canada (PHAC). (2016b). Social Determinants of Health. Canadian Best Practices Portal. Retrieved from http://web.hc-sc.gc.ca.

Public Health Agency of Canada (PHAC). (2016c) Stop Family Violence. Retrieved from http://www.phac-aspc.gc.ca/sfv-avf/index-eng.php.

Public Health Agency of Canada. (2016d). Childhood Obesity. Retrieved from http://www.phac-aspc.gc.ca/hp-ps/hl-mvs/framework-cadre/2011/index-eng.php.

Public Safety Canada. (2009). Bullying prevention in schools. Retrieved from http://www.publicsafety.gc.ca/

Puccini, D., & Liszkowski, U. (2012). 15-month- old infants fast map words but not representational gestures of multimodal labels. *Frontiers in Psychology, 3*, 101.

Puchalski, C. M., Vitillo, R., Hull, S. K., & Reller, N. (2014). Improving the spiritual dimension of whole person care: Reaching national and international consensus. *Journal of Palliative Medicine, 17*(6), 642–656.

Pudrovska, T. (2009). Midlife crises and transitions. In D. Carr (Ed.), *Encyclopedia of the life course and human development.* Boston: Gale Cengage.

Pudrovska, T., Schieman, S., & Carr, D. (2006). Strains of singlehood in later life: Do race and gender matter? *Journals of Gerontology B: Psychological Sciences and Social Sciences, 61*, S315–S322.

Pugh, A. (2004). CrossCurrents. Centre for Addiction and Mental Health (CAMH). Retrieved from http://www.camh.net/

Pujazon-Zazik, M., & Park, M. (2010). To tweet, or not to tweet: Gender differences and potential positive and negative health outcomes of adolescents' social Internet use. *American Journal of Men's Health, 4*, 77–85.

Purnell, L. (2013). *Transcultural health care: A culturally competent approach* (4th ed.). Philadelphia: Davis.

Putallaz, M., Grimes, C. L., Foster, K. J., Kupersmidt, J. B., Clie, J. D., & Dearing, K. (2007). Overt and relational aggression and victimization: Multiple perspectives within the school setting. *Journal of School Psychology, 45*, 523–547.

Putnam, S. P., Sanson, A. V., & Rothbart, M. K. (2002). Child temperament and parenting. In M. H. Bornstein (Ed.), *Handbook of parenting* (2nd ed.). Mahwah, NJ: Erlbaum.

Putnam, S., Sanson, A., & Rothbart, M. (2002). Child temperament and parenting In M. Bornstein (Ed.) *Handbook of parenting*, (vol 1) , (pp. 255–277). Mahwah, NJ: Lawrence Erlbaum.

Q

Qamar, D. (2015). Difficult immigration journey can cause depression in newcomers. *Canadian Immigrant*. Retrieved from http://canadianimmigrant.ca/category/immigrant-stories.

Qin, L., Pomerantz, E., & Wang, Q. (2009). Are gains in the decision - making autonomy during early adolescence beneficial for emotional functioning? The case of the United States and China. *Child Development, 80*, 1705–1721.

Quebec Insurance Plan. (2015). Questions and answers about Quebec Parental Insurance Plan for Employers. Retrieved from http://www.cra-gc-.ca/

Quesnel, C., Fulgencio, J. P., Drie, C., Marro, B., Payen, L., Lembert, N., et al. (2007). Limitations of computed tomographic angiography in the diagnosis of brain death. *Intensive Care Medicine, 33*, 2129–2135.

Quigley, C., & Muller, M. M. (2014). Feature-selective attention in healthy old age: A selective decline in selective attention. *Journal of Neuroscience, 34*, 2471–2476.

Quinn, J. (2011). Introductory essay: Canada's own brand of Truth and Reconciliation? *The International Indigenous Policy Journal, 2*(3). Article 1.

Quinn, P. C., Bhatt, R. S., & Hayden, A. (2008). What goes with what: Development of perceptual grouping in infancy. In B. H. Ross (Ed.), *Motivation* (Vol. 49). London: Elsevier.

Quoidbach, J., Gilbert, D., & Wilson, T. D. (2013). The end of history illusion. *Science, 339*, 96–98.

R

Raabe, A., & Muller, W. U. (2008). Radiation exposure during pregnancy. *Neurosurgery Review, 31*(3), 351–352.

Rachner, T. D., Khosia, S., & Hofbauer, L. C. (2011). Osteoporosis: Now and the future. *Lancet, 377*, 1276–1287.

Racine, T., & Carpendale, J. (2007). The role of shared practice in joint attention. *British Journal of Developmental Psychology, 25*, 3–25.

Rahnema, C. D., et al. (2014, in press). Anabolic steroid-induced hypogonadism: Diagnosis and treatment. *Fertility and Sterility*.

Raikes, H., & Thompson, R. (2008). Attachment security and parenting quality predict children's problem-solving, attributions, and loneliness with peers. *Attachment and Human Development, 10*(3), 319–344.

Rainbow Health Ontario. (2011). RHO Fact Sheet. Rainbow Health Ontario. Retrieved from http://www.rainbowhealthontario.ca/wp-content/uploads/woocommerce_uploads/2014/08/Intersex.pdf.

Raj, T., et al. (2014, in press). CD33: Increased inclusion of exon 2 implicates the Ig V0set domain in Alzheimer's disease susceptibility. *Human Molecular Genetics*.

Ram, N., Morelli, S., Lindberg, C., & Carstensen, L. L. (2008). From static to dynamic: The ongoing dialetic about human development. In K. W. Schaie & R. P. Abeles (Eds.), *Social structures and aging individuals: Continuing challenges*. Mahwah, NJ: Erlbaum.

Ramage-Morin, P. (2009). Medication use among senior Canadians. Statistics Canada Catalogue no. 82-003-X. Retrieved from http://www.statcan.gc.ca/pub/82-003-x/2009001/article/10801-eng.pdf

Ramirez-Rodriquez, G., et al. (2014). Environmental enrichment induces neuroplastic changes in middle age female BalbC mice and increases the hippocampal levels of BDNF, p-Akt, and p-MAPK1/2. *Neuroscience*.

Ramlau-Hansen, C., Toft, G., Jensen, M., Strandberg-Larsen, K., Hansen, M., & Olsen, J. (2010). Maternal consumption during pregnancy and semen quality in the male offspring: two decades of follow-up. *Human Reproduction, 25*,1372–1379.

Rangul, V., Holmen, T., Bauman, A. Bratberg, G., Kurtze, N., & Midthjell, K. (2011), Factors predicating changes in physical activity through adolescence: The Young-HUNT study, Norway. *Journal of Adolescent Health, 48*, 616–624.

Ransmayr, G. (2011). Physical, occupational, speech, and swallowing therapies and exercise in Parkinson's disease. *Journal of Neural Transmission, 118*, 773–781.

Rapaport, S. (1994, November 28). Interview. *U.S. News and World Report*, p. 94.

Raphael, B., Taylor, M., & McAndrew, V. (2008). Women, catastrophe, and mental health. *Australia and New Zealand Journal of Psychiatry, 42*, 13–23.

Raphael, D. (Ed.). (2010). *Health promotion and quality of life in Canada: Essential readings*. Toronto: Canadian Scholars' Press.

Rasmussen, C., Ho, E., Nicoladis, E., Leung, J., & Bisanz, J. (2006). Is the Chinese number-naming system transparent? Evidence from Chinese-English bilingual children. *Canadian Journal of Experimental Psychology, 60*, 60–67.

Ratey, J. (2006, March 27). Commentary in L. Szabo, ADHD treatment is getting a workout. *USA Today*, 6D.

Ratzan, S. (2011). Our new "social" communication age in health. *Journal of Health Communication: International Perspectives, 16*(8), 803–804.

Raudenbush, S. W. (2001). Comparing personal trajectories and drawing causal inferences from longitudinal data. *Annual Review of Psychology, 52*, 501–25.

Raven, P. H., Johnson, G. B., Mason, K. A., Loscos, J., & Singer, S. (2014). *Biology* (10th ed.). New York: McGraw-Hill.

Ravenera, Z. (2008). Profiles of Fathers in Canada. Retrieved from http://www.fira.ca.

Rawlins, W. K. (2009). *The compass of friendship*. Thousand Oaks, CA: Sage.

Ray, G., Mertens, J., & Weisner, C. (2009). Family members of people with alcohol or drug dependence: Health problems and medical cost compared to family members of people with diabetes and asthma. *Addiction, 104*, 203–214.

Raymo, J. M., & Sweeney, M. M. (2006). Work-family conflict and retirement preferences. *Journals of Gerontology B: Psychological Sciences and Social Sciences, 61*, S161–S169.

Raznahan, A., Shaw, P., Lerch, J., Clasen, L., Greenstein, D., Berman, R., ... Giedd, J. (2014). Longitudinal four-dimensional mapping of subcortical anatomy in human development. *Proceedings of the National Academy of Sciences of the United States of America, 111*(4), 1592–1597.

Razza, R. A., Martin, A., & Brooks-Gunn, J. (2012). The implications of early attentional regulational for school success among low-income children. *Journal of Applied Developmental Psychology, 33*, 311–319.

Read, S., & Elliott, D. (2007). Exploring a continuum of support for bereaved people with intellectual disabilities: A strategic approach. *Journal of Intellectual Disabilities, 11*, 167–181.

Real, T. (1997). *I don't want to talk about it: Overcoming the secret legacy of male depression.* New York: Simon and Schuster.

Ream, G. L., & Savin-Williams, R. (2003). Religious development in adolescence. In G. Adams & M. Berzonsky (Eds.), *Blackwell handbook of adolescence.* Malden, MA: Blackwell.

Reeb, B. C., Fox, N. A. Nelson, C. A., & Zeanah, C. H. (2008). The effects of early institutionalization of social behavior and underlying neural correlates. In M. de Haan & M. Gunnar (Eds.), *Handbook of social developmental neuroscience.* Malden, MA: Blackwell.

Reece, E. A. (2008). Obesity, diabetes, and links to congenital defects: A review of the evidence and recommendations for intervention. *Journal of Maternal-Fetal and Neonatal Medicine, 21*, 173–180.

Reeskin, T. & Wright, M. (2011). Subjective well-being and national satisfaction: Taking seriously the "Proud of what" question. *Psychological Science, 22*, 1460–1462.

Reeve, C. L., & Charles, J. E. (2008). Survey of opinions on the primacy of g and social consequences of ability testing: A comparison of expert and non-expert views. *Intelligence, 36*, 681–688.

Regan, P. C. (2008). *The mating game* (2nd ed.). Thousand Oaks, CA: Sage.

Regev, R. H., Lusky, A., Dolfin, T., Litmanovitz, I., Arnon, S., Reichman, B., & Israel Neonatal Network. (2003). Excess mortality and morbidity among small-for-gestational-age premature infants: A population based study. *Journal of Pediatrics, 143*, 186–191.

Rehm, J., et al. (2010). The relation between different dimensions of alcohol consumption and burden of disease—an overview. *Addiction, 105*, 817–843.

Reichstadt, J., Depp, C. A., Palinkas, L. A., Folsom, D. P., & Jeste, D. V. (2007). Building blocks of successful aging: A focus group study of older adults' perceived contributors to successful aging. *American Journal of Geriatric Psychiatry, 15*, 194–201.

Reid, J., Rynard, V., Czoli, C., & Hammond, D. (2015). Who is using e-cigarettes in Canada? Nationally representative data on the prevalence of e-cigarette use among Canadians. *Preventative Medicine, 81*, 18–183.

Reiger, G., & Savin-Williams, R. (2012). Gender nonconformity, sexual orientation, and psychological well-being. *Archives of Sex Behaviour, 41*, 611–621.

Reijmerink, N. E., et al. (2011). Toll-like receptors and microbial exposure: Gene-gene and gene-environment interaction in the development of atopy. *European Respiratory Journal, 128*, 948–955.

Reilly, D. E., Hastings, R. P., Vaughan, F. L., & Huws, J. C. (2008). Parental bereavement and the loss of a child with intellectual disabilities: A review of the literature. *Intellectual and Developmental Disabilities, 46*, 27–43.

Reinders, H., & Youniss, J. (2006). School-based required community service and civic development in adolescence. *Applied Developmental Science, 10*, 2–12.

Reindollar, R. H., & Goldman, M. B. (2012). Gonadotropin therapy: A 20th century relic. *Fertility and Sterility, 97*, 813–818.

Reis, S. M., & Renzulli, J. S. (2014). Challenging gifted and talented learners with a continuum of research-based intervention strategies. In M. A. Bray & T. J. Kehle (Eds.), *Oxford handbook of school psychology*. New York: Oxford University Press.

Rejeski, W. J., et al. (2011). Translating weight loss and physical activity programs into the community to preserve mobility in older, obese adults in poor cardiovascular health. *Archives of Internal Medicine, 171*(10), 880–886.

Rendall, M., Weden, M., Faveault, M., & Waldron, H. (2011). The protective effect of marriage for survival: A review and update. *Demography, 48*, 481–506.

Repacholi, B. M., & Gopnik, A. (1997). Early reasoning about desires: Evidence from 14- and 18-month-olds. *Developmental Psychology, 33*, 12–21.

Responsible Gambling Council. (2015). Canadian gambling digest, 2013-2014. Retrieved from http://www.responsiblegambling.org.

Reuter-Lorenz, P. A. (2013). Aging and cognitive neuroimaging: A fertile union. *Perspectives on Psychological Science, 8*, 68–77.

Reutzel, D. R., & Cooter, R. B. (2015, in press). *Teaching children to read* (7th ed.). Upper Saddle River, NJ: Pearson.

Reyes, S., Algarin, C., Burnout, D., & Peirano, P. (2013). Sleep/wake patterns and physical performance in older adults. *Aging: Clinical and Experimental Research, 25*, 175–181.

Reyna, V. F. (2004). How people make decisions that involve risk: A dual-process approach. *Current Directions in Psychological Science, 13*, 60–66.

Reyna, V. F., & Rivers, S. E. (2008). Current theories and rational decision making. *Developmental Review, 28*, 1–11.

Reynolds, M. (2012). *The legacy of child abuse.* McGill Publications, Headway, Vol. 4., No. 1.

Reznick, J. S. (2014). Working memory in infancy. In P. Bauer & R. Fivush (Eds.), *Wiley-Blackwell handbook of children's memory*. New York: Wiley.

Rhoades, G., Kamp Dusch, C., Atkins, D., Stanley, S., & Markman, H. (2011). Breaking up is hard to do: The impact of unmarried relationship dissolution on mental health and life satisfaction. *Journal of Family Psychology, 25*, 366–374.

Rhoades, G., Stanley, S., & Markman, H. (2009). Couples' reasons for cohabitation and marital instability. *Journal of Family Issues, 30*, 233–258.

Rhodes, A., et al. (2008). The impact of rural residence on medically serious medicinal self-poisonings. *General Hospital Psychiatry, 30*(6), 552–560.

Rholes, W. S., & Simpson, J. A. (2007). Introduction: New directions and emerging issues in adult attachment. In W. S. Rholes & J. A. Simpson (Eds.), *Adult attachment.* New York: Guilford.

Richards, J. (2009). Dropouts: The Achilles Heel of Canada's school system. Commentary 298. Toronto: C.D. Howe Institute. Retrieved from http://www.cdhowe.org

Richardson, G. A., Goldschmidt, L., & Larkby, C. (2008). Effects of prenatal cocaine exposure on growth: A longitudinal analysis. *Pediatrics, 120*, e1017–e1027.

Richardson, G. A., Goldschmidt, L., & Willford, J. (2008). The effects of prenatal cocaine use on infant development. *Neurotoxicology and Teratology, 30*, 96–106.

Richardson, R., & Hayne, H. (2007). You can't take it with you: The translation of memory across development. *Current Directions in Psychological Science, 16*, 223–227.

Richardson, V. E. (2007). A dual process model of grief counseling: Findings from the Changing Lives of Older Couples

(CLOC) Study. *Journal of Gerontological Social Work, 48*, 311–329.

Richens, J. L., Morgan, K., & O'Shea, P. (2014, in press). Reverse engineering of Alzheimer's disease based on biomarker pathways analysis. *Neurobiology of Aging*.

Richmond, E. J., & Rogol, A. D. (2007). Male pubertal development and the role of androgen therapy. *Nature Clinical Practice: Endocrinology and Metabolism, 3*, 338–344.

Riebe, D., Garber, C. E., Rossi, J. S., Greaney, M. L., Nigg, C. R., Lees, F. D., et al. (2005). Physical activity, physical function, and stages of change in older adults. *American Journal of Health Behavior, 29*, 70–80.

Rifas-Shiman, S. L., Rich - Edwards, J. W., Willett, W. C., Kleinman, K. P., Oken, E., & Gillman, M. W. (2006). Changes in dietary intake from the first to the second trimester of pregnancy. *Pediatric and Perinatal Epidemiology, 20*, 35–42.

Rifkin, J. (2005, Spring). Ultimate therapy: Commercial eugenics in the 21st century. *Harvard International Review, 29*(1), 44–48.

Rigaud, D., Verges, B., Colas - Linhart, N., Petiet, A., Moukkaddem, M., Van Wymelbeke, V., et al. (2007). Hormonal and psychological factors linked to the increased thermic effect of food in malnourished fasting anorexia nervosa. *Journal of Clinical Endocrinology and Metabolism, 92*, 1623–1629.

Riley, K. P., Snowdon, D. A., Derosiers, M. F., & Markesbery, W. R. (2005). Early life linguistic ability, late life cognitive function, and neuropathology: Findings from the Nun Study. *Neurobiology of Aging, 26*, 341–347.

Rimsza, M. E., & Kirk, G. M. (2005). Common medical problems of the college student. *Pediatric Clinics of North America, 52*, 9–24.

Ritchie, S., Maxwell, K. L., & Bredekamp, S. (2009). Rethinking early schooling: Using developmental science to transform children's early experiences. In O. A. Babarin & B. H. Wasik (Eds.), *Handbook of child development and early education*. New York: Guilford.

Ritzmann, R., Kramer, A., Bernhardt, S., & Gollhofer, A. (2014). Whole body vibration training—improving balance control and muscle endurance. *PLoS One, 9*(2), e89905.

Rivers, S. E., Reyna, V. F., & Mills, B. (2008). Risk taking under the influence: A fuzzy-trace theory of emotion in adolescence. *Developmental Review, 28*, 107–144.

Rizzuto, D., & Fratiglioni, L. (2014, in press). Lifestyle factors related to mortality and survival: A mini-review. *Gerontology*.

Robbins, G., Powers, D., & Burgess, S. (2008). *A fit way of life*. New York: McGraw-Hill.

Roberie, D. R., & Elliott, W. J. (2012). What is the prevalence of resistant hypertension in the United States? *Current Opinion in Cardiology, 27*, 386–391.

Roberto, K. A., & Skoglund, R. R. (1996). Interactions with grandparents and great-grandparents: A comparison of activities, influences, and relationships. *International Journal of Aging and Human Development, 43*, 107–117.

Roberts, B. W., & Mroczek, D. (2008). Personality trait change in adulthood. *Current Directions in Psychological Science, 17*, 31–35.

Roberts, B. W., & Wood, D. (2006). Personality development in the context of the neo-socioanalytic model of personality. In D. Mroczek & T. Little (Eds.), *Handbook of personality development*. Mahwah, NJ: Erlbaum.

Roberts, B. W., Jackson, J. J., Fayard, J. V., Edmonds, G., & Meints, J. (2009). Conscientiousness. In M. Leary & R. Hoyle (Eds.), *Handbook of individual differences in social behavior*. New York: Guilford.

Roberts, D., Henriksen, L., & Foehr, U. (2009). Adolescence, adolescents, and media. In R.M. Lerner & L. Strinberg (Eds.), *Handbook of adolescent psychology* (3rd ed., Vol. 2, pp. 314–344). New York, NY: Wiley.

Roberts, L. W., Clifton, R. A., Ferguson, B., Kampen, K., & Langlois, S. (Eds.). (2004). *Recent social trends in Canada, 1960–2000*. Montreal: McGill-Queen's University Press.

Robertson, L. T., & Mitchell, J. R. (2013). Benefits of short-term dietary restriction in mammals. *Experimental Gerontology, 48*, 1043–1048.

Robins, R. W., Trzesniewski, K. H., Tracey, J. L., Potter, J., & Gosling, S. D. (2002). Age differences in self-esteem from age 9 to 90. *Psychology and Aging, 17*, 423–434.

Robinson, K. (2009). *The element: How finding your passion changes everything*. London, England: Penguin Books.

Robinson, K. M., & Dube, A. K. (2008). A Microgenetic Study of the Multiplcation and Division Inversion Concept. *Canadian Journal of Experimental Psychology*, 62(3), 1156–1162.

Robinson, K. M., & Dube, A. K. (2009). A Microgenetic Study of Simple Division. *Canadian Journal of Experimental Psychology*, 63(3), 193–200.

Robitaille, A., Cappeliez, P., Coulombe, D., & Webster, J. D. (2010). Factorial structure and psychometric properties of the reminiscence functions scale. *Aging and Mental Health, 14*, 184–192.

Robitaille, A., et al. (2013). Longitudinal mediation of processing speed on age-related change in memory and fluid intelligence. *Psychology and Aging, 28*, 887–901.

Rochlen, A. B., McKelley, R. A., Suizzo, M. A., & Scaringi, V. (2008). Predictors of relationship satisfaction, psychological well-being, and life-satisfaction among stay-at-home fathers. *Psychology of Men and Masculinity, 9*, 17–28.

Rock Hall. (2013). Leonard Cohen biography. Retrieved from http://rockhall.com/inductees/leonard-cohen/bio/

Rocker, G., & Heyland, D. (2003). New research initiatives in Canada for end-of-life and palliative care. *CMAJ, 169*(4), 300–301.

Rode, S. S., Chang, P., Fisch, R. O., & Sroufe, L. A. (1981). Attachment patterns of infants separated at birth. *Developmental Psychology, 17*, 188–191.

Rodrigues, A. E., Hall, J. H., & Fincham, F. D. (2006). What predicts divorce and relationship dissolution. In M. A. Fine & J. H. Harvey (Eds.), *Handbook of divorce and relationship dissolution*. Mahwah, NJ: Erlbaum.

Rodriguez, E. T., Tamis-LeMonda, C. S., Spellman, M. E., Pan, B. A., Riakes, H., Lugo-Gil, J., et al. (2009). The formative role of home literacy experiences across the first three years of life in children from low-income families. *Journal of Applied Developmental Psychology, 30*(6), 677–694.

Rodrique, K. M., & Kennedy, K. M. (2011). The cognitive consequences of structural changes to the aging brain. In K. W. Schaie & S. L.Willis (Eds.), *Handbook of the psychology of aging* (7th ed.). New York: Elsevier.

Roefs, A., Herman, C. P., MacLeod, C. M., Smulders, F. T. Y., & Jansen, A. (2005). At first sight: How do restrained eaters evaluate high-fat palatable foods? *Appetite, 44*, 103–114.

Rogers, A., Willoughby, B., & Nelson, L. (2016). Young adults' perceived purposes of emerging adulthood: Implications for cohabitation. *The Journal of Psychology, 150*(4), 485–501.

Rogers, C. (1961 & 1965). *On becoming a person—A therapist's view of psychotherapy*. Boston: Houghton Mifflin.

Rogers, S., Estes, A. Lord, C., Vismara, L., Winter, J., Fitzpatrick, A., & Dawson, G. (2012). Effects of a brief Early Start Denver Model (ESDM)-based parent intervention on toddlers at risk for autism spectrum disorders: A randomized controlled trial. *Journal of American*

Academy of Child and Adolescent Psychiatry, 51, 1052–1065.

Rogers, S., Vismara, L., Wagner, A. McCormick, C., Young, G., & Ozonoff, S. (2014). Autism treatment in the first year of life: A Pilot study on infant start, a parent implemented intervention for symptomatic infants. *Journal of Autism Developmental Disorders, 44*, 2981–2995.

Rogoff, B. (2001, April). *Examining cultural processes in developmental research.* Paper presented at the meeting of the Society for Research in Child Development, Minneapolis.

Rogoff, B., Moore, L., Najafi, B., Dexter, A., Correa-Chavez, M., & Solis, J. (2007). Children's development of cultural repertoires through participation in everyday routines and practices. In J. E. Grusec & P. D. Hastings (Eds.), *Handbook of socialization.* New York: Guilford.

Roher, E., & Casement, T. (2011). Suffering in silence: Teenagers and suicide. *Principal Connections, 15*(2), 9–11.

Rohr, M. K., & Lang, F. R. (2009). Aging well together—A mini-review. *Gerontology, 55*, 333–343.

Rohrer, J., Egloff, B., & Schmikle, S. (2015). Examining the effects of birth order on personality. *PNAS, 112*, 14224–14229. Retrieved from http://www.pnas.org/content/112/46/14224.abstract.

Roisman, G. I., Clausell, E., Holland, A., Fortuna, K., & Elieff, C. (2008). Adult romantic relationships as contexts of human development: A multimethod comparison of same-sex couples with opposite-sex dating, engaged, and married dyads. *Developmental Psychology, 44*, 91–101.

Rolando, C., & Taylor, V. (2014). Neural stem cell of the hippocampus: Development, physiology regulation, and dysfunction in disease. *Current Topics in Developmental Biology, 107*, 183–206.

Rolland, Y., et al. (2011). Treatment strategies for sarcopenia and frailty. *Medical Clinics of North America, 95*, 427–438.

Romano, A. D., Greco, E., Vendemiale, G., & Serviddio, G. (2014, in press). Bioenergetics and mitochondrial dysfunction in aging: Recent insights for a therapeutical approach. *Current Pharmaceutical Design.*

Romano, A. M., & Lothian, J. A. (2008). Promoting, protecting and supporting normal birth: A look at the evidence. *Journal of Obstetric and Gynecological Neonatal Nursing, 37*, 94–105.

Romanow, R. J. (2002). *Building on values: The future of health care in Canada.* Retrieved from http://publications.gc.ca/site/eng/237274/publication.html

Ronfard, S., & Harris, P. L. (2014). When will Little Red Riding Hood become scared? Children's attribution of mental states to a story character. *Developmental Psychology, 50*(1), 283–292.

Rosander, K., & von Hofsten, C. (2004). Infants' emerging ability to represent occluded object motion. *Cognition, 91*, 1–22.

Rosano, C., et al. (2012). Slower gait, slower information processing, and smaller prefrontal area in older adults. *Age and Aging, 41*, 58–64.

Rose, A., Asher, S., Swenson, L., Carlson, W., & Waller, E. (2012). How girls and boys expect disclosure about problems will make them feel: Implications for friendships. *Child Development, 83*(3), 844–863.

Rose, E. (February 4, 2013). Raising a Canadian: Immigrant children develop different views. Canadian Immigrant. Retrieved from http://canadianimmigrant.ca/slider/raising-a-canadian-immigrant-children-develop-different-views.

Rosenberg, L., Kottorp, A., Winblad, B., & Nygard, L. (2009). Perceived difficulty in everyday technology use among older adults with or without cognitive deficits. *Scandinavian Journal of Occupational Therapy, 16*, 1–11.

Rosenberg, T. J., Garbers, S., Lipkind, H., & Chiasson, M. A. (2005). Maternal obesity and diabetes as risk factors for adverse pregnancy outcomes: Differences among 4 racial/ethnic groups. *American Journal of Public Health, 95*, 1545–1551.

Rosenblith, J. F. (1992). *In the beginning* (2nd ed.). Newbury Park, CA: Sage.

Rosenfeld, A., & Stark, E. (1987, May). The prime of our lives. *Psychology Today*, 62–72.

Rosenfeld, M., & Thomas, R. (2012). Searching for a mate: The rise of the internet as a social intermediary. *American Sociological Review, 77*(4), 523–547.

Rosenn, B. (2009). Obesity and diabetes: a recipe for obstetric complications. *Journal of Fetal Neonatal Medicine*, 21, 159–164.

Rosenthal, C., & Gladstone, J. (2000, September 1). *Grandparenthood in Canada.* The Vanier Institute of the Family.

Rosnow, R. L., & Rosenthal, R. (2008). *Beginning behavioral research* (6th ed.). Upper Saddle River, NJ: Prentice Hall.

Rospenda, K. M., Richman, J. A., & Shannon, C. A. (2008). Prevalence and mental health correlates of harassment and discrimination in the workplace: Results from a national study. *Journal of Interpersonal Violence, 24*, 819–843.

Ross, L. A., Schmidt, E. L., & Ball, K. (2013). Interventions to maintain mobility: What works? *Accident Analysis and Prevention, 61*, 167–196.

Rossi, S., et al. (2005). Age-related functional changes of prefrontal cortex in long-term memory: A repetitive transcranial magnetic stimulation study. *Journal of Neuroscience, 24*, 7939–7944.

Rossi, S., Miniussi, C., Pasqualetti, P., Babilioni, C., Rossini, P. M., & Cappa, S. F. (2005). Age-related functional changes of prefrontal cortex in long-term memory: A repetitive transcranial magnetic stimulation study. *Journal of Neuroscience, 24*, 7939–7944.

Rossignol, M., Moutquin, J., Boughrassa, F., Bédard, M., Chaillet, N., Charest, C.,...Senikas, V. (2013). Preventable obstetrical interventions: How many caesarean sections can be prevented in Canada. *Journal of Obstetricians and Gynaecologists, 35*(5), 434–443.

Roterman, M. (2005). Seniors' health care use. *Supplement to Health Reports, 16*, 33–45.

Rotermann, M. (2008). Trends in sexual behaviour and condom use. Components of Statistics Canada Catalogue no. 82-003-X. http://www.statcan.gc.ca/pub/82-003-x/2008003/article/10664-eng.pdf

Rotermann, M. (2012). Sexual behaviour and condom use of 15- to 24-year-olds in 2003 and 2009/2010. *Health Reports, 23*(1), 1–5 (No. 82-003-XPE). Retrieved from http://www.statcan.gc.ca

Rothbart, M. (2011). *Becoming who we are.* New York, NY: Guilford.

Rothbart, M. K. (2004). Temperament and the pursuit of an integrated developmental psychology. *Merrill-Palmer Quarterly, 50*, 492–505.

Rothbart, M. K. (2007). Temperament, development, and personality. *Current Directions in Psychological Science, 16*, 207–212.

Rothbart, M. K., & Bates, J. E. (2006a). Temperament. In W. Damon & R. Lerner (Eds.), *Handbook of child psychology* (6th ed.). New York: Wiley.

Rothbart, M. K., & Bates, J. E. (2006b). In W. Damon, R. Lerner & N. Eisenberg, N. (Eds.). *Handbook of child psychology: Vol 3, Social, emotional and personality development* (6th ed.). (pp. 96–166). New York, NY: Wiley.

Rothbart, M. K., & Putnam, S. P. (2002). Temperament and socialization. In L. Pulkkinen & A. Caspi (Eds.), *Paths to successful development.* New York: Cambridge University Press.

Rothbart, M. K., & Sheese, B. E. (2007). Temperament and emotion regulation. In J. J. Gross (Ed.), *Handbook of emotion regulation.* New York: Guilford Press.

Rothbaum, F., & Trommsdorff, G. (2007). Do roots and wings complement or oppose one another? The socialization of relatedness and autonomy in cultural context. In J. E. Grusec & P. D. Hastings (Eds.), *Handbook of socialization.* New York: Guilford.

Rothbaum, F., Kakinuma, M., Nagaoka, R., & Azuma., H. (2007). Attachment and Amae: Parent-child closeness in the United States and Japan. *Journal of Cross-Cultural Psychology, 38*(4), 465–486.

Rothman, M. S., Miller, P. D., Lewiecki, E. M., & Bilezikian, J. P. (2014, in press). Bone density testing: Science, the media, and patient care. *Current Osteoporosis Reports.*

Rothman, S. M., & Mattson, M. P. (2012). Sleep disturbances in Alzheimer's and Parkinson's diseases. *Neuromolecular Medicine, 14*(3), 194–204.

Rouse, D. J., et al. (2007). A trial of 17 alpha-hyroxyprogesterone caproate to prevent prematurity in twins. *New England Journal of Medicine, 357,* 454–461.

Routasalo, P. E., Savikko, N., Tilvis, R. S., Strandberg, T. E., & Pitkala, K. H. (2006). Social contacts and their relationship to loneliness among aged people—a population-based study. *Gerontology, 52,* 181–187.

Rovee-Collier, C. (1987). Learning and memory in children. In J. D. Osofsky (Ed.), *Handbook of infant development* (2nd ed.). New York: Wiley.

Rovee-Collier, C. (2008). The development of infant memory. In N. Cowan & M. Courage (Eds.), *The development of memory in childhood.* Philadelphia: Psychology Press.

Rovers, M. M., de Kok, I. M., & Schilder, A. G. (2006). Risk factors for otitis media: An international perspective. *International Journal of Otorhinolaryngology, 70,* 1251–1256.

Rowley, S. R., Kurtz-Costes, B., & Cooper, S. M. (2009). The role of schooling in ethnic minority achievement and attainment. In J. Meece & J. Eccles (Eds.), *Handbook of research on schools, schooling, and human development.* Clifton, NJ: Psychology Press.

Roy, J., Chakraborty, S., & Chakraborty, Y. (2009). Estrogen - like endocrine disrupting chemicals affecting puberty in humans—a review. *Medical Science Monitor: International Medical Journal of Experimental and Clinical Research, 15*(6), RA137–45.

Royal Canadian Mounted Police (RCMP). (2012). Elder abuse. Retrieved from http://www.rcmp-grc.gc.ca/

Rozzini, R., Ranhoff, A., & Trabucchi, M. (2007). Alcoholic beverage and long-term mortality in elderly people living at home. *Journals of Gerontology: Biological Sciences and Medical Sciences, 62A,* M1313–M1314.

Ruan, L., et al. (2014). Neurogenesis in neurological and psychiatric diseases and brain injury: From bench to bedside. *Progress in Neurobiology, 115C,* 116–137.

Rubin, K. H., Bowker, J. C., McDonald, K. L., & Menzer, M. (2013). Peer relationships in childhood. In P. D. Zelazo (Ed.), *Oxford handbook of developmental psychology.* New York: Oxford University Press.

Rubin, K. H., Bukowski, W., & Parker, J. G. (1998). Peer interactions, relationships, and groups. In N. Eisenberg (Ed.), *Handbook of child psychology* (5th ed., Vol. 3). New York: Wiley.

Rubin, K., Fredstrom, B., & Bowker, J. (2008). Future directions in friendship in childhood and early adolescence. *Social Development.*

Rubin, K. H., & Barstead, M. G. (2015). Gender Differences in Child and Adolescent Social Withdrawal: A Commentary. National Center for Biotechnology Information, U.S. National Library of Medicine. Retrieved from http://www.ncbi.nlm.nih.gov/pmc/articles/PMC4335803/

Rubio-Aurioles, E., Casabe, A., Torres, L. O., Quinzanos, L., Glina, S., Filimon, I., et al. (2008). Efficacy and safety of tadalafil in the treatment of Latin American men with erectile dysfunction: Results of integrated analysis. *Journal of Sexual Medicine, 5*(8), 1965–1976.

Ruble, D. (2010). Social development and achievement motivation. Retrieved from http://www.psych.nyu.edu/ruble/

Rudavets, J., Ducimetiè, P., Evans, A., Montaye, M., Haas, B., Bingham, A.,... Ferrères, J. (2010). Patterns of alcohol consumption and ischaemic heart disease in culturally divergent countries: the prospective epidemiological study of myocardial infarction (PRIME). *British Medical Journal, 341,* 1–11.

Rudy, D., & Grusec, J. (2006, March). Authoritarian parenting in individualist and collectivist groups: Associations with maternal emotion and cognition and children's self-esteem. *Journal of Family Psychology, 20*(1).

Rueda, M. R., & Posner, M. I. (2013). Development of attentional networks. In P. D. Zelazo (Ed.), *Oxford handbook of developmental psychology.* New York: Oxford University Press.

Rueda, M. R., Posner, M. I., & Rothbart, M. K. (2005). The development of executive attention: Contributions to the emergence of self-regulation. *Developmental Neuropsychology, 28,* 573–594.

Ruff, H. A., & Capozzoli, M. C. (2003). Development of attention and distractibility in the first 4 years of life. *Developmental Psychology, 39,* 877–890.

Ruiter, M., et al. (2012, June 11). *Short sleep predicts stroke symptoms in persons of normal weight.* Paper presented at the annual meeting of the Associated Professional Sleep Societies (APSS), Boston.

Runciman, S. (2012). *Breaking the cycle of violence: An exploration into dating violence prevention curriculum.* (Master's thesis). Retrieved from http://www.qspace.library.queensu.ca

Rupp, D. E., Vodanovich, S. J., & Crede, M. (2005). The multidimensional nature of ageism: Construct validity and group differences. *Journal of Social Psychology, 145,* 335–362.

Rusen, I. D., Liu, S., Sauve, R., Joseph, K. S., & Kramer, M. S. (2004). Sudden infant death syndrome in Canada: Trends in rates and risk factors, 1985–1998. *Chronic Diseases in Canada, 25*(1), 1–6.

Rusk, T. N., & Rusk, N. (2007, Winter). Not by genes alone: New hope for prevention. *Bulletin of the Menninger Clinic, 71*(1), 1–21.

Rutter, J., & Thapar, A. (2014). Genetics of autism spectrum disorders. In F. R. Volkmar et al. (Eds.), *Handbook of autism and pervasive developmental disorders.* New York: Wiley.

Ruys, J. H., Jonge, G. A., Brand, R., Engelberts, A., & Semmekrot, B. A. (2007). Bed-sharing in the first four months of life: A risk factor for sudden infant death. *Acta Paediatric, 96,* 13099–1403.

Ryan, C., Huebner, D., Diaz, R., & Sanchez, J. (2009). Family rejection as a predictor of negative health outcomes in white and Latino lesbian, gay, and bisexual young adults. *Pediatrics, 123*(1), 346.

Ryan, C., Russel, S., Huebner, D., Diaz, R. & Sanchez, J. (2010). Family acceptance in adolescence and the health of LGBT young adults. *Journal of Child and Adolescent Psychiatric Nursing, 23*(4), 205–213.

Ryan-Harshman, M., & Aldoori, W. (2008). Folic acid in pregnancy of neural tube defects. *Canadian Family Physician, 54,* 36–38.

Ryff, C. D. (1991). Possible selves in adulthood and old age: A tale of shifting horizons. *Psychology and Aging, 6,* 286–295.

Rypma, B., Eldreth, D. A., & Rebbechi, D. (2007). Age-related differences in activation-performance relations in delayed-response tasks: A multiple component analyses. *Cortex, 43,* 65–76.

S

Sabbagh, M. A., Xu, F., Carlson, S. M., Moses, L. J., & Lee, K. (2006). The development of executive functioning and theory of mind: A comparison of Chinese and U.S. preschoolers. *Psychological Science, 17*, 74–81.

Sabeti, P. C., Varilly, P., Fry, B., Lohmueller, J., Hostetter, E., Cotsapas, C., et al. (2007, October 18). Genome-wide detection and characterization of positive selection in human populations. *Nature, 449*, 913–918.

Sable, M., Danis, D., Mauzy, D., & Gallagher, S. (2006). Barriers to reporting sexual assault for women and men: Perspectives of college students. *Journal of American College Health, 55*(3), 157–161.

Sadeh, A. (2008). Sleep. In M. M. Haith & J. B. Benson (Eds.), *Encyclopedia of infant and early childhood development.* Oxford, UK: Elsevier.

Saewyc, E., et al. (2007). Suicidal ideation and attempts among adolescents in North American school-based surveys: Are bisexual youth at increasing risk? *Journal of LGBT Health Research, 3*, 25–36.

Saffran, J. R., Werker, J. F., & Werner, L. A. (2006). The infant's auditory world: Hearing, speech, and the beginning of language. In W. Damon & R. Lerner (Eds.), *Handbook of child psychology* (6th ed.). New York: Wiley.

Sai, F. (2005). The role of the mother's voice in developing mother's face preference: Evidence for intermodal perception at birth. *Infant and Child Development, 14*, 29–50.

Saint Onge, J. M. (2009). Mortality. In D. Carr (Ed.), *Encyclopedia of the life course and human development.* Boston: Gale Cengage.

Sakraida, T. J. (2005). Divorce transition differences of midlife women. *Issues in Mental Health Nursing, 26*, 225–249.

Salkind, N. (2003). *Statistics for people who (think they) hate statistics.* Paperback, Revised.

Salmivalli, C., Peets, K., & Hodges, E. V. E. (2011). Bullying. In P. K. Smith & C. H. Hart (Eds.), *Wiley-Blackwell handbook of childhood social development* (2nd ed.). New York: Wiley.

Salthouse, T. A. (2009). When does age-related cognitive decline begin? *Neurobiology of Aging, 30*, 507–514.

Salthouse, T. A. (2012). Consequences of age-related cognitive declines. *Annual Review of Psychology* (Vol. 63). Palo Alto, CA: Annual Reviews.

Salthouse, T. A. (2013a). Executive functioning. In D. C. Park & N. Schwartz (Eds.), *Cognitive aging* (2nd ed.). New York: Psychology Press.

Salthouse, T. A. (2013b). Within cohort age differences in cognitive functioning. *Psychological Science*.

Salthouse, T. A., & Mandell, A. R. (2013). Do age-related increases in tip-of-the-tongue experiences signify episodic memory deficits? *Psychological Science, 24*, 2489–2497.

Salthouse, T. A., & Skovronek, E. (1992). Within context assessment of working memory. *Journal of Gerontology, 47*, P110–P117.

Samson, S. L., & Garber, A. J. (2014). Metabolic syndrome. *Endocrinology and Metabolism Clinics of North America, 43*, 1–23.

Sandall, J., Devane, D., Soltani, H., Hatem, M., & Gates, S. (2010). Improving quality and safety in maternity care: The contribution if midwife-led care. *Journal of Midwifery & Women's Health, 55*, 255–261.

Sangree, W. H. (1989). Age and power: Life-course trajectories and age structuring of power relations in East and West Africa. In D. I. Kertzer & K. W. Schaie (Eds.), *Age structuring in comparative perspective.* Hillsdale, NJ: Erlbaum.

Sann, C., & Streri, A. (2007). Perception of object shape and texture in human newborns: Evidence from cross-modal tasks. *Developmental Science, 10*, 399–410.

Sanson, A., & Rothbart, M. K. (1995). Child temperament and parenting. In M. H. Bornstein (Ed.), *Handbook of parenting* (Vol. 4). Hillsdale, NJ: Erlbaum.

Santilli, F., et al. (2013). Effects of high-amount-high-intensity exercise on in vivo platelet activation: Modulation by lipid peroxidation and AGE/RAGE axis. *Thrombosis and Hemostasis, 110*(6), 1232–1240.

Sarifakioglu, B., et al. (2014, in press). Effects of a 12-week combined exercise therapy on oxidative stress in female fibromyalgia patients. *Rheumatology International.*

Sarlos, P., et al. (2014, in press). Susceptibility to ulcerative colitis in Hungarian patients determined by gene-gene interaction. *World Journal of Gastroenterology.*

Sasidharan, K., Dutta, S. & Narang, A. (2009). Valididty of new Ballard Score until 7th day of postnatal life in moderately preterm neonates. *Archives of Disease in Childhood Fetal Neonatal Edition, 94*, F39–F44.

Sato, R. L., Li, G. G., & Shaha, S. (2006). Antepartum seafood consumption and mercury levels in newborn cord blood. *American Journal of Obstetrics and Gynecology, 194*(6), 1683–1688.

Sault History Online (2008) Biography. Retrieved from *http://www.cityssm.on.ca/library/Bondar_Bio.html.*

Sauvé, R. (2002). *Connections: Tracking the links between jobs and family.* Ottawa: The Vanier Institute of the Family. Retrieved from http://www.vifamily.ca

Savin-Williams, R. (2015). The new sexual minority teenager. In D.A. Powell & J. S. Kaufman (Eds.), *The meaning of sexual identity in the 21st century.* New York, NY: Cambridge.

Savin-Williams, R. C. (2006). *The new gay teenager.* Cambridge, MA: Harvard University Press.

Savin-Williams, R. C. (2008). Who's gay? It depends on how you measure it. In D. A. Hope (Ed.), *Nebraska Symposium on Motivation: Contemporary perspectives on lesbian, gay, and bisexual identities.* Lincoln, NE: University of Nebraska Press.

Savin-Williams, R. C., & Cohen, K. M. (2007). Development of same-sex attracted youth. In I. H. Meyer & M. E. Northridge (Eds.), *The health of sexual minorities: Public health perspectives on lesbian, gay, bisexual and transgender populations* (pp. 27–47). New York: Springer.

Savin-Williams, R. C., & Cohen, K. M. (2015). Gay, lesbian, and bisexual youth. In J.D. Wright (Ed.), *International encyclopedia of the social and behavioural sciences.* New York, NY: Oxford University Press.

Savin-Williams, R. C., & Diamond, L. (2004). Sex. In R. Lerner & L. Steinberg (Eds.), *Handbook of adolescent psychology.* New York: Wiley.

Savin-Williams, R. C., & Ream, G. L. (2007). Prevalence and stability of sexual orientation components during adolescence and young adulthood. *Archives of Sexual Behavior, 36*, 385–394.

Sayal, K., Heron, J., Golding, J., & Emond, A. (2007). Prenatal alcohol exposure and gender differences in childhood mental health problems: A longitudinal population-based study. *Pediatrics, 119*, e426–e434.

Sayer, A. A., et al. (2013). New horizons in the pathogenesis, diagnosis, and management of sarcopenia. *Age and Aging, 42*(2), 145–150.

Sayer, L. C. (2006). Economic aspects of divorce and relationship dissolution. In M. A. Fine & J. H. Harvey (Eds.), *Handbook of divorce and relationship dissolution.* Mahwah, NJ: Erlbaum.

Sbarra, D. (2012). Marital dissolution and physical health outcomes: A review of mechanisms. *The Science of the Couple:*

The Ontario Symposium (Vol 12). New York, NY: Psychology Press.

Scales, P., Benson, P., & Roehlkepartain, E. (2011). Adolescent thriving: The role of sparks, relationships, and empowerment, *Journal of Youth and Adolescence, 40*, 263–277.

Scarr, S. (1993). Biological and cultural diversity: The legacy of Darwin for development. *Child Development, 64*, 1333–1353.

Schacter, D., Gilbert, D., Wegner, D., Nock, M., & Johnsrude, I. (2014). *Psychology* (3rd Canadian ed.). New York: Worth.

Schacter, E. P., & Ventura, J. J. (2008). Identity agents: Parents as active and reflective participants in their children's identity formation. *Journal of Research on Adolescence, 18*, 449–476.

Schafer, A. (2013). Physician assisted suicide: The great Canadian euthanasia debate. *International Journal of Law and Psychiatry, 36*(5–6), 522–531.

Schaie, K. W. (1994). The life course of adult intellectual abilities. *American Psychologist, 49*, 304–313.

Schaie, K. W. (1996). *Intellectual development in adulthood: The Seattle Longitudinal Study.* New York: Cambridge University Press.

Schaie, K. W. (2007). Generational differences: The age-cohort period model. In J. E. Birren (Ed.), *Encyclopedia of gerontology* (2nd ed.). Oxford, UK: Elsevier.

Schaie, K. W. (2011a). Historical influences on aging and behavior. In K.W. Schaie & S. L. Willis (Eds.), *Handbook of the psychology of aging* (7th ed.). New York: Elsevier.

Schaie, K. W. (2011b). *Developmental influences on adult intellectual development.* New York: Oxford University Press.

Schaie, K. W. (2013). The Seattle Longitudinal Study: Developmental influences on adult intellectual development (2nd Ed.). New York: Oxford University Press.

Schaie, K. W., & Willis, S. L. (1994). Assessing the elderly. In C. B. Fisher & R. M. Lerner (Eds.), *Applied developmental psychology* (pp. 339–372). New York: McGraw Hill.

Schaie, K. W., & Willis, S. L. (2000). *Adult development and aging* (5th ed.). Upper Saddle River, NJ: Prentice Hall.

Scheerings, M. S., Cobham, V. E., & McDermott, B. (2014). Policy and administrative issues for large-scale clinical interventions following disasters. *Journal of Child and Adolescent Psychopharmacology, 24*, 39–46.

Scheibe, S., & Carstensen, L. L. (2010). Emotional aging: Recent findings and future trends. *Journal of Gerontology: Psychological Sciences, 65*(B), 135–144.

Scheibe, S., Freund, A. M., & Baltes, P. B. (2007). Toward a developmental psychology of *Sehnsucht* (life-longings): The optimal (utopian) life. *Developmental Psychology, 43*, 778–795.

Schellenberg, E. G. (2004). Music lessons enhance IQ. *Psychological Science, 15*, 511–514.

Schellenberg, E. G. (2006). Long-term positive associations between music lessons and IQ. *Journal of Experimental Psychology, 98*, 457–468.

Schellenberg, G., & Ostrovsky, Y. (2008a). The retirement puzzle: Sorting the pieces. *Canadian Social Trends, 86*(Winter), 35–47.

Schellenberg, G., & Ostrovsky, Y. (2008b). The retirement plans and expectations of older workers. *Canadian Social Trends, 86*(Winter), 11–34.

Scher, A., & Harel, J. (2008). Separation and stranger anxiety. In M. M. Haith & J. B. Benson (Eds.), *Encyclopedia of infant and early childhood development.* Oxford, UK: Elsevier.

Schiavi, A., & Ventura, N. (2014, in press). The interplay between mitochondria and autophagy and its role in the aging process. *Experimental Gerontology.*

Schiff, W. J. (2009). *Nutrition for healthy living.* New York: McGraw-Hill.

Schiff, W. J. (2015). *Nutrition essentials*. New York: McGraw-Hill.

Schiffman, R. (2012, January 18). Why people who pray are healthier than those who don't. *The Huffington Post*. Retrieved from http://www.huffingtonpost.com/richard-schiffman/why-people-who-pray-areheathier_b_1197313.html

Schiffman, S. S. (2007). Smell and taste. In J. E. Birren (Ed.), *Encyclopedia of gerontology* (2nd ed.). San Diego: Academic Press.

Schindler, A. E. (2006). Climacteric symptoms and hormones. *Gynecological Endocrinology, 22*, 151–154.

Schlesinger, J. (2013). Quest for the cure. Winnipeg Health Region. Retrieved from http://www.wrha.mb.ca/wave/2013/11/quest-for-the-cure.php

Schmidt, K. L., & Schulz, R. (2007). Emotions. In J. E. Birren (Ed.), *Encyclopedia of gerontology* (2nd ed.). San Diego: Academic Press.

Schmidt, L., Fox, N., Perez-Edgar, K., & Hamer, D. (2009). Linking gene, brain, and behavior: DRD4, frontal asymmetry, and temperament. *Psychological Science, 20*, 831–837.

Schmidt, S., et al. (2006). Cigarette smoking strongly modifies the association of LOC387715 and age-related macular degeneration. *American Journal of Human Genetics, 78*, 852–864.

Schmidt, U. (2003). Aetiology of eating disorders in the 21st century: New answers to old questions. *European Child and Adolescent Psychiatry, 12* (Suppl. 1), 1130–1137.

Schmitt, D. P., Allik, J., McCrae, R., & Benet-Martinez, V. (2007). The geographic distribution of big five personality traits: Patterns and profiles of human self-description across 56 nations. *Journal of Cross-Cultural Psychology, 38*(2), 173–212. Retrieved from http://biculturalism.ucr.edu/pdfs/Schmitt%20et%20al_JCCP2007.pdf

Schneider, E., et al. (2014, in press). Widespread differences in cortex DNA methylation of the "language gene" CNTNAP2 between humans and chimpanzees. *Epigenetics*.

Schneider, J. M., et al. (2011). Dual sensory impairment in older age. *Journal of Aging and Health, 23*, 1309–1324.

Schneider, M. (2013). Does education pay? *Issues in Science and Technology, XXX*(1), 33–38.

Schneider, W. (2011). Memory development in childhood. In U. Goswami (Ed.), *Wiley-Blackwell handbook of childhood cognitive development* (2nd ed.). New York: Wiley-Blackwell.

Schnittker, J. (2007). Look (closely) at all the lonely people: Age and social psychology of social support. *Journal of Aging and Health, 19*, 659–682

Schnurer, F. (2008). "But in death he has found victory": The funeral ceremonies for the "knights of the sky" during the Great War as transnational media events. *European Review of History, 15*(6).

Schoenfeld, T. J., & Gould, E. (2013). Differential effects of stress and gludocorticoids on adult neurogenesis. *Current Topics in Behavioral Neuroscience, 15*, 139–164.

Schoenfeld, T. J., et al. (2013). Physical exercise prevents stress-induced activation of granule neurons and enhances local inhibitory mechanisms in the dentate gyrus. *Journal of Neuroscience, 33*, 7770–7777.

Scholnick, E. K. (2008). Reasoning in early development. In M. M. Haith & J. B. Benson (Eds.), *Encyclopedia of infant and early childhood development.* Oxford, UK: Elsevier.

Schonert-Reichl, K. A. & Hymel, S. (Spring, 2007) Educating the Heart as well as the Mind - Social and Emotional Learning for School and Life Success. Education Canada - Canadian Education Association. Retrieved from http://www.jcsh-cces.ca/upload/Educating_Heart_Spring07-1.pdf.

Schooler, C. (2007). Use it—and keep it, longer, probably: A reply to Salthouse (2006). *Perspectives on Psychological Science, 2*, 24–29.

Schoppe-Sullivan, S. J., Mangelsdorf, S. C., Brown, G. L., & Sokolowski, M. S. (2007). Goodness-of-fit in family context: Infant temperament, marital quality, and early coparenting behavior. *Infant Behavior and Development, 30*, 82–96.

Schroer, W. (2016). Generations X, Y, Z, and others. The Social Librarian. Retrieved from http://www.socialmarketing.org/newsletter/features/generations3.htm

Schuklenk, U., Van Delden, J. J. M., Downie, J., McLean, S. A. M., Upshur, R., Weinstock, D. (2011, November 25). End-of-life decision-making in Canada: The report by the Royal Society of Canada expert panel on end-of-life decision-making. *Bioethics.* Retrieved from http://www.ncbi. nlm.nih.gov/pmc/articles/PMC3265521/

Schulenberg, J. E., & Zarett, N. R. (2006). Mental health during emerging adulthood: Continuity and discontinuity in courses, causes, and functions. In J. J. Arnett & J. L. Tanner (Eds.), *Emerging adults in America.* Washington, DC: American Psychological Association.

Schulenberg, J. E., Bryant, A., & O'Malley, P. (2004). Taking hold of some kind of life: How developmental tasks relate to trajectories of well-being during the transition to adulthood. *Development and Psychopathology, 16*, 1119–1140.

Schultz, T. R. (2010). Computational modeling of infant concept learning: The developmental shift from features to correlations. In L. Oakes, C. Cashon, M. Casasola, & D. Rakison (Eds.), *Infant perception and cognition*. New York: Oxford University Press.

Schulz, E., Wenzel, P., Munzel, T., & Daiber, A. (2014). Mitochondrial redox signaling: Interaction of mitochondrial reactive oxygen species with other sources of oxidative stress. *Antioxidants and Redox Signaling, 20*(2), 308–324.

Schulz, R., Hebert, R., & Boerner, K. (2008). Bereavement after caregiving. *Geriatrics, 63*, 20–22.

Schunk, D. H. (2012). Learning theories: An educational perspective (5th ed.). Upper Saddle River, NJ: Prentice Hall.

Schunk, D. H., & Zimmerman, B. J. (2013). Self-regulation and learning. In I. B. Weiner et al. (Eds.), *Handbook of psychology* (2nd ed., Vol. 7). New York: Wiley.

Schuurmans, N., Senikas, V., & Lalonde, A. (2009). *Healthy beginnings: Giving your baby the best start from preconception to birth* (4th ed). Hoboken, NJ: Wiley.

Schwalfenberg, G. (2013). Not enough vitamin D: Health consequences for Canadians. *Canadian Family Physician, 53*(5), 841–854. Retrieved from http://www.cfp.ca/content/53/5/841.abstract

Schwartz, B., Stutz, M., & Lederman, T. (2012). Perceived interparental conflict and early adolescents' friendships: The role of attachment security and emotion regulation. *Journal of Youth and Adolescence, 41*, 1240–1252.

Schwartz, D. L., Lin, X., Brophy, J., & Bransford, J. D. (1999). Toward the development of flexibly adaptive instructional designs. In C. M. Reigelut (Ed.), *Instructional design theories and models* (Vol. II). Mahwah, NJ: Erlbaum.

Schwartz, M. A., & Scott, B. (2007). *Marriages and families* (5th ed.). Upper Saddle River, NJ: Prentice Hall.

Schwartz, M. A., & Scott, B. (2012). *Marriages and families, census update* (6th ed). Upper Saddle River, NJ: Pearson.

Schwartz, S., et al. (2011). Examining the light and dark sides of emerging adults' identity: A study of identity status differences in positive and negative psychosocial functioning. *Journal of Youth and Adolescence, 40*, 839–859.

Schwarzer, R., & Luszczynska, A. (2013). Stressful life events. In I. B. Weiner et al. (Eds.), *Handbook of psychology* (2nd ed., Vol. 9). New York: Wiley.

Scollon, C., & King, L. (2004). Is the good life the easy life? *Social Indicators Research, 68*, 127–162.

Scott, D., et al. (2014, in press). Sarcopenic obesity and dynamic obesity: 5-year associations with falls risk in middle-aged and older adults. *Obesity.*

Scullin, M. K., Bugg, J. M., & McDaniel, M. A. (2012). Whoops, I did it again: Commission errors in prospective memory. *Psychology of Aging, 27*, 46–53.

Scuteri, A., et al. (2014, in press). Metabolic syndrome across Europe: Different clusters of risk factors. *European Journal of Preventive Cardiology.*

Seabrook, J. A., & Avison, W. R. (2015), Family Structure and Children's Socioeconomic Attainment: A Canadian Sample. *Canadian Review of Sociology/Revue Canadienne de Sociologie, 52*, 66–88.

Sebastian-Galles, N. (2007). Biased to learn language. *Developmental Science, 10*, 713–718.

Sebastiani, P., & Perls, T. T. (2012). The genetics of extreme longevity: Lessons from the New England Centenarian study. *Frontiers in Genetics, 30*(3), 277.

Sebastiani, P., et al. (2012). Whole genome sequences of a male and female supercentenarian, ages greater than 114 years. *Frontiers in Genetics, 2*, 90.

Sebastiani, P., et al. (2013). Meta-analysis of genetic variants associated with human exceptional longevity. *Aging, 5*, 653–661.

Seeman, T. E., & Chen, X. (2002). Risk and protective factors for physical functioning in older adults with and without chronic conditions: MacArthur Studies of Successful Aging. *Journal of Gerontology: Social Sciences, 57B*, S135–S144.

Selim, A. J., Fincke, G., Berlowitz, D. R., Miller, D. R., Qian, S. X., Lee, A., Cong, Z., Rogers, W., Sileim, B. J., Ren, X. S., Spiro, A., & Kazis, L. E. (2005). Comprehensive health status assessment of centenarians: Results from the 1999 Large Health Survey of Veteran Enrollees. *Journals of Gerontology A: Biological Sciences and Medical Sciences, 60*, 515–519.

Selye, H. (2013). *Canadian Medical Hall of Fame.* Retrieved from http://www.cdnmedhall.org/dr-hans-selye

Semmler, C., Ashcroft, J., van Jaarsveld, C. H., Carnell, S., & Wardle, J. (2009). Development of overweight in children in relation to parental weight and socioeconomic status. *Obesity, 17*(4), 814–820.

Senechal, M., & Lefevre, J. A. (2014, in press). Continuity and change in the home literacy environment as predictors of growth in vocabulary and reading. *Child Development.*

Sener, A., Terzioglu, R. G., & Karabulut E. (2007). Life satisfaction and leisure activities during men's retirement: A Turkish sample. *Aging and Mental Health, 11*, 30–36.

Seniors' Council of Canada. (2014). Social Isolation of Seniors. Government of Canada. Retrieved from http://www.seniorscouncil.gc.ca/eng/research_publications/social_isolation/page00.shtml.

Serido, J. (2009). Life events. In D. Carr (Ed.), *Encyclopedia of the life course and human development.* Boston: Gale Cengage.

Settersen, R. & Cancel-Tirado, C. (2010). Fatherhood as a hidden variable in men's development and life course. *Research in Human Development, 7*(2), 83–102.

Settersten, R., & Ray, B. (2010). What's going on with young people today? The long twisting path to adulthood. *The Future Children, 20*, 19–41.

Sexual Assault and Rape Statistics. (2014). *Sexual assault in Canada: Information for Canadian victims of sexual abuse*. Retrieved from http://www.sexualassault.ca.

Sexual Identity Centre. (2012). Retrieved from http://www.mcgill.ca/cosum/

Shah, A. (2011). Today, around 21,000 children died around the world. Global Issues, Social, Political, Economic, and Environmental Issues that Affect Us All. Retrieved from http://www.globalissues.org/article/715/today-21000-children-died-around-the-world#AboutChildDeaths

Shah, S. M., Carey, I. M., Harris, T., Dewilde, S., & Cook, D. G. (2012). Quality of prescribing in care homes and the community in England and Wales. *British Journal of General Practice, 62*, 329–336.

Shan, Z. Y., Liu, J. Z., Sahgal, V., Wang, B., & Yue, G. H. (2005). Selective atrophy of left hemisphere and frontal lobe of the brain in older men. *Journals of Gerontology A: Biological Sciences and Medical Sciences, 60*, A165–A174.

Shanahan, M. J., Hill, P. L., Roberts, B. W., Eccles, J., & Friedman, H. S. (2014, in press). Conscientiousness, health, and aging: The life course of personality model. *Developmental Psychology.*

Shank, P. (April 5, 2011). Identical twins are genetically different. *Biopolitical Times* - The webblog of the Center for Genetics and Society. Retrieved from http://www.biopoliticaltimes.org/article.php?id=5660

Shapiro, D., & Walsh R. (Eds.). (2008). *Meditation: Classical and contemporary perspectives.* Rutgers, New Jersey: Aldine Transaction.

Shariff, S. (2005). Cyber-dilemmas in the new millennium: School obligations to provide student safety in a virtual school environment. *McGill Journal of Education, 40*, 467–487.

Sharlip, I. D., Shumaker, B. P., Hakim, L. S., Goldfischer, E., Natanegra, F., & Wong, D. G. (2008). Tadalafil is efficacious and well tolerated in the treatment of erectile dysfunction (ED) in men over 65 years of age: Results from multiple observations in men with ED in national tadalafil study in the United States. *Journal of Sexual Medicine, 5*, 716–725.

Sharma, S. & Ford-Jones, E. (May, 2015). Child poverty. Ways forward for the paediatrician: A comprehensive overview of poverty reduction strategies requiring paediatric support. Paediatrics & Child Health v. 20(4); 203-207 Retrieved from http://www.ncbi.nlm.nih.gov/pmc/articles/PMC4443829/.

Sharma, V. & Sharma, P. (2012). Postpartum depression: Diagnostic and treatment issues. *Journal of Obstetrics and Gynaecology, 34*(5), 436–442.

Sharp, E., Tucker, C., Baril, M., Van Gundy, K., & Rebellion, C. (2015). Breadth of participation in organized and unstructured leisure activities over time and rural adolescents' functioning. *Journal of Youth and Adolescence, 44*, 62–76.

Shaughnessy, J. J., Zechmeister, E. B., & Zechmeister, J. S. (2003). *Research methods in psychology* (6th ed.). New York: McGraw-Hill.

Shaver, P. R., & Mikulincer, M. (2007). Attachment theory and research. In A. W. Kruglanski, & E. T. Higgins (Eds.), *Social psychology* (2nd ed.). New York: Guilford.

Shaver, P., & Mikulincer, M. (2013). Attachment related contributions to the study of psychopathology. In P. Luyten, L. Mayes, P. Fongay, M. Target & S. Blatt (Eds.) *Handbook of Psychodynamic Approaches to Psychopathology* (pp. 27–46). New York, NY: Guilford.

Shay, J. W., Reddel, R. R., & Wright, W. E. (2012). Cancer and telomeres—an alternative to telomerase. *Science, 336*, 1388–1390.

Shaywitz, S. E., Morris, R., & Shaywitz, B. A. (2008). The education of dyslexic children from childhood to young adulthood. *Annual Review of Psychology, 59.* Palo Alto, CA: Annual Reviews.

Shea, A. K., & Steiner, M. (2008). Cigarette smoking during pregnancy. *Nicotine and Tobacco Research, 10*, 267–278.

Shema, L, Ore, L., Ben-Shachar, M., Haj, M., & Linn, S. (2007). The association between breastfeeding and breast cancer occurrence among Jewish women: A case control study. *Journal of Cancer Research and Clinical Oncology, 133*, 903.

Shepherd, M. (2012). Omar Khadr repatriated to Canada. *The Star.* Retrieved from http://www.thestar.com

Sheridan, M., & Nelson, C. A. (2008). Neurobiology of fetal and infant development: Implications for mental health. In C. H. Zeanah (Ed.), *Handbook of infant mental health* (3rd ed.). New York: Guilford.

Shernoff, D., Kelly, S., Tonks, S., Anderson, B., Cavanagh, R., Sinha, S., & Abdi, B. (2016). Student engagement as a function of environmental complexity in high school classrooms. *Learning and Instruction, 43*, 52–60.

Sherwood, C. C., et al. (2011). Aging of the cerebral cortex differs between humans and chimpanzees. *Proceedings of the National Academy of Sciences U.S.A., 108*, 13029–13034.

Shi, R., & Werker, J. (2001). Six-month-old infants' preference for lexical words. *Psychological Science, 12*, 70–75.

Shi, R., & Werker, J. F. (2003). The basis of preference for lexical words in 6-month-old infants. *Developmental Science, 6*, 484–488.

Shibata, Y., et al. (2012). Extrachromosomal microDNAs and chromosomal microdeletions in normal tissues. *Science, 336*, 82–86.

Shield, K., Taylor, B., Kehoe, T., Patra, J., & Rehm, J. (2012). *BMC Public Health, 12*(91), 1–12.

Shields, M., & Martel, L. (2005). Healthy living among seniors. *Supplement to Health Reports, 16*, 7–20.

Shields, M., & Tremblay, M. (2008, June). Sedentary behaviour and obesity. Catalogue no. 82-003-X Health Reports. Retrieved from http://www.statcan.gc.ca/pub/82-003-x/2008002/article/10599-eng.pdf

Shimazu, A., Kubota, K., Bakker, A., Demerouti, E., Shimada, K. & Kawakami, N. (2013). Work-to-family conflict and family-to-work conflict among Japanese dual-earner couples with prescholl children: A Spillover-crossover perspective. *Journal of Occupational Health, 55*, 234–243.

Shin, S. H., Hong, H. G., & Hazen, A. L. (2010). Childhood sexual abuse and adolescence substance use: A latent class analysis. *Drug and Alcohol Dependence, 109*(1), 226–235.

Shipley, B.A., Der, G., Taylor, M. D., & Deary, I. J. (2007). Association between mortality and cognitive change over 7 years in a large representative sample of UK residents. *Psychosomatic Medicine, 69*, 640–650.

Shiraev, E., & Levy, D. (2007). *Cross-cultural psychology* (3rd ed.). Boston: Allyn & Bacon.

Shokhirev, M. N., & Johnson, A. A. (2014). Effects of extrinsic mortality on the evolution of aging: A stochastic modeling approach. *PLoS One, 9*(1), e86602.

Shor, E., Roelfs, D., Bugyi, P., & Schwartz, J. (2012). Meta-analysis of marital dissolution and mortality: Re-evaluating the interaction of gender and age. *Social Science and Medicine, 75*, 46–59.

Shors, T. J. (2009). Saving new brain cells. *Scientific American, 300*, 46–52.

Shriver, T. (2007, November 9). Silent eugenics: Abortion & Down Syndrome. *Commonweal, 134*, 10–11.

Sick Kids. (2012). Paediatric Consultation Clinic (PCC). Retrieved from http://www.sickkids.ca/

SIECCAN Newsletter. (2011). Sexting: Considerations for Canadian youth. *The Canadian Journal of Human Sexuality, 20*(3), 111–113.

SIECCAN. (2012). Trends in sexual intercourse experience among Canadian teens. Retrieved from http://www.sexualityandu.ca

Siedlecki, K. L. (2007). Investigating the structure and age invariance of episodic memory across the adult life span. *Psychology and Aging, 22*, 251–268.

Siegel, D. H. (2013). Open adoption: Adoptive parents' reactions two decades later. *Social Work, 58*, 43–52.

Siegler, I. C., & Costa, P. T. (1999, August). *Personality change and continuity in midlife: UNC Alumni Heart Study.* Paper presented at the meeting of the American Psychological Association, Boston.

Siegler, I. C., Poon, L. W., Madden, D. J., Dilworth-Anderson, P., Schaie, K. W., Willis, S. L., et al. (2009). Psychological aspects of normal aging. In D. G. Blazer & D. Steffens (Eds.), *Textbook of geriatric psychiatry* (4th ed.) Arlington, VA: American Psychiatric Publishing.

Siegler, R. S. (2006). Microgenetic analysis of learning. In W. Damon & R. Lerner (Eds.), *Handbook of child psychology* (6th ed.). New York: Wiley.

Siegler, R. S. (2007). Cognitive variability. *Developmental Science, 10*, 104–109.

Siegler, R. S. (2012). From theory to application and back: Following in the giant footsteps of David Klahr. In S. M. Carver & J. Shrager (Eds.), *The journey from child to scientist: Integrating cognitive development and the education sciences.* Thousand Oaks, CA: Sage.

Siener, S., & Kerns, K. A. (2012). Emotion regulation and depressive symptoms in preadolescence. *Child Psychiatry and Human Development, 43*, 414–430.

Sievert, L. L., & Obermeyer, C. M. (2012). Symptom clusters at midlife: A four-country comparison of checklist and qualitative responses. *Menopause, 19*, 133–144.

Sigman, M., Cohen, S. E., & Beckwith, L. (2000). Why does infant attention predict adolescent intelligence? In D. Muir & A. Slater (Eds.), *Infant development: Essential readings.* Malden, MA: Blackwell.

Signal, T. L., Gander, P. H., Sangalli, M. R., Travier, N., Firestone, R. T., & Tuohy, J. F. (2007). Sleep duration and quality in healthy nulliparous and multiparous women across pregnancy and post-partum. *Australian and New Zealand Journal of Obstetrics and Gynecology, 47*, 16–22.

Sikder, M. & Fleer, M. (2014). Small science: Infants and toddlers experiencing science in everyday family play. *Research in Science Education, 45*(3), 445–464.

Silk, T. & Wood, A. (2011). Lessons about neurodevelopment from anatomical magnetic resonance imaging. *Journal of Development and Behavioral Pediatrics, 32*, 158–168.

Silverman, I. (2003). Confessions of a closet sociobiologist: Personal perspectives on the Darwinian movement in psychology. *Evolutionary Psychology, 1*, 1–9.

Silverslides, A. (2012). Blogging the nursing life. *Canadian Nurse, 108*(1), 22–27.

Silverstein, M. (2009). Caregiving. In D. Carr (Ed.), *Encyclopedia of the life course and human development.* Boston: Gale Cengage.

Silverstein, M., Conroy, S. J., Wang, H., Giarrusso, R., & Bengtsson, V. L. (2002). Reciprocity in parent-child relation over the adult life course. *Journals of Gerontology: Psychological Sciences and Social Sciences, 57*(B), S3–S13.

Sim, M. P. Y., & Lamb, M. E. (2014, in press). Children's disclosure about sexual abuse: How motivational factors affect linguistic categories related to deception detection. *Psychology, Crime, and Law.*

Simmons, E. S., Lanter, E., & Lyons, M. (2014). Supporting mainstream educational success. In F. R. Volkmer et al. (Eds.), *Handbook of autism and pervasive developmental disorders.* New York: Wiley.

Simon, R., & Barrett, A. (2010). Nonmarital romantic relationships and mental health in early adulthood: Does association differ for women and men? *Journal of Health and Social Behavior, 51*, 168–182.

Simonetti, G. D., et al. (2011). Determinants of blood pressure in preschool children: the role of parental smoking. *Circulation, 123*, 292–298.

Simonton, D. K. (1996). Creativity. In J. E. Birren (Ed.), *Encyclopedia of aging.* San Diego: Academic Press.

Simpkins, S. D., Fredricks, J. A., Davis-Kean, P. E., & Eccles, J. S. (2006). Healthy mind, healthy habits: The influence of activity involvement in middle childhood. In A. C. Huston & M. N. Ripke (Eds.), *Developmental contexts in middle childhood.* New York: Cambridge University Press.

Simpson, K. R. (2010). Reconsideration of the costs of convenience: Quality, operational, and fiscal strategies to minimize elective labor induction. *Journal of Perinatal and Neonatal Nursing, 24*(1), 43–52.

Sinah, M. (Ed.). (2013). *Measuring violence against women: Statistical trends.* Retrieved from http://www.statcan.gc.ca.

Sinclair, S., & Chochinov, H. M. (2012). Communicating with patients about existential and spiritual issues: SACR-D work. *Progress in Palliative Care, 20*(2), 72–78.

Singer L., et al. (2004). Cognitive outcomes of preschool children with prenatal cocaine exposure. *Journal of the American Medical Association, 291*(20), 2448–2456.

Singer, D., Golinkoff, R. M., & Hirsh-Pasek, K. (Eds.) (2006). *Play = learning: How play motivates and enhances children's cognitive and social-emotional growth.* New York: Oxford University Press.

Singer, L., et al. (2012). Neurobehavioral outcomes of infants exposed to MDMA (ecstasy) and other recreational drugs during pregnancy. *Neurotoxicology and Teratology, 34*(3), 303–310.

Sinha, J. W., Cnaan, R. A., & Gelles, R. J. (2007). Adolescent risk behaviors and religion: Findings from a national study. *Journal of Adolescence, 30*, 231–249.

Sinha, M. (2012). Victimization among visible minority and immigrant populations. *National Clearing House on Family Violence E- Bulletin, February 2012.* Retrieved from http://www.phac-aspc.gc.ca/ncfv-cnivf/EB/2012/february-fevrier/1-eng.php#anchor1

Sinha, M. (2014). Child care in Canada (Report No. 89-652-X – No. 005) Retrieved from http://www.statcan.gc.ca

Sinha, M. (2015a). *Parenting and child support after separation or divorce.* Statistics Canada. Retrieved from http://www.statcan.gc.ca/pub/89-652-x/89-652-x2014001-eng.htm.

Sinha, M. (2015b). *Section 3: Family violence against children and youth.* Statistics Canada. Retrieved from http://www.statcan.gc.ca/pub/85-002-x/2012001/article/11643/11643-3-eng.htm.

Sirard, J. R., & Barr-Anderson, D. J. (2008). Editorial: Physical activity in adolescents: From associations to interventions. *Journal of Adolescent Health, 42*, 327–328.

Skider, S. (2015). Social situation of development: parents perspectives on infant-toddlers' concept formation in science. *Early Child Development and Care, 185*(10), 1658–1677.

Skinner, B. F. (1957). *Verbal behavior.* New York: Appleton-Century-Crofts.

Skinner, E. I., & Fernandes, M. (2009). Illusory recollection in older adults and younger adults under divided attention. *Psychology and Aging, 24*(1), 211–216. Retrieved from http://cogneurolab.uwaterloo.ca/publications/Erin_Skinner/Illusory_recollection_in_older_adults.pdf

Skinner, R., & McFaull, S. (2012). Suicide among children and adolescents in Canada: Trends and sex difference, 1980–2008. *Canadian Medical Association Journal, 184*(9), 1029–1034.

Skipper, J. I., Goldin-Meadow, S., Nusbaum, H. C., & Small, S. L. (2007). Speech-associated gestures, Broca's area, and the human mirror system. *Brain and Language, 101,* 260–277.

Skolnick, A. S. (2007). Grounds for marriage: How relationships succeed or fail. In A. S. Skolnick & J. H. Skolnick (Eds.), *Family in transition* (14th ed.). Boston: Allyn & Bacon.

Slack, T., & Jensen, L. (2008). Employment hardship among older workers: Does residential and gender inequality extend into old age? *Journals of Gerontology B: Psychological Sciences and Social Sciences, 63,* S15–S24.

Slater, A. (2002). Visual perception in the newborn infant: Issues and debates. *Intellectica, 1*(34), 57–76.

Slater, A., Quinn, P., Kelly, D., Lee, K., Longmore, C. McDonald, P. & Pascalis, O. (2010). The shaping of the face space in early infancy: Becoming a native face processor. *Child Development Perspectives, 4*(3), 205–211.

Slaughter, V. (2005). Young children's understanding of death. *American Psychologists, 40*(3), 179–186.

Slaughter, V., & Griffiths, M. (2007). Death understanding and fear of death in young children. *Clinical Child Psychology and Psychiatry, 12*(4), 525–535.

Slomkowski, C., Rende, R., Conger, K. J., Simons, R. L., & Conger, R. D. (2001). Sisters, brothers, and delinquency: Social influence during early and middle adolescence. *Child Development, 72,* 271–283.

Slutsky, I., et al. (January, 2010). Enhancement of learning and memory by elevating brain magnesium. Neuron article. Cell Press. Retrieved from http://ac.els-cdn.com/S0896627309010447/1-s2.0-S0896627309010447-main.pdf?_tid=237c0b46-2d86-11e6-95d4-00000aacb362&acdnat=1465396662_74abe0219ee8405b88e6347b482936a9.

Small, B. J., Dixon, R. A., McArdle, J. J., & Grimm, K. J. (2012a). Do changes in lifestyle engagement moderate cognitive decline in normal aging? Evidence from the Victoria Longitudinal Study. *Neuropsychology, 26,* 144–155.

Small, B. J., Rawson, K. S., Eisel, S., & McEvoy, C. L. (2012). Memory and aging. In S. K. Whitbourne & M. Sliwinski (Eds.), *Wiley-Blackwell handbook of adulthood and aging.* New York: Wiley.

Smetana, J., Metzger, A., & Campione-Barr, N. (2004). African American late adolescents' relationships with parents: Developmental transitions and longitudinal patterns. *Child Development, 75,* 932–947.

Smid, M., Bourgeous,P. & Auerswald, C. (2010). The challenge of pregnancy among homeless youth: Reclaiming a lost opportunity. *Journal of Health care for the Poor and Underserved, 21,* 140–156.

Smigielski, J., Bielecki, W., & Drygas, W. (2013). Health and lifestyle-related determinants of survival rate in the male residents of the city of Lodz. *International Journal of Occupational Medicine and Environmental Health, 26,* 337–348.

Smith, A. D. (2007). Memory, In J. E. Birren (Ed.), *Encyclopedia of gerontology* (2nd ed.). San Diego: Academic Press.

Smith, B. (2007). *The psychology of sex and gender.* Boston: Allyn & Bacon.

Smith, D. L. (2008). Birth complications and outcomes. In M. M. Haith & J. B. Benson (Eds.), *Encyclopedia of infancy and early childhood. development* Oxford, UK: Elsevier.

Smith, E. (2005). Fathers of stem cell research win prestigious prize—Laker Award known as America's Nobel Prize. *University of Toronto News.*

Smith, J. (2009). Self. In D. Carr (Ed.), *Encyclopedia of the life course and human development.* Boston: Gale Cengage.

Smith, J., & Freund, A. M. (2002). The dynamics of possible selves in old age. *Journals of Gerontology B: Psychological Sciences and Social Sciences, 57,* P492–P500.

Smith, L. B., & Breazeal, C. (2007). The dynamic lift of developmental processes. *Developmental Science, 10,* 61–68.

Smith, L. M., LaGasse, L., Derauf, C., Grant, P., Shah, R., Arria, A., et al. (2008). Prenatal methamphetamine use and neonatal neurobehavioral outcome. *Neurotoxicology and Teratology, 30,* 20–28.

Smith, P. J., Blumenthal, J., Hoffman, B. M., Cooper, H., Strauman, T. A., Welsh-Bohmer, K., Browndyke, J. N., & Sherwood, A. (2010). Aerobic exercise and neurocognitive performance: A metaanalytic review of randomized controlled trials. *Psychosomatic Medicine: Journal of Biobehavioural Medicine.* Retrieved from http://www.psychosomaticmedicine.org/content/72/3/239.short

Smith, R. E., & Hunt, R. R. (2014). Prospective memory in young and older adults: The effects of task importance and ongoing task load. *Aging, Neuropsychology, and Cognition, 21,* 411–431.

Smith, R. L., Rose, A. J., & Schwartz-Mette, R. A. (2010). Relational and overt aggression in childhood and adolescence: Clarifying mean-level gender differences and associations with peer acceptance. *Social Development, 19,* 243–269.

Smith, T. B., McCullough, M. E., & Poll, J. (2003). Religiousness and depression: Evidence for a main effect and the moderating influence of stressful life events. *Psychological Bulletin, 129,* 614–636.

Smithbattle, L. (2007). Legacies of advantage and disadvantage: The case of teen mothers. *Public Health Nursing, 24,* 409–420.

Smithers, L. (2012, August 7). Children's healthy diets lead to healthier IQ. University of Adelaide: Health Sciences, Media Release, Research Story. Retrieved from http://www.adelaide.edu.au/news/print55161.html

Smokowski, P. R., & Bacallao, M. (2007). Acculturation, internalizing mental health symptoms, and self-esteem: Cultural experiences of Latino adolescents in North Carolina. *Child Psychiatry and Human Development, 37*(3), 273–292.

Snarey, J. (1987, June). A question of morality. *Psychology Today,* pp. 6–8.

Snijders, B. E., et al. (2007). Breast-feeding duration and infant atopic manifestations, by maternal allergic status, in the first two years of life (KOALA study). *Journal of Pediatrics, 151,* 347–351.

Snow, C. E., & Yang, J. Y. (2006). Becoming bilingual, biliterate, and bicultural. In W. Damon & R. Lerner (Eds.), *Handbook of child psychology* (6th ed.). New York: Wiley.

Snowdon, D. A. (2002). *Aging with grace: What the Nun Study teaches us about leading longer, healthier, and more meaningful lives.* New York: Bantam.

Snowdon, D. A. (2003). Healthy aging and dementia: Findings from the Nun Study. *Annals of Internal Medicine, 139,* 450–454.

Snyder, K. A., & Torrence, C. M. (2008). Habituation and novelty. In M. M. Haith & J. B. Benson (Eds.), *Encyclopedia of infant and early childhood development.* Oxford, UK: Elsevier.

Soares, N. S., & Patel, D. R. (2012). Office screening and early identification of children with autism. *Pediatric Clinics of North America, 59,* 89–102.

Sobralske, M. & Gruber, M. (2009). Risks and benefits of parent/child bed sharing. *Journal of the American Academy of Nurse Practitioners, 21,* 474–479.

Society of Obstetricians and Gynaecologists (SOGC). (2003). Midwifery. *Journal of Obstetrics and Gynaecology Canada, 25,* 239.

Society of Obstetricians and Gynaecologists (SOGC). (2008a). Joint Policy Statement on Normal Childbirth. *Journal of Obstetricians and Gynaecologists, 30*(12), 1163–1165.

Society of Obstetricians and Gynaecologists (SOGC). (2008b). *Media advisories: Rising c-section*. Retrieved from http://www.sogc.org/

Society of Obstetricians and Gynaecologists (SOGC). (2009). Policy statement on midwifery. Retrieved from http://www.sogc.org/

Society of Obstetricians and Gynaecologists (SOGC). (2011a). Sexuality and U. Ottawa: Author. Retrieved from http://www.sogc.org

Society of Obstetricians and Gynaecologists (SOGC). (2011b). Women's health information: Birth plan. Retrieved from http://www.sogc.org/

Society of Obstetricians and Gynaecologists (SOGC). (2011c). Women's health information: Medications and drugs before and during pregnancy. Retrieved from http://www.sogc.org/

Society of Obstetricians and Gynaecologists (SOGC). (2012). Sexual health: Statistics on sexual intercourse experience among Canadian teenagers. Retrieved from http://www.sexualityandu.ca.

Soderstrom, M. (2007). Beyond babytalk: Re-evaluating the nature and content of speech input to preverbal infants. *Developmental Review, 27*, 501–532.

Soderstrom, M., et al. (2012). Insufficient sleep predicts clinical burnout. *Journal of Occupational Health Psychology, 17*, 175–183.

Soenens, B., Vansteenkiste, M., Lens, W., Luyckx, K., Goossens, L., Beyers, W., et al. (2007). Conceptualizing parental autonomy support: Adolescent perceptions of promotion of independence versus promotion of volitional functioning. *Developmental Psychology, 43*, 633–646.

Soergel, P., Pruggmayer, M., Schwerdtfeger, R., Mulhaus, K., & Scharf, A. (2006). Screening for trisomy 21 with maternal age, fetal nuchal translucency, and maternal serum biochemistry at 11–14 weeks: A regional experience from Germany. *Fetal Diagnosis and Therapy, 21*, 264–268.

Solana, R., et al. (2012). Innate immunosenescence: Effect of aging on cells and receptors of the innate immune system in humans. *Seminars in Immunology, 24*, 331–341.

Song, H., Thompson, R., & Ferrer, E. (2009). Attachment and self-evaluation in Chinese adolescents: Age and gender differences. *Journal of Adolescence, 32*, 1267–1286.

Sonon, K., Richardson, G., Cornelius, J., Kim, K. & Day, N. (2015). Prenatal marijuana exposure predicts marijuana use in young adulthood. *Neurotoxicology and Teratology*, 47, 10–15.

Sontag, L. M., Graber, J., Brooks - Gunn, J., & Warren, M. P. (2008). Coping with social stress: Implications for psychopathology in young adolescent girls. *Journal of Abnormal Child Psychology.*

Sood, A. B., Razdan, A., Weller, E. B., & Weller, R. A. (2006). Children's reactions to parental and sibling death. *Current Psychiatry Reports, 8*, 115–120.

Sorensen, T. L., & Kemp, H. (2010). Ranibizumab treatment in patients with neovascular age-related macular degeneration and very low vision. *Acta Ophthalmologica, 89*(1), e97.

Sorenson, M. (2011). Vitamin D seminar, Edmonton. Retrieved from http://www.vitamindsociety.org/video.php?id=116

Sorte, J., Daeschel, I., & Amador, C. (2014). *Nutrition, health, and safety for young children* (2nd ed.). Upper Saddle River, NJ: Pearson.

Soto, C. J. (2014, in press). Is happiness good for your personality? Concurrent and prospective relations of the Big Five with subjective well-being. *Journal of Personality*.

Soto, C. J., John, O. P., Gosling, S. D., & Potter, J. (2011). Age differences in personality traits from 10 to 65: Big Five domains and facets in a large cross-sectional sample. *Journal of Personality and Social Psychology, 100*, 333–348.

Sowah, L. A., Busse, S., & Amoroso, A. (2013). HIV, tobacco use, and poverty: A potential cause of disparities in health status by race and social status. *Journal of Health Care for the Poor and Underserved, 24*, 1215–1225.

Sowell, E. R., Thompson, P. M., Leonard, C. M., Welcome, S. E., Kan, E., & Toga, A. W. (2004). Longitudinal mapping of cortical thickness and brain growth in children. *Journal of Neuroscience, 24*, 8223–8231.

SPA. (2010). Alan Ross award. Retrieved from http://www.cps.ca/awards-prix/details/#recipients

Spear, L. P. (2004). Adolescence and the trajectory of alcohol use. *Annals of the New York Academy of Sciences, 1021*, 202–205.

Specht, J., Egloff, B., & Schukle, S. C. (2011). Stability and change of personality across the life course: The impact of age and major life events on mean-level and rank-order stability of the Big Five. *Journal of Personality and Social Psychology, 101*, 862–882.

Special Senate Committee on Aging. (2009). *Canada's aging population: Seizing the opportunity final report.* Ottawa: Senate of Canada. Retrieved from http://www.senatesenat.ca/age.asp

Spelke, E. S. (1991). Physical knowledge in infancy: Reflections on Piaget's theory. In S. Carey & R. Gelman (Eds.), *The epigenesis of mind: Essays on biology and cognition.* Hillsdale, NJ: Erlbaum.

Spelke, E. S., & Kinzler, K. D. (2007a). Core knowledge. *Developmental Science, 10*, 89–96.

Spelke, E. S., & Kinzler, K. D. (2007b). Core systems in human cognition. *Progress in Brain Research, 164*, 257–264.

Spence, A. P. (1989). *Biology of human aging.* Englewood Cliffs, NJ: Prentice Hall.

Spence, J. T., & Helmreich, R. (1978). *Masculinity and feminity: Their psychological dimensions.* Austin: University of Texas Press.

Sperling, H., Debruyne, F., Boermans, A., Beneke, M., Ulbrich, E., & Ewald, S. (2010, in press). The POTENT I randomized trial: Efficacy and safety of an orodispersible vardenafil formulation of the treatment of erectile dysfunction. *Journal of Sexual Medicine, 8*, 261–71.

Sperling, R. A., Richmond, A. S., Ramsay, C. M., & Klapp, M. (2012). The measurement and predictive ability of metacognition in middle school learners. *Journal of Educational Research, 105*, 1–7.

Spielmann, G., et al. (2011). Aerobic fitness is associated with lower proportions of senescent blood T cells in man. *Brain, Behavior, and Immunity, 25*, 1521–1529.

Spinks, N., & Battams, N. (2016). Families and Work in Canada. The Vanier Institute of the Family. Retrieved from http://vanierinstitute.ca/families-work-canada/.

Spironelli, C., & Angrilli, A. (2008). Developmental aspects of automatic word processing: Language lateralization of early ERP components in children, young adults, and middle-aged adults. *Biological Psychology.*

Spruijt, E., & Duindam, V. (2010). Joint physical custody in the Netherlands and the well-being of children. *Journal of Divorce and Remarriage, 51*, 65–82.

Squire W. (2008). Shaken baby syndrome: The quest for evidence. *Developmental Medicine and Child Neurology, 50*, 10–14.

Sroufe, L. A., Egeland, B., Carlson, E., & Collins, W. A. (2005). The place of early attachment in developmental context. In K. E. Grossman, K. Krossman, & E. Waters (Eds.), *The power of longitudinal attachment research: From infancy and childhood to adulthood.* New York: Guilford Press.

St. George-Hyslop, P. (2012). Tanz Centre for Research in Neurodegenerative Diseases, University of Toronto. Retrieved from http://tanz.med.utoronto.ca/profile/peter-st-george-hyslop-director

St. John, P. D., Montgomery, P. R., & Tyas, S. L. (2008, Oct. 6). Alcohol misuse, gender, and depressive symptoms in community dwelling seniors. *International Journal of Geriatric Psychiatry.* Retrieved from https://www.ncbi.nlm.nih.gov/pubmed/18837057

Stadler, Z. K., Scharder, K. A., Vijai, J., Robson, M. E., & Offit, K. (2014, in press). Cancer genomics and inherited risk. *Journal of Clinical Oncology.*

Staff, J., & Schulenberg, J. (2010). Millennials and the World of work: Experiences in paid work during adolescence. *Journal of Business Psychology, 25*, 247–255.

Stajduhar, K. I., Allan, D. E., Cohen, S. R., & Heyland, D. K. (2008). Preferences for location of death of seriously ill hospitalized patients: Perspectives from Canadian patients and their family caregivers. *Palliative Medicine, 22*, 85–88.

Stanford Center for Longevity. (2011). Experts consensus on brain health. Retrieved from http://longevity.stanford.edu/mymind/cognitiveagingstatement

Stanton, K. (2011). Canada's Truth and Reconciliation Commission: Settling the past? *The International Indigenous Policy Journal, 2*(3), 2.

Star Staff. (2015, October, 19). 7 Key Trudeau promises show what you can expect. *Toronto Star.* Retrieved from http://www.thestar.com/

Starr, C., Evers, C., & Starr, L. (2010). *Biology today and tomorrow with physiology* (3rd ed.). Boston: Cengage.

Starr, C., Evers, C., & Start, L. (2015, in press). *Biology* (9th ed.). Boston: Cengage

Starr, L. R., & Davila, J. (2008). Clarifying co-rumination: Association with internalizing symptoms and romantic involvement among adolescent girls. *Journal of Adolescence.*

Starr, L., Davila, J., Stroud, C., Li, C., Ching, P., Yoneda, A.,... & Miller Ramsay, M. (2012). Love hurts (in more ways than one): Specificity of psychological symptoms as predictors and consequences of romantic activity among early adolescent girls. *Journal of Clinical Psychology, 68*(4), 373–381.

Stassen Berger, K., & Chuang, S. (2014). *Invitation to the life span* (Canadian edition). New York, NY: Worth Publishers.

Statistics Canada. (2000). *Research paper: High school dropouts returning to school.* Catalogue no. 81-595-M—No. 055. Retrieved from http://www.statcan.gc.ca/pub/81-595-m/81-595-m2008055-eng.pdf

Statistics Canada. (2001a). Target groups project: Women in Canada: Work chapter updates. Catalogue no. 89F0133XIE. Ottawa: Minister of Industry.

Statistics Canada. (2001b). Trends in the use of private education: 1987/88 to 1998/99. *The Daily.* Retrieved from http://www.statcan.ca

Statistics Canada. (2003a). *Canadian roulette.* Canada Safety Council. Retrieved from https://canadasafetycouncil.org/community-safety/canadian-roulette

Statistics Canada. (2003b). How times have changed! Canadian smoking patterns in the 20th century. Catalogue no. 82-005-XIE.

Statistics Canada. (2003c, May 23). Relationship between working while in high school and dropping out. Retrieved from http://www.statcan.ca/

Statistics Canada. (2004a). *National Longitudinal Survey of Children and Youth.* Statistics Canada.

Statistics Canada. (2004b). Trends in drug offences and the role of alcohol and drugs in crime. *The Daily* (February 23, 2004). Retrieved from http://www.statcan.ca

Statistics Canada. (2005a). *Report on seniors' falls in Canada, 2005.* Retrieved from publications.gc.ca/collections/Collection/HP25-1-2005E.pdf

Statistics Canada. (2005b). Secondary school graduates. *The Daily.* Retrieved from http://www.statcan.gc.ca/daily-quotidien/050202/dq050202b-eng.htm

Statistics Canada. (2006a). *Census families in private households by family structure, 1991 and 1996 censuses.* Retrieved from http://www.statcan.ca/

Statistics Canada. (2006b). *Divorces by province and territory.*

Statistics Canada. (2006c). National Longitudinal Survey of Children and Youth (NLSCY). Retrieved from http://www.statcan.ca/

Statistics Canada. (2007a). Components of population growth. Retrieved from http://www.statcan.gc.ca/pub/91-003-X/2007001/4129903-eng.htm

Statistics Canada. (2007b). *Family portrait: Continuity and change in Canadian families and households in 2006, 2006 census.* Catalogue no. 97-553-XIE. Retrieved from http://www12.statcan.ca/

Statistics Canada. (2008a). Eldercare - What we know today. Retrieved from http://www.statcan.gc.ca/pub/11-008-x/2008002/article/10689-eng.htm.

Statistics Canada. (2008b). Sexual assault in Canada 2004 and 2007 (Catalogue no. 85F0033M-No.19). Retrieved from http://www.statcan.gc.ca

Statistics Canada. (2009a). Canada's population by age and sex. Retrieved from http://www.statcan.gc.ca/dailyquotidien/090115/dq090115c-eng.htm

Statistics Canada. (2009b). *Family violence in Canada: A statistical profile.* Ottawa: Author. Catalogue no. 85-224-X.

Statistics Canada. (2010a). Arthritis. Retrieved on September 15, 2013 from http://www.statcan.gc.ca/pub/82-229-x/2009001/status/art-eng.htm

Statistics Canada. (2010b). Gap in life expectancy projected to decrease between Aboriginal people and the total Canadian population. Retrieved from http://www.statcan.gc.ca/

Statistics Canada. (2010c). Leading causes of death (Table 1, 2). http://statcan.gc.ca

Statistics Canada. (2010d). Paid work. Catalogue no. 89-503-X. Retrieved from http://www.statcan.gc.ca/pub/89-503-x/2010001/article/11387-eng.htm

Statistics Canada. (2011a). Canada's population estimates: Age and sex. *The Daily,* Wednesday, September 28, 2011. Retrieved from http://www.statcan.gc.ca/

Statistics Canada. (2011b). Families reference guide (Catalogue no. 98-312-X2011005). Retrieved from http://www.statcan.gc.ca

Statistics Canada. (2011c). Study: Projected trends to 2031 for the Canadian labour force. *The Daily,* Wednesday, August 17, 2011. Retrieved from http://www.statcan.gc.ca/daily-quotidien/110817/dq110817b-eng.htm

Statistics Canada. (2011d). Statistical profile on the health of First Nations in Canada: Leading causes of death (Table 3). Retrieved from http://statcan.gc.ca

Statistics Canada. (2012a). Age-standardized mortality rates by selected causes. Retrieved from http://www.statcan.gc.ca/tables-tableaux/sum-som/l01/cst01/health30a-eng.htm

Statistics Canada. (2012b). Deaths, 2009 (Table 1). Retrieved from http://statcan.gc.ca

Statistics Canada. (2012c). Eating disorders (Section D) (Catalogue no. 82-619-M). Retrieved from http://www.statcan.gc.ca/pub/82-619-m/82-619-m2012004-eng.pdf

Statistics Canada. (2012d). *Health at a glance: Suicide rates: An overview* (Catalogue no. 82-624-X). Retrieved from http://www.statcan.gc.ca

Statistics Canada. (2012e). Highlights (Catalogue no. 84-215-X). Retrieved from http://statcan.gc.ca

Statistics Canada. (2012f). Leading causes of death, infants, by sex, Canada (Table

102–0562). Retrieved from http://statcan.gc.ca

Statistics Canada. (2012g). Life expectancy at birth by sex and by province, May 31, 2012. Retrieved from http://www.statcan.gc.ca/tables-tableaux/sum-som/l01/cst01/health26-eng.htm

Statistics Canada. (2012h). 2011 census: Population and dwelling counts. *The Daily*, Wednesday, February 8, 2012. Retrieved from http://www.statcan.gc.ca/

Statistics Canada. (2012i). *Visible minority of a person.* Retrieved from http://www.statcan.gc.ca

Statistics Canada. (2012j). *Youth court statistics in Canada, 2010/2011.* Retrieved from http://www.statcan.gc.ca

Statistics Canada. (2012k). Overview of family violence. Retrieved from http://www.statcan.gc.ca/pub/85-002-x/2012001/article/11643/hl-fs-eng.htm#a4

Statistics Canada. (2012l). Deaths and mortality rates, by age group and sex, Canada, provinces and territories. Retrieved from http://www.statcan.gc.ca.

Statistics Canada. (2012m). Infant mortality rates, by province and territory. Retrieved from http://www.statcan.gc.ca/tables-tableaux/sum-som/l01/cst01/health21c-eng.htm.

Statistics Canada. (2013a). *Directly measured physical activity of Canadian adults, 2007 to 2011.* Retrieved from https://www.statcan.gc.ca

Statistics Canada. (2013b). Life Tables, Canada, Provinces and Territories, 2009-2011. (Catalogue no. 84-537-X — No. 005). Retrieved from http://www.statcan.gc.ca/

Statistics Canada. (2014a). Findings. Statistics Canada. Retrieved from http://www.statcan.gc.ca/pub/82-003-x/2006008/article/phys/10307-eng.htm.

Statistics Canada. (2014b). Income Survey, 2012. Retrieved from http://www.statcan.gc.ca/daily-quotidien/141210/dq141210a-eng.htm

Statistics Canada. (2015a). Body mass index of children and youth 2012 to 2013. Retrieved from http://www.statcan.gc.ca/pub/82-625-x/2014001/article/14105-eng.htm

Statistics Canada. (2015b). *Family violence in Canada: A statistical profile, 2013.* Retrieved from http://www.statcan.gc.ca.

Statistics Canada. (2015c). *Health at a glance.* Retrieved from https://www.statcan.gc.ca.

Statistics Canada. (2015d). Immigration and Ethnocultural Diversity in Canada. Retrieved from https://www12.statcan.gc.ca/nhs-enm/2011/as-sa/99-010-x/99-010-x2011001-eng.cfm

Statistics Canada. (2015e). Leading Causes of Death by Sex. Retrieved from http://www.statcan.gc.ca/tables-tableaux/sum-som/l01/cst01/hlth36a-eng.htm.

Statistics Canada. (2015f). Portrait of Families and Living Arrangements in Canada Retrieved from http://www12.statcan.gc.ca/census-recensement/2011/as-sa/98-312-x/98-312-x2011001-eng.cfm.

Statistics Canada. (2015g). Section E - Mental Retardation. Retrieved from http://www.statcan.gc.ca/pub/82-619-m/2012004/sections/sectione-eng.htm

Statistics Canada. (2015h). Study: Employment patterns of families with children, 1976–2014. Retrieved from http://www.statcan.gc.ca.

Statistics Canada. (2015i). Centenarians in Canada. Retrieved from https://www12.statcan.gc.ca/census-recensement/2011/as-sa/98-311-x/98-311-x2011003_1-eng.cfm

Statistics Canada. (2015j). Section C - Childhood Conditions. Retrieved from http://www.statcan.gc.ca/pub/82-619-m/2012004/sections/sectionc-eng.htm

Statistics Canada. (2015k). Directly measured physical activity of Canadian children and youth, 2007 to 2011 Retrieved from http://www.statcan.gc.ca/pub/82-625-x/2013001/article/11817-eng.htm.

Statistics Canada. (2015l). Life Expectancy. Statistics Canada Retrieved from http://www.statcan.gc.ca/pub/82-229-x/2009001/demo/lif-eng.htm

Statistics Canada. (2015m). Living arrangements for seniors. Retrieved from https://www12.statcan.gc.ca/census-recensement/2011/as-sa/98-312-x/98-312-x2011003_4-eng.cfm.

Statistics Canada. (2015n). Section 2: Population by age and sex. Statistics Canada. Retrieved from http://www.statcan.gc.ca/pub/91-215-x/2012000/part-partie2-eng.htm.

Statistics Canada. (2015o). *Arthritis.* Retrieved from http://www.statcan.gc.ca/pub/82-229-x/2009001/status/art-eng.htm.

Statistics Canada. (2016a). Fertility: Fewer children, older moms. Retrieved from http://www.statcan.gc.ca/pub/11-630-x/11-630-x2014002-eng.htm.

Statistics Canada. (2016b). *Labour force survey, February 2016.* Retrieved from http://www.statcan.gc.ca.

Statistics Canada. (2016c). National Household Survey: Data tables. Religion (108), Status and Period of Immigration (11), Age Groups (10) and Sex (3) for the Population in Private Households of Canada, Provinces, Territories, Census Metropolitan Areas and Census Agglomerations, 2011 National Household Survey. Retrieved from http://www12.statcan.gc.ca/nhs-enm/2011/dp-pd/dt-td/Rp-eng.cfm?LANG=E&APATH=3&DETAIL=0&DIM=0&FL=A&FREE=0&GC=0&GID=0&GK=0&GRP=0&PID=105399&PRID=0&PTYPE=105277&S=0&SHOWALL=0&SUB=0&Temporal=2013&THEME=95&VID=0&VNAMEE=&VNAMEF=.

Statistics Canada. (2016d). Notice-Supplementary Information to the 2015 Immigration Plan. Retrieved from http://www.cic.gc.ca/english/department/media/notices/2014-11-06.asp

Staudinger, U. M. (1996). Psychologische produktivitat und selbstenfaltung im alter. In M. M. Baltes & L. Montada (Eds.), *Produktives leben im alter.* Frankfurt, Germany: Campus.

Staudinger, U. M., & Dorner, J. (2007). Wisdom. In J. E. Birren (Ed.), *Encyclopedia of gerontology* (2nd ed.). San Diego Academic Press.

Staudinger, U. M., & Gluck, J. (2011, in press). Psychological wisdom research. *Annual review of psychology* (Vol. 62). Palo Alto, CA: Annual Reviews.

Staudinger, U. M., & Jacobs, C. B. (2011). Life-span perspectives on positive personality development in adulthood and old age. In R. M. Lerner, W. F. Overton, A. M. Freund, & M. E. Lamb (Eds.), *Handbook of life-span development.* New York: Wiley.

Stavrinos, D., et al. (2013). Impact of distracted driving on safety and traffic flow. *Accident Analysis and Prevention, 61*, 63–70.

Steeves, V. (2014). *Young Canadians in a Wired World, Phase III: Trends and Recommendations.* Ottawa: MediaSmarts.

Steffener, J., Barulli, D., Habeck, C., & Stern, Y. (2014). Neuroimaging explanations of age-related differences in task performance. *Frontiers in Aging Neuroscience, 6*, 46.

Steiger, A. E., Allemand, M., Robins, R. W., & Fend, H. A. (2014). Low and decreasing self-esteem during adolescence predict adult depression two decades later. *Journal of Personality and Social Psychology, 106*, 325–338.

Stein, M. T., Kennell, J. H., & Fulcher, A. (2004). Benefits of a doula present at the birth of a child. *Journal of Developmental and Behavioral Pediatrics, 25* (Suppl. 5), S89–S92.

Stein, P. K., et al. (2012). Caloric restriction may reverse age-related autonomic decline in humans. *Aging Cell, 11*(4), 644–650.

Steinberg, L. (2008a). *Adolescence.* New York, NY: McGraw-Hill

Steinberg, L. (2008b). A social neuroscience perspective on adolescent risk-taking. *Developmental Review, 28,* 78–106.

Steinberg, L. (2009). Adolescent development and juvenile justice. *Annual Review of Clinical Psychology* (Vol. 5). Palo Alto, CA: Annual Reviews.

Steinberg, L. (2011). Adolescent risk-taking: A social neuroscience perspective. In E. Amsel & J. Smetana (Eds.), *Adolescent vulnerabilities and opportunities: Constructivist developmental perspectives.* New York: Cambridge University Press.

Steinberg, L. (2015a, in press). How should the science of adolescent brain pathology inform legal policy? In J. Bhabba (Ed.), *Coming of age.* Philadelphia: University of Pennsylvania Press.

Steinberg, L. (2015b, in press). The neural underpinnings of adolescent risk-taking: The roles of reward-seeking, impulse control, and peers. In G. Oettigen & P. Gollwitzer (Eds.), *Self-regulation in adolescence.* New York: Cambridge University Press.

Steinberg, L., & Chein, J. (2015). Multiple accounts of adolescent impulsivity. *Proceedings of the National Academy of Science of the United States of America, 112*(29), 8807–8808.

Steinberg, L., & Monahan, K. C. (2007). Age differences in resistance to peer influence. *Developmental Psychology, 43,* 1531–1543.

Steinberg, S. J., & Davila, J. (2008). Romantic functioning and depressive symptoms among early adolescent girls: The moderating role of parental emotional availability. *Journal of Clinical Child and Adolescent Psychology, 37,* 350–362.

Steinhausen, H. C., Blattmann, B., & Pfund, F. (2007). Developmental outcome in children with intrauterine exposure to substances. *European Addiction Research, 13,* 94–100.

Steinstra, D., & Chochinov, M. (2012). Palliative care for vulnerable populations. *Palliative and Supportive Care, 10,* 37–42.

Steptoe, A., & Kivimaki, M. (2012). Stress and cardiovascular disease. Nature Reviews. *Cardiology, 9,* 360–370.

Steptoe, A., de Oliveira, C., Demakakos, P., & Zaninotto, P. (2014). Enjoyment of life and declining physical function at older ages: a latitudinal cohort study. *Canadian Medical Association Journal.*

Sterin, J. C. (2014). *Mass media revolution,* (2nd ed.). Upper Saddle River, NJ: Pearson

Sternberg, K., & Sternberg, R. (2013). Love. In H. Pashler (Ed.) *Encyclopedia of the mind* (pp. 473-476). Thousand Oaks, CA: Sage.

Sternberg, R. J. (1986). *Intelligence applied.* San Diego: Harcourt Brace Jovanovich.

Sternberg, R. J. (2000). Wisdom as a form of giftedness. *Gifted Child Quarterly, 44*(4), 252–259.

Sternberg, R. J. (2002). Intelligence: The triarchic theory of intelligence. In J. W. Gutherie (Ed.), *Encyclopedia of education* (2nd ed.). New York: Macmillan.

Sternberg, R. J. (2004). Individual differences in cognitive development. In U. Goswami (Ed.), *Blackwell handbook of childhood cognitive development.* Malden, MA: Blackwell.

Sternberg, R. J. (2007a). *g, g's,* or jeez: Which is the best model for developing abilities, competencies, and expertise? In P. C. Kyllonen, R. D. Roberts, & L. Stankov (Eds.), *Extending intelligence: Enhancement and New Constructs* (pp. 250–265). Mahwah, NJ: Lawrence Erlbaum Associates.

Sternberg, R. J. (2007b). Finding students who are wise, practical, and creative. *The Chronicle of Higher Education, 53*(44), B11.

Sternberg, R. J. (2010a). A triarchic view of intelligence in cross-cultural perspective. In S. H. Irvine & J. H. Berry (Eds.), *Human abilities in cultural contexts.* New York: Cambridge University Press.

Sternberg, R. J. (2010b). Human intelligence. In V. S. Ramachandran (Ed.), *Encyclopedia of human behavior* (2nd ed.). New York: Elsevier.

Sternberg, R. J. (2010c). Intelligence. In B. McGaw, P. Peterson, & E. Baker (Eds.), *International encyclopedia of education* (3rd ed.). New York: Elseiver.

Sternberg, R. J. (2010d). Teaching for creativity. In R. A. Beghetto & J. C. Kaufman (Eds.), *Nurturing creativity in the classroom.* New York: Cambridge University Press.

Sternberg, R. J., & Bridges, S. L. (2014). Varieties of genius. In D. K. Simonton (Ed.), *Wiley-Blackwell handbook of genius.* New York: Wiley.

Sternberg, R. J., Kaufman, J. C., & Grigorenko, E. (2008). *Applied intelligence.* New York: Cambridge University Press.

Stetsone, B. (2002). *Living victims, stolen lives: Parents of murdered children speak to Americans about death value.* New York: Baywood.

Stevens, C., & Bavelier, D. (2012). The role of selective attention on academic foundations: A cognitive neuroscience perspective. *Developmental Cognitive Neuroscience, 15*(1, Suppl.), S30–S48.

Stevenson, H. W., & Newman, R. S. (1986). Longterm prediction of achievements and attitudes in mathematics and reading. *Child Development, 57,* 646–659.

Stewart, A. J., Ostrove, J. M., & Helson, R. (2001). Middle aging in women: Patterns of personality change from the 30s to the 50s. *Journal of Adult Development, 8,* 23–37.

Stewart, D., MacMillan, H. & Wathen, N. (2013). "Intimate partner violence," *Canadian Journal of Psychiatry, 58*(6), 1–15.

Stewart-Archer, L., Afghani, A., Toye, C., & Gomez, F. (2015). Dialogue on ideal end-of-life care for those with dementia. *American Journal of Hospice & Palliative Medicine, 32*(6), 620–630.

Stice, E., Presnell, K., & Spangler, D. (2002). Risk factors for binge eating onset in adolescent girls: A 2-year prospective investigation. *Health Psychology, 21,* 131–138.

Stice, E., Presnell, K., Gau, J., & Shaw, H. (2007). Testing mediators of intervention effects in randomized controlled trials: An evaluation of two eating disorder programs. *Journal of Consulting and Clinical Psychology, 75,* 20–32.

Stikkelbroek, Y., Prinzie, P., de Graaf, R., ten Have, M., & Cuijpers, P. (2012). Parental death during childhood and psychopathology in adulthood. *Psychiatry Research, 198*(3), 516–520.

Stine-Morrow, E. A. L., & Basak, C. (2011). Cognitive interventions. In K. W. Schaie & S. L. Willis (Eds.), *Handbook of the psychology of aging* (7th ed.). New York: Elsevier.

Stirling, E. (2011). *Valuing older people.* New York: Wiley.

Stone, Jay. (2011). Study shows that 'identical' twins are not genetically identical. *Bio News.* Retrieved from http://www.bionews.org.uk/page_92288.asp.

Stone, L. (2015). Supreme Court strikes down Canada's assisted suicide laws. *Global News.* Retrieved from http://globalnews.ca/news/1815749/supreme-court-strikes-down-canadas-assisted-suicide-laws/.

Stone, R. I. (2006). Emerging issues in long-term care. In R. H. Binstock & L. K. George (Eds.), *Handbook of aging and the social sciences* (6th ed.). San Diego: Academic Press.

Stowell, J. R., Robles, T., & Kane, H. S. (2013). Psychoneuroimmunology: Mechanisms, individual differences, and interventions. In I. B. Weiner et al. (Eds.), *Handbook of psychology* (2nd ed., Vol. 9). New York: Wiley.

Strandberg, T. E., Strandberg, A. Y., Slaomaa, V. V., Pitkala, K., Tilvis, R. S., & Miettinen, T. A. (2007). Alcoholic beverage preference, 29-year mortality, and quality of life in men in old age. *Journals of Gerontology: Biological Sciences and Medical Sciences, 62A,* M213–M218.

Strauss, R. S. (2001). Environmental tobacco smoke and serum vitamin C levels in children. *Pediatrics, 107,* 540–542.

Strehle, E., Gray,W., Gopisetti, S., Richardson, J., McGuire, J & Malone, S. (2011). Can home monitoring reduce mortality in infants at increased risk of infant death syndrome? A systematic review. *Acta Paediatrica, 101,* 8–13.

Striegel, R., Bedrosian, R., Wang, C., & Schwartz, S. (2012). Why men should be included in research on binge eating. Results from a comparison of psychosocial impairment in men and women. *International Journal of Eating Disorders, 45,* 233–240.

Striegel-Moore, R. H., & Bulik, C. M. (2007). Risk factors for eating disorders. *American Psychologist, 62,* 181–198.

Strinberg, L., & Kathryn, M. (2010). Adolescents' exposure to sexy media does not hasten the initiation of sexual intercourse. *American Psychological Association, 47*(2), 562–576.

Stroebe, M., Schut, H., & Stroebe, W. (2007). Health outcomes of bereavement. *Lancet, 370,* 1960–1973.

Strohmeier, D., & Schmitt-Rodermund, E. (Eds.). (2008). *Immigrant youth in European countries.* Clifton, NJ: Psychology Press.

Strong, B., Yarber, W., Sayad, B., & De Vault, C. (2008). *Human sexuality* (6th ed.). New York: McGraw-Hill.

Sturman, M. C. (2003). Searching for the inverted U-shaped relationship between time and performance: Meta-analyses of the experience/performance, tenure/performance, and age-performance relationships. *Journal of Management, 29,* 609–640.

Su, Y., et al. (2013). Identification of novel human glioblastoma-specific transcripts by serial analysis of gene expression data mining. *Cancer Biomarkers, 13,* 367–375.

Sudheimer, E. (2009). Appreciating both sides of the generation gap: Baby boomers and Generation X nurses working together. *Nursing Forum, 44*(1), 57–63.

Suehs, B. T., et al. (2014). Household members of persons with Alzheimer's disease: Health conditions, healthcare resource use, and healthcare costs. *Journal of the American Geriatrics Society, 62,* 435–441.

Sugden, N., Mohamed-Ali, M. & Moulson, M. (2014). I spy with my little eye: Typical, daily exposure to faces documented from a first-person infant perspective. *Developmental Psychology, 56,* 249–261.

Sugita, Y. (2004). Experience in early infancy is indispensable for color perception. *Current Biology, 14,* 1267–1271.

Sullivan, H. S. (1953). *The interpersonal theory of psychiatry.* New York: W. W. Norton.

Sultan-Taieb, H., Chastang, J. F., Mansouri, M., & Niedhammer, I. (2013). The annual costs of cardiovascular diseases and mental disorders attributable to job strain in France. *BMC Public Health, 13,* 748.

Sumter, S., Bokhorst, C., Steinberg, L., & Westenberg, M. (2009). The developmental pattern of resistance to peer influence in adolescence: Will the teenager ever be able to resist? *Journal of Adolescence, 32,* 1009–1021.

Sun, F., et al. (2012). Predicting the trajectories of depressive symptoms among southern community-dwelling older adults: The role of religiosity. *Aging and Mental Health, 16,* 189–198.

Sunstein, C. R. (2008). Adolescent risk-taking and social meaning: A commentary. *Developmental Review, 28,* 145–152.

Supreme Court of Canada. (2015). *Carter v. Canada (Attorney General).* Retrieved from http://www.scc-csc.ca/WebDocuments-DocumentsWeb/35591/FM190_Intervener_Council-of-Canadians-with-Disabilities-and-the-Canadian-Association-for-Community-Living.pdf

Suris, J. C., Jeannin, A., Chossis, I., & Michaud, P. A. (2007). Piercing among adolescents: Body art as a risk marker: A population-based study. *Journal of Family Practice, 56,* 126–130.

Sussman, S., & Arnet, J. (2014). Emerging adulthood: Developmental period facilitative of the addictions. *Research in Emerging Adulthood and Risky Behavior, 37*(2), 147–155.

Sveen, C. A., & Walby, F. A. (2008). Suicide survivors' mental health and grief reactions: A systematic review of controlled studies. *Suicide and Life Threatening Behavior, 38,* 13–29.

Svihula, J., & Estes, C. L. (2008). Social security politics: Ideology and reform. *Journals of Gerontology B: Psychological Sciences and Social Sciences, 62,* S79–S89.

Swamy, G. K., Ostbye, T., & Skjaerven, R. (2008). Association of preterm birth with long-term survival, reproduction, and next generation preterm birth. *Journal of the American Medical Association, 299,* 1429–1436.

Swanson, A., Ramos, E., & Snyder, H. (2014, in press). Next generation sequencing is the impetus for the next generation of laboratory-based genetic counselors. *Journal of Genetic Counseling.*

Swanson, D. P. (1997, April). *Identity and coping styles among African-American females.* Paper presented at the meeting of the Society for Research in Child Development, Washington, DC.

Sweeney, M. (2009). Remarriage. IN D. Carr (Ed.) *Encyclopedia of the life course and human development.* Boston, MA: Gale Cengage.

Sweeney, M. (2010). Remarriage and stepfamilies: strategic sites for family scholarship in the 21st century. *Journal of Marriage and the Family, 72,* 667–684.

Sweeney, M. S. (2009). *Brain: The complete mind, how it develops, how it works, and how to keep it sharp.* Washington, DC: National Geographic.

Swing, E. L., Gentile, D. A., Anderson, C. A., & Walsh, D. A. (2010). Television and video game exposure and the development of attention problems. *Pediatrics, 126,* 214–221.

Syed, M., & Azmitia, M. (2008). A narrative approach to ethnic identity in emerging adulthood: Bringing life to the identity status model. *Developmental Psychology, 44*(4), 1012.

Sylvain-Roy, S., Lungu, O., & Belleville, S. (2014, in press). Normal aging of the attentional control functions that underlie working memory. *Journals of Gerontology B: Psychological Sciences and Social Sciences.*

Szanton, S. L., Seplaki, C. L., Thorpe, R. J., Allen, J. K., & Fried, L. P. (2010). Socioeconomic status is associated with frailty: The women's health and aging studies. *Journal of Epidemiology and Community Health, 64,* 63–67.

Szinovacz, M. E. (2009). Grandparenthood. In D. Carr (Ed.), *Encyclopedia of the life course and human development.* Boston: Gale Cengage.

Szmaus, C. (2013). 90 Canadian cities proclaim intergenerational day. BC Care Provincial Association. Retrieved from http://www.bccare.ca/90-canadian-cities-proclaim-intergenerational-day/.

T

Tabuchi, M., Nakagawa, T., Miura, A., & Gondo, Y. (2014, in press). Generativity and interaction between the old and young: The role of perceived respect and perceived rejection. *Gerontologist.*

Tafoya, M., & Spitzberg, B. H. (2007). The dark side of infidelity. In B. H. Spitzberg & W. R. Cupach (Eds.), *The dark side of*

interpersonal communication. Mahwah, NJ: Erlbaum.

Taher, N., et al. (2014). Amyloid-b alters the DNA methylation status of cell-fate genes in an Alzheimer's disease model. *Journal of Alzheimer's Disease, 38*, 831–844.

Taige, N. M., Neal, C., Glover, V., & Early Stress, Translational Research and Prevention Science Network: Fetal and Neonatal Experience on Child and Adolescent Mental Health. (2007). Antenatal maternal stress and long-term effects on neurodevelopment: How and why? *Journal of Child Psychology and Psychiatry, 48*, 245–261.

Takeuchi, H., et al. (2012). Neural correlates of the differences between working memory speed and simple sensorimotor speed: An fMRI study. *PLoS One, 7*(1), e30579.

Taler, S. J. (2009). Hypertension in women. *Current Hypertension Reports, 11*, 23–28.

Talwar, V., & Lee, K. (2002). Development of lying to conceal a transgression: Children's control of expressive behaviour during verbal deception. *International Journal of Behaviour Development, 26*(5), 436–444.

Talwar, V., Lee, K., Bala, N., & Lindsay, R. C. L. (2006). Adults' judgments of children's coached reports. *Law and Human Behavior, 30*(5), 561–570.

Talwar, V., Murphy, S. M., & Lee, K. (2007). White lie-telling in children for politeness purposes. *International Journal of Behavioral Development, 31*, 1–11.

Tam, W. H., & Chung, T. (2007). Psychosomatic disorders in pregnancy. *Current Opinion in Obstetrics and Gynecology, 19*, 126–132.

Tan, L. J., et al. (2012). Molecular genetic studies of gene identification for sarcopenia. *Human Genetics, 131*, 1–31.

Tang, C., Curran, M., & Arroyo, A. (2014). Cohabitors' reasons for living together, satisfaction with sacrifices, and relationship quality. *Family Review, 50*(7), 598–620.

Tang, K. L. (2008). Taking older people's rights seriously: The role of international law. *Journal of Aging and Social Policy, 20*, 99–117.

Tang, M., et al. (2014). GSK-3/CREB pathway involved in the gx-50's effect on Alzheimer's disease. *Neuropharmacology, 81C*, 256–266.

Tang, Y., & Posner, M. I. (2009). Attention training and attention state training. *Trends in Cognitive Science, 13*, 222–227.

Tanik, S., et al. (2014). Cardiometabolic risk factors in patients with erectile dysfunction. *Scientific World Journal, 89*, 2091.

Tanner, J., Warren, A. & Bellack, D. (2015). *Visualizing the lifespan.* (1st ed.). Hoboken: NJ:Wiley.

Tantillo, M., Keswick, C. M., Hynd, G. W., & Dishman, R. K. (2002). The effects of exercise on children with attention-deficit hyperactivity disorder. *Medical Science and Sports Exercise, 34*, 203–212.

Tappan, M. B. (1998). Sociocultural psychology and caring psychology: Exploring Vygotsky's "hidden curriculum." *Educational Psychologist, 33*, 23–33.

Tarabulsy, G. M., et al. (2008). Similarities and differences in mothers' and observers' ratings of infant security on the attachment Q-sort. *Infant Behavior and Development, 31*(1), 10–22.

Tarabulsy, G. M., Provost, M. A., Deslandes, J., St-Lautenr, D., Moss, E., Lemelin, J. P., et al. (2003). Individual differences in infant still-face response at 6 months. *Infant Behavior & Development, 26*, 421–438.

Tardif, C., & Geva, E. (2006). The link between acculturation disparity and conflict among the Chinese Canadian immigrant mother-adolescent dyads. *Journal of Cross-Cultural Psychology, 37*(2), 191–211.

Tashiro, T., & Frazier, P. (2003). "I'll never be in a relationship like that again": Personal growth following romantic relationship breakups. *Personal Relationships, 10*, 113–128.

Tashiro, T., Frazier, P. & Berman, M. (2006). Stress-related post-traumatic growth following divorce and relationship dissolution. In M. Fine & T. Harvey (Eds), *Handbook of divorce and relationship dissolution* (pp. 361–384). Mahwah, NJ: Erlbaum.

Tate, R. B., Lah L., & Cuddy, T. E. (2003). Definition of successful aging by elderly Canadian males: The Manitoba follow up. *The Gerontologist, 43*(5), 735–744. Retrieved from http://gerontologist.oxfordjournals.org/content/43/5/735.short.

Tavassoli, N., et al. (2013). Factors associated with the undertreatment of atrial fibrillation in geriatric outpatients with Alzheimer's disease. *American Journal of Cardiovascular Drugs, 13*(6), 425–433.

Taveras, E. M., Rifas-Shiman, S. L., Oken, E., Gunderson, E. P., & Gillman, M. W. (2008). Short sleep duration in infancy and risk of childhood overweight. *Archives of Pediatric and Adolescent Medicine, 162*, 305–311.

Tavernier, R., & Willoughby, T. (2014). Bidirectional associations between sleep (quality and duration) and psychological functioning across the university years. *Developmental Psychology, 50*(3), 1395–1405.

Taylor, A. (2012). Introduction to the issue regarding research on age related macular degeneration. *Molecular Aspects of Medicine, 33*(4), 291–294.

Taylor, B. (2005). The little Winnipeg girl who charmed Bay Street. *Toronto Star*, E1, E9.

Taylor, C., & Peter, T. (2011). Every class in every school: Final report on the first National climate survey on homophobia, biphobia, and transphobia in Canadian schools. *Egael Canada Human Rights Trust*. Retrieved from http://www.egale.ca

Taylor, C., Manganello, J., Lee, S., & Rice, J. (2010) Mothers' Spanking of 3-Year-Old children and Subsequent Risk of Aggressive Behaviour. *American Academy of Pediatrics*. Retrieved from http://pediatrics.aappublications.org/content/125/5/e1057.short

Taylor, G. (2013). Forward - Message from the Deputy Chief Public Health Officer. *Congenital Anomalies in Canada 2013 - A Perinatal Health Surveillance Report- Protecting Canadians from Illness.* Public Health Agency of Canada. Retrieved from http://www.aphp.ca/pdf/CAC%20report%202013%20EN.pdf.

Taylor, L. (2012). Why Canada is hazardous to their health. *Ottawa Citizen*. Retrieved from http://www.ottawacitizen.com/health/Canada+hazardous+their+health/6206262/story.html

Taylor, L. S., & Whittaker, C. R. (2009). *Bridging multiple worlds* (2nd ed.). Boston: Allyn & Bacon.

Taylor, M. (2013). International Report: Over 11,000 Syrian children killed in war, most by explosives. *Aljaeera,America.* Retrieved from http://america.aljazeera.com/articles/2013/11/24/report-over-11-000syrianchildrenkilledinwarmostbyexplosives.html

Taylor, P. S. (2007). The wealth report: Celebrating the RRSP miracle. *MacLean's*. Retrieved from http://www.macleans.ca/article.jsp?content=20070226_102281_102281

Taylor, S. E. (2011a). *Health psychology* (8th ed.). New York: McGraw-Hill.

Taylor, S. E. (2011b). Tend and befriend theory. In A. M. van Lange, A. W. Kruglanski, & E. T. Higgins (Eds.), *Handbook of theories of social psychology*. Thousand Oaks, CA: Sage.

Taylor, S. E. (2011c). Affiliation and stress. In S. S. Folkman (Ed.), *Oxford handbook of stress, health, and coping*. New York: Oxford University Press.

Taylor, S. E., et al. (2000). Biobehavioral responses to stress in females: Tend-and-befriend, not fight-or-flight. *Psychological Review, 107*, 411–429.

Teague, M. L., Mackenzie, S. L. C., & Rosenthal, D. M. (2009). *Your health today* (brief ed.). New York: McGraw-Hill.

Teller, D., Pereverzeva,M. & Zemach, I. (2006), Infant color perception and discrete trial preferential looking paradigms. *Progress in Color Studies, 2,* 69–90.

Templeton, J. L., & Eccles, J. S. (2006). The relation between spiritual development and identity processes. In E. Roehlkepartain, P. E. King, L. Wagener, & P. L. Benson (Eds.), *The handbook of spirituality in childhood and adolescence.* Thousand Oaks, CA: Sage.

Templeton, S., & Gehsmann, K. (2014). *Teaching reading and writing*. Upper Saddle River, NJ: Pearson.

Tenenbaum, H., & May, D. (2014). Gender in parent-child relationships. In P. Leman & H. Tenenbaum (Eds.), *Gender and development.* New York: Psychology Press.

Terrion, J. L. (2013). The experience of post-secondary education for students in recovery from addiction to drugs or alcohol: Relationships and recovery capital. *Journal of Social and Personal Relationships, 30*(1), 3–23.

Terry, D. F., Nolan, V. G., Andersen, S. L., Perls, T. T., & Cawthon, R. (2008). Association of longer telomeres with better health in centenarians. *Journals of Gerontology A: Biological Sciences and Medical Sciences, 63,* 809–812.

Terry, D. F., Sebastian, P., Andersen, P. S., & Perls, T. T. (2008). Disentangling the roles of disability and morbidity in survival to exceptional old age. *Archives of Internal Medicine, 168,* 277–283.

Terry, M. B., & Tehranifar, P. (2013). Hormone replacement therapy and breast cancer risk: More evidence of risk stratification? *Journal of the National Cancer Institute, 105*(18), 1342–1343.

Terry, W., Olson, L. G., Wilss, L., & Boulton-Lewis, G. (2006). Experience of dying: Concerns of dying patients and of carers. *Internal Medicine Journal, 36,* 338–346.

Teti, D. M., & Towe-Goodman, N. (2008). Postpartum depression, effects on infant. In M. M. Haith & J. B. Benson (Eds.), *Encyclopedia of infancy and early childhood.* Oxford, UK: Elsevier.

Teunissen, H., Spijkerman, R., Cohen, G., Prinstein, M., Engels, R., & Scholte, R. (2014). An experimental study on the effects of peer drinking norms on adolescents' drinker prototypes. *Addictive Behaviours, 39,* 85–93.

Tezil, T., & Basaga, H. (2014, in press). Modulation of death cell in age-related diseases. *Current Pharmaceutical Design.*

Thagard, P. (2014). Artistic genius and creative cognition. In D. K. Simonton (Ed.), *Wiley-Blackwell handbook of genius.* New York: Wiley.

Thapar, A., Fowler, T., Rice, F., Scourfield, J., Van Den Bree, M., Thomas, S., Harold, G., & Hay, D. (2003). Maternal smoking during pregnancy and attention deficit hyperactivity disorder symptoms in offspring. *American Journal of Psychiatry, 160,* 1985–1989.

Tharp, R. G. (1994). Intergroup differences among Native Americans in socialization and child cognition: An erthogenetic analysis. In P. M. Greenfield & R. Cocking (Eds.), *Cross-cultural roots of minority child development.* Mahwah, NJ: Erlbaum.

The Canadian Association of Genetic Counsellors. (2016). What is CAGC? Retrieved from https://www.cagc-accg.ca/index.php?page=1

The Canadian Encyclopedia. (2015a). Chantal Petitclerc. Retrieved from *http://www.thecanadianencyclopedia.ca/en/article/chantal-petitclerc/*

The Canadian Encyclopedia. (2015b). First Nations and Religion. Retrieved from http://www.thecanadianencyclopedia.ca/en/article/religion-of-aboriginal-people/.

The Canadian Encyclopedia. (2016). Religion. Retrieved from http://www.thecanadianencyclopedia.ca/en/article/religion/.

The Canadian Press. (2012). Census shows new face of the Canadian family. Retrieved from http://www.cbc.ca.

The Canadian Press. (2013). *Women's hockey team preparing for Olympic boot camp.* Retrieved from http://www.cbc.ca

The Canadian Press. (2016). Government wraps consultations on inquiry into murdered indigenous women. *CBC News.* Retrieved from http://www.cbc.ca.

The DANA Foundation. (2012). Brain Awareness Week. Retrieved from http://dana.org/news/.

The New England centenarian study. (2012). Boston University School of Medicine New England Centenarian Study. Retrieved from http://www.bumc.bu.edu/centenarian/

Thelen, E., & Smith, L. B. (2006). Dynamic development of action and thought. In W. Damon & R. Lerner (Eds.), *Handbook of child psychology* (6th ed.). New York: Wiley.

Theurer, W. M., & Bhavsar, A. K. (2013). Prevention of unintentional childhood injury. *American Family Physician, 87,* 502–509.

Thiele, D. M., & Whelan, T. A. (2008). The relationship between grandparent satisfaction, reaming, and generativity. *International Journal of Aging and Human Development, 66,* 21–48.

Thomann, C. R., & Carter, A. S. (2008). Social and emotional development theories. In M. M. Haith & J. B. Benson (Eds.), *Encyclopedia of infant and early childhood development.* Oxford, UK: Elsevier.

Thomas, A., & Chess, S. (1991). Temperament in adolescence and its functional significance. In R. M. Lerner, A. C. Petersen, & J. Brooks-Gunn (Eds.), *Encyclopedia of adolescence* (Vol. 2). New York: Garland.

Thomas, E. M. (2006). Readiness to learn at school among five-year-old children in Canada. Catalogue no. 89-599-MIE – No. 004. Ottawa: Statistics Canada.

Thomas, S., & Kunzmann, U. (2014, in press). Age differences in wisdom-related knowledge: Does the age relevance of the task matter? *Journals of Gerontology B: Psychological Sciences and Social Sciences.*

Thomason, M. E., & Thompson, P. M. (2011). Diffusion imaging, white matter, and psychopathology. *Annual Review of Clinical Psychology* (Vol. 7). Palo Alto, CA: Annual Reviews.

Thompson, J., & Manroe, M. (2015). *Nutrition* (4th ed.) Upper Saddle River, NJ: Pearson.

Thompson, R. (2006). The development of the person: Social understanding, relationships. conscience, self. In N. Eisenberg (Ed.). *Handbook of child psychology: Vol 3 Social emotional and personality development* (6th ed. pp 24–98). Hoboken, NJ: Wiley.

Thompson, R. (2011). Emotion and emotion regulation: Two sides of the developing coin. *Emotion Review, 3*(1), 53–61.

Thompson, R. A. (2006). The development of the person. In W. Damon & R. Lerner (Eds.), *Handbook of child psychology* (6th ed.). New York: Wiley.

Thompson, R. A. (2007). Unpublished review of J. W. Santrock's *Children* (10th ed.). New York: McGraw-Hill.

Thompson, R. A. (2009). Early attachment and later development: Familiar questions, new answers. In J. Cassidy & P. R. Shaver (Eds.), *Handbook of attachment* (2nd ed.). New York: Guilford.

Thompson, R. A. (2011). The emotionate child. In D. Cicchetti & G. I. Roissman (Eds.), *The origins and organization of adaptation and maladaptation.* Minnesota Symposium on Child Psychology (Vol. 36). New York: Wiley.

Thompson, R. A. (2012a). Whither the preoperational child? Toward a lifespan moral development theory. *Child Development.*

Thompson, R. A. (2013). Attachment and its development: Precis and prospect. In P.

Zelazo (Ed.), *Oxford handbook of developmental psychology*. New York: Oxford University Press.

Thompson, R. A. (2014a). Conscience development in early childhood. In M. Killen & J. G. Smetana (Eds.), *Handbook of moral development* (2nd ed.). New York: Psychology Press.

Thompson, R. A. (2014b). Why are relationships important to children's well-being? In A. Ben-Arieh, I. Frones, F. Cases, & J. Korbin (Eds.), *Handbook of child well-being*. New York: Springer.

Thompson, R. A. (2014c, in press). Early attachment and later development: New questions. In J. Cassidy & P. R. Shaver (Eds.), *Handbook of attachment* (3rd ed.). New York: Guilford.

Thompson, R. (2015a). Doing it with feeling: The emotion in early socioemotional development. *Emotion Review, 7*(2), 121–125.

Thompson, R. (2015b). Relationships, regulation, and early development. In R. Learner (Ed.) *Handbook of Child Psychology and Developmental Science* (7th ed., vol 3) (pp. 201–246). New York, NY: Wiley.

Thompson, R. A., & Goodvin, R. (2007). Taming the tempest in the teapot: Emotion regulation in toddlers. In C. A. Brownell & C. B. Kopp (Eds.), *Socioemotional development in toddlers*. New York: Guilford.

Thompson, R. A., & Newton, E. (2009). Infant-caregiver communication. In H. T. Reis & S. Sprecher (Eds.), *Encyclopedia of human relationships*. Thousand Oaks, CA: Sage.

Thompson, R. A., & Virmani, E. A. (2009). Creating persons: Culture, self and personality development. In M. H. Bornstein (Ed.), *Handbook of cross-cultural developmental science*. Clifton, NJ: Psychology Press.

Thompson, R., & Virmani, E. (2010). Self and personality. In M. Bornstein, (Ed.) Self and personality. *Handbook of cultural developmental science* (pp. 195–207). New York, NY: Psychology Press.

Thompson, R. A., Meyer, S., & Jochem, R. (2008). Emotion regulation. In M. M. Haith & J. B. Benson (Eds.), *Encyclopedia of infant and early childhood development*. Oxford, UK: Elsevier.

Thornton, J. G. (2007). Progesterone and preterm labor—Still no definite answers. *New England Journal of Medicine, 357*, 499–501.

Thygesen, K. L., & Hodgins, D. C. (2003). Quitting again: Motivations and strategies for terminating gambling relapses. *Journal of Gambling Issues, 9.*

Tiedemann, M. (2008). Health care at the Supreme Court of Canada. *Library of Parliament Research Publications.* Retrieved from http://www2.parl.gc.ca/Content/LOP/ResearchPublications/prb0519-e.htm

Tielsch-Goddard, A. (2008). Adolescent body art: Piercings and tattoos in the school nurse's office. *NASN Newsletter, 23(3)*, 16–17.

Tildo, T., et al. (2005). Exposure to persisitent organchlorine pollutants associates with human sperm Y-X chromosome ratio. *Human Reproduction, 20*(7), 1903–1909.

Tjepkema, M., Wilkins, R., Senécal, S., Guimond, É., & Penny, C. (2009). Mortality of Métis and Registered Indian adults in Canada: An 11-year follow-up study. *Health Reports, 20*(4), 1–21.

Toepper, M., et al. (2014). The impact of age on load-related dorsolateral prefrontal cortex. *Frontiers in Aging Neuroscience, 6*, 9.

Tomasello, M. (2006). Acquiring linguistic constructions. In W. Damon & R. Lerner (Eds.), *Handbook of child psychology* (6th ed.). New York: Wiley.

Tomasello, M. (2014). *A natural history of human thinking*. Cambridge, MA: Harvard University Press.

Tomasello, M., & Carpenter, M. (2007). Shared intentionality. *Developmental Science, 10*, 121–125.

Tomasello, M., & Hamann, K. (2012). Collaboration in young children. *Quarterly Journal of Experimental Psychology, 65*, 1–12.

Tomasello, M., Carpenter, M., & Liszkowski, U. (2007). A new look at infant pointing. *Child Development, 78*, 705–722.

Tomiyama, A. J., et al. (2012). Does cellular aging relate to patterns of allostasis? An examination of basal and stress reactive HPA axis activity and telomere length. *Physiology and Behavior, 106*, 40–45.

Tompkins, G. E. (2015, in press). *Literacy in the early grades* (4th ed.). Upper Saddle River, NJ: Pearson.

Tong, X., Deacon, S. H., & Cain, K. (2014). Morphological and syntactic awareness in poor comprehenders: Another piece of the puzzle. *Journal of Learning Disabilities, 47*, 22–33.

Tonks, R. G. (1992). *Identity and generativity in the Canadian context.*

Torges, C. M., Stewart, A. J., & Nolen-Hoeksema, S. (2008). Regret resolution, aging, and adapting to loss. *Psychology and Aging, 23*, 169–180.

Toth, S. L. (2009). Attachment-based interventions: Comments on Dozier, Egeland, and Benoit. In R. E. Tremblay, R. deV Peters, M. Boivin, & R. G. Barr (Eds.), *Encyclopedia on early childhood development.* Montreal: Centre of Excellence for Early Childhood Development.

Totten, M. (2004). Safe school study. Retrieved from http://www.cpha.ca.

Tough, S., Siever, J., Leew, S., Johnston, D., Benzier, K. & Clark, D. (2008). Maternal mental health predicts risk of developmental problems at 3 years of age: follow up of a community based trial. *BMC Pregnancy and Childbirth, 8*, 16.

Towle, H. (2015). Special Education Policies Across Canada Need Update, Renewal: Report. Canadian Centre fro Policy Alternative. Retrieved from https://www.policyalternatives.ca/newsroom/news-releases/special-education-policies-across-canada-need-update-renewal-report.

Trahan, L., Steubing, K., Hiscock, M., & Fletcher, J. (2014). The Flynn Effect: A Meta-analysis. *Psycholological Bulletin, 140*(5), 1332–1360. Retrieved from http://www.ncbi.nlm.nih.gov/pmc/articles/PMC4152423/.

Trautner, H. M., Ruble, D. N., Cyphers, L., Kirsten, B., Behrendt, R., & Hartmann, P. (2005). Rigidity and flexibility of gender stereotypes in children: Developmental or differential? *Infant and Child Development, 14*, 365–381.

Trefler, D. (2009). Quality is free: A cost-benefit analysis of early child development initiatives. *Journal of Paediatric and Child Health, 14*(10), 681–684.

Trehub, S. & Hannon, E. (2009). Conventional rhythms enhance infants' and adults' perception of musical patterns. *Cortex, 45*, 110-118.

Trehub, S.E., Plantinga, J., & Brcic, J. (2009). Infants detect cross-modal cues to identity in speech and singing. *Annals of the New York Academy of Science, 1169*, 508–511.

Tremblay, M. S., et al. (2012). Canadian sedentary behavior guidelines for the early years (0–4 years). *Applied Physiology, Nutrition, and Metabolism, 37*, 370–380.

Tremblay, R. E., Gervais, J., & Petitclerc, A. (2008). *Early learning prevents youth violence.* Quebec: Canadian Council on Learning.

Tremblay, S., & Pierce, T. (2011). Perceptions of fatherhood: Longitudinal reciprocal associations within the couple. *Canadian Journal of Behavioural Science, 43*(2), 99–110.

Trezesniewski, K., Donnellan, M., & Robins, R. (2013). Development of self-esteem. In V. Zeigler-Hill (Ed.), *Self-esteem* (pp. 60–79). London, UK: Psychology Press.

Trifunov, W. (2009, May 15). *The practice of bed sharing: A systematic literature and policy review.* Prepared for the Public Health Agency of Canada. Retrieved from http://www.phac-aspc.gc.ca/dca-dea/prenatal/pbs-ppl-eng.php

Trocmé, N. et al. (2010) Canadian Incidence Study of Reported Child Abuse and Neglect 2008. Public Health Agency of Canada. Canadian Incidence Study (CIS) 2010. Retrieved from http://www.repeal43.org/docs/CIS%20Study%202010.pdf.

Trocmé, N., Fallon, B., MacLaurin, B., Sinha, V., Black, T., Fast, E., et al. (2012). Canadian Incidence Study of Reported Child Abuse and Neglect 2008. Public Health Agency of Canada. Retrieved from http://www.phac-aspc.gc.ca/cm-vee/csca-ecve/2008/cis-eci-07-eng.php#c3-1

Troll, L. E. (2000). Transmission and transmutation. In J. E. Birren & J. J. F. Schroots (Eds.), *A history of geropsychology in autobiography.* Washington, DC: American Psychological Association.

Trommsdorff, G. (2002). An eco-cultural and interpersonal relations approach to development of the lifespan. In W. J. Lonner, D. L. Dinnel, S. A. Hayes, & D. N. Sattler (Eds.), *Online readings in psychology and culture* (unit 12, chapter 1). Bellingham, WA: Center for Cross-Cultural Research, Western Washington University. Retrieved from http://www.wwu.edu/

Trottier, J. (2010). Atheists and agnostics, stand up and be counted in the 2011 census! Curently, most of us are not. *Center for Inquiry.* Retrieved from www.centerforinquiry.net/blogs/entry/canadian_atheists_and_agnostics_stand_up_and_be_counted_in_the_2011_census/

True, M., Pisani, L., & Oumar, F. (2001). Infant-mother attachment among the dogon of Mali. *Child Development,* (5), 1451–1466.

Trueswell, J. C., Median, T. N., Hafri, A., & Gleitman, L. R. (2013). Propose but verify: Fast mapping meets cross-situational word learning. *Cognitive Psychology, 66,* 126–156.

Truog, R. D. (2007). Brain death—Too flawed to endure, too ingrained to abandon. *Journal of Law, Medicine, and Ethics, 35,* 273–281.

Truog, R. D. (2008). End-of-life decision-making in the United States. *European Journal of Anesthesiology, 42* (Suppl. 1), S43–S50.

Truth and Reconciliation Commission of Canada. (2012). Residential schools. Retrieved from http://www.trc.ca/websites/trcinstitution/index.php?p=4

Trzesniewski, K. H., Donnellan, M. B., & Robins, R. W. (2003). Stability of self-esteem across the life span. *Journal of Personality and Social Psychology, 84,* 205–220.

Trzesniewski, K. H., Donnellan, M. B., Caspi, A., Moffitt, T. E., Robins, R. W., & Poultin, R. (2006). Adolescent low self-esteem is a risk factor for adult poor health, criminal behavior, and limited economic prospects. *Developmental Psychology, 42,* 381–390.

Tsai, T., Levenson, R., & McCoy, K. (2006). Cultural and temperamental variations in emotional response. *Emotion, 6,* 484–497.

Tsang, A., et al. (2008). Common persistent pain conditions in developed and developing countries: Gender and age differences and comorbidity with depression-anxiety disorders. *Journal of Pain, 9,* 883–891.

Tselepis, A. D. (2014). Cilostazol-based triple antiplatelet therapy in the era of generic clopidogrel and new potent antiplatelet agents. *Current Medical Research and Opinion, 30,* 51–54.

Tubman, J. G., & Windle, M. (1995). Continuity of difficult temperament in adolescence: Relations with depression, life events, family support, and substance abuse. *Journal of Youth and Adolescence, 24,* 133–152.

Tudge, J. (2004). Practice and discourse as the intersection of individual and social in human development. In A. N. Perret-Clermont, L. Resnick, C. Pontecorvo, & B. Burge (Eds.), *Joining society: Social interactions and learning in adolescence and youth.* New York: Cambridge University Press.

Tulsky, J. (2005). Beyond advanced directives: Importance of communication skills at the end of life. *Journal of the American Medical Association, 294*(3), 359–365.

Tulving, E. (2000). Concepts of memory. In E. Tulving & F. I. M. Craik (Eds.), *The Oxford handbook of memory.* New York: Oxford University Press.

Tulviste, T., & Ahtonen, M. (2007). Child-rearing values of Estonian and Finnish mothers and fathers. *Journal of Cross-Cultural Psychology, 38,* 137.

Turati, C., Montirosso, R., Brenna, V., Ferrara, V. & Borgatti, R. (2011). A smile enhances 3-month-olds' recognition of an individual face. *Infancy, 16*(3), 306–317.

Turecki, S., & Tonner, L. (1989). *The difficult child.* New York: Bantam.

Turiano, N. A., et al. (2012). Personality trait level and change as predictors of health outcomes: Findings of a national study of Americans (MIDUS). *Journals of Gerontology B: Psychological Sciences and Social Sciences, 67,* 4–12.

Turner, B. F. (1982). Sex-related differences in aging. In B. B. Wolman (Ed.), *Handbook of developmental psychology.* Englewood Cliffs, NJ: Prentice Hall.

Twells, L., & Newhook, L. (2010). Can exclusive breastfeeding reduce the likelihood of childhood obesity in some regions in Canada? *Canadian Journal of Public Health, 101*(1), 36–39.

Tyas, S. L., et al. (2007). Transitions to mild cognitive impairments, dementia, and death: Findings from the Nun Study. *American Journal of Epidemiology, 165,* 1231–1238.

Tzourio, C., Laurent, S., & Debette, S. (2014, in press). Is hypertension associated with an accelerated aging in the brain? *Hypertension.*

U

UBC. (2010). http://educ.ubc.ca

Uchino, B. N., et al. (2012). Social relationships and health: Is feeling positive, negative, or both (ambivalent) about your social ties related to telomeres? *Health Psychology, 31*(6), 789–796.

Ullah, M. I., Riche, D. M., & Koch, C. A. (2014). Transdermal testosterone replacement therapy in men. *Drug Design, Development, and Therapy, 8,* 101–112.

Ulloa, A., Chen, J., Vergara, V., Calhoun, V., & Liu, J. (2014). Association between copy number variation losses and alcohol dependence across African American and European American ethnic groups. *Alcoholism: Clinical and Experimental Research, 38*(5), 1266–1274.

Umana-Taylor, A. J. (2006, March). *Ethnic identity, acculturation, and enculturation: Considerations in methodology and theory.* Paper presented at the meeting of the Society for Research on Adolescence, San Francisco.

Umaña-Taylor, A., Lee, R., Rivas-Drake, D., Syed, M., Seaton, E., Quintana, S.,... Yip, T. (2014). Ethnic and racial identity during adolescence and into young adulthood: An integrated conceptualization. *Journal of Child Development, 85*(1), 21–39.

UNAIDS. (2006). *2006 report on the global AIDS epidemic.* Geneva: SWIT: UNICEF.

Underwood, M. (2004). Sticks and stones and social exclusion: Aggression among boys and girls. In P. K. Smith & C. H. Hart (Eds.), *Blackwell handbook of childhood social development.* Malden, MA: Blackwell.

Uneo, K. (2010). Mental health differences between young adults with and without same-sex contact: A simultaneous examination of underlying mechanisms. *Journal of Health and Social Behaviour, 51*(4), 391–407.

UNESCO. (2008). *Global education digest 2008: Comparing education statistics across the world.* Retrieved from http://www.uis.UNESCO.org/

UNESCO. (2011a). *Global education digest 2011: Focus on secondary education.* Retrieved from http://www.uis.UNESCO.org/

UNESCO. (2011b). *UNESCO and education: Everyone has the right to education.* Retrieved from http://www.unesdoc.unesco.org

UNICEF. (2011c). The state of the world's children 2011. Geneva, Switzerland: UNICEF. Switzerland.

UNICEF. (2014). *Reimagine the future: Innovation for every child - The State of the Worlds Children 2015: Executive Summary.* Retrieved from http://www.sowc.2015.unicef.org

United Nations. (1948). The Universal Declaration of Human Rights. Retrieved from http://www.un.org/en/universal-declaration-human-rights/.

United Nations. (2004). *Declaration on the elimination of violence against women.* Retrieved from http://www.un.org/documents/ga/res/48/a48r104.htm

United Nations. (2011). *The United Nations Human Development Index report.* New York: United Nations.

United Nations. (2015). The United Nations Human Development Index Report. Retrieved from http://www.hdr.undp.org/sites/default/2015_human_development_report_1.pdf

United Nations. (2016). Human rights demension of poverty. Retrieved from *http://www.ohchr.org/EN/Issues/Poverty/DimensionOfPoverty/Pages/Index.aspx*

University Health Netwook. (2006). Stem Cell Research at UHN. Retrieved from http://www.uhnresearch.ca/news/NR/NRSummer2006.pdf

University of Ottawa. (2015). Legal aspects of abortion in Canada. Society, the Individual, and Medicine. Retrieved from http://www.med.uottawa.ca/sim/data/Abortion_Law_e.htm.

Unterberger, R. (2016). Buffy Saite-Marie, Artist Biography. Retrieved from http://www.allmusic.com/artist/buffy-sainte-marie-mn0000626268/biography.

Upitis, R., Smithrim, K., Patteson, A., MacDonald, J., & Finkle, J. (2003). *Improving math scores: Lessons of engagement.* Paper presented at the Canadian Society for the Study of Education Annual Conference, Halifax.

Uppal, S. (2015) Employment patterns of families with children. Statistics Canada. http://www.statcan.gc.ca/pub/75-006-x/2015001/article/14202-eng.htm

Uppal, S., Kohen, D., & Khan, S. (2006). *Educational services and the disabled child.* Catalogue no. 81-004-XIE. Retrieved from http://www.statcan.ca/

Urban, J., Lewin-Bizan, S., & Lerner, R. (2010). The role of intentional self - regulation, lower neighbourhood ecological assets, and activity involvement in youth developmental outcomes. *Journal of Youth and Adolescence, 39,* 783–800.

Ursula Franklin Academy. (2008–2013). Ursula Franklin biography. Retrieved from http://www.ufacademy.org/v5/school/bio.php

Usalcas, J. (2011). *The Aboriginal labour force analysis series: Aboriginal People and the labour market—Estimates from labour force survey 2008–2010.* Statistics Canada Catalogue no.71-588-X, no.3. Retrieved from http://www.statcan.gc.ca/pub/71-588-x/71-588-x2011003-eng.pdf

V

Vaillancourt, T. (2008). Bullying: Names will never hurt me ... or will they? Canada Research Chairs. Retrieved from http://www.chairs-chaires.gc.ca/chairholders-titulaires/profile-eng.aspx?profileID=2350

Vaillant, G. E. (1977) *Adaptation to life.* Boston: Little, Brown.

Vaillant, G. E. (2002). *Aging well.* Boston: Little, Brown.

Vaish, A., Carpenter, M., & Tomasello, M. (2010). Young children selectively avoid helping people with harmful intentions. *Child Development, 81,* 1661–1669.

Valcarel-Ares, M. N., et al. (2014, in press). Mitochondrial dysfunction promotes and aggravates the inflammatory response in normal human synoviocytes. *Rheumatology.*

Valentini, P. (2013). Newborn of mother with syphilis in pregnancy. *Early Human Development, 8954,* S68–S69.

Valiakalayil, A., Paulson, L. A., & Tibbo, P. (2004). Burden in adolescent children of parents with schizophrenia: The Edmonton High Risk Project. *Social Psychiatry and Psychiatic Epidemiology, 39,* 528–535.

Valkanova, V., & Ebmeier, K. P. (2014, in press). Neuroimaging in dementia. *Maturitas.*

Vallotton, C. D., & Fischer, K. W. (2008). Cognitive development. In M. M. Haith & J. B. Benson (Eds.), *Encyclopedia of infancy and early childhood.* Oxford, UK: Elsevier.

Vallurupalli, M., Lauderdale, K., Balboni, M. J., Phelps, A. C., Block, S. D., Ng, A. Kachnic, L. VanderWeele, T., & Balboni, T. A. (2012). The role of spirituality and religious coping in the quality of life of patients with advanced cancer receiving palliative radiation therapy. *Journal of Supportive Oncology, 10*(2), 81–87.

Van Buren, E., & Graham, S. (2003). *Redefining ethnic identity: Its relationship to positive and negative school adjustment outcomes for minority youth.* Paper presented at the meeting of the Society for Research in Child Development, Tampa.

van de Weijer-Bergsma, E., Wijnroks, L., & Jongmans, M. J. (2008). Attention development in infants and preschool children born preterm: A review. *Infant Behavior and Development.*

van den Berg, P., Neumark-Sztainer, D., Hannan, P. J., & Haines, J. (2007). Is dieting advice from magazines helpful or harmful? Five-year associations with weight-control behaviors and psychological outcomes in adolescents. *Pediatrics, 119,* e30–e37.

van den Kommer, T. N., et al. (2013). Depression and cognition: How do they interrelate in old age? *American Journal of Geriatric Psychiatry, 21,* 398–410.

Van Dyk, J., Ramanjam, V., Church, P., Korean, G. & Donald, K. (2014). Maternal methamphetamine use in pregnancy and long-term neurodevelopmental and behavioural deficits in children. *Journal Popular Therapy Clinical Pharmacology, 21*(2), e185–e196.

Van Hof, P., van der Kamp, J., & Savelsbergh, G. J. (2008). The relation between infants' perception of catchableness and the control of catching. *Developmental Psychology, 44,* 182–194.

Van Hooft, E. (2014). Motivating and hindering factors during the reemployment process: The added value of employment counsellors' assessment. *Journal of Occupational Health Psychology, 19,* 1–17.

van Hooren, S. A., Valentijn, S. A., Bosma, H., Ponds, R. W., van Boxtel, M. P., & Jolles, J. (2005). Relation between health status and cognitive functioning: A 6-year follow-up of the Maastricht Aging Study. *Journals of Gerontology B: Psychological Sciences and Social Sciences, 60,* 57–60.

van IJzendoorn, M. H., & Kroonenberg, P. M. (1988). Crosscultural patterns of attachment: A meta-analysis of the Strange Situation. *Child Development, 59,* 147–156.

van IJzendoorn, M. H., & Sagi-Schwartz, A. (2009). Cross-cultural patterns of attachment: Universal and contextual dimensions. In J. Cassidy & P. R. Shaver (Eds.), *Handbook of attachment* (2nd ed.). New York: Guilford.

van Leijenhorst, L., Zanolie, K., Van Meel, C., Westernberg, P., Rombouts, S., & Crone, E. (2010). What motivates the adolescent? Brain regions mediating reward sensitivity across adolescence. *Cerebral Cortex, 20,* 61–69.

Van Petegem, S., Beyers, W., Brenning, K., & Vansteenkiste, M. (2013). Exploring the association between insecure attachment styles and adolescent autonomy in family decision making: A different approach. *Journal of Youth Adolescence, 42*, 1837–1846.

Van Ryzin, M., Carlson, E. & Sroufe, L. (2011). Attachment discontinuity in a high-risk sample. *Attachment and Human Development, 13,* 381–401.

van Solinge, H., & Henkens, K. (2005). Couples' adjustment to retirement: A multiactor panel study. *Journals of Gerontology B: Psychological Sciences and Social Sciences, 60*, S11–S20.

van Wormer, K., & McKinney, R. (2003). What schools can do to help gay/lesbian/ bisexual youth. A harm reduction approach. *Adolescence, 38*, 409–420.

Vanier Institute of the Family. (2015). Lone Mothers and Their Families in Canada: Diverse, Resilient and Strong. Retrieved from http://vanierinstitute.ca/lone-mothers-families-canada-diverse-resilient-strong/

Vanier Institute of the Family. (2105) Sharing a roof: Multi-generational Homes in Canada. Retrieved from http://blog.vanierinstitute.ca/multigenerational-homes-canada/

Vanier Institute. (2010). *Families count: Profiling Canada's families.* Retrieved from http://www.vanierinstitute.ca/include/get.php?nodeid=1907

Vanier Institute. (2012). *Transition: Family roles and responsibilities.* Retrieved from http://www.vanierinstitute.ca/include/get.php?nodeid=2231

VanKim, N., & Laska, M. (2012). Socioeconomic disparities in emerging adult weight and weight behaviors. *American Journal of Health Behavior, 146*, 259–276.

Vanpee, D., & Swine, C. (2004). Scale of levels of care versus DNR orders. *Journal of Medical Ethics, 30*, 351–352.

Vasdev, G. (2008). *Obstetric anesthesia.* Oxford, UK: Elsevier.

Vasiliadis, H. M., Forget, H., & Preville, M. (2013). The association between self-reported daily hassles and cortisol levels in depression and anxiety in community living older adults. *International Journal of Geriatric Psychiatry, 28*, 991–997.

Vaughn Van Hecke, A., Mundy, P. C., Acra, C. F., Block, J. J., Delgado, E. F., Paralde, M. V., et al. (2007). Infant joint attention, temperament, and social competence in preschool children. *Child Development, 78*, 53–69.

Vaughn, S. R., & Bos, C. S. (2015, in press). *Strategies for teaching students with learning and behavior problems* (9th ed.). Upper Saddle River, NJ: Pearson.

Vazsonyi, A. T., & Huang, L. (2010). Where self-control comes from: On the development of self-control and its relationship to deviance over time. *Developmental Psychology, 46*, 245–257.

Vedam-Mai, V., et al. (2014). Increased precursor cell proliferation after deep brain stimulation for Parkinson's disease: A human study. *PLoS One, 9*(3), e88770.

Veenhof, B & Timusk, P. (2014) Online activities of Canadian boomers and seniors. Retrieved from http://www.statcan.gc.ca/pub/11-008-x/2009002/article/10910-eng.htm

Veenhof, B., & Timusk, P. (2009). Online activities of Canadian boomers and seniors. *Canadian Social Trends, 88*(Winter), 26–33.

Veenstra, A., Lindenberg, S., Munniksma, A., & Dijkstra, J. K. (2010). The complex relationship between bullying, victimization, acceptance, and rejection: Giving special attention status, affection, and sex differences. *Social Development, 19*, 480–486.

Velders, M., & Diel, P. (2013). How sex hormones promote skeletal muscle regeneration. *Sports Medicine, 43*(11), 1089–1100.

Vellutino, F. R., Scanlon, D. M., Small, S., & Fanuele, D. P. (2006). Response to intervention as a vehicle for distinguishing between children with and without reading disabilities: Evidence for the role of kindergarten and first-grade interventions. *Journal of Learning Disabilities, 39*(2), 157–169.

Vendittelli, F., Riviere, O., Crenn-Herbert, C., Rozan, M.A., Maria, B., Jacquetin, B., & the AUDIPOG Sentinel Network. (2008). Is a breech presentation at term more frequent in women with a history of caesarean delivery? *American Journal of Obstetrics and Gynecology, 198*, e1–e6.

Vennemann, M., Bajanowski, T. Blair, P., Complojer, C. & Moon, R. & Kiechl-Kohlendorfer, U. (2012). Bed sharing and SIDS: Understanding the risks. *The Journal of Pediatrics, 160*(1), 44–48.

Venners, S. A., Wang, X., Chen, C., Wang, L., Chen, D., Guang, W., et al. (2004). Paternal smoking and pregnancy loss: A prospective study using a biomarker of pregnancy. *American Journal of Epidemiology, 159*, 993–1001.

Vera, E., et al. (2013). Telomerase reverse transcriptase synergizes with calorie restriction to increase health span and extend mouse longevity. *PLoS One, 8*(1), e53760.

Verghese, J., Ambrose, A. F., Lipton, R. B., & Wang, C. (2010). Neurological gait abnormalities and risk of falls in older adults. *Journal of Neurology, 257*, 392–398.

Verly, M., et al. (2014). Altered functional connectivity of the language network in ASD: Role of classical language areas and cerebellum. *Neuroimage Clinical, 4*, 374–382.

Vermeersch, H., T'Sjoen, G., Kaufman, J.M., & Vincke, J. (2008). The role of testosterone in aggressive and non-aggressive risk-taking in boys. *Hormones and Behavior, 53*, 463–471.

Verster, J. C., van Duin, D., Volkerts, E. R., Schreueder, A. H., & Verbaten, M. N. (2003). Alcohol hangover effects on memory functioning and vigilance performance after an evening of binge drinking. *Neuropsychopharmacology, 28*, 740–746.

Vespa, J. (2014). Historical trends in the marital intentions of one-time and serial cohabiters. *Journal of Marriage and Family, 76*, 207–217.

Vetter, N. C., et al. (2014, in press). Ongoing development of social cognition in adolescence. *Child Neuropsychology*.

Vézina, M. (2015). Being a parent in a stepfamily. Statistics Canada. Retrieved from http://www.statcan.gc.ca/pub/89-650-x/89-650-x2012002-eng.htm.

Vézina, M., & Turcotte, M. (2009). Forty-year-old mothers of pre-school children: A profile. *Canadian Social Trends, 88*, 34–45.

Vézina, M., & Turcotte, M. (2010). Caring for a parent who lives far away: The consequences. *Canadian Social Trends, 89*(Summer), 3–13.

Vieno, A., Nation, M., Pastore, M., & Santinello, M. (2009). Parenting and antisocial behaviour: A model of the relationship between adolescents' self-disclosure, parental closeness, parental control, and adolescent antisocial behaviour. *Developmental Psychology, 45*, 1509–1519.

Vigorito, C., & Giallauria, F. (2014). Effects of exercise on cardiovascular performance in the elderly. *Frontiers in Physiology, 5*, 51.

Vihman, M. M. (2014). Phonological development (2nd ed.). New York: Wiley.

Viken, M., Sollid, H., Joner, G., Dahl -Jorgensen, K., Ronningen, K., Undlien, D., et al. (2007). Polymorphisms in the cathepsin L2 (CTSL2) gene show association with type 1 diabetes and early onset myasthenia gravis. *Human Immunology, 68*(9), 748–755.

Villaverde Gutierrez, C., et al. (2012). Influence of exercise on mood in postmenopausal women. *Journal of Clinical Nursing, 21*, 923–928.

Villegas, R., Gao, Y. T., Yang, G., Li, H. L., Elasy, T., Zheng, W., & Shu, X. O. (2008). Duration of breast-feeding and the incidence of type 2 diabetes mellitus in the Shanghai Women's Health Study. *Diabetologia, 51*(2), 258–266.

Vincent, H. K., Raiser, S. N., & Vincent, K. R. (2012). The aging musculoskeletal system and obesity-related considerations with exercise. *Aging Research and Reviews, 11*, 361–373.

Vinik, J., Almas, A., & Grusec, J. (2011). Mothers' knowledge of what distresses and comforts their children predicts children's coping, empathy, and prosocial behavior. *Parenting: Science and Practice, 11*, 56–71.

Virta, J. J., et al. (2013). Midlife cardiovascular risk factors and late cognitive impairment. European Journal of Epidemiology, 28, 405–416.

Vissers, D., et al. (2013). The effect of exercise on visceral adipose tissue in overweight adults: A systematic review and meta-analysis. *PLoS One, 8*(2), e56415.

Vitaro, F., Boivin, M., & Bukowski, W. M. (2009). The role of friendship in child and adolescent psychological development. In K. H. Rubin, W. M. Bukowski, & B. Laursen (Eds.), *Handbook of peer interaction, relationships, and groups*. New York: Guilford.

Vitaro, F., Pedersen, S., & Brendgen, M. (2007). Children's disruptiveness, peer rejection, friends' deviancy, and delinquent behaviors: A process-oriented approach. *Development and Psychopathology, 19*, 433–453.

Vivona, J. (2012). Is there a nonverbal period of development? *Journal of American Psychiatric Association, 60*(2), 231–265.

Vliegen, N., & Luyten, P. (2009). Dependency and self-criticism in postpartum depression and anxiety: A case control study. *Clinical Psychology & Psychotherapy, 16*(1), 22–32.

Vogel, L. (2011). Advance directives: Obstacles in preparing for the worst. *Canadian Medical Association Journal, 183*(1), E39–E40.

Volberg, R., Gupta, R., Griffiths, M., Olason, D., & Delfabbro, P. (2010). An international perspective on youth gambling prevalence studies. *International Journal of Adolescent Medicine and Health, 22*(1), 3–38.

Volbrecht, M. & Goldsmith, H. (2010). Early temperamental and family predictors of shyness and anxiety. *Developmental Psychology, 46*, 1192–1205.

Volpe, R. (2013). Child Abuse. Canadian Encyclopedia. Retrieved from http://www.thecanadianencyclopedia.ca/en/article/child-abuse/.

Von Beveren, T. T. (1999). *Prenatal development and the newborn*. Unpublished manuscript, University of Texas at Dallas, Richardson.

von Bonsdorff, M. B., et al. (2011). Work ability in midlife as a predictor of mortality and disability in later life: A 28-year prospective follow-up study. *Canadian Medical Association Journal, 183*, E235–E242.

von Bonsdorff, M. B., et al. (2012). Work ability as a determinant of old age disability severity: Evidence from the 28-year Finnish longitudinal study on municipal employees. *Aging: Clinical and Experimental Research, 24*, 354–360.

von Tilburg, T. (2009). Social integration/isolation, later life. In D. Carr (Ed.), *Encyclopedia of the life course and human development*. Boston: Gale Cengage.

Vonderheid, S., Kishi, R., Norr, K. & Klima, C. (2011). Group prenatal care and doula care for pregnant women. In A. Handler, J. Kennelly, & N. Peacock (Rds.). *Reducing racial/ethnic disparities in reproductive and perinatal outcomes: The evidence from population-based interventions* (pp. 369–400). New York, NY: Springer.

Vong, K-I. (2012). Play—A multimodal manifestation in kindergarten education in China. *Early Years: An International Journal of Research and Development, 32*(1), 35–48.

Voorpostel, M., & Blieszner, R. (2008). Intergenerational solidarity and support between adult siblings. *Journal of Marriage and the Family, 70*, 157–167.

Voss, C., Sandercock, G., Wharf Higgins, J., Macdonald, H., Nettleforld, L., Naylor, P. & McKay, H. (2014). A cross-cultural; comparison of body composition, physical fitness and physical activity between regional samples of Canadian and English children and adolescents. *Canadian Journal of Public Health, 105*(4), 245–250.

Voss, M. W., Vivar, C., Kramer, A. F., & van Praag, H. (2013). Bridging animal and human models of exercise-induced brain plasticity. *Trends in Cognitive Science, 17*, 525–544.

Votruba-Drzal, E., Coley, R. L., & Chase-Lansdale, P. L. (2004). Child care and low-income children's development: Direct and moderated effects. *Child Development, 75*, 296–312.

Vouloumanos, A., & Werker, J. F. (2004). Tuned to the signal: The privileged status of speech for young infants. *Developmental Science, 7*, 270–276.

Vreeman, R. C., & Carroll, A. E. (2007). A systematic review of school-based interventions to prevent bullying. *Archives of Pediatric and Adolescent Medicine, 161*, 78–88.

Vurpillot, E. (1968). The development of scanning strategies and their relation to visual differentiation. *Journal of Experimental Child Psychology, 6*.

Vygotsky, L. S. (1962). *Thought and language*. Cambridge, MA: MIT Press.

W

Wachs, T. D. (1994). Fit, context and the transition between temperament and personality. In C. Halverson, G. Kohnstamm, & R. Martin (Eds.), *The developing structure of personality from infancy to adulthood*. Hillsdale, NJ: Erlbaum.

Wachs, T. D. (2000). *Necessary but not sufficient*. Washington, DC: American Psychological Association.

Wade, C., Tavris, C., Saucier, D. M., & Elias, L. J. (2007). *Psychology* (2nd Canadian ed.). Toronto: Prentice Hall.

Wagner, L., & Hoff, E. (2013). Language development. In I. B. Weiner et al. (Eds.), Handbook of psychology (2nd ed.). New York: Wiley.

Waite, L. (2005, June). *The case for marriage*. Paper presented at the 9th annual Smart Marriages conference, Dallas.

Waite, L. (2009). Marriage. In D. Carr (Ed) *Encyclopedia of the life course and human development*. Boston, MA: Gale Cengage.

Waite, L. J., Das, A., & Laumann, E. O. (2009). Sexual activity, later life. In D. Carr (Ed.), *Encyclopedia of the life course and human development*. Boston: Gale Cengage.

Waite, L. J., Laumann, E. O., Das, A., & Schumm, L. P. (2009). Sexuality: Measures of partnerships, practices, attitudes, and problems in the National Social Life, Health, and Aging Project. *The Journals of Gerontology: Psychological Sciences and Social Sciences, 64B* (Suppl. 1), S56–S66.

Wakai, K., Marugame, T., Kuriyama, S., Sobue, T., Tamakoshi, A., Satoh, H., et al. (2007). Decrease in risk of lung cancer death in Japanese men after smoking cessation by age at quitting: Pooled analysis of three large-scale cohort studies. *Cancer Science, 98*, 584–589.

Waldinger, R. J., Vaillant, G. E., & Orav, E. J. (2007). Childhood sibling relationships as a predictor of major depression in adulthood: A 30-year prospective study. *American Journal of Psychiatry, 164*, 949–954.

Waldron, J., & Dieser, R. (2010). Perspectives of fitness and health in college men and women. *Journal of College Student Development, 51*, 65–78.

Walker, L. J. (2004). Progress and prospects in the psychology of moral development. *Merrill-Palmer Quarterly, 50*, 546–557.

Walker, L. J. (2006). Gender and morality. In M. Killen & J. G. Smetana (Eds.), *Handbook of moral development.* Mahwah, NJ: Erlbaum.

Walker, L. J., & Frimer, J. A. (2009b). Moral personality exemplified. In D. Narvaez & D. K. Lapsley (Eds.), *Moral personality, identity and character: An interdisciplinary future.* New York: Cambridge University Press.

Walker, L. J., Frimer, J. A., & Dunlop, W. L. (2010). Varieties of moral personality: Beyond the banality of heroism. *Journal of Personality, 78*(3), 907–942.

Walker, P., Bremner, G., Mason, U., Spring, J., Mattock, K., Slater, A. & Johnson, S. (2010). Preverbal infants' sensitivity to synaesthetic cross-modality correspondences. *Psychological Science. 21*(1), 21–25.

Wallace-Bell, M. (2003). The effects of passive smoking on adult and child health. *Professional Nurse, 19*, 217–219.

Wallenborg, K., et al. (2009). Red wine triggers cell death and thiroredoxin reductase inhibition: Effects beyond resveratrol and SIRT 1. *Experimental Cell Research, 315,* 1360–1371.

Walls, M., Hautala, D., & Hurley, J. (2014). "Rebuilding our community": Hearing silenced voices on Aboriginal youth suicide. *Transcultural Psychiatry, 51*(1), 47–72.

Walsh, H. C. (2008). Caring for bereaved people 2: Nursing management. *Nursing Times, 104*, 32–33.

Walsh, L. V. (2006). Beliefs and rituals in traditional birth attendant practice in Guatemala. *Journal of Transcultural Nursing, 17*, 148–154.

Walter, T. (2005). Three ways to arrange a funeral: Mortuary variation in the modern West. *Mortality, 10*(3), 173–192.

Walters, M. W., Boggs, K. M., Ludington-Hoe, S., & Price, K. M. (2007). Kangaroo care at birth for full term infants: A pilot study. *MCN, The American Journal of Maternal Child Nursing, 32*, 375–381.

Wan, M. & Wong, R. (2014) Benefits of Exercise in the Elderly. *CGS Journal of CME 4*(1), 5. Retrieved from http://www.canadiangeriatrics.ca/default/index.cfm/journals/canadian-geriatrics-society-journal-of-cme/cme-journal-vol-4-issue-1-2014/benefits-of-exercise-in-the-elderly/.

Wandell, P. E., Carlsson, A. C., & Theobald, H. (2009). The association between BMI value and long-term mortality. *International Journal of Obesity, 33*, 577–582.

Wang, B., & Jin, K. (2014, in press). Current perspectives on the link between neuroinflammation and neurogenesis. *Metabolic Brain Disease*.

Wang, B., et al. (2014). The impact of youth, family, peer, and neighborhood risk factors on developmental trajectories of risk involvement from early through middle adolescence. *Social Science Medicine, 106*, 43–52.

Wang, F., et al. (2014, in press). The effects of tai chi on depression, anxiety, and psychological well-being: A systematic review and meta-analysis. *International Journal of Behavioral Medicine*.

Wang, S., Baillargeon, R., & Brueckner, L. (2004). Young infants' reasoning about hidden objects: Evidence from violation-of-expectation tasks with test trials only. *Cognition, 93*, 167–198.

Ward, E. V., Berry, C. J., & Shanks, D. R. (2013). Age effects on explicit and implicit memory. *Frontiers in Psychology, 4*, 639.

Ward, L. M., & Friedman, K. (2006). Using TV as a guide: Associations between television viewing and adolescents' sexual attitudes and behavior. *Journal of Research on Adolescence, 16*, 133–156.

Ward-Griffin, C., Oudshoorn, A., Clark, K., & Bol, N. (2007). Mother-adult daughter relationship within dementia care: A critical analysis. *Journal of Family Nursing, 13*, 13–32.

Wardlaw, G. M., & Hampl, J. (2007). *Perspectives in nutrition* (7th ed.). New York: McGraw-Hill.

Wardlaw, G. M., & Smith, A. M. (2009). *Contemporary nutrition* (7th ed.). New York: McGraw-Hill.

Ward-Ritacco, C. L., et al. (2014, in press). Adiposity, physical activity, and muscle quality are independently related to physical function performance in middle-aged postmenopausal women. Menopause.

Waring, J. D., Addis, D. R., & Kensinger, E. A. (2013). Effects of aging on neural connectivity underlying selective memory for emotional scenes. *Neurobiology of Aging, 34*(2), 451–467.

Wark, G. R., & Krebs, D. L. (2000). The construction of moral dilemmas in everyday life. *Journal of Moral Education, 29*, 5–21.

Warr, P. (2004). Work, well-being, and mental health. In J. Baring, E. K. Kelloway, & M. R. Frone (Eds.), *Handbook of work stress.* Thousand Oaks, CA: Sage.

Warrier, V., Baron-Cohen, S., & Chakrabarti, B. (2014, in press). Genetic variations in GABRB3 is associated with Asperger syndrome and multiple endophenotypes relevant to autism. *Molecular Autism.*

Warshawski, T. (2010). Overweight and obesity in Canadian youth. *National Post.* Retrieved from http://www.nationalpost.com.

Waters, E., & Beauchaine, T. P. (2003). Are there really patterns of attachment? Comment on Fraley and Spieker (2003). *Developmental Psychology, 39*, 417–422.

Watkins, N., Larson, R., & Sullivan, P. (2008). Learning to bridge difference: Community youth programs as contexts for developing multicultural competencies. *American Behavioral Scientist, 51*, 380–402.

Watson, D. L., & Tharp, R. G. (2007). *Self-directed behavior* (9th ed.). Belmont, CA: Wadsworth.

Watson, G. L., Arcona, A. P., Antonuccio, D. O., & Healy, D. (2014). Shooting the messenger: The case of ADHD. *Journal of Contemporary Psychotherapy, 44*, 43–52.

Watson, J. B. (1928). *Psychological care of infant and child.* New York: W. W. Norton.

Way, N., Santos, C., Niwa, E. Y., & Kim-Gervy, C. (2008). To be or not to be: An exploration of ethnic identity development in context. In M. Asmitia, M. Syed, & K. Radmacher (Eds.), *The intersections of personal and social identities. New Directions for Child and Adolescent Development, 120*, 61–79.

Webb, S., Jones, E., Kelly, J. & Dawson, G. (2014). The motivation for very early intervention for infants at high risk for autism spectrum disorders. *International Journal of Speech-Language-Pathology, 16*(1), 36–42.

WebMD. (2016). Parents, Kids & Discipline. WebMD. Retrieved from http://www.webmd.com/parenting/guide/discipline-tactics

Webster, J. D., Westerhof, G. J., & Bohlmeijer, E. T. (2014). Wisdom and mental health across the lifespan. *Journals of Gerontology B: Psychological Sciences and Social Sciences, 69*, 209–218.

Wei, Y., et al. (2014, in press). *Paternally induced transgenerational inheritance of susceptibility to diabetes in mammals.* Proceedings of the National Academy of Sciences U.S.A.

Weinberg, A. E., et al. (2013). Diabetes severity, metabolic syndrome, and the risk of erectile dysfunction. *Journal of Sexual Medicine, 10*(12), 3102–3109.

Weinfield, N. S., Sroufe, L. A., Egeland, B., & Carlson, E. (2009). Individual differences in infant-caregiver attachment: Conceptual and empirical aspects of security. In J. Cassidy & P. R. Shaver

(Eds.), *Handbook of attachment* (2nd ed.). New York: Guilford.

Weis, K., & Sternberg, R. J. (2008). The nature of love. In S. F. Davis & W. Buskist (Eds.), *21st century psychology: A reference handbook* (Vol. 2). Thousand Oaks, CA: Sage.

Weiss, R. (1973). *Loneliness: The experience of emotional and social isolation.* Cambridge, MA: MIT Press.

Weiss, S. K., & Corkum, P. (2012). Pediatric behavioural insomnia–"good night, sleep tight" for child and parent. Insomnia rounds, offered by the Canadian Sleep Society for the Continuing Education of Physician Colleagues. Retrieved from http://css-scs.ca/downloadfolder/150-005_Eng.pdf.

Weissman, P., & Hendrick, J. (2014). The whole child: Developmental education for the early years (10th ed.). Upper Saddle River, NJ: Pearson.

Weisz, A. N., & Black, B. M. (2002). Gender and moral reasoning: African American youth respond to dating dilemmas. *Journal of Human Behavior in the Social Environment, 5*, 35–52.

Wekerle, C., & Tanaka, M. (2010). Adolescent dating violence research and violence prevention: An opportunity to support health outcomes. *Journal of Aggression, Maltreatment & Trauma, 19*(6), 681–698.

Wekerle, C., Leung, E., Wall, A. M., Macmillan, H., Boyle, M., Trocme, N., et al. (2009). The contribution of childhood emotional abuse to teen dating violence among child protective services-involved youth. *Child Abuse and Neglect: The International Journal, 33*, 45–58.

Welch, A. A., & Hardcastle, A. C. (2014, in press). The effects of flavonoids on bone. *Current Osteoporosis Reports.*

Wellman, H. M. (2011). Developing a theory of mind. In U. Goswami (Ed.), *Wiley-Blackwell handbook of childhood cognitive development* (2nd ed.). New York: Wiley.

Wellman, H. M., Cross, D., & Watson, J. (2001). Meta-analysis of theory-of-mind development: The truth about false belief. *Child Development, 72*, 655–684.

Wellman, H. M., Lopez-Duran, S., Labounty, J., & Hamilton, B. (2008). Infant attention to intentional action predicts preschool theory of mind. *Developmental Psychology, 44*, 618–623.

Weltzin, T., Cornella-Carlson, T., Fitzpatrick, M., Kennington, B., Bean, P., & Jeffries, C. (2012). Treatment issues and outcomes for males with eating disorders. *Eating Disorders: The Journal of Treatment & Prevention, 20*, 444–459.

Wen, X., et al. (2014). In vivo monitoring of neural stem cells after transplantation in acute cerebral infarction with dual-modal MR imaging and optical imaging. *Biomaterials, 35*, 4627–4635.

Weng, X., Odouli, R., & Li, D. K. (2008). Maternal caffeine consumption during pregnancy and the risk of miscarriage: A prospective cohort study. *American Journal of Obstetrics and Gynecology, 198*(3), 279.

Wentzel, K. R. (2013). School adjustment. In I. B. Weiner et al. (Eds.), *Handbook of psychology* (2nd ed., Vol. 7). New York: Oxford University Press.

Wentzel, K. R., Barry, C. M., & Caldwell, K. A. (2004). Friendships in middle schools: Influences on motivation and school adjustment. *Journal of Educational Psychology, 96*, 195–203.

Werker, J. & Hensch, T. (2015). Critical periods in speech perception: New Directions. *Annual Review of Psychology, 66*, 173–196.

Wermter, A. K., et al. (2010). From nature versus nurture, via nature and nurture, to gene x environment interaction in mental disorders. *European Journal of Child and Adolescent Psychiatry, 19*, 199–210.

West, K., Mathews, B., & Kerns, K. A. (2013). Mother-child attachment and cognitive performance in middle childhood: An examination of mediating mechanisms. **Early Childhood Research Quarterly, 28**, 259–270.

Westlake, C., Evangelista, L. S., Stromberg, A., Ter-Galstanyan, A., Vazirani, S., & Dracup, K. (2007). Evaluation of a web-based education and counseling pilot for older heart failure patients. *Progress in Cardiovascular Nursing, 22*, 20–26.

Weston, K. (2007). Exiles from kinship. In S. J. Ferguson (Ed.), *Shifting the center: Understanding contemporary families* (3rd ed.). New York: McGraw-Hill.

Weston, M. J. (2010). Magnetic resonance imaging in fetal medicine: A pictorial review of current and developing indications. *Postgraduate Medicine Journal, 86*, 42–51.

Wethington, E., Kessler, R. C., & Pixley, J. E. (2004). Turning points in adulthood. In O. G. Brim, C. D. Ryff, & R. C. Kessler (Eds.), *How healthy are we?* Chicago: University of Chicago Press.

Wetzel, I. (April 25, 2012) Bad news for magnesium supplement users. Retrieved from http://healthstudio.com/bad-news-for-magnesium-supplement-users/ HealthStudio.

Whaley, S., Sigman, M., Beckwith, L., Cohen, S., & Espinosa, M. (2002). Infant-caregiver interaction in Kenya and the United States: The importance of multiple caregivers and adequate comparison samples. *Journal of Cross-Cultural Psychology, 33*(3), 236–247.

Wheatley, R., Kelley, M., Peacock, N. & Delgado, J. (2008). Women's narrative on equality of prenatal care: a multicultural perspective. *Qualitative Health Research*, 18, 1586–1598.

Wheeler, B. (2015). Health promotion in the newborn and family. In M. Hockenberry & D. Wilson (Eds.), *Wong's nursing care of infants and children* (10th ed.). (pp. 243–293). St. Louis: Elsevier.

Wheeler, M. (2008). Braving the no-go zone: Canada's sub-replacement fertility rate. *Transition 38*(4), 3–8.

Whipple, N., Bernier, A., & Mageau, G. A. (2009). Attending to the exploration side of infant attachment: Contributions from self-determination theory. *Canadian Psychology, 50*(4), 219–229.

Whitbourne, S. (2013). Is Birth Order Destiny? Why you shouldn't let stereotypes dictate your fate. *Psychology Today*. Retrieved from https://www.psychologytoday.com/blog/fulfillment-any-age/201305/is-birth-order-destiny.

Whitbourne, S. K., Sneed, J. R., & Sayer, A. (2009). Psychosocial development from college through midlife: A 34-year sequential study. *Developmental Psychology, 45*, 1328–1340.

White, C. D., Hardy, J. R., Gilshenan, K. S., Charles, M. A., & Pinkerton, C. R. (2008). Randomized controlled trials of palliative care—A survey of the views of advanced cancer patients and their relatives. *European Journal of Cancer.*

White, E., Slane, J. D., Klump, K. L., Burt, S. A., & Pivarnik, J. (2014, in press). Sex differences in genetic and environmental influences on percent body fatness and physical activity. *Journal of Physical Activity and Health*.

White, J. W. (2001). Aggression and gender. In J. Worell (Ed.), *Encyclopedia of gender and women.* San Diego: Academic Press.

White, R., Wyn, J., & Albanese, P. (2011). *Youth and society: Exploring the social dynamics of youth experience* (Canadian ed). Don Mills: Oxford University Press.

Whitehead, K., Ainsworth, A., Wittig, M., & Gadino, B. (2009). Implications of ethnic identity exploration and ethnic identity affirmation and belonging for intergroup attitudes among adolescents. *Journal of Research on Adolescence, 19*, 123–135.

Whiteman, S. D., McHale, S. M., & Soli, A. (2011). Theoretical perspectives on sibling relationships. *Journal of Family Theory and Review, 3*, 124–139.

Whiting, P. (2007). Student mental health at Simon Fraser University. *Visions: BC's*

Mental Health and Addiction Journal, 4(3), 10–11.

Whitley, B. E. (2002). *Principles of research in behavioral science* (2nd ed.). New York: McGraw-Hill.

Whitton, S., Stanley, S., Markman, H., & Johnson, C. (2013). Attitudes toward divorce, commitment, and divorce proneness in first marriages and remarriages. *Journal of Marriage and Family, 75*, 276–287.

WHO. (2014). *Global status report on alcohol and health 2014*. Retrieved from http://www.who.int.

WHO. (2016). *Global health observatory: HIV/AIDS*. Retrieved from http://www.who.int.

Wiener, J., & Siegel, L. (2010). A Canadian perspective on learning disabilities. *Journal of Learning Disabilities*. Retrieved from http://ldx.sagepub.com/content/25/6/340

Wiersman, W., & Jurs, S. G. (2009). *Research methods in education* (9th ed.). Upper Saddle River, NJ: Prentice Hall.

Wigle, D. T., Arbuckle, T. E., Turner, M. C., Berube, A., Yang, Q., Liu, S. (2008). Epidemiologic evidence of relationships between reproductive and child health outcomes and environmental chemical contaminants. *Journal of Toxicology and Environmental Health, Part B, 11*, 373–517.

Wijngaards-de Meij, L., Stroebe, M., Schut, H., Stroebe, W., van den Bout, J., van der Heijden, P. G., et al. (2008). Parents grieving the loss of their child: Interdependence in coping. *British Journal of Clinical Psychology, 47*, 31–42.

Wilder-Smith, A., Mustafa, F. B., Earnest, A., Gen, L., & Macary, P. A. (2013). Impact of partial sleep deprivation on immune markers. *Sleep Medicine, 14*(10), 1031–1034.

Wilhelmus, M. M., de Jager, M., Bakker, E. N., & Drukarch, B. (2014, in press). Tissue transglutaminase in Alzheimer's disease: Involvement in pathogenesis and its potential as a therapeutic target. *Journal of Alzheimer's Disease*.

Willey, J., Sherwood, L., & Woolverton, C. (2014). *Prescott's microbiology* (9th ed.). New York: McGraw-Hill.

Williams, A., Franche, R. L., Ibrahim, S., Mustard, C. A., & Layton, F. R. (2006). Examining the relationhip between work-family spillover and sleep quality. *Journal of Occupational Health Psychology, 1*, 27–37.

Williams, B., Sawyer, S., & Wahlstrom, C. (2012). *Marriages, families, and intimate relationships* (2nd ed.). Upper Saddle River, NJ: Pearson.

Williams, D. R., & Sternthal, M. J. (2007). Spirituality, religion, and health: Evidence and research directions. *Medical Journal of Australia, 186* (Suppl.), S47–S50.

Williams, J. H., & Ross, L. (2007). Consequences of prenatal toxin exposure for mental health in children and adolescents: A systematic review. *European Child and Adolescent Psychiatry, 16*, 243–253.

Williams, L., et al. (2010). Early temperament, propensity for risk-taking and adolescence substance-related problems. *Addictive Behaviors, 35*, 1148–1151.

Williams, M. H. (2005). *Nutrition for health, fitness, and sport* (7th ed.). New York: McGraw-Hill.

Williams, P., & Fletcher, S. (2010). Health effects of prenatal radiation exposure. *American Family Physician, 82*(5), 488–493.

Willis, C. (2002). The grieving process in children: Strategies for understanding, educating, and reconciling children's perceptions of death. *Early Childhood Education Journal, 29*, 221–226.

Willis, S. L., & Caskie, G. (2013). Reasoning training in the ACTIVE study: Who benefits. *Journal of Aging and Health, 25*, 8.

Willis, S. L., & Schaie, K. W. (2006). A co-constructionist view of the third age: The case of cognition. *Annual Review of Gerontology and Geriatrics, 26*, 131–152.

Willis, S. L., Temstedt, S. L., Marsiske, M., Ball, K., Elias, J., Koepke, K. M., et al. for the ACTIVE Study Group. (2006). Long-term effects of cognitive training on everyday functional outcomes in older adults. *Journal of the American Medical Association, 296*, 2805–2814.

Willms, J. D. (2002). Implications of the findings for social policy renewal. In D. Willms (Ed.), *Vulnerable children* (pp. 359–377). Edmonton: The University of Alberta Press.

Willoughby, B., Carrol, J., & Busby, D. (2011). The different effects of "living together": Determining and comparing types of cohabiting couples. *Journal of Social and Personal Relationships, 23*, 397–419.

Willoughby, K. A., Desrocher, M., Levine, B., & Rovet, J. F. (2012). Episodic and semantic autobiographical memory and everyday memory during late childhood and early adolescence. *Frontiers in Psychology, 3*, 53.

Willoughby, T., Good, M., Adachi, P., Hamza, C., & Tavernier, R. (2013). Examining the link between adolescent brain development and risk taking from a social-developmental perspective. *Brain and Cognition, 83*, 315–323.

Wilson, A. E., Shuey, K. M., & Elder, G. H. (2003). Ambivalence in relationships of adult children to aging parents and in-laws. *Journal of Marriage and the Family, 65*, 1055–1072.

Wilson, B., & Smallwood, S. (2008). The proportion of marriages ending in divorce. *Population Trends, 131*, 28–36.

Wilson, D., & Wilson, K. (2015). Radiation. In In M. Hockenberry & D. Wilson (Eds.) *Wong's nursing care of infants and children* (10th ed.). (pp. 294–335). St. Louis: Elsevier.

Wilson, D., Bruening, M. & Lowdermilk, D. (2015). Health problems in the adolescence. In M. Hockenberry & D. Wilson (Eds.) *Wong's nursing care of infants and children* (10th ed.). (pp. 687–760). St. Louis: Elsevier.

Wilson, J. (2016) Spanking children could become illegal in Canada. *Global News*. Retrieved from http://globalnews.ca/news/2444188/spanking-children-could-soon-be-illegal-in-canada/.

Wilson, K. G., et al. (2007). Desire for euthanasia or physician-assisted suicide in palliative cancer care. *Health Psychology, 26*, 314–323.

Wilson, R. D. (2007). Principles of human teratology: Drug, chemical, and infectious exposure. *Journal of Obstetrics and Gynecology of Canada, 199*, 911–917.

Wilson, R. S., et al. (2009). Educational attainment and cognitive decline in old age. *Neurology, 72*, 460–465.

Wilson, R. S., et al. (2012). Terminal dedifferentiation of cognitive abilities. *Neurology, 78*, 1116–1122.

Wilson, R. S., Mendes de Leon, C. F., Bienas, J. L., Evans, D. A., & Bennett, D. A. (2004). Personality and mortality in old age. *Journal of Gerontology Psychological Sciences and Social Sciences, 59*, P110–P116.

Windsor, T. D., & Butterworth, P. (2010). Supportive, aversive, ambivalent, and indifferent partner evaluations in midlife and young-old adulthood. *Journals of Gerontology B: Psychological Sciences and Social Sciences, 65B*, 287–295.

Winett, R. A., et al. (2014). Developing a new treatment paradigm for disease prevention and healthy aging. *Translational Behavioral Medicine, 4*, 117–123.

Wing, R., Tate, D. F., Gorin, A. A., Raynor, H. A., Fava, J. L., & Machan, J. (2007). "STOP Regain": Are there negative effects of daily weighing? *Journal of Consulting and Clinical Psychology, 75*, 652–656.

Winner, E. (1996). *Gifted children: Myths and realities*. New York: Basic Books.

Winner, E. (2006). Development in the arts. In W. Damon & R. Lerner (Eds.), *Handbook of child psychology* (6th ed.). New York: Wiley.

Winner, E. (2009). Toward broadening our understanding of giftedness: The spatial domain. In F. D. Horowitz, R. F. Subotnik, & D. J. Matthews (Eds.), *The development of giftedness and talent across the life span.* Washington, DC: American Psychological Association.

Winner, E. (2014). Child prodigies and adult genius: A weak link. In D. K. Simonton (Ed.), *Wiley-Blackwell handbook of genius.* New York: Wiley.

Winning, J., Claus, R., Huse, K. & Bauer, M. (2006). Molecular biology on the ICU. From understanding to treating sepsis. *Minerva Anestesiologica, 72*(5), 255–267.

Winnipeg Regional Health Authority. (nd). Advance care planning workbook. Retrieved from http://www.wrha.mb/ca/acp/files/Workbook.pdf

Winsler, A., Carlton, M. P., & Barry, M. J. (2000). Age-related changes in preschool children's systematic use of private speech in a natural setting. *Journal of Child Language, 27*, 665–687.

Wirth, M., et al. (2014, in press). Neuroprotective pathways: Lifestyle activity, brain pathology, and cognition in cognitively normal older adults. *Neurobiology of Aging.*

Wiseman, H., Mayseless, O., & Sharabany, R. (2006). Why are they lonely? Perceived quality of early relationships with parents, attachment, personality predispositions and loneliness in first year university students. *Personality and Individual Differences, 40*, 237–248.

Wishart, P. M. (2006). Letting go of preconceptions: A novel approach to creating memorial services. *Health Care for Women International, 27*(5), 513–529.

Wisse, L. E., et al. (2014, in press). Hippocampal subfield volumes at 7T in early Alzheimer's disease and normal aging. *Neurobiology of Aging.*

Wister, A. & Speechley, M. (2015). Inherent tensions between population aging and health care systems: What might the Canadian health care system look like in twenty years. *Population Ageing, 8*, 227–243.

Witte, A. V., Fobker, M., Gellner, R., Knecht, S., & Fioel, A. (2009). Caloric restriction improves memory in elderly humans. *Proceedings of the National Academy of Sciences U.S.A., 106*, 1255–1260.

Wivliet, M., et al. (2010). Peer group affiliation in children: The role of perceived popularity, likeability, and behavioral similarity in bullying. *Social Development, 19*, 285–303.

Wolfe, D., et al. (2009). A school-based program to prevent adolescent dating violence. *Archives of Pediatrics & Adolescent Medicine, 163*, 692–699.

Wolfinger, N. H. (2011). More evidence for trends in the intergenerational transmission of divorce: A completed cohort approach using data from the general social survey. *Demography, 48*, 581–592.

Wolinsky, F. D., Vander Weg, M. W., Howren, M. B., Jones, M. P., & Dotson, M. M. (2013). A randomized controlled trial of cognitive training using a visual speed of processing intervention in middle aged and older adults. *PLoS One,8*(5), e61624.

Wong, D. L. (2006). *Maternal child nursing and virtual clinical excursions: 3.0 package* (3rd ed.). St. Louis: Mosby.

Wong, D., Hockenberry, M., Wilson, D., Perry, S., & Lowdermilk, D. (2006). *Maternal child nursing care* (3rd ed). St. Louis: Mosby Elsevier.

Wong, S., Ordean, A., & Kahan, M. (2011). Substance use in pregnancy. *Journal of Obstetrics and Gynaecology Canada, 33*(4), 367–384.

Wood, M. D., Read, J. P., Mitchell, R. E., & Brand, N. H. (2004). Do parents still matter? Parent and peer influences on alcohol involvement among recent high school graduates. *Psychology of Addictive Behaviors, 18*, 19–30.

Woodgate, R. (2006). Living in the shadow of fear: Adolescents' lived experience of depression. *Journal of Advanced Nursing, 56*(3), 261–269.

Woodgate, R., Edwards, M., & Ripat, J. (2012). How families of children with complex care needs participate in everyday life. *Social Sciences & Medicine, 75*, 1912–1920.

Woodward, A. L., & Markman, E. M. (1998). Early word learning. In D. Kuhn & R. S. Siegler (Eds.), *Handbook of child psychology* (5th ed., Vol. 2). New York: Wiley.

Woodward, A., Markman, E., & Fitzsimmons, C. (1994). Rapid word learning in 13- and 18-month-olds. *Developmental Psychology, 30*, 553–556.

Woolhouse, H., McDonald, E. & Brown, S. (2014). Changes to sexual and intimate relationships in the postnatal period: women's experience with health professionals. *Australian Journal of Primary Health. 20*(3), 298–304.

World Health Organization (WHO). (2005). Alcohol use and sexual risk behaviour: A cross-cultural study in eight countries (WHO, Geneva). Retrieved from http://www.who.int/substance_abuse/publications/alcohol_sexual_risk_crosscultural.pdf

World Health Organization (WHO). (2008a). What are the key health indicators for children? Retrieved from http://www.who.int/features/qa/13/en/print.html

World Health Organization (WHO). (2008b). Preventable injuries kill 2000 children every day. Retrieved from http://www.who.int/mediacentre/news/release/2008/pr46/en/index.html

World Health Organization (WHO). (2009). *World health statistics, 2009.* Geneva, Switzerland: Author.

World Health Organization (WHO). (2010). *Global strategy to reduce the harmful use of alcohol.* Retrieved from http://www.who.int/substance_abuse

World Health Organization (WHO). (2012). *Preventing early unwanted pregnancy & pregnancy-related mortality & morbidity in adolescents.* Retrieved from http://www.gfmer.ch/SRH-Course-2012/adolescent-health/Adolescent-pregnancy-WHO-2012

World Health Organization (WHO). (2014). Child maltreatment Fact Sheet. Retrieved from http://www.who.int/mediacentre/factsheets/fs150/en/.

World Health Organization (WHO). (2016a). Life expectancy increased by 5 years since 2000, but health inequities persist. Retrieved from http://www.who.int/mediacentre/news/releases/2016/health-inequalities-persist/en/.

World Health Organization (WHO). (2016b). Child Maltreatment. Retrieved from http://www.who.int/topics/child_abuse/en/.

World Health Organization (WHO). (2016c). Childhood overweight and obesity. Retrieved from http://www.who.int/dietphysicalactivity/childhood/en/

World Health Organization (WHO). (2016d). Global Health Observatory data - Number of deaths due to HIV/AIDS. Retrieved from http://www.who.int/gho/hiv/epidemic_status/deaths_text/en/

Wortman, C. B., & Boerner, K. (2007). Reactions to death of a loved one: Beyond the myths of coping with loss. In H. S. Friedman & R. C. Silver (Eds.), *Foundations of health psychology.* New York: Oxford University Press.

Wright S. (n.d.). *The power of student driven learning.* TED.com. Retrieved from https://www.youtube.com/watch?v=3fMC-z7K0r4&feature=player_embedded#t=12

Wright, J. (2006, March 16). Boomers in the bedroom: Sexual attitudes and behaviours in the boomer generation. Ipsos Reid survey. Retrieved from http://www.ipsos-na-com

Wright, J., Briggs, S., & Behringer, J. (2005). Attachment and the body in suicidal adolescents: A pilot study. *Clinical Child Psychology and Psychiatry, 10*(4), 477–491.

Wright, L., & Leahey, M. (2013). *Nurses and families: A guide to family assessment*

and intervention (6th ed.). Philadelphia: Davis.

Wright, S. (2013). Start with why: the power of student driven learning. Wright's Room. Retrieved from http://shelleywright.wordpress.com

Wu, L. T., Pilowsky, D. J., Schlenger, W. E., & Hasin, D. (2007). Alcohol use disorders and the use of treatment services among college-age young adults. *Psychiatric Services, 58*, 192–200.

Wu, T., Gao, X., Chen, M., & van Dam, R. (2009). Long-term effectiveness of diet-plus-exercise interventions vs. diet-only interventions for weight loss: A meta-analysis. *Obesity Review, 10*, 313–323.

Wu, Y. H., Cheng, M. L., Ho, H. Y., Chiu, D. T., & Wang, T. C. (2009). Telomerase prevents accelerated senescence in glucose-6-phosphate dehydrogenase (G6PD)-deficient human fibroblasts. *Journal of Biomedical Science, 16*, 18.

Wyse, R. D., Dunbar, G. L., & Rossignol, J. (2014). Use of genetically modified mesenchymal stem cells to treat neurodegenerative diseases. *International Journal of Molecular Sciences, 15*, 1719–1745.

X

Xiao, O., et al. (2013). A large prospective investigation of sleep duration, weight change, and obesity in the NIH-AARP Diet and Health Study cohort. *American Journal of Epidemiology, 178*, 1600–1610.

Xu, F., & Baker, A. (2005). Object individuation in 10-month-old infants using a simplified manual search method. *Journal of Cognition and Development, 6*(3), 307–323.

Xu, F., & Garcia, V. (2008), Intuitive statistics by 8-month-olds infants. *PNAS, 105*(3), 5012–5015.

Xu, Q., Parks, C. G., Deroo, L. A., Cawthon, R. M., Sandler, D. P., & Chen, H. (2009). Multivitamin use and telomere length in women. *American Journal of Clinical Nutrition, 89*, 1857–1863.

Xu, X., Hudspeth, C. D., & Bartkowski, J. P. (2006). The role of cohabitation in remarriage. *Journal of Marriage and the Family, 68*, 261–274.

Y

Yaffe, K., Barnes, D., Nevitt, M., Lui, L., & Covinsky, K. (2001). A prospective study of physical activity and cognitive decline in elderly women. *Archives of Internal Medicine, 161*, 1703–1708.

Yan, L., et al. (2013). Calorie restriction can reverse, as well as prevent, aging cardiomyopathy. *Age, 35*, 2177–2182.

Yanchar, N. et al. (2012) Child and youth injury prevention: A public health approach. Canadian Paediatric Society. Retrieved from http://www.cps.ca/documents/position/child-and-youth-injury-prevention.

Yang, Q., Wen, S. W., Leader, A., Chen, X. K., Lipson, J. & Walker, M. (2007). Paternal age and birth defects: How strong is the association. *Human Reproduction, 22*, 696–701.

Yang, Y. (2008). Social inequalities in happiness in the United States, 1972–2004: An age-period-cohort analysis. *American Sociological Review, 73*, 204–226.

Yang, Y., & Lee, L. C. (2010). Dynamics and heterogeneity in the process of human frailty and aging: Evidence from the U.S. older adult population. *Journals of Gerontology B: Psychological Sciences and Social Sciences, 65B*, 246–255.

Yanof, J. A. (2013). Play technique in psychodynamic psychotherapy. *Child and Adolescent Psychiatric Clinics of North America, 22*, 261–282.

Yassine, H. N., Marchetti, C. M., Krishna, R. K., Vrobel, T. R., Gonzalez, F., & Kirwin, J. P. (2009). Effects of exercise and caloric restriction on insulin resistance and cardiometabolic risk factors in older obese adults—A randomized trial. *Journals of Gerontology A: Biological Sciences and Medical Sciences, 64*, 90–95.

Yates, D. (2014). Myelination: Switching modes of myelination. *Nature Reviews Neuroscience, 15*, 66–67.

Yates, L. B., Djuousse, L., Kurth, T., Buring, J. E., & Gaziano, J. M. (2008). Exceptional longevity in men: Modifiable factors associated with survival and function to age 90 years. *Archives of Internal Medicine, 168*, 284–290.

Yen, S., & Martin, S. (2013). Contraception for adolescents. *Pediatric Annals, 42*(2), 21–25.

Yezierski, R. P. (2012). The effects of age on pain sensitivity: Preclinical studies. *Pain Medicine, 13*(2, Suppl.), S27–S36.

Yokoyama, A., et al. (2013). Trends in gastrectomy and ADH1B and ALDH2 genotypes in Japanese alcoholic men and their gene-gastrectomy, gene-gene, and gene-age interactions. *Alcohol and Alcoholism, 48*, 146–152.

Yoo, H. J., Choi, K. M., Ryu, O. H., Suh, S. I., Kim, N. H., Baik, S. H., et al. (2006). Delayed puberty due to pituitary stalk dysgenesis and ectopic neurophyophysis. *Korean Journal of Internal Medicine, 21*, 68–72.

Yoo, H., Feng, X., & Day, R. (2013). Adolescents' empathy and prosocial behavior in the family context: A longitudinal study. *Journal of Youth and Adolescence*.

You, J., Fowler, R. & Heyland, D. Just ask: discussing the goals of care with patients in hospitals with serious illness. *Canadian Medical Association Journal, 186*(6), 425–432.

Young, G. (2011). *Development and causality.* Springer; New York.

Young, K. T. (1990). American conceptions of infant development from 1955 to 1984: What the experts are telling parents. *Child Development, 61*, 17–28.

Youngblade, L, Theokas, C., Schulenberg, J., Curry, L., Huang, I., & Novak, M. (2007). Risk and promotive factors in families, schools, and communities: A contextual model of positive youth development in adolescence. *Pediatrics, 119*(1), S47–S53.

Youniss, J., McLellan, J. A., & Yates, M. (1999). Religion, community service, and identity in American youth. *Journal of Adolescence, 22*, 243–253.

Yu, R., Branje, S., Keijsers, L., Koot, H., & Meeus, W. (2013). Pals, problems, and personality: The moderating role of personality in the longitudinal association between adolescents' and best friends' delinquency. *Journal of Personality, 81*, 499–509.

Yuan, P., & Raz, N. (2014). Prefrontal cortex and executive functions in healthy adults: A meta-analysis of structural neuroimaging studies. *Neuroscience and Biobehavioral Reviews, 42C*, 180–192.

Yun, Y.H., et al. (2011). Attitudes of cancer patients, family caregivers, oncologists and members of the general public towards critical interventions at the end of life of terminally ill patients. *Canadian Medical Association Journal, 183*(10), E673–E679.

Z

Zalc, B. (2006). The acquisition of myelin: A success story. *Novartis Foundation Symposium, 276*, 15–21.

Zalli, A., et al. (2014, in press). Shorter telomeres with high telomerase activity are associated with raised allostatic load and impoverished psychosocial resources. Proceedings of the National Academy of Sciences U.S.A.

Zeifman, D., & Hazan, C. (2009). Pair bonds as attachments: Reevaluating the evidence. In J. Cassidy & P. R. Shaver (Eds.), *Handbook of attachment* (2nd ed.). New York: Guilford.

Zelazo, P. D., & Müller, U. (2004). Executive function in typical and atypical development. In U. Goswami (Ed.), *Blackwell handbook of cognitive development.* Malden, MA: Blackwell.

Zemach, I., Chang, S. & Teller, D. (2007). Infant color vision: Prediction of infants spontaneous color preferences. *Vision Research, 47,* 1368–1381.

Zeng, L., Yu, X., Yu, T., Xiao, J., & Huang, Y. (2015). Interventions for smoking cessation in people with lung cancer (Review). *Cochrane Database of Systematic Reviews, Issue 12*. Retrieved from http://www.cochranelibrary.com

Zerwekh, J. (2006). *Nursing care at the end of life.* Philadelphia: Davis.

Zeskind, P. S. (2009). Impact of the cry of the infant at risk on psychosocial development. In R. E. Tremblay, R. deV Peters, M. Boivan, & R. G. Barr (Eds.), *Encyclopedia on Early Childhood Development.* Montreal: Center of Excellence for Early Childhood Development.

Zeskind, P. S., Klein, L., & Marshall, T. R. (1992). Adults perceptions of experimental modifications of durations and expiratory sounds in infant crying. *Developmental Psychology, 28,* 1153–1162.

Zettel-Watson, L., & Rook, K. S. (2009). Friendship, later life. In D. Carr (Ed.), *Encyclopedia of the life course and human development.* Boston: Gale Cengage.

Zhang, L., Zhang, X. H., Liang, M. Y., & Ren, M. H. (2010). Prenatal cytogenetic diagnosis study of 2782 cases of high-risk pregnant women. *China Medicine (English), 123,* 423–430.

Zhang, L-F., & Sternberg, R. J. (2011). Learning in a cross-cultural perspective. In T. Husen & T. N. Postlewaite (Eds.), *International encyclopedia of education* (3rd ed.). New York: Elsevier.

Zhang, Y. X., Zhang, Z. C., & Xie, L. (2014, in press). Distribution curve of waist-to-height ratio and its association with blood pressure among children and adolescents: Study in a large population in an eastern coastal province, China. *European Journal of Pediatrics.*

Zhao, H., Seibert, S. E., & Lumpkin, G. T. (2010). The relationship of personality to entrepreneurial intentions and performance: A meta-analytic review. *Journal of Management, 36,* 381–404.

Zhao, J., et al. (2014). Association of plasma glucose, insulin, and cardiovascular risk factors in overweight and obese children. *Saudi Medical Journal, 35,* 132–137.

Zhao, M., Kong, L., & Qu, H. (2014, in press). A systems biology approach to identify intelligence quotient score-related genomic regions and pathways relevant to potential therapeutic targets. *Scientific Reports.*

Zhou, P., Su, Y. E., Crain, S., Gao, L., & Zhan, L. (2012). Children's use of phonological information in ambiguity resolution: A view from Mandarin Chinese. *Journal of Child Language, 39*(4), 687–730.

Zhu, D. C., Zacks, R. T., & Slade, J. M. (2010). Brain activation during interference resolution in young and older adults: An fMRI study. *Neuroimage, 50,* 810–817.

Ziegler-Hill, V. (2013). The current state of research concerning self-esteem. In V. Ziegler-Hill (Ed.), *Self-esteem.* New York: Psychology Press."

Zimmer-Gembeck, M. J., & Helfand, M. (2008). Ten years of longitudinal research on U. S. adolescent sexual behavior: Developmental correlates of sexual intercourse, and the importance of age, gender, and ethnic background. *Developmental Review, 28,* 153–224.

Ziso, B., & Larner, A. (2013). CODEX (Cognitive Disorders Examination) for the detection of dementia and mild cognitive impairment: Diagnostic utility. *Journal of Neurology, Neurosurgery, and Psychiatry, 84,* e2.

Zisook, S., & Kendler, K. S. (2007). Is bereavement-related depression different than non-bereavement-related depression? *Psychological Medicine, 19,* 1–31.

Zitouni, D. & Guinhouya, B. (2012). Maturity negates the gender-related differences in physical activity among youth: is this equally justified whatever the accelerometer cut0off point used? *Journal of Science and Medicine in Sport, 15,* 327–333.

Zittleman, K. (2006, April). *Being a girl and being a boy: The voices of middle schoolers.* Paper presented at the meeting of the American Educational Research Association, San Francisco.

Zozuls, K., Martin, C., England, D., Andrews, N., & Borders, A. (2012, April). "I don't want to talk to them because I don't know how to": The role of relationship efficacy in children's gender-related intergroup processes. Paper presented at the Gender Development Research conference, San Francisco.

Zuckoff, A., Shear, K., Frank, E., Daley, D. C., Seligman, K., & Silowash, R. (2006). Treating complicated grief and substance use disorders: A pilot study. *Journal of Substance Abuse and Treatment, 30,* 205–211.

Zuk, C. V., & Zuk, G. H. (2002). Origins of dreaming. *American Journal of Psychiatry, 159,* 495–496.

Zukerman, P. (2005). Top fifty countries with the largest atheist/agnostic populations. Retrieved from http://www.adherents.com/

Zunzunegui, M., Alvarado, B. E., Del Ser, T., & Vtero, A. (2003). Social networks, social integration, and social engagement determine cognitive decline in community-dwelling Spanish older adults. *Journals of Gerontology B: Psychological Sciences and Social Sciences, 58,* S93–S100.

Zwicker, J., Shin Won, Y., MacKay, M., Petrie-Thomas, J., Rogers, M., & Synnes, A. (2013). Perinatal and neonatal predictors of developmental coordination disorder in very low birthweight children. *Archives of Disease in Childhood, 98,* 118–122.

Name Index

A

Aaker, J., 672
Abar, B., 123
Abebe, F., 92
Abdou, C., 144
Abel, T., 518
Abeykoon, H., 526
Aboud, F.E., 361
Abougoush, M., 416
Abouguendia, M., 554
Abramov, A. Y., 599
Abrams, L., 528
Abruscato, J.A., 305, 320
Abyzov, A., 88
Acevedo, B., 489
Adamson, P., 322, 294
Addis, D. R., 617
Adkins, 246
Adler, A., 51, 53, 54*f*, 76, 342
Adolph, K.E., 162, 172, 173, 206
Adomako, P., 158
Aducci, C., 500
Afifi, T. O., 359, 360
Afifi, W., 486, 490
Agbakwu, 424
Agrali, 608
grillo, C., 496
Aguiar, C., 143
Ahern, E. C., 244
Ahlin, E., 419
Ahrons, C., 277
Ahtonen, M., 144
Ailshire, J. A., 515
Aina, O.E., 268, 269
Ainsworth, M., 197, 209, 210, 211, 220
Aisen, P.S., 604
Aizawa, K., 596
Ajdacic-Gross, V., 681
Ajrouch, 648, 652
Akhtar, N., 251
Akiyama, H., 642, 643, 681
Akpek, E. K., 590
Aksan, N., 267
Akyar, 608
Albanese, P., 372, 396
Albert, 400
Albury, K., 433
Aldoori, W., 117, 129
Alexander, K.W., 244
Alfermann, D., 615
Allain, P., 612
Allaire, J.C., 532
Allard, Y.E., 670
Allemand, M., 560, 634
Allen, J.P., 375, 418, 421
Allen, M., 319
Allen, M.C., 138
Alleyne, E., 59
Ali, M., 611
Allison, D.B., 151
Allwood, 306
Alm, B., 160
Almas, A., 194, 264
Almeida, D.M., 520, 553, 555, 583
Al-Safi, Z.A., 524
Al-Sahab, B., 121, 383, 384
Altimer, L., 153
Aly, M., 589
Al-Yagon, M., 418
Alzheimer, A., 85
Amabile, T.M., 303
Amador, C., 231
Amato, P.R., 277, 494, 495, 570
Ambert, A., 501
Ambert, A.M., 101, 435, 565
Ambrose, D., 315
Amoroso, A., 521
Amoroso, J., 217
Amos, H., 87, 89
Ancoli-Israel, S., 589
Andersen, 490
Andersen, S. L., 579, 581
Anderson, 645, 649
Anderson, G. J., 610
Anderson, H.C., 466
Anderson, J., 500
Anderson, K., 120
Anderson, P., 486
Andersson, D. K., 590
Andersson, U., 299
Angel, L., 587, 617
Angrilli, A., 154
Anguera, J. A., 616
Angus, R., 428
Anita, J., 500
Annweiler, 614
Ansado, J., 586
Anspaugh, D.J., 453
Anton, 598
Antonenko, D., 617
Antonishak, J., 421
Antonucci, T.C., 642, 643, 648, 652, 681
Apostoleris, N.H., 271
Applebaum, M., 452
Arai, B., 324
Arbeau, K. A., 283
Archacki, M. A., 262, 339
Archibald, M., 29
Arck, P.C., 130
Arens, A., 411
Argyri, 603
Argys, L., 493
Armer, M., 263
Arneric, 592
Arnett, J., 449
Arnett, J.J., 376, 445, 446
Arnold, A., 268
Arnsburg, K., 583
Aron, A., 33, 489
Aron, E.N., 33
Arpanantikul, M., 552
Arseth, A., 487
Arterberry, M.E., 169, 399
Arvidsson, A., 339
Asagwara, O., 662
Asbury, K., 107
Asendorph, J., 480
Asendorph, J.B., 199
Ash, J. A., 617
Asher, S.R., 361
Asian, Y., 526
Aslan, A., 299
Aslin, R.N., 168
Asscher, J., 663
Astington, J. W., 247, 248
Ata, R.N., 387
Atchley, R.C., 638
Atienza, M., 589
Atkinson, 230
Atleo, S., 192
Attems, J., 585
Aubin, S., 641
Aubry, T., 30
Auerswald, C., 30
Auger, D., 546
Augustine, S., 431
Autexier, C., 583
Averett, S., 493
Avila, J., 603
Avison, W.R., 277
Axelsson, B., 378
Ayduk, O., 21, 23, 395
Azagba, 630
Azmitia, M., 423

B

Baboscai, L., 172
Bacallao, M., 424
Bachman, J.G., 394
Bachschmid, M. M., 583
Backhaus, 472
Backman, L., 531, 587
Bacon, B., 277
Bacon, F., 598
Badawi, A., 599
Baddeley, A.D., 298, 299, 395, 531, 612
Badger, J. L., 605
Bae, J.Y., 124
Baehr, T.A., 638
Baer, J., 303
Baghurst, T., 447
Baglow, J.S., 668
Bahrick, L.E., 172
Bailes, C.N., 254
Bailey, D. M., 596
Bailey, H.N., 31
Bailey, H. R., 613, 615
Baillargeon, R., 176, 177
Bain, N., 375
Bajoghli, H., 488
Baker, 383
Baker, B., 566
Baker, J., 376
Baker, J. K., 264
Baker, M., 638
Bakermans-Kranenburg, M.J., 212, 484
Bakken, J., 420
Bakker, 630
Balarajah, S., 585
Ball, 351
Ball, J. W., 228
Ball, K., 593
Bally, J., 681
Balsano, A., 372
Baltes, P.B., 7, 8, 9, 10, 17, 22, 85, 107, 515, 581, 582, 609, 610, 613, 615, 632, 633
Banasik, J., 124, 375
Bandura, A., 61, 62–63, 74, 75*f*, 77, 85, 107, 186, 267, 270, 303, 341, 349, 541, 653
Band-Winterstein, 644
Banerjee, S., 517
Bangen, K. J., 613
Bangerter, 642
Banja, J., 676
Bank, L., 280, 435
Banks, J.A., 27, 41, 425

Banuelos, C., 616
Barbarin, O.A., 254
Bar-Charma, 525
Barger, J. L., 601
Baringa, M., 154
Barker, E.D., 199
Barker, E.T., 376, 395
Barnett, J. E., 302
Barnett, M.M., 638
Barnett, W., 215
Baron, C., 517
Baron, E., 431
Baron-Cohen, S., 88
Barr-Anderson, D.J., 385
Barrett, A., 17
Barrett, A., 490
Barron, J., 122
Barry, C. M., 361
Barry, M.J., 241
Barstead, M. G., 263, 264
Bart, W.M., 32
Bartel, M. A., 91
Bartholomew, A. N., 612
Bartoletti, M., 340
Basaga, H., 583
Basak, C., 615
Basham, P., 324
Bass, J.E., 305
Bassett, H.H., 343
Bates, J.E., 200, 201, 220, 481
Bateson, 486
Battams, N., 536, 639
Bauer, 583
Bauer, I, 630
Bauer, P.J., 180, 244, 245, 298, 300, 301, 306
Bauman, R. W., 90
Baumeister, R.F., 340, 540
Bauml, K. H., 299
Baumrind, D., 272, 274, 285, 341, 417
Bavelier, D., 244
Bayley, N., 181, 189
Bays, P. M., 612
Baysinger, C.L., 98
Bazzano, L.A., 517
Beach, J., 218
Beach, S.R.H., 495
Bear, M., 568
Beardslee, M.R., 342
Bearman, S.K., 376
Beaupré, P., 276
Beauregard, M., 618
Beck, C.T., 35, 36
Beddor, P., 182, 186
Bedford, V. H., 566
Bednar, 341
Begley, T. H., 96
Behrens, H., 317
Behrens, K., 195
Behrens, R., 417
Behrman, S., 453
Bell, M., 194
Bell, M.A., 194, 226, 243, 246
Bell, N., 431
Bell, R., 610
Bell, R.D., 603
Bell, S.M., 210
Bellack, D., 118
Belleau, L., 277
Belleville, S., 610
Belsky, J., 197, 213, 220, 373, 484
Bem, S.L., 355, 356
Benarroch, E. E., 586
Ben-David, B. M., 611
Bender, W.N., 325
Benenson, J.F., 271
Bener, A., 518
Bengtson, H., 339
Bengtson, V.L., 635
Bennett, C., 464
Bennett, P. W., 321
Bennett, S., 130, 219
Bennetts, B., 95
Benoit, C.M., 28, 39
Benoit, D., 211, 359
Benokraitis, N., 488
Benowitz-Fredericks, C., 376
Benson, H., 619
Benson, J. E., 247
Benson, M., 418
Benson, P.L., 417, 423
Berardi, N., 378
Berchicci, 653
Berenbaum, S.A., 268, 271, 351, 352, 353, 354, 355
Bereti, E., 323
Bergen, D., 282, 283
Berger, J.T., 427, 428
Berger, K., 371, 380, 418, 419, 458, 459, 472
Berger, M., 172
Berger, P.L., 21, 23
Bergeson, T.R., 172, 182, 187, 214
Berhane, E., 336, 337, 338, 339
Berk, L.E., 241
Berko, J., 250, 257
Berko-Gleason, J., 249
Berman, M., 244, 245, 502
Berman, S., 123
Bernard, K., 99, 101, 211
Berndt, T.J., 361
Bernie, A. M., 525
Bernier, A., 246
Berninger, V.W., 321, 326
Bernstein, A., 104
Berookhim, 525
Berridge, 393
Berry, C. J., 612
Berry, D. J., 272
Berscheid, E., 486, 487, 488
Berthelot, J.M., 670
Berthiaume, L., 660
Bertorelle, R., 583
Bertrand, J., 218
Bertrand, R., 516, 521, 562, 653
Best, D., 456
Beta, 295
Betterham, 397
Beyene, Y., 524
Beyers, E., 487
Beyers, W., 417
Bhavsar, A. K., 233
Bherer, 614, 618
Bialek, 615
Bialystok, E., 246
Bianchi, S.M., 500
Bianco, I.H., 154
Bibby, R., 419, 422, 423
Bibok, M.B., 55, 246
Bidell, T.R., 466
Bieber, J., 468
Bielak, A.A.M., 630
Bielecki, W., 601
Bierman, K.L., 361, 362
Biggs, 631
Bigler, R. S., 270, 352, 356
Billari, F.C., 128
Bindler, R. C., 228
Binet, A., 19, 306, 331
Birch, S., 247
Bird, 596
Birditt, K.S., 569, 571, 642, 648, 652
Birkeland, M. S., 430
Birkin, S., 295
Bischof, G., 532, 615
Bisiacchi, P.S., 612
Bisson, M., 491
Bitternose, N., 568
Bjorklund, D.F., 242, 246, 298
Black, B., 351
Blackstone, A., 495
Blair, 599
Blair, B., 430
Blair, C., 272, 302
Blair, M., 300
Blair, P., 158
Blair, S.N., 599
Blake, J., 449
Blakemore, J.E.O., 27, 268, 271, 351, 352, 353, 354, 355
Blanck, H.M., 452
Bland, C. G., 350
Blank, R., 667, 668
Blandon, A., 201
Blankson, A., 484
Blaustein, J., 375
Blavin, M., 486, 487
Blieszner, R., 491, 563, 641, 648
Block, J., 481
Bloomgarden, Z.T., 517
Bloor, C., 598
Blumel, J. E., 525
Blümi, S., 98
Blustein, D.L., 471
Boden, J., 412
Boege, 391
Boelen, P.A., 677, 678
Boelens, C., 589
Boeree, C.G., 54*f*, 504*f*
Boerner, K., 678, 681
Bogetz, J.E., 677
Bogle, K., 491
Bohlin, G., 200, 480
Bohlmeijer, E. T., 613
Bohr, Y., 345, 346
Boisvert, J., 387
Boivin, M., 361
Bombak, A., 451
Bonanno, G.A., 678, 680
Bondar, R.L., 578, 609
Bondare, W., 585
Bondmass, M.D., 680, 681
Bonell, C., 402
Bonura, 636
Booker, J. A., 264
Booth, D., 354
Booth, M., 428
Bor, W., 435
Borella, E., 613
Bornstein, M.H., 186, 345, 346
Boron, J.B., 615
Borzage, M.S., 98
Bos, A., 412
Bos, C. S., 325
Bos, H., 427, 504
Bos, H. M. W., 380

Botek, A., 650
Bouchard, T., 86
Boukydis, C.F., 140
Bourbeau, R., 579
Bourgeous, P., 30
Bowatte, 160
Bowen, 645
Bowen, A., 130
Bowen, R., 130, 142
Bowker, A., 295, 340
Bowker, J., 430
Bowlby, J., 47, 64, 65, 74, 77, 197, 198, 207, 208, 211, 220, 482, 484, 671
Bowles, J., 91
Bowling, 653
Bowman, M.A., 435
Bowman, N., 447
Boyce, W., 379, 382
Boyd, M., 372, 378
Boyer, K., 180
Boyle, P. A., 613
Bozhovich, L., 180
Bozzo, P., 126
Braak, H., 531
Braddick, 230
Bradley, L., 523
Brainerd, C., 301
Brancazio, L.R., 120
Brand, J., 537
Brand, M., 583
Brandon, 383
Brandys, 386
Brannen, P.A., 142
Bransford, J., 320
Branswell, H., 461
Brant, D., 660
Brassard, A., 484
Braun, K.L., 645
Brausch, A., 391
Braver, S., 501
Bravo, G., 662
Bravo, I., 131, 144
Bray, M. A., 306
Brazelton, B., 140
Brazil, K., 667
Breazeal, C., 162, 173
Brechwald, W. A., 360
Bredekamp, S., 254, 312
Bregman, H., 429
Breheny, 648
Bremner, G., 177
Brendgen, M., 281, 421, 435
Brennan, S., 207
Brennan, S., 465
Brenner-Shuman, A., 376
Bresette, L.M., 466
Breslau, J., 501
Bretherton, I., 357
Bretscher, P., 96
Brez, C., 179
Bridges, J.S., 570, 571
Bridges, S. L., 315
Briem, V., 295
Brim, G., 515, 551
Brink, P., 666
Brittain, D., 449
Brkic, S., 454
Broadie, K., 328
Brock, L.J., 594
Brockhuizen, 518
Brockie, J., 524
Brockmeyer, S., 570
Broderick, R., 445
Brody, N., 310
Boerleider, A., 144
Bronfenbrenner, U., 51, 68–70, 75*f*, 78, 107, 273, 323, 339, 357, 383, 416, 505–506, 510, 552, 555
Bronstein, P., 270
Brooker, R., 198, 269
Brooker, R. J., 83, 88, 96
Brookfield, S., 401
Brooks-Gunn, J., 203, 244, 312, 375
Brown, 88, 616
Brown, B.B., 420, 428, 648
Brown, B.V., 372, 421
Brown, C.S., 464
Brown, D.W., 452
Brown, J.D., 433
Brown, K., 396
Brown, L., 451
Brown, M., 324, 431
Brown, S., 141
Brown, S.L., 212, 640, 680, 681
Brownawell, A. M., 616
Browne, C.V., 645
Brownell, C.A., 205, 206
Bruce, A., 668
Bruck, M., 244, 245
Bruening, M., 125
Bruin, J.E., 122
Brumariu, L. E., 357
Brummelman, E., 340
Brune, C.W., 207
Brus, M., 586
Bryant, C., 524
Bryant, J.A., 284
Bryant, J.B., 317
Brym, B., 28, 40
Brym, R., 429, 503
Buchman, 581
Buchman, S., 596
Buchner, A., 610
Buckner, J.C., 342
Buckwalter, J., 486
Bucur, B., 611, 612
Budworth, M., 472
Buehler, C., 418, 430
Bugg, J. M., 612
Buhling, K. J., 524
Buhrmester, D., 430, 432
Buhs, E.S., 362
Bukowski, W.M., 281, 361, 421
Bulanda, J.R., 640
Bulik, C.M., 387, 389
Bumpass, L., 500
Burati, 306
Burdge, 127
Burgard, S., 472
Burgard, S. A., 515
Burgess, S., 449
Burney, R.V., 203
Burns, C., 157, 226, 228
Burns, E., 152
Burns, R. A., 615
Burr, J., 650
Burraston, B., 435
Burt, K.B., 445
Burt, S. A., 104, 105
Burton, P., 277, 329
Busby, D., 500
Busch, H., 547
Bush, K. R., 274
Busolo, 391
Buss, D.M., 84, 269
Buss, K.A., 194, 200
Busse, S., 521
Bussey, K., 270
Butler, R.N., 628, 629
Butterworth, P., 565
Bynner, J., 471
Byrnes, H.F., 435
Byrnes, J.P., 55, 399

C

Caban-Holt, A., 611
Cabeza, R., 587, 617
Cabrera, N., 215
Cacho, I., 590
Cacioppo, J. T., 648
Cahill, K.E., 536
Cain, K., 317
Cain, S., 311, 320
Caldwell, K.A., 361
Calear, 396
Calkins, S.D., 194, 198
Callaghan, M. E., 585, 617
Callwood, J., 576
Cameron, B.A., 659
Cameron, P.A., 268, 269
Camp, J., 143
Campanella, J.L., 178
Campbell, F.A., 311
Campbell, K. L., 610, 617
Campos, J.J., 170, 194, 195
Cancel-Tirado, C., 507
Candow, 596
Canfield, J., 609
Cansino, S., 611, 612
Canterino, J.C., 128
Cantero, J. L., 589
Cantor, N., 245
Cappeliez, P., 629
Cappella, E., 360
Capponi, P., 522
Carbone, P., 219
Cardin, J. F., 277
Cardinal, B., 448
Cardinal, M., 448
Carin, A.A., 305
Carling-Jenkins, R., 604
Carlisle, J., 326
Carlo, G., 351
Carlson, N. Makokis, 568
Carlson, S.M., 177, 228, 245, 246, 264, 302, 341
Carlsson, A. C., 598
Carlsson, N., 233
Carlton, M.P., 241
Carolan, M., 128
Carpendale, J., 55, 246
Carpendale, J.I.M., 206
Carpenter, M., 162, 187, 207, 262, 266
Carrington, H.A., 196
Carrington, N.A., 677
Carrizzo, A., 601
Carroll, D., 519, 597
Carrol, J., 500
Carroll, J.L., 382
Carroll, M.H., 463
Carskadon, M., 386
Carstairs, S., 666
Carstensen, L.L., 597, 613, 630, 631, 632, 635, 643, 648, 653
Carter, A.S., 196
Carter, B., 496, 566
Carter, S., 486
Caruso, D.R., 308, 309, 310, 313, 331
Carver, C. S., 560
Carver, L.J., 180

Casals, P., 609
Case, R., 56, 76, 297
Casement, T., 396
Casey, B.J., 291, 377
Casey, P.H., 138
Casey, R.E., 120
Caskie, G., 615
Casper, L.M., 500
Caspers, K., 484
Caspi, A., 562
Cassidy, J., 211, 482
Cassidy, W., 396
Catalan, M. J., 605
Catarino, A., 328
Caulfield, L.E., 151
Cavanaugh, M. M., 589
Cavanna, A. E., 585
Caylak, E., 88
Ceci, S.J., 70, 244, 245, 311
Cederborg, A-C., 244
Cerqueira, F. M., 583
Cha, 635
Chae, S., 215
Chakrabarti, B., 88
Chakraborty, S., 373
Chakraborty, Y., 373
Chalmers, B., 135, 150
Chalupa, L.M., 586
Chambaere, K., 663
Champagne, M., 425
Chan, C., 381
Chan, H. C., 518
Chance, 60
Chandler, M., 396
Chang, 275
Chang, C., 579
Chang, L.S., 323
Chang, S., 169
Charles, J.E., 310
Charles, S., 480
Charles, S.T., 553, 555, 631, 640, 643
Charness, N., 532
Chassin, L., 391, 570
Chaudhury, H., 629
Chaudhary, J., 92
Cheadle, J., 570
Chehab, O., 583
Chein, J., 378
Chen, 102, 648
Chen, H., 282
Chen, J. J., 516
Chen, K.H., 201
Chen, T.J., 375
Chen, X., 270, 595
Chen, X.K., 127, 383
Chen, Z., 246
Cheng, 648
Cherlin, A.J., 500
Cherry, K., 48, 49, 309, 343
Chess, A., 199, 220
Chess, S., 480
Chevan, 640
Chevret-Measson, M., 641
Chevreul, H., 467
Chi, M.T., 300
Chiang, K.J., 630
Chiffriller, S.H., 377
Childers, J. B., 251
Chinn, P.C., 27
Chochinov, H., 666
Chochinov, H. M., 675
Chochinov, M., 666
Choi, N.G., 629
Chomsky, N., 185, 190
Chow, 648
Chow, J., 152
Chrétien, A., 18
Chrétien, J., 18
Christakis, N.A., 681
Christensen, 397
Christensen, K., 640, 643
Christian, B. E., 583
Christie, J.F., 252
Christodoulidou, A., 583
Chuang, S., 27, 215, 472
Chuang, Y. F., 614
Chugani. H.T., 156
Chui, T., 345
Chung, J. K., 590
Cicchetti, D., 107, 275, 480
Ciccola, A., 612
Cicirelli, V., 672
Cicirelli, V.G., 566
Cillessen, A.H.N., 361
Claes, 526
Clapp, W. C., 612
Clare, L., 602
Clark, D.J., 590
Clark, E., 251
Clark, E. V., 317
Clark, F., 459
Clark, M.D., 463
Clark, W., 446, 539, 540, 618, 639
Clarke, B., 430
Clarke-Stewart, A.K., 272, 273, 357
Clausen, J., 561
Claxton, L.J., 246, 302
Clearfield, M., 162
Cleveland, L.M., 125
Cloutier, E., 276
Cnaan, R.A., 423
Cobb, K.A., 96
Cobb, M., 500
Cobham, V. E., 344
Coffey, V. G., 517
Coffman, J.L., 301
Coghlan, K., 275
Cohen, D., 298, 484, 515
Cohen, F., 472
Cohen, J., 665
Cohen, K.M., 380
Cohen, L., 179, 641
Cohen, S., 520
Cohen-Mansfield, 649
Cohen-Woods, S., 88
Coie, J.D., 282, 435
Colcombe, S.J., 618
Cole, C.A., 613
Cole, P.M., 263, 264, 265
Coleman, M., 358, 502, 641
Coleman, P.D., 586
Coley, R., 381
Collaku, A., 451
Colley, R., 284
Collier, R., 269, 666
Collins, W., 418, 433
Collins, W.A., 339, 418
Colombo, J., 179
Coloroso, B., 364
Colpitts, E., 464
Commons, M.L., 466
Conel, J. LeRoy, 153
Conger, K. J., 560
Connell, 435
Connolly, J.A., 431, 432, 433
Connor, S., 102
Connor-Smith, J., 560
Conry-Murray, C., 271
Contant, T.L., 305
Conte, J., 472
Cook, 660
Cook, E., 430
Cook, T.D., 430
Coolbear, J., 359
Cooper, A.R., 122
Cooper, C.R., 417
Cooper, S.M., 425
Cope, M.B., 151
Coplan, R.J., 263, 283
Copple, C., 253
Copstead, L., 124
Corbetta, D., 173
Corbin, C.B., 450
Cordier, S., 130
Corkum, P., 231
Cornew, L., 207
Cornwell, B., 17, 650
Corona, G., 593
Corsi, D., 455
Corso, J.F., 592
Cortina, K.S., 643
Cory, E., 161
Costa, P.T., 551, 559, 560, 561, 572
Costa, R., 203
Costa-Glomi, E., 310
Cote, J., 414
Cote, J.E., 446
Cotelli, M., 587, 617
Cotten, 649
Coulombe, D., 30
Coupos, E.J., 33
Courage, M.L., 179, 180
Court, F., 91
Cousineau, T., 449
Cowan, 298, 299
Cowen, K. J., 228
Cowan, M. K., 87
Cox, M., 670
Craft, 96
Craft, S., 602
Craig, I. W., 88
Craig, W., 363, 364
Craik, F., 612
Crain, S., 317
Crane, J.D., 589
Craparo, G., 483
Craven, R., 262
Crawford, A., 359
Crawford, D.A., 293
Crawford, K., 433
Creanga, 526
Crede, M., 645
Cresci, M.K., 638
Creswell, J.W., 32
Cribbet, 589
Criger, 568, 614
Cristi, C., 596
Crnic, K. A., 264
Crocetti, E., 413
Crocker, B., 159
Crompton, S., 128
Crone, E.A., 362
Crosby, D. A., 356
Crosnoe, R., 216, 372, 430
Cross, D., 247
Crow, S.M., 464
Crowell, J.A., 570
Crowley, K., 31, 32
Croyle, R.T., 93
Cruchaga, C., 88
Csikszentmihalyi, M., 9, 49, 51, 71, 72, 74, 75*f*, 303, 532, 533, 534, 535
Cuenca-Garcia, M., 518

Cuevas, K., 178, 226, 243, 246
Cui, 525
Cummings, E., 23
Cummings, M., 88, 96
Cunningham, P.M., 318
Cunningham, S. A., 232
Cunningham, W., 452
Cupach, W.R., 490
Currie, C., 375
Currier, J.M., 672, 680
Curtin, S., 182
Curtis, L., 277
Curto, V., 536
Cutler, S.J., 638
Cuzon, V.C., 120
Czoli, C., 455
Czyzewski, K., 28

D

Da Costa, L. A., 599
da Cruz, A. C., 583
da Vinci, L., 14
Daddis, C., 431
Daeschel, I., 231
Dahl, R.E., 362, 378
Dainkeh, S., 426
Daltro, P., 98
Damon, A., 227
Daniels, H., 240
Danner, D.D., 588
Dariotis, J., 378
Darwin, C., 47, 63, 72, 74, 77, 82, 95, 105, 107, 541
Das, A., 464
Das, D.K., 641
Das, S., 526
Dashtipour, K., 516
Dastani, Z., 92
Daubenmier, J.J., 452
David, P., 494
Davidson, 402
Davidson, J., 315
Davidson, M.C., 135
Davidson, P. S., 612
Davies, A. P. C., 358
Davies, G., 310
Davies, P., 23
Davila, J., 433
Davis, 130
Davis, K., 633
Davis, M.C., 590
Davis, S. W., 617
Davis-Kean, P.E., 339
Davis-Unger, A.C., 246, 264, 302
Davison, G., 454
Dawber, T., 295, 354, 361
Dawes, N., 428
Dawkins, R., 540
Dawson, G., 219
Dawson, J. D., 592
Day, N.L., 123
Day, R., 417
De Brouwer, W., 533
de Frias, C. M., 615
de Haan, M., 152, 180
de Jong Gierveld, J., 358, 641
de la Cuesta-Benjumea, C., 604
de Lauzon-Guillain, B., 452
DeLamater, J., 279, 380
DeLoache, J., 235
de Luis, D.A., 451
De Meyer, 604
de Villiers, J., 250
de Villiers, P., 250
de Wind, A. W., 536
de Wit, M.L., 233
Deacon, S. H., 317
Deák, G., 206
Deary, I.J., 310
DeBecker, T., 431
Debette, S., 518
DeCasper, A.J., 171
Decety, J., 350
Declaire, J., 494
Declercq, E., 135
Dedon, P. C., 96
Deeg, D.J.H., 515
De Guzman, N., 376
Deiner, 447
Del Guidice, M., 488
Del Tredici, K., 531
DeLuca, S., 466
Dement, W.C., 157
Dempsey, D., 662
den Hollander, B., 392, 598
Denard, 592
Deng, J. W., 92
Deng, Y., 430
Denham, S., 596
Denham, S.A., 263, 265, 343
Denissen, J., 480
Dennis, N.A., 617
Dennison, S., 171
DePaulo, B., 500
Depestre, R., 627
Derbyshire, E., 128
DeRosa, D.A., 305, 320
DeRose, L., 375
Deshpande-Kamat, N., 532
DesMeules, M., 11
D'souza, B., 345
DeSpelder, L.A., 676
Desrosiers, H., 277
Destin, M., 431
Devlieger, R., 129
DeVries, 418
DeYoung, 480
Diamond, A., 180, 226, 227, 283, 291, 302, 305, 484
Diamond, A. D., 205
Diamond, L., 380
Diamond, L. M., 342
Dick-Read, G., 135
Dickens, B. M., 99
Dickinson, 648
Diehl, M., 466
Diel, P., 524
Dieser, R., 449
Dietz, P.M., 122
Dimmitt, C., 305, 306, 319
Dine, A., 141
Ding, Z., 582
Dinger, M., 449
Dion, C., 468
Dirk, J., 613
Dishion, T.J., 282, 435
Divecha, D., 274
Dixon, R.A., 515, 609, 615
Doane, 386
Dobbs, J.B., 164
Dobson, J., 345
Dobson, K.S., 666
Dodge, K.A., 281, 282, 362, 435
Dodson, L. J., 358
Doey, L., 263
Doherty, M., 247, 248, 249
Dohnt, H., 294
Doidge, N., 48, 50, 57, 58, 364
Doll, C. A., 328
Donaldson, G., 527
Donaldson, T., 638
Donmez, 583
Donnellan, M.B., 412, 560, 562, 634
Donohue, M.R., 267
Dontigny, L., 125
Dorey, E., 603
Dorius, C., 277
Dorn, L.D., 375
Dorner, J., 613
Dorszewska, J., 583
Dorval, V., 126
Doty, R.L., 172
Dougall, A. L., 520
Douglas, 608
Douglas, T., 28
Doumen, S., 412
Dow, B.J., 491
Downie, J., 665
Dozier, M., 101
Draghi-Lorenz R., 195
Drake, 468
Drygas, W., 601
Du, D., 372, 378
Duarte, A., 616
Dube, A. K., 59
Dube, D.A., 150
Dube, M., 661, 662
Dube, S., 160
Duberstein, 634
Dublin, S., 603
Duchesne, D., 637
Duczkowska, A., 98
Dudgeon, G., 602, 604
Duffy, 390
Dufour-Rainfray, D., 124
Duggleby, W., 681
Duindam, V., 277
Duke, 400
Duku, E., 253
Dumas, T.M., 431
Dumont, S., 667
Dunbar, G. L., 605
Dunbar, L., 653
Duncan, E., 120, 121
Duncan, J., 671
Dunlop, W.L., 352
Dunlosky, J., 613, 615
Dunn, M., 326, 472
Dunn, J., 280, 567
Dunn, S., 363
Dunsmore, J. C., 264
Dupre, M.E., 495
Durrant, R., 83
Durston, S., 291
Dutta, S., 140
Dutton, Y., 680
Duvalier, F., 627
Dvornyk, V., 375
Dworkin, R., 649
Dys, S.P., 351
Dysart-Gale, D., 381

E

Eagly, A., 270
Earl, J.K., 638
Easterbrooks, M. A., 261, 263
Eastwick, P.W., 486
Ebemeier, K., 453
Ebmeier, K. P., 602
Eby, J.W., 320

Eccles, J.S., 357, 372, 422
Edeas, M., 583
Edison, T., 466
Edney, D., 416
Edwards, M., 215
Edwards, P., 596
Edwardson, 293
Egan, K., 671
Egan, S. K., 268
Egeland, B., 211
Egloff, B., 280, 560
Eichorn, D.H., 561
Eidelman, A.I., 197
Eiferman, R. R., 283
Einarson, A., 126, 143
Eisenberg, N., 266, 351, 352, 355
Ekeblad, S., 92
El Haj, M., 612
Elashi, F. B., 262, 339
Elavsky, 653
Elder, Jr. G., 372
Elder, G.H., 642
Eldreth, D.A., 585
El-Gabalawy, 595
Eliasieh, K., 586
Elkind, D., 55, 74, 236, 342, 400, 415, 438
Elliot, 526
Elliott, D., 678
Elliott, E. M., 612
Elliott, W. J., 518
Ellis, 610
Ellis, B., 375
Ellis, B. J., 83
Ellis, L., 262
Ellis, W.E., 431
Else-Quest, N., 269, 270, 354, 356
El-Sheikh, M., 231
El-Sohemy, A., 599
Elwert, F., 681
Emerson, R.W., 370
Emery, C. F., 518, 520, 521
Emke, I., 682
English, 631, 632, 653
Ennett, S.T., 394
Enns, J., 472
Ensor, R., 246, 248, 263
Eppinger, B., 613
Erickson, K.I., 586, 597, 614, 618
Ericsson, K. A., 300
Eriksen, S. H., 538, 649
Erikson, E., 51*f*, 74, 75, 75*f*, 105, 203, 204, 208, 220, 261, 282, 286, 342, 412, 413, 416, 423, 429, 435, 438, 439, 487, 488, 492, 496 546, 547, 548, 549, 572, 628, 629–630
Erixon-Lindroth, N., 531
Erol, R., 412
Esmaili, M., 669
Esposito, K., 526
Estabrooks, C.A., 606
Estell, D.B., 310
Etaugh, C., 570, 571
Evaldsson, A-C., 225
Evanoo, G., 197
Evans, M., 134
Evans, S.E., 95
Evans, W.J., 589
Eveleth, D. D., 590
Everett, 598
Everingham, C., 506
Evers, A. W., 520
Evers, C., 84, 90
Eymard, 608
Ezkurdia, L., 96

F

Fabes, R., 351, 352
Fabian, S. G., 583
Fagan, A.A., 435
Fagan, J., 215
Fagan, J.F., 181, 189
Fagot, B.I., 270
Fagundes, C. P., 521
Fahey, T., 25
Fahey, T.D., 452
Fair, D.A., 117, 154
Faja, S., 228, 245, 246, 264, 302, 341
Fakhoury, J., 583
Falci, D., 412
Falk, M.C., 616
Fallows, M., 519
Fang, L., 517
Fantz, Robert, 168, 169
Farajinia, 589
Farb, 383
Farer, M., 228
Farr, R., 279, 280, 504
Farrell, 596
Farrell, S.W., 592
Farrie, A., 215
Farioli-Vecchioli, S., 586
Fatusi, N., 449
Fausto-Sterling, A., 72, 297
Feeney, B., 482
Feeney, J.A., 483, 484, 501
Feeney, S., 282
Feig, D., 126
Feinberg, M.E., 435
Feldman, R., 128, 197, 214, 242, 423, 449, 489
Feldman, S., 245
Feldon, J.M., 677
Fell, 596
Felmlee, D., 491
Fenesi, B., 472
Feng, X., 417, 603
Fenigsen, R., 663
Fenning, R. M., 264
Ferber, S.G., 138
Ferguson, H.B., 322
Ferguson, K., 30
Fergusson, D., 412
Fernandes, M.A., 611
Ferrari, M., 613
Ferrer, E., 419
Ferris, M., 233
Fiedorowicz, C., 325
Field, R. D., 271
Field, T., 130, 138, 139, 143, 172, 205
Field, T. M., 214
Fielding, K., 30
Fiese, B.H., 213, 214
Figueiredo, B., 203
Figueiredo, R., 30
Fillion, L., 667
Finch, C.E., 531, 583, 610
Fincham, F.D., 491, 495
Fine, M., 358
Finer, 382
Finger, B., 210
Fingerhut, A.W., 459, 460, 504
Fingerman, K.L., 566, 569, 571, 642, 648
Finkel, E.J., 486
Finnegan, L., 122, 123
Finnie, R., 472
Fiocco, A. J., 593
Fiori, K.L., 643
Firbank, O., 29
Firth, K., 555
Fischer, K.W., 59, 154, 466
Fischhoff, 400
Fisher, 240
Fisher, M., 54*f*
Fisk, A.D., 638
Fiske, A., 630
Fitzgerald, D., 275
Fitzsimmons, C., 251
Fivush, R., 244, 245, 300
Fjell, 585
Flagel, 393
Flavell, J.H., 247, 305, 306
Fleer, M., 180
Flegal, K. E., 612
Flegel, K., 454
Fletcher, A.C., 393
Fletcher, B. R., 616
Fletcher, G., 493
Fletcher, J. M., 88, 95
Fletcher, S., 124
Flint, J., 96
Floel, A., 617
Flom, R., 179
Flouri, E., 341
Flynn, J.R., 311, 331
Foehr, U., 379
Follari, L., 312
Fontana, L., 598
Forbes, 596
Forbes, J., 126
Forbes-McKay, K., 120, 121
Forchuk, C., 30
Ford-Jones, E.L., 322, 323
Foreman, T., 665
Foresta, C., 126
Forget, H., 553
Forget-Dubois, N., 252
Fosco, 435
Foster, H., 375
Foster-Cohen, S., 137
Fouad, N.A., 471
Fowler, C.G., 517
Fowler, J., 619
Fowler, R., 662
Fox, 318
Fox, M.J., 605
Fox, N., 480
Fox, T., 14
Fozard, J.L., 593
Francescutti, L.H., 666
Francis, A. L., 302
Francis, J., 415
Francis, Pope, 618
Franco, D., 449
Frank, J., 435
Franke, 636
Franke, S., 428
Frankel, L., 380
Frankenburg, W.K., 164
Frankl, V., 540, 541
Franklin, C., 507
Franklin, U.M., 606, 607
Fraser, G., 415
Fraser, K., 29
Fratiglioni, L., 598
Frazier, P., 490, 502
Frederick, I.O., 129
Frederikse, M., 353
Fredstrom, B., 430

Freeman, 225, 315, 386, 635
Freeman, J., 314
French, D.C., 423
Fretts, R. C., 128
Freud, A., 54, 53, 54*f,* 76
Freud, S., 48–53, 74, 75, 75*f,* 270, 282, 285, 286, 416, 429, 439, 537
Freund, A. M., 17, 581, 597, 632, 633, 636, 644, 653
Frey, 632
Freyer-Adam, J., 472
Freytag. S., 92
Fried, 631, 632
Friederici, A.D., 184
Friedman, 246, 613
Friedman, D., 611
Friedman, E.M., 595
Friedman, H.S., 634
Friedman, R., 396
Friedman, W. J., 298, 300
Friedrichs, A., 306
Friend, 325
Friesen, J., 637
Friesen, W.V., 588
Frimer, J., 351, 352
Frisen, J., 586
Fritsch, T., 613
Fritschmann, N.S., 325
Fromm, E., 40, 76, 479, 485
Fry, P.S., 681
Frye, D., 246
Fu, G., 339, 350
Fuchs, D., 299
Fujita, A., 95
Fuligni, A.J., 420
Fuller-Thomson, E., 642, 643
Funai, E.F., 134
Furman, E., 566
Furman, W.C., 431, 433
Furth, H.G., 296
Futris, T., 507

G

Gaff, C., 118
Gaffin, E., 206
Gage, F.H., 586
Gagnon, A., 579
Gainer, J., 401
Gaines, J. F., 560
Gaines, J. M., 593
Gajdos, Z., 373
Galambos, N., 447
Galambos, N.L., 376, 395
Gallagher, J., 96
Gallicano, G. I., 121
Galliher, R.V., 424
Gallo, D. A., 611
Galton, F., 86, 95
Galvan, A., 377
Galvao, 395
Gamino, L.A., 680
Gandhi, M., 48, 290, 363, 611
Gandhi, S., 599
Ganguli, M., 614
Ganiban, J., 481
Ganong, L., 358, 502, 641
Garasen, H., 646
Garber, A. J., 518
Garcia, J.R., 593
Garcia, V., 170
Garcia Coll, C., 424
Garcia-Bournissen, F., 119
Garcia-Preto, N., 496
Garcia-Sierra, A., 185
Gardner, H., 308, 309, 310, 313, 331
Garofalo, R., 381
Garolla, A., 126
Garrett, E., 670
Garriguet, D., 232
Gartstein, M., 196, 243
Garvey, C., 283
Gates, B., 315, 316
Gathercole, V.C.M., 187
Gatz, M., 630
Gauvain, M., 58, 59, 70, 194, 201, 238, 239, 241, 242
Gauri, C, 323
Gavrilova, N., 594
Gawande, A., 67, 606, 649
Geary-Martin, C., 607
Gee, C. L., 262
Geers, A., 419
Gehsmann, K., 326
Gelles, R.J., 423
Gelman, R., 237
Gelman, S.A., 235, 247, 251
Gems, D., 582
Genesee, F., 319
George, L. G., 561
George, L.K., 618, 628
George, M., 23
Georges, J.J., 663
Gerards, F.A., 97
Gerber, L., 424, 426, 458, 472, 500, 503
Gerena, 570
Gerrard, M., 401
Gershoff, E.T., 356
Gerst-Emerson, 649
Gerstein, H.C., 122
Gerstel, N., 570
Gerstenberg, F. X., 340
Gervain, J., 182
Gervais, J., 282
Getz, S., 377
Geva, E., 420
Gewirtz, J., 207
Ghetti, S., 244
Giallauria, F., 596
Giandrea, M.D., 536
Giarrusso, R., 635
Gibbs, J.C., 349, 350
Gibson, E., 170, 177, 189, 230
Giedd, J.N., 154, 226, 353, 377, 378, 401
Gielen, S., 596
Gilbert, 158
Gilbert, D., 560, 562
Gilbert, S., 617
Gilbertson, 293
Giles, A., 178
Gill, T., 644
Gillanders, D., 553
Gillespie, C., 452
Gilliametal, 377
Gilligan, C., 40, 41, 74, 351, 505, 506, 557
Gilliland, A. L., 134
Gillum, R.F., 541
Gilmore, J., 403, 536
Gilstrap, L.L., 311
Gimovsky, A., 97
Ginsberg, 400
Gionet, L., 160
Giovanello, 612
Gjerdingen, D., 142
Gladstone, J., 643
Gladwell, M., 355
Glaser, R., 521
Glazer, J., 671
Glossop, R., 100
Glozah, F., 426
Gluck, J., 613
Glynn, L., 130
Gogtay, N., 228
Goh, J. O., 617
Goh, Y.I., 129
Goldberg, A., 504
Golden, 387
Goldman, M. B., 99
Goldman-Rakic, P.S., 227
Goldsmith, H.H., 102, 194, 200
Goldstein, 123
Goldstein, M., 449
Goldyn, D.T., 214
Golinkoff, R. M., 251, 282, 283
Gollnick, D.M., 27
Golombok, S., 268, 279
Gomez-Pinilla, F., 597, 610, 615
Goni, 603
Gonsalves, 402
Gonzales-Backen, M., 424
Gonzalez-Barcala, F. J., 233
Good, M., 423
Goodall, J., 47, 65, 77
Goodman, J.M., 518
Goodvin, R., 198, 262, 263
Goossens, L., 417
Gopinath, 591
Gopnik, A., 247
Gorby, H. E., 616
Gorchoff, S.M., 566
Gordith, A., 454
Gordon, 615
Gorely, 293
Goritz, C., 586
Goronzy, J. J., 589
Gosselin, J., 358
Gottlieb, G., 94, 96, 106
Gottman, J.M., 264, 360, 494, 495, 509, 565
Gottman, J.S., 494
Gottman, P., 565, 566
Gouin, K., 123
Gould, E., 586
Gould, M., 396, 431
Goulet, C., 153
Goyal, M., 119
Graber, J.A., 375, 376
Grady, C.L., 617
Grafenhain, M., 262
Graham, A., 263
Graham, E.K., 653
Graham, G. M., 231
Graham, J., 670
Graham, J.A., 425, 488
Graham, S., 340
Grambs, J.D., 557
Grammas, P., 603
Grammatikaki, E., 160
Grammer, J.K., 301
Grandner, M. A., 518
Grant, L., 675
Grant, N., 449
Graven, S., 158
Graves, 293
Graves, L., 124
Gray, P.B., 593
Gredler, M.E., 238
Green, M. J., 518

Green, R.J., 504
Greenberg, L., 482, 484
Greener, J.M., 119, 120, 129
Greenman, P., 484
Greenough, A., 138
Greer, F.R., 160
Gregoire, C. A., 586
Greig, 386
Griffin, K., 343
Griffin, P.W., 562
Griffiths, M., 671
Griffiths, R., 648
Grigorenko, E.L., 311, 312
Grigsby, T., 437
Grill, J. D., 602
Grodin, S., 355
Groen, R.S., 124
Grossman, K., 212
Grossman, K. E., 212
Grosz, E., 355
Grotevant, H.D., 101
Gruber, M., 157
Gruber, N., 590
Gruman, J., 49
Grünendahl, M., 551
Grusec, J., 264, 272, 350, 357
Gruslin, A., 126
Grych, J., 417
Gu, D., 596
Gudmundson, J., 211
Gueguen, J., 387
Guelinckx, I., 129
Guerrero, L., 486, 490
Guffanti, G., 91
Guinhouya, B., 376
Guilford, J.P., 303
Guirado, G. N., 597
Gump, B., 538
Gunderson, 354
Gunderson, E.P., 141
Gunes, C., 583
Gunnar, M., 198
Gunning, T. G., 282
Guo, 88
Gupta, R., 669
Gupta, R.P., 233
Gurdon, J., 103
Gurwitch, R.H., 344
Gustafson, T., 652
Gustafsson, J.E., 311
Gutchess, A.H., 617
Gutmann, D.L., 651
Guzzo, K., 500

H

Ha, J.H., 468
Haaf, W., 100
Habel, C., 142
Haber, J., 33
Hadders-Algra, M., 154, 157
Hagekull, B., 200, 480
Hagopian, A., 160
Hahn, B., 154
Hahn, D.B., 25, 450, 451
Hajdu, P., 464
Hajek, P., 455
Halchuk, R., 484
Halford, K.W., 59
Hall, C.B., 615
Hall, D.P., 318
Hall, S. E., 264
Hallinan, E.V., 207
Halliwell, J.O., 260
Halonen, J., 447
Halpern, D., 401
Halpern, D.F., 353, 354
Halseth, R., 464, 465
Haltiwanger, E. P., 581
Hamamura, T., 560
Hamann, J., 662
Hamilton, J., 376
Hamilton, L. D., 553
Hamlin, J.K., 207
Hammond, 246
Hammond, D., 455
Hampl, J., 452
Hampton, M., 668
Hamrick, M.H., 453
Han, 597, 653
Hanger, D. P., 603
Hannon, E.E., 172, 187
Hans, J., 502
Hansen, M.V., 609
Hansson, R., 670, 671, 672, 678
Hanusaik, N., 455
Hanvey, L., 328, 329
Harari, Y., 582
Harden, 102
Harder, G., 396
Harder, K., 396, 376
Hardy, M., 637
Harel, S., 198
Harley, T.A., 325
Harlow, H., 207, 208
Harman, S.M., 526
Harms, R., 207
Harootyan, R.A., 650
Harper, S., 323
Harrell, W., 387
Harrington, S.E., 666
Harris, G., 643
Harris, J., 282
Harris, K.R., 319, 386
Harris, P.L., 247, 249, 251
Harris, Y.R., 425
Harrison, C., 583
Harrison, H.M., 433
Harrison, T., 671
Hart, C.L., 455
Hart, S.L., 195, 196
Harter, S., 261, 262, 338, 339, 341, 411
Hartley, A., 610
Hartup, W., 360
Hasher, L., 612, 613
Hass, J., 470
Hasselhorn, M., 411
Hastings, P.D., 355, 372
Hatcher, C., 636
Hatfield, E., 488
Hatzenbuehler, M., 459
Hauser Kunz, J., 417
Hautala, D., 415
Havighurst, R.J., 630
Hawkes, C., 592
Hawling, S., 533
Hawkley, L.C., 648
Hawley, J. A., 517
Hayatbakhsh, R., 233
Hayflick, L., 582, 620
Hayne, H., 180
Hayslip, B., 670, 671, 672
Hayward, I., 122
Hayward, R. D., 618
Hazan, C., 483
He, C., 185
He, N., 88, 586
He, X., 517
Healey, J.F., 425
Healey, M.K., 613
Heaney, J. L. J., 597
Heath, 451
Heath, A., 271
Hebert, P., 454
Hebert, R., 681
Heffner, L.J., 128
Heidelbaugh, J.J., 526
Heidrich, D., 680
Heine, C., 591
Heine, S.J., 560
Hekman, E. E., 589
Helfand, M., 381
Helgeson, V., 491
Helman, C., 587
Helmreich, R., 355
Helson, R., 548, 561, 566, 572
Helwig, C. C., 351
Hemmingsson, 472
Hemmy, L. S., 588
Henchoz, Y., 453
Hendershot, C., 456
Henderson, J., 122
Henderson, V. W., 524
Hendrick, J., 253
Hendriks, A.A.J., 634
Henkens, K., 638
Hennessey, B.A., 303
Henninger, M. L., 282
Henretta, J., 495
Henrich, J., 582
Henriksen, L., 379
Henry, N.J.M., 640
Hensch, T., 182
Hepper, P.G., 117
Herbison, A.E., 375
Herd, 648
Herd, P., 595
Herdt, G., 379
Herek, G.M., 459
Herman, C.P., 452
Hernandez-Reif, M., 116, 138, 172
Herold, K., 251
Héroux, G., 238
Herrell, A.L., 320
Hertzman, C., 218
Hertzog, C., 613, 615, 616
Hertz-Picciotto, I., 129
Hetherington, E.M., 277, 358, 501, 502
Hewitt, 596
Heyerdahl, S., 276
Heyland, D., 662
Heyman, G.D., 262, 339
Hibbert, L., 456
Hickey, M., 524
Hickman, J.M., 638
Hicks, J., 629
Higginbotham, B., 358
Hilbrecht, M., 428
Hill, 634
Hill, M., 118
Hill, P.L., 560, 562, 634
Hilliard, L. J., 270, 352, 356
Hillman, C., 597, 610, 615
Hindin, M., 449
Hinduja, S., 396, 430
Hines, M., 268
Hirschhorn, J., 373
Hirsh, J., 607
Hirsh-Pasek, K., 251, 282, 283
Hita-Yanez, E., 589
Ho, 518
Ho, M., 433

Hochberg, C., 590
Hock, R., 380
Hockenberry, M., 152, 159, 161, 163, 172, 226, 295
Hodapp, R. M., 313
Hodge, 653
Hodgson, J., 118
Hoefnagels, M., 83
Hoeger, S.A., 453
Hoeger, W.W.K., 453
Hoelter, L., 501
Hofbauer, L. C., 517
Hofer, A., 353
Hofer, J., 547
Hofer, S. M., 614
Hofer, T., 177
Hoff, E., 187, 249
Hofferth, S., 215
Hofmann, 395
Hoffmeyer, K., 583
Hofheimer, J.A., 33
Hogan, 631
Hogan, C.L., 597, 613, 615
Hogerbrugge, M. J., 570, 642
Hohenberger, A., 176, 177
Holahan, C. J., 601
Holden, K., 636
Holden, T., 456
Holder, M., 375
Holland, C.R., 181
Holland, J.M., 672, 680
Hollich, G., 172
Hollier, L.M., 125
Holloway, A.C., 122
Holmes, L.B., 119
Holmes, T.H., 552
Holmin, J. S., 612
Holsen, I., 376
Holt-Hale, S., 231
Holtslander, L., 681
Holtz, M., 29
Holzman, L., 242
Hong, K.L., 423
Hoogendam, Y. Y., 610, 613
Hooley, J., 391
Hopkins, J.R., 52
Hoppmann, C., 635
Horn, J.L., 527, 530
Horn, M., 555
Horney, K., 40, 41, 51, 53, 54*f*, 74, 76
Horwood, L., 412
Hoshino, O., 585
Hosseini, H., 669
Hotson, L., 185
Hou, F., 326, 522
Houston, D., 182
How, N., 216
Howard, 640
Howard, A., 90, 447, 454
Howe, M., 180
Howell, D., 33
Howes, C., 281
Hoyer, W., 14
Hoyer, W.J., 516, 537, 592, 601, 602
Hoyt, J., 306
Hoyt, M. A., 520
Hreljac, R., 349
Hsu, H.C., 213
Hsu, J.L., 531
Hsu, W.L., 596
Hu, 525
Hu, F. B., 598
Hu, J. K., 92
Huang, G., 88
Huang, J., 454
Huang, K., 422
Huang, L., 341
Huart, C., 586
Hudson, A., 30
Hughes, C., 14, 246, 247, 248, 263
Hughes, T.F., 589
Hulton, L., 524
Hultsch, D.F., 556, 615
Hulur, G., 615
Hummel, T., 586
Hunt, R. R., 612
Hur, K., 233
Hurd Clarke, L., 594
Hurley, J., 415
Hurston, Z. Neale, 468
Hurwitz, C., 671
Husain, M., 612
Hussain, M., 558
Huston, A.C., 164, 357, 360
Hutchins, A., 422
Hutchinson, 633
Hutchinson, D.M., 389
Hutchinson, S., 449
Hutton, E., 136
Huxhold, 643
Hwang, 390
Hwang, S., 30
Hwang, S.W., 522
Hyde, J., 279, 380
Hyde, J.S., 85, 269, 270, 351, 352, 354, 356, 366, 505
Hymel, S., 343
Hynes, M., 443
Hyson, D., 452
Hyson, M.C., 253

I

Iciaszczyk, N., 514
Ickovics, J.R., 131
Igarashi, H., 569
Ikeda, A., 495
Immordino-Yang, M.H., 154
Ingram, D.D., 541
Inhelder, B., 235
Insel, 396
Insel, P.M., 25, 452
Ip, S., 160
Iranmanesh, S., 669
Irwing, 310
Isayama, T., 137
Isidori, A. M., 525
Ito, S., 143
Iwasa, H., 634
Izard, C., 194

J

Jackson, G., 496
Jackson, J.J., 634
Jackson, M., 396
Jackson, S.L., 31, 33, 56
Jacob, 553
Jacobs, C.B., 632, 633
Jacobs, J.M., 615
Jaddoe, V.W., 122
Jaeggi, S.M., 244
Jaffee, S., 351
Jager, J., 339
Jain, M.M., 541
Jalbert, J., 201
Jalongo, M. R., 252
Jambon, 351
James, A.H., 120
James, W.H., 459
Janacek, R.J., 452
Janicki-Deverts, D., 520
Janssen, P.A., 134, 135
Jansson, M., 28, 39
Janus, M., 253
Janz, T., 517
Jared, D., 319
Jaremka, L. M., 521
Jarosinka, D., 233
Jarry, V., 579
Jasik, C.B., 374
Javo, C., 276
Jean, M., 627
Jellinger, K.A., 585
Jennings, G., 594
Jennings, L., 143
Jeschonek, S., 172
Jeste, D.V., 581, 613
Jha, A., 228
Ji, 648
Ji, C.Y., 375
Ji, H.F., 599
Jiang, 516
Jiang, T., 602, 603
Jimeno, C., 345
Jimmieson, 646
Jin, K., 586
Jinyao, Y., 484
Jirikowic, T., 120
Jobin, J., 630
Jochem, R., 198, 202
Joh, A.S., 162, 172, 173
Johansson, 306
John, O.P., 561, 566
Johnsen, R., 646
Johnson, A. A., 582
Johnson, G. B., 83
Johnson, H., 464
Johnson, J. A., 320
Johnson, M., 372, 500
Johnson, M.H., 291
Johnson, S., 106, 378, 482, 483, 484, 678
John-Steiner, V., 59, 239, 240
Johnston, 294, 644
Johnston, A.M., 262
Johnston, C.C., 138
Johnston, K.E., 117
Johnston, L.D., 454
Jones, 642
Jones, B. F., 532
Jones, D.C., 375
Jones, J., 253, 431
Jones, M.D., 424
Jones, M.H., 310
Jones, N., 195, 196, 200
Jongmans, M.J., 137
Jonides, J., 244
Jonson, 644
Joosten, H., 614
Jordan, C. H., 340
Jordan, K., 382, 395, 396
Jordan, M.L., 320
Jordan, S.J., 160
Joseph, J., 86
Joseph, K.S., 128
Joshi, H., 341
Joshi, S., 138
Josselson, R., 412
Joubert, J., 336
Juang, L., 9
Judd, F. K., 524
Julian, A. M., 553
Julian, M.M., 101
Jumah, N., 124

Jun, J., 629
Jung, C., 53, 54*f*, 76, 515
Jung, Y., 650
Juraska, J. M., 585
Jurs, S.G., 31
Just, M. A., 328
Jutras-Aswald, D., 123

K

Kaasa, S., 666
Kaeppeler, 383
Kagan, J., 198, 199, 200, 211, 220, 327, 480
Kagan, L., 600
Kagitani, H., 524
Kahan, M., 122, 123, 124
Kalb, L., 219
Kalish, C.W., 251
Kalladka, D., 588
Kalousova, L., 472
Kambhavi, R., 644, 651
Kamiya, M., 604
Kan, P. F., 251
Kandel, E., 48
Kane, H. S., 520, 589
Kane, R.L., 645
Kang, 597, 653
Kantak, C., 99
Kaplan, 525
Kaplan, D. L., 381
Karabulut, E., 638
Karahuta, E., 351
Karasik, L., 162, 167
Karatsoreos, I. N., 586
Karavia, E. A., 518
Karlamangia, A. S., 520
Karney, B., 486
Karniol, R., 355
Kaski, D., 605
Kaszniak, 631
Kassahn, K. S., 88, 95
Kastenbaum, R.J., 671, 673, 674, 677, 682, 683
Kato, T., 490
Katon, W., 142
Kats, 278
Kattenstroth, J. C., 615
Katz, L.M., 596
Katzmarzyk, 598
Kaufman, J.C., 303, 304, 311, 532
Kaufman, L., 176
Kaufman, S.R., 666
Kavanaugh, R. D., 247
Kawagoe, T., 613
Keating, D.P., 315, 401, 465
Keen, S. M., 275
Kehle, T. J., 306
Kekewich, M., 665
Kell, H. J., 315
Keller, M., 586
Keller, S., 433
Kelley, B., 447
Kellman, P., 169, 399
Kelly, 386
Kelly, D., 207
Kelly, E., 215
Kelly, G.F., 379
Kelly, J., 358, 502
Kelly, M., 165
Kelly, M.B., 565
Kelly, P., 29
Kelly, S., 612
Kelly, Y., 135
Kemp, H., 590
Kemp, J., 592
Kempermann, 586
Kempner, 357
Kendall, G., 194
Kendall, M., 661
Kendler, K.S., 680
Kennedy, K.M., 585
Kennedy, S., 500
Kennedy-Moore, E., 339
Kennell, J.H., 144
Kenney, C., 326
Kennis, E., 596
Kenny, 383
Kensinger, E.A., 617
Keown, L., 128
Kercher, G., 507
Kerns, K.A., 357
Kessler, R., 551
Keyes, C., 551, 552
Khadr, O., 415, 416
Khalil, A., 121
Khan, S., 330
Khashan, 383
Khera, M., 525
Khosia, S., 517
Kiang, L., 425
Kiecolt-Glaser, J.K., 521
Kielberger, C., 349, 350
Kielberger, M., 349, 350
Kielsmeier, 402
Kilkenny C., 345
Killen, M., 349
Kim, 390, 526, 605, 642
Kim, H., 426
Kim, J. M., 271
Kim, S., 267
Kim, Su Yeong, 27
Kim-Fuchs, C., 520
King, 598, 640
King, B., 379
King, G., 120
King, K.M., 391
King, L., 629, 672
King, P.M., 366
King, S., 375
Kingsbury, M., 263
Kingston, N.M., 32
Kinney, J., 454
Kinsey, A.C., 459
Kinzler, K.D., 177
Kirby, 526
Kirk, G.M., 449
Kirk, R.E., 34
Kirk, S., 450
Kirk-Sanchez, 597, 614, 618, 653
Kirstein-Miles, J., 583
Kirwan, L.D., 518
Kisilevsky, B.S., 171
Kit, B. K., 233
Kitchener, K.S., 466
Kivimaki, M., 583
Kizilkaya Beji, N., 141
Klahr, A. M., 104
Klassen, T.R., 645
Klemfuss, J.Z., 245
Klieger, C., 115
Kliegman, R.M., 290
Kline, D.W., 517, 590
Klinenberg, E., 500
Klinger, D.A., 312
Klodawsky, F., 30
Klomek, A.B., 431
Klonsky, 390
Klosterman, 435
Knight, B.G., 85
Knight, G., 424
Knoche, L., 215
Knowlton, T., 364
Ko, P. C., 612
Kobo, M., 87
Koch, C. A., 525
Kochanska, G., 267
Koehn, S., 652
Koenig, H.G., 541, 618
Kohen, D., 325, 330
Kohlberg, L., 267, 268, 346–351, 366, 403, 416, 505
Kohut, R., 93
Koien, C.M., 464
Kollar, L., 382, 395, 396
Kolovou, G., 583
Komter, A. E., 570, 642
Kong, L.L., 310
Konik, J., 380
Konopka, A. R., 596
Koo, 653
Koolhof, R., 435
Koopman, P., 91
Kopp, C.B., 198
Koran, M. E., 92
Korat, O., 252
Koren, G., 115, 118, 129
Kornelsen, J., 136
Koorevaar, 634
Korrick, S.A., 129, 130
Korten, N. C., 614
Kostelnik, M.J., 253, 254
Kostenuik, M., 396, 397
Kotecha, S., 138
Kotovsky, L., 176
Kowalski, S.D., 680, 681
Kowaltowski, A. J., 583
Kozbelt, A., 532
Kozey, M., 325
Kozier, B.J., 423, 424
Kraft, E., 586, 614
Krahn, H., 447
Krakoff, L.R., 593
Kral, T., 452
Kramer, A.F., 9
Kramer, K., 215
Kramer, L., 280
Kramer, M.S., 160
Krampe, R. T., 532
Kranz Graham, E., 521, 560, 562
Kraska, M., 33
Krause, N., 618
Krauss, S., 423
Krebs, D.L., 351
Kreklewetz, 391
Kretch, K., 206
Kreutzer, M., 306
Kriebs, J.M., 129
Kriemler, 293
Krimer, L.S., 227
Krist, H., 177
Kristjuhan, U., 614
Kroger, J., 412, 414, 422, 430, 446
Kroonenberg, P.M., 212
Kross, 395
Krowitz, A., 170
Krueger, J.I., 340
Kruger, J., 452
Krüger, M., 177
Krushkal, J., 102
Ksir, C.J., 455
Kübler-Ross, E., 673–674
Kuczynski, L., 417, 419
Kuebli, J., 343

Kuhl, P., 182, 184, 185, 186
Kuhn, D., 304, 306, 400
Kuipers, S., 586
Kulkarni, G., 159
Kulkarni, H., 140
Kulkofsky, S., 245
Kulmala, J., 520
Kumar, N., 92, 612
Kuntz, 117
Kunzmann, U., 8, 613
Kuo, M. C., 612, 613
Kurdek, L.A., 504
Kurtz-Costes, B., 425
Kutcher, S., 396, 397
Kwok, S., 428

L

La Greca, A.M., 433
Labouvie-Vief, G., 465, 466
Lachman, M.E., 515, 516, 521, 551, 552, 555, 560, 562, 613, 653
Lacour, D.E., 126
Ladd, G.W., 362
Ladewig, P.W., 135
Lafasse, L., 123
Laflamme, N., 567, 569, 639
Lafreniere, D., 592
Lagae, O., 299
Lagercrantz, H., 160
Laible, D.J., 203, 205, 206, 262, 351
Lalley, P. M., 593
Lally, M.M., 387
Lalonde, C., 396
Lama, D., 618
Lamaze, F., 135
Lamb, M., 501
Lamb, M.E., 215, 244, 245
Lambert, C., 71
LaMarre, 388
Lampard, 390
Lamy, S., 521
Lan, 246
Landa, R., 219
Landau, A.S., 122
Landoll, R., 430
Landry, J. T., 665
Landry, O., 128, 423, 449, 489
Landesman-Dwyer, S., 121
Landsberg, L., 518
Landrum, A. R., 262
Landy, F., 472
Lange, B. S., 616
Langer, A., 170
Langer, E., 302
Langille, D., 384, 391
Langlois, 388, 389
Langlois, J.H., 205
Lango Allen, H., 88
Lanius, R., 378
Lansford, J.E., 435, 643, 652
Lanter, E., 328
Lapsley, D., 349
Lapsley, D. K., 346
Larimer, M., 456
Larner, A., 602
Larsen-Rife, 560
Larson, F.B., 604
Larson, R., 427, 428
Larson, R.W., 427, 428, 429
Laska, M., 449
Lathrop, A.L., 168
Latt, E., 376
Lau, 449
Laumann, E.O., 17, 426, 641, 650
Laumann, S., 293
Laurent, C., 580
Laurent, S., 518
Laursen, B., 361, 418
Lavalliere, M., 592
Lavender, 390
Lawani, S., 426
Lawler, 644
Lawson, 524
Lawson, C., 170, 171
Lawson, J., 666
Lazaruk, W., 319
Le Couteur, D. G., 582
Leadbeater, B.J., 395
Leahey, M., 213, 502
Leahy-Warren, P,, 140
Leaper, C., 270, 352, 356, 464
Leboyer, F., 135
Lederman, T., 418
Lee, 648
Lee, G.R., 640
Lee, J., 670
Lee, J. H., 92
Lee, K., 59, 238, 248, 251, 262, 302, 339, 350, 613
Lee, K. Y., 96
Lee, L.C., 595
Lee, S., 230, 454
Leerkes, E.M., 194, 203, 211, 484
Lefevre, J. A., 252
Lefkowitz, E. S., 458, 569
Legare, C.H., 339
Legge, G. E., 592
Lehman, E.B., 244
Lei, Hsien-Hsien, 96
Leifheit-Limson, E., 651
Leigh-Paffenroth, E.D., 517
Leighton, S., 681
Leinbach, M.D., 270
Leitzel, J. D., 340
Lemstra, M.E., 431
Lennon, E.M., 181
Lenon, P., 314
Lenroot, R.K., 226
Leon, J., 614
Leonard, C., 306
Leonardi-Bee, J., 122
Leon-Guerrero, A., 425
Leppanen, J.M., 205
Lerner, H., 40, 41, 505
Lerner, R.M., 372, 378, 417, 423
Lerner-Geva, L., 524
Leshikar, E.D., 616, 618
Leslie, 383
Lester, B., 33, 123, 140
Lethbridge, L., 329
Leuschen, J., 590
Levenson, R., 495, 565
Leventhal, E.A., 653
Leventhal, H., 653
Levetown, M., 671
Levin, M. F., 57
Levine, 429
LeVine, S., 557
Levine, T., 491
Levinson, D., 547, 549, 550, 572
Levitt, C., 151
Levy, B.R., 644, 651
Levy, D., 60
Levy, F., 586
Lewin-Bizan, S., 417
Lewis, A., 417
Lewis, C., 215, 263, 264
Lewis, M., 72, 194, 195, 203
Lewis, M.D., 636
Lewis, S., 462
Lewis, T.L., 169
Li, 518, 648
Li, B., 124
Li, C., 451
Li, D.K., 120
Li, F.J., 599
Li, J., 422
Li, P. Q., 99
Li, S.C., 632
Li, X., 461
Li, Y., 88, 681
Liang, J., 233
Liben, L.S., 27, 268, 270, 271, 351, 352, 353, 354, 355, 356
Licata, M., 186
Lickliter, R., 94, 96
Lie, E., 180
Liégeois, F., 154
Liets, L.C., 586
Lieven, E., 182
Li-Korotky, H. S., 591
Lillard, A., 247, 283
Lillenes, M. S., 603
Lim, K.J., 124
Lim, J. H., 99
Lin, 570
Lin, J., 591, 639
Lin, F.R., 555, 585
Lin, S. Y., 233
Lindau, S.T., 594
Linde, K., 615
Lindberg, 354
Lindenberger, U., 8, 9, 515, 609, 615, 632, 633
Lindsay, C., 648
Lindwall, M., 616
Linebarger, J., 671
Lira, F. S., 589
Lisonkova, S., 165
Liston, F., 135
Liszkowski, U., 187, 251
Little, 596
Little, T., 372
Liu, 518, 586, 635
Liu, G., 585
Liu, R., 459
Liu, S., 88
Liu, W., 672
Liu-Ambrose, T., 614, 618
Lliffe, 653
Lo, B., 666
Loaiza, V. M., 531
LoBiondo, G., 33
Lobo Antunes, M., 419
Lobsinger, T., 639
LoBue, V., 206
Lockwood, C.J., 135
Loeber, R., 434, 435
Lofmark, R., 666
Logan, A. G., 518
Lok, 632
Loker, T., 101
Lombardo, P.A., 95
London, M.L., 135, 141
Londono-Vallejo, J. A., 583
Loos, R.J., 92
Lopez, L., 300
Loponen, M., 518

Lorenz, K., 47, 63, 64, 74, 75*f*, 77
Lothian, J.A., 136
Loutfy, M.R., 126, 127
Lovden, M., 609
Love, J. M., 312
Low, J., 247
Low, S., 433
Lowdermilk, D., 125
Lowe, J., 205
Lowe, M., 452
Lowenstein, A., 216
Lowry, N. C., 585
Lu, C. J., 92
Lu, M.C., 131
Lu, W., 131
Lu, P. H., 585, 613
Lubinski, D., 315
Lucas, E.B., 25, 450, 451
Lucas, R.E., 560
Lucchetti, A. L., 541, 618
Lucchetti, G., 541, 618
Lucignani, G., 124
Lucyk, K., 526
Ludden, A.B., 387
Luders, 353
Ludington-Hoe, S.M., 138
Luhmann, M., 552
Lukowski, A. F., 306
Lumpkin, G. T., 560
Luna, B., 378, 395
Lunau, K., 14
Lund, D.A., 677, 681
Lundis, 472
Lung, F., 167
Lungu, O., 610
Luo, 449, 649
Luo, L., 176, 612
Luong, G., 480
Lupart, J.L., 329
Lurye, L.E., 27
Lusardi, A., 536
Lustig, C., 612, 613
Lustig, R.H., 374
Luszczynska, A., 520, 552
Luyckx, K., 414, 417
Luyten, P., 142
Lyall, J., 666
Lye, J., 558, 559
Lynam, D.R., 282, 435
Lynch, T., 682, 683
Lunchard, 632
Lyndaker, C., 524
Lyon, 88
Lyon, G.R., 325
Lyon, T.D., 306
Lyons, 586
Lyons, J.L., 567
Lyons, M., 328

M

Ma, X., 312
Ma, Y.-Y., 315
Maas, J., 141
Macartney, 640
Maccoby, E.E., 273
MacDonald, H., 491
Macdonald, J.A., 14
MacDonald, N., 454
MacDonald, R., 644
Machado-Vidotti, H. G., 596
Maciejewski, P.K., 677, 678
Macionis, J.J., 28, 39, 424, 426, 458, 500, 503
MacKeigan, K., 491
MacKenzie, C.S., 667
MacKenzie, S., 650
Mackin, R. S., 614
Mackoff, R.L., 118
MacMillan, H., 507
Macmillan, H.L., 329
Macneil, L. G., 589
MacNeil, M., 415
Maconochie, N., 127
Mactier, H., 124
Maddaus, M., 445
Madden, D.J., 587, 611, 612
Mader, S., 83, 90, 98
Madigan, S., 211
Maestre, L.A., 98
Maffei, L., 378
Maggs, J., 454
Magnussen, P., 143
Maher, J., 453
Maheux, H., 345
Mahler, M., 204, 220
Mahn, H., 59, 239
Maholmes, V., 312
Mahoney, J. R., 611
Maillard, P., 518
Maimoun, L., 596
Main, R., 252
Maines, D.R., 556
Maiti, S., 87
Makadon, H., 381
Makhoul, I.R., 138
Maki, A., 444
Makinen, J., 484
Malik, N., 88
Malinen, 644
Maloney, 391
Maloy, R. W., 283
Malti, T., 351
Mamtani, M., 140
Mandal, S., 92
Mandela, N., 611
Mandell, A. R., 612
Mandler, J., 180
Mandler, J. M., 235
Manenti, R., 587, 617
Mang, C. S., 57
Mangeni, J., 145
Manios, Y., 160
Mann, N., 592
Mann, T., 451
Mannell, C., 428
Manore, M., 451, 453
Mansvelt, 648
Mantyh, P. W., 592
Manzoli, L., 640
Marano, H. E., 604
Marceau, K., 375
Marcell, J.J., 517
Marcello, 585
Marcia, J., 412, 413, 415, 416, 422, 430, 438
Marcotte, 390
Mares, M-L., 284
Margolis, R., 514
Margrett, J.A., 532
Marin, L., 401
Markant, J. C., 226, 291, 342
Markides, 649
Markman, E.M., 251
Marks, A.K., 424
Marks, B.L., 596
Markus, H. R., 563
Marlatt, G., 456
Maroney, T., 378
Marquart, B., 382
Marques, 387
Marsh, H., 262
Marsh, H. W., 339
Marsh, I., 19
Marshall, K., 216, 272
Marshall, R., 679
Marshall, W., 492
Martel, L., 488, 581
Martin, A., 244
Martin, A. J., 339
Martin, C., 225
Martin, C.L., 278, 352, 551
Martin, J.A., 273
Martin, J.C., 121
Martin, L.R., 634
Martin, M., 551
Martin, P., 627
Martin, S., 383
Martinez, M.E., 300
Martinos, M., 152
Martins, W. P., 524
Martinussen, M., 430
Marx, K., 54*f*
Masche, J., 428
Maslany, G., 130
Maslow, A., 49, 51, 66–67, 74, 78, 416, 437
Mason, 596
Mason, K. A., 88
Masoro, E.J., 517
Massey, Z., 131
Masten, A.S., 302, 344, 445
Mastergeorge, A., 202
Masters, 598
Masui, Y., 580
Mata, J., 597, 613, 615
Maté, G., 105
Mather, 631
Matheson, 598
Matlin, M.W., 27, 505
Matsumoto, D., 9
Mathews, B., 357
Matthews, C.E., 596
Matthews, K., 538
Matthey, S., 358
Mattson, M.P., 589
Maurer, D., 169
Mawani, A., 596
Maxmen, A., 103, 104
Maxson, S. C., 102
Maxwell, K.L., 254
May, D., 270
May, R., 532, 533
May, V., 646
Mayas, J., 615
Mayer, A., 364
Mayer, D., 471
Mayer, J.D., 307, 308, 309, 310, 313, 318, 331, 343
Mayer, K., 381
Mayers, L.B., 377
Mayseless, O., 418, 492
Mbonye, A.K., 143
McAdams, D.P., 563
McAlister, A., 248
McAnarney, E.R., 377
McAndrew, V., 678
McAuley, 599, 630
McBride, D., 661
McCabe, A., 238
McCabe, D. P., 531
McCall, J., 126
McCarron, A., 661, 662
McCarthy, G., 140
McCartney, K., 216
McClelland, K., 91
McCloskey, D., 358
McClung, N., 558

McCormick, C.B., 305, 306, 319
McCoy, M. L., 275
McCrae, R.R., 551, 559, 560, 561, 572
McCuaig, K., 253
McCulloch, E., 102, 103
McCulloch, J., 215
McCullough, 649
McDaniel, M.A., 612
McDermott, B., 344
McDermott, J. M., 101
McDonald, A.B., 577, 609
McDonald, E., 141
McDonald, S.D., 101
McDonough, I. M., 611
McEwen, B. S., 586
McFaull, S., 396
McGabe, J., 142
McGee, T.R., 435
McGoldrick, M., 496, 566
McGough, 597, 614, 618, 653
McGowan, P., 106
McGuffin, P., 88
McHale, S. M., 566
McIntosh, E., 553
McIntyre, M., 447
McIsaac, C., 431, 432, 433
McKay, A., 127
McKay, A. S., 532
McKenna, L., 518
McKenny, E., 142
McKenzie, B., 277
McKenzie, Marika., 64
McKeown, D., 233
McKeown, J., 500
McLaughlin, K., 459
McLeod, S., 66
McMahon, 526
McMillan, C. T., 602
McMillan, J.H., 31
McMillen, C., 129
McNulty, J., 486
McPherson, M., 219
McRae, K., 343
McShane, K., 158
Meadows, S.O., 495
Meaney, M.J., 106
Mebert, C.J., 275
Meeks, T.W., 613
Meerlo, P., 141
Mehler, J., 182
Mehrotra, C. M., 9, 40
Meikle, J., 596
Meili, D., 568
Meins, E., 206, 207, 248
Mellon, N., 182
Meltzer, A., 486
Meltzoff, A.N., 177, 179, 180
Menchola, 631
Mendelson, M., 322
Mendelson, M.J., 361
Mendle, 102
Mendel, J., 376
Menec, V.H., 649
Menias, C.O., 125
Menn, L., 250
Menna, R., 214
Mennecke, A., 455
Menon, M., 340
Menon, R., 97
Mensah, G.A., 452
Merad, M., 585
Mercer, M., 169, 170
Meristo, M., 254
Merrill, D.M., 566, 570
Mertens, J., 456
Merz, E-M., 358
Mesalum, 602
Mesch, G., 26
Messinger, D., 198
Mestre, T. A., 605
Metcalfe, J., 306
Metts, S., 490
Meyer, 293, 651
Meyer, M. J., 329
Meyer, S., 198, 202
Mezzacappa, E., 342
Michalska-Malecka, K., 590
Miche, 643
Midouhas, E., 341
Miech, R., 454
Mikkonen, J., 424, 634, 636, 637
Mikulincer, M., 418, 483, 484
Milan, A., 326, 464, 494, 500, 501, 567, 569, 639, 640
Milberg, A., 678
Miles, M.F., 454
Millar, W.J., 591
Miller, B. J., 40, 41, 505
Miller, C.F., 352
Miller, J. G., 350
Miller, K., 254
Miller, P.H., 245
Miller, R., 165
Miller, R. B., 271, 495
Miller, S., 134
Milligan, K., 636
Mills, A., 127
Mills, B., 400
Mills, C.M., 244, 262, 339
Mills, D., 244
Milte, 653
Minde, K., 137
Mindell, J.A., 157
Miner, M. M., 525
Miniussi, C., 587, 617
Minnotte, K., 473
Minnotte, M., 473
Minzi, M., 211
Miotto, E. C., 611
Miranda, M.L., 254
Mischel, W., 21, 23, 61, 245, 246
Mishra, G.D., 524
Mistry, R. S., 356
Mitchell, 616
Mitchell, D., 179
Mitchell, J. R., 598
Mitchell, M.S., 464
Mitchell, O. S., 536
Mitchell, V., 504
Miyashita, M., 666
Mize, K., 195, 200
Mobley, A. S., 586
Moen, P., 472, 637, 638
Mohamed-Ali, M., 205
Mohr, J.J., 504
Moilanen, 524
Moise, K.J., 99
Moley, K.H., 122
Molina, 384
Mollee, P., 95
Molnar, B.E., 435
Molton, I. R., 592
Monahan, K.C., 379, 431
Monette, M., 600
Monin, J.K., 501
Monsell, S. E., 602
Monserud, M.A., 470
Montessori, M., 253
Montgomery, P.R., 601
Moon, C., 182
Moon, S., 670
Moore, B., 245
Moore, C., 676
Moore, D. S., 90, 92, 95, 96
Moore, S., 294, 376
Moorefield, B.S., 358
Moos, B., 608
Moos, M.K., 131
Moraes, W., 589
Moran, G., 211
Moran, S., 309
Morasch, K., 194
Moravcik, E., 282
Moreau, C., 490
Moreira, S. R., 597
Moreno, A., 214
Morgan, E., 380
Morgano, E., 430
Morin, C. M., 589
Morra, L., 614
Morra, S., 297
Morrell, R.W., 638
Morris, A.S., 266, 351, 355
Morris, D., 81
Morris, P., 70, 107
Morris, R. J., 344
Morris, Y. P., 344
Morrison, G.S., 253, 297, 312
Morrongiello, B., 295, 354, 361
Morrow, D., 9
Morrow-Howell, 630
Mortensen, J., 202
Morton, D., 558
Moschonis, G., 160
Moscovitch, M., 589
Mosenthal, A.C., 666
Moses, L. J., 246, 302
Moshman, D., 466
Mosing, 635
Moss, E.L., 666
Mota, P., 141
Moules, N.J., 677
Moulson, M.C., 33, 117, 118, 205
Mowafaghian, D., 89
Moyer, A., 500
Mozart, W.A., 466
Mroczek, D., 562, 563
Muehlenkamp, J., 391
Mueller, M.P., 297
Muhajarine, N., 130
Muir, K. W., 588
Muller, M. M., 611
Mullen, S. P., 590
Muller, P., 124
Müller, U., 246
Muller, U., 55, 245, 246
Mullet, H. G., 612
Mullinax, M., 462, 463
Mullis, P.E., 115
Mulvaney, M.K., 275
Munakata, Y., 291
Mund, I., 610
Mundt, M., 454
Mungas, D., 603
Muniz-Terrera, G., 614, 615
Munoz, K., 449
Munro, S., 136

Muratore, A.M., 638
Murphy, 522, 592
Murphy, D., 435
Murphy, N., 219
Murphy, R.A., 590
Murphy, S.A., 678
Murr, 603
Murray, J.P., 284
Murray, S., 142
Murray, S.A., 675
Musa, I., 662
Musch, J., 355
Mustanski, B., 459
Mustard, J.F., 216
Mutchler, J.E., 641
Muzio, J.N., 157
Myatchin, I., 299
Myers, M.W., 282
Mykyta, 640
Myles, J., 636

N

Nag, T.C., 590
Nagamatsu, 597, 653
Nagy, A., 103
Nagy, R., 28
Nakamura, K., 130
Nakata, T., 187
Nakayama, H., 197
Nannini, A., 661, 662
Nanovskaya, T.N., 115
Narang, A., 140
Narayan, C., 182, 186
Narayan, A. J., 344
Narberhaus, A., 138
Nardone, R., 602
Narducci, A., 126
Narvaez, D., 349
Nascimento Dda, C., 596
Natalizia, A., 517
Navaneelan, T., 517
Nava-Ocampo, A.A., 118
Neal, J. W., 360
Neal, Z. P., 360
Nechita, A., 316
Needham, A., 167
Neema, S., 143
Neikrug, A. B., 589
Neimeyer, R.A., 672, 680
Nelson, C.A., 33, 117, 118, 152, 156, 180, 262, 263, 291, 378, 446
Nelson, H., 194
Nelson, J., 662
Nelson, J.M., 423, 426
Nelson, R.J., 154, 431
Nelson, S., 128
Nelson, S.D., 344
Nelson, T.D., 423, 426
Nelson, T., 662
Nesse, R.M., 680
Nesteruk, O., 640
Netini, C., 496
Neufeld, G., 105
Neugarten, B.L., 555, 556, 567, 572, 630, 645
Neupert, S.D., 555
Newall, 649
Newburg, D.S., 160
Newcombe, N.S., 180, 211
Newell, F.N., 165
Newhook, L.A., 159
Newman, A.B., 590
Newman, E., 344
Newman, R., 252
Newton, E.K., 196, 205, 214
Newton, N. J., 548
Nicolaisen, M., 538, 649
Nielson, D., 671, 672
Nikitin, 597, 632, 633, 653
Nilsson, L. G.., 610, 612
Nimmo, G.A., 583
Nimrod, 633
Nisbett, R., 312
Nisenblat, V., 120
Nishina, A., 376
Noble, J.M., 613
Noble, W., 603
Noel-Miller, 640, 641
Noels, K.A., 554
Noftle, E. E., 560
Nolen-Hoeksema, S., 459, 630
Nolte, S., 282
Nomoto, M., 605
Nordqvist, C., 599
Nores, M., 215
Nørgård, B., 120
Norman, J. F., 612
Norman, R., 120
Norris, S., 200, 328
Norton, W., 463
Nouchi, R., 616
Nowakowski, M.E., 206
Noya, M., 131, 144
Nutt, S., 469, 470, 471
Nutting, P.A., 646
Nyberg, L., 587, 612, 613
Nygard, C.-H., 536

O

Obenauer, S., 98
Obermeyer, C. M., 524
Obradovic, J., 246, 445
O'Brien, B., 262
O'Brien, E. J., 340
O'Brien, K., 472
O'Brien, M., 507, 611
O'Brien, P., 121
O'Connor, A.B., 124
O'Connor, D.B., 553
O'Dea, 397
O'Donnell, E., 518
Odom, S., 328
Odouli, R., 120
Oiestad, B. E., 596
Oerlemans, 630
Ofen, N., 612
Ogden, C. L., 232
Ogrodnik, L., 646
O'Halloran, A. M., 611
O'Hara, W., 142
Oishi, S., 426
Okada, H. C., 516, 525
O'Kane, J., 471
O'Keefe, 601
Okun, N., 91
Olafsdottir, E., 590
O'Leary, K., 500
Olesen, J., 596
Ollendick, T. H., 264
Olmstead, S., 507
Olson, 396
Olson, B.D., 563
Olson, H.C., 120
Olszewski-Kibilius, P., 314
Olyan, S.M., 679
O'Neill, D.K., 252
Ong, A., 424
Opfer, J., 235
Opitz, A., 184
Orav, 567
Orbe, M.P., 412
Ordean, A., 122, 123, 124
Orecchia, R., 124
O'Reilly, R., 86
Orford, J., 456
Ornstein, K, 604
Ornstein, P.A., 301
O'Rourke, N., 629
Orrange, R.M., 472
Orth, U., 412
Ory, M. G., 520
Osorio, R. S., 603
Ossher, L., 612
Ostbye, T., 137
Osterberg, E. C., 525
Ostfeld, B.M., 158, 159
Ostrove, J.M., 548, 561
Ostrovsky, Y., 637, 638, 652
O'Sullivan, L.F., 432
Oswald, A. J., 613
Otaegui-Arrazola, A., 599
Ott, C.H., 680
Ouellet, M-C., 589
Ouellette-Kuntz, H., 328
Ouellet-Morin, I., 121
Ougrin, 391
Ouyang, 524
Owen, J., 491
Oyserman, D., 431

P

Pacala, J. T., 591
Pace-Schott, E. F., 589
Padilla-Walker, L., 351
Padmanabhan, A., 378
Pagani, L.S., 254
Pageon, H., 516
Paikin, S., 344
Pakhomov, S. V., 588
Palmer, R., 456
Palmert, M., 373
Palmore, E.B., 645
Pan, B. Alexander, 183
Pan, B.A., 317
Pan, Z., 284, 579
Panigrahy, A., 98
Panizzon, M. S., 525
Panscofar, N., 215
Papastavrou, E., 604
Papp, 610
Parade, S., 211, 484
Paré, J.R., 328
Parish-Morris, J., 251
Parisi, 653
Park, 585, 597, 615, 616, 653
Park, C. J., 250
Park, D., 531, 532, 587, 618
Park, D.C., 7, 615
Park, M.J., 385, 449
Park, N., 4886
Park, N. S., 517
Park, S. Y., 99
Parkay, F.W., 320
Parke, R.D., 242, 272, 273, 357
Parker, 651
Parker, J.G., 360
Parker, M. A., 231
Parkin, C., 417, 419
Parnass, J., 271
Parodi, V., 589
Parr, E. B., 517
Parra-Cardona, 570
Parsons, R., 364
Pascoal, A., 141
Pasiak, C., 214

Pasley, K., 358
Pasoli, K., 217
Passini, S., 437
Passuth, P.M., 556
Patchin, J.W., 396, 430
Patel, A., 140
Pathman, T., 245, 300
Patrick, M., 454
Patterson, C., 279, 280, 504
Patterson, C.J., 279, 280, 372
Patton, F., 424
Pauen, S., 172
Pauley, S., 591
Paulhus, D.L., 280, 560
Paus, T., 378
Pavlov, I.P., 60, 74, 75*f*, 77
Pavol, 447
Pawson, T., 96
Payne, W.A., 25, 450, 451
Pearce, T., 101
Pearlman, L., 105
Pearson, L.B., 522
Peck, R., 630
Pedersen, D., 473
Pedersen, S., 430, 435
Pederson, D., 211
Peek, M.K., 640, 641
Peich, M. C., 612
Pelaez, M., 207
Pellicano, E., 248
Pellitier, M., 354
Pendakur, R., 557
Peng, P., 299
Peng, X.D., 630
Peplau, L.A., 459, 460, 504
Pepler, D., 363, 364
Perach, 649
Pereverzeva, M., 169
Perez, 598
Perez, S.M., 194, 201
Perkins, T., 349
Perlman, M., 280
Perls, T.T., 579, 580
Perrault, S., 463
Perrelli-Harris, 500
Perrin, J., 218
Perry, B., 378, 393
Perry, D. G., 268
Perry, N. B., 264, 265
Perry, T.B., 361
Perry, W., 466
Perry-Jenkins, M., 504
Peter, J., 486
Peter, T., 429
Peterson, 341
Peterson, C., 71, 238, 244, 245, 248, 249
Peterson, G. W., 274
Peterson, J.B., 32
Petitclerc, A., 282
Petitclerc, C., 546, 547, 548
Petitto, L.A., 185
Petrick-Steward, E., 239
Pettit, G.S., 201
Pfeffer, J., 472
Pfefferbaum, B., 344
Pfeifer, J., 200
Phelps, E., 423
Philbin, 382
Phillips, D., 216
Phillips, 630
Phillips, A.C., 597
Phinney, J.S., 412, 414, 423
Phinney, S., 424
Phipps, S., 277, 329
Piaget, J., 55–57, 74, 75*f*, 76, 173, 174, 175, 177, 235, 236, 237, 238, 241, 242, 262, 266, 267, 268, 269, 282, 285, 286, 295–298, 346, 399, 400, 403, 415, 416, 465–468, 474
Piazza, J.R., 553, 640, 643
Picard, A., 292
Picasso, P., 224
Pick, A., 179
Pickell, D., 260
Pickens, T. Boone, 587
Piccinin, A. M., 614
Picot, G., 522, 636
Piehler, T., 282
Pieperhoff, P., 531
Pierce, R. S., 610
Pierce, T., 143
Ping, L., 160
Pipe, M., 244
Piper, W.E., 678
Pitman, E., 358
Pitzer, L. M., 569
Pixley, J.E., 551
Pizzol, D., 126
Plomin, R., 104, 105, 107, 201
Pohlhaus, J. Reineke, 40
Poil, S. S., 604
Polan, E., 371, 373, 374, 423, 458
Polat, U., 590
Polen-Petit, N., 379
Polit, D.F., 35, 36
Polivy, J., 452
Pollack, P., 605
Pollack, W., 355
Pollex, E., 115
Polley, S., 467
Polo-Kantola, P., 518
Poltorak, D., 671
Pomerantz, 357
Pomerantz, E., 428
Pomfrey, E., 554
Ponton, L., 390
Pooler, A. M., 603
Popenoe, D., 494, 500
Poranganel, L., 159
Porath-Walker, A., 123
Porterfield, S., 126
Posada, G.E., 212, 214
Posner, M.I., 179, 244
Poulin, F., 430
Poulin-Dubois, D., 238
Powell, B., 210
Power, T. G., 283
Powers, C.J., 361, 362
Powers, D., 449
Prakash, R.S., 615
Prelow, H.M., 435
Prentice, J., 322
Pressley, M., 246, 306
Preston, S.H., 598
Preville, M., 553
Price, 570
Price, C.A., 640
Price, P., 326
Price, T., 120
Prigerson, H.G., 678
Prince-Paul, M., 675
Prinstein, M., 421
Prinstein, M.J., 281, 360
Priyadarshi, B., 612
Proulx, C., 495
Pryor, J.H.Y., 447
Puccini, D., 251
Puchalski, C. M., 675
Pudrovska, T., 551, 471
Pugh, D., 58
Purdy, K.T., 361
Purnell, L., 494
Pursell, G., 361
Putnam, S.P., 202

Q

Qamar, D., 522
Qin, L., 428
Qu, H., 310
Quan-Haase, A., 26
Quesnel, C., 661
Quesnelle, H., 29
Quevedo, K., 198
Quigley, C., 611
Quinn, J., 28
Quinn, J.F., 536
Quiñonez, C., 30
Quoidbach, J., 560, 562

R

Raabe, G., 124
Rachner, T. D., 517
Racine, T.P., 206
Radvansky, 632
Rahe, R.H., 552
Rahnema, C. D., 525
Raikes, H., 208
Raiser, S. N., 590
Raj, T., 88
Rakison, D., 170, 171
Ram, N., 17
Ramage-Morin, P., 606
Ramani, G.B., 205, 206
Ramasamy, R., 525
Ramirez-Rodriquez, G., 586
Ramlau-Hansen, C., 120
Ramos, E., 95
Ramsey-Rennels, J.L., 205
Randolph, S.M., 567
Rangul, V., 376
Ranhoff, A., 601
Ransmayr, G., 605
Rapaport, S., 587
Rapee, R.M., 389
Raphael, B., 678
Raphael, D., 30, 424, 634, 636, 637
Rapoport, J., 5
Rapp, P. R., 616, 617
Rapson, R., 488
Rasmussen, C., 319
Rast, P., 614
Rasulo, D., 640, 643
Ratey, J., 328
Rathunde, K., 9
Ratnapalan, M., 396, 397
Ratzan, S., 25
Ravanera, 503
Raven, P. H., 88
Raver, C. C., 272
Rawlins, W.K., 491
Ray, B., 500
Ray, G., 456
Ray, O.S., 455
Raymo, J.M., 638
Raymond, 392, 403
Raynauld, E., 541
Raynauld, I., 618
Raz, N., 585, 616
Razza, R. A., 244
Razza, R. P., 302
Raznahan, A., 226, 291, 377
Read, S., 678

Reading, J., 523
Ream, G.L., 380, 460
Rebbechi, D., 585
Rebok 616, 653
Reddel, R. R., 583
Reeb, B.C., 156
Reece, M., 129
Reed, 524
Reedy, E. J., 532
Reeskin, T., 26
Reeve, C.L., 310
Regan, P., 379
Regan, P.C., 486, 488
Rehbein, M., 156
Rehm, J., 456
Reichstadt, J., 638
Reid, G., 325
Reid, J., 455
Reiger, G., 429
Reijmerink, N. E., 92
Reilly, 354
Reilly, D.E., 678
Reindollar, R. H., 99
Reis, S. M., 315
Reitman, 427
Rejeski, W. J., 590
Rena, 400
Rendall, M., 495
Renzulli, J. S., 315
Repacholi, B. M., 247
Restak, Richard, 7
Reuter-Lorenz, P.A., 8, 9, 615, 616, 617, 618
Reyes, S., 589
Reyna, V., 301, 400, 401
Reynolds, C.A., 604
Reynolds, R., 106
Reznick, J. S., 299
Rhoades, G., 490, 500
Rhodes, A., 396
Rice, 388
Rich, D.E., 142
Richards, J.E., 179
Richardson, 648
Richardson, G., 123
Richardson, R., 180
Richardson, V.E., 678
Riche, D.M., 525
Richens, J. L., 604
Richman, J.A., 464
Richmond, E.J., 375
Rickman, A., 427, 428
Riediger, M., 597, 632, 633, 653
Rifas-Shiman, S.L., 118
Riley, K.P., 588
Rimsza, M.E., 449
Ripke, M.N., 357, 360
Rippon, 644
Rising, S.S., 131
Ritchie, K., 126
Ritchie, S., 254
Ritzmann, R., 596
Riva Crugnola, 384
Rivers, S.E., 400, 401
Rizzuto, D., 598
Robbins, G., 449
Roberie, D. R., 518
Roberto, K.A., 491, 563, 567, 641,
Roberts, B.W., 562, 563, 634
Roberts, D., 379
Robertson, L. T., 598
Robine, 579
Robins, R.W., 412, 560
Robinson, K., 315
Robinson, K. M., 59, 315, 327
Robitaille, A., 628
Robles, T., 520, 589
Roche, D., 486, 487
Rochette, L. M., 233
Rocke, C., 521
Rodd, E., 619
Rodgers, S., 553
Rodriguez, E.T., 252
Rodriguez, S., 663
Rodrique, K. M., 858
Roehlkepartain, E.C., 417, 423
Roeser, R., 423
Roffwarg, H.P., 157
Rogers, A. N., 90
Rogers, C., 47, 49, 66, 74, 78, 270, 437
Rogers, S., 219
Rogers, W.A., 638
Rogoff, B., 399
Rogol, A.D., 375
Roher, E., 396
Rohrer, J., 280
Roisman, G.I., 460
Rolando, C., 586
Rolland, Y., 517
Roma, 418
Romano, A. D., 583
Romano, A.M., 136
Romanow, R., 28
Romanow, R.J., 646
Rombaux, O. P., 586
Rønning, J.A., 276
Roodin, P., 516, 537, 592, 601, 602
Rook, K.S., 643, 648
Rosano, C., 585
Rosato, F.D., 453
Rose, A., 360, 430
Rosenberg, L., 638
Rosenfeld, A., 561
Rosenfeld, M., 486
Rosenn, B., 126
Rosenthal, C., 643
Rosenthal, R., 31
Rösler, F., 8, 9
Rosnick, C., 521
Rosnow, R.L., 31
Rospenda, K.M., 464
Ross, H., 280
Ross, J., 416
Ross, L. A., 593
Rossi, S., 587
Rossignol, J., 605
Rossignol, M., 135
Rossiter, 159, 160
Rotermann, M., 381, 381*f*, 458, 501, 608
Roth, W., 25, 452
Rothbart, M.K., 179, 198, 200, 201, 202, 220, 243, 244, 481
Rothbaum, F., 144, 194
Rothman, S. M., 589
Rouleau, J., 93
Rovee-Collier, C., 178, 180
Rowbotham, K., 472
Rowley, S.R., 425
Roy, C., 124
Roy, J., 373
Rozzini, R., 601
Ruan, L., 586
Rubenfeld, G., 666
Rubin, K.H., 263, 264, 362, 430
Rubinstein, A., 632, 633
Ruble, D.N., 27, 339, 352
Rudolph, K. L., 583
Rueda, M.R., 244
Ruidavets, 454
Ruiter, M., 518
Runciman, S., 382
Rupp, D.E., 645
Russel, D., 20
Rutter, 390
Ruys, J.H., 158
Ryan, C., 429
Ryan-Harshman, M., 117, 129
Ryff, C., 551, 552
Ryff, C.D., 636
Rypma, B., 585
Ryu, H. M., 99

S

Saarni, C., 194, 344
Sabbagh, M.A., 246, 247, 248
Sadeh, A., 157
Saewyc, E., 396
Saffran, J.R., 171, 172
Sagiv, S. K., 129, 130
Sahler, O., 672
Sainte-Marie, B., 577, 609
Saint Onge, J. M., 579
Sakamoto, Y., 596
Sakraida, T.J., 565
Salat, D.H., 531
Sale, A., 378
Salovey, P., 307, 308, 309, 310, 313, 331
Salthouse, T.A., 8, 530, 531, 532, 536, 609, 610, 612, 613, 616
Samjoo, 583
Samson, S. L., 518
Sana, F., 472
Sandell, 134
Sangree, W.H., 652
Sann, C., 172
Sanson, A.V., 202
Santilli, F., 518
Santoro, N., 524
Santrock, J.W., 87, 116, 152, 176, 185, 228, 235, 353, 374, 436, 447, 644
Sarifakioglu, B., 583
Sarkisian, N., 570
Sarlos, P., 92
Sasidharan, K., 140
Sassenberg, 644
Sauvé, R., 565
Savard, J., 589
Savin-Williams, R.C., 380, 429, 460
Sayegh, P., 85
Sayer, A., 548
Sayer, L.C., 278
Sbarra, D., 490
Scales, P., 417, 423
Scarr, S., 104, 105, 109
Schachar, R., 260
Schacter, D., 180
Schacter, E.P., 417
Schafer, A., 665
Schaffer, D., 384
Schaffer, D. V., 91
Schaie, K. Warner, 7, 10, 17, 36, 465, 515, 528, 529, 530, 531, 543, 603, 613, 614, 615, 617, 651

Scharf, M., 418
Schattschneider, C., 252
Scheerings, M. S., 344
Scheibe, S., 17, 581
Schell, A., 253
Schellenberg, E.G., 310
Schellenberg, G., 539, 540, 601, 608, 618, 637, 636, 639, 641, 645, 647, 650, 651, 652
Scher, A., 198
Scherer, S., 96
Schiavi, A., 583
Schiff, W.J., 231, 385, 451
Schiffman, R., 619
Schiffman, S.S., 592
Schimmack, U., 426
Schirmer, G.J., 229, 230
Schlaggar, B.L., 117, 154
Schlam, T.R., 245, 246
Schlesinger, J., 595
Schmeicchel, 395
Schmidt, E. L., 593
Schmidt, L., 201
Schmidt, S., 590
Schmikle, S., 280
Schmitt, D.P., 560
Schmitt-Rodermund, E., 426
Schneider, E., 91
Schneider, J. M., 590
Schneider, M., 301, 472
Schneider, W., 244, 306
Schnittker, J., 648
Schnurer, F., 682
Schoenfeld, T. J., 586, 597
Scholnick, E.K., 399
Schonert-Reichl, K. A., 343
Schooler, C., 637
Schorr, I., 355
Schroer, W., 18
Schukle, S. C., 560
Schulenberg, J., 428
Schulenberg, J.E., 446
Schulz, E., 583
Schulz, R., 640, 681
Schumm, L.P., 17, 650
Schunk, D., 341
Schut, H., 678, 681
Schuz, 643
Schwalfenberg, G., 599
Schwartz, B., 418
Schwartz, J.E., 634
Schwartz, M.A., 500
Schwartz, S., 413
Schwarz, N., 7
Schwarzer, R., 520, 552
Scialfa, C.T., 517, 590
Scollon, C., 672
Scott, 640
Scott, B., 500
Scott, D., 517
Scott, H. S., 88, 95
Scott, T., 626
Scullin, M. K., 612
Scuteri, A., 518
Seabrook, J.A., 277
Sebastian-Galles, N., 182
Sebastiani, P., 579
Sechrist, 569, 571, 642
Seeman, T.E., 583, 595
Seibert, A. C., 357
Seibert, S. E., 560
Seiffge-Krenke, I. 487
Sekiyama, K., 613
Seligman, M., 49, 51, 71, 74, 75*f*
Selye, H., 554
Senechal, M., 252
Sener, A., 638
Seo, 635
Serido, J., 552
Serra, M.J., 306
Settersten, R., 500, 507
Setliff, A., 180
Sewell, K.W., 680
Sgoifo, A., 141
Shachar, I., 520
Shadel, G. S., 583
Shaffer, D., 49
Shah, A., 234
Shah, M., 172
Shanahan, M.J., 562
Shank, P., 87
Shankar, 649
Shanks, D. R., 612
Shannon, 125, 129
Shannon, C.A., 464
Shapiro, D., 539, 541
Sharabany, R., 492
Sharaf, 630
Sharma, P. 142.
Sharma, V., 142
Sharp, E., 428
Shaver, P.R., 418, 483, 484
Shaw, P., 327
Shay, J. W., 583
Shaywitz, B.A., 325
Shaywitz, S.E., 325
Shea, A.K., 158
Sheese, B.E., 201
Sheikh, A., 675
Shek, D., 428
Shema, L., 160
Shen, L., 599
Sheps, S., 130
Sheridan, J.F., 156
Sheridan, S., 215
Sherman, A.M., 643, 681
Sherwood, C.C., 585
Sherwood, L., 87
Shibata, Y., 88
Shield, K., 456
Shields, L., 194
Shields, M., 387, 581, 596
Shih, 583
Shimazu, A., 472
Shiner, R. L., 480
Shing, Y. L., 612
Shipley, B.A., 519
Shivalingham, H., 410
Shoda, Y., 21, 23
Shokhirev, M. N., 582
Shor, E., 495
Shors, T.J., 586
Short, M., 244
Shovali, 649
Shuey, K.M., 642
Siedlecki, K.L., 611
Siegel, 383
Siegel, D. H., 101
Siegel, L., 325
Siegler, 300, 306, 399, 653
Siegler, I. C., 551
Siegler, R., 59, 246
Siegler, R. S., 298
Siener, S., 357
Sievert, L. L., 524
Signal, T.L., 141
Sikder, M., 180
Silk, T., 154
Silverslides, A., 402
Silverstein, M., 570
Sim, M. P. Y., 245
Simmons, E. S., 328
Simon, R., 490
Simon, T., 306
Simon, V.A., 431
Simonetti, G. D., 233
Simonton, D. K., 466
Simpkins, 570
Simpkins, S.D., 357
Simpson, J.L., 136
Simpson, S., 247
Simpson, S. J., 582
Sinclair, H., 491
Sinclair, S., 675
Singer, D., 283
Singer, L.T., 124
Singh, M., 33
Singh, S., 86, 87
Sinha, J.W., 423
Sinha, M., 215, 216, 217, 276, 359, 463, 464, 465, 503
Sirard, J.R., 385
Skider, S., 180
Skingley, 649
Skinner, B.F., 60, 61, 74, 75*f*, 77, 186
Skinner, E.I., 611
Skinner, R., 396
Skipper, J.I., 184
Skirbekk, 645
Skjaerven, R., 137
Skolnick, A.S., 493
Skovronek, E., 531
Sky, A., 260, 261
Slade, J.M., 587
Slade, M.D., 644
Slater, A., 207
Slaughter, V., 670, 671
Slutsky, I., 585
Small, B.J., 531, 532, 612, 614, 615
Smetana, J., 349, 351
Smid, M., 30
Smigielski, J., 601
Smith, A., 162
Smith, A.D., 617
Smith, B., 270
Smith, C.L., 355
Smith, D.L., 132, 137
Smith, D.W., 121
Smith, E., 103
Smith, G.A., 233
Smith, J., 17, 504, 613, 635, 636
Smith, J.K., 596
Smith, L., 123, 159, 164
Smith, L. B., 162, 172, 172
Smith, M.D., 140
Smith, P.J., 610
Smith, R. A., 590
Smith, R. E., 612
Smith, T.F., 666
Smith, T.J., 666
Smithbattle, L., 127
Smith-Cheine, 401
Smithers, L., 232
Smokowski, P.R., 424
Smylie, J., 158
Snapp-Childs, W., 173
Snarey, J., 350
Sneed, J.R., 548
Snijders, B.E., 160
Snowdon, D.A., 588
Snyder, H., 95
Snyder, J., 435

Snyder, P.J., 179
Snyder-Rivas, L., 495
Sobralske, M., 157
Socrates, 419
Soderman, A.K., 254
Soderstrom, M., 187, 518
Soderpalm, B., 454
Soenens, B., 418
Sok, 635
Solana, R., 589
Solari, E.J., 325
Solberg, 630, 653
Soli, A., 566
Solomon, 90
Somerville, S., 300
Song, H., 419
Sonon, K., 123
Sontag, L.M., 375
Sood, A.B., 671
Sorensen, S., 448
Sorenson, M., 590, 599
Sorkin, J., 493
Sorte, J., 231
Soto, C. J., 560
Sourander, A., 431
Sowah, L. A., 521
Sowden, A., 295
Sowell, E.R., 291, 378
Specht, J., 560
Speechley, M., 29
Spelke, E., 177
Spence, A.P., 585
Spence, J.T., 355
Spence, M.J., 171
Spencer, D., 263, 637
Spencer, J., 80
Spencer, R. M., 589
Sperling, R. A., 306
Spielmann, G., 589
Spinks, N., 536
Spinrad, T., 266, 351, 352, 355
Spiro, A., 562
Spironelli, C., 154
Spitzberg, B.H., 490
Spruijt, E., 277
Spuhl, S.T., 241
Squire, W., 153
Sriraman, B., 315
St. George-Hyslop, P., 603
St. Jacques, P. L., 245, 300
St. John, P.D., 601
Stadler, Z. K., 90
Staff, J., 428
Stafford, L., 494
Stajduhar, K.I., 675
Stanford, B.H., 320, 331
Stanley, S., 495
Stanley- Hagan, M., 277
Stansbury, 117
Stanton, A., 520
Stanton, K., 28
Stark, E., 561
Starkey, S., 328
Starr, C., 84, 90
Starr, L., 84, 90
Starr, L.R., 433
Stassen Berger, K., 27
Staudinger, U.M., 8, 9, 515, 609, 613, 615, 632, 633
Stavrinos, D., 592
Stawski, 553
Stecher, 526
Steeves, M., 681
Steeves, V., 361, 365
Stefansson, E., 590
Steffener, J., 614, 617
Steiger, A. E., 340
Stein, P.K., 598
Steinberg, L., 228, 378, 379, 393, 401, 411, 415, 416, 418, 431
Steinberg, L.D., 377
Steinberg, S.J., 433
Steinem, G., 365
Steiner, M., 158
Steinstra, D., 666
Stenekes, S., 675
Stephens, 648
Steptoe, A., 449, 649, 653
Sterin, J. C., 284
Stern, S., 433
Stern, W., 307
Sternberg, K., 488, 489
Sternberg, R.J., 303, 304, 308, 309, 310, 311, 312, 313, 315, 331, 487, 488–489
Sternthal, M.J., 541
Stessman, 649
Stetsone, B., 672
Stevens, C., 244
Stevenson, D., 506
Stevenson, H.W., 252
Stewart, 388
Stewart, A., 380
Stewart, A.J., 548, 561, 630
Stewart, D., 507
Stewart, M., 495
Stewart-Archer, L., 662
Stikkelbroek, Y., 672
Stiles-Shield, 389
Stine-Morrow, E.A.L., 615
Stipek, 340
Stoel-Gammon, C., 250
Stokes, A., 598
Stone, 632
Stone, Jay., 87
Stone, R.I., 646
Stormshak, 435
Stowell, J. R., 520, 589
Streeter, L., 675
Strehle, E., 158
Streissguth, A.P., 121
Streri, A., 172
Strickland, A.L., 676
Striegel, R., 387
Striegel-Moore, R.H., 387, 389
Stroebe, M., 678, 681
Stroebe, W., 678, 681
Strohmeier, D., 426
Strong, B., 379, 382, 458, 462
Strout, 640
Sturman, M. C., 536
Stutz, M., 418
Su, Y., 88, 215
Suchecki, D., 141
Sudheimer, E., 14
Suehs, B. T., 603
Sugden, N., 205
Sugita, Y., 170
Sullivan, C.E., 355
Sullivan, F.R., 305, 306, 319
Sullivan, H.S., 430, 440
Sullivan, P., 428
Sultan, C., 596
Sultan-Taieb, H., 521
Sumter, S., 431
Sun, F., 618
Sunstein, C.R., 400
Suris, J.C., 377
Susman, E., 375
Sussman, S., 449
Sutherland, P., 679
Sutton, J., 111
Suzuki, D., 513
Sveen, C.A., 678
Swamy, G.K., 137
Swanson, A., 95
Sweeney, M., 502
Sweeney, M.M., 638
Sweeney, M.S., 7
Sweet, E., 491
Swing, E. L., 243
Syed, M., 423
Sylvain-Roy, S., 610
Szanton, S.L., 595
Szinovacz, M.E., 57
Szmaus, C., 650
Szumilas, M., 396, 397
Szyf, M., 106

T

Tabuchi, M., 547
Tafoya, M., 490
Taher, N., 603
Taidre, E., 614
Taige, N.M., 130
Takanishi, R., 312
Takeuchi, H., 617
Taler, S.J., 518
Talmud, I, 26
Talwar, V., 238, 248
Tamir, L.M., 536
Tamis-LeMonda, C., 162
Tan, L. J., 517
Tanaka, M., 382
Tang, M., 603
Tang, Y., 244
Tanik, S., 526
Tanner, J., 118
Tantillo, M., 328
Tappan, M.B., 240
Tarabulsy, G.M., 212
Tarantino, V., 612
Tardif, C., 420
Tarnopolsky, M. A., 589
Tashiro, T., 490, 502
Tasker, F., 279
Tavassoli, N., 603
Taveras, E.M., 157
Tavernier, R., 449
Taylor, A., 523, 590
Taylor, C., 429
Taylor, D., 371, 373, 374, 423, 458
Taylor, G., 95
Taylor, H., 349
Taylor, L., 26
Taylor, M., 234, 678
Taylor, P.S., 645
Taylor, S. E., 555
Taylor, V., 586
Teague, M.L., 449
Tehranifar, P., 524
Teller, D.Y., 169
Telzer, 386
Templeton, J., 372, 422
Templeton, S., 326
Tenenbaum, H., 270
Tennenbaum, 636
Terrill, A. L., 592
Terrion, J.L., 456
Terry, D.F., 579, 580, 582
Terry, M. B., 524
Terry, W., 666, 673

Tezil, T., 583
Terzioglu, R.G., 638
Teti, D.M., 143
Thagard, P., 315
Tharp, R.G., 241
Thelen, E., 72, 162, 164, 172, 713, 297
Theobald, H., 598
Theurer, W. M., 233
Thiele, D.M., 567
Thomann, J., 196
Thomas, A., 480
Thomas, E.M., 255
Thomas, K.M., 180, 226, 291, 342
Thomas, R., 486
Thomas, S., 199, 220, 613
Thomas, W., 649
Thomason, M. E., 291
Thompson, J., 451, 453
Thompson, K. C., 344
Thompson, P.M., 5, 228, 291, 378
Thompson, R., 262, 419, 480, 481
Thompson, R.A., 194, 196, 198, 202, 203, 205, 206, 207, 208, 210, 211, 212, 214, 262, 263, 264, 266, 267, 340, 341, 343, 350, 357
Thomson, D.L., 314
Thorsen, K., 538, 649
Thrush, R., 482
Thurston, 386
Tian, 603
Tiedemann, M., 329
Tielsch-Goddard, A., 377
Tiggemann, M., 294
Tighe, S., 467
Till, J., 102, 103
Tilton-Weaver, L.C., 376
Timusk, P., 638
Titley, K., 159
Tjepkema, M., 670
Tobin, S.S., 630
Todd, A., 364
Todd, R., 636
Toepper, M., 616, 617
Toga, A.W., 378
Tomasello, M., 186, 187, 207, 251, 262, 266
Tomassini, C., 640, 643
Tomiyama, A. J., 583
Tompkins, G.E., 318
Tonella, P., 115
Tong, X., 317
Tonkin, R., 387, 388
Tonks, R.C., 548
Torges, C.M., 630
Torrence, C.M., 179
Tosi, G., 124
Toth, S.L., 107, 211, 275, 480
Tough, S., 167
Towe-Goodman, N., 143
Towle, H., 321, 330
Trabucchi, M., 601
Trahan, L., 311
Trainor, L.J., 185
Tramonte, L., 24
Traskowski, 310
Trautner, H.M., 352
Treboux, D., 570
Trefler, D., 218
Trehub, S.E., 172, 187, 214
Tremblay, M., 292, 387
Tremblay, M. S., 284
Tremblay , R.E., 143, 282
Trifunov, W., 158
Trimble, C., 126
Trinh, N., 417
Trocmé, N., 276, 359
Troll, L.E., 643
Trommsdorff, G., 194
Tronick, E.Z., 140
Troop, 362
Trottier, J., 540
Trudeau, J., 14, 18, 29, 464, 516, 547, 611, 665
Trudeau, P.E., 95, 458
Trueswell, J. C., 251
Trukeschitz, 646
Truog, R.D., 661, 663
Trzesniewski, K.H., 411, 412
Tsang, A., 592
Tselepis, A. D., 593
Tudge, R.H., 59
Tully, E.C., 267
Tulsky, J., 676
Tulving, E., 611
Tulviste, T., 144
Turati, C., 207
Turcotte, M., 128, 601, 608, 638, 639, 641, 645, 646, 647, 650, 651, 652
Turecki, G., 106
Turiano, N. A., 560
Turiel, E., 271, 351
Turkeltaub, P.E., 291
Turner, B.F., 651
Twain, M., 289
Twells, L., 159
Tyas, S.L., 588, 601
Tzourio, C., 518

U

Uccelli, P., 183, 317
Uchino, B. N., 582
Uher, 390
Ullah, M. I., 525
Umana-Taylor, A.J., 420, 423, 424
Upitis, R., 309
Uppal, S., 330
Urban, J., 417
Usalcas, J., 536
Utendale, W.T., 355

V

Vaillant. G., 548, 550, 561, 562, 567, 572
Vaish, A., 266
Valcarel-Ares, M. N., 583
Valdiviezo, 524
Valentini, P., 125
Valkanova, V., 602
Valkenburg, P., 486
Vallotton, C.D., 59
Vallurupalli, M., 675
van Aken, M., 480
van Balen, F., 504
van de Weijer-Bergsma, E., 137
van den Berg, P., 387
van den Berg, Y. H. M., 361
van den Boom, D., 504
van den Bout, J., 677
van den Hout, M.A., 677
van den Kommer, T. N., 614
Van Dyk, J., 123
Van Goethem, 402
van Hof, P., 165
Van Hooft, E., 472
van Ijzendoorn, M.H., 212
van Leijenhorst, L., 378
van Lizendoorn, 484
van Praag, H., 596
Van Petegem, S., 418
Van Ryzin, M., 381
van Solinge, H., 638
van Strien, T., 452
Vanderhaeghe, G., 478
Vandewater, E.A., 652
VanKim, N., 449
Vansant, G., 129
Vasdev, N., 134
Vasiliadis, H. M., 553
Vaughan, A., 207
Vaughn, S. R., 325
Vazsonyi, A.T., 341
Vedam-Mai, V., 605
Veenhof, B., 63
Veenhoven, 630
Velasquez, A.M., 421
Velders, M., 524
Vellas, B., 604
Vellutino, F.R., 254
Vendittelli, M., 135
Vennemann, M., 158
Ventura, J.J., 417
Ventura, N., 583
Vera, E., 598
Vereb, A., 326
Verghese, J., 596
Verkerke, G. J., 589
Verly, M., 328
Vermeersch, H., 375
Vernon-Feagans, L., 215
Vespa, J., 500
Vest, 570
Vetter, N. C., 362
Vézina, M., 128, 278, 646
Vicol, L., 126
Vidal, F., 56
Viechtbauer, W., 562
Vieno, A., 420
Vigorito, C., 596
Vihman, M. M., 249
Vijayakumar, 394, 395
Villaverde Gutierrez, C., 597
Villegas, R., 160
Vimaleswaran, K.S., 92
Vincent, H. K., 590
Vincent, K. R., 590
Vinik, J., 264
Virmani, E.A., 194, 203
Virues-Ortega, J., 207
Virta, J. J., 518, 614
Vissers, D., 518
Vitaro, F., 281, 361, 435
Vivona, J., 184
Vliegen, N., 142
Vodanovich, S.J., 645
Vohs, K.D., 340, 540
Volberg, R., 393
Volbrecht, M., 200
Volpe, R., 276, 382
Volpe, S., 449
Von Beveren, T.T., 132
von Bonsdorff, M. B., 536
Vonderheid, S., 134
Von Goethe, J.W., 444
Vong, K-I., 282
Voorpostel, M., 567
Voss, C., 27
Voss, M. W., 597

Vouloumanos, A., 182
Vromman, 603
Vurpillot, E., 243
Vygotsky, L., 55, 58–59, 74, 75*f*, 76, 238, 239, 240, 241, 242, 256, 268, 282, 286, 416

W

Wachs, H., 296
Wachs, T.D., 481
Wade, C., 21
Wadhwa, S., 590
Wagner, L., 249
Wagner, L.S., 9, 40
Wahlin, A., 531
Wahlsten, D., 94, 96
Waite, L., 502, 641
Waite, L. J., 526
Wakai, K., 455
Walby, F.A., 678
Waldinger, R. J., 567, 640
Waldron, J., 449
Walhovd, 585
Walk, R., 170, 189
Walker, 640
Walker, L.J., 349, 351, 352
Walker, P., 172
Walker, W.A., 160
Wallenborg, K., 601
Walls, M., 415
Walsh, H.C., 681
Walsh, L.V., 143
Walsh, R., 539, 541
Walter, T., 668, 679
Walters, M.W., 138
Walton, K.E., 562
Wan, M., 596, 597
Wandell, P. E., 598
Wang, 88, 603
Wang, B., 586, 597
Wang, C., 378
Wang, P., 92
Wang, Q., 428
Wang, S., 177
Wang, X., 92
Wang, Y., 517
Waqar-ul-Haq, H., 375
Ward, E. V., 612
Ward-Griffin, C., 642
Wardjiman, E., 569, 571, 642
Wardlaw, G.M., 159, 452
Wardle, J., 449
Ward-Ritacco, C. L., 524
Waring, J. D., 617
Wark, G.R., 351
Warner-Smith, P., 506
Warr, P., 637
Warren, K., 244
Warren, W., 376
Warrier, V., 88
Warshawski, T., 390, 450
Wathen, N., 507
Watkins, N., 428
Watson, G. L., 327
Watson, J.A., 567
Watson, J.B., 60, 197, 247
Waxman, 251
Way, N., 423
Weaver, A., 491
Weaver, S.R., 435
Webb, S., 219
Webster, J. D., 613
Wechsler, D., 307, 331
Wehling, E., 531
Wei, Y., 90
Weinberg, A. E., 526
Weinberg, B. A., 532
Weinfeld, M., 558
Weinfield, N.S., 482
Weinstein, J. R., 91
Weinstein, K.K., 567
Weis, K., 487
Weisner, C., 456
Weiss, 644
Weiss, R., 492
Weiss, S. K., 231
Weissig, V., 583
Weissman, P., 253
Weisz, A.N., 351
Wekerle, C., 382
Wellinger, R. J., 583
Wellington, M. A., 560
Wellman, H.M., 247
Wells, 341
Welsh, D., 433
Weltzin, T., 387
Wen, X., 588
Wendel, G.D., 125
Weng, X., 120
Wenger, 518
Wennergren, G., 160
Wentzel, K.R., 361
Werker, J.F., 171, 172, 182, 186
Werner, L.A., 171, 172
West, 590
West, K., 357
West, S.D., 310
Westerhof, G. J., 613, 635
Weston, K., 504
Weston, M.J., 98
Weststrate, N., 613
Wetherell, J.L., 630
Wethington, E., 551
Wetzel, I., 604
Weyand, C. M., 589
Wexler, B., 57
Wexler, N.S., 107
Whaley, S.E., 144
Wheatley, R., 144
Wheeler, B., 133, 159, 172
Wheeler, K., 181
Whelan, T.A., 567
Whipple, N., 210, 246
Whiren, A.P., 254
Whitbourne, S., 280
Whitbourne, S.K., 548, 635
White C., 455
White, C.D., 666
White, E., 105
White, F., 598
White, J.W., 354
White, R., 246, 264, 302, 372, 396
Whitehead, K., 424
Whiteman, S.D., 566
Whiting, P., 447
Whittaker, C., 26
Whitton, S., 502
Wiener, J., 325
Wiersma, W., 31
Wiggins, 386
Wigle, D.T., 125
Wijngaards-de Meij, L., 678
Wijnroks, L., 137
Wilder-Smith, A., 518
Wilhelmsen, 593
Wilhelmus, M. M., 602
Wilkins, R., 670
Wilkinson-Lee, 570
Willey, J., 87
Willette, 598
Willford, J.A., 123
Williams, A., 214
Williams, D.R., 541
Williams, L., 480
Williams, P.M., 124
Williams, R.W., 454
Williamson, R.A., 179, 267
Williams-Wheeler, M., 394
Willis, C., 670
Willis, S.L., 17, 465, 528, 529, 530, 531, 543, 615, 616
Willms, J.D., 23–24
Willoughby, B., 500
Willoughby, K. A., 298, 300
Willoughby, T., 378, 423, 449
Wilson, 117
Wilson, A.E., 642
Wilson, B.J., 284
Wilson, D., 125, 130, 152, 159, 161, 163, 172, 226, 295, 382, 395, 396
Wilson, J., 275
Wilson, K., 130
Wilson, K.G., 664
Wilson, M., 364
Wilson, R.S., 634
Wilson, S., 427, 428, 429
Wilson, T. D., 560, 562
Wilson-Rabbould, J., 464
Windsor, T. D., 565
Windspoll, R., 646
Winer, A. C., 263
Winett, 598
Wink, P., 561
Winner, E., 315
Winsler, A., 241
Winter, 646
Winter, M.A., 213, 214
Wirth, M., 588
Wiseman, H., 492
Wishart, P.M., 682, 683
Wisnewski, 603
Wisse, L. E., 602
Wister, A., 29
Witkow, M., 425
Witte, A.V., 598, 616
Wojcicki, 630
Wolfe, C. D., 194, 246
Wolfe, D., 382
Wolfe, D.A., 431
Wolfe, J., 671
Wolfinger, N. H., 570
Wolfson, 386
Wolinsky, F. D., 613, 616
Wollschlager, D., 531
Wong, 632
Wong, I., 326, 567, 569, 639
Wong, R., 596, 597
Wong, S., 122, 123, 124
Wood, A., 154
Wood, D., 563
Wood, J., 491
Woodgate, R., 219, 391, 395
Woodward, A.L., 141, 207, 251
Woolhouse, H., 141
Woolverton, C., 87
Wortman, C.B., 678, 681
Wright, J., 526
Wright, L., 213, 502
Wright, M., 26
Wright, S., 320
Wright, W. E., 583

Wrosch, C., 630, 635
Wrzus, 631
Wu, 518
Wu, T., 452
Wyatt, T., 343
Wyn, J., 372, 396
Wyse, R. D., 605

X

Xiao, O., 589
Xu, F., 170
Xu, M., 339
Xu, Q., 582
Xu, X., 636
Xu, Y., 496

Y

Yaffe, K., 615
Yalcin, O., 141
Yamakawa, 160
Yamanaka, S., 103
Yan, L., 598
Yanchar, N., 295
Yang, Y., 17, 595
Yanoff, 282
Yanofsky, N., 467, 468
Yarandi, H.N., 638
Yassine, H.N., 596
Yates, D., 226
Yeager, D., 349
Yen, S., 383
Yeuh, B., 591
Yeung, 632
Yezierski, R. P., 592
Yi, 613
Yokoyama, A., 92
Yoo, H.J., 417
Yoon, C., 613
You, J., 662
Young, K.T., 177
Youngblade, L, 417
Yu, J. J., 92
Yu, R., 143, 430
Yuan, P., 616
Yun, Y.H., 664

Z

Zacher, 646
Zacks, R.T., 587
Zalli, A., 582
Zarett, N.R., 354, 446
Zarit, 569
Zavos, P., 102
Zayas, 400
Zeifman, D., 483
Zeigler-Hill, V., 340
Zelazo, P.D., 177, 228, 245, 246, 264, 298, 302, 341
Zelkowitz, P., 137
Zellner, M., 299
Zemach, I., 169
Zeng, L., 455
Zera, C., 128
Zerwas, S., 205, 206
Zerwekh, J., 675, 677, 680
Zeskind, P.S., 197
Zettel-Watson, L., 643
Zhao, J., 88
Zhang, L., 97
Zhang, L.F., 312
Zhang, Y. X., 582
Zhao, H., 310, 560
Zhao, M., 582
Zhou, P., 249
Zhu, D.C., 587
Zielinski, A.E., 233
Ziemski, R., 252
Zimmer-Gembeck, M.J., 381
Zimmerman, B. J., 341
Zimprich, D., 634
Zins, J.E., 343
Ziso, B., 602
Zisook, S., 680
Zitouni, D., 376
Zlater, 602
Zosuls, K.M., 27
Zozuls, K., 271
Zuckoff, A., 678
Zuffianò, A., 351
Zukerman, P., 540
Zuzanek, J., 428
Zwicker, J., 137

Subject Index

A

Aboriginal peoples, 52, 394, 423
afterlife and, 679
aging and, 595
arthritis, incidence of, 596
attachment theory and, 213
average age of, 652
cancer, incidence of, 670
children's education and, 322, 323
culture-fair tests and, 311
death and, 668, 670
education for, 255, 258, 322
elders, role of, 568–569, 614
employment and, 536
ethical research and, 38–39
Fetal alcohol spectrum disorder (FASD), incidence of, 121
gambling and, 393
grandparents, role of, 567–569, 642–643
health and wellness of, 233
heart disease, incidence of, 670
high school drop-outs, incidence of, 403, 407
HIV infection, incidence of, 462
identity, 639
Internet usage by, 638
iron deficiency, incidence of, 159
learning disabilities, 324
life expectancy and, 12, 514, 578, 579
multi-generational homes, 639
parent-infant interactions, 215
PCBs in infants, 129
poverty and, 233, 322, 521
social policy and, 28
spirituality, 639
stress of, 554, 572
suicide among, 394, 395–396, 415, 424
teenage pregnancy, incidence of, 127
violence against women, 464–465
Acceptance, 673–674, 674*f*, 685
Accidents, 295, 330, 595, 596, 621
Accommodation, 55, 173, 398, 407
Achondroplasia, 93
Acquired immune deficiency syndrome (AIDS). *See* AIDS
Active (niche-picking) genotype environment correlations, 105
Active euthanasia, 663, 683
Active Healthy Kids Canada, 292, 293, 385
Activity theory, 630, 654
Acuity and colour, 168–170, 169*f*, 189
Snellen chart and, 168
Adaptation, 83, 84, 107
Adaptive behaviour, 83, 107
Addiction, 455–456, 474
Adler, Alfred, 54*f*, 342
Adolescence, physical and cognitive development in, 15*f*, 16, 43, 369–408
accidents, 390
adolescence, defined, 16
adolescence, nature of, 371–372, 403
alcohol and drug use, 390, 406
body image, 375, 376
brain changes, 377–378, 377*f*, 401, 405, 407
cognition, 397–403, 407
criminal activity, 390, 391, 406
critical thinking, 400
decision making, 400–401, 407
eating disorders, 386–390, 406
education, 401–403, 407
effective schools, 402–403, 408
egocentrism, 400
exuberance, 4
health problems and wellness, 385–395, 406, 448, 473–474
hormonal changes, 375
information processing, 400–401, 407
maturity, teen perspectives on, 376–377, 405
nutrition and exercise, 385, 406
obesity, 88, 450–451
physical performance, 448–449
Piaget's cognitive development theory, 398–400
pregnancy, 127–128, 136, 383–384, 405
puberty, physical changes in, 372–378, 404
risk and vulnerability, 390–391, 406
risk taking, 378
self-injury, 390–391
service-learning, 402, 407
sex problems, risk factors and, 382–383, 406
sexual identity, development of, 380, 405
sexual maturation, height, and weight, 373, 404
sexuality, 379–384, 404–406
sleep, 386, 406
stress, coping with, 447–448
substance use and addiction, 391–394, 406
suicide, 390
teen depression, 394–395
time of firsts, 371
top-dog phenomenon, 402, 430, 447
Adolescence, socio-emotional development in, 4, 409–441
addictions, 434
adolescent versus children's groups, 430
assimilation, 424
autonomy and attachment, 418, 419, 420, 439
Baumrind's parenting styles and, 417
dating and romantic relationships, 431–433, 440
delinquency, 410, 419
depression, 410, 412, 424, 425, 428, 429
education, 428
emerging adulthood and beyond, 415
employment, 428
Erikson's theory of identity development, 412–413
ethnicity, race, and socio-economic status, 425, 439
family, identity and, 416–423, 428, 439
freedom versus control, 418–419, 439
friendship, 429–433
gender and, 427
health, 427
identity, 411, 412–429. *See also* Identity
identity confusion, 412
immigrant and refugee youth, 345–346, 435
Marcia's identity status and development, 413–414
multiculturalism, 424
online social networking, 430
parent-adolescent conflict, 419–420, 428, 439
peer groups, 430–431
peer relationships, 419, 421–422, 428
perspective on death, 671, 672, 685
prevention and intervention programs, successful, 437–438, 440

problems associated with, 433
psychosocial moratorium, 413
racial identity, 423, 439
religion, identity and, 422–423, 439
rites of passage, 426, 439
self-understanding, 411
sex trade workers, 434
sexual orientation and identity, and, 429
social exclusion, 424
spiritual development, 422
street youth, 434
traditions and global changes in adolescence, 426–428, 439
young offenders, 434–435, 440
youth violence, 434
Adolescent egocentrism, 400, 407
imaginary audience, 400, 407
invincibility, 400
personal fable, 400, 407
personal uniqueness, 400
Adoption, 101, 109
Adult lifestyles, diversity of, 499–504, 510
Adulthood, stages of, 547–552, 572
age and well-being, 552*f*
Erikson's stage of generativity versus stagnation, 547–548, 572
individual variations, 552
Levinson's periods of adult development, 549–550, 550*f*, 561, 572
midlife crises, 550–551, 572
Adulthood perspective on death, 672, 685
Advance care planning, 661
Advanced directives, 661, 662
Aerobic exercise, defined, 453
Aesthetic needs, 67
Affectionate love, 488, 489, 508
Afterbirth, 132, 146
Afterlife, 668, 669, 678–679, 683
Age
biological, 18, 19, 43, 515
chronological, 18, 43, 515
concept of, 18, 19, 43
defined, 18, 19
emotional stability, 551*f*
happiness and, 17–18
maternal, prenatal development and, 127–128
mental, 18, 19, 43
periods, development and, 7, 18, 19
psychological, 18, 19, 43, 515
social, 18, 19, 43, 515
well-being, 552*f*
Age dynamisms, 415, 438
Ageism, 637–638, 651, 655
Aggression, social media and, 284, 286
Aging, 655
accidents, 595, 596, 621
adaptation of brain in, 586–587, 620
adult children and older adult parents, 642, 655
age and well-being, 552*f*
altruism, 650–651, 656
antioxidants, 599, 621
arthritis, 595, 596, 599, 621
attention, 610–611, 622
autonomy, 606–607
biological theories of, 581–584, 620
brain, 585–587, 588, 620
care options, 605–606, 622
caregivers, 646
cellular clock theory of aging, 581, 582, 620
circulatory system and lungs, 593, 621
cognitive neuroscience and, 616–618, 623
couples and, 640–641, 655
culture and, 652, 656
death, causes of, 595, 622
decision making and, 613
depression and, 600, 621, 622
eldercare, 646
evolutionary theory of, 581, 582, 620
exercise and, 596–597, 621
fear of victimization, crime, and elder maltreatment, 644–645, 656
free radical theory of, 581, 583, 620
friendship and, 643, 644, 656
gender roles, 651, 656
generational inequity, 646, 655
grandparenting and great grandparenting, 642–643, 656
health-care costs, 645, 646, 655
health-care providers and, 608, 622
hearing, changes in, 591, 592*f*, 620
hormone stress theory of, 581, 583, 620
immune system, 589, 620
income, 636–637, 655
lateralization, decrease in, 587, 587*f*
living arrangements, 638–639, 655
meeting needs of, 607
memory and, 611–613, 622, 623
mild cognitive impairment (MCI) and, 604
mitochondrial theory of, 581, 583, 620
neurogenesis, 586
neurotransmitters, reduction in, 585, 586
nutrition and weight and, 598–599, 621
osteoporosis and, 595, 596, 621
perceptual speed and, 612, 623
physical and mental health and wellness, 594–606, 621–622
physical appearance and movement, 589–590, 620
policy issues in an aging society, 645–646, 655
prescription drug use, 606
reflexes, loss of, 585
retirement, 637–638
romance and sex and, 641
sensory changes in, 590–593
sexuality and, 593–594
smell and taste, changes in, 592, 621
social support and social integration, 648–650, 656
stereotypes re older adults, 644–645
substance abuse, 601
successful, 652–653, 656
technology and social media, 638
telomeres and, 582, 582*f*, 620
touch and pain and, 592, 621
Vaillant's longitudinal studies of, 548
visible signs of in middle adulthood, 516, 542
vision, changes in, 590, 591*f*, 620
vitamins and, 599, 621
volunteering, 637, 650–651, 656
wisdom and, 613–614, 623
work and, 637, 654, 655
Agnostic, 540
AIDS, 41, 462, 474
antiretroviral therapy, 126, 127*f*
breastfeeding and, 462
global reach of, 462, 474
pregnancy and, 126, 127*f*, 462
Ainsworth Strange Situation, 209–210, 209–210*f*, 221
Alberta Council on Aging, 645
Alcohol related birth defects, 121
Alcohol use, early adulthood, in, 454–455, 474
addiction, 455–456
binge drinking, 454
risks of, 456, 474
sexual behaviour and, 454
Alcohol use, pregnancy, in, 120

Fetal alcohol spectrum disorder (FASD), 120–121, 121*f*
Alcoholism
Alcoholics Anonymous (AA), 456
defined, 454
early adulthood, in, 454
genetics and, 455
heredity and, 455
late adulthood, in, 601, 622
Alfred Adler, 51, 53, 54*f*, 76, 342
Allergies, 160
Alphabetic principle, 317
Altruism, 349
volunteerism and, 650–651, 656
Alzheimer's disease, 25, 58, 72, 85, 88, 89, 92, 93, 579, 580, 582, 585, 586, 588, 589, 602–604, 622, 634
apolipoprotein E (apoE), 603
brain of, 603*f*
care for those with, 604, 622
causes and treatments of, 602–604, 622
defined, 602
drug treatment of, 604
early detection of, 604
mild cognitive impairment (MCI) and, 604
American Institute for Psychoanalysis, 40
Amniocentesis, 97, 98*f*, 109
Amnion, 114
Amniotic fluid, 97, 98*f*, 114, 115, 117*f*, 268
Amygdala, 4, 194, 200, 219, 377, 377*f*, 378
Anal stage, Freud and, 50, 51*f*
Analytical intelligence, 308–309
Androgyny, 355, 367
Bem Sex-Role Inventory, 355, 356*f*
Anemia, 93, 124, 127, 159, 383
Anencephaly, 117
Anger, Kübler-Ross's stage of, 673, 674*f*, 685
Anger cry, 196, 219
Animism, 235, 236, 256
Aninut, 679
Anogenital warts, 126, 382
Anorexia nervosa, 294, 386, 387–388, 406, 411, 437, 450
characteristics of, 390
media, effect of on, 390
treatment of, 390
Anoxia, 132
Antidepressants, 119, 142, 455
Antioxidants, 599, 603, 621
Antisocial behaviour, adolescent, 434
Antisperm secretions, 100*f*
Anxiety, 50, 54*f*, 67, 75, 101, 130, 135, 140, 142, 263, 264, 274, 275, 286, 326, 333, 340, 343, 357, 359, 364, 390, 433, 448, 453, 472, 473, 480, 484, 488, 495, 501, 558, 593, 666, 672, 677, 678
Anxious attachment style, 483, 484
Apgar scale, 139, 139*f*, 146
Apolipoprotein E (apoE), 603
Arthritis, 85, 92, 520, 520*f*, 542, 583, 595, 596, 597, 599, 621
Asperger syndrome, 328, 333
Aspirin, 120
Assimilation, 55, 76, 173, 191, 398, 399, 407, 424
Assisted insemination (AI), 99, 100
Assisted suicide, 663
Asthma, 88, 92, 93, 138, 160, 232, 233, 456
Atheists, 540
Atopic dermatitis, 160
Attachment, 144, 207–211, 267, 482–485, 508, 638, 671
Ainsworth Strange Situation, 212, 212*f*, 221
attachment injuries, 483, 484
autonomy in adolescence and, 418, 419, 420, 439
Bowlby's four phases of, 208–209, 221
Classic Contact Comfort study, Harlow's, 207, 208*f*
classifications of and caregiving styles, 210–211, 221
criticism of theory of, 212
death and, 671
development of, 207–208, 221
Erikson's theory of, 208
individual differences in, 209–210, 221
secure, 144
self-determination theory, 212
styles of, 483–484
temperament and wider social world and, 211–212, 212*f*, 221
Attention, 4, 179, 243–244, 257
aging and, 610–611, 622
divided, 611, 622
executive, 243, 611
orienting/investigation process, 179
planfulness, 243, 243*f*
salient versus relevant dimensions, 243
selective, 611, 622
sustained, 180, 243, 611, 622
Attention deficit hyperactivity disorder (ADHD), 88, 130, 305, 326–328, 333
brain changes in, 327*f*
causes of, 88, 327
diagnosis of, 327, 333
exercise and, 327
genetics, 88
social impact of, 327–328
treatment of, 327–328, 333
Attraction, 485–487, 508
consensual validation, 486
familiarity and similarity, 486
online dating, 486
physical, 486, 487, 508
Authoritarian parenting, 272, 273, 273*f*, 285
Authority-oriented morality, 505*f*, 506
Autism Genome Project, 96
Autism spectrum disorders (ASD), 88, 124, 249, 320, 322, 324, 328, 333
causes of, 328
genetics and, 88, 328
social and cognitive deficits, 249
theory of the mind and, 249
Autistic disorder, 328
Autonomous morality, 266, 346
Autonomy versus shame and doubt, Erikson's stage of, 51*f*, 629*f*
Autosomal-dominant, 93
colon cancer, 93
neurofibromatosis I, 93
Autosomal-recessive, 93
cystic fibrosis, 93, 94*f*
phenylketonuria, 93, 94*f*, 108
sickle-cell anemia, 93, 94*f*
Tay-Sachs disease, 93, 94*f*
Autosomes, 93
Avelut, 679
Average children, 361, 362
Avoidant attachment style, 483, 484
Azoospermia, 99

B

Babbling and other vocalizations, 182, 185, 190
Babinski reflex, 163*f*
Baby blues, 142
Baby boomers, 10, 13, 14, 17, 29, 33
Baby-Friendly Hospital Initiative (BFHI), 150
Back-to-bedroom (B2B) kids, 566
Baltes's view of evolution and culture, 85, 85*f*, 108
Baltimore study, Costa and McCrae, 559–560
Bandura's social cognitive theory, 60, 74, 75*f*, 77, 85, 108, 194, 205, 267, 270
Bargaining, Kübler-Ross's stage of, 673, 674*f*, 685
Basal Metabolic Indices (BMI), 27
Basic cry, 196, 219

Basic-skills-and-phonetics approach, 318
Baumrind's parenting styles, 272–273, 273*f*, 285
  adolescence, 417
  authoritarian parenting, 272, 273, 273*f*, 285
  authoritative parenting, 272, 273, 273*f*, 285
  indulgent parenting, 272, 273, 273*f*, 285
  neglectful parenting, 272, 273, 273*f*
Bayley Scales of Infant Development, 181, 189
Bayley-III, 181
Beckwith-Wiedemann syndrome, 91
Becoming One's Own Man (BOOM), Levinson's, 549
Becoming parents and a family with children, 498, 510
Bed sharing, 157, 158
Behaviour genetics, 102–104, 105, 109
Behavioural and social cognitive approach, 37, 60, 61–63, 77, 267
Bandura's social cognitive theory. *See* Bandura's social cognitive theory
  evaluation of, 63, 77
  Pavlov's classical conditioning. *See* Pavlov's classical conditioning
  Skinner's operant conditioning. *See* Skinner's operant conditioning
Behaviourism, 60
Being needs (B-needs), 67
Belsky's Model, 213, 222
Bem Sex-Role Inventory, 355, 356*f*
Bereaved Families of Ontario, 681
Bergen's classification of play, 282–283
Berkeley longitudinal studies, 561, 573
Bias, research and, 40–41, 45
Bicultural identity, 424, 439
Big five factors of personality, 559–560, 560*f*, 573, 634–635
Bilingualism, 319, 332, 399
Binge drinking, 454
Bio-ecological approach, Bronfenbrenner's, 68–70, 74, 75*f*, 78, 273, 357, 505, 552, 555
  evaluation of, 70, 78
Biological age, 18, 19, 43
Biological beginnings, 80–110
  evolutionary perspective, 82–86, 107–108
  genetic foundations, 86–96, 87*f*, 108
  heredity-environment interaction:nature-nurture debate, 103–107, 109–110
  reproduction challenges and choices, 97–101
Biological foundations of language
  Broca's area, 184, 185*f*, 190
  language acquisition device (LAD), Chomsky's, 185, 190
  Wernicke's area, 184, 185*f*, 190
Biological process, development, of, 8, 15, 15*f*
Birth, 131–136, 146
  birth plans, 134–136, 146
  breech position, 135
  caesarean delivery, 135
  childbirth settings and attendants, 133–134, 146
  doula, 134
  fetus to newborn, transition of, 134–136, 146
  kangaroo care and massage therapy, 138
  natural childbirth, 135
  neonatal considerations, 136–138, 146
  neonatal health and responsiveness, measures of, 139–140, 146
  postpartum period, 140–141, 147
  prepared childbirth, 135
  preterm and low-birth-weight infants, 136–138, 146
  process of, 131–136, 146
  stages of, 132, 146
Birth order, 280, 286
Bisexuality, 269, 381, 396, 412, 429, 458, 459, 459*f*
Blastocyst, 114
Blended families, 358, 367, 502, 510
Blind infants, self-recognition and, 203
Blinking reflex, 163*f*
Blood types, incompatible, prenatal development and, 124
  Rh-negative, 124
  RhoGAM, 124
  Rh-positive, 124
Body art, 377
Body image, 294, 371, 372, 375–376, 401, 404, 411, 412, 458
  depression and, 395
  eating disorders and, 386, 387
  gender differences in, 376, 395
  non-suicidal injury (NSSI) and, 391
  obesity and, 390
Body mass index (BMI), 129, 232, 232*f*, 390, 406, 450, 450*f*, 598, 599
Body transcendence versus body preoccupation, 630
Bonding, postpartum, 144
  global responses to, 144
BOOM, 549
Boomerang kids, 566
Bottle feeding, 25
Bowlby's theory of attachment, 47, 64–65, 74, 75*f*, 77, 198, 208–209, 210, 211, 222, 418, 483–484
Brain
  abstract thinking, 6
  adolescence, changes in, 377–378, 377*f*, 401, 405, 407, 434
  aging, 585–587, 588, 618, 620
  Alzheimer's disease versus normal aging, 85, 585, 586, 602, 603*f*
  analytical thinking, 6
  birth to ten years, 2
  Broca's area, 185*f*
  cerebral cortex, mapping of, 154–155, 188
  child care and development of, 216
  childhood nutrition and development of, 233
  computers, influence of on, 25
  dendritic growth in, 586
  dopamine in the, 393, 605
  drug abuse and, 391–392
  early childhood, in, 226–227, 227*f*, 255
  early experiences and, 156, 156*f*, 188
  ecstacy and, 392*f*
  forebrain, mapping of, 154
  four lobes of, 155*f*
  gender and structure of, 353–354, 366
  hemispheres, development of, 155*f*
  infancy, in, 152–157, 158, 180, 188, 194, 200, 201
  language and, 184–185
  learning disabilities and brain scans, 326, 326*f*, 327, 327*f*
  left-brained, 154
  life span development and, 3–6, 14, 15
  lying and brain activity, 59
  mapping of, 154–155
  middle/late childhood, in, 291, 330
  myelination, 153–154, 188
  neurogenesis, 586
  neurons, development of, 153–154, 153*f*, 188
  neuroplasticity of, 44, 57, 72
  prayer and meditation, impact of on, 541, 616, 619, 623
  prenatal period and, 3–4, 117–118, 121*f*, 130, 145
  REM sleep, development and, 158, 188
  right-brained, 154

shaken baby syndrome, 153
shrinking and slowing in, 585, 620
sixty-five to 120 years, 6
stem, 5
stimulation of during aging, 586
suicide and, 106
ten to twenty-five years, 4
twenty-five to sixty-five years, 5–6
Wernicke's area, 185*f*

Brain death, 661, 683
Brain size in primates versus humans, 83*f*
Brain stem, 5, 661
Brainstorming, 303
Brazelton Neonatal Behavioral Assessment Scale (NBAS), 140, 146
Breaking the Cycle of Violence, 437
Breastfeeding, 25, 150–151, 159–161, 188
acquired immune deficiency syndrome (AIDS) and, 462
benefits of, 160
bottle feeding versus, 150
contraindications of, 160
human immunodeficiency virus (HIV) and, 150
postpartum depression and, 143

Breast cancer, 160, 479, 524, 525, 538, 596
Breech position, defined, 135
British Columbia Integrated Youth Services Initiative, 437
Broca's area, 184, 185*f*, 190
Bronfenbrenner's bio-ecological theory, 68–70, 74, 75*f*, 78, 273, 323, 357–358, 416, 552, 555
chronosystem, 68*f*, 69
exosystem, 68*f*, 69
five environmental systems, 68–70, 68*f*
five moral orientations of, 505–506, 505*f*, 510
macrosystem, 68*f*, 69
mesosystem, 68*f*, 69
microsystem, 68*f*, 69

Bulimia nervosa, 386, 390, 406
Bullying, 363–364, 367
adolescent, 431
bullied, 363, 367
bully, 363, 367
bystander, 363, 367
cyberbullying, 364, 368, 431
impact of, 363–364
most likely to bully, traits of, 363–364, 367
most likely victims of, traits, of, 363
reduction of, 364, 367
relational aggression, 363–364
restitution, resolution, and reconciliation, 364, 431
social contexts and, 363
upstander, 363, 367

C

Caesarean section, 135
Caffeine
adolescents, high-caffeine drinks and, 392, 407
prenatal development and, 120

Calorie restriction, life expectancy and, 598–599, 621
Canada, generations in, 13–14
Canada Food Guide, 293
Canada Pension Plan, 636
Canada Standards Association Group (CSA), 523
Canada's Food Guide, 161, 385
Canadian Association for Neuroscience, 72
Canadian Association of Retired Persons (CARP), 645
Canadian Cancer Society (CCS), 524
Canadian Caregiver Coalition, 571
Canadian Council for Refugees (CCR), 29
Canadian Fertility and Andrology Society (CFAS), 100
Canadian Fitness and Lifestyle Research Institute, 385, 386
Canadian Grandparents Rights Association, 643
Canadian Hospice Society Palliative Care Association (CHPCA), 665
Canadian Human Rights Act, 555, 637
Canadian Institute of Health Information, 666
Canadian Institute of Health Research (CIHR), 24, 38, 77, 450
Canadian International Development Agency (CIDA), 290
Canadian Labour Code, 637
Canadian Labour Congress, 651
Canadian Maternity Experiences Survey, 135
Canadian Mental Health Association, 448, 607
Canadian Midwifery Regulators Consortium, 134
Canadian Network for the Prevention of Elder Abuse (CNPEA), 647
Canadian Paediatric Society, 160, 292
Canadian Pension Plan (CPP), 636
Canadian Perinatal Surveillance System (CPSS), 131
Canadian Physical Activity Guideline, 292
Canadian Psychological Association (CPA), 41, 45
Canadian Research for Social Policy, 24
Canadian Research Institute for SocialPolicy (CRISP), 24, 28
Canadian Society for Exercise Physiology, 449
Canadian Stem Cell Foundation, 77
Canadian Virtual Hospice, 667
Cancer, 88, 92, 93, 579
Cancer, childhood, 295, 330
Cancer, incidence of, 523, 524, 670
Carbon monoxide, pregnancy and, 125
Cardiovascular disease, 88, 92
Cardiovascular system
aging and, 593, 621
middle adulthood, changes in, 517–518, 542
strategies for healthy, 518
stress and, 520, 521

Care, 547, 555
Care-ghettos, 649
Care perspective, 351
Careers and work, early adulthood, in, 469–473, 475
developmental changes, 469, 475
impact of work, 471–473, 475
occupational outlook, 471, 475
values and careers, 469–471, 475

Careers and work, late adulthood,
cognitive function and, 614, 622

Careers and work, middle adulthood, in barriers to, 538
challenges of, 538–539, 543

Carriers, 91, 93
Carter v. Canada, 665
Case, Robert, 56, 76
Case study, 33, 37*f*, 44
Cataracts, 590
children and, 169

Categorization, 180, 189
conceptual categories, 189

Causality, 176–177
Celebrations of life, 682, 683, 685
Cellular clock theory of aging, 581, 582, 620
Centenarians, 579–580
functioning of, 580
gender and, 580
health of, 579
life expectancy and, 12, 13, 13*f*

Centration, 236, 256

Centre for Addiction and Mental Health (CAMH), 393–394, 523
Cephalocaudal pattern, 152, 188, 226
Cerebellum. 5
Cerebral cortex, 154–155
  lateralization, 154, 188
Cervical cancer, 126, 382, 460
  vaccines, 382, 383
Charter of Rights and Freedoms, 637, 644, 665
Chemical pollutants, pregnancy and, 125
Chess and Thomas's temperament classification, 199, 221
  difficult child, 199, 221
  easy child, 199, 221
  slow-to-warm-up child, 199, 221
Child care, 216–218
  brain development and, 216
  daycare, child development and, 216–217
  poverty, impact of on, 216
  world policy of, 218
Child maltreatment, 358–360, 367
  child neglect, 359, 367
  context of maltreatment and abuse, 359–360
  developmental consequences of, 359, 367
  prevalence of, 359–360
  prevention of, 359
  sexual abuse, 359
Child rearing, culture and, 56
Childbirth settings and attendants, 133–134
  doulas, 134
  midwifery, 133–134
Child-centred kinder garten, 253, 257
  developmentally appropriate and inappropriate practices, 254, 258
  education for the disadvantaged, 254–255, 258
  literacy and numeracy, young child's, 254, 258
  Montessori approach, 253, 257
Child-directed speech, 187, 190
Childhood, early, physical and cognitive development in, 223–258
  body growth, 226, 255
  brain, 226–227, 255
  child-centred kinder garten, 253, 257
  developmentally appropriate and inappropriate practices, 254, 258
  disadvantaged children, education for, 254–255, 258
  early childhood education, 252–255, 257–258
  health and wellness, 231–234, 256
  information processing, 242–247, 257
  language development, 249–252, 257
  literacy and numeracy, 254, 258
  motor development, 228–229, 255
  nutrition and exercise, 231–234, 256
  physical development, 226–230, 255
  Piaget's preoperational stage, 234–238, 256
  Vygotsky's theory, 238–242, 256
  wellness in Canada, 232–233, 256
  wellness outside Canada, 233, 256
Childhood perspective on death, 670–671, 684
  death of a parent, 671
  terminally ill children, 671
Childhood, early, socio-emotional development in, 259–287
  divorce, 277–278, 285
  emotional development, 263–265, 284
  families, 272–280, 285–286
  gender, 268–271, 285
  moral development, 265–271, 285
  parenting, 272–280, 285
  peer relations, 281, 282, 286
  play, 282–283, 286
  self, 261–262, 284
  sibling relationships and birth order, 280–281, 286
  social media, 283–284, 286
Childhood, middle and late, physical and cognitive development in, 4, 288–334
  attention deficit hyperactivity disorder (ADHD), 326–328, 333
  autism spectrum disorders (ASD), 328, 333
  bilingualism, 319, 332
  body growth and change, 290–291, 330
  brain, 291, 330
  cognitive development, 295–316, 331
  disabilities, children with, 324–330, 333–266
  disabilities, effect on families, 329, 266
  educational approaches and issues, 320–330, 333, 266
  educational issues, 321–323, 329–330
  exercise, 292–293, 330
  exuberance, 4
  health, illness, and disease, 293–294, 330
  information processing, 298–305, 331
  intelligence, 306–316, 331
  international comparisons, 333
  language development, 317–319, 332
  learning disabilities, 324–330
  motor development, 292, 330
  physical changes and health, 290–295, 330
  physical disabilities, 329, 333
  Piaget's concrete operational stage, 295–297
  private schools and home education, 324, 333
  reading, 317–318, 332
  student learning, approaches to, 320–321, 333
  vocabulary, grammar, and metalinguistic awareness, 317–319, 332
Childhood, middle/late, socio-emotional development in, 4, 335–368
  bullying, 363–364, 367
  child maltreatment, 358–360, 367
  emotional and personality development, 338–346, 366
  families, 356–360, 367
  friends, 360–361, 367
  gender, 352–356, 366
  moral development, 346–352, 366
  parent-child relationships, developmental changes in, 357–358, 367
  peer statuses, 361–362, 367
  peers, technology, and social media, 361, 364–365, 367
  self, 338–342, 366
  social cognition, 362, 367
  social media, 364–365, 368
Chlamydia, 382, 461, 474
  pelvic inflammatory disease (PID) and, 461
Cholesterol, 385, 452, 518, 526, 593
Chorionic villus sampling, 97, 98*f*, 109
Chromosomes, 87, 87*f*, 88, 108
  gender and, 91, 91*f*, 268
  genes and, 87, 89–90, 108
  gene-linked variations and, 92–95, 92*f*, 94*f*, 108
  prenatal testing of, 97, 98*f*
Chronic disorders, 520, 520*f*, 542

Chronic stress, 554, 572
Chronological age, 18, 43
Chronosystem, 68*f*, 69
Cigarette smoking, 391, 406, 455
addiction to, 455–456, 474
effects of, 455
incidence of, 455
Circadian rhythm, 386
Circulatory system and lungs, aging and, 593, 621
Classic Contact Comfort study, Harlow's, 207, 208*f*
Classical conditioning. *See* Pavlov's classical conditioning
Classification, 296, 296*f*
Climacteric, 524, 542
Cliques, adolescents and, 431, 440
Close relationships, midlife, 563–571, 573–574
development of, 564*f*
empty nest syndrome, 566, 573
grandparenting, 567–569, 574
intergenerational relationships, 569–571, 574
love and marriage, 563–565, 573
sibling relationships and friendships, 566–567, 574
Club drugs, 392
Cocaine, prenatal development and, 123
Cognitive approach, 55–59, 76
Case's neo-Piagetian theory, 56, 76
evaluation of, 59, 76
information-processing approach, 56, 59, 76
Piaget's cognitive development theory, 55–58, 76
Vygotsky's socio-cultural cognitive theory, 55, 56–58, 76
Cognitive development, adolescence, in, 397–403, 407–408
adolescent egocentrism, 400, 407
critical thinking, 401, 407
hypothetical-deductive reasoning, 398, 407
Piaget's formal operational stage, 398–400, 407
Cognitive development, early adulthood, in, 465–468
formal operational stage, 465–466, 475
Piaget's cognitive developmenttheory, 465–467
postformal thought stage, 466
realistic and pragmatic thinking, 465–466
Cognitive development, early childhood brain and, 227
Piaget's preoperational stage, 234–238, 256
Vygotsky's socio-cultural cognitive theory, 238–242
Cognitive development, infancy, in infant intelligence, 181
information processing, 177–180, 189
sensorimotor stage, Piaget's, 173–177, 174*f*, 189, 234
Cognitive development, middle adulthood, in, 527–535, 543
information processing, 531–533, 543
intelligence, 527–531
Seattle longitudinal study on, 528–531, 543
Cognitive development, middle/late childhood, in, 295–316
information processing, 298–305, 331
intelligence, 306–316
Piaget's concrete operational stage, 295–297, 330
Cognitive influences, gender and, 271
Cognitive mechanics, 609, 610*f*, 622
Cognitive neuroscience, aging and, 616–618, 623
Cognitive performance, late adulthood, in, 609–613, 622–623
attention, 610–611, 622
cognitive mechanics, 609, 610*f*, 622
cognitive neuroscience and, 616–618, 623
cognitive pragmatics, 609, 610*f*, 622
decision making, 612, 613
education, work, and health, 614–615, 623
memory, 611–613, 622, 623
multi-dimensional and multidirectional nature of cognition, 609–613, 622–623
speed-of-processing dimensions, 610, 622
use it or lose it, 615–616, 623
vitamins and, 599
wisdom, 613–614, 623
Cognitive pragmatics, 609, 610*f*, 622
Cognitive process, development, of, 6, 7, 15, 15*f*
Cognitive theory, 55
Cohabitation, 494, 500, 510
Cohabiting adults, 494, 500, 510
Cohort effects, life-span development and, 36–37, 44, 528, 529, 555–556, 572
cognitive aging and, 613
divorce and, 641
gender roles and, 651
right age for life events, 556
right age for life events, conceptions of, 556*f*
social clock, 556
Collective unconscious, 54*f*
Collective-oriented morality, 505*f*, 506
Colon cancer, 93
Commission on the Future of Health Care in Canada, 646
Commitment, 413, 414
Committee on Hospital Care, 219
Communicating with a dying person, 676–677, 685
strategies for, 676–677
Companionate love, 488
Compensation, 632, 633
Competent loners, 502
Complicated grief, 678, 685
Concept formation, 180, 189
Conceptual categories, 180
Concrete operational stage, Piaget's 56, 56*f*, 76, 234, 242, 295–297, 330, 398, 399, 407, 465–466
Conditioning, 177–178
Rovee-Collier's memory study, 178, 178*f*
Conference Board of Canada, 637
Congruence, defined, 66
Connectedness, 417
Conscience, 261, 267
Consensual validation, 486
Conservation, 236–237
dimensions of, 237*f*
Constructivist approach, 320, 333
Consummate love, 488, 489, 508
Contemporary approaches to psychology, 70–73, 78
dynamic systems (DS), 72, 78
evolutionary psychology, 72–73, 78
neuroscience, 73, 78
positive psychology, 70–72, 78
Contemporary life-events approach, 552–553, 555–556, 572
daily hassles and uplifts of middle adulthood, 553, 554*f*
drawbacks of, 553
framework of for interpretation of adult development change, 553*f*
Context, development and, 9, 10–14, 26, 42, 69, 423
culture and, 555, 557–558, 572
context, defined, 9, 26
gender and, 555, 556–557, 572
historical, 555–556, 572
life expectancy and, 11

midlife, in, 555–559, 572
non-normative/highly individualized life events, 11, 42
normative age-graded influences, 10, 42
normative history-graded influences, 10, 42
Continuity and discontinuity issue, 21–22, 21*f*, 43, 60, 181, 189, 589, 600
Contraceptives, use of, 126, 127, 381, 382–383, 384, 405
Controversial children, 362
Conventional reasoning, 347–348
Convergent thinking, 303
Convoy model of social relations, 648
Cooing, 182, 185, 190
Co-parenting, 272
Corporal punishment, 273
Corpus callosum, 377, 377*f*
Correlational research, 33–34, 44, 274, 340
causation versus, 33, 340
correlation coefficient, 33
interpretation of, 33, 34*f*
theories, connection between, 37*f*
Corticotropin-releasing hormone (CRH), 130
Cortisol, pregnancy and, 130
Costa and McCrae's Baltimore study, 559–560, 573
big five factors of personality, 559–560, 560*f*, 634–635, 654
Creative intelligence, 308, 309
Creative thinking, 303, 331
brainstorming, 303
convergent thinking, 303
divergent thinking, 303
strategies for increase in, 303–304
Creativity, 6, 72, 466–467, 475, 532–533, 543
Crime, elderly and, 644, 645, 656
Criminal Code, 665
Crisis, 413, 414
Critical period, 50
Critical thinking, 302, 331, 401, 407
Cross-cultural studies, 26, 69
Cross-gender friendships, 491, 508
Cross-sectional approach, research and, 35, 36*f*, 44, 527–531
cohort effects, 36–37
longitudinal approach versus, 37*f*
theories, connection between, 37*f*
Crowds, adolescents and, 431, 440
Crying, 182, 190, 196–198, 219
anger cry, 196, 172
basic cry, 196, 172
fake, 197
pain cry, 196, 172
Crystallized intelligence, 527–530, 527*f*, 543
Csikszentmihalyi, M., creativity and, 533–535
Cultural-familial intellectual disability, 313–314
Culture, 26, 69, 423–424
adolescent dating and, 433
adult obesity and, 88, 451, 473
cardiovascular disease and, 542
child-rearing and, 56
context and development and, 555, 557–558, 572
cross-cultural studies, 26
death and, 668–669, 684
development and, 26
evolution and, Baltes's view, 85, 85*f*, 108
freedom versus control, 418–419, 439
grieving and, 679–680, 685
identity development and, 413, 414, 415, 419, 423, 426, 439
intelligence and, 311, 332
locus of control, 419, 439
marriage and, 493–494, 509
midlife development and, 555, 557–558, 572
moral development and, 345, 346, 349, 350, 354, 366
mourning and, 681, 682, 685
older adults, status of, 652, 656
parent-adolescent conflict, 419–420
religious identity and, 422–423
temperament and, 201, 481
traditions and, 426
Culture-fair tests, 311, 332
Culture-reduced tests, 312
Cumulative personality model, 562
Cyberbullying, 364, 368, 431
Cyberdating, adolescent, 432, 433
sexting, 432, 433, 440
Cystic fibrosis, 93, 94*f*, 99

D

Dana Alliance, 535
Dark adaptation, 590
Darwin, Charles, 47, 63, 72, 74, 77, 82
epigenetic view of, 105–106
natural selection, 82, 83, 85, 107, 541
Data collection, methods of, 31–33
case studies, 33
laboratory research, 31, 32
naturalistic observation, 31, 32*f*, 44
observation, 31–32, 44
physiological measures, 33, 44
standardized tests, 32–33
surveys and interviews, 32
Date rape, 434
Dating and romantic relationships
adolescent, 431–433, 440
adjustment and, 433
culture and, 433
cyberdating, 432–433
dating violence, 382
developmental changes in dating, 432
functions of, 431
onset of romantic activity, 432*f*
pregnancy and, 433
problems associated with, 433
religion and, 433
socio-cultural contexts and, 433
Daycare, child development and, 216–218, 217*f*
Deaf infants, 182
Deaf young children, 254
education of, 254
Death and grieving, 658–686
causes of and expectations about death, 670
communicating with a dying person, 676–677, 685
contexts in which people die, 675, 684
coping with death of someone else, 676–683, 685
cultural variations, 668–669, 684
death denial, 668, 669
defining death and life/death issues, 661–667, 683
developmental perspective on death, 669–673, 684
euthanasia, 663–665, 683
facing one's own death, 673–675
forms of mourning, the funeral, and celebration of life, 681–682, 685
grieving, 677–680, 685
historical circumstances, changing, 667–668, 684
issues in determining death, 661, 683
Kübler-Ross's stages of dying, 673–674
life, death, and health care, decisions regarding, 661–667
life partner, loss of a, 680–681, 685
life span perspective on death, 670–673
living wills and do not resuscitate (DNR) orders, 661–662

making sense of the world, 680, 685
national mourning, 660
palliative care, 665–667, 683
perceived control and denial, 675, 685
socio-historical cultural contexts, death and, 668–669

Decision making, 4, 407
aging and, 612, 613
factors affecting, 400–401
social context and, 401

Defeated, 502
Deferred imitation, 180
Deficit needs (D-needs), 67
Delinquency, adolescent, 411, 419, 433
causes of, 435–437, 436*f*, 440
cognitive factors, 436
family support systems and, 435
peer influence and, 435, 436
poverty and, 435
sibling influence and, 435
techniques to reduce, 437–438, 440

Delusions, 72
Dementia, 6, 25, 44, 85, 542, 580, 583, 602, 622, 644, 664
multi-infarct dementia, 602, 622

Dendritic
growth in adulthood, 586–587, 620
spreading, 155*f*, 188

Denial, death and, 675, 685
Denial and isolation, 673, 674*f*, 685
Deoxyribonucleic acid (DNA), 86, 87, 87*f*, 88, 89, 90, 96, 105, 108, 328, 582, 583
manipulation and cloning of, 112
repair of and aging, 601
variations of, 93

Dependent variables, 34*f*, 35
Depression, 67, 72, 88, 142, 359, 361, 394–395, 447, 453, 472, 488, 490, 495, 501, 519, 522, 526, 622, 653, 673
attachment and, 64–65, 484
bereavement and, 680
caregiver, 210, 604
causes of, 21
children and, 281, 294, 359, 361, 364
exercise and reduction of, 453
gender and, 269, 600
grieving and, 628, 629, 673, 677, 678, 680
immigrants and, 274, 554
insomnia and, 519
Kübler-Ross's stage of, 673–674, 674*f*, 685
late adulthood, in, 628, 641, 643
major, 600
marital breakup and, 277, 501
marital happiness and, 495, 501
men and, 507
menopause and, 524
postpartum, 101, 136, 142–143
predictors of, 600
reducing, 362
remarriage and, 502
seniors and, 597, 600, 607, 614, 618, 628, 629, 643, 645, 650
suicide and, 600
terminally ill and, 664, 665, 672
theories of, 21
unemployment and, 472
violence against women and, 464–465

Depression, teen, 375, 381, 389, 391, 393, 394, 395, 400, 411, 412, 425, 425, 423, 424, 428, 429, 447, 453, 472
dating and, 433
genetics and, 395
low self-esteem and, 411, 412
negative body image and, 376
predictors of, 395, 406
reasons for, 395
suicide and, 395, 428

Deprived environment, brain activity and, 156*f*
Depth perception, 170, 170*f*, 189
Descriptive research, 33, 34, 35
Development, periods of, 16–17
age, concept of, 17–19
eight-period sequence, 15*f*, 16–17
four ages of, 17

Developmental delay, 313
Developmental processes, 14–15, 43
biological, 15, 15*f*, 43
cognitive, 15, 15*f*, 43
periods of development and, 15*f*
socio-emotional, 15, 15*f*, 43

Developmentally appropriate practice (DAP), 254, 258
Diabetes, 88, 92, 93, 94*f*, 126, 160, 385, 451, 453, 456, 517, 518, 519, 526, 579, 583, 593, 596, 614, 670
gestational, 126
Type 1, 160
Type 2, 160, 232, 233, 596

Diclectin, 119
Dietary fats, obesity and, 451
Dieting, 451–452, 473
restrained eating, 452
successful versus unsuccessful strategies, 452*f*

Differentiation versus role preoccupation, 630, 654
Difficult child, 199
Diffusion tensor imaging (DTI), 616
Dipartimento di Scienzedella Formazione (DISFOR), 24
Direct instruction approach, 320, 333
Disabilities, children with, 324–330
attention deficit hyperactivity disorder (ADHD), 88, 326–328, 333
autism spectrum disorders (ASD), 328, 333
educational issues, 329
family, effect on, 329
learning disabilities, 325–326, 333
mainstreaming, 321
physical disabilities, 328, 333

Disenfranchised grief, 678
Disengagement, 6
Dishabituation, 179
Divergent thinking, 303
Divided attention, 611, 622
Divorce, 14, 277–278, 286, 358, 372, 435, 495, 498, 499, 500–501, 503, 504, 509, 510, 552, 565–566, 567, 569, 570, 573, 574, 640, 641
attachment and, 213
adult children and, 570
causes of, 502, 565
child custody and support, 277
children, effect on, 203, 214, 277–278, 286, 395
dealing with, 501–502
gay and lesbian parents and, 279, 280
grandparent visitation, 569, 574
late adulthood, in, 641
midlife, 565–566, 573
pathways from, 501–502
positivity and negativity ratio and, 565–566
rate of versus length of marriage, 501*f*
relationship identity and, 412
remarriage and, 641
socio-cultural and demographic factors leading to, 565
socio-economic status (SES) and, 278
stepfamilies, 278

Dizygotic twins, 90
Doctors, Engineers, or Teachers Without Borders, 469
Do not resuscitate (DNR) order, 661, 662, 683
Dominant-recessive genes, 90–91, 108
Dopamine, 393
incentive value of, 393

Dose, teratogen, 118, 145
Doulas, 134

Down syndrome, 81, 92, 92*f*, 93, 99, 118, 130, 314, 324, 410
Dual-career couples, 472–473, 475
Dual-income families, 503
Dual-process model of coping with bereavement, 678, 685
Duchenne markers, 198
Dwarfism, 130
Dynamic systems (DS), 72, 74, 297
  self-organization, 72
Dynamic systems theory, 162
Dyslexia, 325, 333

E

Early adulthood, physical and cognitive development in, 442–476
  addiction, 455–456, 474
  adolescence to adulthood, transition from, 445–448, 473
  alcohol use, 454, 474
  careers and work, 469–473, 475
  cigarette smoking, 455
  cognitive development, 465–468
  See also Cognitive development, early adulthood, in
  creativity, 6, 466–467, 475
  criteria for adulthood, 446–447, 473
  early adulthood, defined, 16
  emerging adulthood, 445, 473
  high school to college, university, or work, 447–448, 473
  impact of work, 471–473, 475
  occupational outlook, 471, 475
  Piaget's cognitive development theory, 465–467
  postformal thought stage, 466, 475
  sexual activity in emerging adulthood, 458–460
  sexuality, 457–465
  sexually transmitted infections (STIs), 460–463
  stress, 447–448
  substance abuse, 453–457, 474
  values and careers, 469–471, 475
  violence against women, 463–465
Early adulthood, socio-emotional development in, 477–511
  adult lifestyles, diversity of, 499–504, 510
  attachment, 482–485, 508
  attraction, 485–486, 508
  benefits of a good marriage, 495, 509
  cohabiting adults, 500, 510
  divorced adults, 501–502, 510
  Erikson: intimacy versus isolation, 487–488, 492, 508
  falling out of love, 490–491, 508
  family life cycle, 496–498, 497*f*, 509
  friendship, 491–492, 508
  gay and lesbian adults, 504, 510
  intimacy and independence, 488
  intimate relationships: marriage and the family cycle, 493–499
  loneliness, 492, 500, 501, 502, 509
  lone-parent adults, 503–504, 510
  love, faces of, 487–489, 508
  marital trends, Canadian, 493, 509
  marriages, successful, principles of, 494–495, 509
  men's moral development, 507, 510
  moral development, 505–506, 510
  parenting adults, 503, 510
  parenting myths and realities, 499, 509
  remarried adults, 502, 510
  single adults, 500, 510
  stability and change from childhood to adulthood, 480–485, 508
  temperament, 480–481, 508
  women's moral development, 506, 510
Early childhood, 15*f*, 16, 43
  death, perspective on, 670–671, 684
Early childhood education, 252–255, 257–258
  child-centred kinder garten, 253, 257
Early childhood, physical and cognitive development in, 223–258
  attention, 243–244, 257
  brain and cognitive development, 227
  brain myelination, 226
  brain size and growth, 226, 227*f*, 255
  death, leading cause of, 234, 256
  eating behaviour, 234
  education, early childhood, 252–254, 257–258
  fine motor skill development, 228–229, 229*f*, 255
  gross motor skill development, 228, 229*f*, 255
  information-processing approach, 242–246, 257
  language development, 249–252, 257
  memory, 244–246, 257
  nutrition and exercise, 231–234, 256
  physical development, 226–230
  Piaget's preoperational stage, 234–238, 256
  prefrontal cortex, 227, 228*f*
  theory of mind, young child's, 247–249, 257
  Vygotsky's socio-cultural cognitive theory, 238–242
  wellness in Canada, 232–233, 256
  wellness in other countries, 233, 256
Early childhood, socio-emotional development in, 259–287
  emotional development, 263–265, 284
  families and, 272–280, 285
  gender, 268–271, 285
  moral development, 265–271, 285
  peer relations, play, and social media, 283–284, 286
  self, 261–262, 284
  self-recognition, 261
  self-understanding, 261–262, 266
Early emotions
  other-conscious emotions, 194
  primary emotions, 194, 219
  self-conscious emotions, 194–196, 195*f*, 219
Early experiences, brain and, 154, 188
  early deprivation and brain activity, 156*f*
Early Years Evaluation (EYE), 23
Easy child, 199, 202
Eating disorders, 72, 294, 330
  adolescence, in, 386–390, 406
  anorexia nervosa, 387, 388–389, 406
  bulimia nervosa, 387, 390, 406
  factors affecting, 387
  gender and, 386, 387
  obesity, 390, 406
Eating Well, 161
Echoing, 187, 190
Eclectic theoretical orientation, 74–75, 79
  eclectic approach, 74–75
Ecstasy/ Methylenedioxymethyl

amphetamine (MDMA), pregnancy and, 124
Education, life-span perspective and, 25, 44, 69
Education, middle/late childhood, 320–330
  Aboriginal children, 322, 323, 333
  adolescence and, 428
  cognitive function and, 614, 615, 623
  constructivist approach, 320, 333
  direct instruction approach, 320, 333
  disabled children and, 329
  ethnicity in schools, 323, 333
  gifted children, of, 321
  immigrant children, 323, 333, 345–346
  international comparisons, 333
  poverty and, 322, 333
  private schools and home education, 324, 333
Education, adolescent, 401–403, 407
  effective schools, 402–403, 408
  hidden curriculum, 402
  high school drop-outs, 403, 408
  innovative curriculum, 403, 408
  Katimavik, 402, 407
  service-learning, 402, 407
  top-dog phenomenon, 402
Effective schools, 402–403, 408
  hidden curriculum, 402
Efficacy, need for sense of, 541
Effortful control/self-regulation, 200, 221
Ego, 50, 54*f*, 75
Ego transcendence versus ego preoccupation, 630, 654
Egocentrism, 235, 237*f*, 236, 256
Elaboration, 301
Elder abuse, 647, 656
Eldercare, 646, 655
Elderly. *See also* Late adulthood, physical and cognitive development in;Late adulthood, socio-emotional development in
  abuse of, 29
  home care for, 29
Elkind's age dynamisms, 415, 438
Embryonic period, 114–115, 117, 118, 119*f*, 145
Emerging adulthood, 445, 446, 447
  assets leading to well-being during, 446
  features of, 446
Emotion language and understanding of emotion, 263
Emotion regulation, 198, 264, 359
  coping and, 198–199, 221
Emotional and psychological adjustments, postpartum, 142–143, 147
  baby blues, 142
  father, adjustment of, 143
  postpartum depression, 101, 136, 142–143
Emotional development, early childhood, in, 263–265, 284
  emotion language and understanding emotion, 263
  emotion-coaching and emotion-dismissing parents, 264, 284
  emotions, regulating of, 265
  self-conscious emotions, 263, 284
  shyness, 263
Emotional development, infancy, in, 194–199
  biological and environmental influences, 194, 219
  crying, 195, 219
  early emotions, 194–196, 195*f*, 219
  emotion, defined, 194, 219
  emotion expression and social relationships, 196–198, 219
  emotion regulation and coping, 198–199, 220
  fear, 195, 220
Emotional development, middle/late childhood, 4, 343–345, 354–355, 366
  coping with stress, 344
  developmental changes, 343
  emotional intelligence (EI), 343, 366
  relative age effect (RAE), 355
Emotional intelligence (EI), 343, 366, 403
Emotional stability and age, 551*f*
Emotional states and stress, maternal, prenatal development and, 130
  corticotropin-releasing hormone (CRH), 130
Emotionally focused therapy (EFT), 482, 483, 484
Emotion-coaching and emotion-dismissing, 264, 284
Emotion-related goals, 631, 631*f*, 655
Empathy, 144, 194, 198, 207, 219, 266, 267, 343, 350, 351, 355, 363, 417, 506, 565, 629
Employer-sponsored pension plans (EPPs), 636
Employment, adolescence and, 428
Empty nest syndrome, 566, 573
  refilling of nest, 566, 573
End-of-life (EOL) care, 661, 662, 666, 667
Endometriosis, 100*f*, 458
Engagement, 72, 243, 253, 273, 417, 424, 431, 601, 616, 618
Enhancers, 502
Enterobacter sakazakii, 160
Environment
  intelligence and, 311–312, 331
  temperament and, 201
Environmental hazards, prenatal development and, 125, 130
Epidural block, 134
Epigenetics, 105–106, 109
Episodic memory, 300, 611, 613, 622
Episodic stress, 554, 572
Equilibration, defined, 173
Erectile dysfunction, 525–526
Erikson's psychoanalytic theory, 37, 40, 51, 52, 53, 74, 75, 75*f*, 208, 343, 416, 430, 436*f*, 438, 628
  adolescent delinquency, 435
  adolescent sexuality and, 429, 439
  autonomy versus shame and doubt, 51*f*, 629*f*, 630
  conflict resolution leading to integrity and wisdom, 628, 629*f*
  culture, identity development and, 422, 439
  eight psychosocial stages, 51–52*f*, 342, 412–413, 628, 629, 629*f*
  ethnicity, 439
  Freud's five psychosexual stages versus, 51*f*
  generativity versus stagnation, 52*f*, 547–548, 572, 629*f*
  identity development, 412, 413
  identity versus identity confusion, 51*f*, 413, 629*f*
  independence, 204, 439
  industry versus inferiority, 51*f*, 342, 366, 629*f*
  initiative versus guilt, 51*f*, 261, 284, 629*f*
  integrity versus despair, 51*f*, 628, 629–630, 629*f*, 654
  intimacy versus isolation, 52*f*, 487–488, 492, 496, 508, 547, 629*f*
  Peck's reworking of final stage of, 630, 654
  play and, 282, 286
  psychosocial moratorium, 413
  religion and, 422
  self-understanding, 261–262
  sexuality, 429, 439

statuses of identity, 414
trust versus mistrust, 51*f*, 203, 207, 221, 629*f*
Estradiol, 375, 404
Estrogen, synthetic, 119
Ethics, research and, 38–39
concern for welfare, 38
justice, 38
respect for persons, 38
stem cell research, 102–104
Ethnic diversity, 26, 27
Ethnic gloss, 41
Ethnicity, 26, 27, 28, 40, 44, 333, 423, 479, 651–652, 656
adolescence, impact of on, 423, 424
defined, 27, 423
education and, 319, 323, 323, 333
identity development and, 423, 424, 426, 439
immigrant children, 323, 333, 345–346
late adulthood, impact of in, 651–652, 656
life review, impact of on, 628, 629
parenting and, 274
race, and socio-economic status and, 425, 439, 595
Ethological approach, 37*f*, 63–65, 74, 75*f*, 77, 179, 207
Charles Darwin, 63
evaluation of, 65, 77
Jane Goodall, 65
John Bowlby, 64–65, 207, 222
Konrad Lorenz, 63–64
Ethologists, 399, 407
Ethology, 63
Eugenics, social policy and, 95–96
European Council for High Ability, 314
Euthanasia, 663–665, 683
active, 663, 683
passive, 663, 683
Evocative genotype-environment correlations, 104
Evolutionary perspective, 82–86, 107–108
evolutionary psychology, 83, 84–86
natural selection and adaptive behaviour, 82–83, 85, 197
Evolutionary psychology, 72–73, 78, 83, 84–86, 108, 184, 194, 196, 213, 333, 375, 541
adaptation, 83, 108
Baltes's view of evolution and culture, 85, 85*f*, 81
bi-directional view, 85
evaluation of, 85–86
evolution and development, 83–84
gender and, 268–271, 285
natural selection and adaptive behaviour, 83
one-sided evolutionism, 85
reproduction, 83, 108
Evolutionary theory of aging, 581, 582, 620
Evolved biology, 85, 108
Executive attention, 243
Executive function, 247–249
Exercise
activity, classifications of, 385
adolescence, in, 385, 406
aerobic, 453
Alzheimer's disease and, 603
benefits of, 453, 596–597
cognitive function and, 614, 615, 623
early childhood, 231, 258
health and, 453, 473, 596–597, 598*f*
immune system and, 589
late adulthood, in, 596–597, 621
longevity and, 596
middle/late childhood, in, 292–293, 330
moderate versus vigorous, 453*f*
obesity and, 452, 473
pregnancy and, 128–129
successful aging and, 656
Exosystem, 68*f*, 69, 78
Expanding, 187, 190
Experiment, 34
Experimental research, 34–35, 44, 248, 249, 340, 616
experimental and control groups, 34*f*, 35, 36
independent and dependent variables, 34*f*, 35
principles of, 34*f*
random assignment, 34*f*, 35
theories, connection between, 37*f*
Expertise, 256, 300, 300*f*, 494, 532, 533, 543, 609
knowledge and, 300
memory, role of in, 300*f*, 331
Explicit memory, 180, 189, 193, 612, 623
Exploration, 413
External locus of control, 419, 420
Extraversion, 54*f*, 200, 221, 401, 559, 560, 560*f*, 573, 634
Extremely preterm, 137
Eye constriction, smiling and, 198

F

Facebook, 25
Face-to-face play, 205, 206
Fagan Test of Infant Intelligence, 181, 189
Failure to thrive (FTT), 161
Fake crying, infant's, 197
Fallopian tubes, blocked, 100*f*
Family
adolescent identity, influence of on, 417, 439
autonomy and attachment and, 418, 419, 420, 428, 439
birth order, 280, 286
blended, 502, 510
child maltreatment and, 358–360, 367
child-parent interactions, direct and indirect effects of, 213*f*
children's disabilities, effect on, 329
defined, 213
divorce, 277–278, 285
freedom versus control, 418–419, 439
gay and lesbian parents and, 279–280
identity development and, 416–423
late adulthood, and, 640–645, 655
maternal and paternal caregiving, 215
moral development and, 350, 366
nuclear, 493
parent-adolescent conflict, 419–420, 428, 439
parent-adolescent relationship, 419–420, 420*f*, 439
parent-child relationships, 357–358, 367
parenthood, transition to, 214, 222
parenting, 272–276, 285
parents as managers, 357
parents with mental disorders, 358
reciprocal socialization, 214
sibling relationships, 280–281, 286
socio-emotional development and, 272–280, 285–286
stepfamilies/ blended families, 279, 280, 285, 358, 367, 445, 493, 502, 567
Family Caregivers Association of Nova Scotia (FCgANS), 571
Family caregiving, 571, 574
Family in later life, 498, 509
Family life cycle, 496–498, 509
becoming parents and a family with children, 498, 509
family in later life, 498, 509
family with adolescents, 498
launching, 496
launching children and moving on, 498, 509
leaving home and becoming singleadult, 498
new couple, 498

stages in, 497*f*
Family Reunification Program, 569
Family with adolescents, 498, 509
Father Involvement Initiative–OntarioNetwork (FII-ON), 143
Father Involvement Research Alliance (FIRA), 143
Fathers, postpartum adjustment of, 143
father-infant attachment, 143–144
Fatuous love, 490
Fear, 198, 220
separation protest, 198
stranger anxiety, 198, 220
Fencer's pose, 163*f*
Fertility, rates of, 28
Fertility drugs, 99, 100, 109
Fertilization, 88, 89, 89*f*, 97, 108, 113, 114*f*
Fetal alcohol spectrum disorder (FASD), 120–121, 121*f*
Fetal development, 3
Fetal MRI, 98, 98*f*
Fetal period, 115–116, 118
Fetus to newborn, transition of, 132
Fidelity, 547
Fine motor skills, 165–167, 165–166*f*, 188
early childhood, 229–230, 230*f*, 255
hand-eye coordination, 165
pincer grip, 164
First words, infant's, 182, 190
overextension, 183
receptive vocabulary, 182
spoken vocabulary, 182
underextension, 183
Flow, 72
Fluid intelligence, 527–530, 527*f*, 543
Flynn effect, intelligence and, 311, 331
Focused attention, 179
Folic acid supplementation, 117
pregnancy and, 131
Forebrain, 154
Formal operational stage, Piaget's, 56, 56*f*, 76, 238*f*, 398–400, 407, 423, 465–466, 467, 474, 535
Four ages of development, 17
Fragile X syndrome, 91, 92*f*, 108
Frankl's theory on meaning of life, 541, 544
Fraternal twins, 86, 87, 90, 101, 104
Free radical theory of aging, 581, 583, 603, 620
Freud, Anna, 53, 54*f*, 76
Freud, Sigmund's psychoanalytic theory, 37*f*, 40, 49, 50–52, 74, 75, 75*f*, 207, 270, 416, 537
adolescent sexuality and, 429, 439
data collection, methods of, 44
ego, 50
Electra complex, 51*f*, 270
five psychosexual stages of development, 50, 51–53, 51*f*
gender and, 270
id, 50
morality and, 266
Oedipus complex, 51*f*, 270, 285
play and, 282, 286
superego, 50
Friends, adolescence and, 429–433, 440
adolescent versus children's groups, 430, 440
dating and romantic relationships, 431–433, 440
online social networking, 430, 431, 440
peer groups, 430–431, 440
similarity in, 431
Sullivan's theory on friendship, 430, 440
Friends, early adulthood, in, 491–492
cross-gender friendships, 491, 508
friends with benefits relationships (FWBRs), 491, 508
gender differences in, 491, 508
Friends, late adulthood, in, 643, 644, 656
Friends, middle/late childhood, in
five-level framework, 361
importance of in, 360–361, 367, 429
intimacy in friendships, 361
similarity among, 361
Fromm, Eric, 40, 54*f*, 76, 479, 485
Frontal lobe, 5, 154, 180, 184, 185, 200, 227, 255, 291, 331, 377, 401, 405, 407, 617
Functional magnetic resonance imaging (fMRI), 33, 44, 616
Funerals, 668, 669, 681–682, 685
personalization of, 682–683
Fuzzy trace theory, 301
gist, 301
verbatim memory trace, 301

G

Gambling, 371, 393, 403
addiction, 455, 456
Gametes, 89, 92
Gangs, 434, 435
Gardner's eight frames of mind, 308, 331
Gastrointestinal infections, 160
Gay males and lesbians, 269, 429
adolescence, 380, 381, 382, 390, 396
adults, 504, 510
attitudes re and behaviours towards, 460
eating disorders and, 387
marriage, 563
misconceptions re, 504
parents, divorce and, 279
stereotypes re, 504
Gender
adolescent body image and, 375–376
adolescent self-esteem and, 412
aggression and, 354, 366
androgyny, 355
attachment and, 418
bias, 32, 40, 351
biological influences, 268–269
brain structure and, 353–354, 366
centenarians, 580
chromosomes and hormones and, 268
cognitive development and, 354
cognitive influences and, 271
conceptions of right age for major life events and achievements and, 556, 572
context, influence of on gender differences, 356, 366, 555–556, 572
defined, 27, 268
depression and, 600
eating disorders and, 386, 387
educational opportunities and, 428
elderly poverty and, 637, 655
emotion and, 354, 366
evolutionary psychology view, 268–269, 285
gender identity, 268, 285
gender role, 268
gender schema theory, 271, 285
gender-role classification, 355–356
intergenerational relationships and, 569–571, 574
life expectancy and, 11, 580, 581
midlife development and, 555–556, 572
morality and, 351, 366
parental influences and, 270
parent-child relationships, late adulthood, and, 642, 655
peers and, 270–271
prosocial behaviour, 355, 366
reading skill and, 355, 366

risk taking and, 354
roles of, late adulthood, in, 651, 656
self-esteem and, 635
sexual expression in adolescence and, 427
similarities and differences between, 353–355
social cognitive theory of, 270
social influences and, 270–271, 285
social role theory, 270
social theories of, 270
socio-emotional development in middle/late children and, 353–355
socio-emotional development in young children and, 268–271
stereotypes, 352, 366
temperament and, 201, 481
Gender identity, 268, 285, 352, 429, 439
Gender Inequality Index (GII), 27
Gender role, 268
Gender schema theory, 271, 285
Gender stereotypes, defined, 352, 367
Gender typing, 268
Gene Expression Collaborative for Kids Only Project (GECKO), 89
Gene-gene interaction, 92
Generation squeeze, 571, 574
Generation X, 14, 18
Generation Y, 14
Generation Z, 14
Generational inequity, 29, 646, 655
Generational overload, 571, 574
Generativity versus stagnation, Erikson's stage of, 52*f*, 75, 547–548, 572, 629*f*
assessment of generativity and identity certainty, 548*f*
Genes, 4, 15, 80, 81, 83, 84, 87–88, 89–95, 96, 97, 99, 100, 104, 105, 106, 108, 154, 268, 274, 311, 371–372, 373, 481, 484, 524, 579, 603, 604
dominant-recessive gene principle, 90–91
gene-linked variations, 92–95, 94*f*
imprinting of, 92
sex-linked, 91
temperament and, 200–201
Genetic counselling, 25, 95, 97, 118
Genetic expression, 96, 107
Genetic foundations, 87–95
cells, 87, 87*f*
chromosome and gene-linked variations, 92–95, 108
collaborative gene, 87–88, 108
deoxyribonucleic acid (DNA), 87, 87*f*, 88
genes and chromosomes, 87–90, 87*f*
genetic principles, 90–92
Human Genome Project, 93, 96, 108
mitosis, meiosis, and fertilization, 87, 89
variability, sources of, 90
Genetic principles
dominant-recessive genes, 90–91, 108
genetic imprinting, 92
polygenically inherited characteristics, 90, 108
sex-linked genes, 90, 91–92, 108
Genetic susceptibility, teratogen response and, 118, 145
Genetics, 72
alcoholism and, 455
Alzheimer's disease and, 603
centenarians, 579
disease and, 542
intelligence and, 310–311, 331
learning disabilities and, 325, 333
menopause and, 524
middle adulthood, physical changes in, and, 516–519, 542
obesity and, 88, 390
puberty and, 375
teen depression and, 395
temperament and, 481
Genital herpes, 461, 474
pregnancy and, 125, 127*f*
Genital stage, Freud and, 50, 51*f*
Genomes, 88, 93, 96, 104, 108, 451
Genotype, 90
Geography, 26, 69, 160, 372, 382, 423, 679, 680
Germinal period, 114, 114*f*, 118, 145
Gestational diabetes, 126
Gestures, infant, 182, 190
Giftedness, 314, 321
Gist, 301
Glaucoma, 590
Gonadotropins, 375
Gonads, 375
Gonorrhea, 382, 460, 461, 474, 526
Goodall, Jane, 65, 77
Good-enoughs, 502
Goodness of fit
co-parenting, 203
defined, 202, 221
mother-infant interactions, 203
parenting and, 202–203, 221
sensitive caregiving, 202
temperament and, 481
Grammar, 317, 332
Grandparenting, 567–569, 574
changing profile of, 569, 574, 642–643, 656
roles and styles of, 567, 574
visitation rights of, 643
Grandparents Requesting Access and Dignity (GRAND), 643
Grant Study, 550, 559, 561, 573
Grasping reflex, 163, 163*f*
Great-grandparenting, 643, 656
Grief, 677–680, 685
complicated, 678, 685
coping versus circumstances of death, 678, 685
culture and, 679–680, 685
depression and, 677
disenfranchised, 678
dual-process model of coping with bereavement, 678
long term, 677, 678
post-traumatic stress disorder (PTSD), occurrence of, 678
prolonged, 678
suicide and, 677
Gross motor skills, 164–165, 165*f*, 188, 206
early childhood, development in, 228, 229*f*, 255
Growth, physical, 9, 152, 152*f*, 188
Growth failure, 161
Growth spurts, adolescent, 374, 374*f*, 404
Guaranteed income supplement (GIS), 651
Guilt, feelings of, 160, 194, 195, 198, 266, 285, 628, 629*f*, 647, 677, 678
initiative versus, 51*f*, 75, 261

H

Habits, first, primary circular reactions and, 174
Habituation, 177, 179, 180, 189
Hand-eye coordination, 165
Happiness, 72, 78, 473, 485, 489, 508, 534, 613, 669
activity and, 630
age and, 17–18
characteristics at age 50 versus, 561–562, 562*f*
marital, 641
Hassles and uplifts of middle adulthood, 552–553, 554*f*
evaluation of, 553
Hate/bias crimes, 434
Head Start, 255, 258
Health-adjusted life expectancy (HALE), 579, 619
Health, adolescent, 427
Health, early adulthood, 449, 473
Health, infant, 159–161
breastfeeding, 150–151, 159–161

malnutrition, 161
nutritional needs, 159
Health, men's, 507
Health and wellness, early childhood, in, 231–234, 256
nutrition and exercise, 231–234, 256
poverty and, 234, 256
smoking, exposure to and, 233–234, 256
wellness in Canada, 232–234, 256
wellness in other countries, 234, 256
Health and wellness, late adulthood, in, 594–608, 621
accidents, 595, 596, 621
arthritis, 595, 621
cognitive function and, 614, 615, 623
death, causes of, 595, 621
dementia, 602, 621
depression, 600, 621, 622
exercise, 596–597, 621
health problems, 595–596, 621
health promotion, 605–607, 622
mental health, nature of, 600–601, 621, 622
multi-infarct dementia, 602, 622
nutrition and weight, 598–599, 621
osteoporosis, 595, 621
Parkinson's disease, 602, 605, 622
substance abuse, 601
Health and wellness, middle adulthood, in, 541, 544
Health care, 28, 29, 30, 66, 69, 96, 131, 233, 306, 357, 381, 455, 558, 645
access to, 232, 233, 590, 651
adolescent, 395, 411
adulthood, 514, 533, 537–538
elderly, 605, 606, 607, 608, 623, 634, 645–646, 647, 654, 655, 661, 662, 665, 666, 667
infant, 198
life expectancy and, 514
postpartum, 140
pregnancy, 131, 134, 135, 136, 143–144
Health care directives, 661, 662
Health care tourists, 29
Hearing, 171–172, 171*f*, 189
aging and, 591, 592*f*, 620
cochlear implants, 591
hearing aids, 591, 620
middle adulthood, changes in, 517
rhythm, acquisition of, 171–172
Heart disease, 385, 451, 453, 495, 517, 519, 520, 523, 538, 542, 579, 593, 595, 596, 601, 614, 621, 649, 670
Helson's Mills College study, 561, 573
Hemophilia, 91, 93, 94*f*
Heredity
life expectancy and, 11, 579–580
menopause and, 524
obesity and, 88, 451, 473
temperament and, 201
Heredity-environment interaction: nature-nurture debate. *See* Nature-nurture controversy
Heritability, 310–311
Heroin
methadone treatment, 124
prenatal development and, 124
Heteronomous morality, 266, 267, 346
imminent justice, 266
Hidden curriculum, 402, 408
Hierarchy of needs, 66
Hippocampus, 617
Historical contexts. *See* Cohort effects, life-span development and
Home births, 135
Homelessness, 30
Homeostasis, 66
Home-schooling, 324, 333
Homophobia, 429, 439
Homosexuality, 82, 429, 460, 460*f*, 504
Hormonal changes, puberty, in, 375
estradiol, 375, 404
gonadotropins, 375
gonads, 375
hormones, 375
hypothalamus, 375
pituitary gland, 375
testosterone, 375, 404
Hormone replacement therapy (HRT), 524, 542
Hormone stress theory of aging, 581, 583, 620
Hormones, 96, 100*f*, 115, 118, 132, 200, 201, 268, 354, 375, 459, 583
androgens, 268
chromosomes and, 268
corticotropin-releasing hormone (CRH), 130
estrogens, 268
gender and, 268
gonads, 268
leptin, 451
oxytocics, 134
puberty, in, 375, 386, 401, 404
sex, 333, 524, 525, 526
stress, 198
therapy, 92*f*, 100*f*, 112
Horn's theory on intelligence, 527, 527*f*, 528, 528*f*, 530, 543
Horney, Karen, 40, 51, 53, 54*f*, 74, 76, 79
Hospice, 666, 667
Hospital deliveries, 135
Human Cloning Foundation, 102
Human Development Index (HDI), 11
Human Development Report, 11, 27
Human Genome Project, 88, 93, 102, 108, 603
Human immunodeficiency virus (HIV), 126, 462, 474
breastfeeding and, 150
children and, 234, 256
pregnancy and, 126
Human papillomavirus (HPV), 126, 127*f*, 382, 405, 460–461, 474
anogenital warts, 382, 460
cervical cancer, 382, 460
pregnancy and, 126
Human Resources and Skills Development Canada (HRSDC), 536, 537, 538
Humanist approach, 66–67, 74, 78
Abraham Maslow, 66–67, 78
Carl Rogers, 66, 78
evaluation of, 67, 78
Huntington's disease, 88, 93, 94*f*, 99, 586
Hypertension, 88, 93, 383, 386, 451, 514, 517, 518, 519, 520, 520*f*, 526, 541, 542, 583, 595, 596, 596, 614
Hypothalamus, 375
Hypotheses, 31
Hypothetical-deductive reasoning, 398, 407

I

Id, 50
Identical twins, 86, 87, 90, 101, 104, 105, 106
Identity
adolescent, 411, 412–416, 438
autonomy and attachment, 418, 439
bicultural identity, 424, 439
components of, 412
confusion, 412, 487
connectedness, 417
culture and, 413, 414, 415, 418, 423–424, 426
defined, 412
development of, 413–414, 431
Elkind's age dynamisms, 415
emerging adulthood and beyond, 414–415
Erikson's theory of identity development. *See* Erikson's psychoanalytic theory
ethnicity and, 423, 424, 425, 439
families, 416–423, 439
freedom versus control, 418–419, 439
individuality, 417
locus of control, 419, 439
MAMA cycles, 415
Marcia's four statuses of, 413–414, 414*f*, 438

parent-adolescent conflict, 419–420, 439
psychosocial moratorium, 413
racial, 423, 425, 439
religion and, 422–423, 439
rites of passage, 426, 439
sexual orientation and, 429
social exclusion, assimilation, and multiculturalism, 424–425
socio-economic status and, 425
traditions and global changes in adolescence, 426–428, 439
Identity achievement, 414, 414*f*, 438
Identity certainty, assessment of, 560*f*, 561
Identity diffusion, 414, 414*f*, 438
Identity foreclosure, 414, 414*f*, 438
Identity moratorium, 414, 414*f*, 438
Identity versus identity confusion, Erikson's stage of, 51*f*, 413, 629*f*
Imaginary audience, 400
Imitation, 61, 179–180
deferred imitation, 180
Immigration, 29–30
education of children, 323, 333
effects of, 558–559
rates of, 28, 29–30
Imminent justice, 266
Immune system, 589, 620
stress and, 520–521
Immunizations, 188
Implicit memory, 180, 612, 623
Imprinting, 63, 77
genetic, 91
In vitro fertilization (IVF), 82, 99, 100, 109
Income, late adulthood, in, 636–637, 654, 655
Canadian Pension Plan (CPP), 636, 637
employer-sponsored pension plans (EPPs), 636, 637
Old Age Security (OAS), 636, 651
pension funds, 636
registered retirement savings plans (RRSPs), 636, 637, 645
Incongruity, defined, 49
Independence, 204, 220
autonomy versus shame, 75, 204, 220
Independent variables, 34*f*, 35
Individual differences
attachment and, 209–210, 221
intelligence and, 306
Individuality, 203, 417
Indulgent parenting, 272, 273, 273*f*
Industry versus inferiority, Erikson's stage of, 51*f*, 342, 366, 629*f*
Inequities and Inequalities in Education, 24
Infancy, health of, 159–161, 188
breastfeeding, 150–151, 159–161
failure to thrive (FTT), 161
immunizations, 188
malnutrition, 161, 188
oral health, 145
powdered infant formula (PIF), 160
solid foods, 160
Infancy, physical and cognitive development in, 148–190
brain, 152–157, 156*f*
breast versus bottle feeding, 150, 159–160, 188
cephalocaudal pattern, 152
cognitive development, 173–181. *See also* Cognitive development, infancy, in
health. *See* Infancy, health of
infancy, defined, 15*f*, 16
language development, 181–185, 183*f*, 190
motor, sensory, and perceptual development, 161–173, 163*f*, 164–165*f*, 168*f*, 169*f*, 170*f*, 171*f*, 188, 189
physical development, 151–161, 154*f*, 156*f*, 188, 226
physical growth, 152, 152*f*
proximodistal pattern, 162
sleep, 157–158, 157*f*
social contexts, 213–219
Infancy, socio-emotional development in, 191–222
emotional development, 193–199, 196*f*, 219
social contexts, 213–219
social orientation/understanding and attachment, 205–210, 221
temperament and personality development, 199–204, 220
Infant and Toddler Growth and Feeding Program, 161
Infant intelligence, 181, 189
Infantile amnesia, 180
Infertility and reproductive technology, 99–101
azoospermia, 99
fertility drugs, 99, 100, 109
fetal MRI, 98, 98*f*
infertility, defined, 99
oligospermia, 99
replacement rate, 99
in vitro fertilization (IVF), 99, 100, 109
Infinite generativity, 182
Information processing, novelty, 180
Information processing, adolescence, in, 407
critical thinking, 401
decision making, 400–401
Information processing, early childhood, in, 242–247, 257
attention, 243–244, 257
memory, 244–246
strategies and problem solving, 246, 247*f*, 257
theory of mind, young child's, 247–249, 257
Information processing, infancy, in, 177–180, 189
attention, 179
concept formation and categorization, 180, 189
conditioning, 177–178
deferred imitation, 180
explicit memory, 180, 189
habituation and dishabituation, 179, 189
imitation and memory, 179–180, 189
implicit memory, 180
infantile amnesia, 180
novelty, 174
Information processing, middle adulthood, in, 531–535, 543
creativity, 532–533, 543
expertise, 532
memory, 531
practical problem solving, 531–532, 543
speed of, 531
working memory, 531
Information processing, middle/late childhood, in, 298–303, 331
memory, 298–301, 331
metacognition, 305–306, 331
thinking, 302–305, 331
Information-processing approach, 59, 74, 75*f*, 76, 242–247, 253, 257, 298
Inhibition, 480
Inhibition to the unfamiliar, 199, 220
Initiative versus guilt, Erikson's stage of, 51*f*, 75, 261, 284, 629*f*
conscience, 261
Injuries, 295, 330
Insecure avoidant babies, 210, 221
Insecure disorganized babies, 210, 221
Insecure resistant babies, 210, 221
Insomnia, 519

Instant messaging (IM), 25, 26
Institute of Child Study, 56
Institute for Patient and Family-Centred Care, 219
Institutional daycare, 14
Integrity versus despair, Erikson's stage of, 52*f*, 628, 629–630, 629*f*, 654
  life review and, 628–629, 654
Intellectual disability, 313
Intelligence, 306–316, 331
  analytical, 308
  creative, 308, 309
  cross-sectional versus longitudinal comparison of in middle adulthood, 529*f*
  crystallized, 527–531, 527*f*, 543
  cultural-familial intellectual disability, 313
  culture-fair tests, 311, 331
  culture-reduced tests, 312
  environmental influences, 311–312, 331
  extremes of, 313–316
  fluid, 527–531, 527*f*, 543
  Flynn effect, 311, 331
  Gardner's eight frames of mind, 308, 331
  genetics and, 310–311, 331
  giftedness, 314–316, 321
  heritability and, 310–311, 331
  Horn's theory of, 527, 527*f*, 528, 528*f*, 531, 543
  individual differences in, 306
  intellectual disability/developmental delay, 313–314
  intelligence quotient (IQ), 19, 307
  Mayer-Salovey-Caruso emotional intelligence (EI), 309, 331
  mental age, 307
  multiple intelligence approaches, evaluation of, 308
  music and, 310, 332
  practical, 308, 309
  Seattle longitudinal study on, 527, 528–530, 528*f*, 529*f*, 543
  Stanford-Binet intelligence test, 306–307, 307*f*, 311, 331
  tests, use and misuse of, 312–313
  triarchic theory of, Sternberg's, 308, 331
  types of, 308–310
  Wechsler scales, 307
Intelligence quotient (IQ), 19, 307
Intelligent design, 541, 544
Intention, goal-directed behaviour and, 206
Interactional model, development and, 21
Inter-American Development Bank (IADB), 24
Intergenerational Day, 650
Intergenerational relationships, 569–571, 574
  family caregiving, 570, 574
  gender and, 570
  importance of, 570
Intergenerational Society, 650
Intermodal perception, 172, 189
Internal locus of control, 419
Internalization, 347
International Labour Organization, 536
International Network for the Preventionof Elder Abuse (INPEA), 647
International Task Force, 536
Internet generation, 14
Internet usage, 638
Intersex, 429, 439
Intimacy
  commitment and, 488
  independence and, 488
Intimacy in friendships, 361
  online communication, effect on, 361, 364–365
Intimacy versus isolation, Erikson's stage of, 52*f*, 487–488, 492, 496, 508, 547, 629*f*
Intuitive thought substage, 236, 256
Invincibility, adolescent, 400
Iron deficiency, 159, 188
Issues in life-span development
  continuity and discontinuity, 43
  evaluation of, 23, 43
  interactional model, 21, 43
  stability-change, 43

J

Jealousy, 194, 195, 196, 219, 277, 484, 488, 673
  Hart's assessment of, 196, 196*f*, 219
Jean Baker Miller Training Institute, 41
Joint attention, 206, 207
Joint Statement on Shaken Baby Syndrome (SBS), 153
Jung, Carl, 40, 51, 53, 54*f*, 76, 515
Justice perspective, 351

K

Kagan's behavioural inhibition, 199–200, 220
  inhibition to the unfamiliar, 199, 200
Kangaroo care, 138
Katimavik, 402, 407
Klinefelter syndrome, 92*f*, 108, 269
Knowledge-related goals, 631, 631*f*, 654
Kohlberg's theory and stages of moral development, 267, 346–352, 348*f*
  critics of, 349–351
Kübler-Ross's stages of dying, 673–674, 674*f*
  acceptance, 673–674, 674*f*, 685
  anger, 673, 674*f*, 685
  bargaining, 673, 674*f*, 685
  criticisms of, 674
  denial and isolation, 673, 674*f*, 685
  depression, 673, 674*f*, 685
Kwashiorkor, 161

L

Labelling, 187, 190
Laboratory, 31
Laboratory research, 31, 33
Language acquisition
  babbling and other vocalizations, 182, 190
  first words, 182–183, 190
  language milestones in infancy, 182*f*
  language sounds, recognition of, 182
  two-word utterances, 183, 190
Language acquisition device (LAD), Chomsky's, 185, 190
Language and thought, Vygotsky's theory on, 238–242
Language development, early childhood, 249–252, 257
  literacy, 252, 257
  phonology and morphology, 249, 250*f*, 257
  pragmatics, advances in, 251, 257
  syntax and semantics, changes in, 250–250, 257
Language development, infancy, in, 181–185, 190
  behavioural and environmental influences, 186, 190
  biological foundations of language, 184–185, 190
  child-directed speech, 187
  echoing, 187, 190
  expanding, 187, 190
  infinite generativity, 180
  labelling, 187, 190
  language, defined, 182
  language acquisition, 182–183, 190
  organizational rules, 182
  recasting, 187
Language development, middle/late childhood, in, 317–319, 332
  alphabetic principle, 317
  bilingualism, 319, 332
  pragmatics, 317
  reading, 317–318

vocabulary, grammar, and metalinguistic awareness, 317–319
Late adulthood, physical and cognitive development in, 575–624
aging brain, 585–587, 620
alcoholism, 601, 622
biological theories of aging, 581–584, 620
cancer, 579
cardiovascular disease, 579
circulatory system and lungs, 593, 621
cognition, nature of, 609–613, 622, 623
cognitive functioning, 609–618, 622–623
cognitive neuroscience and aging, 616–618, 623
culture, status and, 652, 656
dementia, Alzheimer's disease, and related disorders, 602–605, 622
diabetes, 579
education, work, and health, cognitive function and, 614–615, 623
exercise, nutrition, and weight, 596–599, 623
health problems, 595–596, 621
health promotion, 605–607, 622
hearing, 591, 592*f*, 620
heart disease, 579
immune system, 589, 620
late adulthood, defined, 15*f*, 16
life expectancy and life span, 578–580, 619
longevity and biological theories of aging, 578–584
meditation, religion, and spirituality, 618–619, 623
mental health, nature of, 600–601, 621
multi-infarct dementia, 602, 622
Parkinson's disease, 585, 586, 602, 605, 622
physical and mental health and wellness, 594–606, 622–623
physical appearance and movement, 589–590, 620
promoting cognitive skills: use it or lose it, 615–616, 623
robust oldest old, 581, 620
sensory changes in, 590–593, 620
sexuality, 593–594, 621
sleep, 589
smell and taste, 592, 621
substance abuse, 601
successful aging, 653–654, 656
touch and pain, 592, 621
vision, 590, 591*f*, 620
young old, old old, and oldest old, 581, 620
Late adulthood, socio-emotional development in, 625–657
activity theory, 630, 654
adult children and older adult parents, 642, 655
ageism, 637, 655
aging couple, 640, 655
caregivers, 646
convoy model of social relations, 648
eldercare, 646, 655
Erikson's theory on, 628–630, 654
families and social relationships, 640–645, 655–656
fear of victimization, crime, and elder maltreatment, 644, 645, 646, 647, 656
friendship, 643, 644, 656
grandparenting and great grandparenting, 642–643, 656
obesity, 580, 593
Peck's reworking of Erikson's final stage, 630, 654
personality and mortality, 634
regrets of, 629
reminiscence therapy, 629, 630
selective optimization with compensation theory, 632–633, 633*f*, 654
social determinants of health, 633–634, 654
social support and social integration, 648–650, 656
socio-emotional selectivity theory, 630–632, 643, 654
stereotypes re older adults, 644–645, 655
Latency period, Freud and, 50, 51*f*, 429
Lateralization, 154, 185*f*, 188, 587, 587*f*
Launching, 496, 498
Launching children and moving on, 498, 509
defined, 498
Lead exposure, pregnancy and, 125, 130
Learning disabilities, 137, 325–326, 333, 355
brain scans and, 326*f*
causes of, 325, 333
diagnosis of, 325, 333
dyslexia, 325
genetics and, 325, 333
social development and, 325–326, 333
Learning Through the Arts™ (LTTA), 309
Leaving home and becoming single adult, 496
Leisure, 538, 543
Leptin, obesity and, 451, 473
Lesbian, gay, and bisexuals (LGBs), 458
Lesbian attitudes and behaviours, 460
Levinson's periods of adult development, 547, 549, 550*f*, 550, 561, 572
Seasons of a Man's Life, 549–550
Libertines, 502
Life expectancy, 11–14, 28, 514, 578–580, 595, 596, 619, 670
Aboriginal Canadians, of, 12, 578, 579
context and, 11
health-adjusted, 579
median age and centenarians, 12, 13
world variation of, 11, 12, 12*f*
Life review, 628–629, 654
Life span, 578–580, 619
Life-events approach, 552–553, 572
Life-history records, 33
Lifelong development, 7
Life-span development, 1–45
age, concept of, 17–19, 43
behavioural and social cognitive approach, 60–63
bio-ecological approach, 68–70
biological, cognitive, and socio emotional processes, 14, 15*f*, 42
cognitive approach, 55–58, 76
cohort effects, 36–37, 44
contemporary approaches to psychology, 70–73, 78
context and, 9, 42
continuity and discontinuity, 21–22, 21*f*, 43
data collection, methods of, 31–33, 44
defined, 7, 14
developmental processes, 14–15, 42
dynamic systems, 72
eclectic theoretical orientation, 74–75, 79
ethological approach, 63–65
evaluating issues of, 23, 43
evolution and, 84–85, 85*f*, 108
evolutionary perspective, 82–86
evolutionary psychology, 72–73
generations in Canada, 13–14
humanist approach, 66–67
importance of studying, 7–10, 42

interactional model, 21, 43
issues in, 23, 43
life expectancy, 11–14, 43
neuroscience, 72
periods of development and, 16–17, 43
positive psychology, 70–72, 78, 534
prominent approaches in, 46–79
psychoanalytic approach, 50–53, 75
research challenges, 38–41, 45
research designs, 33–38, 44
research methods and challenges, 30–41, 44
socio-economic status (SES), life-span development and, 14, 42
stability-change, 22, 43
timeline for major developmental theories, 75*f*

Life-span perspective, 1–6, 7, 8–45
biology, culture, and the individual, co-construction of, 9, 42
brain, changes in, 3–6
characteristics of, 7–10, 42
contemporary concerns, 25–30, 44
contextual development, 9, 42
education and, 25, 44
growth, maintenance, and regulation, involvement of, 9, 42
health and well-being and, 25, 44
lifelong development, 7
life-span approach, 7
life-span development. *See* Life-span development
multidimensional development, 8, 42
multidirectional development, 8, 42
multidisciplinary development, 9, 42
plasticity in development, 8–9, 22, 42
social policy and, 28–30, 44
socio-cultural contexts and, 26–28, 44

Literacy, early childhood, 252, 254–255, 258
Living arrangements, late adulthood, in, 638–639, 655
Living wills, 661–662, 683
Locomotion, infancy, in, 206, 220
Locus of control, 419, 439
external, 419
internal, 419
Loneliness, 492, 509, 648, 649, 655, 656
Lone-parent adults, 503–504, 510
Longitudinal approach, research and, 35–36, 36*f*, 37, 44, 527–531
Berkeley longitudinal studies, 561, 573
cohort effects, 36–37
Costa and McCrae's Baltimore study, 559–560, 573
cross-sectional approach versus, 37*f*
Helson's Mills College study, 561, 573
National Longitudinal Survey of Children and Youth (NLSCY), 37, 37*f*
stability and change, 559–563, 573
theories, connection between, 37*f*
Vaillant's studies, 561–562, 562*f*, 573
Youth in Transition Survey (YITS), 38
Long-term memory, 244–245, 257
Lorenz, Konrad's ethological theory, 63–64, 74, 75*f*, 77
imprinting, 63–64
Loss, adaptation to, 633, 655
Loss oriented stressors, bereavement and, 678, 685
Love, 485–490, 508
affectionate, 488, 489, 508
consummate, 488, 489, 508
falling out of, 489–490, 508
fatuous, 489
intimacy, 487–488
main dimensions of, 488, 489
romantic, 488, 489, 508
triangular theory of, 488, 489*f*
Low-birth-weight infant, 136, 137, 146
long-term outcome, 137–138, 146
Lower respiratory infections, 160
Lungs, 519
aging and, 593, 621
lung capacity and cigarette smoking, 519*f*
Lying, 59
white lies, children's, 247, 248

M

Macrosystem, 68*f*, 69
Macular degeneration, 590, 591*f*
Magnetic resonance imaging (MRI), 4
Mainstreaming, 321, 266
Maintenance, goal of, 9
Major depression, 600
Male menopause, 526
Male-female relationships, 506
Male hypogonadism, 525
Male-male relationships, 506
Malnutrition
immune system and, 589
infancy and, 161, 188
late adulthood, in, 599
pregnancy and, 128–129
MAMA cycles, 415, 422
Mapping, brain, 154–155, 155*f*
cerebral cortex, 154–155
forebrain, 154
Marasmus, 161
Marcia's identity status and development, 413–414, 415, 438
commitment, 413, 438
crisis, 413
four statuses of identity, 414, 414*f*, 438
religious identity, 422, 439
Marfan syndrome, 130
Marijuana, prenatal development and, 123
Marriage, 493–494
benefits of a good, 495, 509
Canadian marital trends, 493, 509
conflict resolution in, 494–495
joining of families through: new couple, 498
midlife marital trends, 563–565, 573
quality of in late adulthood, 640, 641, 655
remarried adults, 502, 510
social contexts, 493–494, 509
solvable versus perpetual problems in, 494–495
successful, principles of, 494–495, 509
Maslow, Abraham, 51, 66–67, 74, 78, 416
aesthetic needs, 67
being needs (B-needs), 67
deficit needs (D-needs), 67
hierarchy of needs, 66
homeostasis, 66
identity development, 416
self-actualization, 67
Massage therapy, preterm infants, 138
Maternal age, prenatal development and, 127–128
Maternal caregiving, 215, 221
Maternal diseases, pregnancy and, 125–127, 127*f*
AIDS, pregnancy and, 126
antiretroviral therapy, 126
diabetes, 126
genital herpes, 125
human immunodeficiency virus (HIV), 126
human papillomavirus (HPV), 126

rubella, 125
syphilis, 125
Maternal serum screening, 97
triple screen, 99
Maternal singing, 214
Maternal weight gain, 129, 129*f*, 130
Maternity Experiences Survey (MES), 122
Maternity leave, 129
Mayer-Salovey-Caruso emotional intelligence (EI), 309, 331
McGill Group for Suicide Studies, 106
Meadows School Project, 650
Meaning in life, 538–541, 544
four main needs for meaning, 540–541, 544
Frankl's theory of, 541, 544
intelligent design, 541, 544
Meaningfulness, 72
Median age, life expectancy and, 12, 13, 28
Meditation, 135, 448, 539, 541, 544, 618, 619, 623
Meiosis, 87, 89, 108
Melatonin, 386
Memory, 4, 244–246, 611-613
aging and, 611–613, 623
autobiographical, 611
beliefs, expectations, and feelings, impact of on, 613, 623
decline of, 531–532
elaboration, 301
episodic, 300, 611, 613, 622
explicit, 180, 189, 612, 623
factors affecting young child's, 247, 257
focused attention, 180
fuzzy trace theory, 301
implicit, 180, 612, 623
infant, 180
infantile amnesia, 180
knowledge and expertise, 300, 300*f*
limiting decline of, 613
long-term, middle/late childhood, 298, 331
long-term, early childhood, 244–245, 257
mental imagery, 301
middle adulthood, in, 531–532
non-cognitive factors, impact of on, 613, 623
perceptual speed and working memory, 612, 623
prospective, 612, 623
semantic, 300, 611–612, 613, 622
short-term, middle/late childhood, 298, 331
short-term, early childhood, 245, 257
source, 612
strategies, 301, 331
working, 531
Menarche, 373, 404
median age of, 373*f*
Menopause, 524–525, 542, 561
biological process, 10
hormone replacement therapies (HRT), 524
perimenopause, 524
Men's moral development, 507, 510
role-strain view, 507
Mental age, 18, 19, 43, 307
Mental health
cognitive function and, 614–615
late adulthood, in, 600–601, 621–622
meeting needs of older adults, 607
middle adulthood, in, 523, 542
Mental Health Commission of Canada, 523
Mercury exposure, pregnancy and, 125, 130
Mercy killing, 663
Mesosystem, 68*f*, 69
Metabolic syndrome, 518
Metacognition, 305–306, 332
metamemory, 305, 306
strategies, 305, 306
Metalinguistic awareness, 317, 332
Metamemory, 305, 306
Methadone, effect on fetus, 124
Methamphetamine, pregnancy and, 123
Methylene dioxy methylamphetamine (MDMA), pregnancy and, 124
Michael Meaney Lab, 106
Michaëlle Jean Foundation, 627
Microsystem, 68*f*, 69
Middle adulthood, 515
Middle adulthood, physical and cognitive development in, 512–544
aging, visible signs of, 516, 542
arthritis, 520, 542
cardiovascular system, 517–518, 542
career challenges and changes, 537–538, 543
careers, work, and leisure, 535–538, 543
changing midlife, 515, 541
chronic disorders, 520, 520*f*, 542
cognitive development, 527–535
culture, relationships, and health, 523, 543
defining middle adulthood, 15*f*, 16, 515
erectile dysfunction, 525–526
health concerns and wellness strategies, 520–523, 541, 544
height and weight, 516–517, 542
hormonal changes in men, 525–526
hormone replacement therapy (HRT), 524, 542
hypertension, 517, 518, 519, 520, 521, 541
information processing, 531–533, 543
intelligence, 527–531, 543
leisure, 538, 543
lungs, 519
male menopause, 526
meaning in life, 538–541, 544
meditation, religion, and spirituality, 538–540, 544
menopause, 524–525
mental health, 523, 544
metabolic syndrome, 518
mortality, rates of, 523, 542
nature of middle adulthood, 514–515, 541
physical changes, 516, 542
physical development, 515–526, 542
poverty and health, 521–523
sexuality, 524–526, 542
sexually transmitted infections (STIs), 526, 542
sleep, 518–519, 542
strength, joints, and bones, 517, 542
stress and disease, 520–521, 542
vision and hearing, 517, 542
work, midlife, 535–538, 537*f*, 543
Middle adulthood, socio-emotional development in, 545–574
adulthood, stages of, 547–552, 572
close relationships, 563–571, 573–574
contexts of midlife development, 555–559, 572
empty nest syndrome, 566, 573
grandparenting, 567–569, 574
intergenerational relationships, 569–571
life-events approach, 552–553, 572
longitudinal studies of stability and change, 559–563, 573
love and marriage, 563–566, 573
midlife consciousness, 561, 573

personality theories and development, 547–559, 572
relationships, development of, 564*f*, 573–574
sibling relationships and friendships, 566–567, 574
stability and change, 559–563, 573
stress in, 554–555, 572
Middle/late childhood, physical and cognitive development in, 288–334
accidents and injuries, 295, 330
attention deficit hyperactivity disorder (ADHD), 88, 321, 326–328, 333
autism spectrum disorders (ASD), 321, 328, 333
bilingualism, 319, 332
body growth and change, 290–291, 330
brain development, 291, 330
cancer, 295, 330
children with disabilities, 324–330, 333
cognitive development, 295–316
middle/late childhood, defined, 15*f*, 16
diet, balance in, 293, 330
eating disorders, thinness obsession and, 294, 330
educational approaches and issues, 320–330, 333
exercise, 292–293, 330
health, illness, and disease, 293–294
information processing, 298–303, 331
intelligence, 306–316, 331
language development, 317–319, 332
learning disabilities, 324–330, 333
motor development, 292, 330
obesity, 294, 330
physical changes and health, 290–295
physical disabilities, 328, 333
Piaget's concrete operational stage, 295–297, 331
reading, 317–318, 332
screen time and, 292, 330
social media, 364–365, 365*f*, 368
vocabulary, grammar, and metalinguistic awareness, 317–319, 332
Middle/late childhood, socio-emotional development, 335–368
bullying, 363–364, 367
child maltreatment, 358–360, 367
emotional and personality development, 338–342, 366
emotional development, 4, 343–345, 366
families, 356–360, 367
friends, 360–361, 367
gender and, 352–355, 366
moral development, 346–352, 366
parent-child relationships, developmental changes in, 357–358, 367
peer relations, technology, and social media, 361, 364–365, 367–368
peer statuses, 361–362, 367
self, 338–340, 366
social cognition, 362, 367
social media, 364–365, 368
Midlife consciousness, 561, 573
Midlife crises, 550–551, 572
age and well-being, 552*f*
Midwife, 134
Midwifery, 133–134
Mild cognitive impairment (MCI), 604
Minnesota Study of Twins Reared Apart, 86
Mitochondrial theory of aging, 581, 583, 620
Mitosis, 87, 89, 108
Modelling, 61
Monozygotic twins, 90
Montessori schools, 252–255, 257
approach of, defined, 253
Moral behaviour, 267, 285
self-control, 267
situational approach to, 267
Moral
character, 352
exemplars, 352
identity, 352
personality, 352
Moral development, early adulthood, in, 505–506
Bronfrenbrenner's five moral orientations, 506*f*
Moral development, early childhood, in, 265, 266–271, 285
anxiety, 266
conscience, 261, 267
empathy, 266
guilt, 266, 284
Kohlberg's theory and stages of, 267
moral behaviour, 267, 285
moral feelings, 266
moral reasoning, 266–267
parenting and young children's, 267
peers and, 268
perspective talking, 266
secure attachment and, 144, 267
superego, 285
Moral development, middle/late childhood, in, 346–352, 366
altruism, 349
autonomous morality, 346
care perspective, 351, 366
conventional reasoning, 347–348
culture and, 349, 350, 354, 366
family and, 350, 367
gender and, 351, 352–355, 366–367
heteronomous morality, 346
justice perspective, 351
Kohlberg's theory and stages of, 346–352, 348*f*, 366, 539
moral personality, 352
moral reasoning, 351
moral thought versus moral behaviour, 349–350
Piaget's cognitive development theory, 346
postconventional reasoning, 348, 539
preconventional reasoning, 347
prosocial behaviour, 351–352
social conventional reasoning, 351
Moral development, adolescence, in, 423
religion and, 423
Moral reasoning, 266–267, 351
autonomous morality, 266
heteronomous morality, 266, 267
imminent justice, 266
Morality and modesty, 350
Moro reflex, 163, 163*f*
Morphology, rules of, 249, 250*f*, 257
Motherrisk Program, Hospital for Sick Children, Toronto, 119
Mothers Against Drunk Driving (MADD), 390
Motor development, early childhood, in, 228–229, 255
fine motor skills, 229–230, 230*f*, 255
gross motor skills, 228, 229*f*, 255
Motor development, infancy, in, 161–167, 228
dynamic systems theory, 162
fine motor skills, 165–167, 229
gross motor skills, 164–165, 228
reflexes, 162–163, 228
Motor development, middle/late childhood, in, 292, 330
gender differences, 292, 330
Multiculturalism, 424
Multidimensional development, 8, 42

Multidirectional development, 8, 42
Multidisciplinary development, 9, 42
Multi-generational living, 639, 643
Multi-infarct dementia, 602, 622
Multiple births, 101
Multiple sclerosis, 72
Music, intelligence and, 310, 332
Mutated gene, 90, 91, 92, 328
Myelin sheath, 6, 154, 585
Myelination, 153–154, 188, 226, 292, 330
Myers-Briggs Personality Inventory, 54*f*

N

National Aboriginal Health Organization (NAHO), 134
National Advisory Council on Aging, 644
National Institute on Aging, 587
National Investigators Network, 24
National Longitudinal Survey of Children and Youth (NLSCY), 23, 24, 37, 37*f*, 275
National Seniors Council, 650
Natural childbirth, 135, 136
  Dick-Read, 135
  Leboyer method, 135
Natural Sciences and Engineering Research Council of Canada (NSERC), 38
Natural selection, 63, 72, 77, 83, 90, 105, 268, 541, 581, 582, 620
  adaptive behaviour and, 83
  defined, 83
  survival of the fittest, 83, 107
Naturalistic observation, 31, 32*f*, 44, 115
Nature, 21
Nature-nurture controversy, 21, 72, 102–107, 109–110, 177, 202, 311, 312, 354, 378
  conclusions about, 107
  epigenetic view, 105–106, 109
  heredity-environment correlations, 104, 109
  shared and nonshared environmental experiences, 105, 109
Negative affectivity, 200, 220
Neglected children, 361, 362
Neglectful parenting, 272, 273, 273*f*, 285
Neo-Freudians, 53
  Alfred Adler, 54*f*, 76
  Anna Freud, 54*f*, 76
  Carl Jung, 54*f*, 76
  Eric Fromm, 54*f*, 76
  Karen Horney, 54*f*, 76
  major contributions of, 54*f*
Neonatal abstinence syndrome, 123
Neonatal considerations, 136–138, 146
  preterm and low-birth-weight infants, 136–138, 139, 146
Neonatal health and responsiveness, measures of, 139–140, 146
  Apgar scale, 139, 139*f*, 146
  Brazelton Neonatal Behavioral Assessment Scale (NBAS), 140, 146
  New Ballard Score, 146
Neonatal Intensive Care Unit Network Neuro behavioral Scale (NNNS), 140, 146
Neonatal intensive-care unit (NICU), 136, 140
  kangaroo care and massage therapy, 138
Nervous system, development of, 117–118, 119, 129, 145
Neural tube, 117, 117*f*
Neurofibromatosis I, 93
Neurogenesis, 117, 586
Neuroimaging, 33
Neuronal migration, 117
Neurons, 4, 117, 145, 153–154, 156
  connectivity of, 117
  dendritic spreading, 153*f*
Neuroplasticity, 8–9, 57, 72
Neuroscience, 72, 75
New Ballard Score, 140, 146
New Brunswick Senior Citizens Federation, 645
New couple, 498
New England Centenarian Study, 579
New Horizons for Seniors, 651
Niche-picking, 105
Nicotine, 120, 136
Nicotine, prenatal development and, 122
  fetal birth weight and, 122, 122*f*
  nicotine replacement therapy (NRT), 122
  sudden infant death syndrome (SIDS), 122
Nicotine replacement therapy (NRT), 122
Noninvasive prenatal diagnosis (NIPD), 97, 99
Non-normative/highly individualized life events, 11
Neo-Piagetians, 56, 76, 297
Non-prescription drugs, prenatal development and, 119–124
Non-shared environmental experiences, 105, 109
Normal distribution, 307
Normative age-graded influences, 10
Normative history-graded influences, 10
Novelty, 174, 180
Nuclear family, 493
Numeracy, early childhood, 254, 258
Nun Study, 588
Nursing homes, 605, 622
Nurture, 21
Nutrition, adolescence, in, 385, 406
Nutrition, infancy, in, 159–161, 188
  malnutrition, 161
Nutrition, late adulthood, in, 598–599, 621
  vitamins, use of, 599, 621
Nutrition, pregnancy, in, 128–129, 146
Nutrition and exercise, early childhood, in, 231–234, 257
  body mass index (BMI), 232, 232*f*
  culture and, 232
  overweight/obese children, 232
Nutrition, middle/late childhood, in, 293, 330

O

Obesity, 88, 390, 406, 450–451, 452
  adulthood, in, 450–451, 473
  body mass index (BMI), 390, 450, 450*f*
  breastfeeding and, 160
  causes of, 390
  childhood, 88
  dietary fats, 451–452
  dieting, 451–452, 473
  environmental factors, 451, 473
  exercise, impact of on, 452, 473
  factors leading to, 450, 451
  genetics and, 390
  health risks of, 390
  heredity and, 451, 474
  late adulthood, 580, 593
  leptin, 451, 473
  middle adulthood, in, 517, 518, 523, 526, 542
  middle/late childhood, in, 294, 330
  pregnancy and, 129
  risk associated with, 450
  set point, 451, 473
  socio-cultural factors, 451, 473
Object permanence, 175, 175*f*, 189
Objectively-oriented morality, 505*f*, 506
Observation, scientific, 31–32, 33, 44
  naturalistic, 31
  theories, connection between, 37*f*
Observational learning, 61

Occipital lobe, 5
OCEAN, 559
Oedipus conflict, 51*f*, 270, 285, 333
Old Age Security (OAS), 636, 651
Old old, 581, 620
Oldest old, 581, 620
  robust, 581, 620
Oligospermia, 99
One-sided evolutionism, 85
Online dating, 486
Operant conditioning. *See* Skinner's operant conditioning
Operations, 234
Optimization, 632, 633
Optimism, 72
Oral health, 160, 188
Oral stage, Freud and, 50, 51*f*, 75
Organic intellectual disability, 313
Organisation for Economic Co-operation and Development (OECD), 23, 38
Organization, defined, 173
Organizational rules, 182
Organogenesis, 115, 119
Origins Canada (2010), 101
Osteoporosis, 595, 596, 599, 621
Otitis media, 160
Ovarian cancer, 160
Overextension, 183
Ovulation problems, 99, 100*f*
Oxytocics, 134

P

Paediatric Consultation Clinic (PCC), 161
Pain cry, 196, 220
Palliative care, 665, 666–667, 676
Parent-adolescent relationships, impact of, 417, 439
  autonomy and attachment, 418, 439
  conflict, 419–420, 439
  freedom versus control, 418–419, 439
  old versus new models of, 421*f*
Parental attitudes, 276
Parental influences, gender and, 270
Parenthood, transition to, 214, 222
Parent-infant synchrony, 214
Parenting, myths and realities of, 499, 509
Parenting, socio-emotional development in early childhood and, 272–276, 285
  Baumrind's parenting styles, 272–273, 273*f*, 285
  child's temperament and, 481
  co-parenting, 272, 285
  culture and ethnicity, 274, 285
  diversity, 274, 285
  economic level, 274, 285
  education, 274
  environment, 274, 285
  parenting styles in context, 273
  punishment, 273, 285
  shifting parental roles, 272, 285
  working parents, 272
Parenting adults, 503
  dual-income families, 503
  trends in, 503
Parkinson's disease, 72, 89, 585, 586, 602, 605, 622
Parietal lobe, 5, 617
Passionate love, 488, 489
Passive euthanasia, 663, 683
Passive genotype-environment correlations, 104
Paternal caregiving, 215, 221
Paternal factors, prenatal development and, 130
  age, 130
  environmental hazards, 130
  secondhand smoke, prenatal development and, 130
Paternal leave, 215, 216
Pavlov's classical conditioning, 60, 74, 75*f*, 77, 177
Peck's reworking of Erikson's final stage, 630, 654
  body transcendence versus body preoccupation, 630, 654
  differentiation versus role preoccupation, 630, 654
  ego transcendence versus ego preoccupation, 630, 654
Peer relations, adolescence in, 421–422, 435, 436
  bullying and, 431
  cliques and crowds, 431, 440
  high-risk behaviour and, 431
  peer groups, 430–431, 440
  peer pressure, 431, 440
Peer relations, middle/late childhood, in
  friends, 360–361, 367
  peer statuses, 361–362
Peer relations, early childhood, in, 281, 282, 286
  culture and, 283
  play, 282, 286
Peer-oriented morality, 505*f*, 506
Pelvic inflammatory disease (PID), 461
Pension plans, 29, 636, 637–638
  registered pension plans (RPPs), 636, 637, 638
  registered retirement savings plans (RRSPs), 636, 637, 638
Perceived control, death and, 675, 685
Perception, 167, 168, 169, 170, 172
  depth, 170, 170*f*, 189
  intermodal, 172, 189
  visual, 168–170. *See also* Visual perception
Perceptual speed, 612, 623
Perceptual-motor coupling, 172, 189
Perimenopause, 524
Perinatal Shaken Baby Syndrome Prevention Program (PSBSPP), 153
Permissive parenting, 14, 33
Personal fable, 400, 407
Personal life investment, 632–633, 633*f*
Personal unconscious, 54*f*
Personal uniqueness, adolescent, 400
Personality, mortality and, 634, 655
  big five factors of personality, 634–635, 654
Personality development, 203–204, 220
  adulthood, in, 562, 573
  autonomy versus shame, 204, 220
  cumulative personality model, 562
  independence, 204, 220
  self, 203–204, 220
  self-recognition, development of, 204*f*
  trust, 203, 220
Perspective talking, 266, 339
Petrochemicals, prenatal development and, 130
Phallic stage, Freud and, 50, 51*f*, 75
Phenotype, 90, 107
Phenylketonuria, 93, 94*f*, 108, 305
Phonology, 185, 249, 250, 257
  morphology and, 249
Physical adjustments, postpartum, 141, 147
  exercise, 141, 147
  sexual intercourse, 141, 147
  sleep, 140, 141, 147
Physical and cognitive development
  adolescence, 369–408
  early adulthood, 442–476
  early childhood, 223–258
  infancy, 148–190
  late adulthood, 575–624
  middle adulthood, 512–544
  middle/late childhood, 288–334
Physical attraction, 486, 487, 508
Physical development and health, infancy, in
  brain, 155*f*, 156, 188
  health, 159–161, 188

Physical development, early childhood, in body growth, 226, 255
brain, 226–227, 255
height and weight, 226
Physical disabilities, children and, 328, 333
Physical growth, infancy, in, 152, 152*f*, 157*f*, 188
cephalocaudal pattern, 152
proximodistal pattern, 152
Physician-assisted dying, 663–664
Physiological measures, 33, 44
functional magnetic resonance imaging (fMRI), 33, 616
neuroimaging, 33
Piaget's cognitive development theory, 55–58, 74, 75, 75*f*, 77, 190, 242, 254, 266, 267, 398–400, 402–403, 415, 416
accommodation, 55
assimilation, 55
concrete operational stage. *See* Piaget's concrete operational stage
equilibration, 173
formal operational stage. *See* Piaget's formal operational stage
four stages of cognitive development, 55–58, 56*f*
morality and, 266, 346
organization, 173
play and, 282
preoperational stage. *See* Piaget's preoperational stage
realistic and pragmatic thinking, 465–466
reflective and relativistic thinking, 466
scheme, 173
sensorimotor stage. *See* Piaget's sensorimotor stage
Vygotsky's socio-cultural cognitive theory versus, 239–232, 240*f*
Piaget's concrete operational stage, 56, 56*f*, 76, 234, 235*f*, 295–297, 331, 398, 399, 407, 465–466
characteristics of, 297*f*
classification, 296, 296*f*, 331
evaluation of, 297
reversibility, 296
seriation, 296, 331
transitivity, 297, 299, 331
Piaget's formal operational stage, 56, 56*f*, 76, 238*f*, 398–400, 407, 423, 465–466, 467, 474, 539
abstract thinking, 398
accommodation, 398, 407
assimilation, 398, 407
characteristics of, 398*f*
evaluation of, 399
hypothetical-deductive reasoning, 398, 407
idealism, 398
Piaget's preoperational stage, 56, 56*f*, 76, 234–238, 235*f*, 242, 296, 297, 399, 407
animism, 235, 236, 256
centration and limits of preoperational thought, 236–238, 256
children's drawings during, 235, 236*f*
conservation and, 236, 237*f*, 256
defined, 234
egocentrism, 235, 236*f*, 236, 256
evaluation of, 237
intuitive thought substage, 236, 256
operations, 234
symbolic function substage, 235, 256
Piaget's sensorimotor stage, 56, 56*f*, 76, 173–181, 174*f*, 189, 234, 238*f*, 399, 407
causality, 176–177, 189
critiques of, 177, 189
first habits and primary circular reactions, 174
internalization of schemes, 174
object permanence, 175, 175*f*, 189
secondary circular reactions, 174
simple reflexes, 174
tertiary circular reactions, novelty, and curiosity, 174
Pincer grip, 164
Pituitary gland, 375
Placenta, 97, 99, 114, 115, 115*f*, 119, 132, 146
Planfulness, 242, 242*f*
Plasticity, 8–9, 17, 22, 353, 354, 583, 615, 620, 623
Play, effect on young children, 282–283
Erikson and, 282
Freud and, 282
functions of, 282
Piaget and, 282, 286
types of, 282–283
Vygotsky's socio-cultural cognitive theory and, 282
Pleasure, 50, 51*f*, 72, 184, 273, 283, 303, 364, 378, 393, 453, 472
Polychlorinated biphenyls (PCBs), prenatal development and, 130
Polygenic inheritance, 90, 92, 108
gene-gene interaction, 92
Popular children, 361, 362
Positive psychology, 70–72, 74, 75*f*
Martin Seligman, 70–72, 74, 75*f*
Positron Emission tomography (PET) scans, 616
Postconventional reasoning, 348, 366, 539
Postformal thought stage, 466, 475
Postpartum depression, 101, 136, 142–143, 147
breastfeeding and, 143
Postpartum perceptions versus experience, 136
Postpartum period, 140–143, 147
bonding, 144
defined, 140
emotional and psychological adjustments, 142–143, 147
father's adjustment, 143
fourth trimester, 140
physical adjustments, 141, 147
rooming-in, postpartum, 141
sleep, 140, 141, 142
Postsecondary education
access to, 472
working after, 472, 476
Post-traumatic stress disorder (PTSD), 378
death and, 678
Poverty
child care and, 215
children's behaviour and, 322
education and, 322, 333
health and, 521–523, 633–634
late adulthood, in, 637, 638, 651, 654, 655
widows and, 680, 681
Powdered infant formula (PIF), 160
Power of attorney for personal care, 661, 662
Practical intelligence, 308, 309
Practical problem solving, 532, 543
Pragmatics, 251–252, 257, 317
Preconventional reasoning, 347, 348*f*, 366
Prefrontal cortex, 4, 6, 291, 302, 327, 328, 330, 342, 377, 377*f*, 378, 416, 531, 585, 587, 587*f*, 617, 618
attention deficit hyperactivity disorder (ADHD), in, 327, 327*f*
early childhood, development in, 227, 228*f*
middle/late childhood, development in, 291, 291*f*, 331
shrinking of with aging, 585, 617, 620
Pregnancy
diet, nutrition, and exercise during, 128–129
emotional states and stress, 130
suggested weight gain during, 129*f*

Pregnancy, adolescent, 383–384, 405, 433
consequences of, 384, 384f
rates of: Canada, 383
rates of: global, 383
reduction of, 384, 405
Prenatal alcohol exposure, 121
Prenatal development, 111–147, 145–146
alcohol and, 120–121, 145
amnion, 114
blastocyst, 114
blood types, incompatible and effecton, 124
blood types, incompatible and effecton prenatal development, 124
brain, 117–118, 145
caffeine and, 120
cigarette smoking, 122
cocaine, 123
course of, 114–118, 145
diet, nutrition, and exercise, 128–129, 129f
dose-response relationship, 118
ecstacy and, 124
embryonic period, 114–115, 145
emotional states and stress, maternal, 130, 146
environmental hazards, 124, 125, 145
fetal period, 115–116, 145
genetic susceptibility to disease, 118
germinal period, 114–115, 115f, 145
heroin, 124
marijuana and, 123
maternal age and, 127–129
maternal diseases, 124–125, 127f
maternal weight gain, 129, 129
methamphetamine, 123
nervous system, 117, 117f
nicotine and, 122
organogenesis, 115
paternal factors, 100
placenta, 114, 115f, 146
positive prenatal development, 131, 146
prenatal care, 131, 146
prescription and non-prescription drugs, 119
teratology and hazards to prenatal development, 118–119, 119f, 130, 145
three trimesters of, 116f, 145
time of teratogen exposure, 118, 145
trophoblast, 114
umbilical cord, 114
Prenatal development and birth, 111–147
Prenatal diagnostic tests, 97–99, 109
amniocentesis, 97, 98f, 109
chorionic villus sampling, 97, 98f, 99, 109
fetal MRI, 98, 99
maternal blood screening, 97, 99, 108
noninvasive prenatal diagnosis (NIPD), 97, 99
ultrasonography, 97, 98f, 99, 109
Prenatal methamphetamine exposure, 123
Prenatal period, 15f, 16, 43
Preoperational stage, Piaget's, 56, 56f, 234–238, 256
Prepared childbirth, 135, 136
Lamaze, 135
Prescription and non-prescription drugs, teratology and, 119, 120
psychoactive drugs, 120
Preterm infant, 136–137, 146
evaluation of, 139, 140
extremely preterm, 137
kangaroo care and massage therapy, 138
neonatal intensive-care unit (NICU), 138
school drop-out rate, effect on, 137, 138f
very preterm, 137
Primary emotions, 194, 219
Private schools, 324, 333
Private speech, 189, 190
Progestin, 119
Program for Student International Assessment (PISA), 23
Project OASIS, 437
Project Teen, 422
Prolonged grief, 678
Prosocial behaviour
morality and, 351–352
young children's, social media and, 284, 286
Prospective memory, 612, 613, 623
Proximodistal pattern, 152, 188, 226
Psychic inheritance, 54f
Psychoactive drugs, 120
alcohol, 120–121, 121f
caffeine, 120
cocaine, 123
ecstasy, 124
heroin, 124
marijuana, 123
methamphetamine, 123
nicotine, 122, 122f
Psychoanalytic approach, 37f, 48, 49–53, 74, 75, 75f, 76, 207, 266, 270
characteristics of, 49, 75
cognitive approach versus, 55
defined, 50
Erikson, Erik. *See* Erikson's psychoanalytic theory
Freud. *See* Freud, Sigmund's psychoanalytic theory
evaluation of, 53, 75
morality and, 266, 333
neo-Freudians, 53, 54f
Psychoanalytic theory of gender, 270, 285
Psychological age, 18, 19, 43
Psychology, contemporary approach esto, 70–73, 78
dynamic systems, 72, 78
evolutionary psychology, 72–73, 78
neuroscience, 72, 78
positive psychology, 70–72, 78
Psychosexual stages of development, Freud's five, 48, 50–52, 51f, 75
critical period, 50
Psychosocial moratorium, 413
Psychosocial stages of development, Erikson's eight, 51–52f, 52, 75, 628
Puberty
biological process, 10
body art, 377
body image, 376
brain changes in, 377–378, 377f, 404
cognitive performance versus psychosocial maturity, 377, 404
defined, 374
growth spurts in, 374f
hormonal changes in, 373, 374
maturity, teen perspectives on, 375–376, 405
menarche, 373, 373f, 404
physical changes in, 372–378
sexual maturation, height, and weight, 373, 404
timing of and variations, 375, 404
Public Health Agency of Canada (PHAC), 120, 121, 122, 129, 131, 140, 141, 142, 153, 158, 159, 161, 293, 294, 295, 382, 384, 385, 390, 431, 453, 455, 460, 461, 462, 519, 520, 523, 593, 594, 595, 596, 599, 600, 601
Punishment, parenting and, 275, 285
Purpose, need for, 540–541

Q

Quality of life, 12, 14, 390, 462, 514, 524, 579, 588, 589, 590, 597, 638, 648, 663, 673
Quality of Life Research Center (QLRC), 534
Quebec Pension Plan (QPP), 636
Quebec Suicide Brain Bank, 106
Quintland, 112
Quintuplets, Dione, 112

R

Race, 27, 423
ethnicity versus, 27, 423, 424
ethnicity and socio-economic status and 424
Racial identity, adolescence, in, 423, 424, 439
Racial profiling, 425, 554
Radiation exposure, pregnancy and, 124–125, 130
Random assignment, 34*f*, 35
Rapid eye movement (REM) sleep, 158, 188
Reading, 317–318, 332
basic-skills-and-phonetics approach, 318, 332
convergence of skills in, 318, 332
whole-language approach, 318, 332
Realistic and pragmatic thinking, 465–466
Recasting, 187, 190
Receptive vocabulary, 182
Recessive genes, 90
Reciprocal interactions, 196
Reciprocal socialization, 214
maternal singing, effect of, 214
mother's state of mind and, 210–211
parent-infant synchrony, 214
scaffolding, 214
Reconciliation, bullying and, 364
Red wine, benefits of, 601
Reflective and relativistic thinking, 466
Reflexes, 162–163, 163*f*, 188
grasping, 163
Moro, 163
rooting, 163
sucking, 163
Reflexive smile, 198, 220
Registered retirement savings plans (RRSPs), 636, 637, 638
Regulation, goal of, 9
Rejected children, 361, 362
aggression and in boys, 362
Relapse Prevention (RP) Model, 456
Relational aggression, 363–364
Relationships, development of in middle adulthood, 564*f*
Relative age, 355
Relative age effect (RAE), 355
Religion, 539, 541, 683
afterlife, and, 678–679
death and, 668, 669
defined, 539, 544
dimensions of, 539–540
grieving and, 680, 681
identity and, 422–423, 439
late adulthood, in, 618, 619
marriage and, 493, 494, 509
moral development, 423
positive role of, 423
spiritual development, 422
Remarried adults, 502, 510
late adulthood, in, 641
Reminiscence therapy, 629, 630
Replacement rate, 99
Reproduction
adoption alternative, 101
challenges and choices, 97–101, 109
infertility and reproductive technology, 99–101
natural selection and, 80, 82, 83, 107
Research challenges, 38–41, 45
bias, minimizing, 40, 45
Canadian Psychological Association (CPA), ethical guidelines of, 41, 45
ethics and, 38–39, 41, 45
ethnic and cultural bias, 40–41, 45
gender bias, 40, 41, 45
Research designs, 33–38, 44
cohort effects, 36–37, 44
connections between research methods and theories, 37*f*
correlational research, 33–34, 34*f*, 44
cross-sectional approach, 35, 36*f*, 44
descriptive research, 33, 34, 44
experimental and control groups, 34*f*, 35
experimental research, 34–35, 34*f*, 44
independent and dependent variables, 34*f*, 35
longitudinal approach, 35–36, 36*f*, 37, 44, 167
sequential approach, 37*f*, 44
time span, research, 35–37
Research methods, challenges and, 30–41, 45, 527
bias, minimizing, 40–41, 45
Canadian Psychological Association (CPA), 41, 45
case studies, 33
data collection, methods of, 31–33, 44
ethics and, 38–39, 45
hypotheses, 31, 44
laboratory, 31
naturalistic observation, 31, 44
physiological measures, 33
research challenges. *See* Research challenges
research designs. *See* Research designs
scientific observation, 31, 44
standardized tests, 32–33
surveys and interviews, 32
theories, connection with, 37*f*
theory, 31, 44
Resolution, bullying and, 364
Restitution, bullying and, 364
Restoration-oriented stressors, 678, 685
Restrained eating, 452
defined, 452
Retirement, 10, 498, 515, 536, 536, 556, 600, 636, 637, 638, 640, 655, 656
adjustment to, 515, 536, 543, 614, 630, 638, 655
age of, 29
Canada and other countries, in, 637–638
Canadian Association of Retired Persons (CARP), 645
income, 636, 637, 645
mandatory, 637, 645
Reversibility, action, 296
Rh-negative blood, 124
RhoGAM, 124
Rh-positive blood, 124
Rhythm, acquisition of, 171–172
Right to Play, 293
Rites of passage, 426, 439
defined, 426
Robson Classification System, 135
Rogers, Carl, 66, 74, 78
congruence, 66
incongruity, 66
Role-strain view of men's development, 507
Romanow Commission, 28
Romantic breakups, 489, 490, 508
positive changes in aftermath of, 491*f*, 508
Romantic love, 488, 489, 508
defined, 488
Rooting reflex, 163, 163*f*
Rothbart and Bates's classification of temperament, 200, 220
extraversion/surgency, 200, 220
Royal Commission on Aboriginal Peoples, 28
Royal Commission on New Reproductive Technologies, 99
Rubella, pregnancy and, 125, 127*f*

S

Sackler Program for Epigenetics and Psychobiology, 106
Sadness, 21, 142, 194, 195, 195*f*, 200, 219, 343, 355,

358, 600, 601, 670, 676, 677, 685
Salient versus relevant dimensions, 243
Salmonella enterica, 160
Samuel Lunenfeld Research Institute, Mt. Sinai hospital, Toronto, 103
Sandwich generation, 571, 574
Sarcopenia, 517
Scaffolding, 214, 238, 240, 256, 268, 275, 302, 305, 357, 618
Schaie, K. Warner's theory on cognition
  adult cognitive change, 466
  intellectual abilities and, 528–531, 543
  diseases related to mental decline, 615
  Seattle Longitudinal Study. *See* Seattle Longitudinal study of Intellectual Development
Schemes, 173
  internalization of, 173
Scientific thinking, 304–305, 332
  constructivist teaching, 320, 321
Seasons of a Man's Life, Levinson's, 549–550, 550*f*, 572
Seattle Longitudinal study of Intellectual Development, 527, 528–531, 528*f*, 529*f*, 543
  cross-sectional versus longitudinal comparison of in middle adulthood, 529*f*
  evaluation of, 530–531
Secondary circular reactions, coordination of, 174
Secondhand smoke, prenatal development and, 130, 131
Secure attachment style, 144, 483–484, 492, 509
Securely attached babies, 209–210, 221
Seekers, 502
Selection, 632, 633
Selective attention, 611, 622
Selective optimization with compensation theory, 628, 632–633, 633*f*, 654
  personal life investment, 632–633, 633*f*
  SOC, factors of, 632, 654
Self, early childhood, in, 261–262, 284
  initiative versus guilt, Erikson, 261, 284
  self-understanding, 261–262
  theory of mind, young child's, 262
  understanding others, 262
Self, late adulthood, in, 634–636, 655
  self-acceptance, 635*f*, 636, 655
  self-control, 636, 655
  self-esteem, 635, 655
Self, middle/late childhood, in, 338–341, 366
  industry versus inferiority, Erikson's, 342, 366
  perspective talking, 339
  self-efficacy, 341, 366
  self-esteem and self-concept, 340, 366
  self-evaluations, 339, 366
  self-regulation, 341–342
  self-understanding, development of, 338–339
  understanding others, 339
Self science classes, 343
Self-absorption, 547
Self-acceptance, 484, 552*f*, 635*f*, 636, 655
Self-actualization, 67, 78, 167
Self-concept, 340, 366
Self-conscious emotions, 194–195, 219, 263, 264, 284
  jealousy, 195*f*, 219
Self-control, 636, 655
  assimilative control strategies, 636
Self-descriptions, 261–262, 339, 561
Self-determination theory, attachment and, 210
Self-efficacy, 303, 339, 341, 366, 436, 484, 613, 638, 655, 656, 667, 681
Self-esteem, 23, 67, 142, 213, 322, 338, 339, 340–341, 355, 358, 360, 364, 366, 458, 465, 472, 484, 541
  adolescent, 382, 402, 411, 412, 415, 423, 424, 425, 428, 429, 435, 439, 440, 635
  community service and, 402
  divorce and, 501
  early childhood, in, 261, 264, 266, 273, 275, 635
  eating disorders and, 294, 386, 387
  exercise and, 292–293, 385
  friends and, 491
  gender and in adolescence, 379, 411, 412
  immigrants and, 554
  late adulthood, in, 618, 619, 635, 655
  middle adulthood, in, 554
  work and, 471, 522, 541
Self-image. *See* Self-esteem
Self-injury, adolescent, 390, 391
Self-organization, 72
Self-oriented morality, 505*f*, 506
Self-recognition, development of, 204*f*, 261
Self-regulation, 6, 341–342, 354, 357, 632, 636, 655
Self-understanding, 203, 261–262, 338–339, 411, 412, 429, 629
  adolescent, 412
  self-descriptions, 261–262
  self-recognition, 261
Self-worth, need for, 541
  See also Self-esteem
Selye's theory of stress, 554
Semantic memory, 300, 611–612, 622
  tip-of-the-tongue (TOT) phenomenon, 612
Semantics, 185, 251, 257
Seniors' Council of Canada, 600
Sensation, 167, 189
Sensorimotor stage, Piaget's, 56, 173–177, 174*f*, 189, 234, 398
Sensory and perceptual development,
  infancy, in, 167–173, 189, 261
  hearing, 170–171, 189
  intermodal perception, 172, 189
  other senses, 172, 189
  perceptual-motor coupling, 172, 189
  sensation and perception, 167, 189
  visual perception, 168–170, 189
Separation, 14
Separation protest, 198
Sequential approach, research and, 37, 44
  cohort effects, 36
  theories, connection between, 37*f*
Seriation, 296, 331
Service-learning, 402, 407, 422
Set point, obesity and, 451, 473
Sexism, 54*f*, 651, 655, 656
Sex-linked genes, 91, 107
  carriers, 91
  fraternal/dizygotic twins, 90
  genetic differences between males and females, 91, 91*f*
  X-linked inheritance, 91
Sexting, 432, 433, 440
Sexual abuse, children, of, 359
Sexual assault, 434, 463, 464, 474, 646, 647, 656
  factors contributing to, 464
Sexual harassment, 464
Sexual health, 128, 379, 380, 383
Sexual identity, 380, 405, 412, 429, 430, 439
Sexual orientation, 28, 279, 380, 381, 405, 416, 429, 433, 439, 458–459, 459*f*, 474
  continuum of, 459
  defined, 429
  determinants of, 458

identity and, 412, 413, 429, 430, 439
self-esteem and, 429, 439
Sexuality, adolescent, 379–384, 405–406
contraceptives, use of, 382, 405
dating violence, 382
HIV/AIDS, 379, 381
pregnancy and health, 383–384, 405
sex problems, risk factors and, 382–383, 405
sexual behaviours, timing of, 381, 381*f*, 405
sexual health, 379
sexual identity, development of, 380–381, 405
sexually transmitted infections (STIs), 379, 381, 382
Sexuality, early adulthood, in, 457–465, 474
sexual activity in emerging adulthood, 458–460, 474
sexual orientation, 458–460, 474
sexually transmitted infections (STIs), 460–463, 474
violence against women, 463–465, 474
Sexuality, late adulthood, in, 593–594, 621, 641
Sexuality, middle adulthood, in, 524–526, 543
climacteric, 524
dimensions of sexual intimacy, 526
sexual attitudes and behaviour, 526, 543
Sexually transmitted infections (STIs)
adolescence, in, 379, 381, 382
chlamydia, 382, 461, 474
defined, 382, 460
early adulthood, in, 460–463, 474
genital herpes, 461, 474
gonorrhea, 382, 461, 474
HIV and AIDS, 462, 474
human papillomavirus (HPV), 382, 460–461, 474
lying about, 462
protection against, 462–463, 474
syphilis, 461, 474
Shaken baby syndrome, 153
Joint Statement on Shaken BabySyndrome (SBS), 153
Perinatal Shaken Baby Syndrome Prevention Program (PSBSPP), 153
Shared environmental experiences, 105, 109
Shared sleeping, 157, 158
Sheloshim, 679
Shivah, 679
Short-term memory, 245, 257
Shyness, 198, 263, 284, 362, 480
Sibling relationships
friendship and, 566–567, 574
young children's, 280–281, 286
Sickle-cell anemia, 93, 94*f*, 108
Simple reflexes, defined, 174
Simplifying Mental Illness plus Life Enhancement Skills (SMILES), 358
Single adults, 500, 510
Skinner's operant conditioning, 60, 61, 74, 75*f*, 77, 177, 185
Sleep, 157–158, 188
adolescence, in, 386, 406
bed sharing, 157, 158
insomnia, 519
middle adulthood, in, 518–519, 542
patterns of and circadian rhythms, 386
rapid eye movement (REM) sleep, 158, 188
sleep apnea, 518–519
sleep patterns and arrangements, 157–158
sudden infant death syndrome (SIDS), 157–158
Sleep apnea, 518–519
Sleep disorders, 72
Sleep patterns
cultural differences, 157
rapid eye movement (REM) sleep, 157, 158, 188
Slow-to-warm-up child, defined, 199
Small-for-date infants, 136
Small-for-gestational-age infants, 136
Smell and taste, changes in adulthood, 592, 621
Smiling, 198, 220
reflexive smile, 198, 220
social smile, 198, 220
Snellen chart, 168
Social age, 18, 19, 43
Social clock, 556, 572
Social cognition, middle/late childhood, in, 362, 367
five stages of, 362
Social cognitive theory of gender, 270, 285
Social constructivist approach, 242
Social contexts, physical and cognitive development in infancy and, 213–219, 222
child care, 216–218
child-parent interactions, direct and indirect effects, 215, 222
family, 213–219, 222
special needs infants, 213, 222
Social conventional reasoning, 351
Social determinants of health, 633–634, 654
Social exclusion, 424
Social influences, gender differences and, 270–271, 285
Social integration, late adulthood, in, 648–650, 656
altruism and volunteerism, 650–651, 656
culture and, 652, 656
ethnicity and, 651–652, 656
gender and, 651, 656
Social media, 283–284, 286
aggression in children, impact on 284, 286
children's prosocial behaviour, impact on, 283–284, 286
family violence, impact on, 360, 364–365
middle/late childhood, impact in, 364–365, 365*f*, 367
Social orientation/understanding and
attachment, infancy, in, 144, 205–210, 221
attachment, development of, 207–210, 221
attachment, individual differences in, 210–211, 221
attachment, temperament and wider social world and, 211–212, 221
caregiving styles and attachment classification, 210–211, 221
face-to-face play, 206
intention, goal-directed behaviour, and cooperation, 206, 221
locomotion, 206, 221
social orientation/understanding, 205, 221
social referencing, 207, 221
social sophistication and insight, infants', 207, 221
Social policy, 23–24, 28–30, 38, 41, 44
assisted insemination (AI), 99, 100
contemporary concerns, 25–30, 44
education, 25–26, 44
eugenics and, 95–96
generational inequity, 29
health and well-being, 25, 44
socio-cultural contexts, 26–28, 44
stem cell research and genetic screening, ethical considerations of, 102–104
Social referencing, 207, 221
Social role theory, 270
Social Sciences and Humanities Research Council (SSHRC), 24, 38
Social smile, 198, 220

Social support, late adulthood, in, 648, 656
convoy model of social relations, 648
Society for Research in Child Development, 72
Society of Obstetricians and Gynaecologists of Canada (SOGC), 112, 119, 134, 135
Socio-cultural contexts, 26–28, 44
context, 26
cross-cultural studies, 26–27, 44
culture, 26
ethnicity, 26, 27, 44
gender, 26, 27, 44
race, 26, 27, 44
Socio-economic status (SES), 9, 14, 42, 69, 121, 127, 274, 278, 294, 322, 325, 360, 417, 418, 423, 425–426, 436*f*, 439, 579, 595, 600, 613, 623
health problems and, 595
Socio-emotional development
adolescence, 409–441
early adulthood, 477–511
early childhood, 259–287
infancy, 191–222
late adulthood, 625–657
middle adulthood, 545–574
middle/late childhood, 4, 335–368
Socio-emotional process, development of, 7, 15, 15*f*, 16, 42, 411
Socio-emotional selectivity theory, 630–632, 643, 650, 654
goals, realization of, 631, 654
model of, 631*f*
Socio-historical conditions, development and, 68*f*, 69
Sociometric status, 361
Solid foods, introduction of, 161
Source memory, 612
Special needs, care of infants with, 219, 222
Special Senate Committee on Aging, 637, 650, 651
Sperm
abnormal shape of, 100*f*
antibodies against, 100*f*
antisperm secretions, 100*f*
azoospermia, 99
fertilization and, 89, 89*f*, 107, 113, 114
immobile, 99, 100*f*
in vitro fertilization, 99, 100
low count of, 99*f*, 525
oligospermia, 99
teratogens and, 124, 130
Spina bifida, 93, 94*f*, 99, 117, 129, 324
folic acid supplementation, 117
Spirituality, 539–540, 541, 544, 618, 619
afterlife, and, 678–679
death, attitudes on, 673
development of, 422–423
Spoken vocabulary, 182
St. Christopher's Hospice, 666
Stability-change issue, development and, 22, 36, 43, 156, 199, 213, 251–252, 480–485, 508, 527, 559–563, 573–574, 581, 585, 593, 632, 638
Berkeley longitudinal studies, 561
big five factors of personality, 559–560, 560*f*
conclusions about, 562–563, 573, 574
Costa and McCrae's Baltimore study, 559–560, 573
Helson's Mills College study, 561, 573
longitudinal studies, 559–563, 573
middle adulthood, in, 559–563, 573
Vaillant's studies, 561–562, 573
Stagnation, 472
generativity versus, 52*f*, 75, 546, 547–548, 572, 629
Standardized tests, 32–33
Stanford-Binet intelligence test, 19, 32, 306–307, 307*f*, 311, 331
Startle reflex, 163*f*
Step Up and Step In, 437
Stepfamilies, 278, 358, 367
Stepping reflex, 163*f*
Sternberg's triarchic theory of intelligence, 308, 331
Strange Situation, 209, 210
Stranger anxiety, 198, 222
Street youth, 434
Stress, 72, 447–448, 473, 554
cardiovascular system and, 520, 521
chronic, 554, 572
coping with, 344–345, 366
disease and, 520–521, 542
episodic, 554, 572
immune system and, 520–521
maternal, pregnancy and, 130
middle adulthood, in, 554–555, 572
negative coping mechanisms, 447
positive coping mechanisms, 447
Stroke, 593
Substance abuse, adulthood, in, 359, 453–457, 465, 474, 479, 495, 601, 622
Substance abuse during pregnancy, 122, 123, 124, 136
Substance use and addiction, adolescent, 359, 391–395, 396, 406, 435, 436
cigarette smoking, 391, 406
club drugs, 392
combating, 393–394
dopamine in the brain, 393
ecstasy, 392, 392*f*, 406
gambling, 393
prescription and non-prescription drugs, 391–392, 406
suicide and, 394
Sucking reflex, 163, 163*f*
Sudden infant death syndrome (SIDS), 122, 157, 158–159
bed sharing and, 157, 158
risk factors for, 158, 188
Sue Rodriguez vs. British Columbia, 663
Suicide, 14, 106, 680
adolescent, 390, 395–397, 406, 671
assisted, 663
bullying and, 364, 367, 431
cyberbullying and, 396
defined, 395
intervention, teen, 396
late adulthood, in, 600
reasons for, 396–397
risk factors for, teen, 396, 406
teen rates of, 395, 396
Superego, 50, 75, 285
Surgency, 200, 221
Surveys and interviews, 32, 33
theories, connection between, 37*f*
Survival of the fittest, 63, 72, 83, 107
Sustained attention, 180, 207, 243, 435, 611, 622
Swarming, 434
Swimming reflex, 163*f*
Symbolic function substage, 235, 256
Synchronous interactions, 196
Syntax, 185, 250–251, 257
Syphilis, 125, 127*f*, 460, 461, 474, 526
pregnancy and, 125

T

Tay-Sachs disease, 93, 94*f*
Telegraphic speech, 183, 190
Telomeres, aging and, 582–583, 582*f*, 620
Temporal lobe, 5
Temperament and personality development, 199–204, 221
ability to control emotions, 481
defining and classifying temperaments, 199–200, 221
early adulthood, in, 480–481, 508
goodness of fit and parenting and, 202–203, 221

inhibition, 480
intervening contexts, 481f
personality development, 203–204, 221
temperament defined, 199, 221
Ten Steps to Successful Breastfeeding (TenSteps), 150
Teratogen, 118, 119, 130, 145, 146
Teratology, hazards to prenatal
development and, 118–119, 119f, 145
dose-response relationship, 118
genetic susceptibility, 118
prescription and non-prescription drugs, 119
time of exposure, 118, 119f
Terminal decline, 615
Tertiary circular reactions, novelty, and curiosity, defined, 174
Testosterone, 375, 404
Tetracycline, 119
Thalidomide, 119, 120
Theory, 31
Theory of mind, child's, 247–249, 257, 262
autism and, 249
culture and, 247
genetics and, 247
individual differences in, 248–249
Thinking, 302–305, 331
convergent, 303
creative, 303, 331
critical, 302, 331
divergent, 303
scientific, 304–305
Time of exposure, teratogen, 119, 119f, 120, 145
Time span, research
cross-sectional approach, 35, 36f, 44
longitudinal approach, 35–36, 36f, 37, 44
sequential approach, 37, 44
Tip-of-the-tongue (TOT) phenomenon, 612
Tonic neck reflex, 163f
Top-dog phenomenon, 402, 430, 447
Toronto District School Board (TDSB), 290
Toronto Intergenerational Partnerships (TIGP), 650
Touch and pain, 590, 592, 621
Toxic waste, pregnancy and, 125
Transgender, 269, 381, 429, 439
Transitivity, 297, 299, 331
Triangular theory of love, 488, 489f, 508
Triarchic theory of intelligence, Sternberg's, 308, 331
Triple screen maternal blood screening, 99
Trophoblast, 114
Trust versus mistrust, Erikson's stage of, 51f, 208, 221, 629f
Truth and Reconciliation Commission, 28
Tuberculosis, 160
Turner syndrome, 92f, 108, 269
Twins, 86
fraternal/dizygotic twins, 86, 87, 90, 101, 103, 104, 105
identical/monozygotic, 86, 87, 90, 101, 103, 104, 105
Minnesota Study of Twins Reared Apart, 86
Two-parent working family, 14
Two-word utterances, infant's, 183, 190
telegraphic speech, 183, 190

U

Ultrasonography, 97, 99, 109
Umbilical cord, 114, 115f, 132
Underextension, 183
Unemployment, early adulthood, in, 472, 475
problems associated with, 472
UNICEF, 150
Uplifts and hassles of middle adulthood, 553, 554f
Urban Native Teacher Education Program, 323

V

Vaillant's longitudinal studies of aging, 548, 550–551, 561–562, 573
characteristics of 50-year olds and happiness, 561–562, 562f
Values, need for, 541
Vanier Institute of the Family, 100, 636, 639
Variability, sources of genetic deoxyribonucleic acid (DNA), 90
genotype, 90
mutated genes, 90
phenotype, 90
Verbatim memory trace, 301
Vernix caseosa, 132
Very preterm, 137
Victimization, elderly, of, 644–645, 656
Violation-of-expectation (VOE), 177
Violence against women, 463–465
depression and, 464
global reach of, 464
sexual assault, 463
sexual harassment, 464
Visible minority, 45, 423, 424, 425, 651
Vision, 590, 591f
aging and, 590
cataracts, 590
dark adaptation, 590
eye disease, 590
glaucoma, 590
late adulthood, 590
macular degeneration, 590
middle adulthood, changes in, 517
Visual expectations, 170, 170, 189
motor, sensory, and perceptual development, 168–169
Visual perception, 168–170
acuity and colour, 168–169, 189
depth perception, 170, 170f, 189
visual expectations, 170–171, 170f
Vitamin D deficiency, 159, 188, 599
Vitamins, aging and, 599, 621
antioxidants, 599, 621
Vocabulary, 317–319, 332
Vygotsky's socio-cultural cognitive theory, 58–59, 74, 75f, 76, 238–242, 253, 256, 416
evaluation of, 242
language and thought, 240–241
Piaget's cognitive development theory versus, 241
play and, 282, 286
scaffolding, 238, 240
social constructivist approach, 242
teaching strategies, 241, 256
zone of proximal development (ZPD), 238, 239, 239f, 256, 268

W

War Child, 470–471
Wechsler scales, 307
Weight gain during pregnancy, 129, 129f
Well-being, dimensions of, 552f
Wernicke's area, 184, 185f, 190
Whole-language approach, 318
Wilding, 434
Willis' intellectual abilities and, 528–531, 543
Wilms' tumour, 91
Wisdom, 613–614, 623
predictors of, 613
Women's moral development, 506, 510
Work, early adulthood, in, 471–473, 475
dual-career couples, 472–473, 475
postsecondary education, after during, 472, 475

unemployment, 472, 475
Work, late adulthood, in, 637, 655
Work, middle adulthood, in, 535–538
age and job satisfaction, 537*f*
Working memory, 298–299, 299*f*, 531, 612, 613, 623
perceptual speed and, 612
World Elder Abuse Day, 647
World Health Organization (WHO), 41, 150, 325, 358, 359, 383, 390, 394, 456, 541, 544
World Literacy Canada (WLC), 290

X

X-linked inheritance, 91
XYY syndrome, 92*f*, 108

Y

Youth at Risk Development (YARD), 437
Young offenders, 434–435, 440
Young old, 581, 620
Youth Criminal Justice Act, 434, 435
Youth in Transition Survey (YITS), 38
Youth violence, 434

Z

Zone of proximal development (ZPD), 238, 239, 239*f*, 268
Zygote, 4, 89, 90, 108, 113